Sears List of
Subject Headings

Sears List of Subject Headings

19th Edition

JOSEPH MILLER

Editor

BARBARA A. BRISTOW

Associate Editor

New York • Dublin

The H. W. Wilson Company

2007

Printed in the United States of America

ISBN 978-0-8242-1076-2

Contents

CONTENTS

Preface

Since the first edition in 1923, the Sears List has served the unique needs of small and medium-sized libraries, suggesting headings appropriate for use in their catalogs and providing patterns and instructions for adding new headings as they are required. The successive editors of the List have faced the need to accommodate change while maintaining a sound continuity. The new and revised headings in each edition reflect developments in the material catalogued and in the use of the English language, aiming always to make library collections as easily available as possible to library users.

The major feature of this new edition of the Sears List is the inclusion of more than four hundred and forty new subject headings. Of special note is the development of new headings in two areas: Islam and Graphic novels. The growing interest in Islam among the general public and in school curricula is reflected in the new material published, for which the Sears List now provides heading such as **Islam and politics**, **Islamic music**, **Muslim women**, **Shiites**, **Sunnis**, and **Dervishes**, among others.

The extraordinary growth in the publication and collection of graphic novels is the impetus for the addition of more than thirty new headings, among them: **Adventure graphic novels**, **Romance graphic novels**, **Superhero graphic novels**, **Manga**, **Komodo**, and **Mecha**. These new headings were suggested to us by Katherine L. Kan, a noted expert in the field. These headings are all genre headings and follow the patterns set by other literary form and genre headings already in the List.

New subject headings in a variety of other areas as well represent a major enhancement to the List in this edition. New headings have been added in the fields of science and technology, such as **Computer animation**, **Open access publishing**, and **Stem cell research**; in lifestyle and entertainment, such as **Neopaganism**, **Reality television programs**, and **Body piercing**; in politics and world affairs, such as **War reparations**, **Suicide bombers**, and **Border patrols**; and in literature and the arts, such as **Urban fiction** and **Art pottery**. Many provisions have been added for creating other new headings as needed. Many of the headings new to this edition were suggested by librarians representing various sizes and types of libraries, by commercial vendors of bibliographic records, and by the catalogers, indexers, and subject specialists at the H.W. Wilson Company.

A limited number of subject headings have been revised in this edition. For the convenience of librarians maintaining their catalogs, these revisions are spelled out in the List of Canceled and Replacement Headings found on page xlii.

The Principles of the Sears List, which follows this Preface, is intended both as a statement of the theoretical foundations of the Sears List and as a concise introduction to subject cataloging in general. It has been expanded in this edition to provide guidance to catalogers in creating headings for topics relating to Native American, government policy, and mythology and folkore.

The List of Commonly Used Subdivisions, which follows the Principles, lists, for the purpose of easy reference, every subdivision for which there is a provision in the List, no matter how specialized. At the same time, for every subdivision there is an entry in the alphabetical List with full instructions for the use of that particular subdivision. There are also many examples of the use of subdivisions, emphasizing that the use of subdivisions is an essential method of expanding and adapting the List to a library's particular needs.

A History of the Sears List

Minnie Earl Sears prepared the first edition of this work in response to demands for a list of subject headings that was better suited to the needs of the small library than the existing American Library Association and Library of Congress lists. Published in 1923, the *List of Subject Headings for Small Libraries* was based on the headings used by nine small libraries that were known to be well cataloged. Minnie Sears used only *See* and "refer from" references in the first edition. In the second edition (1926) she added *See also* references at the request of teachers of cataloging who were using the List as a textbook. To make the List more useful for that purpose, she wrote a chapter on "Practical Suggestions for the Beginner in Subject Heading Work" for the third edition (1933).

Isabel Stevenson Monro edited the fourth (1939) and fifth (1944) editions. A new feature of the fourth edition was the inclusion of Dewey Decimal Classification numbers as applied in the *Standard Catalog for Public Libraries*. The new subjects added to the List were based on those used in the Standard Catalog Series and on the catalog cards issued by the H.W. Wilson Company. Consequently, the original subtitle "Compiled from Lists used in Nine Representative Small Libraries" was dropped.

The sixth (1950), seventh (1954), and eighth (1959) editions were prepared by Bertha M. Frick. In recognition of the pioneering and fundamental contribution made by Minnie Sears the title was changed to *Sears List of Subject Headings* with the sixth edition. Since the List was being used by medium-sized libraries as well as small ones, the phrase "for Small Libraries" was deleted from the title. The symbols x and xx were substituted for the "Refer from (see ref.)" and "Refer from (see also ref.)" phrases to conform to the format adopted by the Library of Congress.

The ninth edition (1965), the first of four to be prepared by Barbara M. Westby, continued the policies of the earlier editions. With the eleventh edition, the "Practical Suggestions for the Beginner in Subject Heading Work" was retitled "Principles of the Sears List of Subject Headings" to emphasize "principles," and a section dealing with nonbook materials was added.

The thirteenth edition (1986), prepared by Carmen Rovira and Caroline Reyes, was the first to take advantage of computer validation capabilities. It also responded to the changing theory in subject analysis occasioned by the development of online public access catalogs. This effort was taken further in the fourteenth edition (1991) under the editorship of Martha T. Mooney, who reduced the number of compound terms, simplified many subdivisions, and advanced the work of uninverting inverted headings.

In accord with a suggestion of the Cataloging of Children's Materials Committee of the American Library Association, many of the headings from *Subject Headings for Children's Literature* (Library of Congress) were incorporated into the Sears List with the thirteenth edition. Since the Sears List is intended for both adult and juvenile collections, wherever the Library of Congress has two different headings for adult and juvenile approaches to a single subject, a choice of a single term was made for Sears. In cases where the Sears List uses the adult form, the cataloger of children's materials may prefer to use the juvenile form found in *Subject Headings for Children's Literature*.

PREFACE

In the fifteenth edition (1994), the first edited by Joseph Miller, the interval between publication of editions was shortened to provide a more timely updating of subject headings. In keeping with prevailing thinking in the field of library and information science, all remaining inverted headings were canceled in favor of the uninverted form. Likewise, the display of the List on the page was changed to conform to the NISO standards for thesauri approved in 1993. While Sears remains a list of subject headings and not a true thesaurus, it uses the labels BT, NT, RT, SA, and UF for broader terms, narrower terms, related terms, See Also, and Used for. A List of Canceled and Replacement Headings was added to facilitate the updating of catalogs. Also in the fifteenth edition many headings were added to enhance access to individual works of fiction, poetry, drama, and other imaginative works, such as films and radio and television programs, based on the *Guidelines on Subject Access to Individual Works of Fiction, Drama, etc.* prepared by a subcommittee of the Subject Analysis Committee of the ALA. These headings have since been updated in accordance with the Second edition of the *Guidelines* (2000).

In the sixteenth edition (1997) further instructions were added for the application of subdivisions, and the headings in the field of religion were extensively revised to reduce their exclusively Christian application and make them more useful for cataloging materials on other religions.

The major feature of the seventeenth edition (2000) was the revision of the headings for the native peoples of the Western Hemisphere. The headings **Indians**, **Indians of North America**, **Indians of Mexico**, etc., were cancelled in favor of **Native Americans**, which may be subdivided geographically by continent, region, country, state, or city. In further revisions in the seventeenth edition, many headings that formerly incorporated the word "modern" were simplified and clarified, such as **Modern history** and **Modern art**, and headings for various kinds of government policy were revised and regularized.

The 18th edition of the Sears List (2004) saw the inclusion of five hundred new subject headings and a significant addition to the Principles of the Sears List regarding the treatment of individual works of fiction, drama, and poetry.

The Scope of the Sears List

No list can possibly provide a heading for every idea, object, process, or relationship, especially not within the scope of a single volume. What Sears hopes to offer instead is a basic list that includes many of the headings most likely to be needed in small libraries together with patterns and examples that will guide the cataloger in creating additional headings as needed. New topics appear every day, and books on those topics require new subject headings. Headings for new topics can be developed from the Sears List in two ways, by establishing new terms as needed and by subdividing the headings already in the List. Instructions for creating new headings based on the pattern in Sears and sources for establishing the wording of new headings are given in the Principles of the Sears List. The various kinds of subdivisions and the rules for their application are also discussed in the Principles of the Sears List.

It is only by being flexible and expandable that Sears has been able over the years to fill the needs of various kinds of libraries. The degree or level of specificity required for a collection depends entirely on the material being collected. While a small library is unlikely to need very narrow topics of a technical or scientific nature, it is not at all unlikely that a small library might have a children's book on a single concept such as **Triangle** or a gardening book on **Irises**. Neither of these terms is in Sears, but the first would be added as a narrower term under **Shape** and the second as a narrower term under **Flowers**.

PREFACE

Form of Headings

It was the policy of Minnie Sears to use the Library of Congress form of subject headings with some modification, chiefly the simplification of phrasing. The Sears List still reflects the usage of the Library of Congress unless there is some compelling reason to vary, but those instances of variation have become numerous over the years. A major difference between the two lists is that in Sears the direct form of entry has replaced the inverted form, on the theory that most library users search for multiple-word terms in the order in which they occur naturally in the language. In most cases cross-references have been made from the inverted form and from the Library of Congress form where it otherwise varies.

Scope Notes

As in previous editions, all the new and revised headings in this edition have been provided with scope notes where such notes are required. Scope notes are intended to clarify the specialized use of a term or to distinguish between terms that might be confused. If there is any question of what a term means, the cataloger should simply consult a dictionary. There are times, however, when subject headings require a stricter limitation of a term than the common usage given in a dictionary would allow, as in the case of **Marketing**, a term in business and economics, not to be confused with **Grocery shopping**. Here a scope note is required. Some scope notes distinguish between topics and forms, such as **Encyclopedias and dictionaries** for critical and historical materials and the subdivisions *Encyclopedias* and *Dictionaries* under topics for items that are themselves encyclopedias or dictionaries. There are also scope notes in Sears that identify any headings in the area of literature that may be assigned to individual works of drama, fiction, poetry, etc.

Classification

The classification numbers in this edition of Sears are taken from the 14th edition of the *Abridged Dewey Decimal Classification* (2004). The numbers are intended only to direct the cataloger to a place in the DDC schedules where material on that subject is often found. They are not intended as a substitute for consulting the schedules, notes, and manual of the DDC itself when classifying a particular item. The relationship between subject headings and classification is further discussed in the Principles of the Sears List.

Usually only one number is assigned to a subject heading. In some cases, however, when a subject can be treated in more than one discipline, the subject is then given more than one number in the List. The heading **Chemical industry**, for example, is given two numbers, **338.4** and **660**, which represent possible classification numbers for materials dealing with the chemical industry from the viewpoints of economics and technology respectively. Classification numbers are not assigned to a few very general subject headings, such as **Charters**, **Exhibitions**, **Hallmarks**, and **Identification**, which cannot be classified unless a specific application is identified. The alphabetic notation of B for individual biographies is occasionally provided in addition to Dewey classification numbers for such materials. Numbers in the 810s and 840s prefixed by a C are given as optional numbers for topics in Canadian literature.

The Dewey numbers given in Sears are extended as far as is authorized by the *Abridged Dewey Decimal Classification*, which is seldom more than four places beyond the decimal point. When an item being classified has a particular form or geographic specificity, the number may be extended by adding form and geographic subdivisions from the Dewey tables. Only a few examples of built numbers are given in Sears, such as **940.53022** for **World War, 1939-1945—Pictorial works**. No library should feel the need to extend classification numbers beyond what is practical for the size of the library's collection. For a discussion of close and broad classification and for instructions on building numbers from the Dewey tables, the cataloger should consult the introduction to the most recent edition of the *Abridged Dewey Decimal Classification and Relative Index.*

Style, Filing, Etc.

For spelling and definitions the editor has relied upon *Webster's Third New International Dictionary of the English Language, Unabridged* (1961) and the *Random House Webster's Unabridged Dictionary*, 2nd ed., revised and updated (1997). Capitalization and the forms of corporate and geographic names used as examples are based on the *Anglo-American Cataloguing Rules*, 2nd ed., 2002 revision. The filing of entries follows the *ALA Filing Rules* (1980).

Every term in the List that may be used as a subject heading is printed in boldface type whether it is a main term; a term in a USE reference; a broader, narrower, or related term; or an example in a scope note or general reference. If a term is not printed in boldface type, it is not used as a heading.

Acknowledgments

The editors wish to acknowledge with gratitude the contributions to this edition of the individual catalogers, reference librarians, and vendors of cataloging services who have offered suggestions for headings to be added to the List.

The Cataloging of Children's Materials Committee of the American Library Association has been, as ever, an important source of advice in the editorial work on the Sears List. ALA's Subject Analysis Committee and its various subcommittees have also been a constant source of advice and guidance in the continuing development of the Sears List.

Thanks are extended to the editors and catalogers of the H.W. Wilson Company; especially to Patricia Kuhr, Editor, Subject Authority Files, for her help in formulating subject headings, and to Joan Goodsell, Assistant Editor, Subject Authority Files, for her research and editorial assistance.

The classification numbers given in this edition of Sears conform to the *Abridged Dewey Decimal Classification Edition 14*, published in 2004, by OCLC. We extend special thanks to Joan S. Mitchell, editor in chief of the Dewey Decimal Classification (DDC), and to the assistant editors of the DDC for their generous help and advice.

Every edition of the Sears List represents the work of many hands, especially those of the previous editors over the years. The contributions of the users of the List have also been invaluable. Every comment, suggestion, question, or request from a user represents an opportunity for improvement and is greatly valued.

J. Miller
B. Bristow

Principles of the Sears List of
Subject Headings

Certain principles and practices of subject cataloging should be understood before an attempt is made to assign subject headings to library materials. The discussion that follows makes reference to the *Sears List of Subject Headings*, henceforth referred to as the Sears List or the List, but the principles are applicable to other lists of subject headings as well.

1. THE PURPOSE OF SUBJECT CATALOGING

All library work is a matter of the storage and retrieval of information, and cataloging is that aspect of library work devoted to storage. The best cataloging is simply that which facilitates the most accurate and complete retrieval. The two basic branches of cataloging are descriptive cataloging and subject cataloging. Descriptive cataloging makes possible the retrieval of materials in a library by title, author, date, etc.—in short all the searchable elements of a cataloging record except the subjects. Only by conforming to the standards for descriptive cataloging can a librarian assure the user accurate retrieval on the descriptive elements, and those standards are codified in the *Anglo-American Cataloguing Rules*, which is now in its second revised edition (commonly known as *AACR2*).

Until the second half of the nineteenth century, descriptive cataloging was the only library cataloging that was found necessary. Libraries were much smaller than they are today, and scholarly librarians then were able, with the aid of printed bibliographies, to be familiar with everything available on a given subject and guide the users to it. With the rapid growth of knowledge in many fields in the course of the nineteenth century and the resulting increase in the volume of books and other library materials, it became desirable to do a preliminary subject analysis of such works and then to represent them in the catalog in such a way that they would be retrievable by subject.

Subject cataloging deals with what a book or other library item is about, and the purpose of subject cataloging is to list under one uniform word or phrase all the materials on a given topic that a library has in its collection. A subject heading is that uniform word or phrase used in the library catalog to express a topic. The use of authorized words or phrases only, with cross-references from unauthorized synonyms, is the essence of bibliographic control in subject cataloging. The purpose of a subject authority, such as the Sears List, is to provide a basic vocabulary of authorized terms together with suggestions for useful cross-references.

The two most common types of subject authorities are the thesaurus and the subject heading list. A true thesaurus, in the realm of information science, is a comprehensive controlled vocabulary of discrete unit terms, called descriptors, arranged is such a way as to display the hierarchical and associative relationships among terms. It is usually limited to a particular realm of knowledge, as in the case of the *Art and Architecture Thesaurus*. The American national standards for thesauri are spelled out in the NISO *Guidelines for the Construction, Format, and Management of Monolingual Thesauri*. A subject heading list, such as the Sears List or the *Library of Congress Subject Headings*, is simply an alphabetical list of terms that have been established over time as warranted by the materials being cataloged. A subject heading list also indicates relationships among terms but does not attempt to establish any comprehensive hierarchies. In addition to simple descriptors, a subject heading list can include pre-coordinated strings composed of subject terms with subdivisions.

The *Library of Congress Subject Headings*, which in print now comprises five large volumes, is primarily a list of headings that have been used in the Library. Likewise *Medical Subject Headings* derives from the holdings of the National Library of Medicine. The Sears List is unique among subject heading lists in that it does not attempt to be a complete list of terms used in any single library but only a list of headings most likely to be needed in a typical small library and a skeleton or pattern for creating other headings as needed. By using the Sears List as a foundation, the cataloger in a small library can develop a local authority list that is consistent in form and comprehensive for that library. This has proven over the years to be a practical and economical solution to the cataloging needs of small libraries. In other ways, such as the use of uninverted headings only and of popular rather than technical vocabulary, the Sears List is specifically tailored to the needs of small libraries of any kind, including school libraries, small public libraries, church libraries, etc.

Because the Sears List is not a complete authority list, the cataloger using the Sears List must take an active part in developing a larger vocabulary of terms. As an aid in this process we offer the following discussion of the basic principles of subject analysis and the construction and control of subject headings.

2. DETERMINING THE SUBJECT OF THE WORK

The first and most important step in subject cataloging is to ascertain the true subject of the material being cataloged. This concept of "aboutness" should never be far from a subject cataloger's thoughts. It is a serious mistake to think of subject analysis as a matter of sorting through material and fitting it into the available categories, like sorting the mail, rather than focusing first on the material and determining what it is really about.

Many times the subject of a work is readily determined. **Hummingbirds** is obviously the subject of a book entitled *The Complete Book of Hummingbirds*. In others cases the subject is not so easy to discern, because it may be a complex one or the author may not express it in a manner clear to someone unfamiliar with the subject. The subject of a work cannot always be determined from the title alone, which is often uninformative or misleading, and undue dependence on it can result in error. A book entitled *Great Masters in Art* immediately suggests the subject **Artists**, but closer examination may reveal the book to be only about painters, not about artists in general. After reading the title page, the cataloger should examine the table of contents and skim the preface and introduction, and then, if the subject is still not clear, examine the text carefully and read parts of it, if necessary. In the case of nonbook materials, the cataloger should examine the container, the label, any accompanying guides, etc., and view or listen to the contents if possible. Only after this preliminary examination has been made is it possible to determine the subject of a work. If the meaning of technical terminology is not clearly understood, reference sources should be consulted, not only an unabridged dictionary and general encyclopedia, but specialized reference books as well.

Only when the cataloger has determined the subject content of a work and identified it with explicit words can the Sears List be used to advantage. The List is consulted to determine one of three possibilities. If the word the cataloger chose to describe the subject content of the work is an established heading in the List, then that heading should be assigned to the work. If the word the cataloger chose is a synonym or alternate form of an established heading in the List, then the cataloger forgoes the word that first came to mind in favor of the term from the List. A third possibility is that there is no heading in the List for the subject of the work at hand, in which case the cataloger must formulate the appropriate heading, add it to the library's subject authority file with its attendant references, and then assign it to the work.

Many books are about more than one subject. In that case a second or third subject heading is necessary. Theoretically there is no limit to the number of subject entries that could be made for one work, but in practice an excess of entries is a disservice to the user of the catalog. More than three subject headings should be assigned to a single item only after careful consideration. The need for more than three may be due to the cataloger's inability to identify precisely the single broader heading that would cover all the topics in the work. Similarly, a subject heading should not be assigned for a topic that comprises less than one third of a work. The commonest practice, known as the Rule of Three, may be stated as follows: As many as three specific subject headings in a given area may be assigned to a work, but if the work treats of more than three subjects, then a broader heading is used instead and the specific headings are omitted. A work about snakes and lizards, for example, would be assigned the headings **Snakes** and **Lizards**. If the work also included material on turtles, a third heading **Turtles** would be added. But if the work discussed alligators and crocodiles as well, the only subject heading assigned would be **Reptiles**.

Subject headings are used for materials that have definite, definable subjects. There are always a few works so indefinite in their subject content that it is better not to assign a heading at all. Such a work might be a collection of materials produced by several individuals on a variety of topics or one person's random thoughts and ideas. If a cataloger cannot determine a definite subject, the reader is unlikely to find the item under a makeshift or general heading. The headings **Human behavior** and **Happiness**, for example, would be misleading when assigned to a book titled *Appreciation*, which is a personal account of the sources of the author's pleasure in life. The book has no specific subject and so it should be assigned no subject headings.

3. SPECIFIC AND DIRECT ENTRY

The principle of specific and direct entry is fundamental in modern subject cataloging. According to that rule a work is entered in the catalog directly under the most specific subject heading that accurately represents its content. This term should be neither broader nor narrower but co-extensive in scope with the subject of the work cataloged. The principle was definitively formulated by Charles A. Cutter (1837-1903) in his *Rules for a Dictionary Catalog*. Cutter wrote: "Enter a work under its subject-heading, not under the heading of a class which includes that subject." His example is: "Put Lady Cust's book on 'The Cat' under Cat, not under Zoology or Mammals, or Domestic animals; and put Garnier's 'Le Fer' under Iron, not under Metals or Metallurgy." The reason this principle has become sacred to modern cataloging is simply that there is no other way to insure uniformity. In subject cataloging uniformity means simply that all materials on a single topic are assigned the same subject heading. If the headings **Cats**, **Zoology**, **Mammals**, and **Domestic animals** were all equally correct for a book on cats, as they would be without Cutter's rule, there would be no single heading for that topic and consequently no assurance of uniformity. One cataloger could assign the heading **Cats** to Lady Cust's book, another cataloger could assign the heading **Mammals** to another book on cats, and a third cataloguer could assign the heading **Domestic animals** or **Pets** to yet another book on cats. There would then be no simple way to retrieve all the materials on cats in the library's collection.

The principle of specific entry holds that a work is always entered under a specific term rather than under a broader heading that includes the specific concept. This principle is of particular importance to the cataloguer using the Sears List, since the heading of appropriate specificity must be added if it is not already there. If, for example, a work being catalogued is about penguins, it should be entered only under the most specific term that is not narrower than the scope of the book itself, that is, **Penguins**. It should not be assigned the heading **Birds** or **Water birds**. This is true even though the heading **Penguins** does not appear in the List. When a specific subject is not found in the List, the heading for the larger group or category to which it belongs should be consulted, in this case **Birds**. There the cataloger finds a general reference that reads: "SA [See also] types of birds, e.g. **Birds of prey**; **Canaries**; etc. {to be added as needed}." The cataloger must establish the heading **Penguins** as a narrower term under the heading **Birds** and then assign it to the book on penguins. In many cases the most specific entry will be a general subject. A book entitled *Birds of the World* would have the subject heading **Birds**. Even though **Birds** is a very broad term, it is the narrowest term that comprehends the subject content of that work.

Having assigned a work the most specific subject heading that is applicable, the cataloger should not then make an additional entry under a broader heading. A work with the title *Birds of the Ocean* should not be entered under both **Birds** and **Water birds** but only under **Water birds**. To eliminate this duplication, the *See also* references in the public catalog direct the user from the broader subject headings to the more specific ones. At **Birds**, for example, the reference would read: "See also **Birds of prey; Canaries; Pelicans; Penguins; Water birds**," etc.

The principle of direct entry holds that a subject heading should stand as a separate term rather than as a subdivision under a broader heading. If the reader wants information about owls, the direct approach is to consult the catalog under the heading **Owls**, not under the broader subject **Birds** subdivided by the narrower topic **Owls**. In other words, the cataloger has entered the book directly under **Owls**, not indirectly under "Birds—Owls," or under "Birds—Birds of prey—Owls." The latter two subject strings are both specific, but they are not direct.

4. TYPES OF SUBJECT HEADINGS

There are four types of subject headings: topical headings, form headings, geographic headings, and proper names.

4. A. TOPICAL HEADINGS

Topical subject headings are simply the words or phrases for common things or concepts that represent the content of various works. In choosing the word or phrase that makes the best subject heading several things should be considered. The first and most obvious is the literary warrant, or the language of the material being cataloged. The word most commonly used in the literature is most likely the word that best represents the item cataloged. If nine out of ten books on the subject use the phrase "Gun control," there is no reason to use any word or phrase other than **Gun control** as a subject heading, so long as that phrase meets certain other criteria.

A second consideration, and one of the criteria that a subject heading should meet, is that of common usage. In so far as possible a subject heading should represent the common usage of the English language. In American libraries this means current American spelling and terminology: **Labor** not Labour; **Elevators** not Lifts. (In British libraries these choices would be reversed.) Foreign terms such as **Film noir** are not used unless they have been fully incorporated into the English language. By the same token contemporary usage gradually should replace antiquated words or phrases. The heading **Blacks**, for example, replaced **Negroes** as common usage changed. In time the heading **African Americans** was added to the Sears List for greater specificity, as the use of that term stabilized. What is common usage depends, in part, upon who the users of a library are. In most small libraries the popular or common word for a thing is to be preferred to the scientific or technical word, when the two are truly synonymous. For example, **Desert animals** is preferable in most small libraries to **Desert fauna**. In such a case the scientific term should be a *See* reference to the established term.

In order to maintain uniformity in a library catalog two things are necessary. The first is abiding by Cutter's rule of specificity, and the second is choosing a single word or phrase from among its synonyms or near-synonyms in establishing a subject heading. If **Desert animals** and Desert fauna were both allowed as established headings, the material on one subject would end up in two places. Sometimes a single word or phrase must be chosen from among several choices that do not mean exactly the same thing but are too close to be easily distinguished. In the Sears List, for example, **Regional planning** is an established heading with *See* references from County planning, Metropolitan planning, and State planning. The term chosen as the established heading is the one that is most inclusive.

Another important consideration in establishing topical subject headings is that they should be clear and unambiguous. Sometimes the most common term for a topic is not suitable as a subject heading because it is ambiguous. Civil War, for example, must be rejected in favor of **United States—History—1861-1865, Civil War**, since not all civil wars are the American Civil War. The term **Civil wars** could itself become a heading, if it were needed for general materials on rebellions or internal revolutions.

When a single word has several meanings, that word can be used as a subject heading only when it is somehow rendered unambiguous. The word Depression, for example, can mean either an economic or a mental state, but as subject headings one is formulated **Depressions** and the other **Depression (Psychology)**. Stress can mean either stress on materials or stress on the mind, and the two headings are **Strength of materials** and **Stress (Psychology)**. Notice that the ambiguous word is qualified even when the other meaning is expressed in other words. Furthermore, an ambiguous term such as Feedback should be qualified, **Feedback (Psychology)**, even when the other meaning, **Feedback (Electronics)**, does not yet exist in the catalog. Whenever identical words with different meanings are used in the catalog, both require a parenthetical qualifier, which is usually either a broader term or discipline of study, as in the case of **Seals (Animals)** and **Seals (Numismatics)**.

In choosing one term as a subject heading from among several possibilities the cataloger must also think of the spelling, number, and connotations of the various forms. When variant spellings are in use, one must be selected and uniformly applied, such as **Archeology** rather than Archaeology. A decision also must be made between the singular and plural form, which will be further discussed under Grammar of Subject Headings below. Sometimes variant forms of words can have different connotations, as with Arab, Arabian, and Arabic. It may seem inconsistent to use all three forms in subject headings, but, in fact, they are used consistently in the following ways: Arab relating to the people; Arabian referring to the geographical area and to horses; and Arabic for the language, script, or literature.

4. B. FORM HEADINGS

The second kind of heading that is found in a library catalog is the form heading, which describes not the subject content of a work but its form. In other words, a form heading tells us not what a work is about but what it is. Form in this context means intellectual form of the materials rather than the physical form of the item. The physical forms of such nonbook materials as videorecordings, electronic resources, etc., are considered general material designations (GMD), a part of the descriptive cataloging, rather than subject headings.

Some form headings describe the general arrangement of the material and the purpose of the work, such as **Almanacs**, **Directories**, **Gazetteers**, and **Encyclopedias and dictionaries**. These headings are customarily assigned to individual works as well as to materials about such forms. Theoretically, at least, any form can also be a topic, since it is possible for someone to write a book about almanacs or gazetteers.

Other form headings are the names of literary forms and genres. Headings for the major literary forms, **Fiction**, **Poetry**, **Drama**, and **Essays**, are usually used as topical subject headings. As form headings they are used for collections only rather than for individual literary works. Minor literary forms, also known as genres, such as **Science fiction**, **Epistolary poetry**, and **Children's plays**, are much more numerous and are often assigned to individual literary works. These headings will be discussed at greater length below under Literature. The distinction between form headings and topical headings in literature can sometimes be made by using the singular form for the topical heading and the plural for the form heading. **Short story**, for example, is topical, for materials about the short story as a literary form, while **Short stories** is a form. Likewise, **Essay** is topical, while **Essays** is a form. The peculiarities of language, however, do not always permit this distinction.

4. C. GEOGRAPHIC HEADINGS

Many works in a library's collection are about geographic areas, countries, cities, etc. The appropriate subject heading for such a work is the name of the place in question. Geographic headings are the established names of individual places, from places as large as **Africa** to places as small as **Walden Pond (Mass.)**. They signify not only physical places but also political jurisdictions. These headings differ from topical subject headings in that they refer to a unique entity rather than to an abstraction or category of things.

The Sears List does not attempt to provide geographic headings, which are numerous far beyond the scope of a single volume. The geographic headings that are found in Sears, such as **United States**, **Ohio**, and **Chicago (Ill.)**, are offered only as examples. The cataloger using the Sears List must establish geographic headings as needed with the aid of standard references sources. Some suggested sources are the most current editions of *The Columbia Gazetteer of the World*; *National Geographic Atlas of the World*; *Statesman's Year-book*; *Times Atlas of the World*; and *Merriam-Webster's Geographical Dictionary* and the Web site of the U.S. Board of Geographic Names. The geographic headings and geographic subdivisions found in Sears follow the form of abbreviation for qualifying states, provinces, etc., found in Appendix B (Abbreviations) of *AACR2*.

4. D. NAMES

Still other materials in a library's collection are about individual persons, families, corporate bodies, literary works, motion pictures, etc. The appropriate heading for such material is the unique name of the entity in question. The three major types of name headings are personal names, corporate names, and uniform titles. Individual or personal name headings are usually established in the inverted form, with dates if necessary, and with *See* references from alternate forms. The heading **Clinton, Bill**, for example, would require a *See* reference from "Clinton, William Jefferson," and if the library had material about any other person called Bill Clinton, the name heading for the president would need to take the form **Clinton, Bill, 1946-** . Corporate name headings are the commonly established names of corporate bodies, such as business firms, institutions, buildings, sports teams, performing groups, etc. Materials about a corporate body, such as **Rockefeller Center** or **Fort Lauderdale International Boat Show**, are entered directly under the corporate name heading as a subject. Uniform titles are the established names of sacred scriptures, anonymous literary works, periodicals, motion pictures, radio and television programs, etc. Materials about a particular motion picture or about an anonymous literary work, for example, are entered directly under the uniform title, such as **Gone with the wind (Motion picture)** or **Beowulf**, as a subject. Materials about a literary work with a known author are entered under a name-title heading consisting of the author's name followed by the title, such as **Shakespeare, William, 1564-1616. Hamlet** for a book about Shakespeare's play.

Like geographic headings, name headings are numerous beyond the scope of the Sears List and must be established by the cataloger as needed. Suggested sources for personal and corporate names are *Who's Who*; *Who's Who in America*; *Merriam-Webster's Biographical Dictionary*; *The Dictionary of National Biography*; and the *Encyclopedia of Associations* and the Library of Congress Name Authories on the Web. General encyclopedias and standard reference works limited to specific fields are also useful sources for names.

5. THE GRAMMAR OF SUBJECT HEADINGS

While many subject headings are simple terms like **Reptiles** or **Electricity**, other subjects can be very complex, in some cases involving several levels of subdivision. In order to construct subject headings consistently the cataloger should understand the grammar of subject headings.

5. A. THE FORMS OF HEADINGS

5. A. i. Single Nouns

A single noun is the ideal type of subject heading when the language supplies it. Such terms are not only the simplest in form but often the easiest to comprehend. A choice must be made between the singular and plural forms of a noun. The plural is the more common, but in practice both are used. Abstract ideas and the names of disciplines of study are usually stated in the singular, such as **Biology** or **Existentialism**. An action, such as **Editing** or **Fraud**, is also expressed in the singular. Headings for concrete things are most commonly in the plural form, when those things can be counted, such as **Playgrounds** or **Children**. Concrete things that cannot be counted, such as **Steel** or **Milk**, obviously remain in the singular. In most cases common sense can be relied upon. In some instances both the singular and the plural of a word can be subject headings when they have two different meanings, such as **Theater** for the activity and **Theaters** for the buildings. In the case of **Arts** and **Art**, the one means the arts in general, while the other means the fine and decorative arts specifically.

5. A. ii. Compound Headings

Subject headings that consist of two nouns joined by "and" are of several types. Some headings link two things because together they form a single concept or topic, such as **Bow and arrow** or **Good and evil**; because they are so closely related they are rarely treated separately, such as **Forests and forestry** or **Publishers and publishing**; or because they are so closely synonymous they are seldom distinguished, such as **Cities and towns** or **Rugs and carpets**. Other headings that link two words with "and" stand for the relationship between the two things, such as **Church and state** or **Television and children**. Compound headings of this type should not be made without careful consideration. Often there is a better way to formulate the heading. A heading like "Medicine and religion," for example, is less accurate than the form established in Sears, which is **Medicine—Religious aspects**. (There is not likely to be material on the medical aspects of religion.) One question that arises in forming compound headings is word order. The only rule is that common usage takes precedence (no one says "Arrow and bow"), and, where there is no established common usage, alphabetic order is preferred. Whatever the order, a *See* reference should be made from either the second term or from the pair of terms reversed, as in Forestry, *See* **Forests and forestry**, or Children and television, *See* **Television and children**.

5. A. iii. Adjectives with Nouns

Often a specific concept is best expressed by a noun with an adjective, such as **Unemployment insurance** or **Buddhist art**. In the past the expression was frequently inverted (Insurance, Unemployment; Art, Buddhist). There were two possible reasons for inversion: 1) an assumption was made that the searcher would think first of the noun; or 2) the noun was placed first in order to keep all aspects of a broad subject together in an alphabetical listing, as in a card catalog. In recent years these arguments have been abandoned in favor of the direct order because users have become more and more accustomed to searching in the order of natural language. The only headings that have been retained in Sears in the inverted form are proper names, including the names of battles and massacres.

5. A. iv. Phrase Headings

Some concepts that involve two or more elements can be expressed only by more or less complex phrases. These are the least satisfactory headings, as they offer the greatest variation in wording, are often the longest, and may not be thought of readily by either the maker or the user of the catalog, but for many topics the English language seems to offer no more compact terminology. Examples are **Insects as carriers of disease** and **Violence in popular culture**.

5. B. SUBDIVISIONS

Specific entry in subject headings is achieved in two basic ways. The first, as noted above, is the creation of narrower terms as needed. The second is the use of subdivisions under an established term to designate aspects of that term, such as **Birds—Eggs** or **Food—Analysis**, or the form of the item itself, such as **Agriculture—Bibliography**. The scope of the Sears List can be expanded far beyond the actual headings printed through the use of subdivisions. Some subdivisions are applicable to only a few subjects. *Eggs*, for example, is applicable only under headings for oviparous animals. Other subdivisions, such as *Analysis*, are applicable under many subjects. Still other subdivisions, such as *Bibliography*, are applicable under nearly any heading. The Sears List does not attempt to list all possible subdivisions, but all those that are most likely to be used in a small library are included. For every subdivision included there is an instruction in the List for the use of that subdivision. Some subdivisions are also headings, such as **Bibliography**, and in such cases the instruction is given in a general reference as part of the entry for that heading. Other subdivisions, such as *Economic aspects*, are not themselves headings, and in such cases the instruction for the use of the subdivision is a free-standing general reference in the alphabetical List.

5. B. i. Topical Subdivisions

Topical subdivisions are those subdivisions that brings out the aspect of a subject or point of view presented in a particular work. A work may be a history of the subject, as in **Clothing and dress—History**; or it may deal with the philosophy of the subject, as in **Religion—Philosophy**; research in the field, as in **Oceanography—Research**; the laws about it, as in **Automobiles—Law and legislation**; or how to study or teach the subject, as in **Mathematics—Study and teaching**. The advantage of subdivisions over phrase headings for complex subjects is that uniformity can be more readily achieved with subdivisions. Once the subdivisions have been established, they can be appended to any applicable subject heading without guessing or straining the language for a suitable phrase. Subject strings with topical subdivisions can be read backwards: **Clothing and dress—History**, for example, means the history of clothing and dress, and **Oceanography—Research—Ethical aspects** means ethical aspects of research in the field of oceanography.

5. B. ii. Geographic Subdivisions

Another aspect of subjects that can be brought out in subdivisions is geographic specificity. The unit used as a subdivision may be the name of a country, state, city, or other geographic area. A topical heading with a geographic subdivision means simply that topic in a particular place. **Bridges—France**, for example, is the appropriate subject string for a work on bridges in France, and **Agriculture—Ohio** for a work on agriculture in Ohio.

Not every topical heading lends itself logically or practically to geographic subdivision. Some topics, such as **Fractions** or **Intuition**, are either non-physical or too abstract to have a geographic location. Other headings, such as **Pet therapy** or **Parenting**, are unlikely to be dealt with geographically, at least in works that would be found in a small library. Still other headings, such as **Exploration** or **Church history**, are not subdivided geographically because the same term is used instead as a subdivision under the geographic heading, as in **Arctic regions—Exploration** or **United States—Church history**.

Many subject headings in the Sears List are followed by the parenthetical phrase (May subdiv. geog.). In application this means that if the work in hand deals with that subject in general, only the heading itself is used; but if it deals with the subject in a particular place, the heading may be subdivided geographically. Some small libraries limit the use of geographic subdivision to countries other than the United States, since most of their material will be concerned with the United States. Furthermore, if a library prefers geographic subdivisions for subjects that are not so indicated in the List, the library should feel free to add them, provided, of course, that the heading is not itself used as a subdivision under geographic headings.

Some subjects, mostly in the fields of art and music, have general references that read: "SA [See also] art of particular countries or regions, e.g. **Greek art**." For these headings the geographic qualification is conveyed by a modifying adjective rather than by a subdivision. The Sears List historically has never distinguished between French art and Art in France (which is not necessarily French). Should a library have sufficient material to warrant such a distinction, **Art—France** could be established in addition to **French art**, which is suggested, and the art of particular countries could also be subdivided by other countries, as in **Italian art—Great Britain**. Such a decision should be based on the materials at hand and the purpose and needs of the library.

Geographic subdivisions can be either direct or indirect. The Sears List uses the direct form of subdivision, whereby topics are subdivided directly by cities, counties, metropolitan areas, etc., as in **Theater—Paris (France)** or **Hospitals—Chicago (Ill.)**. The indirect form of subdivision, used by the Library of Congress and certain other subject heading systems, interposes the name of the country or state (the larger geographic area) between the topical subject and the smaller area, as in "Theater—France—Paris" and "Hospitals—Illinois—Chicago."

5. B. iii. Chronological Subdivisions

In any catalog, large or small, there will be many works on American history. If these works are all entered under the general heading **United States—History**, the library user is required to look through many entries to find materials about any specific period of American history. Chronological subdivisions, which correspond to generally accepted periods of a country's history or to the spans of time most frequently treated in the literature, make such a search much simpler by bringing together all works on a single period of history, such as **United States—History—1945-1953**. If a chronological period has been given a name, this name is included in the heading following the dates, as in **United States—History—1600-1775, Colonial period**.

Historical periods vary from one country to another and usually correspond to major dynastic or governmental changes. The Sears List includes chronological subdivisions only for those countries about which a small library is likely to have much historical material, with the greatest number of period subdivisions under **United States**, **Canada**, **Great Britain**, **France**, **Germany**, and **Italy**, and a few subdivisions only under several other countries. Whenever there is only a small amount of material on the history of a country, it should simply be entered under the name of the country with the subdivision *History*, without a chronological subdivision. For most small libraries in North America the heading **Turkey—History** will suffice for all historical material about Turkey, even though Turkey has a very long history. If, however, a library should acquire a large amount of historical material about any such country or region, period subdivisions should be established beyond those spelled out in the Sears List. For these the cataloger may wish to consult *LC Period Subdivisions under Names of Places*.

The subdivision *Politics and government* under countries should be reserved for general and theoretical material. Historical material on the politics and government of a country are entered under the name of the country subdivided by *History* with or without a further chronological subdivision. Other kinds of subjects, especially those relating to literature and the arts, may also be subdivided chronologically as appropriate, usually by century.

5. B. iv. Form Subdivisions

The most common item found in a library is an expository prose treatise on a subject. Many works, however, present their material in other forms, such as lists, tables, maps, pictures, etc. Form subdivisions specify the form an item takes. Like form headings they tell what an item is rather than what it is about. Some of the most common form subdivisions are *Bibliography*; *Catalogs*; *Dictionaries*; *Directories*; *Gazetteers*; *Handbooks, manuals, etc.*; *Indexes*; *Maps*; *Pictorial works*; *Portraits*; *Registers*; and *Statistics*.

Topical headings with form subdivisions, such as **Children's literature—Bibliography** or **Geology—Maps**, render such works retrievable by form and separate them from expository treatises. Apart from a few examples, these combinations of subject heading with form subdivision are not given in the Sears List but are to be added by the cataloger as needed. Form subdivisions are particularly valuable under headings for the large fields of knowledge that are represented by many entries in a library's catalog. In applying form subdivisions the cataloger should be guided by the character of an item itself, not by the title. Many works with titles beginning with Outline of, Handbook of, or Manual of, are in fact expository works. For example, H. G. Wells's *Outline of History* and H. J. Rose's *Handbook of Latin Literature* are lengthy, comprehensive treatises, and to use the form subdivisions that the titles suggest would be inaccurate. Other so-titled Outlines or Manuals or Handbooks may prove to be bibliographies, dictionaries, or statistics of the subject.

5. B. v. The Order of Subdivisions

At the Subject Subdivision Conference that took place at Airlie House, Virginia, in May 1991, organized by the Library of Congress, it was recommended that subdivisions follow the standard order of **[Topical]—[Geographic]—[Chronological]—[Form]**. Since that time the library community has endeavored to implement that recommendation. Only in a few subject areas, especially in the field of art, have exceptions been made. A cataloger using the Sears List can safely assume that subject strings made in the recommended order will provide the greatest uniformity. By following this standard the cataloger will know, for example, to prefer **Elderly—Housing—United States** to "Elderly—United States—Housing," and **Sports—United States—Statistics** to "Sports—Statistics—United States." (*Housing* is a topical subdivision, and *Statistics* is a form subdivision.)

5. B. vi. Geographic Headings Subdivided by Topic

A longstanding exception to the practice of subdividing topics geographically, and one that remains apart from the Airlie House recommendation, is that of subdividing geographic headings by topics, when those topics pertain to the history, geography, or politics of a place. For works discussing the history of California, a census of Peru, the government of Italy, the boundaries of Bolivia, the population of Paris, or the climate of Alaska, the appropriate subject strings would be **California—History**; **Peru—Census**; **Italy—Politics and government**; **Bolivia—Boundaries**; **Paris (France)—Population**; and **Alaska—Climate**.

Many subdivisions, such as *Defenses* or *Description and travel*, are used only under geographic headings; many subdivisions are never used under geographic headings; and others, such as *History* or *Biography*, are used under geographic headings exactly as they are under topical subjects. Specific instructions for the application of subdivisions are given at the general reference for the subdivision in the List. For example, at **Census** in the List the general reference reads: "SA [See also] names of countries, cities, etc., with the subdivision *Census* {to be added as needed}." Similar instructions appear under **Boundaries**; **Climate**; **Population**; etc. Some topics that are used as subdivisions under geographic headings are applicable to countries only. The subdivision *Foreign relations*, for example, can be used only under countries, since only countries have foreign relations. The instructions for applications are explicit. At *Foreign relations* in the List, for example, the general reference reads: "USE names of countries with the subdivision *Foreign relations*, e.g. **United States—Foreign relations** {to be added as needed}."

A list of suggested topical subdivisions that may be used under the name of any city is given in the List under **Chicago (Ill.)**; those that may be used under the name of any state are listed under **Ohio**; and those that may be used under the name of any country or region, except for *History* further subdivided chronologically, are given under **United States**. Since each country's history is unique, the period subdivisions for its history are also unique.

5. B. vii. Local Materials

If for any reason a library wishes to keep state, local, or community area materials together in the catalog, those materials may constitute an exception to the practice of geographic subdivision. All local materials are then entered under the name of the place with all topics as subdivisions. If, for example, a library in Honolulu chose this option, the headings **Public buildings—Honolulu (Hawaii)** and **Bridges—Honolulu (Hawaii)** would become **Honolulu (Hawaii)—Public buildings** and **Honolulu (Hawaii)—Bridges**. Materials with geographic specificity other than local materials would still be treated in the ordinary way, with most topics subdivided geographically.

6. SOME DIFFICULT AREAS OF APPLICATION

In many areas the application of subject headings and their appropriate subdivisions is a simple and straightforward matter. There are, however, areas in which either the complexity of the material or the vagaries of the English language create persistent problems. Even in these areas, by maintaining sound principles, following instructions carefully, and using common sense, it is possible to catalog library materials in such a way that users can find what they need. Some of these problem areas are dealt with here.

6. A. BIOGRAPHY

Discussions of biography as a form of writing are given the topical subject heading **Biography as a literary form**. Works that are themselves biographies are given either the form heading **Biography** or the form subdivision *Biography*. Such works are considered here in two groups, collective biographies and individual biographies.

6. A. i. Collective Biographies

Collective biographies are works containing biographies of more than three persons. Works consisting of biographies of three persons or fewer are treated as individual biographies and given headings for the names of the persons individually. Collective biographies not limited to any area or to any class of persons, such as *Lives of Famous Men and Women*, are simply assigned the heading **Biography**. Often collective biographies are devoted to persons of a single country or geographic area, such as *Leaders of the Arab World*, or *Dictionary of*

American Biography; or to ethnic groups, such as *Who's Who among Hispanic Americans*. For such works the appropriate subject heading is the name of the geographic area or ethnic group with the subdivision *Biography*, in this case **Arab countries—Biography**; **United States—Biography**; and **Hispanic Americans—Biography**. If there are many entries under any such heading, the biographical dictionaries, which list a large number of names in alphabetical order, may be separated from the works with longer articles intended for continuous reading by adding the form subdivision *Dictionaries*. The heading for such a work as *Dictionary of American Biography* or *Who's Who in America* would then be **United States—Biography—Dictionaries**.

Some collective biographies are devoted to lives of a particular class of persons, such as women, or persons of a particular occupation or profession, such as librarians. These are entered under the heading for the class of persons or occupational group with the subdivision *Biography*, such as **Women—Biography** or **Librarians—Biography**. Still other collective biographies are devoted to any or all persons connected with a particular industry, institution, or field of endeavor. For these works the appropriate heading is the heading for that industry, institution, or field with the subdivision *Biography*, such as **Computer industry—Biography**; **Catholic Church—Biography**; or **Baseball—Biography**. A subject is usually broader in scope than a single category of persons associated with that subject, and likewise **Baseball—Biography** is broader than **Baseball players—Biography** and would be more suitable for a collective biography that includes managers, owners of teams, and other persons associated with the sport.

6. A. ii. Individual Biographies

Usually the only subject heading needed for the life of an individual is the name of the person, established in the same way as an author entry. The rules for establishing names are in *AACR2*. If a work is an autobiography, the author's name is entered in the bibliographic record twice, once as the author and again as the subject. There are a few individual persons about whom much has been written other than biographical material, such as works about their writings or other activities. In such cases, subdivisions are added to the person's name to specify the various aspects treated, among them *Biography*. As examples of such persons, the Sears List includes **Jesus Christ** and **Shakespeare, William, 1564-1616**, with subdivisions appropriate to material written about them. The subdivisions listed under Shakespeare may also be used, if needed, under the name of any voluminous author. The subdivisions provided under **Presidents—United States** may also be used under the name of any president or other ruler, if applicable. The subdivisions needed will vary from one individual to another. Different topics will be applicable, for example, to the material on Martin Luther, Napoleon, and Sigmund Freud. It should be noted that this use of subdivisions represents the exceptional, not the usual, treatment. For most individual biographies the name alone is sufficient.

Occasionally a biography will include enough material about the field in which the person worked that a second subject heading is required in addition to the personal name. A life of Mary Baker Eddy, for example, may include an account of the development of Christian Science substantial enough to warrant the subject heading **Christian Science—History**. The additional subject headings should be used only when the work contains a significant amount of material about the field of endeavor in addition to the subject's personal life, not simply because the subject was prominent in that field.

It is not customary practice to categorize the subjects of individual biographies by race, sex, occupation, etc. with the subdivision *Biography*. Headings such as **African American musicians—Biography** or **Women politicians—Biography** are appropriate only to collective biographies. Some catalogers are tempted to assign such headings to individual biographies as well, but there are several compelling reasons for not doing so. The first and most obvious is that in the case of a collective biography it is the author or compiler of the work who classifies or categorizes the persons included, not the cataloger. For a book such as

Black Women Scientists in the United States, the subject heading **African American women scientists** is applicable because the author has selected the subjects of the biographies expressly for being African Americans, women, and scientists. For a collective biography entitled *Just as I Am: Famous Men and Women with Disabilities*, the subject string **Handicapped—Biography** would be appropriate because the author has written about several handicapped persons with their handicapped condition as the common feature. It would be impertinent labeling, however, for a cataloger to assign the subject string **Handicapped—Biography** to a biography of an individual person who happened to be handicapped, even if that condition were an important element of the person's story. In other words, three or more handicapped persons constitute the category Handicapped, but a single person can never constitute a category. Entering individual biographies under categories of persons violates the principle of specific entry. The only heading that is neither broader nor narrower but is co-extensive in scope with the subject content of the work is the personal name heading for the person written about. *See also* references can be made, if such references are deemed useful, from a category of persons to the names of individuals about whom the library has material. At the heading **African American women authors**, for example, one would then find any books that are really about African American women authors, followed by a reference: "See also **Angelou, Maya; McMillan, Terry; Morrison, Toni**," etc. Increasingly, in an online environment, tagging or bookmarking is used to identify examples of things. Tag are typically flexible and uncontrolled and serve local needs. As such they can be inconsistent without compromising the essential integrity of the catalog.

6. B. NATIONALITIES

An aspect of subject headings fraught with confusion is that of nationalities. Even though some headings are given national adjectives, the general rule is that the national aspects of subjects are expressed by geographic subdivisions under the topical subject headings. Headings for things that are always stationary are never given national adjectives but are instead subdivided geographically, such as **Architecture—France**. Things that are not stationary are also usually expressed as topical headings with a geographic subdivision, such as **Automobiles—Germany** or **Corporations—Japan**. When those things are replicated or transported to foreign countries, however, they are given national adjectives to express national style, ownership, or origin, and subdivided by the place where they are found, such as **German automobiles—United States** or **Japanese corporations—France**.

Headings for topics in literature and the arts are given national adjectives to express national character, such as **American literature**, **Spanish art**, etc. These headings may then be subdivided geographically by any place except for the country expressed in the national adjective. **American literature—Southern States** is therefore allowable, but not "Spanish art—Spain."

In the area of people, all headings for categories of persons are subdivided geographically in the Sears List with the exception of **Authors**, **Novelists**, **Dramatists**, and **Poets**, which are given national adjectives. All other categories of writers, such as **Biographers, Journalists**, etc., are subdivided geographically. A collective biography of American poets would be entered under **American poets—Biography**, but a collective biography of American composers or journalists would be given the heading **Composers—United States—Biography** or **Journalists—United States—Biography**. When a book deals with a category of persons from one country living or working in a foreign country, such as American composers in France, the book requires two subject strings rather than one, in this case **Composers—United States** and **Americans—France**.

6. C. LITERATURE

The field of literature presents special difficulties in cataloging because it includes two distinct types of material. The first consists of works about literature, and such works are assigned topical subject headings for whatever they are about. The second consists of literary works themselves, and those works are assigned form headings to describe what the item is rather than what it is about.

6. C. i. Works about Literature

The subject headings for works about the various literary forms are the headings for those forms, such as **Drama**, **Fiction**, and **Poetry**. A work about poetry is simply given the heading **Poetry**. Topical subdivisions are added to such headings as needed. A work about the history of poetry or about the criticism of poetry would be entered under **Poetry—History and criticism**. A work about the technique of writing plays would be entered under **Drama—Technique**. Form subdivisions may also be used under these headings to indicate the form the work takes, such as **Drama—Dictionaries** or **Poetry—Indexes**. In addition to the major forms of literature there are also lesser genres, which are subsets of the major literary forms, such as **Science fiction** or **Epic poetry**. These headings are also applicable to works about literature, with topical and form subdivisions added as needed.

Literary works are commonly studied and written about according to categories characterized by nationality, language, religions, etc. The primary consideration in discussing literature is nationality, as in **American literature**, **Mexican literature**, and **Brazilian literature**. These topics are never dealt with as subsets of **English literature**, **Spanish literature**, or **Portuguese literature** simply because they are written in the English, Spanish, and Portuguese languages. Nationality takes precedence over language. Only a few national literatures are included in the List, and others are to be added as needed. Works about the major literary forms of national literatures are entered under the direct phrase, such as **Italian poetry** or **Russian fiction**, and again specific aspects or forms are expressed by subdivisions, as in **Italian poetry—History and criticism** or **Russian fiction—Dictionaries**. The subdivisions that appear under **English literature** may be used under any national literature, and headings for the major literary forms for any national literature may be formulated by substituting its national name for the word English.

Apart from national literatures there are also literatures characterized by areas larger than countries, such as **Latin American literature** or **African literature**; by languages not limited to or identified with a single country, such as **Latin literature** or **Arabic literature**; or by religions, such as **Catholic literature** or **Buddhist literature**. All these kinds of literature are treated in the same way as national literatures. Where a national literature is written in two or more prominent languages, the language is identified in parentheses after the name of the literature for material specifically limited to literature in that language, such as **Canadian literature (French)**. Materials about the literatures of minority groups within a country, written in the predominant language of that country's literature, are identified by subdivisions indicating the author group under the name of the literature, such as **American literature—African American authors**. Materials about the literatures of indigenous minority groups written in their own language are given the name of the language, such as **Navajo literature**.

6. C. ii. Literary Works

Items that are literary works themselves are of two types: collections of several authors, or anthologies, and works by a single author, or individual literary works. Literary anthologies are given a heading for the most specific literary form that includes every item in the anthology. Very general anthologies are given broad headings, such as **Literature—Collections**; **Poetry—Collections**; or **Drama—Collections**. Anthologies of national literatures and the forms of national literatures are given the headings for those literatures or forms with the subdivision *Collections*, such as **American literature—Collections** and **Italian poetry—Collections**. Headings for minor literary genres, such as **Science fiction** or **Pastoral poetry**, are usually assigned to anthologies without any subdivision.

Traditionally the literary works of individual authors receive no subject headings. Literary works are best known by author and title, and readers usually want a specific novel or play, or poetry by a specific poet—material that can be located in the catalog by the author and title entries. Headings describing the major literary forms (such as **Drama**, **Fiction**, and **Poetry**) and the headings for the major forms of a national literature (such as **Irish drama**, **Russian fiction**, and **Italian poetry**) are never assigned to an individual work or to a collection by a single author. It would be counterproductive, for example, to assign the heading **Fiction** to every novel in a library's collection, since the numbers of records with the same heading would be impractically large. Furthermore, the form and national origin of a work are expressed in the classification.

In recent years, however, many libraries have felt the need for access by genre to individual works of imaginative literature. In the Sears List the headings for minor literary forms and genres—such as **Ballads**, **Fables**, **Fairy tales**, **Horror fiction**, **Science fiction**, etc.—are identified in the scope notes as applicable to individual works as well as to collections and materials about the topic. If there is no scope note indicating that a literature heading can be applied to an individual work, it can be assumed that it is not intended to be so applied. This policy is in accordance with the *Guidelines on Subject Access to Individual Works of Fiction, Drama, etc.* prepared by the Subcommittee on Subject Access to Individual Works of Fiction, Drama, etc., of the ALA Subject Analysis Committee (ALA, 1990; 2nd ed., 2000). It varies from the usage of the Library of Congress *Subject Cataloging Manual* in that it allows form and genre access to certain kinds of literary works that are often requested in libraries. Genre headings with national or linguistic adjectives, such as **Australian science fiction** or **Latin epic poetry**, are applicable to collections but are never assigned to individual works. If they were assigned to individual works, since all authors fall into the purview of one nationality or another, there would be nothing remaining under the heading **Science fiction** or **Epic poetry** but collections of international scope. Likewise, the cataloger is discouraged from adding the qualifier "juvenile" to the genre headings. The subdivision *—Juvenile literature* may be added to genre headings in libraries where it is necessary to distinguish juvenile materials from adult materials, that is, in libraries not devoted exclusively or primarily to children's materials, or where juvenile material is not indicated in the shelf number. No other subdivision is ever applicable to genre headings, as applied to individual works.

The cataloger is also discouraged, except in the most unusual cases, from devising new genre terms. The *Guidelines on Subject Access* of the ALA aim to limit the number of genre terms in order to bring like material together, while the proliferation of genres and sub-genres would only scatter like material and do the user a disservice. As stated on page 4 of the *Guidelines*, "Genre terms are determined by convention, as set by the bibliographic community of publishers, booksellers, librarians, and readers." It is only by conforming to these conventions that the application of genre headings to individual works is really useful.

In some libraries subject access is provided to works of literature by using any applicable subject heading from the List with the subdivision *Fiction*, *Drama*, or *Poetry*. Hence a collection of stories all set in Los Angeles could be assigned the heading **Los Angeles (Calif.)—Fiction**; a collections of plays in which the main characters are all nurses could be assigned the heading **Nurses—Drama**; and a volume of poems by several authors all on the theme of baseball could be assigned the heading **Baseball—Poetry**. Personal and corporate names can always be added to the List in order to be used with the subdivisions *Fiction*, *Drama*, and *Poetry* to provide subject access to literary collections that deal with real persons or corporate entities.

Providing the same kind of access by setting, character, or theme to individual works of fiction, drama, or poetry is more problematic. For the collection of stories set in Los Angeles, the appropriate level of specificity can be determined by finding what is common to all the stories. The plays about nurses may be about a variety of nurses, one elderly, one

Hispanic American, one male, etc., but their being nurses is what they have in common. The topic **Nurses**, then, is of equal specificity with the collection itself. In individual stories or plays, however, the characters and settings are unique. All subject headings are all less specific than a unique character or a unique situation, and to assign any of them is to violate the principle of specificity and abandon uniformity in cataloging.

It is the case, nonetheless, that some libraries, for the purpose of readers' advisory or for curriculum enhancement, require the application of topical subjects and geographic headings to individual works of fiction, drama, and poetry. In this endeavor they leave behind the logic of subject analysis and embrace a kind of tagging or labeling that is approximate and pragmatic and not subject to hard rules. Even without the principles of specificity and uniformity, however, there are still some guidelines that may be useful in the application of topical subject and geographic headings to individual literary works:

1)   Use only terms that come readily to mind. Only if a novel is extensively set in the milieu of the motion picture industry, for example, would the heading **Motion picture industry—Fiction** be suitable.

2)   Use only terms that are specific enough to limit retrieval in a meaningful way. Headings such as **Family life—Fiction** or **Popular culture—Fiction** are dubiously useful, since they would apply equally to innumerable novels.

3)   Use only discrete terms, not terms that combine two or more concepts. Use two headings, such as **Hispanic Americans—Fiction** and **Nurses—Fiction** instead of **Hispanic American nurses—Fiction**.

4)   Apply headings for categories of persons only when the main character or several principal characters are representative of that category in a more than incidental way.

5)   Use geographic headings only when the setting of a novel is prominent and central to the work. All novels are set somewhere, but many novels have very little in the way of local color.

6)   In applying geographic headings, use only place names of intermediate specificity. Headings for countries are usually too broad for purposes of setting or local color. Only a few novels of epic scope ever deal with the history and geography of an entire country, and the concept of local color implies something more limited than a country. On the other hand the names of most towns and villages are unknown outside their own region. For most novels the most useful geographic headings will be the names of states or regions and certain large cities.

7)   If both a topical subject and a geographic location are central to a work, they should be expressed separately rather than as a subject string.

8)   Historical novels should be given headings only for the broadest historical periods under a place name, usually a century. The only exception to this rule would be for a few distinct periods or events that have stimulated a great number of literary works, such as **United States—History—1861-1865, Civil War—Fiction**.

9)   Do not hesitate to catalog an individual work of fiction, drama, or poetry without topical or geographic headings. Many literary works do not lend themselves to this kind of treatment, and to go beyond the obvious will only lead users to items that do not satisfy their needs.

In applying topical and geographic headings to individual works of fiction, drama, and poetry, the most important rule is to remember or imagine the needs of the users in a particular library setting, either readers who want novels, plays, etc., with a particular theme or setting, or teachers who need fictional materials on curriculum topics.

6. C. iii. Themes in Literature

Some libraries have a significant amount of material about topics, locales, or themes in imaginative literature. The appropriate headings for such material is simply "Topic in literature," according to the pattern found in the Sears List under **Literature—Themes**, such as **Dogs in literature**, **Ohio in literature**, etc. Headings of this type are for critical discussions only, not for literary works. Materials about the depiction of historical persons in drama, fiction, or poetry are entered under the person's name with the subdivision *In literature*, such as **Napoleon I, Emperor of the French, 1769-1821—In literature**. Materials about the depiction of a particular war in drama, fiction, or poetry are entered under the heading for the war with the subdivision *Literature and the war*, such as **World War, 1939-1945—Literature and the war**.

6. D. WARS AND EVENTS

Catalogers are often called upon to formulate headings as needed for wars and current events, when those wars or events generate books and other library materials. Wars fought between two or more nations are given a name, followed by a date or dates, as appropriate, such as **War of 1812**; **Israel-Arab War, 1967**; **World War, 1939-1945**; etc. Civil wars, insurrections, and invasions are entered under the history of the country involved (following the dates, as with other historical periods), such as **United States—History—1861-1865, Civil War**; **Cuba—History—1961, Invasion**; etc.

Events of short duration, including battles, are dealt with as isolated topics rather than as periods in a country's history. Events that have names are given a heading for the name, followed by the place, and then by the date, such as **Tiananmen Square Incident, Beijing (China), 1989**. Battles are entered under the name of the battle, but in the inverted form, with the place of the battle qualified as needed, such as **Hastings (East Sussex, England), Battle of, 1066**. Recurring events, such as games, festivals, etc., are given the recurring name, followed by the date, with the place in parentheses, if the place changes, such as **Olympic Games, 1996 (Atlanta, Ga.)**. Unnamed events, such as individual tornadoes, are entered under the kind of event subdivided by the place of the event, such as **Tornadoes—Moore (Okla.)**.

6. E. NATIVE AMERICANS

The heading **Native Americans** may be subdivided geographically by continent, region, country, state, or city. Headings for individual nations or tribes of Native Americans may be established as needed according to the traditional formulation, such as **Aztecs** and **Navajo Indians**. Headings for classes of persons among the Native Americans, such as Women or Children, and for things distinctly ethnic, such as Medicine or Music, are expressed as phrase headings, such as **Native American women**, **Native American children**, **Native American medicine**, and **Native American music**. Topics not of an ethnic nature, such as Housing or Social conditions, are expressed as subdivisions under **Native Americans**, such as **Native Americans—Housing** and **Native Americans—Social conditions**.

6. F. GOVERNMENT POLICY

Following the principle that subject headings ought to reflect the common usage, subject headings relating to government policy are phrase headings when they apply to something general or when there is a common phrase available, such as **Fiscal policy** or **Social policy**.

Where there is not a ready phrase available, the heading is formulated by the thing the policy applies to with the subdivision —*Government policy*, such as **Genetic engineering—Government policy**.

6. G. MYTHOLOGY AND FOLKLORE

In general, deities that are still worshipped in the modern world are treated as religion rather than mythology. Ancient mythologies are expressed in phrase headings, such as **Celtic mythology** or **Roman mythology**. Materials on individual deities or legendary characters are given the name of the deity or character appropriately qualified, such as **Vesta (Roman deity)** or **Paris (Legendary character)**. Materials on a theme in mythology are assigned a heading for that theme, similar to a theme in literature, such as **Fire in mythology**. Unlike mythology, folklore pertains to modern peoples as well as ancient. The folklore of a people, that is, stories based on oral rather than written traditions, is expressed in subject headings by the name of the people subdivided by *Folklore*, such as **Inuit—Folklore**. Topics in folklore are expressed by the topic subdivided by *Folklore*, such as **Plants—Folklore**. Materials on the collective folklore of a place are assigned the heading **Folklore** subdivided by the continent, region, country, etc.

6. H. NONBOOK MATERIALS

The assignment of subject headings for electronic media and for audiovisual and special instructional materials should follow the same principles that are applied to books. The uniform application of the same headings to book and nonbook materials alike is especially important in an integrated catalog, which brings all materials on one subject together regardless of format. Because nonbook materials often concentrate on very small aspects of larger subjects, the cataloger may not find in the List the specific heading that should be used. In such instances the cataloger should be generous in adding new subjects as needed. There are many form and genre headings that apply equally to nonbook materials and to books about such materials, such as **Biographical films**; **Comedy television programs**; and **Science fiction comic books, strips, etc**.

Topical subject headings assigned to nonbook materials should not include form subdivisions to describe physical format, such as motion pictures, slides, sound recordings, etc. Information on format as an aspect of descriptive cataloging can be found in the most recent edition of AACR2.

7. CLASSIFICATION AND SUBJECT HEADINGS

The cataloger should recognize a fundamental difference between classification and subject headings for the library catalog. In any system of classification that determines the arrangement of items on the shelves, a work can obviously have only one class number and stand in only one place, but in a catalog the same work can be entered, if necessary, under as many different points of entry as there are distinct subjects in the work (usually, however, not more than three). Classification is used to gather in one numerical place on the shelf works that give similar treatment to a subject. Subject headings gather in one alphabetical place in a catalog all treatments of a subject regardless of shelf location.

Another difference between classification and subject cataloging is that classification is frequently less precise than the subject entries for the catalog. Material on floriculture in general as well as on specific kinds of garden flowers are classed together in 635.9 in the Dewey Decimal Classification. A book on flower gardening, one on perennial gardening, and one on rose gardening will all three be classified in one number, while in the catalog each book will have its own specific subject heading: **Flower gardening**, **Perennials**, or **Roses**.

Library materials are classified by discipline, not by subject. A single subject may be dealt with in many disciplines. The Dewey classification numbers given with a heading in the Sears List are intended only to direct the cataloger to the disciplines where that subject is most likely to be treated. They are not meant to be absolute or cover all possibilities and should be used together with the Dewey Decimal Classification schedules. The cataloger must examine the work at hand and determine the discipline in which the author is writing. On the basis of that decision the cataloger classifies the work, not by the subject of the work alone.

8. MAINTAINING A CATALOG

The library catalog is a vital function at the very center of a library, and as such it is always growing and changing to reflect the growing collection and to meet the changing needs of the users. It is a challenge to the cataloger to add new records, revise existing records, and make all the appropriate references, and at the same time maintain the integrity of the catalog.

8. A. ADDING NEW HEADINGS

When a cataloger has determined what an item to be cataloged is about and formulated that concept into words, the next step is to find the subject heading that expresses that concept. The first thing to be determined is whether or not there is already an existing heading in the List for that concept. If, for example, there is a book on lawsuits, the cataloger may think of the terms Lawsuits, Suing, and Suits. Upon consulting the List it becomes clear that those words are not headings but references to the established heading **Litigation**. **Litigation** is slightly broader than Suing but is more suitable as a subject heading because it includes the matter of defending oneself against lawsuits. In this case the cataloger enters the book into the catalog under the heading **Litigation**. A new heading is not necessary.

At other times the appropriate heading for a book is not a new heading but a new combination of an established heading and a subdivision. If, for example, there is a book on the use and abuse of alcohol on college campuses, the cataloger may first think of the term Drunkenness. In the Sears List Drunkenness is an unpreferred term and a reference to two established headings: **Alcoholism** and **Temperance**. The scope note at **Temperance** reads: "Use for materials on the virtue of temperance or on the temperance movement." The book is not about drunkenness in relation to either vice and virtue or the temperance movement, so that heading can be eliminated. Neither is the book really about alcoholism, but at the heading **Alcoholism**, there is a general reference that reads: "SA [See also] classes of persons with the subdivision *Alcohol use*, e.g. **Employees—Alcohol use**; **Youth—Alcohol use**; etc., {to be added as needed}." At this point the cataloger realizes that the appropriate Sears subject heading for the book at hand would be **College students—Alcohol use**. **College students** is already an established heading in the List, but it could be added if it were not.

The cataloger should always keep in mind that it is not only appropriate but essential that types of things and examples of things not found in the List be established as headings and added to the List locally as needed. If there is a book on gloves, for example, and there is no heading in the Sears List for Gloves, the cataloger thinks of the concept or category of thing that would include gloves. Clothing comes to mind. At the heading **Clothing and dress** in the List there is a general reference: "SA [See also] types of clothing articles and accessories {to be added as needed}." The cataloger then establishes the heading **Gloves** and enters the book into the catalog under **Gloves**. It would be inappropriate to enter the book under the heading **Clothing and dress** simply because **Clothing and dress** is in the List and **Gloves** is not. It would mean that a user looking in the catalog under Gloves would find nothing. The general references in the List should reinforce the point that the List does not aim at completeness and must be expanded. Even where there is no general reference, narrower terms for types of things and examples and instances of things must be added as needed.

At times it is nearly impossible to determine what broader concept or category a new subject might be included under. This should not deter the cataloger from establishing any heading that is needed. Take, for example, the case of a book on thumb sucking, a common phenomenon among small children. The nearest terms in the List might be **Child psychology**, **Child rearing**, or **Human behavior**, but they are none too near. Nowhere is there a general reference instructing the cataloger to add headings for common childhood phenomena, and still the only appropriate heading for the book would be **Thumb sucking**. Here the intrepid cataloger, thinking how useless the headings **Child psychology**, **Child rearing**, or **Human behavior** would be on such a book, adds the heading **Thumb sucking** to the List and enters the book into the catalog under that heading.

There are resources that a cataloger can turn to for help in establishing subject headings that are not in the List. Other available databases and catalogs in which books are listed by subject can always be consulted, such as the Web site of any large library whose catalog is online. Periodical indexes, such as *Readers' Guide to Periodical Literature* or *Applied Science & Technology Index,* are especially helpful in establishing headings for current events and very new topics and trends and for technical headings. The index and the schedules of the *Dewey Decimal Classification* are a useful source of subject terminology as well as a way of seeing a topic in its relation to other topics. The Library of Congress issues lists of new subject headings in *Library of Congress Subject Headings Weekly Lists* on its Web site and includes new subject headings of current interest in its quarterly *Cataloging Service Bulletin.* Library of Congress cataloging information, including subject headings, emanating from its Cataloging in Publication (CIP) program, is available in various online databases and is also printed on the title page verso of many books.

8. B. REVISING SUBJECT HEADINGS

Because the English language does not stand still, neither do subject headings. It would be impossible today for a catalog to maintain the headings Negroes or Dinosauria, since common usage has relegated these terms to history. The prevailing thinking about the form of subject headings also changes, and as a result whole groups of headings need to be revised. All the inverted headings in the Sears List, for example, were eventually revised to the uninverted form, such as **Health insurance** for "Insurance, Health." With each new edition of the Sears List a library should consult the List of Canceled and Replacement Headings in the front of the volume and revise its catalog accordingly. Any headings created locally based on the pattern set by a Sears heading, and strings consisting of a Sears heading and a subdivision, must also be revised if that heading is revised in Sears. If, for example, a library had added the headings "Insurance, Title" and "Insurance, Health—Law and legislation," those headings would need to be revised to **Title insurance** and **Health insurance—Law and legislation**.

How a library revises its catalog depends upon the kind of catalog. In an online catalog the revision process depends upon the software employed in the catalog. If the software provides global update capability, the revision of many bibliographic records at once is simple. If they must be revised one by one, the process is still immensely easier than revising cards in a card catalog. In a card catalog the subjects are physically erased and retyped, either on all the cards on which they appear or on the subject entry cards alone. If in a card catalog replacement of a term is desirable but the number of bibliographic records to be revised is prohibitive, a history note can be used instead. A history note is simply a card at both the old and the new form indicating the change. When, for example, the heading "Insurance, Health" is changed in Sears to **Health insurance**, the two cards would read as follows:

Insurance, Health. For materials issued after [date] consult the following heading:
Health insurance

and

Health insurance. For materials issued before [date] consult the following heading:
Insurance, Health.

There is also the option, provided the software allows for it, of displaying a history note in an online catalog in lieu of revising the bibliographic records.

8. C. MAKING REFERENCES

Once an item has been assigned a subject heading, either a heading found in the List or one added as needed, attention must be directed to insuring that the reader who is searching for this material will not fail to find it because of insufficient references to the proper heading. References direct the user from terms not used as headings to the term that is used, and from broader and related terms to the term chosen to represent a given subject. The Sears List uses the symbols found in most thesauri to point out the relationships among the terms found in the List and to assist the cataloger in establishing appropriate references in the public catalog based upon these relationships. There are three types of references: *See* references, *See also* references, and general references.

8. C. i. *See* References

In the public catalog *See* references direct the user from unpreferred or unestablished terms and phrases to the preferred or established terms that are used as subject headings. Under most headings in the Sears List, following the UF [Used for] label, is one or more suggested terms for *See* references in the public catalog. A cataloger may want to use some or all of them as references, and many catalogers add other *See* references they deem useful. In theory there is no limit to the number of *See* references to a particular term, but in practice there may well be, especially in a card catalog. The references will be more useful if the cataloger considers materials from the reader's point of view. The reader's profile depends on age, background, education, occupation, and geographical location, and takes into account the type of library, such as school, public, university, or special.

The following are some types of unpreferred terms that might be used as *See* references in a catalog:

1) Synonyms or terms so nearly synonymous that they would cover the same material. For example, **Instructional materials centers** requires a reference from School media centers.

2) The second part of compound headings. For example, **Antique and vintage motorcycles** requires a reference from Vintage motorcycles.

3) The inverted form of a heading, either an adjective-noun combination or a phrase heading, especially if the word brought forward is not also the broader term. For example, **Theory of knowledge** requires a reference from "Knowledge, Theory of," there being no heading Knowledge.

4) Variant spellings. For example, **Archeology** requires a reference from Archaeology.

5) The opposite of a term, when it is included in the meaning of a term without being specifically mentioned. For example, **School attendance** requires a reference

from Absence from school and from Absenteeism (Schools), and **Equality** requires a reference from Inequality.

6)   The former forms of headings revised to reflect common usage, when the older term still has any currency. For example, Negroes remains as a reference to **Blacks** and to **African Americans**, but Dinosauria is no longer retained as a reference to **Dinosaurs**.

The first time a heading from the List is assigned to a work in the collection, the terms in the UF field in the List are entered, at the cataloger's discretion, as *See* references in the public catalog. When the same heading is subsequently assigned to other works, the references are already in place. When the cataloger adds a heading to the authority file as needed, all the appropriate *See* references are entered as well the first time the heading is used. For the heading **College students—Alcohol use**, for example, suitable *See* references might be Campus drinking, College drinking, and Drinking on campus.

8. C. ii. *See also* References

In the public catalog *See also* references direct the user from one established heading to another established heading. Under most headings in the Sears List, following the BT [Broader term] label, is a term that is broader in scope than the heading itself. As a rule, a term has only one broader term, unless it is an example or aspect of two or more things. The broader term serves two functions in the List. The first is to aid the cataloger in finding the best term to assign to a work. If the first term the cataloger thinks of to describe the contents of the work does not cover all aspects of work, the broader term may be the more appropriate heading for that work. The second function is to indicate where *See also* references should be made in the public catalog. A *See also* reference is made from a broader term to a narrower term, but not from a narrower term to a broader term. Take, for example, the broader term **Clothing and dress** on the heading **Gloves**. When the heading **Gloves** is assigned for the first time to a work in the collection, a reference is made at **Clothing and dress** "See also **Gloves**." If **Clothing and dress** has never been assigned to a work in the collection, it is entered in the catalog for the sake of the reference, and the reference "See also **Gloves**" is made. The point is that the user who is interested in works on clothing and dress in general may also be interested in works limited to gloves. The book on gloves need not be entered under both **Clothing and dress** and **Gloves**, but only under the appropriately specific heading, because the *See also* reference will direct the user from the broader to the narrower term. If the book on gloves were entered under both **Clothing and dress** and **Gloves**, the catalog would first list the book under the heading **Clothing and dress** and then direct the user to look as well under **Gloves** only to find the same book.

Under many headings in the Sears List, following the RT [Related term] label, one or more terms are listed that represent similar or associated subjects. These related terms are neither broader nor narrower than the main term but roughly equal in specificity. The term **Pardon**, for example, is related to **Amnesty**. The cataloger or the user may easily look first to one term only to realize that the other is the more precise term for the material being cataloged or being sought in the catalog. Related terms are reciprocal. When the term **Pardon** is assigned for the first time to a work in the collection, a reference is made in the catalog at **Amnesty** "See also **Pardon**." The reciprocal reference at **Pardon** "See also **Amnesty**" is also made, but only if **Amnesty** has also been assigned to a work in the collection. A reference is never made to a heading until there is a work entered under that heading in the collection, and if the only work entered under a heading is lost or discarded the references to that heading must be deleted. References to headings under which there is no material in the collection are called blind references and are to be avoided.

8. C. iii. General References

Under many headings in the Sears List, following the SA [See also] label, there is what is called a general reference, not to a specific heading but to a general group or category of things that may be established as headings as needed. In the example of **Clothing and dress** given above, the general reference is to "types of clothing articles and accessories, {to be added as needed}." This reference is addressed to the cataloger as a reminder not to be limited to the types of clothing and dress items given as examples in the List—**Hats**, **Hosiery**, **Shoes**, etc.—but to create a heading for any other clothing item, such as **Gloves**, when the need arises.

A second function of general references is to provide instruction in the application of subdivisions. Only a few subdivisions are universally applicable. All others apply only to certain types of headings. For every subdivision provided in the List, except those of unique application, there is a general reference spelling out the use of that subdivision. If the subdivision is also a heading, the general reference is given under the heading. **Folklore**, for example, is both a heading and a subdivision. Under the heading **Folklore** the general reference reads: "SA [See also] topics as themes in folklore with the subdivision *Folklore*, e.g. **Plants—Folklore**; names of ethnic or occupational groups with the subdivision *Folklore*, e.g. **Inuit—Folklore**; and names of individual legendary characters, e.g. **Bunyan, Paul (Legendary character)** {to be added as needed}." When the subdivision is not also a heading, there is a free-standing general reference in the alphabetical List with instructions on the use of that subdivision. For example, at *Industrial applications*, which is not a heading but only a subdivision, there is a general reference that reads: "USE types of scientific phenomena, chemicals, plants, and crops with the subdivision *Industrial applications*, e.g. **Ultrasonic waves—Industrial applications** {to be added as needed}."

Some libraries also display general references in the public catalog. Rather than make a specific *See also* reference from the broader term to every narrower term, they adapt the general reference in the List to address it to the user of the catalog. At **Flowers**, for example, rather than a specific *See also* reference to **Day lilies**, **Orchids**, **Peonies**, **Poppies**, **Roses**, **Tulips**, and **Violets**, there would be a general reference "See also types of flowers." The drawback of this procedure and the reason it is not recommended is that the user who wants to see all the books on specific flower types would have to think of every type of flower and look in dozens of places in the catalog. Many online catalogs are now able to provide the user with an expanded display of all the narrower terms under **Flowers** that have been used in the catalog.

8. D. RECORDING HEADINGS AND REFERENCES

The cataloger should keep a record of all the subject headings used in the catalog and all the references made to and from them. This local authority file may be kept on cards or on a computer. Some catalogers are tempted to forgo this process and merely consult the catalog whenever there is a question of previous practice. Without a local authority file, however, there can be no consistency in the cataloging. It is not possible to consult the catalog at the heading **Teachers—Ethics**, for example, and find what *See also* references were made to that term from any broader or related terms or what *See* references were made from unpreferred terms. Since **Teachers—Ethics** is not in the Sears List but was added as needed, consulting the List is not the answer. When a book appears on the ethics of psychologists, the cataloger will create **Psychologists—Ethics**, but without knowing what references were made to the heading **Teachers—Ethics**, there is no way the cataloger can create similar and consistent references for the new term. Likewise, if there is only one book entered under **Teachers— Ethics**, and if that book is lost or discarded, without a local authority file there would be no way of knowing what to delete in order to avoid blind references.

Many libraries today do little original cataloging but instead get their cataloging records from outside sources, either from computerized cooperative cataloging utilities or from vendors, often the same companies that sell them their books and other library materials. This procurement of cataloging from outside sources can save libraries a great deal of money, but it does not mean that there is no work for the cataloger in the library. Someone must order the cataloging, specifying to the vendor the particular needs of the library. If a library is devoted largely or entirely to children's materials, for example, a librarian will need to specify that the library does not want the subdivision —*Juvenile literature* on every subject heading. A library using Sears subject headings will need to apprise the vendor of that fact. When the cataloging records arrive in the library, only a cataloger can check them to be sure they are what was ordered. And lastly, only a cataloger can make the appropriate references in the local catalog, tailored to that library's particular collection, which make the records useful to the users.

9. CATALOGING IN THE TWENTY-FIRST CENTURY

It is useful to view modern cataloging practice in an historical perspective. In the nineteenth century, as libraries grew and cataloging became more thorough, it was clear that some form of cooperation among libraries was desirable. For many years the distribution of printed library cards was the principal method of cooperative cataloging. Later computerized utilities replaced printed cards. From the beginning it was clear that without principles and standards guaranteeing uniformity, cooperative cataloging would be impossible. In the very first volume of the American Library Association's *Library Journal* (1876-77) there are several lengthy discussions of cooperative cataloging, including an article on the topic by Melvil Dewey. It was out of these discussions and the voluminous correspondence that ensued that the modern standards of cataloging developed, both the rules for descriptive cataloging and Cutter's *Rules for a Dictionary Catalog*. These rules are not arbitrary but are firmly grounded in logic. They have stood unchallenged for over a hundred years because they have served to facilitate accurate and comprehensive retrieval in the modern library.

The world of libraries in the twenty-first century is already quite different from what it was only recently. More information is available in machine-readable form, and ready access to the Internet has changed the way many users seek and find information. Traditional methods of storage and retrieval in libraries will increasingly be supplemented by new methods engendered by artificial intelligence. The challenge of catalogers in the future is to approach every new technology and theory knowledgeably and fearlessly, judge them against what we know are the soundest principles, and embrace the good and reject the spurious, always keeping in mind the ultimate goal of meeting, even anticipating, the changing needs of the library users.

10. BIBLIOGRAPHY

American Library Association. Filing Committee. *ALA Filing Rules*. Chicago: American Library Association, 1980.

American Library Association. Subject Analysis Committee. *Guidelines on Subject Access to Individual Works of Fiction, Drama, etc*. 2nd ed. Chicago: American Library Association, 2000.

Anglo-American Cataloguing Rules. 2nd ed., 2002 Revision. Chicago: American Library Association, 2002.

Chan, Lois Mai. *Cataloging and Classification: an Introduction*. 2nd ed. New York: McGraw-Hill, 1994.

Chan, Lois Mai, Phyllis A. Richmond, and Elaine Svenonius, eds. *Theory of Subject Analysis: a Sourcebook*. Englewood, Colo.: Libraries Unlimited, 1985. [Contains excerpts from Charles A. Cutter's *Rules for a Dictionary Catalog*]

Dewey, Melvil. *Abridged Dewey Decimal Classification and Relative Index*. 14th ed. Edited by Joan S. Mitchell, et al. Dublin, Ohio: OCLC, 2004.

Hoffman, Herbert H. *Small Library Cataloging*. 3rd ed. Lanham, Md.: Scarecrow Press, 2002.

Intner, Sheila S., and Jean Riddle Weihs. *Standard Cataloging for School and Public Libraries*. 3rd ed. Englewood, Colo.: Libraries Unlimited, 2001.

Intner, Sheila S. Joanna F. Fountain, and Jane E. Gilchrist, eds. *Cataloging Correctly for Kids: An Introduction to the Tools*. 4th ed. Chicago: American Library Association, 2006.

Library Literature & Information Science. New York: The H. W. Wilson Co., 1921-

Library of Congress. Cataloging Policy and Support Office. *Subject Cataloging Manual: Subject Headings*. 5th ed. Washington, D.C.: Library of Congress, 1996-

Library of Congress. Office for Subject Cataloging Policy. *LC Period Subdivisions under Names of Places*. 5th ed. Washington, D.C.: Library of Congress, 1994.

Lighthall, Lynne, ed. *Sears List of Subject Headings: Canadian Companion*. 6th ed. New York: The H. W. Wilson Co., 2001.

Taylor, Arlene G. *The Organization of Information*. 2nd ed. Westport, Conn.: Libraries Unlimited, 2004.

Taylor, Arlene G. *Introduction to Cataloging and Classification*. 10th ed. Westport, Conn.: Libraries Unlimited, 2006.

Headings to be Added by the Cataloger

Sears is not intended to be a complete list of subject headings but only a list of many of the most commonly used headings and a pattern for creating other headings as needed. Types of things and names of individual things must always be added when they are not already provided in the List. The general references in the List explicitly instruct the cataloger to create headings in areas where the need for such additions is most obvious (such as under **Flowers**, where the general reference reads "SA [See also] types of flowers, e.g. **Roses** {to be added as needed}"). Where there is no general reference the same instruction is implicit. A further discussion of adding headings can be found in the Principles of the Sears List. Some of the additional headings most likely to be needed are the following:

Topical Subjects
  1. Types of common things—foods, tools, sports, musical instruments, etc.
  2. Types of plants and animals—fruits, flowers, birds, fishes, etc.
  3. Types of chemicals and minerals
  4. Types of enterprises and industries
  5. Types of diseases
  6. Names of organs and regions of the body
  7. Names of languages, language groups, and national literatures
  8. Names of ethnic groups and nationalities
  9. Names of wars, battles, treaties, etc.

Geographic Headings
  1. Names of political jurisdictions—countries, states, cities, provinces, etc.
  2. Groups of states, groups of countries, alliances, etc.
  3. Names of geographic features—regions, mountain ranges, island groups, individual mountains, individual islands, rivers, river valleys, oceans, lakes, etc.

Names
  1. Personal names—individual persons and families
  2. Corporate names—associations, societies, government bodies, religious denominations, business firms, performing groups, colleges, libraries, hospitals, hotels, ships, etc.
  3. Uniform titles—anonymous literary works, newspapers, periodicals, sacred scriptures, motion pictures, etc.

The Key Headings on the following page can be used as a guide in applying subdivisions to any similar headings. Subdivisions not provided for in the Sears List may also be established and used as needed.

"Key" Headings

Certain headings in the Sears List have been chosen to serve as examples, at which the subdivisions particularly applicable to certain categories of headings are given. If a subdivision is provided under the "key" heading, it may also be used under any heading of that type.

Authors: **Shakespeare, William, 1564-1616** (to illustrate the subdivisions that may be used under any voluminous author, and in some cases other individual persons)

Ethnic groups: **Native Americans** (to illustrate the subdivisions that may be used under any ethnic group or native people)

Languages: **English language** (to illustrate the subdivisions that may be used under any language or group of languages)

Literature: **English literature** (to illustrate the subdivisions that may be used under any literature)

Places: **United States**
Ohio
Chicago (Ill.)
(to illustrate the subdivisions—except for historical periods—that may be used under any country, state, or city)

Public figures: **Presidents—United States** (to illustrate the subdivisions that may be used under the presidents, prime ministers, governors, and rulers of any country, state, etc., and in some cases under the names of individual presidents, prime ministers, etc.)

Wars: **World War, 1939-1945** (to illustrate the subdivisions that may be used under any war, and in some cases individual battles)

List of Canceled and Replacement Headings

CANCELED HEADINGS	REPLACEMENT HEADINGS
Alcohol as fuel	Alcohol fuels
Ardennes, Battle of the, 1944-1945	Ardennes (France), Battle of the, 1944-1945
Atlantis	Atlantis (Legendary place)
Biological diversity	Biodiversity
Biological diversity conservation	Biodiversity conservation
Libraries and the elderly	Elderly—Library services
Holmes, Sherlock (Fictitious character)	Holmes, Sherlock (Fictional character)
Native peoples	Indigenous peoples
Intifada, 1987-	Intifada, 1987-1992
Microcomputers	Personal computers
Popular music—Texts	Popular song lyrics
Sexual behavior	Sex
Stereotype (Psychology)	Stereotype (Social psychology)
Super Bowl	Super Bowl (Game)
Libraries and students	Students—Library services
Teacher exchange	Teacher exchange programs
United States—History—1783-1809	United States—History—1783-1815
Vigilance committees	Vigilantes

The Use of Subdivisions in the Sears List

To allow for a standardized formulation of many complex subjects, there are a large number of topical and form subdivisions that may be used under a variety of subjects as needed. There are provisions and examples for more than five hundred subdivisions in the Sears List. The List of Subdivisions found on the following pages is meant for handy reference only. For each of the subdivisions provided for in Sears there is also a general reference in the alphabetical List with specific instructions as to what types of headings that subdivision can be used under.

SUBDIVISIONS OF BROAD APPLICATION

Some subdivisions are of very broad application and can be used under nearly any subject heading. The following are examples of two general references for such subdivisions—one for a topical subdivision, *Computer simulation*, which is also a heading, and one for a form subdivision, *Interactive multimedia*, which is only a subdivision:

> **Computer simulation**
> SA   subjects with the subdivision *Computer simulation*, e.g. **Psychology— Computer simulation** [to be added as needed]

> Interactive multimedia
> USE   subjects with the subdivision *Interactive multimedia*, e.g. **Geology— Interactive multimedia** [to be added as needed]

SUBDIVISIONS OF LIMITED APPLICATION

Some subdivisions are of limited application and can be used only under certain categories of subject heading. The following are examples of two general references for such subdivisions—one for a topical subdivision, *Satellites*, which is also a heading, and one for a form subdivision, *Facsimiles*, which is only a subdivision:

> **Satellites**
> SA   names of planets with the subdivision *Satellites*, e.g. **Mars (Planet)— Satellites** [to be added as needed]

> Facsimiles
> USE   types of printed or written materials, documents, etc., with the subdivision *Facsimiles*, e.g. **Autographs—Facsimiles** [to be added as needed]

List of Subdivisions Provided for in the Sears List

The following is a list of every subdivision for which there is a specific provision in the Sears List. This list is meant for handy reference only. For instructions on the use of a particular subdivision, see the entry for that subdivision in the main body of the alphabetical List. The following list is not exhaustive. It does not, for example, contain geographic or chronological subdivisions, which should be established by the cataloger as needed. Further topical and form subdivisions may also be required in libraries that contain specialized material, and they too should be established as needed and used consistently.

Accidents
Accounting
Accreditation
Adaptations
Administration
Aerial operations
African American authors
Age
Aging
Agriculture
Air conditioning
Alcohol use
Allusions
Alphabet
Amphibious operations
Analysis
Anatomy
Anecdotes
Anniversaries
Antiquities
Apologetic works
Appointment
Appointments and retirements
Appropriations and expenditures
Archives
Armed forces
Armistices
Army
Art and the war
Art collections
Assassination
Atlases
Atrocities
Attitudes
Audiences
Audiovisual aids
Auditing
Autographs
Authorship

Automation
Autonomy and independence
    movements
Awards
Battlefields
Behavior
Biblical teaching
Bibliography
Bio-bibliography
Biography
Bishops
Black authors
Blockades
Book reviews
Books and reading
Boundaries
Brakes
Breeding
Buildings
Calendars
Campaigns
Captivities
Care
Cartoons and caricatures
Case studies
Casualties
Catalogs
Catechisms
Catholic Church
Causes
Censorship
Census
Centennial celebrations, etc.
Chaplains
Characters
Charities
Charts, diagrams, etc.
Chemical warfare
Children

LIST OF SUBDIVISIONS PROVIDED FOR IN THE SEARS LIST

Christian missions
Chronology
Church history
Citizen participation
Civil rights
Civilian relief
Civilization
Claims
Classification
Cleaning
Clergy
Climate
Clothing
Coaching
Collaborationists
Collectibles
Collection and preservation
Collections
Collectors and collecting
Colonies
Color
Comic books, strips, etc.
Commentaries
Commerce
Communication systems
Comparative studies
Comparison
Competitions
Composition
Composition and exercises
Computer networks
Computer software
Computer simulation
Computer-assisted instruction
Concordances
Conduct of life
Conference proceedings
Conferences
Conscientious objectors
Conservation and restoration
Control
Controversial literature
Conversation and phrase books
Correspondence
Corrupt practices
Cost effectiveness
Costs
Counseling of
Courts and courtiers
Creeds
Cross-cultural studies
Curricula
Customs and practices
Data processing

Databases
Death
Death and burial
Defenses
Demobilization
Dental care
Deregulation
Description and travel
Desertions
Design
Design and construction
Designs and plans
Destruction and pillage
Dialects
Diaries
Dictionaries
Diet therapy
Diplomatic history
Directories
Discography
Diseases
Diseases and pests
Doctrines
Documentation
Draft resisters
Drama
Dramatic production
Drug testing
Drug therapy
Drug use
Drying
Dwellings
Early works to 1800
Earthquake effects
Ecology
Economic aspects
Economic conditions
Economic policy
Editing
Education
Education and the war
Eggs
Election
Employees
Employment
Encyclopedias
Endowments
Engineering and construction
Entrance examinations
Entrance requirements
Environmental aspects
Equipment and supplies
Errors of usage
Estimates

LIST OF SUBDIVISIONS PROVIDED FOR IN THE SEARS LIST

Ethical aspects
Ethics
Ethnic identity
Ethnic relations
Ethnobiology
Ethnobotany
Ethnozoology
Etymology
Evacuation of civilians
Evaluation
Evidences, authority, etc.
Evolution
Examinations
Exhibitions
Experiments
Exploration
Exploring expeditions
Facsimiles
Faculty
Family
Fiction
Filmography
Finance
Finishing
Fires and fire prevention
First editions
Flight
Folklore
Food
Food supply
Forced repatriation
Forecasting
Foreign countries
Foreign economic relations
Foreign influences
Foreign opinion
Foreign relations
Foreign words and phrases
Forgeries
Friends and associates
Fuel consumption
Funeral customs and rites
Gazetteers
Genealogy
Genetic aspects
Geographical distribution
Geography
Geology
Gold discoveries
Government
Government ownership
Government policy
Government relations
Governments in exile

Grammar
Graphic novels
Grooming
Growth
Guidebooks
Habitations
Handbooks, manuals, etc.
Health and hygiene
Health aspects
Heating and ventilation
Hispanic American authors
Historical geography
Historiography
History
History and criticism
History of doctrines
Home care
Homes
Homonyms
Housing
Humor
Hunting
Identification
Identity
Idioms
Illustrations
Immigration and emigration
Impeachment
In art
Inaugural addresses
Inauguration
Indexes
Industrial applications
Industries
Infinitive
Influence
Information resources
Information services
In literature
In-service training
Insignia
Inspection
Institutional care
Intellectual life
Interactive multimedia
International cooperation
Internet resources
Interviews
Jargon
Journalists
Juvenile drama
Juvenile fiction
Juvenile literature
Juvenile poetry

LIST OF SUBDIVISIONS PROVIDED FOR IN THE SEARS LIST

Kings and rulers
Kinship
Knowledge
Labeling
Laboratory manuals
Labor productivity
Language
Languages
Law and legislation
Legal status, laws, etc.
Legends
Library resources
Licenses
Life cycles
Life skills guides
Lighting
Lists
Literary collections
Literature and the war
Liturgy
Local history
Localisms
Maintenance and repair
Malpractice
Management
Manpower
Manuscripts
Maps
Marketing
Marks
Material culture
Materials
Mathematical models
Mathematics
Measurement
Medals, badges, decorations, etc.
Medical care
Medical examinations
Meditations
Memorizing
Mental health
Mental health services
Mergers
Messages
Metamorphosis
Methodology
Mexican American authors
Microbiology
Migration
Military history
Military intelligence
Military life
Militia
Miscellanea

Missing in action
Missions
Models
Monuments
Moral conditions
Morphology
Mortality
Motion pictures and the war
Motors
Museums
Name
Names
Naval history
Naval operations
Navy
Nazi persecution
Nests
Noise
Nomenclature
Nomenclature (Popular)
Nomination
Nursing
Nutrition
Obituaries
Occupied territories
Ordnance
Officers
Officials and employees
Origin
Outlines, syllabi, etc.
Packaging
Painting
Parachute troops
Paralysis
Parasites
Parodies, imitations, etc.
Parts of speech
Patients
Patterns
Peace
Pensions
Periodicals
Persecutions
Personal finance
Personal narratives
Personnel management
Philosophy
Physical fitness
Physical therapy
Physiological aspects
Physiological effect
Physiology
Pictorial works
Piloting

Planning
Poetry
Political activity
Political aspects
Politics and government
Population
Portraits
Posters
Practice
Prayers
Preservation
Press coverage
Press relations
Prevention
Price guides
Prices
Prisoners and prisons
Problems, exercises, etc.
Production standards
Programmed instruction
Pronunciation
Propaganda
Prophecies
Protection
Protest movements
Provincialisms
Psychological aspects
Psychology
Public opinion
Publishing
Purchasing
Quality control
Queens
Quotations
Race identity
Race relations
Rates
Rating
Reading materials
Recruiting
Recruiting, enlistment, etc.
Recycling
Refugees
Regimental histories
Registers
Rehabilitation
Relations with Congress
Religion
Religious aspects
Religious life
Relocation
Remedial teaching
Remodeling
Repairing

Reparations
Research
Reservations
Resignation
Reviews
Rhyme
Riots
Rites and ceremonies
Romances
Rural conditions
Safety devices
Safety measures
Safety regulations
Salaries, wages, etc.
Sanitation
Satellites
Scholarships
Secret service
Security measures
Segregation
Sermons
Services for
Sexual behavior
Signaling
Slang
Social aspects
Social conditions
Social life and customs
Societies
Songs
Sound recordings
Sources
Specifications
Spelling
Staff
Stage history
Standards
Statistics
Storage
Stories
Stories, plots, etc.
Strategic aspects
Study and teaching
Study guides
Succession
Suffrage
Suicide
Supply and demand
Surgery
Surveys
Synonyms and antonyms
Tables
Tank warfare
Taxation

LIST OF SUBDIVISIONS PROVIDED FOR IN THE SEARS LIST

Technique
Technological innovations
Telephone directories
Terminology
Terms and phrases
Territorial expansion
Territorial questions
Territories and possessions
Testing
Textbooks
Texts
Theater and the war
Therapeutic use
Thermodynamics
Tombs
Tournaments
Toxicology
Trademarks
Training
Transplantation

Transportation
Travel
Treaties
Tropical conditions
Tropics
Tuning
Underground movements
Uniforms
Usage
Vaccination
Vital statistics
Vocational guidance
War use
War work
Wars
Waste disposal
Weight
Women authors
Wounds and injuries
Writing

Symbols Used

UF = Used for

SA = See also

BT = Broader term

NT = Narrower term

RT = Related term

[Former heading] = Term that was once used as a heading and is no longer

(May subdiv. geog.) = Heading that may be subdivided by name of place

Sears List of Subject Headings

3-D photography
    USE **Three dimensional photography**

4-H clubs   630.6
    UF   Four-H clubs
    BT   **Agriculture—Societies**
          Agriculture—Study and teaching
          Boys' clubs
          Girls' clubs

4th of July
    USE **Fourth of July**

100 years' war
    USE **Hundred Years' War, 1339-1453**

401(k) plans   332.024
    BT   **Individual retirement accounts**

1920s
    USE **Nineteen twenties**

1930s
    USE **Nineteen thirties**

1940s
    USE **Nineteen forties**

1950s
    USE **Nineteen fifties**

1960s
    USE **Nineteen sixties**

1970s
    USE **Nineteen seventies**

1980s
    USE **Nineteen eighties**

1990s
    USE **Nineteen nineties**

Abacus   513.028
    BT   **Calculators**

Abandoned children (May subdiv. geog.)
    362.73
    UF   Exposed children
    BT   **Child welfare**
          Children
    RT   **Orphans**

Abandoned towns
    USE **Extinct cities**
          Ghost towns

Abandonment of family
    USE **Desertion and nonsupport**

Abbeys (May subdiv. geog.)   **271; 726**
    SA   names of individual abbeys [to be added as needed]
    BT   **Church architecture**
          Monasteries
    NT   **Westminster Abbey**
    RT   **Cathedrals**

Abbreviations   411
    UF   Contractions
    BT   **Writing**
    NT   **Acronyms**
          Code names
    RT   **Ciphers**
          Shorthand
          Signs and symbols

ABCs
    USE **Alphabet**

Abduction
    USE **Kidnapping**

Abduction of humans by aliens
    USE **Alien abduction**

Abilities
    USE **Ability**

Ability   153.9
    UF   Abilities
          Aptitude
          Skill
          Skills
          Talent
          Talents
    SA   types of ability [to be added as needed]
    NT   **Creative ability**
          Executive ability
          Leadership
          Mathematical ability
          Musical ability
    RT   **Success**

Ability grouping in education   371.2
    UF   Grouping by ability
    BT   **Education**
          Educational psychology

Ability grouping in education—*Continued*
>>Grading and marking (Education)
- NT **Nongraded schools**

Ability—Testing 153.9; 371.26
- UF Aptitude testing
- BT **Educational tests and measurements**
  >>**Intelligence tests**
  >>**Psychological tests**

ABMs
- USE **Antimissile missiles**

Abnormal children
- USE **Exceptional children**
  >>**Handicapped children**

Abnormal growth
- USE **Growth disorders**

Abnormal psychology 616.89

Use for systematic descriptions of mental disorders. Materials on clinical aspects of mental disorders, including therapy, are entered under **Psychiatry**. Popular materials and materials on regional or social aspects of mental disorders are entered under **Mental illness**.

- UF Mental diseases
  >>Pathological psychology
  >>Psychology, Pathological
  >>Psychopathology
  >>Psychopathy
- BT **Mind and body**
  >>**Nervous system**
- NT **Affective disorders**
  >>**Attention deficit disorder**
  >>**Codependency**
  >>**Compulsive behavior**
  >>**Depression (Psychology)**
  >>**Eating disorders**
  >>**Hallucinations and illusions**
  >>**Mental illness**
  >>**Mental retardation**
  >>**Multiple personality**
  >>**Neuroses**
  >>**Panic disorders**
  >>**Personality disorders**
  >>**Psychosomatic medicine**
  >>**Self-mutilation**
- RT **Criminal psychology**
  >>**Mental health**
  >>**Psychiatry**
  >>**Psychoanalysis**

Abnormalities, Human
- USE **Birth defects**
  >>**Growth disorders**

Abolition of capital punishment
- USE **Capital punishment**

Abolition of slavery
- USE **Abolitionists**
  >>**Slavery**
  >>**Slaves—Emancipation**

Abolitionists (May subdiv. geog.) **326; 920**
- UF Abolition of slavery
  >>Antislavery
- BT **Reformers**
- RT **Slavery**
  >>**Slaves—Emancipation**

Abominable snowman
- USE **Yeti**

Aboriginal Australians 305.89
- UF Australian aborigines
- BT **Australians**
  >>**Indigenous peoples**

Aborigines
- USE **Indigenous peoples**

Abortion (May subdiv. geog.) **618.8**
- UF Induced abortion
  >>Termination of pregnancy

Abortion—Ethical aspects 179.7
- UF Abortion—Moral and religious aspects
- BT **Ethics**
- RT **Pro-choice movement**
  >>**Pro-life movement**

Abortion—Law and legislation (May subdiv. geog.) **344; 363.46**
- BT **Law**
  >>**Legislation**

Abortion—Moral and religious aspects
- USE **Abortion—Ethical aspects**
  >>**Abortion—Religious aspects**

Abortion—Religious aspects 205

May be further subdivided by religion or sect.

- UF Abortion—Moral and religious aspects
- RT **Pro-choice movement**
  >>**Pro-life movement**

Abortion—Religious aspects—Catholic Church 241

Abortion rights movement
- USE **Pro-choice movement**

Abrasives 553.6

Abrasives—*Continued*
    BT   **Ceramics**
Absence from school
    USE   **School attendance**
Absenteeism (Labor)   **331.25; 658.3**
    UF   Employee absenteeism
           Labor absenteeism
    BT   **Hours of labor**
          Personnel management
    RT   **Employee morale**
Absenteeism (Schools)
    USE   **School attendance**
Abstinence
    USE   **Fasting**
         Temperance
Abstinence, Sexual
    USE   **Sexual abstinence**
Abstract art (May subdiv. geog.)
        709.04; 759.06
    UF   Abstract painting
           Geometric art
           Nonobjective art
    BT   **Art**
Abstract painting
    USE   **Abstract art**
Abuse of animals
    USE   **Animal welfare**
Abuse of children
    USE   **Child abuse**
Abuse of medications
    USE   **Medication abuse**
Abuse of medicines
    USE   **Medication abuse**
Abuse of persons
    USE   **Offenses against the person**
Abuse of the elderly
    USE   **Elderly abuse**
Abuse of wives
    USE   **Wife abuse**
Abuse, Verbal
    USE   **Invective**
Abused aged
    USE   **Elderly abuse**
Abused children
    USE   **Child abuse**
Abused wives
    USE   **Abused women**
         Wife abuse
Abused women   **362.82**
    UF   Abused wives
           Battered wives
           Battered women

    BT   **Victims of crimes**
         Women
    RT   **Wife abuse**
Academic achievement (May subdiv.
    geog.)   **370.1; 371.2**
    UF   Academic failure
           Achievement, Academic
           Educational achievement
           Scholastic achievement
           Student achievement
    BT   **Success**
    NT   **Achievement tests**
Academic advising
    USE   **Educational counseling**
Academic degrees   **378.2**
    UF   College degrees
           Degrees, Academic
           Doctors' degrees
           Honorary degrees
           University degrees
    BT   **Colleges and universities**
Academic dishonesty
    USE   **Cheating (Education)**
Academic dissertations
    USE   **Dissertations**
Academic failure
    USE   **Academic achievement**
Academic freedom (May subdiv. geog.)
        371.1; 378.1
    Use for materials on the freedom of teach-
    ers and students to teach, discuss, or investi-
    gate controversial subjects without penalty or
    restraint from officials, governments, or orga-
    nized groups.
    UF   Educational freedom
           Freedom, Academic
           Freedom of teaching
           Teaching, Freedom of
    BT   **Intellectual freedom**
         Toleration
Academic libraries (May subdiv. geog.)
        027.7
    UF   College and university libraries
           College libraries
           University libraries
    BT   **Libraries**
Academy Awards (Motion pictures)
        791.43
    UF   Oscars (Motion pictures)
    BT   **Motion pictures**
Acadians—Louisiana
    USE   **Cajuns**

Accelerated reading
USE **Speed reading**
Access to health care (May subdiv. geog.)
362.1
UF Accessibility of health services
Availability of health services
Health services accessibility
Medical care—Access
BT **Medical care**
Accessibility of health services
USE **Access to health care**
Accident insurance   368.38
UF Insurance, Accident
BT **Casualty insurance**
NT **Workers' compensation**
Accidents (May subdiv. geog.)   **363.1**
UF Emergencies
Injuries
Wrecks
SA types of accidents, e.g. **Railroad
accidents**; subjects with the
subdivision *Accidents*, e.g.
**Chemical industry—Acci-
dents; Nuclear power
plants—Accidents**; etc.; and
groups and classes of persons,
animals, organs of the body,
and plants and crops with the
subdivision *Wounds and inju-
ries*, e.g. **Horses—Wounds
and injuries; Foot—Wounds
and injuries** [to be added as
needed]
NT **Aircraft accidents
Explosions
Fires
Home accidents
Industrial accidents
Poisons and poisoning
Railroad accidents
Shipwrecks
Space vehicle accidents
Traffic accidents
Wounds and injuries**
RT **Disasters
First aid**
Accidents—Prevention   363.1; 658.3
UF Prevention of accidents
Safety measures

SA subjects with the subdivision
Safety devices or *Safety mea-
sures*, e.g. **Railroads—Safety
devices; Radiation—Safety
measures**; etc. [to be added
as needed]
NT **Aeronautics—Safety measures
Radiation—Safety measures
Railroads—Safety devices
Safety education
Safety regulations
Water safety**
RT **Safety devices**
Acclimatization
USE **Adaptation (Biology)
Environmental influence on
humans**
Accompaniment, Musical
USE **Musical accompaniment**
Accountability
USE **Liability (Law)
Responsibility**
Accountants   657.092; 920
UF Bookkeepers
Certified public accountants
RT **Accounting**
Accounting (May subdiv. geog.)   **657**
UF Financial accounting
SA types of industries, professions,
and organizations with the
subdivision *Accounting* [to be
added as needed]
BT **Business
Business education
Business mathematics**
NT **Corporations—Accounting
Cost accounting**
RT **Accountants
Auditing
Bookkeeping**
Accounting machines
USE **Calculators**
Accounts, Collecting of
USE **Collecting of accounts**
Accreditation
USE types of hospitals and service
institutions, types of educa-
tional institutions, and names
of individual institutions with
the subdivision *Accreditation,*
e.g. **Colleges and universi-**

Accreditation—*Continued*

ties—**Accreditation;** and subjects with the subdivision *Study and teaching,* for accreditation of programs of study in those subjects, e.g. **Mathematics—Study and teaching** [to be added as needed]

Accreditation (Education)
USE **Schools—Accreditation**

Acculturation (May subdiv. geog.)
303.48
UF Culture contact
BT **Anthropology**
Civilization
Culture
Ethnology
NT **Ethnic relations**
Multicultural education
Race relations
Socialization
RT **East and West**

Achievement, Academic
USE **Academic achievement**

Achievement motivation 153.8
UF Performance motivation
BT **Educational psychology**
Motivation (Psychology)
Performance

Achievement tests (May subdiv. geog.)
371.26
UF Scholastic achievement tests
School achievement tests
BT **Academic achievement**
Educational tests and measurements

Acid (Drug)
USE **LSD (Drug)**

Acid precipitation
USE **Acid rain**

Acid rain 363.738; 628.5
UF Acid precipitation
BT **Rain**
Water pollution

Acids 546; 661
SA types of acids [to be added as needed]
BT **Chemicals**
Chemistry
NT **Carbolic acid**

Acne 616.5

UF Blackheads (Acne)
Pimples (Acne)
BT **Skin—Diseases**

ACOAs
USE **Adult children of alcoholics**

Acoustics
USE **Architectural acoustics**
Hearing
Music—Acoustics and physics
Sound

Acquaintance rape
USE **Date rape**

Acquired immune deficiency syndrome
USE **AIDS (Disease)**

Acquisitions, Corporate
USE **Corporate mergers and acquisitions**

Acquisitions (Libraries)
USE **Libraries—Acquisitions**

Acrobats and acrobatics 791.3; 796.47
SA types of acrobatic activities, e.g. **Tumbling** [to be added as needed]
BT **Circus**
NT **Tumbling**
RT **Gymnastics**

Acronyms 411
UF English language—Acronyms
Initialisms
BT **Abbreviations**
Code names

Acting 791.4; 792

Use for materials on the art and technique of acting in any medium (stage, television, etc.) and on acting as a profession. Materials limited to the presentation of plays are entered under **Amateur theater** or **Theater—Production and direction**.

UF Dramatic art
Stage
BT **Drama**
Public speaking
NT **Commedia dell'arte**
Mime
Pageants
Pantomimes
RT **Actors**
Amateur theater
Drama in education
Theater

Acting—Costume
USE **Costume**

Actions and defenses
  USE **Litigation**
Activities curriculum
  USE **Creative activities**
Activity schools
  USE **Education—Experimental
    methods**
Actors (May subdiv. geog.)   **791.4; 792;
    920**
  Use for materials on several persons of the
  acting profession, whether male or female.
  Materials on several female actors that empha-
  size their identity as women are entered under
  Actresses. Materials on several male actors
  that emphasize their identity as men are en-
  tered under **Male actors**.
  UF   Actors and actresses
       Motion picture actors and ac-
         tresses
       Television actors
  SA   names of individual actors [to
         be added as needed]
  BT   **Entertainers**
  NT   **Actors—United States**
       Actresses
       African American actors
       Black actors
       Child actors
       Comedians
       Male actors
       Stunt performers
  RT   **Acting**
Actors and actresses
  USE **Actors**
Actors, Black
  USE **Black actors**
Actors—United States   **791.4; 792; 920**
  UF   American actors
       American actors and actresses
  BT   **Actors**
Actresses (May subdiv. geog.)   **791.4;
    792; 920**
  Use for materials on several female actors
  that emphasize their identity as women. Gen-
  eral materials on persons of the acting profes-
  sion, whether male or female, are entered un-
  der **Actors**.
  UF   Female actors
       Women actors
  BT   **Actors**
Acupressure   615.8
  UF   Finger pressure therapy
       Myotherapy

  BT   **Alternative medicine
       Massage**
Acupuncture   615.8
  BT   **Alternative medicine**
Adages
  USE **Proverbs**
Adaptability (Psychology)
  USE **Adjustment (Psychology)**
**Adaptation (Biology)   578.4; 581.4;
    591.4**
  UF   Acclimatization
  BT   **Biology
       Ecology
       Genetics
       Variation (Biology)**
  NT   **Environmental influence on
       humans
       Stress (Physiology)**
Adaptation (Psychology)
  USE **Adjustment (Psychology)**
Adaptations
  USE **Film adaptations
       Television adaptations**
       and names of authors, titles of
         anonymous literary works,
         types of literature, and types
         of musical compositions with
         the subdivision *Adaptations,*
         for individual works, collec-
         tions, or criticism and inter-
         pretation of literary, cinemat-
         ic, video, or television adapta-
         tions, e.g., **Shakespeare, Wil-
         liam, 1564-1616—Adapta-
         tions; Beowulf—Adaptations;
         Arthurian romances—Adap-
         tations;** etc. [to be added as
         needed]
ADD (Child behavior disorder)
  USE **Attention deficit disorder**
Addiction
  USE types of addiction, e.g. **Alcohol-
         ism; Drug abuse; Exercise
         addiction;** etc. [to be added
         as needed]
Addiction to alcohol
  USE **Alcoholism**
Addiction to drugs
  USE **Drug abuse**
Addiction to exercise
  USE **Exercise addiction**

Addiction to gambling
    USE **Compulsive gambling**
Addiction to nicotine
    USE **Tobacco habit**
Addiction to tobacco
    USE **Tobacco habit**
Addiction to work
    USE **Workaholism**
Addictive behavior
    USE **Compulsive behavior**
Addicts
    USE **Drug addicts**
Adding machines
    USE **Calculators**
Addition   **513.2**
    BT   **Arithmetic**
Additives, Food
    USE **Food additives**
Addresses
    USE **Lectures and lecturing**
          Speeches
Adhesives   **620.1; 668; 691**
    SA   types of adhesives [to be added
          as needed]
    BT   **Materials**
    NT   **Cement**
          Glue
          Mortar
Adjustment (Psychology)   **155.2**
    UF   Adaptability (Psychology)
          Adaptation (Psychology)
          Coping behavior
          Maladjustment (Psychology)
    BT   **Psychology**
Adjustment, Social
    USE **Social adjustment**
Administration
    USE **Civil service**
          Management
          Public administration
          and types of institutions in the
          sphere of health, education,
          and social services, and
          names of individual institu-
          tions with the subdivision *Ad-*
          ministration, e.g. **Libraries—**
          Administration; Schools—
          Administration; etc.; types of
          management, e.g. **Office man-**
          agement; types of industries,
          types of industrial plants and

processes, and names of individual corporate bodies, with
the subdivision *Management,*
e.g. **Information systems—**
Management; and names of
countries, cities, etc., with the
subdivision *Politics and gov-*
ernment, e.g. **United States—**
Politics and government [to
be added as needed]
Administration of criminal justice (May
    subdiv. geog.)   **353.4**
    UF   Criminal justice, Administration
          of
    BT   **Administration of justice**
          Criminal law
    NT   **Amnesty**
          Clemency
          Corrections
          Crime
          Law enforcement
          Pardon
          Parole
          Police
          Prisons
          Punishment
Administration of justice (May subdiv.
    geog.)   **347; 353.4**
    UF   Justice, Administration of
    BT   **Law**
    NT   **Administration of criminal jus-**
          tice
          Due process of law
          Governmental investigations
          Impeachments
    RT   **Courts**
Administrative ability
    USE **Executive ability**
Administrative agencies (May subdiv.
    geog.)   **351**
    Use for materials on governmental bodies,
    such as boards, commissions, departments,
    etc., responsible for implementing and admin-
    istering legislation.
    UF   Administrative agencies—Law
          and legislation
          Executive agencies
          Government agencies
          Regulatory agencies
    SA   names of administrative agencies
          [to be added as needed]

Administrative agencies—*Continued*
　BT　**Administrative law**
　　　Public administration
　NT　**Executive departments**
Administrative agencies—Law and legislation
　USE　**Administrative agencies**
Administrative agencies—Reorganization
　　　(May subdiv. geog.)　**351**
　UF　Executive departments—Reorganization
　　　Executive reorganization
　　　Government reorganization
　　　Reorganization of administrative agencies
Administrative agencies—Reorganization—Ohio　352.2
　UF　Ohio—Executive departments—Reorganization
Administrative agencies—Reorganization—United States　352.2
　UF　United States—Executive departments—Reorganization
Administrative law (May subdiv. geog.)　**342**
　BT　**Law**
　NT　**Administrative agencies**
　　　Civil service
　　　Local government
　　　Ombudsman
　RT　**Constitutional law**
　　　Public administration
Administrators and executors
　USE　**Executors and administrators**
Admirals　359.0092; 920
　BT　**Military personnel**
　　　Navies
Admissions applications
　USE　**College applications**
Admissions essays
　USE　**College applications**
Adolescence　155.5; 305.235
　　　Use for materials on the process or the state of growing to maturity. Materials on the time of life between thirteen and twenty-five years, and on people in this general age range, are entered under **Youth**. Materials limited to teen youth are entered under **Teenagers**. Materials limited to people in the general age range of eighteen through twenty-five years are entered under **Young men** or **Young women**.
　UF　Teen age
　　　Teenagers—Development
　BT　**Age**

　RT　**Puberty**
　　　Youth
Adolescence—Psychology
　USE　**Adolescent psychology**
Adolescent fathers
　USE　**Teenage fathers**
Adolescent mothers
　USE　**Teenage mothers**
Adolescent pregnancy
　USE　**Teenage pregnancy**
Adolescent prostitution
　USE　**Juvenile prostitution**
Adolescent psychiatry　616.89
　UF　Teenagers—Psychiatry
　BT　**Psychiatry**
Adolescent psychology　155.5
　UF　Adolescence—Psychology
　　　Behavior of teenagers
　　　Teenage behavior
　　　Teenagers—Psychology
　BT　**Psychology**
Adolescents
　USE　**Teenagers**
Adopted children　306.87; 362.82
　BT　**Adoptees**
　　　Children
　RT　**Adoption**
　　　Orphans
Adoptees　346.01; 362.73
　　　Use for materials on anyone formally adopted as a dependent.
　UF　Adult adoptees
　NT　**Adopted children**
　RT　**Adoption**
　　　Birthparents
Adoption (May subdiv. geog.)　**346.01; 362.734**
　UF　Child placing
　　　Children—Adoption
　　　Children—Placing out
　BT　**Parent-child relationship**
　NT　**International adoption**
　　　Interracial adoption
　RT　**Adopted children**
　　　Adoptees
　　　Foster home care
Adoption—Corrupt practices　364.1
　UF　Black market children
　　　Sale of infants
　　　Selling of infants
　BT　**Criminal law**

Adult adoptees
USE **Adoptees**
Adult child abuse victims   362.76
UF   Adult survivors of child abuse
Adults abused as children
Child abuse survivors
Grown-up abused children
BT   **Victims of crimes**
NT   **Adult child sexual abuse victims**
RT   **Child abuse**
**Adult child sexual abuse victims
362.76**
UF   Adult survivors of child sexual abuse
Adults sexually abused as children
BT   **Adult child abuse victims**
RT   **Child sexual abuse**
Adult children of alcoholics   362.292
UF   ACOAs
Alcoholic parents
BT   **Children of alcoholics**
RT   **Alcoholics**
Adult education (May subdiv. geog.)
374
UF   Education of adults
Lifelong education
BT   **Education**
Higher education
Secondary education
University extension
NT   **Agricultural extension work**
Prisoners—Education
RT   **Continuing education**
Evening and continuation schools
Adult fiction
USE   **Erotic fiction**
Adult films
USE   **Erotic films**
Adult survivors of child abuse
USE   **Adult child abuse victims**
Adult survivors of child sexual abuse
USE   **Adult child sexual abuse victims**
Adulteration of food
USE   **Food adulteration and inspection**
Adultery   176; 306.73; 363.4

UF   Extramarital relationships
Marital infidelity
BT   **Sexual ethics**
Adults (May subdiv. geog.)   **305.26**
UF   Grown-ups
Grownups
BT   **Age**
Adults abused as children
USE   **Adult child abuse victims**
Adults and children
USE   **Child-adult relationship**
Adults sexually abused as children
USE   **Adult child sexual abuse victims**
Adventure and adventurers (May subdiv.
geog.)   **904; 904.092; 910.4; 920**
NT   **Escapes**
Exploration
Explorers
Frontier and pioneer life
Heroes and heroines
Safaris
Sea stories
Seafaring life
Shipwrecks
RT   **Voyages and travels**
Adventure and adventurers—Fiction
USE   **Adventure fiction**
Adventure fiction   808.3; 808.83
Use for individual works, collections, or materials about adventure fiction.
UF   Adventure and adventurers—Fiction
Adventure stories
Suspense novels
Swashbucklers
Thrillers
BT   **Fiction**
NT   **Robinsonades**
Romantic suspense novels
Science fiction
Sea stories
Spy stories
Western stories
Adventure films   791.43
Use for individual works, collections, or materials about adventure films.
UF   Suspense films
Swashbucklers
Thrillers
BT   **Motion pictures**

Adventure films—*Continued*
    NT   Superhero films
         Western films
    RT   Adventure television programs
Adventure graphic novels   741.5
    Use for individual works, collections, or materials about adventure graphic novels.
    BT   Graphic novels
Adventure radio programs   791.44
    Use for individual works, collections, or materials about adventure radio programs.
    BT   Radio programs
    NT   Superhero radio programs
Adventure stories
    USE   Adventure fiction
Adventure television programs   791.45
    Use for individual works, collections, or materials about adventure television programs.
    BT   Television programs
    NT   Superhero television programs
    RT   Adventure films
Adventure travel (May subdiv. geog.)
         904
    Use for materials on travel to remote and sometimes dangerous places without normal tourist amenities.
    BT   Travel
         Voyages and travels
Advertisement writing
    USE   Advertising copy
Advertising (May subdiv. geog.)   659.1
    May be subdivided by topic, e.g. **Advertising—Cosmetics**; to specify the thing advertised.
    BT   Business
         Retail trade
    NT   Advertising and children
         Advertising copy
         Advertising layout and typography
         Commercial art
         Commercial catalogs
         Coupons (Retail trade)
         Deceptive advertising
         Electric signs
         Fashion models
         Market surveys
         Newspaper advertising
         Packaging
         Posters
         Printing—Specimens
         Radio advertising
         Show windows
         Sign painting

         Signs and signboards
         Television advertising
    RT   Marketing
         Propaganda
         Public relations
         Publicity
         Selling
Advertising and children   659.1
    UF   Children and advertising
    BT   Advertising
         Children
Advertising art
    USE   Commercial art
Advertising copy   659.13
    UF   Advertisement writing
         Copy writing
    BT   Advertising
         Authorship
Advertising—Cosmetics   659.1
    UF   Cosmetics—Advertising
Advertising layout and typography
         659.13
    BT   Advertising
         Printing
         Typography
Advertising, Newspaper
    USE   Newspaper advertising
Advertising—Newspapers   659.1
    Use for materials on the advertising of newspapers. Materials on advertising in newspapers are entered under **Newspaper advertising**.
    UF   Newspapers—Advertising
Advice columns   070.4
    BT   Counseling
         Newspapers—Sections, columns, etc.
Advisors
    USE   Consultants
Aerial bombs
    USE   Bombs
Aerial navigation
    USE   Navigation (Aeronautics)
Aerial operations
    USE   names of wars with the subdivision *Aerial operations,* e.g. **World War, 1939-1945—Aerial operations** [to be added as needed]
Aerial photography   778.3
    BT   Photography
    NT   Remote sensing

Aerial propellers   629.134
  UF Airplanes—Propellers
      Propellers, Aerial
  BT **Airplanes**
Aerial reconnaissance   355.4; 358.4
  UF Reconnaissance, Aerial
  BT **Military aeronautics**
      Remote sensing
Aerial rockets
  USE **Rockets (Aeronautics)**
Aerial spraying and dusting
  USE **Aeronautics in agriculture**
Aerobatics
  USE **Stunt flying**
Aerobic dancing
  USE **Aerobics**
Aerobic exercises
  USE **Aerobics**
Aerobics   613.7
  UF Aerobic dancing
      Aerobic exercises
  BT **Exercise**
  NT **Walking**
  RT **Dance**
Aerobiology
  USE **Air—Microbiology**
Aerodromes
  USE **Airports**
Aerodynamics   533; 629.132
  UF Streamlining
  BT **Air**
      Dynamics
      Pneumatics
  NT **Supersonic aerodynamics**
  RT **Aeronautics**
Aerodynamics, Supersonic
  USE **Supersonic aerodynamics**
Aeronautical instruments   629.135
  UF Airplanes—Instruments
      Instruments, Aeronautical
  SA types of instruments, e.g. **Gyro-
      scope** [to be added as need-
      ed]
  BT **Scientific apparatus and in-
      struments**
  NT **Airplanes—Electric equipment**
      Gyroscope
      Instrument flying
Aeronautical sports   797.5
  SA types of aeronautical sports [to
      be added as needed]

  BT **Aeronautics**
      Sports
  NT **Airplane racing**
      Skydiving
Aeronautics (May subdiv. geog.)   **629.13**
    Use for materials dealing collectively with
  various types of aircraft and for materials on
  the scientific or technical aspects of aircraft
  and their construction and operation. Materials
  on companies engaged in commercial aviation
  are entered under **Airlines**.
  UF Air routes
      Airways
      Aviation
  SA aeronautics in particular indus-
      tries or fields of endeavor,
        e.g. **Aeronautics in agricul-
        ture** [to be added as needed]
  BT **Engineering**
      Locomotion
  NT **Aeronautical sports**
      Aeronautics and civilization
      Aeronautics in agriculture
      Air pilots
      Airplanes
      Airports
      Airships
      Astronautics
      Balloons
      Gliders (Aeronautics)
      Gliding and soaring
      Helicopters
      High speed aeronautics
      Kites
      Lasers in aeronautics
      Meteorology in aeronautics
      Military aeronautics
      Navigation (Aeronautics)
      Parachutes
      Radio in aeronautics
      Rocketry
      Rockets (Aeronautics)
      Unidentified flying objects
  RT **Aerodynamics**
      Flight
Aeronautics—Accidents
  USE **Aircraft accidents**
Aeronautics and civilization   306
  UF Civilization and aeronautics
  BT **Aeronautics**
      Civilization
  NT **Astronautics and civilization**

Aeronautics, Commercial
  USE **Commercial aeronautics**
Aeronautics—Flights   387.7; 629.13
  UF   Aeronautics—Voyages
        Flights around the world
        Transatlantic flights
  BT   **Voyages and travels**
  NT   **Space flight**
Aeronautics in agriculture   631.3
  UF   Aerial spraying and dusting
        Airplanes in agriculture
        Crop dusting
        Crop spraying
  BT   **Aeronautics**
        Agriculture
        Spraying and dusting
  RT   **Agricultural pests**
Aeronautics—Medical aspects
  USE **Aviation medicine**
Aeronautics, Military
  USE **Military aeronautics**
Aeronautics—Navigation
  USE **Navigation (Aeronautics)**
Aeronautics—Piloting
  USE **Airplanes—Piloting**
Aeronautics—Safety measures   387.7;
        629.134
  BT   **Accidents—Prevention**
  NT   **Air traffic control**
Aeronautics—Study and teaching
        629.1307
  UF   Flight training
  NT   **Airplanes—Piloting**
Aeronautics—Voyages
  USE **Aeronautics—Flights**
Aeroplanes
  USE **Airplanes**
Aerosol sniffing
  USE **Solvent abuse**
Aerosols   541; 551.51; 660
  BT   **Air pollution**
Aerospace industries
  USE **Aerospace industry**
Aerospace industry (May subdiv. geog.)
        338.4
  UF   Aerospace industries
        Aircraft production
  BT   **Industries**
  NT   **Airplane industry**
Aerospace law
  USE **Space law**

Aerospace medicine
  USE **Aviation medicine**
        Space medicine
Aerothermodynamics   629.132; 629.4
  UF   Thermoaerodynamics
  BT   **Astronautics**
        High speed aeronautics
        Supersonic aerodynamics
        Thermodynamics
Aesthetics   111; 701; 801
  UF   Beauty
        Esthetics
        Taste (Aesthetics)
  SA   styles and movements in the
        arts, e.g. **Classicism**;
        Postmodernism; etc., and
        aesthetics of particular coun-
        tries, e.g. **Japanese aesthetics**
        [to be added as needed]
  BT   **Philosophy**
  NT   **Art appreciation**
        Avant-garde (Aesthetics)
        Classicism
        Color
        Criticism
        Japanese aesthetics
        Kitsch
        Modernism (Aesthetics)
        Postmodernism
        Rhythm
        Romanticism
        Values
  RT   **Arts**
Aesthetics, Japanese
  USE **Japanese aesthetics**
Affection
  USE **Friendship**
        Love
Affective disorders   616.85
  UF   Mood disorders
  BT   **Abnormal psychology**
  NT   **Depression (Psychology)**
        Manic-depressive illness
Affirmations   158.1
  BT   **Self-help techniques**
Affirmative action programs (May
        subdiv. geog.)   **331.13; 658.3**
  UF   Equal employment opportunity
        Equal opportunity in employ-
        ment

Affirmative action programs—*Continued*
- BT **Discrimination in employment**
  Personnel management

Affliction
- USE **Joy and sorrow**
  Suffering

Affluent people
- USE **Rich**

Affordable housing
- USE **Housing**

Afghanistan   958.1

  May be subdivided like **United States** except for *History*.

Africa   960
- NT **Central Africa**
  East Africa
  North Africa
  Northeast Africa
  Northwest Africa
  South Africa
  Southern Africa
  Sub-Saharan Africa
  West Africa
- RT **Africans**

Africa, Central
- USE **Central Africa**

Africa—Civilization   306.096; 960
- UF African civilization
- BT **Civilization**

Africa, East
- USE **East Africa**

Africa, Eastern
- USE **East Africa**

Africa, French-speaking Equatorial
- USE **French-speaking Equatorial Africa**

Africa, French-speaking West
- USE **French-speaking West Africa**

Africa—History   960
Africa—History—1960-   960.3
Africa, North
- USE **North Africa**

Africa, Northeast
- USE **Northeast Africa**

Africa, Northwest
- USE **Northwest Africa**

Africa—Politics and government   320.96
- NT **Pan-Africanism**

Africa, Southern
- USE **Southern Africa**

Africa—Study and teaching   960.07
- UF African studies

- BT **Area studies**

Africa, Sub-Saharan
- USE **Sub-Saharan Africa**

Africa, West
- USE **West Africa**

African American actors   791.4; 792; 920
- UF African American actors and actresses
  Afro-American actors
- BT **Actors**
  Black actors

African American actors and actresses
- USE **African American actors**

African American art (May subdiv. geog.)   **704**

  Use for materials on works of art by several African American artists. Materials on African Americans depicted in works of art are entered under **African Americans in art**.
- UF Afro-American art
- BT **Art**
  Black art
- NT **Harlem Renaissance**
- RT **African American artists**

African American artists   709.2; 920

  Use for materials on several African Americans artists.
- UF Afro-American artists
- BT **Artists**
  Black artists
- RT **African American art**

African American athletes   796.092; 920
- UF Afro-American athletes
- BT **Athletes**
  Black athletes

African American authors   810.9; 920

  Use for materials on several African American authors.
- UF Afro-American authors
- SA genres of American literature with the subdivision *African American authors*, e.g. **American poetry—African American authors**; etc. [to be added as needed]
- BT **American authors**
  Black authors

African American business people
- USE **African American businesspeople**

African American businesspeople   338.092; 658.0092; 920

13

African American businesspeople—*Continued*

UF   African American business people

Afro-American businesspeople

BT   **Black businesspeople**

Businesspeople

African American children 305.23

UF   Afro-American children

BT   **Black children**

Children

African American dancers (May subdiv. geog.) **792.8092; 793.3092; 920**

BT   **African Americans**

Dancers

African American educators (May subdiv. geog.) **370.92; 920**

BT   **African Americans**

Educators

African American elderly 305.26

BT   **Elderly**

African American folklore

USE   **African Americans—Folklore**

African American History Month

USE   **Black History Month**

African American inventors (May subdiv. geog.) **609.2; 920**

BT   **African Americans**

Inventors

African American librarians 020.92; 920

UF   Afro-American librarians

BT   **Black librarians**

Librarians

African American literature

USE   **American literature—African American authors**

African American men 305.38

UF   Afro-American men

BT **Men**

African American music (May subdiv. geog.) **780.089**

Use for materials on the music of African Americans. Materials on the music of Blacks not limited to the United States are entered under **Black music**.

UF   African American songs

Afro-Americans—Music

Songs, African American

BT   **Black music**

Music

NT   **Blues music**

Gospel music

Harlem Renaissance

Rap music

RT   **African American musicians**

Spirituals (Songs)

African American musicians 780.92; 920

UF   Afro-American musicians

BT   **Black musicians**

Musicians

RT   **African American music**

African American poetry

USE   **American poetry—African American authors**

African American singers (May subdiv. geog.) **782.0092; 920**

BT   **African Americans**

Singers

African American songs

USE   **African American music**

African American suffrage

USE   **African Americans—Suffrage**

African American women 305.48

UF   Afro-American women

BT   **Black women**

Women

African American youth 305.235

BT   **Youth**

African Americans (May subdiv. geog. by cities, states, or regions of the U.S.) **305.896; 973**

Use for materials dealing collectively with Blacks in the United States. General materials and materials on Blacks in places other than the United States are entered under **Blacks**.

UF   Afro-Americans

Black Americans

Blacks—United States

Negroes

SA   African Americans in various occupations and professions, e.g. **African American artists**; **African American librarians**; etc. [to be added as needed]

BT   **Blacks**

NT   **African American dancers**

African American educators

African American inventors

African American singers

Libraries and African Americans

African Americans—*Continued*
    World War, 1939-1945—African Americans
African Americans and libraries
    USE   **Libraries and African Americans**
African Americans—Biography   920
    BT   **Blacks—Biography**
African Americans—Chicago (Ill.)
        305.896; 977.3
African Americans—Civil rights (May subdiv. geog.)   **323.1196; 342**
    BT   **Blacks—Civil rights**
        Civil rights
    NT   **African Americans—Suffrage**
African Americans—Economic conditions
        (May subdiv. geog.)   **330.973**
    BT   **Blacks—Economic conditions**
        Economic conditions
African Americans—Education (May subdiv. geog.)   **370.89; 371.829**
    BT   **Blacks—Education**
        Education
African Americans—Employment (May subdiv. geog.)   **331.6**
    BT   **Blacks—Employment**
        Employment
African Americans—Folklore   398
    UF   African American folklore
    BT   **Blacks—Folklore**
        Folklore
African Americans—Housing (May subdiv. geog.)   **307.3; 363.5**
    BT   **Blacks—Housing**
        Housing
African Americans in art   **704.9**

Use for materials on African Americans depicted in works of art. Materials on the attainments of several African Americans in the area of art are entered under **African American artists**. Materials on works of art by several African American artists are entered under **African American art**.

    UF   Afro-Americans in art
    BT   **Art—Themes**
African Americans in literature   809

Use for materials on the theme of African Americans in works of literature. Materials on several African American authors are entered under **African American authors**. Materials on works of literature by several African American authors are entered under **American literature—African American authors** and the various forms of American literature with the subdivision *African American authors*, e.g.

American poetry—African American authors.
    UF   Afro-Americans in literature
    BT   **Literature—Themes**
African Americans in motion pictures
        791.43

Use for materials on the depiction of African Americans in motion pictures. Materials on several African American actors are entered under **African American actors**. Materials discussing all aspects of African Americans' involvement in motion pictures are entered under **African Americans in the motion picture industry**.

    BT   **Blacks in motion pictures**
        Motion pictures
African Americans in television
    USE   **African Americans on television**
African Americans in television broadcasting   **791.45; 384.55**

Use for materials on all aspects of African Americans' involvement in the television industry. Materials on the portrayal of African Americans in television programs are entered under **African Americans on television**.

    UF   African Americans in the television industry
        Afro-Americans in television broadcasting
    BT   **Television broadcasting**
African Americans in the motion picture industry   **791.43092**

Use for materials on all aspects of African Americans' involvement in motion pictures. Materials on the depiction of African Americans in motion pictures are entered under **African Americans in motion pictures**.

    BT   **Blacks in the motion picture industry**
        Motion picture industry
African Americans in the television industry
    USE   **African Americans in television broadcasting**
African Americans—Intellectual life
        (May subdiv. geog.)   **305.896**
    BT   **Blacks—Intellectual life**
        Intellectual life
African Americans—Ohio   **305.896; 977.1**
African Americans on television   **791.45**

Use for materials on the portrayal of African Americans in television programs. Materials on all aspects of African Americans' involvement in the television industry are entered under **African Americans in television broadcasting**.

African Americans on television—*Continued*

UF African Americans in television
Afro-Americans on television
BT **Television**
African Americans—Political activity
(May subdiv. geog.) **322.4; 324**
BT **Blacks—Political activity**
Political participation
NT **Black nationalism**
Black power
African Americans—Race identity
305.896
BT **Blacks—Race identity**
Race awareness
NT **Black nationalism**
African Americans—Religion **270.089;**
299.6
BT **Blacks—Religion**
Religion
NT **Black Muslims**
African Americans—Segregation (May
subdiv. geog.) **305.896**
BT **Blacks—Segregation**
Segregation
African Americans—Social conditions
(May subdiv. geog.) **305.896**
BT **Blacks—Social conditions**
Social conditions
African Americans—Social life and cus-
toms (May subdiv. geog.)
305.896
BT **Blacks—Social life and cus-**
toms
Manners and customs
African Americans—Southern States
305.896; 975
UF Southern States—African Ameri-
cans
African Americans—Suffrage (May
subdiv. geog.) **324.6**
UF African American suffrage
BT **African Americans—Civil**
rights
Blacks—Suffrage
Suffrage
African art **709.6**
BT **Art**
African civilization
USE **Africa—Civilization**
African diaspora **304.8096**

UF Black diaspora
Diaspora, African
BT **Human geography**
African literature **896**
BT **Literature**
African literature (English) **820**
BT **Literature**
African mythology **398.2096**
BT **Mythology**
African peoples
USE **Africans**
African relations
USE **Pan-Africanism**
African songs **782.42096**
UF Songs, African
BT **Songs**
African studies
USE **Africa—Study and teaching**
Africans **305.896; 960**
UF African peoples
SA names of African peoples, e.g.
Yoruba (African people) [to
be added as needed]
NT **Blacks—Africa**
Yoruba (African people)
RT **Africa**
Afrikaaners
USE **Afrikaners**
Afrikaners **305.83; 968**
UF Afrikaaners
Boers
South African Dutch
South Africans, Afrikaans-
speaking
Afro-American actors
USE **African American actors**
Afro-American art
USE **African American art**
Afro-American artists
USE **African American artists**
Afro-American athletes
USE **African American athletes**
Afro-American authors
USE **African American authors**
Afro-American businesspeople
USE **African American**
businesspeople
Afro-American children
USE **African American children**
Afro-American librarians
USE **African American librarians**

Afro-American men
  USE **African American men**
Afro-American musicians
  USE **African American musicians**
Afro-American women
  USE **African American women**
Afro-Americans
  USE **African Americans**
Afro-Americans and libraries
  USE **Libraries and African Americans**
Afro-Americans in art
  USE **African Americans in art**
Afro-Americans in literature
  USE **African Americans in literature**
Afro-Americans in television broadcasting
  USE **African Americans in television broadcasting**
Afro-Americans—Music
  USE **African American music**
Afro-Americans on television
  USE **African Americans on television**
After dinner speeches   808.5; 808.85
  BT **Speeches**
  RT **Toasts**
After school day care
  USE **After school programs**
After school programs   362.71; 372.12
  UF After school day care
  BT **Student activities**
Afterlife
  USE **Future life**
Afternoon teas   641.5
  UF Teas
  BT **Cooking**
  RT **Entertaining**
      Tea
Age   305.2
  UF Age groups
  SA types of animals, plants, and
      crops with the subdivision
      Age [to be added as needed]
  NT **Adolescence**
      Adults
      Age and employment
      Aging
      Children
      Drinking age
      Elderly

Life expectancy
Longevity
Middle age
Middle aged persons
Old age
Teenagers
Youth
Age and employment   331.3
  UF Employment and age
  BT **Age**
      Employment
  NT **Career changes**
      Child labor
      Teenagers—Employment
      Youth—Employment
Age discrimination   305.2
  BT **Discrimination**
Age groups
  USE **Age**
Age—Physiological effect
  USE **Aging**
Aged
  USE **Elderly**
Aged men
  USE **Elderly men**
Aged parents
  USE **Aging parents**
Aged—Pensions
  USE **Old age pensions**
Aged women
  USE **Elderly women**
Ageing
  USE **Aging**
Agent Orange   363.17; 615.9
  BT **Herbicides**
Aggregates
  USE **Set theory**
Aggressive behavior
  USE **Aggressiveness (Psychology)**
Aggressiveness (Psychology)   152.4; 155.2
  UF Aggressive behavior
  BT **Human behavior**
      Psychology
  NT **Assertiveness (Psychology)**
      Bullies
      Teasing
      Violence
Aging   571.8; 612.6
  UF Age—Physiological effect
      Ageing

Aging—*Continued*
    Senescence
  SA   types of animals, organs of the
       body, plants, and crops with
       the subdivision *Aging* [to be
       added as needed]
  BT   **Age**
       Elderly
       Gerontology
       Longevity
       Middle age
       Old age
  NT   **Male climacteric**
       Menopause
Aging parents (May subdiv. geog.)
    306.874
  UF   Aged parents
       Elderly parents
  BT   **Elderly**
       Parents
Aging persons
  USE **Elderly**
Agnosticism   149; 211
  BT   **Free thought**
       Religion
  RT   **Atheism**
       Belief and doubt
       Positivism
       Rationalism
       Skepticism
Agoraphobia   616.85
  UF   Fear of open spaces
  BT   **Phobias**
Agrarian question
  USE **Agriculture—Economic aspects**
       Agriculture—Government poli-
       cy
       Land tenure
Agrarian reform
  USE **Land reform**
Agreements
  USE **Contracts**
       Covenants
Agribusiness
  USE **Agricultural industry**
Agricultural bacteriology   630.2
  UF   Bacteriology, Agricultural
       Diseases and pests
  SA   types of crops, plants, trees, etc.,
       with the subdivision *Diseases*
       and pests, e.g. **Fruit—Diseas-**

       es and pests [to be added as
       needed]
  BT   **Bacteriology**
  RT   **Soil microbiology**
Agricultural botany
  USE **Economic botany**
Agricultural chemicals   631.8; 668
  SA   types of agricultural chemicals
       and names of individual
       chemicals [to be added as
       needed]
  BT   **Agricultural chemistry**
       Chemicals
  NT   **Fertilizers**
       Herbicides
       Insecticides
       Pesticides
Agricultural chemistry   630.2
  BT   **Chemistry**
  NT   **Agricultural chemicals**
  RT   **Soils**
Agricultural clubs
  USE **Agriculture—Societies**
Agricultural cooperation
  USE **Cooperative agriculture**
Agricultural credit (May subdiv. geog.)
    332.7
  UF   Farm credit
       Farm loans
       Rural credit
  BT   **Agriculture—Economic aspects**
       Banks and banking
       Credit
Agricultural economics
  USE **Agriculture—Economic aspects**
Agricultural education
  USE **Agriculture—Study and teach-**
       ing
Agricultural engineering (May subdiv.
    geog.)   **630**
  UF   Agricultural mechanics
       Farm mechanics
  BT   **Engineering**
  NT   **Drainage**
       Electricity in agriculture
       Irrigation
  RT   **Agricultural machinery**
Agricultural experiment stations (May
    subdiv. geog.)   **630.7**
  UF   Experimental farms

Agricultural experiment stations—*Continued*

   BT   **Agriculture—Government policy**

         Agriculture—Research

         Agriculture—Study and teaching

   RT   **Agricultural extension work**

Agricultural extension work (May subdiv. geog.)   **630.7**

   BT   **Adult education**

         Agriculture—Government policy

   NT   **County agricultural agents**

   RT   **Agricultural experiment stations**

         Agriculture—Study and teaching

         Community development

Agricultural industries

   USE   **Agricultural industry**

Agricultural industry (May subdiv. geog.)   **338.1**

   UF   Agribusiness

         Agricultural industries

   BT   **Agriculture—Economic aspects**

         Industries

   NT   **Food industry**

Agricultural innovations (May subdiv. geog.)   **631**

   UF   Agriculture—Innovations

   BT   **Technological innovations**

Agricultural laborers (May subdiv. geog.)   **331.7**

   UF   Farm laborers

   BT   **Labor**

   RT   **Migrant labor**

         Peasantry

Agricultural machinery   **631.3**

   UF   Agricultural tools

         Farm engines

         Farm equipment

         Farm implements

         Farm machinery

         Farm mechanics

   SA   types of farm machinery [to be added as needed]

   BT   **Machinery**

         Tools

   NT   **Electricity in agriculture**

         Harvesting machinery

         Plows

         Tractors

   RT   **Agricultural engineering**

Agricultural mechanics

   USE   **Agricultural engineering**

Agricultural pests   **632**

   UF   Diseases and pests

         Garden pests

   SA   types of crops, plants, trees, etc., with the subdivision *Diseases and pests*, e.g. **Fruit—Diseases and pests** [to be added as needed]

   BT   **Economic zoology**

         Pests

   NT   **Fruit—Diseases and pests**

         Fungi

         Pest control

         Plant diseases

         Spraying and dusting

         Weeds

   RT   **Aeronautics in agriculture**

         Insect pests

Agricultural policy

   USE   **Agriculture—Government policy**

Agricultural products

   USE   **Farm produce**

Agricultural research

   USE   **Agriculture—Research**

Agricultural societies

   USE   **Agriculture—Societies**

Agricultural subsidies (May subdiv. geog.)   **338.9**

   UF   Farm subsidies

   BT   **Subsidies**

   RT   **Agriculture—Government policy**

Agricultural tools

   USE   **Agricultural machinery**

Agriculture (May subdiv. geog.)   **338.1; 630**

   UF   Agronomy

         Farming

         Planting

   SA   types of agriculture, e.g. **Truck farming**; types of agricultural products, e.g. **Corn**; and ethnic groups with the subdivision *Agriculture*, e.g. **Native Americans—Agriculture** [to be added as needed]

Agriculture—*Continued*
- BT   **Life sciences**
- NT   **Aeronautics in agriculture**
  Aquaculture
  Beekeeping
  Cooperative agriculture
  Crop rotation
  Cultivated plants
  Dairying
  Dry farming
  Economic botany
  Farmers
  Forests and forestry
  Fruit culture
  Gardening
  Horticulture
  Livestock industry
  Native Americans—Agriculture
  Organic farming
  Pastures
  Plant breeding
  Reclamation of land
  Soils
  Truck farming
- RT   **Farms**
  Food supply

Agriculture and state
- USE   **Agriculture—Government poli-cy**

Agriculture—Bibliography   016.63

Agriculture, Cooperative
- USE   **Cooperative agriculture**

Agriculture—Documentation   025
- BT   **Documentation**

Agriculture—Economic aspects (May subdiv. geog.)   **338.1**
- UF   Agrarian question
  Agricultural economics
- BT   **Economics**
- NT   **Agricultural credit**
  Agricultural industry
  Land tenure
- RT   **Farm management**
  Farm produce—Marketing

Agriculture—Government policy (May subdiv. geog.)   **338.9**
- UF   Agrarian question
  Agricultural policy
  Agriculture and state
  State and agriculture
- BT   **Industrial policy**

- NT   **Agricultural experiment sta-tions**
  Agricultural extension work
  Rural development
- RT   **Agricultural subsidies**
  Land reform

Agriculture—Innovations
- USE   **Agricultural innovations**

Agriculture—Research   630.7
- UF   Agricultural research
- BT   **Research**
- NT   **Agricultural experiment sta-tions**

Agriculture—Societies   630.6
- UF   Agricultural clubs
  Agricultural societies
- SA   names of agricultural societies [to be added as needed]
- BT   **Associations**
  Country life
  Societies
- NT   **4-H clubs**
  Grange

Agriculture—Statistics   338.1; 630.2
- UF   Crop reports
- BT   **Statistics**

Agriculture—Study and teaching   630.7
- UF   Agricultural education
- BT   **Vocational education**
- NT   **4-H clubs**
  Agricultural experiment sta-tions
  County agricultural agents
- RT   **Agricultural extension work**

Agriculture—Tenant farming
- USE   **Farm tenancy**

Agriculture—Tropics   630.913
- BT   **Tropics**

Agriculture—United States   630.973

Agronomy
- USE   **Agriculture**

AI (Artificial intelligence)
- USE   **Artificial intelligence**

Aid to dependent children
- USE   **Child welfare**

Aid to developing areas
- USE   **Foreign aid**
  Technical assistance

AIDS (Disease) (May subdiv. geog.)   **616.97**

AIDS (Disease)—*Continued*
- UF   Acquired immune deficiency syndrome
  - HIV disease
- BT   **Communicable diseases**
  - **Diseases**

AIDS (Disease)—Prevention   616.97

Use for materials on AIDS prevention in general not limited to safe sexual practices. Materials limited to safe sexual practices in the prevention of AIDS are entered under **Safe sex in AIDS prevention**.
- NT   **Safe sex in AIDS prevention**

AIDS (Disease)—Treatment   615.5
- BT   **Therapeutics**

Air   533; 546

Use for materials dealing with air in general and with its chemical and physical properties. Materials on the body of air surrounding the earth are entered under **Atmosphere**.
- BT   **Meteorology**
- NT   **Aerodynamics**
  - **Atmosphere**
  - **Bubbles**
  - **Ventilation**
- RT   **Atmosphere**

Air bases (May subdiv. geog.)   **358.4**
- UF   Military air bases
  - Naval air bases
- BT   **Airports**
  - **Military aeronautics**

Air cargo
- USE   **Commercial aeronautics**

Air carriers
- USE   **Airlines**

Air charters
- USE   **Airlines—Chartering**

Air conditioning   644; 697.9
- SA   subjects with the subdivision *Air conditioning* [to be added as needed]
- NT   **Automobiles—Air conditioning**
- RT   **Refrigeration**
  - **Ventilation**

Air crashes
- USE   **Aircraft accidents**

Air-cushion vehicles   629.3
- UF   Ground effect machines
  - Hovercraft
- BT   **Vehicles**

Air defenses (May subdiv. geog.)   **363.3**

Use for materials on military defense against air attack. Materials on the protection of civilians from enemy attack are entered under **Civil defense**.

- UF   Air raid defensive measures
- BT   **Military aeronautics**
- NT   **Radar defense networks**

Air freight
- USE   **Commercial aeronautics**

Air guitar   787.87
- BT   **Guitars**

Air lines
- USE   **Airlines**

Air mail service   383
- BT   **Commercial aeronautics**
  - **Postal service**

Air—Microbiology   579
- UF   Aerobiology
- BT   **Microbiology**

Air, Moisture of
- USE   **Humidity**

Air navigation
- USE   **Navigation (Aeronautics)**

Air pilots   629.13092; 920
- UF   Airplane pilots
  - Aviators
  - Pilots
  - Test pilots
- BT   **Aeronautics**
- NT   **Astronauts**
  - **Women air pilots**

Air piracy
- USE   **Hijacking of airplanes**

Air pollution (May subdiv. geog.)   **363.739; 628.5**
- UF   Atmosphere—Pollution
  - Pollution of air
- BT   **Environmental health**
  - **Pollution**
- NT   **Aerosols**
  - **Dust**
  - **Indoor air pollution**

Air pollution—Measurement   363.739; 628.5
- BT   **Measurement**

Air pollution—United States   363.739; 628.5

Air power   358.4
- BT   **Military aeronautics**

Air raid defensive measures
- USE   **Air defenses**

Air raid shelters   363.3
- UF   Blast shelters
  - Bomb shelters
  - Fallout shelters

Air raid shelters—*Continued*
>Nuclear bomb shelters
>Public shelters
>Shelters, Air raid
>BT   **Civil defense**

Air rights law
>USE   **Airspace law**

Air routes
>USE   **Aeronautics**

Air-ships
>USE   **Airships**

Air space law
>USE   **Airspace law**

Air surfing
>USE   **Gliding and soaring**

Air terminals
>USE   **Airports**

Air traffic control   **387.7**
>UF   Airports—Traffic control
>BT   **Aeronautics—Safety measures**

Air transport
>USE   **Commercial aeronautics**

Air travel (May subdiv. geog.)   **387.7**
>BT   **Transportation**
>**Travel**
>**Voyages and travels**

Air warfare
>USE   **Military aeronautics**
>**Military airplanes**

Aircraft
>USE   **Airplanes**
>**Airships**
>**Balloons**
>**Gliders (Aeronautics)**
>**Helicopters**

Aircraft accidents (May subdiv. geog.)   **363.12; 629.13**
>UF   Aeronautics—Accidents
>Air crashes
>Airplane accidents
>Airplane crashes
>Airplanes—Accidents
>Aviation accidents
>Plane crashes
>BT   **Accidents**
>RT   **Survival after airplane accidents, shipwrecks, etc.**

Aircraft carriers   **359.3; 623**
>UF   Airplane carriers
>BT   **Military aeronautics**
>**Warships**

Aircraft industry
>USE   **Airplane industry**

Aircraft production
>USE   **Aerospace industry**
>**Airplane industry**

Airdromes
>USE   **Airports**

Airline hostesses
>USE   **Flight attendants**

Airline stewardesses
>USE   **Flight attendants**

Airline stewards
>USE   **Flight attendants**

Airlines (May subdiv. geog.)   **387.7**
>Use for materials on companies engaged in commercial aviation. Materials on various types of aircraft and on the scientific or technical aspects of aircraft and their construction and operation are entered under **Aeronautics**.
>UF   Air carriers
>Air lines
>BT   **Commercial aeronautics**
>NT   **Flight attendants**

Airlines—Chartering   **387.7**
>UF   Air charters
>Airplanes—Chartering
>Charter flights

Airlines—Hijacking
>USE   **Hijacking of airplanes**

Airplane accidents
>USE   **Aircraft accidents**

Airplane carriers
>USE   **Aircraft carriers**

Airplane crashes
>USE   **Aircraft accidents**

Airplane engines   **629.134**
>UF   Airplane motors
>Airplanes—Engines
>Airplanes—Motors
>BT   **Engines**
>NT   **Jet propulsion**

Airplane hijacking
>USE   **Hijacking of airplanes**

Airplane industry (May subdiv. geog.)   **338.4; 387.7**
>UF   Aircraft industry
>Aircraft production
>BT   **Aerospace industry**

Airplane motors
>USE   **Airplane engines**

Airplane pilots
>USE   **Air pilots**

Airplane racing   **797.5**

Airplane racing—*Continued*
  UF   Airplanes—Racing
  BT   **Aeronautical sports**
        Racing
Airplane spotting
  USE   **Airplanes—Identification**
Airplanes   387.7; 629.133
  UF   Aeroplanes
        Aircraft
  SA   types of airplanes and specific
          makes of airplanes [to be
          added as needed]
  BT   **Aeronautics**
  NT   **Aerial propellers**
        Bombers
        Gliders (Aeronautics)
        Helicopters
        Jet planes
        Military airplanes
Airplanes—Accidents
  USE   **Aircraft accidents**
Airplanes—Chartering
  USE   **Airlines—Chartering**
Airplanes—Design and construction
        629.134
Airplanes—Electric equipment   629.135
  UF   Airplanes—Instruments
  BT   **Aeronautical instruments**
Airplanes—Engines
  USE   **Airplane engines**
Airplanes—Flight testing
  USE   **Airplanes—Testing**
Airplanes—Hijacking
  USE   **Hijacking of airplanes**
Airplanes—Identification   623.74;
        629.133
  UF   Airplane spotting
        Airplanes—Recognition
  BT   **Identification**
Airplanes in agriculture
  USE   **Aeronautics in agriculture**
Airplanes—Inspection   387.7; 629.134
Airplanes—Instruments
  USE   **Aeronautical instruments**
        Airplanes—Electric equipment
Airplanes—Maintenance and repair
        629.134
  UF   Airplanes—Repair
Airplanes—Materials   629.134
  BT   **Materials**
Airplanes, Military
  USE   **Military airplanes**

Airplanes—Models   629.133
  UF   Model airplanes
        Paper airplanes
  BT   **Models and modelmaking**
Airplanes—Motors
  USE   **Airplane engines**
Airplanes—Noise   629.132
  BT   **Noise**
        Noise pollution
Airplanes—Operation
  USE   **Airplanes—Piloting**
Airplanes—Piloting   629.132
  UF   Aeronautics—Piloting
        Airplanes—Operation
        Flight training
  SA   types and names of airplanes
          with the subdivision *Piloting*
          [to be added as needed]
  BT   **Aeronautics—Study and teach-
          ing**
        Navigation (Aeronautics)
  NT   **Helicopters—Piloting**
        Instrument flying
        Stunt flying
Airplanes—Propellers
  USE   **Aerial propellers**
Airplanes—Racing
  USE   **Airplane racing**
Airplanes—Recognition
  USE   **Airplanes—Identification**
Airplanes—Repair
  USE   **Airplanes—Maintenance and
          repair**
Airplanes, Rocket propelled
  USE   **Rocket planes**
Airplanes—Testing   629.134
  UF   Airplanes—Flight testing
        Test pilots
Airports (May subdiv. geog.)   **387.7;**
        629.136
  UF   Aerodromes
        Air terminals
        Airdromes
  SA   names of individual airports [to
          be added as needed]
  BT   **Aeronautics**
  NT   **Air bases**
        Heliports
Airports—Security measures   363.28
Airports—Traffic control
  USE   **Air traffic control**

Airships   629.133

Use for materials on self-propelled aircraft that are lighter than air and steerable. Materials on aircraft held aloft by hot air or light gases that are nondirigible and propelled only by the wind are entered under **Balloons**.

UF   Air-ships

Aircraft

Balloons, Dirigible

Blimps

Dirigible balloons

Zeppelins

BT   **Aeronautics**

RT   **Balloons**

Airspace law   341.4

UF   Air rights law

Air space law

BT   **Property**

Airways

USE   **Aeronautics**

Alaska Highway (Alaska and Canada)
      388.1; 979.8

BT   **Roads**

Alchemy   540.1

Use for materials on medieval attempts to change base metals into gold. Materials on the transmutation of metals in nuclear physics are entered under **Transmutation (Chemistry)**.

UF   Hermetic art and philosophy

Philosophers' stone

Transmutation of metals

BT   **Chemistry**

Occultism

RT   **Transmutation (Chemistry)**

Alcohol   547; 661

UF   Alcohol use

Intoxicants

SA   classes of persons with the subdivision *Alcohol use*, e.g. **Employees—Alcohol use; Youth—Alcohol use**; etc. [to be added as needed]

BT   **Chemicals**

NT   **Alcohol fuels**

Alcoholic beverages

Denatured alcohol

RT   **Alcoholism**

Distillation

Alcohol and employees

USE   **Employees—Alcohol use**

Alcohol and teenagers

USE   **Teenagers—Alcohol use**

Alcohol and youth

USE   **Youth—Alcohol use**

Alcohol consumption

USE   **Drinking of alcoholic beverages**

Alcohol, Denatured

USE   **Denatured alcohol**

Alcohol fuels   662

UF   Ethanol as fuel [*Former heading*]

Ethyl alcohol fuel

BT   **Alcohol**

Fuel

Alcohol in the workplace

USE   **Employees—Alcohol use**

Alcohol—Physiological effect   615

Alcohol use

USE   **Alcohol**

Alcoholism

Drinking of alcoholic beverages

and classes of persons with the subdivision *Alcohol use*, e.g. **Employees—Alcohol use; Youth—Alcohol use**; etc. [to be added as needed]

Alcoholic beverage consumption

USE   **Drinking of alcoholic beverages**

Alcoholic beverages   641.2

UF   Drinks

Intoxicants

BT   **Alcohol**

Beverages

NT   **Liquors**

Wine and wine making

RT   **Drinking of alcoholic beverages**

Alcoholic parents

USE   **Adult children of alcoholics**

Children of alcoholics

Alcoholics   362.292; 616.86

UF   Drunkards

NT   **Recovering alcoholics**

RT   **Adult children of alcoholics**

Alcoholism

Children of alcoholics

Alcoholism (May subdiv. geog.)
      362.292; 616.86

UF   Addiction to alcohol

Alcohol use

Drinking problem

Drunkenness

Intemperance

Intoxication

Liquor problem

Problem drinking

Alcoholism—*Continued*

SA classes of persons with the subdivision *Alcohol use*, e.g. **Employees—Alcohol use**; **Youth—Alcohol use**; etc. [to be added as needed]

BT **Social problems**

RT **Alcohol**
Alcoholics
Drinking of alcoholic beverages
Temperance
Twelve-step programs

Alfalfa 583; 633.3

BT **Forage plants**

Algae 579.8

UF Sea mosses
Seaweeds

BT **Marine plants**

Algebra 512

BT **Mathematical analysis**
Mathematics

NT **Graph theory**
Group theory
Linear algebra
Logarithms
Number theory
Probabilities
Sequences (Mathematics)

Algebra, Boolean

USE **Boolean algebra**

Algeria 965

May be subdivided like **United States** except for *History*.

Alien abduction (May subdiv. geog.) 001.942

UF Abduction of humans by aliens
Extraterrestrial abduction
UFO abduction

BT **Human-alien encounters**

Alien encounters with humans

USE **Human-alien encounters**

Alien labor (May subdiv. geog.) 331.6

BT **Labor**

RT **Migrant labor**

Alienation (Social psychology) 302.5

UF Estrangement (Social psychology)
Rebels (Social psychology)
Social alienation

BT **Social psychology**

Aliens (May subdiv. geog.) 323.6

UF Foreign population
Foreigners
Noncitizens
Nonnationals

SA national groups subdivided by the place of their residence, e.g. **Mexicans—United States** [to be added as needed]

BT **Minorities**

NT **Illegal aliens**
Refugees

RT **Citizenship**
Immigrants
Immigration and emigration
Naturalization

Aliens from outer space

USE **Extraterrestrial beings**

Aliens—United States 325.73

UF United States—Foreign population

NT **Mexicans—United States**

RT **United States—Immigration and emigration**

Alimony (May subdiv. geog.) 346.01

BT **Divorce**

All Fools' Day

USE **April Fools' Day**

All Hallows' Eve

USE **Halloween**

All terrain bicycles

USE **Mountain bikes**

All terrain cycling

USE **Mountain biking**

All terrain vehicles 629.22

UF ATVs

SA types of vehicles, e.g. **Snowmobiles** [to be added as needed]

BT **Vehicles**

NT **Mountain bikes**
Snowmobiles

Allegories 808.88

Use for individual works or for collections of allegories. Materials on allegory as a literary form or on allegory in the fine and decorative arts are entered under **Allegory**.

BT **Fiction**

RT **Fables**
Parables

Allegory 704.9; 808

Use for materials on allegory as a literary form as well as for allegory in the fine and decorative arts. Individual allegories and collections of allegories are entered under **Allegories**.

Allegory—*Continued*
- BT **Arts**
- **Fiction**
- RT **Symbolism in literature**

Allergies
- USE **Allergy**

Allergies, Food
- USE **Food allergy**

Allergy   616.97
- UF Allergies
- SA types of allergies [to be added as needed]
- BT **Immunity**
- NT **Asthma**
- **Food allergy**
- **Hay fever**

Allergy, Food
- USE **Food allergy**

Alleys
- USE **Streets**

Allied health personnel   610.69
- UF Paramedical personnel
- SA types of allied health personnel [to be added as needed]
- NT **Emergency medical technicians**
- **Medical technologists**
- **Nurse practitioners**

Alligators   597.98
- BT **Reptiles**
- RT **Crocodiles**

Allocation of time
- USE **Time management**

Allowances, Children's
- USE **Children's allowances**

Alloys   669
- SA types of alloys [to be added as needed]
- BT **Industrial chemistry**
- **Metals**
- NT **Aluminum alloys**
- **Brass**
- **Pewter**
- RT **Metallurgy**

Allusions   031.02; 803
- SA names of individual persons with the subdivision *Allusions*, for materials on allusions to that person, e.g. **Shakespeare, William, 1564-1616—Allusions** [to be added as needed]
- RT **Terms and phrases**

Almanacs   030
- UF Annuals
- BT **Serial publications**
- NT **Nautical almanacs**
- RT **Calendars**
- **Chronology**
- **Yearbooks**

Alphabet   411

Use for materials on the series of characters that form the elements of a written language and for materials to be used in teaching children the ABCs. Materials on the styles of alphabets used by artists, etc., are entered under **Alphabets**.
- UF ABCs
- Alphabet books
- Letters of the alphabet
- SA names of languages with the subdivision *Alphabet*, e.g. **English language—Alphabet** [to be added as needed]
- BT **Writing**
- NT **Alphabets**

Alphabet books
- USE **Alphabet**

Alphabetizing
- USE **Files and filing**

Alphabets   745.6

Use for materials on the styles of alphabets used by artists, etc. Materials on the series of characters that form the elements of a written language and for materials to be used in teaching children the ABCs are entered under **Alphabet**.
- UF Ornamental alphabets
- BT **Alphabet**
- **Sign painting**
- NT **Monograms**
- RT **Illumination of books and manuscripts**
- **Initials**
- **Lettering**

Alpine animals
- USE **Mountain animals**

Alpine fauna
- USE **Mountain animals**

Alpine flora
- USE **Mountain plants**

Alpine plants
- USE **Mountain plants**

Alternate energy resources
- USE **Renewable energy resources**

Alternate work sites
- USE **Telecommuting**

Alternating current machinery
  USE   **Electric machinery—Alternating current**
Alternating currents
  USE   **Alternating electric currents**
Alternating electric currents   621.31
  UF   Alternating currents
        Electric currents, Alternating
  BT   **Electric currents**
Alternative energy resources
  USE   **Renewable energy resources**
Alternative histories   808.3; 808.83
  Use for individual works, collections, or materials about imaginative works featuring key changes in historical facts.
  BT   **Fantasy fiction**
Alternative lifestyles (May subdiv. geog.)
        306
  Use for materials on ways of living regarded as unacceptable by conventional standards, especially those that reject consumerism, the work ethic, etc.
  BT   **Lifestyles**
  RT   **Counter culture**
Alternative medicine (May subdiv. geog.)
        610; 613; 615.5
  UF   Therapeutic systems
  SA   types of alternative medicine [to be added as needed]
  BT   **Medicine**
  NT   **Acupressure**
        Acupuncture
        Chiropractic
        Health self-care
        Holistic medicine
        Homeopathy
        Mental healing
        Naturopathy
        Reflexology
Alternative military service
  USE   **National service**
Alternative press (May subdiv. geog.)
        070.4
  Use for materials about publications issued clandestinely and contrary to government regulation and for materials about publications issued legally (and usually serially) and produced by radical, anti-establishment, or counter-culture groups.
  UF   Underground literature
        Underground press
  BT   **Press**
Alternative schools
  USE   **Experimental schools**

Alternative universities
  USE   **Free universities**
Alternative work schedules
  USE   **Flexible hours of labor**
        Part-time employment
Altitude, Influence of
  USE   **Environmental influence on humans**
Altruism   171
  UF   Altruistic behavior
        Unselfishness
  BT   **Conduct of life**
  RT   **Charity**
        Helping behavior
Altruistic behavior
  USE   **Altruism**
Altruists
  USE   **Philanthropists**
Aluminum   669; 673
  BT   **Metals**
  NT   **Aluminum foil**
Aluminum alloys   669; 673
  BT   **Alloys**
Aluminum foil   673
  BT   **Aluminum**
        Packaging
Aluminum—Recycling   628.4; 673
  BT   **Recycling**
Alzheimer's disease   616.8
  BT   **Brain—Diseases**
Amateur films   778.5; 791.43
  Use for individual works, collections, or materials about amateur films.
  UF   Amateur motion pictures
        Home movies
        Home video movies
        Personal films
  BT   **Motion pictures**
  RT   **Camcorders**
        Motion picture cameras
Amateur motion pictures
  USE   **Amateur films**
Amateur radio stations   384.54; 621.3841
  UF   Ham radio stations
  BT   **Radio stations**
        Shortwave radio
Amateur theater (May subdiv. geog.)
        792
  UF   Non-professional theater
        Play production
        Private theater

Amateur theater—*Continued*

   BT   **Amusements**
          Theater
   NT   **Charades**
          Children's plays
          College and school drama
          One act plays
          Pantomimes
          Shadow pantomimes and plays
   RT   **Acting**
          Drama in education
          Little theater movement

Ambassadors (May subdiv. geog.)
      327.2092
   BT   **Diplomats**

Ambition   302.5
   BT   **Social psychology**

Amendments, Equal rights
   USE   **Equal rights amendments**

America   970

   Use for general materials on the Western Hemisphere.
   UF   Western Hemisphere
   SA   names of individual countries of the Western Hemisphere [to be added as needed]
   NT   **Caribbean Region**
          Latin America
          North America
          South America

America—Antiquities   970.01
   BT   **Antiquities**

America—Civilization   970; 980

   Use for general materials on the civilization of the Western Hemisphere in modern times. Materials on ancient civilizations in America are entered under **America—Antiquities**; under a region, country, city, etc., with the subdivision *Antiquities*; or under the name of an ancient people. Materials limited to the civilization of the United States are entered under **United States—Civilization**.
   UF   American civilization
   BT   **Civilization**

America—Discovery and exploration
   USE   **America—Exploration**

America—Exploration   970.01
   UF   America—Discovery and exploration
   BT   **Exploration**
   NT   **Northwest Passage**
          United States—Exploration

America—History   970
   UF   American history

America—Politics and government   970
   NT   **Pan-Americanism**

American actors
   USE   **Actors—United States**

American actors and actresses
   USE   **Actors—United States**

American architecture
   USE   **Architecture—United States**

American art   709.73
   UF   Art, American
   BT   **Art**
   NT   **American folk art**

American artificial satellites   629.43; 629.46
   UF   Artificial satellites, American
   BT   **Artificial satellites**

American artists
   USE   **Artists—United States**

American arts
   USE   **Arts—United States**

American authors   810.9; 920
   UF   Authors, American
   BT   **Authors**
   NT   **African American authors**
          American dramatists
          American novelists
          American poets
          Hispanic American authors

American ballads   811
   BT   **American poetry**

American Bicentennial
   USE   **American Revolution Bicentennial, 1776-1976**

American Bill of rights
   USE   **United States. Constitution. 1st-10th amendments**

American bison
   USE   **Bison**

American characteristics
   USE   **American national characteristics**

American Civil War
   USE   **United States—History—1861-1865, Civil War**

American civilization
   USE   **America—Civilization**

American colonial style in architecture   724
   UF   Colonial architecture
   BT   **Architecture**

American colonies
    USE   **United States—History—1600-**
            1775, Colonial period
American color prints   769.973
    UF   Color prints, American
    BT   **Color prints**
American composers
    USE   **Composers—United States**
American constitution
    USE   **United States. Constitution**
American cooking   641.5973
    Use for materials on cooking limited to American national and regional styles.
    UF   Cookery, American
    SA   styles of regional American
          cooking, e.g. **Southern cook-**
          ing [to be added as needed]
    BT   **Cooking**
American decoration and ornament
    USE   **Decoration and ornament—**
          United States
American diaries   809; 920
    Use for collections of American diaries and for materials about American diaries.
    BT   **American literature**
          Diaries
American diplomatic and consular ser-
    vice (May subdiv. geog.)   **327.73;**
    353.1
    UF   Diplomatic and consular service,
          American
          United States—Diplomatic and
          consular service
    BT   **Diplomatic and consular ser-**
          vice
American drama   812
    Use for general materials about American drama, not for individual works.
    BT   **American literature**
          Drama
    NT   **American folk drama**
American drama—Collections   812.008
American drama—History and criticism
    812.009
American dramatists   812.009; 920
    UF   Dramatists, American
    BT   **American authors**
          Dramatists
American drawing   741.973
    UF   Drawing, American
    BT   **Drawing**

American economic assistance
    USE   **American foreign aid**
American engraving   760; 769
    UF   Engraving, American
    BT   **Engraving**
American espionage   327.127; 355.3
    UF   Espionage, American
    BT   **Espionage**
American essays   814; 814.008
    BT   **American literature**
          Essays
American ethics
    USE   **Ethics—United States**
American exploring expeditions
    USE   **United States—Exploring expe-**
          ditions
American fables   813
    BT   **Fables**
American fiction   813
    Use for collections or materials about American fiction, not for individual works.
    BT   **American literature**
          Fiction
American films
    USE   **Motion pictures—United States**
American flag
    USE   **Flags—United States**
American folk art   745.0973
    UF   Folk art, American
    BT   **American art**
          Folk art
American folk dancing
    USE   **Folk dancing—United States**
American folk drama   812
    BT   **American drama**
          Folk drama
American folk music
    USE   **Folk music—United States**
American folk songs
    USE   **Folk songs—United States**
American foreign aid (May subdiv. geog.)
    338.91; 361.6
    UF   American economic assistance
          Economic assistance, American
    BT   **Foreign aid**
American furniture   684.100973;
    749.09073
    UF   Furniture, American
    SA   styles of American furniture o
          be added as needed]
    BT   **Furniture**

American government
  USE **United States—Politics and government**
American graphic arts
  USE **Graphic arts—United States**
American historians
  USE **Historians—United States**
American history
  USE **America—History**
      United States—History
American hostages (May subdiv. geog. except U.S.) **920**
  BT **Hostages**
American hostages—Iran   920
  NT **Iran hostage crisis, 1979-1981**
American illustrators
  USE **Illustrators—United States**
American Indian authors
  USE **Native American authors**
American Indians
  USE **Native Americans**
American letters   816; 816.008
  BT **American literature**
      Letters
American literature (May subdiv. geog. by state or region)   **810**
  May be subdivided by the topical subdivisions and literary forms used under **English literature**; or geographically by states or regions of the United States for works by or about several authors from a state or region or writing about a state or region, e.g. **American literature—Massachusetts**; **American literature—Southern States**; etc.
  SA various forms of American literature, e.g. **American poetry**; **American satire**; etc. [to be added as needed]
  BT **Literature**
  NT **American diaries**
      American drama
      American essays
      American fiction
      American letters
      American literature (Spanish)
      American poetry
      American prose literature
      American satire
      American speeches
      American wit and humor
      Beat generation
American literature—17th and 18th centuries   810

  UF American literature—Colonial period
American literature—19th century   810
American literature—20th century   810
American literature—21st century   810
American literature—African American authors   810.8; 810.9
  Use for collections or materials about American literature by several African American authors, not for individual works. Use same pattern for literatures and literary forms written by other ethnic groups or classes of authors.
  UF African American literature
     American literature—Afro-American authors
     American literature—Black authors
     Black literature (American)
  SA particular forms of American literature with the subdivision *African American authors*; e.g., **American poetry—African American authors** [to be added as needed]
  NT **Harlem Renaissance**
American literature—Afro-American authors
  USE **American literature—African American authors**
American literature—American Indian authors
  USE **American literature—Native American authors**
American literature—Black authors
  USE **American literature—African American authors**
American literature—Collections   810.8
  Use for collections of both poetry and prose by several American authors. Collections consisting of prose only are entered under **American prose literature**; collections of poetry are entered under **American poetry—Collections**.
American literature—Colonial period
  USE **American literature—17th and 18th centuries**
American literature—Hispanic American authors   810
  Use for materials on American literature in English written by American authors of Spanish or Latin American origins. Materials on American literature written in Spanish are entered under **American literature (Spanish)**.
  UF American literature—Latin American authors

American literature—Hispanic American authors—*Continued*

Hispanic American literature (English)

SA   genres of American literature with the subdivision *Hispanic American authors*; and **American literature** and genres of American literature with subdivisions for specific groups of Hispanic American authors, e.g. **American literature—Mexican American authors** [to be added as needed]

NT   **American literature—Mexican American authors**

American literature—Latin American authors

USE   **American literature—Hispanic American authors**

American literature—Massachusetts   810

American literature—Mexican American authors   810

Use for materials on American literature written in English by American authors of Mexican origins.

UF   Chicano literature (English)

Mexican American literature (English)

SA   genres of American literature with the subdivision *Mexican American authors* [to be added as needed]

BT   **American literature—Hispanic American authors**

American literature—Native American authors   810.8; 810.9

Use for collections or materials about American literature written in English by several Native American authors, not for individual works. Collections or materials about literature written in Native American languages by several Native American authors are entered under **Native American literature**.

UF   American literature—American Indian authors

American literature—Southern States   810

UF   Southern literature

American literature (Spanish)   860

Use for materials on American literature written in Spanish. Materials on American literature in English written by American au-

thors of Spanish or Latin American origins are entered under **American literature—Hispanic American authors**.

UF   Hispanic American literature (Spanish)

Spanish American literature

SA   genres of American literature with the qualifier (Spanish) [to be added as needed]

BT   **American literature**

American literature—Women authors   810.8; 810.9

Use for collections or for materials about several American women authors.

American Loyalists   973.3

UF   Loyalists, American

Tories, American

BT   **United States—History—1775-1783, Revolution**

American military assistance (May subdiv. geog.)   **355**

UF   Military assistance, American

BT   **Military assistance**

American motion pictures

USE   **Motion pictures—United States**

American music   780.973

UF   Music, American

BT   **Music**

American musicians

USE   **Musicians—United States**

American national characteristics   306.0973; 973

UF   American characteristics

National characteristics, American

United States—National characteristics

BT   **National characteristics**

American national songs

USE   **National songs—United States**

American newspapers

USE   **Newspapers—United States**

American novelists   813.009; 920

UF   Novelists, American

BT   **American authors**

Novelists

American orations

USE   **American speeches**

American painters

USE   **Painters—United States**

American painting   759.13

UF   Painting, American

BT   **Painting**

American periodicals
USE **Periodicals—United States**
American personal names
USE **Personal names—United States**
American philosophers
USE **Philosophers—United States**
American philosophy   191
UF   Philosophy, American
BT   **Philosophy**
American poetry   811
Use for general materials about American poetry, not for individual works.
BT   **American literature**
   Poetry
NT   **American ballads**
American poetry—African American authors   811
Use for collections or materials about American poetry by several African American authors, not for individual works.
UF   African American poetry
   American poetry—Afro-American authors
   American poetry—Black authors
   Black poetry (American)
American poetry—Afro-American authors
USE   **American poetry—African American authors**
American poetry—Black authors
USE   **American poetry—African American authors**
American poetry—Collections   811.008
American poetry—History and criticism 811.009
American poets   811.009; 920
UF   Poets, American
BT   **American authors**
   Poets
American politicians
USE   **Politicians—United States**
American politics
USE   **United States—Politics and government**
American pottery   738.0973
UF   Pottery, American
BT   **Pottery**
American prints   769.973
UF   Prints, American
BT   **Prints**
American propaganda   303.3; 327.1
UF   Propaganda, American
BT   **Propaganda**

American prose literature   818
Use for collections of prose writings by several American authors that may include a variety of literary forms, such as essays, fiction, orations, etc. May also be used for general materials about such prose writings.
UF   Prose literature, American
BT   **American literature**
American Revolution
USE   **United States—History—1775-1783, Revolution**
American Revolution Bicentennial, 1776-1976   973.3
UF   American Bicentennial
   Bicentennial celebrations—United States—1976
   United States—Bicentennial celebrations
   United States—History—1775-1783, Revolution—Centennial celebrations, etc.
BT   **United States—Centennial celebrations, etc.**
American Revolution Bicentennial, 1776-1976—Collectibles   973.3075
BT   **Collectors and collecting**
American satire   817; 817.008
UF   Satire, American
BT   **American literature**
   Satire
American schools
USE   **Schools—United States**
American sculptors
USE   **Sculptors—United States**
American sculpture   730.973
BT   **Sculpture**
American songs   782.420973
BT   **Songs**
NT   **Folk songs—United States**
   National songs—United States
American-Spanish War, 1898
USE   **Spanish-American War, 1898**
American speeches   815; 815.008
UF   American orations
   Speeches, addresses, etc., American
BT   **American literature**
   Speeches
American technical assistance (May subdiv. geog.)   **338.91; 361.6**
UF   Technical assistance, American
BT   **Technical assistance**

American teenagers

    USE   **Teenagers—United States**

American tourists

    USE   **American travelers**

American travelers   910.92; 920

    UF   American tourists

    BT   **Travelers**

American wit and humor   817; 817.008; 817.009

    Use for collections by several authors or for materials about American wit and humor. Individual works by American humorists are entered under **Wit and humor**.

    BT   **American literature**

           Wit and humor

American youth

    USE   **Youth—United States**

Americana   069; 973

    Use for materials about American objects of interest to collectors for their historical value, such as documents, relics, etc., including items of little intrinsic value. Materials about old American objects that have aesthetic as well as financial value, usually furniture or decorative arts, are entered under **Antiques—United States**.

    BT   **Collectors and collecting**

           Popular culture—United States

           United States—Civilization

           United States—History

    RT   **Antiques—United States**

Americanisms   427

    Use for materials on words and expressions peculiar to the United States.

    UF   English language—Americanisms

    BT   **English language—Dialects**

Americanization   305.813; 306.0973

    BT   **Socialization**

    NT   **United States—Immigration and emigration**

    RT   **Immigration and emigration**

           Naturalization

Americans (May subdiv. geog. except U.S.)   305.813; 920; 973

    Use for materials on citizens of the United States.

    NT   **Japanese Americans**

    RT   **United States**

Americans—Foreign countries   305.813; 920; 973

Americans—Greece   305.813

Amish   289.7

    BT   **Christian sects**

           Mennonites

Ammunition   623.4

    SA   types of ammunition, e.g. **Bombs** [to be added as needed]

    BT   **Explosives**

           Ordnance

           Projectiles

    NT   **Bombs**

    RT   **Firearms**

           Gunpowder

Amnesia   616.85

    BT   **Memory**

Amnesty   364.6

    BT   **Administration of criminal justice**

           Executive power

    RT   **Clemency**

           Forgiveness

           Pardon

Amniocentesis   618.3

    BT   **Prenatal diagnosis**

Amphetamines   615

    UF   Pep pills

    SA   types of amphetamines, e.g. **Methamphetamine** [to be added as needed]

    BT   **Stimulants**

    NT   **Methamphetamine**

Amphibians (May subdiv. geog.)   567; 597.8

    SA   types of amphibians [to be added as needed]

    BT   **Animals**

    NT   **Frogs**

           Salamanders

Amphibious operations

    USE   names of wars with the subdivision *Amphibious operations,* e.g. **World War, 1939-1945—Amphibious operations** [to be added as needed]

Amplifiers (Electronics)   621.3815

    SA   types of amplifiers [to be added as needed]

    BT   **Electronics**

    NT   **Masers**

           Transistor amplifiers

Amplifiers, Transistor

    USE   **Transistor amplifiers**

Amusement parks (May subdiv. geog.)   791.06

    UF   Theme parks

Amusement parks—*Continued*
- SA   names of specific parks [to be added as needed]
- BT   **Parks**
- NT   **Walt Disney World (Fla.)**
- RT   **Carnivals**

Amusements (May subdiv. geog.)   **790**
- UF   Entertainments
       Pastimes
- SA   types of amusements, e.g. **Carnivals** [to be added as needed]
- NT   **Amateur theater**
       Carnivals
       Charades
       Children's parties
       Christmas entertainments
       Church entertainments
       Circus
       Concerts
       Creative activities
       Dance
       Fireworks
       Fortune telling
       Hobbies
       Juggling
       Literary recreations
       Magic tricks
       Mathematical recreations
       Puzzles
       Riddles
       Roller coasters
       Scientific recreations
       Shadow pictures
       Skits
       String figures
       Theater
       Toys
       Tricks
       Vaudeville
       Ventriloquism
- RT   **Entertaining**
       Games
       Indoor games
       Play
       Recreation
       Sports

Anabolic steroids
- USE   **Steroids**

Anaesthetics
- USE   **Anesthetics**

Analysis
- USE   types of chemicals and substances with the subdivision *Analysis,* e.g. **Water—Analysis; Milk—Analysis;** etc., for materials on methods of analyzing those items [to be added as needed]

Analysis (Chemistry)
- USE   **Analytical chemistry**

Analysis (Mathematics)
- USE   **Calculus**
        Functions
        Mathematical analysis

Analysis of food
- USE   **Food adulteration and inspection**
        Food—Analysis

Analytic geometry   516.3
- UF   Geometry, Analytic
- BT   **Geometry**

Analytical chemistry   543
- UF   Analysis (Chemistry)
       Chemical analysis
       Chemistry, Analytic
       Qualitative analysis
       Quantitative analysis
- SA   types of substances with the subdivision *Analysis*, e.g. **Water—Analysis** [to be added as needed]
- BT   **Chemistry**
- NT   **Distillation**
       Food—Analysis
       Water—Analysis

Anarchism and anarchists   320.5; 335
- BT   **Freedom**
       Political crimes and offenses
       Political science
- RT   **Terrorism**

Anatomy   571.3; 611
- SA   names of organs and regions of the body and subjects with the subdivision *Anatomy*, e.g. **Heart—Anatomy; Birds—Anatomy;** etc. [to be added as needed]
- BT   **Biology**
       Medicine
- NT   **Animals—Anatomy**
       Artistic anatomy

Anatomy—*Continued*
>> Birds—Anatomy
>> Cardiovascular system
>> Comparative anatomy
>> Digestive system
>> Foot
>> Glands
>> Head
>> Heart—Anatomy
>> Human anatomy
>> Immune system
>> Musculoskeletal system
>> Nervous system
>> Plants—Anatomy
>> Reproductive system
>> Respiratory system
>> Skin
>> Stomach
>> Throat
> RT Physiology

Anatomy, Artistic
> USE **Artistic anatomy**

Anatomy, Comparative
> USE **Comparative anatomy**

Anatomy of animals
> USE **Animals—Anatomy**

Anatomy of plants
> USE **Plants—Anatomy**

Ancestor worship (May subdiv. geog.) **202**
> UF Worship of the dead
> BT **Religion**

Ancestry
> USE **Genealogy**
> **Heredity**

Ancient architecture (May subdiv. geog.) **722**
> UF Architecture, Ancient
> BT **Archeology**
> **Architecture**
> NT **Byzantine architecture**
> **Greek architecture**
> **Pyramids**
> **Roman architecture**

Ancient art (May subdiv. geog.) **709.01**
> UF Art, Ancient
> BT **Art**
> NT **Byzantine art**
> **Greek art**
> **Roman art**

Ancient civilization **306.093; 930**
> UF Civilization, Ancient

> BT **Ancient history**
> **Civilization**
> NT **Classical civilization**

Ancient geography **913**

Use for materials on the geography of the ancient world in general. Materials on the ancient geography of one country or region still existing in modern times are entered under the name of the place with the subdivision *Historical geography*. Materials on the geography of regions or countries of antiquity that no longer exist as such in modern times are entered under the name of the place with the subdivision *Geography*.

> UF Classical geography
> Geography, Ancient
> SA names of modern countries with the subdivision *Historical geography*, e.g. **Greece—Historical geography**; and names of places of antiquity with the subdivision *Geography*, e.g. **Gaul—Geography** [to be added as needed]
> BT **Ancient history**
> **Historical geography**
> NT **Gaul—Geography**
> **Greece—Historical geography**
> **Rome—Geography**

Ancient Greece
> USE **Greece—History—0-323**

Ancient Greece—Description
> USE **Greece—Description and travel—0-323**

Ancient history **930**

Use for materials on the history of the ancient world up to the fall of Rome not limited to a single country or region.

> UF History, Ancient
> SA names of ancient peoples, e.g. **Hittites**; and names of countries of antiquity, with the subdivision *History* [to be added as needed]
> BT **World history**
> NT **Ancient civilization**
> **Ancient geography**
> **Bible**
> **Classical dictionaries**
> **Hittites**
> **Inscriptions**
> **Numismatics**

Ancient philosophy **180**
> UF Greek philosophy
> Philosophy, Ancient

Ancient philosophy—*Continued*
    Roman philosophy
    BT   **Philosophy**
    NT   **Stoics**
Androgyny   155.3; 305.3
    BT   **Sex differences (Psychology)**
          Sex role
Anecdotes   808.88
    Use for collections of anecdotes and for materials about anecdotes.
    UF   Facetiae
          Stories
    SA   subjects with the subdivision *Anecdotes* [to be added as needed]
    NT   **Music—Anecdotes**
    RT   **Wit and humor**
Anesthetics   615; 617.9
    UF   Anaesthetics
    BT   **Materia medica**
    RT   **Pain**
          Surgery
Angels   235
    BT   **Heaven**
          Spirits
Anger   152.4
    UF   Rage
          Wrath
    BT   **Emotions**
Angina pectoris   616.1
    BT   **Heart diseases**
Anglican Church
    USE   **Church of England**
Angling
    USE   **Fishing**
Anglo-American law
    USE   **Common law**
Anglo-French intervention in Egypt, 1956
    USE   **Sinai Campaign, 1956**
Anglo-Saxon language
    USE   **English language—Old English period**
Anglo-Saxon literature
    USE   **English literature—Old English period**
Anglo-Saxons   305.82; 941.01
    BT   **Great Britain—History—0-1066**
          Teutonic peoples
Animal abuse
    USE   **Animal welfare**
Animal attacks   591.6
    UF   Attacks by animals

    BT   **Dangerous animals**
Animal babies   591.3
    Use for materials on baby animals of several species. Baby animals of a particular species are entered under the name of the species.
    UF   Animals—Infancy
          Baby animals
    BT   **Animals**
Animal behavior   591.5
    UF   Animals—Behavior
          Behavior
          Habits of animals
    SA   types of specific behavior, e.g. **Animals—Migration; Hibernation; Sexual behavior in animals**; etc.; and types of animals with the subdivision *Behavior*, e.g. **Birds—Behavior** [to be added as needed]
    BT   **Animals**
          Zoology
    NT   **Animal communication**
          Animal courtship
          Animal defenses
          Animal sounds
          Animals—Food
          Animals—Migration
          Birds—Behavior
          Hibernation
          Instinct
          Monkeys—Behavior
          Nest building
          Primates—Behavior
          Sexual behavior in animals
    RT   **Animal intelligence**
          Tracking and trailing
Animal camouflage
    USE   **Camouflage (Biology)**
Animal communication   591.59
    UF   Animal language
          Animals—Language
          Communication among animals
    BT   **Animal behavior**
    RT   **Animal sounds**
Animal courtship   591.56
    UF   Animals—Courtship
          Courtship (Animal behavior)
          Courtship of animals
          Mate selection in animals
          Mating behavior

Animal courtship—*Continued*
    BT   **Animal behavior**
        Sexual behavior in animals
Animal defenses   591.47
    UF   Defense mechanisms of animals
        Self-defense in animals
        Self-protection in animals
    BT   **Animal behavior**
    NT   **Camouflage (Biology)**
Animal drawing
    USE   **Animal painting and illustra-
        tion**
Animal embryos, Frozen
    USE   **Frozen embryos**
Animal experimentation   616
    UF   Experimentation on animals
        Laboratory animal experimenta-
        tion
    BT   **Research**
    NT   **Vivisection**
    RT   **Animal welfare**
Animal exploitation
    USE   **Animal welfare**
Animal-facilitated therapy
    USE   **Pet therapy**
Animal flight   573.7
    UF   Animals—Flight
    SA   types of animals with the subdi-
        vision *Flight*, e.g. **Birds—
        Flight** [to be added as need-
        ed]
    BT   **Animal locomotion**
        Flight
    NT   **Birds—Flight**
Animal food
    USE   **Animals—Food**
        Food of animal origin
Animal habitations
    USE   **Animals—Habitations**
Animal homes
    USE   **Animals—Habitations**
Animal housing   636.08
    Use for materials on houses or habitations
provided by humans for either wild or domes-
tic animals. Materials on the natural shelters
and homes animals build for themselves, such
as burrows, dens, lairs, etc., are entered under
Animals—Habitations.
    UF   Animals—Housing
        Domestic animal dwellings
        Domestic animals—Housing
        Habitations of domestic animals

    SA   types of animals with the subdi-
        vision *Housing*, e.g. **Pets—
        Housing** [to be added as
        needed]
    BT   **Animals**
    NT   **Beehives**
        Birdhouses
        Pets—Housing
    RT   **Animals—Habitations**
Animal husbandry
    USE   **Livestock industry**
Animal industry
    USE   **Livestock industry**
Animal instinct
    USE   **Instinct**
Animal intelligence   591.5
    UF   Animal psychology
        Intelligence of animals
    SA   types of animals with the subdi-
        vision *Psychology* [to be add-
        ed as needed]
    BT   **Animals**
    NT   **Dogs—Psychology**
        Psychology of learning
    RT   **Animal behavior**
        Comparative psychology
        Instinct
Animal kingdom
    USE   **Zoology**
Animal language
    USE   **Animal communication**
        Animal sounds
Animal light
    USE   **Bioluminescence**
Animal locomotion   573.7; 591.57
    UF   Animals—Movements
        Movements of animals
    BT   **Animals**
        Locomotion
    NT   **Animal flight**
Animal lore
    USE   **Animals—Folklore**
        Animals in literature
        Mythical animals
        Natural history
Animal luminescence
    USE   **Bioluminescence**
Animal magnetism
    USE   **Hypnotism**
Animal migration
    USE   **Animals—Migration**

Animal oils

    USE   **Oils and fats**

Animal painting and illustration   704.9;
    743.6; 758

    Use for materials on the art of painting or drawing animals. Materials on the depiction of animals in works of art are entered under **Animals in art**. Popular materials consisting chiefly of photographs or illustrations of animals are entered under **Animals—Pictorial works**.

    UF   Animal drawing

    BT   **Painting**

    RT   **Animals in art**

          Animals—Pictorial works

          Photography of animals

Animal parasites

    USE   **Parasites**

Animal photography

    USE   **Photography of animals**

Animal physiology

    USE   **Zoology**

Animal pictures

    USE   **Animals—Pictorial works**

Animal pounds

    USE   **Animal shelters**

Animal products   338.1; 338.4

    UF   Products, Animal

    SA   types of animal products [to be
          added as needed]

    BT   **Commercial products**

    NT   **Dairy products**

          Hides and skins

          Ivory

          Leather

          Wool

Animal psychology

    USE   **Animal intelligence**

          Comparative psychology

Animal reproduction   571.8

    UF   Animals—Birth

          Animals—Reproduction

    BT   **Animals**

          Reproduction

Animal rights (May subdiv. geog.)   **179**

    Use for materials on the inherent rights attributed to animals. Materials on the protection and treatment of animals are entered under **Animal welfare**. Materials on the political movement to promote the idea of animal rights are entered under **Animal rights movement**.

    UF   Animals' rights

          Rights of animals

    RT   **Animal rights movement**

          Animal welfare

Animal rights movement (May subdiv.
    geog.)   **179**

    UF   Animal rights movements

          Animal welfare movement

          Antivivisection movement

    BT   **Social movements**

    RT   **Animal rights**

          Animal welfare

Animal rights movements

    USE   **Animal rights movement**

Animal senses

    USE   **Senses and sensation in animals**

Animal sexual behavior

    USE   **Sexual behavior in animals**

Animal shelters   179; 636.08

    UF   Animal pounds

    BT   **Animal welfare**

Animal signs

    USE   **Animal tracks**

Animal sounds   573.9; 591.59

    UF   Animal language

          Animals—Sounds

    BT   **Animal behavior**

    NT   **Birdsongs**

    RT   **Animal communication**

Animal stories

    USE   **Animals—Fiction**

Animal tracks   590

    UF   Animal signs

          Tracks of animals

    BT   **Tracking and trailing**

Animal training

    USE   **Animals—Training**

Animal welfare   179

    Use for materials on the protection and treatment of animals. Materials on the inherent rights attributed to animals are entered under **Animal rights**. Materials on the political movement to promote the idea of animal rights are entered under **Animal rights movement**.

    UF   Abuse of animals

          Animal abuse

          Animal exploitation

          Animals—Mistreatment

          Animals—Protection

          Animals—Treatment

          Cruelty to animals

          Humane treatment of animals

          Laboratory animal welfare

Animal welfare—*Continued*

        Prevention of cruelty to animals

        Protection of animals

  NT **Animal shelters**

  RT **Animal experimentation**

        Animal rights

        Animal rights movement

Animal welfare movement

  USE **Animal rights movement**

Animals (May subdiv. geog.)   **590**

    Use for nonscientific materials. Materials on the science of animals are entered under **Zoology**. Subdivisions used under this heading may be used under the names of orders, classes, or individual species of animals.

  UF Beasts

        Fauna

        Wild animals

  SA names of orders and classes of the animal kingdom; kinds of animals characterized by their environments; names of individual species; and names of individual animals [to be added as needed]

  NT **Amphibians**

        Animal babies

        Animal behavior

        Animal housing

        Animal intelligence

        Animal locomotion

        Animal reproduction

        Aquatic animals

        Arachnids

        Birds

        Carnivorous animals

        Dangerous animals

        Desert animals

        Domestic animals

        Extinct animals

        Forest animals

        Furbearing animals

        Game and game birds

        Insects

        Invertebrates

        Jungle animals

        Mammals

        Mountain animals

        Pets

        Poisonous animals

        Predatory animals

        Prehistoric animals

        Rare animals

        Reptiles

        Stream animals

        Swamp animals

        Vertebrates

        Wildlife

        Wildlife attracting

        Working animals

        Worms

  RT **Zoology**

        Zoos

Animals—Anatomy   **571.3**

  UF Anatomy of animals

        Structural zoology

        Zoology—Anatomy

  BT **Anatomy**

        Zoology

  NT **Fur**

Animals and the handicapped   **636.088**

  UF Handicapped and animals

        Pets and the handicapped

  BT **Animals—Training**

  NT **Guide dogs**

        Hearing ear dogs

        Pet therapy

Animals as food

  USE **Food of animal origin**

Animals—Behavior

  USE **Animal behavior**

Animals—Birth

  USE **Animal reproduction**

Animals—Camouflage

  USE **Camouflage (Biology)**

Animals—Color   **573.5; 591.47**

  BT **Color**

Animals—Courtship

  USE **Animal courtship**

Animals—Diseases   **571.9; 636.089**

  UF Diseases of animals

        Domestic animals—Diseases

  SA types of animals with the subdivision *Diseases* [to be added as needed]

  BT **Diseases**

  NT **Horses—Diseases**

  RT **Veterinary medicine**

Animals, Edible

  USE **Food of animal origin**

Animals—Fiction   **808.83**

    Use for collections of stories about animals. Materials about the portrayal of animals in literature are entered under **Animals in literature**.

Animals—Fiction—*Continued*
- UF   Animal stories
- SA   types of animals with the subdivision *Fiction*, e.g. **Dogs—Fiction** [to be added as needed]
- RT   **Animals in literature**
       Fables

Animals—Filmography   016.591

Animals—Flight
- USE   **Animal flight**

Animals—Folklore   398.24
- UF   Animal lore
- BT   **Folklore**
- NT   **Dragons**
       Ethnozoology
       Monsters
- RT   **Mythical animals**

Animals—Food   591.5

Use for materials on the food and food habits of animals. Materials on human food of animal origin are entered under **Food of animal origin**.
- UF   Animal food
       Feeding behavior in animals
- SA   types of animals and species of animals with the subdivision *Food* [to be added as needed]
- BT   **Animal behavior**
       Food
- NT   **Feeds**
       Food chains (Ecology)

Animals—Habitations   591.56

Use for materials on the natural shelters and homes animals build for themselves, such as burrows, dens, lairs, etc. Materials on houses or habitations provided by humans for either wild or domestic animals are entered under **Animal housing**.
- UF   Animal habitations
       Animal homes
       Habitations of wild animals
       Wild animal dwellings
- SA   types of animals and individual species of animals with the subdivision *Habitations*, or *Nests*, e.g. **Beavers—Habitations**; **Birds—Nests**; etc. [to be added as needed]
- NT   **Nest building**
- RT   **Animal housing**

Animals—Hearing
- USE   **Hearing in animals**

Animals—Hibernation
- USE   **Hibernation**

Animals—Housing
- USE   **Animal housing**

Animals in art   704.9

Use for materials on the depiction of animals in works of art. Materials on the art of painting or drawing animals are entered under **Animal painting and illustration**. Materials consisting chiefly of photographs or illustrations of animals are entered under **Animals—Pictorial works**.
- BT   **Art—Themes**
- RT   **Animal painting and illustration**
       Animals—Pictorial works

Animals in literature   809

Use for materials on the theme of animals in literature. Collections of poems or stories about animals are entered under **Animals—Poetry** or **Animals—Fiction**.
- UF   Animal lore
- SA   phrase headings for specific animals in literature, e.g. **Dogs in literature** [to be added as needed]
- BT   **Literature—Themes**
- RT   **Animals—Fiction**
       Animals—Poetry

Animals in motion pictures   791.43
- BT   **Motion pictures**

Animals in police work   363.2; 636.088
- BT   **Police**
       Working animals

Animals—Infancy
- USE   **Animal babies**

Animals—Language
- USE   **Animal communication**

Animals—Migration   591.56
- UF   Animal migration
       Migration
- SA   types of animals with the subdivision *Migration*, e.g. **Birds—Migration** [to be added as needed]
- BT   **Animal behavior**

Animals—Mistreatment
- USE   **Animal welfare**

Animals—Movements
- USE   **Animal locomotion**

Animals, Mythical
- USE   **Mythical animals**

Animals—Photography
- USE   **Photography of animals**

Animals—Pictorial works   590.22

Use for popular materials consisting chiefly of photographs or illustrations of animals. Materials on the art of painting or drawing animals are entered under **Animal painting and illustration**. Materials on the depiction of animals in works of art are entered under **Animals in art**.

UF   Animal pictures

RT   **Animal painting and illustration**

Animals in art

Photography of animals

Animals—Poetry   808.81

Use for collections of poetry about animals. Materials on the theme of animals in literature are entered under **Animals in literature**.

RT   **Animals in literature**

Animals, Prehistoric

USE   **Prehistoric animals**

Animals—Protection

USE   **Animal welfare**

Animals—Reproduction

USE   **Animal reproduction**

Animals' rights

USE   **Animal rights**

Animals—Senses and sensation

USE   **Senses and sensation in animals**

Animals—Sexual behavior

USE   **Sexual behavior in animals**

Animals—Sounds

USE   **Animal sounds**

Animals—Temperature

USE   **Body temperature**

Animals—Training   636.088

UF   Animal training

Training of animals

SA   types of animals with the subdivision *Training*, e.g. **Horses—Training** [to be added as needed]

NT   **Animals and the handicapped**

Dogs—Training

Animals—Treatment

USE   **Animal welfare**

Animals—United States   591.973

UF   Zoology—United States

Animals, Useful and harmful

USE   **Economic zoology**

Animals—Vision

USE   **Vision in animals**

Animals—War use   355.4

UF   War use of animals

BT   **Working animals**

NT   **Dogs—War use**

Animated cartoons

USE   **Animated films**

Animated films   741.5; 791.43

Use for individual works, collections, or materials about animated films.

UF   Animated cartoons

Cartoons, Animated

Motion picture cartoons

BT   **Cartoons and caricatures**

Motion pictures

NT   **Anime**

RT   **Animation (Cinematography)**

Animated television programs   791.45

Use for individual works, collections, or materials about animated television programs.

UF   Cartoons, Television

Television cartoons

BT   **Television programs**

NT   **Anime**

Animation (Cinematography)   741.5; 778.5

BT   **Cinematography**

NT   **Computer animation**

RT   **Animated films**

Anime   791.4

BT   **Animated films**

Animated television programs

Anniversaries   394.2

UF   Celebrations, anniversaries, etc.

Commemorations

SA   ethnic groups, classes of persons, individuals, corporate bodies, places, religious denominations, historic or social movements, and historic events with the subdivision *Anniversaries*, for materials about anniversary celebrations, e.g. **Shakespeare, William, 1564-1616—Anniversaries**, and names of places, corporate bodies, and historical events with the subdivision *Centennial celebrations, etc.*, e.g. **United States—History—1861-1865, Civil War—Centennial celebrations, etc.** [to be added as needed]

BT   **Manners and customs**

NT   **Birthdays**

Anniversaries—*Continued*
- RT **Days**
- **Festivals**
- **Holidays**

Annual income guarantee
- USE **Guaranteed annual income**

Annuals
- USE **Almanacs**
- **Calendars**
- **Periodicals**
- **School yearbooks**
- **Yearbooks**

  and subjects and names of countries, cities, etc., individual persons, families, and corporate bodies with the subdivision *Periodicals,* e.g. **Engineering—Periodicals** [to be added as needed]

Annuals (Plants)   582.1; 635.9
- BT **Cultivated plants**
- **Flower gardening**
- **Flowers**

Annuities   368.3
- BT **Investments**
- **Retirement income**
- NT **Pensions**
- RT **Life insurance**

Annulment of marriage
- USE **Marriage—Annulment**

Anointing of the sick   265
- UF Extreme unction
- Last rites (Sacraments)
- Last sacraments
- BT **Sacraments**

Anonyms
- USE **Pseudonyms**

Anorexia nervosa   616.85
- BT **Eating disorders**

Answers to questions
- USE **Questions and answers**

Antarctic expeditions
- USE **Antarctica—Exploration**

Antarctic regions
- USE **Antarctica**

Antarctica   998

  Use for materials on the continent of Antarctica and the regions adjacent to it.
- UF Antarctic regions
- BT **Earth**
- **Polar regions**
- RT **South Pole**

Antarctica—Exploration   919.8
- UF Antarctic expeditions
- Polar expeditions
- SA names of expeditions, e.g. **Byrd Antarctic Expedition** [to be added as needed]
- BT **Exploration**
- **Scientific expeditions**
- NT **Byrd Antarctic Expedition**

Antenuptial contracts
- USE **Marriage contracts**

Anthologies   080; 808.8

  Use for collections of general interest by several authors not limited to works of literature or focused on a single subject.
- UF Collected papers (Anthologies)
- Collected works
- Collections (Anthologies)
- Collections of literature
- Literary collections
- Readings (Anthologies)
- SA form headings for minor literary forms that represent collections of works of several authors, e.g. **Essays; American essays; Parodies; Short stories**; etc.; major literary forms and national literatures with the subdivision *Collections,* e.g. **Poetry—Collections; English literature—Collections**; etc.; and subjects with the subdivision *Literary collections,* for collections focused on a single subject by two or more authors involving two or more literary forms, e.g. **Cats—Literary collections** [to be added as needed]
- BT **Books**

Anthropogeography
- USE **Human geography**

Anthropology (May subdiv. geog.)   301; 599.9
- UF Human race
- SA names of races and peoples, e.g. **Navajo Indians** [to be added as needed]
- BT **Social sciences**
- NT **Acculturation**
- **Anthropometry**
- **Ethnopsychology**

Anthropology—*Continued*
      Human geography
      Language and languages
      National characteristics
      Physical anthropology
      Social change
  RT **Civilization**
      Culture
      Ethnology
      Human beings
Anthropometry 599.9
  UF Skeletal remains
  BT **Anthropology**
      Ethnology
      Human beings
  NT **Fingerprints**
Anti-abortion movement
  USE **Pro-life movement**
Anti-Americanism
  USE **United States—Foreign opinion**
Anti-apartheid movement 172; 320.5; 323.1
  BT **Civil rights**
      Social movements
      South Africa—Race relations
  RT **Apartheid**
Anti-fascist movements
  USE **World War, 1939-1945—Underground movements**
Anti-Nazi movement
  USE **World War, 1939-1945—Underground movements**
Anti-poverty programs
  USE **Domestic economic assistance**
Anti-Reformation
  USE **Counter-Reformation**
Anti-terrorism
  USE **Terrorism—Prevention**
Anti-utopias
  USE **Dystopias**
Anti-war films
  USE **War films**
Anti-war poetry
  USE **War poetry**
Anti-war stories
  USE **War stories**
Antiabortion movement
  USE **Pro-life movement**
Antiamericanism
  USE **United States—Foreign opinion**
Antiballistic missiles
  USE **Antimissile missiles**

Antibiotic resistance in microorganisms
  USE **Drug resistance in microorganisms**
Antibiotics 615
  SA names of specific antibiotics [to be added as needed]
  BT **Drug therapy**
  NT **Penicillin**
Antibusing
  USE **Busing (School integration)**
Anticommunist movements (May subdiv. geog.) **322.4**
  BT **Communism**
Anticorrosive paint
  USE **Corrosion and anticorrosives**
Antidepressants 615
  BT **Psychotropic drugs**
Antimissile missiles 358.1; 623.4
  UF ABMs
      Antiballistic missiles
  BT **Guided missiles**
Antinuclear movement (May subdiv. geog.) **303.48; 327.1; 363.17**
  UF Nuclear freeze movement
  BT **Arms control**
      Nuclear weapons
      Social movements
  RT **Nuclear power plants—Environmental aspects**
Antipoverty programs
  USE **Domestic economic assistance**
Antiquarian books
  USE **Rare books**
Antique and classic cars (May subdiv. geog.) **629.222**
  UF Antique automobiles
      Antique cars
      Classic automobiles
      Classic cars
      Vintage automobiles
      Vintage cars
  BT **Automobiles**
Antique and vintage motorcycles (May subdiv. geog.) **629.227**
  UF Antique motorcycles
      Classic motorcycles
      Vintage motorcycles
  BT **Motorcycles**
Antique automobiles
  USE **Antique and classic cars**

Antique cars
USE **Antique and classic cars**
Antique motorcycles
USE **Antique and vintage motorcycles**
Antiques (May subdiv. geog.) **745.1**

Use for materials on old decorative or utilitarian objects that have aesthetic or historical importance and financial value. Materials on any objects of interest to collectors, including mass produced items of little intrinsic value, are entered under **Collectibles**.

SA   subjects and names with the subdivision *Collectibles*, e.g. **American Revolution Bicentennial, 1776-1976—Collectibles**; and types of objects collected, excluding antiquities and natural objects, with the subdivision *Collectors and collecting*, e.g. **Boxes—Collectors and collecting** [to be added as needed]

BT   **Antiquities**
      Collectors and collecting
      Decoration and ornament
      Decorative arts
NT   **Art objects**
      Collectors and collecting
      Victoriana
Antiques—Price guides   745.075
Antiques—United States   745.10973

Use for materials about old American objects that have aesthetic as well as financial value, usually furniture or decorative arts. Materials about American objects of interest to collectors for their historical value, such as documents, relics, etc., including items of little intrinsic value, are entered under **Americana**.

RT   **Americana**
Antiquities   930.1

Use for general materials on the relics or monuments of ancient times. Materials on the relics or monuments of an extinct city or town are entered under the name of the city or town.

UF   Archeological specimens
      Ruins
SA   names of extinct cities, e.g. **Delphi (Extinct city)**; and names of groups of people extant in modern times and names of cities (except extinct cities), countries, regions, etc., with the subdivision *Antiquities*, e.g. **Native Americans—Antiquities**; **United States—Antiquities**; etc. [to be added as needed]

NT   **America—Antiquities**
      Antiques
      Bible—Antiquities
      Chicago (Ill.)—Antiquities
      Christian antiquities
      Classical antiquities
      Egypt—Antiquities
      Italy—Antiquities
      Jews—Antiquities
      Native Americans—Antiquities
      Ohio—Antiquities
      Prehistoric peoples
      Turkey—Antiquities
      United States—Antiquities
RT   **Archeology**
Antiquities—Collection and preservation 069
UF   Preservation of antiquities
BT   **Collectors and collecting**
Antiquity of man
USE   **Human origins**
Antisemitism (May subdiv. geog.) **305.892**
BT   **Prejudices**
NT   **Holocaust, 1933-1945**
      Jews—Persecutions
Antiseptics   614.4; 617.9
BT   **Therapeutics**
RT   **Disinfection and disinfectants**
      Surgery
Antislavery
USE   **Abolitionists**
      Slavery
      Slaves—Emancipation
Antistalking laws
USE   **Stalking**
Antitank warfare
USE   **Tank warfare**
Antitrust law (May subdiv. geog.) **343.07**
UF   Industrial trusts—Law and legislation
BT   **Commercial law**
RT   **Industrial trusts**
Antivivisection movement
USE   **Animal rights movement**

Antiwar movements
  USE **Peace movements**
Antonyms
  USE **Opposites**
      and names of languages with
      the subdivision *Synonyms and
      antonyms,* e.g. **English lan-
      guage—Synonyms and ant-
      onyms** [to be added as need-
      ed]
Ants   595.79
  BT **Insects**
Anxieties
  USE **Anxiety**
Anxiety   152.4
  UF Anxieties
      Anxiousness
  BT **Emotions
      Neuroses
      Stress (Psychology)**
  NT **Post-traumatic stress disorder
      Separation anxiety in children**
  RT **Fear
      Worry**
Anxiousness
  USE **Anxiety**
Apartheid   320.5
      Use for materials on the economic, political,
      and social policies of the government of
      South Africa designed to segregate racial
      groups in South Africa and Namibia.
  UF Separate development (Race re-
      lations)
  BT **Segregation
      South Africa—Race relations**
  RT **Anti-apartheid movement**
Apartment houses (May subdiv. geog.)
      647; 728
  BT **Buildings
      Domestic architecture
      Houses
      Housing**
  NT **Apartments
      Condominiums
      Tenement houses**
Apartments (May subdiv. geog.)   **643**
  UF Flats
  BT **Apartment houses**
Apes (May subdiv. geog.)   **599.88**
  BT **Primates**
  NT **Baboons
      Chimpanzees**

Gorillas
Aphasia   371.91; 616.85
      Use for materials that discuss language in-
      abilities.
  UF **Speech problems**
  BT **Brain—Diseases
      Language disorders
      Speech disorders**
Apiculture
  USE **Beekeeping**
Apocalyptic fiction   808.3; 808.83
      Use for individual works, collections, or
      materials about apocalyptic fiction
  UF End-of-the-world fiction
  BT **Fiction**
Apocalyptic films   791.43
      Use for individual works, collections, or
      materials about apocalyptic films.
  UF End-of-the-world films
  BT **Motion pictures**
Apollo project   629.45
  UF Project Apollo
  BT **Life support systems (Space
      environment)
      Orbital rendezvous (Space
      flight)
      Space flight to the moon**
Apologetic works
  USE **Apologetics**
      and religions and denominations
      with the subdivision *Apologet-
      ic works,* for materials de-
      fending those religions or de-
      nominations, e.g. **Christiani-
      ty—Apologetic works** for
      materials defending Christiani-
      ty; and religions, denomina-
      tions, religious orders, and sa-
      cred works with the subdivi-
      sion *Controversial literature,*
      for materials that argue
      against or express opposition
      to those groups or works, e.g.
      **Christianity—Controversial
      literature** for materials attack-
      ing Christianity [to be added
      as needed]
Apologetics   202; 239
  UF Apologetic works
  SA religions and denominations with
      the subdivision *Apologetic
      works*, for materials defending

45

Apologetics—*Continued*
those religions or denominations, e.g. **Christianity—Apologetic works** for materials defending Christianity; and religions, denominations, religious orders, and sacred works with the subdivision *Controversial literature*, for materials that argue against or express opposition to those groups or works, e.g. **Christianity—Controversial literature** for materials attacking Christianity [to be added as needed]
  BT **Theology**
  NT **Christianity—Apologetic works**
        Natural theology

Apoplexy
  USE **Stroke**

Apostles **225.92**
  UF Disciples, Twelve
  BT **Christian saints**
        Church history—30-600, Early church

Apostles' Creed **238**
  BT **Creeds**

Apostolic Church
  USE **Church history—30-600, Early church**

Appalachia
  USE **Appalachian Region**

Appalachian Mountains Region
  USE **Appalachian Region**

Appalachian Region **974**
  UF Appalachia
        Appalachian Mountains Region
  BT **United States**

Apparatus, Chemical
  USE **Chemical apparatus**

Apparatus, Electric
  USE **Electric apparatus and appliances**

Apparatus, Electronic
  USE **Electronic apparatus and appliances**

Apparatus, Scientific
  USE **Scientific apparatus and instruments**

Apparitions **133.1**

  UF Phantoms
        Specters
  BT **Parapsychology**
        Spirits
  NT **Ghosts**
  RT **Hallucinations and illusions**
        Spiritualism
        Visions

Appearance, Personal
  USE **Personal appearance**

Apperception **153.7**
  BT **Educational psychology**
        Psychology
  NT **Attention**
        Consciousness
        Number concept
  RT **Perception**
        Theory of knowledge

Appetizers **641.812**
  UF Canapés
        Hors d'oeuvres
  BT **Cooking**

Apple
  USE **Apples**

Apple Macintosh (Computer)
  USE **Macintosh (Computer)**

Apples **641.3**
  UF Apple
  BT **Fruit**

Appliances, Electric
  USE **Electric apparatus and appliances**
        Electric household appliances

Appliances, Electronic
  USE **Electronic apparatus and appliances**

Applications for college
  USE **College applications**

Applications for positions **331.12; 650.14**
  UF Employment applications
        Employment references
        Job applications
        Letters of recommendation
        Recommendations for positions
  BT **Job hunting**
        Personnel management
  NT **Job interviews**
        Résumés (Employment)

Applied arts
  USE **Decorative arts**

Applied mechanics   620.1

Use for materials on the application of the principles of mechanics to engineering structures other than machinery. Materials on the application of the principles of mechanics to the design, construction, and operation of machinery are entered under **Mechanical engineering**.

UF   Mechanics, Applied

BT   **Mechanics**

Applied psychology   158

UF   Industrial psychology
Practical psychology
Psychology, Applied

SA   subjects with the subdivision
Psychological aspects, e.g.
Drugs—Psychological aspects
[to be added as needed]

BT   **Psychology**

NT   **Behavior modification**
Counseling
Drugs—Psychological aspects
Employee morale
Human engineering
Negotiation
Organizational behavior
Pastoral psychology
Psychological warfare
Self-help techniques

RT   **Educational psychology**
Interviewing
Social psychology

Applied science

USE   **Technology**

Appliqué   746.44

BT   **Needlework**

Appointment

USE   types of public officials and
names of individual public officials with the subdivision
Appointment, e.g. **Presidents—United States—Appointment** [to be added as needed]

Appointments and retirements

USE   names of armed forces with the
subdivision *Appointments and retirements,* e.g. **United States. Army—Appointments and retirements** [to be added as needed]

Apportionment (Election law) (May subdiv. geog.)   **324; 328.3; 342**

UF   Legislative reapportionment
Reapportionment (Election law)

BT   **Representative government and representation**

Appraisal

USE   **Tax assessment**
Valuation

Appraisal of books

USE   **Book reviewing**
Books and reading
Criticism
Literature—History and criticism

Appreciation of art

USE   **Art appreciation**

Appreciation of music

USE   **Music appreciation**

Apprentices   331.5

BT   **Labor**
Technical education

RT   **Employees—Training**

Apprenticeship novels

USE   **Bildungsromans**

Appropriations and expenditures

USE   names of countries and names
of individual government departments, agencies, etc., with the subdivision *Appropriations and expenditures,* e.g. **United States—Appropriations and expenditures** [to be added as needed]

Approximate computation   372.7; 511

UF   Arithmetic—Estimation
Computation, Approximate
Estimation (Mathematics)

BT   **Numerical analysis**

April First

USE   **April Fools' Day**

April Fools' Day   394.262

UF   All Fools' Day
April First

BT   **Holidays**

Aptitude

USE   **Ability**

Aptitude testing

USE   **Ability—Testing**

Aquaculture   639

UF   Aquiculture
Freshwater aquaculture
Mariculture

Aquaculture—*Continued*
        Marine aquaculture
        Ocean farming
        Sea farming
  BT **Agriculture**
       Marine resources
  NT **Fish culture**
Aquarian Age movement
  USE **New Age movement**
Aquariums 597.073; 639.34
  SA names of specific aquariums [to
       be added as needed]
  BT **Freshwater biology**
       Natural history
  NT **Marine aquariums**
  RT **Fish culture**
       Fishes
Aquatic animals (May subdiv. geog.)
      591.76
  UF Aquatic fauna
       Water animals
  BT **Animals**
  NT **Fishes**
       Freshwater animals
       Marine animals
       Shellfish
       Sponges
Aquatic birds
  USE **Water birds**
Aquatic fauna
  USE **Aquatic animals**
Aquatic plants
  USE **Freshwater plants**
       Marine plants
Aquatic sports
  USE **Water sports**
Aquatic sports—Safety measures
  USE **Water safety**
Aqueducts 628.1
  UF Water conduits
  BT **Civil engineering**
       Hydraulic structures
       Water supply
Aquiculture
  USE **Aquaculture**
Arab countries 956
  Use for materials on several Arabic-speaking countries. Materials on the region consisting of northeastern Africa and Asia west of Afghanistan are entered under **Middle East**.
  BT **Islamic countries**
       Middle East

Arab countries—Foreign relations—Israel
    956
  UF Arab-Israel relations
       Arab-Israeli relations
       Israel-Arab relations
       Israeli-Arab relations
  NT **Israel-Arab conflicts**
  RT **Israel—Foreign relations—**
       Arab countries
       Jewish-Arab relations
Arab countries—Politics and government
    956
  BT **Politics**
  NT **Pan-Arabism**
Arab-Israel conflicts
  USE **Israel-Arab conflicts**
Arab-Israel relations
  USE **Arab countries—Foreign rela-**
         tions—Israel
       Israel—Foreign relations—
         Arab countries
Arab-Israel War, 1948-1949
  USE **Israel-Arab War, 1948-1949**
Arab-Israel War, 1956
  USE **Sinai Campaign, 1956**
Arab-Israel War, 1967
  USE **Israel-Arab War, 1967**
Arab-Israel War, 1973
  USE **Israel-Arab War, 1973**
Arab-Israeli conflict, 1987-1992
  USE **Intifada, 1987-1992**
Arab-Israeli conflict, 2000-
  USE **Intifada, 2000-**
Arab-Israeli conflicts
  USE **Israel-Arab conflicts**
Arab-Israeli relations
  USE **Arab countries—Foreign rela-**
         tions—Israel
       Israel—Foreign relations—
         Arab countries
Arab-Jewish relations
  USE **Jewish-Arab relations**
Arab refugees (May subdiv. geog.)
    305.9
  UF Refugees, Arab
  BT **Refugees**
Arab science
  USE **Science—Islamic countries**
Arabia
  USE **Arabian Peninsula**
Arabian Peninsula 953

Arabian Peninsula—*Continued*
> UF   Arabia
> BT   **Peninsulas**

Arabic civilization   306.0917; 909
> UF   Civilization, Arab
> BT   **Civilization**

Arabic language   492.7
> BT   **Language and languages**

Arabic literature   892.7
> BT   **Literature**

Arabs (May subdiv. geog.)   305.892; 909
> SA   names of specific Arab peoples
> [to be added as needed]
> NT   **Bedouins**
>   **Jewish-Arab relations**
>   **Palestinian Arabs**

Arabs—Palestine
> USE   **Palestinian Arabs**

Arachnida
> USE   **Arachnids**

Arachnids (May subdiv. geog.)   595.4
> UF   Arachnida
> BT   **Animals**
> NT   **Spiders**
>   **Ticks**

Arbitration and award   347
> Use for materials on the settlement of civil disputes by arbitration instead of a court trial.
> UF   Awards (Law)
>   Mediation
> BT   **Commercial law**
>   **Courts**
> RT   **Litigation**

Arbitration, Industrial
> USE   **Industrial arbitration**

Arbitration, International
> USE   **International arbitration**

Arboriculture
> USE   **Forests and forestry**
>   **Fruit culture**
>   **Trees**

Arc light
> USE   **Electric lighting**

Arc welding
> USE   **Electric welding**

Archaeology
> USE   **Archeology**

Archbishops
> USE   **Bishops**

Archeological specimens
> USE   **Antiquities**

Archeologists   920; 930.1092
> BT   **Historians**

Archeology (May subdiv. geog.)   930.1
> Use for materials on the discipline of archeology. General materials on the relics or monuments of ancient times are entered under **Antiquities**. Materials on the relics or monuments of an extinct city or town are entered under the name of the city or town.
> UF   Archaeology
>   Prehistory
> SA   names of extinct cities, e.g. **Delphi (Extinct city)**; and names of groups of people and of cities (except extinct cities), countries, regions, etc., with the subdivision *Antiquities*, e.g. **Native Americans—Antiquities**; **United States—Antiquities**; etc. [to be added as needed]
> BT   **History**
> NT   **Ancient architecture**
>   **Bible—Antiquities**
>   **Brasses**
>   **Bronzes**
>   **Burial**
>   **Buried treasure**
>   **Cliff dwellers and cliff dwellings**
>   **Excavations (Archeology)**
>   **Extinct cities**
>   **Fossil hominids**
>   **Gems**
>   **Heraldry**
>   **Historic sites**
>   **Industrial archeology**
>   **Inscriptions**
>   **Mounds and mound builders**
>   **Mummies**
>   **Numismatics**
>   **Obelisks**
>   **Prehistoric peoples**
>   **Pyramids**
>   **Radiocarbon dating**
>   **Rock drawings, paintings, and engravings**
>   **Tombs**
> RT   **Antiquities**

Archery   799.3
> BT   **Martial arts**
>   **Shooting**
> RT   **Bow and arrow**

Architects (May subdiv. geog.) **720.92; 920**
   BT   **Artists**
Architectural acoustics **729; 690**
   UF   Acoustics
   BT   **Sound**
   NT   **Soundproofing**
Architectural decoration and ornament
   729
   UF   Architecture—Decoration and or-
          nament
          Decoration and ornament, Archi-
          tectural
   BT   **Architecture**
        Decoration and ornament
   NT   **Gargoyles**
Architectural design **720**
   Use for materials on the process and meth-
odology of designing buildings.
   BT   **Architecture**
        Design
Architectural designs
   USE   **Architecture—Designs and**
          plans
Architectural details
   USE   **Architecture—Details**
Architectural drawing **720.28**
   BT   **Drawing**
Architectural engineering
   USE   **Building**
        Structural analysis (Engineer-
          ing)
        Structural engineering
Architectural features
   USE   **Architecture—Details**
Architectural metalwork **721**
   BT   **Metalwork**
Architectural perspective
   USE   **Perspective**
Architecture (May subdiv. geog.) **720**
   Use for materials on the design and style of
structures. Materials on the process of con-
struction are entered under **Building**. General
materials on buildings are entered under
Buildings.
   UF   Building design
          Construction
   SA   styles of architecture, e.g. **By-**
          zantine architecture; and
          types of buildings, e.g. **Farm**
          buildings [to be added as
          needed]
   BT   **Art**

   NT   **American colonial style in ar-**
          chitecture
        Ancient architecture
        Architectural decoration and
          ornament
        Architectural design
        Asian architecture
        Baroque architecture
        Byzantine architecture
        Church architecture
        Classicism in architecture
        Domestic architecture
        Gothic revival (Architecture)
        Greek architecture
        Industrial buildings—Design
          and construction
        Islamic architecture
        Landscape architecture
        Library architecture
        Lost architecture
        Medieval architecture
        Modernism in architecture
        Monuments
        Native American architecture
        Naval architecture
        Obelisks
        Roman architecture
        Romanesque architecture
        Spires
        Sustainable architecture
        Tombs
        Underground architecture
   RT   **Building**
        Buildings
Architecture—15th and 16th centuries
   (May subdiv. geog.) **724**
   UF   Architecture, Renaissance
          Renaissance architecture
Architecture—17th and 18th centuries
   (May subdiv. geog.) **724**
   UF   Architecture, Modern—17th-18th
          centuries
          Modern architecture—1600-1799
          (17th and 18th centuries)
Architecture—19th century (May subdiv.
   geog.) **724**
   UF   Architecture, Modern—19th cen-
          tury
          Modern architecture—1800-1899
          (19th century)
   NT   **Victorian architecture**

Architecture—20th century (May subdiv. geog.) **724**

    UF   Architecture, Modern—20th century

         Modern architecture—1900-1999 (20th century)

Architecture—21st century (May subdiv. geog.) **724**

    UF   Architecture, Modern—21st century

         Modern architecture—2000-2099 (21st century)

Architecture, American

    USE **Architecture—United States**

Architecture, Ancient

    USE **Ancient architecture**

Architecture and the handicapped   **720**

    UF   Barrier free design

         Handicapped and architecture

    BT   **Handicapped**

Architecture—Awards   **720.79**

Architecture, Baroque

    USE **Baroque architecture**

Architecture, Byzantine

    USE **Byzantine architecture**

Architecture—Composition, proportion, etc.   **720; 729**

    UF   Architecture—Proportion

         Proportion (Architecture)

    BT   **Composition (Art)**

Architecture—Conservation and restoration   **690; 720.28**

    UF   Architecture—Restoration

         Buildings, Restoration of

         Conservation of buildings

         Preservation of buildings

         Restoration of buildings

    RT   **Buildings—Maintenance and repair**

Architecture—Decoration and ornament

    USE **Architectural decoration and ornament**

Architecture—Designs and plans   **720.28; 729**

    UF   Architectural designs

         Architecture—Plans

         Designs, Architectural

    NT   **Domestic architecture—Designs and plans**

Architecture—Details   **721; 729**

    UF   Architectural details

         Architectural features

    SA   types of architectural features, e.g. **Windows**; **Fireplaces**; etc. [to be added as needed]

    NT   **Chimneys**

         Doors

         Fireplaces

         Floors

         Foundations

         Gargoyles

         Roofs

         Windows

         Woodwork

Architecture, Domestic

    USE **Domestic architecture**

Architecture, Gothic

    USE **Gothic architecture**

Architecture, Greek

    USE **Greek architecture**

Architecture, Islamic

    USE **Islamic architecture**

Architecture, Medieval

    USE **Medieval architecture**

Architecture, Modern

    USE **Modernism in architecture**

Architecture, Modern—17th-18th centuries

    USE **Architecture—17th and 18th centuries**

Architecture, Modern—19th century

    USE **Architecture—19th century**

Architecture, Modern—20th century

    USE **Architecture—20th century**

Architecture, Modern—21st century

    USE **Architecture—21st century**

Architecture—Plans

    USE **Architecture—Designs and plans**

Architecture—Proportion

    USE **Architecture—Composition, proportion, etc.**

Architecture, Renaissance

    USE **Architecture—15th and 16th centuries**

Architecture—Restoration

    USE **Architecture—Conservation and restoration**

Architecture, Roman

    USE **Roman architecture**

Architecture, Romanesque

    USE **Romanesque architecture**

Architecture, Rural
USE **Farm buildings**
Architecture—United States 720.973
UF American architecture
Architecture, American
**Architecture—United States—1600-1775,
Colonial period 720.973**
UF Colonial architecture
Archives (May subdiv. geog.) **026; 027**
UF Documents
Government records—Preservation
Historical records—Preservation
Preservation of historical records
Public records—Preservation
Records—Preservation
SA subjects, ethnic groups, classes
of persons, individuals, families, schools, and military services with the subdivision *Archives* [to be added as needed]
BT **Bibliography**
Documentation
History—Sources
Information services
NT **Manuscripts**
Presidents—United States—Archives
RT **Charters**
Libraries
**Archives—United States 027.0973;
353.0071**
UF United States—Archives
Arctic expeditions
USE **Arctic regions—Exploration**
Arctic regions 919.8; 998
UF Far north
BT **Earth**
Polar regions
NT **Northeast Passage**
Northwest Passage
RT **North Pole**
Arctic regions—Exploration 919.8
UF Arctic expeditions
Polar expeditions
SA names of expeditions [to be added as needed]
BT **Exploration**
Scientific expeditions

**Ardennes (France), Battle of the, 1944-
1945 940.54**
UF Bastogne, Battle of
Battle of the Bulge
Bulge, Battle of the
BT **World War, 1939-1945—Campaigns**
Area studies 940-999
Use for general materials on area studies.
UF Foreign area studies
SA continents, countries, and geographic regions with the subdivision *Study and teaching* [to be added as needed]
BT **Education**
NT **Africa—Study and teaching**
Arena theater 725; 792
UF Round stage
Theater-in-the-round
BT **Theater**
Argentina 982
May be subdivided like **United States** except for *History*.
Argentine rummy
USE **Canasta (Game)**
Argumentation
USE **Debates and debating**
Logic
Arid regions (May subdiv. geog.)
551.41
UF Arid zones
Semiarid regions
BT **Earth**
Arid zones
USE **Arid regions**
Aristocracy (May subdiv. geog.) **305.5**
BT **Political science**
Upper class
RT **Nobility**
Arithmetic 513
UF Computation (Mathematics)
SA types of arithmetic operations [to be added as needed]
BT **Mathematics**
Set theory
NT **Addition**
Average
Cube root
Division
Fractions
Mental arithmetic
Metric system

Arithmetic—*Continued*
>> **Multiplication**
>> **Percentage**
>> **Ratio and proportion**
>> **Square root**
>> **Subtraction**
> RT **Numbers**

Arithmetic, Commercial
> USE **Business mathematics**

Arithmetic—Estimation
> USE **Approximate computation**

Arithmetic—Study and teaching   372.7; 513.07
> NT **Counting**
>> **Mathematical readiness**
>> **Number games**

Arithmetic—Textbooks   513

Arithmetical ability
> USE **Mathematical ability**

Arithmetical readiness
> USE **Mathematical readiness**

Armada, 1588
> USE **Spanish Armada, 1588**

Armaments
> USE **Military readiness**
>> **Military weapons**

Armaments industries
> USE **Defense industry**

Armed forces   343; 355
> UF Armed services
>> Military forces
> SA specific branches of the armed forces under names of countries, e.g. **United States. Army**; and names of countries, regions, and international organizations with the subdivision *Armed forces*, e.g. **United States—Armed forces; United Nations—Armed forces**; etc. [to be added as needed]
> BT **Military art and science**
> NT **Armies**
>> **Military personnel**
>> **Navies**
>> **Ohio—Militia**
>> **Recruiting and enlistment**
>> **United Nations—Armed forces**
>> **United States—Armed forces**
>> **United States—Militia**
>> **Voluntary military service**

> RT **Military readiness**
>> **War**

Armed forces—Recruiting, enlistment, etc.
> USE **Recruiting and enlistment**

Armed forces—Women
> USE **Women in the military**

Armed services
> USE **Armed forces**

Armies   355.3
> UF Army
>> Military power
> SA names of countries with the subhead *Army*, e.g. **United States. Army** [to be added as needed]
> BT **Armed forces**
>> **Military personnel**
> NT **Draft**
>> **Soldiers**
>> **United States. Army**
> RT **Military art and science**

Armies—Medical care   355.3
> SA names of wars with the subdivision *Health aspects* or *Medical care*, e.g. **World War, 1939-1945—Health aspects; World War, 1939-1945—Medical care**; etc. [to be added as needed]
> BT **Medical care**
>> **Military medicine**
> RT **Military personnel—Health and hygiene**

Armistice Day
> USE **Veterans Day**

Armistices
> USE names of wars with the subdivision *Armistices*, e.g. **World War, 1939-1945—Armistices** [to be added as needed]

Armor   355.8; 623.4; 739.7
> Use for materials on protective covering worn as a defense against weapons.
> UF Arms and armor
>> Suits of armor
> BT **Art metalwork**
>> **Costume**
>> **Military art and science**
> RT **Weapons**

Armored cars (Tanks)
> USE **Military tanks**

Arms and armor
    USE   **Armor**
          Weapons
Arms control (May subdiv. geog.)
       327.1; 341.7
    UF   Disarmament
          Limitation of armament
          Non-proliferation of nuclear
             weapons
          Nuclear non-proliferation
          Nuclear test ban
    BT   **International relations**
          International security
          War
    NT   **Antinuclear movement**
          Arms race
    RT   **International arbitration**
          Military readiness
          Peace
Arms proliferation
    USE   **Arms race**
Arms race (May subdiv. geog.)   **327.1;**
       355
    Use for materials on the competitive in-
    crease in the military power of two or more
    nations or blocs.
    UF   Arms proliferation
          Proliferation of arms
    BT   **Arms control**
          International security
    RT   **Arms transfers**
          Military readiness
          Military weapons
Arms sales
    USE   **Arms transfers**
          Defense industry
          Military assistance
          Military weapons
Arms traffic
    USE   **Arms transfers**
Arms transfers (May subdiv. geog.)
       327.1; 382
    UF   Arms sales
          Arms traffic
          Foreign military sales
          Military sales
    BT   **International trade**
    RT   **Arms race**
          Defense industry
          Military assistance

Army
    USE   **Armies**
          Military art and science
          and names of countries with the
            subhead *Army,* e.g. **United
            States. Army** [to be added as
            needed]
Army bases
    USE   **Military bases**
Army desertion
    USE   **Military desertion**
Army life
    USE   **Soldiers**
          and names of armies with the
            subdivision *Military life,* e.g.
            **United States. Army—Mili-
            tary life** [to be added as
            needed]
Army posts
    USE   **Military bases**
Army schools
    USE   **Military education**
Army tests
    USE   **United States. Army—Exami-
            nations**
Army vehicles
    USE   **Military vehicles**
Aromatherapy   615
    BT   **Therapeutics**
Aromatic plant products
    USE   **Essences and essential oils**
Aromatic plants (May subdiv. geog.)
       582; 635.9
    BT   **Plants**
    RT   **Essences and essential oils**
          Fragrant gardens
Arrow
    USE   **Bow and arrow**
Arson (May subdiv. geog.)   **364.16**
    BT   **Offenses against property**
Art   700
    Use for materials on the visual arts only
    (architecture, painting, etc.). Materials on the
    arts in general, including the visual arts, liter-
    ature, and the performing arts, are entered un-
    der **Arts**.
    SA   types of art, e.g. **Commercial
          art**; art of particular religions,
          e.g. **Christian art**; move-
          ments in art, e.g. **Romanti-
          cism in art**; art and other
          subjects, e.g. **Art and my-**

thology; subjects and themes in art, e.g. **Animals in art**; and art of particular countries, regions, or ethnic groups, e.g. **American art; Greek art; Native American art**; etc. [to be added as needed]

BT   **Arts**

NT   **Abstract art**
African American art
African art
American art
Ancient art
Architecture
Art and mythology
Art and religion
Art and society
Art objects
Artistic anatomy
Artistic photography
Artists' models
Arts and crafts movement
Asian art
Baroque art
Black art
Botanical illustration
Bronzes
Buddhist art
Byzantine art
Celtic art
Children's art
Christian art
Collage
Collectors and collecting
Commercial art
Composition (Art)
Computer art
Copy art
Cubism
Decoration and ornament
Drawing
Earthworks (Art)
Engraving
Erotic art
Etching
Ethnic art
Expressionism (Art)
Folk art
Futurism (Art)
Gems
Gothic revival (Art)
Graphic arts
Greek art
Illumination of books and manuscripts
Illustration of books
Impressionism (Art)
Interior design
Islamic art
Kinetic art
Medieval art
Modernism in art
Municipal art
Native American art
Painting
Performance art
Pictures
Portraits
Postimpressionism (Art)
Prehistoric art
Realism in art
Religious art
Roman art
Romanticism in art
Sculpture
Symbolism
Video art
World War, 1939-1945—Art and the war

RT   **Artists**

Art—15th and 16th centuries   709.02; 709.03

UF   Art, Renaissance
Renaissance art

Art—17th and 18th centuries   709.03

UF   Art, Modern—17th-18th centuries

Art—19th century   709.03

UF   Art, Modern—19th century
Modern art—1800-1899 (19th century)

NT   **Art nouveau**

Art—20th century   709.04

UF   Art, Modern—20th century
Modern art—1900-1999 (20th century)

SA   types of twentieth-century art, e.g. **Cubism** [to be added as needed]

NT   **Art deco**

Art—21st century   709.05

Art—21st century—*Continued*
    UF   Art, Modern—21st century
           Modern art—2000-2099 (21st
           century)
Art, American
    USE   **American art**
Art—Analysis, interpretation, appreciation
    USE   **Art appreciation**
           Art criticism
           Art—Study and teaching
Art, Ancient
    USE   **Ancient art**
Art and mythology   704.9
    UF   Mythology in art
    BT   **Art**
           Mythology
    RT   **Art and religion**
Art and religion   201; 246; 701
    UF   Arts in the church
           Religion and art
    BT   **Art**
           Religion
    RT   **Art and mythology**
           Religious art
Art and society (May subdiv. geog.)
    701
    UF   Art and sociology
           Society and art
           Sociology and art
    BT   **Art**
    NT   **Art patronage**
           Art—Political aspects
           Folk art
Art and sociology
    USE   **Art and society**
Art and the war
    USE   names of wars with the subdivi-
           sion *Art and the war,* e.g.
           World War, 1939-1945—Art
           and the war [to be added as
           needed]
Art appreciation   701
    UF   Appreciation of art
           Art—Analysis, interpretation, ap-
           preciation
    BT   **Aesthetics**
           Art criticism
Art, Asian
    USE   **Asian art**
Art, Baroque
    USE   **Baroque art**

Art, Black
    USE   **Black art**
Art, Buddhist
    USE   **Buddhist art**
Art, Byzantine
    USE   **Byzantine art**
Art collections (May subdiv. geog.)   **708**
    UF   Art—Collections
           Art—Private collections
           Collections of art, painting, etc.
           Private art collections
    SA   names of collectors or of the
           original owners of private art
           collections with the subdivi-
           sion *Art collections* [to be
           added as needed]
    RT   **Art museums**
           Collectors and collecting
Art—Collections
    USE   **Art collections**
Art—Composition
    USE   **Composition (Art)**
Art criticism   701; 709
    UF   Art—Analysis, interpretation, ap-
           preciation
    BT   **Criticism**
    NT   **Art appreciation**
Art deco   709.04
    BT   **Art—20th century**
Art education
    USE   **Art—Study and teaching**
Art—Exhibitions   707.4
    BT   **Exhibitions**
Art—Federal aid
    USE   **Federal aid to the arts**
Art—Forgeries   702.8; 751.5
    UF   Art forgeries
           Forgery of works of art
    BT   **Counterfeits and counterfeiting**
           Forgery
Art forgeries
    USE   **Art—Forgeries**
Art galleries
    USE   **Art museums**
           Commercial art galleries
Art, Gothic
    USE   **Gothic art**
Art, Greek
    USE   **Greek art**
Art—History   709
    BT   **History**

Art in advertising
USE **Commercial art**
Art in motion
USE **Kinetic art**
Art industries and trade
USE **Decorative arts**
Art, Islamic
USE **Islamic art**
Art, Kinetic
USE **Kinetic art**
Art, Medieval
USE **Medieval art**
Art metalwork   739; 745.56
UF   Decorative metalwork
SA   types of art metalwork [to be
        added as needed]
BT   **Decorative arts**
        Metalwork
NT   **Armor**
        Brasses
        Bronzes
        Goldwork
        Pewter
        Silverwork
Art, Modern—17th-18th centuries
USE   **Art—17th and 18th centuries**
Art, Modern—19th century
USE   **Art—19th century**
Art, Modern—20th century
USE   **Art—20th century**
Art, Modern—21st century
USE   **Art—21st century**
Art, Municipal
USE   **Municipal art**
Art museums (May subdiv. geog.)   **708**
UF   Art galleries
        Collections of art, painting, etc.
        Picture galleries
SA   names of individual art museums
        [to be added as needed]
BT   **Museums**
RT   **Art collections**
Art nouveau   709.03
UF   Jugendstil
BT   **Art—19th century**
Art objects   700; 745
Use for general materials about decorative
articles of artistic merit such as snuff boxes,
brasses, pottery, needlework, glassware, etc.
Materials on old decorative objects having
historical or financial value are entered under
Antiques.
UF   Objets d'art

SA   types of art objects, e.g. **Furni-
        ture**; **Pottery**; etc. [to be add-
        ed as needed]
BT   **Antiques**
        Art
        Decoration and ornament
        Decorative arts
NT   **Miniature objects**
Art, Oriental
USE   **Asian art**
Art patronage (May subdiv. geog.)   **700**
Use for materials on patronage of the arts
by individuals or corporations. Materials on
government support of the arts are entered un-
der **Arts—Government policy** or **Federal aid
to the arts**.
UF   Art patrons
        Business patronage of the arts
        Corporate patronage of the arts
        Corporations—Art patronage
        Funding for the arts
        Patronage of the arts
        Private funding of the arts
BT   **Art and society**
RT   **Arts—Government policy**
        Federal aid to the arts
Art patrons
USE   **Art patronage**
Art—Political aspects (May subdiv. geog.)
        701
BT   **Art and society**
Art pottery   738
UF   Studio pottery
SA   types of art pottery, e.g.
        Rookwood pottery [to be
        added as needed]
BT   **Pottery**
NT   **Rookwood pottery**
Art, Prehistoric
USE   **Prehistoric art**
Art—Prices   707.5
BT   **Prices**
Art—Private collections
USE   **Art collections**
Art, Renaissance
USE   **Art—15th and 16th centuries**
Art robberies
USE   **Art thefts**
Art, Roman
USE   **Roman art**
Art, Romanesque
USE   **Romanesque art**

Art schools
　USE **Art—Study and teaching**
Art—Study and teaching　707
　　UF　Art—Analysis, interpretation, appreciation
　　　　Art education
　　　　Art schools
Art—Technique　702.8
Art thefts (May subdiv. geog.)　364.16
　　UF　Art robberies
　　BT　**Theft**
Art—Themes　704.9
　　UF　Iconography
　　　　Themes in art
　　SA　topics in art, e.g. **Dogs in art**; and names of persons, families, and corporate bodies with the subdivision *In art*, e.g. **Napoleon I, Emperor of the French, 1769-1821—In art** [to be added as needed]
　　NT　**African Americans in art**
　　　　Animals in art
　　　　Blacks in art
　　　　Children in art
　　　　Dogs in art
　　　　Flowers in art
　　　　Napoleon I, Emperor of the French, 1769-1821—In art
　　　　Nude in art
　　　　Plants in art
　　　　Women in art
Art—Therapeutic use
　USE **Art therapy**
Art therapy　615.8; 616.89
　　UF　Art—Therapeutic use
　　BT　**Therapeutics**
Arthritis　616.7
　　BT　**Diseases**
　　NT　**Gout**
Arthritis—Physical therapy　616.7
Arthurian romances　398.22; 808.8; 809
　　Use for individual works, collections, or materials about Arthurian romances.
　　UF　Knights of the Round Table
　　BT　**Romances**
　　RT　**Grail—Legends**
Arthurian romances—Adaptations
　　808.8
Articles of war
　USE **Military law**

Articulation (Education)　371.2
　　Use for materials that discuss the integration of various elements of the school system, between levels, between schools, between subjects, or between the school's programs and outside activities, aimed at promoting a continuous advancement by the student.
　　BT　**Education—Curricula**
　　　　Schools—Administration
Artificial flies　688.7; 799.1
　　UF　Fishing flies
　　　　Flies, Artificial
　　BT　**Fishing—Equipment and supplies**
　　　　Fly casting
Artificial flowers　745.594
　　UF　Flowers, Artificial
　　BT　**Decoration and ornament**
Artificial foods　641.3; 664
　　UF　Synthetic foods
　　BT　**Food**
　　　　Synthetic products
Artificial fuels
　USE **Synthetic fuels**
Artificial heart　617.4
　　BT　**Artificial organs**
　　　　Heart
Artificial insemination　636.08
　　Use for general materials on artificial insemination and materials specifically on the artificial insemination of livestock and other animals. Materials limited to artificial insemination in humans are entered under **Human artificial insemination**.
　　BT　**Reproduction**
　　NT　**Human artificial insemination**
Artificial insemination, Human
　USE **Human artificial insemination**
Artificial intelligence　006.3
　　UF　AI (Artificial intelligence)
　　　　Machine intelligence
　　BT　**Computer science**
　　NT　**Expert systems (Computer science)**
Artificial limbs　617.5
　　UF　Limbs, Artificial
　　　　Prosthesis
　　BT　**Orthopedics**
Artificial organs　617.9
　　UF　Organs, Artificial
　　　　Prosthesis
　　SA　names of artificial organs, e.g. **Artificial heart** [to be added as needed]

Artificial organs—*Continued*
    BT   **Surgery**
    NT   **Artificial heart**
Artificial reality
    USE **Virtual reality**
Artificial respiration   617.1
    UF   Pulmonary resuscitation
         Respiration, Artificial
         Resuscitation, Pulmonary
    BT   **First aid**
Artificial satellites   629.43; 629.46
    UF   Orbiting vehicles
         Satellites, Artificial
    SA   satellites of particular countries,
         e.g. **American artificial satel-**
         lites; types of satellites; and
         names of specific satellites [to
         be added as needed]
    BT   **Astronautics**
    NT   **American artificial satellites**
         Explorer (Artificial satellite)
         Meteorological satellites
         Space stations
    RT   **Space vehicles**
Artificial satellites, American
    USE **American artificial satellites**
Artificial satellites—Control systems
    629.46
Artificial satellites in telecommunication
    384.5; 621.382
    UF   Communication satellites
         Communications relay satellites
         Global satellite communications
           systems
         Satellite communication systems
    SA   names of specific satellites or
         projects [to be added as need-
         ed]
    BT   **Telecommunication**
    NT   **Telstar project**
Artificial satellites—Launching   629.43
    UF   Launching of satellites
    BT   **Rockets (Aeronautics)**
Artificial satellites—Law and legislation
    USE **Space law**
Artificial satellites—Orbits   629.4
    BT   **Astrodynamics**
Artificial satellites—Tracking   629.43
    UF   Tracking of satellites
Artificial selection
    USE **Breeding**

Artificial sweeteners
    USE **Sugar substitutes**
Artificial weather control
    USE **Weather control**
Artillery   355.8; 623.4
    BT   **Military art and science**
    RT   **Ordnance**
Artistic anatomy   704.9; 743.4
    UF   Anatomy, Artistic
         Human anatomy in art
         Human figure in art
    BT   **Anatomy**
         Art
         Drawing
         Nude in art
    NT   **Figure drawing**
         Figure painting
Artistic photography   770; 779
    UF   Photography—Aesthetics
         Photography, Artistic
    BT   **Art**
         Photography
Artists (May subdiv. geog.)   **709.2; 920**
    SA   types of artists and names of in-
         dividual artists [to be added
         as needed]
    NT   **African American artists**
         Architects
         Black artists
         Child artists
         Designers
         Engravers
         Etchers
         Illustrators
         Lithographers
         Painters
         Photographers
         Potters
         Sculptors
         Women artists
    RT   **Art**
         Arts
Artists, American
    USE **Artists—United States**
Artists, Black
    USE **Black artists**
Artists' materials   741.2; 751.2
    UF   Drawing materials
         Painters' materials
    SA   types of artists' materials [to be
         added as needed]

Artists' materials—*Continued*
  BT **Materials**
Artists' models 702.8
  UF Models
      Models, Artists'
      Models (Persons)
  BT **Art**
Artists—United States 709.2; 920
  UF American artists
      Artists, American
Arts (May subdiv. geog.) **700**
  Use for materials on the arts in general, including the visual arts, literature, and the performing arts. Materials on the visual arts only (architecture, painting, etc.) are entered under **Art.**
  BT **Humanities**
  NT **Allegory**
      Art
      Decorative arts
      Handicraft
      Performing arts
      Surrealism
      Visual literacy
  RT **Aesthetics**
      Artists
Arts, American
  USE **Arts—United States**
Arts and crafts movement (May subdiv. geog.) **745**
  Use for materials on the movement originating in England in the nineteenth century that promoted a return to craftsmanship in the applied and decorative arts.
  UF Crafts (Arts)
  BT **Art**
      Decoration and ornament
      Decorative arts
      Industrial arts
  RT **Folk art**
      Handicraft
Arts and state
  USE **Arts—Government policy**
       Federal aid to the arts
Arts—Federal aid
  USE **Federal aid to the arts**
Arts—Government policy (May subdiv. geog.) **353.7; 700**
  UF Arts and state
      Funding for the arts
      State encouragement of the arts
  BT **Social policy**
  RT **Art patronage**
      Federal aid to the arts

Arts, Graphic
  USE **Graphic arts**
Arts in the church
  USE **Art and religion**
Arts—United States 700.973
  UF American arts
      Arts, American
Aryans
  USE **Indo-Europeans**
Asbestos 553.6; 620.1; 666; 691
  BT **Minerals**
Asceticism 204; 248.4
  May be subdivided by religion or sect.
  BT **Ethics**
      Religious life
  NT **Fasting**
      Sexual abstinence
Asceticism—Catholic Church 248.4
Asia 950
  UF East
      Orient
  SA areas of Asia [to be added as needed]
  NT **Central Asia**
      East Asia
      Middle East
      Southeast Asia
Asia, Central
  USE **Central Asia**
Asia—Civilization 306.095; 950
  UF Asian civilization
      Civilization, Oriental
      Oriental civilization
  BT **Civilization**
      East and West
Asia—Politics and government 950
  BT **Politics**
Asia, Southeastern
  USE **Southeast Asia**
Asian Americans 305.895
  BT **Ethnic groups**
Asian architecture 720.95
  UF Oriental architecture
  BT **Architecture**
Asian art 709.5
  UF Art, Asian
      Art, Oriental
      Oriental art
  BT **Art**
Asian civilization
  USE **Asia—Civilization**

Asperger's syndrome   616.85; 618.92
    BT   **Autism**
Asphyxiating gases
    USE   **Poisonous gases**
Assassination   364.15
    SA   classes of persons and names of
          individuals with the subdivi-
          sion *Assassination* [to be add-
          ed as needed]
    BT   **Crime**
          Homicide
          Political crimes and offenses
    NT   **Presidents—United States—As-**
          sassination
Assault, Criminal
    USE   **Offenses against the person**
Assault, Sexual
    USE   **Rape**
Assembly programs, School
    USE   **School assembly programs**
Assembly, Right of
    USE   **Freedom of assembly**
Assertive behavior
    USE   **Assertiveness (Psychology)**
Assertiveness (Psychology)   155.2; 158.2
    UF   Assertive behavior
    BT   **Aggressiveness (Psychology)**
          Psychology
    RT   **Self-confidence**
Assessment
    USE   **Tax assessment**
Assessment, Tax
    USE   **Tax assessment**
Assistance in emergencies
    USE   **Helping behavior**
Assistance to developing areas
    USE   **Foreign aid**
          Technical assistance
Assisted independent residential living
    USE   **Assisted living**
Assisted living (May subdiv. geog.)
    362.6; 363.5
    UF   Assisted independent residential
          living
          Congregate housing
    BT   **Housing**
    RT   **Elderly—Housing**
Assisted reproduction
    USE   **Reproductive technology**
Association, Freedom of
    USE   **Freedom of association**

Associations (May subdiv. geog.)   **060;**
    302.3; 366
    UF   Associations, institutions, etc.
          Networks (Associations, institu-
          tions, etc.)
          Organizations
          Voluntary associations
          Voluntary organizations
    SA   types of associations; subjects,
          classes of persons, ethnic
          groups, and names of individ-
          ual persons, families, and cor-
          porate bodies, with the subdi-
          vision *Societies*; and names of
          specific associations [to be
          added as needed]
    NT   **Agriculture—Societies**
          Charity organization
          Clubs
          Community life
          Cooperation
          Financial institutions
          Nonprofit organizations
          Religious institutions
          Societies
          Trade and professional associa-
          tions
Associations, institutions, etc.
    USE   **Associations**
Associations, International
    USE   **International agencies**
Asteroids   523.44
    UF   Minor planets
          Planetoids
    BT   **Astronomy**
          Solar system
    RT   **Planets**
Asthma (May subdiv. geog.)   **616.2**
    UF   Bronchial asthma
    BT   **Allergy**
          Lungs—Diseases
Astral projection   133.9
    UF   Astral travel
          Out-of-body experiences
    BT   **Parapsychology**
Astral travel
    USE   **Astral projection**
Astrobiology
    USE   **Life on other planets**
          Space biology

Astrochemistry
USE **Space chemistry**
Astrodynamics   521; 629.4
    BT **Dynamics**
    NT **Artificial satellites—Orbits**
        Navigation (Astronautics)
    RT **Astronautics**
        Space flight
Astrogeology   559.9
    SA names of planets with the subdi-
        vision *Geology* [to be added
        as needed]
    BT **Geology**
    NT **Lunar geology**
        Mars (Planet)—Geology
Astrology   133.5
    UF Hermetic art and philosophy
    BT **Astronomy**
        Divination
        Occultism
    NT **Horoscopes**
        Zodiac
    RT **Constellations**
Astronautical accidents
    USE **Space vehicle accidents**
Astronautical communication systems
    USE **Astronautics—Communication**
        systems
Astronautical instruments   629.4
    UF Instruments, Astronautical
        Space vehicles—Instruments
    BT **Navigation (Astronautics)**
        Space optics
    RT **Astronautics—Communication**
        systems
Astronautics (May subdiv. geog.)   **629.4**
    BT **Aeronautics**
    NT **Aerothermodynamics**
        Artificial satellites
        Astronautics and civilization
        Interplanetary voyages
        Navigation (Astronautics)
        Outer space
        Rocketry
        Space flight
        Space flight to the moon
        Space stations
        Unidentified flying objects
    RT **Astrodynamics**
        Space sciences
        Space vehicles

Astronautics—Accidents
    USE **Space vehicle accidents**
Astronautics and civilization   306.4
    UF Civilization and astronautics
        Outer space and civilization
        Space age
        Space power
    BT **Aeronautics and civilization**
        Astronautics
        Civilization
    NT **Space colonies**
        Space law
Astronautics—Communication systems
    629.47
    UF Astronautical communication sys-
        tems
        Space communication
    BT **Interstellar communication**
        Telecommunication
    NT **Radio in astronautics**
    RT **Astronautical instruments**
Astronautics—International cooperation
    629.4
    UF International space cooperation
    BT **International cooperation**
Astronautics—Law and legislation
    USE **Space law**
Astronautics—United States   629.40973
    NT **Project Voyager**
Astronauts   629.450092; 920
    UF Cosmonauts
    BT **Air pilots**
        Space flight
    NT **Space vehicles—Piloting**
        Women astronauts
Astronauts—Clothing
    USE **Space suits**
Astronauts—Nutrition   629.47
    UF Space nutrition
    BT **Nutrition**
Astronavigation
    USE **Navigation (Astronautics)**
Astronomers   520.92; 920
    BT **Scientists**
Astronomical instruments   522
    UF Instruments, Astronomical
    SA types of instruments, e.g. **Tele-**
        scopes [to be added as need-
        ed]
    BT **Scientific apparatus and in-**
        struments

Astronomical instruments—*Continued*
        Space optics
    NT   Astronomical photography
        Telescopes
Astronomical observatories   522
    UF   Observatories, Astronomical
    RT   Astronomy
Astronomical photography   522
    UF   Astrophotography
    BT   Astronomical instruments
        Photography
Astronomical physics
    USE   Astrophysics
Astronomy   520
    BT   Physical sciences
        Science
        Universe
    NT   Asteroids
        Astrology
        Astrophysics
        Bible—Astronomy
        Black holes (Astronomy)
        Chronology
        Comets
        Galaxies
        Life on other planets
        Lunar eclipses
        Meteorites
        Meteors
        Moon
        Nautical astronomy
        Outer space
        Planetariums
        Planets
        Pulsars
        Quasars
        Radio astronomy
        Seasons
        Sky
        Solar eclipses
        Solar system
        Space environment
        Spectrum analysis
        Sun
        Zodiac
    RT   Astronomical observatories
        Constellations
        Space sciences
        Stars
Astronomy—Atlases
    USE   Stars—Atlases
Astronomy—Mathematics   520.1

    BT   Mathematics
Astrophotography
    USE   Astronomical photography
Astrophysics   523.01
    UF   Astronomical physics
    BT   Astronomy
        Physics
    NT   Black holes (Astronomy)
        Spectrum analysis
Astros (Baseball team)
    USE   Houston Astros (Baseball
        team)
Asylum   323.6; 342.08
    UF   Asylum, Right of
        Political asylum
        Right of asylum
        Sanctuary (Law)
    BT   International law
    NT   Political refugees
        Sanctuary movement
Asylum, Right of
    USE   Asylum
Asylums
    USE   Institutional care
At-home employment
    USE   Home-based business
At risk students   371.93
      Use for materials on students considered
    prone to academic failure or other problems.
    UF   Disadvantaged students
        High risk students
        Students with problems
        Underprivileged students
    BT   Students
    RT   Dropouts
        Socially handicapped children
Atheism   211
    BT   Religion
        Secularism
        Theology
    RT   Agnosticism
        Deism
        Rationalism
        Theism
Athletes (May subdiv. geog.)   796.092;
    920
    SA   types of athletes, e.g. Baseball
        players [to be added as need-
        ed]
    NT   African American athletes
        Baseball players
        Black athletes

Athletes—*Continued*
> **Women athletes**
> RT   **Sports**

Athletes, Black
> USE   **Black athletes**

Athletes—Drug use   362.29; 796
> UF   Drugs and sports
>   Sports and drugs
> RT   **Steroids**

Athletic coaching
> USE   **Coaching (Athletics)**

Athletic medicine
> USE   **Sports medicine**

Athletics (May subdiv. geog.)   **796**
> SA   types of athletic activities [to be added as needed]
> NT   **Boxing**
>   **Coaching (Athletics)**
>   **Gymnastics**
>   **Martial arts**
>   **Olympic games**
>   **Rowing**
>   **Track athletics**
>   **Walking**
>   **Weight lifting**
>   **Wrestling**
> RT   **Physical education**
>   **Sports**

Atlantic Ocean   910.9163
> BT   **Ocean**
> NT   **Bermuda Triangle**

Atlantic States   974; 975
> UF   Eastern Seaboard
>   Middle Atlantic States
>   South Atlantic States
> BT   **United States**

Atlantis (Legendary place)   001.94; 398.23
> BT   **Geographical myths**
>   **Lost continents**

Atlas (Missile)   623.4; 629.47
> BT   **Ballistic missiles**
>   **Intercontinental ballistic missiles**

Atlases   912
> Use as a form heading for geographical atlases of world coverage. General materials about maps and their history are entered under **Maps**.
> UF   Geographical atlases

> SA   scientific and technical subjects with the subdivision *Atlases*, for materials consisting of comprehensive, often systematically arranged, collections of illustrative plates, charts, etc., usually with explanatory captions, e.g. **Human anatomy—Atlases**; and names of countries, cities, etc., with the subdivision *Maps*, e.g. **United States—Maps** [to be added as needed]
> BT   **Geography**
>   **Maps**
> NT   **Bible—Geography**
>   **Historical atlases**
>   **Human anatomy—Atlases**
>   **Stars—Atlases**
>   **United States—Maps**

Atlases, Astronomical
> USE   **Stars—Atlases**

Atmosphere   551.5
> Use for materials on the body of air surrounding the earth. Materials on the chemical and physical properties of air are entered under **Air**.
> BT   **Air**
>   **Earth**
> NT   **Clouds**
>   **Fog**
>   **Sky**
>   **Upper atmosphere**
> RT   **Meteorology**

Atmosphere—Pollution
> USE   **Air pollution**

Atmosphere, Upper
> USE   **Upper atmosphere**

Atmospheric chemistry   551.51
> BT   **Physical chemistry**

Atmospheric dust
> USE   **Dust**

Atmospheric greenhouse effect
> USE   **Greenhouse effect**

Atmospheric humidity
> USE   **Humidity**

Atolls
> USE   **Coral reefs and islands**

Atom smashing
> USE   **Cyclotrons**

Atomic bomb   355.8; 623.4

Atomic bomb—*Continued*
  BT **Bombs**
      Nuclear weapons
  NT **Radioactive fallout**
  RT **Hydrogen bomb**
Atomic bomb—Physiological effect
    616.9
  RT **Radiation—Physiological effect**
Atomic bomb—Testing 623.4
Atomic bomb victims 940.54
  UF Victims of atomic bombings
Atomic energy
  USE **Nuclear energy**
Atomic industry
  USE **Nuclear industry**
Atomic medicine
  USE **Nuclear medicine**
Atomic nuclei
  USE **Nuclear physics**
Atomic power
  USE **Nuclear energy**
Atomic power plants
  USE **Nuclear power plants**
Atomic-powered vehicles
  USE **Nuclear propulsion**
Atomic submarines
  USE **Nuclear submarines**
Atomic theory 539.7; 541
  BT **Physical chemistry**
  RT **Quantum theory**
Atomic warfare
  USE **Nuclear warfare**
Atomic weapons
  USE **Nuclear weapons**
Atoms 539.7; 541
  BT **Physical chemistry**
  NT **Cyclotrons**
      Electrons
      Isotopes
      Neutrons
      Protons
      Transmutation (Chemistry)
Atonement—Christianity 232; 234
  UF Vicarious atonement
  BT **Christianity**
      Sacrifice
      Salvation
Atonement, Day of
  USE **Yom Kippur**
Atonement—Judaism 296.3
  UF Atonement (Judaism)
  BT **Judaism**

Atonement (Judaism)
  USE **Atonement—Judaism**
Atrocities (May subdiv. geog.) **909**
  UF Military atrocities
  SA names of wars with the subdivision *Atrocities*, e.g. **World War, 1939-1945—Atrocities**; and names of specific atrocities [to be added as needed]
  BT **Crime**
      Cruelty
  NT **Massacres**
      Persecution
      World War, 1939-1945—Atrocities
Attacks by animals
  USE **Animal attacks**
Attempted suicide
  USE **Suicide**
Attendance, School
  USE **School attendance**
Attention 153.1; 153.7
  UF Concentration
  BT **Apperception**
      Educational psychology
      Memory
      Psychology
      Thought and thinking
  NT **Listening**
Attention deficit disorder 616.85
  UF ADD (Child behavior disorder)
      Attention deficit disorder in adolescence
      Attention deficit disorder in adults
      Attention-deficit hyperactivity disorder
      Hyperactivity disorder
      Hyperkinesia
  BT **Abnormal psychology**
Attention deficit disorder in adolescence
  USE **Attention deficit disorder**
Attention deficit disorder in adults
  USE **Attention deficit disorder**
Attention-deficit hyperactivity disorder
  USE **Attention deficit disorder**
Attention-seeking
  USE **Showing off**
Attitude (Psychology) 152.4
  UF Attitudes

Attitude (Psychology)—*Continued*
- SA   ethnic groups and classes of persons with the subdivision *Attitudes*, e.g. **Teenagers—Attitudes** [to be added as needed]
- BT   **Emotions**
  - **Psychology**
- NT   **Conformity**
  - **Empathy**
  - **Frustration**
  - **Job satisfaction**
  - **Prejudices**
  - **Racism**
  - **Sexism**
  - **Stereotype (Social psychology)**
  - **Teenagers—Attitudes**
  - **Trust**
- RT   **Public opinion**

Attitudes
- USE   **Attitude (Psychology)**
  - and ethnic groups and classes of persons with the subdivision *Attitudes*, e.g. **Teenagers—Attitudes** [to be added as needed]

Attorneys
- USE   **Lawyers**

Attracting birds
- USE   **Bird attracting**

Attracting wildlife
- USE   **Wildlife attracting**

ATVs
- USE   **All terrain vehicles**

Auction bridge
- USE   **Bridge (Game)**

Auctions   **658.8**
- UF   Sales, Auction
- BT   **Selling**
- NT   **Internet auctions**

Audiences (May subdiv. geog.)   **302.3**
- SA   types of performances or events with the subdivision *Audiences*, e.g. **Performing arts—Audiences** [to be added as needed]
- BT   **Communication**
  - **Social psychology**
- NT   **Performing arts—Audiences**
  - **Sports spectators**
  - **Television viewers**

Audio amplifiers, Transistor
- USE   **Transistor amplifiers**

Audio cassettes
- USE   **Sound recordings**

Audiobooks   **028**
> Use for materials on sound recordings of books, including but not limited to materials recorded specifically for the blind.

- UF   Books on cassette
  - Books on tape
  - Cassette books
  - Recorded books
  - Talking books
- BT   **Sound recordings**
- RT   **Blind—Books and reading**

Audiodisc players
- USE   **Compact disc players**

Audiotapes
- USE   **Sound recordings**

Audiovisual aids
- USE   subjects with the subdivision *Audiovisual aids,* e.g. **Library education—Audiovisual aids;** and subjects with the subdivisions *Study and teaching—Audiovisual aids,* for the use of audiovisual aids in the teaching of those subjects, e.g. **Science—Study and teaching—Audiovisual aids** [to be added as needed]

Audiovisual education   **371.33**
- UF   Visual instruction
- SA   subjects with the subdivision *Audiovisual aids* to be added as needed]
- BT   **Education**
- NT   **Audiovisual materials**
  - **Library education—Audiovisual aids**
  - **Motion pictures in education**
  - **Radio in education**
  - **Television in education**

Audiovisual equipment   **621.389**
- NT   **Audiovisual materials**
- RT   **Audiovisual materials**

Audiovisual materials   **025.17; 371.33**
- UF   Multimedia materials
  - Nonbook materials
  - Nonprint materials
- SA   subjects with the subdivision *Audiovisual aids*; and names of specific audiovisual materials [to be added as needed]

Audiovisual materials—*Continued*
- BT **Audiovisual education**
  Audiovisual equipment
  Teaching—Aids and devices
- NT **Filmstrips**
  Library education—Audiovisual aids
  Manipulatives
  Motion pictures
  Sound recordings
  Videodiscs
  Videotapes

Audiovisual materials centers
- USE **Instructional materials centers**

Auditing (May subdiv. geog.) **657**
- SA topics and names of corporate bodies with the subdivision *Auditing* [to be added as needed]
- BT **Bookkeeping**
- RT **Accounting**

Auditoriums (May subdiv. geog.) **725**
- BT **Buildings**
  Centers for the performing arts
- NT **Concert halls**

Aunts (May subdiv. geog.) **306.87**
- BT **Family**

Auricular confession
- USE **Confession**

Aurora australis
- USE **Auroras**

Aurora borealis
- USE **Auroras**

Auroras **538**
- UF Aurora australis
  Aurora borealis
  Northern lights
  Polar lights
  Southern lights
- BT **Geophysics**
  Meteorology

Australia **994**
  May be subdivided like **United States** except for *History*.
- NT **Australians**

Australian aborigines
- USE **Aboriginal Australians**

Australians **305.82; 994**
- BT **Australia**
- NT **Aboriginal Australians**

Austria **943.6**
  May be subdivided like **United States** except for *History*.

Author and publisher
- USE **Authors and publishers**

Authoring programs for computer-assisted instruction
- USE **Computer-assisted instruction— Authoring programs**

Authoritarianism
- USE **Fascism**
  Totalitarianism

Authority **303.3**
- BT **Political science**

Authors **809; 920**
- UF Writers
- SA authors of particular countries, e.g. **American authors**; types of writers, e.g. **Poets**; names of national literatures with the subdivision for a particular kind of author, e.g. **American literature—Women authors**; **American literature—African American authors**; etc.; subjects and names of countries, cities, etc. with the subdivision *Bio-bibliography*; and names of individual authors [to be added as needed]
- NT **American authors**
  Black authors
  Child authors
  Dramatists
  English authors
  Historians
  Journalists
  Native American authors
  Novelists
  Poets
  Women authors
- RT **Books**
  Literature—Bio-bibliography

Authors, American
- USE **American authors**

Authors and publishers **070.5**
  Use for materials on the relations between author and publisher.
- UF Author and publisher
  Publishers and authors
- BT **Authorship**
  Contracts

Authors and publishers—*Continued*
> Publishers and publishing
>> RT **Copyright**

Authors, Black
>> USE **Black authors**

Authors—Correspondence   808.6; 808.86
>> BT **Letters**

Authors, English
>> USE **English authors**

Authors—Homes and haunts
>> USE **Literary landmarks**

Authors—Interviews   809
>> BT **Interviews**

Authorship   808
> Use for general materials on being or becoming an author. Materials concerning the composition of special types of literature are entered under more specific headings such as **Fiction—Technique**; **Biography as a literary form**; **Short story**; etc.
>> UF Writing (Authorship)
>> SA individual writers, titles of literary works, and sacred works with the subdivision *Authorship*; e.g. **Shakespeare, William, 1564-1616—Authorship** [to be added as needed]
>> BT **Literature**
>> NT **Advertising copy**
>>> **Authors and publishers**
>>> **Biography as a literary form**
>>> **Creative writing**
>>> **Drama—Technique**
>>> **Editing**
>>> **Fiction—Technique**
>>> **Historiography**
>>> **Journaling**
>>> **Journalism**
>>> **Love stories—Technique**
>>> **Radio authorship**
>>> **Report writing**
>>> **Short story**
>>> **Technical writing**
>>> **Television authorship**
>>> **Travel writing**
>>> **Versification**

Authorship—Handbooks, manuals, etc.   808
>> RT **Printing—Style manuals**

Autism   616.85; 618.92
>> UF Autism spectrum disorders
>>> Autistic spectrum disorders

>> BT **Child psychiatry**
>> NT **Asperger's syndrome**

Autism spectrum disorders
>> USE **Autism**

Autistic spectrum disorders
>> USE **Autism**

Autobiographical fiction   808.3; 808.83
> Use for individual works, collections, or materials about autobiographical fiction.
>> UF Autobiographical novels
>> BT **Biographical fiction**

Autobiographical graphic novels   741.5
> Use for individual works, collections, or materials about autobiographical graphic novels.
>> BT **Graphic novels**

Autobiographical novels
>> USE **Autobiographical fiction**

Autobiographies   920
> Use for collections of autobiographies. Materials about autobiography as a literary form are entered under **Autobiography**.
>> UF Memoirs
>>> Personal narratives
>> SA ethnic groups, classes of persons, and subjects with the subdivision *Biography* or *Correspondence*, e.g. **Women—Biography**; **Authors—Correspondence**; etc.; and names of diseases, events, and wars with the subdivision *Personal narratives* [to be added as needed]
>> BT **Biography**
>> NT **Holocaust, 1933-1945—Personal narratives**
>>> **United States—History—1861-1865, Civil War—Personal narratives**
>>> **World War, 1939-1945—Personal narratives**
>> RT **Diaries**

Autobiography   809
> Use for materials on autobiography as a literary form. Collections of autobiographies are entered under **Autobiographies**.
>> UF Autobiography as a literary form
>>> Autobiography—History and criticism
>>> Autobiography—Technique
>>> Memoirs
>> BT **Biography as a literary form**
>> NT **Slave narratives**

Autobiography as a literary form
USE **Autobiography**
Autobiography—History and criticism
USE **Autobiography**
Autobiography—Technique
USE **Autobiography**
Autographed copies
USE **Autographed editions**
Autographed editions   016
UF   Autographed copies
Signed editions
BT   **Autographs**
Editions
Autographs   929.8
SA   classes of persons, ethnic
groups, wars, and names of
individual persons with the
subdivision *Autographs*, or
Autographs—Facsimiles [to be
added as needed]
BT   **Biography**
Writing
NT   **Autographed editions**
RT   **Manuscripts**
Autographs—Facsimiles   929.8
SA   classes of persons, ethnic
groups, wars, and names of
individual persons with the
subdivisions *Autographs—Fac-*
similes [to be added as need-
ed]
Automata
USE   **Robots**
Automated cataloging   025.3
UF   Cataloging—Data processing
BT   **Cataloging**
Automatic bread machines
USE   **Bread machines**
Automatic control
USE   **Cybernetics**
Electric controllers
Servomechanisms
Automatic data processing
USE   **Data processing**
Automatic drafting
USE   **Computer graphics**
Automatic drawing
USE   **Computer graphics**
Automatic machinery
USE   **Automation**
Automatic speech recognition   006.4

UF   Mechanical speech recognition
Speech recognition, Automatic
BT   **Speech processing systems**
Voice
Automation   629.8; 670.42
UF   Automatic machinery
Computer control
SA   subjects with the subdivision *Au-*
tomation, e.g. **Libraries—Au-**
tomation [to be added as
needed]
BT   **Industrial equipment**
Machinery in the workplace
NT   **Feedback control systems**
Industrial robots
Libraries—Automation
Servomechanisms
Systems engineering
Telecommuting
Automatons
USE   **Robots**
Automobile accidents
USE   **Traffic accidents**
Automobile design
USE   **Automobiles—Design and con-**
struction
Automobile driver education (May
subdiv. geog.)   **629.28**
UF   Automobile drivers—Education
Car driver education
Driver education
BT   **Education**
Automobile drivers   629.28
UF   Automobile driving
Automobiles—Driving
Car drivers
Drivers, Automobile
Automobile drivers—Education
USE   **Automobile driver education**
Automobile drivers' licenses
USE   **Drivers' licenses**
Automobile driving
USE   **Automobile drivers**
Automobile engines
USE   **Automobiles—Motors**
Automobile guides
USE   **Automobile travel—Guidebooks**
Automobile industry (May subdiv. geog.)
338.4; 388.3
UF   Automotive industry
Car industry

Automobile industry—*Continued*

    Motor vehicle industry

  BT **Industries**

  NT **Service stations**

Automobile industry—Production standards 658.5

  BT **Production standards**

Automobile insurance 368

  UF Car insurance

    Insurance, Automobile

  BT **Insurance**

Automobile motors

  USE **Automobiles—Motors**

Automobile parts 629.28

  UF Automobiles—Parts

    Car parts

  BT **Automobiles**

Automobile pools

  USE **Car pools**

Automobile racing (May subdiv. geog.) **796.72**

  UF Automobiles—Racing

    Car racing

  SA types of automobile racing and names of specific races, e.g. **Indianapolis 500 (Race)** [to be added as needed]

  BT **Racing**

  NT **Karts and karting**

    Stock car racing

Automobile repairs

  USE **Automobiles—Maintenance and repair**

Automobile touring

  USE **Automobile travel**

Automobile transmission

  USE **Automobiles—Transmission devices**

Automobile travel (May subdiv. geog.) **796.7**

  UF Automobile touring

    Automobiles—Touring

    Car travel

    Motoring

  BT **Transportation**

    Travel

    Voyages and travels

Automobile travel—Guidebooks 912

  UF Automobile guides

    Automobiles—Road guides

    Travel guides

  BT **Maps**

  RT **Road maps**

Automobiles (May subdiv. geog.) **388.3; 629.222**

  UF Cars (Automobiles)

    Motor cars

  SA names of specific makes and models of automobiles, e.g. **Ford automobile** [to be added as needed]

  BT **Highway transportation**

    Vehicles

  NT **Antique and classic cars**

    Automobile parts

    Buses

    Compact cars

    Diesel automobiles

    Electric automobiles

    Ford automobile

    Foreign automobiles

    Sports cars

    Trucks

Automobiles—Accidents

  USE **Traffic accidents**

Automobiles—Air conditioning 629.2

  BT **Air conditioning**

Automobiles—Brakes 629.2

  BT **Brakes**

Automobiles—Conservation and restoration 629.28

  UF Automobiles—Restoration

    Restoration of automobiles

Automobiles—Construction

  USE **Automobiles—Design and construction**

Automobiles—Design

  USE **Automobiles—Design and construction**

Automobiles—Design and construction 629.222

  UF Automobile design

    Automobiles—Construction

    Automobiles—Design

    Automotive engineering

    Car design

  BT **Industrial design**

Automobiles—Drivers' licenses

  USE **Drivers' licenses**

Automobiles—Driving

  USE **Automobile drivers**

Automobiles, Electric

  USE **Electric automobiles**

Automobiles—Electric equipment
629.25
UF   Electric equipment of automobiles
Automobiles—Engines
USE   **Automobiles—Motors**
Automobiles, Foreign
USE   **Foreign automobiles**
Automobiles—Fuel consumption   629.28
BT   **Energy consumption**
Fuel
Automobiles—Gearing
USE   **Automobiles—Transmission devices**
Automobiles—Inspection (May subdiv. geog.)   **353.9**
Automobiles—Law and legislation (May subdiv. geog.)   **343.09**
BT   **Law**
Legislation
RT   **Traffic regulations**
Automobiles—Maintenance and repair
629.28
UF   Automobile repairs
Automobiles—Repairing
Car maintenance
Car repair
Automobiles—Models   629.22
UF   Model cars
BT   **Models and modelmaking**
Automobiles—Motors   629.25
UF   Automobile engines
Automobile motors
Automobiles—Engines
Car engines
SA   types of automobiles and makes and models of automobiles with the subdivision *Motors* [to be added as needed]
BT   **Engines**
Automobiles—Painting   667
UF   Car painting
BT   **Industrial painting**
Automobiles—Parts
USE   **Automobile parts**
Automobiles—Pollution control devices
629.25
UF   Pollution control devices (Motor vehicles)
BT   **Pollution control industry**

Automobiles—Purchasing (May subdiv. geog.)   **381**
Automobiles—Racing
USE   **Automobile racing**
Automobiles—Repairing
USE   **Automobiles—Maintenance and repair**
Automobiles—Restoration
USE   **Automobiles—Conservation and restoration**
Automobiles—Road guides
USE   **Automobile travel—Guidebooks**
Automobiles—Technological innovations
629.22
BT   **Technological innovations**
Automobiles—Touring
USE   **Automobile travel**
Automobiles—Trailers
USE   **Travel trailers and campers**
Automobiles—Transmission devices
629.2
UF   Automobile transmission
Automobiles—Gearing
Car transmissions
Transmissions, Automobile
BT   **Gearing**
Automotive engineering
USE   **Automobiles—Design and construction**
Automotive industry
USE   **Automobile industry**
Autosuggestion
USE   **Hypnotism**
Mental suggestion
Autumn   508; 525
UF   Fall
BT   **Seasons**
Availability of health services
USE   **Access to health care**
Avalanches (May subdiv. geog.)   **553.1**
BT   **Snow**
Avant-garde (Aesthetics) (May subdiv. geog.)   **700.1**
BT   **Aesthetics**
Modernism (Aesthetics)
Avant-garde churches
USE   **Non-institutional churches**
Avant-garde films
USE   **Experimental films**
Avant-garde theater
USE   **Experimental theater**

Avarice   178; 205
    Use for materials on an inordinate desire
    for wealth. Materials on any excessive desire
    for food, personal possessions, etc. are entered
    under **Greed**.
    UF   Covetousness
    BT   **Sin**
    RT   **Greed**
Avenues
    USE   **Streets**
Average   519.5
    BT   **Arithmetic**
          Probabilities
          Statistics
Aviation
    USE   **Aeronautics**
Aviation accidents
    USE   **Aircraft accidents**
Aviation medicine   616.9
    UF   Aeronautics—Medical aspects
          Aerospace medicine
    BT   **Medicine**
    NT   **Jet lag**
    RT   **Space medicine**
Aviators
    USE   **Air pilots**
Avocations
    USE   **Hobbies**
Awakening, Religious
    USE   **Religious awakening**
Awards   001.4
    UF   Competitions
          Prizes (Rewards)
          Rewards (Prizes, etc.)
    SA   types of awards and prizes; sub-
          jects, corporate entities, per-
          sons, and military services
          with the subdivision *Awards*,
          e.g. **Architecture—Awards**;
          and names of specific awards
          and prizes, e.g. **Nobel Prizes**
          [to be added as needed]
    NT   **Literary prizes**
          Nobel Prizes
    RT   **Contests**
Awards (Law)
    USE   **Arbitration and award**
Axiology
    USE   **Values**
Aztecs   972.004
    BT   **Native Americans—Mexico**
B-52 bomber   623.74

    BT   **Bombers**
B and B accommodations
    USE   **Bed and breakfast accommo-
            dations**
Babies
    USE   **Infants**
Baboons (May subdiv. geog.)   **599.8**
    BT   **Apes**
Baby animals
    USE   **Animal babies**
Baby boom generation (May subdiv.
    geog.)   **305.2**
    UF   Baby boomers
    BT   **Population**
Baby boomers
    USE   **Baby boom generation**
Baby care
    USE   **Infants—Care**
Baby clothes
    USE   **Infants' clothing**
Baby names
    USE   **Personal names**
Baby showers
    USE   **Showers (Parties)**
Baby sitters
    USE   **Babysitters**
Baby sitting
    USE   **Babysitting**
Babysitters   649
    UF   Baby sitters
          Sitters (Babysitters)
    RT   **Babysitting**
Babysitting   649
    UF   Baby sitting
    BT   **Child care**
          Infants—Care
    RT   **Babysitters**
Bachelors
    USE   **Single men**
Back packing
    USE   **Backpacking**
Backpack cycling
    USE   **Bicycle touring**
Backpacking   796.51
    UF   Back packing
          Pack transportation
    BT   **Camping**
          Hiking
Bacon-Shakespeare controversy
    USE   **Shakespeare, William, 1564-
            1616—Authorship**

Bacon's Rebellion, 1676   973.2
>   BT   **United States—History—1600-**
>   **1775, Colonial period**

Bacteria   579.3

> Use for general materials on bacteria. Materials on the science of studying bacteria are entered under **Bacteriology**.

>   UF   Disease germs
>
>   Germs
>
>   Microbes
>
>   BT   **Microorganisms**
>
>   **Parasites**
>
>   RT   **Bacteriology**

Bacterial resistance to antibiotics
>   USE   **Drug resistance in microorganisms**

Bacterial warfare
>   USE   **Biological warfare**

Bacteriology   579.3

> Use for materials on the science of studying bacteria. General materials on bacteria are entered under **Bacteria**.

>   SA   types of bacteriology, e.g. **Agricultural bacteriology**; types of microbiology, e.g. **Soil microbiology**; and subjects with the subdivision *Microbiology*, e.g. **Cheese—Microbiology** [to be added as needed]
>
>   BT   **Microbiology**
>
>   NT   **Agricultural bacteriology**
>
>   RT   **Bacteria**

Bacteriology, Agricultural
>   USE   **Agricultural bacteriology**

Bad behavior   179; 302.3; 395

>   UF   Meanness
>
>   Rudeness
>
>   BT   **Human behavior**

Bad breath   616.3

>   UF   Halitosis
>
>   BT   **Mouth—Diseases**

Bad sportsmanship
>   USE   **Sportsmanship**

Badgers (May subdiv. geog.)   **599.76**

>   BT   **Mammals**

Badges   355.1; 737; 929.9

>   BT   **Heraldry**
>
>   **Insignia**

Badges of honor
>   USE   **Decorations of honor**
>
>   **Insignia**
>
>   **Medals**

Baggage
>   USE   **Luggage**

Bahai Faith   297.9

>   UF   Bahaism
>
>   BT   **Religions**

Bahaism
>   USE   **Bahai Faith**

Baking   641.7

>   SA   types of baked products [to be added as needed]
>
>   BT   **Cooking**
>
>   NT   **Bread**
>
>   **Cake**
>
>   **Cookies**
>
>   **Pastry**
>
>   **Pies**
>
>   RT   **Bread machines**

Balance of nature
>   USE   **Ecology**

Balance of payments (May subdiv. geog.)   **382**

>   BT   **International economic relations**
>
>   RT   **Balance of trade**

Balance of power   327.1

>   UF   Power politics
>
>   BT   **International relations**

Balance of trade (May subdiv. geog.)   **382**

>   UF   Trade, Balance of
>
>   Trade deficits
>
>   Trade surpluses
>
>   BT   **International trade**
>
>   RT   **Balance of payments**

Ball bearings
>   USE   **Bearings (Machinery)**

Ball games   796.3

>   SA   types of games, e.g. **Baseball**; and names of competitions [to be added as needed]
>
>   BT   **Games**
>
>   NT   **Baseball**
>
>   **Basketball**
>
>   **Billiards**
>
>   **Bowling**
>
>   **Football**
>
>   **Soccer**
>
>   **Softball**
>
>   **Table tennis**
>
>   **Volleyball**

Ball room dancing
USE **Ballroom dancing**
Ballads   808.1; 808.81

Use for individual works, collections, or materials about ballads. Materials on the folk tunes associated with these ballads and collections that include both words and music are entered under **Folk songs**.

BT **Literature**
Poetry
Songs
RT **Folk songs**

Ballet (May subdiv. geog.)   **792.8**

Use for musical works composed for the ballet and for materials about the ballet. Individual ballet plots or collections of ballet plots are entered under **Ballet—Stories, plots, etc.**

UF Ballets
BT **Dance**
Drama
Performing arts
Theater
RT **Pantomimes**

Ballet dancers   792.8092; 920
BT **Dancers**

Ballet plots
USE **Ballet—Stories, plots, etc.**

Ballet—Stories, plots, etc.   792.8
UF Ballet plots

Ballets
USE **Ballet**

Ballistic missiles   358.1; 623.4

Use for materials on high-altitude, high-speed missiles that are self-propelled and guided in the first stage of flight only and later have a natural and uncontrolled trajectory.

UF Missiles, Ballistic
SA types of ballistic missiles and names of specific missiles [to be added as needed]
BT **Guided missiles**
Nuclear weapons
Rockets (Aeronautics)
NT **Atlas (Missile)**
Intercontinental ballistic missiles

Balloons   629.133

Use for materials on aircraft held aloft by hot air or light gases that are nondirigible and propelled only by the wind. Materials on self-propelled aircraft that are lighter than air and steerable are entered under **Airships**.

UF Aircraft
BT **Aeronautics**
RT **Airships**

Balloons, Dirigible
USE **Airships**

Ballot
USE **Elections**

Ballparks
USE **Stadiums**

Ballroom dancing (May subdiv. geog.)   **793.3**
UF Ball room dancing
BT **Dance**

Band music   784
BT **Instrumental music**
Military music

Bandages   616.02
UF Bandages and bandaging
BT **First aid**

Bandages and bandaging
USE **Bandages**

Bandits
USE **Thieves**

Bandmasters
USE **Conductors (Music)**

Bands (Music)   784
SA types of bands and names of individual bands [to be added as needed]
NT **Drum majoring**
Instrumentation and orchestration
RT **Conducting**
Orchestra

Bangladesh   954.92

May be subdivided like **United States** except for *History*.

Bank credit cards
USE **Credit cards**

Bank debit cards
USE **Debit cards**

Bank failures (May subdiv. geog.)   **332.1**
UF Failure of banks
BT **Bankruptcy**
Banks and banking
Business failures

Bank robberies (May subdiv. geog.)   **364.15**
BT **Theft**

Banking
USE **Banks and banking**

Bankruptcy (May subdiv. geog.)   **332.7; 336.3; 346.07**
UF Business mortality
Failure in business

Bankruptcy—*Continued*
      Insolvency
  BT **Business failures**
      Commercial law
      Debtor and creditor
      Finance
  NT **Bank failures**
Banks and banking (May subdiv. geog.)
      332.1
  UF Banking
      Savings banks
  SA names of individual banks [to be
      added as needed]
  BT **Business**
      Capital
      Commerce
      Finance
  NT **Agricultural credit**
      Bank failures
      Consumer credit
      Cooperative banks
      Debit cards
      Federal Reserve banks
      Foreign exchange
      Interest (Economics)
      Investments
      Negotiable instruments
      Savings and loan associations
  RT **Credit**
      Money
      Trust companies
Banks and banking, Cooperative
  USE **Cooperative banks**
Banks and banking—Credit cards
  USE **Credit cards**
Banks and banking—Data processing
      332.10285
  BT **Data processing**
Banks and banking—United States
      332.10973
Banned books
  USE **Books—Censorship**
Banners
  USE **Flags**
Banquets
  USE **Dining**
      Dinners
Baptism **234; 265**
  UF Christening
  BT **Sacraments**
Baptists **286**
  BT **Christian sects**

Bar
  USE **Lawyers**
Bar coding **006.4; 658.7**
  BT **Identification**
Bar mitzvah (May subdiv. geog.) **296.4**
  BT **Judaism—Customs and prac-**
        tices
Barbary States
  USE **North Africa**
Barbecue cookery
  USE **Barbecue cooking**
Barbecue cooking **641.7**
  UF Barbecue cookery
      Grill cooking
      Grilling
  BT **Outdoor cooking**
Barbering
  USE **Hair**
Barbie dolls **688.7**
  BT **Dolls**
Bargaining
  USE **Negotiation**
Barns **631.2; 728**
  BT **Farm buildings**
Barometers **551.5; 681**
  BT **Meteorological instruments**
Baroque architecture (May subdiv. geog.)
      724
  UF Architecture, Baroque
  BT **Architecture**
Baroque art (May subdiv. geog.) **709.03**
  UF Art, Baroque
  BT **Art**
Barrier free design
  USE **Architecture and the handi-**
        capped
Barristers
  USE **Lawyers**
Barrooms
  USE **Bars**
Barrows
  USE **Mounds and mound builders**
Bars (May subdiv. geog.) **647.95**
    Use for materials on public drinking estab-
  lishments.
  UF Barrooms
      Pubs
      Restaurants, bars, etc.
      Saloons
      Taverns
  BT **Liquor industry**
  RT **Restaurants**

Bartending   641.8
- UF   Mixology
- BT   **Food service**

Barter (May subdiv. geog.)   **332**
- UF   Exchange, Barter
- BT   **Commerce**
  - **Economics**
  - **Money**
  - **Subsistence economy**
  - **Underground economy**

Basal readers   372.41; 418

Use for readers providing controlled vocabulary in a series of books intended to be read sequentially and for materials about such readers.

- UF   English language—Basal readers
- BT   **Reading materials**

Baseball (May subdiv. geog.)   **796.357**
- BT   **Ball games**
  - **Sports**
- NT   **Baseball teams**
  - **Little League baseball**
  - **Negro leagues**
  - **Softball**
- RT   **Baseball players**

Baseball cards   769
- BT   **Sports cards**

Baseball clubs
- USE   **Baseball teams**

Baseball—Fiction   808.83

Use for collections of baseball stories.
- UF   Baseball stories

Baseball players (May subdiv. geog.)
  796.357; 920
- BT   **Athletes**
- RT   **Baseball**

Baseball stories
- USE   **Baseball—Fiction**

Baseball teams (May subdiv. geog.)
  796.35706
- UF   Baseball clubs
- SA   names of individual baseball teams, e.g. **Houston Astros (Baseball team)** [to be added as needed]
- BT   **Baseball**
  - **Sports teams**
- NT   **Houston Astros (Baseball team)**

Basements   721
- UF   Cellars

- BT   **Foundations**
  - **Underground architecture**

Bases (Chemistry)   546; 661
- BT   **Chemistry**

Bashfulness
- USE   **Shyness**

Basic education (May subdiv. geog.)
  370.11
- UF   Basic skills education
  - Fundamental education
- BT   **Education**

Basic life skills
- USE   **Life skills**

Basic needs (May subdiv. geog.)   **306**

Use for materials on human needs such as food, shelter, education, health, water, employment, etc., that provide a minimum quality of life.
- RT   **Poverty**
  - **Quality of life**

Basic rights
- USE   **Civil rights**
  - **Human rights**

Basic skills education
- USE   **Basic education**

Basket making   746.41
- BT   **Weaving**

Basketball (May subdiv. geog.)   **796.323**
- BT   **Ball games**
  - **Sports**
- NT   **Basketball teams**
  - **Wheelchair basketball**

Basketball for women (May subdiv. geog.)   **796.323**
- BT   **Sports for women**

Basketball teams (May subdiv. geog.)
  796.323
- SA   names of individual basketball teams, e.g. **New York Knicks (Basketball team)** [to be added as needed]
- BT   **Basketball**
  - **Sports teams**
- NT   **New York Knicks (Basketball team)**

Baskets (May subdiv. geog.)   **746.41**
- BT   **Containers**

Bastogne, Battle of
- USE   **Ardennes (France), Battle of the, 1944-1945**

Bat mitzvah (May subdiv. geog.)   **296.4**

Bat mitzvah—*Continued*
> BT **Judaism—Customs and prac-**
> **tices**

Bathrooms 643
> BT **Rooms**

Baths 613; 615.8
> BT **Cleanliness**
> **Hygiene**
> **Physical therapy**
> RT **Hydrotherapy**

Bathyscaphe 387.2; 623.8
> BT **Oceanography—Research**
> **Submersibles**

Batik 746.6
> BT **Dyes and dyeing**

Baton twirling 791.6
> RT **Drum majoring**

Bats 599.4
> BT **Mammals**

Battered elderly
> USE **Elderly abuse**

Battered wives
> USE **Abused women**

Battered women
> USE **Abused women**

Batteries, Electric
> USE **Electric batteries**
> **Storage batteries**

Batteries, Solar
> USE **Solar batteries**

Battering of wives
> USE **Wife abuse**

Battle of the Bulge
> USE **Ardennes (France), Battle of**
> **the, 1944-1945**

Battle ships
> USE **Warships**

Battle songs
> USE **War songs**

Battlefields (May subdiv. geog.) **904**
> UF Battlegrounds
> SA names of wars with the subdivi-
> sion *Battlefields*, e.g. **World**
> **War, 1939-1945—Battle-**
> **fields**; and names of individu-
> al battlefields [to be added as
> needed]
> BT **Battles**

Battlegrounds
> USE **Battlefields**

Battles (May subdiv. geog.) **355.4; 904;**
> **909**

> UF Fighting
> Sieges
> SA names of wars with the subdivi-
> sion *Campaigns*, e.g. **United**
> **States—History—1861-1865,**
> **Civil War—Campaigns**; and
> names of individual battles,
> e.g. **Ardennes, Battle of the,**
> **1944-1945** [to be added as
> needed]
> BT **Military art and science**
> **Military history**
> **War**
> NT **Battlefields**
> **Naval battles**

Battleships
> USE **Warships**

Bay of Pigs invasion
> USE **Cuba—History—1961, Invasion**

Bazaars
> USE **Fairs**

BBBs (Better business bureaus)
> USE **Better business bureaus**

Beaches (May subdiv. geog.) **551.45**
> BT **Seashore**

Beads 745.58
> BT **Decoration and ornament**
> RT **Jewelry**

Beadwork 746.5
> BT **Handicraft**

Bearings (Machinery) 621.8
> UF Ball bearings
> BT **Machinery**
> RT **Lubrication and lubricants**

Bears (May subdiv. geog.) **599.78**
> BT **Mammals**

Beasts
> USE **Animals**

Beat generation 810.9
> UF Beatniks
> Beats
> BT **American literature**
> **Bohemianism**

Beatniks
> USE **Beat generation**

Beats
> USE **Beat generation**

Beautification of landscape
> USE **Landscape protection**

Beauty
> USE **Aesthetics**

Beauty contests (May subdiv. geog.)
    791.6
  UF Beauty pageants
  BT **Contests**
Beauty pageants
  USE **Beauty contests**
Beauty parlors
  USE **Beauty shops**
Beauty, Personal
  USE **Personal appearance**
       Personal grooming
Beauty salons
  USE **Beauty shops**
Beauty shops 646.7
  UF Beauty parlors
       Beauty salons
  BT **Business enterprises**
Beavers 599.37
  BT **Furbearing animals**
       Mammals
Beavers—Habitations 599.37
Bed and breakfast accommodations (May
    subdiv. geog.) **910.46**
  UF B and B accommodations
  BT **Hotels and motels**
Bedouins (May subdiv. geog.) **305.892;**
    909
  BT **Arabs**
Bedspreads 643; 746.9
  UF Coverlets
  BT **Interior design**
Bedtime 306.4; 392.3
  UF Getting ready for bed
  BT **Night**
       Sleep
  NT **Lullabies**
Bee culture
  USE **Beekeeping**
Bee hives
  USE **Beehives**
Bee houses
  USE **Beehives**
Beef 641.3; 664
  BT **Meat**
Beef cattle 636.2
  UF Steers
  SA names of breeds of beef cattle
       [to be added as needed]
  BT **Cattle**
  NT **Hereford cattle**
Beehives 638

  UF Bee hives
       Bee houses
       Bees—Housing
  BT **Animal housing**
  RT **Beekeeping**
Beekeeping 638
  UF Apiculture
       Bee culture
       Honeybee culture
  BT **Agriculture**
  RT **Beehives**
       Bees
Beer making
  USE **Brewing**
Bees 595.79; 638
  BT **Insects**
  RT **Beekeeping**
       Honey
Bees—Housing
  USE **Beehives**
Beetles (May subdiv. geog.) **595.76**
  BT **Insects**
Begging 362.5
  UF Mendicancy
       Panhandling
  BT **Poor**
  RT **Tramps**
Beginning reading materials
  USE **Easy reading materials**
Behavior
  USE **Animal behavior**
       Human behavior
       and types of specific behavior,
       e.g. **Helping behavior;** and
       types of animals with the
       subdivision *Behavior,* e.g.
       Birds—Behavior [to be add-
       ed as needed]
Behavior genetics 155.7
  UF Psychogenetics
  BT **Genetics**
       Psychology
Behavior, Helping
  USE **Helping behavior**
Behavior in organizations
  USE **Organizational behavior**
Behavior modification 153.8
  BT **Applied psychology**
       Human behavior
       Psychology of learning

Behavior modification—*Continued*
   NT   **Brainwashing**
         Twelve-step programs
Behavior of children
   USE **Child psychology**
         Children—Conduct of life
         Etiquette for children and
            teenagers
Behavior of teenagers
   USE **Adolescent psychology**
         Etiquette for children and
            teenagers
         Teenagers—Conduct of life
Behavior problems (Children)
   USE **Emotionally disturbed children**
Behavioral psychology
   USE **Psychophysiology**
Behaviorism   150.19
    Use for materials on empirical psychology dealing with the observable actions of organisms rather than with mental phenomena.
   UF Behavioristic psychology
        Interbehaviorial psychology
   BT **Human behavior**
       Psychology
       Psychophysiology
Behavioristic psychology
   USE **Behaviorism**
Beijing Massacre, 1989
   USE **Tiananmen Square Incident,**
          Beijing (China), 1989
Belgium   949.3
    May be subdivided like **United States** except for *History*.
Belief and doubt   121
    Use for materials on belief and doubt from the philosophical standpoint. Materials on religious belief and doubt are entered under **Faith**.
   UF Doubt
   BT **Philosophy**
       Theory of knowledge
   NT **Truth**
   RT **Agnosticism**
       Faith
       Rationalism
       Skepticism
Bell System Telstar satellite
   USE **Telstar project**
Belles lettres
   USE **Literature**
Bells   786.8

   UF Carillons
       Chimes
       Church bells
   BT **Musical instruments**
Belly dancing (May subdiv. geog.)   793.3
   BT **Dance**
Belts and belting   621.8
   UF Chain belting
   BT **Machinery**
   RT **Power transmission**
Beneficial insects   591.6
   UF Helpful insects
       Useful insects
   SA types of beneficial insects, e.g.
       Silkworms [to be added as
         needed]
   BT **Economic zoology**
       Insects
   NT **Silkworms**
Benefit cost analysis
   USE **Cost effectiveness**
Benefits, Employee
   USE **Fringe benefits**
Benefits, Fringe
   USE **Fringe benefits**
Benevolent institutions
   USE **Institutional care**
Beowulf—Adaptations   829
Bequests
   USE **Gifts**
       Inheritance and succession
       Wills
Bereavement   155.9; 248.8
    Use for materials on the suffering of those who have lost a loved one. Materials on mental suffering or sorrow from other causes, especially loss or remorse, are entered under **Grief**.
   UF Mourning
       Sorrow
   BT **Emotions**
   RT **Consolation**
       Grief
Bermuda Triangle   001.9
   UF Devil's Triangle
   BT **Atlantic Ocean**
Berries   634
   SA types of berries, e.g. **Strawberries** [to be added as needed],
       in the plural form
   BT **Fruit**
       Fruit culture
   NT **Strawberries**

Best-book lists

USE **Best books**

Best books 011

Use for lists of recommended books and materials about recommended books. Materials on the principles of book selection for libraries are entered under **Book selection**.

UF Best-book lists

Bibliography—Best books

Book lists

Books and reading—Best books

Choice of books

Evaluation of literature

Literature—Evaluation

BT **Books**

RT **Book selection**

Best sellers (Books) 028; 070.5

UF Books—Best sellers

BT **Books and reading**

Betrothal (May subdiv. geog.) **392.4**

UF Engagement

BT **Courtship**

Marriage

Better business bureaus (May subdiv. geog.) **381.3**

UF BBBs (Better business bureaus)

BT **Consumer protection**

Betting

USE **Gambling**

Bevel gearing

USE **Gearing**

Beverage industry (May subdiv. geog.) **338.4**

SA types of beverage industries, e.g. **Coffee industry** [to be added as needed]

BT **Food industry**

NT **Coffee industry**

Liquor industry

Tea industry

Beverages 613; 641.2; 641.8; 663

UF Drinks

SA types of beverages and names of specific beverages [to be added as needed]

BT **Diet**

Food

NT **Alcoholic beverages**

Cocoa

Coffee

Liquors

Tea

Bi-racial people

USE **Racially mixed people**

Bias attacks

USE **Hate crimes**

Bias crimes

USE **Hate crimes**

Bias in testing

USE **Test bias**

Bias (Psychology)

USE **Prejudices**

Bible 220

The subdivisions provided under Bible may also be used with any part of the Bible, with single books of the Bible, and with groups of books, e.g. **Bible. O.T.—Biography**; **Bible. O.T. Pentateuch—Commentaries**; **Bible. O.T. Psalms—History**; **Bible. N.T. Gospels—Inspiration**; etc.

UF Holy Scriptures

Scriptures, Holy

BT **Ancient history**

Hebrew literature

Jewish literature

Sacred books

Bible. N.T. 225

Use same subdivisions as those given under **Bible**. They may also be used for groups of books, e.g. **Bible. N.T. Gospels—Inspiration**; and for single books, e.g. **Bible. N.T. Matthew—Commentaries**.

UF New Testament

Bible. O.T. 221

Use same subdivisions as those given under **Bible**. They may also be used for groups of books, e.g. **Bible. O.T. Pentateuch—Commentaries**; and for single books, e.g. **Bible. O.T. Psalms—History**.

UF Old Testament

NT **Ten commandments**

Bible and science 220.8

UF Science and the Bible

BT **Religion and science**

Science

RT **Creationism**

Bible—Animals

USE **Bible—Natural history**

Bible—Antiquities 220.9

UF Biblical archeology

BT **Antiquities**

Archeology

Bible as literature 809

UF Bible—Language, style, etc.

Bible—Literary character

NT **Bible—Criticism**

Bible—Parables

RT **Religious literature**

Bible—Astronomy   220.8
>   BT   **Astronomy**
Bible—Biography   220.92
>   UF   Biblical characters
>   BT   **Biography**
Bible—Birds
>   USE   **Bible—Natural history**
Bible—Botany
>   USE   **Bible—Natural history**
Bible—Catechism, question books
>   USE   **Bible—Catechisms**
Bible—Catechisms   220
>   UF   Bible—Catechism, question
>   books
>   Bible—Question books
>   BT   **Bible—Study and teaching**
>   **Catechisms**
Bible—Chronology   220.9
>   Use for materials on the dates of events related in the Bible and their correlation with the dates of general history.
>   UF   Bible—History of biblical
>   events—Chronology
>   Biblical chronology
>   BT   **Chronology**
Bible classes
>   USE   **Bible—Study and teaching**
>   **Religious summer schools**
>   **Sunday schools**
Bible—Commentaries   220.7
>   UF   Bible—Interpretation
>   Commentaries, Biblical
Bible—Concordances   220.3
>   Use for works that list the words of the Bible and give the passages where each word occurs. Works that list topics or names found in the Bible and give the passages where those topics or names rather than exact words are found are entered under **Bible—Indexes**.
Bible—Cosmology
>   USE   **Biblical cosmology**
Bible—Criticism   220.6
>   UF   Bible—Criticism, interpretation,
>   etc.
>   Bible—Exegesis
>   Bible—Hermeneutics
>   Bible—Interpretation
>   Exegesis, Biblical
>   Hermeneutics, Biblical
>   Higher criticism
>   BT   **Bible as literature**
Bible—Criticism, interpretation, etc.
>   USE   **Bible—Criticism**
Bible—Dictionaries   220.3

>   BT   **Encyclopedias and dictionaries**
Bible—Drama
>   USE   **Bible plays**
Bible—Evidences, authority, etc.   220.1
>   Use for materials that attempt to establish the truth of statements in the Bible or the authority of its precepts. Materials on the divine inspiration of the Bible are entered under **Bible—Inspiration**.
>   UF   Evidences of the Bible
Bible—Exegesis
>   USE   **Bible—Criticism**
Bible fiction   808.3; 808.83
>   Use for individual works, collections, or materials about imaginative fiction in which characters and settings are taken from the Bible. Stories that are retold or adapted from the Bible while remaining faithful to the original are entered under **Bible stories**.
>   SA   names of biblical characters with
>   the subdivision *Fiction* [to be
>   added as needed]
>   BT   **Fiction**
>   RT   **Bible stories**
Bible films   791.43
>   Use for individual works, collections, or materials about bible films.
>   UF   Biblical films
>   BT   **Motion pictures**
Bible—Flowers
>   USE   **Bible—Natural history**
Bible games and puzzles   220.07;
>   793.73
>   UF   Bible puzzles
>   BT   **Games**
>   **Puzzles**
Bible—Gardens
>   USE   **Bible—Natural history**
Bible—Geography   220.91
>   UF   Bible—Maps
>   Biblical geography
>   BT   **Atlases**
>   **Geography**
Bible—Hermeneutics
>   USE   **Bible—Criticism**
Bible—History   220.9
>   Use for materials on the origin, authorship, and composition of the Bible as a book. Materials on historical events as described in the Bible are entered under **Bible—History of biblical events**.
Bible—History of biblical events   220.9
>   Use for materials on historical events as described in the Bible. Materials on the origin, authorship, and composition of the Bible as a book are entered under **Bible—History**.

Bible—History of biblical events—*Continued*

    UF   History, Biblical

Bible—History of biblical events—Chronology

    USE   **Bible—Chronology**

Bible—Illustrations

    USE   **Bible—Pictorial works**

Bible in literature   809

    Use for materials that discuss the Bible as a theme in literature.

    BT   **Literature**

    RT   **Religion in literature**

Bible in the schools

    USE   **Religion in the public schools**

Bible—Indexes   220.3

    Use for works that list topics or names found in the Bible and give the passages where those topics or names rather than exact words are found. Works that list the words of the Bible and give the passages where the exact word occurs are entered under **Bible—Concordances**.

Bible—Inspiration   220.1

    Use for materials on the divine inspiration of the Bible. Materials that attempt to establish the truth of statements in the Bible or the authority of its precepts are entered under **Bible—Evidence, authority, etc.**

    UF   Inspiration, Biblical

Bible—Interpretation

    USE   **Bible—Commentaries**

            Bible—Criticism

Bible—Introductions

    USE   **Bible—Study and teaching**

Bible—Language, style, etc.

    USE   **Bible as literature**

Bible—Literary character

    USE   **Bible as literature**

Bible—Maps

    USE   **Bible—Geography**

Bible—Natural history   220.8

    UF   Bible—Animals

            Bible—Birds

            Bible—Botany

            Bible—Flowers

            Bible—Gardens

            Bible—Plants

            Bible—Zoology

            Botany of the Bible

            Nature in the bible

            Zoology of the Bible

    BT   **Natural history**

Bible—Parables   226.8

    BT   **Bible as literature**

            Parables

Bible—Pictorial works   220.022

    UF   Bible—Illustrations

    RT   **Jesus Christ—Art**

Bible—Plants

    USE   **Bible—Natural history**

Bible plays   808.82

    Use for individual plays, collections, or materials about dramatizations of biblical events.

    UF   Bible—Drama

            Biblical plays

    SA   names of biblical characters with the subdivision *Drama* [to be added as needed]

    BT   **Religious drama**

    NT   **Mysteries and miracle plays**

            Passion plays

Bible—Prophecies   220.1

    UF   Prophecies (Bible)

    NT   **Jesus Christ—Prophecies**

Bible—Psychology   220.8

    UF   Biblical psychology

    BT   **Psychology**

Bible puzzles

    USE   **Bible games and puzzles**

Bible—Question books

    USE   **Bible—Catechisms**

Bible—Reading   220.5

    BT   **Books and reading**

Bible stories   220.9

    Use for individual works, collections, or materials about stories that are retold or adapted from the Bible while remaining faithful to the original. Imaginative fiction in which characters and settings are taken from the Bible is entered under **Bible fiction**.

    UF   Stories

    RT   **Bible fiction**

Bible—Study

    USE   **Bible—Study and teaching**

Bible—Study and teaching   220.07

    UF   Bible classes

            Bible—Introductions

            Bible—Study

    BT   **Sunday schools**

    NT   **Bible—Catechisms**

Bible—Use   220.6

    Use for materials that show how the Bible is used as a guide to living, to cultivation of a spiritual life, and to problems of doctrine.

Bible—Versions   220.4; 220.5

    Use for materials on the various versions and translations of the Bible.

Bible—Women
USE **Women in the Bible**
Bible—Zoology
USE **Bible—Natural history**
Biblical archeology
USE **Bible—Antiquities**
Biblical characters
USE **Bible—Biography**
Biblical chronology
USE **Bible—Chronology**
Biblical cosmology   202; 231.7; 296.3
UF   Bible—Cosmology
BT   **Cosmology**
RT   **Creation**
Biblical films
USE **Bible films**
Biblical geography
USE **Bible—Geography**
Biblical plays
USE **Bible plays**
Biblical psychology
USE **Bible—Psychology**
Biblical teaching
USE   religious or secular topics with
the subdivision *Biblical teach-ing,* e.g. **Salvation—Biblical teaching; Family—Biblical teaching;** etc. [to be added as needed]
Bibliographic control   025.3
UF   Universal bibliographic control
BT   **Documentation**
NT   **Cataloging**
Indexing
Information systems
MARC formats
Bibliographic data in machine readable form
USE   **Machine readable bibliographic data**
Bibliographic instruction   025.5
Use for materials on the instruction of readers in library use. Materials on the education of librarians are entered under **Library education.**
UF   Library instruction
Library orientation
Library skills
Library user orientation
BT   **Library services**
Bibliography   010

SA   subjects and names of persons and places with the subdivision *Bibliography,* e.g. **Agriculture—Bibliography; Shakespeare, William, 1564-1616—Bibliography; United States—Bibliography;** etc. [to be added as needed]
BT   **Documentation**
NT   **Archives**
Editions
Indexes
Indexing
Manuscripts
Printing
Reference books
Serial publications
RT   **Books**
Cataloging
Library science
Bibliography—Best books
USE   **Best books**
Bibliography—Bilingual books
USE   **Bilingual books**
Bibliography—Editions
USE   **Editions**
Bibliography—First editions
USE   **First editions**
Bibliography—Rare books
USE   **Rare books**
Bibliography—Reprint editions
USE   **Reprints (Publications)**
Bibliomania
USE   **Book collecting**
Bibliophily
USE   **Book collecting**
Bicentennial celebrations—United States—1976
USE   **American Revolution Bicentennial, 1776-1976**
Biculturalism (May subdiv. geog.)
305.8; 306.44
Use for materials on the presence of two distinct cultures within a single country or region. Materials on the coexistence of several distinct ethnic, religious, or cultural groups within one society are entered under **Pluralism (Social sciences)**. Materials on policies or programs that foster the preservation of various cultures or cultural identities within a unified society are entered under **Multiculturalism**.
BT   **Pluralism (Social sciences)**
RT   **Multiculturalism**

Biculturalism—United States   305.8;
   306.44

Bicycle camping
   USE   **Bicycle touring**

Bicycle racing (May subdiv. geog.)
   796.6
   BT   **Cycling**
      Racing
   RT   **Bicycle touring**
      Bicycles

Bicycle touring (May subdiv. geog.)
   796.6
   UF   Backpack cycling
      Bicycle camping
      Touring, Bicycle
   BT   **Camping**
      Cycling
      Travel
   RT   **Bicycle racing**
      Bicycles

Bicycles   629.227
   UF   Bicycles and bicycling
      Bikes
   BT   **Vehicles**
   NT   **Minibikes**
      Motorcycles
      Mountain bikes
   RT   **Bicycle racing**
      Bicycle touring
      Cycling

Bicycles and bicycling
   USE   **Bicycles**
      Cycling

Bicycling
   USE   **Cycling**

Big bang cosmology
   USE   **Big bang theory**

Big bang theory   523.1
   UF   Big bang cosmology
   BT   **Cosmology**

Big books   372.41
   Use for books produced in an oversize format and intended for use in shared-reading learning experiences or for materials about such books.
   UF   Enlarged texts for shared reading
      Oversize books
      Oversized books for shared reading
      Shared reading books
   BT   **Children's literature**
      Reading materials

RT   **Large print books**

Big foot
   USE   **Sasquatch**

Big game hunting (May subdiv. geog.)
   799.2
   BT   **Hunting**

Bigfoot
   USE   **Sasquatch**

Bigotry
   USE   **Prejudices**
      Toleration

Bigotry-motivated crimes
   USE   **Hate crimes**

Bikes
   USE   **Bicycles**

Biking
   USE   **Cycling**

Bildungsromans   808.3
   Use for individual works, collections, or materials about fiction in which the theme is the development of a character from youth to adulthood.
   UF   Apprenticeship novels
      Coming of age stories
   BT   **Fiction**

Bilingual books   002; 011
   Use for materials about bilingual books. As a form heading for the bilingual materials themselves, use this heading subdivided by the languages, e.g. **Bilingual books—English-Spanish**.
   UF   Bibliography—Bilingual books
      Books—Bilingual editions
   BT   **Books**
      Editions

Bilingual books—English-Spanish
   Use as a form heading for bilingual materials in English and Spanish.
   UF   Bilingual books—Spanish-English

Bilingual books—Spanish-English
   USE   **Bilingual books—English-Spanish**

Bilingual education (May subdiv. geog.)
   370.117
   UF   Education, Bilingual
   BT   **Bilingualism**
      Multicultural education

Bilingualism (May subdiv. geog.)
   306.44; 400
   BT   **Language and languages**
   NT   **Bilingual education**

Bilingualism—United States   306.44;
   420

Bill collecting
    USE   **Collecting of accounts**
Bill of rights (U.S.)
    USE   **United States. Constitution.
          1st-10th amendments**
Billboards
    USE   **Signs and signboards**
Billiards   794.92
    BT   **Ball games**
    NT   **Pool (Game)**
Bills and notes
    USE   **Negotiable instruments**
Bills of credit
    USE   **Credit
          Negotiable instruments**
Bills of fare
    USE   **Menus**
Binary system (Mathematics)   513.5
    UF   Pair system
    BT   **Mathematics
          Numbers**
Binding of books
    USE   **Bookbinding**
Binge eating behavior
    USE   **Bulimia**
Binge-purge behavior
    USE   **Bulimia**
Bio-bibliography
    USE   subjects, groups and classes of
          persons, names of places, and
          names of individual persons
          with the subdivision *Bio-
          bibliography,* e.g. **English lit-
          erature—Bio-bibliography;
          United States—Bio-
          bibliography;** etc. [to be add-
          ed as needed]
Bioastronautics
    USE   **Space medicine**
Biochemistry   572
    UF   Biological chemistry
          Physiological chemistry
    BT   **Biology
          Chemistry
          Medicine**
    NT   **Carbohydrates
          Clinical chemistry
          Metabolism
          Molecular biology
          Nucleic acids
          Proteins**

          Steroids
Bioconversion
    USE   **Biomass energy**
Biodiversity (May subdiv. geog.)   **333.95**
    Use for materials on the variety and vari-
    ability among living organisms and the eco-
    logical complexes in which they occur, includ-
    ing ecosystem diversity, species diversity, and
    genetic diversity.
    UF   Biological diversification
          Biological diversity [*Former
            heading*]
          Diversity, Biological
    BT   **Biology**
    RT   **Ecology**
Biodiversity conservation (May subdiv.
    geog.)   **333.95**
    UF   Biological diversity conservation
          [*Former heading*]
          Conservation of biodiversity
          Maintenance of biodiversity
          Preservation of biodiversity
    BT   **Conservation of natural re-
          sources**
Bioethics   174
    UF   Biological ethics
          Biology—Ethical aspects
          Biomedical ethics
          Life sciences ethics
    BT   **Ethics**
    NT   **Medical ethics
          Transplantation of organs, tis-
          sues, etc.—Ethical aspects**
Biofeedback training   152.1
    UF   Visceral learning
    BT   **Feedback (Psychology)
          Mind and body
          Psychology of learning
          Psychotherapy**
Biogeography (May subdiv. geog.)
    578.09
    Use for materials on the geographical distri-
    bution of animals and plants collectively or of
    animals only. Materials on the geographical
    distribution of plants are entered under
    Plants—Geographical distribution.
    UF   Distribution of animals and
          plants
          Geographical distribution of ani-
          mals and plants
    SA   types of plants and animals with
          the subdivision *Geographical
          distribution,* e.g. **Fishes—Geo-**

Biogeography—*Continued*

       graphical distribution [to be added as needed]

  BT **Ecology**

       Geography

  NT **Fishes—Geographical distribution**

       Plants—Geographical distribution

  RT **Natural history**

Biographical dictionaries

  USE **Biography—Dictionaries**

Biographical fiction   808.3; 808.83

Use for individual works, collections, or materials about fictionalized accounts of the lives of real persons.

  UF Biographical novels

  SA names of real persons with the subdivision *Fiction*, e.g. **Napoleon I, Emperor of the French, 1769-1821—Fiction**; or *In literature*, e.g. **Napoleon I, Emperor of the French, 1769-1821—In literature**; [to be added as needed]

  BT **Fiction**

  NT **Autobiographical fiction**

  RT **Historical fiction**

Biographical films   791.43

Use for individual works, collections, or materials about films depicting the lives of real persons.

  BT **Motion pictures**

Biographical graphic novels   741.5

Use for individual works, collections, or materials about biographical graphic novels.

  BT **Graphic novels**

Biographical novels

  USE **Biographical fiction**

Biographical radio programs   791.44

Use for individual works, collections, or materials about radio programs recounting the lives of real persons.

  BT **Radio programs**

Biographical television programs   791.45

Use for individual works, collections, or materials about television programs depicting the lives of real persons.

  BT **Television programs**

Biography   920

Use for collections of biographies not limited to one country or to one group or class of persons. Materials on the writing of biography are entered under **Biography as a literary form**.

  UF Life histories

       Memoirs

       Personal narratives

  SA subjects and names of places and corporate bodies with the subdivision *Biography*; ethnic groups and classes of persons with the subdivision *Biography* or *Correspondence*; and names of diseases, events, and wars with the subdivision *Personal narratives* [to be added as needed]

  BT **History**

  NT **Autobiographies**

       Autographs

       Bible—Biography

       Blacks—Biography

       Chicago (Ill.)—Biography

       Christian biography

       Epitaphs

       Greece—Biography

       Medicine—Biography

       Men—Biography

       Motion pictures—Biography

       Musicians—Biography

       Obituaries

       Ohio—Biography

       Portraits

       Religious biography

       Rome—Biography

       United States. Army—Biography

       United States. Navy—Biography

       United States. Supreme Court—Biography

       United States—Biography

       United States—History—1861-1865, Civil War—Biography

       United States—History—1861-1865, Civil War—Personal narratives

       Women—Biography

       World War, 1939-1945—Biography

       World War, 1939-1945—Personal narratives

  RT **Genealogy**

Biography (as a literary form)

  USE **Biography as a literary form**

Biography as a literary form   809

Use for materials on the writing of biography.

  UF   Biography (as a literary form)

        Biography—History and criticism

        Biography—Technique

  BT   **Authorship**

        Literature

  NT   **Autobiography**

Biography—Dictionaries   920.02

Use for collections of biographies in dictionary form not limited to one group or class of persons.

  UF   Biographical dictionaries

        Dictionaries, Biographical

  SA   subjects, groups or classes of

        persons, and names of places

        with the subdivisions *Biography—Dictionaries*, e.g. **Women—Biography—Dictionaries**;

        United States—Biography—Dictionaries; etc. [to be added as needed]

  BT   **Encyclopedias and dictionaries**

Biography—History and criticism

  USE   **Biography as a literary form**

Biography—Technique

  USE   **Biography as a literary form**

Biological anthropology

  USE   **Physical anthropology**

Biological chemistry

  USE   **Biochemistry**

Biological clocks

  USE   **Biological rhythms**

Biological diversification

  USE   **Biodiversity**

Biological diversity

  USE   **Biodiversity**

Biological diversity conservation

  USE   **Biodiversity conservation**

Biological ethics

  USE   **Bioethics**

Biological form

  USE   **Morphology**

Biological parents

  USE   **Birthparents**

Biological physics

  USE   **Biophysics**

Biological rhythms   571.7

  UF   Biological clocks

        Biology—Periodicity

        Biorhythms

  BT   **Cycles**

  NT   **Jet lag**

Biological structure

  USE   **Morphology**

Biological warfare (May subdiv. geog.)

        358; 623.4

  UF   Bacterial warfare

        Germ warfare

  BT   **Military art and science**

        Tactics

Biologists (May subdiv. geog.)   **570.92;**

        920

  BT   **Naturalists**

        Scientists

Biology   570

  BT   **Life sciences**

        Science

  NT   **Adaptation (Biology)**

        Anatomy

        Biochemistry

        Biodiversity

        Biomathematics

        Biophysics

        Botany

        Cells

        Cryobiology

        Death

        Ecology

        Embryology

        Ethnobiology

        Fossils

        Freshwater biology

        Gaia hypothesis

        Genetics

        Heredity

        Life (Biology)

        Life cycles (Biology)

        Marine biology

        Microbiology

        Physiology

        Protoplasm

        Radiobiology

        Reproduction

        Sex (Biology)

        Space biology

        Symbiosis

        Variation (Biology)

        Zoology

  RT   **Evolution**

Biology—Ecology

  USE   **Ecology**

Biology—Ethical aspects
  USE **Bioethics**
Biology, Molecular
  USE **Molecular biology**
Biology—Periodicity
  USE **Biological rhythms**
Biology—Social aspects
  USE **Sociobiology**
Bioluminescence 572
  UF Animal light
      Animal luminescence
      Light production in animals
  BT **Luminescence**
Biomass energy 333.95
  Use for materials on organic matter that can be converted to fuel and is therefore regarded as a potential energy source.
  UF Bioconversion
      Energy, Biomass
      Energy conversion, Microbial
      Microbial energy conversion
  SA types of matter as fuels, e.g.
      Waste products as fuel [to be added as needed]
  BT **Energy resources**
      Fuel
  RT **Waste products as fuel**
Biomathematics 570.1
  BT **Biology**
      Mathematics
Biomechanics
  USE **Human engineering**
      Human locomotion
Biomedical ethics
  USE **Bioethics**
Bionics 003
  Use for materials on the science of technological systems that function in the manner of living systems.
  BT **Biophysics**
      Cybernetics
      Systems engineering
Biophysics 571.4
  UF Biological physics
  BT **Biology**
      Physics
  NT **Bionics**
      Molecular biology
      Radiobiology
Biorhythms
  USE **Biological rhythms**
Biosciences
  USE **Life sciences**

Biotechnology 620.8; 660.6
  Use for materials on the application of living organisms or their biological systems or processes to the manufacture of products.
  BT **Chemical engineering**
      Microbiology
  NT **Reproductive technology**
  RT **Genetic engineering**
Bipolar depression
  USE **Manic-depressive illness**
Bipolar disorder
  USE **Manic-depressive illness**
Bird attracting 639.9
  UF Attracting birds
  BT **Wildlife attracting**
Bird decoys (Hunting)
  USE **Decoys (Hunting)**
Bird eggs
  USE **Birds—Eggs**
Bird houses
  USE **Birdhouses**
Bird photography
  USE **Photography of birds**
Bird song
  USE **Birdsongs**
Bird watching 598.07
  UF Birding
  BT **Natural history**
Birdbanding 598.07
  UF Birds—Banding
      Birds—Marking
  BT **Wildlife conservation**
Birdhouses 690
  UF Bird houses
  BT **Animal housing**
Birding
  USE **Bird watching**
Birds (May subdiv. geog.) **598**
  SA types of birds, e.g. **Birds of prey**; **Canaries**; etc. [to be added as needed]
  BT **Animals**
  NT **Birds of prey**
      Cage birds
      Canaries
      Ducks
      Eagles
      Game and game birds
      Geese
      Peacocks
      Pheasants
      Poultry

Birds—*Continued*
> **Robins**
> **State birds**
> **Terns**
> **Turkeys**
> **Water birds**

Birds—Anatomy 598
> BT **Anatomy**

Birds—Banding
> USE **Birdbanding**

Birds—Behavior 598.15
> UF Birds—Habits and behavior
> BT **Animal behavior**

Birds—Collection and preservation 598.075
> BT **Zoological specimens—Collection and preservation**

Birds—Color 598.147
> BT **Color**

Birds—Eggs 598.14
> UF Bird eggs
> Birds' eggs
> Birds—Eggs and nests
> BT **Eggs**

Birds' eggs
> USE **Birds—Eggs**

Birds—Eggs and nests
> USE **Birds—Eggs**
> **Birds—Nests**

Birds—Flight 591.5; 598.15
> BT **Animal flight**

Birds—Habits and behavior
> USE **Birds—Behavior**

Birds—Marking
> USE **Birdbanding**

Birds—Migration 598.156
> UF Migration of birds

Birds—Nests 598.156
> UF Birds—Eggs and nests
> Birds' nests

Birds' nests
> USE **Birds—Nests**

Birds of prey 598.9
> SA names of specific birds of prey
> [to be added as needed]
> BT **Birds**
> **Predatory animals**
> NT **Eagles**

Birds—Photography
> USE **Photography of birds**

Birds—Protection 333.95; 639.9
> UF Protection of birds
> BT **Wildlife conservation**
> RT **Game protection**

Birds—Song
> USE **Birdsongs**

Birds—United States 598.0973

Birdsongs 598.159
> UF Bird song
> Birds—Song
> BT **Animal sounds**

Birth
> USE **Childbirth**

Birth attendants
> USE **Midwives**

Birth control (May subdiv. geog.)
> **353.5; 363.9; 613.9**
> UF Conception—Prevention
> Contraception
> Family planning
> Fertility control
> Planned parenthood
> BT **Population**
> **Sexual hygiene**
> NT **Sterilization (Birth control)**
> RT **Birth rate**
> **Childlessness**
> **Family size**
> **Human fertility**
> **Infertility**

Birth control—Ethical aspects 176
> UF Birth control—Moral and religious aspects
> BT **Ethics**

Birth control—Moral and religious aspects
> USE **Birth control—Ethical aspects**
> **Birth control—Religious aspects**

Birth control—Religious aspects 205; 248.4
> UF Birth control—Moral and religious aspects

Birth customs
> USE **Childbirth**

Birth defects 616
> UF Abnormalities, Human
> Birth injuries
> Deformities
> Human abnormalities
> Infants—Birth defects
> Malformations, Congenital
> BT **Medical genetics**
> **Pathology**

Birth defects—*Continued*
    RT   **Fetal alcohol syndrome**
          Growth disorders
Birth injuries
    USE **Birth defects**
Birth, Multiple
    USE **Multiple birth**
Birth order   306.87
    UF   Firstborn child
          Middle child
          Oldest child
          Sibling sequence
          Youngest child
    BT   **Children**
          Family
Birth rate (May subdiv. geog.)   **304.6**
    UF   Birthrate
    BT   **Vital statistics**
    NT   **Human fertility**
    RT   **Birth control**
          Population
Birth records
    USE **Registers of births, etc.**
Birthday books   394.2
    Use for books with birthdays of famous persons for every day or month of the year and for similar books with space for recording birthdays of acquaintances.
    BT   **Birthdays**
          Calendars
Birthdays   394.2
    BT   **Anniversaries**
          Days
    NT   **Birthday books**
Birthparents   306.874
    Use for materials on natural, i.e. biological, parents who relinquished their children for adoption.
    UF   Biological parents
          Natural parents
          Parents, Biological
    BT   **Parents**
    RT   **Adoptees**
Birthrate
    USE **Birth rate**
Births, Registers of
    USE **Registers of births, etc.**
Bisexuality   306.76
    BT   **Sex**
Bishops (May subdiv. geog.)   **270.092**
    UF   Archbishops

    SA   church denominations with the subdivision *Bishops*, e.g. **Catholic Church—Bishops** [to be added as needed]
    BT   **Clergy**
    NT   **Catholic Church—Bishops**
Bison   599.64; 636.2
    UF   American bison
          Buffalo, American
    BT   **Mammals**
Black actors   791.4; 792; 920
    UF   Actors, Black
          Black actors and actresses
    BT   **Actors**
    NT   **African American actors**
Black actors and actresses
    USE **Black actors**
Black Africa
    USE **Sub-Saharan Africa**
Black Americans
    USE **African Americans**
Black art (May subdiv. geog.)   **704.03**
    Use for materials on works of art by several Black artists. Materials on Blacks depicted in works of art are entered under **Blacks in art**.
    UF   Art, Black
          Blacks—Art
    BT   **Art**
    NT   **African American art**
    RT   **Black artists**
Black art (Magic)
    USE **Magic**
          Witchcraft
Black artists (May subdiv. geog.)   **709.2; 920**
    Use for materials on several Black artists.
    UF   Artists, Black
    BT   **Artists**
    NT   **African American artists**
    RT   **Black art**
Black athletes (May subdiv. geog.)   **796.092; 920**
    UF   Athletes, Black
    BT   **Athletes**
    NT   **African American athletes**
Black authors   809; 920
    Use for collections and for materials on several Black authors not limited to a single national literature or literary form.
    UF   Authors, Black
    SA   names of national literatures other than American literature and forms of literature with

Black authors—*Continued*
the subdivision *Black authors*,
e.g. **French literature—Black
authors**; **French poetry—
Black authors**; etc. [to be
added as needed]
  BT **Authors**
  NT **African American authors**
Black business people
  USE **Black businesspeople**
Black businesspeople (May subdiv. geog.)
    338.092; 658.0092; 920
  UF Black business people
  BT **Businesspeople**
  NT **African American
businesspeople**
Black children (May subdiv. geog.)
    305.23
  UF Blacks—Children
Children, Black
  BT **Children**
  NT **African American children**
Black comedy (Literature)
  USE **Black humor (Literature)**
Black death
  USE **Plague**
Black diaspora
  USE **African diaspora**
Black folk songs
  USE **Black music**
Black folklore
  USE **Blacks—Folklore**
Black Hawk War, 1832   **973.5**
  BT **Native Americans—Wars
United States—History—1815-
1861**
Black History Month   **394.261**
  UF African American History Month
  BT **Special months**
Black holes (Astronomy)   **523.8**
  UF Frozen stars
  BT **Astronomy
Astrophysics
Stars**
Black humor (Literature)   **808.7; 808.87**
Use for individual works, collections, or materials about literary works characterized by a desperate, sardonic humor intended to induce laughter as the appropriate response to the apparent meaninglessness and absurdity of existence.
  UF Black comedy (Literature)
Dark humor (Literature)

  BT **Fiction
Literature
Wit and humor**
Black lead
  USE **Graphite**
Black librarians   **020.92; 920**
  BT **Librarians**
  NT **African American librarians**
Black literature (American)
  USE **American literature—African
American authors**
Black literature (French)
  USE **French literature—Black au-
thors**
Black magic (Witchcraft)
  USE **Magic
Witchcraft**
Black market (May subdiv. geog.)   **381**
Use for materials on illegal trade aimed at avoiding government regulations, such as fixed prices or rationing. Materials on goods and services that are produced and sold legally but not reported or taxed are entered under **Underground economy**.
  UF Grey market
  BT **Commerce**
  RT **Underground economy**
Black market children
  USE **Adoption—Corrupt practices**
Black music (May subdiv. geog.)
    780.089
Use for general materials and for materials on the music of Blacks not in the United States. Materials on the music of African Americans are entered under **African American music**.
  UF Black folk songs
Black songs
Blacks—Music
Blacks—Songs and music
  BT **Music**
  NT **African American music**
  RT **Black musicians**
Black musicians (May subdiv. geog.)
    780.92; 920
  UF Musicians, Black
  BT **Musicians**
  NT **African American musicians**
  RT **Black music**
Black Muslims   **297.8**
  UF Nation of Islam
  BT **African Americans—Religion
Black nationalism
Muslims—United States**

Black nationalism 320.54
>   UF Black separatism
>   Nationalism, Black
>   Separatism, Black
>   BT **African Americans—Political activity**
>   **African Americans—Race identity**
>   **Blacks—Political activity**
>   **Blacks—Race identity**
>   NT **Black Muslims**
>   RT **Black power**

Black poetry (American)
>   USE **American poetry—African American authors**

Black poetry (French)
>   USE **French poetry—Black authors**

Black power 322.4
>   BT **African Americans—Political activity**
>   **Blacks—Political activity**
>   RT **Black nationalism**

Black separatism
>   USE **Black nationalism**

Black songs
>   USE **Black music**

Black suffrage
>   USE **Blacks—Suffrage**

Black women (May subdiv. geog.) 305.48
>   UF Women, Black
>   BT **Women**
>   NT **African American women**

Blackboard drawing
>   USE **Chalk talks**
>   **Crayon drawing**

Blackheads (Acne)
>   USE **Acne**

Blackmail
>   USE **Extortion**

Blackouts, Electric power
>   USE **Electric power failures**

Blacks (May subdiv. geog. except U.S.) 305.896

Use for materials on the Black race in general or for materials on Blacks as an element in the population, especially in countries where they are a minority. Works on Black people in countries with a population predominantly Black are assigned headings appropriate for the country without the use of the heading **Blacks**, except when the works discuss Blacks as distinct from other groups in the country. Materials on Blacks in the United States are entered under **African Americans**.
>   UF Negroes
>   SA Blacks in various occupations and professions, e.g. **Black artists**; **Black librarians**; etc. [to be added as needed]
>   NT **African Americans**

Blacks—Africa 305.896; 960
>   BT **Africans**

Blacks—Art
>   USE **Black art**

Blacks—Biography 920
>   BT **Biography**
>   NT **African Americans—Biography**

Blacks—Children
>   USE **Black children**

Blacks—Civil rights (May subdiv. geog.) 323.1196; 342
>   BT **Blacks—Political activity**
>   **Civil rights**
>   NT **African Americans—Civil rights**

Blacks—Economic conditions (May subdiv. geog.) 330.9
>   BT **Economic conditions**
>   NT **African Americans—Economic conditions**

Blacks—Education (May subdiv. geog.) 370.89; 371.829
>   BT **Education**
>   NT **African Americans—Education**

Blacks—Employment (May subdiv. geog.) 331.6
>   BT **Employment**
>   NT **African Americans—Employment**

Blacks—Folklore 398
>   UF Black folklore
>   BT **Folklore**
>   NT **African Americans—Folklore**

Blacks—France 305.896; 944
>   UF France—Blacks

Blacks—Housing (May subdiv. geog.) 307.3; 363.5
>   BT **Housing**
>   NT **African Americans—Housing**

Blacks in art 704.9

Use for materials on Blacks depicted in works of art. Materials on African Americans depicted in works of art are entered under **African Americans in art**. Materials on the at-

Blacks in art—*Continued*

tainments of several Blacks in the area of art are entered under **Black artists**. Materials on the attainments of several African Americans in the area of art are entered under **African American artists**. Materials on works of art by several Black artists are entered under **Black art**. Materials on works of art by several African American artists are entered under **African American art**.

BT   Art—Themes

Blacks in literature   809

Use for materials on the theme of Blacks in works of literature. Materials on the attainments of several Blacks in the area of literature are entered under **Black authors**. Materials on works of literature by several Black authors are entered under individual literatures and forms of literature with the subdivision *Black authors*, e.g. **French literature—Black authors**; **French poetry—Black authors**; etc. Materials on the theme of African Americans in works of literature are entered under **African Americans in literature**. Materials on the attainments of several African Americans in the area of literature are entered under **African American authors**. Materials on works of literature by several African American authors are entered under **American literature—African American authors** and the various forms of American literature with the subdivision *African American authors*, e.g. **American poetry—African American authors**.

BT   Literature—Themes

Blacks in motion pictures   791.43

Use for materials on the depiction of Blacks in motion pictures. Materials on several Black actors are entered under **Black actors**. Materials discussing all aspects of Blacks' involvement in motion pictures are entered under **Blacks in the motion picture industry**.

BT   **Motion pictures**

NT   **African Americans in motion pictures**

Blacks in the motion picture industry 791.43092

Use for materials on all aspects of Blacks' involvement in motion pictures. Materials on the depiction of Blacks in motion pictures are entered under **Blacks in motion pictures**.

BT   **Motion picture industry**

NT   **African Americans in the motion picture industry**

Blacks—Intellectual life (May subdiv. geog.)   **305.896**

BT   **Intellectual life**

NT   **African Americans—Intellectual life**

Blacks—Music

USE   **Black music**

Blacks—Political activity (May subdiv. geog.)   **322.4; 324**

BT   **Political participation**

NT   **African Americans—Political activity**

Black nationalism

Black power

Blacks—Civil rights

Blacks—Race identity   305.896

UF   Negritude

BT   **Race awareness**

NT   **African Americans—Race identity**

Black nationalism

Blacks—Religion   270.089; 299.6

BT   **Religion**

NT   **African Americans—Religion**

Blacks—Segregation (May subdiv. geog.)   **305.896**

BT   **Segregation**

NT   **African Americans—Segregation**

Blacks—Social conditions (May subdiv. geog.)   **305.896**

BT   **Social conditions**

NT   **African Americans—Social conditions**

Blacks—Social life and customs (May subdiv. geog.)   **305.896**

BT   **Manners and customs**

NT   **African Americans—Social life and customs**

Blacks—Songs and music

USE   **Black music**

Blacks—Suffrage   324.6

UF   Black suffrage

BT   **Suffrage**

NT   **African Americans—Suffrage**

Blacks—United States

USE   **African Americans**

Blacksmithing   682

BT   **Ironwork**

NT   **Welding**

RT   **Forging**

Blast furnaces   669

BT   **Furnaces**

Smelting

Blast shelters

USE   **Air raid shelters**

Bleaching   667

Bleaching—*Continued*
  BT **Cleaning**
      Industrial chemistry
      Textile industry
  RT **Dyes and dyeing**
Blessed Virgin Mary
  USE **Mary, Blessed Virgin, Saint**
Blimps
  USE **Airships**
Blind 362.4
  BT **Physically handicapped**
  RT **Blindness**
**Blind—Books and reading 011.63;
      027.6; 028**
  UF Books for the blind
  BT **Books and reading**
  NT **Large print books**
  RT **Audiobooks**
      Braille books
Blind—Education (May subdiv. geog.)
      371.91
  UF Education of the blind
  BT **Education**
Blind—Institutional care 362.4
  BT **Institutional care**
Blindness 617.7
  BT **Vision disorders**
  RT **Blind**
      Vision
Blizzards 551.55
  BT **Storms**
  RT **Snow**
Block printing
  USE **Color prints**
      Linoleum block printing
      Textile printing
      Wood engraving
      Woodcuts
Block signal systems
  USE **Railroads—Signaling**
Blockades
  USE names of wars with the subdivi-
      sion *Blockades,* e.g. **World
      War, 1939-1945—Blockades**
      [to be added as needed]
Blogs
  USE **Weblogs**
Blood 573.1; 612.1
  BT **Physiology**
  NT **Blood groups**
      Blood pressure
Blood—Circulation 573.1; 612.1

  UF Circulation of the blood
  RT **Blood pressure**
      Cardiovascular system
Blood—Diseases 616.1
  UF Diseases of the blood
  SA types of blood diseases, e.g.
      Leukemia [to be added as
      needed]
  BT **Diseases**
  NT **Leukemia**
Blood feuds
  USE **Vendetta**
Blood groups 612.1
  UF Rh factor
  BT **Blood**
  RT **Blood—Transfusion**
Blood pressure 612.1
  BT **Blood**
  NT **Hypertension**
  RT **Blood—Circulation**
Blood—Transfusion 615
  RT **Blood groups**
Blowing the whistle
  USE **Whistle blowing**
Blowouts, Oil well
  USE **Oil wells—Blowouts**
Blue collar workers
  USE **Labor**
      Working class
Blue prints
  USE **Blueprints**
Blueprints 604.2; 692
  UF Blue prints
  BT **Mechanical drawing**
Blues music 781.643; 782.421643
  UF Blues songs
  BT **African American music**
      Folk music—United States
      Popular music
  RT **Jazz music**
Blues songs
  USE **Blues music**
Board games 794
  BT **Games**
  NT **Checkers**
      Chess
Board sailing
  USE **Windsurfing**
Boarding houses
  USE **Hotels and motels**

Boarding schools
USE **Private schools**
Boards of education
USE **School boards**
Boards of health
USE **Health boards**
Boards of trade
USE **Chambers of commerce**
Boards of trustees
USE **Trusts and trustees**
Boat building
USE **Boatbuilding**
Boat racing (May subdiv. geog.) **797.1**
UF Regattas
SA types of boat racing and names
of specific races [to be added
as needed]
BT **Boats and boating**
Racing
Boatbuilding 623.8
UF Boat building
Boats—Construction
BT **Naval architecture**
NT **Yachts and yachting**
RT **Boats and boating**
Shipbuilding
Boating
USE **Boats and boating**
Boats and boating 797.1
UF Boating
BT **Water sports**
NT **Boat racing**
Canoes and canoeing
Catamarans
Houseboats
Hydrofoil boats
Iceboats
Marinas
Motorboats
Rowing
Steamboats
Tugboats
Yachts and yachting
RT **Boatbuilding**
Sailing
Ships
Boats—Construction
USE **Boatbuilding**
Body
USE **Human body**

Body and mind
USE **Mind and body**
Body building
USE **Bodybuilding**
Body care
USE **Hygiene**
Body heat
USE **Body temperature**
Body image 128; 155.2
Use for materials on the visual, mental, or
memory image of one's own body or anoth-
er's body, and one's attitude towards that im-
age.
BT **Human body**
Mind and body
Personality
Self-perception
Body language 153.6; 302.2
BT **Nonverbal communication**
Body piercing 391.6
BT **Personal appearance**
Body surfing
USE **Surfing**
Body temperature 571.7; 612
UF Animals—Temperature
Body heat
Temperature, Animal and human
Temperature, Body
BT **Diagnosis**
Physiology
RT **Fever**
Body weight 613
BT **Human body**
Weight
NT **Obesity**
Weight gain
Weight loss
Bodybuilding 646.7
UF Body building
Physique
BT **Exercise**
Physical fitness
RT **Weight lifting**
Boers
USE **Afrikaners**
Bogs (May subdiv. geog.) **551.41**
BT **Wetlands**
Bohemianism (May subdiv. geog.) **306**
BT **Counter culture**
Manners and customs
NT **Beat generation**
Hippies

Bolshevism
USE **Communism**
Bomb attacks
USE **Bombings**
Bomb shelters
USE **Air raid shelters**
Bombers   358.4; 623.74
SA   types of bombers, e.g. **B-52 bomber** [to be added as needed]
BT   **Airplanes**
Military airplanes
NT   **B-52 bomber**
Bombings (May subdiv. geog.)   **364.1**
Use for materials on the use of explosive devices for the purposes of political terrorism or protest. Materials on bombs in general and on bombs launched from aircraft are entered under **Bombs**.
UF   Bomb attacks
Terrorist bombings
SA   names of individual bombings incidents [to be added as needed]
BT   **Offenses against public safety**
Political crimes and offenses
Terrorism
Bombs   355.8; 623.4
Use for materials on bombs in general and and on bombs launched from aircraft. Materials on the use of explosive devices for the purposes of political terrorism or protest are entered under **Bombings**.
UF   Aerial bombs
SA   types of bombs, e.g. **Atomic bomb** [to be added as needed]
BT   **Ammunition**
Explosives
Ordnance
Projectiles
NT   **Atomic bomb**
Guided missiles
Hydrogen bomb
Incendiary bombs
Neutron bomb
Bonds   332.63
BT   **Finance**
Investments
Negotiable instruments
Securities
Stock exchanges
NT   **Junk bonds**

RT   **Public debts**
Stocks
Bonds—Rating   332.63
Bones   573.7; 611; 612.7
Use for comprehensive and systematic materials on the anatomy of bones. Materials limited to the morphology or mechanics of the skeleton, human or animal, are entered under **Skeleton**.
BT   **Musculoskeletal system**
NT   **Fractures**
RT   **Skeleton**
Bones—Diseases   616.7
BT   **Diseases**
NT   **Osteoporosis**
Bonsai   635.9
BT   **Dwarf trees**
Book arts—Exhibitions
USE   **Books—Exhibitions**
Book awards
USE   **Literary prizes**
and   names of awards, e.g.
Caldecott Medal; Newbery Medal; etc. [to be added as needed]
Book buying (Libraries)
USE   **Libraries—Acquisitions**
Book clubs (Discussion groups) (May subdiv. geog.)   **028**
UF   Book discussion groups
BT   **Clubs**
Book collecting   002.075
UF   Bibliomania
Bibliophily
Books—Collectors and collecting
BT   **Book selection**
Collectors and collecting
RT   **Bookplates**
Books
Book discussion groups
USE   **Book clubs (Discussion groups)**
Book fairs
USE   **Books—Exhibitions**
Book illustration
USE   **Illustration of books**
Book industries
USE   **Book industry**
Book industries and trade
USE   **Book industry**
Book industries—Exhibitions
USE   **Books—Exhibitions**
Book industry (May subdiv. geog.)   **686**

Book industry—*Continued*
  UF Book industries
       Book industries and trade
       Book trade
  BT **Industries**
  NT **Bookbinding**
       Booksellers and bookselling
       Printing
  RT **Publishers and publishing**
Book lending
  USE **Library circulation**
Book lists
  USE **Best books**
Book numbers, Publishers' standard
  USE **Publishers' standard book
        numbers**
Book plates
  USE **Bookplates**
Book prices
  USE **Books—Prices**
Book prizes
  USE **Literary prizes**
        and names of prizes, e.g.
        **Caldecott Medal; Newbery
        Medal;** etc. [to be added as
        needed]
Book rarities
  USE **Rare books**
Book reviewing   028.1; 808
  Use for materials on the technique of re-
  viewing books. Collections of miscellaneous
  book reviews are entered under **Book re-
  views**.
  UF Appraisal of books
       Books—Appraisal
       Evaluation of books
       Literature—Evaluation
       Reviewing (Books)
  SA types of books with the subdivi-
       sion *Reviews*, and topics,
       types of literature, ethnic
       groups, classes of persons,
       and names of places with the
       subdivision *Book reviews*; for
       collections of book reviews
       devoted to a particular type
       of book or subject, e.g. **Ref-
       erence books—Reviews; So-
       ciology—Book reviews; Chil-
       dren's literature—Book re-
       views;** etc. [to be added as
       needed]

  BT **Books and reading
       Criticism**
  RT **Book reviews**
Book reviews   028.1; 808.8
  Use for collections of book reviews. Materi-
  als on the technique of reviewing books are
  entered under **Book reviewing**.
  UF Books—Reviews
  SA types of books with the subdivi-
       sion *Reviews*, and topics,
       types of literature, ethnic
       groups, classes of persons,
       and names of places with the
       subdivision *Book reviews*; for
       collections of book reviews
       devoted to a particular type
       of book or subject, e.g. **Ref-
       erence books—Reviews; So-
       ciology—Book reviews; Chil-
       dren's literature—Book re-
       views;** etc. [to be added as
       needed]
  NT **Book talks**
  RT **Book reviewing**
Book sales
  USE **Books—Prices**
Book selection   025.2
  Use for materials on the principles of book
  selection for libraries. Lists of recommended
  books and materials about recommended
  books are entered under **Best books**.
  UF Books—Selection
       Choice of books
  BT **Libraries—Acquisitions
       Libraries—Collection develop-
       ment**
  NT **Book collecting**
  RT **Best books**
Book talks   021.7; 028.1
  UF Booktalking
       Booktalks
  BT **Book reviews
       Libraries—Public relations
       Public speaking**
Book trade
  USE **Book industry
        Booksellers and bookselling
        Publishers and publishing**
Book trade—Exhibitions
  USE **Books—Exhibitions**
Book Week, National
  USE **National Book Week**

Bookbinding (May subdiv. geog.)   **025.7; 095; 686.3**
   UF Binding of books
   BT **Book industry**
        Books
Bookkeepers
   USE **Accountants**
Bookkeeping   **657**
   SA types of industries, professions,
         and organizations with the
         subdivision *Accounting* [to be
         added as needed]
   BT **Business**
        Business education
        Business mathematics
   NT **Auditing**
        Corporations—Accounting
        Cost accounting
        Office equipment and supplies
   RT **Accounting**
Bookmaking (Betting)
   USE **Gambling**
Bookmobiles   **027.4**
   BT **Library extension**
Bookplates   **025.7; 769.5**
   UF Book plates
        Ex libris
   BT **Prints**
   RT **Book collecting**
Books   **002**
   NT **Anthologies**
        Best books
        Bilingual books
        Bookbinding
        Books of hours
        Braille books
        Chapbooks
        Early printed books
        Electronic books
        Illumination of books and
          manuscripts
        Illustration of books
        Incunabula
        Librettos
        Manuscripts
        Paperback books
        Rare books
        Reference books
        Reprints (Publications)
        Textbooks

   RT **Authors**
        Bibliography
        Book collecting
        Literature
        Printing
        Publishers and publishing
Books and reading (May subdiv. geog.)
        028
    Use for general materials on reading for information and culture, advice to readers, and surveys of reading habits.
   UF Appraisal of books
        Books—Appraisal
        Choice of books
        Evaluation of literature
        Literature—Evaluation
        Reading interests
   SA names of individuals and classes
         of persons with the subdivi-
         sion *Books and reading*, e.g.
         Blind—Books and reading
         [to be added as needed]
   BT **Communication**
        Education
        Reading
   NT **Best sellers (Books)**
        Bible—Reading
        Blind—Books and reading
        Book reviewing
        Children—Books and reading
        National Book Week
        Reference books
        Teenagers—Books and reading
   RT **Reading materials**
Books and reading—Best books
   USE **Best books**
Books and reading for children
   USE **Children—Books and reading**
Books and reading for teenagers
   USE **Teenagers—Books and reading**
Books and reading for young adults
   USE **Teenagers—Books and reading**
Books—Appraisal
   USE **Book reviewing**
        Books and reading
        Criticism
        Literature—History and criti-
          cism
Books—Best sellers
   USE **Best sellers (Books)**
Books—Bilingual editions
   USE **Bilingual books**

Books—Catalogs
USE **Booksellers' catalogs**
Publishers' catalogs
Books—Censorship   025.2; 323.44
UF   Banned books
Index librorum prohibitorum
Prohibited books
BT   **Censorship**
Books—Classification
USE **Library classification**
Books—Collectors and collecting
USE **Book collecting**
Books—Exhibitions (May subdiv. geog.)
070.5074; 686.074
UF   Book arts—Exhibitions
Book fairs
Book industries—Exhibitions
Book trade—Exhibitions
Library book fairs
Publishers and publishing—Exhibitions
BT   **Exhibitions**
Books—First editions
USE **First editions**
Books for children
USE **Children's literature**
Books for sight saving
USE **Large print books**
Books for teenagers
USE **Young adult literature**
Books for the blind
USE **Blind—Books and reading**
Braille books
Books in machine-readable form
USE **Electronic books**
Books—Large print
USE **Large print books**
Books of hours (May subdiv. geog.)
242; 745.6
BT   **Books**
RT   **Illumination of books and manuscripts**
Books of lists   030
Use as a form heading for books consisting of miscellaneous lists of facts, names, etc.
UF   Facts, Miscellaneous
List books
Lists
Miscellanea
Miscellaneous facts

SA   topics with the subdivision *Lists*, e.g. **Sports—Lists** [to be added as needed]
Books on cassette
USE **Audiobooks**
Books on tape
USE **Audiobooks**
Books—Preservation
USE **Library resources—Conservation and restoration**
Books—Prices   002.075
UF   Book prices
Book sales
BT   **Booksellers and bookselling**
Prices
Books—Reviews
USE **Book reviews**
Books—Selection
USE **Book selection**
Booksellers and bookselling (May subdiv. geog.)   **070.5; 381; 658.8**
UF   Book trade
BT   **Book industry**
NT   **Books—Prices**
Booksellers' catalogs
RT   **Publishers and publishing**
Booksellers' catalogs   017
Use for retail book catalogs and book auction catalogs and materials about such catalogs. Materials on library catalogs in book form are entered under **Book catalogs**. Publishers' book catalogs and materials about such catalogs are entered under **Publishers' catalogs**.
UF   Books—Catalogs
Catalogs
Catalogs, Booksellers'
BT   **Booksellers and bookselling**
Booktalking
USE **Book talks**
Booktalks
USE **Book talks**
Boolean algebra   511.3
UF   Algebra, Boolean
BT   **Group theory**
Set theory
Symbolic logic
Boots
USE **Shoes**
Border life
USE **Frontier and pioneer life**
Border patrols (May subdiv. geog.)
363.28

Border patrols—*Continued*
    BT   **Police**
Borders (Geography)
    USE **Boundaries**
Boring
    USE **Drilling and boring (Earth and rocks)**
           Drilling and boring (Metal, wood, etc.)
Born again Christianity
    USE **Regeneration (Christianity)**
Borrowing
    USE **Loans**
Boss rule
    USE **Political corruption**
Bossiness   155.2
    BT   **Personality**
Botanic gardens
    USE **Botanical gardens**
Botanical chemistry   572
    UF   Plant chemistry
    BT   **Chemistry**
    NT   **Plants—Analysis**
Botanical classification
    USE **Botany—Classification**
Botanical gardens (May subdiv. geog.)   580.73
    UF   Botanic gardens
    SA   names of individual botanical gardens [to be added as needed]
    BT   **Gardens**
           Parks
Botanical illustration (May subdiv. geog.)   758
    UF   Flower painting and illustration
           Fruit painting and illustration
    BT   **Art**
           Illustration of books
    RT   **Botany**
           Plants in art
Botanical specimens—Collection and preservation
    USE **Plants—Collection and preservation**
Botanists (May subdiv. geog.)   580.92; 920
    BT   **Naturalists**
Botany   580
    Use for materials on the science of plants. Nonscientific materials on plants are entered under **Plants**.

    UF   Flora
           Vegetable kingdom
    BT   **Biology**
           Science
    NT   **Economic botany**
           Medical botany
           Photosynthesis
           Plant physiology
           Plants—Anatomy
    RT   **Botanical illustration**
           Natural history
           Plants
Botany—Anatomy
    USE **Plants—Anatomy**
Botany—Classification   580.1
    UF   Botanical classification
           Botany—Taxonomy
           Classification—Botany
           Classification—Plants
           Plant classification
           Plant taxonomy
           Plants—Classification
           Systematic botany
           Taxonomy (Botany)
    BT   **Classification**
Botany—Ecology
    USE **Plant ecology**
Botany, Economic
    USE **Economic botany**
Botany, Medical
    USE **Medical botany**
Botany—Nomenclature   580.1
    Use for systematically derived lists of names or designations of plants and for materials about such names. Materials on the common or vernacular names of plants are entered under **Popular plant names**.
    UF   Plants—Names
           Plants—Nomenclature
           Scientific names of plants
           Scientific plant names
    RT   **Botany—Terminology**
           Popular plant names
Botany of the Bible
    USE **Bible—Natural history**
Botany—Pathology
    USE **Plant diseases**
Botany—Physiology
    USE **Plant physiology**
Botany—Structure
    USE **Plants—Anatomy**
Botany—Taxonomy
    USE **Botany—Classification**

Botany—Terminology 580.1

Use for lists or discussions of words and expressions in the field of botany. Systematically derived lists of names or designations of plants and materials about such names are entered under **Botany—Nomenclature**. Materials on the common or vernacular names of plants are entered under **Popular plant names**.

    RT   **Botany—Nomenclature**
           Popular plant names

Botany—United States
    USE **Plants—United States**

Boulder Dam (Ariz. and Nev.)
    USE **Hoover Dam (Ariz. and Nev.)**

Boulevards
    USE **Streets**

Boundaries 320.1; 341.4
    UF   Borders (Geography)
          Frontiers
          Political boundaries
          Political geography
    SA   names of wars with the subdivision *Territorial questions*, and countries, cities, etc., with the subdivision *Boundaries* [to be added as needed]
    BT   **Geography**
          International law
          International relations
    NT   **Chicago (Ill.)—Boundaries**
          Ohio—Boundaries
          United States—Boundaries
          World War, 1914-1918—Territorial questions
          World War, 1939-1945—Territorial questions
    RT   **Geopolitics**

Bourgeoisie
    USE **Middle class**

Boutique breweries
    USE **Microbreweries**

Bow and arrow 799.2028
    UF   Arrow
    BT   **Weapons**
    RT   **Archery**

Bow and arrow hunting
    USE **Bowhunting**

Bowed instruments
    USE **Stringed instruments**

Bowhunting (May subdiv. geog.)
    799.2028
    UF   Bow and arrow hunting

    BT   **Hunting**

Bowling 794.6; 796.31
    UF   Tenpins
    BT   **Ball games**

Boxes 688.8; 745.593
    UF   Crates
    BT   **Containers**

Boxes—Collectors and collecting
    745.593
    BT   **Collectors and collecting**

Boxing 796.83
    UF   Fighting
          Prize fighting
          Pugilism
          Sparring
    BT   **Athletics**
          Self-defense

Boy-love manga
    USE **Shonen-ai**

Boy Scouts (May subdiv. geog.) 369.43
    UF   Cub Scouts
    BT   **Boys' clubs**
          Scouts and scouting

Boycott
    USE **Boycotts**

Boycotts (May subdiv. geog.) **331.89; 338.6; 341.5; 327.1**
    UF   Boycott
          Consumer boycotts
    BT   **Commerce**
          Consumers
          Passive resistance
    RT   **Restraint of trade**

Boys 155.43; 305.23081
    BT   **Children**
    RT   **Teenagers**
          Young men

Boys' clubs 369.42
    UF   Boys—Societies
    BT   **Clubs**
          Societies
    NT   **4-H clubs**
          Boy Scouts

Boys—Education (May subdiv. geog.)
    371.823
    BT   **Education**
    RT   **Coeducation**

Boys—Employment
    USE **Youth—Employment**

Boys—Societies
    USE **Boys' clubs**

Boys' towns
USE **Children—Institutional care**
Brahmanism 294.5
BT **Religions**
RT **Hinduism**
Braids (Hairstyling) 646.7
BT **Hair**
Braille 411
BT **Writing**
Braille books 011.63; 411
UF Books for the blind
BT **Books**
RT **Blind—Books and reading**
Brain 573.8; 611; 612.8
BT **Head**
Nervous system
NT **Memory**
Mind and body
Phrenology
Psychology
Sleep
Brain damaged children 618.92
BT **Exceptional children**
Handicapped children
Brain death 616.07
UF Irreversible coma
BT **Death**
Brain—Diseases 616.8
BT **Diseases**
NT **Alzheimer's disease**
Aphasia
Cerebral palsy
Dementia
Stroke
Brain storming
USE **Group problem solving**
Brainwashing 153.8
Use for materials on the forcible indoctrination of an individual or group in order to alter basic political, social, religious, or moral beliefs.
UF Deprogramming
Forced indoctrination
Indoctrination, Forced
Mind control
Thought control
Will
BT **Behavior modification**
Mental suggestion
Psychological warfare
Psychology of learning
Brakes 625.2; 629.2

SA types of vehicles with the subdivision *Brakes*, e.g. **Automobiles—Brakes** [to be added as needed]
NT **Automobiles—Brakes**
Branch stores
USE **Chain stores**
Brand name products 381; 658.8
UF Branded merchandise
BT **Commercial products**
Manufactures
RT **Trademarks**
Branded merchandise
USE **Brand name products**
Brass 669; 673
BT **Alloys**
Metals
NT **Brasses**
Brass instruments 788.9
BT **Wind instruments**
Brasses 739.5
UF Monumental brasses
Sepulchral brasses
BT **Archeology**
Art metalwork
Brass
Inscriptions
Sculpture
Tombs
Bravery
USE **Courage**
Brazil 981
May be subdivided like **United States** except for *History*.
Brazilian literature 869
May use same subdivisions and names of literary forms as for **English literature**.
BT **Latin American literature**
Literature
Bread 641.8; 664
BT **Baking**
Cooking
Food
RT **Bread machines**
Bread machines 641.7
UF Automatic bread machines
BT **Kitchen utensils**
RT **Baking**
Bread
Break dancing 793.3
BT **Dance**

Breakers
USE **Ocean waves**
Breakfast cereals
USE **Prepared cereals**
Breakfasts 642
BT **Cooking**
Menus
NT **Prepared cereals**
Breakthroughs, Scientific
USE **Discoveries in science**
Breast—Cancer
USE **Breast cancer**
Breast cancer 616.99
UF Breast—Cancer
BT **Cancer**
Women—Diseases
Breast feeding 649
UF Nursing (Infant feeding)
BT **Infants—Nutrition**
Breathing
USE **Respiration**
Breeding (May subdiv. geog.) **631.5;
636.08**

Use for materials on the controlled propagation of plants and animals with the purpose of
producing or maintaining desired characteristics.

UF Artificial selection
Selection, Artificial
SA types of animals with the subdi-
vision *Breeding* [to be added
as needed]
BT **Reproduction**
NT **Dogs—Breeding**
Heredity
Horses—Breeding
Livestock breeding
Mendel's law
Plant breeding
RT **Genetics**
Breeding behavior
USE **Sexual behavior in animals**
Breweries (May subdiv. geog.) **663**
BT **Factories**
NT **Microbreweries**
RT **Brewing**
Brewing 641.8; 663
UF Beer making
RT **Breweries**
Liquors
Bricklaying 693
BT **Building**

RT **Bricks**
Masonry
Bricks 666; 691
BT **Building materials**
RT **Bricklaying**
Bridal customs
USE **Marriage customs and rites**
Bridal showers
USE **Showers (Parties)**
Bridge (Game) 795.41
UF Auction bridge
Contract bridge
Duplicate bridge
BT **Card games**
Bridges (May subdiv. geog.) **624.2; 725**

This heading may be subdivided by the
names of rivers, lakes, canals, etc. as well as
by countries, states, cities, etc.

UF Viaducts
SA types of bridges and names of
individual bridges, e.g. **Gol-
den Gate Bridge (San Fran-
cisco, Calif.)** [to be added as
needed]
BT **Civil engineering**
Transportation
NT **Golden Gate Bridge (San
Francisco, Calif.)**
Bridges—Chicago (Ill.) 624.209773
UF Chicago (Ill.)—Bridges
**Bridges—Hudson River (N.Y. and N.J.)
624.20973**
UF Hudson River (N.Y. and N.J.)—
Bridges
Brigands
USE **Thieves**
Bright children
USE **Gifted children**
British Commonwealth countries
USE **Commonwealth countries**
British Commonwealth of Nations
USE **Commonwealth countries**
British Dominions
USE **Commonwealth countries**
British Empire
USE **Great Britain—Colonies**
Broadcast journalism (May subdiv. geog.)
070.4
UF Radio journalism
Television journalism
BT **Broadcasting**
Journalism

Broadcast journalism—*Continued*
      Press
  NT **Radio broadcasting of sports**
      Television broadcasting of news
      Television broadcasting of sports
Broadcasting (May subdiv. geog.) **384.54**
  BT **Telecommunication**
  NT **Broadcast journalism**
      Equal time rule (Broadcasting)
      Fairness doctrine (Broadcasting)
      Minorities in broadcasting
      Radio broadcasting
      Television broadcasting
Brokers (May subdiv. geog.)
  NT **Stockbrokers**
Brokers (Stocks)
  USE **Stockbrokers**
Bronchial asthma
  USE **Asthma**
Bronze Age (May subdiv. geog.) **930.1**
  BT **Civilization**
Bronzes (May subdiv. geog.) **739.5**
  BT **Archeology**
      Art
      Art metalwork
      Decoration and ornament
      Metalwork
      Sculpture
Brothers **306.875**
  BT **Men**
      Siblings
Brothers and sisters
  USE **Siblings**
Brownies (Girl Scouts)
  USE **Girl Scouts**
Brownouts
  USE **Electric power failures**
Brutality
  USE **Cruelty**
Bubbles **530.4**
  BT **Air**
      Gases
Bubonic plague
  USE **Plague**
Buccaneers
  USE **Pirates**
Bucolic poetry
  USE **Pastoral poetry**

Buddhism (May subdiv. geog.) **294.3**
  BT **Religions**
  NT **Zen Buddhism**
Buddhism—Prayers **294.3**
  UF Buddhist prayers
  BT **Prayers**
Buddhist art (May subdiv. geog.) **294.3; 704.9**
  UF Art, Buddhist
  BT **Art**
Buddhist prayers
  USE **Buddhism—Prayers**
Budget (May subdiv. geog.) **352.4**
    Use for materials on government budgets or reports on governmental appropriations and expenditures. Materials on business budgets are entered under **Business budgets**. Materials on household budgets are entered under **Household budgets**. Materials on personal budgets are entered under **Personal finance**.
  UF Government budgets
  SA names of countries and names of individual government departments, agencies, etc., with the subdivision *Appropriations and expenditures*, e.g. **United States—Appropriations and expenditures** [to be added as needed]
  BT **Public finance**
Budget—United States **352.4**
  UF Federal budget
      United States—Budget
  NT **United States—Appropriations and expenditures**
Budgets, Business
  USE **Business budgets**
Budgets, Household
  USE **Household budgets**
Budgets, Personal
  USE **Personal finance**
Buffalo, American
  USE **Bison**
Buffing
  USE **Grinding and polishing**
Bugging, Electronic
  USE **Eavesdropping**
Building **690**
    Use for materials on the process of constructing buildings and other structures. Materials on the design and style of structures are entered under **Architecture**. General materials on buildings and materials on buildings in a particular place are entered under **Buildings**.

Building—*Continued*
    UF   Architectural engineering
            Construction
    SA   types of buildings with the sub-
            division *Design and construc-
            tion*, e.g. **Industrial build-
            ings—Design and construc-
            tion** [to be added as needed]
    BT   **Structural engineering**
    NT   **Bricklaying**
            Carpentry
            Concrete construction
            House construction
            **Industrial buildings—Design
              and construction**
            Masonry
            Plumbing
            Steel construction
    RT   **Architecture**
            Building materials
Building and earthquakes
    USE   **Buildings—Earthquake effects**
Building and loan associations
    USE   **Savings and loan associations**
Building contracts
    USE   **Construction contracts**
Building—Contracts and specifications
    USE   **Construction contracts**
Building design
    USE   **Architecture**
Building—Estimates 692
Building failures 690
    BT   **Structural failures**
Building, Iron and steel
    USE   **Steel construction**
Building machinery
    USE   **Construction equipment**
Building materials 691
    UF   Structural materials
    SA   types of building materials, e.g.
            Bricks [to be added as need-
            ed]
    BT   **Materials**
    NT   **Bricks**
            Cement
            Concrete
            Glass
            Glass construction
            Reinforced concrete
            Stone
            Structural steel
            Stucco

            Terra cotta
            Tiles
            Wood
    RT   **Building**
            Strength of materials
Building nests
    USE   **Nest building**
Building repair
    USE   **Buildings—Maintenance and
            repair**
Building—Repair and reconstruction
    USE   **Buildings—Maintenance and
            repair**
Building security
    USE   **Burglary protection**
Building—Tropical conditions 690
Buildings (May subdiv. geog.) **690; 720**
    Use for general materials on buildings and,
with geographic subdivisions, for materials on
buildings in a particular place. Materials on
the design and style of structures are entered
under **Architecture**. Materials on the process
of constructing buildings and other structures
are entered under **Building**.
    UF   Edifices
            Structures
    SA   types of building features, e.g.
            Doors; **Windows**; etc.; types
            of buildings and construction,
            e.g. **Farm buildings**; types of
            institutions and names of indi-
            vidual institutions and corpo-
            rate bodies with the subdivi-
            sion *Buildings*, e.g. **Colleges
            and universities—Buildings**;
            and names of specific build-
            ings [to be added as needed]
    NT   **Apartment houses**
            Auditoriums
            Castles
            Children's playhouses
            Chimneys
            Church buildings
            **Colleges and universities—
              Buildings**
            Commercial buildings
            Doors
            Farm buildings
            Fireplaces
            Floors
            Foundations
            Garden structures
            Historic buildings

Buildings—*Continued*

> **Houses**
> **Industrial buildings**
> **Office buildings**
> **Palaces**
> **Prefabricated buildings**
> **Public buildings**
> **Roofs**
> **Rooms**
> **School buildings**
> **Skyscrapers**
> **Synagogues**
> **Temples**
> **Theaters**
> **Tree houses**
> **Walls**
> **Windows**

RT **Architecture**

Buildings—Earthquake effects   693.8

Use for materials on the design and construction of buildings to withstand earthquakes.

UF Building and earthquakes
Earthquakes and building
BT **Earthquakes**
NT **Skyscrapers—Earthquake effects**

Buildings, Industrial
USE **Industrial buildings**

**Buildings—Maintenance and repair
690**

UF Building repair
Building—Repair and reconstruction
Buildings—Remodeling
SA types of buildings with the subdivision *Maintenance and repair*, e.g. **Houses—Maintenance and repair**; and types of buildings and parts of buildings with the subdivision *Remodeling*, e.g. **Houses—Remodeling; Kitchens—Remodeling**; etc. [to be added as needed]
RT **Architecture—Conservation and restoration**

Buildings, Office
USE **Office buildings**

Buildings, Prefabricated
USE **Prefabricated buildings**

Buildings—Remodeling
USE **Buildings—Maintenance and repair**

Buildings, Restoration of
USE **Architecture—Conservation and restoration**

Buildings, School
USE **School buildings**

Buildings—Security
USE **Burglary protection**

Built-in furniture   645; 684.1; 749
BT **Furniture**

Bulbs   584; 635.9
BT **Flower gardening**
Plants

Bulge, Battle of the
USE **Ardennes (France), Battle of the, 1944-1945**

Bulimia   616.85
UF Binge eating behavior
Binge-purge behavior
Gorge-purge syndrome
BT **Eating disorders**

Bulletin boards   371.33
BT **Teaching—Aids and devices**
NT **Computer bulletin boards**

Bullfights   791.8
UF Fighting
BT **Sports**

Bullies   155.4; 302.3
UF Bullying
Bullyism
BT **Aggressiveness (Psychology)**
NT **Cyberbullying**

Bullion
USE **Precious metals**

Bullying
USE **Bullies**

Bullyism
USE **Bullies**

Bunnies
USE **Rabbits**

Bunny rabbits
USE **Rabbits**

**Bunyan, Paul (Legendary character)
398.22**
UF Paul Bunyan
BT **Folklore—United States**

Bureaucracy (May subdiv. geog.)   **302.3**
BT **Political science**
Public administration

Bureaucracy—*Continued*
RT **Civil service**
Organizational sociology
Burglar alarms 621.389
BT **Burglary protection**
Electric apparatus and appliances
Burglars
USE **Thieves**
Burglary protection 621.389; 643
UF Building security
Buildings—Security
Protection against burglary
Residential security
SA types of protective devices, e.g.
Burglar alarms; and types of
buildings with the subdivision
Security measures, e.g. **Nuclear power plants—Security measures** [to be added as needed]
BT **Crime prevention**
NT **Burglar alarms**
Locks and keys
Burial (May subdiv. geog.) 363.7; 393
UF Burial customs
Burying grounds
Graves
Interment
SA names of individual persons and
groups of notable persons
with the subdivision *Death and burial*, e.g. **Presidents—United States—Death and burial** [to be added as needed]
BT **Archeology**
Public health
NT **Catacombs**
Cemeteries
Cryonics
Mounds and mound builders
Mummies
Premature burial
Tombs
RT **Cremation**
Death
Funeral rites and ceremonies
Burial customs
USE **Burial**
Burial, Premature
USE **Premature burial**

Burial statistics
USE **Mortality**
Registers of births, etc.
Vital statistics
Buried cities
USE **Extinct cities**
Buried treasure 622; 910.4
UF Hidden treasure
Sunken treasure
Treasure trove
BT **Archeology**
Underwater exploration
Burlesque (Literature) 808.7
Use for materials on burlesque as a literary
composition. Materials on burlesque as a theatrical entertainment are entered under **Burlesque (Theater)**.
UF Comic literature
BT **Comedy**
Parody
Satire
Burlesque (Theater) 792.7
Use for materials on burlesque as a theatrical entertainment. Materials on burlesque as a
literary composition are entered under **Burlesque (Literature)**.
UF Travesty
BT **Theater**
Burma
USE **Myanmar**
Burn out (Psychology) 158.7
UF Burnout syndrome
BT **Job satisfaction**
Job stress
Mental health
Motivation (Psychology)
Occupational health and safety
Stress (Psychology)
Burnout syndrome
USE **Burn out (Psychology)**
Burnt offering
USE **Sacrifice**
Bursaries
USE **Scholarships**
Burying grounds
USE **Burial**
Cemeteries
Buses 388.4; 629.222
UF Motor buses
BT **Automobiles**
Highway transportation
Local transit

Bush survival
 USE **Wilderness survival**
Business 650
 UF Trade
 BT **Commerce**
   Economics
 NT **Accounting**
   Advertising
   Banks and banking
   Bookkeeping
   Business budgets
   Business enterprises
   Business failures
   Businesspeople
   Competition
   Customer relations
   Department stores
   Economic conditions
   Entrepreneurship
   Home-based business
   Installment plan
   Mail-order business
   Management
   Marketing
   Markets
   Office management
   Profit
   Real estate business
   Selling
   Small business
   Social responsibility of business
   Trust companies
Business administration
 USE **Management**
Business and government
 USE **Economic policy**
Business and politics (May subdiv. geog.)
   322
 UF Business—Political activity
   Politics and business
 BT **Politics**
Business arithmetic
 USE **Business mathematics**
Business budgets 658.15
 UF Budgets, Business
 BT **Business**
Business colleges
 USE **Business schools**
Business consultants 658.4
 UF Management consultants
 BT **Consultants**

Business correspondence
 USE **Business letters**
Business cycles (May subdiv. geog.)
   338.5
 UF Economic cycles
   Stabilization in industry
 SA types of business cycles, e.g.
   Depressions [to be added as
   needed]
 BT **Cycles**
   Economic conditions
 NT **Depressions**
   Economic forecasting
   Recessions
 RT **Financial crises**
Business—Databases 650
 BT **Databases**
Business depression, 1929-1939
 USE **Great Depression, 1929-1939**
Business depressions
 USE **Depressions**
Business education (May subdiv. geog.)
   650.07
 UF Business—Study and teaching
   Clerical work—Training
   Commercial education
   Office work—Training
 BT **Education**
 NT **Accounting**
   Bookkeeping
   Keyboarding (Electronics)
   Shorthand
   Typewriting
Business English
 USE **English language—Business
   English**
Business enterprises (May subdiv. geog.)
   338.7
 Use for materials on business concerns as
 legal entities, regardless of the form of organi-
 zation.
 UF Business organizations
   Businesses
   Companies
   Enterprises
   Firms
 SA types of businesses [to be added
   as needed]
 BT **Business**
 NT **Beauty shops**
   **Christian-owned business en-
   terprises**

Business enterprises—*Continued*
      Commercial art galleries
      Corporations
      **Government business enter-
        prises**
      Joint ventures
      Minority business enterprises
      **Money-making projects for
        children**
      Multinational corporations
      New business enterprises
      Partnership
Business enterprises—**Computer net-
    works   004.6; 658**
   BT   **Computer networks**
   NT   **Intranets**
Business entertaining   395.3; 658
   BT   **Entertaining**
       Public relations
Business ethics (May subdiv. geog.)   **174**
   BT   **Ethics**
       Professional ethics
   NT   **Competition**
       Deceptive advertising
       Social responsibility of business
       Success
Business etiquette   395.5
   UF   Office etiquette
   BT   **Etiquette**
Business failures (May subdiv. geog.)
    338; 658
   UF   Business mortality
       Failure in business
   BT   **Business**
   NT   **Bank failures**
       Bankruptcy
Business forecasting (May subdiv. geog.)
    338.5
   BT   **Economic forecasting**
       Forecasting
Business—**Government policy**
   USE **Economic policy**
Business—**Information resources   650**
   BT   **Information resources**
Business—**Information services** (May
    subdiv. geog.)   **658.4**
   BT   **Information services**
Business—**International aspects**
   USE **Multinational corporations**
Business—**Internet resources   650**
   BT   **Internet resources**

Business—**Internet resources**—**Directories
    650.025**
Business Japanese
   USE **Japanese language**—**Business
       Japanese**
Business language
   USE names of languages with unique
       language subdivisions, e.g.
       English language—**Business
       English; Japanese lan-
       guage**—**Business Japanese;**
       etc. [to be added as needed]
Business law
   USE **Commercial law**
Business—**Law and legislation**
   USE **Commercial law**
Business letters   651.7
   UF   Business correspondence
       Commercial correspondence
       Correspondence
   BT   **Letter writing**
Business libraries   026
   Use for materials on libraries with a subject
focus on business. Materials on libraries locat-
ed within companies, firms, or private busi-
nesses, covering any subject area, are entered
under **Corporate libraries**.
   UF   Libraries, Business
   BT   **Special libraries**
Business machines
   USE **Office equipment and supplies**
Business management
   USE **Management**
Business math
   USE **Business mathematics**
Business mathematics   650.01
   UF   Arithmetic, Commercial
       Business arithmetic
       Business math
       Commercial arithmetic
       Commercial mathematics
       Finance—Mathematics
   BT   **Mathematics**
   NT   **Accounting**
       Bookkeeping
       Interest (Economics)
Business mortality
   USE **Bankruptcy**
       Business failures
Business organizations
   USE **Business enterprises**
Business patronage of the arts
   USE **Art patronage**

Business people
  USE **Businesspeople**
Business—Political activity
  USE **Business and politics**
Business recessions
  USE **Recessions**
Business schools 650.071
  UF Business colleges
  BT **Schools**
Business secrets
  USE **Trade secrets**
Business—Social responsibility
  USE **Social responsibility of business**
Business—Study and teaching
  USE **Business education**
Businesses
  USE **Business enterprises**
Businessmen (May subdiv. geog.)
      338.092; 658.0092; 920
  UF Men in business
  BT **Businesspeople**
Businesspeople (May subdiv. geog.)
      338.092; 658.0092; 920
  UF Business people
  BT **Business**
  NT **African American
        businesspeople**
      Black businesspeople
      Businessmen
      Businesswomen
      Capitalists and financiers
      Entrepreneurs
      Merchants
      Self-employed
Businesswomen (May subdiv. geog.)
      338.092; 658.0092; 920
  UF Women in business
  BT **Businesspeople**
      Women
Busing (School integration) 379.2
  UF Antibusing
      School busing
      Student busing
  BT **School children—Transporta-
        tion**
      School integration
Butter 637; 641.3
  BT **Dairy products**
Butterflies 595.78
  UF Cocoons
      Lepidoptera

  BT **Insects**
  NT **Caterpillars**
  RT **Moths**
Buttons 646; 687
  BT **Clothing and dress**
Buy American policy
  USE **Buy national policy—United
        States**
Buy national policy (May subdiv. geog.)
      352.5
      Use for materials on the requirement that a
      national government procure goods produced
      domestically.
  UF Government policy
  BT **Commercial policy**
      Government purchasing
Buy national policy—United States
      352.5
  UF Buy American policy
Buyers' guides
  USE **Consumer education**
      Shopping
Buying
  USE **Purchasing**
Buyouts, Corporate
  USE **Corporate mergers and acqui-
        sitions**
Buyouts, Leveraged
  USE **Leveraged buyouts**
By-products
  USE **Waste products**
Byrd Antarctic Expedition 919.8
  BT **Antarctica—Exploration**
Byzantine architecture (May subdiv.
      geog.) 723
  UF Architecture, Byzantine
  BT **Ancient architecture**
      Architecture
      Medieval architecture
Byzantine art 709.02
  UF Art, Byzantine
  BT **Ancient art**
      Art
      Medieval art
Byzantine Empire 949.5
  UF Eastern Empire
Cabala 135; 296.1
  UF Cabbala
      Kabbala
  BT **Hebrew literature**
      Jewish literature
      Judaism

Cabala—*Continued*
>
> Mysticism
>
> Occultism
>
> RT   Symbolism of numbers

Cabarets
> USE   Night clubs, cabarets, etc.

Cabbala
> USE   Cabala

Cabinet officers (May subdiv. geog.)
> 352.24; 920
>
> UF   Ministers of state
>
> NT   Prime ministers

Cabinet work
> USE   Cabinetwork

Cabinetwork   684.1
> Use for materials on the making and finish-
> ing of fine woodwork, such as furniture or in-
> terior details. Materials on the construction of
> a wooden building or the wooden portion of
> any building are entered under **Carpentry**.
>
> UF   Cabinet work
>
> BT   Carpentry
>
> NT   Veneers and veneering
>
> RT   Furniture
>
> Woodwork

Cabins
> USE   Log cabins and houses

Cable railroads (May subdiv. geog.)
> 385; 625.5
>
> UF   Funicular railroads
>
> Railroads, Cable
>
> BT   Railroads
>
> RT   Street railroads

Cable television (May subdiv. geog.)
> 384.55
>
> BT   Television broadcasting

Cables   384.6; 621.319; 624.1
> BT   Power transmission
>
> Rope

Cables, Submarine
> USE   Submarine cables

Cabs
> USE   Taxicabs

Cactus   583; 635.9
> BT   Desert plants

CAD
> USE   Computer-aided design

CAD/CAM software
> USE   Computer-aided design soft-
> ware

CAD software
> USE   Computer-aided design soft-
> ware

Cafes
> USE   Coffeehouses
>
> Restaurants

Cage birds   636.6
> SA   types of cage birds [to be added
> as needed]
>
> BT   Birds
>
> NT   Canaries

CAI
> USE   Computer-assisted instruction

Cajuns (May subdiv. geog.)   976.3
> UF   Acadians—Louisiana
>
> BT   Ethnic groups

Cake   641.8; 664
> BT   Baking
>
> Confectionery
>
> Cooking
>
> Desserts
>
> NT   Cheesecake (Cooking)
>
> RT   Pastry

Cake decorating   641.8
> BT   Confectionery

Calculating machines
> USE   Calculators

Calculators   510.28; 651.8; 681
> Use for materials on present-day calculators
> or on calculators and mechanical computers
> made before 1945. Materials on modern elec-
> tronic computers developed after 1945 are en-
> tered under **Computers**.
>
> UF   Accounting machines
>
> Adding machines
>
> Calculating machines
>
> Pocket calculators
>
> BT   Office equipment and supplies
>
> NT   Abacus
>
> Slide rule
>
> RT   Computers

Calculus   515
> UF   Analysis (Mathematics)
>
> BT   Mathematical analysis
>
> Mathematics
>
> NT   Differential equations
>
> RT   Functions

Caldecott Awards
> USE   Caldecott Medal

Caldecott Medal   028.5
> UF   Caldecott Awards
>
> Caldecott Medal books
>
> BT   Children's literature
>
> Illustration of books
>
> Literary prizes

Caldecott Medal books
USE **Caldecott Medal**
Calendars 529
UF Annuals
SA subjects, corporate bodies, and
names of countries, cities,
etc., with the subdivision *Cal-
endars*, for works that list re-
curring, coming, or past
events in those places or re-
lated to those topics or orga-
nizations [to be added as
needed]
BT **Time**
NT **Birthday books**
Church year
Days
Devotional calendars
Months
Week
RT **Almanacs**
California—Gold discoveries 979.4
UF California gold rush
California gold rush
USE **California—Gold discoveries**
Calisthenics
USE **Gymnastics**
Physical education
Calligraphy 745.6
BT **Decorative arts**
Handwriting
Writing
Caloric content of foods
USE **Food—Caloric content**
Calories (Food)
USE **Food—Caloric content**
Calvinism (May subdiv. geog.) **284**
BT **Reformation**
RT **Congregationalism**
Puritans
Cambodia 959.6
May be subdivided like **United States** ex-
cept for *History.*
UF Kampuchea
Camcorders 621.388; 778.59
UF Home video cameras
Video cameras, Home
BT **Cameras**
Home video systems
Video recording
RT **Amateur films**
Camels 599.63; 636.2

UF Dromedaries
BT **Desert animals**
Mammals
Cameras 681; 771.3
SA types of cameras and names of
individual makes of cameras
[to be added as needed]
BT **Photography**
**Photography—Equipment and
supplies**
NT **Camcorders**
Digital cameras
Kodak camera
Motion picture cameras
Camouflage (Biology) 591.47
UF Animal camouflage
Animals—Camouflage
BT **Animal defenses**
**Camouflage (Military science) 355.4;
623**
BT **Military art and science**
Naval art and science
Camp cooking
USE **Outdoor cooking**
Camp Fire Girls 369.47
BT **Girls' clubs**
Camp sites
USE **Campgrounds**
Campaign funds (May subdiv. geog.)
324.7
UF Elections—Finance
Political parties—Finance
BT **Elections**
Politics
Campaign funds—United States 324.7
UF Elections—United States—Fi-
nance
United States—Campaign funds
Campaign literature (May subdiv. geog.)
324.2
UF Political campaign literature
BT **Literature**
Politics
Campaigns
USE names of wars with the subdivi-
sion *Campaigns,* e.g. **World
War, 1939-1945—Cam-
paigns;** which may be further
subdivided geographically [to
be added as needed]

Campaigns, Political
  USE **Politics**
Campaigns, Presidential—United States
  USE **Presidents—United States—
     Election**
Campers and trailers
  USE **Travel trailers and campers**
Campgrounds (May subdiv. geog.)
  796.54
  UF Camp sites
  NT **Trailer parks**
  RT **Camping**
Camping (May subdiv. geog.) **796.54**
  Use for materials on the technique of camp-
  ing. Materials on camps with a definite pro-
  gram of activities are entered under **Camps**.
  BT **Outdoor recreation**
  NT **Backpacking**
      Bicycle touring
      Outdoor cooking
      Tents
      Travel trailers and campers
      Wilderness survival
  RT **Campgrounds**
      Outdoor life
Camps (May subdiv. geog.) **796.54**
  Use for materials on camps with a definite
  program of activities. Materials on the tech-
  nique of camping are entered under **Camping**.
  UF Summer camps
  BT **Recreation**
Camps (Military)
  USE **Military camps**
Campus disorders
  USE **College students—Political ac-
     tivity**
Canada **971**
  May be subdivided like **United States** ex-
  cept for *History*.
  SA names of individual provinces,
     territories, or regions [to be
     added as needed]
Canada—English-French relations
  305.811; 306.44
  UF Canada—French-English relations
Canada—French-English relations
  USE **Canada—English-French rela-
     tions**
Canada—History—0-1763 (New France)
  971.01
  UF New France—History
Canada—History—1755-1763 **971.01**
Canada—History—1763-1791 **971.02**

Canada—History—1763-1867 **971.02**
Canada—History—1775-1783 **971.02**
Canada—History—1791-1841 **971.03**
Canada—History—19th century **971.03**
Canada—History—1841-1867 **971.04**
Canada—History—1867- **971.05**
Canada—History—1867-1914 **971.05**
Canada—History—20th century **971.06**
Canada—History—1914-1945 **971.06**
Canada—History—1945- **971.06**
Canada—History—21st century **971.07**
Canadian Indians
  USE **Native Americans—Canada**
Canadian Invasion, 1775-1776 **973.3**
  BT **United States—History—1775-
     1783, Revolution**
Canadian literature (May subdiv. geog.)
  810; C810
  Use for general materials not limited to lit-
  erature in a particular language or form. May
  use same subdivision and names of literary
  forms as for **English literature**; e.g. **Canadi-
  an poetry**; etc.
  BT **Literature**
  NT **Canadian literature (English)**
      Canadian literature (French)
      Canadian poetry
Canadian literature (English) (May
  subdiv. geog.) **810; C810**
  May use same subdivisions and names of
  literary forms as for **English literature**; e.g.
  Canadian poetry (English); etc.
  UF English Canadian literature
  BT **Canadian literature**
  NT **Canadian poetry (English)**
Canadian literature (French) (May
  subdiv. geog.) **C840; 840**
  May use same subdivisions and names of
  literary forms as for **English literature**; e.g.
  Canadian poetry (French); etc.
  UF French Canadian literature
     French literature—Canada
  BT **Canadian literature**
  NT **Canadian poetry (French)**
Canadian poetry (May subdiv. geog.)
  811; C811
  Use for general materials about Canadian
  poetry not limited to a particular language, not
  for individual works.
  BT **Canadian literature**
  NT **Canadian poetry (English)**
      Canadian poetry (French)

Canadian poetry (English) (May subdiv. geog.) **811; C811**

Use for general materials about Canadian poetry in English, not for individual works.

UF English Canadian poetry

BT **Canadian literature (English)**
Canadian poetry

Canadian poetry (French) (May subdiv. geog.) **841; C841**

Use for general materials about Canadian poetry in French, not for individual works.

UF French Canadian poetry

BT **Canadian literature (French)**
Canadian poetry

Canadians **305.811; 971**

NT **French Canadians**

Canals (May subdiv. geog.) **386; 627**

SA names of individual canals [to be added as needed]

BT **Civil engineering**
Hydraulic structures
Transportation
Waterways

NT **Panama Canal**

RT **Inland navigation**

Canapés

USE **Appetizers**

Canaries **598.8; 636.6**

BT **Birds**
Cage birds

Canasta (Game) **795.41**

UF Argentine rummy

BT **Card games**

Cancer (May subdiv. geog.) **616.99**

UF Carcinoma
Malignant tumors

SA types of cancer [to be added as needed]

BT **Diseases**
Tumors

NT **Breast cancer**
Leukemia
Lung cancer

Cancer—Chemotherapy **616.99**

UF Chemotherapy

BT **Drug therapy**

Cancer—Diet therapy **616.99**

BT **Diet therapy**

Cancer—Environmental aspects **616.07**

BT **Environmentally induced diseases**

Cancer—Genetic aspects **616.99**

BT **Medical genetics**

Cancer—Nursing **616.99**

BT **Nursing**

Cancer patients

USE **Cancer—Patients**

Cancer—Patients **616.99**

UF Cancer patients

BT **Patients**

Cancer—Surgery **616.99**

BT **Surgery**

Candies

USE **Candy**

Candles **621.32; 745.593**

BT **Lighting**

Candy **641.8**

UF Candies
Sweets

BT **Confectionery**

Caning of chairs

USE **Chair caning**

Cannabis

USE **Marijuana**

Canned goods

USE **Canning and preserving**

Cannibalism **394**

BT **Ethnology**
Human behavior

Canning and preserving **641.4; 664**

UF Canned goods
Food, Canned
Pickling
Preserving

SA types of foods with the subdivision *Preservation* [to be added as needed]

BT **Cooking**
Food—Preservation
Industrial chemistry

NT **Fruit—Preservation**
Vegetables—Preservation

Cannon

USE **Ordnance**

Canoes and canoeing **797.122**

BT **Boats and boating**
Water sports

NT **Kayaking**

Canon law

USE **Ecclesiastical law**

Canonization (May subdiv. geog.) **235**

BT **Christian saints**
Rites and ceremonies

Canons, fugues, etc.
USE **Fugue**
Cantatas 782.2
Use for musical scores and for materials on the cantata as a musical form.
BT **Choral music**
Vocal music
Canvas embroidery
USE **Needlepoint**
Capital (May subdiv. geog.) **332**
BT **Economics**
Finance
NT **Banks and banking**
Human capital
Industrial trusts
Interest (Economics)
Investments
Profit
Saving and investment
Venture capital
RT **Capitalism**
Wealth
Capital accumulation
USE **Saving and investment**
Capital and labor
USE **Industrial relations**
Capital equipment
USE **Industrial equipment**
Capital formation
USE **Saving and investment**
Capital goods
USE **Industrial equipment**
Capital market 332
BT **Finance**
Financial institutions
Loans
Securities
NT **Euro**
Capital punishment (May subdiv. geog.)
179.7; 364.6
UF Abolition of capital punishment
Death penalty
Hanging
BT **Criminal law**
Punishment
RT **Executions and executioners**
Capital punishment—United States
364.6
Capitalism (May subdiv. geog.) **330.12**
BT **Economics**
Labor
Profit

NT **Entrepreneurship**
RT **Capital**
Capitalists and financiers
Free enterprise
Capitalists and financiers (May subdiv. geog.) **332.092; 920**
UF Financiers
BT **Businesspeople**
RT **Capitalism**
Capitalization (Finance)
USE **Corporations—Finance**
Securities
Valuation
Capitals (Cities) 307.76
Use for materials on the capital cities of several countries or states.
BT **Cities and towns**
NT **Capitols**
Capitols 725
BT **Capitals (Cities)**
Public buildings
Captivities
USE ethnic groups with the subdivision *Captivities,* e.g. **Native Americans—Captivities** [to be added as needed]
Car accidents
USE **Traffic accidents**
Car design
USE **Automobiles—Design and construction**
Car driver education
USE **Automobile driver education**
Car drivers
USE **Automobile drivers**
Car engines
USE **Automobiles—Motors**
Car industry
USE **Automobile industry**
Car insurance
USE **Automobile insurance**
Car maintenance
USE **Automobiles—Maintenance and repair**
Car painting
USE **Automobiles—Painting**
Car parts
USE **Automobile parts**
Car pools 388.4
UF Automobile pools
Carpools
Ride sharing

Car pools—*Continued*
      Van pools
  BT **Traffic engineering**
      Transportation
Car racing
  USE **Automobile racing**
Car repair
  USE **Automobiles—Maintenance and repair**
Car transmissions
  USE **Automobiles—Transmission devices**
Car travel
  USE **Automobile travel**
Car wheels
  USE **Wheels**
Car wrecks
  USE **Traffic accidents**
Carbines
  USE **Rifles**
Carbohydrates 613.2
  BT **Biochemistry**
      Nutrition
  RT **High-carbohydrate diet**
      Low-carbohydrate diet
Carbolic acid 547; 661
  BT **Acids**
      Chemicals
Carbon 540; 660
  BT **Chemical elements**
  NT **Diamonds**
      Graphite
Carbon 14 dating
  USE **Radiocarbon dating**
Carbon dioxide greenhouse effect
  USE **Greenhouse effect**
Carburetors 621.43
  BT **Internal combustion engines**
Carcinoma
  USE **Cancer**
Card catalogs 025.3
  UF Catalogs, Card
  BT **Library catalogs**
Card games 795.4
  SA types of card games [to be added as needed]
  BT **Games**
  NT **Bridge (Game)**
      Canasta (Game)
      Card tricks
      Collectible card games
      Poker

      Solitaire (Game)
      Tarot
  RT **Playing cards**
Card tricks 795.4
  BT **Card games**
      Magic tricks
      Tricks
Cardiac diseases
  USE **Heart diseases**
Cardiac resuscitation 616.1
  UF Heart resuscitation
      Resuscitation, Heart
  BT **Emergency medicine**
  RT **CPR (First aid)**
Cardinals 262
  BT **Catholic Church—Clergy**
Cardiopulmonary resuscitation
  USE **CPR (First aid)**
Cardiovascular system 612.1
  UF Circulatory system
      Vascular system
  BT **Anatomy**
      Physiology
  NT **Heart**
  RT **Blood—Circulation**
Cards, Debit
  USE **Debit cards**
Cards, Greeting
  USE **Greeting cards**
Cards, Playing
  USE **Playing cards**
Cards, Sports
  USE **Sports cards**
Care
  USE parts of the body, classes of persons, and types of animals with the subdivision *Care*, e.g. **Foot—Care; Infants—Care; Dogs—Care;** etc.; classes of persons with the subdivisions *Medical care, Institutional care,* and *Home care,* e.g. **Elderly—Medical care; Elderly—Institutional care; Elderly—Home care;** etc.; ethnic groups and classes of persons with the subdivision *Health and hygiene,* e.g. **Infants—Health and hygiene;** and inanimate things with the subdivision *Mainte-*

Care—*Continued*

> *nance and repair,* e.g. **Automobiles—Maintenance and repair** [to be added as needed]

Care givers
> USE **Caregivers**

Care of children
> USE **Child care**

Care of the dying
> USE **Terminal care**

Career changes   650.14; 658.4
> UF Changing careers
> Mid-career changes
> SA fields of knowledge, professions, industries, and trades with the subdivision *Vocational guidance* [to be added as needed]
> BT **Age and employment**
> **Vocational guidance**

Career counseling
> USE **Vocational guidance**

Career development
> USE **Personnel management**
> **Vocational guidance**

Career education
> USE **Vocational education**

Career guidance
> USE **Vocational guidance**

Careers
> USE **Occupations**
> **Professions**
> **Vocational guidance**

Caregivers   362; 649.8
> Use for materials on family and friends who on a voluntary basis provide personal home care for the elderly, ill, or handicapped.
> UF Care givers
> Family caregivers
> BT **Volunteer work**
> RT **Home care services**

Caribbean Area
> USE **Caribbean Region**

Caribbean Region   972.9
> UF Caribbean Area
> Caribbean Sea Region
> West Indies Region
> BT **America**

Caribbean Sea Region
> USE **Caribbean Region**

Caricatures and cartoons
> USE **Cartoons and caricatures**

Carillons
> USE **Bells**

Carnival (May subdiv. geog.)   **394.25**
> Use for materials on festivals, merrymaking, and revelry before Lent. Materials on traveling amusement enterprises, consisting of sideshows, games of chance, etc., are entered under **Carnivals**.
> UF Mardi Gras
> Pre-Lenten festivities
> BT **Festivals**

Carnivals (May subdiv. geog.)   **394.26; 791**
> Use for materials on traveling amusement enterprises, consisting of sideshows, games of chance, merry-go-rounds, etc. Materials on festivals, merrymaking, and revelry before Lent are entered under **Carnival**.
> BT **Amusements**
> **Festivals**
> RT **Amusement parks**
> **Circus**
> **Fairs**

Carnivora
> USE **Carnivorous animals**

Carnivores
> USE **Carnivorous animals**

Carnivorous animals   599.7
> UF Carnivora
> Carnivores
> Meat-eating animals
> SA types of carnivorous animals [to be added as needed]
> BT **Animals**

Carnivorous plants   583; 635.9
> UF Insect-eating plants
> Insectivorous plants
> BT **Plants**

Carols   782.28
> UF Christmas carols
> Easter carols
> BT **Church music**
> **Folk songs**
> **Hymns**
> **Songs**
> **Vocal music**

Carpentry   694
> Use for materials on the construction of a wooden building or the wooden portion of any building. Materials on the making and finishing of fine woodwork, such as furniture or interior details, are entered under **Cabinetwork**.
> BT **Building**

Carpentry—*Continued*
    NT   **Cabinetwork**
          Turning
    RT   **Woodwork**
Carpentry—Tools
    USE **Carpentry tools**
Carpentry tools 694
    UF   Carpentry—Tools
    SA   types of carpentry tools [to be
          added as needed]
    BT   **Tools**
    NT   **Saws**
Carpet cleaning
    USE **Rugs and carpets—Cleaning**
Carpetbag rule
    USE **Reconstruction (1865-1876)**
Carpets
    USE **Rugs and carpets**
Carpools
    USE **Car pools**
Carriages and carts 388.3; 688.6
    UF   Carts
          Stagecoaches
          Wagons
    BT   **Vehicles**
Cars (Automobiles)
    USE **Automobiles**
Cartels
    USE **Industrial trusts**
Cartography
    USE **Map drawing**
         Maps
Cartooning 741.5
    BT   **Cartoons and caricatures**
         Wit and humor
Cartoons and caricatures 741.5
    Use for collections of pictorial humor and
for materials about cartoons and caricatures.
    UF   Caricatures and cartoons
    SA   subjects, classes of persons,
         names of individuals, and
         names of wars with the sub-
         division *Cartoons and carica-*
         tures [to be added as needed]
    BT   **Pictures**
         Portraits
    NT   **Animated films**
         Cartooning
         Computers—Cartoons and car-
         icatures
         World War, 1939-1945—Car-
         toons and caricatures

    RT   **Comic books, strips, etc.**
Cartoons, Animated
    USE **Animated films**
Cartoons, Television
    USE **Animated television programs**
Carts
    USE **Carriages and carts**
Carts (Midget cars)
    USE **Karts and karting**
Carving (Arts)
    USE **Carving (Decorative arts)**
Carving (Decorative arts) (May subdiv.
    geog.) **731.4; 736**
    UF   Carving (Arts)
    SA   types of carving, e.g. **Wood**
         carving [to be added as need-
         ed]
    BT   **Decorative arts**
    NT   **Wood carving**
    RT   **Sculpture**
Carving (Meat, etc.) 642
    BT   **Dining**
         Entertaining
         Meat
Carving, Wood
    USE **Wood carving**
Case studies
    USE subjects with the subdivision
         Case studies, e.g. **Juvenile**
         delinquency—Case studies
         [to be added as needed]
Case work, Social
    USE **Social case work**
Cassette books
    USE **Audiobooks**
Cassette recorders and recording
    USE **Magnetic recorders and re-**
         cording
Cassette tapes, Audio
    USE **Sound recordings**
Castaways
    USE **Survival after airplane acci-**
         dents, shipwrecks, etc.
Caste (May subdiv. geog.) **305.5**
    BT   **Manners and customs**
    NT   **Social classes**
Casting
    USE **Founding**
         Plaster casts
Castles (May subdiv. geog.) **728.8**
    UF   Chateaux

Castles—*Continued*
    BT   **Buildings**
    RT   **Medieval architecture**
Casts, Plaster
    USE **Plaster casts**
Casualty insurance   368.5
    UF   Insurance, Casualty
    BT   **Insurance**
    NT   **Accident insurance**
CAT scan
    USE **Tomography**
Catacombs   393; 726
    BT   **Burial**
          Cemeteries
          Christian antiquities
          Tombs
    RT   **Church history—30-600, Early church**
Cataloging   025.3
    UF   Cataloguing
          Libraries—Cataloging
          Library cataloging
    SA   cataloging of particular subjects, e.g., **Cataloging of music** [to be added as needed]
    BT   **Bibliographic control**
          Documentation
          Library science
          Library technical processes
    NT   **Automated cataloging**
          Cataloging of music
          International Standard Bibliographic Description
          Library classification
          Machine readable bibliographic data
          Subject headings
    RT   **Bibliography**
          Indexing
          Library catalogs
Cataloging data in machine readable form
    USE **Machine readable bibliographic data**
Cataloging—Data processing
    USE **Automated cataloging**
Cataloging—Music
    USE **Cataloging of music**
Cataloging of music   025.3
    UF   Cataloging—Music
          Music—Cataloging
    BT   **Cataloging**

Catalogs
    USE **Booksellers' catalogs**
           Commercial catalogs
           Library catalogs
           Publishers' catalogs
           and subjects and names of museums with the subdivision *Catalogs,* e.g. **Motion pictures—Catalogs** [to be added as needed]
Catalogs, Booksellers'
    USE **Booksellers' catalogs**
Catalogs, Card
    USE **Card catalogs**
Catalogs, Classified
    USE **Classified catalogs**
Catalogs, Film
    USE **Motion pictures—Catalogs**
Catalogs, Library
    USE **Library catalogs**
Catalogs, Online
    USE **Online catalogs**
Catalogs, Publishers'
    USE **Publishers' catalogs**
Catalogs, Subject
    USE **Subject catalogs**
Cataloguing
    USE **Cataloging**
Catalysis   541
    BT   **Physical chemistry**
    RT   **Catalytic RNA**
Catalytic RNA   572.8
    UF   Ribozymes
    BT   **Enzymes**
          RNA
    RT   **Catalysis**
Catamarans   797.1
    BT   **Boats and boating**
Catastrophes
    USE **Disasters**
Catechisms   202; 238
    SA   names of religions and sects and titles of sacred works with the subdivision *Catechisms* [to be added as needed]
    BT   **Theology—Study and teaching**
    NT   **Bible—Catechisms**
    RT   **Creeds**

Categories of persons
　USE　**Persons**
　　　and classes of persons, e.g. **El-
　　　derly; Handicapped; Explor-
　　　ers; Drug addicts;** etc. [to be
　　　added as needed]
Caterers and catering
　USE　**Catering**
Catering　642
　UF　Caterers and catering
　BT　**Cooking**
　　　Food service
　RT　**Menus**
Caterpillars　595.78
　UF　Cocoons
　BT　**Butterflies**
　　　Moths
Cathedrals (May subdiv. geog.)　**726.6**
　SA　names of individual cathedrals
　　　[to be added as needed]
　BT　**Church buildings**
　RT　**Abbeys**
　　　Church architecture
　　　Gothic architecture
　　　Medieval architecture
Cathedrals—United States　726.60973
Cathode ray tubes　537.5; 621.3815
　UF　CRTs
　BT　**Vacuum tubes**
Catholic charismatic movement　282
　UF　Charismatic movement
　　　Charismatic renewal movement
　BT　**Catholic Church**
　　　Episcopal Church
　RT　**Pentecostalism**
　　　Spiritual gifts
Catholic Church (May subdiv. geog.)
　　　282
　UF　Roman Catholic Church
　SA　religious subjects with the subdi-
　　　vision *Catholic Church*, e.g.
　　　**Asceticism—Catholic
　　　Church; Laity—Catholic
　　　Church;** etc., and other sub-
　　　jects with the subdivisions
　　　*Religious aspects—Catholic
　　　Church*; e.g. **Abortion—Reli-
　　　gious aspects—Catholic
　　　Church** [to be added as
　　　needed]

　BT　**Christian sects**
　　　Christianity
　NT　**Catholic charismatic movement**
　　　Inquisition
　　　Laity—Catholic Church
　　　Papacy
　RT　**Catholics**
Catholic Church—Bishops (May subdiv.
　　　geog.)　**280**
　BT　**Bishops**
Catholic Church—Charities　361.7
　BT　**Charities**
Catholic Church—Clergy　253
　BT　**Clergy**
　　　Priests
　NT　**Cardinals**
　　　Ex-priests
Catholic Church—Converts
　USE　**Converts to Catholicism**
Catholic Church—Creeds　238
　　　Use for materials about the concise, formal,
　　　authorized statements of Catholic doctrine and
　　　for the texts of such statements.
　UF　Catholic creeds
　BT　**Creeds**
Catholic Church—Foreign relations (May
　　　subdiv. geog.)　**282; 327.456**
　　　Use for materials on diplomatic relations
　　　between the Catholic Church and various gov-
　　　ernments or political bodies. When this head-
　　　ing is subdivided geographically, an additional
　　　entry is provided with the Catholic Church
　　　and the place in reversed positions. Materials
　　　on the relations between the Catholic Church
　　　and other churches or religions are entered
　　　under **Catholic Church—Relations**.
　UF　Catholic Church—Relations
　　　　(Diplomatic)
　　　Vatican City—Foreign relations
　BT　**International relations**
Catholic Church—Liturgy　264
　　　Use for materials on the forms of prayers,
　　　rituals, and ceremonies used in the official
　　　public worship of the Catholic Church. Texts
　　　of Catholic liturgies are entered under **Catho-
　　　lic Church—Liturgy—Texts**.
　UF　Catholic liturgies
　BT　**Liturgies**
　　　Rites and ceremonies
Catholic Church—Liturgy—Texts　264
Catholic Church—Missions　266
　BT　**Christian missions**
Catholic Church—Relations　282
　　　Use for materials on relations between the
　　　Catholic Church and other churches or reli-

Catholic Church—Relations—*Continued*
gions. This heading may be further subdivided by church or religion, in which case an additional entry is provided with the two churches or religions in reversed positions. Materials on diplomatic relations between the Catholic Church and various governments or political bodies are entered under **Catholic Church—Foreign relations**.

Catholic Church—Relations (Diplomatic)
    USE   **Catholic Church—Foreign relations**

Catholic Church—United States   282
Catholic colleges and universities (May subdiv. geog.)   **378**
    UF   Catholic universities and colleges
    BT   **Colleges and universities**
Catholic converts
    USE   **Converts to Catholicism**
Catholic creeds
    USE   **Catholic Church—Creeds**
Catholic ex-nuns
    USE   **Ex-nuns**
Catholic ex-priests
    USE   **Ex-priests**
Catholic laity
    USE   **Laity—Catholic Church**
Catholic literature   282; 808; 809
    BT   **Christian literature**
         Literature
Catholic liturgies
    USE   **Catholic Church—Liturgy**
Catholic universities and colleges
    USE   **Catholic colleges and universities**
Catholics (May subdiv. geog.)   **282.092; 305.6**
    NT   **Converts to Catholicism**
    RT   **Catholic Church**
Catholics—United States   282.092; 305.6
Cats   599.75; 636.8
    UF   Felines
         Kittens
    SA   names of specific breeds of cat [to be added as needed]
    BT   **Domestic animals**
         Mammals
    RT   **Wild cats**
Cat's cradle
    USE   **String figures**
Cats—Literary collections   808.8
Cattle   599.64; 636.2
    UF   Cows

    BT   **Domestic animals**
         Mammals
    NT   **Beef cattle**
         Dairy cattle
Cattle brands   636.2
Cattle—Vaccination   636.089
    BT   **Vaccination**
Causality
    USE   **Causation**
Causation   122
    UF   Causality
         Cause and effect
    BT   **Metaphysics**
         Philosophy
Cause and effect
    USE   **Causation**
Causes
    USE   names of wars with the subdivision *Causes,* e.g. **World War, 1939-1945—Causes** [to be added as needed]
Causes of diseases
    USE   **Diseases—Causes**
Cautionary tales and verses
    USE   **Didactic fiction**
         Didactic poetry
         Fables
         Parables
Cave drawings
    USE   **Cave drawings and paintings**
Cave drawings and paintings (May subdiv. geog.)   **743; 759.01**
    UF   Cave drawings
         Cave paintings
    BT   **Rock drawings, paintings, and engravings**
Cave dwellers   569.9; 930.1
    BT   **Prehistoric peoples**
Cave paintings
    USE   **Cave drawings and paintings**
Caves   551.44
    UF   Grottoes
         Speleology
CB radio
    USE   **Citizens band radio**
CD-I technology   006.7
    UF   CDI technology
         Compact disc interactive technology
         Interactive CD technology

CD-I technology—*Continued*
    BT   **Compact discs**
          Optical storage devices
CD players
    USE **Compact disc players**
CD-ROM
    USE **CD-ROMs**
CD-ROMs   **004.5**
    UF   CD-ROM
          CDROM
          CDROMs
          Compact disc read-only memory
    BT   **Compact discs**
          Optical storage devices
CDI technology
    USE **CD-I technology**
CDROM
    USE **CD-ROMs**
CDROMs
    USE **CD-ROMs**
CDs (Compact discs)
    USE **Compact discs**
Celebrations, anniversaries, etc.
    USE **Anniversaries**
Celebrities (May subdiv. geog.)   **920**
    UF   Famous people
          Public figures
    SA   types of celebrities, e.g. **Actors**;
          Television personalities; and
          names of individual celebrities
          [to be added as needed]
    BT   **Persons**
    NT   **Television personalities**
    RT   **Fame**
Celebrity
    USE **Fame**
Celery   **635; 641.3**
    BT   **Vegetables**
Celibacy   **204; 248.4**
    Use for materials on the renunciation of
marriage for religious reasons. Materials on
the virtue that moderates and regulates the
sexual appetite in human beings are entered
under **Chastity**. Materials on abstinence from
sexual activity are entered under **Sexual abstinence**.
    UF   Clerical celibacy
    BT   **Clergy**
          Religious life
    RT   **Chastity**
          Sexual abstinence
Cell phones
    USE **Cellular telephones**

Cellars
    USE **Basements**
Cellists
    USE **Violoncellists**
Cello
    USE **Violoncellos**
Cello players
    USE **Violoncellists**
Cells   **571.6**
    UF   Cytology
    BT   **Biology**
          Physiology
          Reproduction
    NT   **DNA**
    RT   **Embryology**
          Protoplasm
Cells, Electric
    USE **Electric batteries**
Cellular phones
    USE **Cellular telephones**
Cellular telephones   **384.5**
    UF   Cell phones
          Cellular phones
    BT   **Telephone**
Celtic art   **709.01**
    BT   **Art**
Celtic civilization   **936.4**
    BT   **Civilization**
Celtic legends   **398.208991**
    BT   **Legends**
Celtic mythology   **299; 936.4**
    UF   Mythology, Celtic
    BT   **Mythology**
Celts (May subdiv. geog.)   **305.891;
936.4**
    UF   Gaels
    BT   **France—History—0-1328**
          Great Britain—History—0-1066
    NT   **Druids and Druidism**
Cement   **691; 620.1; 666**
    UF   Hydraulic cement
    BT   **Adhesives**
          Building materials
          Ceramics
          Masonry
          Plaster and plastering
    RT   **Concrete**
Cemeteries (May subdiv. geog.)   **393;
718**
    UF   Burying grounds
          Churchyards

Cemeteries—*Continued*
> Graves
> Graveyards
>
> SA   types of cemeteries and names of individual cemeteries [to be added as needed]
>
> BT   **Burial**
> **Public health**
> **Sanitation**
>
> NT   **Catacombs**
> **Epitaphs**
>
> RT   **Tombs**

Censorship (May subdiv. geog.)   **303.3; 363.31**
> Use for general materials on the limitation of freedom of expression in various fields.
>
> SA   subjects and names of wars with the subdivision *Censorship*, e.g. **Books—Censorship** [to be added as needed]
>
> BT   **Intellectual freedom**
>
> NT   **Books—Censorship**
> **Freedom of speech**
> **Libraries—Censorship**
> **Motion pictures—Censorship**
> **Television—Censorship**
> **World War, 1939-1945—Censorship**
>
> RT   **Freedom of information**
> **Freedom of the press**

Census   **304.6; 310; 352.7**
> SA   names of countries, cities, etc., with the subdivision *Census* [to be added as needed]
>
> BT   **Population**
> **Statistics**
> **Vital statistics**
>
> NT   **Chicago (Ill.)—Census**
> **Ohio—Census**
> **United States—Census**

Centennial celebrations, etc.
> USE   names of places, wars, and historical events with the subdivision *Centennial celebrations, etc.*, e.g. **United States—History—1861-1865, Civil War—Centennial celebrations, etc.**; and ethnic groups, classes of persons, individuals, corporate bodies, places, religious denominations, historic or social movements, and historic events with the subdivision *Anniversaries,* for materials about anniversary celebrations, e.g. **Shakespeare, William, 1564-1616—Anniversaries** [to be added as needed]

Centers for older people
> USE   **Senior centers**

Centers for the elderly
> USE   **Senior centers**

Centers for the performing arts   **725; 790.2**
> SA   names of individual centers [to be added as needed]
>
> BT   **Performing arts**
>
> NT   **Auditoriums**
> **Theaters**

Central Africa   **967**
> Use for materials dealing collectively with the region of Africa that includes the Central African Republic, Equatorial Guinea, Gabon, Congo (Republic), and Congo (Democratic Republic).
>
> UF   Africa, Central
>
> BT   **Africa**
>
> NT   **French-speaking Equatorial Africa**

Central America   **972.8**
> BT   **North America**

Central Asia   **958**
> UF   Asia, Central
>
> BT   **Asia**

Central Asia—History   **958**
Central Asia—History—1991-   **958**
Central Europe   **943**
> Use for materials on the area included in the basins of the Danube, Elbe and Rhine rivers.
>
> UF   Europe, Central

Central planning
> USE   **Economic policy**

Central States
> USE   **Middle West**

Centralization of schools
> USE   **Schools—Centralization**

Centralized processing (Libraries)
> USE   **Library technical processes**

Ceramic industries
> USE   **Ceramic industry**

Ceramic industry (May subdiv. geog.)   **338.4**
> UF   Ceramic industries

Ceramic industry—*Continued*

    SA   types of ceramic industries, e.g.
           Glass manufacture [to be
           added as needed]

    BT   **Industries**

    NT   **Clay industry**

           Glass manufacture

    RT   **Ceramics**

Ceramic materials

    USE   **Ceramics**

Ceramic tiles

    USE   **Tiles**

Ceramics   666

    Use for materials on the technology of fired earth products or on ceramic products intended for industrial use. Materials on ceramic products intended for the table or decorative use are entered under **Pottery** or **Porcelain**.

    UF   Ceramic materials

    BT   **Industrial chemistry**

           Materials

    NT   **Abrasives**

           Cement

           Clay

           Glass

           Glazes

           Pottery

           Tiles

    RT   **Ceramic industry**

Cereals

    USE   **Grain**

Cereals, Prepared

    USE   **Prepared cereals**

Cerebral palsy   616.8

    UF   Paralysis, Cerebral

    BT   **Brain—Diseases**

Cerebrovascular disease

    USE   **Stroke**

Ceremonies

    USE   **Etiquette**

           Manners and customs

           Rites and ceremonies

Certainty   121

    BT   **Logic**

           Theory of knowledge

    RT   **Truth**

Certified public accountants

    USE   **Accountants**

Ceylon

    USE   **Sri Lanka**

CGI (Cinematography)

    USE   **Computer animation**

Chain belting

    USE   **Belts and belting**

Chain stores   658.8

    UF   Branch stores

    BT   **Retail trade**

           Stores

Chair caning   684.1

    UF   Caning of chairs

    BT   **Handicraft**

Chairs   645; 684.1; 749

    BT   **Furniture**

    NT   **Wheelchairs**

Chakras   131; 181

    BT   **Yoga**

Chalk talks   741.2

    UF   Blackboard drawing

    BT   **Public speaking**

Chamber music   785

    BT   **Instrumental music**

           Music

    NT   **Quintets**

Chambers of commerce (May subdiv. geog.)   **380.106; 381.06**

    UF   Boards of trade

           Trade, Boards of

    BT   **Commerce**

Change   116

    BT   **Metaphysics**

    NT   **Metamorphosis**

Change of life in men

    USE   **Male climacteric**

Change of life in women

    USE   **Menopause**

Change of sex

    USE   **Transsexualism**

Change, Organizational

    USE   **Organizational change**

Change, Social

    USE   **Social change**

Changing careers

    USE   **Career changes**

Chanties

    USE   **Sea songs**

Chants (Plain, Gregorian, etc.)   782.32

    Use for books of chants and for materials about chants.

    UF   Gregorian chant

           Plain chant

           Plainsong

    BT   **Church music**

Chanukah

    USE   **Hanukkah**

Chaos (Science)   003
  UF Chaotic behavior in systems
  BT **Dynamics**
      Science
      System theory
Chaotic behavior in systems
  USE **Chaos (Science)**
Chap-books
  USE **Chapbooks**
Chapbooks   398
  Use for individual works, collections, or materials about chapbooks.
  UF Chap-books
      Jestbooks
  BT **Books**
      Folklore
      Literature
      Pamphlets
      Periodicals
      Wit and humor
  NT **Tracts**
  RT **Comic books, strips, etc.**
Chaplains   253
  SA corporate bodies and institutions with the subdivision *Chaplains*, e.g. **United States. Army—Chaplains** [to be added as needed]
  BT **Clergy**
  NT **United States. Army—Chaplains**
Character   155.2
  BT **Ethics**
      Personality
  NT **Human behavior**
  RT **Temperament**
Character assassination
  USE **Libel and slander**
Character education
  USE **Moral education**
Characters
  USE **Characters and characteristics in literature**
      and names of authors with the subdivision *Characters;* e.g. **Shakespeare, William, 1564-1616—Characters** [to be added as needed]
Characters and characteristics in literature   809
  UF Characters
      Literary characters

  SA names of authors with the subdivision *Characters*; e.g. **Shakespeare, William, 1564-1616—Characters**; racial and ethnic groups and classes of persons in literature, e.g. **African Americans in literature**; **Children in literature**; etc.; names of persons, families, and corporate bodies with the subdivision *In literature*, e.g. **Napoleon I, Emperor of the French, 1769-1821—In literature** [to be added as needed]
  BT **Literature**
  NT **Fictional characters**
  RT **Literature—Themes**
Charades   793.2
  BT **Amateur theater**
      Amusements
      Literary recreations
      Riddles
Charcoal   662
  BT **Fuel**
Charismata
  USE **Spiritual gifts**
Charismatic movement
  USE **Catholic charismatic movement**
      Pentecostalism
Charismatic renewal movement
  USE **Catholic charismatic movement**
      Pentecostalism
Charitable institutions
  USE **Charities**
      Institutional care
      Orphanages
Charities (May subdiv. geog.)   **361.7**
  Use for materials on privately supported welfare activities. Materials on tax supported welfare activities are entered under **Public welfare**. Materials on the methods employed in welfare work, public or private, are entered under **Social work**. General materials on the various policies, programs, services, and facilities to meet basic human needs, such as health, education, and welfare, are entered under **Human services**.
  UF Charitable institutions
      Endowed charities
      Homes (Institutions)
      Institutions, Charitable and philanthropic
      Poor relief
      Social welfare

Charities—*Continued*
    Welfare agencies
    Welfare work
  SA names of appropriate corporate
      bodies with the subdivision
      Charities, e.g. **Catholic**
      Church—Charities; and
      names of wars with the sub-
      division *Civilian relief*, e.g.
      World War, 1939-1945—Ci-
      vilian relief [to be added as
      needed]
  BT **Human services**
      Social work
  NT **Catholic Church—Charities**
      Child welfare
      Disaster relief
      Food relief
      Institutional care
      Medical charities
      Orphanages
      Social settlements
      World War, 1939-1945—Civil-
      ian relief
  RT **Charity organization**
      Endowments
      Philanthropy
      Public welfare
      Volunteer work
Charities, Medical
  USE **Medical charities**
Charity 177
  BT **Ethics**
      Virtue
  RT **Altruism**
      Love—Religious aspects
Charity organization 361
  BT **Associations**
  RT **Charities**
      Philanthropy
Charity shops
  USE **Thrift shops**
Charlatans
  USE **Impostors and imposture**
Charms 133.4
  UF Spells
      Talismans
  BT **Folklore**
      Superstition
Charter flights
  USE **Airlines—Chartering**

Charter schools (May subdiv. geog.)
    371.01
    Use for materials on legislatively autho-
rized, independent, and innovative public
schools that operate under the authority of a
charter.
  BT **Schools**
Charters
  UF Documents
  BT **History—Sources**
  NT **Magna Carta**
  RT **Archives**
      Manuscripts
Chartography
  USE **Maps**
Charts
  USE **Charts, diagrams, etc.**
Charts, diagrams, etc. 912
  UF Charts
  SA topics with the subdivision
      Charts, diagrams, etc., for
      works consisting of charts or
      diagrams illustrating those
      topics, e.g. **Electric wiring—**
      Charts, diagrams, etc. [to be
      added as needed]
  RT **Maps**
Charts, Nautical
  USE **Nautical charts**
Chasidism
  USE **Hasidism**
Chastity 176
    Use for materials on the virtue that moder-
ates and regulates the sexual appetite in hu-
man beings. Materials on the renunciation of
marriage for religious reasons are entered un-
der **Celibacy**. Materials on abstinence from
sexual activity are entered under **Sexual absti-**
nence.
  BT **Sexual ethics**
      Virtue
  RT **Celibacy**
      Sexual abstinence
Chat groups, Online
  USE **Online chat groups**
Chat rooms, Online
  USE **Online chat groups**
Chateaux
  USE **Castles**
Cheating (Education) (May subdiv. geog.)
    371.26; 371.5
  UF Academic dishonesty
      Student cheating
      Student dishonesty

Cheating (Education)—*Continued*
  BT **Honesty**
Cheating in sports
  USE **Sports—Corrupt practices**
Checkers 794.2
  UF Draughts
  BT **Board games**
Cheerleaders
  USE **Cheerleading**
Cheerleading 371.8; 791.6
  UF Cheerleaders
       Cheers and cheerleading
  BT **Student activities**
Cheers and cheerleading
  USE **Cheerleading**
Cheese 637; 641.3
  BT **Dairy products**
Cheese—Bacteriology
  USE **Cheese—Microbiology**
Cheese—Microbiology 637
  UF Cheese—Bacteriology
  BT **Microbiology**
Cheesecake (Cooking) 641.8653
  BT **Cake**
Chemical analysis
  USE **Analytical chemistry**
Chemical apparatus 542
  UF Apparatus, Chemical
       Chemistry—Apparatus
  BT **Scientific apparatus and in-**
       struments
Chemical elements 546
  UF Elements, Chemical
  SA names of chemical elements [to
       be added as needed]
  BT **Chemistry**
  NT **Carbon**
       Gold
       Helium
       Hydrogen
       Iron
       Mercury
       Oxygen
       Radium
       Silver
       Sulphur
       Tin
       Uranium
       Zinc
  RT **Periodic law**
Chemical engineering (May subdiv. geog.)
    660

  UF Chemistry, Industrial
       Chemistry, Technical
  BT **Engineering**
  NT **Biotechnology**
       Fermentation
  RT **Industrial chemistry**
       Metallurgy
Chemical equations 540
  UF Equations, Chemical
  BT **Chemical reactions**
Chemical geology
  USE **Geochemistry**
Chemical industries
  USE **Chemical industry**
Chemical industry (May subdiv. geog.)
    338.4; 660
    Use for materials about industries that pro-
    duce chemicals or are based on chemical pro-
    cesses. General materials on chemicals, in-
    cluding their manufacture, are entered under
    Chemicals.
  UF Chemical industries
       Chemistry, Industrial
       Chemistry, Technical
  SA types of industries, e.g. **Plastics**
       industry [to be added as
       needed]
  BT **Industries**
  NT **Plastics industry**
  RT **Chemicals**
       Industrial chemistry
Chemical industry—Accidents 363.11
  BT **Industrial accidents**
Chemical industry—Employees 331.11
  UF Chemical workers
  BT **Employees**
Chemical industry—Employees—Diseases
    616.9
  UF Chemical workers' diseases
  BT **Occupational diseases**
Chemical industry—Employees—Pensions
    331.25
Chemical industry—Employees—Salaries,
    wages, etc. (May subdiv. geog.)
    331.2
  BT **Salaries, wages, etc.**
Chemical industry—Employees—Supply
    and demand 331.12
  BT **Supply and demand**
Chemical industry—Law and legislation
    (May subdiv. geog.) **343**
  BT **Law**
       Legislation

**Chemical industry—Waste disposal
363.72; 628.4**
    BT   **Refuse and refuse disposal**
Chemical landfills
    USE **Hazardous waste sites**
Chemical pollution
    USE **Pollution**
Chemical reactions   541
    UF   Reactions, Chemical
    BT   **Chemistry**
    NT   **Chemical equations**
Chemical societies
    USE **Chemistry—Societies**
Chemical technology
    USE **Industrial chemistry**
Chemical warfare   358; 623.4
    UF   Gas warfare
          Poisonous gases—War use
    SA   names of wars with the subdivi-
          sion *Chemical warfare* [to be
          added as needed]
    BT   **Military art and science
          War**
    NT   **Incendiary weapons
          World War, 1914-1918—Chem-
          ical warfare
          World War, 1939-1945—Chem-
          ical warfare**
Chemical workers
    USE **Chemical industry—Employees**
Chemical workers' diseases
    USE **Chemical industry—Employ-
           ees—Diseases**
Chemicals   540; 661
    Use for general materials on chemicals, in-
   cluding their manufacture. Materials about in-
   dustries that produce chemicals or are based
   on chemical processes are entered under
   Chemical industry.
    SA   types of chemicals, e.g. **Acids**;
          Agricultural chemicals; etc.;
          and names of individual
          chemicals [to be added as
          needed]
    NT   **Acids
          Agricultural chemicals
          Alcohol
          Carbolic acid
          Deuterium oxide
          Nitrates
          Organic compounds
          Petrochemicals**

    RT   **Chemical industry
          Industrial chemistry**
Chemicals—Toxicology
    USE **Toxicology**
Chemistry   540
    BT   **Physical sciences
          Science**
    NT   **Acids
          Agricultural chemistry
          Alchemy
          Analytical chemistry
          Bases (Chemistry)
          Biochemistry
          Botanical chemistry
          Chemical elements
          Chemical reactions
          Color
          Combustion
          Explosives
          Fermentation
          Fire
          Geochemistry
          Industrial chemistry
          Inorganic chemistry
          Microchemistry
          Organic chemistry
          Pharmaceutical chemistry
          Pharmacy
          Photographic chemistry
          Physical chemistry
          Space chemistry
          Spectrum analysis**
Chemistry, Analytic
    USE **Analytical chemistry**
Chemistry—Apparatus
    USE **Chemical apparatus**
Chemistry, Diagnostic
    USE **Clinical chemistry**
Chemistry—Dictionaries   540.3
    BT   **Encyclopedias and dictionaries**
Chemistry—Experiments   540; 542
Chemistry, Industrial
    USE **Chemical engineering
          Chemical industry**
Chemistry, Inorganic
    USE **Inorganic chemistry**
**Chemistry—Laboratory manuals
540.78**
Chemistry, Medical
    USE **Clinical chemistry**

Chemistry of food
    USE   **Food—Analysis**
            Food—Composition
Chemistry, Organic
    USE   **Organic chemistry**
Chemistry, Physical and theoretical
    USE   **Physical chemistry**
Chemistry—Problems, exercises, etc.
    540.76
Chemistry—Societies 540.6
    UF   Chemical societies
    BT   **Societies**
Chemistry, Synthetic
    USE   **Organic compounds—Synthesis**
Chemistry, Technical
    USE   **Chemical engineering**
            Chemical industry
            Industrial chemistry
Chemistry, Textile
    USE   **Textile chemistry**
Chemists (May subdiv. geog.) **540.92;**
    920
    BT   **Scientists**
Chemists' shops
    USE   **Drugstores**
Chemotherapy
    USE   **Cancer—Chemotherapy**
            Drug therapy
Chess 794.1
    BT   **Board games**
Chests (May subdiv. geog.) **749**
    BT   **Furniture**
Chicago (Ill.) 917.73; 977.3
    The subdivisions under **Chicago (Ill.)** may
    be used under the name of any city. The sub-
    divisions under **United States** may be further
    consulted as a guide for formulating other
    headings as needed.
Chicago (Ill.)—Antiquities 977.3
    BT   **Antiquities**
Chicago (Ill.)—Bibliography 015.773;
    016.9773
Chicago (Ill.)—Bio-bibliography 012
Chicago (Ill.)—Biography 920.0773
    BT   **Biography**
Chicago (Ill.)—Biography—Portraits
    920.0773
Chicago (Ill.)—Boundaries 977.3
    BT   **Boundaries**
Chicago (Ill.)—Bridges
    USE   **Bridges—Chicago (Ill.)**
Chicago (Ill.)—Census 317.73
    BT   **Census**

Chicago (Ill.)—City planning
    USE   **City planning—Chicago (Ill.)**
Chicago (Ill.)—Civil defense
    USE   **Civil defense—Chicago (Ill.)**
Chicago (Ill.)—Climate 551.69773
    BT   **Climate**
Chicago (Ill.)—Commerce 381
    BT   **Commerce**
Chicago (Ill.)—Description
    USE   **Chicago (Ill.)—Description and**
            travel
Chicago (Ill.)—Description and travel
    917.73
    UF   Chicago (Ill.)—Description
Chicago (Ill.)—Description and travel—
    Guidebooks
    USE   **Chicago (Ill.)—Guidebooks**
Chicago (Ill.)—Description and travel—
    Views
    USE   **Chicago (Ill.)—Pictorial works**
Chicago (Ill.)—Directories 917.73
    Use for lists of names and addresses. Lists
    of names without addresses are entered under
    Chicago (Ill.)—Registers.
    BT   **Directories**
    NT   **Chicago (Ill.)—Telephone di-**
            rectories
    RT   **Chicago (Ill.)—Registers**
Chicago (Ill.)—Directories—Telephone
    USE   **Chicago (Ill.)—Telephone di-**
            rectories
Chicago (Ill.)—Economic conditions
    330.9773
    BT   **Economic conditions**
Chicago (Ill.)—Employees
    USE   **Chicago (Ill.)—Officials and**
            employees
Chicago (Ill.)—Government
    USE   **Chicago (Ill.)—Politics and**
            government
Chicago (Ill.)—Government employees
    USE   **Chicago (Ill.)—Officials and**
            employees
Chicago (Ill.)—Government publications
    USE   **Government publications—Chi-**
            cago (Ill.)
Chicago (Ill.)—Guidebooks 917.73
    UF   Chicago (Ill.)—Description and
            travel—Guidebooks
Chicago (Ill.)—Historic buildings
    USE   **Historic buildings—Chicago**
            (Ill.)

Chicago (Ill.)—History   977.3

Chicago (Ill.)—History—Societies
    977.3006
    BT   History—Societies

Chicago (Ill.)—Industries
    USE   Industries—Chicago (Ill.)

Chicago (Ill.)—Intellectual life   977.3
    BT   Intellectual life

Chicago (Ill.)—Manufactures
    USE   Manufactures—Chicago (Ill.)

Chicago (Ill.)—Maps   912.773
    BT   Maps

Chicago (Ill.)—Moral conditions   977.3
    BT   Moral conditions

Chicago (Ill.)—Occupations
    USE   Occupations—Chicago (Ill.)

Chicago (Ill.)—Officials and employees
    352.1773
    UF   Chicago (Ill.)—Employees
        Chicago (Ill.)—Government em-
        ployees

Chicago (Ill.)—Pictorial works   917.73
    UF   Chicago (Ill.)—Description and
        travel—Views

Chicago (Ill.)—Politics and government
    977.3
    UF   Chicago (Ill.)—Government
    BT   Municipal government
        Politics

Chicago (Ill.)—Popular culture
    USE   Popular culture—Chicago (Ill.)

Chicago (Ill.)—Population   304.609773
    BT   Population

Chicago (Ill.)—Public buildings
    USE   Public buildings—Chicago (Ill.)

Chicago (Ill.)—Public works
    USE   Public works—Chicago (Ill.)

Chicago (Ill.)—Race relations
    305.8009773
    BT   Race relations

Chicago (Ill.)—Registers   917.73
    Use for lists of names without addresses.
    Lists of names that include addresses are en-
    tered under Chicago (Ill.)—Directories.
    RT   Chicago (Ill.)—Directories

Chicago (Ill.)—Social conditions   977.3
    BT   Social conditions

Chicago (Ill.)—Social life and customs
    977.3
    BT   Manners and customs

Chicago (Ill.)—Social policy
    USE   Social policy—Chicago (Ill.)

Chicago (Ill.)—Statistics   317.73
    BT   Statistics

Chicago (Ill.)—Streets
    USE   Streets—Chicago (Ill.)

Chicago (Ill.)—Suburbs and environs
    USE   Chicago Suburban Area (Ill.)

Chicago (Ill.)—Telephone directories
    917.73
    UF   Chicago (Ill.)—Directories—
        Telephone
    BT   Chicago (Ill.)—Directories

Chicago (Ill.)—Urban renewal
    USE   Urban renewal—Chicago (Ill.)

Chicago Metropolitan Area (Ill.)   977.3
    RT   Chicago Suburban Area (Ill.)

Chicago Metropolitan Area (Ill.)—Poli-
    tics and government   977.3
    BT   Metropolitan government

Chicago Suburban Area (Ill.)   977.3
    UF   Chicago (Ill.)—Suburbs and en-
        virons
    RT   Chicago Metropolitan Area
        (Ill.)

Chicanas
    USE   Mexican American women

Chicanery
    USE   Deception

Chicano literature (English)
    USE   American literature—Mexican
        American authors

Chicanos
    USE   Mexican Americans

Chicken pox
    USE   Chickenpox

Chickenpox   616.9
    UF   Chicken pox
    BT   Diseases
        Viruses

Chickens (May subdiv. geog.)   598.6;
    636.5
    BT   Poultry

Chief justices
    USE   Judges

Child abuse (May subdiv. geog.)
    305.23086; 362.76; 364.15
    UF   Abuse of children
        Abused children
        Child neglect
        Children—Abuse
        Cruelty to children

Child abuse—*Continued*
- BT **Child welfare**
  Domestic violence
  Parent-child relationship
- NT **Child sexual abuse**
- RT **Adult child abuse victims**

Child abuse survivors
- USE **Adult child abuse victims**

Child actors (May subdiv. geog.)
792.02; 791.4302
- BT **Actors**

Child-adult relationship   305.23; 362.7;
649
- UF Adults and children
  Children and adults
- BT **Children**
- NT **Child rearing**
  Children and strangers
  Conflict of generations
  Parent-child relationship
  Teacher-student relationship

Child and father
- USE **Father-child relationship**

Child and mother
- USE **Mother-child relationship**

Child and parent
- USE **Parent-child relationship**

Child artists   704; 709.2; 920
> Use for materials on children as artists and on works of art by children.
- UF Children as artists
- BT **Artists**
  Gifted children
- NT **Finger painting**

Child authors   809; 920
> Use for materials on children as authors and discussions of literary works written by children. Individual literary works and collections of literary works written by children are entered under the form heading **Children's writings**.
- UF Children as authors
- BT **Authors**
  Gifted children
- RT **Children's writings**

Child behavior
- USE **Child psychology**
  Children—Conduct of life
  Etiquette for children and
    teenagers

Child birth
- USE **Childbirth**

Child care (May subdiv. geog.)   **649**

- UF Care of children
  Children—Care
- NT **Babysitting**
  Child rearing
  Day care centers
  Infants—Care
  Nannies

Child care centers
- USE **Day care centers**

Child custody   306.89; 346.01; 362.7
- UF Children—Custody
  Custody of children
  Joint custody of children
  Parental custody
  Shared custody
- BT **Divorce mediation**
  Parent-child relationship
- NT **Parental kidnapping**
- RT **Visitation rights (Domestic relations)**

Child death
- USE **Children—Death**

Child development   155.4; 305.231;
612.6
- UF Child study
  Children—Development
- BT **Children**
- NT **Children—Growth**
- RT **Child psychology**
  Child rearing

Child labor (May subdiv. geog.)   331.3
- UF Children—Employment
  Employment of children
  Working children
- BT **Age and employment**
  Child welfare
  Labor
  Social problems

Child labor—United States   331.3

Child molesting
- USE **Child sexual abuse**

Child mortality
- USE **Children—Mortality**

Child neglect
- USE **Child abuse**

Child placing
- USE **Adoption**
  Foster home care

Child pornography (May subdiv. geog.)
363.4
- BT **Pornography**

Child prostitution
USE **Juvenile prostitution**
Child psychiatry   616.89; 618.92
　　Use for materials on the clinical and thera-
　peutic aspects of mental disorders in children.
　Materials on children suffering from mental or
　emotional illnesses are entered under **Emo-
　tionally distrubed children**.
　　UF　Children—Mental health
　　　　Pediatric psychiatry
　　BT　**Psychiatry**
　　NT　**Autism**
　　　　Mentally handicapped children
　　RT　**Child psychology**
　　　　Emotionally disturbed children
Child psychology   155.4
　　UF　Behavior of children
　　　　Child behavior
　　　　Child study
　　　　Children—Psychology
　　BT　**Psychology**
　　NT　**Cognitive styles in children**
　　　　Emotions in children
　　　　Fear in children
　　　　Imaginary playmates
　　　　Intelligence tests
　　　　Moral development
　　　　Psychology of learning
　　　　Separation anxiety in children
　　　　Sibling rivalry
　　RT　**Child development**
　　　　Child psychiatry
　　　　Child rearing
　　　　Educational psychology
Child raising
USE **Child rearing**
Child rearing   392.1; 649
　　Use for materials on the principles and
　techniques of rearing children. Materials on
　the psychological and social interaction be-
　tween parents and their minor children are en-
　tered under **Parent-child relationship**. Mate-
　rials on the skills, attributes, and attitudes
　needed for parenthood are entered under **Par-
　enting**.
　　UF　Child raising
　　　　Children—Management
　　　　Children—Training
　　　　Discipline of children
　　　　Training of children
　　BT　**Child-adult relationship**
　　　　Child care
　　　　Parent-child relationship
　　NT　**Children's allowances**
　　　　Socialization

Toilet training
　　RT　**Child development**
　　　　Child psychology
　　　　Parenting
Child sex abuse
USE **Child sexual abuse**
Child sexual abuse (May subdiv. geog.)
　　　　362.76; 364.15
　　UF　Child molesting
　　　　Child sex abuse
　　　　Children—Molesting
　　　　Molesting of children
　　　　Sexual abuse
　　　　Sexually abused children
　　BT　**Child abuse**
　　　　Incest
　　　　Sex crimes
　　RT　**Adult child sexual abuse vic-
　　　　tims**
Child snatching by parents
USE **Parental kidnapping**
Child study
USE **Child development**
　　　　Child psychology
Child support   346.01
　　UF　Support of children
　　BT　**Child welfare**
　　　　Desertion and nonsupport
　　　　Divorce mediation
Child welfare (May subdiv. geog.)   **362.7**
　　Use for materials on the aid, support, and
　protection of children, by the state or by pri-
　vate welfare organizations.
　　UF　Aid to dependent children
　　　　Children—Charities, protection,
　　　　　etc.
　　　　Mothers' pensions
　　　　Protection of children
　　BT　**Charities**
　　　　Public welfare
　　　　Social work
　　NT　**Abandoned children**
　　　　Child abuse
　　　　Child labor
　　　　Child support
　　　　Children—Institutional care
　　　　Day care centers
　　　　Foster home care
　　RT　**Children's hospitals**
　　　　Juvenile delinquency
　　　　Orphanages

Childbirth (May subdiv. geog.)   612.6; 618.2
- UF   Birth
  - Birth customs
  - Child birth
  - Labor (Childbirth)
  - Obstetrics
- NT   **Midwives**
  - **Multiple birth**
  - **Natural childbirth**
- RT   **Pregnancy**

Childhood diseases
- USE   **Children—Diseases**

Childlessness   306.85
- BT   **Children**
  - **Family size**
- RT   **Birth control**
  - **Human fertility**
  - **Infertility**

Children (May subdiv. geog.)   **305.23**

Use for materials on people from birth through age twelve. Materials limited to the first two years of a child's life are entered under **Infants**.

- UF   Preschool children
- SA   children of particular racial or ethnic groups, e.g. **African American children**; children and other subjects, e.g. **Children and war**; and names of wars with the subdivision *Children*, e.g. **World War, 1939-1945—Children** [to be added as needed]
- BT   **Age**
  - **Family**
- NT   **Abandoned children**
  - **Adopted children**
  - **Advertising and children**
  - **African American children**
  - **Birth order**
  - **Black children**
  - **Boys**
  - **Child-adult relationship**
  - **Child development**
  - **Childlessness**
  - **Children and war**
  - **Children of alcoholics**
  - **Children of drug addicts**
  - **Children of immigrants**
  - **Computers and children**
  - **Exceptional children**

- **Father-child relationship**
- **Foster children**
- **Girls**
- **Handicapped children**
- **Infants**
- **Internet and children**
- **Missing children**
- **Mother-child relationship**
- **Motion pictures and children**
- **Native American children**
- **Only child**
- **Orphans**
- **Parent-child relationship**
- **Runaway children**
- **School children**
- **Television and children**

Children, Abnormal
- USE   **Handicapped children**

Children—Abuse
- USE   **Child abuse**

Children—Adoption
- USE   **Adoption**

Children and adults
- USE   **Child-adult relationship**

Children and advertising
- USE   **Advertising and children**

Children and death   155.9

Use for materials on children's experiences with, conceptions of, and reactions to death. Materials on the death of children are entered under **Children—Death**. Materials on children's death rates and causes are entered under **Children—Mortality**.

- UF   Death and children
- BT   **Death**

Children and motion pictures
- USE   **Motion pictures and children**

Children and strangers   362.7
- UF   Infants and strangers
  - Strangers and children
- BT   **Child-adult relationship**

Children and television
- USE   **Television and children**

Children and the Internet
- USE   **Internet and children**

Children and war (May subdiv. geog.)   **305.23**
- UF   War and children
- SA   names of particular wars with the subdivision *Children*, e.g. **World War, 1939-1945—Children** [to be added as needed]

Children and war—*Continued*

BT **Children**
War

NT **World War, 1939-1945—Children**

Children as artists
USE **Child artists**

Children as authors
USE **Child authors**

Children as consumers
USE **Young consumers**

Children, Black
USE **Black children**

Children—Books and reading   011.62; 028.5

Use for materials on the reading interests of children and lists of books for children. Collections or materials about literature published for children are entered under **Children's literature**. Individual literary works and collections of literary works written by children are entered under **Children's writings**. Materials about works written by children and materials about children as authors are entered under **Child authors**.

UF Books and reading for children
Children's reading
Reading interests of children

BT **Books and reading**

Children—Care
USE **Child care**

Children—Charities, protection, etc.
USE **Child welfare**

Children—Civil rights   323.3; 342

BT **Civil rights**

Children—Clothing
USE **Children's clothing**

Children—Conduct of life   173

UF Behavior of children
Child behavior

BT **Conduct of life**

NT **Etiquette for children and teenagers**

Children—Costume
USE **Children's costumes**

Children, Crippled
USE **Physically handicapped children**

Children—Custody
USE **Child custody**

Children—Day care
USE **Day care centers**

Children—Death   306.9

Use for materials on the death of children. Materials on children's experiences with, conceptions of, and reactions to death are entered under **Children and death**. Materials on children's death rates and causes are entered under **Children—Mortality**.

UF Child death

BT **Death**

RT **Terminally ill children**

Children—Death—Causes
USE **Children—Mortality**

Children—Death rate
USE **Children—Mortality**

Children—Defense
USE **Self-defense for children**

Children—Dental care   617.6

Children—Development
USE **Child development**

Children—Diseases   618.92

UF Childhood diseases
Children's diseases
Diseases of children
Medicine, Pediatric
Pediatrics

SA types of diseases, e.g.
Chickenpox [to be added as needed]

BT **Diseases**

RT **Children—Health and hygiene**

Children—Education
USE **Elementary education**
Preschool education

Children—Employment
USE **Child labor**

Children—Etiquette
USE **Etiquette for children and teenagers**

Children—Food
USE **Children—Nutrition**

Children, Gifted
USE **Gifted children**

Children—Growth   155.4; 612.6

BT **Child development**

Children—Health and hygiene (May subdiv. geog.) **613**

UF Children—Hygiene
Pediatrics

BT **Health**
Hygiene

NT **Children—Nutrition**
Children—Physical fitness
School hygiene

Children—Health and hygiene—*Continued*
> RT   **Children—Diseases**
> **Children's hospitals**
> **Health education**

Children—Hospitals
> USE   **Children's hospitals**

Children—Hygiene
> USE   **Children—Health and hygiene**

Children, Hyperactive
> USE   **Hyperactive children**

Children in art   704.9
> Use for materials on children depicted in works of art. Materials on children as artists are entered under **Child artists**.
> BT   **Art—Themes**

Children in literature   809
> Use for materials on the theme of children in works of literature. Individual literary works or collections of literary works written by children are entered under the form heading **Children's writings**. Materials about children as authors and about works written by children are entered under **Child authors**.
> BT   **Literature—Themes**

Children—Institutional care (May subdiv. geog.)   **362.73**
> UF   Boys' towns
> Children's homes
> BT   **Child welfare**
> **Institutional care**
> NT   **Day care centers**
> **Orphanages**
> **Reformatories**
> RT   **Foster home care**

Children—Language   155.4
> BT   **Language and languages**

Children—Management
> USE   **Child rearing**

Children—Medical examinations   616.07
> UF   Medical inspection in schools
> School children—Medical examinations
>
Children—Mental health
> USE   **Child psychiatry**

Children—Molesting
> USE   **Child sexual abuse**

Children—Mortality (May subdiv. geog.)   **304.6**
> Use for material on children's death rates and causes. Material on children's experiences with, conceptions of, and reactions to death are entered under **Children and death**. Materials on the death of children are entered under **Children—Death**.

> UF   Child mortality
> Children—Death—Causes
> Children—Death rate
> BT   **Mortality**

Children—Nutrition   613.2083; 641.1083; 649
> UF   Children—Food
> Children's food
> BT   **Children—Health and hygiene**
> **Nutrition**
> NT   **School children—Food**

Children of alcoholics   362.292
> UF   Alcoholic parents
> COAs
> BT   **Children**
> NT   **Adult children of alcoholics**
> RT   **Alcoholics**

Children of divorced parents   306.874; 646.7
> BT   **Divorce**
> **Parent-child relationship**
> RT   **Part-time parenting**

Children of drug addicts   362.29
> UF   Children of narcotic addicts
> Cocaine babies
> Crack babies
> BT   **Children**
> **Drug addicts**

Children of immigrants   305.23
> UF   First generation children
> BT   **Children**
> **Immigration and emigration**

Children of narcotic addicts
> USE   **Children of drug addicts**

Children of single fathers
> USE   **Children of single parents**

Children of single mothers
> USE   **Children of single parents**

Children of single parents   306.874
> UF   Children of single fathers
> Children of single mothers
> Single parents' children
> BT   **Single parents**

Children of working parents   306.874; 362.7
> UF   Working parents' children
> BT   **Parent-child relationship**
> NT   **Latchkey children**

Children—Physical fitness   613.7
> BT   **Children—Health and hygiene**
> **Physical fitness**

Children—Placing out
  USE **Adoption**
      Foster home care
Children—Psychology
  USE **Child psychology**
Children, Retarded
  USE **Mentally handicapped children**
Children—Self-defense
  USE **Self-defense for children**
Children—Socialization
  USE **Socialization**
Children—Surgery   617
  UF Pediatric surgery
  BT **Surgery**
Children—Training
  USE **Child rearing**
Children—United States   305.230973
Children's allowances   332.024; 649
  UF Allowances, Children's
  BT **Child rearing**
      Money
      Personal finance
  RT **Money-making projects for
      children**
Children's art (May subdiv. geog.)
   704.083
  BT **Art**
Children's books
  USE **Children's literature**
Children's clothing   391; 646.4

Use for materials on children's clothing that is worn from day to day, including historical materials. Works on children's costumes for fancy dress or theatricals are entered under **Children's costumes**.

  UF Children—Clothing
  BT **Clothing and dress**
  NT **Infants' clothing**
  RT **Children's costumes**
Children's costumes   646.4; 792

Use for materials on children's costumes for fancy dress or theatricals. Materials on children's clothing that is worn from day to day are entered under **Children's clothing**.

  UF Children—Costume
  BT **Costume**
  RT **Children's clothing**
Children's courts
  USE **Juvenile courts**
Children's day care centers
  USE **Day care centers**
Children's diseases
  USE **Children—Diseases**

Children's food
  USE **Children—Nutrition**
Children's homes
  USE **Children—Institutional care**
Children's hospitals   362.11
  UF Children—Hospitals
  BT **Hospitals**
  RT **Child welfare**
      Children—Health and hygiene
Children's libraries   027.62
  UF Libraries and children
      Library services to children
  BT **Libraries**
  RT **Libraries and schools**
Children's literature   808.8

Use for collections or materials about literature published for children. Materials on the reading interests of children and lists of books for children are entered under **Children—Books and reading**. Individual literary works and collections of literary works written by children are entered under **Children's writings**. Materials about works written by children and materials about children as authors are entered under **Child authors**.

  UF Books for children
      Children's books
      Juvenile literature
  SA subjects and personal, corporate,
      and place names with the
      subdivision *Juvenile literature*,
      for non-fiction materials e.g.
      **Computers—Juvenile litera-
      ture**; and with the subdivi-
      sions *Juvenile fiction*; *Juvenile
      poetry*; and *Juvenile drama*;
      for materials in those forms,
      e.g. **Christmas—Juvenile fic-
      tion**; **Christmas—Juvenile
      poetry**; **Christmas—Juvenile
      drama**; etc. [to be added as
      needed]
  BT **Literature**
  NT **Big books**
      Caldecott Medal
      Children's plays
      Children's poetry
      Children's stories
      Coretta Scott King Award
      Easy reading materials
      Fairy tales
      Newbery Medal
      Picture books for children
      Plot-your-own stories

Children's literature—*Continued*
 Reading materials
 Storytelling
Children's literature—Book reviews
 808.8
Children's literature—History and criticism 809
Children's moneymaking projects
 USE Money-making projects for children
Children's parties 395.3; 793.2
 BT Amusements
  Entertaining
  Parties
Children's playhouses 690
 BT Buildings
Children's plays 808.82
 Use for individual works, collections, or materials about plays for children. Materials about plays for production in colleges and schools are entered under **College and school drama**. Individual works and collections of plays written by children are entered under **Children's writings**. Materials about plays written by children are entered under **Child authors**.
 UF Plays for children
  School plays
 SA subjects and personal, corporate, and place names with the subdivision *Juvenile drama*, e.g. **Christmas—Juvenile drama** [to be added as needed]
 BT Amateur theater
  Children's literature
  Drama
  Theater
Children's poetry 808.81
 Use for individual poems, collections, or materials about poetry written for children. Individual works and collections of poetry written by children are entered under **Children's writings**. Materials about poetry written by children are entered under **Child authors**.
 UF Poetry for children
 SA subjects and personal, corporate, and place names with the subdivision *Juvenile poetry*; e.g. **Christmas—Juvenile poetry** [to be added as needed]
 BT Children's literature
  Poetry
 NT Children's songs
  Lullabies

  Nonsense verses
  Nursery rhymes
  Tongue twisters
Children's reading
 USE Children—Books and reading
  Reading
Children's secrets 155.4
 BT Secrecy
Children's songs 782.42
 Use for collections of songs that contain both words and music, and for materials about songs for children. Collections of songs without the music are entered under **Children's poetry**.
 UF Songs for children
 BT Children's poetry
  School songbooks
  Songs
 NT Lullabies
  Nursery rhymes
Children's stories 808.3; 808.83
 Use for individual stories and collections of stories written for children. Individual works and collections of stories written by children are entered under **Children's writings**. Materials about stories written by children are entered under **Child authors**.
 UF Fiction for children
  Stories for children
 SA subjects and personal, corporate, and place names with the subdivision *Juvenile fiction*, e.g. **Christmas—Juvenile fiction** [to be added as needed]
 BT Children's literature
  Fiction
Children's writings 808.8
 Use for individual literary works or collections of literary works written by children. Materials on children as authors and discussions of literary works written by children are entered under **Child authors**. Collections of works published for children are entered under **Children's literature**.
 UF School prose
  School verse
 RT Child authors
  College and school journalism
Chile 983
 May be subdivided like **United States** except for *History*.
Chimes
 USE Bells
Chimneys 697; 721
 UF Smoke stacks

Chimneys—*Continued*
  BT Architecture—Details
      Buildings
  RT Fireplaces
Chimpanzees (May subdiv. geog.)
      599.85
  UF Chimps
  BT Apes
Chimps
  USE Chimpanzees
China 951
  Use as a heading or as a geographic subdi-
  vision for materials dealing with mainland
  China, regardless of time period, or with the
  People's Republic of China, or for compre-
  hensive materials on China including Taiwan.
  Materials dealing with the island of Taiwan,
  regardless of time period, or with the post-
  1948 Republic of China are entered under
  Taiwan. May be subdivided like **United
  States** except for *History*.
  UF China (People's Republic of
        China)
      People's Republic of China
China—History 951
China—History—1912-1949 951.04
China—History—1949- 951.05
China—History—1949-1976 951.05
China—History—1976- 951.05
China—History—1989, Tiananmen Square
      Incident
  USE Tiananmen Square Incident,
        Beijing (China), 1989
China painting 738.1
  UF Porcelain painting
  BT Decoration and ornament
      Painting
      Porcelain
China (People's Republic of China)
  USE China
China (Porcelain)
  USE Porcelain
China (Republic)
  USE Taiwan
Chinaware
  USE Porcelain
Chinese Americans (May subdiv. geog.)
      305.895; 973
  BT Ethnic groups
Chinese cooking 641.5953
  BT Cooking
Chinese New Year (May subdiv. geog.)
      394.261
  BT Holidays

Chipmunks 599.36
  BT Mammals
      Squirrels
Chiropody
  USE Podiatry
Chiropractic 615.5
  BT Alternative medicine
      Massage
  RT Naturopathy
      Osteopathic medicine
Chivalry 394
  BT Manners and customs
  NT Medieval tournaments
  RT Crusades
      Feudalism
      Heraldry
      Knights and knighthood
      Medieval civilization
      Romances
Chivalry—Romances
  USE Romances
Chocolate 641.3
  BT Food
  RT Cocoa
      Desserts
Choice, Freedom of
  USE Free will and determinism
Choice of books
  USE Best books
      Book selection
      Books and reading
Choice of college
  USE College choice
Choice of profession, occupation, vocation,
      etc.
  USE Vocational guidance
Choice of school
  USE School choice
Choice (Psychology) 153.8
  BT Psychology
  RT Decision making
Choirs (Music) 782.5
  BT Church music
  RT Choral conducting
      Choral music
      Choral societies
      Singing
Cholesterol 572
  RT Low-cholesterol diet
Cholesterol content of food
  USE Food—Cholesterol content

Choose-your-own story plots
USE **Plot-your-own stories**
Choral conducting **782.5**
UF Conducting, Choral
BT **Conducting**
RT **Choirs (Music)**
Choral music
Conductors (Music)
Choral music **782.5**
UF Music, Choral
BT **Church music**
Vocal music
NT **Cantatas**
RT **Choirs (Music)**
Choral conducting
Choral societies
Choral societies **782.506**
UF Singing societies
BT **Societies**
RT **Choirs (Music)**
Choral music
Choral speaking **808.5**
UF Speaking choirs
Unison speaking
BT **Drama**
Recitations
Christ
USE **Jesus Christ**
Christening
USE **Baptism**
Christian antiquities (May subdiv. geog.)
225.9; 270; 930.1
UF Christian archeology
Church antiquities
Ecclesiastical antiquities
BT **Antiquities**
NT **Catacombs**
RT **Christian art**
Christian archeology
USE **Christian antiquities**
Christian art (May subdiv. geog.) **246;**
704.9
UF Christian art and symbolism
Ecclesiastical art
BT **Art**
Religious art
NT **Icons (Religion)**
Jesus Christ—Art
Mary, Blessed Virgin, Saint—
Art

RT **Christian antiquities**
Christian symbolism
Gothic art
Christian art and symbolism
USE **Christian art**
Christian symbolism
Christian biography **270.092; 920**
UF Christianity—Biography
Christians—Biography
Ecclesiastical biography
BT **Biography**
Religious biography
NT **Fathers of the church**
Christian civilization **270; 909**
UF Civilization, Christian
BT **Christianity**
Civilization
Christian denominations
USE **Christian sects**
Christian devotional calendars
USE **Devotional calendars**
Christian doctrinal theology
USE **Christianity—Doctrines**
Christian doctrine
USE **Christianity—Doctrines**
Christian education (May subdiv. geog.)
268
Use for materials on the instruction of
Christian religion in schools and private life.
General materials on the instruction of reli-
gion in schools and private life are entered
under **Religious education**. Materials on the
relation of the church to education and materi-
als on the history of the part that the church
has taken in secular education are entered un-
der **Church and education**. Materials on
church supported and controlled elementary
and secondary schools are entered under
Church schools.
UF Education, Christian
BT **Religious education**
RT **Church and education**
Christian ethics **241**
UF Christian moral theology
Moral theology, Christian
BT **Ethics**
NT **Conscience**
RT **Christian life**
Christian fasts and feasts
USE **Christian holidays**
Christian fiction **808.83**
Use for individual works, collections, or
materials about fiction that promotes Christian
teachings or exemplifies a Christian way of
life.

Christian fiction—*Continued*
  BT **Fiction**
      Religious fiction
Christian fundamentalism   230; 270.8
  Use for materials on the modern conservative movement in Protestantism emphasizing literal interpretation of the Bible, as opposed to religious liberalism, modernism, or evolutionism.
  UF Fundamentalism
      Modernist-fundamentalist controversy
  BT **Christianity—Doctrines**
      Religious fundamentalism
  RT **Modernism (Theology)**
Christian heresies (May subdiv. geog.)
      273
  UF Heresies, Christian
  BT **Doctrinal theology**
      Heresy
Christian holidays   263; 394.266
  UF Christian fasts and feasts
      Christian holy days
      Fasts and feasts—Christianity
  SA names of Christian holidays, e.g.
      Christmas [to be added as needed]
  BT **Church year**
      Religious holidays
  NT **Christmas**
      Easter
      Good Friday
Christian holy days
  USE **Christian holidays**
Christian-Jewish relations
  USE **Christianity—Relations—Judaism**
      Judaism—Relations—Christianity
Christian legends   270.9; 398.2
  BT **Legends**
Christian life   248.4
  UF Religious life (Christian)
  BT **Religious life**
  RT **Christian ethics**
Christian life—Sermons   252
  BT **Sermons**
Christian literature   230
  BT **Religious literature**
  NT **Catholic literature**
      Early Christian literature
      Papal encyclicals
      Sermons

Christian literature—30-600, Early
  USE **Early Christian literature**
Christian literature, Early
  USE **Early Christian literature**
Christian ministry   253
  BT **Ministry**
Christian missionaries   266.0092; 920
  UF Missionaries, Christian
  RT **Christian missions**
Christian missions (May subdiv. geog.)
      266
  UF Foreign missions, Christian
      Home missions, Christian
      Missions, Christian
  SA names of Christian churches, denominations, religious orders, etc., with the subdivision *Missions*, e.g. **Catholic Church—Missions**; and names of peoples evangelized with the subdivision *Christian missions*, e.g. **Native Americans—Christian missions** [to be added as needed]
  BT **Christianity**
      Church history
      Church work
  NT **Catholic Church—Missions**
      Native Americans—Christian missions
      Salvation Army
  RT **Christian missionaries**
      Evangelistic work
Christian moral theology
  USE **Christian ethics**
Christian names
  USE **Personal names**
Christian-owned business enterprises (May subdiv. geog.)   **338.7**
  BT **Business enterprises**
Christian philosophy   190; 230.01
  Use for materials on philosophy as practiced by Christian philosophers or on the nature, origins, or validity of Christian beliefs from a philosophical point of view.
  UF Christianity—Philosophy
  BT **Philosophy**
Christian saints   270.092; 920
  BT **Saints**
  NT **Apostles**
      Canonization
Christian Science   289.5

Christian Science—*Continued*

UF   Church of Christ, Scientist

BT   **Christian sects**

RT   **Spiritual healing**

Christian sects (May subdiv. geog.)   **280**

UF   Christian denominations

        Church denominations

        Denominations, Christian

SA   names of Christian sects, e.g.

        Presbyterian Church [to be

        added as needed]

BT   **Christianity**

        Church history

        Sects

NT   **Amish**

        Baptists

        Catholic Church

        Christian Science

        Christian union

        Church of England

        Church of Jesus Christ of Lat-

        ter-day Saints

        Community churches

        Congregationalism

        Eastern churches

        Ecumenical movement

        Episcopal Church

        Greek Orthodox Church

        Huguenots

        Interdenominational coopera-

        tion

        Mennonites

        Moravians

        Non-institutional churches

        Orthodox Eastern Church

        Pentecostal churches

        Presbyterian Church

        Protestant churches

        Puritans

        Russian Orthodox Church

        Salvation Army

        Shakers

        Society of Friends

        Unitarianism

Christian sects—Government

USE   **Church polity**

Christian sociology (May subdiv. geog.)

    261

Use for materials on social theory from a Christian point of view. Materials on religious sociology in general are entered under **Religion and sociology**. Materials on the practical treatment of social problems from the point of view of the church are entered under **Church and social problems**.

UF   Sociology, Christian

BT   **Religion and sociology**

        Sociology

RT   **Christianity and economics**

        Church and social problems

Christian symbolism (May subdiv. geog.)

    246; 704.9

UF   Christian art and symbolism

BT   **Symbolism**

RT   **Christian art**

Christian union (May subdiv. geog.)

    280

Use for materials on prospective and actual mergers within and across denominational lines. Materials on unity as one of the marks of the church are entered under **Church—Unity**. Materials on a movement originating in the twentieth century aimed at promoting church cooperation and unity are entered under **Ecumenical movement**. Materials on religious activities planned and conducted cooperatively by two or more Christian sects are entered under **Interdenominational cooperation**.

UF   Christian unity

        Christianity—Union between

        churches

        Ecumenism

BT   **Christian sects**

        Church

RT   **Ecumenical movement**

Christian unity

USE   **Christian union**

        Church—Unity

        Ecumenical movement

        Interdenominational coopera-

        tion

Christian year

USE   **Church year**

Christianity (May subdiv. geog.)   **230**

SA   names of Christian churches and

        sects, e.g. **Catholic Church**;

        Huguenots; etc.; and Chris-

        tianity and other subjects, e.g.

        Christianity and economics

        [to be added as needed]

BT   **Religions**

NT   **Atonement—Christianity**

        Catholic Church

        Christian civilization

        Christian missions

        Christian sects

Christianity—*Continued*
>### Christianity and economics
>### Councils and synods
>### Counter-Reformation
>### Eastern churches
>### Pentecostalism
>### Protestantism
>### Reformation
>RT **Christians**
>**Church**

Christianity and economics   261.8
>UF   Economics and Christianity
>BT   **Christianity**
>**Economics**
>RT   **Christian sociology**
>**Church and labor**

Christianity and evolution
>USE   **Creationism**

Christianity and other religions   261.2
>Use for materials on the relations between Christianity and several other religions. Materials on the relations between Christianity and one other religion are entered under **Christianity** subdivided by *Relations* further subdivided by the other religion, and also under the other religion subdivided by *Relations—Christianity*, e.g. **Christianity—Relations—Judaism** and **Judaism—Relations—Christianity**. The same pattern is followed for sects and denominations.
>UF   Comparative religion
>BT   **Religions**
>NT   **Christianity—Relations—Judaism**
>**Judaism—Relations—Christianity**
>**Paganism**

Christianity and other religions—Judaism
>USE   **Christianity—Relations—Judaism**
>**Judaism—Relations—Christianity**

Christianity and politics   261.7; 322
>UF   Christianity—Political aspects
>Politics and Christianity
>BT   **Church and state**
>**Religion and politics**

Christianity—Apologetic works   239
>Use for materials defending Christianity. Materials attacking Christianity are entered under **Christianity—Controversial literature**.
>BT   **Apologetics**

Christianity—Biography
>USE   **Christian biography**

Christianity—Controversial literature   239
>Use for materials attacking Christianity. Materials defending Christianity are entered under **Christianity—Apologetic works**.

Christianity—Doctrines   230
>UF   Christian doctrinal theology
>Christian doctrine
>BT   **Doctrinal theology**
>NT   **Christian fundamentalism**
>**Creationism**
>**God—Christianity**
>**Liberation theology**
>**Modernism (Theology)**
>**Regeneration (Christianity)**
>**Trinity**

Christianity—Government
>USE   **Church polity**

Christianity—History
>USE   **Church history**

Christianity—Origin
>USE   **Church history—30-600, Early church**

Christianity—Philosophy
>USE   **Christian philosophy**

Christianity—Political aspects
>USE   **Christianity and politics**

Christianity—Polity
>USE   **Church polity**

Christianity—Psychology   230.01; 253.5
>BT   **Psychology of religion**

Christianity—Relations—Judaism   261.2; 296.3
>Use for materials on the relations between Christianity and Judaism. When assigning this heading, provide an additional subject entry under **Judaism—Relations—Christianity**.
>UF   Christian-Jewish relations
>Christianity and other religions—Judaism
>Jewish-Christian relations
>BT   **Christianity and other religions**
>**Judaism**

Christianity—Union between churches
>USE   **Christian union**

Christians (May subdiv. geog.)   270.092
>RT   **Christianity**

Christians—Biography
>USE   **Christian biography**

Christians—Persecutions (May subdiv. geog.)   272
>BT   **Church history**
>**Persecution**

Christmas (May subdiv. geog.) **263;
394.2663**
  BT **Christian holidays
Holidays**
  NT **Christmas entertainments
Santa Claus**
Christmas cards **741.6; 745.594**
  BT **Greeting cards**
Christmas carols
  USE **Carols**
Christmas cooking (May subdiv. geog.)
641.5
  BT **Cooking**
Christmas decorations **394.2663;
745.594**
  UF Christmas ornaments
  BT **Decoration and ornament**
  NT **Christmas trees**
Christmas—Drama **394.2663; 792;
808.82**
  Use for collections of plays about Christmas.
  UF Christmas plays
Christmas entertainments **394.2663;
791**
  BT **Amusements
Christmas**
Christmas—Fiction **808.83**
  Use for collections of stories about Christmas.
  UF Christmas stories
Christmas—Juvenile drama **808.82**
  Use for collections of plays about Christmas written for children.
Christmas—Juvenile fiction **808.83**
  Use for collections of stories about Christmas written for children.
Christmas—Juvenile poetry **808.81**
  Use for collections of poems about Christmas written for children.
Christmas ornaments
  USE **Christmas decorations**
Christmas plays
  USE **Christmas—Drama**
Christmas poetry
  USE **Christmas—Poetry**
Christmas—Poetry **808.81**
  Use for collections of poems about Christmas.
  UF Christmas poetry
Christmas stories
  USE **Christmas—Fiction**
Christmas tree growing **635.9**

  UF Growing of Christmas trees
  BT **Forests and forestry**
  RT **Christmas trees**
Christmas trees **394.2663; 745.594**
  BT **Christmas decorations
Trees**
  RT **Christmas tree growing**
Christmas—United States **394.2663**
Christology
  USE **Jesus Christ**
Chromosome mapping
  USE **Gene mapping**
Chromosomes **572.8**
  BT **Genetics
Heredity**
  NT **Genetic recombination**
Chronic diseases **616**
  UF Diseases, Chronic
  BT **Diseases**
  NT **Chronic pain**
Chronic pain **616**
  UF Persistent pain
  BT **Chronic diseases
Pain**
Chronicle history (Drama)
  USE **Historical drama**
Chronicle plays
  USE **Historical drama**
Chronology **529**
  Use for materials on the science that deals with measuring time by regular divisions and that assigns proper dates to events.
  SA individual persons, wars, sacred works, topics that are inherently historical, and topics not subdivided by *History*, such as art, music, literature, etc., with the subdivision *Chronology*, e.g. **Bible—Chronology**; and ethnic groups, corporate bodies, military services, topics not inherently historical, and names of places with the subdivision *History—Chronology*, e.g. **Native Americans—History—Chronology** [to be added as needed]
  BT **Astronomy
History
Time**
  NT **Bible—Chronology
Day**

Chronology—*Continued*
>> Historical chronology
>> Months
>> Night
>> Week
> RT Almanacs

Chronology, Historical
> USE Historical chronology

Church 260
> Use for materials on the concept and function of the Christian Church as a whole.
> SA church and other subjects, e.g. Church and education [to be added as needed]
> BT Theology
> NT Christian union
>> Church and education
>> Church and social problems
>> Church and state
>> Church polity
>> Church work
>> Clergy
>> Ecclesiastical law
>> Ecumenical movement
>> Laity
>> Sacraments
> RT Christianity

Church and education 261
> Use for materials on the relation of the church to education in general, and for materials on the history of the part that the church has taken in secular education. Materials on church supported and controlled elementary and secondary schools are entered under Church schools. Materials on the instruction of religion in schools and private life are entered under Religious education, and of Christian religion under Christian education.
> UF Education and church
>> Education and religion
>> Fundamentalism and education
>> Religion and education
> BT Church
>> Education
> NT Religion in the public schools
> RT Christian education

Church and labor 261.8
> UF Labor and the church
> BT Labor
> RT Christianity and economics

Church and race relations 261.8
> UF Integrated churches
>> Race relations and the church
> BT Church work

Church and social problems 261.8
> Use for materials on the practical treatment of social problems from the point of view of the church. Materials on social theory from a Christian point of view are entered under Christian sociology. Materials on religious sociology in general are entered under Religion and sociology.
> UF Religion and social problems
>> Social problems and the church
> BT Church
>> Social problems
> NT Liberation theology
>> Sanctuary movement
> RT Christian sociology
>> Church work

Church and state (May subdiv. geog.) 201; 261.7; 322
> UF Church—Government policy
>> Religion and state
>> Religion—Government policy
>> Separation of church and state
> BT Church
>> State, The
> NT Christianity and politics
>> Religion in the public schools

Church and state—United States 322
> UF United States—Church and state

Church antiquities
> USE Christian antiquities

Church architecture (May subdiv. geog.) 726.5
> UF Ecclesiastical architecture
> BT Architecture
> NT Abbeys
>> Monasteries
>> Spires
> RT Cathedrals
>> Church buildings
>> Gothic architecture

Church attendance
> USE Public worship

Church bells
> USE Bells

Church buildings (May subdiv. geog.) 726.5
> Use for general descriptive and historical materials on church buildings that cannot be entered under Church architecture.
> UF Churches
> SA names of individual churches, e.g. Westminster Abbey [to be added as needed]
> BT Buildings

Church buildings—*Continued*
    NT   **Cathedrals**
          Westminster Abbey
    RT   **Church architecture**
Church buildings—United States
    726.50973
Church councils
    USE **Councils and synods**
Church denominations
    USE **Christian sects**
          Sects
Church entertainments   253.7
    UF   Church sociables
          Socials
    BT   **Amusements**
          Church work
Church fathers
    USE **Fathers of the church**
Church festivals
    USE **Religious holidays**
Church finance   254; 262.0068
    BT   **Finance**
    NT   **Tithes**
Church furniture   247
    UF   Ecclesiastical furniture
    BT   **Furniture**
Church government
    USE **Church polity**
Church—Government policy
    USE **Church and state**
Church history   270
    Use for materials dealing with the development of Christianity and church organization.
    UF   Christianity—History
          Ecclesiastical history
          Religious history
    SA   names of countries, states, etc. with the subdivision *Church history*, e.g. **United States—Church history**; and names of individual denominations, sects, churches, etc. [to be added as needed]
    BT   **History**
    NT   **Christian missions**
          Christian sects
          Christians—Persecutions
          Councils and synods
          Martyrs
          Monasteries
          Ohio—Church history
          Papacy

          Popes
          Popes—Temporal power
          Protestant churches
          Protestantism
          Sects
          United States—Church history
Church history—30-600, Early church
    270.1
    UF   Apostolic Church
          Christianity—Origin
          Early church history
          Primitive Christianity
    NT   **Apostles**
          Gnosticism
    RT   **Catacombs**
          Early Christian literature
Church history—600-1500, Middle Ages
    270.3
    UF   Medieval church history
    BT   **Middle Ages**
    NT   **Crusades**
Church history—1500-, Modern period
    270.6
    UF   Modern church history
    NT   **Counter-Reformation**
          Reformation
Church history—Ohio
    USE **Ohio—Church history**
Church history—United States
    USE **United States—Church history**
Church law
    USE **Ecclesiastical law**
Church libraries   027.6
    UF   Parish libraries
    BT   **Libraries**
Church music (May subdiv. geog.)
    781.71
    This heading may be subdivided by religion or denomination as needed.
    UF   Religious music
          Sacred music
    SA   types of church music, e.g. **Hymns** [to be added as needed]
    BT   **Music**
    NT   **Carols**
          Chants (Plain, Gregorian, etc.)
          Choirs (Music)
          Choral music
          Gospel music
          Hymnals
          Hymns

Church music—*Continued*
>> Oratorio
>> Organ music
> RT Liturgies

Church of Christ, Scientist
> USE Christian Science

Church of England (May subdiv. geog.)
>> 283
> UF Anglican Church
>> England, Church of
> BT Christian sects

Church of England—Government 283

Church of England—United States 283
> Use for materials on the Episcopal Church in the United States prior to 1789. Materials on the Episcopal Church in the United States after 1789 are entered under **Episcopal Church**.
> RT Episcopal Church
>> Puritans

Church of Jesus Christ of Latter-day
>> Saints (May subdiv. geog.) 289.3
> UF Latter-day Saints
>> Mormon Church
> BT Christian sects
> RT Mormons

Church polity 262
> UF Christian sects—Government
>> Christianity—Government
>> Christianity—Polity
>> Church government
>> Ecclesiastical polity
>> Polity, Ecclesiastical
> SA names of church denominations with the subdivision *Government*, e.g. **Church of England—Government** [to be added as needed]
> BT Church

Church schools (May subdiv. geog.)
>> 371.07
> Use for materials on church supported and controlled elementary and secondary schools. Materials on the relation of the church to education and on the history of the part that the church has taken in secular education are entered under **Church and education**. Materials on the instruction of religion in schools and private life are entered under **Religious education**, and of Christian religion under **Christian education**.
> UF Denominational schools
>> Nonpublic schools
>> Parochial schools

> BT Private schools
>> Schools

Church service books
> USE Liturgies

Church settlements
> USE Social settlements

Church sociables
> USE Church entertainments

Church—Unity 262
> Use for materials on unity as one of the marks of the church. Materials on prospective and actual mergers within and across denominational lines are entered under **Christian union**. Materials on a movement originating in the twentieth century aimed at promoting church cooperation and unity are entered under **Ecumenical movement**. Materials on religious activities planned and conducted cooperatively by two or more Christian sects are entered under **Interdenominational cooperation**.
> UF Christian unity

Church work 200; 253
> SA church work with particular groups of persons, e.g.
>> **Church work with the sick** [to be added as needed]
> BT Church
> NT Christian missions
>> Church and race relations
>> Church entertainments
>> Church work with the sick
>> Church work with youth
>> Evangelistic work
>> Interdenominational cooperation
>> Lay ministry
>> Ministry
>> Pastoral psychology
>> Rural churches
>> Sunday schools
> RT Church and social problems
>> Pastoral theology

Church work with the sick 259;
>> 362.1023
> BT Church work
>> Sick

Church work with youth 259
> BT Church work
>> Youth

Church year 263
> Use for materials on the seasons of observance and Christian festivals with their cycles, as making up the Christian or church year. Works on the origins of Christian festivals

Church year—*Continued*
and fasts are entered under **Christian holidays**.

- UF Christian year
  - Ecclesiastical year
  - Liturgical year
- SA festival seasons and seasons of the church year, e.g. **Lent** [to be added as needed]
- BT **Calendars**
  - **Religious holidays**
  - **Worship**
- NT **Christian holidays**
  - **Holy Week**
  - **Lent**

Churches
- USE **Church buildings**
  - **Religious institutions**

Churches, Community
- USE **Community churches**

Churches, Country
- USE **Rural churches**

Churches, Non-institutional
- USE **Non-institutional churches**

Churches, Rural
- USE **Rural churches**

Churches, Undenominational
- USE **Community churches**

Churchyards
- USE **Cemeteries**

Cigarettes 679
- BT **Smoking**
  - **Tobacco**

Cigars 679
- BT **Smoking**
  - **Tobacco**

Cinco de Mayo (Holiday) (May subdiv. geog.) **391.262**
- UF Fifth of May (Holiday)
- BT **Holidays**

Cinema
- USE **Motion pictures**

Cinemas
- USE **Motion picture theaters**

Cinematography 778.5

Use for materials on the technical aspects of making motion pictures and their projection onto a screen. General materials on motion pictures, including motion pictures as an art form, are entered under **Motion pictures**.

- UF Motion picture photography
  - Photography—Motion pictures
- BT **Photography**

- NT **Animation (Cinematography)**
  - **Motion picture cameras**

Cinesiology
- USE **Kinesiology**

Cipher and telegraph codes 384.1
- UF Codes, Telegraph
  - Morse code
  - Telegraph codes
- BT **Ciphers**
  - **Telegraph**

Ciphers 652
- UF Codes
  - Contractions
- BT **Signs and symbols**
- NT **Cipher and telegraph codes**
- RT **Abbreviations**
  - **Cryptography**
  - **Writing**

Ciphers (Lettering)
- USE **Monograms**

Circuits, Electric
- USE **Electric circuits**

Circulation of library materials
- USE **Library circulation**

Circulation of the blood
- USE **Blood—Circulation**

Circulatory system
- USE **Cardiovascular system**

Circumcision (May subdiv. geog.) **392.1**
- UF Male circumcision
- BT **Initiation rites**

Circumcision, Female
- USE **Female circumcision**

Circumnavigation
- USE **Voyages around the world**

Circus (May subdiv. geog.) **791.3**
- BT **Amusements**
- NT **Acrobats and acrobatics**
  - **Clowns**
- RT **Carnivals**

CIS
- USE **Commonwealth of Independent States**

Cities and towns (May subdiv. geog.) **307.76**

Use for general materials on cities and towns. For materials on large cities and their surrounding areas use **Metropolitan areas**. General materials on the government of cities are entered under **Municipal government**. General materials on local government other than that of cities are entered under **Local government**.

Cities and towns—*Continued*
    UF   Municipalities
          Towns
          Urban areas
    SA   names of individual cities and
          towns [to be added as need-
          ed]
    BT   **Sociology**
    NT   **Capitals (Cities)**
          City and town life
          Extinct cities
          Inner cities
          Markets
          Municipal art
          Parks
          Streets
          Urbanization
          Villages
    RT   **Urban sociology**
Cities and towns—Civic improvement
    307.3; 354.3
    UF   Civic improvement
          Municipal improvements
    NT   **City planning**
          Community centers
Cities and towns—Finance
    USE **Municipal finance**
Cities and towns—Government
    USE **Municipal government**
Cities and towns—Growth   **307.76**
    UF   Cities and towns, Movement to
          Urban development
    BT   **Internal migration**
          Population
    NT   **Metropolitan areas**
          Suburbs
    RT   **Urbanization**
Cities and towns—Lighting
    USE **Streets—Lighting**
Cities and towns, Movement to
    USE **Cities and towns—Growth**
         Urbanization
Cities and towns—Planning
    USE **City planning**
Cities and towns—United States
    307.760973; 973
    UF   United States—Cities and towns
Cities, Imaginary
    USE **Geographical myths**

Citizen participation
    USE **Political participation**
         and subjects designating govern-
         ment activity with the subdi-
         vision *Citizen participation,*
         e.g. **City planning—Citizen**
         participation [to be added as
         needed]
Citizens band radio   **384.5; 621.3845**
    UF   CB radio
          Citizens radio service
    BT   **Shortwave radio**
Citizen's defender
    USE **Ombudsman**
Citizens radio service
    USE **Citizens band radio**
Citizenship (May subdiv. geog.)   **172;**
    323.6
    UF   Civics
          Franchise
          Nationality (Citizenship)
    BT   **Constitutional law**
          Political ethics
          Political science
    NT   **Patriotism**
          Suffrage
    RT   **Aliens**
          Naturalization
Citrus
    USE **Citrus fruits**
Citrus fruit
    USE **Citrus fruits**
Citrus fruits   **634**
   Names of particular fruits may be used for
either the fruit or the tree.
    UF   Citrus
          Citrus fruit
    SA   types of citrus fruits, e.g. **Lem-**
         ons [to be added as needed]
    BT   **Fruit**
    NT   **Lemons**
          Limes
          Oranges
City and town life (May subdiv. geog.)
    307.76
    UF   City life
          Town life
          Urban life
    BT   **Cities and towns**
          Urban sociology
    NT   **Street life**
          Urban policy

City-federal relations
    USE   **Federal-city relations**
City government
    USE   **Municipal government**
City life
    USE   **City and town life**
City manager
    USE   **Municipal government by city manager**

City planning (May subdiv. geog.)
    307.1; 354.3; 711

Use for materials on the architectural and engineering aspects of urban redevelopment. Materials on the economic, sociological, and political aspects are entered under **Urban renewal**.

    UF   Cities and towns—Planning
          Municipal planning
          Town planning
          Urban development
          Urban planning
    BT   **Cities and towns—Civic improvement**
          Planning
    NT   **Planned communities**
          Suburbs
          Zoning
    RT   **Community development**
          Housing
          Municipal art
          Public works
          Regional planning
          Urban policy
          Urban renewal

City planning—Chicago (Ill.)   **307.1; 354.3; 711**
    UF   Chicago (Ill.)—City planning

City planning—Citizen participation (May subdiv. geog.)   **307.1**
    BT   **Political participation**
          Social action

City planning—United States   **307.1; 354.3; 711**

City planning—Zone system
    USE   **Zoning**
City schools
    USE   **Urban schools**
City-state relations
    USE   **State-local relations**

City traffic   **388.4**
    UF   Local traffic
          Street traffic
          Traffic, City

          Urban traffic
    BT   **Streets**
          Traffic engineering
City transit
    USE   **Local transit**
Civic art
    USE   **Municipal art**
Civic improvement
    USE   **Cities and towns—Civic improvement**
Civic involvement
    USE   **Political participation**
          and subjects with the subdivision *Citizen participation,* e.g.
          City planning—United States—Citizen participation
          [to be added as needed]
Civics
    USE   **Citizenship**
          Political science

Civil defense (May subdiv. geog.)
    363.35

Use for materials on the protection of civilians from enemy attack. Materials on military defenses against air attack are entered under **Air defenses**.

    UF   Civilian defense
    SA   names of wars with the subdivision *Evacuation of civilians* [to be added as needed]
    BT   **Military art and science**
    NT   **Air raid shelters**
          Evacuation of civilians
          Rescue work
          Survival skills
          World War, 1939-1945—Evacuation of civilians

Civil defense—Chicago (Ill.)   **363.35**
    UF   Chicago (Ill.)—Civil defense

Civil defense—United States   **363.35**
    UF   United States—Civil defense

Civil disobedience (May subdiv. geog.)
    303.6; 322.4
    BT   **Resistance to government**
Civil disorders
    USE   **Riots**

Civil engineering (May subdiv. geog.)
    624
    BT   **Engineering**
    NT   **Aqueducts**
          Bridges
          Canals

Civil engineering—*Continued*
>Dams
>Drainage
>Dredging
>Excavation
>Extraterrestrial bases
>Harbors
>Highway engineering
>Hydraulic engineering
>Lunar bases
>Marine engineering
>Mechanical engineering
>Military engineering
>Mining engineering
>Public works
>Railroad engineering
>Reclamation of land
>Roads
>Streets
>Structural engineering
>Structural steel
>Surveying
>Tunnels
>Walls
>Water supply engineering

Civil government
>USE **Political science**

Civil law suits
>USE **Litigation**

Civil liberty
>USE **Freedom**

Civil procedure (May subdiv. geog.)
>**347**
>BT **Courts**
>NT **Probate law and practice**
>**Small claims courts**
>RT **Litigation**

Civil rights (May subdiv. geog.)   **323;**
>**342**

>Use for materials on citizens' rights as established by law or protected by a constitution. Materials on the rights of persons regardless of their legal, socioeconomic, or cultural status and as recognized by the international community are entered under **Human rights**.

>UF   Basic rights
>Constitutional rights
>Fundamental rights
>SA   ethnic groups and classes of persons with the subdivision *Civil rights* [to be added as needed]

>BT   **Constitutional law**
>**Human rights**
>**Political science**
>NT   **African Americans—Civil rights**
>**Anti-apartheid movement**
>**Blacks—Civil rights**
>**Children—Civil rights**
>**Due process of law**
>**Employee rights**
>**Fair trial**
>**Freedom of assembly**
>**Freedom of association**
>**Freedom of information**
>**Freedom of movement**
>**Freedom of religion**
>**Freedom of speech**
>**Freedom of the press**
>**Gay rights**
>**Habeas corpus**
>**Right of privacy**
>**Right of property**
>**Women's rights**
>RT   **Civil rights demonstrations**
>**Discrimination**
>**Freedom**

Civil rights demonstrations (May subdiv. geog.)   **322.4**
>UF   Demonstrations for civil rights
>Freedom marches for civil rights
>Marches for civil rights
>Sit-ins for civil rights
>BT   **Demonstrations**
>RT   **Civil rights**

Civil rights (International law)
>USE   **Human rights**

Civil servants
>USE   **Civil service**

Civil service (May subdiv. geog.)   **351;**
>**352.6; 342**

>Use for general materials on career government service and the laws governing it. Materials on civil service employees are entered under the name of the country, state, city, corporate body, or government agency with the subdivision *Officials and employees*.

>UF   Administration
>Civil servants
>Employees and officials
>Government employees
>Government service
>Officials and employees
>Tenure of office

Civil service—*Continued*
    SA   names of countries, states, cities, etc., and corporate bodies with the subdivision *Officials and employees*, e.g. **United States—Officials and employees**; **Ohio—Officials and employees**; **Chicago (Ill.)—Officials and employees**; **United Nations—Officials and employees**; etc. [to be added as needed]
    BT   **Administrative law**
          Political science
          Public administration
    NT   **Municipal officials and employees**
    RT   **Bureaucracy**
          Public officers

Civil service—Examinations   351.076
    BT   **Examinations**

Civil service—United States   351.73
    UF   United States—Civil service
    RT   **United States—Officials and employees**

Civil War—England
    USE   **Great Britain—History—1642-1660, Civil War and Commonwealth**

Civil War—United States
    USE   **United States—History—1861-1865, Civil War**

Civilian defense
    USE   **Civil defense**

Civilian evacuation
    USE   **Evacuation of civilians**
          World War, 1939-1945—Evacuation of civilians

Civilian relief
    USE   names of wars with the subdivision *Civilian relief,* e.g. **World War, 1939-1945—Civilian relief** [to be added as needed]

Civilization   306; 909
    Use for materials on civilization in general and on the development of social customs, art, industry, religion, etc., of several countries or peoples.
    SA   names of continents, regions, countries, states, etc., with the subdivision *Civilization,* e.g. **United States—Civilization**; and the civilizations of peoples not confined to a single place, e.g. **Arab civilization**; **Western civilization**; etc. [to be added as needed]
    NT   **Acculturation**
          Aeronautics and civilization
          Africa—Civilization
          America—Civilization
          Ancient civilization
          Arabic civilization
          Asia—Civilization
          Astronautics and civilization
          Bronze Age
          Celtic civilization
          Christian civilization
          Computers and civilization
          Education
          Iron Age
          Islamic civilization
          Jewish civilization
          Learning and scholarship
          Manners and customs
          Medieval civilization
          Modern civilization
          Ohio—Civilization
          Primitive societies
          Progress
          Religions
          Renaissance
          Science and civilization
          Social sciences
          Stone Age
          Technology and civilization
          United States—Civilization
          War and civilization
          Western civilization
    RT   **Anthropology**
          Culture
          Ethnology
          History
          Sociology

Civilization, Ancient
    USE   **Ancient civilization**

Civilization and aeronautics
    USE   **Aeronautics and civilization**

Civilization and astronautics
    USE   **Astronautics and civilization**

Civilization and computers
    USE   **Computers and civilization**

Civilization and science
    USE   **Science and civilization**
Civilization and technology
    USE   **Technology and civilization**
Civilization and war
    USE   **War and civilization**
Civilization, Arab
    USE   **Arabic civilization**
Civilization, Christian
    USE   **Christian civilization**
Civilization, Classical
    USE   **Classical civilization**
Civilization, Greek
    USE   **Greece—Civilization**
Civilization, Medieval
    USE   **Medieval civilization**
Civilization, Modern
    USE   **Modern civilization**
Civilization, Oriental
    USE   **Asia—Civilization**
Civilization, Western
    USE   **Western civilization**
Claims
    USE   ethnic groups, places, and wars
          with the subdivision *Claims,*
          e.g. **Native Americans—**
          Claims [to be added as need-
          ed]

Clairvoyance   133.8
    BT   **Extrasensory perception**
          Occultism
    RT   **Telepathy**
Clairvoyants
    USE   **Psychics**
Clans (May subdiv. geog.)   **306.85; 941.1**
    SA   names of clans or of families
          [to be added as needed]
    BT   **Family**
    NT   **Tribes**
    RT   **Kinship**
Clans—Scotland   941.1
    UF   Highland clans
          Scottish clans
    NT   **Tartans**
Class action lawsuits
    USE   **Class actions (Civil procedure)**
Class actions (Civil procedure) (May
    subdiv. geog.)   **347**
    UF   Class action lawsuits
    BT   **Litigation**

Class conflict
    USE   **Social conflict**
Class consciousness   305.5
    BT   **Social classes**
          Social psychology
    RT   **Marxism**
Class distinction
    USE   **Social classes**
Class struggle
    USE   **Social conflict**
Classed catalogs
    USE   **Classified catalogs**
Classes (Mathematics)
    USE   **Set theory**
Classes of persons
    USE   **Persons**
          and classes of persons, e.g. **El-**
          derly; Handicapped; Explor-
          ers; Drug addicts; etc. [to be
          added as needed]
Classic automobiles
    USE   **Antique and classic cars**
Classic cars
    USE   **Antique and classic cars**
Classic motorcycles
    USE   **Antique and vintage motorcy-**
          cles
Classical antiquities   937; 938
    UF   Classical archeology
          Greek antiquities
          Roman antiquities
    SA   names of extinct cities of Greek
          and Roman antiquity e.g. **Del-**
          phi (Extinct city); and names
          of groups of people extant in
          modern times and names of
          cities (except extinct cities),
          countries, regions, etc., with
          the subdivision *Antiquities* [to
          be added as needed]
    BT   **Antiquities**
    NT   **Greece—Antiquities**
          Greek art
          Roman art
          Rome—Antiquities
          Rome (Italy)—Antiquities
Classical antiquities—Dictionaries
    USE   **Classical dictionaries**
Classical archeology
    USE   **Classical antiquities**

Classical art
  USE   **Greek art**
        Roman art
Classical biography
  USE   **Greece—Biography**
        Rome—Biography
Classical civilization (May subdiv. geog.)
        937

  Use for materials on both ancient Greek and Roman civilizations. Materials on the spread of Greek civilization throughout the ancient world following the conquests of Alexander the Great are entered under **Hellenism**.

  UF   Civilization, Classical
  BT   **Ancient civilization**
  NT   **Greece—Civilization**
       Rome—Civilization
  RT   **Classicism**
Classical dictionaries   937.003; 938.003
  UF   Classical antiquities—Dictionaries
       Dictionaries, Classical
  BT   **Ancient history**
       Encyclopedias and dictionaries
Classical drama   882
  UF   Greek and Latin drama
  BT   **Classical literature**
       Drama
Classical education   370.11
  BT   **Education**
  RT   **Humanism**
       Humanities
Classical geography
  USE   **Ancient geography**
        Greece—Historical geography
        Rome—Geography
Classical languages
  USE   **Greek language**
        Latin language
Classical literature   870; 880
  BT   **Literature**
  NT   **Classical drama**
  RT   **Greek literature**
       Latin literature
Classical music
  USE   **Music**
Classical mythology   292.1
  UF   Mythology, Classical
  BT   **Mythology**
  NT   **Greek mythology**
       Roman mythology
Classicism   709; 809

  BT   **Aesthetics**
       Literature
  NT   **Classicism in architecture**
  RT   **Classical civilization**
Classicism in architecture   723; 724
  BT   **Architecture**
       Classicism
Classification   001

  Use for materials on the organization of knowledge into a systematic arrangement of topics or categories. Materials on the classification of library materials are entered under **Library classification**, which may be subdivided by the type of literature or the subject of the materials classified.

  UF   Classification of knowledge
  SA   subjects with the subdivision
       Classification, e.g. **Botany—Classification** [to be added as needed]
  NT   **Botany—Classification**
       Library classification
Classification—Books
  USE   **Library classification**
Classification—Botany
  USE   **Botany—Classification**
Classification, Dewey Decimal
  USE   **Dewey Decimal Classification**
Classification of knowledge
  USE   **Classification**
Classification—Plants
  USE   **Botany—Classification**
Classified catalogs   017; 025.3
  UF   Catalogs, Classified
       Classed catalogs
  BT   **Library catalogs**
  RT   **Library classification**
Classroom management   371.102
  BT   **School discipline**
       Teaching
Clay   553.6; 666; 738.1
  BT   **Ceramics**
       Soils
  NT   **Modeling**
Clay industries
  USE   **Clay industry**
Clay industry (May subdiv. geog.)
        338.4; 666
  UF   Clay industries
  BT   **Ceramic industry**
  NT   **Pottery**
Clay modeling
  USE   **Modeling**

Cleaning   648; 667
SA   topics with the subdivision
     Cleaning, e.g. **Rugs and car-
     pets—Cleaning** [to be added
     as needed]
BT   **Sanitation**
NT   **Bleaching**
     Cleaning compounds
     Dry cleaning
     House cleaning
     Laundry
     Street cleaning
Cleaning compounds   648; 667
BT   **Cleaning**
NT   **Detergents**
     Soap
Cleanliness   391.6; 613
UF   Neatness
BT   **Hygiene**
     Sanitation
NT   **Baths**
Clearing of land
USE   **Reclamation of land**
Clemency   364.6
BT   **Administration of criminal jus-
     tice**
     Executive power
RT   **Amnesty**
     Forgiveness
     Pardon
Clergy (May subdiv. geog.)   **200.92;
     270.092**
UF   Curates
     Ministers of the gospel
     Pastors
     Preachers
     Rectors
SA   church denominations with the
     subdivision *Clergy*, e.g. **Cath-
     olic Church—Clergy** [to be
     added as needed]
BT   **Church**
NT   **Bishops**
     Catholic Church—Clergy
     Celibacy
     Chaplains
     Priests
     Rabbis
     Televangelists
     Women clergy

RT   **Ministry**
     Ordination
     Pastoral theology
Clergy—Office
USE   **Ministry**
Clergy—Political activity   201; 261.7
BT   **Political participation**
Clerical celibacy
USE   **Celibacy**
Clerical employees
USE   **Office workers**
Clerical personnel
USE   **Office workers**
Clerical psychology
USE   **Pastoral psychology**
Clerical work—Training
USE   **Business education**
Clerks
USE   **Office workers**
Clerks (Retail trade)
USE   **Sales personnel**
Cliff dwellers and cliff dwellings (May
     subdiv. geog.)   **979**
BT   **Archeology**
     **Native Americans—Southwest-
     ern States**
Climacteric, Female
USE   **Menopause**
Climacteric, Male
USE   **Male climacteric**
Climate   551.6
Use for materials on climate as it relates to
humans and to plant and animal life, including
the effects of changes of climate. Materials
limited to the climate of a particular region
are entered under the name of the place with
the subdivision **Climate**. Materials on the
state of the atmosphere at a given time and
place with respect to heat or cold, wetness or
dryness, calm or storm, are entered under
Weather. Scientific materials on the atmosphere, especially weather factors, are entered
under **Meteorology**.
UF   Climatology
SA   names of countries, cities, etc.,
     with the subdivision *Climate*
     [to be added as needed]
BT   **Earth sciences**
NT   **Chicago (Ill.)—Climate**
     Desertification
     Forest influences
     Greenhouse effect
     Ohio—Climate
     Seasons
     United States—Climate

Climate—*Continued*
>RT **Meteorology**
>**Weather**

Climate and forests
>USE **Forest influences**

Climatology
>USE **Climate**

Climbing plants   582.1; 635.9
>UF Vines
>BT **Gardening**
>**Plants**

Clinical chemistry   616.07
>Use for materials on the chemical diagnosis of disease and health monitoring.
>UF Chemistry, Diagnostic
>Chemistry, Medical
>Diagnostic chemistry
>Medical chemistry
>BT **Biochemistry**
>**Diagnosis**

Clinical drug trials
>USE **Drugs—Testing**

Clinical genetics
>USE **Medical genetics**

Clinical records
>USE **Medical records**

Clinical trials of drugs
>USE **Drugs—Testing**

Clinics
>USE **Health facilities**
>**Medical practice**

Clip art   741.6
>Use for materials on clipping art work from published sources to use in creating documents, posters, newsletters, etc. Materials on the use of photocopying machines to create original works of art are entered under **Copy art**.
>BT **Graphic arts**

Clipper ships   387.2; 623.82
>BT **Ships**

Clippings (Books, newspapers, etc.)
>025.17
>UF Newspaper clippings
>Press clippings
>BT **Newspapers**

Clitoridotomy
>USE **Female circumcision**

Clocks and watches (May subdiv. geog.)
>681.1; 739.3
>UF Horology
>Watches
>BT **Time**

NT **Sundials**

Clog dancing   793.3
>UF Clog-dancing
>Clogging (Dance)
>BT **Dance**

Clog-dancing
>USE **Clog dancing**

Clogging (Dance)
>USE **Clog dancing**

Cloisters
>USE **Convents**
>**Monasteries**

Clones and cloning
>USE **Cloning**

Cloning   571.8; 660.6
>UF Clones and cloning
>BT **Genetic engineering**
>NT **Human cloning**
>**Molecular cloning**

Cloning—Ethical aspects   174
>BT **Ethics**

Closed caption television   384.55
>BT **Deaf**
>**Television**

Closed caption video recordings   384.55
>UF Video recordings, Closed caption
>Video recordings for the hearing impaired
>BT **Deaf**
>**Videodiscs**
>**Videotapes**

Closed-circuit television   384.55
>UF Television, Closed-circuit
>BT **Intercommunication systems**
>**Microwave communication systems**
>**Television**

Closed shop
>USE **Open and closed shop**

Closing of factories
>USE **Plant shutdowns**

Cloth
>USE **Fabrics**

Clothes
>USE **Clothing and dress**

Clothiers
>USE **Clothing industry**

Clothing
>USE types of clothing articles and accessories; costume of particular ethnic groups, e.g. **Native**

Clothing—*Continued*

American costume; and professions and classes of persons with the subdivision *Clothing,* e.g. **Handicapped—Clothing** [to be added as needed]

Clothing and dress (May subdiv. geog.) **391; 646.4**

Use for materials on clothing and the art of dress from day to day in practical situations, including historical dress and the clothing of various professions or classes of persons. Materials on the characteristic costume of ethnic groups and on fancy dress and theatrical costumes are entered under **Costume**. Materials on the prevailing mode or style of dress are entered under **Fashion**.

UF Clothes

Dress

Garments

Style in dress

SA types of clothing articles and accessories; costume of particular ethnic groups, e.g. **Native American costume**; and professions and classes of persons with the subdivision *Clothing,* e.g. **Handicapped—Clothing** [to be added as needed]

BT **Manners and customs**

NT **Buttons**

Children's clothing

Dress accessories

Dressmaking

Fans

Fashion

Handicapped—Clothing

Hats

Hosiery

Infants' clothing

Jewelry

Leather garments

Men's clothing

Shoes

T-shirts

Tailoring

Umbrellas and parasols

Uniforms

Wigs

Women's clothing

RT **Clothing industry**

Costume

Personal appearance

Personal grooming

Clothing and dress—Dry cleaning

USE **Dry cleaning**

Clothing and dress—France 391

Use for materials on day to day dress in France.

Clothing and dress—France—History 391

Use for materials on day to day dress in France in the past.

Clothing and dress—History 391

Use for materials on day to day dress in the past.

Clothing and dress—Repairing 646.2

UF Mending

Clothing and dress—Social aspects 391

NT **Dress codes**

Clothing designers

USE **Fashion designers**

Clothing industry (May subdiv. geog.) **338.4; 687**

UF Clothiers

Clothing trade

Fashion industry

Garment industry

BT **Industries**

NT **Dressmaking**

Fashion design

Shoe industry

Tailoring

RT **Clothing and dress**

Clothing trade

USE **Clothing industry**

Cloud seeding

USE **Weather control**

Clouds 551.57

BT **Atmosphere**

Meteorology

Clowns 791.3; 791.3092; 920

BT **Circus**

Entertainers

Clubs (May subdiv. geog.) **367**

BT **Associations**

NT **Book clubs (Discussion groups)**

Boys' clubs

Girls' clubs

Men—Societies

Scouts and scouting

Women—Societies

RT **Societies**

Co-dependence
USE **Codependency**
Co-dependency
USE **Codependency**
Co-ops
USE **Cooperative societies**
Co-ops (Housing)
USE **Cooperative housing**
Co-parenting
USE **Part-time parenting**
Coaching
USE **Coaching (Athletics)**
Horsemanship
and types of sports with the subdivision *Coaching* [to be added as needed]
Coaching (Athletics)   796.07
UF   Athletic coaching
Coaching
Sports coaching
SA   types of sports with the subdivision *Coaching* [to be added as needed]
BT   **Athletics**
Physical education
Sports
NT   **Football—Coaching**
Coal (May subdiv. geog.)   **553.2**
BT   **Fuel**
NT   **Coal gasification**
Coal liquefaction
Coal mines and mining
Coal gas
USE   **Gas**
Coal gasification   **665.7**
UF   Gasification of coal
BT   **Coal**
Coal liquefaction   **622**
UF   Liquefaction of coal
BT   **Coal**
Coal miners   **622; 920**
BT   **Miners**
Coal mines and mining (May subdiv. geog.)   **622**
BT   **Coal**
Mines and mineral resources
NT   **Mining engineering**
Coal oil
USE   **Petroleum**
Coal tar products   547; 661
BT   **Petroleum**

RT   **Gas**
COAs
USE   **Children of alcoholics**
Coast ecology
USE   **Coastal ecology**
Coast pilot guides
USE   **Pilot guides**
Coastal ecology (May subdiv. geog.)
577.5
UF   Coast ecology
Coastal zone ecology
BT   **Ecology**
Coastal landforms
USE   **Coasts**
Coastal signals
USE   **Signals and signaling**
Coastal zone ecology
USE   **Coastal ecology**
Coastal zone management (May subdiv. geog.)   **333.91**
BT   **Coasts**
Regional planning
Coasts (May subdiv. geog.)   **551.45**
UF   Coastal landforms
BT   **Landforms**
NT   **Coastal zone management**
RT   **Seashore**
Coats of arms
USE   **Heraldry**
Cocaine   362.29; 615
BT   **Narcotics**
NT   **Crack (Drug)**
Cocaine babies
USE   **Children of drug addicts**
Cockroaches (May subdiv. geog.)   **595.7**
UF   Roaches (Insects)
BT   **Insects**
Cocoa   633.7; 641.3
BT   **Beverages**
RT   **Chocolate**
Cocoons
USE   **Butterflies**
Caterpillars
Moths
Silkworms
Code deciphering
USE   **Cryptography**
Code enciphering
USE   **Cryptography**
Code names   423

Code names—*Continued*
  BT **Abbreviations**
      Names
  NT **Acronyms**
Codependency 616.86
  UF Co-dependence
      Co-dependency
      Codependent behavior
  BT **Abnormal psychology**
Codependent behavior
  USE **Codependency**
Codes
  USE **Ciphers**
Codes, Penal
  USE **Criminal law**
Codes, Telegraph
  USE **Cipher and telegraph codes**
Coeducation (May subdiv. geog.)
      371.822
  BT **Education**
  RT **Boys—Education**
      Girls—Education
      Men—Education
      Women—Education
Coffee 633.7; 641.8
  BT **Beverages**
  RT **Coffee industry**
Coffee bars
  USE **Coffeehouses**
Coffee houses
  USE **Coffeehouses**
Coffee industry (May subdiv. geog.)
      338.1; 338.4
  UF Coffee trade
  BT **Beverage industry**
  NT **Coffeehouses**
  RT **Coffee**
Coffee shops
  USE **Restaurants**
Coffee trade
  USE **Coffee industry**
Coffeehouses (May subdiv. geog.)
      647.95
  Use for materials on public establishments
  devoted primarily to serving coffee. Materials
  on coffee shops and cafes as small inexpen-
  sive restaurants are entered under **Restau-
  rants.**
  UF Cafes
      Coffee bars
      Coffee houses
  BT **Coffee industry**
      Restaurants

Cog wheels
  USE **Gearing**
Cognition
  USE **Theory of knowledge**
Cognitive styles 153; 370.15
  BT **Intellect**
      Theory of knowledge
**Cognitive styles in children 155.4;
      370.15**
  BT **Child psychology**
Cohabitation
  USE **Unmarried couples**
Cohousing
  USE **Cooperative housing**
Coiffure
  USE **Hair**
Coin collecting
  USE **Coins—Collectors and collect-
        ing**
Coinage (May subdiv. geog.) **332.4**
  Use for materials on the processing and his-
  tory of metal money. Lists of coins and gener-
  al materials about coins are entered under
  Coins.
  BT **Money**
  NT **Counterfeits and counterfeiting**
  RT **Gold**
      Mints
      Silver
Coinage of words
  USE **New words**
Coins (May subdiv. geog.) **737.4**
  Use for lists of coins and general materials
  about coins. Materials on coins from the point
  of view of art and archeology are entered un-
  der **Numismatics.** Materials on the processing
  of metal money are entered under **Coinage.**
  UF Specie
  BT **Money**
Coins—Collectors and collecting 737.4
  UF Coin collecting
  RT **Numismatics**
Cold 536; 551.5
  NT **Cryobiology**
      Ice
  RT **Low temperatures**
      Temperature
Cold (Disease) 616.2
  UF Common cold
  BT **Communicable diseases**
      Diseases
Cold—Physiological effect 613
  BT **Cryobiology**
Cold storage 641.4; 664

Cold storage—*Continued*

    BT   **Food—Preservation**

    NT   **Compressed air**

    RT   **Refrigeration**

Cold—Therapeutic use   **615.8**

    UF   Cryotherapy

    BT   **Therapeutics**

    NT   **Cryosurgery**

Cold war   **909.82**

    UF   Power politics

    BT   **World politics—1945-1991**

Collaborationists (May subdiv. geog.) **364.1**

    UF   Collaborators (Traitors)

    SA   names of wars with the subdivision *Collaborationists*, e.g. **World War, 1939-1945—Collaborationists** [to be added as needed]

    BT   **Traitors**

    NT   **World War, 1939-1945—Collaborationists**

Collaborators (Traitors)

    USE   **Collaborationists**

Collage   **702.8; 751.4**

    BT   **Art**

           Handicraft

Collapse of structures

    USE   **Structural failures**

Collectables

    USE   **Collectibles**

Collected papers (Anthologies)

    USE   **Anthologies**

Collected works

    USE   **Anthologies**

           Literature—Collections

           Storytelling—Collections

           and form headings for minor literary forms that represent collections of works of several authors, e.g. **Essays; American essays; Parodies; Short stories;** etc.; major literary forms and national literatures with the subdivision *Collections,* e.g. **Poetry—Collections; English literature—Collections;** etc.; and subjects with the subdivision *Literary collections,* for collections focused on a single subject by

two or more authors involving two or more literary forms, e.g. **Cats—Literary collections** [to be added as needed]

Collectible card games   **795.4**

    UF   Trading card games

    BT   **Card games**

Collectibles (May subdiv. geog.) **745.1**

    Use for materials on any objects of interest to collectors, including mass produced items of little intrinsic value. Materials on old decorative or utilitarian objects that have aesthetic or historical importance and financial value are entered under **Antiques**.

    UF   Collectables

           Memorabilia

    SA   subjects and names with the subdivision *Collectibles*, e.g. **American Revolution Bicentennial, 1776-1976—Collectibles**; and types of objects collected, excluding antiquities and natural objects, with the subdivision *Collectors and collecting,* e.g. **Boxes—Collectors and collecting** [to be added as needed]

    BT   **Collectors and collecting**

    NT   **Trading cards**

           Victoriana

Collecting

    USE   **Collectors and collecting**

Collecting of accounts   **658.8**

    UF   Accounts, Collecting of

           Bill collecting

           Collection of accounts

    BT   **Commercial law**

           Credit

           Debt

           Debtor and creditor

Collection and preservation

    USE   types of antiquities and types of natural objects, including animal specimens and plant specimens, with the subdivision *Collection and preservation,* e.g. **Birds—Collection and preservation;** for materials on methods of collecting and preserving those objects [to be added as needed]

Collection development (Libraries)
USE **Libraries—Collection development**
Collection of accounts
USE **Collecting of accounts**
Collections
USE form headings for minor literary
forms that represent collections of works of several authors, e.g. **Essays; American
essays; Parodies; Short stories;** etc.; major literary forms
and national literatures with
the subdivision *Collections,*
e.g. **Poetry—Collections; English literature—Collections;**
etc.; and subjects with the
subdivision *Literary collections,* for collections focused
on a single subject by two or
more authors involving two or
more literary forms, e.g.
Cats—Literary collections [to
be added as needed]
Collections (Anthologies)
USE **Anthologies**
Collections of art, painting, etc.
USE **Art collections
Art museums**
Collections of literature
USE **Anthologies
Literature—Collections
Storytelling—Collections**
and form headings for minor
literary forms that represent
collections of works of several authors, e.g. **Essays;
American essays; Parodies;
Short stories;** etc.; major literary forms and national literatures with the subdivision
Collections, e.g. **Poetry—Collections; English literature—
Collections;** etc.; and subjects
with the subdivision *Literary
collections,* for collections focused on a single subject by
two or more authors involving
two or more literary forms,
e.g. **Cats—Literary collections** [to be added as needed]

Collections of natural specimens
USE **Plants—Collection and preservation
Zoological specimens—Collection and preservation**
and types of natural specimens
with the subdivision *Collection and preservation,* e.g.
**Birds—Collection and pres-
ervation** [to be added as
needed]
Collections of objects
USE **Collectors and collecting**
and subjects and names with
the subdivision *Collectibles,*
e.g. **American Revolution Bicentennial, 1776-1976—Collectibles;** and types of objects
collected, excluding antiquities
and natural objects, with the
subdivision *Collectors and
collecting,* e.g. **Boxes—Collectors and collecting** [to be
added as needed]
Collective bargaining (May subdiv. geog.)
331.89; 658.3
May be subdivided by groups of profession-
al or nonprofessional workers, e.g. **Collective
bargaining—Librarians**.
UF Labor negotiations
BT **Industrial relations
Labor
Labor disputes
Negotiation**
RT **Industrial arbitration
Labor contract
Labor unions
Participative management
Strikes**
**Collective bargaining—Librarians
331.89**
UF Librarians—Collective bargaining
Libraries—Collective bargaining
Collective farms
USE **Collective settlements
Cooperative agriculture**
Collective identity
USE **Group identity**
Collective labor agreements
USE **Labor contract**
Collective security
USE **International security**

Collective settlements (May subdiv. geog.)
307.77; 335

Use for materials on traditional, formally organized communal ventures, usually based on ideological, political, or religious affiliation. Materials on arrangements in voluntary cooperative living, usually informal, are entered under **Communal living**.

- UF Collective farms
  Communal settlements
  Communes
  Cooperative living
- SA names of individual collective settlements [to be added as needed]
- BT **Communism**
  Cooperation
  Socialism
- RT **Communal living**
  Cooperative agriculture
  Counter culture
  Utopias

Collective settlements—Israel   307.77

- UF Israel—Collective settlements
  Kibbutz

**Collective settlements—United States
307.77**

Collectivism (May subdiv. geog.)
320.53; 335

- BT **Economics**
  Political science
- NT **Communism**
  Socialism

Collectors and collecting (May subdiv.
geog.)   **790.1**

- UF Collecting
  Collections of objects
- SA types of collecting, e.g. **Book collecting**; types of objects collected, excluding antiquities and natural objects, with the subdivision *Collectors and collecting*, e.g. **Postcards—Collectors and collecting**; names of original owners of private art collections with the subdivision *Art collections*; subjects and names with the subdivision *Collectibles*, e.g. **American Revolution Bicentennial, 1776-1976—Collectibles**; and antiquities and types of natural objects with the subdivision *Collection and preservation*, e.g. **Birds—Collection and preservation** [to be added as needed]

- BT **Antiques**
  Art
  Hobbies
- NT **American Revolution Bicentennial, 1776-1976—Collectibles**
  Americana
  Antiques
  Antiquities—Collection and preservation
  Book collecting
  Boxes—Collectors and collecting
  Collectibles
  Plants—Collection and preservation
  Stamp collecting
  Zoological specimens—Collection and preservation
- RT **Art collections**

Collects
- USE **Prayers**

College admissions essays
- USE **College applications**

College and school drama   371.8; 792

Use for materials about college and school drama. Individual works, collections, and materials about plays for children are entered under **Children's plays**. Plays for children on a particular theme are entered under subjects and personal, corporate, and place names with the subdivision *Juvenile drama*.

- UF College drama
  School plays
- BT **Amateur theater**
  Drama
  Student activities
- RT **Drama in education**

College and school journalism   371.8

- UF College journalism
  College periodicals
  School journalism
  School newspapers
- BT **Journalism**
  Student activities
- RT **Children's writings**

College and university libraries
- USE **Academic libraries**

College applications   378.1

College applications—*Continued*
    UF   Admissions applications
          Admissions essays
          Applications for college
          College admissions essays
          Colleges and universities—Applications
    RT   **Colleges and universities—Entrance requirements**
College athletics
    USE **College sports**
College choice   378
    UF   Choice of college
          Colleges and universities—Selection
    BT   **Colleges and universities**
          School choice
College costs   378.3
    UF   Tuition
    BT   **Colleges and universities—Finance**
    NT   **Student aid**
          Student loan funds
College degrees
    USE **Academic degrees**
College drama
    USE **College and school drama**
College dropouts
    USE **Dropouts**
College entrance examinations
    USE **Colleges and universities—Entrance examinations**
College entrance requirements
    USE **Colleges and universities—Entrance requirements**
College fraternities
    USE **Fraternities and sororities**
College graduates (May subdiv. geog.)
    305.5; 378
    UF   Graduates, College
          University graduates
    BT   **Professions**
    RT   **College students**
College journalism
    USE **College and school journalism**
College libraries
    USE **Academic libraries**
College life
    USE **College students**
College periodicals
    USE **College and school journalism**

College songs
    USE **Students' songs**
College sororities
    USE **Fraternities and sororities**
College sports (May subdiv. geog.)
    371.8; 796
    UF   College athletics
          Intercollegiate athletics
          Varsity sports
    SA   types of sports [to be added as needed]
    BT   **Sports**
          Student activities
    RT   **School sports**
College students (May subdiv. geog.)
    371.8; 378
    UF   College life
          Colleges and universities—Students
          Student life
          Undergraduates
          University students
    BT   **Students**
    RT   **College graduates**
College students, Foreign
    USE **Foreign students**
College students—Political activity
    371.8; 378
    UF   Campus disorders
    BT   **Political participation**
College students—Sexual behavior
    371.8; 378
    BT   **Sex**
College teachers
    USE **Colleges and universities—Faculty**
          Educators
          Teachers
College yearbooks
    USE **School yearbooks**
Colleges and universities (May subdiv. geog.)   **378**
    UF   Universities
          Universities and colleges
    SA   types of colleges and universities, e.g. **Catholic colleges and universities**; and names of individual colleges and universities [to be added as needed]

Colleges and universities—*Continued*
- BT **Education**
   Higher education
   Professional education
   Schools
- NT **Academic degrees**
   Catholic colleges and universities
   College choice
   Commencements
   Fraternities and sororities
   Free universities
   Junior colleges
   Law schools
   Medical colleges
   Teachers colleges
   United States Military Academy
   University extension

Colleges and universities—Accreditation 378; 379.1

Colleges and universities—Applications
- USE **College applications**

Colleges and universities—Buildings 727
- BT **Buildings**

Colleges and universities—Curricula 378.1
- UF Core curriculum
- SA types of education and schools with the subdivision *Curricula*, e.g. **Library education—Curricula** [to be added as needed]
- BT **Education—Curricula**

Colleges and universities—Employees (May subdiv. geog.) **378.1**
- BT **Employees**

Colleges and universities—Employees—Salaries, wages, etc. (May subdiv. geog.) **331.2**
- BT **Salaries, wages, etc.**

Colleges and universities—Endowments 378
- BT **Endowments**

Colleges and universities—Entrance examinations 378.1
- UF College entrance examinations
   Entrance examinations for colleges
- BT **Educational tests and measurements**

Examinations
- NT **Graduate Record Examination**
   Scholastic Assessment Test

Colleges and universities—Entrance requirements 378.1
- UF College entrance requirements
   Entrance requirements for colleges and universities
- SA names of individual colleges and universities with the subdivision *Entrance requirements* [to be added as needed]
- BT **Examinations**
- RT **College applications**

Colleges and universities—Faculty 378.1
- UF College teachers
   Faculty (Education)
- BT **Teachers**

Colleges and universities—Faculty—Pensions 331.25

Colleges and universities—Finance 378.1
- UF Tuition
- BT **Finance**
- NT **College costs**
- RT **Federal aid to education**

Colleges and universities—Insignia 378.2
- BT **Insignia**

Colleges and universities—Selection
- USE **College choice**

Colleges and universities—Students
- USE **College students**

Colleges and universities—United States 378.73

Collies 636.737
- BT **Dogs**

Collisions, Railroad
- USE **Railroad accidents**

Colloids 541
- BT **Physical chemistry**

Colombia 986.1
   May be subdivided like **United States** except for *History.*

Colonial architecture
- USE **American colonial style in architecture**
   Architecture—United States—1600-1775, Colonial period

Colonial history (U.S.)
　　USE　**United States—History—1600-1775, Colonial period**
Colonialism
　　USE　**Colonies**
　　　　　Imperialism
Colonies　321; 325
　　Use for materials on general colonial policy. Materials on the policy of settling immigrants or nationals abroad are entered under **Colonization**. Materials on migration from one country to another are entered under **Immigration and emigration**. Materials on the movement of population within a country for permanent settlement are entered under **Internal migration**.
　　UF　Colonialism
　　　　　Dependencies
　　SA　names of countries with the subdivision *Colonies*, or *Territories and possessions*, e.g.
　　　　　Great Britain—Colonies;
　　　　　United States—Territories and possessions; etc. [to be added as needed]
　　BT　**Imperialism**
　　NT　**Great Britain—Colonies**
　　　　　Land settlement
　　　　　Penal colonies
　　RT　**Colonization**
Colonies, Space
　　USE　**Space colonies**
Colonization　325
　　Use for materials on the policy of settling immigrants or nationals abroad. Materials on general colonial policy are entered under **Colonies**. Materials on migration from one country to another are entered under **Immigration and emigration**. Materials on the movement of population within a country for permanent settlement are entered under **Internal migration**.
　　SA　names of countries with the subdivision *Immigration and emigration*, e.g. **United States—Immigration and emigration** [to be added as needed]
　　BT　**Imperialism**
　　　　　Land settlement
　　NT　**Internal migration**
　　　　　Land grants
　　　　　Public lands
　　RT　**Colonies**
　　　　　Immigration and emigration
Color　752; 535.6; 701
　　UF　Colour

　　SA　subjects with the subdivision *Color*, and names of specific colors [to be added as needed]
　　BT　**Aesthetics**
　　　　　Chemistry
　　　　　Light
　　　　　Optics
　　　　　Painting
　　　　　Photometry
　　NT　**Animals—Color**
　　　　　Birds—Color
　　　　　Dyes and dyeing
　　　　　Red
　　RT　**Pigments**
Color blindness　617.7
　　BT　**Color sense**
　　　　　Vision disorders
Color etchings
　　USE　**Color prints**
Color photography　778.6
　　UF　Color slides
　　　　　Photography, Color
　　BT　**Photography**
Color printing　686.2
　　Use for materials on practical printing in color. Materials on hand-colored prints or on pictures printed in color are entered under **Color prints**.
　　SA　types of color printing processes [to be added as needed]
　　BT　**Printing**
　　NT　**Illustration of books**
　　　　　Lithography
　　　　　Silk screen printing
　　RT　**Color prints**
Color prints　769
　　Use for materials on hand-colored prints or on pictures printed in color. Materials on practical printing in color are entered under **Color printing**.
　　UF　Block printing
　　　　　Color etchings
　　　　　Painting—Color reproductions
　　SA　color prints of particular countries, e.g. **American color prints** [to be added as needed]
　　BT　**Prints**
　　NT　**American color prints**
　　　　　Japanese color prints
　　RT　**Color printing**

Color prints, American
  USE **American color prints**
Color prints, Japanese
  USE **Japanese color prints**
Color—Psychological aspects   **152.14**
  UF Psychology of color
  BT **Color sense**
      Psychology
Color sense   **152.14**
  BT **Psychophysiology**
      Senses and sensation
      Vision
  NT **Color blindness**
      Color—Psychological aspects
Color slides
  USE **Color photography**
       Slides (Photography)
Color television   **621.388**
  BT **Television**
Colorado River—Hoover Dam
  USE **Hoover Dam (Ariz. and Nev.)**
Coloring books   **372.5**
  UF Painting books
  BT **Picture books for children**
Colour
  USE **Color**
Columnists
  USE **Journalists**
Combustion   **541; 621.402**
  BT **Chemistry**
  NT **Fuel**
  RT **Fire**
      Heat
Comedians (May subdiv. geog.)   **791;**
      792.2; 920
  BT **Actors**
      Entertainers
  NT **Fools and jesters**
Comedies   **808.82**
  Use for individual works or for collections.
  Materials about comedy as a literary form are
  entered under **Comedy**.
  UF Comic drama
      Comic plays
      Humorous plays
      Slapstick comedies
  BT **Drama**
      Wit and humor
  NT **Comedy films**
      Comedy television programs
      Farces

Comedy   **792.2; 809.2**
  Use for materials on comedy as a literary
  form. Individual works and collections of
  comedies are entered under **Comedies**.
  UF Comic drama
      Comic literature
  BT **Drama**
      Wit and humor
  NT **Burlesque (Literature)**
      Commedia dell'arte
  RT **Tragicomedy**
Comedy films   **791.43**
  Use for individual works, collections, or
  materials about comedy films.
  UF Comic films
      Humorous films
      Slapstick comedies
  SA types of comedy films, e.g.
      Three Stooges films [to be
      added as needed]
  BT **Comedies**
      Motion pictures
  NT **Three Stooges films**
  RT **Comedy television programs**
Comedy radio programs   **791.44**
  Use for individual works, collections, or
  materials about comedy radio programs.
  UF Radio comedies
      Radio comedy programs
  BT **Radio programs**
Comedy television programs   **791.45**
  Use for individual works, collections, or
  materials about television comedies.
  UF Comic television programs
      Sitcoms
      Situation comedies
      Slapstick comedies
      Television comedies
      Television comedy programs
  BT **Comedies**
      Television programs
  RT **Comedy films**
Comets   **523.6**
  BT **Astronomy**
      Solar system
  NT **Halley's comet**
Comic book novels
  USE **Graphic novels**
Comic books, strips, etc. (May subdiv.
      geog.)   **741.5**
  Use for individual works, collections, or
  materials about printed comic strips, i.e.
  groups of cartoons in narrative sequence, and

Comic books, strips, etc.—*Continued*
books and magazines consisting of comic strips, etc.
    UF   Comic strips
           Funnies
           Humorous pictures
    SA   ethnic groups, classes of persons, corporate bodies, individual persons, literary authors, or sacred works with the subdivision *Comic books, strips, etc.*; and names of comic books, comic strips, and comic strip characters [to be added as needed]
    BT   **Wit and humor**
    NT   **Graphic novels**
           Mystery comic books, strips, etc.
           Science fiction comic books, strips, etc.
           Superhero comic books, strips, etc.
           Western comic books, strips, etc.
    RT   **Cartoons and caricatures**
           Chapbooks
Comic drama
    USE **Comedies**
           Comedy
Comic epic literature
    USE **Mock-heroic literature**
Comic films
    USE **Comedy films**
Comic literature
    USE **Burlesque (Literature)**
           Comedy
           Parody
           Satire
Comic novels
    USE **Humorous fiction**
Comic opera
    USE **Opera**
           Operetta
Comic plays
    USE **Comedies**
Comic strips
    USE **Comic books, strips, etc.**
Comic television programs
    USE **Comedy television programs**
Comic verse
    USE **Humorous poetry**

Coming of age stories
    USE **Bildungsromans**
Commedia dell'arte   792.2
    BT   **Acting**
           Comedy
           Farces
Commemorations
    USE **Anniversaries**
Commencements   394.2
    UF   Graduation
    BT   **Colleges and universities**
           High schools
           School assembly programs
Commentaries
    USE names of sacred works, including named parts of sacred works, with the subdivision *Commentaries,* e.g. **Bible—Commentaries** [to be added as needed]
Commentaries, Biblical
    USE **Bible—Commentaries**
Commerce   381
    Use for general materials on foreign and domestic commerce. Materials limited to commerce between states are entered under **Interstate commerce**.
    UF   Distribution (Economics)
           Trade
    SA   names of countries, cities, etc., with the subdivision *Commerce,* e.g. **United States—Commerce**; and names of articles of commerce, e.g. **Cotton** [to be added as needed]
    BT   **Economics**
           Finance
    NT   **Banks and banking**
           Barter
           Black market
           Boycotts
           Business
           Chambers of commerce
           Chicago (Ill.)—Commerce
           Commercial geography
           Commercial products
           Competition
           Contracts
           Cooperation
           Developing countries—Commerce
           Electronic commerce

Commerce—*Continued*
    Exchange
    Industrial trusts
    International trade
    Interstate commerce
    Marine insurance
    Markets
    Monopolies
    Multinational corporations
    Ohio—Commerce
    Prices
    Profit sharing
    Restraint of trade
    Retail trade
    Stocks
    Tourist trade
    Trade routes
    Trademarks
    United States—Commerce
  RT Transportation
Commerce—Law and legislation
  USE Commercial law
Commercial aeronautics (May subdiv.
    geog.) 387.7
  UF Aeronautics, Commercial
      Air cargo
      Air freight
      Air transport
      Commercial aviation
  BT Freight
      Transportation
  NT Air mail service
      Airlines
Commercial arithmetic
  USE Business mathematics
Commercial art (May subdiv. geog.)
    741.6
  UF Advertising art
      Art in advertising
  BT Advertising
      Art
      Drawing
  NT Fashion design
      Posters
      Textile design
Commercial art galleries (May subdiv.
    geog.) 338.7; 708
  UF Art galleries
      Picture galleries
  BT Business enterprises
Commercial aviation
  USE Commercial aeronautics

Commercial buildings (May subdiv.
    geog.) 333.33; 725
  UF Mercantile buildings
      Store buildings
  BT Buildings
  NT Shopping centers and malls
      Stores
Commercial catalogs 380.1029; 659.13
  UF Catalogs
      Commercial products—Catalogs
      Mail order catalogs
      Trade catalogs
  SA types of merchandise, objects,
      products, etc., and names of
      individual companies with the
      subdivision *Catalogs* [to be
      added as needed]
  BT Advertising
Commercial correspondence
  USE Business letters
Commercial education
  USE Business education
Commercial employees
  USE Office workers
Commercial endeavors in space
  USE Space industrialization
Commercial fishing (May subdiv. geog.)
    338.3; 639.2
    Use for materials on the fishing industry.
    Materials on the cultivation of fish in captivi-
    ty are entered under **Fish culture**. Materials
    on fishing as a sport are entered under **Fish-
    ing**.
  UF Fisheries
      Fishing, Commercial
      Fishing industry
      Sea fisheries
  BT Industries
  NT Pearl fisheries
      Whaling
Commercial fishing—United States
    338.3; 639.2
Commercial geography 330.9
  UF Economic geography
      World economics
  BT Commerce
      Geography
  NT Trade routes
  RT Economic conditions
Commercial law (May subdiv. geog.)
    346.07
  UF Business law
      Business—Law and legislation

167

Commercial law—*Continued*

Commerce—Law and legislation

Mercantile law

BT **Law**

NT **Antitrust law**

Arbitration and award

Bankruptcy

Collecting of accounts

Contracts

Corporation law

Debtor and creditor

Fraud

Insider trading

Landlord and tenant

Licenses

Negotiable instruments

Restraint of trade

Unfair competition

RT **Maritime law**

Commercial mathematics

USE **Business mathematics**

Commercial paper

USE **Negotiable instruments**

Commercial photography   778

BT **Photography**

NT **Photojournalism**

Commercial policy (May subdiv. geog.)
381.3; 382

Use for general materials on the various regulations by which governments seek to protect and increase the commerce of a country, such as subsidies, tariffs, free ports, etc.

UF Government policy

Government regulation of commerce

Reciprocity

Trade barriers

World economics

BT **Economic policy**

International economic relations

NT **Buy national policy**

Free trade

Protectionism

Tariff

Commercial policy—United States
381.3; 382

UF United States—Commercial policy

Commercial products (May subdiv. geog.)
338; 381

UF Merchandise

Products, Commercial

SA types of products and names of specific products [to be added as needed]

BT **Commerce**

NT **Animal products**

Brand name products

Consumer goods

Forest products

Generic products

Manufactures

Marine resources

New products

Raw materials

Substitute products

Commercial products—Catalogs

USE **Commercial catalogs**

Commercial products recall

USE **Product recall**

Commercial secrets

USE **Trade secrets**

Commercials, Radio

USE **Radio advertising**

Commercials, Television

USE **Television advertising**

Commission government

USE **Municipal government by commission**

Commission government with city manager

USE **Municipal government by city manager**

Common cold

USE **Cold (Disease)**

Common currencies

USE **Monetary unions**

Common law (May subdiv. geog.)   **340.5**

UF Anglo-American law

BT **Law**

Common law marriage

USE **Unmarried couples**

Common market

USE **European Union**

Commonplaces

USE **Terms and phrases**

Commonwealth countries   909

Use for materials dealing collectively with the member countries of the international organization that was founded in 1931 as the British Commonwealth of Nations, changed its name to the Commonwealth of Nations in 1950, and became known as the Commonwealth in 1969.

Commonwealth countries—*Continued*
- UF   British Commonwealth countries
British Commonwealth of Nations
British Dominions
Commonwealth of Nations
Dominions, British
- RT   **Great Britain—Colonies**

Commonwealth of England
- USE   **Great Britain—History—1642-1660, Civil War and Commonwealth**

Commonwealth of Independent States
947.086

Use for materials specifically on the federation of independent former Soviet republics that was established in December 1991 and does not include the Baltic states. General materials on several or all of the countries that emerged from the dissolution of the Soviet Union in 1991 are entered under **Former Soviet republics**.
- UF   CIS
- RT   **Former Soviet republics**
Russia (Federation)
Soviet Union

Commonwealth of Nations
- USE   **Commonwealth countries**

Commonwealth, The
- USE   **Political science**
Republics
State, The

Communal living (May subdiv. geog.)
307.77

Use for materials on arrangements in voluntary cooperative living, usually informal. Materials on traditional, formally organized communal ventures, usually based on ideological, political, or religious affiliation are entered under **Collective settlements**.
- UF   Communal settlements
Communes
Cooperative living
Group living
- BT   **Cooperation**
- RT   **Collective settlements**
Cooperative housing
Counter culture

Communal settlements
- USE   **Collective settlements**
Communal living

Communes
- USE   **Collective settlements**
Communal living

Communicable diseases (May subdiv. geog.) **614.4; 616.9**
- UF   Contagion and contagious diseases
Contagious diseases
Infection and infectious diseases
Quarantine
- SA   names of communicable diseases [to be added as needed]
- BT   **Diseases**
Public health
- NT   **AIDS (Disease)**
Cold (Disease)
Fumigation
Germ theory of disease
Influenza
Plague
Rabies
Sexually transmitted diseases
- RT   **Epidemics**
Immunity
Insects as carriers of disease

Communicable diseases—Prevention
614.4
- BT   **Preventive medicine**

Communication **302.2**

Use for general materials on communication in its broadest sense, including the use of the spoken and written word, signs, symbols, or behavior.
- UF   Mass communication
- BT   **Sociology**
- NT   **Audiences**
Books and reading
Conversation
Cybernetics
Deaf—Means of communication
Information science
Language and languages
Language arts
Mass media
Nonverbal communication
Persuasion (Psychology)
Popular culture
Postal service
Public speaking
Signals and signaling
Signs and symbols
Social networking
Telecommunication
Writing

Communication among animals
USE **Animal communication**
Communication arts
USE **Language arts**
Communication disorders (Medicine)
USE **Communicative disorders**
Communication in marriage 646.7
UF Marital communication
BT **Marriage**
Communication satellites
USE **Artificial satellites in telecommunication**
Communication systems
USE subjects with the subdivision
Communication systems, e.g.
Astronautics—Communication systems [to be added as needed]
Communication systems, Wireless
USE **Wireless communication systems**
Communications relay satellites
USE **Artificial satellites in telecommunication**
Communicative disorders 616.85
UF Communication disorders (Medicine)
Disorders of communication
BT **Nervous system—Diseases**
NT **Language disorders**
Speech disorders
Communion
USE **Eucharist**
Communism (May subdiv. geog.) 320.5;
321.9; 324.1; 335.43
UF Bolshevism
SA communism and other subjects,
e.g. **Communism and literature** [to be added as needed]
BT **Collectivism**
Political science
Totalitarianism
NT **Anticommunist movements**
Collective settlements
Communism and literature
Communism and religion
Dialectical materialism
RT **Communist countries**
Marxism
Socialism
Communism and literature 335.4; 809

UF Literature and communism
BT **Communism**
Literature
Communism and religion 261.7; 335.4
UF Communism—Religious aspects
Religion and communism
BT **Communism**
Religion
Communism—Religious aspects
USE **Communism and religion**
Communism—Soviet Union 320.5;
335.430947; 947.084
UF Russian communism
Soviet communism
Soviet Union—Communism
Communism—United States 320.5;
335.43; 973
Communist countries 909
RT **Communism**
Communities, Space
USE **Space colonies**
Community action
USE **Political participation**
Community and libraries
USE **Libraries and community**
Community and school (May subdiv.
geog.) 371.19
UF School and community
BT **Community life**
NT **Parent-teacher associations**
Community based residences
USE **Group homes**
Community centers (May subdiv. geog.)
374; 790.06
UF Neighborhood centers
Play centers
Recreation centers
BT **Cities and towns—Civic improvement**
Community life
Community organization
Recreation
Social settlements
NT **Senior centers**
Youth hostels
RT **Playgrounds**
Community chests
USE **Fund raising**
Community churches (May subdiv. geog.)
254
Use for materials on local churches that
have no denominational affiliations.

Community churches—*Continued*
UF   Churches, Community
     Churches, Undenominational
     Nondenominational churches
     Undenominational churches
     Union churches
BT   **Christian sects**
Community colleges
   USE   **Junior colleges**
Community councils
   USE   **Community organization**
Community development (May subdiv. geog.)   **307.1; 361.6**
UF   Neighborhood development
     Regional development
BT   **Domestic economic assistance**
     Social change
     Urban renewal
NT   **Rural development**
RT   **Agricultural extension work**
     City planning
     Technical assistance
Community health services (May subdiv. geog.)   **362.12**
BT   **Community services**
     Public health
Community history
   USE   **Local history**
Community identity
   USE   **Group identity**
Community life (May subdiv. geog.)   **307**
BT   **Associations**
NT   **Community and school**
     Community centers
     Community organization
     Neighborhood
     Scouts and scouting
Community organization (May subdiv. geog.)   **307**
UF   Community councils
BT   **Community life**
     Social work
NT   **Community centers**
     Local government
RT   **Urban renewal**
Community services (May subdiv. geog.)   **361.7; 361.8**
SA   types of services, e.g. **Community health services** [to be added as needed]
BT   **Social work**

NT   **Community health services**
Community surveys
   USE   **Social surveys**
Community theater
   USE   **Little theater movement**
Compact automobiles
   USE   **Compact cars**
Compact cars   **629.222**
UF   Compact automobiles
     Compacts (Automobiles)
     Economy cars
     Small cars
SA   names of specific makes and models of compact cars [to be added as needed]
BT   **Automobiles**
Compact disc interactive technology
   USE   **CD-I technology**
Compact disc players   **621.389**
UF   Audiodisc players
     CD players
     Digital audio disc players
BT   **Phonograph**
     Sound—Recording and reproducing
Compact disc read-only memory
   USE   **CD-ROMs**
Compact discs   **621.389; 780.26**
   Use for materials on small optical discs in general and on the compact disc format for sound recordings. Materials about sound recordings that emphasize the content of the recording rather than the format are entered under **Sound recordings**.
UF   CDs (Compact discs)
     Compact disks
     Digital compact discs
BT   **Optical storage devices**
     Sound recordings
NT   **CD-I technology**
     CD-ROMs
Compact disks
   USE   **Compact discs**
Compacts (Automobiles)
   USE   **Compact cars**
Companies
   USE   **Business enterprises**
     Corporations
     Partnership
Companion-animal partnership
   USE   **Pet therapy**
Company libraries
   USE   **Corporate libraries**

Company symbols
USE **Trademarks**
Comparative anatomy   571.3
UF   Anatomy, Comparative
BT   **Anatomy**
       Zoology
NT   **Morphology**
Comparative government   320.3
UF   Government, Comparative
SA   names of countries, cities, etc.,
       with the subdivision *Politics
       and government,* e.g. **United
       States—Politics and govern-
       ment** [to be added as needed]
BT   **Political science**
Comparative linguistics
USE **Linguistics**
Comparative literature   809
   This heading may be subdivided by the na-
   tionalities of literatures compared, with dupli-
   cate entry, e.g.**Comparative literature—En-
   glish and German** and **Comparative litera-
   ture—German and English**.
UF   Literature, Comparative
BT   **Literature**
**Comparative literature—English and
   German   809**
**Comparative literature—German and
   English   809**
Comparative morphology
USE **Morphology**
Comparative philology
USE **Linguistics**
Comparative philosophy   100
BT   **Philosophy**
Comparative physiology   571.1
UF   Physiology, Comparative
BT   **Physiology**
Comparative psychology   156
UF   Animal psychology
       Psychology, Comparative
SA   types of animals with the subdi-
       vision *Psychology*, e.g.
       Dogs—Psychology [to be
       added as needed]
BT   **Zoology**
NT   **Dogs—Psychology**
       Sociobiology
RT   **Animal intelligence**
       Instinct
Comparative religion
USE **Christianity and other religions**
       Religions

Comparative studies
USE religious topics and names of
       sacred works and individual
       Christian denominations with
       the subdivision *Comparative
       studies,* e.g. **Mysticism—
       Comparative studies** [to be
       added as needed]
Comparison
USE names of languages with the
       subdivision *Comparison,* e.g.
       **English language—Compari-
       son** [to be added as needed]
Comparison (English grammar)
USE **English language—Comparison**
Comparison of cultures
USE **Cross-cultural studies**
Compass   538; 623.8
UF   Magnetic needle
       Mariner's compass
BT   **Magnetism**
       Navigation
Compassion   177
BT   **Emotions**
Compensation
USE **Pensions**
       Salaries, wages, etc.
       Workers' compensation
Compensatory spending
USE **Deficit financing**
Competence
USE **Performance**
Competition (May subdiv. geog.)   338.6
BT   **Business**
       Business ethics
       Commerce
RT   **Industrial trusts**
       Monopolies
       Supply and demand
Competition, International
USE **International competition**
Competition, Unfair
USE **Unfair competition**
Competitions
USE **Awards**
       Contests
       and subjects with the subdivi-
       sion *Competitions,* e.g. **Liter-
       ature—Competitions** [to be
       added as needed]

Composers (May subdiv. geog.)   **780.92; 920**
  UF   Songwriters
  BT   **Musicians**
Composers, American
  USE **Composers—United States**
Composers—United States   **780.92; 920**
  UF   American composers
       Composers, American
Composition
  USE types of natural substances of
       unfixed composition, including
       soils, plants and crops, ani-
       mals, farm products, etc., with
       the subdivision *Composition,*
       for the results of analyses of
       those substances, e.g. **Food—**
       Composition [to be added as
       needed]
Composition and exercises
  USE names of languages with the
       subdivision *Composition and*
       exercises, e.g. **English lan-**
       guage—Composition and ex-
       ercises [to be added as need-
       ed]
Composition (Art)   **701**
  UF   Art—Composition
  BT   **Art**
  NT   **Architecture—Composition,**
       proportion, etc.
  RT   **Painting**
Composition (Music)   **781.3**
  UF   Music—Composition
       Musical composition
       Song writing
       Songwriting
  BT   **Music**
       Music—Theory
  NT   **Counterpoint**
       Harmony
       Instrumentation and orchestra-
       tion
       Musical accompaniment
       Musical form
       Popular music—Writing and
       publishing
Composition of natural substances
  USE types of natural substances of
       unfixed composition, including
       soils, plants and crops, ani-

mals, farm products, etc., with
       the subdivision *Composition*
       for the results of analyses of
       those substances, e.g. **Food—**
       Composition [to be added as
       needed]
Composition (Printing)
  USE **Typesetting**
Composition (Rhetoric)
  USE **Rhetoric**
       and names of languages with
       the subdivision *Composition*
       and exercises, e.g. **English**
       language—Composition and
       exercises [to be added as
       needed]
Compost   **631.8**
  BT   **Fertilizers**
       Soils
  RT   **Organic gardening**
Comprehensive health care organizations
  USE **Health maintenance organiza-**
       tions
Compressed air   **621.5**
  UF   Pneumatic transmission
  BT   **Cold storage**
       Pneumatics
       Power (Mechanics)
Compulsion (Psychology)
  USE **Compulsive behavior**
Compulsive behavior   **616.85**
  UF   Addictive behavior
       Compulsion (Psychology)
  SA   types of compulsive behavior [to
       be added as needed]
  BT   **Abnormal psychology**
       Human behavior
  NT   **Compulsive gambling**
       Exercise addiction
       Workaholism
  RT   **Obsessive-compulsive disorder**
       Twelve-step programs
Compulsive exercising
  USE **Exercise addiction**
Compulsive gambling   **616.85**
  UF   Addiction to gambling
  BT   **Compulsive behavior**
       Gambling
Compulsive working
  USE **Workaholism**
Compulsory education   **379.2**

Compulsory education—*Continued*
- UF   Compulsory school attendance
  - Education, Compulsory
- BT   **Education—Government policy**
- NT   **Evening and continuation schools**
- RT   **School attendance**

Compulsory labor
- USE   **Forced labor**

Compulsory military service
- USE   **Draft**

Compulsory school attendance
- USE   **Compulsory education**
  - **School attendance**

Computation, Approximate
- USE   **Approximate computation**

Computation (Mathematics)
- USE   **Arithmetic**

Computer-aided design   620

Use for materials on the use of computer graphics to design tools, vehicles, buildings, etc.
- UF   CAD
  - Computer aided design
  - Computer-assisted design
  - Electronic design
- BT   **Computer graphics**
  - **Design**
- RT   **Computer-aided design software**

Computer aided design
- USE   **Computer-aided design**

Computer-aided design software   006.6
- UF   CAD/CAM software
  - CAD software
- BT   **Computer software**
- RT   **Computer-aided design**

Computer animation   741.5
- UF   CGI (Cinematography)
  - Computer-generated animation
- BT   **Animation (Cinematography)**

Computer art (May subdiv. geog.)   **776; 700; 760**

Use for materials on the use of computer graphics to create artistic designs, drawings, or other works of art.
- BT   **Art**
  - **Computer graphics**

Computer-assisted design
- USE   **Computer-aided design**

Computer-assisted instruction   371.33

Use for materials on automated instruction in which a student interacts directly with a computer.
- UF   CAI
  - Computer assisted instruction
  - Computers—Educational use
  - Education—Automation
  - Education—Data processing
  - Teaching—Data processing
- SA   subjects with the subdivision *Computer-assisted instruction* [to be added as needed]
- BT   **Programmed instruction**
- NT   **Mathematics—Computer-assisted instruction**

Computer assisted instruction
- USE   **Computer-assisted instruction**

Computer-assisted instruction—Authoring programs   005.5; 371.33

Use for materials on computer programs that allow the user with comparatively little expertise to design customized computer programs for educational purposes.
- UF   Authoring programs for computer-assisted instruction
- BT   **Computer software**

Computer awareness
- USE   **Computer literacy**

Computer-based information systems
- USE   **Information systems**
  - **Management information systems**

Computer-based multimedia information systems
- USE   **Multimedia**

Computer bulletin boards   004.693; 384.3

Use for materials on services that allow users to post messages and retrieve messages from others who have some common interest. Materials on services that allow users to engage in conversations in real time are entered under **Online chat groups**. Materials on services, commonly called electronic mailing lists, that allow subscribers to post messages that are then distributed to other subscribers are entered under **Electronic discussion groups**.
- UF   Electronic bulletin boards
- BT   **Bulletin boards**
- RT   **Electronic discussion groups**
  - **Online chat groups**

Computer control
- USE   **Automation**

Computer crimes (May subdiv. geog.)
    364.16
    UF   Computer fraud
    BT   **Crime**
    NT   **Computer hackers**
          Computer viruses
          Cyberbullying
    RT   **Computer security**
Computer drafting
    USE   **Computer graphics**
Computer drawing
    USE   **Computer graphics**
Computer fonts   **686.2**
    BT   **Type and type-founding**
Computer fraud
    USE   **Computer crimes**
Computer games   **794.8**
    BT   **Computer software**
          Games
Computer-generated animation
    USE   **Computer animation**
Computer graphics   **006.6**
    Use for materials on the production of drawings, pictures, or diagrams, as distinct from letters and numbers, on a computer screen or hard-copy output devices. Materials on the use of computer graphics to create artistic designs, drawings, or other works of art are entered under **Computer art**. Materials on the use of computer graphics to design tools, vehicles, buildings, etc., are entered under **Computer-aided design**.
    UF   Automatic drafting
          Automatic drawing
          Computer drafting
          Computer drawing
          Electronic drafting
          Electronic drawing
          Graphics, Computer
    BT   **Data processing**
    NT   **Computer-aided design**
          Computer art
          Icons (Computer graphics)
Computer hackers   **005.8092**
    BT   **Computer crimes**
          Criminals
Computer hardware
    USE   **Computers**
Computer icons
    USE   **Icons (Computer graphics)**
Computer industry (May subdiv. geog.)
    338.7
    BT   **Industries**
    RT   **Computers**

Computer input-output equipment
    USE   **Computer peripherals**
Computer interfaces   **004.6; 621.39**
    Use for materials on equipment and techniques linking computers to peripheral devices or to other computers.
    UF   Interfaces, Computer
    BT   **Computer peripherals**
Computer keyboarding
    USE   **Keyboarding (Electronics)**
Computer keyboards
    USE   **Keyboards (Electronics)**
Computer languages
    USE   **Programming languages**
Computer literacy   **004**
    Use for materials on the basic knowledge of computers a person needs in order to function in a computer-based society.
    UF   Computer awareness
    BT   **Computers and civilization**
          Literacy
Computer memory systems
    USE   **Computer storage devices**
Computer modeling
    USE   **Computer simulation**
Computer models
    USE   **Computer simulation**
Computer monitors   **004.7**
    Use for materials on video display devices connected to a personal computer.
    UF   CRT display terminals
          Video display terminals
    BT   **Computer peripherals**
Computer music   **786.7**
    BT   **Music**
    RT   **Computer sound processing**
          Electronic music
Computer network resources
    USE   **Internet resources**
Computer networks   **004.6; 384.3**
    Use for materials on systems consisting of two or more interconnected computers.
    UF   Information superhighway
          Networks, Computer
    SA   types of computer networks, names of specific computer networks, and subjects with the subdivision *Computer networks*, e.g. **Business enterprises—Computer networks** [to be added as needed]
    BT   **Data transmission systems**
          Telecommunication

Computer networks—*Continued*
- NT **Business enterprises—Computer networks**
  Cyberspace
  Internet
  Local area networks
- RT **Information networks**

Computer operating systems   005.4
- UF Computers—Operating systems
  Operating systems (Computers)
- BT **Computer software**

Computer peripherals   004.7; 621.39
- UF Computer input-output equipment
  Input equipment (Computers)
  Output equipment (Computers)
- SA types of computer peripherals [to be added as needed]
- BT **Computers**
- NT **Computer interfaces**
  Computer monitors
  Computer storage devices
  Computer terminals
  Keyboards (Electronics)
  Optical scanners

Computer program languages
- USE **Programming languages**

Computer programming   005.1
- UF Computers—Programming
  Programming (Computers)
- SA subjects with the subdivision *Computer software*, e.g. **Database management—Computer software** [to be added as needed]
- BT **Computer science**
  Data processing
- RT **Computer software**
  Programming languages

Computer programs
- USE **Computer software**

Computer science   004

Use for materials discussing collectively the disciplines that deal with the general theory and application of computers.
- BT **Science**
- NT **Artificial intelligence**
  Computer programming
  Database management
- RT **Computers**

Computer science—Dictionaries   004.03
- UF Computer terms
  Computers—Dictionaries

- BT **Encyclopedias and dictionaries**

Computer security   005.8

Use for materials on protecting computer hardware and software from accidental or malicious access, use, modification, disclosure, or destruction.
- UF Computers—Access control
  Computers—Security measures
- BT **Computers**
- RT **Computer crimes**
  Computer viruses

Computer sex   306.7
- UF Cybersex
  On-line sex
  Online sex
- BT **Sex**

Computer simulation   003
- UF Computer modeling
  Computer models
  Simulation, Computer
- SA subjects with the subdivision *Computer simulation*, e.g. **Psychology—Computer simulation** [to be added as needed]
- BT **Mathematical models**
- NT **Psychology—Computer simulation**
  Virtual reality

Computer software   005.3
- UF Computer programs
  Programs, Computer
  Software, Computer
- SA types of computer software, e.g. **Computer games**; **Spreadsheet software**; etc.; subjects with the subdivision *Computer software*, e.g. **Oceanography—Computer software**; and names of individual computer programs qualified by *(Computer software)*, e.g. **Microsoft Word (Computer software)** [to be added as needed]
- NT **Computer-aided design software**
  Computer-assisted instruction—Authoring programs
  Computer games
  Computer operating systems
  Computer viruses

Computer software—*Continued*
       Database management—Computer software
       Educational software
       Free computer software
       Image processing software
       Internet software
       Microsoft Word (Computer software)
       Multimedia
       Oceanography—Computer software
       Open source software
       Programming languages
       Shareware (Computer software)
       Spreadsheet software
       Utilities (Computer software)
       Word processing software
  RT Computer programming
       Computer software industry
       Computers

Computer software industry (May subdiv. geog.) **338.4**
  BT Industries
  RT Computer software

Computer sound processing **006.5**
  UF Sound processing, Computer
  BT Computers
       Sound
  NT MP3 players
  RT Computer music
       Speech processing systems

Computer speech processing systems
  USE Speech processing systems

Computer storage devices **004.5; 621.39**
  UF Computer memory systems
       Computers—Memory systems
       Computers—Storage devices
       Memory devices (Computers)
       Storage devices, Computer
  BT Computer peripherals
  NT Optical storage devices

Computer terminals **004.7; 621.39**
    Use for materials on video display devices connected to a mainframe computer.
  UF Terminals, Computer
  BT Computer peripherals

Computer terms
  USE Computer science—Dictionaries

Computer utility programs
  USE Utilities (Computer software)

Computer viruses **005.8**
  UF Software viruses
       Viruses, Computer
  BT Computer crimes
       Computer software
  RT Computer security

Computerized tomography
  USE Tomography

Computers **004; 621.39**
    Use for materials on modern electronic computers developed after 1945. Materials on present-day calculators and on calculating machines and mechanical computers made before 1945 are entered under **Calculators**.
  UF Computer hardware
  SA types of computers, e.g. **Personal computers**; and names of specific computers [to be added as needed]
  BT Electronic apparatus and appliances
  NT Computer peripherals
       Computer security
       Computer sound processing
       Computers and children
       Computers and civilization
       Computers and the handicapped
       Data processing
       Information systems
       Macintosh (Computer)
       Microprocessors
       Personal computers
       Portable computers
       Supercomputers
  RT Calculators
       Computer industry
       Computer science
       Computer software

Computers—Access control
  USE Computer security

Computers and children **004.083**
  BT Children
       Computers

Computers and civilization **004; 303.48**
  UF Civilization and computers
  BT Civilization
       Computers
       Technology and civilization
  NT Computer literacy

Computers and the handicapped 004.6;
362.4
> BT **Computers**
> **Handicapped**

Computers—Cartoons and caricatures
621.39; 741.5
> BT **Cartoons and caricatures**

Computers—Dictionaries
> USE **Computer science—Dictionaries**

Computers—Educational use
> USE **Computer-assisted instruction**

Computers—Juvenile literature 004

Computers—Memory systems
> USE **Computer storage devices**

Computers—Operating systems
> USE **Computer operating systems**

Computers—Programming
> USE **Computer programming**

Computers—Security measures
> USE **Computer security**

Computers—Storage devices
> USE **Computer storage devices**

Computers—Utility programs
> USE **Utilities (Computer software)**

Con artists
> USE **Swindlers and swindling**

Con game
> USE **Swindlers and swindling**

Concealment
> USE **Secrecy**

Concentration
> USE **Attention**

Concentration camps (May subdiv. geog.)
365
> UF Internment camps
> SA names of wars with the subdivision *Prisoners and prisons*; and names of individual camps [to be added as needed]
> BT **Military camps**
> **Political crimes and offenses**
> NT **World War, 1939-1945—Prisoners and prisons**
> RT **Prisoners of war**

Concept formation
> USE **Concept learning**

Concept learning 153.2; 370.15
> Use for materials on the process of discovering the distinguishing features of particular concepts and the ensuing ability to use the concepts appropriately.

> UF Concept formation
> BT **Concepts**
> **Psychology of learning**

Conception—Prevention
> USE **Birth control**

Concepts 153.2
> SA types of concepts and images, e.g. **Size**; **Shape**; etc. [to be added as needed]
> BT **Perception**
> NT **Concept learning**
> **Opposites**
> **Shape**
> **Size**

Concert halls (May subdiv. geog.) 725
> UF Music-halls
> BT **Auditoriums**

Concerto 784.18
> Use for musical scores and for materials on the concerto as a musical form.
> UF Concertos
> BT **Musical form**
> **Orchestral music**

Concertos
> USE **Concerto**

Concerts 780.78
> BT **Amusements**
> **Music**
> RT **Music festivals**

Concordances 010
> Use for works that list words with references to passages in a text where the exact word occurs. Works that list topics or names with references to books, articles, or passages where those topics or name are to be found are entered under **Indexes**.

> SA names of individual authors, literary works, sacred works, literatures, and literary forms, with the subdivision *Concordances*, e.g. **Shakespeare, William, 1564-1616—Concordances**; **Bible—Concordances**; etc. [to be added as needed]
> BT **Indexes**

Concrete 691; 693
> BT **Building materials**
> **Foundations**
> **Masonry**
> **Plaster and plastering**
> NT **Reinforced concrete**

Concrete—*Continued*

RT Cement

Concrete construction

Concrete building

USE Concrete construction

Concrete construction 693

UF Concrete building

Construction, Concrete

BT Building

RT Concrete

Concrete—Testing 620.1

BT Strength of materials

Condemnation of land

USE Eminent domain

Condensers (Electricity) 621.31

UF Electric condensers

BT Induction coils

Condensers (Steam) 621.1

BT Steam engines

Condominium timesharing

USE Timesharing (Real estate)

Condominiums (May subdiv. geog.)
346.04; 643

BT Apartment houses

NT Timesharing (Real estate)

Conduct of life 170

Use for materials on standards of behavior and materials containing moral guidance and advice to the individual.

UF Morals

Personal conduct

SA classes of persons with the subdivision *Conduct of life*, e.g. **Children—Conduct of life**; and names of vices and virtues [to be added as needed]

BT Ethics

Human behavior

Life skills

NT Altruism

Children—Conduct of life

Fairness

Honor

Pride and vanity

Simplicity

Sympathy

Teenagers—Conduct of life

Vice

Virtue

Conducting 781.45

Use for materials on orchestral conducting or a combination of orchestral and choral con-

ducting. Materials limited to choral conducting are entered under **Choral conducting**.

BT Music

NT Choral conducting

RT Bands (Music)

Conductors (Music)

Orchestra

Conducting, Choral

USE Choral conducting

Conductors, Electric

USE Electric conductors

Conductors (Music) (May subdiv. geog.)
784.2092; 920

UF Bandmasters

Music conductors

BT Musicians

Orchestra

RT Choral conducting

Conducting

Confectionary

USE Confectionery

Confectionery 641.8; 664

UF Confectionary

Sweets

BT Cooking

NT Cake

Cake decorating

Candy

Confederacies

USE Federal government

Confederate States of America 973.7

BT United States—History—1861-1865, Civil War

Confederation of American colonies

USE United States—History—1783-1815

Conference calls (Teleconferencing)

USE Teleconferencing

Conference papers

USE Conference proceedings

Conference proceedings (May subdiv. geog.) 060

Use for materials about the papers and other documents stemming from a conference and for collections of various conference proceedings. Materials about conferences apart from the proceedings are entered under **Conferences**.

UF Conference papers

SA topics and names of corporate bodies with the subdivision *Conference proceedings* [to be added as needed]

Conference proceedings—*Continued*
  BT **Documentation**
  RT **Conferences**
Conferences   060
  Use for materials about conferences, congresses, or conventions. Materials about the papers and other documents stemming from a conference and collections of various conference proceedings are entered under **Conference proceedings**.
  UF Congresses
    Congresses and conventions
    Conventions
    International conferences
  SA subjects and names of corporate bodies with the subdivision *Conferences*, e.g. **World War, 1939-1945—Conferences**; **Physics—Conferences**; names of specific conferences, congresses, or conventions; and subjects and names of corporate bodies with the subdivision *Conference proceedings* [to be added as needed]
  BT **Intellectual cooperation**
    International cooperation
  NT **Constitutional conventions**
    Political conventions
    World War, 1939-1945—Conferences
  RT **Conference proceedings**
Conferences, Parent-teacher
  USE **Parent-teacher conferences**
Confession   265
  UF Auricular confession
  RT **Forgiveness of sin**
    Penance
Confessions of faith
  USE **Creeds**
Confidence game
  USE **Swindlers and swindling**
Configuration (Psychology)
  USE **Gestalt psychology**
Confirmation   265
  BT **Sacraments**
Conflict management (May subdiv. geog.)
  303.6
  UF Conflict resolution
    Dispute settlement
    Management of conflict
  BT **Management**
    Negotiation

Problem solving
    Social conflict
  RT **Crisis management**
Conflict of cultures
  USE **Culture conflict**
Conflict of generations   306.874
  UF Generation gap
  BT **Child-adult relationship**
    Interpersonal relations
    Parent-child relationship
    Social conflict
Conflict of interests (May subdiv. geog.)
  172; 353.4
  BT **Political ethics**
  NT **Misconduct in office**
    Political corruption
Conflict resolution
  USE **Conflict management**
Conflict, Social
  USE **Social conflict**
Conformity   153.8; 302.5; 303.3
  UF Nonconformity
    Social conformity
  BT **Attitude (Psychology)**
    Freedom
  NT **Persuasion (Psychology)**
  RT **Deviant behavior**
    Dissent
    Individuality
Confucianism (May subdiv. geog.)   **181; 299.5**
  BT **Religions**
Congenital diseases
  USE **Medical genetics**
Conglomerate corporations (May subdiv. geog.)   **338.8**
  UF Diversified corporations
  BT **Corporations**
  RT **Corporate mergers and acquisitions**
Congo (Democratic Republic)   967.5
  May be subdivided like **United States** except for *History*.
  UF Democratic Republic of the Congo
    Zaire
Congo (Republic)   967.2
  May be subdivided like **United States** except for *History*.
  UF Republic of the Congo
Congregate housing
  USE **Assisted living**

Congregationalism (May subdiv. geog.)
  285.8
  BT **Christian sects**
  NT **Unitarianism**
  RT **Calvinism**
      Puritans
Congregations
  USE **Religious institutions**
Congress (U.S.)
  USE **United States. Congress**
Congresses
  USE **Conferences**
      and subjects with the subdivision *Conferences,* e.g. **World War, 1939-1945—Conferences; Physics—Conferences;** and names of specific conferences, congresses, or conventions [to be added as needed]
Congresses and conventions
  USE **Conferences**
Congressional investigations
  USE **Governmental investigations**
Conjuring
  USE **Magic tricks**
Conscience **170; 241**
  BT **Christian ethics**
      Duty
      Ethics
  NT **Freedom of conscience**
      Guilt
Conscientious objectors (May subdiv. geog.) **343; 355.2**
  SA names of wars with the subdivision *Conscientious objectors* [to be added as needed]
  BT **Freedom of conscience**
      War—Religious aspects
  NT **World War, 1939-1945—Conscientious objectors**
  RT **Draft resisters**
      Pacifism
Consciousness **126; 153**
  BT **Apperception**
      Mind and body
      Perception
      Psychology
  NT **Gestalt psychology**
      Individuality
      Personality
      Self

      Theory of knowledge
  RT **Subconsciousness**
Consciousness expanding drugs
  USE **Hallucinogens**
Conscript labor
  USE **Forced labor**
Conscription, Military
  USE **Draft**
Conservation and restoration
  USE types of art objects, library materials, architecture, and land vehicles with the subdivision *Conservation and restoration,* e.g. **Automobiles—Conservation and restoration** [to be added as needed]
Conservation movement
  USE **Environmental movement**
Conservation of biodiversity
  USE **Biodiversity conservation**
Conservation of buildings
  USE **Architecture—Conservation and restoration**
Conservation of energy
  USE **Energy conservation**
      Force and energy
Conservation of forests
  USE **Forest conservation**
Conservation of natural resources (May subdiv. geog.) **333.72; 639.9**
  UF Preservation of natural resources
      Resource management
  SA types of conservation, e.g. **Soil conservation** [to be added as needed]
  BT **Environmental protection**
      Natural resources
  NT **Biodiversity conservation**
      Energy conservation
      Forest conservation
      Nature conservation
      Plant conservation
      Soil conservation
      Water conservation
      Wildlife conservation
  RT **Environmental policy**
      National parks and reserves
      Wilderness areas
Conservation of nature
  USE **Nature conservation**

Conservation of photographs
 USE **Photographs—Conservation
  and restoration**
Conservation of plants
 USE **Plant conservation**
Conservation of power resources
 USE **Energy conservation**
Conservation of the soil
 USE **Soil conservation**
Conservation of water
 USE **Water conservation**
Conservation of wildlife
 USE **Wildlife conservation**
Conservation of works of art, books, etc.
 USE subjects with the subdivision
  Conservation and restoration,
  e.g. **Library resources—Con-
  servation and restoration;
  Painting—Conservation and
  restoration;** etc. [to be added
  as needed]
Conservatism (May subdiv. geog.) **320.5**
 UF Reaction (Political science)
  Right (Political science)
 BT **Political science
  Social sciences**
 RT **Right and left (Political sci-
  ence)**
Conservatories, Home
 USE **Garden rooms**
Consolation **152.4; 155.9**
 UF Solace
 BT **Emotions
  Human behavior**
 RT **Bereavement
  Grief**
Consolidation and merger of corporations
 USE **Corporate mergers and acqui-
  sitions**
Consolidation of schools
 USE **Schools—Centralization**
Consortia, Library
 USE **Library cooperation**
Constellations **523.8**
 SA names of constellations [to be
  added as needed]
 BT **Sky**
 RT **Astrology
  Astronomy
  Stars**

Constitution (U.S.)
 USE **United States. Constitution**
Constitutional amendments (May subdiv.
 geog.) **342**
 Use for texts of constitutional amendments
 and materials about constitutional amendments
 and the amending process.
 SA subjects dealt with in constitu-
  tional amendments with the
  subdivision *Law and legisla-
  tion,* or *Legal status, laws,
  etc.* [to be added as needed]
 BT **Constitutional law
  Constitutions**
Constitutional conventions (May subdiv.
 geog.) **342**
 UF Conventions, Constitutional
 BT **Conferences**
Constitutional history (May subdiv. geog.)
 342
 Use for materials on the history of constitu-
 tions. Texts of constitutions are entered under
 Constitutions.
 UF Constitutional law—History
 BT **History**
 NT **Democracy
  Monarchy
  Representative government and
  representation
  Republics**
 RT **Constitutions**
Constitutional history—Ohio **342.771;
 977.1**
 UF Ohio—Constitutional history
 BT **Ohio—History**
**Constitutional history—United States
 342.73; 973**
 UF United States—Constitutional
  history
 BT **United States—History**
Constitutional law (May subdiv. geog.)
 342
 Use for materials on constitutions or consti-
 tutional law. Texts of constitutions are entered
 under **Constitutions**.
 BT **Law**
 NT **Citizenship
  Civil rights
  Constitutional amendments
  Democracy
  Election law
  Eminent domain
  Executive power**

Constitutional law—*Continued*

    Federal government

    Habeas corpus

    Injunctions

    Legislative bodies

    Monarchy

    Proportional representation

    Referendum

    Representative government and representation

    Republics

    Separation of powers

    Suffrage

    War and emergency powers

  RT **Administrative law**

    Constitutions

Constitutional law—History

  USE **Constitutional history**

Constitutional law—Ohio 342.771

  UF Ohio—Constitutional law

Constitutional law—United States
    342.73

  UF United States—Constitutional law

Constitutional rights

  USE **Civil rights**

Constitutions (May subdiv. geog.) **342**

  Use for texts of constitutions. Materials about constitutions are entered under either **Constitutional law** or **Constitutional history**.

  UF State constitutions

  BT **Law**

  NT **Constitutional amendments**

    Equal rights amendments

  RT **Constitutional history**

    Constitutional law

Constitutions—Ohio 342.771

  UF Ohio—Constitution

Constitutions—United States 342.73;
    973

  Use for collections of texts of several state or federal constitutions. Materials about constitutions are entered under either **Constitutional history** or **Constitutional law**. Materials on the United States Constitution alone are entered under **United States—Constitution**.

  UF State constitutions

    United States—Constitutions

Construction

  USE **Architecture**

    Building

    Engineering

Construction, Concrete

  USE **Concrete construction**

Construction contracts 692

  UF Building contracts

    Building—Contracts and specifications

  BT **Contracts**

Construction equipment 621.8

  UF Building machinery

  BT **Machinery**

  NT **Road machinery**

Construction, House

  USE **House construction**

Construction of roads

  USE **Roads**

Consular service

  USE **Diplomatic and consular service**

Consulates

  USE **Diplomatic and consular service**

Consuls (May subdiv. geog.) 327.2092

  BT **Diplomats**

Consultants 001

  UF Advisors

  SA types of consultants [to be added as needed]

  BT **Counseling**

  NT **Business consultants**

    Educational consultants

Consultative management

  USE **Participative management**

Consumer behavior

  USE **Consumers**

Consumer boycotts

  USE **Boycotts**

Consumer credit 332.7

  BT **Banks and banking**

    Credit

    Personal finance

  NT **Credit cards**

    Installment plan

    Personal loans

Consumer demand

  USE **Consumption (Economics)**

Consumer education (May subdiv. geog.)
    640.73

  Use for materials on the selection and efficient use of consumer goods and services and on methods of educating consumers. Materials on the decision-making processes, external factors, and individual characteristics of consumers that determine their purchasing behavior are entered under **Consumers**. Materials on the economic theory of consumption and

Consumer education—*Continued*
on consumerism or consumer demand are entered under **Consumption (Economics)**.

UF Buyers' guides

Consumers' guides

Shoppers' guides

BT **Education**

Home economics

RT **Consumers**

Shopping

Consumer goods (May subdiv. geog.)
338.4

Use for materials on products that are purchased for personal or household purposes.

UF Consumer products

Merchandise

BT **Commercial products**

Manufactures

RT **Consumption (Economics)**

Consumer loans

USE **Personal loans**

Consumer organizations

USE **Cooperative societies**

Consumer price indexes **338.5**

UF Cost of living indexes

Price indexes, Consumer

BT **Cost and standard of living**

Prices

Consumer products

USE **Consumer goods**

Consumer protection (May subdiv. geog.)
343.07; 381.3

Use for materials on governmental and private activities that guard consumers against dangers to their health, safety, or economic well-being.

UF Consumerism

BT **Industrial policy**

NT **Better business bureaus**

Drugs—Testing

Food adulteration and inspection

Product recall

Product safety

Consumer spending

USE **Consumption (Economics)**

Consumerism

USE **Consumer protection**

Consumption (Economics)

Consumers (May subdiv. geog.) **640.73;**
658.8

Use for materials on the decision-making processes, external factors, and individual

characteristics of consumers that determine their purchasing behavior. Materials on the selection and efficient use of consumer goods and services and on methods of educating consumers are entered under **Consumer education**. Materials on the economic theory of consumption and on consumerism or consumer demand are entered under **Consumption (Economics)**.

UF Consumer behavior

NT **Boycotts**

Young consumers

RT **Consumer education**

Consumption (Economics)

Shopping

Consumers' cooperative societies

USE **Cooperative societies**

Consumers' guides

USE **Consumer education**

Consumers—Information services (May
subdiv. geog.) **658.8**

BT **Information services**

Consumption (Economics) (May subdiv.
geog.) **339.4**

Use for materials on the economic theory of consumption and on consumerism or consumer demand. Materials on the decision-making processes, external factors, and individual characteristics of consumers that determine their purchasing behavior are entered under **Consumers**. Materials on the selection and efficient use of consumer goods and services and on methods of educating consumers are entered under **Consumer education**.

UF Consumer demand

Consumer spending

Consumerism

BT **Economics**

NT **Prices**

RT **Consumer goods**

Consumers

Consumption of alcoholic beverages

USE **Drinking of alcoholic beverages**

Consumption of energy

USE **Energy consumption**

Contact lenses **617.7**

BT **Eyeglasses**

Lenses

Contagion and contagious diseases

USE **Communicable diseases**

Contagious diseases

USE **Communicable diseases**

Container gardening **635.9**

BT **Gardening**

RT **Flower gardening**

House plants

Indoor gardening

Container gardening—*Continued*
    Miniature gardens
    Window gardening
Containers   688.8
  BT **Implements, utensils, etc.**
  NT **Baskets**
      Boxes
      Luggage
  RT **Packaging**
Contaminated food
  USE **Food contamination**
Contamination of environment
  USE **Pollution**
Contests   001.4; 790.1
  UF Competitions
  SA types of contests and names of
      specific contests, e.g. **Olym-**
      pic games; and subjects with
      the subdivision *Competitions*
      or *Tournaments*, e.g. **Litera-**
      ture—Competitions; Ten-
      nis—Tournaments [to be
      added as needed]
  NT **Beauty contests**
      Literature—Competitions
      Olympic games
      Sports tournaments
  RT **Awards**
Continental drift   551.1
  UF Drifting of continents
  BT **Continents**
      Geology
  RT **Plate tectonics**
Continental shelf   551.41
  BT **Geology**
  RT **Territorial waters**
Continents   551.41
  BT **Earth**
  NT **Continental drift**
      Lost continents
Continuation schools
  USE **Evening and continuation**
      schools
Continuing care communities
  USE **Life care communities**
Continuing care retirement communities
  USE **Life care communities**
Continuing education (May subdiv. geog.)
    374
  UF Lifelong education
      Permanent education
      Recurrent education

  BT **Education**
  NT **Elderhostels**
      Evening and continuation
      schools
  RT **Adult education**
Contraband trade
  USE **Smuggling**
Contraception
  USE **Birth control**
Contract bridge
  USE **Bridge (Game)**
Contract labor (May subdiv. geog.)
    331.5
  UF Indentured servants
  BT **Labor**
  RT **Peonage**
Contracting for services
  USE **Outsourcing**
Contracting out
  USE **Outsourcing**
Contractions
  USE **Abbreviations**
      Ciphers
Contracts   346.02
  UF Agreements
  SA types of contracts, e.g. **Con-**
      struction contracts [to be
      added as needed]
  BT **Commerce**
      Commercial law
  NT **Authors and publishers**
      Construction contracts
      Covenants
      Labor contract
      Liability (Law)
      Marriage contracts
      Negotiable instruments
      Outsourcing
      Trusts and trustees
Contrition
  USE **Penance**
      Repentance
Control
  USE types of control, e.g. **Flood con-**
      trol; Weather control; etc.,
      and animals, plants, or pro-
      cesses with the subdivision
      Control, e.g. **Mosquitoes—**
      Control [to be added as
      needed]

Control of guns
USE **Gun control**
Controversial literature
USE types of religions, denominations, religious orders, and sacred works with the subdivision *Controversial literature,*
for materials that argue
against or express opposition
to those groups or works, e.g.
**Christianity—Controversial
literature** for materials attacking Christianity; and religions
and denominations with the
subdivision *Apologetic works,*
for materials defending those
religions or denominations,
e.g. **Christianity—Apologetic
works** for materials defending
Christianity [to be added as
needed]
Conundrums
USE **Riddles**
Convenience cooking
USE **Quick and easy cooking**
Convenience foods   641.3; 664
Use for materials on prepackaged foods that
are easy to prepare for eating.
UF Fast foods
BT **Food**
NT **Fast food restaurants**
Conventions
USE **Conferences**
and subjects with the subdivi-
sion *Conferences,* e.g. **World
War, 1939-1945—Confer-
ences; Physics—Conferences;**
and names of specific confer-
ences, congresses, or conven-
tions [to be added as needed]
Conventions, Constitutional
USE **Constitutional conventions**
Conventions, Political
USE **Political conventions**
Convents (May subdiv. geog.)   **271; 726**
UF Cloisters
Nunneries
BT **Monasteries**
NT **Monasticism and religious or-
ders for women**
Conversation   808.56

UF Discussion
Table talk
Talking
BT **Communication
Language and languages**
NT **Discussion groups
Interviews
Online chat groups**
Conversation and phrase books
USE **Modern languages—Conversa-
tion and phrase books**
and names of languages and
groups of languages with the
subdivision *Conversation and
phrase books,* e.g. **English
language—Conversation and
phrase books** [to be added as
needed]
Conversation in foreign languages
USE **Modern languages—Conversa-
tion and phrase books**
Conversations and phrases
USE **Modern languages—Conversa-
tion and phrase books**
Conversion   204; 248.2
BT **Evangelistic work
Salvation
Spiritual life**
NT **Converts**
RT **Regeneration (Christianity)**
Conversion of saline water
USE **Sea water conversion**
Conversion of waste products
USE **Recycling**
Converts   204; 248.2
Use for materials on converts from one reli-
gion or denomination to another.
SA converts to a particular religion
or denomination, e.g. **Con-
verts to Catholicism** [to be
added as needed]
BT **Conversion**
NT **Converts to Catholicism**
Converts to Catholicism   282
UF Catholic Church—Converts
Catholic converts
BT **Catholics
Converts**
Conveying machinery   621.8
UF Conveyors
BT **Machinery
Materials handling**

Conveying machinery—*Continued*
  RT **Hoisting machinery**
Conveyors
  USE **Conveying machinery**
Convict labor (May subdiv. geog.)
       331.5; 365
  UF Prison labor
  BT **Forced labor**
       Prisoners
Convicts
  USE **Criminals**
       Prisoners
Cook books
  USE **Cooking**
Cookbooks
  USE **Cooking**
Cookery
  USE **Cooking**
Cookery, American
  USE **American cooking**
Cookery for the sick
  USE **Cooking for the sick**
Cookery, French
  USE **French cooking**
Cookies   641.8654
  BT **Baking**
       Cooking
Cooking (May subdiv. geog.)   **641.5**
  Use a phrase heading, e.g. **French cooking**;
  Southern cooking; etc., for distinctive nation-
  al or regional styles of cooking. For cooking
  as it is practiced in a particular city, state,
  province, etc., subdivide **Cooking** geographi-
  cally.
  UF Cook books
       Cookbooks
       Cookery
       Food preparation
       Recipes
  SA types of cooking, e.g. **Micro-
       wave cooking**; cooking of
       particular countries or regions,
       e.g. **French cooking; Ameri-
       can cooking; Southern cook-
       ing**; etc.; and, for materials
       on the cooking of specific
       foods or kinds of food, **Cook-
       ing** with a subdivision for the
       food, e.g. **Cooking—Vegeta-
       bles; Cooking—Natural
       foods**; etc. [to be added as
       needed]
  BT **Home economics**

  NT **Afternoon teas**
       American cooking
       Appetizers
       Baking
       Bread
       Breakfasts
       Cake
       Canning and preserving
       Catering
       Chinese cooking
       Christmas cooking
       Confectionery
       Cookies
       Cooking for one
       Cooking for the sick
       Cooking for two
       Dairy-free cooking
       Desserts
       Dinners
       Fish as food
       Flavoring essences
       French cooking
       Holiday cooking
       Luncheons
       Menus
       Microwave cooking
       Outdoor cooking
       Pastry
       Pies
       Quantity cooking
       Quick and easy cooking
       Salads
       Salt-free diet
       Sandwiches
       Sauces
       Soups
       Southern cooking
       Vegetarian cooking
       Wok cooking
  RT **Diet**
       Food
       Gastronomy
Cooking—Fish   641.692
  BT **Cooking—Seafood**
  RT **Fish as food**
Cooking for institutions
  USE **Food service**
Cooking for large numbers
  USE **Quantity cooking**
Cooking for one   641.561
  BT **Cooking**

Cooking for the sick   **641.5**

UF   Cookery for the sick
      Food for invalids
      Invalid cooking

SA   types of diets, e.g. **Salt-free diet**
      [to be added as needed]

BT   **Cooking**
      Diet in disease
      Nursing
      Sick

NT   **Diet therapy**

Cooking for two   **641.561**

BT   **Cooking**

Cooking—Meat   **641.66**

BT   **Meat**

Cooking—Natural foods   **641.5**

UF   Natural food cooking

RT   **Natural foods**

Cooking—Poultry   **641.665**

BT   **Poultry**

Cooking—Seafood   **641.692**

BT   **Seafood**

NT   **Cooking—Fish**

Cooking utensils

USE   **Kitchen utensils**

Cooking—Vegetables   **641.6**

BT   **Vegetables**

RT   **Salads**
      Vegetarian cooking

Cooling appliances

USE   **Refrigeration**

Cooperation (May subdiv. geog.)   **334**

Use for general materials on the theory and history of cooperation and the cooperative movement. Materials dealing specifically with cooperative enterprises are entered under **Cooperative societies**.

UF   Cooperative distribution
      Distribution, Cooperative

BT   **Associations**
      Commerce
      Economics

NT   **Collective settlements**
      Communal living
      Cooperative agriculture
      Cooperative banks
      Cooperative housing
      Cooperative societies
      International cooperation
      Savings and loan associations

RT   **Profit sharing**

Cooperation, Intellectual

USE   **Intellectual cooperation**

Cooperation, Interchurch

USE   **Interdenominational cooperation**

Cooperation, Interdenominational

USE   **Interdenominational cooperation**

Cooperation (Psychology)

USE   **Cooperativeness**

Cooperative agriculture (May subdiv. geog.)   **334**

Use for materials on cooperation in the production and disposal of agricultural products.

UF   Agricultural cooperation
      Agriculture, Cooperative
      Collective farms
      Farmers' cooperatives

BT   **Agriculture**
      Cooperation

RT   **Collective settlements**

Cooperative banks (May subdiv. geog.)   **334**

UF   Banks and banking, Cooperative
      People's banks

BT   **Banks and banking**
      Cooperation
      Cooperative societies
      Personal loans

NT   **Credit unions**

RT   **Savings and loan associations**

Cooperative distribution

USE   **Cooperation**
      Cooperative societies

Cooperative education (May subdiv. geog.)   **371.2**

UF   Education, Cooperative
      Study-work plan
      Work-based learning

BT   **Vocational education**

Cooperative housing (May subdiv. geog.)   **334**

UF   Co-ops (Housing)
      Cohousing
      Housing, Cooperative

BT   **Cooperation**
      Housing

RT   **Communal living**

Cooperative learning   **371.3**

Use for materials on the method of education that involves having students work together on projects in a structured manner.

UF   Group method in teaching
      Group teaching

Cooperative learning—*Continued*
    Group work in education
  BT **Education**
        Teaching
Cooperative living
  USE **Collective settlements**
        Communal living
Cooperative societies (May subdiv. geog.)
    334; 658.8
    Use for materials dealing specifically with cooperative enterprises. General materials on the theory and history of cooperation and the cooperative movement are entered under **Co-operation**.
  UF Co-ops
        Consumer organizations
        Consumers' cooperative societies
        Cooperative distribution
        Cooperative stores
        Cooperatives
  SA types of cooperative societies, e.g. **Credit unions** [to be added as needed]
  BT **Cooperation**
        Corporations
        Societies
  NT **Cooperative banks**
        Savings and loan associations
Cooperative stores
  USE **Cooperative societies**
Cooperativeness 158
  UF Cooperation (Psychology)
  BT **Social psychology**
Cooperatives
  USE **Cooperative societies**
Copiers
  USE **Copying machines**
Coping behavior
  USE **Adjustment (Psychology)**
Coping skills
  USE **Life skills**
Copper engraving
  USE **Engraving**
Copperwork 673; 739.5
  BT **Metalwork**
Copy art (May subdiv. geog.) **760**
    Use for materials on the use of photocopying machines to create original works of art. Materials on clipping art work from published sources to use in creating documents, posters, newsletters, etc., are entered under **Clip art**.
  UF Copying machine art
        Reprographic art
        Xerographic art

  BT **Art**
  RT **Photocopying**
Copy writing
  USE **Advertising copy**
Copying machine art
  USE **Copy art**
Copying machines 681
  UF Copiers
        Copying processes and machines
        Duplicating machines
        Photocopying machines
  BT **Office equipment and supplies**
  RT **Copying processes**
Copying processes 686
  UF Copying processes and machines
        Duplicating processes
        Reproduction processes
        Reprography
  SA names of specific processes [to be added as needed]
  BT **Documentation**
  NT **Photocopying**
  RT **Copying machines**
Copying processes and machines
  USE **Copying machines**
        Copying processes
Copyright (May subdiv. geog.) **346.04; 352.7**
    May be subdivided by topic, e.g. **Copyright—Sound recordings**.
  UF International copyright
        Literary property
  NT **Fair use (Copyright)**
  RT **Authors and publishers**
        Intellectual property
Copyright—Sound recordings (May subdiv. geog.) **346.04**
  UF Sound recordings—Copyright
Coral reefs and islands (May subdiv. geog.) **551.42**
  UF Atolls
  BT **Geology**
        Islands
Corals 563; 593.6
  BT **Marine animals**
Cordials (Liquor)
  USE **Liquors**
Core curriculum
  USE **Colleges and universities—Curricula**
        Education—Curricula
Coretta Scott King Award 028.5

Coretta Scott King Award—*Continued*
UF King Award
BT **Children's literature**
Literary prizes

Corn (May subdiv. geog.)   **633.1; 633.2**
UF Maize
BT **Forage plants**
Grain

Coronary diseases
USE **Heart diseases**

Corporate accountability
USE **Social responsibility of business**

Corporate acquisitions
USE **Corporate mergers and acqui-sitions**

Corporate culture (May subdiv. geog.)
302.3
UF Culture, Corporate
Organizational culture
BT **Corporations**

Corporate downsizing
USE **Downsizing of organizations**

Corporate libraries   **027.6**

Use for materials on libraries located within companies, firms, or private businesses, covering any subject areas. Materials on libraries with a subject focus on business are entered under **Business libraries**.

UF Company libraries
Industrial libraries
Libraries, Corporate
BT **Special libraries**

Corporate mergers and acquisitions
(May subdiv. geog.)   **338.8; 658.1**
UF Acquisitions, Corporate
Buyouts, Corporate
Consolidation and merger of corporations
Corporate acquisitions
Corporate takeovers
Industrial mergers
Mergers
Takeovers, Corporate
SA types of institutions and types of industries and businesses with the subdivision *Mergers*, e.g. **Railroads—Mergers** to be added as needed]
NT **Leveraged buyouts**
Railroads—Mergers
RT **Conglomerate corporations**
Industrial trusts

Corporate patronage of the arts
USE **Art patronage**

Corporate responsibility
USE **Social responsibility of business**

Corporate symbols
USE **Trademarks**

Corporate takeovers
USE **Corporate mergers and acqui-sitions**

Corporate welfare
USE **Subsidies**

Corporation law (May subdiv. geog.)
346
BT **Commercial law**
Corporations
Law
NT **Limited liability companies**
Public service commissions
RT **Industrial trusts**
Monopolies
Restraint of trade

Corporations (May subdiv. geog.)
338.7; 658.1
UF Companies
BT **Business enterprises**
NT **Conglomerate corporations**
Cooperative societies
Corporate culture
Corporation law
Limited liability companies
Multinational corporations
Municipal ownership
Public service commissions
Trust companies
RT **Industrial trusts**
Stocks

Corporations—Accounting   **657; 658.15**
BT **Accounting**
Bookkeeping

Corporations—Art patronage
USE **Art patronage**

Corporations—Finance   **658.15**
UF Capitalization (Finance)
BT **Finance**

Corporations, Multinational
USE **Multinational corporations**

Corporations, Nonprofit
USE **Nonprofit organizations**

Corporations—Social responsibility
USE **Social responsibility of business**

Corpulence
USE **Obesity**

Correctional institutions (May subdiv. geog.) **365**
UF Penal institutions
SA types of correctional institutions [to be added as needed]
BT **Punishment**
NT **Halfway houses**
Penal colonies
Prisons
Reformatories

Correctional services
USE **Corrections**

Corrections (May subdiv. geog.) **364.6**
Use for materials on the rehabilitation and treatment of offenders through parole, penal custody, and probation programs, and on the administration of such programs.
UF Correctional services
Criminals—Rehabilitation programs
Penology
Reform of criminals
BT **Administration of criminal justice**
NT **Parole**
Probation
Punishment

Correspondence
USE **Business letters**
Letter writing
Letters
and ethnic groups, classes of persons, and names of individual persons and families with the subdivision *Correspondence,* e.g. **Authors—Correspondence** [to be added as needed]

Correspondence schools and courses (May subdiv. geog.) **374.35**
UF Home education
Home study courses
BT **Distance education**
Schools
Technical education
University extension
RT **Self-instruction**

Corrosion and anticorrosives **620.1**
UF Anticorrosive paint
Rust

Rustless coatings
BT **Industrial chemistry**
RT **Paint**

Corrupt practices
USE subjects with the subdivision *Corrupt practices,* e.g. **Adoption—Corrupt practices; Sports—Corrupt practices;** etc. [to be added as needed]

Corruption in politics
USE **Political corruption**

Corruption in sports
USE **Sports—Corrupt practices**

Corruption, Police
USE **Police corruption**

Corsairs
USE **Pirates**

Cosmetic surgery
USE **Plastic surgery**

Cosmetics **646.7**
UF Makeup (Cosmetics)
SA types of cosmetics [to be added as needed]
BT **Personal grooming**
NT **Perfumes**
Theatrical makeup
RT **Toiletries**

Cosmetics—Advertising
USE **Advertising—Cosmetics**

Cosmic rays **539.7**
UF Millikan rays
BT **Nuclear physics**
Radiation
Radioactivity
Space environment

Cosmobiology
USE **Space biology**

Cosmochemistry
USE **Space chemistry**

Cosmogony
USE **Cosmology**
Universe

Cosmography
USE **Cosmology**
Universe

Cosmology **113; 523.1**
Use for general or theoretical materials on the science or philosophy of the universe. Materials limited to the physical description of the universe are entered under **Universe**.
UF Cosmogony
Cosmography

Cosmology—*Continued*
    BT   **Universe**
    NT   **Biblical cosmology**
           Big bang theory
Cosmonauts
    USE   **Astronauts**
Cost accounting   657
    BT   **Accounting**
           Bookkeeping
Cost and standard of living (May subdiv.
    geog.)   **339.4**
    UF   Cost of living
          Food, Cost of
          Household finances
          Standard of living
    BT   **Economics**
           Home economics
           Quality of life
           Social conditions
           Wealth
    NT   **Consumer price indexes**
           Household budgets
           Subsistence economy
    RT   **Prices**
           Salaries, wages, etc.
Cost benefit analysis
    USE   **Cost effectiveness**
Cost effectiveness   658.15
    UF   Benefit cost analysis
          Cost benefit analysis
    SA   topics with the subdivision *Cost
          effectiveness,* e.g. **Electric au-
          tomobiles—Cost effectiveness**
          [to be added as needed]
    BT   **Economics**
    NT   **Electric automobiles—Cost ef-
          fectiveness**
Cost of living
    USE   **Cost and standard of living**
Cost of living indexes
    USE   **Consumer price indexes**
Cost of medical care
    USE   **Medical care—Costs**
Costs
    USE   subjects with the subdivision
          Costs, e.g. **Medical care—
          Costs** [to be added as need-
          ed]
Costume (May subdiv. geog.)   **391; 792**
    Use for materials on the characteristic cos-
    tume of ethnic or national groups and for ma-
terials on fancy dress and theatrical costumes.
For the traditional national costume of a particular country subdivide geographically. Materials on clothing and the art of dress from
day to day in practical situations, including
historical dress and the clothing of various
professions or classes of persons, are entered
under **Clothing and dress**. Materials on the
prevailing mode or style of dress are entered
under **Fashion**.
    UF   Acting—Costume
          Fancy dress
          Style in dress
          Theatrical costume
    SA   costume of particular ethnic
          groups, e.g. **Native American
          costume**; and professions and
          classes of persons with the
          subdivision *Clothing*, e.g.
          Handicapped—Clothing [to
          be added as needed]
    BT   **Decorative arts**
           Ethnology
           Manners and customs
    NT   **Armor**
           Children's costumes
           Disguise
           Fans
           Hats
           Jewelry
           Masks (Facial)
           Native American costume
           Theatrical makeup
           Uniforms
           Wigs
    RT   **Clothing and dress**
Cot death
    USE   **Sudden infant death syndrome**
Côte d'Ivoire   966.6
    May be subdivided like **United States** ex-
cept for *History.*
    UF   Ivory Coast
Cottage industry
    USE   **Home-based business**
Cotton   633.5; 677
    BT   **Economic botany**
           Fabrics
           Fibers
           Yarn
Cotton manufacture   677
    BT   **Textile industry**
Councils and synods   262
    UF   Church councils
          Ecumenical councils
          Synods

Councils and synods—*Continued*
- SA names of specific councils and synods, e.g. **Vatican Council (2nd: 1962-1965)** [to be added as needed]
- BT **Christianity**
  Church history
- NT **Vatican Council (2nd: 1962-1965)**

Counseling   361; 371.4
- UF Guidance
- SA types of counseling; and ethnic groups and classes of persons with the subdivision *Counseling of*, e.g. **Employees—Counseling of** [to be added as needed]
- BT **Applied psychology**
  Helping behavior
  Personnel management
- NT **Advice columns**
  Consultants
  Crisis centers
  Drug abuse counseling
  Educational counseling
  Elderly—Counseling of
  Employees—Counseling of
  Family therapy
  Health counseling
  Hotlines (Telephone counseling)
  Marriage counseling
  Mentoring
  Peer counseling
  School counseling
  Self-help groups
  Social group work
  Vocational guidance
- RT **Interviewing**
  Social case work

Counseling of
- USE classes of persons and ethnic groups with the subdivision *Counseling of,* e.g. **Elderly—Counseling of** [to be added as needed]

Counseling of the elderly
- USE **Elderly—Counseling of**

Counseling with the aged
- USE **Elderly—Counseling of**

Counter culture (May subdiv. geog.)
  306
- UF Counterculture
  Nonconformity
  Subculture
- BT **Lifestyles**
  Social conditions
- NT **Bohemianism**
- RT **Alternative lifestyles**
  Collective settlements
  Communal living
  Radicalism

Counter-Reformation (May subdiv. geog.)
  270.6
- UF Anti-Reformation
- BT **Christianity**
  Church history—1500-, Modern period
- RT **Reformation**

Counter-terrorism
- USE **Terrorism—Prevention**

Counterculture
- USE **Counter culture**

Counterespionage
- USE **Intelligence service**

Counterfeits and counterfeiting   332; 364.1
- BT **Coinage**
  Crime
  Forgery
  Impostors and imposture
  Money
  Swindlers and swindling
- NT **Art—Forgeries**
  Literary forgeries

Counterintelligence
- USE **Intelligence service**

Counterpoint   781.2
- BT **Composition (Music)**
  Music—Theory
- NT **Fugue**

Counting   513.2

Use for materials on counting, including counting books. Materials on numbers, numbering, and systems of numeration are entered under **Numbers**. Materials on the conceptualization of numbers are entered under **Number concept**.
- UF Counting books
- BT **Arithmetic—Study and teaching**
- NT **Number games**
- RT **Numbers**

Counting books
- USE **Counting**

Countries
USE **Nations**

Country and western music
USE **Country music**

Country churches
USE **Rural churches**

Country life (May subdiv. geog.)
307.72; 630

Use for descriptive, popular, and literary materials on living in the country. Materials on social organization and conditions in rural communities are entered under **Rural sociology**.

UF Rural life
BT **Manners and customs**
NT **Agriculture—Societies**
Farm life
Mountain life
Plantation life
RT **Outdoor life**
Rural sociology

Country life—United States 307.72;
630

Country music 781.642
UF Country and western music
Hillbilly music
BT **Folk music—United States**
Popular music

Country schools
USE **Rural schools**

Country stores
USE **General stores**

County agricultural agents 630.7
BT **Agricultural extension work**
Agriculture—Study and teach-ing

County government (May subdiv. geog.)
320.8; 352.15
UF County officers
BT **Local government**

County libraries
USE **Public libraries**
Regional libraries

County officers
USE **County government**

County planning
USE **Regional planning**

Coupons (Retail trade) 659
BT **Advertising**

Coups d'état
USE **Revolutions**

Courage 179

UF Bravery
Heroism
BT **Virtue**
NT **Encouragement**
Morale
RT **Heroes and heroines**

Courses of study
USE **Education—Curricula**

Court fools
USE **Fools and jesters**

Court life
USE **Courts and courtiers**

Court martial
USE **Courts martial and courts of inquiry**

Courtesy 177; 395
UF Manners
Politeness
BT **Etiquette**
Virtue

Courtiers
USE **Courts and courtiers**

Courting
USE **Courtship**

Courtroom drama
USE **Legal drama (Films)**
Legal drama (Radio programs)
Legal drama (Television pro-grams)

Courts (May subdiv. geog.) **347**
UF Judiciary
BT **Law**
NT **Arbitration and award**
Civil procedure
Courts martial and courts of inquiry
Criminal procedure
Jury
Juvenile courts
Small claims courts
United States. Supreme Court
RT **Administration of justice**
Judges

Courts and courtiers 394; 929.7
UF Court life
Courtiers
SA names of countries, cities, etc., with the subdivision *Courts and courtiers* [to be added as needed]
BT **Manners and customs**

Courts and courtiers—*Continued*
  NT **Fools and jesters**
       Princes
       Princesses
  RT **Kings and rulers**
       Queens
Courts martial and courts of inquiry
    343
  UF Court martial
       Military courts
  BT **Courts**
       Trials
  RT **Military law**
Courts—United States 347.73
  UF Federal courts
       United States—Courts
Courtship (May subdiv. geog.) **306.73;**
    392.4
  UF Courting
  BT **Love**
  NT **Betrothal**
       Dating (Social customs)
  RT **Marriage**
Courtship (Animal behavior)
  USE **Animal courtship**
Courtship of animals
  USE **Animal courtship**
Cousins 306.87
  BT **Family**
Couturiers
  USE **Fashion designers**
Covenants 202; 231.7
    Use for materials on religious covenants. May be subdivided by religion as needed. Materials on non-religious covenants are entered under **Contracts**.
  UF Agreements
       Religious covenants
  BT **Contracts**
       Theology
Covens
  USE **Witches**
Coverlets
  USE **Bedspreads**
       Quilts
Covetousness
  USE **Avarice**
Cowboys
  USE **Cowhands**
Cowgirls
  USE **Cowhands**

Cowhands (May subdiv. geog.) **636.2;**
    978
  UF Cowboys
       Cowgirls
       Gauchos
  BT **Frontier and pioneer life**
       Ranch life
  RT **Rodeos**
Cowhands—Songs 782.42
  UF Cowhands—Songs and music
  BT **Music**
       Songs
Cowhands—Songs and music
  USE **Cowhands—Songs**
Cows
  USE **Cattle**
CPR (First aid) 616.1
  UF Cardiopulmonary resuscitation
  BT **First aid**
  RT **Cardiac resuscitation**
Crabs 565; 595.3
  BT **Crustacea**
       Shellfish
Crack babies
  USE **Children of drug addicts**
Crack cocaine
  USE **Crack (Drug)**
Crack (Drug) 362.29; 615
  UF Crack cocaine
  BT **Cocaine**
Cradle songs
  USE **Lullabies**
Craft festivals
  USE **Craft shows**
Craft shows 745
  UF Craft festivals
  BT **Exhibitions**
       Festivals
       Handicraft
Crafts (Arts)
  USE **Arts and crafts movement**
       Handicraft
Cranes, derricks, etc. 621.8
  UF Derricks
  BT **Hoisting machinery**
Crank (Drug)
  USE **Crystal meth (Drug)**
Cranks
  USE **Eccentrics and eccentricities**
Crashes (Finance)
  USE **Financial crises**

Crates
    USE   **Boxes**

Crayon drawing   741.2
    UF   Blackboard drawing
    BT   **Drawing**
    RT   **Pastel drawing**

Crazes
    USE   **Fads**

Creation   231.7; 213
    BT   **Natural theology**
    RT   **Biblical cosmology**
           Creationism
           Evolution
           Universe

Creation (Literary, artistic, etc.)   153.3
    UF   Inspiration
    BT   **Genius**
           Imagination
           Intellect
           Inventions
    NT   **Creative writing**
           Planning
    RT   **Creative ability**

Creation—Study and teaching
    USE   **Creationism**
           Evolution—Study and teaching

Creationism   231.7
    Use for materials on the doctrine that the universe was created by God out of nothing in the initial seven days of time and that all biological species were created rather than evolving from pre-existing types through modifications in successive generations.
    UF   Christianity and evolution
           Creation—Study and teaching
           Evolution and Christianity
           Fundamentalism and education
           Fundamentalism and evolution
           Scientific creationism
    BT   **Christianity—Doctrines**
    RT   **Bible and science**
           Creation
           Evolution
           Evolution—Study and teaching
           Religion and science

Creative ability   153.3; 701; 801
    UF   Creativity
    BT   **Ability**
    NT   **Creative thinking**
    RT   **Creation (Literary, artistic, etc.)**

Creative activities   372.5
    Use for materials on activities for children that result in some form of personal expression such as painting, cooking, drama, etc.
    UF   Activities curriculum
    BT   **Amusements**
           Elementary education
           Kindergarten
    RT   **Handicraft**

Creative movement
    USE   **Movement education**

Creative thinking   153.4
    BT   **Creative ability**

Creative writing   808
    UF   Writing (Authorship)
    BT   **Authorship**
           Creation (Literary, artistic, etc.)
           Language arts

Creativity
    USE   **Creative ability**

Creature films
    USE   **Horror films**

Credibility
    USE   **Truthfulness and falsehood**

Credit (May subdiv. geog.)   **332.7**
    UF   Bills of credit
           Letters of credit
    BT   **Finance**
           Money
    NT   **Agricultural credit**
           Collecting of accounts
           Consumer credit
           Installment plan
           Negotiable instruments
    RT   **Banks and banking**
           Debtor and creditor
           Loans

Credit card crimes
    USE   **Credit card fraud**

Credit card fraud   364.16
    UF   Credit card crimes
    BT   **Fraud**
           Swindlers and swindling

Credit cards   332.7
    UF   Bank credit cards
           Banks and banking—Credit cards
    BT   **Consumer credit**

Credit unions (May subdiv. geog.)   **334**
    Use for materials on cooperative associations that make small loans to its members at low interest rates.

Credit unions—*Continued*
  BT **Cooperative banks**
Creditor
  USE **Debtor and creditor**
Creeds 202; 238
    Use for materials about the concise, formal, and authorized statements of doctrines and for the texts of those statements.
  UF Confessions of faith
  SA names of religions and individual denominations with the subdivision *Creeds*, e.g. **Catholic Church—Creeds** [to be added as needed]
  BT **Doctrinal theology**
  NT **Apostles' Creed**
      Catholic Church—Creeds
      Nicene Creed
  RT **Catechisms**
Cremation   363.7; 393; 614
  UF Incineration
      Mortuary customs
  BT **Public health**
      Sanitation
  RT **Burial**
      Funeral rites and ceremonies
Creole folk songs   782.42162
  UF Folk songs, Creole
  BT **Folk songs**
Creoles (May subdiv. geog.)   **305.84; 972.9; 976**
  BT **Ethnic groups**
Crests
  USE **Heraldry**
Crew (Rowing)
  USE **Rowing**
Crewelwork   746.44
  BT **Embroidery**
Crib death
  USE **Sudden infant death syndrome**
Crickets (May subdiv. geog.)   **595.7**
  BT **Insects**
Crime (May subdiv. geog.)   **364**
  UF Crimes
      Criminology
      Felony
  SA types of crimes, e.g. **Computer crimes** [to be added as needed]
  BT **Administration of criminal justice**
      Social problems
  NT **Assassination**
      Atrocities
      Computer crimes
      Counterfeits and counterfeiting
      Crime prevention
      Crimes against humanity
      Crimes without victims
      Criminals
      Drugs and crime
      Drunk driving
      Forgery
      Fraud
      Hate crimes
      Homicide
      Impostors and imposture
      Juvenile delinquency
      Lynching
      Offenses against property
      Offenses against public safety
      Offenses against the person
      Organized crime
      Racketeering
      Riots
      School shootings
      Sex crimes
      Smuggling
      Swindlers and swindling
      Theft
      Treason
      Victims of crimes
      Vigilantes
      White collar crimes
  RT **Criminal law**
      Police
      Punishment
      Trials
      Vice
Crime and drugs
  USE **Drugs and crime**
Crime and narcotics
  USE **Drugs and crime**
Crime comics
  USE **Mystery comic books, strips, etc.**
Crime films
  USE **Film noir**
      Gangster films
      Mystery films
Crime plays
  USE **Mystery and detective plays**

Crime prevention (May subdiv. geog.)
   364.4
   UF   Prevention of crime
   BT   **Crime**
   NT   **Burglary protection**
Crime prevention—Citizen participation
   (May subdiv. geog.)   **364.4**
   BT   **Political participation**
Crime programs
   USE   **Mystery radio programs**
           Mystery television programs
Crime stories
   USE   **Mystery fiction**
Crime syndicates
   USE   **Organized crime**
           Racketeering
Crime—United States   364.973
Crime victims
   USE   **Victims of crimes**
Crimean War, 1853-1856   947
   UF   Great Britain—History—1853-
           1856, Crimean War
           Russo-Turkish War, 1853-1856
Crimes
   USE   **Crime**
Crimes against humanity (May subdiv.
   geog.)   **364.1**
   BT   **Crime**
   NT   **Forced labor**
           Genocide
           Slavery
           War crimes
Crimes against property
   USE   **Offenses against property**
Crimes against public safety
   USE   **Offenses against public safety**
Crimes against the person
   USE   **Offenses against the person**
Crimes, Military
   USE   **Military offenses**
Crimes of hate
   USE   **Hate crimes**
Crimes, Political
   USE   **Political crimes and offenses**
Crimes without victims   364.1
   UF   Non-victim crimes
           Nonvictim crimes
           Victimless crimes
   BT   **Crime**
           Criminal law

Criminal assault
   USE   **Offenses against the person**
Criminal behavior
   USE   **Criminal psychology**
Criminal investigation (May subdiv.
   geog.)   **363.25**
   BT   **Law enforcement**
   NT   **Criminals—Identification**
           Eavesdropping
           Fingerprints
           Lie detectors and detection
           Missing persons
           Wiretapping
   RT   **Detectives**
           Forensic sciences
           Police
Criminal justice, Administration of
   USE   **Administration of criminal jus-
           tice**
Criminal law (May subdiv. geog.)   **345**
   UF   Codes, Penal
           Misdemeanors (Law)
           Penal codes
           Penal law
   SA   types of crimes, e.g. **Homicide**
           [to be added as needed]
   BT   **Law**
   NT   **Administration of criminal jus-
           tice**
           Adoption—Corrupt practices
           Capital punishment
           Crimes without victims
           Executions and executioners
           Homicide
           Insanity defense
           Jury
           Kidnapping
           Military offenses
           Misconduct in office
           Obscenity (Law)
           Offenses against property
           Offenses against public safety
           Offenses against the person
           Political crimes and offenses
           Probation
           Prohibition
           Sports—Corrupt practices
           Tax evasion
           Trials
           Vigilantes

Criminal law—*Continued*
RT **Crime**
Criminal procedure
Punishment
Criminal procedure (May subdiv. geog.)
345
BT **Courts**
NT **Executions and executioners**
Habeas corpus
Torture
RT **Criminal law**
Criminal psychiatry
USE **Criminal psychology**
Criminal psychology 364.3
UF Criminal behavior
Criminal psychiatry
BT **Psychology**
RT **Abnormal psychology**
Criminalistics
USE **Forensic sciences**
Criminals (May subdiv. geog.) 364.3;
364.6
UF Convicts
Delinquents
Outlaws
BT **Crime**
NT **Computer hackers**
Gangs
Impostors and imposture
Pirates
Prisoners
Serial killers
Swindlers and swindling
Thieves
Criminals and drugs
USE **Criminals—Drug use**
Criminals and narcotics
USE **Criminals—Drug use**
Criminals—Drug use 362.29; 364.3
UF Criminals and drugs
Criminals and narcotics
Drugs and criminals
Narcotics and criminals
RT **Drugs and crime**
Criminals—Identification 363.25
BT **Criminal investigation**
Identification
NT **Fingerprints**
Criminals—Rehabilitation programs
USE **Corrections**
Criminology
USE **Crime**

Crippled children
USE **Physically handicapped children**
Crippled people
USE **Physically handicapped**
Crisis centers 361.3; 362
UF Crisis intervention centers
SA types of crisis centers, e.g.
Hotlines (Telephone counseling) [to be added as needed]
BT **Counseling**
Social work
RT **Hotlines (Telephone counseling)**
Crisis counseling
USE **Hotlines (Telephone counseling)**
Crisis intervention centers
USE **Crisis centers**
Crisis intervention (Mental health services) (May subdiv. geog.) 362.2;
616.89
UF Crisis intervention (Psychiatry)
Emergency mental health services
BT **Mental health services**
Crisis intervention (Psychiatry)
USE **Crisis intervention (Mental health services)**
Crisis intervention telephone service
USE **Hotlines (Telephone counseling)**
Crisis management 658.4
BT **Management**
Problem solving
RT **Conflict management**
Critical thinking 153.4; 160
Use for materials on thinking that is based on sound logic and the careful evaluation of all pertinent evidence.
BT **Decision making**
Logic
Problem solving
Reasoning
Thought and thinking
Criticism 801
Use for materials on the history, principles, methods, etc., of criticism in general and of literary criticism in particular. Materials that are themselves histories or criticisms of literature are entered under **Literature—History and criticism**. Criticism of the work of an individual author, artist, composer, etc., is entered under that person's name as a subject; only in the case of voluminous authors is it necessary to add the subdivision *Criticism*. Criticism of a single work is entered under

Criticism—*Continued*
the name of the author, artist, or composer, followed by the title of the work.

UF   Appraisal of books
        Books—Appraisal
        Criticism and interpretation
        Criticism, interpretation, etc.
        Evaluation of literature
        Literary criticism
        Literature—Evaluation

SA   literature, film, and music subjects with the subdivision *History and criticism*, e.g. **English poetry—History and criticism**; and names of voluminous authors and of sacred works with the subdivision *Criticism*, e.g. **Shakespeare, William, 1564-1616—Criticism**; **Bible—Criticism**; etc. [to be added as needed]

BT   **Aesthetics**
        Literature
        Rhetoric

NT   **Art criticism**
        Book reviewing
        Dramatic criticism
        Feminist criticism

RT   **Literary style**

Criticism and interpretation
USE   **Criticism**
        and literature, film, and music subjects with the subdivision *History and criticism,* e.g. **English poetry—History and criticism**; and names of voluminous authors and of sacred works with the subdivision *Criticism,* e.g. **Shakespeare, William, 1564-1616—Criticism**; **Bible—Criticism**; etc. [to be added as needed]

Criticism, Feminist
USE   **Feminist criticism**

Criticism, interpretation, etc.
USE   **Criticism**
        and literature, film, and music subjects with the subdivision *History and criticism,* e.g. **English poetry—History and criticism**; and names of volu-

minous authors and of sacred works with the subdivision *Criticism,* e.g. **Shakespeare, William, 1564-1616—Criticism; Bible—Criticism;** etc. [to be added as needed]

Cro-Magnons   569.9; 930.1
UF   Cromagnons
BT   **Prehistoric peoples**

Crocheting   746.43
BT   **Needlework**
NT   **Lace and lace making**

Crockery
USE   **Pottery**

Crocodiles (May subdiv. geog.)   597.98
BT   **Reptiles**
RT   **Alligators**

Cromagnons
USE   **Cro-Magnons**

Crop dusting
USE   **Aeronautics in agriculture**

Crop reports
USE   **Agriculture—Statistics**

Crop rotation   631.5
UF   Rotation of crops
BT   **Agriculture**

Crop spraying
USE   **Aeronautics in agriculture**

Crops
USE   **Farm produce**

Cross cultural conflict
USE   **Culture conflict**

Cross-cultural psychology
USE   **Ethnopsychology**

Cross-cultural studies   306
Use for materials on the systematic comparison of two or more cultural groups, either within the same country or in separate countries.

UF   Comparison of cultures
        Cross cultural studies
        Intercultural studies
        Transcultural studies

SA   topics with the subdivision *Cross-cultural studies*, e.g. **Marriage—Cross-cultural studies** [to be added as needed]

BT   **Culture**
        Social sciences

Cross cultural studies
USE   **Cross-cultural studies**

Cross-examination
   USE **Witnesses**
Cross-stitch 746.44
   BT **Embroidery**
Crossdressers
   USE **Transvestites**
Crossword puzzles 793.73
   BT **Puzzles**
       Word games
Crowds 302.3
   UF Mobs
   NT **Demonstrations**
       Riot control
   RT **Riots**
       Social psychology
Crown lands
   USE **Public lands**
CRT display terminals
   USE **Computer monitors**
CRTs
   USE **Cathode ray tubes**
Crucifixion of Jesus Christ
   USE **Jesus Christ—Crucifixion**
Crude oil
   USE **Petroleum**
Cruelty 179
   UF Brutality
   BT **Ethics**
   NT **Atrocities**
       Torture
Cruelty to animals
   USE **Animal welfare**
Cruelty to children
   USE **Child abuse**
Cruises
   USE **Ocean travel**
Crusades 909.07
   BT **Church history—600-1500,**
       Middle Ages
   RT **Chivalry**
Crushes 152.4; 177
   UF Romantic crushes
   BT **Friendship**
       Love
Crustacea 565; 595.3
   SA names of specific crustaceans,
       e.g. **Lobsters** [to be added as
       needed]
   BT **Shellfish**
   NT **Crabs**
       Lobsters

Cryobiology 571.4
   UF Freezing
       Low temperature biology
   BT **Biology**
       Cold
       Low temperatures
   NT **Cold—Physiological effect**
       Frozen embryos
Cryogenic interment
   USE **Cryonics**
Cryogenic surgery
   USE **Cryosurgery**
Cryogenics
   USE **Low temperatures**
Cryonics 621.5
   UF Cryogenic interment
       Freezing of human bodies
       Human cold storage
   BT **Burial**
Cryosurgery 617
   UF Cryogenic surgery
   BT **Cold—Therapeutic use**
       Surgery
Cryotherapy
   USE **Cold—Therapeutic use**
Cryptography 652
   UF Code deciphering
       Code enciphering
       Secret writing
   BT **Signs and symbols**
       Writing
   RT **Ciphers**
Crystal gazing
   USE **Divination**
Crystal meth (Drug) 362.29; 615
   UF Crank (Drug)
       Ice (Drug)
   BT **Designer drugs**
       Methamphetamine
Crystallization
   USE **Crystals**
Crystallography
   USE **Crystals**
Crystals 548
   UF Crystallization
       Crystallography
   SA types of crystals, e.g. **Quartz** [to
       be added as needed]
   BT **Physical chemistry**
       Solids
   NT **Quartz**

Crystals—*Continued*

    RT   **Minerals**

Cub Scouts

    USE   **Boy Scouts**

Cuba   972.91

    May be subdivided like **United States** except for *History*.

    BT   **Islands**

Cuba—History   972.91

Cuba—History—1958-1959, Revolution
    972.9106

Cuba—History—1959-   972.9106

Cuba—History—1961, Invasion
    972.9106

    UF   Bay of Pigs invasion

           Cuban invasion, 1961

           Invasion of Cuba, 1961

Cuban invasion, 1961

    USE   **Cuba—History—1961, Invasion**

Cube root   513.2

    BT   **Arithmetic**

Cubic measurement

    USE   **Volume (Cubic content)**

Cubism (May subdiv. geog.)   **709.04;**
    759.06

    BT   **Art**

Cultivated plants (May subdiv. geog.)
    581.6; 631.5

    UF   Plants, Cultivated

    BT   **Agriculture**

           Gardening

           Plants

    NT   **Annuals (Plants)**

           House plants

           Ornamental plants

           Perennials

Cultivated plants—United States   **581.6;**
    631.5

Cults (May subdiv. geog.)   **209; 306.6**

    Use for materials on groups or movements whose beliefs or practices differ significantly from the traditional religions and are often focused upon a charismatic leader. Materials on the major world religions are entered under **Religions**. Materials on independent religious groups whose teachings or practices fall within the normative bounds of the major world religions are entered under **Sects**.

    UF   Religious cults

    BT   **Religions**

    NT   **New Age movement**

    RT   **Sects**

Cultural anthropology

    USE   **Ethnology**

Cultural change

    USE   **Social change**

Cultural diversity in the workplace

    USE   **Diversity in the workplace**

Cultural exchange programs

    USE   **Exchange of persons programs**

Cultural heritage

    USE   **Cultural property**

Cultural life

    USE   **Intellectual life**

Cultural patrimony

    USE   **Cultural property**

Cultural policy (May subdiv. geog.)   **306**

    Use for materials on official government policy toward educational, artistic, intellectual, or other cultural activities and organizations in general.

    UF   Government policy

           Intellectual life—Government policy

           State encouragement of science, literature, and art

    SA   types of artistic or intellectual activities with the subdivision *Government policy* [to be added as needed]

    BT   **Culture**

           Intellectual life

    NT   **Cultural property—Protection**

Cultural policy—United States   306

    UF   United States—Cultural policy

Cultural property (May subdiv. geog.)
    344

    Use for materials on property that is considered essential to a nation's cultural heritage.

    UF   Cultural heritage

           Cultural patrimony

           Heritage property

           National heritage

           National patrimony

           National treasure

    BT   **Property**

Cultural property—Protection (May subdiv. geog.)   **344**

    Use for materials on protecting cultural heritage property from theft, misappropriation, or exportation. Materials on identifying and preserving historically important towns, buildings, sites, etc., are entered under **Historic preservation**.

    UF   Cultural property—Protection—Government policy

           Cultural resources management

    BT   **Cultural policy**

Cultural property—Protection—*Continued*
RT **Historic preservation**
Cultural property—Protection—Government policy
USE **Cultural property—Protection**
Cultural relations   303.48; 306; 344
UF Intercultural relations
BT **Intellectual cooperation**
International cooperation
International relations
NT **Exchange of persons programs**
Interfaith relations
Cultural resources management
USE **Cultural property—Protection**
Cultural tourism (May subdiv. geog.)
910
UF Heritage tourism
Historical tourism
History tourism
BT **Tourist trade**
Culturally deprived
USE **Socially handicapped**
Culturally deprived children
USE **Socially handicapped children**
Culturally handicapped
USE **Socially handicapped**
Culturally handicapped children
USE **Socially handicapped children**
Culture   306; 909
Use for materials on the sum total of ways of living or thinking established by a group of human beings and transmitted from one generation to the next, including a concern for what is regarded as excellent in the arts, manners, scholarship, etc.
SA regions, countries, states, etc., with the subdivisions *Intellectual life*; *Civilization*; or *Social life and customs*, e.g. **United States—Intellectual life**; **United States—Civilization**; **United States—Social life and customs**; etc. [to be added as needed]
NT **Acculturation**
Cross-cultural studies
Cultural policy
Humanism
Intellectual life
Language and culture
Material culture
Multiculturalism
Pluralism (Social sciences)

Popular culture
RT **Anthropology**
Civilization
Education
Learning and scholarship
Sociology
Culture conflict (May subdiv. geog.)
155.8; 306; 155.8
UF Conflict of cultures
Cross cultural conflict
Culture shock
Future shock
BT **Ethnic relations**
Ethnopsychology
Race relations
Culture contact
USE **Acculturation**
Culture, Corporate
USE **Corporate culture**
Culture shock
USE **Culture conflict**
Curates
USE **Clergy**
Curiosities and wonders (May subdiv. geog.)   **030**
UF Enigmas
Facts, Miscellaneous
Miscellanea
Miscellaneous facts
Oddities
Trivia
Wonders
SA subjects with the subdivision *Miscellanea*, e.g. **Medicine—Miscellanea** [to be added as needed]
NT **Eccentrics and eccentricities**
Medicine—Miscellanea
Monsters
World records
Curiosity   155.2
UF Exploratory behavior
Inquisitiveness
BT **Human behavior**
Currency
USE **Money**
Currency devaluation
USE **Monetary policy**
Current events   909.82
Use for materials on the study and teaching of current events. Accounts or discussions of

Current events—*Continued*
the events themselves are entered under the appropriate heading for historical period or history of a place. Periodicals and yearbooks devoted to current events are entered under **History—Periodicals**.
    BT   **Modern history—Study and teaching**
Currents, Electric
    USE **Electric currents**
Currents, Ocean
    USE **Ocean currents**
Curricula
    USE **Education—Curricula**
        and types of education and schools with the subdivision *Curricula,* e.g. **Library education—Curricula** [to be added as needed]
Curriculum development
    USE **Curriculum planning**
Curriculum materials centers
    USE **Instructional materials centers**
Curriculum planning (May subdiv. geog.) **375**
    UF   Curriculum development
    BT   **Education—Curricula**
          Planning
    NT   **Interdisciplinary approach in education**
Curtains
    USE **Draperies**
Custody kidnapping
    USE **Parental kidnapping**
Custody of children
    USE **Child custody**
Custom duties
    USE **Tariff**
Customer relations   **658.8**
    BT   **Business**
          Public relations
    NT   **Customer services**
Customer service
    USE **Customer services**
Customer services   **658.8**
    UF   Customer service
          Service, Customer
          Service (in industry)
          Services, Customer
          Technical service
    BT   **Customer relations**

Customs and practices
    USE religions, denominations, religious orders, and religious holidays with the subdivision *Customs and practices,* e.g. **Judaism—Customs and practices** [to be added as needed]
Customs, Social
    USE **Manners and customs**
Customs (Tariff)
    USE **Tariff**
Cyberbullying   **302.3**
    BT   **Bullies**
          Computer crimes
Cybercommerce
    USE **Electronic commerce**
Cybernetics   **003**
    UF   Automatic control
          Mechanical brains
    BT   **Communication**
          Electronics
          System theory
    NT   **Bionics**
          System analysis
          Systems engineering
Cybersex
    USE **Computer sex**
Cybershopping
    USE **Internet shopping**
Cyberspace   **006**
    Use for materials on the non-physical environment created by the Internet or other computer networks.
    BT   **Computer networks**
          Space and time
Cycles   **115**
    UF   Cyclic theory
          Natural cycles
          Periodicity
    NT   **Biological rhythms**
          Business cycles
          Life cycles (Biology)
    RT   **Rhythm**
          Time
Cyclic theory
    USE **Cycles**
Cycling   **796.6**
    UF   Bicycles and bicycling
          Bicycling
          Biking

Cycling—*Continued*
  BT **Exercise**
      Outdoor recreation
      Sports
  NT **Bicycle racing**
      Bicycle touring
      Motorcycling
      Mountain biking
  RT **Bicycles**
      Tricycles
Cyclones (May subdiv. geog.)   **551.55**

Use for materials on large-scale storms that involve high winds rotating around a center of low atmospheric pressure. Materials on the cyclones of the West Indies are entered under **Hurricanes**. Materials on the cyclones of the China Seas and the Philippines are entered under **Typhoons**.

  BT **Meteorology**
      Storms
      Winds
  NT **Hurricanes**
      Typhoons
Cyclopedias
  USE **Encyclopedias and dictionaries**
Cyclotron
  USE **Cyclotrons**
Cyclotrons   **539.7**
  UF Atom smashing
      Cyclotron
      Magnetic resonance accelerator
  BT **Atoms**
      Nuclear physics
      Transmutation (Chemistry)
Cytology
  USE **Cells**
Czech Republic   **943.71**

Use for materials on this part of the former country of Czechoslovakia since its becoming independent on January 1, 1993. May be subdivided like **United States** except for *History*.

  RT **Czechoslovakia**
Czechoslovakia   **943.703**

Use for materials on the former country of Czechoslovakia through December 31, 1992. Materials on the two parts of the former country of Czechoslovakia, which became independent on January 1, 1993, are entered under **Czech Republic** and **Slovakia**.

  RT **Czech Republic**
      Slovakia
Czechoslovakia—History—1918-1968
      943.703
Czechoslovakia—History—1945-1992
      943.704

  UF Czechoslovakia—History—1989-
      1992
Czechoslovakia—History—1968-1989
      943.704
Czechoslovakia—History—1989-1992
  USE **Czechoslovakia—History—1945-1992**
D.D.T. (Insecticide)
  USE **DDT (Insecticide)**
D Day
  USE **Normandy (France), Attack on,**
      1944
Daily readings (Spiritual exercises)
  USE **Devotional calendars**
Dairies
  USE **Dairying**
Dairy cattle   **636.2**
  SA names of breeds of dairy cattle
      [to be added as needed]
  BT **Cattle**
      Dairying
  NT **Holstein-Friesian cattle**
Dairy farming
  USE **Dairying**
Dairy-free cooking   **641.8**
  UF Lactose intolerance—Diet thera-
      py—Recipes
  BT **Cooking**
  RT **Lactose intolerance**
Dairy industry
  USE **Dairying**
Dairy products   **637; 641.3**
  UF Products, Dairy
  SA types of dairy products [to be
      added as needed]
  BT **Animal products**
  NT **Butter**
      Cheese
      Milk
Dairying (May subdiv. geog.)   **636.2;**
      637

Use for materials on the production and marketing of milk and milk products and for general materials on dairy farming.

  UF Dairies
      Dairy farming
      Dairy industry
  BT **Agriculture**
      Livestock industry
  NT **Dairy cattle**
      Milk
Dams (May subdiv. geog.)   **627**

Dams—*Continued*

  SA   names of dams, e.g. **Hoover Dam (Ariz. and Nev.)** [to be added as needed]

  BT   **Civil engineering**
         Hydraulic structures
         Water supply

  NT   **Hoover Dam (Ariz. and Nev.)**

Dance (May subdiv. geog.)   **792.8; 793.3**

Use for materials on recreational dancing as well as performance dance.

  UF   Dances
         Dancing

  SA   types of dances and dancing [to be added as needed]

  BT   **Amusements**
         Performing arts

  NT   **Ballet**
         Ballroom dancing
         Belly dancing
         Break dancing
         Clog dancing
         Folk dancing
         Modern dance
         Step dancing
         Tap dancing

  RT   **Aerobics**
         Dance music

Dance music (May subdiv. geog.)   **781.5; 784.18**

  BT   **Music**

  RT   **Dance**

Dance—United States   **792.80973; 793.30973**

Dancers (May subdiv. geog.)   **792.8092; 793.3092; 920**

  SA   types of dancers, e.g. **Ballet dancers** [to be added as needed]

  BT   **Entertainers**

  NT   **African American dancers**
         Ballet dancers

Dances
  USE   **Dance**

Dancing
  USE   **Dance**

Dangerous animals   **591.6**

  BT   **Animals**

  NT   **Animal attacks**
         Poisonous animals

Dangerous materials
  USE   **Hazardous substances**

Dangerous occupations
  USE   **Hazardous occupations**

Danish language   **439.8**

May be subdivided like **English language**.

  BT   **Language and languages**
         Norwegian language
         Scandinavian languages

Danish literature   **839.81**

May use same subdivisions and names of literary forms as for **English literature**.

  BT   **Literature**
         Scandinavian literature

Dao
  USE   **Tao**

Dark Ages
  USE   **Middle Ages**

Dark humor (Literature)
  USE   **Black humor (Literature)**

Dark matter (Astronomy)   **523.1**

  BT   **Matter**

Dark night of the soul
  USE   **Mysticism**

Darkroom technique in photography
  USE   **Photography—Processing**

Darwinism
  USE   **Evolution**

Data banks
  USE   **Databases**

Data base design
  USE   **Database design**

Data bases
  USE   **Databases**

Data processing (May subdiv. geog.)   **004**

  UF   Automatic data processing
         Electronic data processing

  SA   subjects with the subdivision *Data processing*, e.g. **Banks and banking—Data processing** [to be added as needed]

  BT   **Computers**
         Information systems

  NT   **Banks and banking—Data processing**
         Computer graphics
         Computer programming
         Database management
         Expert systems (Computer science)
         Optical data processing

  RT   **Computer science**

Data processing—Keyboarding
USE **Keyboarding (Electronics)**
Data retrieval
USE **Information retrieval**
Data storage and retrieval systems
USE **Information systems**
**Data transmission systems   004.6;
    621.38; 621.39**
UF   Transmission of data
BT   **Telecommunication**
NT   **Computer networks**
        Electronic mail systems
        Fax transmission
        Instant messaging
        Teletext systems
        Video telephone
        Videotex systems
Databanks
USE **Databases**
Database design   005.74
UF   Data base design
BT   **System design**
Database management   005.74
UF   Systems, Database management
BT   **Computer science**
        Data processing
        Information systems
Database management—Computer programs
USE **Database management—Com-
        puter software**
**Database management—Computer soft-
        ware   005.74**
UF   Database management—Comput-
        er programs
BT   **Computer software**
Databases   025.04
Use for materials on any type of organized
body of information, including written, numer-
ical, and visual information, not limited to a
particular subject.
UF   Data banks
        Data bases
        Databanks
SA   subjects with the subdivision
        Databases, for materials about
        data files on a subject regard-
        less of the medium of distri-
        bution, e.g. **Business—
        Databases**; subjects with the
        subdivision *Information re-
        sources*, for general materials

about information on a subject, e.g. **Business—Information resources**; subjects with
the subdivision *Internet resources*, for materials about
information available on the
Internet on a subject, e.g.
Business—Internet resources;
and headings for the providers
or the users of information
with the subdivision *Information services*, for materials
about organizations that provide information services, e.g.
**United Nations—Information
services**; **Consumers—Infor-
mation services**; etc. [to be
added as needed]
BT   **Information resources**
NT   **Business—Databases**
        Web databases
Date etiquette
USE **Dating (Social customs)**
Date rape   362.883; 364.15
UF   Acquaintance rape
        Dating violence
BT   **Dating (Social customs)**
        Rape
Dates, Historical
USE **Historical chronology**
Dating etiquette
USE **Dating (Social customs)**
Dating, Radiocarbon
USE **Radiocarbon dating**
Dating (Social customs) (May subdiv.
        geog.)   **306.73; 392.4; 646.7**
UF   Date etiquette
        Dating etiquette
BT   **Courtship**
        Etiquette
        Manners and customs
NT   **Date rape**
RT   **Man-woman relationship**
Dating violence
USE **Date rape**
Daughters   306.874
BT   **Family**
        Women
NT   **Father-daughter relationship**
        Mother-daughter relationship

Daughters and fathers
USE **Father-daughter relationship**
Daughters and mothers
USE **Mother-daughter relationship**
Day   529
BT **Chronology**
Time
RT **Night**
Day care centers (May subdiv. geog.)
362.71
UF Child care centers
Children—Day care
Children's day care centers
Day nurseries
Nurseries, Day
BT **Child care**
Child welfare
Children—Institutional care
RT **Nursery schools**
Day dreams
USE **Fantasy**
Day nurseries
USE **Day care centers**
Day of Atonement
USE **Yom Kippur**
Day trading (Securities)   332.64
BT **Securities**
Days   394.2
UF Days of the week
SA types of days and names of par-
ticular days [to be added as
needed]
BT **Calendars**
NT **Birthdays**
Holidays
RT **Anniversaries**
Festivals
Week
Days of the week
USE **Days**
DDT (Insecticide)   668
UF D.D.T. (Insecticide)
Dichloro-diphenyl-trichloroethane
BT **Insecticides**
Dead Sea scrolls   221.4; 229; 296.1
UF Qumran texts
RT **Essenes**
Deaf (May subdiv. geog.)   **362.4**
BT **Hearing impaired**
Physically handicapped

NT **Closed caption television**
**Closed caption video record-
ings**
RT **Deafness**
Deaf—Education (May subdiv. geog.)
371.91
UF Education of the deaf
BT **Education**
Deaf—Institutional care   362.4
BT **Institutional care**
**Deaf—Means of communication   362.4;
419**
Use for general materials on communication
in the broadest sense by people who are deaf.
Materials on language systems based on hand
gestures are entered under **Sign language**.
BT **Communication**
NT **Hearing ear dogs**
Lipreading
RT **Nonverbal communication**
Sign language
Deaf—Sign language
USE **Sign language**
Deafness   362.4; 617.8
NT **Hearing aids**
RT **Deaf**
Hearing
Death (May subdiv. geog.)   **128; 236;
306.9; 571.9**
SA ethnic groups and classes of per-
sons with the subdivision
Death, e.g. **Infants—Death**;
and names of individual per-
sons and groups of notable
persons with the subdivision
Death and burial, e.g. **Presi-
dents—United States—Death
and burial** [to be added as
needed]
BT **Biology**
Eschatology
Life
NT **Brain death**
Children and death
Children—Death
Future life
Infants—Death
Near-death experiences
Right to die
RT **Burial**
Mortality
Terminal care

Death—*Continued*
> **Terminally ill**

Death and burial
> USE   names of individual persons and
> groups of notable persons
> with the subdivision *Death*
> *and burial,* e.g. **Presidents—**
> **United States—Death and**
> **burial** [to be added as need-
> ed]

Death and children
> USE   **Children and death**

Death masks
> USE   **Masks (Sculpture)**

Death notices
> USE   **Obituaries**

Death penalty
> USE   **Capital punishment**

Death rate
> USE   **Mortality**
> **Vital statistics**

Deaths, Registers of
> USE   **Registers of births, etc.**

Debates and debating   808.53
> UF   Argumentation
> Discussion
> Speaking
> BT   **Public speaking**
> **Rhetoric**
> NT   **Parliamentary practice**
> **Radio addresses, debates, etc.**
> RT   **Discussion groups**

Debit cards   332.1
> UF   Bank debit cards
> Cards, Debit
> BT   **Banks and banking**

Debris in space
> USE   **Space debris**

Debt (May subdiv. geog.)   332.7
> Use for economic and statistical materials
> on debt. Legal materials regarding debtor and
> creditor are entered under **Debtor and credi-**
> **tor.**
> UF   Indebtedness
> BT   **Finance**
> NT   **Collecting of accounts**
> **Public debts**
> RT   **Debtor and creditor**

Debtor
> USE   **Debtor and creditor**

Debtor and creditor (May subdiv. geog.)
> **346.07**
> Use for legal materials regarding debtor and
> creditor. Economic and statistical materials on
> debt are entered under **Debt.**
> UF   Creditor
> Debtor
> BT   **Commercial law**
> NT   **Bankruptcy**
> **Collecting of accounts**
> RT   **Credit**
> **Debt**

Debts, Public
> USE   **Public debts**

Decalogue
> USE   **Ten commandments**

Deceit
> USE   **Deception**
> **Fraud**

Decentralization of schools
> USE   **Schools—Decentralization**

Deception   001.9; 177
> UF   Chicanery
> Deceit
> Subterfuge
> BT   **Truthfulness and falsehood**
> NT   **Disguise**

Deceptive advertising   343.07
> UF   False advertising
> Fraudulent advertising
> Misleading advertising
> Misrepresentation in advertising
> Truth in advertising
> BT   **Advertising**
> **Business ethics**

Decimal system   513.5
> BT   **Numbers**
> RT   **Metric system**

Decision making (May subdiv. geog.)
> **153.8; 302.3; 658.4**
> NT   **Critical thinking**
> **Group decision making**
> RT   **Choice (Psychology)**
> **Problem solving**

Decks (Domestic architecture)
> USE   **Patios**

Declamations
> USE   **Monologues**
> **Recitations**

Declaration of independence (U.S.)
> USE   **United States—Declaration of**
> **independence**

Decoration and ornament (May subdiv. geog.)   **745.4**

Use for general materials on the forms and styles of decoration in various fields of fine arts or applied art and on the history of various styles of ornament. In addition to geographic subdivision, this heading may be subdivided by date or by style of ornament, e.g. **Decoration and ornament—15th and 16th centuries**; **Decoration and ornament—Gothic style**; etc. Materials limited to the decoration of houses are entered under **Interior design**.

UF Decorative art

Decorative design

Decorative painting

Ornament

Painting, Decorative

BT **Art**

Decorative arts

NT **Antiques**

Architectural decoration and ornament

Art objects

Artificial flowers

Arts and crafts movement

Beads

Bronzes

China painting

Christmas decorations

Decoupage

Design

Egg decoration

Embroidery

Enamel and enameling

Flower arrangement

Furniture

Garden ornaments and furniture

Gems

Glass painting and staining

Holiday decorations

Illumination of books and manuscripts

Illustration of books

Interior design

Ironwork

Leather work

Lettering

Metalwork

Monograms

Mosaics

Mural painting and decoration

Needlework

Picture frames and framing

Pottery

Sculpture

Show windows

Stencil work

Stucco

Table setting and decoration

Tapestry

Terra cotta

Textile design

Wood carving

RT **Handicraft**

Painting

Decoration and ornament—15th and 16th centuries (May subdiv. geog.)   **745.4**

UF Decoration and ornament, Renaissance

Renaissance decoration and ornament

Decoration and ornament, American

USE **Decoration and ornament— United States**

Decoration and ornament, Architectural

USE **Architectural decoration and ornament**

Decoration and ornament, Gothic

USE **Decoration and ornament— Gothic style**

Decoration and ornament—Gothic style (May subdiv. geog.)   **745.4**

UF Decoration and ornament, Gothic

Gothic decoration and ornament

Decoration and ornament, Renaissance

USE **Decoration and ornament— 15th and 16th centuries**

Decoration and ornament—United States   **745.4**

UF American decoration and ornament

Decoration and ornament, American

Decoration Day

USE **Memorial Day**

Decorations, Holiday

USE **Holiday decorations**

Decorations of honor (May subdiv. geog.)   **355.1; 929.8**

UF Badges of honor

Emblems

Decorations of honor—*Continued*
  SA names of medals [to be added
      as needed]
  RT **Heraldry**
      Insignia
      Medals
Decorative art
  USE **Decoration and ornament**
      Decorative arts
Decorative arts (May subdiv. geog.) **745**
  Use for general materials on the various ap-
  plied art forms having some utilitarian as well
  as decorative purpose, including furniture, sil-
  verware, the decoration of buildings, etc.
  UF Applied arts
      Art industries and trade
      Decorative art
      Minor arts
  SA types of decorative arts [to be
      added as needed]
  BT **Arts**
  NT **Antiques**
      Art metalwork
      Art objects
      Arts and crafts movement
      Calligraphy
      Carving (Decorative arts)
      Costume
      Decoration and ornament
      Decoupage
      Enamel and enameling
      Fabrics
      Furniture
      Glassware
      Jewelry
      Lacquer and lacquering
      Leather work
      Mosaics
      Needlework
      Porcelain
      Pottery
      Rugs and carpets
      Silverware
      Tapestry
      Woodwork
  RT **Folk art**
      Handicraft
Decorative arts—United States
      745.0973
Decorative design
  USE **Decoration and ornament**

Decorative metalwork
  USE **Art metalwork**
Decorative painting
  USE **Decoration and ornament**
Decoupage **745.54**
  BT **Decoration and ornament**
      Decorative arts
      Paper crafts
Decoys (Hunting) (May subdiv. geog.)
      745.593; 799.2
  UF Bird decoys (Hunting)
  BT **Hunting**
      Shooting
Deduction (Logic)
  USE **Logic**
Deejays
  USE **Disc jockeys**
Deep diving (May subdiv. geog.) **627**
  Use for materials on underwater diving with
  equipment. Materials on diving from a board
  or platform are entered under **Diving**.
  UF Deep sea diving
      Submarine diving
      Underwater diving
  BT **Underwater exploration**
      Water sports
  NT **Scuba diving**
      Skin diving
  RT **Diving**
Deep sea diving
  USE **Deep diving**
Deep sea drilling (Petroleum)
  USE **Offshore oil well drilling**
Deep sea engineering
  USE **Ocean engineering**
Deep sea mining
  USE **Ocean mining**
Deep-sea photography
  USE **Underwater photography**
Deer (May subdiv. geog.) **599.65**
  UF Fawns
  BT **Game and game birds**
      Mammals
  NT **Reindeer**
Defamation
  USE **Libel and slander**
Defective speech
  USE **Speech disorders**
Defective vision
  USE **Vision disorders**
Defectors (May subdiv. geog.) **325;**
      327.12

Defectors—*Continued*
> UF Political defectors
>   Turncoats
> BT **Political refugees**

Defense industries
> USE **Defense industry**

Defense industry (May subdiv. geog.)
     338.4

Use for materials on the industries producing the implements of war. Materials on the implements of war themselves are entered under **Ordnance** or under **Military weapons**.

> UF Armaments industries
>   Arms sales
>   Defense industries
>   Military sales
>   Military supplies industry
>   Munitions
>   Weapons industry
> BT **Industries**
> RT **Arms transfers**
>   **Military readiness**
>   **Military weapons**
>   **Ordnance**

Defense (Law)
> USE **Litigation**

Defense mechanisms of animals
> USE **Animal defenses**

Defense mechanisms of plants
> USE **Plant defenses**

Defense policy
> USE **Military policy**

Defense readiness
> USE **Military readiness**

Defense research
> USE **Military research**

Defenses
> USE types of defenses, e.g. **Air defenses;** and names of continents, regions, countries, and individual colonies with the subdivision *Defenses,* e.g. **United States—Defenses** [to be added as needed]

Defenses, Radar
> USE **Radar defense networks**

Deficit financing (May subdiv. geog.)
     336.3
> UF Compensatory spending
>   Deficit spending
> BT **Public finance**
> RT **Public debts**

Deficit spending
> USE **Deficit financing**

Defoliants
> USE **Herbicides**

Deforestation (May subdiv. geog.)   **634.9**
> UF Forest depletion
> BT **Forests and forestry**

Deformities
> USE **Birth defects**

Degrees, Academic
> USE **Academic degrees**

Degrees of latitude and longitude
> USE **Geodesy**
>   **Latitude**
>   **Longitude**

Dehydrated foods
> USE **Dried foods**

Dehydrated milk
> USE **Dried milk**

Deism (May subdiv. geog.)   **211**
> BT **Religion**
>   **Theology**
> RT **Atheism**
>   **Free thought**
>   **Positivism**
>   **Rationalism**
>   **Theism**

Deities
> USE **Gods and goddesses**

Dejection
> USE **Depression (Psychology)**

Delayed memory
> USE **Recovered memory**

Delinquency, Juvenile
> USE **Juvenile delinquency**

Delinquents
> USE **Criminals**

Delivery of health care
> USE **Medical care**

Delivery of medical care
> USE **Medical care**

Delphi (Ancient city)
> USE **Delphi (Extinct city)**

Delphi (Extinct city)   938
> UF Delphi (Ancient city)
> BT **Extinct cities—Greece**
>   **Greece—Antiquities**

Delusions
> USE **Hallucinations and illusions**

Dementia   616.8
> BT **Brain—Diseases**

Demobilization
USE names of armed forces with the
subdivision *Demobilization,*
e.g. **United States. Army—
Demobilization** [to be added
as needed]
Democracy (May subdiv. geog.)   **321.8**
UF Popular government
Self-government
BT **Constitutional history
Constitutional law
Political science**
NT **Freedom
Referendum
Suffrage**
RT **Equality
Representative government and
representation
Republics**
Democratic Party (U.S.)   324.2736
BT **Political parties**
Democratic Republic of the Congo
USE **Congo (Democratic Republic)**
Demography
USE **Population**
Demoniac possession   133.4
BT **Demonology**
RT **Devil
Exorcism**
Demonology (May subdiv. geog.)   **133.4**
UF Evil spirits
BT **Occultism**
NT **Demoniac possession**
RT **Devil
Exorcism
Spirits**
Demonstrations (May subdiv. geog.)
322.4; 361.2
Use for materials on public gatherings,
marches, etc., organized for nonviolent protest
even though incidental disturbances or rioting
may occur.
UF Marches (Demonstrations)
Protest marches and rallies
Protests, demonstrations, etc.
Public demonstrations
Rallies (Protest)
SA names of specific wars or other
objects of protest with the
subdivision *Protest move-
ments,* e.g. **World War,**

**1939-1945—Protest move-
ments** [to be added as need-
ed]
BT **Crowds
Public meetings**
NT **Civil rights demonstrations
Hunger strikes**
RT **Peace movements
Protest movements
Riots**
**Demonstrations—Chicago (Ill.)
322.409773**
Demonstrations for civil rights
USE **Civil rights demonstrations**
**Demonstrations—United States
322.40973; 361.2**
Denationalization
USE **Privatization**
Denatured alcohol   661
UF Alcohol, Denatured
Industrial alcohol
BT **Alcohol**
Denmark   948.9
May be subdivided like **United States** ex-
cept for *History.*
Denominational schools
USE **Church schools**
Denominations, Christian
USE **Christian sects**
Denominations, Protestant
USE **Protestant churches**
Denominations, Religious
USE **Sects**
Dental care (May subdiv. geog.)   **617.6**
Use for materials on the organization of
services and facilities for dental care. Materi-
als on the technical and medical aspects of
dental care are entered under **Dentistry**.
SA ethnic groups, classes of per-
sons, and military services
with the subdivision *Dental
care,* e.g. **Children—Dental
care** [to be added as needed]
BT **Medical care**
RT **Dentistry**
Dentistry (May subdiv. geog.)   **617.6**
Use for materials on the technical and medical aspects of dental care. Materials on the
organization of services and facilities for dental care are entered under **Dental care**.
SA ethnic groups, classes of persons, and military services
with the subdivision *Dental*

Dentistry—*Continued*
  care, e.g. **Children—Dental care** [to be added as needed]
 BT **Medicine**
 RT **Dental care**
   Teeth
Deoxyribonucleic acid
 USE **DNA**
Department stores (May subdiv. geog.) **658.8**
 BT **Business**
   Retail trade
   Stores
Dependencies
 USE **Colonies**
Depression, Mental
 USE **Depression (Psychology)**
Depression (Psychology) **616.85**
 UF Dejection
   Depression, Mental
   Depressive psychoses
   Melancholia
   Mental depression
   Mentally depressed
 BT **Abnormal psychology**
   Affective disorders
   Neuroses
 NT **Postpartum depression**
 RT **Manic-depressive illness**
Depressions (May subdiv. geog.) **338.5**
 UF Business depressions
   Economic depressions
 SA names of countries, states, cities, etc., with the subdivision *Economic conditions* [to be added as needed]
 BT **Business cycles**
 NT **Great Depression, 1929-1939**
Depressions—1929
 USE **Great Depression, 1929-1939**
Depressive psychoses
 USE **Depression (Psychology)**
Deprogramming
 USE **Brainwashing**
Derailments
 USE **Railroad accidents**
Deregulation (May subdiv. geog.) **338.9; 352.8**
 UF Industries—Deregulation
 SA types of industry with the subdivision *Deregulation*, e.g. **Petroleum industry—**

Deregulation to be added as needed]
 BT **Industrial policy**
Dermatitis
 USE **Skin—Diseases**
Derricks
 USE **Cranes, derricks, etc.**
Dervishes (May subdiv. geog.) **297.4**
 RT **Sufism**
Desalination of water
 USE **Sea water conversion**
Desalting of water
 USE **Sea water conversion**
Descent
 USE **Genealogy**
   Heredity
Description
 USE names of cities (except extinct cities), countries, states, and regions with the subdivision *Description and travel*, e.g. **Chicago (Ill.)—Description and travel; United States—Description and travel;** etc., for descriptive materials and accounts of travel, including the history of travel, in those places; names of places with the subdivision *Geography* for broad geographical materials about a specific place, e.g. **United States—Geography;** and names of extinct cities or towns, without further subdivision, for general descriptive materials on those places, e.g. **Delphi (Extinct city)** [to be added as needed]
Description and travel
 USE names of cities (except extinct cities), countries, states, etc., with the subdivision *Description and travel*, e.g. **Chicago (Ill.)—Description and travel; United States—Description and travel;** etc., for descriptive materials and accounts of travel, including the history of travel, in those places; names of places with the subdivision *Geography* for

Description and travel—*Continued*
  broad geographical materials
  about a specific place, e.g.
  United States—Geography;
  names of extinct cities or
  towns, without further subdivision, for general descriptive
  materials on those places, e.g.
  Delphi (Extinct city); and
  ethnic groups, classes of persons, and names of individuals with the subdivision *Travel,* e.g. **Handicapped—Travel**
  [to be added as needed]

Descriptive geometry   516
  UF Geometry, Descriptive
  BT **Geometrical drawing**
      Geometry
  NT **Perspective**
Desegregated schools
  USE **School integration**
Desegregation
  USE **Segregation**
Desegregation in education
  USE **School integration**
Desert animals (May subdiv. geog.)
      578.754
  UF Desert fauna
  SA types of desert animals, e.g.
      Camels [to be added as need-
      ed]
  BT **Animals**
      Deserts
  NT **Camels**
Desert ecology (May subdiv. geog.)
      577.54
  BT **Ecology**
Desert fauna
  USE **Desert animals**
Desert plants (May subdiv. geog.)   **581.7**
  SA types of desert plants, e.g. **Cac-
      tus** [to be added as needed]
  BT **Deserts**
      Plant ecology
      Plants
  NT **Cactus**
Desertification (May subdiv. geog.)
      333.73
  BT **Climate**
      Deserts

Desertion
  USE **Desertion and nonsupport**
       Military desertion
Desertion and nonsupport   306.88;
      346.01
  UF Abandonment of family
      Desertion
      Nonsupport
  BT **Divorce**
      Domestic relations
  NT **Child support**
      Runaway adults
Desertion, Military
  USE **Military desertion**
Desertions
  USE names of wars with the subdivi-
       sion *Desertions,* e.g. **World
       War, 1939-1945—Desertions**
       [to be added as needed]
Deserts   551.41
  BT **Physical geography**
  NT **Desert animals**
      Desert plants
      Desertification
Design (May subdiv. geog.)   **745.4**
  SA types of design, e.g. **Industrial
      design; Fashion design;** etc.;
      types of objects, structures,
      machines, equipment, etc., and
      types of educational tests and
      examinations with the subdivi-
      sion *Design and construction,*
      e.g. **Automobiles—Design
      and construction;** topical
      headings with which the sub-
      division *Design and construc-
      tion* would be inappropriate
      with the subdivision *Design,*
      e.g. **Quilts—Design; Pam-
      phlets—Design;** etc.; and
      types of architecture and land-
      scape with the form subdivision
      Designs and plans, for
      materials containing designs
      and drawings, e.g. **Domestic
      architecture—Designs and
      plans** [to be added as needed]
  BT **Decoration and ornament**
  NT **Architectural design**
      Computer-aided design
      Fashion design

Design—*Continued*

    Garden design

    Industrial design

    Interior design

    Machine design

    Pamphlets—Design

    Quilts—Design

    Textile design

    Web sites—Design

  RT **Designers**

    Patternmaking

Design and construction

  USE types of objects, structures, machines, equipment, etc., and types of educational tests and examinations with the subdivision *Design and construction,* e.g. **Airplanes—Design and construction** [to be added as needed]

Design, Industrial

  USE **Industrial design**

Design perception

  USE **Pattern perception**

Designed genetic change

  USE **Genetic engineering**

Designer drugs 362.29; 615

  Use for materials on illicit drugs manufactured by altering the molecular structure of existing drugs to mimic the effects of standard narcotics, stimulants, or hallucinogens.

  UF Synthetic drugs of abuse

  SA types of designer drugs, e.g. **Crystal meth (Drug)** [to be added as needed]

  BT **Drugs**

  NT **Crystal meth (Drug)**

Designers (May subdiv. geog.) **709.2**

  BT **Artists**

  NT **Fashion designers**

  RT **Design**

Designs and plans

  USE types of architecture and landscape with the form subdivision *Designs and plans,* for materials containing designs and drawings, e.g. **Domestic architecture—Designs and plans** [to be added as needed]

Designs, Architectural

  USE **Architecture—Designs and plans**

Designs, Floral

  USE **Flower arrangement**

Desktop computers

  USE **Personal computers**

Desktop icons (Computer graphics)

  USE **Icons (Computer graphics)**

Desktop publishing 070.5; 686.2

  Use for materials on the use of a personal computer with writing, graphics, and page layout software to produce printed material for publication. Materials on the process of publishing by which books and articles or any kind of data are made available as an electronic product are entered under **Electronic publishing**.

  RT **Electronic publishing**

    Word processing

Desserts 641.8

  SA types of desserts and names of specific desserts [to be added as needed]

  BT **Cooking**

  NT **Cake**

    Ice cream, ices, etc.

  RT **Chocolate**

Destiny

  USE **Fate and fatalism**

Destitution

  USE **Poverty**

Destruction and pillage

  USE names of wars with the subdivision *Destruction and pillage,* e.g. **World War, 1939-1945—Destruction and pillage** [to be added as needed]

Destruction of property

  USE **Vandalism**

Destructive insects

  USE **Insect pests**

Detective and mystery comic books, strips, etc.

  USE **Mystery comic books, strips, etc.**

Detective and mystery films

  USE **Mystery films**

Detective and mystery plays

  USE **Mystery and detective plays**

Detective and mystery radio programs

  USE **Mystery radio programs**

Detective and mystery stories

  USE **Mystery fiction**

Detective and mystery television programs

  USE **Mystery television programs**

Detective comics
USE **Mystery comic books, strips, etc.**
Detective fiction
USE **Mystery fiction**
Detective stories
USE **Mystery fiction**
Detectives (May subdiv. geog.) **363.25; 920**
BT **Police**
RT **Criminal investigation**
Secret service
Detergent pollution of rivers, lakes, etc.
USE **Water pollution**
Detergents 668
UF Synthetic detergents
BT **Cleaning compounds**
RT **Soap**
Determinism and indeterminism
USE **Free will and determinism**
Deuterium oxide 546
UF Heavy water
BT **Chemicals**
Devaluation of currency
USE **Monetary policy**
Developing countries 330.9
Use for comprehensive materials on countries that are not fully modernized or industrialized. This heading may be subdivided by the topical subdivisions used under countries, regions, etc., and may also be used as a geographic subdivision e.g. **Education—Developing countries**.
UF Less developed countries
Third World
Underdeveloped areas
BT **Economic conditions**
Industrialization
NT **New states**
Developing countries—Commerce 338.91; 382
BT **Commerce**
Developing countries—Education
USE **Education—Developing countries**
Development
USE **Embryology**
Evolution
Growth disorders
Modernization (Sociology)
Development, Economic
USE **Economic development**
Developmental psychology 155

BT **Psychology**
Deviancy
USE **Deviant behavior**
Deviant behavior 155.2; 302.5
UF Deviancy
Social deviance
BT **Human behavior**
RT **Conformity**
Social adjustment
Deviation, Sexual
USE **Sexual deviation**
Devices (Heraldry)
USE **Heraldry**
Insignia
Devil 235
UF Satan
RT **Demoniac possession**
Demonology
Devil's Triangle
USE **Bermuda Triangle**
Devotion
USE **Prayer**
Worship
Devotional calendars 242
UF Christian devotional calendars
Daily readings (Spiritual exercises)
Devotional exercises (Daily readings)
BT **Calendars**
Devotional literature
Devotional exercises 242; 248.3
Use for general materials on acts of private prayer and private worship and for materials on religious practices other than the corporate worship of a congregation. Materials on the religious literature used as aids in devotional exercises are entered under **Devotional literature**.
UF Devotional theology
Devotions
Family devotions
Family prayers
BT **Worship**
NT **Meditation**
RT **Prayer**
Devotional exercises (Daily readings)
USE **Devotional calendars**
Devotional literature 242
Use for materials on the religious literature used as aids in devotional exercises. General materials on acts of private prayer and private worship and materials on religious practices other than the corporate worship of a congre-

Devotional literature—*Continued*
gation are entered under **Devotional exercises**.
- BT **Religious literature**
- NT **Devotional calendars**
  Devotional literature for children
  Meditations
  Prayers

Devotional literature for children   242
- BT **Devotional literature**

Devotional theology
- USE **Devotional exercises**
  Prayer

Devotions
- USE **Devotional exercises**

Dewey Decimal Classification   025.4
- UF Classification, Dewey Decimal
- BT **Library classification**

Diabetes   616.4
- BT **Diseases**

Diagnosis   616.07
- UF Medical diagnosis
  Symptoms
- BT **Medicine**
- NT **Body temperature**
  Clinical chemistry
  Magnetic resonance imaging
  Pain
  Prenatal diagnosis
- RT **Pathology**

Diagnostic chemistry
- USE **Clinical chemistry**

Dialectical materialism   335.4
- UF Historical materialism
- BT **Communism**
  Socialism
- RT **Marxism**

Dialectics
- USE **Logic**

Dialects
- USE names of languages with the subdivision *Dialects,* e.g. **English language—Dialects** [to be added as needed]

Diamonds   553.8
- BT **Carbon**
  Precious stones

Diaries   808; 920
Use for collections of diaries from various countries and for materials about diaries in general.
- UF Journals (Diaries)
- SA diaries of particular countries, e.g. **American diaries**; and classes of persons, ethnic groups, and names of individual persons and families with the subdivision *Diaries* [to be added as needed]
- BT **Literature**
- NT **American diaries**
  Journaling
  Weblogs
- RT **Autobiographies**

Diaspora, African
- USE **African diaspora**

Diaspora, Jewish
- USE **Jewish diaspora**

Dichloro-diphenyl-trichloroethane
- USE **DDT (Insecticide)**

Dictators   321.909; 920
- BT **Heads of state**
  Totalitarianism

Dictionaries
- USE **Encyclopedias and dictionaries** and subjects, names of languages, and names of voluminous authors with the subdivision *Dictionaries,* e.g. **English language—Dictionaries; Biography—Dictionaries; Shakespeare, William, 1564-1616—Dictionaries** etc. [to be added as needed]

Dictionaries, Biographical
- USE **Biography—Dictionaries**

Dictionaries, Classical
- USE **Classical dictionaries**

Dictionaries, Machine readable
- USE **Machine readable dictionaries**

Dictionaries, Multilingual
- USE **Polyglot dictionaries**

Dictionaries, Picture
- USE **Picture dictionaries**

Dictionaries, Polyglot
- USE **Polyglot dictionaries**

Didactic drama   808.82
Use for individual works, collections, or materials about didactic drama.
- BT **Drama**

Didactic fiction   808.3; 808.83
Use for individual works, collections, or materials about didactic fiction.

Didactic fiction—*Continued*
    UF   Cautionary tales and verses
          Moral and philosophic stories
          Morality stories
    BT   **Fiction**
    RT   **Fables**
          Parables
Didactic poetry   808.1; 808.81
    Use for individual works, collections, or materials about didactic poetry.
    UF   Cautionary tales and verses
    BT   **Poetry**
    RT   **Fables**
          Parables
Dies (Metalworking)   621.9; 671.2
    BT   **Metalwork**
Diesel automobiles   629.222
    UF   Diesel cars
    BT   **Automobiles**
Diesel cars
    USE **Diesel automobiles**
Diesel engines   621.43
    BT   **Engines**
          Internal combustion engines
Diet (May subdiv. geog.)   **613.2**
    UF   Dietetics
    SA   types of diets, e.g. **Salt-free diet** [to be added as needed]
    BT   **Health**
          Hygiene
    NT   **Beverages**
          Dietetic foods
          Eating customs
          Fasting
          Gastronomy
          High-carbohydrate diet
          Low-carbohydrate diet
          Low-cholesterol diet
          Low-fat diet
          Menus
          Salt-free diet
          School children—Food
          Vegetarianism
    RT   **Cooking**
          Digestion
          Food
          Nutrition
          Weight gain
          Weight loss
Diet in disease   613.2; 616.3
    SA   types of diets [to be added as needed]

    BT   **Therapeutics**
    NT   **Cooking for the sick**
          Diet therapy
Diet supplements
    USE **Dietary supplements**
Diet—Therapeutic use
    USE **Diet therapy**
Diet therapy   615.8
    UF   Diet—Therapeutic use
          Invalid cooking
    SA   names of diseases with the subdivision *Diet therapy*, e.g. **Cancer—Diet therapy**; and types of food with the subdivision *Therapeutic use*, e.g. **Herbs—Therapeutic use** [to be added as needed]
    BT   **Cooking for the sick**
          Diet in disease
          Therapeutics
    NT   **Cancer—Diet therapy**
Dietary fiber
    USE **Food—Fiber content**
Dietary supplements   613.2; 615.1
    UF   Diet supplements
          Food supplements
          Nutritional supplements
    BT   **Nutrition**
          Vitamins
    NT   **Probiotics**
    RT   **Food additives**
Dietetic foods   641.3; 664
    BT   **Diet**
          Food
Dietetics
    USE **Diet**
Dieting
    USE **Weight loss**
Diets, Reducing
    USE **Weight loss**
Differential equations   515
    BT   **Calculus**
    NT   **Functions**
Digestion   573.3; 612.3
    BT   **Physiology**
    NT   **Indigestion**
    RT   **Diet**
          Nutrition
          Stomach
Digestive system   573.3; 612.3; 616.3
    BT   **Anatomy**

Digital audio disc players
USE **Compact disc players**
Digital cameras   771.3
BT **Cameras**
Digital circuits
USE **Digital electronics**
Digital compact discs
USE **Compact discs**
Digital electronics   621.381
UF Digital circuits
BT **Electronics**
NT **Digital photography**
Digital libraries   025.00285
UF Electronic libraries
Virtual libraries
BT **Information systems**
Libraries
Digital photography   775
UF Photography—Digital techniques
BT **Digital electronics**
Photography
Digital reference services (Libraries)
USE **Electronic reference services**
(Libraries)
Dimension, Fourth
USE **Fourth dimension**
Dining (May subdiv. geog.)   **641.01**
Use for materials on dining customs and gastronomic travel. Materials on menus and recipes for dinners are entered under **Dinners**.
UF Banquets
Dinners and dining
Eating
BT **Food**
NT **Carving (Meat, etc.)**
RT **Dinners**
Eating customs
Entertaining
Gastronomy
Table etiquette
Dinners   642
Use for materials on menus and recipes for dinners. Materials on dining customs and gastronomic travel are entered under **Dining**.
UF Banquets
Dinners and dining
BT **Cooking**
Menus
RT **Dining**
Dinners and dining
USE **Dining**
Dinners

Dinosaur eggs
USE **Dinosaurs—Eggs**
Dinosaurs (May subdiv. geog.)   **567.9**
SA types of dinosaurs and names of specific dinosaurs [to be added as needed]
BT **Fossil reptiles**
Prehistoric animals
Dinosaurs—Eggs   567.9
UF Dinosaur eggs
BT **Eggs**
Dioptrics
USE **Refraction**
Diphtheria   616.9
BT **Diseases**
Diplomacy   327.2; 341.3
SA names of countries with the subdivision *Foreign relations* [to be added as needed]
BT **International relations**
NT **Diplomats**
Treaties
United States—Foreign relations
RT **Diplomatic and consular service**
Diplomatic and consular service (May subdiv. geog.)   **327.2**
Use for materials on diplomatic and consular service in general or on the diplomatic and consular officials of various countries stationed abroad in various countries. Materials on the diplomatic and consular officials of various countries stationed in a specific country are entered under **Diplomatic and consular service** subdivided by the country where they are stationed. Materials on the diplomatic and consular officials of a specific country, regardless of where they are stationed, are entered under the appropriately modified heading, e.g. **American diplomatic and consular service**. Materials on the diplomatic and consular officials of a specific country stationed in a specific country are entered under the appropriately modified heading subdivided by the place where they are stationed.
UF Consular service
Consulates
Embassies
Foreign service
Legations
SA diplomatic and consular services of particular countries, e.g. **American diplomatic and consular service** [to be added as needed]

Diplomatic and consular service—*Continued*
  BT **International relations**
  NT **American diplomatic and consular service**
  RT **Diplomacy**
      Diplomats
Diplomatic and consular service, American
  USE **American diplomatic and consular service**
Diplomatic history
  USE names of wars with the subdivision *Diplomatic history,* e.g. **World War, 1939-1945—Diplomatic history** [to be added as needed]
Diplomats (May subdiv. geog.)
      327.2092; 920
  UF Ministers (Diplomatic agents)
  BT **Diplomacy**
      International relations
      Statesmen
  NT **Ambassadors**
      Consuls
  RT **Diplomatic and consular service**
Direct current machinery
  USE **Electric machinery—Direct current**
Direct legislation
  USE **Referendum**
Direct mail campaigns
  USE **Direct marketing**
Direct marketing (May subdiv. geog.)
      381; 658.8
  UF Direct mail campaigns
  BT **Mail-order business**
      Marketing
  RT **Direct selling**
Direct primaries
  USE **Primaries**
Direct selling   658.8
  BT **Marketing**
      Retail trade
      Selling
  NT **Mail-order business**
      Peddlers and peddling
      Telemarketing
  RT **Direct marketing**
Direct taxation
  USE **Taxation**
Direction sense   152.1; 912

  UF Orientation
      Sense of direction
  NT **Left and right (Direction)**
  RT **Navigation**
      Orienteering
Direction (Theater)
  USE **Theater—Production and direction**
Directories   910.25
    Use for materials about directories and for bibliographies of directories.
  SA subjects and names of countries, cities, etc., with the subdivision *Directories*, for lists of persons, organizations, objects, etc., together with addresses or other identifying data [to be added as needed]
  NT **Chicago (Ill.)—Directories**
      Junior colleges—Directories
      Ohio—Directories
      Physicians—Directories
      United States—Directories
Directories—Telephone
  USE names of cities with the subdivision *Telephone directories,* e.g. **Chicago (Ill.)—Telephone directories** [to be added as needed]
Directors
  USE types of producers and directors in specific media, e.g. **Motion picture producers and directors; Theatrical producers and directors;** etc. [to be added as needed]
Directory, French, 1795-1799
  USE **France—History—1789-1799, Revolution**
Dirigible balloons
  USE **Airships**
Disabilities   362.1
  UF Disabling conditions
      Handicaps
      Impairment
      Physical disabilities
  BT **Diseases**
      Wounds and injuries
  NT **Movement disorders**
Disability income insurance
  USE **Disability insurance**
Disability insurance   368.38

Disability insurance—*Continued*
- UF   Disability income insurance
        Insurance, Disability
- BT   **Insurance**

Disability law
- USE   **Handicapped—Legal status, laws, etc.**

Disabled
- USE   **Handicapped**

Disabling conditions
- USE   **Disabilities**

Disadvantaged
- USE   **Socially handicapped**

Disadvantaged children
- USE   **Socially handicapped children**

Disadvantaged students
- USE   **At risk students**

Disappointment   152.4
- BT   **Emotions**

Disarmament
- USE   **Arms control**

Disaster preparedness
- USE   **Disaster relief**

Disaster relief (May subdiv. geog.)   363.34
- UF   Disaster preparedness
        Emergency preparedness
        Emergency relief
- BT   **Charities**
        Public welfare
- NT   **Evacuation of civilians**
        Food relief

Disasters (May subdiv. geog.)   904
- UF   Catastrophes
        Emergencies
- SA   types of disasters [to be added as needed]
- NT   **Fires**
        Natural disasters
        Railroad accidents
        Shipwrecks
- RT   **Accidents**

Disc jockeys   791.44092; 780.92
- UF   Deejays
        Disk jockeys
        DJs (Disc jockeys)
- BT   **Musicians**
        Radio and music

Disciples, Twelve
- USE   **Apostles**

Discipline
- USE   **Punishment**

Discipline of children
- USE   **Child rearing**
        School discipline

Discography
- USE   **Sound recordings**
        and subjects and names of persons with the subdivision *Discography,* e.g. **Music—Discography; Shakespeare, William, 1564-1616—Discography;** etc., for lists or catalogs of sound recordings [to be added as needed]

Discount stores   381; 658.8
- BT   **Retail trade**
        Stores

Discoverers
- USE   **Explorers**

Discoveries and exploration
- USE   **Exploration**

Discoveries in geography
- USE   **Exploration**

Discoveries in science (May subdiv. geog.)   500
- UF   Breakthroughs, Scientific
        Discoveries, Scientific
        Scientific breakthroughs
        Scientific discoveries
- BT   **Research**
        Science

Discoveries, Scientific
- USE   **Discoveries in science**

Discrimination (May subdiv. geog.)   177; 305

Use for general materials on discrimination by race, religion, sex, age, social status, or other factors, including reverse discrimination.
- SA   phrase headings for discrimination in particular realms of activity, e.g. **Discrimination in employment**; or discrimination against particular ethnic groups or classes of persons, e.g. **Discrimination against the handicapped**; and ethnic groups and classes of persons with the subdivision *Civil rights,* or *Legal status, laws, etc.*, e.g. **African Americans—Civil rights; Handicapped—Legal status, laws, etc.** [to be added as needed]

Discrimination—*Continued*
   BT **Ethnic relations**
       Interpersonal relations
       Prejudices
       Race relations
       Social problems
       Social psychology
   NT **Age discrimination**
       Discrimination against the handicapped
       Discrimination in education
       Discrimination in employment
       Discrimination in housing
       Discrimination in public accommodations
       Hate crimes
       Race discrimination
       Sex discrimination
   RT **Civil rights**
       Minorities
       Segregation
       Toleration

Discrimination against disabled persons
   USE **Discrimination against the handicapped**

Discrimination against handicapped persons
   USE **Discrimination against the handicapped**

Discrimination against the disabled
   USE **Discrimination against the handicapped**

Discrimination against the handicapped
   305.9; 362.4
   UF Discrimination against disabled persons
       Discrimination against handicapped persons
       Discrimination against the disabled
   BT **Discrimination**
       Handicapped

Discrimination in education (May subdiv. geog.) **379.2**
   BT **Discrimination**
   NT **Test bias**
   RT **Segregation in education**

Discrimination in employment (May subdiv. geog.) **331.13**
   UF Employment discrimination
       Equal employment opportunity
       Equal opportunity in employment

       Fair employment practice
       Job discrimination
   SA ethnic groups and classes of persons with the subdivision *Employment*, e.g. **African Americans—Employment** [to be added as needed]
   BT **Discrimination**
   NT **Affirmative action programs**
       Equal pay for equal work

Discrimination in housing (May subdiv. geog.) **363.5**
   UF Fair housing
       Open housing
       Segregation in housing
   BT **Discrimination**
       Housing

Discrimination in public accommodations (May subdiv. geog.) **305**
   UF Public accommodations, Discrimination in
       Segregation in public accommodations
   BT **Discrimination**

Discussion
   USE **Conversation**
       Debates and debating
       Negotiation

Discussion groups **374**
   UF Forums (Discussions)
       Great books program
       Group discussion
       Panel discussions
   BT **Conversation**
   NT **Electronic discussion groups**
   RT **Debates and debating**

Disease germs
   USE **Bacteria**
       Germ theory of disease

Disease (Pathology)
   USE **Pathology**

Diseases (May subdiv. geog.) **616**
   UF Illness
       Sickness
   SA types of diseases, e.g. **Communicable diseases**; names of specific diseases, e.g. **Influenza**; and types of animals, classes of persons, and parts of the body with the subdivision *Diseases*, e.g. **Nervous**

Diseases—*Continued*
      system—Diseases [to be add-
      ed as needed]
  NT **AIDS (Disease)**
      Animals—Diseases
      Arthritis
      Blood—Diseases
      Bones—Diseases
      Brain—Diseases
      Cancer
      Chickenpox
      Children—Diseases
      Chronic diseases
      Cold (Disease)
      Communicable diseases
      Diabetes
      Diphtheria
      Disabilities
      Elderly—Diseases
      Epidemics
      Heart diseases
      Hyperactivity
      Infants—Diseases
      Influenza
      Leprosy
      Lungs—Diseases
      Lyme disease
      Malaria
      Men—Diseases
      Mental illness
      Mouth—Diseases
      Nervous system—Diseases
      Occupational diseases
      Plant diseases
      Poliomyelitis
      Rheumatism
      Skin—Diseases
      Teeth—Diseases
      Typhoid fever
      Women—Diseases
  RT **Health**
      Medicine
      Pathology
      Sick
Diseases and pests
  USE **Agricultural bacteriology**
      Agricultural pests
      Fungi
      Household pests
      Insect pests
      Parasites
      Plant diseases

and names of individual pests,
e.g. **Locusts;** and types of
crops, plants, trees, etc., with
the subdivision *Diseases and
pests,* e.g. **Fruit—Diseases
and pests** [to be added as
needed]

Diseases—Causes   **616.07**
  UF Causes of diseases
  NT **Environmentally induced dis-
      eases**
Diseases, Chronic
  USE **Chronic diseases**
Diseases—Environmental aspects
  USE **Environmentally induced dis-
      eases**
Diseases of animals
  USE **Animals—Diseases**
Diseases of children
  USE **Children—Diseases**
Diseases of plants
  USE **Plant diseases**
Diseases of the blood
  USE **Blood—Diseases**
Diseases of women
  USE **Women—Diseases**
Diseases—Prevention
  USE **Preventive medicine**
Diseases—Treatment
  USE **Therapeutics**
Diseases, Tropical
  USE **Tropical medicine**
Disguise   **306.4**
  BT **Costume**
      Deception
Dishes
  USE **Porcelain**
      Pottery
      Tableware
Dishonesty
  USE **Honesty**
Disinfection and disinfectants   **614.4**
  UF Germicides
  BT **Hygiene**
      Pharmaceutical chemistry
      Public health
      Sanitation
  RT **Antiseptics**
      Fumigation
Disk jockeys
  USE **Disc jockeys**

Diskinesia
USE **Movement disorders**
Disney World (Fla.)
USE **Walt Disney World (Fla.)**
Disobedience
USE **Obedience**
Disorderliness
USE **Messiness**
Disorders of communication
USE **Communicative disorders**
Displaced persons
USE **Political refugees**
Refugees
Disposal of medical waste
USE **Medical wastes**
Disposal of refuse
USE **Refuse and refuse disposal**
Dispute settlement
USE **Conflict management**
Dissent (May subdiv. geog.) **303.48;
361.2**
UF Nonconformity
Protest
BT **Freedom of conscience**
Freedom of religion
RT **Conformity**
Dissertations 378.2; 808
Use for materials about academic theses and
dissertations.
UF Academic dissertations
Dissertations, Academic
Doctoral theses
Theses
BT **Research**
Dissertations, Academic
USE **Dissertations**
Distance education (May subdiv. geog.)
371.35
Use for materials on the various forms of
long-distance instruction, usually in the field
of adult education, made possible by written,
audiovisual, or electronic communication be-
tween a student and a teacher.
UF Distance learning
BT **Education**
NT **Correspondence schools and
courses**
University extension
Distance learning
USE **Distance education**
Distillation 641.2; 663
UF Stills

BT **Analytical chemistry**
Industrial chemistry
Technology
NT **Essences and essential oils**
RT **Alcohol**
Liquors
Distribution, Cooperative
USE **Cooperation**
Distribution (Economics)
USE **Commerce**
Marketing
Distribution of animals and plants
USE **Biogeography**
Distribution of wealth
USE **Economics**
Wealth
District libraries
USE **Regional libraries**
District schools
USE **Rural schools**
Districting (in city planning)
USE **Zoning**
Diversified corporations
USE **Conglomerate corporations**
Diversity, Biological
USE **Biodiversity**
Diversity in the workplace (May subdiv.
geog.) **331.11; 658.3**
UF Cultural diversity in the
workplace
Multicultural diversity in the
workplace
Workforce diversity
BT **Multiculturalism**
Personnel management
Diversity movement
USE **Multiculturalism**
Dividends
USE **Securities**
Stocks
Divination (May subdiv. geog.) **133.3**
UF Crystal gazing
Necromancy
Soothsaying
BT **Occultism**
NT **Astrology**
Feng shui
Fortune telling
Palmistry
RT **Oracles**
Prophecies

Divine healing
USE **Spiritual healing**
Diving 797.2

Use for materials on diving from a board or platform. Materials on underwater diving with equipment are entered under **Deep diving**.

BT **Swimming**
Water sports
RT **Deep diving**
Divinity of Jesus Christ
USE **Jesus Christ—Divinity**
Division 513.2
BT **Arithmetic**
Division of powers
USE **Separation of powers**
Divorce (May subdiv. geog.) **173;**
306.89; 346.01
BT **Family**
NT **Alimony**
Children of divorced parents
Desertion and nonsupport
Divorce mediation
Separation (Law)
RT **Divorced people**
Domestic relations
Divorce counseling
USE **Divorce mediation**
Divorce mediation 362.82
UF Divorce counseling
Mediation, Divorce
BT **Divorce**
NT **Child custody**
Child support
RT **Marriage counseling**
Divorced men (May subdiv. geog.)
306.892
BT **Divorced people**
Single men
Divorced people (May subdiv. geog.)
306.89
UF Divorced persons
BT **Single people**
NT **Divorced men**
Divorced women
RT **Divorce**
Divorced persons
USE **Divorced people**
Divorced women (May subdiv. geog.)
306.893
BT **Divorced people**
Single women

DJs (Disc jockeys)
USE **Disc jockeys**
DNA 572.8
UF Deoxyribonucleic acid
BT **Cells**
Heredity
Nucleic acids
NT **Recombinant DNA**
DNA cloning
USE **Molecular cloning**
DNA fingerprinting 614
UF DNA fingerprints
DNA identification
DNA profiling
Genetic fingerprinting
Genetic fingerprints
Genetic profiling
BT **Identification**
Medical jurisprudence
DNA fingerprints
USE **DNA fingerprinting**
DNA identification
USE **DNA fingerprinting**
DNA profiling
USE **DNA fingerprinting**
Docks 386; 387.1; 627
BT **Hydraulic structures**
Marinas
RT **Harbors**
Doctor films
USE **Medical drama (Films)**
Doctor novels
USE **Medical novels**
Doctor radio programs
USE **Medical drama (Radio programs)**
Doctor television programs
USE **Medical drama (Television programs)**
Doctoral theses
USE **Dissertations**
Doctors
USE **Physicians**
Doctors' degrees
USE **Academic degrees**
Doctrinal theology (May subdiv. geog.)
202; 230
UF Dogmatic theology
Dogmatics
Systematic theology
Theology, Doctrinal

Doctrinal theology—*Continued*
  SA names of religions or individual denominations with the subdivision *Doctrines*, e.g. **Christianity—Doctrines**; **Judaism—Doctrines**; etc., and religious topics with the subdivision *History of doctrines*, e.g. **Salvation—History of doctrines** [to be added as needed]
  BT **Theology**
  NT **Christian heresies**
      Christianity—Doctrines
      Creeds
      Grace (Theology)
      Human beings (Theology)
      Judaism—Doctrines
      Salvation
      Salvation—History of doctrines
Doctrine of fairness (Broadcasting)
  USE **Fairness doctrine (Broadcasting)**
Doctrines
  USE names of religions or individual denominations with the subdivision *Doctrines,* e.g. **Christianity—Doctrines; Judaism—Doctrines;** etc. [to be added as needed]
Documentaries (Motion pictures)
  USE **Documentary films**
Documentary films (May subdiv. geog.) **070.1**
  UF Documentaries (Motion pictures)
      Nonfiction films
  BT **Motion pictures**
Documentation   025
  SA subjects with the subdivision *Documentation*, e.g. **Agriculture—Documentation** [to be added as needed]
  BT **Information science**
  NT **Agriculture—Documentation**
      Archives
      Bibliographic control
      Bibliography
      Cataloging
      Conference proceedings
      Copying processes
      Information retrieval
      Libraries

Library science
  RT **Information services**
Documents
  USE **Archives**
       Charters
       Government publications
Dog
  USE **Dogs**
Dog breeding
  USE **Dogs—Breeding**
Dog care
  USE **Dogs—Care**
Dog guides
  USE **Guide dogs**
Dog sled racing
  USE **Sled dog racing**
Dogmatic theology
  USE **Doctrinal theology**
Dogmatics
  USE **Doctrinal theology**
Dogs (May subdiv. geog.)   **599.77; 636.7**
  UF Dog
      Puppies
  SA types of dogs, e.g. **Guide dogs**; and names of specific breeds of dogs [to be added as needed]
  BT **Domestic animals**
      Mammals
  NT **Collies**
      Working dogs
Dogs—Breeding   636.7
  UF Dog breeding
  BT **Breeding**
Dogs—Care   636.7
  UF Dog care
Dogs—Fiction   808.83
  Use for collections of stories about dogs. Materials about dog stories are entered under **Dogs in literature**.
Dogs for the blind
  USE **Guide dogs**
Dogs for the deaf
  USE **Hearing ear dogs**
Dogs in art   704.9
  BT **Art—Themes**
Dogs in literature   809
  Use for materials about the depiction of dogs in literary works. Collections of dog stories are entered under **Dogs—Fiction**.
  BT **Literature—Themes**
Dogs—Psychology   636.7

Dogs—Psychology—*Continued*
- BT **Animal intelligence**
  Comparative psychology
  Psychology

Dogs—Training 636.7
- BT **Animals—Training**

Dogs—War use 355.4
- UF War use of dogs
- BT **Animals—War use**

Doll
- USE **Dolls**

Doll furniture (May subdiv. geog.)
  688.7; 745.592
- BT **Miniature objects**
  Toys

Dollhouses 688.7
- BT **Miniature objects**
  Toys

Dollmaking 745.592
- BT **Dolls**

Dolls (May subdiv. geog.) **688.7**
- UF Doll
- BT **Toys**
- NT **Barbie dolls**
  Dollmaking

Dolphins (May subdiv. geog.) **599.53**
- BT **Marine mammals**

Domesday book 942.02
- UF Doomsday book
- BT **Great Britain—History—1066-
  1154, Norman period**

Domestic animal dwellings
- USE **Animal housing**

Domestic animals (May subdiv. geog.)
  636

Use for general materials on farm animals. Materials limited to animals as pets are entered under **Pets**. Materials on stock raising as an industry are entered under **Livestock industry**.
- UF Domestication
  Farm animals
  Livestock
- SA types of domestic animals, e.g.
  Cattle [to be added as needed]
- BT **Animals**
- NT **Cats**
  Cattle
  Dogs
  Pigs
  Poultry
  Reindeer

  Sheep
  Working animals
- RT **Livestock industry**
  Pets

Domestic animals—Diseases
- USE **Animals—Diseases**

Domestic animals—Housing
- USE **Animal housing**

Domestic appliances
- USE **Electric household appliances**
  Household equipment and supplies

Domestic architecture (May subdiv.
  geog.) **728**

Use for materials on residential buildings from the standpoint of style and design. General materials on buildings in which people live are entered under **Houses**.
- UF Architecture, Domestic
  Dwellings
  Residences
- SA types of residential buildings,
  e.g. **Apartment houses** [to be added as needed]
- BT **Architecture**
- NT **Apartment houses**
  House construction
  Prefabricated houses
  Solar homes
- RT **Houses**

**Domestic architecture—Designs and
  plans** 728
- UF Home designs
  House plans
- BT **Architecture—Designs and
  plans**

Domestic economic assistance (May
  subdiv. geog.) **338.9**
- UF Anti-poverty programs
  Antipoverty programs
  Economic assistance
  Economic assistance, Domestic
  Poor relief
- BT **Economic policy**
- NT **Community development**
  Government lending
  Public works
  Subsidies
  Transfer payments
- RT **Grants-in-aid**
  Poverty
  Unemployed

Domestic finance
    USE   **Household budgets**
          Personal finance
Domestic relations (May subdiv. geog.)
       346.01
    UF   Family relations
    BT   **Interpersonal relations**
    NT   **Desertion and nonsupport**
          Visitation rights (Domestic relations)
    RT   **Divorce**
          Family
          Family life education
          Marriage
Domestic terrorism (May subdiv. geog.)
       363.325
    BT   **Terrorism**
Domestic violence (May subdiv. geog.)
       362.82
    UF   Family violence
          Household violence
    BT   **Violence**
    NT   **Child abuse**
          Elderly abuse
          Wife abuse
Domestic workers
    USE   **Household employees**
Domestication
    USE   **Domestic animals**
Dominion of the sea
    USE   **Sea power**
Dominions, British
    USE   **Commonwealth countries**
Donation of organs, tissues, etc.   **362.1**
    UF   Organ donation
          Tissue donation
    BT   **Gifts**
    RT   **Transplantation of organs, tissues, etc.**
Donations
    USE   **Gifts**
Doomsday
    USE   **Judgment Day**
Doomsday book
    USE   **Domesday book**
Door to door selling
    USE   **Peddlers and peddling**
Doors   **721**
    BT   **Architecture—Details**
          Buildings

Double consciousness
    USE   **Multiple personality**
Doubt
    USE   **Belief and doubt**
Down syndrome   **616.85**
    UF   Down's syndrome
    BT   **Mental retardation**
Down's syndrome
    USE   **Down syndrome**
Downsizing of organizations   **658.1**
    UF   Corporate downsizing
          Organizational downsizing
          Organizational retrenchment
          Retrenchment of organizations
    BT   **Organizational change**
    RT   **Employees—Dismissal**
Draft   **355.2**
    UF   Compulsory military service
          Conscription, Military
          Military conscription
          Military draft
          Military service, Compulsory
          Military training, Universal
          Selective service
          Universal military training
    BT   **Armies**
          Military law
          Recruiting and enlistment
    RT   **Draft resisters**
Draft dodgers
    USE   **Draft resisters**
Draft evaders
    USE   **Draft resisters**
Draft resisters   **355.2**
    UF   Draft dodgers
          Draft evaders
    SA   names of wars with the subdivision *Draft resisters* [to be added as needed]
    NT   **World War, 1939-1945—Draft resisters**
    RT   **Conscientious objectors**
          Draft
          Military desertion
Drafting, Mechanical
    USE   **Mechanical drawing**
Dragons   **398.24**
    BT   **Animals—Folklore**
          Folklore
          Monsters
          Mythical animals

Drainage (May subdiv. geog.)   **631.6**

Use for materials on land drainage. Materials on house drainage are entered under **House drainage**.

UF   Land drainage

BT   **Agricultural engineering**

Civil engineering

Hydraulic engineering

Municipal engineering

Reclamation of land

Sanitary engineering

RT   **Sewerage**

Drainage, House

USE   **House drainage**

Drama   **808.2; 808.82**

Use for general materials on drama, not for individual works. Materials on the history and criticism of drama as literature are entered under **Drama—History and criticism**. Materials on criticism of drama as presented on the stage are entered under **Dramatic criticism**. Materials on the presentation of plays are entered under **Acting; Amateur theater;** or **Theater—Production and direction**. Collections of plays are entered under **Drama—Collections; American drama—Collections; English drama—Collections;** etc.

UF   Stage

SA   subjects, historical events, names of countries, cities, etc., ethnic groups, classes of persons, and names of individual persons with the subdivision *Drama*, to express the theme or subject content of collections of plays, e.g. **Easter—Drama; United States—History—1861-1865, Civil War—Drama; Napoleon I, Emperor of the French, 1769-1821—Drama**; etc. [to be added as needed]

BT   **Literature**

NT   **Acting**

American drama

Ballet

Children's plays

Choral speaking

Classical drama

College and school drama

Comedies

Comedy

Didactic drama

Drama in education

Dramatists

English drama

Folk drama

Historical drama

Horror plays

Masks (Plays)

Melodrama

Morality plays

Mystery and detective plays

One act plays

Opera

Pantomimes

Pastoral drama

Puppets and puppet plays

Radio plays

Religious drama

Science fiction plays

Screenplays

Television plays

Tragedies

Tragedy

Tragicomedy

RT   **Dramatic criticism**

Theater

Drama—Collections   **808.82**

Use for collections of plays by several authors.

UF   Plays

Drama—History and criticism   **809.2**

Use for materials on criticism of drama as a literary form. Materials on criticism of drama as presented on the stage are entered under **Dramatic criticism**.

NT   **English drama—History and criticism**

RT   **Dramatic criticism**

Drama in education   **372.66**

BT   **Drama**

RT   **Acting**

Amateur theater

College and school drama

School assembly programs

Drama—Technique   **808.2**

UF   Play writing

Playwriting

BT   **Authorship**

NT   **Motion picture plays—Technique**

Radio plays—Technique

Television plays—Technique

Dramatic art

USE   **Acting**

Dramatic criticism   792.9

Use for materials on criticism of drama as presented on the stage. Materials on criticism of drama as a literary form are entered under **Drama—History and criticism**; **American drama—History and criticism**; etc.

UF   Theater criticism

BT   **Criticism**

RT   **Drama**

Drama—History and criticism

Theater

Dramatic music

USE   **Musicals**

Opera

Operetta

Dramatic plots

USE   **Stories, plots, etc.**

Dramatic production

USE   names of dramatists with the subdivision *Dramatic production*, e.g. **Shakespeare, William, 1564-1616—Dramatic production** [to be added as needed]

Dramatists   809.2; 920

Use for materials on the personal lives of several playwrights, not limited to a single national literature. Materials dealing with their literary work are entered under **Drama—History and criticism**; **English drama—History and criticism**; etc.

UF   Playwrights

SA   dramatists of particular countries, e.g. **American dramatists** [to be added as needed]

BT   **Authors**

Drama

NT   **American dramatists**

Dramatists, American

USE   **American dramatists**

Draperies   645; 684

UF   Curtains

Drapery

BT   **Interior design**

Upholstery

Drapery

USE   **Draperies**

Draughts

USE   **Checkers**

Drawing   741; 743

UF   Drawings

Sketching

SA   drawing of particular countries, e.g. **American drawing** [to be added as needed]

BT   **Art**

Graphic arts

NT   **American drawing**

Architectural drawing

Artistic anatomy

Commercial art

Crayon drawing

Figure drawing

Geometrical drawing

Graphic methods

Landscape drawing

Map drawing

Mechanical drawing

Pastel drawing

Pen drawing

Pencil drawing

Shades and shadows

Topographical drawing

RT   **Illustration of books**

Painting

Perspective

Drawing, American

USE   **American drawing**

Drawing materials

USE   **Artists' materials**

Drawings

USE   **Drawing**

Drawn work   746.44

BT   **Embroidery**

Needlework

NT   **Hardanger needlework**

Dream interpretation

USE   **Dreams**

Dreaming

USE   **Dreams**

Dreams   154.6

UF   Dream interpretation

Dreaming

BT   **Visions**

NT   **Fantasy**

RT   **Sleep**

Subconsciousness

Dredging   627

BT   **Civil engineering**

Hydraulic engineering

Dress

USE   **Clothing and dress**

Dress accessories   391.4; 646

Dress accessories—*Continued*

    BT   **Clothing and dress**

Dress codes (May subdiv. geog.)   **391**

    BT   **Clothing and dress—Social aspects**

Dressage

    USE   **Horsemanship**

Dressing of ores

    USE   **Ore dressing**

Dressmaking   **646.4; 687**

    UF   Garment making

    BT   **Clothing and dress**

          Clothing industry

    RT   **Needlework**

          Sewing

          Tailoring

Dressmaking—Patterns   **646.4; 687**

Dried flowers

    USE   **Flowers—Drying**

Dried foods   **641.4; 664**

    UF   Dehydrated foods

    BT   **Food**

    NT   **Dried milk**

          Freeze-dried foods

    RT   **Food—Preservation**

Dried milk   **637**

    UF   Dehydrated milk

          Powdered milk

    BT   **Dried foods**

          Milk

Drifting of continents

    USE   **Continental drift**

Drill and minor tactics   **355.5**

    UF   Military drill

          Minor tactics

    BT   **Tactics**

    RT   **Military art and science**

Drill (Nonmilitary)

    USE   **Marching drills**

Drilling and boring

    USE   **Drilling and boring (Earth and rocks)**

          Drilling and boring (Metal, wood, etc.)

Drilling and boring (Earth and rocks)   **622**

    Use for materials on the operation of cutting holes in earth or rock. Materials on workshop operations in metal, wood, etc., are entered under **Drilling and boring (Metal, wood, etc.)**.

    UF   Boring

          Drilling and boring

Shaft sinking

Well boring

    BT   **Hydraulic engineering**

          Mining engineering

          Water supply engineering

    NT   **Oil well drilling**

    RT   **Tunnels**

          Wells

Drilling and boring (Metal, wood, etc.)   **621.9**

    Use for materials on workshop operations in metal, wood, etc. Materials on the operation of cutting holes in earth or rock are entered under **Drilling and boring (Earth and rocks)**.

    UF   Boring

          Drilling and boring

    BT   **Machine shop practice**

    RT   **Machine tools**

Drilling, Oil well

    USE   **Oil well drilling**

Drilling platforms   **627**

    UF   Marine drilling platforms

          Ocean drilling platforms

          Oil drilling platforms

          Platforms, Drilling

    BT   **Ocean engineering**

          Offshore oil well drilling

Drills, Marching

    USE   **Marching drills**

Drinking age (May subdiv. geog.)   **344; 363.4**

    UF   Minimum drinking age

    BT   **Age**

          Teenagers—Alcohol use

          Youth—Alcohol use

Drinking and employees

    USE   **Employees—Alcohol use**

Drinking and teenagers

    USE   **Teenagers—Alcohol use**

Drinking and youth

    USE   **Youth—Alcohol use**

Drinking in the workplace

    USE   **Employees—Alcohol use**

Drinking of alcoholic beverages (May subdiv. geog.)   **178; 363.4; 394.1; 613.81**

    Use for materials on drinking in its social aspects and as a social problem.

    UF   Alcohol consumption

          Alcohol use

          Alcoholic beverage consumption

Drinking of alcoholic beverages—*Continued*

       Consumption of alcoholic beverages

       Drinking problem

       Liquor problem

       Social drinking

  SA   classes of persons and ethnic groups with the subdivision *Alcohol use*, e.g. **Employees—Alcohol use**; **Youth—Alcohol use**; etc. [to be added as needed]

  NT   **Drunk driving**

  RT   **Alcoholic beverages**

       Alcoholism

       Temperance

Drinking problem

  USE **Alcoholism**

       Drinking of alcoholic beverages

Drinking water (May subdiv. geog.) **363.6; 628.1**

  UF   Potable water

       Tap water

  BT   **Water**

       Water supply

Drinks

  USE **Alcoholic beverages**

       Beverages

       Liquors

Driver education

  USE **Automobile driver education**

Drivers, Automobile

  USE **Automobile drivers**

Drivers' licenses (May subdiv. geog.) **353.9; 629.28**

  UF   Automobile drivers' licenses

       Automobiles—Drivers' licenses

       Motor vehicles—Drivers' licenses

  BT   **Safety regulations**

Driving under the influence of alcohol

  USE **Drunk driving**

Driving while intoxicated

  USE **Drunk driving**

Dromedaries

  USE **Camels**

Drop forging

  USE **Forging**

Dropouts (May subdiv. geog.) **371.2**

  UF   College dropouts

       Elementary school dropouts

       High school dropouts

       School dropouts

       Student dropouts

       Teenage dropouts

  BT   **Students**

       Youth

  RT   **At risk students**

       Educational counseling

       School attendance

Droughts (May subdiv. geog.) **551.57; 632**

  BT   **Meteorology**

  NT   **Dust storms**

  RT   **Rain**

Drowning prevention

  USE **Water safety**

Drug abuse (May subdiv. geog.) **362.29; 613.8; 616.86**

Use for general materials on the misuse or abuse of drugs. Materials on the abuse of a particular drug or kind of drugs are entered under this heading and also under the drug or kind of drugs, e.g. **Cocaine**; **Hallucinogens**; etc.

  UF   Addiction to drugs

       Drug addiction

       Drug habit

       Drug misuse

       Drug use

       Drugs—Abuse

       Drugs—Misuse

       Narcotic abuse

       Narcotic addiction

       Narcotic habit

       Substance abuse

  SA   classes of persons with the subdivision *Drug use*, e.g. **Criminals—Drug use**; and types of drug abuse, e.g. **Medication abuse** [to be added as needed]

  BT   **Social problems**

  NT   **Medication abuse**

  RT   **Drug addicts**

       Drugs

       Solvent abuse

       Twelve-step programs

Drug abuse counseling **362.29; 613.8**

  UF   Drug addiction counseling

       Drug counseling

       Narcotic addiction counseling

  BT   **Counseling**

  NT   **Drug addicts—Rehabilitation**

Drug abuse education
USE **Drug education**
Drug abuse—Physiological effect
USE **Drugs—Physiological effect**
Drug abuse screening
USE **Drug testing**
Drug abuse—Study and teaching
USE **Drug education**
Drug abuse—Testing
USE **Drug testing**
Drug abuse—Treatment   362.29
BT **Therapeutics**
Drug abusing physicians
USE **Physicians—Drug use**
Drug addicted physicians
USE **Physicians—Drug use**
Drug addiction
USE **Drug abuse**
Drug addiction counseling
USE **Drug abuse counseling**
Drug addiction education
USE **Drug education**
Drug addicts (May subdiv. geog.)
362.29; 616.86
UF Addicts
Narcotic addicts
SA classes of persons with the sub-
division *Drug use*, e.g. **Crim-
inals—Drug use** [to be added
as needed]
NT **Children of drug addicts**
Recovering addicts
RT **Drug abuse**
**Drug addicts—Rehabilitation   362.29;
613.8; 616.86**
BT **Drug abuse counseling**
Drug counseling
USE **Drug abuse counseling**
Drug dealing
USE **Drug traffic**
Drug education (May subdiv. geog.)
362.29; 371.7; 613.8
Use for materials on the study of drugs, in-
cluding their source, abuse, chemical composi-
tion, and social, physical, and personal effects.
UF Drug abuse education
Drug abuse—Study and teaching
Drug addiction education
BT **Health education**
Drug habit
USE **Drug abuse**

Drug misuse
USE **Drug abuse**
Drug plants
USE **Medical botany**
Drug pushers
USE **Drug traffic**
**Drug resistance in microorganisms
616.01**
UF Antibiotic resistance in microor-
ganisms
Bacterial resistance to antibiotics
Microbial drug resistance
Resistance to drugs in microor-
ganisms
BT **Microorganisms**
Drug stores
USE **Drugstores**
Drug testing   344; 658.3
Use for materials on testing to identify per-
sonal use or misuse of drugs. Materials on the
testing of drugs for safety or effectiveness are
entered under **Drugs—Testing**.
UF Drug abuse screening
Drug abuse—Testing
Screening for drug abuse
Testing for drug abuse
SA classes of persons with the sub-
division *Drug testing*, e.g.
Employees—Drug testing [to
be added as needed]
NT **Employees—Drug testing**
Drug testing in the workplace
USE **Employees—Drug testing**
Drug therapy   615.5
UF Chemotherapy
Pharmacotherapy
SA names of diseases other than
cancer with the subdivision
Drug therapy, e.g. **Mental ill-
ness—Drug therapy** [to be
added as needed]
BT **Therapeutics**
NT **Antibiotics**
Cancer—Chemotherapy
Mental illness—Drug therapy
RT **Drugs**
Pharmacology
Drug trade, Illicit
USE **Drug traffic**
Drug traffic (May subdiv. geog.)
363.45; 364.1

Drug traffic—*Continued*
- UF Drug dealing
    - Drug pushers
    - Drug trade, Illicit
    - Narcotic traffic
    - Smuggling of drugs
    - Trafficking in drugs
    - Trafficking in narcotics
- BT **Drugs and crime**

Drug use
- USE **Drug abuse**
    - **Drugs**
    - and classes of persons with the subdivision *Drug use,* e.g. **Criminals—Drug use; Employees—Drug use; Teenagers—Drug use; Youth—Drug use;** etc. [to be added as needed]

Drugs   615
- UF Drug use
    - Pharmaceuticals
- SA classes of persons with the subdivision *Drug use*, e.g. **Criminals—Drug use**; types of drugs, e.g. **Amphetamines; Hallucinogens; Narcotics; Stimulants**; etc.; and names of individual drugs, e.g. **Crack (Drug); Marijuana**; etc. [to be added as needed]
- BT **Pharmacy**
    - **Therapeutics**
- NT **Designer drugs**
    - **Drugs and crime**
    - **Generic drugs**
    - **Hallucinogens**
    - **Narcotics**
    - **Nonprescription drugs**
    - **Orphan drugs**
    - **Psychotropic drugs**
    - **Steroids**
    - **Stimulants**
    - **Sulfonamides**
- RT **Drug abuse**
    - **Drug therapy**
    - **Materia medica**
    - **Pharmacology**

Drugs—Abuse
- USE **Drug abuse**

Drugs—Adulteration and analysis
- USE **Pharmacology**

Drugs and crime (May subdiv. geog.)
   364.1

Use for general materials on the relationship of drugs and crime. Materials on the illicit drug trade are entered under **Drug traffic**. Materials on the use of drugs by criminals are entered under **Criminals—Drug use**.
- UF Crime and drugs
    - Crime and narcotics
    - Narcotics and crime
- BT **Crime**
    - **Drugs**
- NT **Drug traffic**
- RT **Criminals—Drug use**

Drugs and criminals
- USE **Criminals—Drug use**

Drugs and employees
- USE **Employees—Drug use**

Drugs and sports
- USE **Athletes—Drug use**

Drugs and teenagers
- USE **Teenagers—Drug use**

Drugs and youth
- USE **Youth—Drug use**

Drugs—Chemistry
- USE **Pharmaceutical chemistry**

Drugs—Generic substitution
- USE **Generic drugs**

Drugs in the workplace
- USE **Employees—Drug use**

Drugs—Misuse
- USE **Drug abuse**

Drugs, Nonprescription
- USE **Nonprescription drugs**

Drugs—Physiological effect   615; 616.86

Use for materials limited to the effect of drugs on the functions of living organisms.
- UF Drug abuse—Physiological effect
- SA names of drugs with the subdivision *Physiological effect* [to be added as needed]
- BT **Pharmacology**
- NT **Opium—Physiological effect**

Drugs—Psychological aspects   615; 616.86
- BT **Applied psychology**

Drugs—Testing   363.19

Use for materials on the testing of drugs for safety or effectiveness. Materials on testing to identify the personal use or misuse or drugs are entered under **Drug testing**.
- UF Clinical drug trials
    - Clinical trials of drugs

Drugs—Testing—*Continued*

> BT **Consumer protection**
>
> **Pharmacology**

Drugstores   381

Use for materials on business establishments that sell drugs. Materials on the art or practice of preparing, preserving, and dispensing drugs are entered under **Pharmacy**.

> UF   Chemists' shops
>
> Drug stores
>
> Pharmacies
>
> BT   **Retail trade**
>
> **Stores**

Druids and Druidism   299

> BT   **Celts**
>
> **Religions**

Drum

> USE   **Drums**

Drum majoring   784.9; 791.6

> BT   **Bands (Music)**
>
> RT   **Baton twirling**

Drums   786.9

> UF   Drum
>
> BT   **Musical instruments**
>
> **Percussion instruments**

Drunk driving   363.12; 364.1

> UF   Driving under the influence of alcohol
>
> Driving while intoxicated
>
> BT   **Crime**
>
> **Drinking of alcoholic beverages**

Drunkards

> USE   **Alcoholics**

Drunkenness

> USE   **Alcoholism**
>
> **Temperance**

Dry cleaning   667

> UF   Clothing and dress—Dry cleaning
>
> BT   **Cleaning**

Dry farming (May subdiv. geog.)   **631.5**

> UF   Farming, Dry
>
> BT   **Agriculture**

Dry goods

> USE   **Fabrics**

Drying   660

> SA   materials, products, or objects dried with the subdivision *Drying*, e.g. **Flowers—Drying** [to be added as needed]
>
> BT   **Industrial chemistry**

Dual-career couples

> USE   **Dual-career families**

Dual-career families   306.85; 646.7

Use for materials on families in which both the husband and wife are pursuing careers.

> UF   Dual-career couples
>
> Dual career family
>
> Dual-career marriage
>
> Dual-income couples
>
> Two-career couples
>
> Two-career families
>
> Two-career family
>
> Two-income families
>
> Working couples
>
> BT   **Family**
>
> RT   **Work and family**

Dual career family

> USE   **Dual-career families**

Dual-career marriage

> USE   **Dual-career families**

Dual-income couples

> USE   **Dual-career families**

Ducks   598.4; 636.5

> BT   **Birds**
>
> **Poultry**

Ductless glands

> USE   **Endocrine glands**

Due process of law (May subdiv. geog.)   **347**

Use for materials on the regular administration of the law, according to which citizens may not be denied their legal rights and all laws must conform to fundamental and accepted legal principles. Materials on legal hearings before an impartial and disinterested tribunal are entered under **Fair trial**.

> UF   Procedural due process
>
> Substantive due process
>
> BT   **Administration of justice**
>
> **Civil rights**
>
> NT   **Fair trial**

Dueling (May subdiv. geog.)   **179.7; 394**

> UF   Fighting
>
> BT   **Manners and customs**
>
> **Martial arts**
>
> NT   **Fencing**

Dumps, Toxic

> USE   **Hazardous waste sites**

Dunes

> USE   **Sand dunes**

Duplicate bridge

> USE   **Bridge (Game)**

Duplicating machines

> USE   **Copying machines**

Duplicating processes
USE **Copying processes**
Durable power of attorney
USE **Power of attorney**
Dust   551.51
UF   Atmospheric dust
Dust particles
BT   **Air pollution**
Dust particles
USE **Dust**
Dust, Radioactive
USE **Radioactive fallout**
Dust storms   551.55
BT   **Droughts**
Erosion
Storms
Dusting and spraying
USE **Spraying and dusting**
Duties
USE **Tariff**
Taxation
Duty   170
BT   **Ethics**
Human behavior
NT   **Conscience**
Vocation
DVDs   004.5
BT   **Optical storage devices**
Dwarf trees   582.16; 635.9
SA   types of dwarf trees, e.g. **Bonsai** [to be added as needed]
BT   **Trees**
NT   **Bonsai**
Dwarfism   616.4
UF   Growth retardation
BT   **Growth disorders**
Dwellings
USE **Domestic architecture**
Houses
Housing
and ethnic groups and classes of persons with the subdivision *Dwellings,* for materials on the residential buildings of a group from the standpoint of architecture, construction, or ethnology, e.g. **Native Americans—Dwellings;** and ethnic groups and classes of persons with the subdivision *Housing,* for materials on the

social and economic aspects of providing housing for the group, e.g. **Physically handicapped—Housing** [to be added as needed]
Dyes and dyeing   646.6; 667; 746.6
SA   types of dyes and types of dyeing [to be added as needed]
BT   **Color**
Pigments
Textile chemistry
Textile industry
NT   **Batik**
Tie dyeing
RT   **Bleaching**
Dying children
USE **Terminally ill children**
Dying patients
USE **Terminally ill**
Dynamics   531
UF   Kinetics
BT   **Mathematics**
Mechanics
NT   **Aerodynamics**
Astrodynamics
Chaos (Science)
Hydrodynamics
Kinematics
Matter
Motion
Quantum theory
Thermodynamics
RT   **Force and energy**
Physics
Statics
Dynamite   662
BT   **Explosives**
Dynamos
USE **Electric generators**
Dyslexia   371.91; 616.85
BT   **Reading disability**
Dyspepsia
USE **Indigestion**
Dysphasia
USE **Language disorders**
Dystopias   808.3
Use for individual works, collections, or materials about dystopias.
UF   Anti-utopias
BT   **Fantasy fiction**
Science fiction
RT   **Utopian fiction**

E-mail
> USE **Electronic mail systems**

E-mail discussion groups
> USE **Electronic discussion groups**

E-mail reference services (Libraries)
> USE **Electronic reference services (Libraries)**

Eagles 598.9
> BT **Birds**
>
> **Birds of prey**

Ear 611; 612.8
> BT **Head**
>
> RT **Hearing**

Early childhood education (May subdiv. geog.) **372.21**
> Use for materials on formal or informal education of children up to grade 3.
>
> BT **Education**

Early Christian literature 270.1
> Use for individual works or collections of the writings of early Christian authors. Materials on the lives and thought of the leaders of the Christian church up to the time of Gregory the Great in the West and John of Damascus in the East are entered under **Fathers of the church**.
>
> UF Christian literature—30-600, Early
>
> Christian literature, Early
>
> BT **Christian literature**
>
> **Literature**
>
> **Medieval literature**
>
> RT **Church history—30-600, Early church**
>
> **Fathers of the church**
>
> **Latin literature**

Early church history
> USE **Church history—30-600, Early church**

Early printed books (May subdiv. geog.) **094**
> SA subjects with the subdivision *Early works to 1800*, for materials on those subjects written before 1800, e.g. **Political science—Early works to 1800** [to be added as needed]
>
> BT **Books**

Early printed books—15th century
> USE **Incunabula**

Early works to 1800
> USE subjects with the subdivision *Early works to 1800,* for materials on those subjects writ-

ten before 1800, e.g. **Political science—Early works to 1800** [to be added as needed]

Earth 525; 550
> Use for general materials on the whole planet. Materials limited to the structure and composition of the earth and the physical changes it has undergone and is still undergoing are entered under **Geology**.
>
> UF World
>
> BT **Planets**
>
> **Solar system**
>
> NT **Antarctica**
>
> **Arctic regions**
>
> **Arid regions**
>
> **Atmosphere**
>
> **Continents**
>
> **Earthquakes**
>
> **Gaia hypothesis**
>
> **Geodesy**
>
> **Geography**
>
> **Ice age**
>
> **Latitude**
>
> **Longitude**
>
> **Ocean**
>
> **Seas**
>
> **Tropics**
>
> RT **Earth sciences**
>
> **Geology**
>
> **Physical geography**

Earth—Age 551.7

Earth—Chemical composition
> USE **Geochemistry**

Earth—Crust 551.1
> BT **Earth—Internal structure**
>
> NT **Plate tectonics**
>
> RT **Earth—Surface**

Earth, Effect of man on
> USE **Human influence on nature**

Earth fills
> USE **Landfills**

Earth-friendly technology
> USE **Green technology**

Earth—Gravity
> USE **Gravity**

Earth—Internal structure 551.1
> NT **Earth—Crust**

Earth magnetic field
> USE **Geomagnetism**

Earth—Magnetism
> USE **Geomagnetism**

Earth sciences 550
> UF Geoscience

Earth sciences—*Continued*
- BT   **Physical sciences**
-      **Science**
- NT   **Climate**
-      **Geochemistry**
-      **Geography**
-      **Geology**
-      **Geophysics**
-      **Meteorology**
-      **Oceanography**
-      **Water**
- RT   **Earth**

Earth sheltered houses   **690; 728**
- UF   Underground houses
- BT   **House construction**
-      **Houses**
-      **Underground architecture**

Earth—Surface   **551.1**
- UF   Surface of the earth
- NT   **Landforms**
- RT   **Earth—Crust**

Earthenware
- USE   **Pottery**

Earthly paradise
- USE   **Paradise**

Earthquake effects
- USE   types of structures with the subdivision *Earthquake effects,* e.g. **Skyscrapers—Earthquake effects** [to be added as needed]

Earthquake sea waves
- USE   **Tsunamis**

Earthquakes (May subdiv. geog.)   **551.22**
- UF   Seismography
-      Seismology
- SA   types of structures subject to earthquake forces with the subdivision *Earthquake effects,* e.g. **Skyscrapers—Earthquake effects** [to be added as needed]
- BT   **Earth**
-      **Geology**
-      **Natural disasters**
-      **Physical geography**
- NT   **Buildings—Earthquake effects**
-      **Skyscrapers—Earthquake effects**

Earthquakes and building
- USE   **Buildings—Earthquake effects**

Earthquakes—California   **551.2209794**

Earthquakes—United States   **551.220973**

Earthworks (Archeology)
- USE   **Excavations (Archeology)**

Earthworks (Art) (May subdiv. geog.)   **709.04**
- UF   Landscape sculpture
-      Site oriented art
- BT   **Art**

East
- USE   **Asia**

East Africa   **967.6**

Use for materials dealing collectively with the eastern regions of Africa. The term usually includes the areas now occupied by Burundi, Kenya, Rwanda, Tanzania, Uganda, and Somalia, and sometimes Malawi and Mozambique as well.
- UF   Africa, East
-      Africa, Eastern
-      Eastern Africa
- BT   **Africa**

East and West   **306; 909**

Use for materials on both acculturation and cultural conflict between Asian and Occidental civilizations.
- BT   **International relations**
- NT   **Asia—Civilization**
-      **Orientalism**
-      **Western civilization**
- RT   **Acculturation**

East Asia   **950**

Use for materials that deal collectively with the eastern regions of Asia including China, Japan, Korea, and Taiwan.
- UF   East (Far East)
-      Far East
-      Orient
- BT   **Asia**
- RT   **Pacific rim**

East (Far East)
- USE   **East Asia**

East Germany
- USE   **Germany (East)**

East Goths
- USE   **Goths**

East Indians   **305.891; 954**
- UF   Indians (of India)

East Timor   **959.87**

May be subdivided like **United States** except for *History.*

Easter (May subdiv. geog.)   **263; 394.2667**
- BT   **Christian holidays**
-      **Holy Week**

Easter—*Continued*
RT **Lent**
Easter carols
USE **Carols**
Easter—Drama   808.82
Use for collections of plays about Easter.
BT **Religious drama**
Easter egg decoration
USE **Egg decoration**
Eastern Africa
USE **East Africa**
Eastern churches   281
BT **Christian sects**
Christianity
NT **Orthodox Eastern Church**
Eastern Empire
USE **Byzantine Empire**
Eastern Europe   947
UF Europe, Eastern
Eastern Europe—History   947
Eastern Europe—History—1989-
947.085; 947.086
Eastern Seaboard
USE **Atlantic States**
Easy and quick cooking
USE **Quick and easy cooking**
Easy reading materials   372.41
UF Beginning reading materials
Preprimers
Preschool reading materials
Primers
BT **Children's literature**
Reading materials
Eating
USE **Dining**
Gastronomy
Eating customs (May subdiv. geog.)
394.1
UF Food customs
Food habits
BT **Diet**
Human behavior
Nutrition
NT **Table etiquette**
RT **Dining**
Eating disorders   616.85
SA types of eating disorders [to be
added as needed]
BT **Abnormal psychology**
NT **Anorexia nervosa**
Bulimia
Eavesdropping   363.25

UF Bugging, Electronic
Electronic bugging
Electronic eavesdropping
Electronic listening devices
Listening devices
BT **Criminal investigation**
Right of privacy
RT **Wiretapping**
Eccentrics and eccentricities (May subdiv.
geog.)   **920**
UF Cranks
BT **Curiosities and wonders**
Personality
NT **Hermits**
Ecclesiastical antiquities
USE **Christian antiquities**
Ecclesiastical architecture
USE **Church architecture**
Ecclesiastical art
USE **Christian art**
Ecclesiastical biography
USE **Christian biography**
Ecclesiastical fasts and feasts
USE **Religious holidays**
Ecclesiastical furniture
USE **Church furniture**
Ecclesiastical history
USE **Church history**
Ecclesiastical institutions
USE **Religious institutions**
Ecclesiastical law   262.9
UF Canon law
Church law
BT **Church**
Law
NT **Tithes**
Ecclesiastical polity
USE **Church polity**
Ecclesiastical rites and ceremonies
USE **Rites and ceremonies**
Ecclesiastical year
USE **Church year**
Eclipses, Lunar
USE **Lunar eclipses**
Eclipses, Solar
USE **Solar eclipses**
Eclogues
USE **Pastoral poetry**
Eco-development
USE **Economic development—Envi-**
ronmental aspects

Ecodevelopment
  USE **Economic development—Environmental aspects**
Ecological movement
  USE **Environmental movement**
Ecological tourism
  USE **Ecotourism**
Ecology (May subdiv. geog.) **577**
  UF Balance of nature
      Biology—Ecology
      Ecosystems
  SA types of ecology, e.g. **Marine ecology**; and types of animals, plants, and crops with the subdivision *Ecology* [to be added as needed]
  BT **Biology**
      Environment
  NT **Adaptation (Biology)**
      Biogeography
      Coastal ecology
      Desert ecology
      Environmental protection
      Fishes—Ecology
      Food chains (Ecology)
      Gaia hypothesis
      Habitat (Ecology)
      Marine ecology
      Plant ecology
      Symbiosis
  RT **Biodiversity**
      Environmental sciences
Ecology, Human
  USE **Human ecology**
Ecology, Social
  USE **Human ecology**
Economic aid
  USE **Foreign aid**
Economic aspects
  USE subjects with the subdivision *Economic aspects,* e.g. **Agriculture—Economic aspects** [to be added as needed]
Economic assistance
  USE **Domestic economic assistance**
      Foreign aid
Economic assistance, American
  USE **American foreign aid**
Economic assistance, Domestic
  USE **Domestic economic assistance**

Economic biology
  USE **Economic botany**
      Economic zoology
Economic botany **581.6**
  UF Agricultural botany
      Botany, Economic
      Economic biology
  BT **Agriculture**
      Botany
  NT **Cotton**
      Edible plants
      Forage plants
      Forest products
      Plant conservation
      Plant introduction
      Poisonous plants
      Weeds
Economic conditions **330.9**
  Use for general materials on some or all of the following: natural resources, business, commerce, industry, labor, manufactures, financial conditions. Materials on the history of the economic development of several countries are entered under **Economic development**.
  UF Economic history
      National resources
      World economics
  SA racial and ethnic groups, classes of persons, and names of countries, cities, areas, etc., with the subdivision *Economic conditions*, e.g. **African Americans—Economic conditions**; **United States—Economic conditions**; etc. [to be added as needed]
  BT **Business**
      Economics
      Social conditions
      Wealth
  NT **African Americans—Economic conditions**
      Blacks—Economic conditions
      Business cycles
      Chicago (Ill.)—Economic conditions
      Developing countries
      Great Depression, 1929-1939
      Industrial revolution
      Jews—Economic conditions
      Labor supply

Economic conditions—*Continued*
>> Native Americans—Economic conditions
>> Natural resources
>> Ohio—Economic conditions
>> Poverty
>> Quality of life
>> United States—Economic conditions
> RT   Commercial geography
>>   Economic development

Economic cycles
> USE   **Business cycles**

Economic depressions
> USE   **Depressions**

Economic development   338.9

Use for materials on the theory and policy of economic development. Materials restricted to a particular place are entered under the name of the country, city, or area with the subdivisions *Economic conditions* or *Industries*.

> UF   Development, Economic
>>   Economic growth
> BT   **Economic policy**
>>   **Economics**
> NT   **Infrastructure (Economics)**
>>   **Rural development**
>>   **Sustainable development**
> RT   **Economic conditions**

Economic development—Environmental aspects   333.71; 338.9

Use for general materials on the environmental impact of economic development. Materials on economic development that satisfies the needs of the present generation without depleting natural resources for the future or having adverse environmental effects are entered under **Sustainable development**.

> UF   Eco-development
>>   Ecodevelopment

Economic equilibrium
> USE   **Equilibrium (Economics)**

Economic forecasting   338.5
> BT   **Business cycles**
>>   **Economics**
>>   **Forecasting**
> NT   **Business forecasting**
>>   **Employment forecasting**

Economic geography
> USE   **Commercial geography**

Economic geology   553
> UF   Geology, Economic

> SA   types of geological products, e.g. **Asbestos**; **Gypsum**; etc. [to be added as needed]
> BT   **Geology**
> NT   **Mines and mineral resources**
>>   **Petroleum geology**
>>   **Quarries and quarrying**
>>   **Soils**
>>   **Stone**

Economic growth
> USE   **Economic development**

Economic history
> USE   **Economic conditions**

Economic mobilization
> USE   **Industrial mobilization**

Economic planning
> USE   **Economic policy**

Economic policy (May subdiv. geog.)   **338.9**

Use for materials on the policy of government in economic affairs.

> UF   Business and government
>>   Business—Government policy
>>   Central planning
>>   Economic planning
>>   Government and business
>>   Government policy
>>   National planning
>>   State planning
> SA   subjects with the subdivision *Government policy*, e.g. **Agriculture—Government policy**; and types of activities, facilities, industries, services, and undertakings with the subdivision *Planning*, e.g. **Transportation—Planning** [to be added as needed]
> BT   **Economics**
>>   **Planning**
> NT   **Commercial policy**
>>   **Domestic economic assistance**
>>   **Economic development**
>>   **Fiscal policy**
>>   **Foreign aid**
>>   **Free enterprise**
>>   **Government lending**
>>   **Government ownership**
>>   **Industrial mobilization**
>>   **Industrial policy**
>>   **Industrialization**

Economic policy—*Continued*
    International economic rela-
      tions
    Labor policy
    Land reform
    Monetary policy
    Municipal ownership
    Privatization
    Sanctions (International law)
    Subsidies
    Tariff
    Transfer payments
    Urban policy
    Welfare state
  RT National security
    Social policy
Economic policy—Ohio   338.9771
  UF Ohio—Economic policy
Economic policy—United States
    338.973
  UF United States—Economic policy
Economic recessions
  USE **Recessions**
Economic relations, Foreign
  USE **International economic rela-
       tions**
Economic sanctions
  USE **Sanctions (International law)**
Economic sustainability
  USE **Sustainable development**
Economic zones (Maritime law)
  USE **Territorial waters**
Economic zoology   591.6
    Use for general materials on animals injuri-
    ous or beneficial to agriculture, and for mate-
    rials on the extermination of wild animals,
    venomous snakes, etc.
  UF Animals, Useful and harmful
    Economic biology
    Zoology, Economic
  BT **Zoology**
  NT **Agricultural pests**
    Beneficial insects
    Furbearing animals
    Insect pests
    Livestock industry
    Pest control
    Pests
    Poisonous animals
    Wildlife conservation
    Working animals

Economics (May subdiv. geog.)   330
    Use for materials on the science of econom-
    ics. This heading may be subdivided geo-
    graphically for materials on this branch of
    learning in a particular place. Materials on the
    economic conditions of a particular place are
    entered under the name of the place with the
    subdivision *Economic conditions*.
  UF Distribution of wealth
    Political economy
    Production
  SA subjects with the subdivision
    Economic aspects, e.g. **Agri-
    culture—Economic aspects**;
    and countries, states, cities,
    regions, etc., with the subdivi-
    sion *Economic conditions*, e.g.
    **United States—Economic
    conditions** [to be added as
    needed]
  BT **Social sciences**
  NT **Agriculture—Economic aspects**
    Barter
    Business
    Capital
    Capitalism
    Christianity and economics
    Collectivism
    Commerce
    Consumption (Economics)
    Cooperation
    Cost and standard of living
    Cost effectiveness
    Economic conditions
    Economic development
    Economic forecasting
    Economic policy
    Employment
    Equilibrium (Economics)
    Finance
    Gross national product
    Income
    Individualism
    Industrial trusts
    Industries
    Labor
    Labor economics
    Land use
    Macroeconomics
    Marxism
    Medical economics
    Microeconomics
    Money

Economics—*Continued*

>> **Monopolies**
>> **Population**
>> **Prices**
>> **Profit**
>> **Property**
>> **Risk**
>> **Saving and investment**
>> **Socialism**
>> **Statistics**
>> **Supply and demand**
>> **Underground economy**
>> **Waste (Economics)**
>> **Wealth**

Economics and Christianity
> USE **Christianity and economics**

Economics—History   330.09; 330.1

> Use for materials describing the development of economic theories. Materials on the economic conditions and development of countries are entered under **Economic conditions**.

Economics of war
> USE **War—Economic aspects**

Economy
> USE **Saving and investment**

Economy cars
> USE **Compact cars**

Economy, Underground
> USE **Underground economy**

Ecosystems
> USE **Ecology**

Ecoterrorism (May subdiv. geog.)
>> **303.625; 364.1**
> BT **Environmental movement**
>> **Terrorism**

Ecotourism (May subdiv. geog.)   **338.4**
> UF   Ecological tourism
>> Environmental tourism
>> Green tourism
>> Nature tourism
> BT **Tourist trade**

Ecumenical councils
> USE **Councils and synods**

Ecumenical movement (May subdiv. geog.)   **280**

> Use for materials on a movement originating in the twentieth century aimed at promoting church cooperation and unity. Materials on unity as one of the marks of the church are entered under **Church—Unity**. Materials on prospective and actual mergers within and across denominational lines are entered under **Christian union**. Materials on religious activ-

ities planned and conducted cooperatively by two or more Christian sects are entered under **Interdenominational cooperation**.

> UF   Christian unity
>> Ecumenism
> BT **Christian sects**
>> **Church**
> RT **Christian union**

Ecumenism
> USE **Christian union**
>> **Ecumenical movement**

Eddas   839

> Use for individual works, collections, or materials about eddas.

> BT **Old Norse literature**
>> **Poetry**
>> **Scandinavian literature**

Eden
> USE **Paradise**

Edgar Allan Poe Awards   808.3
> UF   Edgars
> BT **Literary prizes**
>> **Mystery fiction**

Edgars
> USE **Edgar Allan Poe Awards**

Edible plants   581.6
> UF   Food plants
>> Plants, Edible
> BT **Economic botany**
>> **Food**
>> **Plants**

Edifices
> USE **Buildings**

Editing   070.5; 808

> Use for materials on the editing of books and texts. Materials on the editing of newspapers and periodicals are entered under **Journalism—Editing**.

> SA   subjects and types of literature with the subdivision *Editing*, e.g. **Poetry—Editing**; etc. [to be added as needed]
> BT **Authorship**
>> **Publishers and publishing**
> NT **Journalism—Editing**
>> **Poetry—Editing**

Editions   016
> UF   Bibliography—Editions
> BT **Bibliography**
> NT **Autographed editions**
>> **Bilingual books**
>> **First editions**
>> **Paperback books**
>> **Reprints (Publications)**

Education (May subdiv. geog.)　370

    Subdivisions listed under this heading may be used under other education headings where applicable.

  UF   Instruction
        Pedagogy
        Study and teaching
  SA   types of education, e.g. **Vocational education**; classes of persons and social and ethnic groups with the subdivision *Education*, e.g. **Deaf—Education**; **African Americans—Education**; etc.; and subjects with the subdivision *Study and teaching*, e.g. **Science—Study and teaching** [to be added as needed]
  BT   **Civilization**
  NT   **Ability grouping in education**
        Adult education
        African Americans—Education
        Area studies
        Audiovisual education
        Automobile driver education
        Basic education
        Blacks—Education
        Blind—Education
        Books and reading
        Boys—Education
        Business education
        Church and education
        Classical education
        Coeducation
        Colleges and universities
        Consumer education
        Continuing education
        Cooperative learning
        Deaf—Education
        Distance education
        Early childhood education
        Educational evaluation
        Educational games
        Educational technology
        Educational tests and measurements
        Educators
        Elderly—Education
        Elementary education
        Evening and continuation schools
        Family life education

        Foreign study
        Girls—Education
        Health education
        Higher education
        Home and school
        Home schooling
        International education
        Internet in education
        Labor—Education
        Library education
        Literacy
        Mainstreaming in education
        Men—Education
        Mentally handicapped children—Education
        Military education
        Moral education
        Multicultural education
        Native Americans—Education
        Nature study
        Naval education
        Outdoor education
        Physical education
        Preschool education
        Professional education
        Psychology of learning
        Religious education
        Scholarships
        School choice
        Secondary education
        Self-instruction
        Simulation games in education
        Socialization
        Special education
        Study skills
        Teaching
        Technical education
        Veterans—Education
        Vocational education
        Women—Education
        World War, 1939-1945—Education and the war
  RT   **Culture**
        Learning and scholarship
        Schools

Education—Aims and objectives　370.11

Education and church
  USE **Church and education**
Education and radio
  USE **Radio in education**

Education and religion
  USE **Church and education**
Education and state
  USE **Education—Government policy**
Education and television
  USE **Television in education**
Education and the war
  USE names of wars with the subdivision *Education and the war,* e.g. **World War, 1939-1945—Education and the war** [to be added as needed]
Education associations
  USE **Education—Societies**
Education—Automation
  USE **Computer-assisted instruction**
Education, Bilingual
  USE **Bilingual education**
Education, Christian
  USE **Christian education**
Education, Compulsory
  USE **Compulsory education**
Education—Computer software
  USE **Educational software**
Education, Cooperative
  USE **Cooperative education**
Education—Curricula   375
  UF Core curriculum
     Courses of study
     Curricula
     Schools—Curricula
  SA types of education and schools with the subdivision *Curricula*, e.g. **Library education—Curricula** [to be added as needed]
  NT **Articulation (Education)**
     Colleges and universities—Curricula
     Curriculum planning
     Library education—Curricula
Education—Data processing
  USE **Computer-assisted instruction**
Education—Developing countries   370.9172
  UF Developing countries—Education
Education, Elementary
  USE **Elementary education**
Education—Experimental methods   371.3

  UF Activity schools
     Experimental methods in education
     Progressive education
     Teaching—Experimental methods
  SA types of experimental methods, e.g. **Nongraded schools; Open plan schools**; etc. [to be added as needed]
  NT **Experimental schools**
     Nongraded schools
     Open plan schools
     Whole language
Education—Federal aid
  USE **Federal aid to education**
Education—Finance   371.2; 379.1
  UF School finance
     School taxes
     Tuition
  BT **Finance**
  NT **Educational vouchers**
     Government aid to education
  RT **Federal aid to education**
Education for librarianship
  USE **Library education**
Education—Government aid
  USE **Government aid to education**
Education—Government policy (May subdiv. geog.)   **379**
  UF Education and state
     Educational policy
  BT **Social policy**
  NT **Compulsory education**
     Federal aid to education
     Government aid to education
Education, Higher
  USE **Higher education**
Education, Industrial
  USE **Industrial arts education**
Education—Integration
  USE **School integration**
     Segregation in education
Education of adults
  USE **Adult education**
Education of children
  USE **Elementary education**
Education of criminals
  USE **Prisoners—Education**
Education of men
  USE **Men—Education**

Education of prisoners
USE **Prisoners—Education**
Education of the blind
USE **Blind—Education**
Education of the deaf
USE **Deaf—Education**
Education of veterans
USE **Veterans—Education**
Education of women
USE **Women—Education**
Education of workers
USE **Labor—Education**
Education—Parent participation (May
subdiv. geog.) **371.19**
UF Parent participation in children's
education
Parental involvement in chil-
dren's education
RT **Home schooling**
Education—Personnel service
USE **Educational counseling**
Education, Preschool
USE **Preschool education**
Education, Primary
USE **Elementary education**
Education, Secondary
USE **Secondary education**
Education—Segregation
USE **Segregation in education**
Education—Societies   370.6
UF Education associations
Educational associations
BT **Societies**
NT **Parent-teacher associations**
Education—State aid
USE **Government aid to education**
Education—Statistics   370
BT **Statistics**
Education—Study and teaching   370.7

Use for materials on the study of education
as a discipline. Materials on the history and
methods of training teachers, including the educational functions of teachers colleges, are
entered under **Teachers—Training**. Materials
on the art of teaching and methods of teaching are entered under **Teaching**.

UF Pedagogy
NT **Teachers colleges**
Teachers—Training
Education, Theological
USE **Theology—Study and teaching**
Education—United States   370.973

Educational accreditation
USE **Schools—Accreditation**
Educational achievement
USE **Academic achievement**
Educational administration
USE **Schools—Administration**
Educational assessment
USE **Educational evaluation**
Educational associations
USE **Education—Societies**
Educational consultants (May subdiv.
geog.) **370.7**
BT **Consultants**
Educational counseling (May subdiv.
geog.) **371.4**

Use for materials on the assistance given to
students by schools, colleges, or universities
in the selection of a program of studies suited
to their abilities, interests, future plans, and
general circumstances. Materials on the assistance given to students in understanding and
coping with adjustment problems are entered
under **School counseling**. Materials on the activities and programs designed to help people
plan, choose, and succeed in their careers are
entered under **Vocational guidance**.

UF Academic advising
Education—Personnel service
Educational guidance
Guidance counseling, Educational
Personnel service in education
Student guidance
Students—Counseling
BT **Counseling**
RT **Dropouts**
School counseling
Vocational guidance
Educational evaluation (May subdiv.
geog.) **370.7; 379.1**
UF Educational assessment
Educational program evaluation
Evaluation research in education
Instructional systems analysis
Program evaluation in education
Self-evaluation in education
SA topics in education with the sub-
division *Evaluation*, e.g. **Sci-
ence—Study and teaching—
Evaluation** [to be added as
needed]
BT **Education**
Educational films
USE **Motion pictures in education**

Educational freedom
    USE   **Academic freedom**

Educational games   371.33
    UF   Instructional games
          Instructive games
    BT   **Education**
          Games
    NT   **Simulation games in education**

Educational gaming
    USE   **Simulation games in education**

Educational guidance
    USE   **Educational counseling**

Educational measurements
    USE   **Educational tests and measurements**

Educational media
    USE   **Teaching—Aids and devices**

Educational media centers
    USE   **Instructional materials centers**

Educational policy
    USE   **Education—Government policy**

Educational program evaluation
    USE   **Educational evaluation**

Educational psychology   370.15
    BT   **Psychology**
          Teaching
    NT   **Ability grouping in education**
          Achievement motivation
          Apperception
          Attention
          Imagination
          Intelligence tests
          Listening
          Memory
          Psychology of learning
          Thought and thinking
    RT   **Applied psychology**
          Child psychology

Educational reports
    USE   **School reports**

Educational simulation games
    USE   **Simulation games in education**

Educational sociology (May subdiv. geog.)   306.43
    UF   Social problems in education
    BT   **Sociology**

Educational software   005.3
    UF   Education—Computer software
    BT   **Computer software**

Educational surveys (May subdiv. geog.)   370
    UF   School surveys
    BT   **Surveys**

Educational technology (May subdiv. geog.)   371.33
    UF   Instructional technology
    BT   **Education**
    RT   **Teaching—Aids and devices**

Educational television
    USE   **Public television**
          Television in education

Educational tests and measurements (May subdiv. geog.)   371.26
    UF   Educational measurements
          Tests
    BT   **Education**
    NT   **Ability—Testing**
          Achievement tests
          Colleges and universities—Entrance examinations
          Grading and marking (Education)
          Test bias
    RT   **Examinations**
          Intelligence tests
          Psychological tests

Educational vouchers   379.1
    UF   School vouchers
          Vouchers, Educational
    BT   **Education—Finance**

Educators (May subdiv. geog.)   370.92; 920
    Use for materials on people engaged professionally in the field of education in general. Materials on educators engaged in classroom or other instruction are entered under **Teachers**.
    UF   College teachers
          Faculty (Education)
          Professors
    BT   **Education**
    NT   **African American educators**
          Teachers

EEC
    USE   **European Union**

Efficiency, Industrial
    USE   **Industrial efficiency**

Egg decoration   745.59
    UF   Easter egg decoration
    BT   **Decoration and ornament**
          Handicraft

Eggs   636.5; 641
    Use for materials on chicken eggs or on animal eggs in general.

Eggs—*Continued*
    SA   types of animals other than
          chickens with the subdivision
          Eggs, e.g. **Dinosaurs—Eggs**
          [to be added as needed]
    BT   **Food**
    NT   **Birds—Eggs**
          Dinosaurs—Eggs
Ego (Psychology)   154.2
    BT   **Personality**
          Psychoanalysis
          Psychology
          Self
    RT   **Identity (Psychology)**
Egypt   962
    May be subdivided like **United States** except for *History*.
Egypt—Antiquities   932
    UF   Egyptology
    BT   **Antiquities**
Egypt—History   932; 962
    NT   **Sinai Campaign, 1956**
Egypt—History—1970-   962.05
Egyptian mythology   398.20962
    BT   **Mythology**
Egyptology
    USE   **Egypt—Antiquities**
Eight-hour day
    USE   **Hours of labor**
Eighteenth century
    USE   **World history—18th century**
El Niño Current   551.46
    BT   **Ocean currents**
Elder abuse
    USE   **Elderly abuse**
Elder care
    USE   **Elderly—Care**
Elderhostels (May subdiv. geog.)   **647.94**
    UF   Hostels, Elder
    BT   **Continuing education**
          Elderly—Education
Elderly (May subdiv. geog.)   **155.67; 305.26**
    UF   Aged
          Aging persons
          Elderly persons
          Older persons
          Senior citizens
    SA   elderly of particular racial or
          ethnic groups [to be added as
          needed]

    BT   **Age**
          Gerontology
    NT   **African American elderly**
          Aging
          Aging parents
          Elderly—Library services
          Elderly men
          Elderly women
          Social work with the elderly
    RT   **Old age**
          Retirees
Elderly abuse   362.6
    UF   Abuse of the elderly
          Abused aged
          Battered elderly
          Elder abuse
          Elderly—Mistreatment
          Elderly neglect
          Parent abuse
    BT   **Domestic violence**
Elderly and libraries
    USE   **Elderly—Library services**
Elderly—Care (May subdiv. geog.)   **362.6**
    Use for general materials on the care of the dependent elderly.
    UF   Elder care
    NT   **Elderly—Home care**
          Elderly—Institutional care
          Elderly—Medical care
Elderly centers
    USE   **Senior centers**
Elderly—Counseling of   362.6
    UF   Counseling of the elderly
          Counseling with the aged
    BT   **Counseling**
Elderly—Diseases   618.97
    UF   Geriatrics
    BT   **Diseases**
    RT   **Elderly—Health and hygiene**
Elderly—Education
    BT   **Education**
    NT   **Elderhostels**
Elderly—Health and hygiene (May subdiv. geog.)   **618.97**
    UF   Geriatrics
    BT   **Health**
          Hygiene
    RT   **Elderly—Diseases**
Elderly—Home care (May subdiv. geog.)   **362.14; 362.6; 649.8**

Elderly—Home care—*Continued*
 BT **Elderly—Care**
   Home care services
Elderly—Housing (May subdiv. geog.)
  362.6
 UF Housing for the elderly
 BT **Housing**
 NT **Retirement communities**
 RT **Assisted living**
Elderly—Institutional care (May subdiv.
 geog.) **362.61**
 UF Homes for the elderly
   Old age homes
 BT **Elderly—Care**
   Institutional care
Elderly—Library services **027.6**
 UF Elderly and libraries
   Libraries and the elderly [*Former heading*]
   Library services to the elderly
 BT **Elderly**
   Library services
Elderly—Life skills guides **362.6; 646.7**
 BT **Life skills**
 RT **Retirement**
Elderly—Medical care (May subdiv.
 geog.) **362.1; 618.97**
 UF Medical care for the elderly
 BT **Elderly—Care**
   Medical care
 NT **Medicare**
Elderly men (May subdiv. geog.) **305.26**
 UF Aged men
 BT **Elderly**
Elderly—Mistreatment
 USE **Elderly abuse**
Elderly neglect
 USE **Elderly abuse**
Elderly parents
 USE **Aging parents**
Elderly persons
 USE **Elderly**
Elderly—Recreation **790.084**
 BT **Recreation**
Elderly—Societies **367**
 BT **Societies**
Elderly—United States **305.260973**
Elderly women (May subdiv. geog.)
  305.26
 UF Aged women
 BT **Elderly**

Elected officials
 USE **Public officers**
Election
 USE **Elections**
   and types of public officials
   and names of individual public officials with the subdivision *Election,* e.g. **Presidents—United States—Election** [to be added as needed]
Election law (May subdiv. geog.) **342**
 UF Law, Election
 BT **Constitutional law**
Election (Theology)
 USE **Predestination**
Electioneering
 USE **Politics**
Elections (May subdiv. geog.) **324**
 UF Ballot
   Election
   Franchise
   Polls
   Voting
 SA types of public officials and names of individual public officials with the subdivision *Election*, e.g. **Presidents—United States—Election** [to be added as needed]
 BT **Politics**
 NT **Campaign funds**
   Presidents—United States—Election
   Primaries
   Referendum
   Suffrage
   Voter registration
 RT **Proportional representation**
   Representative government and representation
Elections—Finance
 USE **Campaign funds**
Elections—United States **324.973**
 UF United States—Elections
Elections—United States—Finance
 USE **Campaign funds—United States**
Electoral college
 USE **Presidents—United States—Election**

Electric apparatus and appliances
    621.3028; 643

Use for materials on small electrical machines and appliances. Materials on large machines powered by electricity are entered under **Electric machinery**.

  UF   Apparatus, Electric
        Appliances, Electric
        Electric appliances
  SA   types of electric apparatus and appliances, e.g. **Burglar alarms** [to be added as needed]
  BT   **Scientific apparatus and instruments**
  NT   **Burglar alarms**
        Electric batteries
        Electric generators
        Electric household appliances
        Electric lamps
        Induction coils
        Storage batteries

Electric appliances
  USE **Electric apparatus and appliances**
         Electric household appliances

Electric automobiles   **629.222**
  UF   Automobiles, Electric
        Electric cars
  BT   **Automobiles**

Electric automobiles—Cost effectiveness
    388.3
  BT   **Cost effectiveness**

Electric batteries   **621.31**
  UF   Batteries, Electric
        Cells, Electric
  BT   **Electric apparatus and appliances**
        Electrochemistry
  NT   **Fuel cells**
        Solar batteries
  RT   **Storage batteries**

Electric cars
  USE **Electric automobiles**

Electric circuits   **621.319**
  UF   Circuits, Electric
  BT   **Electric lines**
        Electricity
  NT   **Electronic circuits**

Electric companies
  USE **Electric utilities**

Electric condensers
  USE **Condensers (Electricity)**

Electric conductors   **621.319**
  UF   Conductors, Electric
  BT   **Electronics**
  NT   **Semiconductors**
        Superconductors

Electric controllers   **629.8**
  UF   Automatic control
  BT   **Electric machinery**

Electric currents   **537.6; 621.31**
  UF   Currents, Electric
  BT   **Electricity**
  NT   **Alternating electric currents**
        Electric measurements
        Electric transformers

Electric currents, Alternating
  USE **Alternating electric currents**

Electric distribution
  USE **Electric lines**
         Electric power distribution

Electric engineering
  USE **Electrical engineering**

Electric equipment of automobiles
  USE **Automobiles—Electric equipment**

Electric eye
  USE **Photoelectric cells**

Electric generators   **621.31**
  UF   Dynamos
        Generators, Electric
  BT   **Electric apparatus and appliances**
        Electric machinery

Electric guitar   **787.87**
  BT   **Electronic musical instruments**
        Guitars

Electric heating   **621.402; 644; 697**
  UF   Electricity in the home
  BT   **Heating**

Electric household appliances   **643**
  UF   Appliances, Electric
        Domestic appliances
        Electric appliances
        Electricity in the home
        Household appliances, Electric
        Labor saving devices, Household
  SA   types of specific appliances [to be added as needed]
  BT   **Electric apparatus and appliances**

Electric household appliances—*Continued*
    Household equipment and supplies
Electric industries
    USE **Electric products industry**
Electric lamps   621.32; 645
    UF Incandescent lamps
    BT **Electric apparatus and appliances**
        Lamps
    RT **Electric lighting**
Electric light
    USE **Electric lighting**
          Photometry
          Phototherapy
Electric light and power industry
    USE **Electric utilities**
Electric lighting   621.32
    UF Arc light
        Electric light
        Electricity in the home
        Light, Electric
    BT **Lighting**
    NT **Fluorescent lighting**
    RT **Electric lamps**
Electric lighting, Fluorescent
    USE **Fluorescent lighting**
Electric lines   621.319
> Use for materials on power transmission lines, their construction and properties.

    UF Electric distribution
        Electric power transmission
        Electric transmission
        Electricity—Distribution
        Power transmission, Electric
        Transmission of power
    BT **Electric power distribution**
    NT **Electric circuits**
        Electric wiring
Electric machinery   621.31
> Use for materials on large machines powered by electricity. Materials on smaller machines and appliances are entered under **Electric apparatus and appliances**.

    BT **Machinery**
    NT **Electric controllers**
        Electric generators
        Electric motors
        Electric transformers
Electric machinery—**Alternating current**
    621.319
    UF Alternating current machinery

Electric machinery—**Direct current**
    621.319
    UF Direct current machinery
Electric measurements   621.37
    UF Measurements, Electric
    BT **Electric currents**
        Weights and measures
    NT **Electric meters**
    RT **Electric testing**
Electric meters   621.37
    UF Meters, Electric
    BT **Electric measurements**
Electric motors   621.46
    UF Induction motors
        Motors
    BT **Electric machinery**
    NT **Electric transformers**
Electric power   621.31
    BT **Electricity**
        Energy resources
        Power (Mechanics)
Electric power development
    USE **Electrification**
Electric power distribution   621.319
    UF Electric distribution
        Electric power transmission
        Electric transmission
        Electricity—Distribution
        Power transmission, Electric
        Transmission of power
    BT **Electrical engineering**
        Power transmission
    NT **Electric lines**
        Electric utilities
        Electric wiring
Electric power failures   621.319
    UF Blackouts, Electric power
        Brownouts
        Electric power interruptions
        Power blackouts
        Power failures
Electric power in mining
    USE **Electricity in mining**
Electric power industry
    USE **Electric utilities**
Electric power interruptions
    USE **Electric power failures**
Electric power plants (May subdiv. geog.)
    621.31
    UF Power plants
        Power stations

Electric power plants—*Continued*

 SA types of electric power plants,
   e.g. **Nuclear power plants**
   [to be added as needed]

 NT **Hydroelectric power plants**
   Nuclear power plants
   Steam power plants

Electric power transmission
 USE **Electric lines**
   Electric power distribution

Electric products industry (May subdiv. geog.) **338.4**

 Use for materials on industries producing products that contain electrical motors or otherwise employ electricity.

 UF Electric industries
 BT **Industries**

Electric railroads (May subdiv. geog.) **621.33; 625.1; 385**

 UF Interurban railroads
 BT **Railroads**
 RT **Street railroads**

Electric signs **621.32; 659.13**

 BT **Advertising**
   Signs and signboards
 NT **Neon tubes**

Electric smelting
 USE **Electrometallurgy**

Electric testing **621.37**

 BT **Testing**
 RT **Electric measurements**

Electric toys **688.7**

 BT **Toys**

Electric transformers **621.31**

 UF Transformers, Electric
 BT **Electric currents**
   Electric machinery
   Electric motors

Electric transmission
 USE **Electric lines**
   Electric power distribution

Electric utilities (May subdiv. geog.) **333.793**

 Use for materials on businesses that sell and distribute electricity to customers.

 UF Electric companies
   Electric light and power industry
   Electric power industry
 BT **Electric power distribution**
   Public utilities
 NT **Electrification**

Electric utilities—Government ownership (May subdiv. geog.) **333.793**

Electric waves **537; 621.381**

 UF Hertzian waves
   Radio waves
 BT **Electricity**
   Waves
 NT **Electromagnetic waves**
   Microwaves

Electric welding **671.5**

 UF Arc welding
   Resistance welding
   Spot welding
   Welding, Electric
 BT **Welding**

Electric wiring **621.319**

 UF Wiring, Electric
 BT **Electric lines**
   Electric power distribution

Electric wiring—Charts, diagrams, etc. **621.319**

Electrical engineering (May subdiv. geog.) **621.3**

 UF Electric engineering
 BT **Engineering**
   Mechanical engineering
 NT **Electric power distribution**
   Electricity in mining
   Electrification

Electricity **537; 621.3**

 SA electricity in various endeavors,
   e.g. **Electricity in agriculture**
   [to be added as needed]

 BT **Physics**
 NT **Electric circuits**
   Electric currents
   Electric power
   Electric waves
   Electricity in agriculture
   Electricity in mining
   Lightning
 RT **Magnetism**

Electricity—Distribution
 USE **Electric lines**
   Electric power distribution

Electricity in agriculture **333.79; 631.3**

 UF Electricity on the farm
 BT **Agricultural engineering**
   Agricultural machinery
   Electricity
 RT **Rural electrification**

Electricity in medicine
 USE **Electrotherapeutics**

Electricity in mining   622
 UF Electric power in mining
   Mining, Electric
 BT **Electrical engineering**
   Electricity
 RT **Mining engineering**
Electricity in the home
 USE **Electric heating**
   Electric household appliances
   Electric lighting
Electricity on the farm
 USE **Electricity in agriculture**
Electrification (May subdiv. geog.)
   621.319
 UF Electric power development
 BT **Electric utilities**
   Electrical engineering
 NT **Rural electrification**
Electrochemistry   541; 660
 BT **Industrial chemistry**
   Physical chemistry
 NT **Electric batteries**
   Electrometallurgy
   Electroplating
   Electrotyping
   Fuel cells
Electromagnetic waves   539.2
 UF Waves, Electromagnetic
 BT **Electric waves**
   Radiation
 NT **Gamma rays**
   Heat
   Infrared radiation
   Light
   Microwaves
   Ultraviolet rays
   X-rays
Electromagnetism   621.34
 BT **Magnetism**
 NT **Masers**
Electromagnets   621.34
 UF Magnet winding
 BT **Magnetism**
   Magnets
Electrometallurgy   669.028
 UF Electric smelting
 BT **Electrochemistry**
   Metallurgy
   Smelting
 RT **Electroplating**
   Electrotyping

Electron microscope and microscopy
 USE **Electron microscopes**
Electron microscopes   502.8
 UF Electron microscope and micros-
   copy
 BT **Microscopes**
Electron tubes
 USE **Vacuum tubes**
Electronic apparatus and appliances
   621.381
 UF Apparatus, Electronic
   Appliances, Electronic
 SA types of electronic apparatus and
   appliances, e.g. **Computers**
   [to be added as needed]
 BT **Electronics**
   Scientific apparatus and in-
   struments
 NT **Computers**
   Electronic toys
   Intercommunication systems
   Magnetic recorders and re-
   cording
   Vacuum tubes
Electronic art
 USE **Video art**
Electronic books   070.5
 UF Books in machine-readable form
   Online books
 BT **Books**
Electronic bugging
 USE **Eavesdropping**
Electronic bulletin boards
 USE **Computer bulletin boards**
Electronic circuits   621.319; 621.3815
 BT **Electric circuits**
   Electronics
Electronic commerce (May subdiv. geog.)
   381; 658
   Use for materials on the exchange of goods
   and services and the transfer of funds through
   electronic communications.
 UF Cybercommerce
   Internet commerce
   Online commerce
 BT **Commerce**
 NT **Internet auctions**
   Internet marketing
   Internet shopping
Electronic data processing
 USE **Data processing**

Electronic design

  USE **Computer-aided design**

Electronic discussion groups   004.692

> Use for materials on services, commonly called electronic mailing lists, that allow subscribers to post messages that are then distributed to other subscribers. Materials on services that allow users to engage in conversations in real time are entered under **Online chat groups**. Materials on services that allow users to post messages and retrieve messages from others who have some common interest are entered under **Computer bulletin boards**.

  UF   E-mail discussion groups

        Online discussion groups

  BT   **Discussion groups**

  RT   **Computer bulletin boards**

        Online chat groups

Electronic drafting

  USE **Computer graphics**

Electronic drawing

  USE **Computer graphics**

Electronic eavesdropping

  USE **Eavesdropping**

Electronic games

  USE **Video games**

Electronic journalism

  USE **Online journalism**

Electronic libraries

  USE **Digital libraries**

Electronic listening devices

  USE **Eavesdropping**

Electronic mail reference services (Libraries)

  USE **Electronic reference services (Libraries)**

Electronic mail systems   004.692; 384.3

> Use for materials on the electronic transmission of letters, messages, etc., primarily through the use of computers.

  UF   E-mail

        Email

  BT   **Data transmission systems**

        Telecommunication

Electronic marketing

  USE **Telemarketing**

Electronic music   786.7

  UF   Synthesizer music

  BT   **Music**

  RT   **Computer music**

Electronic musical instruments   786.7

  UF   Musical instruments, Electronic

  SA   types of instruments, e.g. **Synthesizer (Musical instrument)** [to be added as needed]

  BT   **Musical instruments**

  NT   **Electric guitar**

        Synthesizers (Musical instruments)

Electronic publishing (May subdiv. geog.) **070.5; 686.2**

> Use for materials on the process of publishing by which books and articles or any kind of data are made available as an electronic product. Materials on the use of a personal computer with writing, graphics, and page layout software to produce printed material for publication are entered under **Desktop publishing**.

  UF   Online publishing

        Web publishing

  BT   **Information services**

        Publishers and publishing

  NT   **Open access publishing**

        Teletext systems

  RT   **Desktop publishing**

Electronic reference services (Libraries) (May subdiv. geog.) **025.5**

  UF   Digital reference services (Libraries)

        E-mail reference services (Libraries)

        Electronic mail reference services (Libraries)

        Online reference services

  BT   **Reference services (Libraries)**

Electronic speech processing systems

  USE **Speech processing systems**

Electronic spreadsheets

  USE **Spreadsheet software**

Electronic surveillance   621.389

  UF   Surveillance, Electronic

  BT   **Remote sensing**

Electronic toys   688.7

  BT   **Electronic apparatus and appliances**

        Toys

  NT   **Video games**

Electronics   537.5; 621.381

  BT   **Engineering**

        Physics

        Technology

  NT   **Amplifiers (Electronics)**

        Cybernetics

        Digital electronics

        Electric conductors

        Electronic apparatus and appliances

Electronics—*Continued*
>> **Electronic circuits**
>> **High-fidelity sound systems**
>> **Microelectronics**
>> **Semiconductors**
>> **Superconductors**
>> **Transistors**

Electrons   539.7
> BT   **Atoms**
> **Particles (Nuclear physics)**

Electroplating   671.7
> BT   **Electrochemistry**
> **Metalwork**
> RT   **Electrometallurgy**

Electrotherapeutics   615.8
> UF   Electricity in medicine
> Medical electricity
> BT   **Massage**
> **Physical therapy**
> **Therapeutics**
> NT   **Radiotherapy**

Electrotyping   686.2
> BT   **Electrochemistry**
> **Printing**
> RT   **Electrometallurgy**

Elegiac poetry   808.1; 808.81
> Use for individual works, collections, or materials about elegiac poetry.
> UF   Elegies
> Lamentations
> BT   **Poetry**

Elegies
> USE   **Elegiac poetry**

Elementary education (May subdiv. geog.)   372
> UF   Children—Education
> Education, Elementary
> Education of children
> Education, Primary
> Grammar schools
> Primary education
> BT   **Education**
> NT   **Creative activities**
> **Exceptional children**
> **Kindergarten**
> **Montessori method of education**
> **Nursery schools**
> **Readiness for school**

Elementary particles (Physics)
> USE   **Particles (Nuclear physics)**

Elementary school dropouts
> USE   **Dropouts**

Elementary school libraries   027.8
> BT   **School libraries**

Elementary schools (May subdiv. geog.)   373.236
> UF   Grade schools
> BT   **Schools**
> RT   **Middle schools**

Elements, Chemical
> USE   **Chemical elements**

Elephants (May subdiv. geog.)   599.67
> BT   **Mammals**

Elevators   621.8
> UF   Lifts
> BT   **Hoisting machinery**

Elite (Social sciences) (May subdiv. geog.)   305.5
> BT   **Leadership**
> **Power (Social sciences)**
> **Social classes**
> **Social groups**

Elizabeth II, Queen of Great Britain, 1926-   92; B
> BT   **Queens**

Elocution
> USE   **Public speaking**

Elves   398.21
> BT   **Folklore**

Email
> USE   **Electronic mail systems**

Emancipation
> USE   **Freedom**

Emancipation of slaves
> USE   **Slaves—Emancipation**

Emancipation of women
> USE   **Women's rights**

Embarrassment
> USE   **Self-consciousness**

Embassies
> USE   **Diplomatic and consular service**

Emblems
> USE   **Decorations of honor**
> **Heraldry**
> **Insignia**
> **Mottoes**
> **National emblems**
> **Seals (Numismatics)**
> **Signs and symbols**

Emblems, State
   USE **State emblems**

Embracing
   USE **Hugging**

Embroidery (May subdiv. geog.) **746.44**
   SA types of embroidery [to be add-
       ed as needed]
   BT **Decoration and ornament**
       Needlework
       Sewing
   NT **Crewelwork**
       Cross-stitch
       Drawn work
       Hardanger needlework
       Needlepoint
       Samplers

Embryology   **571.8; 612.6**
   UF Development
   BT **Biology**
       Zoology
   NT **Fetus**
       Frozen embryos
       Genetics
   RT **Cells**
       Protoplasm
       Reproduction

Embryos, Frozen
   USE **Frozen embryos**

Emergencies
   USE **Accidents**
       Disasters
       First aid

Emergency assistance
   USE **Helping behavior**

Emergency medical technicians   **610.69;
      616.02**
   UF Emergency paramedics
       EMTs (Medicine)
       Paramedical personnel
       Paramedics, Emergency
   BT **Allied health personnel**

Emergency medicine   **616.02**
   BT **Medicine**
   NT **Cardiac resuscitation**

Emergency mental health services
   USE **Crisis intervention (Mental
       health services)**

Emergency paramedics
   USE **Emergency medical technicians**

Emergency powers
   USE **War and emergency powers**

Emergency preparedness
   USE **Disaster relief**

Emergency relief
   USE **Disaster relief**

Emergency survival
   USE **Survival skills**

Emigrants
   USE **Immigrants**

Emigration
   USE **Immigration and emigration**

Eminent domain   **333.1; 343**
   UF Condemnation of land
       Expropriation
   BT **Constitutional law**
       Land use
       Property

Emmy Awards   **791.45**
   BT **Television broadcasting**

Emotional stress
   USE **Stress (Psychology)**

Emotionally disturbed children   **155.4;
      362.2; 371.94; 618.92**
   Use for general materials on children suffer-
   ing from mental or emotional illnesses. Mate-
   rials on the clinical and therapeutic aspects of
   mental disorders in children are entered under
   Child psychiatry.
   UF Behavior problems (Children)
       Maladjusted children
       Mentally ill children
       Neurotic children
       Problem children
       Psychotic children
   BT **Exceptional children**
       Mentally ill
   RT **Child psychiatry**
       Juvenile delinquency

Emotions   **152.4**
   UF Feelings
       Passions
   SA types of emotions [to be added
       as needed]
   BT **Psychology**
       Psychophysiology
   NT **Anger**
       Anxiety
       Attitude (Psychology)
       Bereavement
       Compassion
       Consolation
       Disappointment
       Emotions in children
       Empathy

Emotions—*Continued*
>> Fanaticism
>> Fear
>> Frustration
>> Gratitude
>> Grief
>> Guilt
>> Happiness
>> Hate
>> Helplessness (Psychology)
>> Hope
>> Horror
>> Jealousy
>> Joy and sorrow
>> Laughter
>> Loneliness
>> Love
>> Pain
>> Pleasure
>> Prejudices
>> Self-confidence
>> Shame
>> Shyness
>> Sympathy
>> Temper tantrums
>> Trust
>> Worry

Emotions in children   155.4
> BT **Child psychology**
>> **Emotions**

Empathy   152.4
> BT **Attitude (Psychology)**
>> **Emotions**
>> **Social psychology**

Emperors (May subdiv. geog.)   **920; 929.7**
> UF Rulers
>> Sovereigns
> SA names of emperors, e.g. **Nero, Emperor of Rome, 37-68** [to be added as needed]
> BT **Kings and rulers**

Emperors—Rome   **920; 937**
> UF Roman emperors
> SA names of Roman emperors, e.g. **Nero, Emperor of Rome, 37-68** [to be added as needed]
> NT **Nero, Emperor of Rome, 37-68**

Empiricism   146
> UF Experience
> BT **Philosophy**
>> **Rationalism**

>> **Theory of knowledge**
> RT **Pragmatism**

Employee absenteeism
> USE **Absenteeism (Labor)**

Employee assistance programs   658.3
> BT **Personnel management**

Employee benefits
> USE **Fringe benefits**

Employee counseling
> USE **Employees—Counseling of**

Employee drinking
> USE **Employees—Alcohol use**

Employee drug testing
> USE **Employees—Drug testing**

Employee fringe benefits
> USE **Fringe benefits**

Employee health services
> USE **Occupational health services**

Employee morale   158.7; 658.3
> BT **Applied psychology**
>> **Morale**
>> **Personnel management**
> NT **Job satisfaction**
> RT **Absenteeism (Labor)**

Employee rights (May subdiv. geog.)   **331.01**
> UF Employees—Civil rights
>> Labor rights
>> Rights of employees
> BT **Civil rights**
>> **Labor laws and legislation**

Employees   331.11; 920
> UF Workers
> SA types of employees, e.g. **Office workers**; types of industries, services, establishments, or institutions, with the subdivision *Employees*; e.g. **Chemical industry—Employees**; **Railroads—Employees**; etc.; and names of countries, states, cities, etc., and corporate bodies with the subdivision *Officials and employees*, e.g. **United States—Officials and employees**; **Ohio—Officials and employees**; **Chicago (Ill.)—Officials and employees**; **United Nations—Officials and employees**; etc. [to be added as needed]

Employees—*Continued*
  BT **Labor**
  NT **Chemical industry—Employees**
      Colleges and universities—Employees
      Medical personnel
      Migrant labor
      Office workers
      Railroads—Employees
  RT **Personnel management**
Employees—Accidents
  USE **Industrial accidents**
Employees—Alcohol use   331.25; 658.3
  UF Alcohol and employees
      Alcohol in the workplace
      Drinking and employees
      Drinking in the workplace
      Employee drinking
      Employees and alcohol
Employees and alcohol
  USE **Employees—Alcohol use**
Employees and drugs
  USE **Employees—Drug use**
Employees and narcotics
  USE **Employees—Drug use**
Employees and officials
  USE **Civil service**
Employees—Civil rights
  USE **Employee rights**
Employees—Counseling of   658.3
  UF Employee counseling
      Industrial counseling
  BT **Counseling**
Employees—Dismissal   331.25; 658.3
  BT **Job security**
      Personnel management
  RT **Downsizing of organizations**
Employees—Drug testing   331.25; 658.3
  UF Drug testing in the workplace
      Employee drug testing
  BT **Drug testing**
Employees—Drug use   331.25; 658.3
  UF Drugs and employees
      Drugs in the workplace
      Employees and drugs
      Employees and narcotics
Employees—Pensions
  USE **Old age pensions**
Employees—Rating   331.25; 658.3
Employees' representation in management
  USE **Participative management**

Employees—Salaries, wages, etc.
  USE **Salaries, wages, etc.**
Employees—Training   331.25; 658.3
    Use for materials discussing on-the-job training. Materials on teaching people a skill during the educational process are entered under **Vocational education**. Materials on teaching people a skill after formal education are entered under **Occupational training**. Materials on retraining are entered under **Occupational retraining**.
  UF In-service training
      Inservice training
      Training of employees
  SA types of employees or personnel
      with the subdivision *Training*,
      e.g. **Teachers—Training**; or
      with the subdivision *In-service
      training*, e.g. **Librarians—In-
      service training** [to be added
      as needed]
  BT **Occupational training**
      Personnel management
      Vocational education
  NT **Internship programs**
      Occupational retraining
  RT **Apprentices**
      Technical education
Employer-employee relations
  USE **Industrial relations**
Employers' liability
  USE **Workers' compensation**
Employment   331.1
    Use for materials on the economic theory of employment.
  SA racial and ethnic groups and
      classes of persons with the
      subdivision *Employment*, e.g.
      **African Americans—Employ-
      ment**; **Veterans—Employ-
      ment**; etc. [to be added as
      needed]
  BT **Economics**
      Labor
  NT **African Americans—Employ-
      ment**
      Age and employment
      Blacks—Employment
      Labor supply
      Men—Employment
      Part-time employment
      Summer employment
      Teenagers—Employment
      Temporary employment

Employment—*Continued*

> Unemployment
> Veterans—Employment
> Women—Employment
> Youth—Employment
RT   Occupations
> Vocational guidance

Employment agencies (May subdiv. geog.) **331.12**

BT   **Labor**
> **Labor turnover**
> **Personnel management**
> **Recruiting of employees**
> **Unemployment**
NT   **Job hunting**
RT   **Labor supply**

Employment and age
USE   **Age and employment**

Employment applications
USE   **Applications for positions**

Employment discrimination
USE   **Discrimination in employment**

Employment forecasting (May subdiv. geog.) **331.1**

UF   Occupational forecasting
BT   **Economic forecasting**
RT   **Labor supply**

Employment guidance
USE   **Vocational guidance**

Employment interviewing
USE   **Job interviews**

Employment management
USE   **Personnel management**

Employment of children
USE   **Child labor**

Employment references
USE   **Applications for positions**

Employment security
USE   **Job security**

Employment, Supplementary
USE   **Supplementary employment**

Employment, Temporary
USE   **Temporary employment**

Empresses (May subdiv. geog.) **920**

SA   names of empresses; and countries, cities, etc., with the subdivision *Kings and rulers* [to be added as needed]
BT   **Monarchy**
RT   **Queens**

EMTs (Medicine)
USE   **Emergency medical technicians**

Enamel and enameling   738.4

UF   Porcelain enamels
BT   **Decoration and ornament**
> **Decorative arts**

Encounter groups
USE   **Group relations training**

Encouragement   158

BT   **Courage**
> **Helping behavior**

Encyclicals, Papal
USE   **Papal encyclicals**

Encyclopedias
USE   **Encyclopedias and dictionaries** and subjects, groups or classes of persons, and names of places with the subdivision *Encyclopedias,* e.g. **Philosophy—Encyclopedias; Jews—Encyclopedias;** etc., for materials that provide topical information usually in alphabetical order [to be added as needed]

Encyclopedias and dictionaries   030; 403

Use for general materials about encyclopedias and dictionaries.

UF   Cyclopedias
> Dictionaries
> Encyclopedias
> Glossaries
> Subject dictionaries
SA   subjects and names of languages with the subdivision *Dictionaries,* for materials in alphabetical order that define terms or identify things, e.g. **Chemistry—Dictionaries; English language—Dictionaries;** etc.; subjects, groups or classes of persons, and names of places with the subdivision *Biography—Dictionaries,* for biographical dictionaries, e.g. **Women—Biography—Dictionaries; Ohio—Biography—Dictionaries;** etc.; and subjects, groups or classes of persons, and names of places with the subdivision *Encyclopedias,* e.g. **Philosophy—En-**

Encyclopedias and dictionaries—*Continued*

> cyclopedias; **Jews—Encyclopedias**; etc., for materials that provide topical information usually in alphabetical order [to be added as needed]

  BT   **Reference books**
  NT   **Bible—Dictionaries**
       Biography—Dictionaries
       Chemistry—Dictionaries
       Classical dictionaries
       Computer science—Dictionaries
       English language—Dictionaries
       English language—Dictionaries—French
       French language—Dictionaries—English
       Geography—Dictionaries
       History—Dictionaries
       Jews—Encyclopedias
       Literature—Dictionaries
       Machine readable dictionaries
       Philosophy—Encyclopedias
       Picture dictionaries
       Polyglot dictionaries
       Shakespeare, William, 1564-1616—Dictionaries
       Technology—Dictionaries

End of the earth
  USE **End of the world**

End of the world   001.9; 202; 236; 523.1

> Use for materials on the end of the world from an eschatological point of view (including Judgment Day, signs, fulfillments of prophecies, etc.) or from a scientific point of view.

  UF   End of the earth
       End of the world (Astronomy)
  BT   **Eschatology**
  NT   **Judgment Day**

End of the world (Astronomy)
  USE **End of the world**

End-of-the-world fiction
  USE **Apocalyptic fiction**

End-of-the-world films
  USE **Apocalyptic films**

Endangered species (May subdiv. geog.) 333.95; 578.68
  UF   Threatened species
       Vanishing species

  BT   **Environmental protection**
       Nature conservation
  NT   **Plant conservation**
       Wildlife conservation
  RT   **Rare animals**
       Rare plants

Endocrine glands   616.4
  UF   Ductless glands
       Glands, Ductless
  BT   **Endocrinology**
  RT   **Hormones**

Endocrinology   616.4
  BT   **Medicine**
  NT   **Endocrine glands**
       Hormones

Endorphins   612.8; 615

Endowed charities
  USE **Charities**
       Endowments

Endowments (May subdiv. geog.)   001.4; 361.6; 361.7
  UF   Endowed charities
       Foundations (Endowments)
  SA   disciplines, types of corporate bodies, and names of individual corporate bodies with the subdivision *Endowments*, e.g. **Colleges and universities—Endowments** [to be added as needed]
  BT   **Finance**
  NT   **Colleges and universities—Endowments**
       Scholarships
  RT   **Charities**
       Philanthropy

Endurance, Physical
  USE **Physical fitness**

Energy
  USE **Energy resources**
       Force and energy

Energy and state
  USE **Energy policy**

Energy, Biomass
  USE **Biomass energy**

Energy conservation (May subdiv. geog.) 333.791
  UF   Conservation of energy
       Conservation of power resources
       Power resources conservation

Energy conservation—*Continued*
- SA types of energy conservation, e.g. **Recycling** [to be added as needed]
- BT **Conservation of natural resources**
  Energy resources
- NT **Recycling**
- RT **Energy consumption**
  Energy policy

Energy consumption (May subdiv. geog.) **333.79**
- UF Consumption of energy
- SA subjects with the subdivision *Fuel consumption*, e.g. **Automobiles—Fuel consumption** [to be added as needed]
- BT **Energy resources**
- NT **Automobiles—Fuel consumption**
- RT **Energy conservation**

Energy consumption—Forecasting 333.79

Energy conversion from waste
- USE **Waste products as fuel**

Energy conversion, Microbial
- USE **Biomass energy**

Energy development (May subdiv. geog.) **333.79**
- UF Energy resources development
  Power resources development
- BT **Energy resources**
- NT **Water resources development**

Energy policy (May subdiv. geog.) **333.79; 354.3**
- UF Energy and state
  Energy resources—Government policy
  Government policy
- BT **Energy resources**
  Industrial policy
- RT **Energy conservation**

Energy resources (May subdiv. geog.) **333.79**

Use for materials on the available sources of mechanical power in general. Materials on the physics and engineering aspects of power are entered under **Power (Mechanics)**.
- UF Energy
  Power resources
  Power supply
- BT **Natural resources**
  Power (Mechanics)
- NT **Biomass energy**
  Electric power
  Energy conservation
  Energy consumption
  Energy development
  Energy policy
  Fuel
  Ocean energy resources
  Renewable energy resources
  Solar energy
  Water power
  Wind power

Energy resources development
- USE **Energy development**

Energy resources—Government policy
- USE **Energy policy**

Energy technology
- USE **Power (Mechanics)**

Engagement
- USE **Betrothal**

Engineering (May subdiv. geog.) **620**
- UF Construction
- SA types of engineering, e.g. **Chemical engineering** [to be added as needed]
- BT **Industrial arts**
  Technology
- NT **Aeronautics**
  Agricultural engineering
  Chemical engineering
  Civil engineering
  Electrical engineering
  Electronics
  Genetic engineering
  Highway engineering
  Human engineering
  Hydraulic engineering
  Marine engineering
  Mechanical drawing
  Military engineering
  Mining engineering
  Minorities in engineering
  Municipal engineering
  Nuclear engineering
  Ocean engineering
  Railroad engineering
  Reliability (Engineering)
  Sanitary engineering
  Steam engineering

Engineering—*Continued*
  Structural engineering
  Systems engineering
  Traffic engineering
  Water supply engineering
 RT **Engineers**
  Materials
Engineering and construction
 USE names of wars with the subdivision *Engineering and construction,* e.g. **World War, 1939-1945—Engineering and construction** [to be added as needed]
Engineering drawing
 USE **Mechanical drawing**
Engineering, Genetic
 USE **Genetic engineering**
Engineering instruments 620.0028
 UF Instruments, Engineering
 BT **Scientific apparatus and instruments**
Engineering materials
 USE **Materials**
Engineering—Periodicals 620.005
Engineering—Study and teaching 620.007
 BT **Technical education**
Engineers (May subdiv. geog.) **620.0092; 920**
 RT **Engineering**
  Inventors
Engines 621.4
 UF Motors
 SA types of engines and motors, e.g. **Steam engines**; **Electric motors**; etc., and types of vehicles and makes and models of vehicles with the subdivision *Motors,* e.g. **Automobiles—Motors** [to be added as needed]
 BT **Machinery**
 NT **Airplane engines**
  Automobiles—Motors
  Diesel engines
  Fire engines
  Fuel
  Heat engines
  Internal combustion engines
  Marine engines
  Pumping machinery

  Solar engines
  Steam engines
  Turbines
England 942
 May be subdivided like **United States** except for *History*, and *Politics and government*, or any subdivisions relating to history or politics and government. Such materials are entered instead under **Great Britain**.
 BT **Great Britain**
England, Church of
 USE **Church of England**
England—History
 USE **Great Britain—History**
English as a foreign language
 USE **English as a second language**
English as a second language 420.7; 428
 UF English as a foreign language
  English for foreigners
  English language as a second language
  English language—Study and teaching, Foreign
  English language—Texts for foreigners
 BT **English language—Study and teaching**
 NT **English language—Conversation and phrase books**
English authors 820.9; 920
 UF Authors, English
 BT **Authors**
English authors—First editions
 USE **English literature—First editions**
English authors—Homes (May subdiv. geog.) **820.9; 920**
 BT **Literary landmarks**
English Canadian literature
 USE **Canadian literature (English)**
English Canadian poetry
 USE **Canadian poetry (English)**
English composition
 USE **English language—Composition and exercises**
English drama 822
 Use for general materials about English drama, not for individual works.
 BT **Drama**
  English literature
 NT **Morality plays**
  Mysteries and miracle plays

English drama—Collections   822.008

English drama—History and criticism
822.009

BT   **Drama—History and criticism**

English essays   824; 824.008

Use for collections of literary essays by several authors.

BT   **English literature**
Essays

English fiction   823

Use for collections or materials about English fiction, not for individual works.

BT   **English literature**
Fiction

English fiction—History and criticism
823.009

English for foreigners

USE   **English as a second language**
English language—Conversation and phrase books

English grammar

USE   **English language—Grammar**

English history

USE   **Great Britain—History**

English language (May subdiv. geog.)
420

Subdivisions used under this heading may be used under other languages unless otherwise specified.

BT   **Language and languages**

English language—0-1100

USE   **English language—Old English period**

English language—Acronyms

USE   **Acronyms**

English language—Alphabet   421

English language—Americanisms

USE   **Americanisms**

English language—Antonyms

USE   **English language—Synonyms and antonyms**

English language as a second language

USE   **English as a second language**

English language—Basal readers

USE   **Basal readers**

English language—Business English
428

Business English is a unique subdivision for **English language**. Use same pattern with unique subdivisions for other languages, e.g. **Japanese language—Business Japanese**; etc.

UF   Business English

English language—Comparison   425

UF   Comparison (English grammar)

English language—Composition and exercises   428

UF   English composition

RT   **Rhetoric**

English language—Conversation and phrase books   428

UF   English for foreigners
English language—Conversations and phrases

BT   **English as a second language**

English language—Conversations and phrases

USE   **English language—Conversation and phrase books**

English language—Dialects   427

NT   **Americanisms**

English language—Dictionaries   423

Use for English language dictionaries. Dictionaries from English to another language are entered under this heading further subdivided by the other language, e.g. **English language—Dictionaries—French**. French-English dictionaries are entered under **French language—Dictionaries—English**. Combined English-French and French-English dictionaries are entered under both headings.

BT   **Encyclopedias and dictionaries**

RT   **English language—Terms and phrases**

English language—Dictionaries—French
443

Use for English-French dictionaries. French-English dictionaries are entered under **French language—Dictionaries—English**. Combined English-French and French-English dictionaries are entered under both headings.

UF   Foreign language dictionaries

BT   **Encyclopedias and dictionaries**

RT   **French language—Dictionaries—English**

English language—Errors

USE   **English language—Errors of usage**

English language—Errors of usage   428

UF   English language—Errors

English language—Etymology   422

BT   **English language—History**

English language—Examinations   420.76

BT   **Examinations**

English language—Examinations—Study guides   420.76

English language—Figures of speech

USE   **Figures of speech**

English language—Foreign words and phrases 422

Use for materials on foreign words and phrases incorporated into the English language.

UF   Foreign language phrases

English language—Grammar   425

UF   English grammar

SA   **English language** subdivided by topics in the study of grammar, e.g. **English language—Parts of speech**; **English language—Infinitive**; etc. [to be added as needed]

BT   **Grammar**

NT   **English language—Usage**

English language—History   420.9

NT   **English language—Etymology**

English language—Homonyms   423

English language—Idioms   428

RT   **English language—Provincialisms**

English language—Infinitive   425

English language—Jargon   427

English language—Middle English period 420

UF   Middle English language

English language—Old English period 429

UF   Anglo-Saxon language
English language—0-1100
Old English language

English language—Orthography

USE   **English language—Spelling**

English language—Parts of speech   425

English language—Phonetics

USE   **English language—Pronunciation**

English language—Phrases and terms

USE   **English language—Terms and phrases**

English language—Programmed instruction   420.7

BT   **Programmed instruction**

English language—Pronunciation   421

UF   English language—Phonetics

BT   **Phonetics**

NT   **Reading—Phonetic method**

English language—Provincialisms   427

RT   **English language—Idioms**

English language—Punctuation

USE   **Punctuation**

English language—Reading materials

USE   **Reading materials**

English language—Rhetoric

USE   **Rhetoric**

English language—Rhyme   428.1

BT   **Rhyme**

English language—Slang   427

English language—Social aspects   420

English language—Spelling   421

UF   English language—Orthography

BT   **Spelling**

NT   **Spellers**

RT   **Word skills**

English language—Spelling reform

USE   **Spelling reform**

English language—Study and teaching 420.7

NT   **English as a second language**

English language—Study and teaching, Foreign

USE   **English as a second language**

English language—Synonyms and antonyms   423

UF   English language—Antonyms

RT   **Opposites**

English language—Terms and phrases 420

Use for general lists of words and phrases and for lists that are applicable to certain situations (collective nouns, curious expressions, etc.) rather than to specific subjects. Lists of words and phrases limited to specific subjects are entered under the subject with the subdivision *Dictionaries*, e.g. **Chemistry—Dictionaries**.

UF   English language—Phrases and terms

RT   **English language—Dictionaries**

English language—Texts for foreigners

USE   **English as a second language**

English language—Usage   428

BT   **English language—Grammar**

English language—Versification

USE   **Versification**

English language—Vocabulary

USE   **Vocabulary**

English letters   826; 826.008

BT   **English literature**
Letters

English literature   820

Subdivisions used under this heading may be used under other literatures.

BT   **Literature**

English literature—*Continued*

NT   English drama

English essays

English fiction

English letters

English poetry

English prose literature

English satire

English sermons

English speeches

English wit and humor

English literature—0-1100

USE   English literature—Old English period

English literature—16th and 17th centuries   820

UF   English literature—Early modern, 1500-1700

Renaissance English literature

English literature—18th century   820

English literature—19th century   820

UF   Victorian literature

English literature—20th century   820

English literature—21st century   820

English literature—Bibliography   016.82

English literature—Bio-bibliography 820.9

English literature—Collections   820.8

Use for collections of English literature by several authors in more than one genre. Collections of prose are entered under **English prose literature**. Collections of poetry are entered under **English poetry—Collections**. Collections of drama are entered under **English drama—Collections**.

English literature—Criticism

USE   English literature—History and criticism

English literature—Dictionaries   820.3

BT   Literature—Dictionaries

English literature—Early modern, 1500-1700

USE   English literature—16th and 17th centuries

English literature—Examinations 820.76

BT   English literature—Study and teaching

English literature—First editions   820

UF   English authors—First editions

English literature—History and criticism 820.9

UF   English literature—Criticism

English literature—Indexes   016.82

English literature—Middle English period   820

UF   Middle English literature

English literature—Old English period 829

UF   Anglo-Saxon literature

English literature—0-1100

Old English literature

English literature—Outlines, syllabi, etc. 820.2

BT   Literature—Outlines, syllabi, etc.

RT   English literature—Study and teaching

English literature—Study and teaching 820.7

NT   English literature—Examinations

RT   English literature—Outlines, syllabi, etc.

English newspapers

USE   Newspapers—Great Britain

English orations

USE   English speeches

English periodicals   052

BT   Periodicals

English poetry   821

Use for general materials about English poetry, not for individual works.

BT   English literature

Poetry

English poetry—Collections   821.008

English poetry—History and criticism 821.009

English prose literature   828

Use for collections of prose writings that may include several literary forms, such as essays, fiction, orations, etc.

UF   Prose literature, English

BT   English literature

English public schools   373.2

Use for materials on British endowed secondary schools that are open to public admission but are not financed or administered by any government body.

UF   Public schools, Endowed (Great Britain)

Public schools, English

BT   Private schools

English satire   827; 827.008

UF   Satire, English

English satire—*Continued*
  BT **English literature**
      Satire
English sermons 252
  BT **English literature**
      Sermons
English speeches 825; 825.008
  UF English orations
      Speeches, addresses, etc., English
  BT **English literature**
      Speeches
English wit and humor 827; 827.008;
      827.009

  Use for collections by several authors or for materials about English wit and humor. Individual works by English humorists are entered under **Wit and humor**.

  BT **English literature**
      Wit and humor
Engravers (May subdiv. geog.) 760.92;
      920
  BT **Artists**
  NT **Etchers**
Engraving 760; 765
  UF Copper engraving
      Engravings
      Line engraving
      Steel engraving
  SA engraving of particular countries,
      e.g. **American engraving** [to
      be added as needed]
  BT **Art**
      Graphic arts
      Illustration of books
      Pictures
  NT **American engraving**
      Gems
      Mezzotint engraving
      Photoengraving
      Wood engraving
  RT **Etching**
Engraving, American
  USE **American engraving**
Engravings
  USE **Engraving**
Enhanced radiation weapons
  USE **Neutron weapons**
Enigmas
  USE **Curiosities and wonders**
       Riddles

Enlarged texts for shared reading
  USE **Big books**
Enlarging (Photography)
  USE **Photography—Enlarging**
Enlightenment (May subdiv. geog.) 190;
      909.7; 940.2

  Use for materials on the philosophic movement of the 18th century marked by the questioning of traditional doctrines and values, naturalistic and individualistic tendencies, and an emphasis on the empirical method in science and the free use of reason.

  BT **Modern civilization**
      Modern philosophy
      Rationalism
Enlistment
  USE **Recruiting and enlistment**
Enneagram 155.2
  BT **Typology (Psychology)**
Ensemble playing
  USE **Ensembles (Music)**
Ensembles (Mathematics)
  USE **Set theory**
Ensembles (Music) 782; 784

  Use for materials on small instrumental or vocal groups and for the music written for such groups.

  UF Ensemble playing
      Instrumental ensembles
      Musical ensembles
      Vocal ensembles
  SA types of vocal or instrumental
      ensembles, e.g. **Jazz ensembles** [to be added as needed]
  BT **Music**
      Musical form
      Musicians
  NT **Jazz ensembles**
  RT **Orchestra**
Ensigns
  USE **Flags**
Enteric fever
  USE **Typhoid fever**
Enterprises
  USE **Business enterprises**
Entertainers (May subdiv. geog.)
      791.092; 920
  SA types of entertainers and names
      of individual entertainers [to
      be added as needed]
  NT **Actors**
      Clowns
      Comedians
      Dancers

Entertainers—*Continued*
    Fools and jesters
    Geishas
Entertaining (May subdiv. geog.)   **395.3;
  642**
    Use for materials on hospitality and the art
of entertaining guests.
    UF   Guests
           Hospitality
    BT   **Etiquette**
           Home economics
    NT   **Business entertaining**
           Carving (Meat, etc.)
           Children's parties
           Games
           Parties
    RT   **Afternoon teas**
           Amusements
           Dining
           Luncheons
Entertainments
    USE **Amusements**
Entozoa
    USE **Parasites**
Entrance examinations
    USE types of educational institutions
          and names of individual insti-
          tutions with the subdivision
          Entrance examinations, e.g.
          **Colleges and universities—
          Entrance examinations** [to
          be added as needed]
Entrance examinations for colleges
    USE **Colleges and universities—En-
          trance examinations**
Entrance requirements
    USE types of educational institutions
          and names of individual insti-
          tutions with the subdivision
          Entrance requirements, e.g
          **Colleges and universities—
          Entrance requirements** [to
          be added as needed]
Entrance requirements for colleges and uni-
    versities
    USE **Colleges and universities—En-
          trance requirements**
Entrepreneurs (May subdiv. geog.)   **338;
  920**
    BT   **Businesspeople**
           Self-employed

Entrepreneurship (May subdiv. geog.)
  338; 658.4
    BT   **Business**
           Capitalism
           Small business
Entropy   **536**
    BT   **Thermodynamics**
Environment (May subdiv. geog.)   **304.2;
  333.7; 363.7**
    Use for materials on the habitat or sur-
roundings of a population or on all factors external to the individual.
    SA   subjects with the subdivision *En-
          vironmental aspects,* e.g. **Nu-
          clear power plants—Envi-
          ronmental aspects** [to be
          added as needed]
    NT   **Ecology**
           Environmental degradation
           Environmental movement
           Environmental policy
           Environmental protection
           **Nuclear power plants—Envi-
          ronmental aspects**
           **Pesticides—Environmental as-
          pects**
           Work environment
    RT   **Environmental sciences**
Environment and pesticides
    USE **Pesticides—Environmental as-
          pects**
Environment and state
    USE **Environmental policy**
Environment—Government policy
    USE **Environmental policy**
Environment, Space
    USE **Space environment**
Environmental aspects
    USE subjects with the subdivision *En-
          vironmental aspects,* e.g. **Nu-
          clear power plants—Envi-
          ronmental aspects; Economic
          development—Environmental
          aspects** [to be added as need-
          ed]
Environmental control
    USE **Environmental law**
Environmental damages, Liability for
    USE **Liability for environmental
          damages**
Environmental degradation (May subdiv.
  geog.)   **333.7; 363.7**

Environmental degradation—*Continued*
   UF   Environmental destruction
         Environmental deterioration
   BT   **Environment**
         Natural disasters
Environmental destruction
   USE   **Environmental degradation**
Environmental deterioration
   USE   **Environmental degradation**
Environmental ethics   179
   UF   Environmental quality—Ethical
         aspects
         Human ecology—Ethical aspects
   BT   **Ethics**
Environmental health (May subdiv. geog.)
         616.9
   UF   Health—Environmental aspects
   SA   subjects with the subdivision *En-*
         vironmental aspects, e.g. **Nu-**
         clear power plants—Envi-
         ronmental aspects [to be
         added as needed]
   BT   **Environmental influence on**
         humans
         Public health
   NT   **Air pollution**
         Environmentally induced dis-
         eases
         Nuclear power plants—Envi-
         ronmental aspects
         Occupational health and safety
         Pollution
         Water pollution
Environmental health engineering
   USE   **Sanitary engineering**
Environmental illness
   USE   **Environmentally induced dis-**
         eases
Environmental influence on humans
         (May subdiv. geog.)   **304.2; 599.9**
   UF   Acclimatization
         Altitude, Influence of
         Man—Influence of environment
   BT   **Adaptation (Biology)**
         Human ecology
         Human geography
   NT   **Environmental health**
         Survival skills
         Weightlessness
Environmental law (May subdiv. geog.)
         344

   UF   Environmental control
         Environmental protection—Law
         and legislation
   BT   **Environmental policy**
         Environmental protection
         Law
   NT   **Liability for environmental**
         damages
Environmental lobby
   USE   **Environmental movement**
Environmental movement (May subdiv.
         geog.)   **320.5; 322.4; 363.7**
   UF   Conservation movement
         Ecological movement
         Environmental lobby
         Environmentalism
         Green movement
   BT   **Environment**
         Social movements
   NT   **Ecoterrorism**
Environmental policy (May subdiv. geog.)
         344; 354.3; 363.7
   UF   Environment and state
         Environment—Government poli-
         cy
         Environmental quality—Govern-
         ment policy
         Government policy
         State and environment
   BT   **Environment**
   NT   **Environmental law**
   RT   **Conservation of natural re-**
         sources
Environmental policy—United States
         344; 354.30973; 363.7
   UF   United States—Environmental
         policy
Environmental pollution
   USE   **Pollution**
Environmental protection (May subdiv.
         geog.)   **344; 363.7**
   UF   Environmentalism
         Protection of environment
   BT   **Ecology**
         Environment
   NT   **Conservation of natural re-**
         sources
         Endangered species
         Environmental law
         Landscape protection
         Soil conservation

Environmental protection—*Continued*
> **Wildlife conservation**
> RT **Pollution**

Environmental protection—Law and legislation
> USE **Environmental law**

Environmental protection—Standards
> (May subdiv. geog.) **354.3**

Environmental quality—Ethical aspects
> USE **Environmental ethics**

Environmental quality—Government policy
> USE **Environmental policy**

Environmental radioactivity
> USE **Radioactive pollution**

Environmental sciences **304.2; 333.7; 363.7**
> BT **Science**
> RT **Ecology**
> **Environment**

Environmental technology
> USE **Green technology**

Environmental tourism
> USE **Ecotourism**

Environmentalism
> USE **Environmental movement**
> **Environmental protection**

Environmentally friendly architecture
> USE **Sustainable architecture**

Environmentally induced diseases **616.07**
> UF Diseases—Environmental aspects
> Environmental illness
> SA names of individual diseases
> with the subdivision *Environmental aspects*, e.g. **Cancer—Environmental aspects** [to be added as needed]
> BT **Diseases—Causes**
> **Environmental health**
> NT **Cancer—Environmental aspects**

Enzymes **547; 572**
> BT **Proteins**
> NT **Catalytic RNA**

Eolithic period
> USE **Stone Age**

Epic films **791.43**
> Use for individual works, collections, or materials about epic films.
> UF Film epics
> BT **Motion pictures**

Epic literature **800**
> Use for individual works, collections, or materials about epic literature.
> BT **Literature**
> NT **Epic poetry**
> RT **Mock-heroic literature**

Epic poetry **808.81; 808.1**
> Use for individual works, collections, or materials about epic poetry.
> BT **Epic literature**
> **Narrative poetry**
> RT **Romances**

Epidemics (May subdiv. geog.) **614.4**
> UF Pestilences
> SA names of contagious diseases, e.g. **AIDS (Disease)** [to be added as needed]
> BT **Diseases**
> **Public health**
> NT **Plague**
> RT **Communicable diseases**

Epigrams **808.88**
> Use for collections of epigrams and for materials about epigrams.
> UF Sayings
> BT **Wit and humor**
> NT **Quotations**
> **Toasts**
> RT **Proverbs**

Epigraphy
> USE **Inscriptions**

Epilepsy **616.8**
> BT **Nervous system—Diseases**

Episcopal Church (May subdiv. geog.) **283**
> Use for materials on the Episcopal Church in the United States after 1789. Materials on the Episcopal Church in the United States prior to 1789 are entered under **Church of England—United States**.
> UF Protestant Episcopal Church in the U.S.A.
> BT **Christian sects**
> NT **Catholic charismatic movement**
> RT **Church of England—United States**

Epistemology
> USE **Theory of knowledge**

Epistolary fiction **808.3**
> Use for individual works, collections, or materials about novels written in the form of a series of letters.
> UF Epistolary novels
> Novels in letters

Epistolary fiction—*Continued*

  BT   **Fiction**

Epistolary novels

  USE **Epistolary fiction**

Epistolary poetry   **808.1; 808.81**

    Use for individual works, collections, or materials about epistolary verse.

  UF   Verse epistles

  BT   **Poetry**

Epitaphs   **929**

  UF   Graves

  BT   **Biography**

        Cemeteries

        Inscriptions

        Tombs

Epithets

  USE **Names**

        Nicknames

Epizoa

  USE **Parasites**

Equal employment opportunity

  USE **Affirmative action programs**

        Discrimination in employment

Equal opportunity in employment

  USE **Affirmative action programs**

        Discrimination in employment

Equal pay for equal work   **331.2; 658.3**

  UF   Pay equity

  BT   **Discrimination in employment**

        Salaries, wages, etc.

        Women—Employment

Equal rights amendments (May subdiv. geog.)   **305.42; 323.4; 342**

  UF   Amendments, Equal rights

        ERAs

  BT   **Constitutions**

        Sex discrimination

Equal time rule (Broadcasting)   **324**

    Use for materials on the requirement that all qualified candidates for public office be granted equal broadcast time if one of one such candidates is permitted to broadcast. Materials on the requirement that, if one side of a controversial issue of public importance is aired, the same opportunity must be given for the presentation of contrasting views are entered under **Fairness doctrine (Broadcasting)**.

  UF   Rule of equal time (Broadcasting)

  BT   **Broadcasting**

        Television and politics

  RT   **Fairness doctrine (Broadcasting)**

Equality (May subdiv. geog.)   **323.42**

  UF   Inequality

        Social equality

  BT   **Political science**

        Sociology

  NT   **Individualism**

        Social justice

  RT   **Democracy**

        Freedom

Equations, Chemical

  USE **Chemical equations**

Equestrianism

  USE **Horsemanship**

Equilibrium (Economics)   **339.5**

  UF   Economic equilibrium

  BT   **Economics**

Equipment and supplies

  USE subjects and names of wars with the subdivision *Equipment and supplies,* e.g. **Television—Equipment and supplies; World War, 1939-1945—Equipment and supplies** [to be added as needed]

ERAs

  USE **Equal rights amendments**

Ergonomics

  USE **Human engineering**

Eritrea   **963.5**

    May be subdivided like **United States** except for *History.*

Erosion   **551.3**

  SA   types of erosion, e.g. **Soil erosion** [to be added as needed]

  BT   **Geology**

  NT   **Dust storms**

        Soil erosion

  RT   **Soil conservation**

Erotic art (May subdiv. geog.)   **704.9**

  UF   Sex in art

  BT   **Art**

        Erotica

Erotic fiction   **808.3; 808.83**

    Use for individual works, collections, or materials about erotic fiction.

  UF   Adult fiction

        Erotic novels

        Erotic stories

  BT   **Erotic literature**

        Fiction

Erotic films   791.43

Use for individual works, collections, or materials about erotic films.

UF   Adult films

BT   **Motion pictures**

Erotic literature   808.8; 809

UF   Literature, Erotic

BT   **Erotica**

Literature

NT   **Erotic fiction**

Erotic poetry

Erotic novels

USE   **Erotic fiction**

Erotic poetry   808.1; 808.81

Use for individual works, collections, or materials about erotic poetry.

BT   **Erotic literature**

Poetry

RT   **Love poetry**

Erotic stories

USE   **Erotic fiction**

Erotica   704.9; 809

SA   types of erotica, e.g. **Erotic art**; **Erotic literature**; etc. [to be added as needed]

NT   **Erotic art**

Erotic literature

RT   **Obscenity (Law)**

Pornography

Errors   001.9; 153.7; 165

Use for materials on errors of judgment, errors of observation, scientific errors, popular misconceptions, etc. Errors in language are entered under names of languages with the subdivision *Errors of usage*, e.g. **English language—Errors of usage**.

UF   Fallacies

Medical errors

Mistakes

Scientific errors

RT   **Superstition**

Errors of usage

USE   names of languages with the subdivision *Errors of usage,* e.g. **English language—Errors of usage** [to be added as needed]

Erudition

USE   **Learning and scholarship**

Eruptions

USE   **Geysers**

Escapes (May subdiv. geog.)   365; 904

UF   Hostage escapes

Prison escapes

BT   **Adventure and adventurers**

Prisons

Eschatology   202; 236

UF   Intermediate state

Last things (Theology)

BT   **Theology**

NT   **Death**

End of the world

Future life

Heaven

Hell

Immortality

Millennium

Purgatory

Second Advent

Eskimos

USE   **Inuit**

ESP

USE   **Extrasensory perception**

Esperanto   499

BT   **Universal language**

Espionage (May subdiv. geog.)   327.12

UF   Spying

SA   espionage practiced by particular countries, e.g. **American espionage** [to be added as needed]

BT   **Intelligence service**

Secret service

Subversive activities

NT   **American espionage**

Spies

Espionage, American

USE   **American espionage**

Espionage films

USE   **Spy films**

Espionage stories

USE   **Spy stories**

Espionage television programs

USE   **Spy television programs**

Esquimaux

USE   **Inuit**

Essay   808.4

Use for materials on the appreciation of the essay and on the technique of writing essays. Collections of essays are entered under **Essays**; **American essays**; etc.

BT   **Literature**

Essays   808.4; 808.84

Use for collections of literary essays by authors of several nationalities. Collections of literary essays by American authors are en-

Essays—*Continued*

tered under **American essays**; by English authors, under **English essays**; etc. Essays limited to a particular subject, by one or more authors, are entered under that subject. Materials on the appreciation of the essay and on the technique of writing essays are entered under **Essay**.

    NT   **American essays**

            English essays

Essences and essential oils   **664; 668**

    UF   Aromatic plant products

            Essential oils

            Vegetable oils

            Volatile oils

    BT   **Distillation**

            Oils and fats

    NT   **Flavoring essences**

            Perfumes

    RT   **Aromatic plants**

Essenes   **296.8**

    BT   **Jews**

    RT   **Dead Sea scrolls**

Essential oils

    USE   **Essences and essential oils**

Estate planning (May subdiv. geog.)

        332.024; 343.05; 346.05

    BT   **Personal finance**

            Planning

    NT   **Inheritance and transfer tax**

            Insurance

    RT   **Investments**

            Tax planning

            Trusts and trustees

Estate tax

    USE   **Inheritance and transfer tax**

Esthetics

    USE   **Aesthetics**

Estimates

    USE   types of engineering, technical processes, industries, etc., with the subdivision *Estimates,* e.g. **Building—Estimates** [to be added as needed]

Estimation (Mathematics)

    USE   **Approximate computation**

Estrangement (Social psychology)

    USE   **Alienation (Social psychology)**

Etchers (May subdiv. geog.)   **769.92; 920**

    BT   **Artists**

            Engravers

Etching   **767**

    UF   Etchings

    BT   **Art**

            Pictures

    NT   **Pyrography**

    RT   **Engraving**

Etchings

    USE   **Etching**

Eternal life

    USE   **Eternity**

            Future life

            Immortality

Eternal punishment

    USE   **Hell**

Eternity   **115**

Use for materials on the philosophical concept of eternity. Materials on the character and form of a future life are entered under **Future life**. Materials on the question of the endless existence of the soul are entered under **Immortality**.

    UF   Eternal life

    RT   **Future life**

Ethanol as fuel

    USE   **Alcohol fuels**

Ethical aspects

    USE   subjects with the subdivision *Ethical aspects,* e.g. **Birth control—Ethical aspects** [to be added as needed]

Ethical development

    USE   **Moral development**

Ethical education

    USE   **Moral education**

Ethics (May subdiv. geog.)   **170**

    UF   Moral philosophy

            Morality

            Morals

    SA   types of ethics, e.g. **Business ethics**; ethics of particular religions, e.g. **Christian ethics**; names of individual persons, classes of persons, types of professions, and types of professional personnel with the subdivision *Ethics,* e.g. **Librarians—Ethics**; **Shakespeare, William, 1564-1616—Ethics**; etc., and subjects with the subdivision *Ethical aspects,* e.g. **Birth control—Ethical aspects** [to be added as needed]

    BT   **Philosophy**

Ethics—*Continued*

NT   **Abortion—Ethical aspects**
      Asceticism
      Bioethics
      Birth control—Ethical aspects
      Business ethics
      Character
      Charity
      Christian ethics
      Cloning—Ethical aspects
      Conduct of life
      Conscience
      Cruelty
      Duty
      Environmental ethics
      Feminist ethics
      Golden rule
      Good and evil
      Guilt
      Honesty
      Human cloning—Ethical aspects
      Jewish ethics
      Justice
      Legal ethics
      Loyalty
      Medical ethics
      Moral education
      Motion pictures—Ethical aspects
      Natural law
      Perseverance
      Political ethics
      Professional ethics
      Promises
      Responsibility
      Secularism
      Sexual ethics
      Sin
      Social ethics
      Stoics
      Utilitarianism
      Values
      Vice
      Virtue
      Vocation
      Work ethic
      World War, 1939-1945—Ethical aspects

RT   **Human behavior**

Ethics—United States 170.973

UF   American ethics

Ethiopia 963

May be subdivided like **United States** except for *History*.

Ethiopian-Italian War, 1935-1936

USE   **Italo-Ethiopian War, 1935-1936**

Ethnic art (May subdiv. geog.) 709

BT   **Art**
      Ethnic groups

Ethnic cleansing

USE   **Genocide**

Ethnic conflict

USE   **Ethnic relations**

Ethnic diversity

USE   **Pluralism (Social sciences)**

Ethnic groups (May subdiv. geog.) 305.8

Use for materials on groups of people bound together by common ancestry and culture. Materials on indigenous minorities are entered under **Indigenous peoples**. Materials on the subjective sense of belonging to a particular ethnic group are entered under **Ethnicity**. Materials on several ethnic groups in a particular region or country are entered under **Ethnology** subdivided geographically. Materials on individual ethnic groups are entered under the name of the group, e.g. **Mexican Americans**.

UF   People

SA   names of individual ethnic groups [to be added as needed]

BT   **Ethnology**

NT   **Asian Americans**
      Cajuns
      Chinese Americans
      Creoles
      Ethnic art
      Hispanic Americans
      Mexican Americans
      Racially mixed people

RT   **Ethnic relations**
      Ethnicity

Ethnic identity

USE   **Ethnicity**
      and ethnic groups with the subdivision *Ethnic identity,* e.g. **Mexican Americans—Ethnic identity** [to be added as needed]

Ethnic psychology

USE   **Ethnopsychology**

Ethnic relations 305.8

UF   Ethnic conflict
      Relations among ethnic groups

Ethnic relations—*Continued*

SA   names of regions, countries, cities, etc., with the subdivision *Ethnic relations*; e.g. **United States—Ethnic relations** [to be added as needed]

BT   **Acculturation**
        Ethnology
        Sociology

NT   **Culture conflict**
        Discrimination

RT   **Ethnic groups**
        Minorities
        Multiculturalism
        Pluralism (Social sciences)
        Race relations

Ethnic relations—Political aspects
    305.8

Ethnic relations—Religious aspects
    305.8

Ethnicity (May subdiv. geog.)   **305.8**

Use for materials on the subjective sense of belonging to a particular ethnic group. Materials on groups of people bound together by a common ancestry or culture are entered under **Ethnic groups**. Materials on several ethnic groups in a particular region or country are entered under **Ethnology**.

UF   Ethnic identity

SA   ethnic groups with the subdivision *Ethnic identity*, e.g. **Mexican Americans—Ethnic identity**; and racial groups with the subdivision *Race identity*, e.g. **African Americans—Race identity** [to be added as needed]

BT   **Identity (Psychology)**

RT   **Ethnic groups**
        Multiculturalism
        Pluralism (Social sciences)

Ethnobiology (May subdiv. geog.)
    306.4; 578.6

UF   Folk biology

SA   names of ethnic groups with the subdivision *Ethnobiology*, e.g. **Native Americans—Ethnobiology** [to be added as needed]

BT   **Biology**
        Ethnology

NT   **Ethnobotany**
        Ethnozoology

Native Americans—Ethnobiology

Ethnobotany (May subdiv. geog.)   **581.6**

SA   names of ethnic groups with the subdivision *Ethnobotany*, e.g. **Native Americans—Ethnobotany** [to be added as needed]

BT   **Ethnobiology**
        Ethnology
        Plants—Folklore

NT   **Native Americans—Ethnobotany**

Ethnocentrism (May subdiv. geog.)
    305.8

BT   **Ethnopsychology**
        Nationalism
        Prejudices
        Race

Ethnocide

USE   **Genocide**

Ethnography

USE   **Ethnology**

Ethnology (May subdiv. geog.)   **305.8; 306; 599.97**

Use for materials on the disciplines of ethnology and cultural anthropology, and, with appropriate geographic subdivisions, for materials on the origin, distribution, and characteristics of the elements of the population of a particular region or country. General materials on groups of people who are bound together by common ties of ancestry and culture are entered under **Ethnic groups**. Materials on individual racial or ethnic groups are entered under the name of the group, e.g. **Aboriginal Australians**.

UF   Cultural anthropology
        Ethnography
        Races of people
        Social anthropology

SA   names of countries with the subdivision *Social life and customs*, e.g. **United States—Social life and customs**; and names of individual ethnic groups [to be added as needed]

BT   **Human beings**

NT   **Acculturation**
        Anthropometry
        Cannibalism
        Costume
        Ethnic groups
        Ethnic relations

Ethnology—*Continued*
    Ethnobiology
    Ethnobotany
    Ethnopsychology
    Ethnozoology
    Folklore
    Human geography
    Indigenous peoples
    Kinship
    Language and languages
    Manners and customs
    Mountain people
    Physical anthropology
    Primitive societies
    Race
    Race relations
    Semitic peoples
    Totems and totemism
RT   Anthropology
    Archeology
    Civilization

Ethnology—United States   **305.813**
UF United States—Ethnology
    United States—Peoples
SA names of individual ethnic
    groups [to be added as need-
    ed]

Ethnopsychology (May subdiv. geog.)
  155.8
UF Cross-cultural psychology
    Ethnic psychology
    Folk psychology
    National psychology
    Race psychology
SA names of racial or ethnic groups
    with the subdivision *Psycholo-*
    gy [to be added as needed]
BT **Anthropology**
    Ethnology
    Psychology
    Sociology
NT **Culture conflict**
    Ethnocentrism
    Native Americans—Psychology
RT **National characteristics**
    Social psychology

Ethnozoology (May subdiv. geog.)   **591.6**
UF Folk zoology
SA names of ethnic groups with the
    subdivision *Ethnozoology,* e.g.
    Native Americans—

Ethnozoology [to be added as
    needed]
BT **Animals—Folklore**
    Ethnobiology
    Ethnology
NT **Native Americans—**
    Ethnozoology

Ethyl alcohol fuel
USE **Alcohol fuels**

Etiquette (May subdiv. geog.)   **395**
UF Ceremonies
    Manners
    Politeness
    Salutations
SA types of etiquette, e.g. **Table et-**
    iquette; and names of coun-
    tries with the subdivision *So-*
    cial life and customs, e.g.
    United States—Social life
    and customs [to be added as
    needed]
BT **Human behavior**
NT **Business etiquette**
    Courtesy
    Dating (Social customs)
    Entertaining
    Excuses
    Letter writing
    Table etiquette
RT **Manners and customs**

Etiquette for children and teenagers
  177.1; 395.1
UF Behavior of children
    Behavior of teenagers
    Child behavior
    Children—Etiquette
    Etiquette for teenagers
    Teenage behavior
    Teenagers—Etiquette
BT **Children—Conduct of life**
    Teenagers—Conduct of life

Etiquette for teenagers
USE **Etiquette for children and**
    teenagers

Etymology
USE **Language and languages—Ety-**
    mology
    and names of languages with
    the subdivision *Etymology,*
    e.g. **English language—Ety-**

Etymology—*Continued*

    mology [to be added as needed]

Eucharist   234; 264

    May be subdivided by Christian sect or denomination.

    UF   Communion

            Holy communion

            Lord's Supper

    BT   **Liturgies**

            Sacraments

    RT   **Mass (Liturgy)**

Eugenics (May subdiv. geog.)   **363.9**

    BT   **Genetics**

            Population

    RT   **Heredity**

Euro   332.4

    BT   **Capital market**

            Money

Europe   940

    UF   Europe, Western

            Western Europe

Europe, Central

    USE   **Central Europe**

Europe, Eastern

    USE   **Eastern Europe**

Europe—History   940

    NT   **Holy Roman Empire**

Europe—History—0-476   936; 937

Europe—History—476-1492   940.1; 940.2

    NT   **Hundred Years' War, 1339-1453**

    RT   **Middle Ages**

Europe—History—1492-1789   940.2

    NT   **Seven Years' War, 1756-1763**

            Thirty Years' War, 1618-1648

Europe—History—18th century   940.2

Europe—History—1789-1815   940.2

    NT   **Napoleonic Wars, 1800-1815**

Europe—History—1789-1900   940.2

    UF   Europe—History—19th century

Europe—History—19th century

    USE   **Europe—History—1789-1900**

Europe—History—1815-1848   940.2

Europe—History—1848-1871   940.2

Europe—History—1871-1918   940.2

    NT   **World War, 1914-1918**

Europe—History—20th century   940.5

Europe—History—1918-1945   940.5

    NT   **Russo-Finnish War, 1939-1940**

            World War, 1939-1945

Europe—History—1945-   940.55

Europe—History—21st century   940.56

Europe—Politics and government   940

    May be subdivided by period using the same subdivisions as are listed under **Europe—History**.

    NT   **European federation**

Europe, Western

    USE   **Europe**

European Common Market

    USE   **European Union**

European Community

    USE   **European Union**

European Economic Community

    USE   **European Union**

European federation   321; 940

    Use for general materials on the political or economic union of European countries. Materials on the corporate body formerly known as the European Economic Community and the European Community, which became known as the European Union upon ratification of the Treaty of European Union on October 29, 1993, are entered under **European Union**.

    UF   Federation of Europe

    BT   **Europe—Politics and government**

            Federal government

            International organization

    NT   **European Union**

European Union   341.242; 382

    Use for materials on the corporate body formerly known as the European Economic Community and the European Community, which became known as the European Union upon ratification of the Treaty on European Union on October 29, 1993. General materials on the political or economic union of European countries are entered under **European federation**.

    UF   Common market

            EEC

            European Common Market

            European Community

            European Economic Community

    BT   **European federation**

Euthanasia (May subdiv. geog.)   **179.7**

    UF   Mercy killing

    BT   **Homicide**

            Medical ethics

    RT   **Right to die**

Evacuation and relocation of Japanese Americans, 1942-1945

    USE   **Japanese Americans—Evacuation and relocation, 1942-1945**

Evacuation of civilians (May subdiv.
  geog.) **363.3**
  UF Civilian evacuation
  SA names of wars with the subdivi-
      sion *Evacuation of civilians*,
      e.g. **World War, 19391945—
      Evacuation of civilians** [to
      be added as needed]
  BT **Civil defense
      Disaster relief**
Evaluation
  USE types of evaluation, e.g. **Educa-
      tional evaluation;** and names
      of corporate bodies and types
      of institutions, products, ser-
      vices, equipment, activities,
      projects, and programs with
      the subdivision *Evaluation,*
      e.g. **Public health—Evalua-
      tion; Science—Study and
      teaching—Evaluation;** etc.
      [to be added as needed]
Evaluation of books
  USE **Book reviewing**
Evaluation of literature
  USE **Best books
      Books and reading
      Criticism
      Literature—History and criti-
      cism**
Evaluation research in education
  USE **Educational evaluation**
Evangelical Protestantism
  USE **Evangelicalism**
Evangelicalism (May subdiv. geog.) **280**
  UF Evangelical Protestantism
  BT **Protestantism**
Evangelism
  USE **Evangelistic work**
Evangelistic healing
  USE **Spiritual healing**
Evangelistic work (May subdiv. geog.)
  253; 269
  UF Evangelism
      Revival (Religion)
  BT **Church work**
  NT **Conversion
      Revivals**
  RT **Christian missions**
Evening and continuation schools 374

  UF Continuation schools
      Evening schools
      Night schools
  BT **Compulsory education
      Continuing education
      Education
      Public schools
      Schools
      Secondary education
      Technical education**
  RT **Adult education**
Evening schools
  USE **Evening and continuation
      schools**
Evergreens 582.1; 635.9
  BT **Landscape gardening
      Shrubs
      Trees**
Evidences of the Bible
  USE **Bible—Evidences, authority,
      etc.**
Evil
  USE **Good and evil**
Evil spirits
  USE **Demonology**
Evolution 576.8
  UF Darwinism
      Development
      Mutation (Biology)
      Origin of species
  SA types of animals, plants, crops,
      chemicals, and organs of the
      body with the subdivision
      Evolution [to be added as
      needed]
  BT **Philosophy**
  NT **Life—Origin**
  RT **Biology
      Creation
      Creationism
      Human origins
      Natural selection
      Religion and science
      Variation (Biology)**
Evolution and Christianity
  USE **Creationism**
Evolution—Study and teaching 576.807
  UF Creation—Study and teaching
  RT **Creationism**
Ex libris
  USE **Bookplates**

Ex-nuns 305.48
   UF   Catholic ex-nuns
         Former nuns
   BT   **Nuns**
Ex-priests 305.33; 920
   UF   Catholic ex-priests
         Former priests
   BT   **Catholic Church—Clergy**
         Priests
Ex-Soviet republics
   USE **Former Soviet republics**
Ex-Soviet states
   USE **Former Soviet republics**
Examinations (May subdiv. geog.)
      371.26

Use for general materials on examinations. Materials discussing the requirements for examinations in particular branches of study, or compilations of questions and answers for such examinations, are entered under the subject with the subdivision *Examinations*.

   UF   Tests
   SA   branches of study with the subdivision *Examinations*, e.g. **English language—Examinations**; and names of individual examinations [to be added as needed]
   BT   **Questions and answers**
         Teaching
   NT   **Civil service—Examinations**
         Colleges and universities—Entrance examinations
         Colleges and universities—Entrance requirements
         English language—Examinations
         Graduate Record Examination
         Music—Examinations
         Scholastic Assessment Test
         United States. Army—Examinations
   RT   **Educational tests and measurements**
Examinations—Design and construction
   371.26
Examinations—Study guides 371.26

Use for materials that provide directions on how to prepare for and pass examinations, usually with practice questions and answers included.

   UF   Preparation guides for examinations
         Study guides for examinations

         Test preparation guides
   SA   subjects, educational levels, and names of educational institutions with the subdivisions *Examinations—Study guides*, e.g. **English language—Examinations—Study guides**; and named examinations with the subdivision *Study guides*, e.g. **Graduate Record Examination—Study guides** [to be added as needed]
   BT   **Study skills**
Excavation 624.1
   BT   **Civil engineering**
         Tunnels
Excavations (Archeology) (May subdiv. geog.) **930.1**
   UF   Earthworks (Archeology)
         Ruins
   BT   **Archeology**
   RT   **Extinct cities**
         Mounds and mound builders
Excavations (Archeology)—United States 973
Exceptional children 155.45
   UF   Abnormal children
   BT   **Children**
         Elementary education
   NT   **Brain damaged children**
         Emotionally disturbed children
         Gifted children
         Handicapped children
         Mainstreaming in education
         Slow learning children
         Wild children
Excess government property
   USE **Surplus government property**
Exchange 332.4; 332.64
   BT   **Commerce**
   NT   **Foreign exchange**
         Money
   RT   **Supply and demand**
Exchange, Barter
   USE **Barter**
Exchange of persons programs 327.1; 370.116
   UF   Cultural exchange programs
         Interchange of visitors
         Specialists exchange programs
         Visitors' exchange programs

Exchange of persons programs—*Continued*

SA   types of exchange programs for particular classes of persons, e.g. **Teacher exchange** [to be added as needed]

BT   **Cultural relations**

       International cooperation

NT   **Student exchange programs**

       Teacher exchange programs

Exchange of prisoners of war

USE   **Prisoners of war**

Exchange of students

USE   **Student exchange programs**

Exchange of teachers

USE   **Teacher exchange programs**

Exchange programs, Student

USE   **Student exchange programs**

Exchange rates

USE   **Foreign exchange**

Excuses   **395**

BT   **Etiquette**

       Manners and customs

Executions and executioners (May subdiv. geog.)   **364.66**

BT   **Criminal law**

       Criminal procedure

RT   **Capital punishment**

Executive ability   **658.4**

UF   Administrative ability

BT   **Ability**

NT   **Leadership**

       Planning

Executive agencies

USE   **Administrative agencies**

Executive departments (May subdiv. geog.)   **351**

Use for materials on major administrative divisions of the executive branch of government, usually headed by an officer of cabinet rank.

UF   Government departments

       Government ministries

       State ministries

SA   names of executive departments [to be added as needed]

BT   **Administrative agencies**

Executive departments—Ohio   **352.2**

UF   Ohio—Executive departments

SA   names of executive departments [to be added as needed]

Executive departments—Reorganization

USE   **Administrative agencies—Reorganization**

Executive departments—United States   **352.2**

UF   United States—Executive departments

SA   names of executive departments [to be added as needed]

NT   **Presidents—United States—Staff**

Executive investigations

USE   **Governmental investigations**

Executive power (May subdiv. geog.)   **351**

Use for materials on the powers of the executive or administrative branch of government.

UF   Presidents—Powers

BT   **Constitutional law**

       Political science

NT   **Amnesty**

       Clemency

       Heads of state

       Monarchy

       Pardon

       Prime ministers

       Separation of powers

       War and emergency powers

RT   **Presidents**

Executive power—United States   **352.230973**

UF   Presidents—United States—Power

       United States—Executive power

Executive reorganization

USE   **Administrative agencies—Reorganization**

Executors and administrators (May subdiv. geog.)   **346.05**

UF   Administrators and executors

BT   **Inheritance and succession**

RT   **Trusts and trustees**

       Wills

Exegesis, Biblical

USE   **Bible—Criticism**

Exemption from taxation

USE   **Tax exemption**

Exercise (May subdiv. geog.)   **613.7**

SA   types of exercises and physical activities [to be added as needed]

Exercise—*Continued*
BT   **Health**
      Hygiene
NT   **Aerobics**
      Bodybuilding
      Cycling
      Gymnastics
      Hatha yoga
      Physical fitness
      Pilates method
      Rowing
      Tai chi
      Weight lifting
RT   **Physical education**
      Weight loss
Exercise addiction   616.85
UF   Addiction to exercise
      Compulsive exercising
BT   **Compulsive behavior**
Exercises, problems, etc.
USE   subjects with the subdivision
      Problems, exercises, etc., for
      compilations of practice prob-
      lems or exercises for use in
      the study of a topic, e.g.
      Chemistry—Problems, exer-
      cises, etc. [to be added as
      needed]
Exhaustion
USE   **Fatigue**
Exhibitions
UF   Exhibits
      Expositions
      International exhibitions
      World's fairs
SA   types of exhibitions, e.g. **Flower**
      shows; subjects and names of
      individual persons with the
      subdivision *Exhibitions,* e.g.
      Printing—Exhibitions; and
      names of particular exhibi-
      tions, e.g. **Expo 92 (Seville,**
      Spain) [to be added as need-
      ed]
NT   **Art—Exhibitions**
      Books—Exhibitions
      Craft shows
      Expo 92 (Seville, Spain)
      Fashion shows
      Flower shows
      Printing—Exhibitions
      Science—Exhibitions

      Trade shows
RT   **Fairs**
Exhibits
USE   **Exhibitions**
Exiles (May subdiv. geog.)   **305.9**
      Use for materials on persons banished from
      their native countries or homes as a punitive
      measure. This heading may be subdivided
      geographically to indicate the country of ori-
      gin or the destination of the exiles.
BT   **Persons**
      Political refugees
Existentialism   142
BT   **Metaphysics**
      Modern philosophy
      Phenomenology
Exorcism   133.4; 203
BT   **Supernatural**
RT   **Demoniac possession**
      Demonology
Expansion (United States politics)
USE   **United States—Territorial ex-**
      pansion
Expectancy of life
USE   **Life expectancy**
Expectation of life
USE   **Life expectancy**
Expeditions, Scientific
USE   **Scientific expeditions**
Experience
USE   **Empiricism**
Experimental farms
USE   **Agricultural experiment sta-**
      tions
Experimental films (May subdiv. geog.)
      791.43
      Use for individual works, collections, or
      materials about experimental films.
UF   Avant-garde films
      Personal films
      Underground films
BT   **Motion pictures**
Experimental medicine (May subdiv.
      geog.)   **619**
BT   **Medicine—Research**
Experimental methods in education
USE   **Education—Experimental**
      methods
Experimental schools (May subdiv. geog.)
      371.04
      Use for materials on schools in which new
      teaching methods, organizations of subject
      matter, educational theories, personnel prac-
      tices, etc., are tested.

Experimental schools—*Continued*
- UF Alternative schools
  Free schools
  Nonformal schools
  Project schools
  Schools, Nonformal
- BT **Education—Experimental methods**
  Schools
- RT **Open plan schools**

Experimental theater (May subdiv. geog.) **792**
- UF Avant-garde theater
- BT **Theater**

Experimental universities
- USE **Free universities**

Experimentation on animals
- USE **Animal experimentation**

Experimentation on humans, Medical
- USE **Human experimentation in medicine**

Experiments
- USE scientific subjects with the subdivision *Experiments,* e.g. **Chemistry—Experiments** [to be added as needed]

Experiments, Scientific
- USE **Science—Experiments**

Expert systems (Computer science) 006.3
- UF Knowledge-based systems (Computer science)
- BT **Artificial intelligence**
  Data processing
  Information systems

Exploration 910.9
Use for materials on voyages and explorations that have advanced geographic knowledge.
- UF Discoveries and exploration
  Discoveries in geography
  Explorations
  Maritime discoveries
- SA names of celestial bodies, continents, regions, countries, states, etc., with the subdivision *Exploration* for materials on the exploration of those areas when they were unsettled or sparsely settled and largely unknown to the world at large, e.g. **America—Exploration**; or with the subdivision *Description and travel* for materials on later and recent travels in those areas, e.g. **United States—Description and travel**; and names of countries, states, etc., with the subdivision *Exploring expeditions* for materials on explorations sponsored by those governments, e.g. **United States—Exploring expeditions** [to be added as needed]
- BT **Adventure and adventurers**
  Geography
  History
- NT **America—Exploration**
  Antarctica—Exploration
  Arctic regions—Exploration
  Northeast Passage
  Outer space—Exploration
  Underwater exploration
  United States—Exploration
- RT **Explorers**
  Scientific expeditions
  Voyages and travels

Exploration of space
- USE **Outer space—Exploration**

Exploration—United States
- USE **United States—Exploration**

Explorations
- USE **Exploration**

Exploratory behavior
- USE **Curiosity**

Explorer (Artificial satellite) 629.46
- BT **Artificial satellites**

Explorers (May subdiv. geog.) **910.92; 920**
- UF Discoverers
  Navigators
  Voyagers
- SA names of places explored with the subdivision *Exploration,* e.g. **America—Exploration**; names of countries with the subdivisions *Description* and *Exploring expeditions*; and names of individual explorers [to be added as needed]

Explorers—*Continued*
　　BT　**Adventure and adventurers**
　　　　　Heroes and heroines
　　NT　**United States—Exploring expeditions**
　　RT　**Exploration**
　　　　　Travelers
　　　　　Voyages and travels
Exploring expeditions
　　USE　names of countries sponsoring
　　　　　exploring expeditions with the
　　　　　subdivision *Exploring expeditions,* e.g. **United States—Exploring expeditions;** etc.; and
　　　　　names of expeditions, e.g.
　　　　　**Lewis and Clark Expedition
　　　　　(1804-1806)** [to be added as
　　　　　needed]
Explosions　904
　　BT　**Accidents**
Explosives　363.17; 363.33; 623.4; 662
　　SA　types of explosives and explosive devices [to be added as
　　　　　needed]
　　BT　**Chemistry**
　　NT　**Ammunition**
　　　　　Bombs
　　　　　Dynamite
　　　　　Gunpowder
　　　　　Land mines
　　　　　Torpedoes
Expo 92 (Seville, Spain)　909.82
　　UF　Seville (Spain). World's Fair,
　　　　　1992
　　　　　World's Fair (1992: Seville,
　　　　　Spain)
　　BT　**Exhibitions**
　　　　　Fairs
Exports (May subdiv. geog.)　**382**
　　BT　**International trade**
Exposed children
　　USE　**Abandoned children**
Expositions
　　USE　**Exhibitions**
Express highways (May subdiv. geog.)
　　388.1; 625.7
　　UF　Freeways
　　　　　Interstate highways
　　　　　Limited access highways
　　　　　Motorways
　　　　　Parkways
　　　　　Superhighways

　　　　　Toll roads
　　　　　Turnpikes (Modern)
　　BT　**Roads**
　　　　　Traffic engineering
Express service　388
　　BT　**Railroads**
　　　　　Transportation
　　NT　**Pony express**
Expressionism (Art) (May subdiv. geog.)
　　709.04; 759.06
　　BT　**Art**
Expropriation
　　USE　**Eminent domain**
Expulsion
　　USE　**Penal colonies**
Extended care facilities
　　USE　**Long-term care facilities**
Extermination of pests
　　USE　**Pest control**
Extinct animals (May subdiv. geog.)
　　560
　　SA　types of extinct animals [to be
　　　　　added as needed]
　　BT　**Animals**
　　NT　**Mastodon**
　　RT　**Fossils**
　　　　　Prehistoric animals
　　　　　Rare animals
Extinct cities (May subdiv. geog.)　**930**
　　UF　Abandoned towns
　　　　　Buried cities
　　　　　Ruins
　　　　　Sunken cities
　　SA　names of extinct cities and
　　　　　towns, e.g. **Delphi (Extinct
　　　　　city)** [to be added as needed]
　　BT　**Archeology**
　　　　　Cities and towns
　　NT　**Ghost towns**
　　RT　**Excavations (Archeology)**
Extinct cities—Greece　938
　　NT　**Delphi (Extinct city)**
Extinct cities—Italy　937
　　NT　**Herculaneum (Extinct city)**
　　　　　Pompeii (Extinct city)
Extinct cities—Turkey　939
　　NT　**Troy (Extinct city)**
Extinct plants
　　USE　**Fossil plants**
Extortion (May subdiv. geog.)　**364.16**
　　UF　Blackmail

Extortion—*Continued*
    BT   **Offenses against property**
           Racketeering
Extracurricular activities
    USE **Student activities**
Extragalactic nebulae
    USE **Galaxies**
Extramarital relationships
    USE **Adultery**
Extrasensory perception   133.8
    UF   ESP
    BT   **Parapsychology**
    NT   **Clairvoyance**
           Telepathy
Extrasolar planetary systems
    USE **Extrasolar planets**
Extrasolar planets   523.2
    UF   Extrasolar planetary systems
    BT   **Planets**
Extraterrestrial abduction
    USE **Alien abduction**
Extraterrestrial bases   629.44
    Use for materials on bases established on natural extraterrestrial bodies for specific functions other than colonization. Materials on communities established in space or on natural extraterrestrial bodies are entered under **Space colonies**. Materials on manned installations orbiting in space for specific functions, such as servicing space ships, are entered under **Space stations**.
    BT   **Civil engineering**
    RT   **Space colonies**
Extraterrestrial beings   576.8
    UF   Aliens from outer space
           Interplanetary visitors
    BT   **Life on other planets**
    RT   **Human-alien encounters**
Extraterrestrial communication
    USE **Interstellar communication**
Extraterrestrial encounters with humans
    USE **Human-alien encounters**
Extraterrestrial environment
    USE **Space environment**
Extraterrestrial life
    USE **Life on other planets**
Extravehicular activity (Space flight)
    629.45
    UF   Space vehicles—Extravehicular
           activity
           Space walk
           Walking in space
    BT   **Space flight**

Extreme sports (May subdiv. geog.)
    796.04
    BT   **Sports**
Extreme unction
    USE **Anointing of the sick**
Extremism (Political science)
    USE **Radicalism**
Eye   611; 612.8
    BT   **Face**
           Head
    RT   **Optometry**
           Vision
Eyeglasses   617.7; 681
    UF   Glasses
           Spectacles
    SA   types of eyeglasses, e.g. **Contact lenses** [to be added as needed]
    NT   **Contact lenses**
Fables   398.24; 808.8
    Use for individual works, collections, or materials about short tales intended to teach moral lessons, often with animals or inanimate objects speaking and acting like human beings, and usually with the lesson stated briefly at the end.
    UF   Cautionary tales and verses
           Moral and philosophic stories
           Tales
    SA   fables of particular countries, e.g. **American fables** [to be added as needed]
    BT   **Fiction**
           Literature
    NT   **American fables**
    RT   **Allegories**
           Animals—Fiction
           Didactic fiction
           Didactic poetry
           Folklore
           Legends
           Parables
           Romances
Fabric design
    USE **Textile design**
Fabrics (May subdiv. geog.)   677
    UF   Cloth
           Dry goods
           Textiles
    SA   types of fabrics [to be added as needed]
    BT   **Decorative arts**

Fabrics—*Continued*
- NT **Cotton**
      Linen
      Silk
      Synthetic fabrics
      Wool
- RT **Weaving**

Face 611; 612
- BT **Head**
- NT **Eye**
      Mouth
      Nose
- RT **Physiognomy**

Facetiae
- USE **Anecdotes**
        Wit and humor

Facsimile transmission
- USE **Fax transmission**

Facsimiles
- USE types of printed or written materials, documents, etc., with the subdivision *Facsimiles,* e.g. **Autographs—Facsimiles** [to be added as needed]

Factories (May subdiv. geog.) **338.6; 670; 725**
- UF Industrial plants
      Mill and factory buildings
      Plants, Industrial
- SA types of factories [to be added as needed]
- BT **Industrial buildings**
- NT **Breweries**
      Plant shutdowns
- RT **Factory management**
      Mills

Factories—Management
- USE **Factory management**

Factory and trade waste
- USE **Industrial waste**

Factory management 658.5

Use for materials on the technical aspects of manufacturing processes. Materials on general principles of management of industries are entered under **Management**.
- UF Factories—Management
      Production engineering
      Shop management
- BT **Management**
- NT **Job analysis**
      Motion study
      Office management

      Participative management
      Supervisors
      Time study
- RT **Factories**
      Personnel management

Factory waste
- USE **Industrial waste**

Factory workers
- USE **Labor**
        Working class

Facts, Miscellaneous
- USE **Books of lists**
        Curiosities and wonders

Faculty
- USE types of educational institutions and names of individual educational institutions with the subdivision *Faculty,* e.g. **Colleges and universities—Faculty** [to be added as needed]

Faculty (Education)
- USE **Colleges and universities—Faculty**
        Educators
        Teachers

Fads 306
- UF Crazes
- BT **Manners and customs**
      Popular culture

Faience
- USE **Pottery**

Failure in business
- USE **Bankruptcy**
        Business failures

Failure of banks
- USE **Bank failures**

Failure to thrive syndrome
- USE **Growth disorders**

Failures, Structural
- USE **Structural failures**

Fair employment practice
- USE **Discrimination in employment**

Fair housing
- USE **Discrimination in housing**

Fair trade
- USE **Unfair competition**

Fair trade (Tariff)
- USE **Free trade**

Fair trial (May subdiv. geog.) **345**

Use for materials on legal hearings before an impartial and disinterested tribunal. Materi-

Fair trial—*Continued*

als on the regular administration of the law, according to which citizens may not be denied their legal rights and all laws must conform to fundamental and accepted legal principles, are entered under **Due process of law**.

UF   Right to a fair trial

BT   **Civil rights**

      Due process of law

NT   **Freedom of the press and fair trial**

Fair trial and free press

USE   **Freedom of the press and fair trial**

Fair use (Copyright) (May subdiv. geog.) **346.04**

BT   **Copyright**

Fairies **398.21**

BT   **Folklore**

Fairness **179**

UF   Impartiality

BT   **Conduct of life**

RT   **Justice**

Fairness doctrine (Broadcasting) **343.09**

Use for materials on the requirement that, if one side of a controversial issue of public importance is aired, the same opportunity must be given for the presentation of contrasting views. Materials on the requirement that all qualified candidates for public office be granted equal broadcast time if any one such candidate is permitted to broadcast are entered under **Equal time rule (Broadcasting)**.

UF   Doctrine of fairness (Broadcasting)

BT   **Broadcasting**

      Television and politics

RT   **Equal time rule (Broadcasting)**

Fairs (May subdiv. geog.) **381; 394; 607; 907.4**

Use for general materials on public showings that suggest a variety of kinds of display and entertainment, usually in an outdoor setting, sometimes for the promotion of sales and sometimes in competition for prizes of excellence.

UF   Bazaars

      World's fairs

SA   names of fairs, e.g. **Expo 92 (Seville, Spain)** [to be added as needed]

NT   **Expo 92 (Seville, Spain)**

      Trade shows

RT   **Carnivals**

      Exhibitions

      Markets

Fairy tales (May subdiv. geog.) **398.2; 808.83**

Use for individual works, collections, or materials about short, simple narratives, often of folk origin and usually intended for children, involving fantastic forces and magical beings such as dragons, elves, fairies, goblins, witches, and wizards.

UF   Stories

      Tales

BT   **Children's literature**

      Fiction

NT   **Fractured fairy tales**

RT   **Folklore**

Fairy tales—Parodies, imitations, etc.

USE   **Fractured fairy tales**

Faith **121; 201; 234**

Use for materials on religious belief and doubt. Materials on belief and doubt from the philosophical standpoint are entered under **Belief and doubt**.

UF   Religious belief

BT   **Religion**

      Salvation

      Spiritual life

      Theology

      Virtue

RT   **Belief and doubt**

Faith cure

USE   **Spiritual healing**

Faith healing

USE   **Spiritual healing**

Faith—Psychology **200.1; 248; 253.5**

BT   **Psychology of religion**

Faithfulness

USE   **Loyalty**

Falconry **799.2**

UF   Hawking

BT   **Game and game birds**

      Hunting

Fall

USE   **Autumn**

Fallacies

USE   **Errors**

      Logic

Falling stars

USE   **Meteors**

Fallout, Radioactive

USE   **Radioactive fallout**

Fallout shelters

USE   **Air raid shelters**

False advertising

USE   **Deceptive advertising**

False memories
USE **False memory syndrome**
False memory syndrome   616.85
UF   False memories
BT   **Memory**
RT   **Recovered memory**
Falsehood
USE   **Truthfulness and falsehood**
Fame   306.4
UF   Celebrity
Renown
RT   **Celebrities**
Family (May subdiv. geog.)   **306.85**
Use for materials stressing the sociological concept and structure of the family. Materials stressing the everyday life, interaction, and relationships of family members are entered under **Family life**.
SA   types of family members, e.g. **Children**; **Fathers**; **Mothers**; etc., types of family relationships, e.g. **Mother-son relationship**; and names of individual persons with the subdivision *Family* [to be added as needed]
BT   **Interpersonal relations**
Sociology
NT   **Aunts**
Birth order
Children
Clans
Cousins
Daughters
Divorce
Dual-career families
Family life
Family size
Farm family
Fathers
Grandparent-grandchild relationship
Grandparents
Husbands
Kinship
Marriage
Married people
Mothers
Parent-child relationship
Parenthood
Parents
Siblings
Single-parent families
Sons
Stepfamilies
Tribes
Uncles
Wives
Work and family
RT   **Domestic relations**
Family reunions
Home
Family and work
USE   **Work and family**
Family—Biblical teaching   248.4; 261.8
Family budget
USE   **Household budgets**
Family caregivers
USE   **Caregivers**
Family counseling
USE   **Family therapy**
Family devotions
USE   **Devotional exercises**
Family—Religious life
Family farms (May subdiv. geog.)   **338.1; 630**
BT   **Farms**
RT   **Farm family**
Farm life
Family finance
USE   **Personal finance**
Family group therapy
USE   **Family therapy**
Family histories
USE   **Genealogy**
Family leave
USE   **Parental leave**
Family life (May subdiv. geog.)   **306.85; 392.3; 646.7**
Use for materials stressing the everyday life, interaction, and relationships of family members. Materials on the sociological concept and structure of the family are entered under **Family**.
UF   Family relations
Home life
BT   **Family**
NT   **Family traditions**
Family life education (May subdiv. geog.)   **306.85; 362.82; 372.82**
BT   **Education**
NT   **Home economics**
Marriage counseling
Sex education
RT   **Domestic relations**
Family medicine   610

Family medicine—*Continued*
    UF   Family practice (Medicine)
            General practice (Medicine)
    BT   **Medicine**
Family names
    USE **Personal names**
Family planning
    USE **Birth control**
Family practice (Medicine)
    USE **Family medicine**
Family prayers
    USE **Devotional exercises**
           Family—Religious life
Family psychotherapy
    USE **Family therapy**
Family relations
    USE **Domestic relations**
           Family life
Family—Religious life   204; 248.4; 249
    UF   Family devotions
            Family prayers
            Family worship
    BT   **Religious life**
Family reunions   394.2
    UF   Reunions, Family
    RT   **Family**
Family size (May subdiv. geog.)   304.6
    BT   **Family**
    NT   **Childlessness**
           Only child
    RT   **Birth control**
Family social work
    USE **Social case work**
Family therapy   616.89
    UF   Family counseling
            Family group therapy
            Family psychotherapy
            Problem families—Counseling of
    BT   **Counseling**
           Psychotherapy
Family traditions (May subdiv. geog.)
      306.85; 392.3
    BT   **Family life**
           Manners and customs
Family trees
    USE **Genealogy**
Family—United States   306.850973
Family violence
    USE **Domestic violence**
Family worship
    USE **Family—Religious life**
Famines (May subdiv. geog.)   904

    BT   **Food supply**
           Starvation
Famines—United States   363.80973; 973
Famous people
    USE **Celebrities**
Fan magazines
    USE **Fanzines**
Fanaticism   152.4; 200.1; 303
    UF   Intolerance
    BT   **Emotions**
Fancy dress
    USE **Costume**
Fans   391.4
    BT   **Clothing and dress**
           Costume
Fantastic fiction
    USE **Fantasy fiction**
Fantastic films
    USE **Fantasy films**
Fantastic poetry
    USE **Fantasy poetry**
Fantastic radio programs
    USE **Fantasy radio programs**
Fantastic television programs
    USE **Fantasy television programs**
Fantasy   154.3
    Use for materials on fantasy as an aspect of psychology. Literary fantasies are entered under **Fantasy fiction**.
    UF   Day dreams
    BT   **Dreams**
           Imagination
    RT   **Hallucinations and illusions**
Fantasy fiction   808.3; 808.83
    Use for individual works, collections, or materials about imaginative fiction with strange settings, grotesque or fanciful characters, and supernatural or impossible events or forces.
    UF   Fantastic fiction
    BT   **Fiction**
    NT   **Alternative histories**
           Dystopias
           Ghost stories
           Imaginary voyages
           Utopian fiction
    RT   **Horror fiction**
           Occult fiction
           Science fiction
Fantasy films   791.43
    Use for individual works, collections, or materials about fantasy films.
    UF   Fantastic films
    BT   **Motion pictures**

Fantasy films—*Continued*
>   RT   **Horror films**
>   **Science fiction films**

Fantasy games   793.93
>   UF   Fantasy role playing games
>   Role playing games
>   BT   **Games**
>   **Role playing**

Fantasy graphic novels   741.5
>   Use for individual works, collections, or materials about fantasy graphic novels.
>   BT   **Graphic novels**

Fantasy poetry   808.1; 808.81
>   Use for individual works, collections, or materials about fantasy poetry.
>   UF   Fantastic poetry
>   BT   **Poetry**

Fantasy radio programs   791.44
>   Use for individual works, collections, or materials about fantasy radio programs.
>   UF   Fantastic radio programs
>   BT   **Radio programs**

Fantasy role playing games
>   USE   **Fantasy games**

Fantasy television programs   791.45
>   Use for individual works, collections, or materials about fantasy television programs.
>   UF   Fantastic television programs
>   BT   **Television programs**
>   RT   **Horror television programs**
>   **Science fiction television programs**

Fanzines (May subdiv. geog.)   070.4
>   UF   Fan magazines
>   Zines
>   BT   **Periodicals**

Far East
>   USE   **East Asia**

Far north
>   USE   **Arctic regions**

Farces   808.2; 808.82
>   Use for individual works, collections, or materials about farces.
>   BT   **Comedies**
>   NT   **Commedia dell'arte**

Farm animals
>   USE   **Domestic animals**

Farm buildings (May subdiv. geog.)   631.2; 728
>   UF   Architecture, Rural
>   Rural architecture
>   SA   types of farm buildings [to be added as needed]

>   BT   **Buildings**
>   NT   **Barns**

Farm credit
>   USE   **Agricultural credit**

Farm crops
>   USE   **Farm produce**

Farm engines
>   USE   **Agricultural machinery**

Farm equipment
>   USE   **Agricultural machinery**

Farm family (May subdiv. geog.)   306.85
>   UF   Rural families
>   BT   **Family**
>   RT   **Family farms**
>   **Farm life**
>   **Rural sociology**

Farm implements
>   USE   **Agricultural machinery**

Farm laborers
>   USE   **Agricultural laborers**

Farm life (May subdiv. geog.)   306.3; 630
>   UF   Rural life
>   BT   **Country life**
>   **Farmers**
>   NT   **Ranch life**
>   RT   **Family farms**
>   **Farm family**
>   **Rural sociology**

Farm life—United States   306.3; 630

Farm loans
>   USE   **Agricultural credit**

Farm machinery
>   USE   **Agricultural machinery**

Farm management   630
>   BT   **Farms**
>   **Management**
>   RT   **Agriculture—Economic aspects**

Farm mechanics
>   USE   **Agricultural engineering**
>   **Agricultural machinery**

Farm produce (May subdiv. geog.)   338.1; 630; 631.5
>   UF   Agricultural products
>   Crops
>   Farm crops
>   Products, Agricultural
>   SA   types of farm products [to be added as needed]

Farm produce—*Continued*

  BT **Food**

        Raw materials

  NT **Hay**

Farm produce—Marketing 338.1

  UF Marketing of farm produce

  BT **Marketing**

        Prices

  RT **Agriculture—Economic aspects**

Farm subsidies

  USE **Agricultural subsidies**

Farm tenancy (May subdiv. geog.)
    333.5

  Use for materials on the economic and social aspects of farm tenancy. Materials on the
legal aspects are entered under **Landlord and
tenant**.

  UF Agriculture—Tenant farming

        Tenant farming

  BT **Farms**

        Land tenure

  NT **Sharecropping**

  RT **Landlord and tenant**

Farmers (May subdiv. geog.) **305.9;
    630.92; 920**

  BT **Agriculture**

  NT **Farm life**

Farmers' cooperatives

  USE **Cooperative agriculture**

Farming

  USE **Agriculture**

Farming, Dry

  USE **Dry farming**

Farming, Organic

  USE **Organic farming**

Farms 333.76; 630; 636

  BT **Land use**

        Real estate

  NT **Family farms**

        Farm management

        Farm tenancy

        Plantations

        Vineyards

  RT **Agriculture**

Fascism (May subdiv. geog.) **320.53;
    321.9; 335.6**

  Use for materials on the political philosophy, movements, or regimes that advocate a
centralized autocratic government, severe economic and social regimentation, and the exal-
tation of nation and race over the individual.
Materials on fascism in Germany during the
Nazi regime are entered under **National socialism**.

  UF Authoritarianism

        Neo-fascism

  BT **Totalitarianism**

  NT **National socialism**

        Neo-Nazis

Fascism—United States 320.5; 973.9

Fashion (May subdiv. geog.) **391**

  Use for materials on the prevailing mode or
style of dress. Materials on the characteristic
costume of ethnic or national groups and for
materials on fancy dress and theatrical costumes are entered under **Costume**. Materials
on clothing and the art of dress from day to
day in practical situations, including historical
dress and the clothing of various professions
or classes of persons, are entered under
Clothing and dress.

  UF Style in dress

  BT **Clothing and dress**

  RT **Fashion design**

Fashion design (May subdiv. geog.)
    746.9

  BT **Clothing industry**

        Commercial art

        Design

  RT **Fashion**

Fashion designers (May subdiv. geog.)
    746.9

  UF Clothing designers

        Couturiers

  BT **Designers**

Fashion industry

  USE **Clothing industry**

Fashion models 659.1; 746.9

  UF Manikins (Fashion models)

        Mannequins (Fashion models)

        Models

        Models (Persons)

        Style manikins

  BT **Advertising**

Fashion shows 391; 659.1

  BT **Exhibitions**

Fashionable society

  USE **Upper class**

Fast food restaurants (May subdiv. geog.)
    647.95

  BT **Convenience foods**

        Restaurants

Fast foods

  USE **Convenience foods**

Faster reading

  USE **Speed reading**

Fasting 178; 204; 248.4; 296.7; 613.2

  UF Abstinence

Fasting—*Continued*
- BT **Asceticism**
- **Diet**
- NT **Hunger strikes**
- RT **Hunger**
- **Religious holidays**
- **Starvation**

Fasts and feasts
- USE **Religious holidays**

Fasts and feasts—Christianity
- USE **Christian holidays**

Fasts and feasts—Islam
- USE **Islamic holidays**

Fasts and feasts—Judaism
- USE **Jewish holidays**

Fatally ill children
- USE **Terminally ill children**

Fatally ill patients
- USE **Terminally ill**

Fate and fatalism 149
- UF Destiny
- Fortune
- BT **Philosophy**
- RT **Free will and determinism**
- **Predestination**

Father and child
- USE **Father-child relationship**

Father-child relationship 306.874
- UF Child and father
- Father and child
- BT **Children**
- **Fathers**
- **Parent-child relationship**
- NT **Father-daughter relationship**
- **Father-son relationship**

Father-daughter relationship 306.874
- UF Daughters and fathers
- Fathers and daughters
- BT **Daughters**
- **Father-child relationship**
- **Fathers**

Father-son relationship 306.874
- UF Fathers and sons
- Sons and fathers
- BT **Father-child relationship**
- **Fathers**
- **Sons**

Fatherhood 306.874
- BT **Parenthood**
- RT **Fathers**

Fathers (May subdiv. geog.) 306.874
- BT **Family**
- **Men**
- NT **Father-child relationship**
- **Father-daughter relationship**
- **Father-son relationship**
- **Stepfathers**
- **Teenage fathers**
- **Unmarried fathers**
- RT **Fatherhood**

Fathers and daughters
- USE **Father-daughter relationship**

Fathers and sons
- USE **Father-son relationship**

Fathers of the church 270.1; 920

Use for materials on the lives and thought of the leaders of the Christian church up to the time of Gregory the Great in the West and John of Damascus in the East. Individual works or collections of the writings of early Christian authors are entered under **Early Christian literature**.
- UF Church fathers
- Patristic philosophy
- Patristics
- BT **Christian biography**
- RT **Early Christian literature**

Fatigue 613.7; 152.1; 612
- UF Exhaustion
- Weariness
- BT **Physiology**
- NT **Jet lag**
- RT **Rest**

Fatness
- USE **Obesity**

Fats
- USE **Oils and fats**

Faults (Geology) (May subdiv. geog.) 551.8
- BT **Geology**

Fauna
- USE **Animals**
- **Zoology**

Fawns
- USE **Deer**

Fax machines
- USE **Fax transmission**

Fax transmission 384.1; 621.382

Use for the machines, the processes, and the products of facsimile transmission.
- UF Facsimile transmission
- Fax machines
- BT **Data transmission systems**
- **Telecommunication**

Fear 152.4

Fear—*Continued*
- BT **Emotions**
- NT **Fear in children**
  Fear of the dark
  Horror
  Phobias
- RT **Anxiety**

Fear in children   155.41246
- BT **Child psychology**
  Fear
- NT **Fear of the dark**

Fear of open spaces
- USE **Agoraphobia**

Fear of the dark   152.4
- BT **Fear**
  Fear in children

Feast days
- USE **Religious holidays**

Feast of Dedication
- USE **Hanukkah**

Feast of Lights
- USE **Hanukkah**

Fecundity
- USE **Fertility**

Federal aid (May subdiv. geog.)   336

Use for materials on central government aid in federal systems. Materials on aid from governments at any level in non-federal systems and on aid from states, provinces, or local governments in federal systems are entered under **Government aid**.

- SA federal aid to specific endeavors, e.g. **Federal aid to the arts** [to be added as needed]
- BT **Public finance**
- NT **Federal aid to education**
  Federal aid to libraries
  Federal aid to minority business enterprises
  Federal aid to the arts
- RT **Government aid**

Federal aid to education (May subdiv. geog.)   379.1
- UF Education—Federal aid
- BT **Education—Government policy**
  Federal aid
- RT **Colleges and universities—Finance**
  Education—Finance

Federal aid to libraries (May subdiv. geog.)   021.8
- UF Libraries—Federal aid

- BT **Federal aid**
  Libraries—Government policy
- RT **Library finance**

Federal aid to minority business enterprises (May subdiv. geog.)   338.6
- UF Minority business enterprises—Federal aid
- BT **Federal aid**
  Subsidies

Federal aid to the arts (May subdiv. geog.)   353.7; 700
- UF Art—Federal aid
  Arts and state
  Arts—Federal aid
  Funding for the arts
  State and the arts
  State encouragement of the arts
- BT **Federal aid**
- RT **Art patronage**
  Arts—Government policy

Federal budget
- USE **Budget—United States**

Federal-city relations   351.09
- UF City-federal relations
  Federal-municipal relations
  Municipal-federal relations
  Urban-federal relations
- BT **Federal government**
  Municipal government

Federal courts
- USE **Courts—United States**

Federal debt
- USE **Public debts**

Federal government   321.02; 351
- UF Confederacies
  Federalism
- BT **Constitutional law**
  Political science
  Republics
- NT **European federation**
  Federal-city relations
  Federal-state relations
- RT **State governments**

Federal-Indian relations
- USE **Native Americans—Government relations**

Federal libraries
- USE **Government libraries**

Federal-municipal relations
- USE **Federal-city relations**

Federal Republic of Germany
USE **Germany**
   Germany (West)
Federal Reserve banks   332.1
   BT **Banks and banking**
Federal revenue sharing
   USE **Revenue sharing**
Federal spending policy
   USE **United States—Appropriations and expenditures**
Federal-state relations   321.02
   UF State-federal relations
   BT **Federal government**
   State governments
Federal-state tax relations
   USE **Intergovernmental tax relations**
Federalism
   USE **Federal government**
Federation of Europe
   USE **European federation**
Feedback control systems   629.8
   BT **Automation**
   NT **Servomechanisms**
Feedback (Psychology)   153.1
   BT **Psychology of learning**
   NT **Biofeedback training**
Feeding behavior in animals
   USE **Animals—Food**
Feeds   633.2; 633.3
   UF Fodder
   SA types of feeds, e.g. **Oats** [to be added as needed]
   BT **Animals—Food**
   NT **Forage plants**
   Oats
   Silage and silos
   RT **Grasses**
   Hay
   Root crops
Feeling
   USE **Perception**
   Touch
Feelings
   USE **Emotions**
Fees
   USE **Salaries, wages, etc.**
Feet
   USE **Foot**
Felidae
   USE **Wild cats**

Felines
   USE **Cats**
Fellowships
   USE **Scholarships**
Felony
   USE **Crime**
Female actors
   USE **Actresses**
Female circumcision (May subdiv. geog.)
   392.1
   UF Circumcision, Female
   Clitoridotomy
   Female genital mutilation
   Genital mutilation, Female
   Mutilation, Female genital
   BT **Initiation rites**
Female climacteric
   USE **Menopause**
Female friendship   302.4
   UF Friendship between women
   Friendship in women
   Women's friendship
   BT **Friendship**
Female genital mutilation
   USE **Female circumcision**
Female identity
   USE **Women—Identity**
Female impersonators   791.4
   Use for materials on men who impersonate women for purposes of entertainment or comic effect. Materials on persons, especially men, who assume the dress of the opposite sex for psychological gratification are entered under **Transvestites**.
   BT **Impostors and imposture**
Female-male relationship
   USE **Man-woman relationship**
Female role
   USE **Sex role**
Female superhero graphic novels   741.5
   Use for individual works, collections, or materials about female superhero graphic novels.
   BT **Female superhero graphic novels**
   Graphic novels
   NT **Female superhero graphic novels**
Feminine identity
   USE **Women—Identity**
Feminine psychology
   USE **Women—Psychology**
Femininity (May subdiv. geog.)   **155.3**
   UF Femininity (Psychology)

Femininity—*Continued*
  BT **Sex (Psychology)**
  RT **Women**
Femininity of God 212; 231
  UF God—Femininity
  BT **God**
Femininity (Psychology)
  USE **Femininity**
Feminism (May subdiv. geog.) 305.42; 323.3

  Use for materials on the theory of the political and social equality of the sexes and women's perspectives on various subjects. Materials on activities aimed at obtaining equal rights and opportunities for women are entered under **Women's movement**.

  UF Feminist theory
  SA types of feminist endeavors, e.g.
      Feminist criticism; **Feminist theology**; etc. [to be added as needed]
  NT **Feminist ethics**
      Women—History
  RT **Suffragists**
      Women's movement
      Women's rights
Feminist criticism 801
  UF Criticism, Feminist
  BT **Criticism**
Feminist ethics (May subdiv. geog.) 170
  BT **Ethics**
      Feminism
Feminist fiction 808.3; 808.83
  BT **Fiction**
Feminist theology 230

  Use for materials on the feminist critique of traditional theology and on alternative theology from a feminist perspective.

  BT **Theology**
Feminist theory
  USE **Feminism**
Fencing 796.86
  UF Fighting
  BT **Dueling**
Feng shui (May subdiv. geog.) 133.3
  BT **Divination**
Feral animals
  USE **Wildlife**
Feral cats
  USE **Wild cats**
Feral children
  USE **Wild children**
Fermentation 547; 660; 663
  UF Ferments

  BT **Chemical engineering**
      Chemistry
      Microbiology
Ferments
  USE **Fermentation**
Ferns 587; 635.9
  BT **Plants**
Fertility 573.6; 591.1

  Use for general materials on fertility in animals, including humans. Materials limited to fertility in humans are entered under **Human fertility**.

  UF Fecundity
  BT **Reproduction**
  NT **Human fertility**
  RT **Infertility**
Fertility control
  USE **Birth control**
Fertility, Human
  USE **Human fertility**
Fertilization in vitro 176; 618.1; 636.089
  UF Fertilization in vitro, Human
      Fertilization, Test tube
      In vitro fertilization
      Laboratory fertilization
      Test tube babies
      Test tube fertilization
  BT **Genetic engineering**
      Reproduction
Fertilization in vitro, Human
  USE **Fertilization in vitro**
Fertilization of plants 575.6
  UF Plants—Fertilization
      Pollination
  BT **Plant physiology**
      Plants
Fertilization, Test tube
  USE **Fertilization in vitro**
Fertilizers 631.8; 668
  UF Fertilizers and manures
      Manures
  BT **Agricultural chemicals**
      Soils
  NT **Compost**
      Lime
      Nitrates
      Phosphates
      Potash
Fertilizers and manures
  USE **Fertilizers**

Festivals (May subdiv. geog.) **394.26**

Use for materials on occasions other than holidays devoted to festive community observances or to programs of cultural events. Materials on days of general exemption from work or days publicly dedicated to the commemoration of some person, event, or principle are entered under **Holidays**. Materials on religious fasts and feasts are entered under **Religious holidays**.

UF Fiestas
SA types of festivals and names of specific festivals, e.g. **Carnival** [to be added as needed]
BT **Manners and customs**
NT **Carnival**
  Carnivals
  Craft shows
  Film festivals
  Music festivals
  Parades
  Powwows
RT **Anniversaries**
  Days
  Holidays
  Pageants
  Religious holidays

Festivals—United States **394.260973**
Fetal alcohol syndrome **618.3**
BT **Social problems**
RT **Birth defects**
  Growth disorders

Fetal death
USE **Miscarriage**
Fetus **571.8; 612.6**
UF Unborn child
BT **Embryology**
  Reproduction

Feudalism (May subdiv. geog.) **321**
UF Fiefs
  Vassals
BT **Land tenure**
  Medieval civilization
NT **Peasantry**
RT **Chivalry**

Feuds
USE **Vendetta**
Fever **616**
BT **Pathology**
RT **Body temperature**

Fiber content of food
USE **Food—Fiber content**
Fiber glass
USE **Glass fibers**

Fiberglass
USE **Glass fibers**
Fibers **677**
UF Textile fibers
NT **Cotton**
  Flax
  Glass fibers
  Hemp
  Linen
  Paper
  Silk
  Wool

Fibers, Glass
USE **Glass fibers**
Fiction **808.3**

Use for collections and materials about fiction from several countries and for materials on fiction as a literary form, not for individual works.

UF Novels
  Stories
SA fiction of particular national literatures, e.g. **American fiction**; genres of fiction, e.g. **Fantasy fiction**; and subjects, names of places, and personal and corporate names with the subdivision *Fiction*, to express the theme or subject content of collections of fiction, e.g. **Slavery—United States—Fiction**; **United States—History—1861-1865, Civil War—Fiction**; **Ohio—Fiction**; **Napoleon I, Emperor of the French, 1769-1821—Fiction**; etc. [to be added as needed]
BT **Literature**
NT **Adventure fiction**
  Allegories
  Allegory
  American fiction
  Apocalyptic fiction
  Bible fiction
  Bildungsromans
  Biographical fiction
  Black humor (Literature)
  Children's stories
  Christian fiction
  Didactic fiction
  English fiction
  Epistolary fiction

Fiction—*Continued*
>> Erotic fiction
>> Fables
>> Fairy tales
>> Fantasy fiction
>> Feminist fiction
>> Folklore
>> Graphic novels
>> Historical fiction
>> Horror fiction
>> Humorous fiction
>> Interplanetary voyages
>> Jewish religious fiction
>> Legal stories
>> Legends
>> Love stories
>> Medical novels
>> Movie novels
>> Mystery fiction
>> Occult fiction
>> Pastoral fiction
>> Picaresque literature
>> Plot-your-own stories
>> Radio and television novels
>> Religious fiction
>> Romances
>> Romans à clef
>> School stories
>> Science fiction
>> Sea stories
>> Short stories
>> Short story
>> Urban fiction
>> War stories
>> Western stories

Fiction for children
> USE **Children's stories**
Fiction—History and criticism   809.3
Fiction—Technique   808.3
> BT **Authorship**
Fictional characters   808.3
> UF Fictitious characters
> SA names of individual literary characters established in the inverted form with the qualifier (Fictional character), e.g. **Holmes, Sherlock (Fictional character)** [to be added as needed]
> BT **Characters and characteristics in literature**
> NT **Fictional robots**

Fictional places
> USE **Imaginary places**
Fictional plots
> USE **Stories, plots, etc.**
Fictional robots   741.5
> SA names of individual fictional robots, e.g. **Neon Genesis Evangelion (Fictional robot)** [to be added as needed]
> BT **Fictional characters**
> **Mecha**
> NT **Gundam (Fictional character)**
> **Neon Genesis Evangelion (Fictional robot)**
Fictitious characters
> USE **Fictional characters**
Fictitious names
> USE **Pseudonyms**
Fictitious places
> USE **Imaginary places**
Fiddle
> USE **Violins**
Fiduciaries
> USE **Trusts and trustees**
Fiefs
> USE **Feudalism**
> **Land tenure**
Field athletics
> USE **Track athletics**
Field hockey   796.35
> BT **Sports**
Field hospitals
> USE **Military hospitals**
> **Military medicine**
Field photography
> USE **Outdoor photography**
Field trips   069; 371.3
> UF School excursions
> School trips
> BT **Student activities**
Fiestas
> USE **Festivals**
Fifteenth century
> USE **World history—15th century**
Fifth column
> USE **Subversive activities**
> **World War, 1939-1945—Collaborationists**
Fifth of May (Holiday)
> USE **Cinco de Mayo (Holiday)**

Fighting
USE **Battles**
Boxing
Bullfights
Dueling
Fencing
Gladiators
Military art and science
Naval art and science
Self-defense
Self-defense for women
War
Figure drawing   743.4
UF   Human figure in art
BT   **Artistic anatomy**
Drawing
RT   **Figure painting**
Figure painting   757
UF   Human figure in art
BT   **Artistic anatomy**
Painting
RT   **Figure drawing**
Portrait painting
Figure skating
USE   **Ice skating**
Figures of speech   808
UF   English language—Figures of
speech
Imagery
Tropes
BT   **Rhetoric**
Symbolism
Files and filing   005.74; 025.3; 651.5
UF   Alphabetizing
Filing systems
BT   **Office management**
RT   **Indexing**
Filing systems
USE   **Files and filing**
Filling stations
USE   **Service stations**
Fills (Earthwork)
USE   **Landfills**
Film adaptations   791.43
Use for individual works, collections, or
materials about film adaptations of material
from other media.
UF   Adaptations
Filmed books
Films from books
Literature—Film and video adap-
tations

Motion picture adaptations
SA   names of authors, titles of anonymous literary works, types of
literature, and types of musical compositions with the
subdivision *Adaptations*, for
individual works, collections,
or criticism and interpretation
of literary, cinematic, video,
or television adaptations, e.g.,
Shakespeare, William, 1564-
1616—Adaptations; **Beo-**
wulf—Adaptations; **Arthuri-**
an romances—Adaptations;
etc. [to be added as needed]
BT   **Motion pictures**
Film catalogs
USE   **Motion pictures—Catalogs**
Film direction
USE   **Motion pictures—Production**
and direction
Film directors
USE   **Motion picture producers and**
directors
Film epics
USE   **Epic films**
Film festivals   791.43
UF   Motion picture festivals
Movie festivals
BT   **Festivals**
Film industry (Motion pictures)
USE   **Motion picture industry**
Film noir   791.43
UF   Crime films
Films noirs
BT   **Motion pictures**
RT   **Mystery films**
Film posters   741.6; 791.43
UF   Motion picture posters
Motion pictures—Posters
Movie posters
Playbills
BT   **Posters**
Film producers
USE   **Motion picture producers and**
directors
Film production
USE   **Motion pictures—Production**
and direction
Film projectors
USE   **Projectors**

Film scripts
USE **Screenplays**
Filmed books
USE **Film adaptations**
Filmmaking
USE **Motion pictures—Production
and direction**
Filmography
USE **Motion pictures—Catalogs**
and types of motion pictures
with the subdivision *Catalogs,*
e.g. **Science fiction films—
Catalogs;** and subjects, class-
es of persons, corporate enti-
ties, and names of individual
persons with the subdivision
Filmography, e.g. **Animals—
Filmography; Shakespeare,
William, 1564-1616—
Filmography;** etc. [to be add-
ed as needed]
Films
USE **Filmstrips
Motion pictures**
Films from books
USE **Film adaptations**
Films noirs
USE **Film noir**
Filmstrips   371.33; 778.2
UF   Films
Strip films
BT   **Audiovisual materials
Photography**
RT   **Slides (Photography)**
Finance (May subdiv. geog.)   **332**
Use for general materials on the manage-
ment of money and credit. Materials on the
raising and expenditure of funds in the public
sector are entered under **Public finance**.
UF   Funding
Funds
SA   subjects, ethnic groups, names of
wars, and names of corporate
bodies with the subdivision
Finance, e.g. **Education—Fi-
nance** [to be added as need-
ed]
BT   **Economics**
NT   **Bankruptcy
Banks and banking
Bonds
Capital**

**Capital market
Church finance
Colleges and universities—Fi-
nance
Commerce
Corporations—Finance
Credit
Debt
Education—Finance
Endowments
Financial crises
Foreign exchange
Fund raising
Income
Inflation (Finance)
Insurance
Interest (Economics)
Investments
Library finance
Loans
Money
Personal finance
Prices
Public finance
Railroads—Finance
Securities
Speculation
Stock exchanges
United Nations—Finance
Wealth**
RT   **Monetary policy**
Finance, Household
USE   **Household budgets**
Finance—Mathematics
USE   **Business mathematics**
Finance, Municipal
USE   **Municipal finance**
Finance, Personal
USE   **Personal finance**
Finance, Public
USE   **Public finance**
**Finance—United States   332.0973;
336.73**
Financial accounting
USE   **Accounting**
Financial aid to students
USE   **Student aid**
Financial crashes
USE   **Financial crises**
Financial crises (May subdiv. geog.)
338 5

Financial crises—*Continued*

UF   Crashes (Finance)
Financial crashes
Financial panics
Panics (Finance)
Stock exchange crashes
Stock market panics

BT   **Finance**

RT   **Business cycles**

Financial institutions (May subdiv. geog.)
332.1

UF   Lending institutions

BT   **Associations**

NT   **Capital market**

Financial panics
USE   **Financial crises**

Financial planning, Personal
USE   **Personal finance**

Financiers
USE   **Capitalists and financiers**

Finding things
USE   **Lost and found possessions**

Finger games
USE   **Finger play**

Finger marks
USE   **Fingerprints**

Finger painting   751.4

UF   Painting, Finger

BT   **Child artists**
Painting

Finger play   793.4

UF   Finger games

BT   **Play**

Finger pressure therapy
USE   **Acupressure**

Finger prints
USE   **Fingerprints**

Fingerprints   363.25

UF   Finger marks
Finger prints

BT   **Anthropometry**
Criminal investigation
Criminals—Identification
Identification

Finishes and finishing   667; 684.1; 698;
745.7

UF   Finishing
Finishing materials

SA   topics with the subdivision *Finishing*, e.g. **Metals—Finishing**; or with the subdivision

Painting, e.g. **Automobiles—Painting** [to be added as needed]

BT   **Materials**

NT   **Industrial painting**
Lacquer and lacquering
Metals—Finishing
Paint
Varnish and varnishing
Wood finishing

Finishing
USE   **Finishes and finishing**
and topics with the subdivision *Finishing*, e.g. **Metals—Finishing** [to be added as needed]

Finishing materials
USE   **Finishes and finishing**

Finno-Russian War, 1939-1940
USE   **Russo-Finnish War, 1939-1940**

Fire   536; 541

BT   **Chemistry**

NT   **Fires**
Fuel

RT   **Combustion**
Heat

Fire bombs
USE   **Incendiary bombs**

Fire departments (May subdiv. geog.)
628.9

UF   Fire stations

RT   **Fire fighters**

Fire engines   628.9

BT   **Engines**
Fire fighting

Fire etching
USE   **Pyrography**

Fire fighters (May subdiv. geog.)
363.37092; 920

UF   Firemen and firewomen

RT   **Fire departments**

Fire fighting (May subdiv. geog.)   628.9

BT   **Fire prevention**
Fires

NT   **Fire engines**

Fire in mythology   398.2

BT   **Mythology**

Fire insurance   368.1

UF   Insurance, Fire

BT   **Insurance**

NT   **Fireproofing**

Fire prevention (May subdiv. geog.)
    363.37; 628.9
  UF Prevention of fire
  SA types of institutions, buildings,
        industries, and vehicles with
        the subdivision *Fires and fire*
        prevention, e.g. **Nuclear pow-**
        er plants—Fires and fire
        prevention [to be added as
        needed]
  BT **Fires**
  NT **Fire fighting**
        Fireproofing
        Nuclear power plants—Fires
        and fire prevention

Fire stations
  USE **Fire departments**

Firearms (May subdiv. geog.) **623.4;**
    739.7
  UF Guns
        Small arms
  SA types of firearms [to be added
        as needed]
  BT **Weapons**
  NT **Gunpowder**
        Handguns
        Rifles
        Shotguns
  RT **Ammunition**
        Shooting

Firearms control
  USE **Gun control**

Firearms industry (May subdiv. geog.)
    338.4; 683.4
    Use for materials on the small arms indus-
    try. Materials on the production of military
    weapons are entered under **Defense industry**.
  UF Firearms industry and trade
        Firearms trade
        Gunsmithing
        Weapons industry
  BT **Industries**

Firearms industry and trade
  USE **Firearms industry**

Firearms—Law and legislation
  USE **Gun control**

Firearms trade
  USE **Firearms industry**

Firemen and firewomen
  USE **Fire fighters**

Fireplaces **697; 749**

  BT **Architecture—Details**
        Buildings
        Heating
        Space heaters
  RT **Chimneys**

Fireproofing **628.9; 693.8**
  BT **Fire insurance**
        Fire prevention

Fires (May subdiv. geog.) **363.37; 904**
  SA types of institutions, buildings,
        industries, and vehicles with
        the subdivision *Fires and fire*
        prevention, e.g. **Nuclear pow-**
        er plants—Fires and fire
        prevention [to be added as
        needed]
  BT **Accidents**
        Disasters
        Fire
  NT **Fire fighting**
        Fire prevention
        Forest fires
        Nuclear power plants—Fires
        and fire prevention

Fires and fire prevention
  USE types of institutions, buildings,
        industries, and vehicles with
        the subdivision *Fires and fire*
        prevention, e.g. **Nuclear pow-**
        er plants—Fires and fire
        prevention [to be added as
        needed]

Fireworks **662**
  BT **Amusements**

Firms
  USE **Business enterprises**

First aid **362.18; 616.02**
  UF Emergencies
        Injuries
        Wounded, First aid to
  BT **Health self-care**
        Home accidents
        Medicine
        Nursing
        Rescue work
        Sick
  NT **Artificial respiration**
        Bandages
        CPR (First aid)
  RT **Accidents**
        Lifesaving

First editions   094
  UF   Bibliography—First editions
       Books—First editions
  SA   types of publications, types of
       literature, and names of au-
       thors and composers with the
       subdivision *First editions*, e.g.
       **English literature—First edi-
       tions** [to be added as needed]
  BT   **Editions**
First generation children
  USE   **Children of immigrants**
First ladies—United States
  USE   **Presidents' spouses—United
        States**
First names
  USE   **Personal names**
First nations
  USE   **Native Americans—Canada**
First World War
  USE   **World War, 1914-1918**
Firstborn child
  USE   **Birth order**
Fiscal policy (May subdiv. geog.)   336.3
  UF   Government policy
  BT   **Economic policy**
       Public finance
  RT   **Monetary policy**
Fiscal policy—United States   336.73
  UF   United States—Fiscal policy
Fish
  USE   **Fish as food**
        Fishes
Fish as food   641.3
  UF   Fish
  BT   **Cooking**
       Fishes
       Food
  RT   **Cooking—Fish**
       Seafood
Fish culture (May subdiv. geog.)   639.3
  Use for materials on the cultivation of fish
  in captivity. Materials on fishing as an indus-
  try are entered under **Commercial fishing**.
  UF   Fish farming
       Fish hatcheries
  BT   **Aquaculture**
  RT   **Aquariums**
Fish farming
  USE   **Fish culture**
Fish hatcheries
  USE   **Fish culture**

Fisheries
  USE   **Commercial fishing**
Fishes (May subdiv. geog.)   597
  UF   Fish
       Ichthyology
  SA   types of fishes, e.g. **Salmon** [to
       be added as needed]
  BT   **Aquatic animals**
  NT   **Fish as food**
       Goldfish
       Salmon
       Tropical fish
  RT   **Aquariums**
Fishes—Ecology (May subdiv. geog.)
       597
  BT   **Ecology**
Fishes—Geographical distribution
       597.09
  BT   **Biogeography**
Fishes—Photography
  USE   **Photography of fishes**
Fishes—United States   597.0973
Fishing (May subdiv. geog.)   799.1
  Use for materials on fishing as a sport. Ma-
  terials on fishing as an industry are entered
  under **Commercial fishing**.
  UF   Angling
  SA   types of fishing [to be added as
       needed]
  BT   **Sports**
  NT   **Fly casting**
       Saltwater fishing
       Spear fishing
       Trout fishing
Fishing, Commercial
  USE   **Commercial fishing**
Fishing—Equipment and supplies   799.1
  UF   Fishing tackle
  NT   **Artificial flies**
Fishing flies
  USE   **Artificial flies**
Fishing industry
  USE   **Commercial fishing**
Fishing tackle
  USE   **Fishing—Equipment and sup-
        plies**
Fishing—United States   799.10973
Fitness
  USE   **Physical fitness**
Five-day work week
  USE   **Hours of labor**

Fixed ideas
USE **Obsessive-compulsive disorder**
Fixing
USE **Repairing**
Flags (May subdiv. geog.)   **929.9**
UF Banners
Ensigns
BT **Heraldry**
RT **National emblems**
Signals and signaling
Flags—United States   929.9
UF American flag
United States—Flags
Flannel boards   371.33
BT **Teaching—Aids and devices**
Flats
USE **Apartments**
Flatware, Silver
USE **Silverware**
Flavoring essences   664
BT **Cooking**
Essences and essential oils
Food
Flax   633.5; 677
BT **Fibers**
Yarn
RT **Linen**
Flea markets (May subdiv. geog.)   **658.8**
BT **Markets**
Secondhand trade
Flexible hours of labor   331.25
UF Alternative work schedules
Flexible work hours
Flextime
Four-day week
Hours of labor, Flexible
BT **Hours of labor**
Flexible work hours
USE **Flexible hours of labor**
Flextime
USE **Flexible hours of labor**
Flies   595.77
UF Fly
House flies
SA types of flies [to be added as needed]
BT **Household pests**
Insects
Pests
NT **Fruit flies**

Flies, Artificial
USE **Artificial flies**
Flight   629.13
UF Flying
SA types of animals with the subdivision *Flight*, e.g. **Birds—Flight** [to be added as needed]
BT **Locomotion**
NT **Animal flight**
RT **Aeronautics**
Flight attendants   387.7
UF Airline hostesses
Airline stewardesses
Airline stewards
Stewardesses, Airline
Stewards, Airline
BT **Airlines**
Flight to the moon
USE **Space flight to the moon**
Flight training
USE **Aeronautics—Study and teaching**
Airplanes—Piloting
Flights around the world
USE **Aeronautics—Flights**
Flint implements
USE **Stone implements**
Floating hospitals
USE **Hospital ships**
Floats (Parades)
USE **Parades**
Flood control (May subdiv. geog.)   **627**
UF Flood prevention
BT **Hydraulic engineering**
RT **Forest influences**
Flood prevention
USE **Flood control**
Floods (May subdiv. geog.)   **363.34; 551.48; 904**
May also be subdivided by names of rivers or river valleys, e.g. **Floods—Mississippi River**.
BT **Meteorology**
Natural disasters
Rain
Water
RT **Rivers**
Floods and forests
USE **Forest influences**
Floods—Mississippi River   363.34
Floors   690; 721

Floors—*Continued*
- BT **Architecture—Details**
  Buildings

Flora
- USE **Botany**
  Plants

Floral decoration
- USE **Flower arrangement**

Floriculture
- USE **Flower gardening**

Florists' designs
- USE **Flower arrangement**

Flour   641.3; 664
- RT **Grain**

Flour mills   664
- UF Grist mills
  Milling (Flour)
- BT **Mills**

Flow charts
- USE **Graphic methods**
  System analysis

Flowcharting
- USE **Graphic methods**
  System analysis

Flower arrangement   745.92

Use for materials on the artistic arrangement of flowers, including decoration of houses, churches, etc., with flowers.
- UF Designs, Floral
  Floral decoration
  Florists' designs
  Flowers—Arrangement
- BT **Decoration and ornament**
  Flowers
  Table setting and decoration

Flower drying
- USE **Flowers—Drying**

Flower gardening (May subdiv. geog.)
  635.9

Use for practical materials on the cultivation of flowering plants for either commercial or private purposes.
- UF Floriculture
- SA types of flowers, e.g. **Roses** [to be added as needed]
- BT **Gardening**
  Horticulture
- NT **Annuals (Plants)**
  Bulbs
  Greenhouses
  House plants
  Ornamental plants
  Perennials

- RT **Container gardening**
  Flowers
  Window gardening

Flower language
- USE **Language of flowers**

Flower painting and illustration
- USE **Botanical illustration**
  Flowers in art

Flower prints
- USE **Flowers in art**

Flower shows   635.9074
- UF Flowers—Exhibitions
- BT **Exhibitions**

Flowers (May subdiv. geog.)   **575.6;**
  582.13

Use for general materials on flowers. Materials limited to the cultivation of flowers are entered under **Flower gardening**.
- SA types of flowers, e.g. **Roses** [to be added as needed]
- BT **Plants**
- NT **Annuals (Plants)**
  Flower arrangement
  Perennials
  Roses
  State flowers
  Wild flowers
- RT **Flower gardening**

Flowers—Arrangement
- USE **Flower arrangement**

Flowers, Artificial
- USE **Artificial flowers**

Flowers, Drying
- USE **Flowers—Drying**

Flowers—Drying   745.92
- UF Dried flowers
  Flower drying
  Flowers, Drying
- BT **Plants—Collection and preservation**

Flowers—Exhibitions
- USE **Flower shows**

Flowers in art   758
- UF Flower painting and illustration
  Flower prints
- BT **Art—Themes**

Flowers—United States   582.130973

Flu
- USE **Influenza**

Fluid mechanics   532; 620.1

Use for materials on the branch of mechanics dealing with the properties of liquids or gases, either at rest or in motion.

Fluid mechanics—*Continued*
UF Hydromechanics
BT **Mechanics**
NT **Gases**
Hydraulic engineering
Hydraulics
Hydrodynamics
Hydrostatics
Liquids
Fluorescent lighting   621.32
UF Electric lighting, Fluorescent
BT **Electric lighting**
Fluoridation of water
USE **Water fluoridation**
Flute
USE **Flutes**
Flutes   788.3
UF Flute
BT **Wind instruments**
Fly
USE **Flies**
Fly casting   799.12
UF Fly fishing
BT **Fishing**
NT **Artificial flies**
Fly fishing
USE **Fly casting**
Flying
USE **Flight**
Flying saucers
USE **Unidentified flying objects**
FM radio
USE **Radio frequency modulation**
Foals
USE **Horses**
Ponies
Fodder
USE **Feeds**
Fog   551.57
BT **Atmosphere**
Meteorology
Fog signals
USE **Signals and signaling**
Folding of napkins
USE **Napkin folding**
Foliage
USE **Leaves**
Folk art   745

Use for materials on objects of fine or decorative art produced in a peasant, popular, or naive style, often in cultural isolation and by unschooled artists or artisans.

UF Peasant art
SA folk art of particular countries or ethnic groups, e.g. **American folk art** [to be added as needed]
BT **Art**
Art and society
NT **American folk art**
RT **Arts and crafts movement**
Decorative arts
Handicraft
Folk art, American
USE **American folk art**
Folk beliefs
USE **Folklore**
Superstition
Folk biology
USE **Ethnobiology**
Folk dances
USE **Folk dancing**
Folk dancing (May subdiv. geog.)   **793.3**
UF Folk dances
National dances
SA dance of particular ethnic groups, e.g. **Native American dance** [to be added as needed]
BT **Dance**
NT **Native American dance**
Square dancing
Folk dancing—United States   793.3
UF American folk dancing
Folk drama   808.2; 808.82

Use for collections or materials about folk drama, not for individual works.

UF Folk plays
SA folk drama of particular countries or ethnic groups, e.g. **American folk drama** [to be added as needed]
BT **Drama**
Folk drama
NT **American folk drama**
Folk drama
Puppets and puppet plays
Folk literature   398.2
SA types of folk literature, e.g. **Jewish folk literature** [to be added as needed]
BT **Folklore**
Literature
NT **Jewish folk literature**

Folk lore
USE **Folklore**
Folk medicine
USE **Traditional medicine**
Folk music (May subdiv. geog.)   **781.62**
BT **Music**
Folk music—United States   781.6200973
UF American folk music
NT **Blues music**
Country music
Folk plays
USE **Folk drama**
Folk psychology
USE **Ethnopsychology**
Folk songs (May subdiv. geog.)
782.42162
Use for materials about folk songs and collections of folk songs that include both words and music. Materials about ballads and collections of ballads without music are entered under **Ballads**.
SA folk songs of particular ethnic
groups, e.g. **Creole folk
songs** [to be added as needed]
BT **Folklore**
Songs
Vocal music
NT **Carols**
Creole folk songs
RT **Ballads**
National songs
Folk songs, Creole
USE **Creole folk songs**
Folk songs—France   782.4216200944
UF Folk songs, French
France—Folk songs
French folk songs
Folk songs, French
USE **Folk songs—France**
Folk songs—Ohio   782.42162009771
Folk songs—United States
782.4216200973
UF American folk songs
BT **American songs**
NT **Spirituals (Songs)**
Folk tales
USE **Folklore**
Legends
Folk zoology
USE **Ethnozoology**

Folklore (May subdiv. geog.)   **398**
Use for general materials on folklore. May also be used for individual works, collections, or materials about stories based on spoken rather than written traditions.
UF Folk beliefs
Folk lore
Folk tales
Tales
Traditions
SA topics as themes in folklore with
the subdivision Folklore, e.g.
Plants—Folklore; names of
ethnic or occupational groups
with the subdivision *Folklore*,
e.g. **Inuit—Folklore**; types of
folkloric creatures, e.g. **Elves**;
and names of individual legendary characters, e.g. **Bunyan, Paul (Legendary character)** [to be added as needed]
BT **Ethnology**
Fiction
Manners and customs
NT **African Americans—Folklore**
Animals—Folklore
Blacks—Folklore
Chapbooks
Charms
Dragons
Elves
Fairies
Folk literature
Folk songs
Ghosts
Giants
Gnomes
Goblins
Grail
Inuit—Folklore
Jews—Folklore
Monsters
Native Americans—Folklore
Nursery rhymes
Plants—Folklore
Proverbs
Roland (Legendary character)
Sagas
Superstition
Tall tales
Tongue twisters

Folklore—*Continued*
        Urban folklore
        Vampires
        Weather—Folklore
        Witchcraft
  RT Fables
        Fairy tales
        Legends
        Material culture
        Mythology
        Storytelling
Folklore, Medical
  USE Traditional medicine
Folklore—United States   398.0973
  NT Bunyan, Paul (Legendary character)
Folkways
  USE Manners and customs
Food   641; 641.3; 664
  SA types of foods, names of specific foods, and subjects with the subdivision *Food* [to be added as needed]
  BT Home economics
  NT Animals—Food
        Artificial foods
        Beverages
        Bread
        Chocolate
        Convenience foods
        Dietetic foods
        Dining
        Dried foods
        Edible plants
        Eggs
        Farm produce
        Fish as food
        Flavoring essences
        Food of animal origin
        Frozen foods
        Fruit
        Honey
        Meat
        Milk
        Minerals in human nutrition
        Natural foods
        Nuts
        Pollen as food
        Prepared cereals
        School children—Food
        Seafood
        Snack foods

        Spices
        Sugar
        Vegetables
        Vitamins
  RT Cooking
        Diet
        Food industry
        Gastronomy
        Grocery trade
        Nutrition
Food additives   641.3; 664
  UF Additives, Food
  BT Food—Analysis
        Food—Preservation
  RT Dietary supplements
Food adulteration and inspection (May subdiv. geog.)   363.19
  UF Adulteration of food
        Analysis of food
        Food inspection
        Inspection of food
        Pure food
  BT Consumer protection
        Public health
  NT Food contamination
        Meat inspection
        Milk supply
  RT Food—Law and legislation
Food allergies
  USE Food allergy
Food allergy   616.97
  UF Allergies, Food
        Allergy, Food
        Food allergies
  SA types of food allergies [to be added as needed]
  BT Allergy
Food—Analysis   664
    Use for materials on methods of analyzing foods. Materials presenting the results of the analysis of foods are entered under **Food—Composition**.
  UF Analysis of food
        Chemistry of food
        Food chemistry
  SA types of foods with the subdivision *Analysis*, e.g. **Milk—Analysis** [to be added as needed]
  BT Analytical chemistry
        Industrial chemistry
  NT Food additives

Food—Analysis—*Continued*
    RT   **Food—Composition**
Food assistance programs
    USE **Food relief**
Food—Bacteriology
    USE **Food—Microbiology**
Food banks (May subdiv. geog.)   **363.8**
    BT   **Food relief**
Food buying
    USE **Grocery shopping**
Food—Caloric content   **613.2**
    UF   Caloric content of foods
         Calories (Food)
         Food calories
    BT   **Food—Composition**
Food calories
    USE **Food—Caloric content**
Food, Canned
    USE **Canning and preserving**
Food chains (Ecology)   **577**
    BT   **Animals—Food**
         Ecology
Food chemistry
    USE **Food—Analysis**
         Food—Composition
Food—Cholesterol content   **613.2**
    UF   Cholesterol content of food
    BT   **Food—Composition**
Food—Composition   **641; 664**
    Use for materials presenting the results of the analysis of foods. Materials on methods of analyzing foods are entered under **Food—Analysis**.
    UF   Chemistry of food
         Food chemistry
    SA   food and types of food with subdivisions to indicate the particular content being analyzed, e.g. **Food—Cholesterol content** [to be added as needed]
    NT   **Food—Caloric content**
         Food—Cholesterol content
         Food—Fiber content
         Food—Sodium content
    RT   **Food—Analysis**
Food contamination (May subdiv. geog.)   **363.19**
    UF   Contaminated food
    BT   **Food adulteration and inspection**

Food contamination—Press coverage (May subdiv. geog.)   **070.4**
Food control
    USE **Food supply**
Food, Cost of
    USE **Cost and standard of living**
Food coupons
    USE **Food stamps**
Food customs
    USE **Eating customs**
Food—Fiber content   **613.2**
    UF   Dietary fiber
         Fiber content of food
         Roughage
    BT   **Food—Composition**
Food for invalids
    USE **Cooking for the sick**
Food for school children
    USE **School children—Food**
Food, Freeze-dried
    USE **Freeze-dried foods**
Food habits
    USE **Eating customs**
Food industry (May subdiv. geog.)   **338.1**
    Use for materials on the processing and marketing of food.
    UF   Food preparation
         Food preparation industry
         Food processing
         Food processing industry
         Food trade
    SA   type of food industries, e.g. **Beverage industry** [to be added as needed]
    BT   **Agricultural industry**
    NT   **Beverage industry**
         Food service
         Grocery trade
         Meat industry
    RT   **Food**
Food inspection
    USE **Food adulteration and inspection**
Food—Labeling   **363.19; 641**
    UF   Food labels
Food labels
    USE **Food—Labeling**
Food—Law and legislation (May subdiv. geog.)   **344**
    UF   Food laws

Food—Law and legislation—*Continued*
- BT **Law**
  Legislation
- RT **Food adulteration and inspection**

Food laws
- USE **Food—Law and legislation**

Food—Microbiology   664
- UF Food—Bacteriology
- BT **Microbiology**

Food of animal origin   641.3

Use for materials on human food of animal origin. Materials on the food and food habits of animals are entered under **Animals—Food**.
- UF Animal food
  Animals as food
  Animals, Edible
- BT **Food**

Food—Packaging   664
- UF Groceries—Packaging
- BT **Packaging**

Food plants
- USE **Edible plants**

Food poisoning   615.9
- BT **Poisons and poisoning**

Food preparation
- USE **Cooking**
  Food industry

Food preparation industry
- USE **Food industry**

Food—Preservation   641.4; 664
- UF Preservation of food
- SA types of foods with the subdivision *Preservation* [to be added as needed]
- NT **Canning and preserving**
  Cold storage
  Food additives
  Fruit—Preservation
- RT **Dried foods**
  Frozen foods

Food processing
- USE **Food industry**

Food processing industry
- USE **Food industry**

Food—Purchasing
- USE **Grocery shopping**

Food relief (May subdiv. geog.)   **363.8**
- UF Food assistance programs
- SA types of food relief, e.g. **Meals on wheels programs**; and names of wars with the sub-

division *Civilian relief* or *Food supply* [to be added as needed]
- BT **Charities**
  Disaster relief
  Public welfare
  Unemployed
- NT **Food banks**
  Food stamps
  Meals on wheels programs
  World War, 1939-1945—Civilian relief
  World War, 1939-1945—Food supply

Food service   642; 647.95

Use for materials on the preparation, delivery, and serving of ready-to-eat foods in large quantities outside of the home. Materials solely on the preparation of food in large quantities are entered under **Quantity cooking**.
- UF Cooking for institutions
  Mass feeding
  Volume feeding
- BT **Food industry**
  Service industries
- NT **Bartending**
  Catering
  Restaurants
  Waiters and waitresses
- RT **Quantity cooking**

Food—Sodium content   613.2
- UF Sodium content of food
- BT **Food—Composition**

Food stamp program
- USE **Food stamps**

Food stamps (May subdiv. geog.)   **363.8**
- UF Food coupons
  Food stamp program
- BT **Food relief**

Food supplements
- USE **Dietary supplements**

Food supply (May subdiv. geog.)   **363.8**

Use for economic materials on the availability of food in general and on the conservation of food in wartime.
- UF Food control
- SA names of wars with the subdivision *Food supply*, e.g. **World War, 1939-1945—Food supply** [to be added as needed]
- NT **Famines**
- RT **Agriculture**

Food trade
USE **Food industry**
Fools and jesters **791.092; 920**
UF Court fools
Jesters
BT **Comedians**
Courts and courtiers
Entertainers
Foot **611; 612**
UF Feet
BT **Anatomy**
Foot—Care **617.5**
UF Foot—Care and hygiene
BT **Podiatry**
Foot—Care and hygiene
USE **Foot—Care**
Foot injuries
USE **Foot—Wounds and injuries**
Foot—Paralysis **616.8**
BT **Paralysis**
Foot—Wounds and injuries **617.5**
UF Foot injuries
RT **Podiatry**
Football (May subdiv. geog.) **796.332**
BT **Ball games**
Sports
NT **Soccer**
Super Bowl (Game)
Football—Coaching **796.33207**
BT **Coaching (Athletics)**
Footwear
USE **Shoes**
Forage plants (May subdiv. geog.)
633.2
SA names of forage plants [to be
added as needed]
BT **Economic botany**
Feeds
Plants
NT **Alfalfa**
Corn
Hay
Silage and silos
Soybean
RT **Grasses**
Force and energy **531**
UF Conservation of energy
Energy
BT **Power (Mechanics)**
RT **Dynamics**
Mechanics

Motion
Quantum theory
Forced indoctrination
USE **Brainwashing**
Forced labor (May subdiv. geog.)
331.11
UF Compulsory labor
Conscript labor
BT **Crimes against humanity**
Labor
NT **Convict labor**
Peonage
RT **Slavery**
Forced migration (May subdiv. geog.)
325
BT **Internal migration**
Forced removal of Indians
USE **Native Americans—Relocation**
Forced repatriation
USE names of wars with the subdivi-
sion *Forced repatriation,* e.g.
World War, 1939-1945—
Forced repatriation [to be
added as needed]
Ford automobile **629.222**
BT **Automobiles**
Forecasting **003**
UF Forecasts
Futurology
Predictions
SA types of forecasting, e.g. **Weath-**
er forecasting; and subjects
and names of countries, cities,
etc., with the subdivision
Forecasting, e.g. **Energy con-**
sumption—Forecasting [to be
added as needed]
NT **Business forecasting**
Economic forecasting
Weather forecasting
Forecasts
USE **Forecasting**
Foreign affairs
USE **International relations**
Foreign aid (May subdiv. geog.) **338.91**
Use for general materials on international
economic aid given in the form of gifts, loans,
relief grants, etc. Materials limited to foreign
aid in the form of technical expertise are en-
tered under **Technical assistance.**
UF Aid to developing areas
Assistance to developing areas
Economic aid

Foreign aid—*Continued*
    Economic assistance
    Foreign aid program
    Foreign assistance
  SA foreign aid from particular countries, e.g. **American foreign aid** [to be added as needed]
  BT **Economic policy**
      International cooperation
      International economic relations
  NT **American foreign aid**
      Technical assistance
      World War, 1939-1945—Civilian relief
  RT **Reconstruction (1914-1939)**
      Reconstruction (1939-1951)

Foreign aid program
  USE **Foreign aid**
      Military assistance
      Technical assistance

Foreign area studies
  USE **Area studies**

Foreign assistance
  USE **Foreign aid**

Foreign automobiles (May subdiv. geog.)
    629.222
  UF Automobiles, Foreign
      Foreign cars
  SA names of specific makes and models [to be added as needed]
  BT **Automobiles**

Foreign cars
  USE **Foreign automobiles**

Foreign commerce
  USE **International trade**

Foreign countries
  USE ethnic and national groups, individual languages and literatures, military services, and types of publications qualified by language or nationality with the subdivision *Foreign countries,* e.g. **Americans—Foreign countries** [to be added as needed]

Foreign economic relations
  USE **International economic relations**

and names of countries with the subdivision *Foreign economic relations,* e.g. **United States—Foreign economic relations** [to be added as needed]

Foreign economic relations—United States
  USE **United States—Foreign economic relations**

Foreign exchange (May subdiv. geog.)
    332.4
  UF Exchange rates
      International exchange
  BT **Banks and banking**
      Exchange
      Finance
      Money

Foreign influences
  USE subjects, ethnic groups, and literatures with the subdivision *Foreign influences,* e.g. **United States—Civilization—Foreign influences** [to be added as needed]

Foreign investments (May subdiv. geog.)
    332.6
  UF International investment
      Investments, Foreign
  BT **Investments**
      Multinational corporations

Foreign language dictionaries
  USE **English language—Dictionaries—French**
      French language—Dictionaries—English

Foreign language laboratories
  USE **Language laboratories**

Foreign language phrases
  USE **English language—Foreign words and phrases**
      Modern languages—Conversation and phrase books

Foreign military sales
  USE **Arms transfers**

Foreign missions, Christian
  USE **Christian missions**

Foreign opinion
  USE names of countries with the subdivision *Foreign opinion,* which may be further subdivided by the country holding

Foreign opinion—*Continued*

the opinion, e.g. **United States—Foreign opinion; United States—Foreign opinion—France;** etc. [to be added as needed]

Foreign policy

USE **International relations**

Foreign population

USE **Aliens**

Immigrants

Immigration and emigration

Minorities

Population

and names of countries with the subdivision *Population,* e.g. **United States—Population;** or with the subdivision *Immigration and emigration,* e.g. **United States—Immigration and emigration** [to be added as needed]

Foreign public opinion

USE names of countries with the subdivision *Foreign opinion,* which may be further subdivided by the country holding the opinion, e.g. **United States—Foreign opinion; United States—Foreign opinion—France;** etc. [to be added as needed]

Foreign relations

USE **International relations**

and names of countries with the subdivision *Foreign relations,* e.g. **United States—Foreign relations** [to be added as needed]

Foreign service

USE **Diplomatic and consular service**

Foreign students (May subdiv. geog.)

370.116

UF College students, Foreign

Students, Foreign

BT **Students**

Foreign study (May subdiv. geog.)

370.116

UF Overseas study

Study abroad

Study, Foreign

Study overseas

BT **Education**

Foreign trade

USE **International trade**

Foreign words and phrases

USE names of languages with the subdivision *Foreign words and phrases,* e.g. **English language—Foreign words and phrases** [to be added as needed]

Foreigners

USE **Aliens**

Immigrants

Foremen

USE **Supervisors**

Forensic medicine

USE **Medical jurisprudence**

Forensic science

USE **Forensic sciences**

Forensic sciences   363.25

Use for materials on science as applied in courts of law or in criminal investigations.

UF Criminalistics

Forensic science

BT **Science**

NT **Medical jurisprudence**

RT **Criminal investigation**

Foreordination

USE **Predestination**

Forest animals (May subdiv. geog.)

578.73

UF Forest fauna

BT **Animals**

NT **Jungle animals**

Forest conservation (May subdiv. geog.)

333.75

UF Conservation of forests

Forest preservation

Preservation of forests

BT **Conservation of natural resources**

RT **Forest reserves**

Forests and forestry

Forest depletion

USE **Deforestation**

Forest fauna

USE **Forest animals**

Forest fires   634.9

BT **Fires**

Forest influences   577.3

311

Forest influences—*Continued*

UF   Climate and forests
      Floods and forests
      Forests and climate
      Forests and floods
      Forests and rainfall
      Forests and water supply
      Rainfall and forests

BT   **Climate**
      Water supply

RT   **Flood control**
      Forests and forestry
      Plant ecology
      Rain

Forest plants (May subdiv. geog.)   **581.7**

BT   **Forests and forestry**
      Plant ecology
      Plants

Forest preservation
  USE   **Forest conservation**

Forest products (May subdiv. geog.)
      634.9; 674

BT   **Commercial products**
      Economic botany
      Raw materials

NT   **Gums and resins**
      Lumber and lumbering
      Rubber
      Wood

Forest reserves (May subdiv. geog.)
      333.75; 719

UF   National forests

BT   **Public lands**

NT   **Wilderness areas**

RT   **Forest conservation**
      Forests and forestry
      National parks and reserves

Forestry
  USE   **Forests and forestry**

Forests and climate
  USE   **Forest influences**

Forests and floods
  USE   **Forest influences**

Forests and forestry (May subdiv. geog.)
      577.3; 578.73; 634.9

UF   Arboriculture
      Forestry
      Timber
      Woods

BT   **Agriculture**
      Natural resources

NT   **Christmas tree growing**
      Deforestation
      Forest plants
      Jungles
      Logging
      Lumber and lumbering
      Pruning
      Rain forests
      Reforestation
      Tree planting

RT   **Forest conservation**
      Forest influences
      Forest reserves
      Trees
      Wood

Forests and forestry—United States
      577.30973; 634.90973

Forests and rainfall
  USE   **Forest influences**

Forests and water supply
  USE   **Forest influences**

Forgeries
  USE   names of individual persons and
        types of art objects, docu-
        ments, etc., with the subdivi-
        sion *Forgeries,* e.g. **Art—**
        Forgeries [to be added as
        needed]

Forgery   **332; 364.16**

SA   names of individual persons and
        types of art objects, docu-
        ments, etc., with the subdivi-
        sion *Forgeries*, e.g. **Art—**
        Forgeries [to be added as
        needed]

BT   **Crime**
      Fraud
      Impostors and imposture

NT   **Art—Forgeries**
      Counterfeits and counterfeiting
      Literary forgeries
      Piltdown forgery

Forgery of works of art
  USE   **Art—Forgeries**

Forgetfulness   **153.1**

BT   **Memory**
      Personality

Forging   **671.3; 682**

UF   Drop forging

BT   **Manufacturing processes**
      Metalwork

Forging—*Continued*
  NT **Welding**
  RT **Blacksmithing**
      Ironwork
Forgiveness   179
  BT **Virtue**
  RT **Amnesty**
      Clemency
      Pardon
Forgiveness of sin   234
  UF Sin, Forgiveness of
  RT **Penance**
      Sin
Form in biology
  USE **Morphology**
Formal gardens
  USE **Gardens**
Former nuns
  USE **Ex-nuns**
Former priests
  USE **Ex-priests**
Former Soviet republics   947.086
    Use for general materials on several or all
  of the countries that emerged from the disso-
  lution of the Soviet Union in 1991. Materials
  specifically on the federation of independent
  former Soviet republics that was established in
  1991 and does not include the Baltic states
  are entered under **Commonwealth of Inde-
  pendent States**.
  UF Ex-Soviet republics
      Ex-Soviet states
      Former Soviet states
  RT **Soviet Union**
Former Soviet states
  USE **Former Soviet republics**
Formosa
  USE **Taiwan**
Formula translation (Computer language)
  USE **FORTRAN (Computer lan-
        guage)**
Fortification (May subdiv. geog.)   **623**
  UF Forts
  SA names of countries with the sub-
      division *Defenses* [to be add-
      ed as needed]
  BT **Military art and science**
  RT **Military engineering**
**FORTRAN (Computer language)
  005.13**
  UF Formula translation (Computer
      language)
      FORTRAN (Computer program
      language)

  BT **Programming languages**
FORTRAN (Computer program language)
  USE **FORTRAN (Computer lan-
        guage)**
Forts
  USE **Fortification**
Fortune
  USE **Fate and fatalism**
        Probabilities
        Success
Fortune telling   133.3
  BT **Amusements**
      Divination
  NT **Palmistry**
      Tarot
Fortunes
  USE **Income**
        Wealth
Forums (Discussions)
  USE **Discussion groups**
Fossil botany
  USE **Fossil plants**
Fossil hominids (May subdiv. geog.)
    569.9
  UF Hominids, Fossil
      Human fossils
      Human paleontology
      Man, Prehistoric
      Prehistoric man
      Prehistory
  BT **Archeology**
      Fossils
  NT **Piltdown forgery**
  RT **Human origins**
Fossil mammals (May subdiv. geog.)
    569
  UF Mammals, Fossil
  SA types of extinct mammals [to be
      added as needed]
  BT **Fossils**
      Mammals
  NT **Mastodon**
Fossil plants (May subdiv. geog.)   **561**
  UF Extinct plants
      Fossil botany
      Paleobotany
      Plants, Extinct
      Plants, Fossil
  BT **Fossils**
      Plants

Fossil reptiles (May subdiv. geog.)
567.9
> UF   Reptiles, Fossil
> SA   types of fossil reptiles, e.g. **Dinosaurs** [to be added as needed]
> BT   **Fossils**
>   **Reptiles**
> NT   **Dinosaurs**

Fossils (May subdiv. geog.)   **560**
> BT   **Biology**
>   **Natural history**
>   **Science**
>   **Stratigraphic geology**
> NT   **Fossil hominids**
>   **Fossil mammals**
>   **Fossil plants**
>   **Fossil reptiles**
>   **Prehistoric animals**
> RT   **Extinct animals**
>   **Paleontology**

Foster children   **306.874**
> BT   **Children**
> RT   **Foster home care**

Foster grandparents   **362.73**
> BT   **Grandparents**
>   **Volunteer work**

Foster home care   **362.73**
> UF   Child placing
>   Children—Placing out
> BT   **Child welfare**
> RT   **Adoption**
>   **Children—Institutional care**
>   **Foster children**
>   **Group homes**

Foundations   **624.1; 721**
> BT   **Architecture—Details**
>   **Buildings**
>   **Structural engineering**
> NT   **Basements**
>   **Concrete**
> RT   **Soil mechanics**

Foundations (Endowments)
> USE   **Endowments**

Founding   **671.2**
> Use for materials on the melting and casting of metals.
> UF   Casting
>   Foundry practice
>   Molding (Metal)
>   Moulding (Metal)

> BT   **Manufacturing processes**
>   **Metalwork**
> NT   **Type and type-founding**
> RT   **Patternmaking**

Founding Fathers of the United States
973.4
> BT   **Statesmen—United States**

Foundlings
> USE   **Orphans**

Foundry practice
> USE   **Founding**

Four-day week
> USE   **Flexible hours of labor**

Four-H clubs
> USE   **4-H clubs**

Fourteenth century
> USE   **World history—14th century**

Fourth dimension   **530.11**
> UF   Dimension, Fourth
>   Hyperspace
> BT   **Mathematics**
> NT   **Space and time**
>   **Time travel**

Fourth of July   **394.2634**
> UF   4th of July
>   Independence Day (United States)
>   July Fourth
> BT   **Holidays**
>   **United States—History—1775-1783, Revolution**

Fractal geometry
> USE   **Fractals**

Fractals   **514**
> Use for materials on shapes or mathematical sets that have fractional, i.e. irregular, dimensions as opposed to the regular dimensions of Euclidean geometry.
> UF   Fractal geometry
>   Sets, Fractal
>   Sets of fractional dimension
> BT   **Geometry**
>   **Mathematical models**
>   **Set theory**
>   **Topology**

Fractions   **513.2**
> BT   **Arithmetic**
>   **Mathematics**

Fractured fairy tales   **398.2; 808.83**
> UF   Fairy tales—Parodies, imitations, etc.

Fractured fairy tales—*Continued*
   BT   **Fairy tales**
       Parodies
Fractures **617.1**
   BT   **Bones**
       Wounds and injuries
Fragrant gardens (May subdiv. geog.)
   635.9
   UF   Gardening for fragrance
       Scented gardens
   BT   **Gardens**
   RT   **Aromatic plants**
Framing of pictures
   USE **Picture frames and framing**
France **944**
      May be subdivided like **United States** except for *History*.
France—Blacks
   USE **Blacks—France**
France—Folk songs
   USE **Folk songs—France**
France—History **944**
France—History—0-1328 **944**
   NT   **Celts**
France—History—1328-1589, House of Valois **944**
   NT   **Hundred Years' War, 1339-1453**
       Saint Bartholomew's Day, Massacre of, 1572
France—History—1589-1789, Bourbons **944**
France—History—1789-1799, Revolution **944.04**
   UF   Directory, French, 1795-1799
       French Revolution
       Reign of Terror
       Revolution, French
       Terror, Reign of
   BT   **Revolutions**
France—History—1799-1815 **944.05**
   NT   **Napoleonic Wars, 1800-1815**
France—History—1815-1914 **944.06**
France—History—20th century **944.081**
France—History—1914-1940 **944.081**
France—History—1940-1945, German occupation **944.081**
   UF   German occupation of France, 1940-1945
France—History—1945- **944.082**
France—History—1945-1958 **944.082**
France—History—1958- **944.083**
   UF   France—History—1958-1969
       France—History—1969-
France—History—1958-1969
   USE **France—History—1958-**
France—History—1969-
   USE **France—History—1958-**
France—History—21st century **944.084**
Franchise
   USE **Citizenship**
       Elections
       Suffrage
Franchises (Retail trade) (May subdiv. geog.) **658.8**
   UF   Franchising
       Retail franchises
   BT   **Retail trade**
Franchising
   USE **Franchises (Retail trade)**
Franciscans **271**
   UF   Friars Minor
       Gray Friars
       Grey Friars
       Mendicant orders
       Minorites
       Saint Francis, Order of
       St. Francis, Order of
   BT   **Monasticism and religious orders**
Fraternities and sororities **371.8**
   UF   College fraternities
       College sororities
       Greek letter societies
       Sororities
   BT   **Colleges and universities**
       Students—Societies
   RT   **Secret societies**
Fraud (May subdiv. geog.) **364.16**
   UF   Deceit
       Ripoffs
   BT   **Commercial law**
       Crime
       Offenses against property
       White collar crimes
   NT   **Credit card fraud**
       Forgery
       Securities fraud
   RT   **Impostors and imposture**
       Swindlers and swindling
Fraud in science **501**
   UF   Scientific fraud
   BT   **Science**

Frauds, Literary
  USE **Literary forgeries**
Fraudulent advertising
  USE **Deceptive advertising**
Free agency
  USE **Free will and determinism**
Free coinage
  USE **Monetary policy**
Free computer software   005.3
  UF Free software
      Freeware
      Public domain software
  BT **Computer software**
      Free material
Free diving
  USE **Scuba diving**
      Skin diving
Free enterprise (May subdiv. geog.)
      330.12
  UF Free markets
      Laissez-faire
      Private enterprise
  BT **Economic policy**
  RT **Capitalism**
Free fall
  USE **Weightlessness**
Free love   176; 306.7
  BT **Sexual ethics**
Free markets
  USE **Free enterprise**
Free material
  UF Freebies
      Giveaways
  BT **Gifts**
  NT **Free computer software**
Free press
  USE **Freedom of the press**
Free press and fair trial
  USE **Freedom of the press and fair trial**
Free schools
  USE **Experimental schools**
Free software
  USE **Free computer software**
Free speech
  USE **Freedom of speech**
Free thought   211
  BT **Freedom of conscience**
  NT **Agnosticism**
      Skepticism

  RT **Deism**
      Rationalism
Free time (Leisure)
  USE **Leisure**
Free trade (May subdiv. geog.)   382
  UF Fair trade (Tariff)
      Free trade and protection
  BT **Commercial policy**
      International trade
  RT **Protectionism**
      Tariff
Free trade and protection
  USE **Free trade**
      Protectionism
Free universities (May subdiv. geog.)
      378
  UF Alternative universities
      Experimental universities
      Open universities
  BT **Colleges and universities**
Free verse   808.1; 808.81
    Use for collections or materials about free
    verse, not for individual works.
  UF Vers libre
  BT **Poetry**
Free will and determinism   123
  UF Choice, Freedom of
      Determinism and indeterminism
      Free agency
      Freedom of choice
      Freedom of the will
      Indeterminism
      Liberty of the will
      Will
  BT **Philosophy**
  RT **Fate and fatalism**
      Predestination
Freebies
  USE **Free material**
Freedom (May subdiv. geog.)   323.4
  UF Civil liberty
      Emancipation
      Liberty
      Personal freedom
  BT **Democracy**
      Political science
  NT **Anarchism and anarchists**
      Conformity
      Freedom of assembly
      Freedom of association
      Freedom of conscience
      Freedom of movement

Freedom—*Continued*
>Freedom of religion
>Freedom of speech
>Freedom of the press
>Intellectual freedom
>Slaves—Emancipation
>RT Civil rights
>>Equality

Freedom, Academic
>USE Academic freedom

Freedom marches for civil rights
>USE Civil rights demonstrations

Freedom of assembly (May subdiv. geog.)
>323.4
>UF Assembly, Right of
>>Right of assembly
>BT Civil rights
>>Freedom
>NT Public meetings
>>Riots
>RT Freedom of association
>>Freedom of speech

Freedom of association (May subdiv. geog.) 323.4
>UF Association, Freedom of
>>Right of association
>BT Civil rights
>>Freedom
>RT Freedom of assembly

Freedom of choice
>USE Free will and determinism

Freedom of choice movement
>USE Pro-choice movement

Freedom of conscience (May subdiv. geog.) 323.44
>UF Liberty of conscience
>BT Conscience
>>Freedom
>>Toleration
>NT Conscientious objectors
>>Dissent
>>Free thought
>>Public opinion
>RT Freedom of religion

Freedom of information (May subdiv. geog.) 323.44
>UF Information, Freedom of
>>Right to know
>BT Civil rights
>>Intellectual freedom
>NT Press—Government policy

>RT Censorship
>>Freedom of speech
>>Freedom of the press

Freedom of movement (May subdiv. geog.) 323.4
>UF Movement, Freedom of
>BT Civil rights
>>Freedom

Freedom of religion (May subdiv. geog.)
>201; 261.7; 323.44
>UF Freedom of worship
>>Religious freedom
>>Religious liberty
>BT Civil rights
>>Freedom
>>Toleration
>NT Dissent
>RT Freedom of conscience
>>Persecution

Freedom of speech (May subdiv. geog.)
>323.44
>UF Free speech
>>Liberty of speech
>>Speech, Freedom of
>BT Censorship
>>Civil rights
>>Freedom
>>Intellectual freedom
>RT Freedom of assembly
>>Freedom of information
>>Libel and slander

Freedom of teaching
>USE Academic freedom

Freedom of the press (May subdiv. geog.)
>323.44
>UF Free press
>>Liberty of the press
>>Press censorship
>BT Civil rights
>>Freedom
>>Intellectual freedom
>>Press
>NT Freedom of the press and fair trial
>RT Censorship
>>Freedom of information
>>Libel and slander

Freedom of the press and fair trial
>323.42; 323.44; 342
>UF Fair trial and free press
>>Free press and fair trial

Freedom of the press and fair trial—*Continued*

        Prejudicial publicity

        Trial by publicity

  BT **Fair trial**

      Freedom of the press

      Press

Freedom of the will

  USE **Free will and determinism**

Freedom of worship

  USE **Freedom of religion**

Freelancers

  USE **Self-employed**

Freemasons 366

  UF Masonic orders

      Masons (Secret order)

  BT **Secret societies**

Freeware

  USE **Free computer software**

Freeways

  USE **Express highways**

Freeze-dried foods 641.4; 664

  UF Food, Freeze-dried

  BT **Dried foods**

Freezing

  USE **Cryobiology**

      Frost

      Ice

      Refrigeration

Freezing of human bodies

  USE **Cryonics**

Freight 388

  UF Freight and freightage

  BT **Maritime law**

      Materials handling

      Railroads

      Transportation

  NT **Commercial aeronautics**

      Trucking

  RT **Railroads—Rates**

Freight and freightage

  USE **Freight**

French and Indian War

  USE **United States—History—1755-1763, French and Indian War**

French Canadian literature

  USE **Canadian literature (French)**

French Canadian poetry

  USE **Canadian poetry (French)**

French Canadians (May subdiv. geog.)
  305.811; 971

  BT **Canadians**

French cookery

  USE **French cooking**

French cooking 641.5944

  UF Cookery, French

      French cookery

  BT **Cooking**

French Equatorial Africa

  USE **French-speaking Equatorial Africa**

French folk songs

  USE **Folk songs—France**

French language 440

    May be subdivided like **English language**.

  BT **Language and languages**

      Romance languages

French language—Conversation and phrase books 448

  UF French language—Conversations and phrases

French language—Conversations and phrases

  USE **French language—Conversation and phrase books**

French language—Dictionaries—English 443

    Use for French-English dictionaries. English-French dictionaries are entered under **English language—Dictionaries—French**. Combined French-English and English-French dictionaries are entered under both headings.

  UF Foreign language dictionaries

  BT **Encyclopedias and dictionaries**

  RT **English language—Dictionaries—French**

French language—Reading materials 448.6

French literature 840

    May use same subdivisions and names of literary forms as for **English literature**.

  BT **Literature**

      Romance literature

  NT **French poetry**

French literature—Black authors 840.8; 840.9

    Use for collections or materials about French literature by several Black authors, not for individual works.

  UF Black literature (French)

French literature—Canada

  USE **Canadian literature (French)**

French poetry 841

  BT **French literature**

      Poetry

French poetry—*Continued*
  NT **Troubadours**
French poetry—Black authors   841
  Use for collections or materials about French poetry by several Black authors, not for individual works.
  UF   Black poetry (French)
French Revolution
  USE   **France—History—1789-1799, Revolution**
French-speaking Equatorial Africa   967
  Use for materials dealing collectively with the region of Africa that includes Central African Republic, Chad, Congo (Republic), and Gabon. The former name for the region was French Equatorial Africa.
  UF   Africa, French-speaking Equatorial
        French Equatorial Africa
  BT   **Central Africa**
French-speaking West Africa   966
  Use for materials dealing collectively with the region of Africa that includes Benin, Burkina Faso, Guinea, Ivory Coast, Mali, Mauritania, Niger, Senegal, and Togo.
  UF   Africa, French-speaking West
        French West Africa
  BT   **West Africa**
French West Africa
  USE   **French-speaking West Africa**
Frequency modulation, Radio
  USE   **Radio frequency modulation**
Fresco painting
  USE   **Mural painting and decoration**
Freshwater animals (May subdiv. geog.) **591.76**
  UF   Freshwater fauna
  SA   types of freshwater animals [to be added as needed]
  BT   **Aquatic animals**
  RT   **Freshwater biology**
Freshwater aquaculture
  USE   **Aquaculture**
Freshwater biology   578.76
  BT   **Biology**
  NT   **Aquariums**
        Freshwater plants
  RT   **Freshwater animals**
Freshwater fauna
  USE   **Freshwater animals**
Freshwater plants (May subdiv. geog.) **581.7**
  UF   Aquatic plants
        Water plants

  BT   **Freshwater biology**
        Plants
  RT   **Marine plants**
Friars Minor
  USE   **Franciscans**
Friendly fire (Military science) (May subdiv. geog.) **355.4**
  BT   **Military art and science**
Friends
  USE   **Friendship**
Friends and associates
  USE   names of individuals with the subdivision *Friends and associates* [to be added as needed]
Friends, Society of
  USE   **Society of Friends**
Friendship   177
  UF   Affection
        Friends
  BT   **Human behavior**
  NT   **Crushes**
        Female friendship
  RT   **Love**
Friendship between women
  USE   **Female friendship**
Friendship in women
  USE   **Female friendship**
Friesian cattle
  USE   **Holstein-Friesian cattle**
Fringe benefits   331.25
  UF   Benefits, Employee
        Benefits, Fringe
        Employee benefits
        Employee fringe benefits
        Non-wage payments
        Nonwage payments
  BT   **Salaries, wages, etc.**
Frogs (May subdiv. geog.) **597.8**
  UF   Tadpoles
  BT   **Amphibians**
Frontier and pioneer life (May subdiv. geog.) **978**
  UF   Border life
        Pioneer life
  BT   **Adventure and adventurers**
  NT   **Cowhands**
        Native Americans—Captivities
        Overland journeys to the Pacific
        Ranch life

Frontiers
USE **Boundaries**
Frost   551.57
UF   Freezing
BT   **Meteorology**
     Water
NT   **Ice**
     Refrigeration
Frozen animal embryos
USE **Frozen embryos**
Frozen embryos   176; 571.8; 612.6
UF   Animal embryos, Frozen
     Embryos, Frozen
     Frozen animal embryos
     Frozen human embryos
     Human embryos, Frozen
BT   **Cryobiology**
     Embryology
Frozen foods   641.4; 664
BT   **Food**
NT   **Ice cream, ices, etc.**
RT   **Food—Preservation**
Frozen human embryos
USE **Frozen embryos**
Frozen stars
USE **Black holes (Astronomy)**
Fruit (May subdiv. geog.)   **634; 641.3**
      Names of tree fruits may be used for either
      the fruit or the tree.
SA   types of fruits, e.g. **Berries; Ap-
     ples; Citrus fruits**; etc. [to be
     added as needed]
BT   **Food**
     Plants
NT   **Apples**
     Berries
     Citrus fruits
     Fruit culture
     Grapes
Fruit—Canning
USE **Fruit—Preservation**
Fruit culture (May subdiv. geog.)   **634**
      Names of tree fruits may be used for either
      the fruit or the tree.
UF   Arboriculture
     Orchards
BT   **Agriculture**
     Fruit
     Gardening
     Horticulture
     Trees

NT   **Berries**
     Nurseries (Horticulture)
     Plant propagation
     Pruning
Fruit—Diseases and pests   634
BT   **Agricultural pests**
     Insect pests
     Pests
     Plant diseases
NT   **Spraying and dusting**
Fruit flies (May subdiv. geog.)   **595.77**
BT   **Flies**
Fruit painting and illustration
USE **Botanical illustration**
Fruit—Preservation   641.4; 664
UF   Fruit—Canning
BT   **Canning and preserving**
     Food—Preservation
Frustration   152.4
UF   Futility
BT   **Attitude (Psychology)**
     Emotions
Fuel (May subdiv. geog.)   **333.8; 662**
SA   types of fuel; and subjects with
     the subdivision **Fuel con-
     sumption** [to be added as
     needed]
BT   **Combustion**
     Energy resources
     Engines
     Fire
     Home economics
NT   **Alcohol fuels**
     **Automobiles—Fuel consump-
     tion**
     Biomass energy
     Charcoal
     Coal
     Gas
     Gasoline
     Natural gas
     Petroleum as fuel
     Synthetic fuels
     Wood
RT   **Heating**
Fuel cells   621.31
BT   **Electric batteries**
     Electrochemistry

Fuel consumption
USE   subjects with the subdivision
Fuel consumption, e.g. **Auto-mobiles—Fuel consumption**
[to be added as needed]

Fuel oil
USE   **Petroleum as fuel**

Fugitive slaves (May subdiv. geog.)
306.3
UF   Runaway slaves
BT   **Slaves**

Fugue   784.18
Use for musical scores and for materials on the fugue as a musical form.
UF   Canons, fugues, etc.
Fugues
Prelude and fugue
Preludes and fugues
BT   **Counterpoint**
Musical form

Fugues
USE   **Fugue**

Fulfillment, Self
USE   **Self-realization**

Fumigation   614.4; 648
BT   **Communicable diseases**
Insecticides
RT   **Disinfection and disinfectants**

Functional competencies
USE   **Life skills**

Functional literacy   302.2; 374
UF   Occupational literacy
BT   **Literacy**

Functions   511.3
UF   Analysis (Mathematics)
BT   **Differential equations**
Mathematical analysis
Mathematics
Set theory
RT   **Calculus**

Fund raising (May subdiv. geog.)
361.7068; 658.15
UF   Community chests
Money raising
BT   **Finance**
RT   **Gifts**

Fundamental education
USE   **Basic education**

Fundamental life skills
USE   **Life skills**

Fundamental rights
USE   **Civil rights**
Human rights

Fundamentalism
USE   **Christian fundamentalism**
Islamic fundamentalism
Religious fundamentalism

Fundamentalism and education
USE   **Church and education**
Creationism
Religion in the public schools

Fundamentalism and evolution
USE   **Creationism**

Fundamentalist movements
USE   **Religious fundamentalism**

Funding
USE   **Finance**

Funding for the arts
USE   **Art patronage**
Arts—Government policy
Federal aid to the arts

Funds
USE   **Finance**

Funeral customs and rites
USE   **Funeral rites and ceremonies**
and ethnic groups and native peoples with the subdivision *Funeral customs and rites* [to be added as needed]

Funeral directors
USE   **Undertakers and undertaking**

Funeral rites and ceremonies (May subdiv. geog.)   **393**
UF   Funeral customs and rites
Graves
Mortuary customs
Mourning customs
SA   ethnic groups and native peoples with the subdivision *Funeral customs and rites* [to be added as needed]
BT   **Manners and customs**
Rites and ceremonies
RT   **Burial**
Cremation

Fungi   579.5
UF   Diseases and pests
Mycology
BT   **Agricultural pests**
Pests
Plants

Fungi—*Continued*
- NT Molds (Fungi)
     Plant diseases
     Yeast
- RT Mushrooms

Fungicides   632; 668
- UF Germicides
- BT **Pesticides**
- RT **Spraying and dusting**

Funicular railroads
- USE **Cable railroads**

Funnies
- USE **Comic books, strips, etc.**

Fur   675; 685
- BT **Animals—Anatomy**
- RT **Hides and skins**

Fur-bearing animals
- USE **Furbearing animals**

Fur trade (May subdiv. geog.)   338.3
- BT **Trapping**

Furbearing animals (May subdiv. geog.)
     599.7; 636.97
- UF Fur-bearing animals
- SA types of furbearing animals, e.g.
     Beavers [to be added as needed]
- BT **Animals**
     Economic zoology
- NT **Beavers**

Furnaces   697
- BT **Heating**
- NT **Blast furnaces**
     Smelting

Furniture   645; 749
- SA furniture of particular countries, e.g. **American furniture**; types of furniture, and names of specific articles of furniture, e.g. **Tables**; **Chairs**; etc. [to be added as needed]
- BT **Decoration and ornament**
     Decorative arts
     Interior design
- NT **American furniture**
     Built-in furniture
     Chairs
     Chests
     Church furniture
     Furniture making
     Garden ornaments and furniture

   Libraries—Equipment and supplies
   Mirrors
   Schools—Equipment and supplies
   Tables
   Veneers and veneering
- RT **Cabinetwork**
   Upholstery

Furniture, American
- USE **American furniture**

Furniture building
- USE **Furniture making**

Furniture—Conservation and restoration
- USE **Furniture finishing**
     Furniture—Repairing

Furniture finishing   684.1; 749
- UF Furniture—Conservation and restoration
     Furniture—Refinishing
     Furniture—Restoration
     Refinishing furniture
     Restoration of furniture
- BT **Furniture making**
     Handicraft
     Wood finishing
- RT **Furniture—Repairing**

Furniture making   684.1; 749
- UF Furniture building
- BT **Furniture**
     Woodwork
- NT **Furniture finishing**
     Furniture—Repairing

Furniture—Refinishing
- USE **Furniture finishing**

Furniture—Repairing   684.1; 749
- UF Furniture—Conservation and restoration
     Furniture—Restoration
     Restoration of furniture
- BT **Furniture making**
- RT **Furniture finishing**

Furniture—Restoration
- USE **Furniture finishing**
     Furniture—Repairing

Futility
- USE **Frustration**

Future life   129; 236

Use for materials on the character and form of a future existence. Materials on the question of the endless existence of the soul are

Future life—*Continued*
entered under **Immortality**. Materials on the
philosophical concept of eternity are entered
under **Eternity**.

　　UF　Afterlife
　　　　Eternal life
　　　　Intermediate state
　　　　Life after death
　　　　Life, Future
　　　　Resurrection
　　BT　**Death**
　　　　Eschatology
　　NT　**Heaven**
　　　　Hell
　　　　Paradise
　　　　Soul
　　RT　**Eternity**
　　　　Immortality
Future shock
　　USE　**Culture conflict**
Futures (May subdiv. geog.)　**332.64**
　　UF　Futures contracts
　　　　Futures trading
　　BT　**Investments**
　　　　Securities
Futures contracts
　　USE　**Futures**
Futures trading
　　USE　**Futures**
Futurism (Art) (May subdiv. geog.)
　　　　709.04; 759.06
　　BT　**Art**
Futurology
　　USE　**Forecasting**
Fuzzy logic
　　USE　**Fuzzy systems**
Fuzzy systems　629.8
　　UF　Fuzzy logic
　　　　Systems, Fuzzy
　　BT　**System analysis**
Gadgets
　　USE　**Implements, utensils, etc.**
Gaels
　　USE　**Celts**
Gaia concept
　　USE　**Gaia hypothesis**
Gaia hypothesis　550.1; 570.1
　　UF　Gaia concept
　　　　Gaia principle
　　　　Gaia theory
　　　　Living earth theory

　　BT　**Biology**
　　　　Earth
　　　　Ecology
　　　　Life (Biology)
Gaia principle
　　USE　**Gaia hypothesis**
Gaia theory
　　USE　**Gaia hypothesis**
Gaining weight
　　USE　**Weight gain**
Galaxies　523.1
　　UF　Extragalactic nebulae
　　　　Nebulae, Extragalactic
　　BT　**Astronomy**
　　　　Stars
　　NT　**Milky Way**
Gales
　　USE　**Winds**
Gambling (May subdiv. geog.)　**306.4;**
　　　　795
　　UF　Betting
　　　　Bookmaking (Betting)
　　　　Gaming
　　SA　types of gambling, e.g. **Lotteries**
　　　　[to be added as needed]
　　BT　**Games**
　　NT　**Compulsive gambling**
　　　　Internet gambling
　　　　Lotteries
　　　　Sports betting
Game and game birds (May subdiv.
　　geog.)　**636.6**
　　UF　Wild fowl
　　SA　types of animals and birds, e.g.
　　　　Deer; **Pheasants**; etc. [to be
　　　　added as needed]
　　BT　**Animals**
　　　　Birds
　　　　Wildlife
　　NT　**Deer**
　　　　Falconry
　　　　Game protection
　　　　Pheasants
　　RT　**Hunting**
　　　　Trapping
Game preserves
　　USE　**Game reserves**
Game protection (May subdiv. geog.)
　　　　333.95; 636.9
　　UF　Game wardens
　　　　Protection of game

Game protection—*Continued*
    BT   **Game and game birds**
           Hunting
           Wildlife conservation
    RT   **Birds—Protection**
Game reserves (May subdiv. geog.)
         333.95
    UF   Game preserves
    BT   **Hunting**
           Wildlife conservation
Game theory   **519.3**
    UF   Games, Theory of
           Theory of games
    BT   **Mathematical models**
           Mathematics
           Probabilities
    NT   **Simulation games**
           Simulation games in education
Game wardens
    USE **Game protection**
Games (May subdiv. geog.)   **790**
    UF   Pastimes
    SA   types of games and names of
           individual games [to be added
           as needed]
    BT   **Entertaining**
           Physical education
           Recreation
    NT   **Ball games**
           Bible games and puzzles
           Board games
           Card games
           Computer games
           Educational games
           Fantasy games
           Gambling
           Indoor games
           Native American games
           Olympic games
           Singing games
           Video games
           Word games
    RT   **Amusements**
           Play
           Sports
Games, Theory of
    USE **Game theory**
Gaming
    USE **Gambling**
Gaming, Educational
    USE **Simulation games in education**

Gaming simulations
    USE **Simulation games**
Gamma rays   **537.5; 539.7**
    BT   **Electromagnetic waves**
           Radiation
           X-rays
Gangs (May subdiv. geog.)   **302.3;**
         364.106
    UF   Gangsters
           Street gangs
           Teenage gangs
    BT   **Criminals**
           Juvenile delinquency
           Organized crime
Gangster films   **791.43**
    Use for individual works, collections, or
  materials about gangster films.
    UF   Crime films
    BT   **Motion pictures**
    RT   **Mystery films**
Gangsters
    USE **Gangs**
Garage sales   **381**
    UF   Yard sales
    BT   **Secondhand trade**
Garbage
    USE **Refuse and refuse disposal**
Garbage disposal
    USE **Refuse and refuse disposal**
Garden architecture
    USE **Garden structures**
Garden design (May subdiv. geog.)   **712**
    UF   Gardens—Design
    BT   **Design**
           Gardening
    RT   **Landscape gardening**
Garden farming
    USE **Truck farming**
Garden furniture
    USE **Garden ornaments and furni-
          ture**
Garden of Eden
    USE **Paradise**
Garden ornaments and furniture   **717**
    UF   Garden furniture
    BT   **Decoration and ornament**
           Furniture
           Gardens
           Landscape architecture
    NT   **Sundials**

Garden pests
USE **Agricultural pests**
Insect pests
Plant diseases
Garden rooms 643
UF Conservatories, Home
Home conservatories
BT **Houses**
Rooms
RT **Greenhouses**
Garden structures 690
UF Garden architecture
Structures, Garden
BT **Buildings**
Landscape architecture
Gardening (May subdiv. geog.) **635**

Use for materials on the practical aspects of creating gardens and cultivating flowers, fruits, vegetables, etc. Materials on the design or rearrangement of extensive gardens or estates are entered under **Landscape gardening**. Materials on the scientific and economic aspects of the cultivation of plants are entered under **Horticulture**. General materials about gardens, the history of gardens, various types of gardens, etc., are entered under **Gardens**.

UF Planting
BT **Agriculture**
NT **Climbing plants**
Container gardening
Cultivated plants
Flower gardening
Fruit culture
Garden design
Gardening in the shade
Greenhouses
Grounds maintenance
Herb gardening
Indoor gardening
Landscape gardening
Nurseries (Horticulture)
Organic gardening
Plant propagation
Pruning
Truck farming
Vegetable gardening
Weeds
Window gardening
Winter gardening
RT **Gardens**
Horticulture
Plants
Gardening for fragrance
USE **Fragrant gardens**

Gardening in the shade 635
UF Gardens, Shade
Shade gardens
Shady gardens
BT **Gardening**
Gardens (May subdiv. geog.) **635; 712**

Use for general materials about gardens, the history of gardens, various types of gardens, etc. Materials on the design or rearrangement of extensive gardens or estates are entered under **Landscape gardening**. Materials on the practical aspects of creating gardens and cultivating flowers, fruits, vegetables, etc., are entered under **Gardening**.

UF Formal gardens
SA types of gardens, e.g. **Botanical gardens**; **Islamic gardens** etc., and names of individual gardens [to be added as needed]
NT **Botanical gardens**
Fragrant gardens
Garden ornaments and furniture
Islamic gardens
Maze gardens
Miniature gardens
Rock gardens
RT **Gardening**
Gardens—Design
USE **Garden design**
Gardens, Miniature
USE **Miniature gardens**
Gardens, Shade
USE **Gardening in the shade**
Gargoyles (May subdiv. geog.) **729**
BT **Architectural decoration and ornament**
Architecture—Details
Garment industry
USE **Clothing industry**
Garment making
USE **Dressmaking**
Tailoring
Garments
USE **Clothing and dress**
Gas 665.7
UF Coal gas
BT **Fuel**
RT **Coal tar products**
Gas and oil engines
USE **Internal combustion engines**

Gas companies (May subdiv. geog.)
363.6

> Use for materials on the sale and distribution of gas to consumers.

   UF   Natural gas companies

         Natural gas utilities

   BT   **Public utilities**

Gas engines

   USE   **Internal combustion engines**

Gas stations

   USE   **Service stations**

Gas turbines   621.43

   BT   **Turbines**

Gas warfare

   USE   **Chemical warfare**

Gases   530.4; 533

   SA   types of gases, e.g. **Nitrogen** [to be added as needed]

   BT   **Fluid mechanics**

         Hydrostatics

         Physics

   NT   **Bubbles**

         Helium

         Natural gas

         Nitrogen

         Oxygen

         Poisonous gases

   RT   **Pneumatics**

Gases, Asphyxiating and poisonous

   USE   **Poisonous gases**

Gasification of coal

   USE   **Coal gasification**

Gasoline   665.5

   BT   **Fuel**

         Petroleum

Gasoline engines

   USE   **Internal combustion engines**

Gastronomy   641.01

   UF   Eating

   BT   **Diet**

   NT   **Slow food movement**

   RT   **Cooking**

         Dining

         Food

Gauchos

   USE   **Cowhands**

Gaul—Geography   914.4

   BT   **Ancient geography**

         Historical geography

Gay and lesbian rights

   USE   **Gay rights**

Gay liberation movement (May subdiv. geog.) **306.76**

   BT   **Homosexuality**

   RT   **Gay rights**

Gay lifestyle

   USE   **Homosexuality**

Gay marriage

   USE   **Same-sex marriage**

Gay men (May subdiv. geog.) **306.76**

   UF   Gays, Male

         Homosexuals, Male

   BT   **Men**

   NT   **Gay parents**

         Gays and lesbians in the military

   RT   **Gay men's writings**

         Homosexuality

Gay men—Civil rights

   USE   **Gay rights**

Gay men—Ordination

   USE   **Ordination of gays and lesbians**

Gay men's writings   808.8

> Use for collections of gay men's writings by more than one author and for materials about such writings.

   UF   Writings of gay men

   BT   **Literature**

   RT   **Gay men**

Gay parents (May subdiv. geog.)
306.85; 649

   UF   Homosexual parents

   BT   **Gay men**

         Lesbians

         Parents

Gay rights (May subdiv. geog.)
323.3264

   UF   Gay and lesbian rights

         Gay men—Civil rights

         Lesbian rights

         Lesbians—Civil rights

         Rights of gays

         Rights of lesbians

   BT   **Civil rights**

   RT   **Gay liberation movement**

Gay women

   USE   **Lesbians**

Gay women's writings

   USE   **Lesbians' writings**

Gays and lesbians in the military (May subdiv. geog.) **355.008**

Gays and lesbians in the military—*Continued*

UF Gays in the military

Lesbians and gays in the military

Lesbians in the military

United States—Armed forces—Gays

BT **Gay men**

Lesbians

Military personnel

Gays, Female

USE **Lesbians**

Gays in the military

USE **Gays and lesbians in the military**

Gays, Male

USE **Gay men**

Gazetteers 910.3

SA names of countries, states, etc., with the subdivision *Gazetteers*, e.g. **United States—Gazetteers** [to be added as needed]

BT **Geography**

NT **Ohio—Gazetteers**

United States—Gazetteers

RT **Geographic names**

Gearing 621.8

UF Bevel gearing

Cog wheels

Gears

Spiral gearing

BT **Machinery**

Power transmission

Wheels

NT **Automobiles—Transmission devices**

RT **Mechanical movements**

Gears

USE **Gearing**

Geese (May subdiv. geog.) 598.4; 636.5

UF Goose

BT **Birds**

Poultry

Water birds

Geishas 792.7

BT **Entertainers**

Gemini project 629.45

UF Project Gemini

BT **Orbital rendezvous (Space flight)**

Space flight

Gems (May subdiv. geog.) 736

Use for materials on cut and polished precious stones treated from the point of view of art or antiquity. Materials on gem stones treated from a mineralogical or technological point of view are entered under **Precious stones**. Materials on gems in which the emphasis is on the setting are entered under **Jewelry**.

UF Jewels

BT **Archeology**

Art

Decoration and ornament

Engraving

Minerals

RT **Jewelry**

Precious stones

Gemstones

USE **Precious stones**

Gender identity

USE **Sex role**

Gene mapping 572.8

UF Chromosome mapping

Genetic mapping

Genome mapping

BT **Genetics**

Gene splicing

USE **Genetic engineering**

Gene therapy 616

Use for materials on therapeutic efforts involving the replacement or supplementation of genes in order to cure diseases caused by genetic defects.

UF Therapy, Gene

BT **Genetic engineering**

Therapeutics

Gene transfer

USE **Genetic engineering**

Genealogy 929

UF Ancestry

Descent

Family histories

Family trees

Pedigrees

SA countries, cities, etc., corporate bodies, ethnic groups, and classes of persons with the subdivision *Genealogy*; names of individual persons with the subdivision *Family*; and names of families, e.g. **Lincoln family** [to be added as needed]

BT **History**

Genealogy—*Continued*
    NT **Registers of births, etc.**
        Wills
    RT **Biography**
        Heraldry
General practice (Medicine)
    USE **Family medicine**
General stores (May subdiv. geog.)
        381.1
    UF Country stores
    BT **Retail trade**
        Stores
Generals (May subdiv. geog.)   355.0092;
        920
    BT **Military personnel**
Generation gap
    USE **Conflict of generations**
Generative organs
    USE **Reproductive system**
Generators, Electric
    USE **Electric generators**
Generic drugs   615
    UF Drugs—Generic substitution
    BT **Drugs**
        Generic products
Generic products   658.8
    UF Products, Generic
    BT **Commercial products**
        Manufactures
    NT **Generic drugs**
Generosity   179
    UF Giving
Genes
    USE **Heredity**
Genetic aspects
    USE types of diseases with the subdi-
        vision *Genetic aspects*, e.g.
        Cancer—Genetic aspects [to
        be added as needed]
Genetic code   572.8
    BT **Molecular biology**
Genetic counseling   616; 618
    BT **Medical genetics**
        Prenatal diagnosis
Genetic engineering (May subdiv. geog.)
        660.6
    UF Designed genetic change
        Engineering, Genetic
        Gene splicing
        Gene transfer
        Genetic intervention
        Genetic surgery

Splicing of genes
        Transgenics
    BT **Engineering**
        Genetic recombination
    NT **Cloning**
        Fertilization in vitro
        Gene therapy
        Molecular cloning
        Recombinant DNA
    RT **Biotechnology**
Genetic engineering—Government policy
        (May subdiv. geog.)   353.7; 660.6
Genetic engineering—Social aspects
        306.4
Genetic fingerprinting
    USE **DNA fingerprinting**
Genetic fingerprints
    USE **DNA fingerprinting**
Genetic intervention
    USE **Genetic engineering**
Genetic mapping
    USE **Gene mapping**
Genetic profiling
    USE **DNA fingerprinting**
Genetic recombination   572.8
    UF Recombination, Genetic
    BT **Chromosomes**
    NT **Genetic engineering**
        Genetic transformation
        Recombinant DNA
Genetic surgery
    USE **Genetic engineering**
Genetic transformation   576.5
    UF Transformation (Genetics)
    BT **Genetic recombination**
Genetics   576.5
    SA types of diseases with the subdi-
        vision *Genetic aspects*, e.g.
        Cancer—Genetic aspects [to
        be added as needed]
    BT **Biology**
        Embryology
        Life (Biology)
        Mendel's law
        Reproduction
    NT **Adaptation (Biology)**
        Behavior genetics
        Chromosomes
        Eugenics
        Gene mapping
        Genomes

Genetics—*Continued*
    Human genome
    Medical genetics
    Natural selection
    Nature and nurture
    Variation (Biology)
  RT **Breeding**
    Heredity
Genetics and environment
  USE **Nature and nurture**
Genital mutilation, Female
  USE **Female circumcision**
Genitalia
  USE **Reproductive system**
Genius **153.9**
  UF Talent
  BT **Psychology**
  NT **Creation (Literary, artistic, etc.)**
Genocide (May subdiv. geog.) **179.7; 364.1**
  UF Ethnic cleansing
    Ethnocide
  BT **Crimes against humanity**
Genome
  USE **Genomes**
Genome mapping
  USE **Gene mapping**
Genomes **572.8**
  UF Genome
  BT **Genetics**
Geochemistry **551.9**
  UF Chemical geology
    Earth—Chemical composition
    Geological chemistry
  BT **Chemistry**
    Earth sciences
    Petrology
  NT **Geothermal resources**
Geodesy **526**
  UF Degrees of latitude and longitude
  BT **Earth**
    Measurement
  NT **Latitude**
    Longitude
  RT **Surveying**
Geographic names (May subdiv. geog.) **910**
  UF Names, Geographical
    Place names
  BT **Names**

  RT **Gazetteers**
Geographic names—United States
    917.3
  UF United States—Geographic names
Geographical atlases
  USE **Atlases**
Geographical distribution
  USE types of plants and animals with the subdivision *Geographical distribution,* e.g. **Fishes—Geographical distribution** [to be added as needed]
Geographical distribution of animals and plants
  USE **Biogeography**
Geographical distribution of people
  USE **Human geography**
Geographical distribution of plants
  USE **Plants—Geographical distribution**
Geographical myths **398.23**
  Use for materials on legendary or mythical places. Materials on imaginary places created for literary or artistic purposes are entered under **Imaginary places.**
  UF Cities, Imaginary
  BT **Mythology**
  NT **Atlantis (Legendary place)**
    Lost continents
Geography **910**
  Use for general materials, frequently school materials, that describe the surface of the earth and its interrelationship with various peoples, animals, natural products, and industries. Materials limited to a particular place are entered under the name of the place with the subdivision *Geography.* General descriptive materials and travel materials limited to a particular place are entered under the name of the place (except extinct cities) with the subdivision *Description and travel.* Materials on the physical features of the earth's surface and its atmosphere are entered under **Physical geography.**
  UF Social studies
  SA names of countries, states, etc., with the subdivisions *Description and travel* and *Geography*; and sacred works with the subdivision *Geography,* e.g. **Bible—Geography** [to be added as needed]
  BT **Earth**
    Earth sciences
    World history

Geography—*Continued*
 NT **Atlases**
 Bible—Geography
 Biogeography
 Boundaries
 Commercial geography
 Exploration
 Gazetteers
 Greece—Geography
 Historical geography
 Human geography
 Maps
 Military geography
 Physical geography
 Regionalism
 Surveying
 United States—Description and travel
 United States—Geography
 Voyages and travels
Geography, Ancient
 USE **Ancient geography**
Geography—Dictionaries 910.3
 Use for dictionaries of geographic terms. Materials listing names and descriptions of places are entered under **Gazetteers**.
 BT **Encyclopedias and dictionaries**
Geography, Historical
 USE **Historical geography**
Geography, Political
 USE **Geopolitics**
Geological chemistry
 USE **Geochemistry**
Geological physics
 USE **Geophysics**
Geologists (May subdiv. geog.) **551.092; 920**
 BT **Scientists**
Geology (May subdiv. geog.) **550**
 Use for materials limited to the structure and composition of the earth and the physical changes it has undergone and is still undergoing. General materials on the whole planet are entered under **Earth**.
 UF Geoscience
 SA names of planets and types of ore with the subdivision *Geology* [to be added as needed]
 BT **Earth sciences**
 Science
 NT **Astrogeology**
 Continental drift
 Continental shelf

 Coral reefs and islands
 Earthquakes
 Economic geology
 Erosion
 Faults (Geology)
 Geysers
 Glaciers
 Historical geology
 Landforms
 Minerals
 Ore deposits
 Physical geography
 Stratigraphic geology
 Submarine geology
 Volcanoes
 RT **Earth**
 Petrology
 Rocks
Geology, Dynamic
 USE **Geophysics**
Geology, Economic
 USE **Economic geology**
Geology—Interactive multimedia 551
Geology, Lunar
 USE **Lunar geology**
Geology—Maps 550.22
 BT **Maps**
Geology—Moon
 USE **Lunar geology**
Geology, Petroleum
 USE **Petroleum geology**
Geology, Stratigraphic
 USE **Stratigraphic geology**
Geology—United States 557.3
Geomagnetic field
 USE **Geomagnetism**
Geomagnetism (May subdiv. geog.) 538
 UF Earth magnetic field
 Earth—Magnetism
 Geomagnetic field
 BT **Geophysics**
 Magnetism
Geometric art
 USE **Abstract art**
Geometric patterns
 USE **Patterns (Mathematics)**
Geometrical drawing 516; 604.2
 UF Mathematical drawing
 Plans
 BT **Drawing**
 Geometry

Geometrical drawing—*Continued*
- NT **Descriptive geometry**
    Graphic methods
    Perspective
- RT **Mechanical drawing**

Geometry   516
- BT **Mathematics**
- NT **Analytic geometry**
    Descriptive geometry
    Fractals
    Geometrical drawing
    Plane geometry
    Projective geometry
    Ratio and proportion
    Shape
    Solid geometry
    Square
    Topology
    Trigonometry
    Volume (Cubic content)

Geometry, Analytic
- USE **Analytic geometry**

Geometry, Descriptive
- USE **Descriptive geometry**

Geometry, Plane
- USE **Plane geometry**

Geometry, Projective
- USE **Projective geometry**

Geometry, Solid
- USE **Solid geometry**

Geophysics   550
- UF Geological physics
    Geology, Dynamic
    Physics, Terrestrial
    Terrestrial physics
- BT **Earth sciences**
    Physics
- NT **Auroras**
    Geomagnetism
    Plate tectonics

Geopolitics   320.1; 327.101
- UF Geography, Political
    Political geography
- BT **International relations**
    Political science
- RT **Boundaries**
    Human geography
    World politics

Geoscience
- USE **Earth sciences**
    Geology

Geothermal resources (May subdiv. geog.)   **333.8**
- UF Natural steam energy
    Thermal waters
- SA types of geothermal resources, e.g. **Geysers** [to be added as needed]
- BT **Geochemistry**
    Ocean energy resources
    Renewable energy resources
- NT **Geysers**

Geriatrics
- USE **Elderly—Diseases**
    Elderly—Health and hygiene

Germ theory
- USE **Life—Origin**

Germ theory of disease   616
- UF Disease germs
    Germs
    Microbes
- BT **Communicable diseases**

Germ warfare
- USE **Biological warfare**

German Democratic Republic
- USE **Germany (East)**

German Federal Republic
- USE **Germany (West)**

German language   430
> May be subdivided like **English language**.
- BT **Language and languages**

German literature   830
> May use same subdivisions and names of literary forms as for **English literature**.
- BT **Literature**

German occupation of France, 1940-1945
- USE **France—History—1940-1945, German occupation**

German occupation of Netherlands, 1940-1945
- USE **Netherlands—History—1940-1945, German occupation**

Germany   943
> Use for materials on Germany before or after the division of the country following World War II and for materials on East and West Germany discussed collectively as occupied zones or countries. Materials limited to the eastern part of Germany from 1945 to 1990, the Russian occupation zone, or the German Democratic Republic, are entered under **Germany (East)**. Materials limited to the western part of Germany from 1945 to 1990, the American, British, and French occupation zones, or the German Federal Republic, are entered under **Germany (West)**. May be subdivided like **United States** except for *History*.

Germany—*Continued*
UF   Federal Republic of Germany
NT   **Germany (East)**
     Germany (West)
Germany (Democratic Republic)
USE   **Germany (East)**
Germany (East)   943

Use for materials limited to the eastern part of Germany from 1945 to 1990, the Russian occupation zone, or the German Democratic Republic. Materials on Germany before or after the division of the country following World War II and materials on East and West Germany discussed collectively as occupied zones or countries are entered under **Germany**.

UF   East Germany
     German Democratic Republic
     Germany (Democratic Republic)
BT   **Germany**
Germany (Federal Republic)
USE   **Germany (West)**
Germany—History   943
Germany—History—0-1517   943
Germany—History—1517-1740   943
NT   **Thirty Years' War, 1618-1648**
Germany—History—1740-1815   943
Germany—History—1815-1866   943
Germany—History—1848-1849, Revolution   943
Germany—History—1866-1918   943.08
Germany—History—1918-1933   943.085
Germany—History—1933-1945   943.086
Germany—History—1945-1990   943.087
Germany—History—1990-   943.088
UF   Germany—History—Unification, 1990
Germany—History—Unification, 1990
USE   **Germany—History—1990-**
Germany (West)   943.087

Use for materials limited to the western part of Germany from 1945 to 1990, the American, British, and French occupation zones, or the German Federal Republic. Materials on Germany before or after the division of the country following World War II and materials on East and West Germany discussed collectively as occupied zones or countries are entered under **Germany**.

UF   Federal Republic of Germany
     German Federal Republic
     Germany (Federal Republic)
     West Germany
BT   **Germany**

Germicides
USE   **Disinfection and disinfectants**
     Fungicides
Germination   571.8
UF   Seeds—Germination
BT   **Plant physiology**
Germs
USE   **Bacteria**
     Germ theory of disease
     Microorganisms
Gerontology   305.26; 362.6; 612.6
BT   **Social sciences**
NT   **Aging**
     Elderly
RT   **Old age**
Gestalt psychology   150.19
UF   Configuration (Psychology)
     Psychology, Structural
     Structural psychology
BT   **Consciousness**
     Perception
     Psychology
     Senses and sensation
     Theory of knowledge
Getting ready for bed
USE   **Bedtime**
Gettysburg (Pa.), Battle of, 1863   973.7
BT   **United States—History—1861-1865, Civil War—Campaigns**
Geysers (May subdiv. geog.)   **551.2**
UF   Eruptions
     Thermal waters
BT   **Geology**
     Geothermal resources
     Physical geography
     Water
Ghettoes, Inner city
USE   **Inner cities**
Ghost stories   808.3; 808.83

Use for individual works, collections, or materials about ghost stories.

UF   Ghosts—Fiction
     Terror tales
BT   **Fantasy fiction**
     Horror fiction
     Occult fiction
RT   **Gothic novels**
     Mystery fiction
Ghost towns (May subdiv. geog.)   **307.76**
UF   Abandoned towns
     Towns, Abandoned
BT   **Extinct cities**

Ghosts (May subdiv. geog.)   **133.1**

   UF   Phantoms

          Poltergeists

          Specters

   BT   **Apparitions**

          Folklore

          Spirits

   RT   **Haunted houses**

          Parapsychology

Ghosts—Fiction

   USE   **Ghost stories**

Giantism   **616.4**

   Use for materials on excessive growth in humans. Materials on beings with a human form but with superhuman size or strength in folklore or imaginative literature are entered under **Giants**.

   UF   Gigantism

   BT   **Growth disorders**

Giants   **398.21**

   Use for materials on beings with a human form but with superhuman size or strength in folklore or imaginative literature. Materials on excessive growth in humans are entered under **Giantism**.

   BT   **Folklore**

          Monsters

Gift of tongues

   USE   **Glossolalia**

Gift wrapping   **745.54**

   UF   Wrapping of gifts

   BT   **Packaging**

          Paper crafts

Gifted children   **155.45**

   UF   Bright children

          Children, Gifted

          Precocious children

   BT   **Exceptional children**

   NT   **Child artists**

          Child authors

Gifts   **306.4; 361.7**

   UF   Bequests

          Donations

          Presents

   BT   **Manners and customs**

   NT   **Donation of organs, tissues, etc.**

          Free material

   RT   **Fund raising**

Gifts of grace

   USE   **Spiritual gifts**

Gifts of the Holy Spirit

   USE   **Spiritual gifts**

Gifts, Spiritual

   USE   **Spiritual gifts**

Gigantism

   USE   **Giantism**

Gipsies

   USE   **Gypsies**

Girl-love manga

   USE   **Shojo-ai**

Girl Scouts (May subdiv. geog.)   **369.463**

   UF   Brownies (Girl Scouts)

   BT   **Girls' clubs**

          Scouts and scouting

Girls (May subdiv. geog.)   **155.43; 305.23082**

   BT   **Children**

   RT   **Teenagers**

          Young women

Girls' clubs (May subdiv. geog.)   **369.46**

   UF   Girls—Societies and clubs

   BT   **Clubs**

          Societies

   NT   **4-H clubs**

          Camp Fire Girls

          Girl Scouts

Girls—Education (May subdiv. geog.)   **371.822**

   BT   **Education**

   RT   **Coeducation**

Girls—Employment

   USE   **Women—Employment**

          Youth—Employment

Girls—Societies and clubs

   USE   **Girls' clubs**

GIs

   USE   **Soldiers—United States**

Giveaways

   USE   **Free material**

Giving

   USE   **Generosity**

Glacial epoch

   USE   **Ice age**

Glaciers (May subdiv. geog.)   **551.3**

   BT   **Geology**

          Ice

          Physical geography

Gladiators   **796.8092; 920**

   UF   Fighting

Gladness

   USE   **Happiness**

Glands   **571.7; 573.4; 611; 612.4**

Glands—*Continued*
    BT   **Anatomy**
           Physiology
Glands, Ductless
    USE **Endocrine glands**
Glass 666
    BT   **Building materials**
           Ceramics
    NT   **Glass fibers**
Glass construction 693
    BT   **Building materials**
Glass fibers 666
    UF   Fiber glass
           Fiberglass
           Fibers, Glass
           Glass, Spun
           Spun glass
    BT   **Fibers**
           Glass
Glass industry
    USE **Glass manufacture**
Glass manufacture (May subdiv. geog.)
    666
    UF   Glass industry
    BT   **Ceramic industry**
Glass painting and staining (May subdiv.
   geog.) **748.5**
    UF   Glass, Stained
           Painted glass
           Stained glass
           Windows, Stained glass
    BT   **Decoration and ornament**
           Painting
Glass, Spun
    USE **Glass fibers**
Glass, Stained
    USE **Glass painting and staining**
Glasses
    USE **Eyeglasses**
Glassware (May subdiv. geog.) **642;**
    748.2
    BT   **Decorative arts**
           Tableware
    RT   **Vases**
Glassware—Trademarks 748.2
    BT   **Trademarks**
Glazes 666; 738.1
    BT   **Ceramics**
           Pottery
Gliders (Aeronautics) 629.133
    UF   Aircraft
           Sailplanes (Aeronautics)

    BT   **Aeronautics**
           Airplanes
Gliding and soaring 797.5
    UF   Air surfing
           Hang gliding
           Soaring flight
    BT   **Aeronautics**
Global Positioning System 526; 623.89
    UF   GPS (Navigation system)
    BT   **Navigation**
Global satellite communications systems
    USE **Artificial satellites in telecom-
          munication**
Global warming
    USE **Greenhouse effect**
Globalization 303.48; 337
    UF   Internationalization
    BT   **International relations**
Globes 912
    BT   **Maps**
Glossaries
    USE **Encyclopedias and dictionaries**
Glossolalia 234
    UF   Gift of tongues
           Speaking in tongues
           Speaking with tongues
    BT   **Spiritual gifts**
    RT   **Pentecostalism**
Glow-in-the-dark books
    UF   Luminescent books
           Luminous books
    BT   **Picture books for children**
           Toy and movable books
Glue 668
    BT   **Adhesives**
Glue sniffing
    USE **Solvent abuse**
Gnomes 398.21
    BT   **Folklore**
Gnosticism 273; 299
    BT   **Church history—30-600, Early
          church**
           Philosophy
           Religions
GNP
    USE **Gross national product**
Go-karts
    USE **Karts and karting**
Goblins 398.21
    BT   **Folklore**

God   211; 212; 231
    May subdivide by religion as needed, e.g.
    God—Christianity.
    NT   **Femininity of God**
          Providence and government of
            God
          Revelation
    RT   **Metaphysics**
          Monotheism
          Religion
          Theism
          Theology

God—Christianity   231
    BT   **Christianity—Doctrines**
    NT   **Holy Spirit**
          Jesus Christ
          Trinity

God—Femininity
    USE   **Femininity of God**
God—Praise
    USE   **Praise of God**
God—Providence and government
    USE   **Providence and government of**
            God
God—Sovereignty
    USE   **Providence and government of**
            God
Goddess movement
    USE   **Goddess religion**

Goddess religion (May subdiv. geog.)
    201
    UF   Goddess movement
          Mother Goddess religion
    BT   **Paganism**
    RT   **Gods and goddesses**
          Wicca
Goddesses
    USE   **Gods and goddesses**
Gods
    USE   **Gods and goddesses**

Gods and goddesses   201
    UF   Deities
          Goddesses
          Gods
    SA   names of gods and goddesses,
          e.g. **Zeus (Greek deity)**; **Vesta (Roman deity)**; etc. [to be
          added as needed]
    NT   **Vesta (Roman deity)**
          Zeus (Greek deity)
    RT   **Goddess religion**
          Mythology

          Religions

Gold (May subdiv. geog.)   **332.4; 553.4;**
    669
    BT   **Chemical elements**
          Precious metals
    NT   **Goldwork**
    RT   **Coinage**
          Gold mines and mining
          Money
Gold articles
    USE   **Goldwork**
Gold discoveries
    USE   names of places with the subdivision *Gold discoveries,* e.g.
          California—Gold discoveries
          [to be added as needed]
Gold fish
    USE   **Goldfish**

Gold mines and mining (May subdiv.
    geog.)   **622**
    UF   Gold rush
          Gold rushes
    SA   names of places with the subdivision *Gold discoveries*, e.g.
          California—Gold discoveries
          [to be added as needed]
    BT   **Mines and mineral resources**
    NT   **Prospecting**
    RT   **Gold**
Gold plate
    USE   **Plate**
Gold rush
    USE   **Gold mines and mining**
Gold rushes
    USE   **Gold mines and mining**
Gold work
    USE   **Goldwork**

Golden Gate Bridge (San Francisco,
    Calif.)   624.209794; 979.4
    BT   **Bridges**

Golden rule   170
    UF   Rule, Golden
    BT   **Ethics**

Goldfish   597.5
    UF   Gold fish
    BT   **Fishes**
Goldsmithing
    USE   **Goldwork**

Goldwork (May subdiv. geog.)   **739.2**
    UF   Gold articles
          Gold work

Goldwork—*Continued*
    Goldsmithing
  BT **Art metalwork**
    Gold
    Metalwork
  NT **Plate**
Golf courses 796.352
  BT **Sports facilities**
Good and evil 170; 214; 241
  UF Evil
    Wickedness
  BT **Ethics**
    Philosophy
    Theology
  NT **Guilt**
    Sin
Good Friday 263
  BT **Christian holidays**
    Holy Week
    Lent
Good grooming
  USE **Personal grooming**
Goose
  USE **Geese**
Gorge-purge syndrome
  USE **Bulimia**
Gorillas (May subdiv. geog.) **599.884**
  BT **Apes**
Gospel music 781.71; 782.25
  UF Music, Gospel
    Revivals—Music
  BT **African American music**
    Church music
    Popular music
  RT **Spirituals (Songs)**
Gossip 070.4; 177; 302.2
  BT **Journalism**
    Libel and slander
  NT **Tattling**
Gothic architecture (May subdiv. geog.)
    723
  UF Architecture, Gothic
  BT **Medieval architecture**
  RT **Cathedrals**
    Church architecture
    Gothic art
Gothic art (May subdiv. geog.) **709.02**
  UF Art, Gothic
  BT **Medieval art**
  RT **Christian art**
    Gothic architecture

Gothic decoration and ornament
  USE **Decoration and ornament—**
      Gothic style
Gothic fiction
  USE **Gothic novels**
Gothic novels 808.3
    Use for individual works, collections, or materials about contemporary novels that have a medieval setting and usually include castles and ghosts. For materials on literature of the eighteenth and nineteenth centuries featuring medieval settings and romantic gloom, use **Gothic revival (Literature)**.
  UF Gothic fiction
  BT **Historical fiction**
    Horror fiction
    Occult fiction
  RT **Ghost stories**
    Love stories
    Romantic suspense novels
Gothic revival (Architecture) (May
    subdiv. geog.) **724.3**
  BT **Architecture**
  NT **Victorian architecture**
  RT **Victorian architecture**
Gothic revival (Art) (May subdiv. geog.)
    700.41
  BT **Art**
Gothic revival (Literature) (May subdiv.
    geog.) **808.83; 823.08**
    Use for materials on literature of the eighteenth and nineteenth centuries featuring medieval settings and romantic gloom. For contemporary novels that have a medieval setting and usually include castles and ghosts use **Gothic novels**.
  BT **Literature**
Goths 305.83
  UF East Goths
    Ostrogoths
  BT **Teutonic peoples**
Gout 616.3
  BT **Arthritis**
    Rheumatism
Government
  USE **Political science**
    and names of countries, cities, etc., with the subdivision *Politics and government,* e.g. **United States—Politics and government** and names of Christian denominations with the subdivision *Government,* e.g. **Church of England—**

Government—*Continued*

Government [to be added as needed]

Government agencies

USE **Administrative agencies**

Government aid (May subdiv. geog.) **336**

Use for materials on aid from governments at any level in non-federal systems and on aid from state, provincial, or local governments in federal systems. Materials on central government aid in federal systems are entered under **Federal aid**.

SA government aid to specific endeavors, e.g. **Government aid to libraries** [to be added as needed]

BT **Government aid**
Public finance

NT **Government aid**
Government aid to education
Government aid to libraries

RT **Federal aid**

Government aid to education (May subdiv. geog.) **379.1**

UF Education—Government aid
Education—State aid
State aid to education

BT **Education—Finance**
Education—Government policy
Government aid

Government aid to libraries (May subdiv. geog.) **021.8**

UF Libraries—Government aid
Libraries—State aid
State aid to libraries

BT **Government aid**
Libraries—Government policy
Library finance

Government and business

USE **Economic policy**

Government and the press

USE **Press—Government policy**

Government budgets

USE **Budget**

Government buildings

USE **Public buildings**

Government business enterprises (May subdiv. geog.) **338.7**

UF Government companies
Nationalized companies
Public enterprises

SA types of industries with the subdivision *Government ownership*, e.g. **Electric utilities—Government ownership**; which may be further subdivided geographically [to be added as needed]

BT **Business enterprises**

Government by commission

USE **Municipal government by commission**

Government companies

USE **Government business enterprises**

Government, Comparative

USE **Comparative government**

Government debts

USE **Public debts**

Government departments

USE **Executive departments**

Government documents

USE **Government publications**

Government employees

USE **Civil service**

Government health insurance

USE **National health insurance**

Government housing

USE **Public housing**

Government investigations

USE **Governmental investigations**

Government lending (May subdiv. geog.) **332.7; 354.8**

BT **Domestic economic assistance**
Economic policy
Loans
Public finance

Government libraries (May subdiv. geog.) **027.5**

Use for materials on special libraries maintained by government funds.

UF Federal libraries
Libraries, Governmental

BT **Special libraries**

NT **National libraries**
State libraries

Government, Local

USE **Local government**

Government, Military

USE **Military government**

Government ministries

USE **Executive departments**

Government, Municipal
  USE **Municipal government**
Government officials
  USE **Public officers**
Government ownership (May subdiv.
    geog.) **333.1; 338.9**
  UF Nationalization
      Public ownership
      Socialization of industry
      State ownership
  SA types of industries with the sub-
      division *Government owner-
      ship*, e.g. **Electric utilities—
      Government ownership**;
      which may be further subdi-
      vided geographically [to be
      added as needed]
  BT **Economic policy**
      Industrial policy
      Socialism
  NT **Municipal ownership**
      Railroads—Government policy
  RT **Privatization**
Government ownership of railroads
  USE **Railroads—Government policy**
Government policy
  USE **Buy national policy**
      Commercial policy
      Cultural policy
      Economic policy
      Energy policy
      Environmental policy
      Fiscal policy
      Industrial policy
      Labor policy
      Medical policy
      Military policy
      Monetary policy
      Social policy
      Wage-price policy
      and subjects, ethnic groups, and
      classes of persons with the
      subdivision *Government poli-
      cy,* e.g. **Genetic engineer-
      ing—Government policy;
      Homeless persons—Govern-
      ment policy;** etc., which may
      be further subdivided geo-
      graphically [to be added as
      needed]

Government procurement
  USE **Government purchasing**
Government property, Surplus
  USE **Surplus government property**
Government publications (May subdiv.
    geog.) **011; 015; 025.17**
  UF Documents
      Government documents
      Official publications
      Public documents
  BT **Library resources**
Government publications—Chicago (Ill.)
    015.773
  UF Chicago (Ill.)—Government pub-
      lications
Government publications—Ohio
    015.771
  UF Ohio—Government publications
Government publications—United States
    015.73; 025.17
  UF United States—Government pub-
      lications
Government purchasing (May subdiv.
    geog.) **352.5**
  UF Government procurement
      Procurement, Government
      Public procurement
      Public purchasing
  BT **Purchasing**
  NT **Buy national policy**
Government records—Preservation
  USE **Archives**
Government regulation of commerce
  USE **Commercial policy**
      Industrial laws and legislation
      Interstate commerce
Government regulation of industry
  USE **Industrial policy**
Government regulation of railroads
  USE **Railroads—Government policy**
Government relations
  USE ethnic groups with the subdivi-
      sion *Government relations,*
      e.g. **Native Americans—Gov-
      ernment relations** [to be add-
      ed as needed]
Government reorganization
  USE **Administrative agencies—Reor-
      ganization**
Government, Resistance to
  USE **Resistance to government**

338

Government service
USE **Civil service**
Government spending policy
USE **United States—Appropriations and expenditures**
Government subsidies
USE **Subsidies**
Government surveys
USE **Surveys**
Government transfer payments
USE **Transfer payments**
Governmental investigations (May subdiv. geog.) **328.3; 353.4**

Use for materials on investigations initiated by the legislative, executive, or judicial branches of the government, usually of some particular problem of public interest.

UF Congressional investigations
Executive investigations
Government investigations
Judicial investigations
Legislative investigations
BT **Administration of justice**
Governmental investigations—United States 328.3; 353.4
UF United States—Governmental investigations
Governments in exile
USE names of wars with the subdivision *Governments in exile,* e.g. **World War, 1939-1945—Governments in exile** [to be added as needed]
Governors (May subdiv. geog.) **352.23; 920**
BT **State governments**
GPS (Navigation system)
USE **Global Positioning System**
Grace (Theology) 202; 234
BT **Doctrinal theology**
Salvation
NT **Sacraments**
Spiritual gifts
Grade repetition
USE **Promotion (School)**
Grade retention
USE **Promotion (School)**
Grade schools
USE **Elementary schools**
Grading and marking (Education) 371.27

UF Grading and marking (Students)
Marking and grading (Education)
Students—Grading and marking
BT **Educational tests and measurements**
NT **Ability grouping in education**
Promotion (School)
RT **School reports**
Grading and marking (Students)
USE **Grading and marking (Education)**
Graduate Record Examination 378.1
UF GRE
BT **Colleges and universities—Entrance examinations**
Examinations
Graduate Record Examination—Study guides 378.1
Graduates, College
USE **College graduates**
Graduation
USE **Commencements**
Graffiti (May subdiv. geog.) **080; 808.88**
BT **Inscriptions**
Vandalism
Graft in politics
USE **Political corruption**
Grafting 631.5
BT **Plant propagation**
Grail 398
UF Holy Grail
BT **Folklore**
Grail—Legends 398; 809
RT **Arthurian romances**
Grain 633.1
UF Cereals
SA types of cereal plants, e.g. **Corn**; **Wheat**; etc. [to be added as needed]
NT **Corn**
Wheat
RT **Flour**
Grain—Storage (May subdiv. geog.) **633.1**
Grammar 415
SA names of languages with the subdivision *Grammar* [to be added as needed]
BT **Language and languages**
Linguistics

Grammar—*Continued*

    NT   **English language—Grammar**

Grammar schools

    USE **Elementary education**

Grammy Awards   780.26

    BT   **Sound recordings**

Gramophone

    USE **Phonograph**

Grandfathers (May subdiv. geog.)
    306.874

    BT   **Grandparents**

Grandmothers (May subdiv. geog.)
    306.874

    BT   **Grandparents**

Grandparent and child

    USE **Grandparent-grandchild relationship**

Grandparent-grandchild relationship
    306.874

Use for materials on the interaction between grandparents and their grandchildren. Materials restricted to the legal right of grandparents to visit their grandchildren are entered under **Visitation rights (Domestic relations)**. Materials on the skills, etc., needed for being an effective grandparent are entered under **Grandparenting**.

    UF   Grandparent and child

    BT   **Family**

           Grandparents

Grandparenting   306.874

Use for materials on the skills, etc., needed for being an effective grandparent. Materials on the interaction between grandparents and their grandchildren are entered under **Grandparent-grandchild relationship**.

    BT   **Grandparents**

           Parenting

Grandparents   306.874

    BT   **Family**

    NT   **Foster grandparents**

           Grandfathers

           Grandmothers

           Grandparent-grandchild relationship

           Grandparenting

           Grandparents as parents

Grandparents as parents   306.874

    UF   Parenting by grandparents

    BT   **Grandparents**

           Parenting

Grange   334

    BT   **Agriculture—Societies**

Granite   552; 553.5

    BT   **Rocks**

           Stone

Grants

    USE **Grants-in-aid**

           Subsidies

Grants-in-aid (May subdiv. geog.)
    336.1; 352.73

Use for materials on grants of money made from a central government to a local government.

    UF   Grants

    SA   federal aid to particular endeavors, e.g. **Federal aid to education** [to be added as needed]

    BT   **Public finance**

    RT   **Domestic economic assistance**

Grapes   634.8; 641.3

    UF   Viticulture

    BT   **Fruit**

    RT   **Vineyards**

           Wine and wine making

Graph theory   511

    UF   Graphs, Theory of

           Theory of graphs

    BT   **Algebra**

           Mathematical analysis

           Topology

Graphic arts (May subdiv. geog.)   760

    UF   Arts, Graphic

    SA   types of graphic arts [to be added as needed]

    BT   **Art**

    NT   **Clip art**

           Drawing

           Engraving

           Painting

           Photography

           Printing

           Prints

           Typography

Graphic arts—United States   760.097

    UF   American graphic arts

Graphic fiction

    USE **Graphic novels**

Graphic methods   001.4; 511

    UF   Flow charts

           Flowcharting

           Graphs

    BT   **Drawing**

           Geometrical drawing

           Mechanical drawing

Graphic methods—*Continued*
  NT Statistics—Graphic methods
Graphic novels 741.5
  UF Comic book novels
      Graphic fiction
  BT **Comic books, strips, etc.**
      Fiction
  NT **Adventure graphic novels**
      Autobiographical graphic novels
      Biographical graphic novels
      Fantasy graphic novels
      Female superhero graphic novels
      Horror graphic novels
      Humorous graphic novels
      Manga
      Mystery graphic novels
      Religious graphic novels
      Romance graphic novels
      Science fiction graphic novels
      Sports—Graphic novels
      Superhero graphic novels
      Supernatural graphic novels
Graphics, Computer
  USE **Computer graphics**
Graphite 553.2
  UF Black lead
  BT **Carbon**
Graphology 137; 155.2
    Use for materials on handwriting as an expression of the writer's character. General materials on the history and art of writing are entered under **Writing**. Materials on writing with a pen or pencil and practical or prescriptive guides to penmanship are entered under **Handwriting**.
  BT **Handwriting**
      Writing
Graphs
  USE **Graphic methods**
Graphs, Theory of
  USE **Graph theory**
Grass (Drug)
  USE **Marijuana**
Grasses (May subdiv. geog.) 584; 633.2
  BT **Plants**
  RT **Feeds**
      Forage plants
      Hay
      Lawns
Grasslands (May subdiv. geog.) 577.4; 578.74

  BT **Land use**
  NT **Prairies**
Gratefulness
  USE **Gratitude**
Gratitude 179
  UF Gratefulness
      Thankfulness
  BT **Emotions**
      Virtue
Graves
  USE **Burial**
      Cemeteries
      Epitaphs
      Funeral rites and ceremonies
      Mounds and mound builders
      Tombs
Graveyards
  USE **Cemeteries**
Gravitation 521; 531
    Use for materials on the phenomenon in physics of attraction between masses. Materials on the gravitational pull of the earth or other planets or celestial bodies on objects at or near their surface are entered under **Gravity**.
  BT **Physics**
  NT **Gravity**
  RT **Relativity (Physics)**
Gravity 531
    Use for materials on the gravitational pull of the earth or other planets or celestial bodies on objects at or near their surface. Materials on the phenomenon in physics of attraction between masses are entered under **Gravitation**.
  UF Earth—Gravity
  BT **Gravitation**
Gravity free state
  USE **Weightlessness**
Gray Friars
  USE **Franciscans**
GRE
  USE **Graduate Record Examination**
Grease
  USE **Lubrication and lubricants**
      Oils and fats
Great books program
  USE **Discussion groups**
Great Britain 941
    Use for materials on the United Kingdom of Great Britain and Northern Ireland, which comprises England, Scotland, Wales, and Northern Ireland, as well as for materials on the island of Great Britain. May be subdivided like **United States** except for *History*. Materi-

Great Britain—*Continued*

als limited to one of the constituent parts of the United Kingdom, apart from materials relating to history or politics and government, are entered under that part, e.g. **England**.

  NT **England**

Great Britain—Colonies 325

  UF British Empire

  BT **Colonies**

  RT **Commonwealth countries**

Great Britain—History 941

  UF England—History

       English history

Great Britain—History—0-1066 941.01

  NT **Anglo-Saxons**

       Celts

Great Britain—History—1066-1154, Norman period 941.02

  NT **Domesday book**

       Hastings (East Sussex, England), Battle of, 1066

       Normans

Great Britain—History—1066-1485, Medieval period 941.03

  NT **Hundred Years' War, 1339-1453**

Great Britain—History—1154-1399, Plantagenets 941.03

  NT **Magna Carta**

Great Britain—History—1399-1485, Lancaster and York 941.04

Great Britain—History—1455-1485, Wars of the Roses 941.04

  UF Wars of the Roses, 1455-1485

Great Britain—History—1485-1603, Tudors 941.05

  NT **Spanish Armada, 1588**

Great Britain—History—1603-1714, Stuarts 941.06

Great Britain—History—1642-1660, Civil War and Commonwealth 941.06

  UF Civil War—England

       Commonwealth of England

Great Britain—History—1714-1837 941.07

  NT **War of 1812**

Great Britain—History—19th century 941.081

  RT **Industrial revolution**

Great Britain—History—1853-1856, Crimean War

  USE **Crimean War, 1853-1856**

Great Britain—History—20th century 941.082

Great Britain—History—1945-1952 941.085

Great Britain—History—1952- 941.085

Great Britain—History—21st century 941.086

Great Britain—Kings and rulers 920; 941.092

  UF Great Britain—Kings, queens, rulers, etc.

  BT **Kings and rulers**

Great Britain—Kings, queens, rulers, etc.

  USE **Great Britain—Kings and rulers**

Great Britain—Prime ministers

  USE **Prime ministers—Great Britain**

Great Britain—Queens

  USE **Queens—Great Britain**

Great Depression, 1929-1939 (May subdiv. geog.) **338.5; 909.82**

  UF Business depression, 1929-1939

       Depressions—1929

  BT **Depressions**

       Economic conditions

Greece 938; 949.5

May be subdivided like **United States** except for *History*.

Greece, Ancient

  USE **Greece—History—0-323**

Greece—Antiquities 938

  BT **Classical antiquities**

  NT **Delphi (Extinct city)**

Greece—Biography 920.038; 920.0495

  UF Classical biography

  BT **Biography**

Greece—Civilization 938

Use for materials on the civilization of Greece, ancient and modern. Materials on the spread of Greek civilization throughout the ancient world following the conquests of Alexander the Great are entered under **Hellenism**. Materials on both ancient Greek and Roman civilizations are entered under **Classical civilization**.

  UF Civilization, Greek

       Greek civilization

  BT **Classical civilization**

  NT **Hellenism**

Greece—Description

  USE **Greece—Description and travel**

Greece—Description—0-323

  USE **Greece—Description and travel—0-323**

Greece—Description and travel   914.95

Use for descriptive materials on modern Greece, including materials for travelers. Descriptive materials on ancient Greece, including accounts by travelers in ancient times, are entered under **Greece—Description and travel—0-323**.

UF   Greece—Description

**Greece—Description and travel—0-323
913.8**

Use for descriptive materials on ancient Greece including accounts by travelers of ancient times.

UF   Ancient Greece—Description

Greece—Description—0-323

Greece—Geography   914.95

Use for materials on the geography of modern Greece. Materials on the geography of ancient Greece are entered under **Greece—Historical geography**.

BT   **Geography**

NT   **Greece—Historical geography**

**Greece—Historical geography   911;
913.8**

UF   Classical geography

BT   **Ancient geography
Greece—Geography
Historical geography**

Greece—History   938; 949.5

Greece—History—0-323   938

UF   Ancient Greece

Greece, Ancient

Greece—History—323-1453   949.5

UF   Medieval Greece

Greece—History—1453-   949.5

UF   Greece, Modern

Greece—History—20th century   949.507

Greece—History—1967-1974   949.507

Greece—History—1974-   949.507

Greece, Modern

USE   **Greece—History—1453-**

Greed   178

Use for materials on any excessive desire for food, personal possessions, etc. Materials on an inordinate desire for wealth are entered under **Avarice**.

BT   **Human behavior**

RT   **Avarice**

Greek and Latin drama

USE   **Classical drama**

Greek antiquities

USE   **Classical antiquities**

Greek architecture (May subdiv. geog.)
722

UF   Architecture, Greek

BT   **Ancient architecture
Architecture**

Greek art   709.38; 709.495

UF   Art, Greek

Classical art

BT   **Ancient art
Art
Classical antiquities**

Greek Church

USE   **Greek Orthodox Church**

Greek civilization

USE   **Greece—Civilization**

Greek language   480

Use for classical Greek. Modern Greek is entered under **Modern Greek language**. May be subdivided like **English language**.

UF   Classical languages

BT   **Language and languages**

RT   **Modern Greek language**

Greek language, Modern

USE   **Modern Greek language**

Greek letter societies

USE   **Fraternities and sororities**

Greek literature   880

May use same subdivisions and names of literary forms as for **English literature**.

BT   **Literature**

RT   **Classical literature**

Greek literature, Modern

USE   **Modern Greek literature**

Greek mythology   292.1

UF   Mythology, Greek

BT   **Classical mythology**

Greek Orthodox Church (May subdiv. geog.)   **281.9**

UF   Greek Church

BT   **Christian sects
Orthodox Eastern Church**

Greek philosophy

USE   **Ancient philosophy**

Greek sculpture   730.938; 730.9495

UF   Sculpture, Greek

BT   **Sculpture**

Green movement

USE   **Environmental movement**

Green technology (May subdiv. geog.)
363.7

UF   Earth-friendly technology

Environmental technology

BT   **Technology**

Green tourism

USE   **Ecotourism**

Greenhouse effect (May subdiv. geog.)
363.738; 551.5; 551.6
- UF Atmospheric greenhouse effect
  Carbon dioxide greenhouse effect
  Global warming
  Greenhouse effect, Atmospheric
- BT **Climate**
  Solar radiation

Greenhouse effect, Atmospheric
- USE **Greenhouse effect**

Greenhouses 631.5
- UF Hothouses
- BT **Flower gardening**
  Gardening
  Horticulture
- RT **Garden rooms**

Greeting cards 741.6; 745.594
- UF Cards, Greeting
- SA types of greeting cards [to be added as needed]
- NT **Christmas cards**

Gregorian chant
- USE **Chants (Plain, Gregorian, etc.)**

Grey Friars
- USE **Franciscans**

Grey market
- USE **Black market**

Grief 152.4; 155.9
  Use for materials on mental suffering or sorrow from causes such as loss or remorse other than the loss of a loved one. Materials on the suffering of those who have lost a loved one are entered under **Bereavement**.
- UF Sorrow
- BT **Emotions**
- RT **Bereavement**
  Consolation
  Joy and sorrow

Grievance procedures (Public administration)
- USE **Ombudsman**

Griffins 398.2454
- UF Gryphons
- BT **Mythical animals**

Grill cooking
- USE **Barbecue cooking**

Grilling
- USE **Barbecue cooking**

Grinding and polishing 621.9
- UF Buffing
  Polishing
- BT **Machine shop practice**

- RT **Machine tools**

Grist mills
- USE **Flour mills**

Groceries—Packaging
- USE **Food—Packaging**

Groceries—Purchasing
- USE **Grocery shopping**

Grocery shopping 641.3
  Use for materials on food buying. Materials on the principles and methods involved in the transfer of merchandise from producer to consumer are entered under **Marketing**.
- UF Food buying
  Food—Purchasing
  Groceries—Purchasing
  Marketing (Home economics)
  Supermarket shopping
- BT **Home economics**
  Shopping

Grocery trade (May subdiv. geog.)
338.4
- BT **Food industry**
- NT **Supermarkets**
- RT **Food**

Grooming
- USE types of animals with the subdivision *Grooming* [to be added as needed]

Grooming, Personal
- USE **Personal grooming**

Gross national product (May subdiv. geog.) **339.3**
- UF GNP
  National product, Gross
- BT **Economics**
  Statistics
  Wealth
- RT **Income**

Grottoes
- USE **Caves**

Ground effect machines
- USE **Air-cushion vehicles**

Ground water
- USE **Groundwater**

Grounds maintenance 712
  Use for materials on maintenance of public, industrial, and institutional grounds and large estates.
- BT **Gardening**
- NT **Roadside improvement**

Groundwater (May subdiv. geog.)
551.49; 553.7

Groundwater—*Continued*
    UF   Ground water
          Subterranean water
          Underground water
    BT   **Water**

Group decision making   302.3; 658.4
    BT   **Decision making**

Group discussion
    USE   **Discussion groups**

Group dynamics
    USE   **Social groups**

Group homes   362; 363.5

    Use for materials on planned housing for groups of unrelated people needing supervision.

    UF   Community based residences
          Group residences
          Residential treatment centers
    BT   **Institutional care**
          Social work
    NT   **Halfway houses**
    RT   **Foster home care**

Group hospitalization
    USE   **Hospitalization insurance**

Group identity   302.4
    UF   Collective identity
          Community identity
          Social identity
    BT   **Identity (Psychology)**

Group insurance   368.3

    Use for materials on group life insurance. Materials on group insurance in other fields are entered under the specific kind of insurance, e.g. **Health insurance.**

    UF   Insurance, Group
    BT   **Life insurance**

Group living
    USE   **Communal living**

Group medical practice
    USE   **Medical practice**

Group medical practice, Prepaid
    USE   **Health maintenance organizations**

Group medical service
    USE   **Health insurance**

Group method in teaching
    USE   **Cooperative learning**

Group problem solving   153.4
    UF   Brain storming
          Team problem solving
          Think tanks
    BT   **Problem solving**

Group relations training   302

    UF   Encounter groups
          Sensitivity training
          T groups
    BT   **Interpersonal relations**

Group residences
    USE   **Group homes**

Group social work
    USE   **Social group work**

Group teaching
    USE   **Cooperative learning**

Group theory   512
    UF   Groups, Theory of
    BT   **Algebra**
          Mathematics
          Number theory
    NT   **Boolean algebra**

Group travel
    USE   **Travel**

Group values
    USE   **Social values**

Group work in education
    USE   **Cooperative learning**

Group work, Social
    USE   **Social group work**

Grouping by ability
    USE   **Ability grouping in education**

Groups of persons
    USE   **Persons**

Groups, Social
    USE   **Social groups**

Groups, Theory of
    USE   **Group theory**

Growing of Christmas trees
    USE   **Christmas tree growing**

Grown-up abused children
    USE   **Adult child abuse victims**

Grown-ups
    USE   **Adults**

Grownups
    USE   **Adults**

Growth   155; 571.8; 612.6
    SA   subjects with the subdivision *Growth*, e.g. **Children—Growth; Cities and towns—Growth; Plants—Growth;** etc. [to be added as needed]
    BT   **Physiology**

Growth disorders   616.4
    UF   Abnormal growth
          Abnormalities, Human
          Development

Growth disorders—*Continued*
>>> Failure to thrive syndrome
>>> Human abnormalities
>> BT **Metabolism**
>> NT **Dwarfism**
>>> **Giantism**
>> RT **Birth defects**
>>> **Fetal alcohol syndrome**

Growth retardation
> USE **Dwarfism**

Gryphons
> USE **Griffins**

Guaranteed annual income (May subdiv. geog.) **362.5**
> Use for materials on compensation provided by a government to anyone whose annual income falls below a specified level.
>> UF Annual income guarantee
>>> Guaranteed income
>> BT **Income**

Guaranteed income
> USE **Guaranteed annual income**

Guerillas
> USE **Guerrillas**

Guerrilla warfare (May subdiv. geog.) **355.02; 355.4**
> Use for materials on the military aspects of irregular warfare. General and historical materials are entered under **Guerrillas**.
>> UF Unconventional warfare
>> BT **Insurgency**
>>> **Military art and science**
>>> **Tactics**
>>> **War**

Guerrillas (May subdiv. geog.) **356**
> Use for general and historical materials. Materials on the military aspects of irregular warfare are entered under **Guerrilla warfare**.
>> UF Guerillas
>>> Partisans
>> SA names of wars with the subdivision *Underground movements,* e.g. **World War, 1939-1945—Underground movements** [to be added as needed]
>> BT **National liberation movements**

Guests
> USE **Entertaining**

Guidance
> USE **Counseling**

Guidance counseling, Educational
> USE **Educational counseling**

Guidance counseling, School
> USE **School counseling**

Guidance, Vocational
> USE **Vocational guidance**

Guide dogs **636.7**
>> UF Dog guides
>>> Dogs for the blind
>>> Seeing eye dogs
>> BT **Animals and the handicapped**
>>> **Working dogs**

Guidebooks
> USE names of cities (except ancient cities), countries, states, etc., with the subdivision *Guidebooks,* e.g. **Chicago (Ill.)—Guidebooks; United States—Guidebooks;** etc. [to be added as needed]

Guided missiles **358.1; 623.4**
>> UF Missiles, Guided
>> SA types of missiles and names of specific missiles [to be added as needed]
>> BT **Bombs**
>>> **Projectiles**
>>> **Rocketry**
>>> **Rockets (Aeronautics)**
>> NT **Antimissile missiles**
>>> **Ballistic missiles**
>>> **Nike rocket**

Guilt **152.4**
>> BT **Conscience**
>>> **Emotions**
>>> **Ethics**
>>> **Good and evil**
>>> **Sin**
>> RT **Shame**

Guitar
> USE **Guitars**

Guitar music **787.87**
>> BT **Instrumental music**

Guitars **787.87**
>> UF Guitar
>> BT **Stringed instruments**
>> NT **Air guitar**
>>> **Electric guitar**

Gulf States (U.S.) **976**
>> BT **United States**

Gulf War, 1991
> USE **Persian Gulf War, 1991**

Gums and resins **547; 668**

Gums and resins—*Continued*

    UF   Resins

          Rosin

    BT   **Forest products**

          Industrial chemistry

          Plastics

Gun control (May subdiv. geog.)   **323.4; 344.05; 363.33**

    Use for materials about existing laws governing the purchase and use of firearms and for materials about the political controversy over limiting legal access to firearms and stopping the traffic in illegal firearms.

    UF   Control of guns

          Firearms control

          Firearms—Law and legislation

          Guns—Control

          Handgun control

          Right to bear arms

    BT   **Law**

          Legislation

Gundam (Fictional character)   **741.5**

    BT   **Fictional robots**

          Manga

          Mecha

Gunpowder   **623.4**

    UF   Powder, Smokeless

          Smokeless powder

    BT   **Explosives**

          Firearms

    RT   **Ammunition**

Guns

    USE **Firearms**

          Ordnance

          Rifles

          Shotguns

Guns—Control

    USE **Gun control**

Gunsmithing

    USE **Firearms industry**

Gymnastics   **613.7; 796.44**

    UF   Calisthenics

    BT   **Athletics**

          Exercise

          Sports

    RT   **Acrobats and acrobatics**

          Physical education

Gynecology

    USE **Women—Diseases**

          Women—Health and hygiene

Gypsies   **305.891**

    UF   Gipsies

          Romanies

Gypsum   **553.6**

    BT   **Minerals**

Gyroscope   **629.135; 681**

    BT   **Aeronautical instruments**

Habeas corpus   **345**

    BT   **Civil rights**

          Constitutional law

          Criminal procedure

          Martial law

Habit   **152.3**

    BT   **Human behavior**

          Psychology

    NT   **Tobacco habit**

    RT   **Instinct**

Habitat (Ecology) (May subdiv. geog.)   **577; 591.7**

    SA   types of ecology, e.g. **Marine ecology**; and types of animals, plants, and crops with the subdivision *Ecology*, e.g. **Fishes—Ecology** [to be added as needed]

    BT   **Ecology**

Habitations

    USE types of animals with the subdivision *Habitations,* for materials on the natural shelters and homes animals build for themselves, such as burrows, dens, lairs, etc., e.g. **Beavers—Habitations** [to be added as needed]

Habitations, Human

    USE **Housing**

Habitations of domestic animals

    USE **Animal housing**

Habitations of wild animals

    USE **Animals—Habitations**

Habits of animals

    USE **Animal behavior**

Hades

    USE **Hell**

Haiku   **808.1; 808.81**

    Use for collections of haiku by one or several authors or for materials about haiku.

    BT   **Poetry**

Hair   **612.7; 646.7**

    Use for general materials on hair as well for as materials on hairdressing and haircutting.

    UF   Barbering

          Coiffure

Hair—*Continued*
Haircutting
Hairdressing
Hairstyles
Hairstyling
BT   **Head**
      Personal grooming
NT   **Braids (Hairstyling)**
      Wigs
Haircutting
USE   **Hair**
Hairdressing
USE   **Hair**
Hairstyles
USE   **Hair**
Hairstyling
USE   **Hair**
Halftone process
USE   **Photoengraving**
Halfway houses (May subdiv. geog.)
    362; 365
> Use for materials on centers for formerly institutionalized individuals, such as mental patients or drug addicts, that are designed to facilitate their readjustment to private life.

BT   **Correctional institutions**
      Group homes
Halitosis
USE   **Bad breath**
Halley's comet   523.6
BT   **Comets**
Hallmarks
UF   Marks
      Marks on plate
SA   types of things with identifying marks, other than plate, with the subdivision *Marks*, e.g. **Pottery—Marks** [to be added as needed]
BT   **Plate**
Halloween   394.2646
UF   All Hallows' Eve
BT   **Holidays**
Hallucinations and illusions   616.85; 616.89
UF   Delusions
      Illusions
BT   **Abnormal psychology**
      Parapsychology
      Subconsciousness
      Visions
NT   **Optical illusions**

RT   **Apparitions**
      Fantasy
      Magic
      Magic tricks
      Personality disorders
Hallucinogenic drugs
USE   **Hallucinogens**
Hallucinogenic plants
USE   **Hallucinogens**
Hallucinogens   615
UF   Consciousness expanding drugs
      Hallucinogenic drugs
      Hallucinogenic plants
SA   types of hallucinogens [to be added as needed]
BT   **Drugs**
      Psychotropic drugs
      Stimulants
NT   **LSD (Drug)**
Ham radio stations
USE   **Amateur radio stations**
Hand shadows
USE   **Shadow pictures**
Hand weaving
USE   **Weaving**
Handbooks, manuals, etc.
USE   subjects, classes of persons, and names of places, corporate bodies, individual literary authors, and sacred works with the subdivision *Handbooks, manuals, etc.*, e.g. **Photography—Handbooks, manuals, etc.; United States. Army—Handbooks, manuals, etc.** [to be added as needed]
Handedness
USE   **Left- and right-handedness**
Handgun control
USE   **Gun control**
Handguns (May subdiv. geog.)   **683.4**
UF   Pistols
      Revolvers
BT   **Firearms**
Handheld computers
USE   **Portable computers**
Handicapped (May subdiv. geog.)   **305.9; 362.4**
UF   Disabled
NT   **Architecture and the handicapped**

Handicapped—*Continued*

>> Computers and the handi-
>> capped
>> Discrimination against the
>> handicapped
>> Handicapped children
>> Mentally handicapped
>> Physically handicapped
>> Sick
>> Socially handicapped
>> Sports for the handicapped
>> Vocational guidance for the
>> handicapped

Handicapped and animals
> USE **Animals and the handicapped**

Handicapped and architecture
> USE **Architecture and the handi-
> capped**

Handicapped children (May subdiv.
> geog.) **362.7**
> UF Abnormal children
> Children, Abnormal
> BT **Children**
> **Exceptional children**
> **Handicapped**
> NT **Brain damaged children**
> **Hyperactive children**
> **Mainstreaming in education**
> **Mentally handicapped children**
> **Parents of handicapped chil-
> dren**
> **Physically handicapped chil-
> dren**
> **Socially handicapped children**

Handicapped—Clothing **646.4**
> BT **Clothing and dress**

Handicapped—Legal status, laws, etc.
> (May subdiv. geog.) **346.01**
> UF Disability law
> BT **Law**

Handicapped—Nazi persecution (May
> subdiv. geog.) **940.53**
> UF Nazi persecution of the handi-
> capped
> BT **Persecution**
> **World War, 1939-1945—Atroc-
> ities**

Handicapped—Salaries, wages, etc. (May
> subdiv. geog.) **331.2**
> BT **Salaries, wages, etc.**

Handicapped—Services for (May subdiv.
> geog.) **362.4**

> UF Services for the handicapped
> BT **Human services**
> **Social work**

Handicapped—Travel **910.2**
> BT **Travel**

Handicaps
> USE **Disabilities**

Handicraft (May subdiv. geog.) **745.5;
> 746**
> Use for materials on creative work done by
> hand, sometimes with the aid of simple tools
> or machines.
> UF Crafts (Arts)
> SA types of handicrafts [to be added
> as needed]
> BT **Arts**
> NT **Beadwork**
> **Chair caning**
> **Collage**
> **Craft shows**
> **Egg decoration**
> **Furniture finishing**
> **Hooked rugs**
> **Industrial arts**
> **Leather work**
> **Models and modelmaking**
> **Nature craft**
> **Paper crafts**
> **Picture frames and framing**
> **Polymer clay craft**
> **Scrapbooking**
> **Toy making**
> **Weaving**
> RT **Arts and crafts movement**
> **Creative activities**
> **Decoration and ornament**
> **Decorative arts**
> **Folk art**
> **Hobbies**
> **Occupational therapy**

Handling of materials
> USE **Materials handling**

Handwriting **652**
> Use for materials on writing with a pen or
> pencil and for practical or prescriptive guides
> to penmanship. General materials on the histo-
> ry and art of writing are entered under **Writ-
> ing**. Materials on handwriting as an expres-
> sion of the writer's character are entered un-
> der **Graphology**.
> UF Legibility of handwriting
> Penmanship
> Writing—Study and teaching
> BT **Writing**

Handwriting—*Continued*
　　NT　**Calligraphy**
　　　　Graphology
　　　　Writing of numerals
Hang gliding
　　USE　**Gliding and soaring**
Hanging
　　USE　**Capital punishment**
Hansen's disease
　　USE　**Leprosy**
Hanukkah (May subdiv. geog.)　**296.4;**
　　394.267
　　UF　Chanukah
　　　　Feast of Dedication
　　　　Feast of Lights
　　BT　**Jewish holidays**
Happening (Art)
　　USE　**Performance art**
Happiness　158
　　UF　Gladness
　　BT　**Emotions**
　　NT　**Mental health**
　　RT　**Joy and sorrow**
　　　　Pleasure
Harassment, Sexual
　　USE　**Sexual harassment**
Harbors (May subdiv. geog.)　**386;**
　　387.1; 627
　　UF　Ports
　　BT　**Civil engineering**
　　　　Hydraulic structures
　　　　Merchant marine
　　　　Navigation
　　　　Shipping
　　　　Transportation
　　NT　**Marinas**
　　RT　**Docks**
Hard-of-hearing
　　USE　**Hearing impaired**
Hardanger needlework　746.44
　　UF　Norwegian drawn work
　　BT　**Drawn work**
　　　　Embroidery
　　　　Needlework
Hardware　683
　　BT　**Iron industry**
　　NT　**Knives**
Hares
　　USE　**Rabbits**
Harlem Renaissance　810.9; 974.7
　　UF　New Negro Movement

　　BT　**African American art**
　　　　African American music
　　　　American literature—African
　　　　　American authors
Harmful insects
　　USE　**Insect pests**
Harmony　781.2
　　BT　**Composition (Music)**
　　　　Music
　　　　Music—Theory
Harry S. Truman Library (Indepen-
　　dence, Mo.)　026
　　BT　**Presidents—United States—Ar-**
　　　　chives
Harvesting machinery　631.3
　　UF　Reapers
　　BT　**Agricultural machinery**
Hashish
　　USE　**Marijuana**
Hasidism (May subdiv. geog.)　**296.8**
　　UF　Chasidism
　　　　Hassidism
　　BT　**Judaism**
Hassidism
　　USE　**Hasidism**
Hastings (East Sussex, England), Battle
　　of, 1066　941.02
　　BT　**Great Britain—History—1066-**
　　　　1154, Norman period
Hate　152.4
　　BT　**Emotions**
Hate crimes (May subdiv. geog.)　**364**
　　UF　Bias attacks
　　　　Bias crimes
　　　　Bigotry-motivated crimes
　　　　Crimes of hate
　　　　Prejudice-motivated crimes
　　BT　**Crime**
　　　　Discrimination
　　　　Violence
Hatha yoga　613.7
　　UF　Yoga exercises
　　　　Yoga, Hatha
　　BT　**Exercise**
　　　　Yoga
Hats (May subdiv. geog.)　**391.4; 646.5;**
　　687
　　UF　Millinery
　　BT　**Clothing and dress**
　　　　Costume

Haunted houses (May subdiv. geog.)
133.1
BT **Houses**
RT **Ghosts**
Hawking
USE **Falconry**
Hay   633.2
SA   types of hay crops, e.g. **Alfalfa**
[to be added as needed]
BT **Farm produce**
Forage plants
RT **Feeds**
Grasses
Hay fever   616.2
BT **Allergy**
Hazardous materials
USE **Hazardous substances**
Hazardous occupations   331.702
UF   Dangerous occupations
BT **Occupations**
RT **Industrial accidents**
Occupational diseases
Occupational health and safety
Hazardous substances   363.17; 604.7
UF   Dangerous materials
Hazardous materials
Inflammable substances
Toxic substances
BT **Materials**
NT **Hazardous wastes**
Poisons and poisoning
Hazardous substances—Transportation
363.17; 604.7
BT **Transportation**
Hazardous waste disposal
USE **Hazardous wastes**
Hazardous waste sites (May subdiv.
geog.)   363.72; 628.4
UF   Chemical landfills
Dumps, Toxic
Toxic dumps
BT **Landfills**
NT **Love Canal Chemical Waste
Landfill (Niagara Falls,
N.Y.)**
Hazardous wastes   363.72
UF   Hazardous waste disposal
Toxic wastes
Wastes, Hazardous
BT **Hazardous substances**
Industrial waste

Refuse and refuse disposal
RT **Medical wastes**
Pollution
HDTV (Television)
USE **High definition television**
Head   611; 612
BT **Anatomy**
NT **Brain**
Ear
Eye
Face
Hair
Mouth
Nose
Phrenology
Teeth
Head pain
USE **Headache**
Headache   616.8
UF   Head pain
BT **Pain**
NT **Migraine**
Heads of state (May subdiv. geog.)
352.23; 920
UF   Rulers
State, Heads of
SA   names of individual heads of
state [to be added as needed]
BT **Executive power**
Statesmen
NT **Dictators**
Kings and rulers
Presidents
Healing   615.5
BT **Therapeutics**
Healing, Mental
USE **Mental healing**
Healing, Spiritual
USE **Spiritual healing**
Health   613
Use for materials on physical, mental, and
social well-being. Materials on personal body
care are entered under **Hygiene**.
UF   Personal health
SA   parts of the body with the sub-
division *Care*, e.g. **Foot—
Care**; classes of persons and
ethnic groups with the subdi-
vision *Health and hygiene*,
e.g. **Women—Health and
hygiene**; and subjects and

Health—*Continued*
  names of wars with the sub-
  division *Health aspects*, e.g.
  World War, 1939-1945—
  Health aspects [to be added
  as needed]
 BT **Medicine**
   Physiology
   Preventive medicine
 NT **Children—Health and hygiene**
   Diet
   Elderly—Health and hygiene
   Exercise
   Health education
   Health self-care
   Infants—Health and hygiene
   Mental health
   Nutrition
   Physical fitness
   Public health
   Rest
   Sleep
   Stress management
   Women—Health and hygiene
 RT **Diseases**
   Holistic medicine
   Hygiene
Health and hygiene
 USE classes of persons and ethnic
   groups with the subdivision
   Health and hygiene, e.g.
   Women—Health and hy-
   giene; and parts of the body
   with the subdivision *Care,*
   e.g. **Foot—Care; Skin—**
   Care; etc. [to be added as
   needed]
Health aspects
 USE subjects, industries, and wars
   with the subdivision *Health*
   aspects, e.g. **World War,**
   1939-1945—Health aspects
   [to be added as needed]
Health boards 614.06
 UF Boards of health
   Public health boards
 BT **Public health**
Health care
 USE **Medical care**
Health care delivery
 USE **Medical care**

Health care facilities
 USE **Health facilities**
Health care personnel
 USE **Medical personnel**
Health care policy
 USE **Medical policy**
Health care reform (May subdiv. geog.)
  362.1
 UF Health reform
   Health system reform
   Medical care reform
   Reform of health care delivery
   Reform of medical care delivery
 RT **Health insurance**
   Medical care
Health care, Right to
 USE **Right to health care**
Health care, Self
 USE **Health self-care**
Health clubs
 USE **Physical fitness centers**
Health counseling 362.1; 613
 BT **Counseling**
   Health education
Health education (May subdiv. geog.)
  372.37; 613.07
 UF Health—Study and teaching
   Hygiene—Study and teaching
 BT **Education**
   Health
 NT **Drug education**
   Health counseling
   School hygiene
 RT **Children—Health and hygiene**
   School nurses
Health—Environmental aspects
 USE **Environmental health**
Health examinations
 USE **Periodic health examinations**
Health facilities (May subdiv. geog.)
  362.11
 UF Clinics
   Health care facilities
   Medical care facilities
 BT **Medical care**
   Public health
Health foods
 USE **Natural foods**
Health, Industrial
 USE **Occupational health and safety**

Health insurance (May subdiv. geog.)
    368.38
    UF   Group medical service
          Insurance, Health
          Medical insurance
    BT   **Insurance**
    NT   **Health maintenance organizations**
          Hospitalization insurance
          National health insurance
          Workers' compensation
    RT   **Health care reform**

Health maintenance organizations (May subdiv. geog.)   **362.1; 368.38; 610.6**
    UF   Comprehensive health care organizations
          Group medical practice, Prepaid
          HMOs
          Prepaid group medical practice
    BT   **Health insurance**
          Medical practice

Health personnel
    USE **Medical personnel**

Health policy
    USE **Medical policy**

Health professions
    USE **Medical personnel**

Health program evaluation
    USE **Public health—Evaluation**

Health records
    USE **Medical records**

Health reform
    USE **Health care reform**

Health resorts (May subdiv. geog.)   **613**
    UF   Health resorts, spas, etc.
          Health spas
          Spas
          Watering places
    BT   **Resorts**
    RT   **Hydrotherapy**

Health resorts, spas, etc.
    USE **Health resorts**

Health sciences personnel
    USE **Medical personnel**

Health self-care   **613; 616**
    UF   Health care, Self
          Medical self-care
          Self-care, Health
          Self-care, Medical
          Self-examination, Medical

          Self health care
          Self-help medical care
          Self-medication
    BT   **Alternative medicine**
          Health
          Medical care
    NT   **First aid**
          Physical fitness
    RT   **Holistic medicine**
          Popular medicine

Health services accessibility
    USE **Access to health care**

Health services personnel
    USE **Medical personnel**

Health spas
    USE **Health resorts**
          Physical fitness centers

Health—Study and teaching
    USE **Health education**

Health system reform
    USE **Health care reform**

Healths, Drinking of
    USE **Toasts**

Hearing   **152.1; 612.8**
    UF   Acoustics
    BT   **Senses and sensation**
          Sound
    NT   **Hearing in animals**
    RT   **Deafness**
          Ear
          Listening

Hearing aids   **617.8**
    BT   **Deafness**

Hearing ear dogs   **636.7**
    UF   Dogs for the deaf
    BT   **Animals and the handicapped**
          Deaf—Means of communication
          Working dogs

Hearing impaired   **362.4; 617.8**
    UF   Hard-of-hearing
          Partial hearing
          Partially hearing
    BT   **Physically handicapped**
    NT   **Deaf**

Hearing in animals   **573.8**
    UF   Animals—Hearing
    BT   **Hearing**
          Senses and sensation in animals

Heart   **573.1; 611; 612.1**

Heart—*Continued*
BT Cardiovascular system
NT Artificial heart
Heart—Anatomy   573.1; 611
BT Anatomy
Heart attack   616.1
UF Heart—Infarction
Myocardial infarction
BT Heart diseases
Heart disease
USE Heart diseases
Heart—Diseases
USE Heart diseases
Heart diseases   616.1
UF Cardiac diseases
Coronary diseases
Heart disease
Heart—Diseases
BT Diseases
NT Angina pectoris
Heart attack
Heart diseases—Prevention   616.1
BT Preventive medicine
Heart—Infarction
USE Heart attack
Heart—Physiology   612.1
BT Physiology
Heart resuscitation
USE Cardiac resuscitation
Heart—Surgery   617.4
UF Open heart surgery
BT Surgery
Heart—Surgery—Nursing   617.4
BT Nursing
Heart—Transplantation   617.4
BT Transplantation of organs, tissues, etc.
Heat   536
BT Electromagnetic waves
NT Steam
Thermometers
RT Combustion
Fire
Temperature
Thermodynamics
Heat—Conduction   536
Heat engines   621.4
UF Hot air engines
BT Engines
Thermodynamics
Heat insulating materials
USE Insulation (Heat)

Heat pumps   621.4
BT Pumping machinery
Thermodynamics
Heat—Transmission   536
Heating   644; 697
SA subjects with the subdivision *Heating and ventilation*, e.g. **Houses—Heating and ventilation** [to be added as needed]
BT Home economics
NT Electric heating
Fireplaces
Furnaces
Hot air heating
Hot water heating
Houses—Heating and ventilation
Insulation (Heat)
Oil burners
Radiant heating
Solar heating
Space heaters
Steam heating
Stoves
RT Fuel
Ventilation
Heating and ventilation
USE types of buildings with the subdivision *Heating and ventilation*, e.g. **Houses—Heating and ventilation** [to be added as needed]
Heaven   202; 236
BT Eschatology
Future life
NT Angels
RT Paradise
Heavy water
USE Deuterium oxide
Hebrew language   492.4
May be subdivided like **English language**.
UF Jewish language
Jews—Language
BT Language and languages
Hebrew literature   892.4
May use same subdivisions and names of literary forms as for **English literature**.
UF Jews—Literature
BT Literature
NT Bible
Cabala

Hebrew literature—*Continued*
    Talmud
    RT **Jewish literature**
Hebrews
    USE **Jews**
Heirs
    USE **Inheritance and succession**
Helicopters 387.7; 629.133
    UF Aircraft
    BT **Aeronautics**
        Airplanes
Helicopters—Piloting 629.132
    BT **Airplanes—Piloting**
Heliports 387.7
    BT **Airports**
Helium 546
    BT **Chemical elements**
        Gases
Hell 202; 236
    UF Eternal punishment
        Hades
    BT **Eschatology**
        Future life
Hellenism 938
    Use for materials on the spread of Greek civilization throughout the ancient world following the conquests of Alexander the Great. Materials limited to the civilization of Greece, ancient and modern, are entered under **Greece—Civilization**. Materials on both ancient Greek and Roman civilizations are entered under **Classical civilization**.
    BT **Greece—Civilization**
Helpful insects
    USE **Beneficial insects**
Helpfulness
    USE **Helping behavior**
Helping behavior 158
    UF Assistance in emergencies
        Behavior, Helping
        Emergency assistance
        Helpfulness
    BT **Human behavior**
        Interpersonal relations
    NT **Counseling**
        Encouragement
    RT **Altruism**
Helplessness (Psychology) 155.2
    BT **Emotions**
Hemp 633.5; 677
    BT **Fibers**
    RT **Rope**
Heraldry (May subdiv. geog.) 929.6

    UF Coats of arms
        Crests
        Devices (Heraldry)
        Emblems
        Pedigrees
    BT **Archeology**
        Signs and symbols
        Symbolism
    NT **Badges**
        Flags
        Insignia
        Mottoes
        Seals (Numismatics)
    RT **Chivalry**
        Decorations of honor
        Genealogy
        Knights and knighthood
        National emblems
        Nobility
Herb gardening (May subdiv. geog.)
    635
    BT **Gardening**
    RT **Herb gardens**
Herb gardens (May subdiv. geog.) 635
    RT **Herb gardening**
Herb remedies
    USE **Herbs—Therapeutic use**
Herbal medicine
    USE **Herbs—Therapeutic use**
        Medical botany
Herbals
    USE **Herbs**
        Materia medica
Herbaria
    USE **Plants—Collection and preservation**
Herbicides 632; 668
    UF Defoliants
        Weed killers
    SA types of herbicides, e.g. **Agent Orange** [to be added as needed]
    BT **Agricultural chemicals**
        Pesticides
    NT **Agent Orange**
    RT **Plants**
        Spraying and dusting
Herbs 581.6; 635
    UF Herbals
    BT **Plants**
    NT **Potpourri**

Herbs—Therapeutic use   615
   UF   Herb remedies
         Herbal medicine
         Medicinal herbs
   BT   **Therapeutics**
Herculaneum (Extinct city)   937
   BT   **Extinct cities—Italy**
         Italy—Antiquities
Hereditary diseases
   USE   **Medical genetics**
Hereditary succession
   USE   **Inheritance and succession**
Heredity   576.5
   UF   Ancestry
         Descent
         Genes
         Inheritance (Biology)
   BT   **Biology**
         Breeding
   NT   **Chromosomes**
         DNA
         Nature and nurture
         Variation (Biology)
   RT   **Eugenics**
         Genetics
         Mendel's law
         Natural selection
Heredity and environment
   USE   **Nature and nurture**
Heredity of diseases
   USE   **Medical genetics**
Hereford cattle   636.2
   BT   **Beef cattle**
Heresies
   USE   **Heresy**
Heresies, Christian
   USE   **Christian heresies**
Heresy   202
   UF   Heresies
   BT   **Religion**
   NT   **Christian heresies**
Heritage property
   USE   **Cultural property**
Heritage tourism
   USE   **Cultural tourism**
Hermeneutics, Biblical
   USE   **Bible—Criticism**
Hermetic art and philosophy
   USE   **Alchemy**
         Astrology
         Occultism

Hermits (May subdiv. geog.)   920
   UF   Recluses
   BT   **Eccentrics and eccentricities**
   RT   **Monasticism and religious or-**
         ders
Heroes and heroines   920
   UF   Heroines
         Heroism
   BT   **Adventure and adventurers**
   NT   **Explorers**
         Martyrs
   RT   **Courage**
         Mythology
Heroin   362.29; 615
   BT   **Morphine**
         Narcotics
Heroines
   USE   **Heroes and heroines**
Heroism
   USE   **Courage**
         Heroes and heroines
Hertzian waves
   USE   **Electric waves**
Hi-fi systems
   USE   **High-fidelity sound systems**
Hibernation   591.56
   UF   Animals—Hibernation
   BT   **Animal behavior**
Hidden children (Holocaust)   940.53
   BT   **Jewish children in the Holo-**
         caust
Hidden economy
   USE   **Underground economy**
Hidden treasure
   USE   **Buried treasure**
Hides and skins   636.088; 675
   UF   Pelts
         Skins
   BT   **Animal products**
   RT   **Fur**
         Leather
         Tanning
Hieroglyphics   411
   BT   **Inscriptions**
         Writing
   NT   **Rosetta stone**
   RT   **Picture writing**
High blood pressure
   USE   **Hypertension**
High-carbohydrate diet   613.2
   BT   **Diet**

Historic buildings—United States   973

UF   United States—Historic buildings

Historic houses

USE   **Historic buildings**

Historic preservation (May subdiv. geog.)
363.6

Use for materials on identifying and preserving historically important towns, buildings, sites, etc. Materials on protecting cultural heritage property from theft, misappropriation, or exportation are entered under **Cultural property—Protection**.

UF   Preservationism (Historic preservation)

SA   types of objects, architecture, etc., with the subdivision *Conservation and restoration*, e.g. **Theaters—Conservation and restoration** [to be added as needed]

NT   **Theaters—Conservation and restoration**

RT   **Cultural property—Protection**

Historic sites (May subdiv. geog.)   **363.6**

UF   Historical sites

BT   **Archeology**
History

NT   **Historic buildings**

RT   **National monuments**

Historical atlases   911

UF   Historical geography—Maps
History—Atlases
Maps, Historical

BT   **Atlases**

RT   **Historical geography**

Historical chronology   902

Use for materials in which historical events are arranged by date.

UF   Chronology, Historical
Dates, Historical
History—Chronology

SA   ethnic groups, corporate bodies, military services, topics not inherently historical, and names of places with the subdivision *History—Chronology*, e.g. **Native Americans—History—Chronology**; **United States—History—Chronology**; and names of individual persons, wars, sacred works, topics that are inherently his-

torical, and topics not subdivided by *History*, such as art, music, literture, etc., with the subdivision *Chronology*, e.g. **Bible—Chronology** [to be added as needed]

BT   **Chronology**
History

Historical dictionaries

USE   **History—Dictionaries**

Historical drama   808.2; 808.82

Use for individual works, collections, or materials about historical drama.

UF   Chronicle history (Drama)
Chronicle plays
History plays

SA   historical topics, events, or personages with the subdivision *Drama*, e.g. **United States—History—1861-1865, Civil War—Drama**; **Napoleon I, Emperor of the French, 1769-1821—Drama** [to be added as needed]

BT   **Drama**

NT   **United States—History—1861-1865, Civil War—Drama**
United States—History—Drama
War films
Western films

Historical fiction   808.3; 808.83

Use for individual works, collections, or materials about fiction set during a time significantly prior to the time in which it was written.

UF   Historical novels
Historical romances

SA   historical topics, events, or personages with the subdivision *Fiction*, e.g. **Slavery—United States—Fiction**; **United States—History—1861-1865, Civil War—Fiction**; **Napoleon I, Emperor of the French, 1769-1821—Fiction**; etc. [to be added as needed]

BT   **Fiction**

NT   **Gothic novels**
Regency novels
War stories
Western stories

RT   **Biographical fiction**
History

Historical geography   911

Use for materials that discuss the extent of territory held by the states or nations at a given period of history. Materials limited to one country or region still existing in modern times are entered under the name of the place with the subdivision *Historical geography*. Materials on the geography of regions or countries of antiquity that no longer exist as such in modern times are entered under the name of the place with the subdivision *Geography*.

UF   Geography, Historical

SA   names of modern countries or regions with the subdivision *Historical geography*, e.g. **Greece—Historical geography; United States—Historical geography**; etc.; and names of places of antiquity with the subdivision *Geography*, e.g. **Gaul—Geography** [to be added as needed]

BT   **Geography**
    History

NT   **Ancient geography**
    Gaul—Geography
    Greece—Historical geography
    Rome—Geography
    United States—Historical geography

RT   **Historical atlases**

Historical geography—Maps
    USE   **Historical atlases**

Historical geology (May subdiv. geog.) **551.7**

BT   **Geology**
NT   **Paleontology**

Historical materialism
    USE   **Dialectical materialism**

Historical novels
    USE   **Historical fiction**

Historical poetry   808.1; 808.81

Use for individual works, collections, or materials about historical poetry.

UF   Poetry, Historical
BT   **Narrative poetry**
NT   **United States—History—Poetry**
    World War, 1939-1945—Poetry

Historical records—Preservation
    USE   **Archives**

Historical reenactments (May subdiv. geog.) **900**

UF   History—Reenactments
    Reenactment of historical events

BT   **History**

Historical romances
    USE   **Historical fiction**

Historical sites
    USE   **Historic sites**

Historical societies
    USE   **History—Societies**

Historical tourism
    USE   **Cultural tourism**

Historiographers
    USE   **Historians**

Historiography   907

Use for materials limited to the study and criticism of sources of history, methods of historical research, and the writing of history. General materials on history as a science, including the principles of history, the influence of various factors on history, and the relation of the science of history to other subjects, are entered under **History**. Materials on the interpretation and meaning of history and on the course of events and their resulting consequences are entered under **History—Philosophy**.

UF   History—Criticism
    History—Historiography

SA   subjects, wars, historical events, and names of countries, cities, etc., with the subdivision *Historiography* [to be added as needed]

BT   **Authorship**
    History

NT   **History—Sources**
    Local history
    Philosophy—Historiography
    United States—Historiography
    United States—History—1861-1865, Civil War—Historiography

RT   **Historians**

History   900

Use for general materials on history as a science, including the principles of history, the influence of various factors on history, and the relation of the science of history to other subjects. Materials on the interpretation and meaning of history and on the course of events and their resulting consequences are entered under **History—Philosophy**. Materials limited to the study and criticism of sources of history, methods of historical research, and the writing of history are entered under **Historiography**. Materials on past events themselves are entered under **World history**; or under the names of regions, countries, cities, etc., with the subdivision *History*.

UF   Social studies

History—*Continued*

SA   countries, states, etc., with the subdivisions *Antiquities*; *Foreign relations*; *History*; or *Politics and government*; and subjects with the subdivision *History*, or, for literature, film, and music headings, *History and criticism*, e.g. **Art—History; English literature—History and criticism** [to be added as needed]

BT   **Humanities**
       Social sciences

NT   **Archeology**
       Art—History
       Biography
       Chronology
       Church history
       Constitutional history
       Exploration
       Genealogy
       Historic sites
       Historical chronology
       Historical geography
       Historical reenactments
       Historiography
       Local history
       Massacres
       Military history
       Naval history
       Numismatics
       Oral history
       Scandals
       Seals (Numismatics)
       Women—History
       World history

RT   **Civilization**
       Historians
       Historical fiction

History, Ancient
USE   **Ancient history**

History and criticism
USE   types of literature, music, and other arts with the subdivision *History and criticism*, e.g. **English literature—History and criticism** [to be added as needed]

History—Atlases
USE   **Historical atlases**

History, Biblical
USE   **Bible—History of biblical events**

History—Chronology
USE   **Historical chronology**

History—Criticism
USE   **Historiography**

History—Dictionaries 903
UF   Historical dictionaries
BT   **Encyclopedias and dictionaries**
NT   **United States—History—Dictionaries**

History—Historiography
USE   **Historiography**

History, Military
USE   **Military history**

History, Modern
USE   **Modern history**

History, Modern—16th century
USE   **World history—16th century**

History, Modern—17th century
USE   **World history—17th century**

History, Modern—18th century
USE   **World history—18th century**

History, Modern—19th century
USE   **World history—19th century**

History, Modern—20th century
USE   **World history—20th century**

History, Modern—1945-
USE   **World history—1945-**

History, Modern—21st century
USE   **World history—21st century**

History of doctrines
USE   religious topics with the subdivision *History of doctrines*, e.g. **Salvation—History of doctrines** [to be added as needed]

History—Periodicals 905
History—Philosophy 901
   Use for materials on the interpretation and meaning of history and on the course of events and their resulting consequences. General materials on history as a science, including the principles of history, the influences of various factors on history, and the relation of the science of history to other subjects, are entered under **History**. Materials limited to the study and criticism of the sources of history, methods of historical research, and the writing of history are entered under **Historiography**.

UF   Philosophy of history
BT   **Philosophy**

History plays
　USE **Historical drama**
History—Reenactments
　USE **Historical reenactments**
History—Societies 906
　UF　Historical societies
　BT　**Societies**
　NT　**Chicago (Ill.)—History—
　　　　Societies**
　　　Ohio—History—Societies
　　　**United States—History—
　　　　Societies**
History—Sources 900
　　Use for collections of documents, records, and other source materials upon which narrative history is based and for materials about such sources.
　SA　historical subjects, periods of history, individual literary and sacred works, and names of wars with the subdivision *Sources*, e.g. **World War, 1939-1945—Sources**; and subjects, ethnic groups, classes of persons, coporate bodies, and names of countries, states, etc., with the subdivision *History—Sources*; e.g. **United States—History—Sources** [to be added as needed]
　BT　**Historiography**
　NT　**Archives**
　　　Charters
History tourism
　USE **Cultural tourism**
Hittites 939
　BT　**Ancient history**
HIV disease
　USE **AIDS (Disease)**
HMOs
　USE **Health maintenance organizations**
Hoaxes
　USE **Impostors and imposture**
Hobbies 790.1
　UF　Avocations
　SA　types of hobbies [to be added as needed]
　BT　**Amusements**
　　　Leisure
　　　Recreation
　NT　**Collectors and collecting**

　RT　**Handicraft**
Hoboes
　USE **Tramps**
Hockey (May subdiv. geog.)　**796.962**
　UF　Ice hockey
　BT　**Winter sports**
Hogs
　USE **Pigs**
Hoisting machinery　621.8
　UF　Lifts
　SA　types of hoisting machinery [to be added as needed]
　BT　**Machinery**
　NT　**Cranes, derricks, etc.**
　　　Elevators
　RT　**Conveying machinery**
Holiday cooking (May subdiv. geog.)　**641.5**
　SA　cooking for particular holidays, e.g. **Christmas cooking** [to be added as needed]
　BT　**Cooking**
Holiday decorations　394.26; 745.5
　UF　Decorations, Holiday
　BT　**Decoration and ornament**
Holidays (May subdiv. geog.)　**394.26**
　　Use for materials on days of general exemption from work or days publicly dedicated to the commemoration of some person, event, or principle. Materials on occasions other than holidays devoted to festive community observances or to programs of cultural events are entered under **Festivals**.
　UF　Legal holidays
　　　National holidays
　SA　names of holidays [to be added as needed]
　BT　**Days**
　　　Manners and customs
　NT　**April Fools' Day**
　　　Chinese New Year
　　　Christmas
　　　Cinco de Mayo (Holiday)
　　　Fourth of July
　　　Halloween
　　　Kwanzaa
　　　Lincoln's Birthday
　　　Martin Luther King Day
　　　Memorial Day
　　　Mother's Day
　　　Religious holidays
　　　Thanksgiving Day
　　　Valentine's Day

Holidays—*Continued*
>> Veterans Day
> RT Anniversaries
>> Festivals
>> Vacations

Holidays, Jewish
> USE Jewish holidays

Holistic health
> USE Holistic medicine

Holistic medicine (May subdiv. geog.)
>> 610; 615.5
> UF Holistic health
>> Wholistic medicine
> BT Alternative medicine
>> Medicine
> RT Health
>> Health self-care
>> Mind and body

Holland
> USE Netherlands

Holmes, Sherlock (Fictional character)
>> 823
> UF Sherlock Holmes (Fictitious character)

Holocaust, 1933-1945   940.53
> UF Holocaust, Jewish (1939-1945)
>> Jewish Holocaust (1933-1945)
> SA names of concentration camps [to be added as needed]
> BT Antisemitism
>> Jews—Persecutions
> NT Holocaust denial
>> Holocaust survivors
>> Jewish children in the Holocaust
>> Righteous Gentiles in the Holocaust
> RT World War, 1939-1945—Jews

Holocaust, 1933-1945—Personal narratives   920
> BT Autobiographies

Holocaust denial   940.53
> BT Holocaust, 1933-1945

Holocaust, Jewish (1939-1945)
> USE Holocaust, 1933-1945

Holocaust survivors (May subdiv. geog.)
>> 940.53

Use for materials on Jews who survived persecution or imprisonment under the Nazis. Accounts by Holocaust survivors are entered under **Holocaust, 1933-1945—Personal narratives**.

> BT Holocaust, 1933-1945

Holography   774
> UF Laser photography
>> Lensless photography
> BT Laser recording
>> Photography
> RT Three dimensional photography

Holstein-Friesian cattle   636.2
> UF Friesian cattle
> BT Dairy cattle

Holy communion
> USE Eucharist

Holy days
> USE Religious holidays

Holy Ghost
> USE Holy Spirit

Holy Grail
> USE Grail

Holy Land
> USE Palestine

Holy Office
> USE Inquisition

Holy Roman Empire   943
> BT Europe—History

Holy Scriptures
> USE Bible

Holy See
> USE Papacy
>> Popes

Holy Shroud   232.96
> UF Shroud, Holy
>> Shroud of Turin
>> Turin Shroud

Holy Spirit   231
> UF Holy Ghost
> BT God—Christianity
>> Trinity
> RT Spiritual gifts

Holy war (Islam)
> USE Jihad

Holy Week   263
> BT Church year
>> Lent
>> Special weeks
> NT Easter
>> Good Friday

Home   306.8; 640
> RT Family
>> Home economics

Home accidents   363.13
> BT Accidents

Home accidents—*Continued*
    NT   **First aid**
Home and school   371.19
    UF   School and home
    BT   **Education**
    RT   **Parent-teacher associations**
          Parent-teacher relationship
Home-based business (May subdiv. geog.)
          338.6; 658
    UF   At-home employment
          Cottage industry
          Home business
          Home labor
          Work at home
          Working at home
    BT   **Business**
          Self-employed
          Small business
Home-based education
    USE   **Home schooling**
Home business
    USE   **Home-based business**
Home buying
    USE   **Houses—Buying and selling**
Home care
    USE   **Home care services**
          and classes of persons with the
          subdivision *Home care,* e.g.
          Elderly—Home care [to be
          added as needed]
Home care services (May subdiv. geog.)
          362.14; 649.8
    UF   Home care
          Home health care
          Home medical care
          Respite care
    SA   classes of persons with the sub-
          division *Home care*, e.g. **El-
          derly—Home care** [to be
          added as needed]
    BT   **Medical care**
    NT   **Elderly—Home care**
          Home nursing
Home computers
    USE   **Personal computers**
Home conservatories
    USE   **Garden rooms**
Home construction
    USE   **House construction**
Home decoration
    USE   **Interior design**

Home delivered meals programs
    USE   **Meals on wheels programs**
Home designs
    USE   **Domestic architecture—Designs
          and plans**
Home economics (May subdiv. geog.)
          640
    UF   Homemaking
          Household management
          Housekeeping
    BT   **Family life education**
    NT   **Consumer education**
          Cooking
          Cost and standard of living
          Entertaining
          Food
          Fuel
          Grocery shopping
          Heating
          House cleaning
          Household employees
          **Household equipment and sup-
          plies**
          Household pests
          Interior design
          Laundry
          Mobile home living
          Moving
          Sewing
          Shopping
          Storage in the home
          Ventilation
    RT   **Home**
          Homemakers
Home economics—Accounting
    USE   **Household budgets**
Home education
    USE   **Correspondence schools and
          courses**
          Home schooling
          Self-instruction
Home equity loans (May subdiv. geog.)
          332.7
    BT   **Loans**
Home health care
    USE   **Home care services**
Home instruction
    USE   **Home schooling**
Home labor
    USE   **Home-based business**

Home life
USE **Family life**
Home loans
USE **Mortgages**
Home medical care
USE **Home care services**
Home missions, Christian
USE **Christian missions**
Home movies
USE **Amateur films**
Home nursing   649.8
BT **Home care services**
Nursing
RT **Sick**
Home purchase
USE **Houses—Buying and selling**
Home remodeling
USE **Houses—Remodeling**
Home repairing
USE **Houses—Maintenance and re-pair**
Home repairs
USE **Houses—Maintenance and re-pair**
Home schooling (May subdiv. geog.)
371.04

Use for materials on the provision of compulsory education in the home as an alternative to traditional public or private schooling. General materials on the instruction of children in the home are entered under **Child rearing**.

UF Home-based education
Home education
Home instruction
Home teaching by parents
Homeschooling
BT **Education**
RT **Education—Parent participation**
Home sharing
USE **Shared housing**
Home storage
USE **Storage in the home**
Home study courses
USE **Correspondence schools and courses**
Self-instruction
Home teaching by parents
USE **Home schooling**
Home video cameras
USE **Camcorders**

Home video movies
USE **Amateur films**
Home video systems   384.55; 621.388; 778.59
BT **Television**
NT **Camcorders**
Videotapes
RT **Video recording**
Homeless
USE **Homeless persons**
Homelessness
Homeless people
USE **Homeless persons**
Homeless persons (May subdiv. geog.)
305.5; 362.5
UF Homeless
Homeless people
Street people
BT **Poor**
NT **Refugees**
Runaway children
Runaway teenagers
Tramps
RT **Homelessness**
Homeless persons—Government policy
(May subdiv. geog.)   **362.5**
BT **Social policy**
Homelessness (May subdiv. geog.)
305.5; 362.5
UF Homeless
BT **Housing**
Poverty
Social problems
RT **Homeless persons**
Homemakers   306.85; 640
UF Househusbands
Housewives
RT **Home economics**
Homemaking
USE **Home economics**
Homeopathy   615.5
BT **Alternative medicine**
Pharmacy
Homes
USE **Houses**
and ethnic groups, classes of persons, and names of corporate bodies, families, and individual persons with the subdivision *Homes,* e.g. **English authors—Homes;** which may

Homes—*Continued*
    be further subdivided geo-
    graphically [to be added as
    needed]
Homes for the elderly
  USE **Elderly—Institutional care**
Homes (Institutions)
  USE **Charities**
      Institutional care
      Orphanages
Homeschooling
  USE **Home schooling**
Homework **371.3028**
  BT **Study skills**
Homicide (May subdiv. geog.) **364.152**
  UF Manslaughter
      Murder
  BT **Crime**
      Criminal law
      Offenses against the person
  NT **Assassination**
      Euthanasia
      Poisons and poisoning
      Serial killers
      Trials (Homicide)
  RT **Suicide**
Homicide trials
  USE **Trials (Homicide)**
Hominids
  USE **Human origins**
Hominids, Fossil
  USE **Fossil hominids**
Homo sapiens
  USE **Human beings**
Homonyms
  USE names of languages with the
      subdivision *Homonyms,* e.g.
      English language—Hom-
      onyms [to be added as need-
      ed]
Homosexual marriage
  USE **Same-sex marriage**
Homosexual parents
  USE **Gay parents**
Homosexuality (May subdiv. geog.)
    306.76
  UF Gay lifestyle
  BT **Sex**
  NT **Gay liberation movement**
      Lesbianism
  RT **Gay men**
      Lesbians

Homosexuals, Female
  USE **Lesbians**
Homosexuals, Male
  USE **Gay men**
Honesty **179**
  UF Dishonesty
  BT **Ethics**
      Human behavior
  NT **Cheating (Education)**
  RT **Truthfulness and falsehood**
Honey **638; 641.3**
  BT **Food**
  RT **Bees**
Honeybee culture
  USE **Beekeeping**
Honor (May subdiv. geog.) **179**
  UF Honour
  BT **Conduct of life**
Honorary degrees
  USE **Academic degrees**
Honour
  USE **Honor**
Hooked rugs **746.7**
  BT **Handicraft**
      Rugs and carpets
Hoover Dam (Ariz. and Nev.) **627**
  UF Boulder Dam (Ariz. and Nev.)
      Colorado River—Hoover Dam
  BT **Dams**
Hope **152.4; 179; 234**
  BT **Emotions**
      Spiritual life
      Virtue
Hormones **571.7; 573.4; 612.4**
  BT **Endocrinology**
  RT **Endocrine glands**
      Steroids
Hornbooks **028.5; 096; 372.41**
  BT **Reading materials**
Horology
  USE **Clocks and watches**
      Sundials
      Time
Horoscopes **133.5**
  BT **Astrology**
Horror **152.4**
  BT **Emotions**
      Fear
Horror—Fiction
  USE **Horror fiction**

Horror fiction   808.3; 808.83

 Use for individual works, collections, or materials about horror fiction.

 UF   Horror—Fiction

 Horror novels

 Horror stories

 Horror tales

 Terror tales

 BT   **Fiction**

 NT   **Ghost stories**

 Gothic novels

 RT   **Fantasy fiction**

 Occult fiction

Horror films   791.43

 Use for individual works, collections, or materials about horror films.

 UF   Creature films

 Horror movies

 Monster films

 SA   types of horror films, e.g. **Vampire films** [to be added as needed]

 BT   **Motion pictures**

 NT   **Vampire films**

 RT   **Fantasy films**

Horror graphic novels   741.5

 Use for individual works, collections, or materials about horror graphic novels.

 BT   **Graphic novels**

Horror movies

 USE   **Horror films**

Horror novels

 USE   **Horror fiction**

Horror plays   808.82

 Use for individual works, collections, or materials about horror plays.

 BT   **Drama**

Horror radio programs   791.44

 Use for individual works, collections, or materials about horror radio programs.

 BT   **Radio programs**

Horror stories

 USE   **Horror fiction**

Horror tales

 USE   **Horror fiction**

Horror television programs   791.45

 Use for individual works, collections, or materials about horror television programs.

 BT   **Television programs**

 RT   **Fantasy television programs**

Hors d'oeuvres

 USE   **Appetizers**

Horse breeding

 USE   **Horses—Breeding**

Horse racing   798.4

 BT   **Racing**

 RT   **Horsemanship**

Horse riding

 USE   **Horsemanship**

Horseback riding

 USE   **Horsemanship**

Horsebreaking

 USE   **Horses—Training**

Horsemanship (May subdiv. geog.)   **798.2**

 UF   Coaching

 Dressage

 Equestrianism

 Horse riding

 Horseback riding

 Riding

 BT   **Locomotion**

 NT   **Horses—Training**

 Trail riding

 RT   **Horse racing**

 Rodeos

Horses (May subdiv. geog.)   **599.665; 636.1**

 UF   Foals

 BT   **Mammals**

 NT   **Ponies**

Horses—Breeding   636.1

 UF   Horse breeding

 BT   **Breeding**

Horses—Diseases   636.089

 BT   **Animals—Diseases**

Horses—Training   636.1

 UF   Horsebreaking

 BT   **Horsemanship**

Horses—Wounds and injuries   636.1

Horticulture (May subdiv. geog.)   **635**

 Use for materials on the scientific and economic aspects of the cultivation of flowers, fruits, vegetables, etc. Materials on the practical aspects of creating gardens and cultivating plants are entered under **Gardening**. General materials about gardens, the history of gardens, various types of gardens, etc., are entered under **Gardens**.

 BT   **Agriculture**

 Plants

 NT   **Flower gardening**

 Fruit culture

 Greenhouses

 Hydroponics

Horticulture—*Continued*
        Landscape gardening
        Organic gardening
        Plant breeding
        Truck farming
        Vegetable gardening
  RT   **Gardening**
Hosiery   391.4; 687
  UF   Stockings
  BT   **Clothing and dress**
        Textile industry
Hospices (May subdiv. geog.)   **362.17**
  BT   **Hospitals**
        Social medicine
        Terminal care
Hospital care records
  USE **Medical records**
Hospital libraries (May subdiv. geog.)
        027.6
  UF   Libraries, Hospital
  BT   **Libraries**
Hospital personnel administration
  USE **Hospitals—Personnel manage-
        ment**
Hospital ships   362.1; 623.826
  UF   Floating hospitals
  BT   **Hospitals**
        Ships
Hospital wastes
  USE **Medical wastes**
Hospitality
  USE **Entertaining**
Hospitality industry (May subdiv. geog.)
        910.46
  BT   **Service industries**
Hospitalization insurance   368.38
  UF   Group hospitalization
        Insurance, Hospitalization
  BT   **Health insurance**
Hospitals (May subdiv. geog.)   **362.11**
  UF   Infirmaries
  SA   types of hospitals and names of
        individual hospitals [to be
        added as needed]
  BT   **Institutional care**
        Public health
  NT   **Children's hospitals**
        Hospices
        Hospital ships
        **Life support systems (Medical
        environment)**
        Long-term care facilities

        Military hospitals
        Nursing homes
        Psychiatric hospitals
  RT   **Medical centers**
        Medical charities
Hospitals—Personnel management (May
        subdiv. geog.)   **362.11**
  UF   Hospital personnel administration
  BT   **Personnel management**
Hospitals—Sanitation   614.4
  BT   **Sanitation**
Hospitals—United States   362.110973
Hostage escapes
  USE **Escapes**
Hostage negotiation   363.3
  BT   **Hostages**
        Negotiation
Hostages (May subdiv. geog.)   **920**
  SA   hostages from a particular coun-
        try, e.g. **American hostages**
        [to be added as needed]
  BT   **Terrorism**
  NT   **American hostages**
        Hostage negotiation
Hostels, Elder
  USE **Elderhostels**
Hostels, Youth
  USE **Youth hostels**
Hot air engines
  USE **Heat engines**
Hot air heating   697
  UF   Warm air heating
  BT   **Heating**
Hot water heating   697
  BT   **Heating**
Hotels and motels (May subdiv. geog.)
        728; 910.46
    Use for materials on public accommoda-
  tions, including inns and guest houses.
  UF   Boarding houses
        Inns
        Motels
        Rooming houses
        Tourist accommodations
  BT   **Service industries**
  NT   **Bed and breakfast accommo-
        dations**
        Youth hostels
**Hotels and motels—United States   728;
        910.460973**
Hothouses
  USE **Greenhouses**

Hotlines (Telephone counseling) 361;
362.2
   UF   Crisis counseling
         Crisis intervention telephone ser-
           vice
         Switchboard hotlines
         Telephone counseling
   BT   **Counseling**
         Information services
         Social work
   RT   **Crisis centers**
Hours of labor 331.25
   UF   Eight-hour day
         Five-day work week
         Overtime
         Working day
         Working hours
   BT   **Labor**
   NT   **Absenteeism (Labor)**
         Flexible hours of labor
         Leave of absence
         Part-time employment
Hours of labor, Flexible
   USE   **Flexible hours of labor**
House boats
   USE   **Houseboats**
House buying
   USE   **Houses—Buying and selling**
House cleaning 648
   BT   **Cleaning**
         Home economics
         Household sanitation
House construction (May subdiv. geog.)
690
   UF   Construction, House
         Home construction
   SA   types of house construction and
           special kinds of houses [to be
           added as needed]
   BT   **Building**
         Domestic architecture
   NT   **Earth sheltered houses**
         House painting
         Houses—Remodeling
         Log cabins and houses
         Prefabricated houses
   RT   **Houses**
House decoration
   USE   **Interior design**

House drainage 690
   Use for materials on house drainage. Mate-
   rials on land drainage are entered under
   Drainage.
   UF   Drainage, House
   BT   **Household sanitation**
   NT   **Sewerage**
   RT   **Plumbing**
House flies
   USE   **Flies**
House furnishing
   USE   **Interior design**
House of Representatives (U.S.)
   USE   **United States. Congress. House**
House painting 698
   BT   **House construction**
   RT   **Industrial painting**
House plans
   USE   **Domestic architecture—Designs
           and plans**
House plants 635.9
   BT   **Cultivated plants**
         Flower gardening
         Plants
         Window gardening
   RT   **Container gardening**
         Indoor gardening
House purchase
   USE   **Houses—Buying and selling**
House repairing
   USE   **Houses—Maintenance and re-
           pair**
House repairs
   USE   **Houses—Maintenance and re-
           pair**
House sanitation
   USE   **Household sanitation**
House selling
   USE   **Houses—Buying and selling**
House sharing
   USE   **Shared housing**
House trailers
   USE   **Mobile homes**
         Travel trailers and campers
Houseboats 728.7
   UF   House boats
   BT   **Boats and boating**
Household appliances
   USE   **Household equipment and sup-
           plies**
Household appliances, Electric
   USE   **Electric household appliances**

Household budgets   640
    UF   Budgets, Household
            Domestic finance
            Family budget
            Finance, Household
            Home economics—Accounting
            Household finances
    BT   **Cost and standard of living**
            Personal finance

Household employees   640
    UF   Domestic workers
            Housemaids
            Servants
    BT   **Home economics**
            Labor

Household equipment and supplies
        643; 683
    UF   Domestic appliances
            Household appliances
            Labor saving devices, Household
    BT   **Home economics**
            Implements, utensils, etc.
    NT   **Electric household appliances**
            Kitchen utensils

Household finances
    USE   **Cost and standard of living**
            Household budgets

Household management
    USE   **Home economics**

Household moving
    USE   **Moving**

Household pests   648
    UF   Diseases and pests
            Vermin
    SA   types of pests, e.g. **Flies** [to be
            added as needed]
    BT   **Home economics**
            Household sanitation
            Pests
    NT   **Flies**
    RT   **Insect pests**

Household repairs
    USE   **Houses—Maintenance and re-
            pair**

Household sanitation   648
    UF   House sanitation
            Sanitation, Household
    BT   **Sanitation**
    NT   **House cleaning**
            House drainage
            Household pests

            Laundry
            Ventilation
    RT   **Plumbing**

Household utensils
    USE   **Kitchen utensils**

Household violence
    USE   **Domestic violence**

Househusbands
    USE   **Homemakers**

Housekeeping
    USE   **Home economics**

Housemaids
    USE   **Household employees**

Houses (May subdiv. geog.)   **643; 728**
    Use for general materials on buildings in
    which people live. Materials on residential
    buildings from the standpoint of style and de-
    sign are entered under **Domestic architecture**.
    UF   Dwellings
            Homes
            Residences
    SA   types of houses, e.g. **Earth shel-
            tered houses**; types of archi-
            tectural features, e.g. **Win-
            dows**; **Fireplaces**; etc.; and
            rooms and parts of the house,
            e.g. **Kitchens** [to be added as
            needed]
    BT   **Buildings**
    NT   **Apartment houses**
            Earth sheltered houses
            Garden rooms
            Haunted houses
            Housing
            Igloos
            Kitchens
            Log cabins and houses
            Prefabricated houses
            Rooms
            Solar homes
            Vacation homes
    RT   **Domestic architecture**
            House construction

Houses—Buying and selling   333.33
    UF   Home buying
            Home purchase
            House buying
            House purchase
            House selling
    BT   **Real estate business**
    NT   **Urban homesteading**

Houses—Heating and ventilation 644; 697
　BT　**Heating**
Houses—Maintenance and repair 643
　UF　Home repairing
　　　Home repairs
　　　House repairing
　　　House repairs
　　　Household repairs
Houses—Remodeling 643
　UF　Home remodeling
　　　Remodeling (Architecture)
　　　Remodeling of houses
　SA　types of houses and parts of
　　　houses with the subdivision
　　　Remodeling, e.g. **Kitchens—**
　　　Remodeling [to be added as
　　　needed]
　BT　**House construction**
Housewives
　USE　**Homemakers**
Housing (May subdiv. geog.) **307.3;
　　　363.5**
　　Use for materials on the social and econom-
　ic aspects of housing. Materials on the social
　and economic aspects of housing as it pertains
　to specific ethnic groups or classes of persons
　are entered under that group or class of per-
　sons with the subdivision *Housing*. Materials
　on the residential buildings of ethnic groups
　or classes of persons from the standpoint of
　architecture, construction, or ethnology are en-
　tered under the name of the ethnic group or
　class of persons with the subdivision *Dwell-
　ings*.
　UF　Affordable housing
　　　Dwellings
　　　Habitations, Human
　　　Housing needs
　　　Urban housing
　SA　ethnic groups, classes of per-
　　　sons, and domestic animals
　　　with the subdivision *Housing*;
　　　e.g. **Native Americans—
　　　Housing**; **Physically handi-
　　　capped—Housing**; etc. [to be
　　　added as needed]
　BT　**Houses**
　　　Landlord and tenant
　NT　**African Americans—Housing**
　　　Apartment houses
　　　Assisted living
　　　Blacks—Housing
　　　Cooperative housing
　　　Discrimination in housing

　　　Elderly—Housing
　　　Homelessness
　　　Labor—Housing
　　　Mobile homes
　　　Native Americans—Housing
　　　**Physically handicapped—Hous-
　　　ing**
　　　Public housing
　　　Shared housing
　　　Timesharing (Real estate)
　　　Urban homesteading
　RT　**City planning**
Housing, Cooperative
　USE　**Cooperative housing**
Housing estates
　USE　**Planned communities**
Housing for the elderly
　USE　**Elderly—Housing**
Housing for the physically handicapped
　USE　**Physically handicapped—Hous-
　　　ing**
Housing needs
　USE　**Housing**
Housing projects, Government
　USE　**Public housing**
**Houston Astros (Baseball team)
　　　796.357**
　UF　Astros (Baseball team)
　　　Houston (Tex.). Baseball Club
　　　(National League)
　BT　**Baseball teams**
Houston (Tex.). Baseball Club (National
　　　League)
　USE　**Houston Astros (Baseball
　　　team)**
Hovercraft
　USE　**Air-cushion vehicles**
How to start a business
　USE　**New business enterprises**
How-to-stop-smoking programs
　USE　**Smoking cessation programs**
How to study
　USE　**Study skills**
**HTML (Document markup language)
　　　006.7**
　UF　HyperText Markup Language
　　　(Document markup language)
　BT　**Programming languages**
Hubble Space Telescope 522
　BT　**Telescopes**

Hudson River (N.Y. and N.J.)—Bridges
USE **Bridges—Hudson River (N.Y. and N.J.)**
Hugging 158; 302.2; 395
UF Embracing
Hugs
BT **Manners and customs**
Nonverbal communication
Touch
Hugo Award 808.3
BT **Literary prizes**
Science fiction
Hugs
USE **Hugging**
Huguenots (May subdiv. geog.) **284**
BT **Christian sects**
Reformation
NT **Saint Bartholomew's Day, Massacre of, 1572**
Hull House
USE **Hull House (Chicago, Ill.)**
Hull House (Chicago, Ill.) 361.4
UF Hull House
BT **Social settlements**
Human abnormalities
USE **Birth defects**
Growth disorders
Human-alien encounters (May subdiv. geog.) **001.942**
UF Alien encounters with humans
Extraterrestrial encounters with humans
Human encounters with aliens
NT **Alien abduction**
RT **Extraterrestrial beings**
Life on other planets
Unidentified flying objects
Human anatomy 611
SA parts of the body, e.g. **Foot**; and names of organs and regions of the body with the subdivision *Anatomy*, e.g. **Heart—Anatomy** [to be added as needed]
BT **Anatomy**
RT **Human body**
Human anatomy—Atlases 611
BT **Atlases**
Human anatomy in art
USE **Artistic anatomy**
Nude in art

Human artificial insemination 346.01; 618.1
UF Artificial insemination, Human
BT **Artificial insemination**
Reproduction
Human assets
USE **Human capital**
Human behavior 150; 302
UF Behavior
Morals
Social behavior
BT **Character**
Psychology
Social sciences
NT **Aggressiveness (Psychology)**
Bad behavior
Behavior modification
Behaviorism
Cannibalism
Compulsive behavior
Conduct of life
Consolation
Curiosity
Deviant behavior
Duty
Eating customs
Etiquette
Friendship
Greed
Habit
Helping behavior
Honesty
Lifestyles
Love
Messiness
Patience
Patriotism
Sex
Showing off
Social adjustment
Sportsmanship
Suicide—Psychological aspects
Temper tantrums
Truthfulness and falsehood
Vice
Virtue
RT **Ethics**
Interpersonal relations
Life skills

Human beings (May subdiv. geog.)   **128; 599.9**

Use for materials on the human species from the point of view of biology or anthropology. Materials on human beings as individuals are entered under **Persons**.

UF   Homo sapiens

Human race

Man

BT   **Primates**

NT   **Anthropometry**

Ethnology

Human body

Persons

Prehistoric peoples

RT   **Anthropology**

Human beings—Sexual behavior

USE   **Sex**

Human beings (Theology)   **202; 218; 233**

UF   Man (Theology)

BT   **Doctrinal theology**

NT   **Soul**

Human body   **612**

Use for materials on the human body not limited to anatomy or physiology.

UF   Body

SA   parts of the body, e.g. **Foot** [to be added as needed]

BT   **Human beings**

Self

NT   **Body image**

Body weight

RT   **Human anatomy**

Mind and body

Physiology

Human capital (May subdiv. geog.)   **658.3**

Use for materials on investments of capital in training and educating employees to improve their productivity. Materials on the strength of a country in terms of available personnel, both military and industrial, are entered under **Manpower**.

UF   Human assets

Human resources

BT   **Capital**

RT   **Labor supply**

Human cloning   **571.8; 660.6**

BT   **Cloning**

Human cloning—Ethical aspects   **174**

BT   **Ethics**

Human cold storage

USE   **Cryonics**

Human ecology (May subdiv. geog.)   **304.2**

UF   Ecology, Human

Ecology, Social

Social ecology

BT   **Sociology**

NT   **Environmental influence on humans**

Human geography

Human influence on nature

Human settlements

Population

Social psychology

Survival skills

Human ecology—Ethical aspects

USE   **Environmental ethics**

Human embryos, Frozen

USE   **Frozen embryos**

Human encounters with aliens

USE   **Human-alien encounters**

Human engineering (May subdiv. geog.)   **620.8**

Use for materials on engineering design as related to human anatomical, physiological, and psychological capabilities and limitations.

UF   Biomechanics

Ergonomics

BT   **Applied psychology**

Engineering

Industrial design

Psychophysiology

NT   **Life support systems (Space environment)**

Life support systems (Submarine environment)

RT   **Machine design**

Human experimentation in medicine (May subdiv. geog.)   **174.2**

UF   Experimentation on humans, Medical

Medical experimentation on humans

BT   **Medical ethics**

Medicine—Research

Human fertility (May subdiv. geog.)   **304.6; 612.6; 616.6**

UF   Fertility, Human

BT   **Birth rate**

Fertility

Population

RT   **Birth control**

Childlessness

Human figure in art
  USE **Artistic anatomy**
          Figure drawing
          Figure painting
          Nude in art
Human fossils
  USE **Fossil hominids**
Human genome **611**
  BT **Genetics**
Human geography (May subdiv. geog.)
    304.2
  UF Anthropogeography
       Geographical distribution of people
       Social geography
  BT **Anthropology**
       Ethnology
       Geography
       Human ecology
       Immigration and emigration
  NT **African diaspora**
       Environmental influence on humans
       Human settlements
       Jewish diaspora
  RT **Geopolitics**
Human habitat
  USE **Human settlements**
Human influence on nature (May subdiv. geog.) **304.2; 363.7**
  UF Earth, Effect of man on
       Man—Influence on nature
       Nature—Effect of human beings on
  BT **Human ecology**
  NT **Pollution**
Human locomotion **152.3; 612.7**
  UF Biomechanics
       Human mechanics
       Human movement
  BT **Locomotion**
       Physiology
  NT **Kinesiology**
       Walking
  RT **Musculoskeletal system**
Human mechanics
  USE **Human locomotion**
Human movement
  USE **Human locomotion**
Human origins **599.9**

  UF Antiquity of man
       Hominids
       Man—Antiquity
       Man—Origin
       Origin of man
  BT **Physical anthropology**
  RT **Evolution**
       Fossil hominids
       Prehistoric peoples
Human paleontology
  USE **Fossil hominids**
Human physiology
  USE **Physiology**
Human race
  USE **Anthropology**
       Human beings
Human records
  USE **World records**
Human relations
  USE **Interpersonal relations**
Human resource management
  USE **Personnel management**
Human resources
  USE **Human capital**
       Manpower
Human rights (May subdiv. geog.) **323; 341.4**
    Use for materials on the rights of persons regardless of their legal, socioeconomic, or cultural status, as recognized by the international community. Materials on citizens' rights as established by law or protected by a constitution are entered under **Civil rights**.
  UF Basic rights
       Civil rights (International law)
       Fundamental rights
       Rights, Human
       Rights of man
  NT **Civil rights**
       Right to health care
Human services (May subdiv. geog.) **361**
    Use for general materials on the various policies, programs, services, and facilities to meet basic human needs, such as health, education, and welfare. Materials on the methods employed in social work, public or private, are entered under **Social work**. Materials on privately supported welfare activities are entered under **Charities**. Materials on tax-supported welfare activities are entered under **Public welfare**.
  SA ethnic groups and classes of persons with the subdivision *Services for*, e.g. **Handicapped—**

Human services—*Continued*

       Services for [to be added as needed]

  NT **Charities**

      Handicapped—Services for

      Public health

      Public welfare

      Social work

Human settlements (May subdiv. geog.) **307**

  UF Human habitat

  BT **Human ecology**

      Human geography

      Population

      Sociology

  RT **Land settlement**

Human sexuality

  USE **Sex**

Human survival skills

  USE **Survival skills**

Human values

  USE **Values**

Humane treatment of animals

  USE **Animal welfare**

Humanism (May subdiv. geog.) **001.2; 880**

Use for materials on culture founded on the study of the classics, or more narrowly on Greek and Roman scholarship. Materials on any intellectual or philosophical movement or set of beliefs that promotes human values as separate and distinct from religious doctrines are entered under **Secularism**.

  BT **Culture**

      Literature

      Philosophy

  NT **Humanities**

  RT **Classical education**

      Learning and scholarship

      Renaissance

      Secularism

Humanism, Secular

  USE **Secularism**

Humanitarians

  USE **Philanthropists**

Humanities (May subdiv. geog.) **001.3**

  BT **Humanism**

      Learning and scholarship

  NT **Arts**

      History

      Literature

      Music

      Philosophy

Science and the humanities

  RT **Classical education**

Humanities and science

  USE **Science and the humanities**

Humans in space

  USE **Space flight**

Humidity **551.57**

  UF Air, Moisture of

      Atmospheric humidity

      Relative humidity

  BT **Meteorology**

      Weather

Humor

  USE **Wit and humor**

      and subjects with the subdivision *Humor,* e.g. **World War, 1939-1945—Humor** [to be added as needed]

Humorists (May subdiv. geog.) **809.7; 920**

  BT **Wit and humor**

Humorous fiction **808.3; 808.83**

Use for individual works, collections, or materials about humorous fiction.

  UF Comic novels

      Humorous stories

  BT **Fiction**

      Wit and humor

  RT **Mock-heroic literature**

Humorous films

  USE **Comedy films**

Humorous graphic novels **741.5**

Use for individual works, collections, or materials about humorous graphic novels.

  BT **Graphic novels**

Humorous pictures

  USE **Comic books, strips, etc.**

Humorous plays

  USE **Comedies**

Humorous poetry **808.1; 808.81**

Use for individual works, collections, or materials about humorous poetry.

  UF Comic verse

      Humorous verse

      Light verse

  BT **Poetry**

      Wit and humor

  NT **Limericks**

      Nonsense verses

Humorous stories

  USE **Humorous fiction**

Humorous verse
    USE **Humorous poetry**
Hundred Years' War, 1339-1453   944
    UF   100 years' war
    BT   **Europe—History—476-1492**
            France—History—1328-1589,
               House of Valois
            Great Britain—History—1066-
               1485, Medieval period
Hungary—History   943.9
Hungary—History—1956, Revolution
    943.905
    BT   **Revolutions**
Hunger (May subdiv. geog.)   **363.8**
    RT   **Fasting**
            Starvation
Hunger strikes (May subdiv. geog.)
    303.6
    BT   **Demonstrations**
            Fasting
            Nonviolence
            Passive resistance
            Resistance to government
Hunting (May subdiv. geog.)   **799.2**
    SA   types of hunting, e.g. **Whaling**;
            and ethnic groups with the
            subdivision *Hunting*, e.g. **Na-**
            tive Americans—Hunting [to
            be added as needed]
    NT   **Big game hunting**
            Bowhunting
            Decoys (Hunting)
            Falconry
            Game protection
            Game reserves
            Native Americans—Hunting
            Tracking and trailing
            Whaling
    RT   **Game and game birds**
            Safaris
            Shooting
            Trapping
Hunting—United States   799.2973
Hurricanes (May subdiv. geog.)   **551.55**
    Use for cyclonic storms originating in the
    region of the West Indies.
    SA   names of specific hurricanes [to
            be added as needed]
    BT   **Cyclones**
            Storms
            Winds
    RT   **Typhoons**

Husbands   306.872
    UF   Married men
            Spouses
    BT   **Family**
            Marriage
            Married people
            Men
Husbands, Runaway
    USE **Runaway adults**
Hybridization
    USE **Plant breeding**
Hydraulic cement
    USE **Cement**
Hydraulic engineering (May subdiv.
    geog.)   **627**
    BT   **Civil engineering**
            Engineering
            Fluid mechanics
            Water power
    NT   **Drainage**
            Dredging
            Drilling and boring (Earth and
               rocks)
            Flood control
            Hydraulic structures
            Hydrodynamics
            Hydrostatics
            Irrigation
            Pumping machinery
            Reclamation of land
            Wells
    RT   **Hydraulics**
            Rivers
            Water
            Water supply engineering
Hydraulic machinery   621.2
    BT   **Machinery**
            Water power
    NT   **Turbines**
Hydraulic structures   627
    SA   types of hydraulic structures [to
            be added as needed]
    BT   **Hydraulic engineering**
            Structural engineering
    NT   **Aqueducts**
            Canals
            Dams
            Docks
            Harbors
            Pipelines
            Reservoirs

Hydraulics   621.2; 627

Use for materials on technical applications of the theory of hydrodynamics.

UF   Water flow

BT   **Fluid mechanics**

Liquids

Mechanics

Physics

NT   **Hydrodynamics**

Hydrostatics

Water

Water power

RT   **Hydraulic engineering**

Hydrodynamics   532

Use for materials on the theory of the motion and action of fluids. Materials on the experimental investigation and technical application of this theory are entered under **Hydraulics.**

BT   **Dynamics**

Fluid mechanics

Hydraulic engineering

Hydraulics

Liquids

Mechanics

NT   **Hydrostatics**

Viscosity

Waves

Hydroelectric power

USE   **Water power**

Hydroelectric power plants (May subdiv. geog.)   **621.31**

UF   Power plants, Hydroelectric

BT   **Electric power plants**

Water power

Hydrofoil boats   623.82

BT   **Boats and boating**

Hydrogen   546

BT   **Chemical elements**

Hydrogen bomb   623.4

BT   **Bombs**

Nuclear weapons

NT   **Radioactive fallout**

RT   **Atomic bomb**

Hydrogen nucleus

USE   **Protons**

Hydrology

USE   **Water**

Hydromechanics

USE   **Fluid mechanics**

Hydropathy

USE   **Hydrotherapy**

Hydrophobia

USE   **Rabies**

Hydroponics   631.5; 635

UF   Plants—Soilless culture

Soilless agriculture

Water farming

BT   **Horticulture**

Hydrostatics   532

BT   **Fluid mechanics**

Hydraulic engineering

Hydraulics

Hydrodynamics

Liquids

Mechanics

Physics

Statics

NT   **Gases**

Hydrotherapy   615.8

UF   Hydropathy

Water cure

BT   **Physical therapy**

Therapeutics

Water

RT   **Baths**

Health resorts

Hygiene   613

UF   Body care

Personal cleanliness

Personal hygiene

SA   parts of the body with the subdivision *Care*, e.g. **Foot— Care**; and classes of persons and ethnic groups with the subdivision *Health and hygiene*, e.g. **Women—Health and hygiene** [to be added as needed]

BT   **Medicine**

Preventive medicine

NT   **Baths**

Children—Health and hygiene

Cleanliness

Diet

Disinfection and disinfectants

Elderly—Health and hygiene

Exercise

Infants—Health and hygiene

Military personnel—Health and hygiene

Personal grooming

Rest

Hygiene—*Continued*
      School hygiene
      Sexual hygiene
      Sleep
      Ventilation
      Women—Health and hygiene
  RT **Health**
      Sanitation
Hygiene, Military
  USE **Military personnel—Health and hygiene**
Hygiene, Sexual
  USE **Sexual hygiene**
Hygiene, Social
  USE **Public health**
Hygiene—Study and teaching
  USE **Health education**
Hymn books
  USE **Hymnals**
Hymnals 782.27
    Use for collections of sacred songs that contain both words and music. Materials about hymns are entered under **Hymns**.
  UF Hymn books
      Hymnbooks
  BT **Church music**
      Hymns
      Songbooks
Hymnbooks
  USE **Hymnals**
Hymnology
  USE **Hymns**
Hymns 264; 782.27
    Use for materials about hymns. Collections of hymns that contain both words and music are entered under **Hymnals**.
  UF Hymnology
  BT **Church music**
      Liturgies
      Songs
      Vocal music
  NT **Carols**
      Hymnals
      Spirituals (Songs)
  RT **Religious poetry**
Hyperactive children 155.4; 618.92
  UF Children, Hyperactive
      Hyperkinetic children
  BT **Handicapped children**
  RT **Hyperactivity**
Hyperactivity 616.85; 616.92
  UF Hyperkinesia
  BT **Diseases**

  RT **Hyperactive children**
Hyperactivity disorder
  USE **Attention deficit disorder**
Hyperkinesia
  USE **Attention deficit disorder**
      Hyperactivity
Hyperkinetic children
  USE **Hyperactive children**
Hyperspace
  USE **Fourth dimension**
Hypertension 616.1
  UF High blood pressure
  BT **Blood pressure**
Hypertext 005.75
    Use for materials on document retrieval networks having text files and dynamic indexes for links among documents.
  UF Hypertext systems
  BT **Multimedia**
HyperText Markup Language (Document markup language)
  USE **HTML (Document markup language)**
Hypertext systems
  USE **Hypertext**
Hypnosis
  USE **Hypnotism**
Hypnotism 154.7
  UF Animal magnetism
      Autosuggestion
      Hypnosis
      Mesmerism
  BT **Mental healing**
      Psychophysiology
  RT **Mental suggestion**
      Mind and body
      Psychoanalysis
      Subconsciousness
      Suggestive therapeutics
ICBM
  USE **Intercontinental ballistic missiles**
Ice (May subdiv. geog.) **551.3**
  UF Freezing
  BT **Cold**
      Frost
      Physical geography
      Water
  NT **Glaciers**
      Icebergs
Ice age 551.7
  UF Glacial epoch

Ice age—*Continued*
   BT   **Earth**
Ice boats
   USE **Iceboats**
Ice cream, ices, etc.   **637; 641.8**
   UF   Ices
   BT   **Desserts**
        Frozen foods
Ice (Drug)
   USE **Crystal meth (Drug)**
Ice hockey
   USE **Hockey**
Ice skating   **796.91**
   UF   Figure skating
        Skating
   BT   **Winter sports**
Ice sports
   USE **Winter sports**
Icebergs   **551.3**
   BT   **Ice**
        Ocean
        Physical geography
Iceboats   **623.82**
   UF   Ice boats
   BT   **Boats and boating**
Icelandic language   **439**
   BT   **Language and languages**
        Scandinavian languages
Icelandic language—0-1500
   USE **Old Norse language**
Icelandic literature   **839**
   UF   Icelandic literature, Modern
   BT   **Literature**
        Scandinavian literature
   RT   **Old Norse literature**
Icelandic literature, Modern
   USE **Icelandic literature**
Ices
   USE **Ice cream, ices, etc.**
Ichthyology
   USE **Fishes**
Iconography
   USE **Art—Themes**
Icons (Computer graphics)   **005.3; 005.4**
   UF   Computer icons
        Desktop icons (Computer graphics)
   BT   **Computer graphics**
Icons (Religion)   **704.9**
   BT   **Christian art**

Ideal states
   USE **Utopian fiction**
        Utopias
Idealism   **141**
   BT   **Philosophy**
   RT   **Materialism**
        Realism
        Transcendentalism
Identification
   SA   subjects with the subdivision *Identification* [to be added as needed]
   NT   **Airplanes—Identification**
        Bar coding
        Criminals—Identification
        DNA fingerprinting
        Fingerprints
Identity
   USE **Identity (Psychology)**
        Individuality
        Personality
        and classes of persons with the subdivision *Identity,* e.g. **Women—Identity;** ethnic groups with the subdivision *Ethnic identity,* e.g. **Mexican Americans—Ethnic identity;** and racial groups with the subdivision *Race identity,* e.g. **African Americans—Race identity** [to be added as needed]
Identity (Psychology)   **126**
   UF   Identity
   SA   classes of persons with the subdivision *Identity,* e.g. **Women—Identity;** ethnic groups with the subdivision *Ethnic identity,* e.g. **Mexican Americans—Ethnic identity;** and racial groups with the subdivision *Race identity,* e.g. **African Americans—Race identity** [to be added as needed]
   BT   **Personality**
        Psychology
        Self
   NT   **Ethnicity**
        Group identity
        Women—Identity
   RT   **Ego (Psychology)**

Identity theft   364.15
    BT **Offenses against the person**
         Theft
Ideology (May subdiv. geog.)   **140**
    BT **Philosophy**
         Political science
         Psychology
         Theory of knowledge
         Thought and thinking
    NT **Political correctness**
Idioms
    USE names of languages with the
         subdivision *Idioms,* e.g. **En-**
         glish language—Idioms [to
         be added as needed]
Idyllic poetry
    USE **Pastoral poetry**
Igloos   643.2
    BT **Houses**
         Inuit
Ilium (Extinct city)
    USE **Troy (Extinct city)**
Illegal aliens (May subdiv. geog.)   **323.6;**
    325; 342
    UF Undocumented aliens
    BT **Aliens**
         Immigration and emigration
         Underground economy
    RT **Sanctuary movement**
Illegitimacy (May subdiv. geog.)
    306.874; 346.01
    UF Illegitimate children
         Legitimacy (Law)
    RT **Unmarried fathers**
         Unmarried mothers
Illegitimate children
    USE **Illegitimacy**
Illiteracy
    USE **Literacy**
Illness
    USE **Diseases**
Illuminated manuscripts
    USE **Illumination of books and**
         manuscripts
Illumination
    USE **Lighting**
Illumination of books and manuscripts
    (May subdiv. geog.)   **096; 745.6**
    UF Illuminated manuscripts
         Manuscripts, Illuminated

         Miniatures (Illumination of
         books and manuscripts)
         Ornamental alphabets
    BT **Art**
         Books
         Decoration and ornament
         Illustration of books
         Manuscripts
         Medieval art
    RT **Alphabets**
         Books of hours
         Initials
Illusions
    USE **Hallucinations and illusions**
         Optical illusions
Illustration of books (May subdiv. geog.)
    741.6
    UF Book illustration
    SA types of illustration, e.g. **Botani-**
         cal illustration [to be added
         as needed]
    BT **Art**
         Books
         Color printing
         Decoration and ornament
    NT **Botanical illustration**
         Caldecott Medal
         Engraving
         Illumination of books and
         manuscripts
         Photomechanical processes
    RT **Drawing**
         Picture books for children
Illustrations
    USE subjects, names, and uniform ti-
         tles with the subdivision *Pic-*
         torial works, e.g. **Animals—**
         Pictorial works; United
         States—History—1861-1865,
         Civil War—Pictorial works;
         etc. [to be added as needed]
Illustrators (May subdiv. geog.)
    741.6092; 920
    BT **Artists**
Illustrators, American
    USE **Illustrators—United States**
Illustrators—United States   741.6092;
    920
    UF American illustrators
         Illustrators, American
Image processing software   006.6

Image processing software—*Continued*
  BT **Computer software**
Imagery
  USE **Figures of speech**
Imaginary animals
  USE **Mythical animals**
Imaginary companions
  USE **Imaginary playmates**
Imaginary creatures
  USE **Mythical animals**
Imaginary friends
  USE **Imaginary playmates**
Imaginary places 809
  Use for materials on imaginary places creat-
  ed for literary or artistic purposes. Materials
  on legendary or mythical places are entered
  under **Geographical myths**.
  UF Fictional places
      Fictitious places
  NT **Narnia (Imaginary place)**
Imaginary playmates 155.4
  UF Imaginary companions
      Imaginary friends
      Make-believe playmates
  BT **Child psychology**
      Imagination
      Play
Imaginary voyages 808.3; 808.83
  Use for individual works, collections, or
  materials about imaginary voyages.
  UF Space flight (Fiction)
      Voyages to the moon
  BT **Fantasy fiction**
      Science fiction
  NT **Robinsonades**
  RT **Interplanetary voyages**
Imagination 153.3
  BT **Educational psychology**
      Intellect
      Psychology
  NT **Creation (Literary, artistic,**
      etc.)
      Fantasy
      Imaginary playmates
Imaging, Magnetic resonance
  USE **Magnetic resonance imaging**
Imitations
  USE types of literature and names of
       prominent authors with the
       subdivision *Parodies, imita-*
       tions, etc., e.g. **Shakespeare,**
       William, 1564-1616—Paro-

dies, imitations, etc. [to be
added as needed]
Immigrants (May subdiv. geog.) **304.8**
  Use for materials on foreign-born persons
  who enter a country intending to become permanent residents or citizens. This heading
  may be locally subdivided by the names of
  places where immigrants have settled.
  UF Emigrants
      Foreign population
      Foreigners
  SA names of immigrant ethnic
      groups, e.g. **Mexican Ameri-**
      cans; and, for immigrants
      who are not citizens, the
      names of national groups with
      the appropriate subdivision for
      the country of their residence,
      e.g. **Mexicans—United States**
      [to be added as needed]
  BT **Minorities**
  RT **Aliens**
      Immigration and emigration
Immigrants—United States 325.73
  UF United States—Foreign popula-
      tion
  NT **Mexican Americans**
  RT **United States—Immigration**
      and emigration
Immigration and emigration 304.8; 325
  Use for materials on migration from one
  country to another. Materials on the move-
  ment of population within a country for per-
  manent settlement are entered under **Internal**
  migration.
  UF Emigration
      Foreign population
      Migration
  SA names of countries with the sub-
      division *Immigration and emi-*
      gration, e.g. **United States—**
      Immigration and emigration;
      and names of immigrant mi-
      norities and national groups,
      e.g. **Mexican Americans**;
      Mexicans—United States;
      etc. [to be added as needed]
  BT **Population**
  NT **Children of immigrants**
      Human geography
      Illegal aliens
      Naturalization
      Refugees
      Return migration

Immigration and emigration—*Continued*

    United States—Immigration
      and emigration

  RT **Aliens**

      Americanization

      Colonization

      Immigrants

      Internal migration

Immortality **129**

Use for materials on the question of the endless existence of the soul. Materials on the character and form of a future existence are entered under **Future life**. Materials on the philosophical concept of eternity are entered under **Eternity**.

  UF Eternal life

      Life after death

  BT **Eschatology**

      Soul

      Theology

  RT **Future life**

Immune system **616.07**

  UF Immunological system

  BT **Anatomy**

      Physiology

  RT **Immunity**

Immunity **571.9; 616.07**

  NT **Allergy**

      Immunization

  RT **Immune system**

Immunization (May subdiv. geog.)
    614.4

Use for materials on any process, active or passive, that leads to increased immunity. Materials on active immunization with a vaccine are entered under **Vaccination**.

  BT **Immunity**

      Public health

  NT **Vaccination**

Immunological system

  USE **Immune system**

Immunology **571.9; 616.07**

  BT **Medicine**

Impaired vision

  USE **Vision disorders**

Impairment

  USE **Disabilities**

Impartiality

  USE **Fairness**

Impeachment

  USE types of public officials and names of individual public officials with the subdivision *Impeachment*, e.g. **Presidents—United States—Impeachment** [to be added as needed]

Impeachments (May subdiv. geog.) **342**

  SA types of public officials and names of individual officials with the subdivision *Impeachment* [to be added as needed]

  BT **Administration of justice**

  NT **Recall (Political science)**

Imperialism **325**

  UF Colonialism

  SA names of countries with the subdivision *Foreign relations* or *Colonies* [to be added as needed]

  BT **Political science**

  NT **Colonies**

      Colonization

Implements, utensils, etc. **683**

  UF Gadgets

      Utensils

  NT **Containers**

      Household equipment and supplies

      Stone implements

      Tools

Imports (May subdiv. geog.) **382**

  BT **International trade**

Impostors and imposture (May subdiv. geog.) **364.1**

  UF Charlatans

      Hoaxes

      Pretenders

  BT **Crime**

      Criminals

  NT **Counterfeits and counterfeiting**

      Female impersonators

      Forgery

      Male impersonators

      Quacks and quackery

  RT **Fraud**

      Swindlers and swindling

Impressionism (Art) (May subdiv. geog.)
    709.03; 759.05

  UF Neo-impressionism (Art)

  BT **Art**

Imprisonment

  USE **Prisons**

In art
USE names of persons, families, and
corporate bodies with the subdivision *In art,* for materials
about the depiction of those
persons or bodies in works of
art, e.g. **Napoleon I, Emper-
or of the French, 1769-
1821—In art;** and phrase
headings denoting particular
themes in art for materials
about those themes, e.g. **Dogs
in art** [to be added as need-
ed]

In-line skating   796.2
UF   Rollerblading
BT   **Roller skating**

In literature
USE names of persons, families, and
corporate bodies with the subdivision *In literature,* for materials about the depiction of
those persons or bodies in literary works, e.g. **Napoleon I,
Emperor of the French,
1769-1821—In literature;** and
phrase headings denoting particular themes in literature for
materials about those themes,
e.g. **Dogs in literature** [to be
added as needed]

In-service training
USE   **Employees—Training**
and types of employees or personnel with the subdivision
In-service training, e.g. **Librarians—In-service training**
[to be added as needed]

In vitro fertilization
USE   **Fertilization in vitro**

Inaudible sound
USE   **Ultrasonics**

Inaugural addresses
USE types of public officials and
names of individual public of-
ficials with the subdivision
Inaugural addresses, e.g.
**Presidents—United States—
Inaugural addresses** [to be
added as needed]

Inauguration
USE types of public officials and
names of individual public officials with the subdivision
Inauguration, e.g. **Presidents—United States—Inau-
guration** [to be added as
needed]

Incandescent lamps
USE   **Electric lamps**

Incas   985
BT   **Native Americans—South
America**

Incendiary bombs   623.4
UF   Fire bombs
BT   **Bombs
Incendiary weapons**

Incendiary weapons   623.4
BT   **Chemical warfare**
NT   **Incendiary bombs**

Incentive (Psychology)
USE   **Motivation (Psychology)**

Incest   306.877; 616.85
BT   **Sex crimes**
NT   **Child sexual abuse**

Incineration
USE   **Cremation
Refuse and refuse disposal**

Income (May subdiv. geog.)   **331.2;
339.3**
UF   Fortunes
BT   **Economics
Finance
Property
Wealth**
NT   **Guaranteed annual income
Retirement income
Salaries, wages, etc.**
RT   **Gross national product
Profit**

Income tax (May subdiv. geog.)   **336.24**
UF   Personal income tax
BT   **Internal revenue
Taxation**
NT   **Tax credits**

Incunabula (May subdiv. geog.)   **093**
Use for materials on books printed before
the year 1501.
UF   Early printed books—15th century

Incunabula—*Continued*

SA subjects with the subdivision *Early works to 1800*, for materials on those subjects written before 1800, e.g. **Political science—Early works to 1800** [to be added as needed]

BT **Books**

Indebtedness

USE **Debt**

Indentured servants

USE **Contract labor**

Independence Day (United States)

USE **Fourth of July**

Independent schools

USE **Private schools**

Independent study   371.39

Use for materials on individual study that may be directed or assisted by instructional staff through periodic consultations.

BT **Study skills**

Tutors and tutoring

Indeterminism

USE **Free will and determinism**

Index librorum prohibitorum

USE **Books—Censorship**

Indexes   016

Use for works that list topics or names with references to books, articles, or passages where those topics or names are to be found. Works that list words with references to passages in a text where the exact word occurs are entered under **Concordances**.

SA subjects with the subdivision *Indexes*, e.g. **Newspapers—Indexes**; **Short stories—Indexes**; **English literature—Indexes**; etc. [to be added as needed]

BT **Bibliography**

NT **Concordances**

Subject headings

Indexing   025.3

BT **Bibliographic control**

Bibliography

RT **Cataloging**

Files and filing

India   954

May be subdivided like **United States** except for *History*.

Indian languages (North American)

USE **Native American languages**

Indian literature (East Indian)

USE **Indic literature**

Indian missions

USE **Native Americans—Christian missions**

Indian Ocean   551.4615

BT **Ocean**

Indian removal

USE **Native Americans—Relocation**

Indian reservations

USE **Native Americans—Reservations**

and names of native peoples, tribes, etc., with the subdivision *Reservations* [to be added as needed]

Indians

USE **Native Americans**

Indians of Canada

USE **Native Americans—Canada**

Indians of Central America

USE **Native Americans—Central America**

Indians of Central America—Guatemala

USE **Native Americans—Guatemala**

Indians (of India)

USE **East Indians**

Indians of Mexico

USE **Native Americans—Mexico**

Indians of North America

USE **Native Americans**

Native Americans—North America

Native Americans—United States

Indians of North America—Agriculture

USE **Native Americans—Agriculture**

Indians of North America—Antiquities

USE **Native Americans—Antiquities**

Indians of North America—Architecture

USE **Native American architecture**

Indians of North America—Art

USE **Native American art**

Indians of North America—Canada

USE **Native Americans—Canada**

Indians of North America—Captivities

USE **Native Americans—Captivities**

Indians of North America—Children

USE **Native American children**

Indians of North America—Christian missions

USE **Native Americans—Christian missions**

Indians of North America—Claims
USE **Native Americans—Claims**
Indians of North America—Costume
USE **Native American costume**
Indians of North America—Dances
USE **Native American dance**
Indians of North America—Dwellings
USE **Native Americans—Dwellings**
Indians of North America—Economic conditions
USE **Native Americans—Economic conditions**
Indians of North America—Education
USE **Native Americans—Education**
Indians of North America—First contact with Europeans
USE **Native Americans—First contact with Europeans**
Indians of North America—Folklore
USE **Native Americans—Folklore**
Indians of North America—Games
USE **Native American games**
Indians of North America—Government relations
USE **Native Americans—Government relations**
Indians of North America—History
USE **Native Americans—History**
Indians of North America—History—Chronology
USE **Native Americans—History—Chronology**
Indians of North America—Industries
USE **Native Americans—Industries**
Indians of North America—Languages
USE **Native American languages**
Indians of North America—Literature
USE **Native American literature**
Indians of North America—Medicine
USE **Native American medicine**
Indians of North America—Music
USE **Native American music**
Indians of North America—Names
USE **Native American names**
Indians of North America—Origin
USE **Native Americans—Origin**
Indians of North America—Politics and government
USE **Native Americans—Politics and government**

Indians of North America—Psychology
USE **Native Americans—Psychology**
Indians of North America—Relations with early settlers
USE **Native Americans—Relations with early settlers**
Indians of North America—Religion
USE **Native Americans—Religion**
Indians of North America—Reservations
USE **Native Americans—Reservations**
Indians of North America—Rites and ceremonies
USE **Native Americans—Rites and ceremonies**
Indians of North America—Schools
USE **Native Americans—Education**
Indians of North America—Sign language
USE **Native American sign language**
Indians of North America—Silverwork
USE **Native American silverwork**
Indians of North America—Social conditions
USE **Native Americans—Social conditions**
Indians of North America—Social life and customs
USE **Native Americans—Social life and customs**
Indians of North America—Wars
USE **Native Americans—Wars**
Indians of North America—Women
USE **Native American women**
Indians of South America
USE **Native Americans—South America**
Indians of South America—Peru
USE **Native Americans—Peru**
Indians of the West Indies
USE **Native Americans—West Indies**
Indic literature 891.4
UF Indian literature (East Indian)
BT **Literature**
Indigenous peoples (May subdiv. geog.)
305.8
Use for materials on indigenous groups within a colonial area or modern state where the group does not control the government. General materials on people bound together by common ancestry and culture are entered under **Ethnic groups**. Materials on the various ethnic groups or native peoples in a particular region or country are entered under **Ethnology** subdivided geographically.

Indigenous peoples—*Continued*
    UF   Aborigines
         Native peoples [*Former heading*]
         Natives
         People
    SA   names of individual indigenous peoples e.g. **Yoruba (African people)** [to be added as needed]
    BT   **Ethnology**
    NT   **Aboriginal Australians**
         Inuit
         Native Americans
         Yoruba (African people)

Indigenous peoples—America
    USE **Native Americans**

Indigestion   616.3
    UF   Dyspepsia
    BT   **Digestion**

Individual retirement accounts   332.024
    UF   IRAs (Pensions)
    BT   **Pensions**
         Retirement income
    NT   **401(k) plans**

Individualism (May subdiv. geog.)   **141; 302.5; 330.1**
    BT   **Economics**
         Equality
         Political science
         Sociology
    RT   **Persons**

Individuality   155.2
    UF   Identity
    BT   **Consciousness**
         Psychology
    NT   **Self**
    RT   **Conformity**
         Personality

Individualized instruction   371.39
    Use for materials on the adaptation of instruction to meet individual needs within a group. General materials on one-on-one instruction are entered under **Tutors and tutoring**.
    BT   **Tutors and tutoring**
    RT   **Open plan schools**

Indo-European civilization
    USE **Indo-Europeans**

Indo-Europeans (May subdiv. geog.)   **305-809**
    UF   Aryans
         Indo-European civilization

Indochina   959
    Use for the area comprising Laos, Cambodia, and Vietnam.
    BT   **Southeast Asia**

Indoctrination, Forced
    USE **Brainwashing**

Indolence
    USE **Laziness**

Indonesia   959.8
    May be subdivided like **United States** except for *History*.

Indoor air pollution (May subdiv. geog.)   **363.739; 628.5**
    BT   **Air pollution**

Indoor games   793
    BT   **Games**
    RT   **Amusements**

Indoor gardening   635.9
    BT   **Gardening**
    NT   **Terrariums**
         Window gardening
    RT   **Container gardening**
         House plants
         Miniature gardens

Induced abortion
    USE **Abortion**

Induction coils   537.6; 621.319
    BT   **Electric apparatus and appliances**
    NT   **Condensers (Electricity)**

Induction (Logic)
    USE **Logic**

Induction motors
    USE **Electric motors**

Industrial accidents (May subdiv. geog.)   **363.11; 658.3**
    UF   Employees—Accidents
         Industrial disasters
         Industrial injuries
         Labor—Accidents
         Occupational accidents
         Occupational injuries
    SA   industries with the subdivision *Accidents*, e.g. **Chemical industry—Accidents** [to be added as needed]
    BT   **Accidents**
    NT   **Chemical industry—Accidents**
    RT   **Hazardous occupations**

Industrial alcohol
    USE **Denatured alcohol**

Industrial antiquities
USE **Industrial archeology**
Industrial applications
USE types of scientific phenomena, chemicals, plants, and crops with the subdivision *Industrial applications*, e.g. **Ultrasonic waves—Industrial applications** [to be added as needed]
Industrial arbitration (May subdiv. geog.) **331.89**
UF Arbitration, Industrial
Industrial conciliation
Labor arbitration
Labor courts
Labor negotiations
Mediation, Industrial
Trade agreements (Labor)
BT **Industrial relations**
Labor
Labor disputes
Labor unions
Negotiation
RT **Collective bargaining**
Strikes
Industrial archaeology
USE **Industrial archeology**
Industrial archeology (May subdiv. geog.) **609**
Use for materials on the study of the physical remains of industries from the eighteenth and nineteenth centuries, including buildings, machinery, and tools.
UF Industrial antiquities
Industrial archaeology
BT **Archeology**
Industries—History
Industrial arts **600**
UF Mechanic arts
Trades
SA types of industries, arts, and trades; and names of countries, cities, etc., with the subdivision *Industries* [to be added as needed]
BT **Handicraft**
NT **Arts and crafts movement**
Engineering
Industrial arts education
Manufacturing processes
Printing
RT **Technology**

Industrial arts education (May subdiv. geog.) **607**
UF Education, Industrial
Industrial education
Industrial schools
Manual training
BT **Industrial arts**
Vocational education
RT **Technical education**
Industrial arts shops
USE **School shops**
Industrial buildings (May subdiv. geog.) **725**
UF Buildings, Industrial
BT **Buildings**
NT **Factories**
Industrial buildings—Design and construction **690**
BT **Architecture**
Building
Industrial chemistry **660**
UF Chemical technology
Chemistry, Technical
Technical chemistry
SA types of industries and products, e.g. **Clay industry; Dyes and dyeing**; etc. [to be added as needed]
BT **Chemistry**
Technology
NT **Alloys**
Bleaching
Canning and preserving
Ceramics
Corrosion and anticorrosives
Distillation
Drying
Electrochemistry
Food—Analysis
Gums and resins
Synthetic products
Tanning
Textile chemistry
Waste products
RT **Chemical engineering**
Chemical industry
Chemicals
Metallurgy
Industrial conciliation
USE **Industrial arbitration**

Industrial councils
USE **Participative management**
Industrial counseling
USE **Employees—Counseling of**
Industrial design (May subdiv. geog.)
745.2
UF Design, Industrial
BT **Design**
NT **Automobiles—Design and construction**
Human engineering
Systems engineering
Industrial disasters
USE **Industrial accidents**
Industrial diseases
USE **Occupational diseases**
Industrial disputes
USE **Labor disputes**
Industrial drawing
USE **Mechanical drawing**
Industrial education
USE **Industrial arts education**
Technical education
Industrial efficiency (May subdiv. geog.)
658

Use for materials on the various means of increasing efficiency and output in business and industries, including time and motion studies and materials on the application of psychological principles to industrial production.

UF Efficiency, Industrial
BT **Management**
NT **Job analysis**
Labor productivity
Motion study
Office management
Time study
Industrial equipment   **621.8**
UF Capital equipment
Capital goods
Industries—Equipment and supplies
Machinery in industry
SA types of industries with the subdivision *Equipment and supplies* [to be added as needed]
BT **Machinery**
NT **Automation**
Industrial robots
Industrial exhibitions
USE **Trade shows**

Industrial health
USE **Occupational health and safety**
Industrial injuries
USE **Industrial accidents**
Industrial laws and legislation (May subdiv. geog.)   **343**
UF Government regulation of commerce
Industries—Law and legislation
SA types of industries with the subdivision *Law and legislation*, e.g. **Chemical industry—Law and legislation** [to be added as needed]
BT **Law**
Legislation
NT **Labor laws and legislation**
Industrial libraries
USE **Corporate libraries**
Industrial management
USE **Management**
Industrial materials
USE **Materials**
Industrial mergers
USE **Corporate mergers and acquisitions**
Industrial mobilization (May subdiv. geog.)   **355.2**

Use for materials on industrial and labor policies and programs for defense mobilization.

UF Economic mobilization
Industry and war
Mobilization, Industrial
National defenses
BT **Economic policy**
Military art and science
War—Economic aspects
RT **Military readiness**
Industrial organization
USE **Management**
Industrial painting   **698**
SA topics with the subdivision *Painting*; e.g. **Automobiles—Painting** [to be added as needed]
BT **Finishes and finishing**
NT **Automobiles—Painting**
Lettering
Sign painting
RT **House painting**

Industrial plants
    USE **Factories**
Industrial policy (May subdiv. geog.)
    338.9; 354
    UF Government policy
        Government regulation of indus-
            try
        Industries—Government policy
        Industries—Organization, control,
            etc.
        Industry and state
        State regulation of industry
    BT **Economic policy**
    NT **Agriculture—Government poli-
            cy**
        Consumer protection
        Deregulation
        Energy policy
        Government ownership
        Privatization
        Public service commissions
        Railroads—Government policy
Industrial policy—United States
    338.973; 354
    UF Industries—Government policy—
            United States
        United States—Industrial policy
Industrial processing
    USE **Manufacturing processes**
Industrial psychology
    USE **Applied psychology**
Industrial relations (May subdiv. geog.)
    331
    Use for general materials on employer-
employee relations. Materials on problems of
personnel and relations from the employer's
point of view are entered under **Personnel
management**.
    UF Capital and labor
        Employer-employee relations
        Labor and capital
        Labor-management relations
        Labor relations
    BT **Labor**
        Management
    NT **Collective bargaining**
        Industrial arbitration
        Labor contract
        Labor disputes
        Labor unions
        Participative management
        Personnel management
        Strikes

Industrial research (May subdiv. geog.)
    607; 658.5
    BT **Research**
    NT **New products**
    RT **Inventions**
        Technological innovations
Industrial revolution (May subdiv. geog.)
    330.9; 909.81
    Use for materials on the historical shift
from home-based industries to large-scale factory production. Materials on the development
of organized productions as industries, especially factory-based industries, are entered under **Industrialization**.
    SA names of countries with the sub-
            division *Economic conditions*
            [to be added as needed]
    BT **Economic conditions**
        Industries—History
    RT **Great Britain—History—19th
            century**
        Industrialization
        Technology and civilization
Industrial robots   629.8
    UF Robots, Industrial
        Working robots
    BT **Automation**
        Industrial equipment
        Robots
Industrial safety
    USE **Occupational health and safety**
Industrial schools
    USE **Industrial arts education**
        Technical education
Industrial secrets
    USE **Trade secrets**
Industrial trusts   338.8; 658
    Use for materials on combinations in re-
straint of trade in which stock ownership is
transferred to trustees, who in turn issue trust
certificates and dividends and who attempt to
achieve monopolistic control over output,
prices, or markets.
    UF Cartels
        Trusts, Industrial
    BT **Capital**
        Commerce
        Economics
    RT **Antitrust law**
        Competition
        **Corporate mergers and acqui-
            sitions**
        Corporation law
        Corporations

Industrial trusts—*Continued*

        Monopolies

        Restraint of trade

Industrial trusts—Law and legislation

    USE   **Antitrust law**

Industrial uses of space

    USE   **Space industrialization**

Industrial waste   363.72; 628.4

    UF   Factory and trade waste

        Factory waste

        Industrial wastes

        Trade waste

    BT   **Refuse and refuse disposal**

        Waste products

    NT   **Hazardous wastes**

    RT   **Pollution**

        Water pollution

Industrial wastes

    USE   **Industrial waste**

Industrial welfare (May subdiv. geog.)

        658.3

    UF   Welfare work in industry

    BT   **Labor**

        Management

        Social work

    NT   **Social settlements**

Industrial workers

    USE   **Labor**

        Working class

Industrialization (May subdiv. geog.)

        338

    Use for materials on the development of organized productions as industries, especially factory-based industries. Materials on the historical shift from home-based industries to large-scale factory production are entered under **Industrial revolution**.

    BT   **Economic policy**

        Industries

    NT   **Developing countries**

        Space industrialization

    RT   **Industrial revolution**

        Modernization (Sociology)

Industries (May subdiv. geog.)   **338**

    Apart from **Manufacturing industries** and **Service industries**, all headings for types of industries are formulated in the singular.

    UF   Industry

        Production

    SA   types of industries, e.g. **Steel industry**; and ethnic groups with the subdivision *Industries*, e.g. **Native Ameri-**

cans—Industries [to be added as needed]

    BT   **Economics**

    NT   **Aerospace industry**

        Agricultural industry

        Automobile industry

        Book industry

        Ceramic industry

        Chemical industry

        Clothing industry

        Commercial fishing

        Computer industry

        Computer software industry

        Defense industry

        Electric products industry

        Firearms industry

        Industrialization

        Internet industry

        Iron industry

        Leather industry

        Management

        Manufactures

        Manufacturing industries

        Motion picture industry

        Native Americans—Industries

        Nuclear industry

        Paper industry

        Petroleum industry

        Pollution control industry

        Radio supplies industry

        Service industries

        Steel industry

        Textile industry

        Tobacco industry

Industries—Chicago (Ill.)   338.09773

    UF   Chicago (Ill.)—Industries

Industries—Deregulation

    USE   **Deregulation**

Industries—Equipment and supplies

    USE   **Industrial equipment**

Industries—Government policy

    USE   **Industrial policy**

Industries—Government policy—United States

    USE   **Industrial policy—United States**

Industries—History (May subdiv. geog.)

        338.09

    NT   **Industrial archeology**

        Industrial revolution

Industries—Law and legislation
USE **Industrial laws and legislation**
Industries—Ohio 338.09771
UF Ohio—Industries
Industries—Organization, control, etc.
USE **Industrial policy**
Industries—Social responsibility
USE **Social responsibility of business**
Industries—United States 338.0973
UF United States—Industries
Industry
USE **Industries**
Industry and state
USE **Industrial policy**
Industry and war
USE **Industrial mobilization**
War—Economic aspects
Inequality
USE **Equality**
Infallibility of the Pope
USE **Popes—Infallibility**
Infant care
USE **Infants—Care**
Infant care leave
USE **Parental leave**
Infant mortality
USE **Infants—Mortality**
Infant sudden death
USE **Sudden infant death syndrome**
Infantile paralysis
USE **Poliomyelitis**
Infants (May subdiv. geog.) **155.42;**
305.232; 362.7; 618.92

Use for materials about children in the earliest period of life, usually the first two years only.

UF Babies
BT **Children**
Infants and strangers
USE **Children and strangers**
Infants—Birth defects
USE **Birth defects**
Infants—Care 649
UF Baby care
Infant care
BT **Child care**
NT **Babysitting**
Infants—Clothing
USE **Infants' clothing**
Infants' clothing 646.4
UF Baby clothes
Infants—Clothing

BT **Children's clothing**
Clothing and dress
Infants—Death 306.9; 618.92

Use for general materials on the death of infants. Materials on infant death rates and causes are entered under **Infants—Mortality**.

BT **Death**
NT **Sudden infant death syndrome**
Infants—Diseases 618.92
UF Pediatrics
BT **Diseases**
RT **Infants—Health and hygiene**
Infants—Education
USE **Preschool education**
Infants—Health and hygiene 613;
618.92
UF Infants—Hygiene
Pediatrics
BT **Health**
Hygiene
RT **Infants—Diseases**
Infants—Hygiene
USE **Infants—Health and hygiene**
Infants—Mortality (May subdiv. geog.)
304.6

Use for materials on infant death rates and causes. General materials on the death of infants are entered under **Infants—Death**.

UF Infant mortality
BT **Mortality**
Infants—Nutrition 613.2; 649
BT **Nutrition**
NT **Breast feeding**
Infection and infectious diseases
USE **Communicable diseases**
Infectious wastes
USE **Medical wastes**
Infertility 616.6

Use for materials on infertility in humans and in animals.

UF Sterility in animals
Sterility in humans
BT **Reproduction**
RT **Birth control**
Childlessness
Fertility
Human fertility
Infinitive
USE names of languages with the subdivision *Infinitive*, e.g. **English language—Infinitive** [to be added as needed]

Infirmaries
  USE **Hospitals**
Inflammable substances
  USE **Hazardous substances**
Inflation (Finance) (May subdiv. geog.)
    332.4
  BT **Finance**
  NT **Wage-price policy**
  RT **Monetary policy**
    Paper money
Influence
  USE subjects, corporate bodies, indi-
    vidual persons, literary au-
    thors, religions, denomina-
    tions, sacred works, and wars
    with the subdivision *Influence,*
    e.g. **World War, 1939-
    1945—Influence; Shake-
    speare, William, 1564-1616—
    Influence** [to be added as
    needed]
Influenza   616.2
  UF Flu
  BT **Communicable diseases**
    Diseases
Informal sector (Economics)
  USE **Underground economy**
Information centers
  USE **Information services**
Information clearinghouses
  USE **Information services**
Information, Freedom of
  USE **Freedom of information**
Information networks   004.6
  Use for materials on the interconnection
  through telecommunications of a geographi-
  cally dispersed group of libraries or informa-
  tion centers for the purpose of sharing their
  total information resources.
  UF Information superhighway
    Networks, Information
  SA types of information networks
    and names of specific net-
    works [to be added as need-
    ed]
  BT **Information systems**
  NT **Internet**
    Library information networks
  RT **Computer networks**
Information resources (May subdiv.
    geog.)   **025.04**
  Use for materials on sources of information
  in general, not limited to a specific topic or

format. Materials on organizations that pro-
vide information services are entered under
Information services.
  UF Information sources
  SA subjects with the subdivision *In-
    formation resources*, for gen-
    eral materials about informa-
    tion on a subject, e.g. **Busi-
    ness—Information resources**;
    subjects with the subdivision
    Internet resources, for materi-
    als about information avail-
    able on the Internet on a sub-
    ject, e.g. **Business—Internet
    resources**; subjects with the
    subdivision *Databases*, for
    materials about data files on a
    subject regardless of the me-
    dium of distribution, e.g.
    Business—Databases; and
    headings for the providers or
    the users of information with
    the subdivision *Information
    services*, for materials about
    organizations that provide in-
    formation services, e.g. **Unit-
    ed Nations—Information ser-
    vices; Consumers—Informa-
    tion services**; etc. [to be add-
    ed as needed]
  BT **Information science**
  NT **Business—Information re-
    sources**
    Databases
    Information services
    Internet resources
Information retrieval   025.5
  UF Data retrieval
    Information storage and retrieval
    Retrieval of information
  BT **Documentation**
    Information science
  NT **Internet searching**
  RT **Information systems**
Information science (May subdiv. geog.)
    020
  BT **Communication**
  NT **Documentation**
    Information resources
    Information retrieval
    Information systems
    Library science

Information services (May subdiv. geog.)
025.5

Use for materials on organizations that provide information services. Materials on sources of information, not limited to a specific topic or format, are entered under **Information resources**.

UF   Information centers

Information clearinghouses

SA   headings for the providers or the users of information with the subdivision *Information services*, for materials about organizatons that provide information services, e.g. **United Nations—Information services**; **Consumers—Information services**; etc.; subjects with the subdivision *Information resources*, for general materials about information on a subject, e.g. **Business—Information resources**; subjects with the subdivision *Internet resources*, for materials about information available on the Internet on a subject, e.g. **Business—Internet resources**; and subjects with the subdivision *Databases*, for materials about data files on a subject regardless of the medium of distribution, e.g. **Business—Databases** [to be added as needed]

BT   **Information resources**

NT   **Archives**

Business—Information services

Consumers—Information services

Electronic publishing

Hotlines (Telephone counseling)

Machine readable bibliographic data

Reference services (Libraries)

United Nations—Information services

RT   **Documentation**

Information systems

Libraries

Research

Information society (May subdiv. geog.)
303.48

Use for materials on a society whose primary activity is the production and communication of information by means of computer networks and other advanced technology.

BT   **Sociology**

Information sources

USE   **Information resources**

Information storage and retrieval

USE   **Information retrieval**

Information storage and retrieval systems

USE   **Information systems**

Information superhighway

USE   **Computer networks**

Information networks

Internet

Information systems   **025.04**

UF   Computer-based information systems

Data storage and retrieval systems

Information storage and retrieval systems

BT   **Bibliographic control**

Computers

Information science

NT   **Data processing**

Database management

Digital libraries

Expert systems (Computer science)

Information networks

Machine readable bibliographic data

Management information systems

Multimedia

Teletext systems

Videotex systems

RT   **Information retrieval**

Information services

Libraries—Automation

Information systems—Management
025.04

Use for materials on the management of information systems.

BT   **Management**

Information technology (May subdiv. geog.)   **004; 303.48**

Use for materials on the acquisition, processing, storage, and dissemination of any type of information by microelectronics, computers, and telecommunication.

Information technology—*Continued*

    BT   **Technology**

    RT   **Knowledge management**

Infrared radiation   **535.01; 621.36**

    BT   **Electromagnetic waves**

         Radiation

Infrastructure (Economics) (May subdiv. geog.)   **363**

    BT   **Economic development**

         Public works

Inhalant abuse

    USE   **Solvent abuse**

Inhalation abuse of solvents

    USE   **Solvent abuse**

Inheritance and succession (May subdiv. geog.)   **346.05**

    UF   Bequests

         Heirs

         Hereditary succession

         Intestacy

         Legacies

    BT   **Wealth**

    NT   **Executors and administrators**

         Inheritance and transfer tax

         Probate law and practice

    RT   **Trusts and trustees**

         Wills

Inheritance and transfer tax (May subdiv. geog.)   **343.05**

    UF   Estate tax

         Taxation of legacies

         Transfer tax

    BT   **Estate planning**

         Inheritance and succession

         Internal revenue

         Taxation

Inheritance (Biology)

    USE   **Heredity**

Initialisms

    USE   **Acronyms**

Initials **745.6**

    NT   **Printing—Specimens**

    RT   **Alphabets**

         Illumination of books and manuscripts

         Lettering

         Monograms

         Type and type-founding

Initiation ceremonies

    USE   **Initiation rites**

Initiation rites (May subdiv. geog.)   **203; 392.1**

    UF   Initiation ceremonies

         Initiations

    BT   **Rites and ceremonies**

    NT   **Circumcision**

         Female circumcision

Initiations

    USE   **Initiation rites**

Initiative and referendum

    USE   **Referendum**

Injunctions (May subdiv. geog.)   **331.89**

    BT   **Constitutional law**

         Labor unions

    RT   **Strikes**

Injuries

    USE   **Accidents**

         First aid

         Wounds and injuries

Injurious insects

    USE   **Insect pests**

Ink drawing

    USE   **Pen drawing**

Inland navigation (May subdiv. geog.)   **386**

    May be subdivided by the names of rivers, lakes, canals, etc., as well as by countries, states, cities, etc.

    BT   **Navigation**

         Shipping

         Transportation

    RT   **Canals**

         Lakes

         Rivers

         Waterways

Inner cities (May subdiv. geog.)   **307.76**

    Use for materials on the densely populated, economically depressed, central areas of large cities.

    UF   Ghettoes, Inner city

         Inner city ghettoes

         Inner city problems

    BT   **Cities and towns**

Inner city ghettoes

    USE   **Inner cities**

Inner city problems

    USE   **Inner cities**

Inner city schools

    USE   **Urban schools**

Innovations, Technological

    USE   **Technological innovations**

Inns

    USE   **Hotels and motels**

Innuit

    USE   **Inuit**

Inoculation
USE **Vaccination**
Inorganic chemistry   546
UF   Chemistry, Inorganic
BT   **Chemistry**
NT   **Metals**
Input equipment (Computers)
USE **Computer peripherals**
Inquisition (May subdiv. geog.)   **272**
UF   Holy Office
BT   **Catholic Church**
Inquisitiveness
USE **Curiosity**
Insane
USE **Mentally ill**
Insanity defense (May subdiv. geog.)
345
UF   Insanity—Jurisprudence
Insanity plea
Mental illness—Jurisprudence
BT   **Criminal law**
Insanity—Jurisprudence
USE **Insanity defense**
Insanity plea
USE **Insanity defense**
Inscriptions (May subdiv. geog.)   **411**
UF   Epigraphy
BT   **Ancient history**
Archeology
NT   **Brasses**
Epitaphs
Graffiti
Hieroglyphics
Seals (Numismatics)
Insect-eating plants
USE **Carnivorous plants**
Insect pests (May subdiv. geog.)   **632**
UF   Destructive insects
Diseases and pests
Garden pests
Harmful insects
Injurious insects
SA   types of insect pests, e.g. **Lo-
custs**; etc.; and types of
crops, plants, trees, etc., with
the subdivision *Diseases and
pests*, e.g. **Fruit—Diseases
and pests** [to be added as
needed]
BT   **Economic zoology**
Insects

Pests
NT   **Fruit—Diseases and pests**
Insects as carriers of disease
Locusts
RT   **Agricultural pests**
Household pests
Parasites
Insecticides   632; 668
SA   types of insecticides [to be add-
ed as needed]
BT   **Agricultural chemicals**
Pesticides
NT   **DDT (Insecticide)**
Fumigation
RT   **Spraying and dusting**
Insecticides—Toxicology   615.9
BT   **Poisons and poisoning**
Insectivorous plants
USE **Carnivorous plants**
Insects (May subdiv. geog.)   **595.7**
SA   types of insects [to be added as
needed]
BT   **Animals**
NT   **Ants**
Bees
Beetles
Beneficial insects
Butterflies
Cockroaches
Crickets
Flies
Insect pests
Locusts
Mosquitoes
Moths
Silkworms
Wasps
Insects as carriers of disease   614.4
BT   **Insect pests**
RT   **Communicable diseases**
Insects—Metamorphosis   592.7
Inservice training
USE **Employees—Training**
Insider trading   346.07; 364.16
UF   Securities trading, Insider
Stocks—Insider trading
BT   **Commercial law**
Securities
Stock exchanges
Insignia   929.9

Insignia—*Continued*
    UF   Badges of honor
          Devices (Heraldry)
          Emblems
    SA   armies, navies, and other appro-
          priate subjects with the subdi-
          vision *Insignia* or *Medals,*
          badges, decorations, etc. [to
          be added as needed]
    BT   **Heraldry**
    NT   **Badges**
          Colleges and universities—In-
             signia
          United States. Army—Insignia
          United States. Army—Medals,
             badges, decorations, etc.
          United States. Navy—Insignia
          United States. Navy—Medals,
             badges, decorations, etc.
    RT   **Decorations of honor**
          Medals
          National emblems

Insolvency
    USE **Bankruptcy**

Insomnia   616.8
    UF   Sleeplessness
          Wakefulness
    RT   **Sleep**

Inspection
    USE topics with the subdivision *In-*
           spection, e.g. **Automobiles—**
           Inspection [to be added as
           needed]

Inspection of food
    USE **Food adulteration and inspec-**
           tion

Inspection of meat
    USE **Meat inspection**

Inspection of schools
    USE **School supervision**
           Schools—Administration

Inspiration
    USE **Creation (Literary, artistic,**
           etc.)

Inspiration, Biblical
    USE **Bible—Inspiration**

Installment plan   658.8
    UF   Instalment plan
    BT   **Business**
          Consumer credit
          Credit
          Purchasing

Instalment plan
    USE **Installment plan**

Instant messaging   004.69; 384.3
    BT   **Data transmission systems**

Instinct   152.3; 156
    UF   Animal instinct
    BT   **Animal behavior**
          Psychology
    RT   **Animal intelligence**
          Comparative psychology
          Habit

Institutional care   361
    UF   Asylums
          Benevolent institutions
          Charitable institutions
          Homes (Institutions)
    SA   classes of persons with the sub-
          division *Institutional care* [to
          be added as needed]
    BT   **Charities**
          Medical charities
          Public welfare
    NT   **Blind—Institutional care**
          Children—Institutional care
          Deaf—Institutional care
          Elderly—Institutional care
          Group homes
          Hospitals
          Mentally ill—Institutional care
          Nursing homes

Institutions, Charitable and philanthropic
    USE **Charities**

Institutions, Ecclesiastical
    USE **Religious institutions**

Institutions, Religious
    USE **Religious institutions**

Instruction
    USE **Education**
          Teaching

Instructional games
    USE **Educational games**

Instructional materials
    USE **Teaching—Aids and devices**

Instructional materials centers (May
    subdiv. geog.)   027.7
    UF   Audiovisual materials centers
          Curriculum materials centers
          Educational media centers
          Learning resource centers
          Media centers (Education)
          Multimedia centers

Instructional materials centers—*Continued*
      School media centers
    BT   **Libraries**
    NT   **School libraries**
Instructional supervision
    USE **School supervision**
Instructional systems analysis
    USE **Educational evaluation**
Instructional technology
    USE **Educational technology**
Instructive games
    USE **Educational games**
Instrument flying   **629.132**
    BT   **Aeronautical instruments**
          Airplanes—Piloting
Instrumental ensembles
    USE **Ensembles (Music)**
Instrumental music   **784**
    SA   types of instrumental music [to
          be added as needed]
    BT   **Music**
    NT   **Band music**
          Chamber music
          Guitar music
          Orchestral music
          Organ music
          Piano music
    RT   **Musical instruments**
Instrumentalists (May subdiv. geog.)
        784
    SA   types of instrumentalists, e.g. **Vi-**
          olinists [to be added as need-
          ed]
    BT   **Musicians**
    NT   **Organists**
          Pianists
          Violinists
          Violoncellists
Instrumentation and orchestration
        781.3; 784.13
    UF   Orchestration
    BT   **Bands (Music)**
          Composition (Music)
          Music
          Orchestra
    RT   **Musical instruments**
Instruments, Aeronautical
    USE **Aeronautical instruments**
Instruments, Astronautical
    USE **Astronautical instruments**
Instruments, Astronomical
    USE **Astronomical instruments**

Instruments, Engineering
    USE **Engineering instruments**
Instruments, Measuring
    USE **Measuring instruments**
Instruments, Meteorological
    USE **Meteorological instruments**
Instruments, Musical
    USE **Musical instruments**
Instruments, Negotiable
    USE **Negotiable instruments**
Instruments, Optical
    USE **Optical instruments**
Instruments, Scientific
    USE **Scientific apparatus and in-**
          struments
Insulation (Heat)   **691; 693.8**
    UF   Heat insulating materials
          Thermal insulation
    BT   **Heating**
Insulation (Sound)
    USE **Soundproofing**
Insults
    USE **Invective**
Insurance (May subdiv. geog.)   **368**
    SA   types of insurance, e.g. **Automo-**
          bile insurance [to be added
          as needed]
    BT   **Estate planning**
          Finance
          Personal finance
    NT   **Automobile insurance**
          Casualty insurance
          Disability insurance
          Fire insurance
          Health insurance
          Life insurance
          Malpractice insurance
          Marine insurance
          Unemployment insurance
Insurance, Accident
    USE **Accident insurance**
Insurance, Automobile
    USE **Automobile insurance**
Insurance, Casualty
    USE **Casualty insurance**
Insurance, Disability
    USE **Disability insurance**
Insurance, Fire
    USE **Fire insurance**
Insurance, Group
    USE **Group insurance**

Insurance, Health
USE **Health insurance**
Insurance, Hospitalization
USE **Hospitalization insurance**
Insurance, Life
USE **Life insurance**
Insurance, Malpractice
USE **Malpractice insurance**
Insurance, Marine
USE **Marine insurance**
Insurance, Professional liability
USE **Malpractice insurance**
Insurance, Social
USE **Social security**
Insurance, Unemployment
USE **Unemployment insurance**
Insurance, Workers' compensation
USE **Workers' compensation**
Insurgency (May subdiv. geog.) **322.4;
355.02**
UF Rebellions
BT **Revolutions**
NT **Guerrilla warfare**
Subversive activities
Terrorism
RT **Internal security**
Resistance to government
Integrated churches
USE **Church and race relations**
Integrated curriculum
USE **Interdisciplinary approach in
education**
Integrated language arts (Holistic)
USE **Whole language**
Integrated schools
USE **School integration**
Integration in education
USE **School integration**
Segregation in education
Integration, Racial
USE **Race relations**
Intellect 153.4
UF Intelligence
Mind
Understanding
BT **Psychology**
NT **Cognitive styles**
**Creation (Literary, artistic,
etc.)**
Imagination
Logic

Memory
Perception
Reason
Senses and sensation
RT **Reasoning**
Theory of knowledge
Thought and thinking
Intellectual cooperation 327.1; 370.116
UF Cooperation, Intellectual
BT **International cooperation**
NT **Conferences**
Cultural relations
RT **International education**
Intellectual freedom 323.44
BT **Freedom**
NT **Academic freedom**
Censorship
Freedom of information
Freedom of speech
Freedom of the press
Intellectual life 001.1
Use for general materials on learning and
scholarship, literature, the arts, etc. Materials
on literature, art, music, motion pictures, etc.
produced for a mass audience are entered un-
der **Popular culture**.
UF Cultural life
SA classes of persons, ethnic
groups, and names of coun-
tries, cities, etc., with the sub-
division *Intellectual life* [to be
added as needed]
BT **Culture**
NT **African Americans—Intellectu-
al life**
Blacks—Intellectual life
Chicago (Ill.)—Intellectual life
Cultural policy
Learning and scholarship
Ohio—Intellectual life
Popular culture
United States—Intellectual life
Intellectual life—Government policy
USE **Cultural policy**
Intellectual property (May subdiv. geog.)
346.04
UF Literary property
Proprietary rights
Rights, Proprietary
BT **Property**
RT **Copyright**
Patents
Intellectuals (May subdiv. geog.) **305.5**

Intellectuals—*Continued*
UF Intelligentsia
SA ethnic groups, classes of persons, and names of countries, cities, etc., with the subdivision *Intellectual life*, e.g. **African Americans—Intellectual life**; **United States—Intellectual life**; etc. [to be added as needed]
BT **Persons**
    Social classes
Intelligence
USE **Intellect**
Intelligence agents
USE **Spies**
Intelligence of animals
USE **Animal intelligence**
Intelligence service (May subdiv. geog.)
    327.12; 355.3
  Use for materials on a government agency that is engaged in obtaining information, usually about an enemy but sometimes about an ally or a neutral country, and also in blocking the attempts by foreign agents to obtain information about one's own national secrets.
UF Counterespionage
    Counterintelligence
BT **Public administration**
    Research
NT **Espionage**
    Military intelligence
RT **Secret service**
Intelligence service—United States
    327.1273; 355.3
UF United States—Intelligence service
Intelligence testing
USE **Intelligence tests**
Intelligence tests   153.9
UF Intelligence testing
    IQ tests
    Mental tests
BT **Child psychology**
    Educational psychology
NT **Ability—Testing**
RT **Educational tests and measurements**
Intelligentsia
USE **Intellectuals**
Intemperance
USE **Alcoholism**
    Temperance

Inter-American relations
USE **Pan-Americanism**
Interactive CD technology
USE **CD-I technology**
Interactive media
USE **Multimedia**
Interactive multimedia
USE **Multimedia**
    and subjects with the subdivision *Interactive multimedia*, e.g. **Geology—Interactive multimedia** [to be added as needed]
Interactive videotex
USE **Videotex systems**
Interbehaviorial psychology
USE **Behaviorism**
Interchange of visitors
USE **Exchange of persons programs**
Interchurch cooperation
USE **Interdenominational cooperation**
Intercollegiate athletics
USE **College sports**
Intercommunication systems   621.38; 651.7
UF Interoffice communication systems
BT **Electronic apparatus and appliances**
    Telecommunication
NT **Closed-circuit television**
    Microwave communication systems
Intercontinental ballistic missiles   623.4
UF ICBM
SA names of specific ICBM missiles, e.g. **Atlas (Missile)** [to be added as needed]
BT **Ballistic missiles**
NT **Atlas (Missile)**
Intercountry adoption
USE **International adoption**
Intercultural education
USE **Multicultural education**
Intercultural relations
USE **Cultural relations**
Intercultural studies
USE **Cross-cultural studies**

Interdenominational cooperation (May subdiv. geog.) **280**

Use for materials on religious activities planned and conducted cooperatively by two or more Christian sects. Materials on unity as one of the marks of the church are entered under **Church—Unity**. Materials on prospective and actual mergers within and across denominational lines are entered under **Christian union**. Materials on a movement originating in the twentieth century aimed at promoting church cooperation and unity are entered under **Ecumenical movement**.

    UF   Christian unity

            Cooperation, Interchurch

            Cooperation, Interdenominational

            Interchurch cooperation

    BT   **Christian sects**

            Church work

Interdisciplinarity in education

    USE   **Interdisciplinary approach in education**

Interdisciplinary approach in education **375**

    UF   Integrated curriculum

            Interdisciplinarity in education

            Interdisciplinary studies

    BT   **Curriculum planning**

Interdisciplinary studies

    USE   **Interdisciplinary approach in education**

Interest centers approach to teaching

    USE   **Open plan schools**

Interest (Economics) **332.8**

    BT   **Banks and banking**

            Business mathematics

            Capital

            Finance

            Loans

Interest groups

    USE   **Lobbying**

             Political action committees

Interfaces, Computer

    USE   **Computer interfaces**

Interfaith marriage **201; 261.8; 306.84**

    UF   Mixed marriage

    BT   **Intermarriage**

Interfaith relations **201; 261.2**

    BT   **Cultural relations**

Interfaith worship **291.172**

    BT   **Worship**

Intergovernmental tax relations (May subdiv. geog.) **336.2**

    UF   Federal-state tax relations

            State-local tax relations

            Tax relations, Intergovernmental

            Tax sharing

    BT   **Taxation**

    NT   **Revenue sharing**

Interior decoration

    USE   **Interior design**

Interior design (May subdiv. geog.) **729; 747**

Use for materials on the art and techniques of planning and supervising the design and execution of architectural interiors and their furnishings.

    UF   Home decoration

            House decoration

            House furnishing

            Interior decoration

    BT   **Art**

            Decoration and ornament

            Design

            Home economics

    NT   **Bedspreads**

            Draperies

            Furniture

            Lighting

            Mural painting and decoration

            Paperhanging

            Quilts

            Rugs and carpets

            Tapestry

            Upholstery

            Wallpaper

    RT   **Rooms**

Interlibrary loans (May subdiv. geog.) **025.6**

    BT   **Library circulation**

            Library cooperation

Interlocking signals

    USE   **Railroads—Signaling**

Intermarriage (May subdiv. geog.) **306.84**

Use for materials that discuss collectively marriage between persons of different religions, religious denominations, races, or ethnic groups.

    UF   Mixed marriage

    BT   **Marriage**

    NT   **Interfaith marriage**

            Interracial marriage

Intermediate schools

    USE   **Middle schools**

Intermediate state
USE **Eschatology**
Future life
Interment
USE **Burial**
Internal combustion engines   621.43
UF   Gas and oil engines
Gas engines
Gasoline engines
Oil engines
Petroleum engines
BT   **Engines**
NT   **Carburetors**
Diesel engines
Internal migration   304.8
Use for materials on the movement of pop-
ulation within a country for permanent settle-
ment. Materials on casual or seasonal workers
who move from place to place in search of
employment are entered under **Migrant labor**.
Materials on migration from one country to
another are entered under **Immigration and
emigration**.
UF   Migration, Internal
Rural-urban migration
Urban-rural migration
BT   **Colonization**
Population
NT   **Cities and towns—Growth**
Forced migration
RT   **Immigration and emigration**
Land settlement
Migrant labor
Internal revenue   336.2
BT   **Taxation**
NT   **Income tax**
Inheritance and transfer tax
Internal revenue law (May subdiv. geog.)
343.04
BT   **Law**
Internal security (May subdiv. geog.)
353.3; 363.2
UF   Loyalty oaths
Security, Internal
RT   **Insurgency**
Subversive activities
**Internal security—United States   353.3;
363.2**
UF   United States—Internal security
International adoption (May subdiv.
geog.)   **362.734**
UF   Intercountry adoption
BT   **Adoption**

RT   **Interracial adoption**
International agencies (May subdiv.
geog.)   **060**
UF   Associations, International
International associations
International organizations
SA   names of individual agencies [to
be added as needed]
BT   **International cooperation**
International arbitration   327.1
UF   Arbitration, International
International mediation
Mediation, International
BT   **International cooperation**
International law
International relations
International security
Treaties
NT   **League of Nations**
United Nations
RT   **Arms control**
Peace
International associations
USE   **International agencies**
International business enterprises
USE   **Multinational corporations**
**International competition   337; 382;
658**
UF   Competition, International
World economics
BT   **International relations**
International trade
RT   **War—Economic aspects**
International conferences
USE   **Conferences**
International cooperation   327.1; 341.7
Use for general materials on international
cooperative activities, with or without the par-
ticipation of governments.
SA   subjects with the subdivision *In-
ternational cooperation*, e.g.
**Astronautics—International
cooperation** [to be added as
needed]
BT   **Cooperation**
International law
International relations
NT   **Astronautics—International co-
operation**
Conferences
Cultural relations
Exchange of persons programs

International cooperation—*Continued*

      Foreign aid
      Intellectual cooperation
      International agencies
      International arbitration
      International police
      League of Nations
      Space sciences—International
        cooperation
      United Nations

RT   International education
      International organization
      Reconstruction (1914-1939)
      Reconstruction (1939-1951)
      Technology transfer

International copyright

USE **Copyright**

International economic relations **382**

UF   Economic relations, Foreign
      Foreign economic relations

BT   Economic policy
      International relations

NT   Balance of payments
      Commercial policy
      Foreign aid
      International trade
      Multinational corporations
      Sanctions (International law)
      Technical assistance
      United States—Foreign eco-
        nomic relations

International education (May subdiv.
     geog.) **370.116**

    Use for materials on education for interna-
tional understanding, world citizenship, etc.

BT   **Education**

NT   **Student exchange programs**
      Teacher exchange programs

RT   **Intellectual cooperation**
      International cooperation
      Multicultural education

International exchange

USE **Foreign exchange**

International exchange of students

USE **Student exchange programs**

International exhibitions

USE **Exhibitions**

International investment

USE **Foreign investments**

International language

USE **Universal language**

International law (May subdiv. geog.)
     341

UF   Law of nations

BT   **Law**

NT   **Asylum**
      Boundaries
      International arbitration
      International cooperation
      Intervention (International law)
      Mandates
      Marine salvage
      Maritime law
      Military law
      Naturalization
      Neutrality
      Pirates
      Political refugees
      Privateering
      Sanctions (International law)
      Slave trade
      Sovereignty
      Space law
      Treaties
      War crimes

RT   **International organization**
      International relations
      Natural law
      War

International mediation

USE **International arbitration**

International organization **341.2**

    Use for materials on plans leading towards
political organization of nations.

UF   World government
      World organization

SA   names of specific organizations,
      e.g. **United Nations** [to be
      added as needed]

BT   **International relations**
      International security

NT   **European federation**
      International police
      League of Nations
      Mandates
      **North Atlantic Treaty Organi-
      zation**
      United Nations

RT   **International cooperation**
      International law
      World politics

International organizations

USE **International agencies**

International police   341.7
   UF   Interpol
        Police, International
   BT   **International cooperation**
        International organization
        International relations
        International security
International politics
   USE   **World politics**
International relations   327; 341.3
   Use for materials on the theory of international relations. Historical accounts are entered under **World politics**; **Europe—Politics and government**; etc. Materials on the foreign relations of an individual country are entered under the name of the country with the subdivison *Foreign relations*. Materials limited to diplomatic relations between two countries are entered under the name of each country with the subdivision *Foreign relations* further subdivided by the name of the other country, e.g. **United States—Foreign relations—Iran** and also **Iran—Foreign relations—United States**.
   UF   Foreign affairs
        Foreign policy
        Foreign relations
        Peaceful coexistence
        World order
   SA   names of countries with the subdivision *Foreign relations*,
        e.g. **United States—Foreign relations** [to be added as needed]
   NT   **Arms control**
        Balance of power
        Boundaries
        Catholic Church—Foreign relations
        Cultural relations
        Diplomacy
        Diplomatic and consular service
        Diplomats
        East and West
        Geopolitics
        Globalization
        International arbitration
        International competition
        International cooperation
        International economic relations
        International organization
        International police
        International security

Isolationism
Jihad
Mandates
Monroe Doctrine
Nationalism
Neutrality
Peace
Political refugees
Treaties
United States—Foreign relations
   RT   **International law**
        National security
        Technology transfer
        World politics
International security   327.1; 341.7
   UF   Collective security
        Security, International
   BT   **International relations**
   NT   **Arms control**
        Arms race
        International arbitration
        International organization
        International police
        Neutrality
   RT   **Peace**
International space cooperation
   USE   **Astronautics—International cooperation**
International Standard Bibliographic Description   025.3
   UF   ISBD
   BT   **Cataloging**
International Standard Book Numbers 070.5
   UF   ISBN
   BT   **Publishers' standard book numbers**
International Standard Serial Numbers 070.5
   UF   ISSN
   RT   **Serial publications**
International trade (May subdiv. geog.) **382**
   Use for general materials about trade among nations. Materials on foreign trade of specific countries, cities, etc., are entered under the name of the place with the subdivision *Commerce*. Materials limited to trade between two countries are entered under the name of each country with the subdivision *Commerce* further subdivided by the name of the other country, i.e. **United States—Commerce—Ja-**

International trade—*Continued*
pan and also **Japan—Commerce—United States**.

UF   Foreign commerce
Foreign trade
Trade, International

BT   **Commerce**
International economic relations

NT   **Arms transfers**
Balance of trade
Exports
Free trade
Imports
International competition

Internationalization
USE   **Globalization**

Internet   004.67

UF   Information superhighway
Internet (Computer network)

BT   **Computer networks**
Information networks

NT   **Internet addresses**
Internet resources
World Wide Web

Internet access providers
USE   **Internet service providers**

Internet addresses   004.67

BT   **Internet**

Internet addresses—Directories   025.04

SA   topics, names of places, categories of persons, ethnic groups, etc., with the subdivisions *Internet resources—Directories*, e.g. **Business—Internet resources—Directories** [to be added as needed]

Internet and children   004.678083

UF   Children and the Internet

BT   **Children**

Internet auctions   381.177

UF   Online auctions

BT   **Auctions**
Electronic commerce

Internet chat groups
USE   **Online chat groups**

Internet commerce
USE   **Electronic commerce**

Internet companies
USE   **Internet industry**

Internet (Computer network)
USE   **Internet**

Internet—Computer software
USE   **Internet software**

Internet gambling (May subdiv. geog.)
795

UF   Online gambling

BT   **Gambling**

Internet—Home shopping services
USE   **Internet marketing**
Internet shopping

Internet in education (May subdiv. geog.)
004.678071

BT   **Education**

Internet industry (May subdiv. geog.)
004.67; 338.7

UF   Internet companies

BT   **Industries**

NT   **Internet service providers**

Internet journalism
USE   **Online journalism**

Internet marketing (May subdiv. geog.)
658.8

UF   Internet—Home shopping services
Online marketing
Online selling

BT   **Electronic commerce**
Marketing

RT   **Internet shopping**

Internet resources   004.67

UF   Computer network resources

SA   subjects with the subdivision *Internet resources*, for materials about information available on the Internet on a subject, e.g. **Business—Internet resources**; subjects with the subdivision *Information resources*, for general materials about information on a subject, e.g. **Business—Information resources**; subjects with the subdivision *Databases*, for materials about data files on a subject regardless of the medium of distribution, e.g. **Business—Databases**; and headings for the providers or the users of information with the subdivision *Information services*, for materials about organizations that provide in-

Internet resources—*Continued*

formation services, e.g. **United Nations—Information services; Consumers—Information services**; etc. [to be added as needed]

  BT **Information resources**
       Internet
  NT **Business—Internet resources**
       Web sites

Internet searching   004.67; 025.5

  UF Searching the Internet
       Web searching
       World Wide Web searching
  BT **Information retrieval**
  NT **Web search engines**

Internet service providers (May subdiv. geog.)   004.67

  UF Internet access providers
  BT **Internet industry**

Internet shopping (May subdiv. geog.)   381; 640

  UF Cybershopping
       Internet—Home shopping services
       Online shopping
       Shopping—Computer network resources
       Shopping—Internet resources
  BT **Electronic commerce**
       Shopping
  RT **Internet marketing**

Internet software   005.7

  UF Internet—Computer software
  BT **Computer software**

Internment camps
  USE **Concentration camps**

Internment of Japanese Americans, 1942-1945
  USE **Japanese Americans—Evacuation and relocation, 1942-1945**

Internship programs   331.25

  UF Internships
  BT **Employees—Training**

Internships
  USE **Internship programs**

Interoffice communication systems
  USE **Intercommunication systems**

Interpersonal competence
  USE **Social skills**

Interpersonal relations (May subdiv. geog.)   158; 302

Use for materials on group behavior, social relations between persons, and problems arising from organizational and interpersonal relations.

  UF Human relations
  SA relations between particular groups of persons or individuals, e.g. **Jewish-Arab relations; Parent-child relationship**; etc. [to be added as needed]
  BT **Social psychology**
  NT **Conflict of generations**
       Discrimination
       Domestic relations
       Family
       Group relations training
       Helping behavior
       Life skills
       Man-woman relationship
       Personal space
       Prejudices
       Social adjustment
       Social skills
       Teacher-student relationship
       Teasing
       Toleration
  RT **Human behavior**

Interplanetary communication
  USE **Interstellar communication**

Interplanetary visitors
  USE **Extraterrestrial beings**

Interplanetary voyages   808.3; 808.83; 919.904

Use for general materials about travel to other planets and for individual works, collections, or materials about imaginary accounts of such travels. Materials on the physics and technical details of flight beyond the earth's atmosphere are entered under **Space flight**.

  UF Interstellar travel
       Space travel
  BT **Astronautics**
       Fiction
  NT **Outer space—Exploration**
  RT **Imaginary voyages**
       Rockets (Aeronautics)
       Science fiction
       Space flight

Interplanetary warfare
  USE **Space warfare**

Interpol
USE **International police**
Interpreting and translating
USE **Translating and interpreting**
Interpretive dance
USE **Modern dance**
Interracial adoption (May subdiv. geog.)
362.73
BT **Adoption**
Race relations
RT **International adoption**
Interracial marriage (May subdiv. geog.)
306.84
UF Marriage, Interracial
Racial intermarriage
BT **Intermarriage**
Interracial relations
USE **Race relations**
Interscholastic sports
USE **School sports**
Interstate commerce 381
Use for materials limited to commerce between states. General materials on foreign and domestic commerce are entered under **Commerce**.
UF Government regulation of commerce
BT **Commerce**
Interstate highways
USE **Express highways**
Interstellar communication 621.382
UF Extraterrestrial communication
Interplanetary communication
Outer space—Communication
Space communication
Space telecommunication
BT **Life on other planets**
Telecommunication
NT **Astronautics—Communication systems**
Radio astronomy
Interstellar travel
USE **Interplanetary voyages**
Interstellar warfare
USE **Space warfare**
Interurban railroads
USE **Electric railroads**
Street railroads
Intervention (International law) 341.5
UF Military intervention
BT **International law**
War

NT **Monroe Doctrine**
RT **Neutrality**
Interviewing 158
BT **Social psychology**
NT **Talk shows**
RT **Applied psychology**
Counseling
Interviews
Interviewing (Journalism) 070.4
BT **Reporters and reporting**
Interviews 920
Use for materials about interviews and for collections of diverse interviews.
SA subjects, ethnic groups, classes of persons, and names of corporate bodies and individual persons with the subdivision *Interviews*, e.g. **Authors—Interviews** [to be added as needed]
BT **Conversation**
NT **Authors—Interviews**
RT **Interviewing**
Interviews, Parent-teacher
USE **Parent-teacher conferences**
Intestacy
USE **Inheritance and succession**
Intifada, 1987-1992 956.940
UF Arab-Israeli conflict, 1987-1992
Israeli-Arab conflict, 1987-1992
Palestinian-Israeli conflict, 1987-1992
Palestinian uprising, 1987-1992
BT **Israel-Arab conflicts**
Intifada, 2000- 956.940
UF Arab-Israeli conflict, 2000-
Israeli-Arab conflict, 2000-
Palestinian-Israeli conflict, 2000-
Palestinian uprising, 2000-
BT **Israel-Arab conflicts**
Intolerance
USE **Fanaticism**
Toleration
Intoxicants
USE **Alcohol**
Alcoholic beverages
Liquors
Intoxication
USE **Alcoholism**
Temperance
Intranets 004.6; 651.7

Intranets—*Continued*
    BT   **Business enterprises—Comput-**
         er networks
Intuition 153.4
    BT   **Philosophy**
         Psychology
         Rationalism
         Theory of knowledge
    RT   **Perception**
Inuit (May subdiv. geog.)   **970.004**

    Use for materials on the native peoples of the arctic regions of Alaska, Canada, and Greenland. If local usage dictates, libraries may establish Eskimos as a broader term than Inuit; and the names of other groups of Arctic peoples may be added as needed.

    UF   Eskimos
         Esquimaux
         Innuit
    BT   **Indigenous peoples**
    NT   **Igloos**
Inuit—Folklore 398
    BT   **Folklore**
Invalid cooking
    USE **Cooking for the sick**
         Diet therapy
Invalids (May subdiv. geog.)   **305.908**
    BT **Sick**
Invasion of Cuba, 1961
    USE **Cuba—History—1961, Invasion**
Invasion of privacy
    USE **Right of privacy**
Invective 808.88
    UF   Abuse, Verbal
         Insults
         Verbal abuse
    BT   **Satire**
Inventions (May subdiv. geog.)   **608**

    Use for materials on original devices or processes. Materials on technological improvements in materials, production methods, processes, organization, or management are entered under **Technological innovations**.

    BT   **Technology**
    NT   **Creation (Literary, artistic,**
         etc.)
         Technological innovations
         Technology transfer
    RT   **Industrial research**
         Inventors
         Patents
Inventors (May subdiv. geog.)   **609.2;**
    920
    NT   **African American inventors**

    RT   **Engineers**
         Inventions
Inventory control 658.7
    UF   Stock control
    BT   **Management**
         Retail trade
Invertebrates 592
    BT   **Animals**
Investment and saving
    USE **Saving and investment**
Investment brokers
    USE **Stockbrokers**
Investment companies
    USE **Mutual funds**
Investment in real estate
    USE **Real estate investment**
Investment trusts
    USE **Mutual funds**
Investments (May subdiv. geog.)   **332.6**
    BT   **Banks and banking**
         Capital
         Finance
    NT   **Annuities**
         Bonds
         Foreign investments
         Futures
         Mutual funds
         Real estate investment
         Savings and loan associations
         Securities
    RT   **Estate planning**
         Loans
         Saving and investment
         Speculation
         Stock exchanges
         Stocks
Investments, Foreign
    USE **Foreign investments**
Invincible Armada
    USE **Spanish Armada, 1588**
Invisible world
    USE **Spirits**
IQ tests
    USE **Intelligence tests**
Iran 935; 955
    May be subdivided like **United States** except for *History.*
    UF   Persia
Iran—Foreign relations—United States
    327.55073
    NT   **Iran hostage crisis, 1979-1981**
Iran—History—1941-1979 955.05

Iran—History—1979-   955.05

Iran hostage crisis, 1979-1981
        327.55073; 327.73055; 955
    BT   **American hostages—Iran**
        **Iran—Foreign relations—Unit-
        ed States**
        **United States—Foreign rela-
        tions—Iran**
Iraq   956.7

> May be subdivided like **United States** ex-
> cept for *History*.

Iraq—History—2003-, Anglo-American in-
    vasion
    USE   **Iraq War, 2003-**
Iraq War, 2003-   956.7044
    UF   Iraq—History—2003-, Anglo-
        American invasion
IRAs (Pensions)
    USE   **Individual retirement accounts**
Ireland   941.5

> May be subdivided like **United States** ex-
> cept for *History*.

Iron   669; 672
    BT   **Chemical elements**
        Metals
    NT   **Iron in the body**
        Iron ores
        Ironwork
        Steel
Iron Age (May subdiv. geog.)   **930.1**
    BT   **Civilization**
Iron and steel building
    USE   **Steel construction**
Iron in the body   612.3; 613.2
    BT   **Iron**
        Minerals in the body
Iron industry (May subdiv. geog.)   **338.2**
    UF   Iron industry and trade
    BT   **Industries**
    NT   **Hardware**
    RT   **Steel industry**
Iron industry and trade
    USE   **Iron industry**
Iron ores   553.3
    BT   **Iron**
        Ores
Ironing
    USE   **Laundry**
Ironwork (May subdiv. geog.)   **672; 682;
    739.4**
    UF   Wrought iron work

    BT   **Decoration and ornament**
        Iron
        Metalwork
    NT   **Blacksmithing**
        Welding
    RT   **Forging**
Irreversible coma
    USE   **Brain death**
Irrigation (May subdiv. geog.)   **333.91;
    627; 631.5**
    BT   **Agricultural engineering**
        Hydraulic engineering
        Water resources development
        Water supply
    RT   **Reclamation of land**
**Irrigation—United States   333.91; 627;
    631.5**
ISBD
    USE   **International Standard Biblio-
        graphic Description**
ISBN
    USE   **International Standard Book
        Numbers**
Islam (May subdiv. geog.)   **297**

> Use for materials on the religion. Materials
> on the believers in this religion are entered
> under **Muslims**.

    BT   **Religions**
    NT   **Islam—Relations—Judaism**
        Islamic fundamentalism
        Islamic sects
        Jihad
        Judaism—Relations—Islam
        Koran
        Mysticism—Islam
    RT   **Islamic law**
        Muslims
Islam and politics (May subdiv. geog.)
    320.5
    UF   Islam—Political aspects
        Politics and Islam
    BT   **Political science**
Islam—Poetry
    USE   **Islamic poetry**
Islam—Political aspects
    USE   **Islam and politics**
Islam—Relations—Judaism   297

> Use for materials on the relations between
> Islam and Judaism. When assigning this head-
> ing, provide an additional subject entry under
> **Judaism—Relations—Islam**. Materials on the
> conflicts between the Arab countries and Isra-
> el are entered under **Israel-Arab conflicts**.

Islam—Relations—Judaism—*Continued*
Materials that discuss collectively the relations between Arabs and Jews, including religious, ethnic, and ideological relations, are entered under **Jewish-Arab relations**.

UF   Islamic-Jewish relations
      Jewish-Islamic relations

BT   **Islam**
      Judaism

RT   **Jewish-Arab relations**

Islam—Sermons
USE **Islamic sermons**

Islamic architecture (May subdiv. geog.) **720.917**

UF   Architecture, Islamic
      Moorish architecture
      Muslim architecture

BT   **Architecture**

NT   **Mosques**

Islamic art (May subdiv. geog.) **709.1**

UF   Art, Islamic
      Muslim art

BT   **Art**

Islamic civilization **909**

UF   Muslim civilization

BT   **Civilization**

Islamic countries **956**

UF   Muslim countries

NT   **Arab countries**

Islamic fundamentalism (May subdiv. geog.) **297.09; 320.557; 322.1**

UF   Fundamentalism

BT   **Islam**
      Religious fundamentalism

Islamic gardens (May subdiv. geog.) **635.9; 712**

BT   **Gardens**

Islamic holidays **297.3**

UF   Fasts and feasts—Islam

BT   **Religious holidays**

NT   **Ramadan**

Islamic holy war
USE **Jihad**

Islamic-Jewish relations
USE **Islam—Relations—Judaism**
      Judaism—Relations—Islam

Islamic law (May subdiv. geog.) **340.5**

UF   Muslim law

BT   **Law**

RT   **Islam**

Islamic literature **297**

UF   Muslim literature

BT   **Religious literature**

NT   **Islamic poetry**
      Islamic sermons

Islamic music (May subdiv. geog.) **780.89**

BT   **Music**

Islamic mysticism
USE **Mysticism—Islam**

Islamic poetry **808.81**

UF   Islam—Poetry

BT   **Islamic literature**
      Poetry

Islamic science
USE **Science—Islamic countries**

Islamic sects **297.8**

BT   **Islam**
      Sects

NT   **Shiites**
      Sunnis

Islamic sermons **297**

UF   Islam—Sermons
      Muslim sermons

SA   individual Islamic sects with the subdivision *Sermons* [to be added as needed]

BT   **Islamic literature**
      Sermons

Islamic women
USE **Muslim women**

Islands (May subdiv. geog.) **551.42**

SA   names of islands and groups of islands [to be added as needed]

NT   **Coral reefs and islands**
      Cuba
      Islands of the Pacific

Islands of the Pacific **990**

Use for comprehensive materials on all the islands of the Pacific Ocean. Materials restricted to comprehensive treatment of the island groups of Melanesia, Micronesia, and Polynesia are entered under **Oceania**.

UF   Pacific Islands
      Pacific Ocean Islands

BT   **Islands**

NT   **Oceania**

RT   **Pacific rim**

Isolationism (May subdiv. geog.) **327.1**

BT   **International relations**

RT   **Neutrality**

Isotopes **539.7; 541**

BT   **Atoms**

NT   **Radioisotopes**

Israel   956.94

May be subdivided like **United States** except for *History.*

BT   **Middle East**

Israel-Arab conflicts   956.05; 965.04

Use for materials on the conflicts between the Arab countries and Israel. Materials that discuss collectively the relations between Arabs and Jews, including religious, ethnic, and ideological relations, are entered under **Jewish-Arab relations**. Materials on relations between the religions of Judaism and Islam are entered under **Judaism—Relations—Islam** and under **Islam—Relations—Judaism**.

UF   Arab-Israel conflicts

Arab-Israeli conflicts

Israeli-Arab conflicts

BT   **Arab countries—Foreign relations—Israel**

Israel—Foreign relations—Arab countries

NT   **Intifada, 1987-1992**

Intifada, 2000-

Israel-Arab War, 1948-1949

Israel-Arab War, 1967

Israel-Arab War, 1973

Sinai Campaign, 1956

RT   **Jewish-Arab relations**

Israel-Arab relations

USE   **Arab countries—Foreign relations—Israel**

Israel—Foreign relations—Arab countries

Israel-Arab War, 1948-1949   956.04

UF   Arab-Israel War, 1948-1949

BT   **Israel-Arab conflicts**

Israel-Arab War, 1956

USE   **Sinai Campaign, 1956**

Israel-Arab War, 1967   956.04

UF   Arab-Israel War, 1967

Six Day War, 1967

BT   **Israel-Arab conflicts**

Israel-Arab War, 1973   956.04

UF   Arab-Israel War, 1973

Yom Kippur War, 1973

BT   **Israel-Arab conflicts**

Israel—Collective settlements

USE   **Collective settlements—Israel**

Israel—Foreign relations—Arab countries   956

UF   Arab-Israel relations

Arab-Israeli relations

Israel-Arab relations

Israeli-Arab relations

NT   **Israel-Arab conflicts**

RT   **Arab countries—Foreign relations—Israel**

Jewish-Arab relations

Israel, Ten lost tribes of

USE   **Lost tribes of Israel**

Israeli-Arab conflict, 1987-1992

USE   **Intifada, 1987-1992**

Israeli-Arab conflict, 2000-

USE   **Intifada, 2000-**

Israeli-Arab conflicts

USE   **Israel-Arab conflicts**

Israeli-Arab relations

USE   **Arab countries—Foreign relations—Israel**

Israel—Foreign relations—Arab countries

Israelis (May subdiv. geog.)   **305.892; 920; 956.94**

BT   **Jews**

Israelites

USE   **Jews**

ISSN

USE   **International Standard Serial Numbers**

Italo-Ethiopian War, 1935-1936   963

UF   Ethiopian-Italian War, 1935-1936

Italy   945

May be subdivided like **United States** except for *History.*

Italy—Antiquities   937

BT   **Antiquities**

NT   **Herculaneum (Extinct city)**

Pompeii (Extinct city)

Italy—History   945

Italy—History—0-1559   945

Italy—History—1559-1789   945

Italy—History—1789-1815   945

Italy—History—1815-1914   945; 945.09

Italy—History—1914-1945   945.091

Italy—History—1945-1976   945.092

Italy—History—1976-   945.092

Ivory   679

BT   **Animal products**

Ivory Coast

USE   **Côte d'Ivoire**

Jack the Ripper murders, London (England), 1888   364.152

UF   Whitechapel murders, 1888

BT   **Serial killers**

Jails

USE   **Prisons**

Jainism 294.4
 BT Religions
Japan 952
 May be subdivided like **United States** except for *History*.
 RT **Japanese**
Japan—Commerce—United States 382
Japan—History 952
Japan—History—0-1868 952
Japan—History—1868-1945 952.03
Japan—History—1945-1952, Allied occupation 952.04
Japan—History—1952- 952.04
Japanese
 NT **Japanese Americans**
 RT **Japan**
Japanese aesthetics 111; 701; 801
 UF Aesthetics, Japanese
 BT **Aesthetics**
Japanese Americans 973.04956
 UF Nisei
 BT **Americans**
  Japanese
Japanese Americans—Evacuation and relocation, 1942-1945 940.5317
 UF Evacuation and relocation of Japanese Americans, 1942-1945
  Internment of Japanese Americans, 1942-1945
  Relocation of Japanese Americans, 1942-1945
 BT **World War, 1939-1945—Evacuation of civilians**
Japanese color prints 769.952
 UF Color prints, Japanese
 BT **Color prints**
Japanese language 495.6
 May be subdivided like **English language**.
 BT **Language and languages**
Japanese language—Business Japanese 495.6
 Business Japanese is a unique subdivision for Japanese language.
 UF Business Japanese
Japanese paper folding
 USE **Origami**
Jargon
 USE subjects and names of languages with the subdivision *Jargon*, e.g. **English language—Jargon** [to be added as needed]

Jazz ensembles 784.4
 BT **Ensembles (Music)**
Jazz music (May subdiv. geog.) 781.65; 782.42165
 BT **Music**
 RT **Blues music**
Jealousy 152.4
 BT **Emotions**
Jestbooks
 USE **Chapbooks**
Jesters
 USE **Fools and jesters**
Jesus Christ 232
 UF Christ
  Christology
 BT **God—Christianity**
 RT **Christianity**
Jesus Christ—Art 704.9
 UF Jesus Christ—Iconography
  Jesus Christ in art
 BT **Christian art**
 RT **Bible—Pictorial works**
Jesus Christ—Birth
 USE **Jesus Christ—Nativity**
Jesus Christ—Crucifixion 232.96
 UF Crucifixion of Jesus Christ
 RT **Good Friday**
Jesus Christ—Divinity 232
 UF Divinity of Jesus Christ
 RT **Trinity**
Jesus Christ—Drama 808.82
 Use for collections of plays about Jesus Christ.
 BT **Religious drama**
Jesus Christ—Historicity 232.9
Jesus Christ—Iconography
 USE **Jesus Christ—Art**
Jesus Christ—Messiahship 232
Jesus Christ—Nativity 232.92
 UF Jesus Christ—Birth
  Nativity of Jesus Christ
 RT **Christmas**
Jesus Christ—Parables 226.8; 232.9
 BT **Parables**
Jesus Christ—Passion 232.96
 UF Passion of Christ
Jesus Christ—Prayers 232.9
Jesus Christ—Prophecies 232
 BT **Bible—Prophecies**
Jesus Christ—Resurrection 232.9
 UF Resurrection of Jesus Christ
Jesus Christ—Teachings 232.9

Jesus Christ—Teachings—*Continued*
  UF Teachings of Jesus Christ
Jesus Christ in art
  USE **Jesus Christ—Art**
Jet airplanes
  USE **Jet planes**
Jet lag   616.9
  BT **Aviation medicine**
      Biological rhythms
      Fatigue
Jet planes   629.133
  UF Jet airplanes
      Jets (Airplanes)
  BT **Airplanes**
  NT **Supersonic transport planes**
Jet propulsion   621.43
  BT **Airplane engines**
  RT **Rockets (Aeronautics)**
Jets (Airplanes)
  USE **Jet planes**
Jewelry (May subdiv. geog.)   **391.7; 739.27**

  Use for general materials on jewelry and for materials on gems in which the emphasis is on the setting. Materials on cut and polished precious stones treated from the point of view of art or antiquity are entered under **Gems**. Materials on gem stones treated from the mineralogical or technological point of view are entered under **Precious stones**.

  UF Jewels
  SA styles of jewelry and types of
          jewelry items [to be added as
          needed]
  BT **Clothing and dress**
      Costume
      Decorative arts
  RT **Beads**
      Gems
Jewels
  USE **Gems**
       Jewelry
       Precious stones
Jewish-Arab relations   956

  Use for materials that discuss collectively the relations between Arabs and Jews, including religious, ethnic, and ideological relations. Materials on the conflicts between the Arab countries and Israel are entered under **Israel-Arab conflicts**. Materials on relations between the religions of Judaism and Islam are entered under **Judaism—Relations—Islam**; and **Islam—Relations—Judaism**.

  UF Arab-Jewish relations
  BT **Arabs**
      Jews

  RT **Arab countries—Foreign rela-
          tions—Israel**
      Islam—Relations—Judaism
      Israel-Arab conflicts
      **Israel—Foreign relations—
          Arab countries**
      Judaism—Relations—Islam
      Palestinian Arabs
Jewish children in the Holocaust (May
    subdiv. geog.)   **940.53**
  BT **Holocaust, 1933-1945**
  NT **Hidden children (Holocaust)**
Jewish-Christian relations
  USE **Christianity—Relations—Juda-
          ism**
       **Judaism—Relations—Christian-
          ity**
Jewish civilization   909
  UF Jews—Civilization
  BT **Civilization**
Jewish customs
  USE **Jews—Social life and customs**
       **Judaism—Customs and prac-
          tices**
Jewish diaspora   909
  UF Diaspora, Jewish
      Jews—Diaspora
  SA the heading **Jews** subdivided
          geographically, e.g. **Jews—
          France** [to be added as need-
          ed]
  BT **Human geography**
      Jews
Jewish doctrines
  USE **Judaism—Doctrines**
Jewish ethics   296.3
  BT **Ethics**
Jewish folk literature   398.2
  BT **Folk literature**
      Jewish literature
Jewish folklore
  USE **Jews—Folklore**
Jewish holidays   296.4; 394.267
  UF Fasts and feasts—Judaism
      Holidays, Jewish
      Jews—Festivals
  SA names of individual holidays,
          e.g. **Hanukkah** [to be added
          as needed]
  BT **Judaism**
      Religious holidays

412

Jewish holidays—*Continued*
NT Hanukkah
Passover
Yom Kippur
Jewish Holocaust (1933-1945)
USE **Holocaust, 1933-1945**
Jewish-Islamic relations
USE **Islam—Relations—Judaism**
Judaism—Relations—Islam
Jewish language
USE **Hebrew language**
Yiddish language
Jewish legends 296.1; 398.2
Use for individual works, collections, or materials about Jewish legends.
UF Jews—Legends
Legends, Jewish
BT **Legends**
Jewish life
USE **Jews—Social life and customs**
Judaism—Customs and practices
Jewish literature 296; 808.8
UF Jews—Literature
BT **Literature**
Religious literature
NT **Bible**
Cabala
Jewish folk literature
Jewish religious fiction
Talmud
Yiddish literature
RT **Hebrew literature**
Jewish liturgies
USE **Judaism—Liturgy**
Jewish men (May subdiv. geog.) 305.38; 305.892
BT **Men**
Jewish religion
USE **Judaism**
Jewish religious fiction 808.3; 808.83
Use for individual works, collections, or materials about fiction that promotes Jewish teachings or exemplifies a Jewish religious way of life.
BT **Fiction**
Jewish literature
Religious fiction
Jewish theology
USE **Judaism—Doctrines**
Jewish wit and humor 808.87
BT **Wit and humor**

Jewish women (May subdiv. geog.) 305.48; 305.892
BT **Women**
Jews (May subdiv. geog.) 305.892; 909; 296.092
UF Hebrews
Israelites
NT **Essenes**
Israelis
Jewish-Arab relations
Jewish diaspora
Lost tribes of Israel
World War, 1939-1945—Jews
RT **Judaism**
Jews—Antiquities 933
BT **Antiquities**
Jews—Civilization
USE **Jewish civilization**
Jews—Customs
USE **Jews—Social life and customs**
Judaism—Customs and practices
Jews—Diaspora
USE **Jewish diaspora**
Jews—Economic conditions 305.892; 330.9
BT **Economic conditions**
Jews—Encyclopedias 909
BT **Encyclopedias and dictionaries**
Jews—Festivals
USE **Jewish holidays**
Jews—Folklore 398
UF Jewish folklore
BT **Folklore**
Jews—France 305.892; 944
Jews—Language
USE **Hebrew language**
Yiddish language
Jews—Legends
USE **Jewish legends**
Jews—Literature
USE **Hebrew literature**
Jewish literature
Jews—Lost tribes
USE **Lost tribes of Israel**
Jews—Persecutions (May subdiv. geog.) 909; 933
BT **Antisemitism**
Persecution

Jews—Persecutions—*Continued*
    NT **Holocaust, 1933-1945**
        World War, 1939-1945—
            Jews—Rescue
Jews—Political activity 909; 956.94
    BT **Political participation**
Jews—Religion
    USE **Judaism**
Jews—Restoration 956.94
    Use for materials on the belief that the
    Jews, in fulfillment of Biblical prophecy,
    would some day return to Palestine.
    RT **Zionism**
Jews—Rites and ceremonies
    USE **Judaism—Customs and prac-
            tices**
Jews—Ritual
    USE **Judaism—Customs and prac-
            tices**
          Judaism—Liturgy
Jews—Social conditions 305.892; 909
    BT **Social conditions**
Jews—Social life and customs 305.892
    Use for materials on Jewish social customs.
    General materials on Jewish religious prac-
    tices are entered under **Judaism—Customs
    and practices**. Materials on the forms of pub-
    lic worship in Judaism are entered under **Ju-
    daism—Liturgy**.
    UF Jewish customs
        Jewish life
        Jews—Customs
    BT **Manners and customs**
Jigsaw puzzles 793.73
    BT **Puzzles**
Jihad 297.7
    UF Holy war (Islam)
        Islamic holy war
        Muslim holy war
    BT **International relations**
        Islam
Jiu-jitsu 796.815
    UF Jujitsu
    BT **Martial arts**
        Self-defense
Job analysis 658.3
    UF Personnel classification
    BT **Factory management**
        Industrial efficiency
        Management
        Occupations
        Personnel management
        Salaries, wages, etc.

    NT **Motion study**
        Time study
Job applications
    USE **Applications for positions**
Job discrimination
    USE **Discrimination in employment**
Job hunting 650.14
    UF Job searching
    SA fields of knowledge, professions,
        industries, and trades with the
        subdivision *Vocational guid-
        ance* [to be added as needed]
    BT **Employment agencies**
        Vocational guidance
    NT **Applications for positions**
        Résumés (Employment)
Job interviews 650.14
    UF Employment interviewing
    BT **Applications for positions**
Job performance standards
    USE **Performance standards**
Job placement guidance
    USE **Vocational guidance**
Job résumés
    USE **Résumés (Employment)**
Job retraining
    USE **Occupational retraining**
Job satisfaction 650.1; 658.3
    UF Work satisfaction
    BT **Attitude (Psychology)**
        Employee morale
        Personnel management
        Work
    NT **Burn out (Psychology)**
Job searching
    USE **Job hunting**
Job security 331.25; 650.1; 658.3
    UF Employment security
    BT **Personnel management**
    NT **Employees—Dismissal**
Job sharing 331.2; 658.3
    UF Sharing of jobs
    BT **Part-time employment**
Job stress 158.7; 658.3
    UF Occupational stress
        Organizational stress
        Work stress
    BT **Stress (Physiology)**
        Stress (Psychology)
    NT **Burn out (Psychology)**

Job training
USE **Occupational training**
Jobless people
USE **Unemployed**
Joblessness
USE **Unemployment**
Jobs
USE **Occupations**
Professions
Jogging 613.7
BT **Running**
Joint custody of children
USE **Child custody**
Part-time parenting
Joint ventures (May subdiv. geog.)
338.7
BT **Business enterprises**
Partnership
Joke books
USE **Jokes**
Jokes 808.7; 808.88
Use for collections of jokes and for materials about jokes.
UF Joke books
BT **Wit and humor**
NT **Practical jokes**
Jordan 956.95
May be subdivided like **United States** except for *History.*
Josei 741.5
Use for individual works, collections, or materials about manga for women ages 18-30.
BT **Manga**
Journaling 808
BT **Authorship**
Diaries
Journalism (May subdiv. geog.) 070.4
Use for materials on writing for the periodical press or on journalism as an occupation. Materials limited to the history, organization, and management of newspapers are entered under **Newspapers.**
SA types of journalism, e.g. **Scientific journalism**; and topics with the subdivision *Press coverage,* e.g. **Food contamination—Press coverage** [to be added as needed]
BT **Authorship**
Literature
NT **Broadcast journalism**
College and school journalism
Gossip
Libel and slander

Newsletters
Online journalism
Photojournalism
Press
Reporters and reporting
Scientific journalism
RT **Journalists**
Newspapers
Periodicals
Journalism—Editing 070.4
UF Magazine editing
News editing
Newspapers—Editing
Periodicals—Editing
BT **Editing**
Journalism—Objectivity 070.4
UF Slanted journalism
BT **Professional ethics**
Journalism, Scientific
USE **Scientific journalism**
Journalistic photography
USE **Photojournalism**
Journalists (May subdiv. geog.) 070.92; 920
UF Columnists
SA names of wars with the subdivision *Journalists,* e.g. **World War, 1939-1945—Journalists** [to be added as needed]
BT **Authors**
NT **World War, 1939-1945—Journalists**
RT **Journalism**
Journals
USE **Periodicals**
Journals (Diaries)
USE **Diaries**
Journeys
USE **Travel**
Voyages and travels
Joy and sorrow 152.4
UF Affliction
Sorrow
BT **Emotions**
NT **Pleasure**
RT **Grief**
Happiness
Suffering
Judaism (May subdiv. geog.) 296
UF Jewish religion
Jews—Religion

Judaism—*Continued*

SA   names of Jewish sects, e.g. **Hasidism** [to be added as needed]

BT   **Religions**

NT   **Atonement—Judaism**

       Cabala

       Christianity—Relations—Judaism

       Hasidism

       Islam—Relations—Judaism

       Jewish holidays

       Judaism—Relations—Christianity

       Judaism—Relations—Islam

       Rabbis

       Sabbath

       Talmud

RT   **Jews**

       Synagogues

Judaism—Customs and practices   **296.4**

Use for materials on Jewish religious practices in general. Materials on the forms of public worship in Judaism are entered under **Judaism—Liturgy**. Materials on Jewish social customs are entered under **Jews—Social life and customs**.

UF   Jewish customs

       Jewish life

       Jews—Customs

       Jews—Rites and ceremonies

       Jews—Ritual

BT   **Rites and ceremonies**

NT   **Bar mitzvah**

       Bat mitzvah

       Seder

RT   **Judaism—Liturgy**

Judaism—Doctrines   **296.3**

UF   Jewish doctrines

       Jewish theology

BT   **Doctrinal theology**

Judaism—Liturgy   **296.4**

Use for materials on the forms of public worship in Judaism. Materials on Jewish religious practices in general are entered under **Judaism—Customs and practices**. Materials on Jewish social customs are entered under **Jews—Social life and customs**.

UF   Jewish liturgies

       Jews—Ritual

BT   **Liturgies**

RT   **Judaism—Customs and practices**

Judaism—Relations—Christianity
    261.2; 296.3

Use for materials on the relations between Judaism and Christianity. When assigning this heading, provide an additional subject entry under **Christianity—Relations—Judaism**.

UF   Christian-Jewish relations

       Christianity and other religions—Judaism

       Jewish-Christian relations

BT   **Christianity and other religions**

       Judaism

Judaism—Relations—Islam   **296.3**

Use for materials on the relations between Judaism and Islam. When assigning this heading, provide an additional subject entry under **Islam—Relations—Judaism**. Materials on the conflicts between the Arab countries and Israel are entered under **Israel-Arab conflicts**. Materials that discuss collectively the relations between Arabs and Jews, including religious, ethnic, and ideological relations, are entered under **Jewish-Arab relations**.

UF   Islamic-Jewish relations

       Jewish-Islamic relations

BT   **Islam**

       Judaism

RT   **Jewish-Arab relations**

Judea and Samaria

USE   **West Bank**

Judges (May subdiv. geog.)   **347; 920**

UF   Chief justices

BT   **Lawyers**

NT   **Women judges**

RT   **Courts**

Judgment Day   **202**

UF   Doomsday

       Last judgment

BT   **End of the world**

       Second Advent

Judicial investigations

USE   **Governmental investigations**

Judiciary

USE   **Courts**

Judo   **796.815**

BT   **Martial arts**

       Self-defense

NT   **Karate**

Jugendstil

USE   **Art nouveau**

Juggling   **793.8**

UF   Legerdemain

       Sleight of hand

BT   **Amusements**

       Tricks

Jujitsu
USE **Jiu-jitsu**
July Fourth
USE **Fourth of July**
Jumble sales
USE **Rummage sales**
Jungle animals (May subdiv. geog.)
578.734
UF Jungle fauna
BT **Animals**
Forest animals
Jungle fauna
USE **Jungle animals**
Jungles (May subdiv. geog.) **634.9**
Use for materials on impenetrable thickets of second-growth vegetation replacing tropical rain forests that have been disturbed or degraded. Materials on forests of broad-leaved, mainly evergreen trees found in moist climates in the tropics, subtropics, and some parts of the temperate zones, are entered under **Rain forests.**
UF Tropical jungles
BT **Forests and forestry**
RT **Rain forests**
Junior colleges (May subdiv. geog.)
378.1
UF Community colleges
Two-year colleges
BT **Colleges and universities**
Higher education
Junior colleges—Directories **378.1**
BT **Directories**
Junior high school libraries
USE **High school libraries**
Junior high schools (May subdiv. geog.)
373.236
UF Secondary schools
BT **High schools**
Public schools
Schools
RT **Middle schools**
Secondary education
Junk
USE **Waste products**
Junk bonds **332.63**
UF High-yield junk bonds
BT **Bonds**
Junk in space
USE **Space debris**
Jupiter (Planet) **523.45**
BT **Planets**

Jurisprudence
USE **Law**
Jurisprudence, Medical
USE **Medical jurisprudence**
Jurists
USE **Lawyers**
Jury **345; 347**
UF Trial by jury
BT **Courts**
Criminal law
Justice **340**
BT **Ethics**
Law
Virtue
NT **Social justice**
RT **Fairness**
Justice, Administration of
USE **Administration of justice**
Justice League (Fictional characters)
741.5
BT **Superheroes**
Juvenile courts (May subdiv. geog.) **345**
UF Children's courts
BT **Courts**
RT **Juvenile delinquency**
Probation
Juvenile delinquency (May subdiv. geog.)
364.3
UF Delinquency, Juvenile
Juvenile delinquents
BT **Crime**
Social problems
NT **Gangs**
Juvenile prostitution
School violence
RT **Child welfare**
Emotionally disturbed children
Juvenile courts
Reformatories
Teenagers—Drug use
Youth—Drug use
Juvenile delinquency—Case studies
364.3
Juvenile delinquents
USE **Juvenile delinquency**
Juvenile drama
USE subjects and names with the subdivision *Juvenile drama*, e.g. **Christmas—Juvenile drama** [to be added as needed]

Juvenile fiction
USE subjects and names with the subdivision *Juvenile fiction,* e.g. **Christmas—Juvenile fiction** [to be added as needed]

Juvenile literature
USE **Children's literature** and subjects and names with the subdivision *Juvenile literature,* e.g. **Computers—Juvenile literature** [to be added as needed]

Juvenile poetry
USE subjects and names with the subdivision *Juvenile poetry,* e.g. **Christmas—Juvenile poetry** [to be added as needed]

Juvenile prostitution (May subdiv. geog.) **176; 306.74; 362.7; 363.4; 364.1**
UF Adolescent prostitution
Child prostitution
Teenage prostitution
BT **Juvenile delinquency**
Prostitution

Kabbala
USE **Cabala**

Kabuki **792.0952**
BT **Theater—Japan**

Kampuchea
USE **Cambodia**

Karate **796.815**
BT **Judo**
Martial arts
Self-defense

Kart racing
USE **Karts and karting**

Karting
USE **Karts and karting**

Karts and karting **796.7**
UF Carts (Midget cars)
Go-karts
Kart racing
Karting
Karts (Midget cars)
Midget cars
BT **Automobile racing**

Karts (Midget cars)
USE **Karts and karting**

Kayaking (May subdiv. geog.) **797.122**
BT **Canoes and canoeing**

Kempo
USE **Kung fu**

Kennels **636**
BT **Pets—Housing**

Kenya **967.62**
May be subdivided like **United States** except for *History.*

Keyboarding (Electronics) **005.72**
UF Computer keyboarding
Data processing—Keyboarding
Word processor keyboarding
BT **Business education**
Office practice
RT **Typewriting**

Keyboards (Electronics) **004.7**
UF Computer keyboards
BT **Computer peripherals**
Office equipment and supplies

Keyboards (Musical instruments) **786**
BT **Organs (Musical instruments)**
Pianos

Keys
USE **Locks and keys**

Kibbutz
USE **Collective settlements—Israel**

Kidnapping (May subdiv. geog.) **364.15**
UF Abduction
BT **Criminal law**
Offenses against the person

Kidnapping, Parental
USE **Parental kidnapping**

Kindergarten (May subdiv. geog.) **372.21**
BT **Elementary education**
Schools
NT **Creative activities**
Montessori method of education
RT **Nursery schools**
Preschool education

Kinematics **531**
BT **Dynamics**
NT **Mechanical movements**
RT **Mechanics**
Motion

Kinesiology **613.7**
UF Cinesiology
BT **Human locomotion**
Physical fitness

Kinetic art (May subdiv. geog.) **709.04**
UF Art in motion
Art, Kinetic

Kinetic art—*Continued*
　　BT　**Art**
　　NT　**Kinetic sculpture**
Kinetic sculpture　731; 735
　　UF　Sculpture in motion
　　BT　**Kinetic art**
　　　　Sculpture
　　NT　**Mobiles (Sculpture)**
Kinetics
　　USE　**Dynamics**
　　　　Motion
King Award
　　USE　**Coretta Scott King Award**
King Philip's War, 1675-1676　973.2
　　UF　United States—History—1675-
　　　　1676, King Philip's War
　　BT　**Native Americans—Wars**
　　　　United States—History—1600-
　　　　1775, Colonial period
King William's War, 1689-1697
　　USE　**United States—History—1689-**
　　　　1697, King William's War
Kings and rulers　352.23; 920; 929.7
　　　Use for materials on monarchs and other
　　heads of state not democratically elected.
　　UF　Kings, queens, rulers, etc.
　　　　Monarchs
　　　　Royal houses
　　　　Royalty
　　　　Rulers
　　　　Sovereigns
　　SA　names of places with the subdi-
　　　　vision *Kings and rulers*, e.g.
　　　　Great Britain—Kings and
　　　　rulers; and names of individ-
　　　　ual monarchs or rulers [to be
　　　　added as needed]
　　BT　**Heads of state**
　　NT　**Emperors**
　　　　Great Britain—Kings and rul-
　　　　ers
　　RT　**Courts and courtiers**
　　　　Monarchy
　　　　Queens
Kings, queens, rulers, etc.
　　USE　**Kings and rulers**
Kinship (May subdiv. geog.)　**306.83**
　　SA　ethnic groups with the subdivi-
　　　　sion *Kinship* [to be added as
　　　　needed]
　　BT　**Ethnology**
　　　　Family

　　RT　**Clans**
Kitchen gardens
　　USE　**Vegetable gardening**
Kitchen remodeling
　　USE　**Kitchens—Remodeling**
Kitchen renovation
　　USE　**Kitchens—Remodeling**
Kitchen utensils　643; 683
　　UF　Cooking utensils
　　　　Household utensils
　　　　Kitchenware
　　　　Utensils, Kitchen
　　SA　types of kitchen utensils, e.g.
　　　　Bread machines [to be added
　　　　as needed]
　　BT　**Household equipment and sup-**
　　　　plies
　　NT　**Bread machines**
Kitchens　643
　　BT　**Houses**
　　　　Rooms
Kitchens—Remodeling　643
　　UF　Kitchen remodeling
　　　　Kitchen renovation
　　　　Remodeling of kitchens
Kitchenware
　　USE　**Kitchen utensils**
Kites　629.133; 796.1
　　BT　**Aeronautics**
Kitsch　709.03
　　BT　**Aesthetics**
Kittens
　　USE　**Cats**
Knicks (Basketball team)
　　USE　**New York Knicks (Basketball**
　　　　team)
Knighthood
　　USE　**Knights and knighthood**
Knights and knighthood (May subdiv.
　　geog.)　**394; 940.1**
　　UF　Knighthood
　　BT　**Middle Ages**
　　　　Nobility
　　RT　**Chivalry**
　　　　Heraldry
Knights of the Round Table
　　USE　**Arthurian romances**
Knitting　677; 746.43
　　BT　**Needlework**
Knives　621.9; 623.4

Knives—*Continued*

   BT   **Hardware**

        Weapons

Knots and splices   623.88

   UF   Splicing

   BT   **Navigation**

        Rope

Knowledge

   USE   names of individual persons with the subdivision *Knowledge,* e.g. **Shakespeare, William, 1564-1616—Knowledge;** which may be further subdivided by the subject known, e.g. **Shakespeare, William, 1564-1616—Knowledge—Animals** [to be added as needed]

Knowledge-based systems (Computer science)

   USE   **Expert systems (Computer science)**

Knowledge management (May subdiv. geog.)   **658.4**

   UF   Management of knowledge assets

   BT   **Management**

   RT   **Information technology**

Knowledge, Theory of

   USE   **Theory of knowledge**

Kodak camera   771.3

   BT   **Cameras**

Kodomo   741.5

   Use for individual works, collections, or materials about manga for children up to age 12.

   BT   **Manga**

Koran   297.1

   UF   Qur'an

   BT   **Islam**

        Sacred books

Koran—Recitation   297.1

   UF   Recitation of the Koran

   BT   **Recitations**

Korea   951.9

   Use for comprehensive materials on all of Korea and for materials on Korea before it was divided in 1948 into two separate republics.

   NT   **Korea (North)**

        Korea (South)

Korea (Democratic People's Republic)

   USE   **Korea (North)**

Korea (North)   951.93

   Use for materials on the Democratic People's Republic of Korea, established in 1948. May be subdivided like **United States** except for *History.*

   UF   Korea (Democratic People's Republic)

        North Korea

   BT   **Korea**

Korea (Republic)

   USE   **Korea (South)**

Korea (South)   951.95

   May be subdivided like **United States** except for *History.* Use for materials on the Republic of Korea, established in 1948.

   UF   Korea (Republic)

        South Korea

   BT   **Korea**

Korean War, 1950-1953   951.904

Ku Klux Klan   322.4

   UF   Ku Klux Klan (1915-)

        Ku Klux Klan (19th cent.)

   BT   **Secret societies**

   RT   **Reconstruction (1865-1876)**

Ku Klux Klan (1915-)

   USE   **Ku Klux Klan**

Ku Klux Klan (19th cent.)

   USE   **Ku Klux Klan**

Kung fu   796.815

   UF   Kempo

        Wing chun

   BT   **Martial arts**

Kwanzaa   394.2612

   BT   **Holidays**

Labeling

   USE   subjects with the subdivision *Labeling,* e.g. **Food—Labeling** [to be added as needed]

Labor (May subdiv. geog.)   **331**

   Use for materials on the collective human activities involved in the production and distribution of goods and services in an economy, especially activities performed by workers for wages as distinguished from those performed by entrepreneurs for profits. Also use for general materials on workers. Materials on laborers as a social class are entered under **Working class**. Materials on the physical or mental exertion of individuals to produce or accomplish something are entered under **Work**.

   UF   Blue collar workers

        Factory workers

        Industrial workers

        Labor and laboring classes

        Laborers

Labor—*Continued*
- Manual workers
- Workers
- SA types of laborers, e.g. **Agricultural laborers**; **Miners**; etc. [to be added as needed]
- BT **Economics**
  Social conditions
  Sociology
- NT **Agricultural laborers**
  Alien labor
  Apprentices
  Capitalism
  Child labor
  Church and labor
  Collective bargaining
  Contract labor
  Employees
  Employment
  Employment agencies
  Forced labor
  Hours of labor
  Household employees
  Industrial arbitration
  Industrial relations
  Industrial welfare
  Labor supply
  Labor unions
  Migrant labor
  Miners
  Open and closed shop
  Part-time employment
  Peasantry
  Proletariat
  Skilled labor
  Supplementary employment
  Unskilled labor
- RT **Labor movement**
  Work
  Working class

Labor absenteeism
  USE **Absenteeism (Labor)**
Labor—Accidents
  USE **Industrial accidents**
Labor and capital
  USE **Industrial relations**
Labor and laboring classes
  USE **Labor**
  Labor movement
  Working class
Labor and state
  USE **Labor policy**

Labor and the church
  USE **Church and labor**
Labor arbitration
  USE **Industrial arbitration**
Labor (Childbirth)
  USE **Childbirth**
Labor contract (May subdiv. geog.)
  331.1; 331.89

> Use for materials on agreements between employer and employee in which the latter agrees to perform work in return for compensation from the former.

- UF Collective labor agreements
  Trade agreements (Labor)
- BT **Contracts**
  Industrial relations
- NT **Open and closed shop**
- RT **Collective bargaining**

Labor courts
  USE **Industrial arbitration**
Labor disputes (May subdiv. geog.)
  331.89
- UF Industrial disputes
- BT **Industrial relations**
- NT **Collective bargaining**
  Industrial arbitration
  Strikes
Labor economics   331
- BT **Economics**
Labor—Education (May subdiv. geog.)
  331.25
- UF Education of workers
- BT **Education**
Labor force
  USE **Labor supply**
Labor—Government policy
  USE **Labor policy**
Labor—Housing (May subdiv. geog.)
  363.5
- BT **Housing**
Labor—Insurance
  USE **Unemployment insurance**
Labor laws and legislation (May subdiv. geog.)   **344.01**
- UF Work—Law and legislation
- BT **Industrial laws and legislation**
- NT **Employee rights**
Labor-management relations
  USE **Industrial relations**
Labor market
  USE **Labor supply**

421

Labor movement (May subdiv. geog.)
    331.8
    Use for materials on the efforts of organizations and individuals to improve conditions for labor.
    UF Labor and laboring classes
    BT **Social movements**
    RT **Labor**
         Labor unions
Labor negotiations
    USE **Collective bargaining**
          Industrial arbitration
Labor organizations
    USE **Labor unions**
Labor output
    USE **Labor productivity**
Labor participation in management
    USE **Participative management**
Labor policy (May subdiv. geog.)   **331**
    UF Government policy
         Labor and state
         Labor—Government policy
         Manpower policy
    BT **Economic policy**
Labor productivity (May subdiv. geog.)
    331.11
    UF Labor output
         Productivity of labor
    SA types of industries, occupations, and processes with the subdivision *Labor productivity*, e.g. **Steel industry—Labor productivity** [to be added as needed]
    BT **Industrial efficiency**
    NT **Production standards**
         Steel industry—Labor productivity
Labor relations
    USE **Industrial relations**
Labor rights
    USE **Employee rights**
Labor saving devices, Household
    USE **Electric household appliances**
         Household equipment and supplies
Labor supply (May subdiv. geog.)
    331.11
    UF Labor force
         Labor market
    BT **Economic conditions**
         Employment

    Labor
    NT **Occupational retraining**
         Unemployed
         Unemployment
    RT **Employment agencies**
         Employment forecasting
         Human capital
         Manpower
Labor turnover   **331.12**
    BT **Personnel management**
    NT **Employment agencies**
Labor unions (May subdiv. geog.)
    331.88
    UF Labor organizations
         Organized labor
         Trade-unions
         Unions, Labor
    SA types of unions and names of individual labor unions [to be added as needed]
    BT **Industrial relations**
         Labor
         Societies
    NT **Industrial arbitration**
         Injunctions
         Librarians' unions
         Open and closed shop
         United Steelworkers of America
    RT **Collective bargaining**
         Labor movement
         Strikes
Labor unions—United States
    331.880973
Labor—United States   **331.0973**
Laboratories (May subdiv. geog.)   **001.4**
    UF Laboratory facilities
         Research buildings
         Science laboratories
         Scientific laboratories
    RT **Science**
Laboratory animal experimentation
    USE **Animal experimentation**
Laboratory animal welfare
    USE **Animal welfare**
Laboratory facilities
    USE **Laboratories**
Laboratory fertilization
    USE **Fertilization in vitro**

Laboratory manuals
    USE   scientific and technical subjects
           with the subdivision *Labora-*
           tory manuals, e.g. **Chemis-**
           try—Laboratory manuals [to
           be added as needed]
Laborers
    USE   **Labor**
          Working class
          and types of laborers, e.g. **Ag-**
          ricultural laborers; Miners;
          etc. [to be added as needed]
Laboring class
    USE   **Working class**
Laboring classes
    USE   **Working class**
Labyrinth gardens
    USE   **Maze gardens**
Labyrinths (May subdiv. geog.)   **291.3;**
    302.2
Lace and lace making (May subdiv.
    geog.)   **677; 746.2**
    BT   **Crocheting**
          Needlework
          Weaving
    NT   **Tatting**
Lacquer and lacquering (May subdiv.
    geog.)   **667; 745.7**
    BT   **Decorative arts**
          Finishes and finishing
Lactose intolerance   **616.3**
    RT   **Dairy-free cooking**
Lactose intolerance—Diet therapy—Recipes
    USE   **Dairy-free cooking**
Laissez-faire
    USE   **Free enterprise**
Laity   **262**
    May be subdivided by religion or sect.
    UF   Laymen
    BT   **Church**
    RT   **Lay ministry**
Laity—Catholic Church   **262**
    UF   Catholic laity
    BT   **Catholic Church**
Lakes (May subdiv. geog.)   **551.48**
    SA   names of lakes [to be added as
          needed]
    BT   **Physical geography**
          Water
          Waterways
    RT   **Inland navigation**

Lakes—United States   **551.48**
Lamaze method of childbirth
    USE   **Natural childbirth**
Lambs
    USE   **Sheep**
Lamentations
    USE   **Elegiac poetry**
Lamps   **621.32; 749**
    BT   **Lighting**
    NT   **Electric lamps**
Land
    USE   **Land use**
          Landforms
Land drainage
    USE   **Drainage**
Land forms
    USE   **Landforms**
Land grants (May subdiv. geog.)   **333.1**
    UF   Land patents
    BT   **Colonization**
          Public lands
Land mines (May subdiv. geog.)   **355.8;**
    623.4
    BT   **Explosives**
          Ordnance
Land patents
    USE   **Land grants**
Land question
    USE   **Land tenure**
Land, Reclamation of
    USE   **Reclamation of land**
Land reform (May subdiv. geog.)   **333.3**
    UF   Agrarian reform
          Reform, Agrarian
    BT   **Economic policy**
          Land use
          Social policy
    NT   **Land tenure**
    RT   **Agriculture—Government poli-**
          cy
Land settlement (May subdiv. geog.)
    304.8; 325
    UF   Resettlement
          Settlement of land
    BT   **Colonies**
          Land use
    NT   **Colonization**
    RT   **Human settlements**
          Internal migration
Land settlement—United States   **304.8;**
    325.73

Land settlement—United States—_Continued_

UF   United States—Land settlement

        Westward movement

Land slides

    USE   **Landslides**

Land surveying

    USE   **Surveying**

Land surveys

    USE   **Surveying**

Land tenure (May subdiv. geog.)   **333.3**

Use for general and historical materials on systems of holding land. Materials on the legal relationships between landlord and tenant are entered under **Landlord and tenant.**

UF   Agrarian question

        Fiefs

        Land question

        Tenure of land

BT   **Agriculture—Economic aspects**

        Land reform

        Land use

NT   **Farm tenancy**

        Feudalism

        Landlord and tenant

RT   **Peasantry**

        Real estate

Land use (May subdiv. geog.)   **333.73**

Use for general materials that cover such topics as types of land; the utilization, distribution, and development of land; and the economic factors affecting the value of land. Materials dealing only with ownership of land are entered under **Real estate.**

UF   Land

BT   **Economics**

NT   **Eminent domain**

        Farms

        Grasslands

        Land reform

        Land settlement

        Land tenure

        Landfills

        Pastures

        Public lands

        Real estate

        Reclamation of land

        Regional planning

Landfills (May subdiv. geog.)   **363.72; 628.3; 628.4**

Use for materials on places for waste disposal in which waste is buried in layers of earth in low ground.

UF   Earth fills

        Fills (Earthwork)

        Sanitary landfills

SA   names of landfills [to be added as needed]

BT   **Land use**

NT   **Hazardous waste sites**

        Love Canal Chemical Waste Landfill (Niagara Falls, N.Y.)

Landforms (May subdiv. geog.)   **551.41**

UF   Land

        Land forms

SA   types of landforms, e.g. **Mountains**; **Coasts**; etc. [to be added as needed]

BT   **Earth—Surface**

        Geology

NT   **Coasts**

        Mountains

        Seashore

        Wetlands

Landlord and tenant (May subdiv. geog.)   **333.5; 346.04**

Use for materials on the legal relationships between landlord and tenant. General and historical materials on systems of holding land are entered under **Land tenure.**

UF   Tenant and landlord

BT   **Commercial law**

        Land tenure

        Real estate

NT   **Housing**

RT   **Farm tenancy**

Landmarks, Literary

    USE   **Literary landmarks**

Landmarks, Preservation of

    USE   **National monuments**

           Natural monuments

Landscape architecture (May subdiv. geog.)   **712**

Use for materials on modifying or arranging the features of a landscape, urban area, etc., for aesthetic or pragmatic purposes.

UF   Landscape design

BT   **Architecture**

NT   **Garden ornaments and furniture**

        Garden structures

        Parks

        Patios

        Roadside improvement

RT   **Landscape gardening**

        Landscape protection

Landscape design
    USE **Landscape architecture**
Landscape drawing   743
    BT   **Drawing**
    RT   **Landscape painting**
Landscape gardening (May subdiv. geog.)
    712
    Use for materials on the design or rearrangement of extensive gardens or estates.
    UF   Planting
    BT   **Gardening**
           Horticulture
    NT   **Evergreens**
           Lawns
           Ornamental plants
           Xeriscaping
    RT   **Garden design**
           Landscape architecture
           Shrubs
           Trees
Landscape painting   758
    BT   **Painting**
    RT   **Landscape drawing**
Landscape protection (May subdiv. geog.)
    333.73
    UF   Beautification of landscape
           Natural beauty conservation
           Preservation of natural scenery
           Protection of natural scenery
           Scenery
    BT   **Environmental protection**
           Nature conservation
    NT   **Natural monuments**
    RT   **Landscape architecture**
           Regional planning
Landscape sculpture
    USE   **Earthworks (Art)**
Landslides (May subdiv. geog.)   **551.3**
    UF   Land slides
    BT   **Natural disasters**
Language
    USE   **Language and languages**
           and disciplines, classes of persons, types of newspapers, and names of individual persons, corporate bodies, and literary works entered under title with the subdivision *Language,* e.g. **Technology—Language; Children—Language;** etc. [to be added as needed]

Language and culture (May subdiv.
    geog.)   **306.44**
    BT   **Culture**
           Language and languages
Language and languages   400
    Use for general materials on the history, philosophy, origin, etc., of language. Materials on the scientific study of speech and comparative studies of language are entered under **Linguistics**.
    UF   Language
           Languages
           Philology
    SA   names of languages or groups of languages, e.g. **English language; Scandinavian languages; Native American languages;** etc.; disciplines, classes of persons, types of newspapers, and names of individual persons, corporate bodies, and literary works entered under title with the subdivison *Language,* e.g. **Technology—Language; Children—Language;** etc.; and names countries, cities, etc., with the subdivison *Languages,* for materials on the several languages spoken in a place, e.g. **United States—Languages;** etc. [to be added as needed]
    BT   **Anthropology**
           Communication
           Ethnology
    NT   **Arabic language**
           Bilingualism
           Children—Language
           Conversation
           Danish language
           English language
           French language
           German language
           Grammar
           Greek language
           Hebrew language
           Icelandic language
           Japanese language
           Language and culture
           Latin language
           Linguistics
           Modern Greek language

Language and languages—*Continued*
>>> Modern languages
>>> Multilingualism
>>> Native American languages
>>> Norwegian language
>>> Old Norse language
>>> Phonetics
>>> Programming languages
>>> Rhetoric
>>> Romance languages
>>> Russian language
>>> Scandinavian languages
>>> Semantics
>>> Sign language
>>> Sociolinguistics
>>> Spanish language
>>> Swedish language
>>> Translating and interpreting
>>> Universal language
>>> Verbal learning
>>> Vocabulary
>>> Voice
>>> Writing
>>> Yiddish language
>> RT **Speech**

Language and languages—Business language
>> USE names of languages with unique language subdivisions, e.g. **English language—Business English; Japanese language—Business Japanese;** etc. [to be added as needed]

Language and languages—Comparative philology
>> USE **Linguistics**

Language and languages—Etymology 412
>> UF Etymology
>>> Word histories
>> SA names of languages with the subdivision *Etymology*, e.g. **English language—Etymology** [to be added as needed]

Language and languages—Government policy (May subdiv. geog) **306.449**
>> UF Language policy
>>> National languages
>>> Official languages

Language and languages—Political aspects 400
>> Use for general materials on the political aspects of languages.
>> SA names of countries, cities, etc., with the subdivision *Languages*, e.g. **United States—Languages**; or with the two subdivisions *Languages—Political aspects*; and names of individual languages and groups of languages with the subdivision *Political aspects* [to be added as needed]

Language and society
>> USE **Sociolinguistics**

Language arts 372.6; 400
>> Use for materials on language and literature considered comprehensively as a school subject at the elementary level.
>> UF Communication arts
>> BT **Communication**
>> NT **Creative writing**
>>> **Literature**
>>> **Reading**
>>> **Speech**
>>> **Whole language**
>>> **Writing**

Language arts (Holistic)
>> USE **Whole language**

Language arts—Patterning 372.6
>> UF Patterns (Language arts)
>>> Reading—Patterning
>>> Writing—Patterning

Language disorders 616.85
>> Use for materials on disorders of the central neurological functions affecting the reception, processing, or expression of language. Materials on disorders of the physiological mechanisms required for speech are entered under **Speech disorders**.
>> UF Dysphasia
>> BT **Communicative disorders**
>> NT **Aphasia**

Language experience approach in education
>> USE **Whole language**

Language games
>> USE **Literary recreations**

Language, International
>> USE **Universal language**

Language laboratories 407
>> UF Foreign language laboratories
>> RT **Modern languages—Study and teaching**

Language of flowers   302.2; 398.24
UF   Flower language
BT   **Plants—Folklore**
Language policy
USE   **Language and languages—Government policy**
Language, Universal
USE   **Universal language**
Languages
USE   **Language and languages**
and countries, cities, etc., with the subdivision *Languages,* for materials on the several languages spoken in a place, e.g. **United States—Languages;** etc. [to be added as needed]
Languages, Modern
USE   **Modern languages**
Languages—Vocabulary
USE   **Vocabulary**
LANs (Computer networks)
USE   **Local area networks**
Lantern slides
USE   **Slides (Photography)**
Laptop computers
USE   **Portable computers**
Larceny
USE   **Theft**
Large and small
USE   **Size**
Large print books   028
UF   Books for sight saving
Books—Large print
Large type books
Sight saving books
BT   **Blind—Books and reading**
RT   **Big books**
Large type books
USE   **Large print books**
Laser-beam recording
USE   **Laser recording**
Laser photography
USE   **Holography**
Laser recording   621.36; 621.38
UF   Laser-beam recording
Recording, Laser
BT   **Optical data processing**
NT   **Holography**
RT   **Lasers**
Optical storage devices
Lasers   621.36

SA   lasers in particular subjects or fields of endeavor, e.g. **Lasers in aeronautics** [to be added as needed]
BT   **Light**
NT   **Lasers in aeronautics**
RT   **Laser recording**
Lasers in aeronautics   629.13
BT   **Aeronautics**
Lasers
Last judgment
USE   **Judgment Day**
Last rites (Sacraments)
USE   **Anointing of the sick**
Last sacraments
USE   **Anointing of the sick**
Last Supper   232.9
Use for materials on the final meal of Jesus with his apostles, where the sacrament of the Eurcharist was instituted.
Last things (Theology)
USE   **Eschatology**
Latchkey children   306.874; 362.7; 640
BT   **Children of working parents**
Lateness
USE   **Punctuality**
Lathe work
USE   **Lathes**
Turning
Lathes   621.9
UF   Lathe work
BT   **Woodworking machinery**
RT   **Turning**
Latin America   980
Use for materials that discuss collectively several or all of the countries of the Western Hemisphere south of the United States in which Spanish, Portuguese, or French is the principal language.
UF   Spanish America
SA   names of individual Latin American countries [to be added as needed]
BT   **America**
NT   **Pan-Americanism**
Latin America—Politics and government   980
BT   **Politics**
Latin American literature   860
Use for materials on the French, Portuguese, or Spanish literature of several Latin American countries. May use same subdivisions and names of literary forms as for **English literature.**

Latin American literature—*Continued*
- UF South American literature
  - Spanish American literature
- SA names of individual Latin American literatures [to be added as needed]
- BT **Literature**
- NT **Brazilian literature**
  - **Mexican literature**

Latin Americans (May subdiv. geog.)
920; 980

Use for materials on citizens of Latin American countries. Materials on United States citizens of Latin American descent are entered under **Hispanic Americans**.

Latin language   470

May be subdivided like **English language**.
- UF Classical languages
- BT **Language and languages**
- RT **Romance languages**

Latin literature   870

May use same subdivisions and names of literary forms as for **English literature**.
- UF Roman literature
- BT **Literature**
- RT **Classical literature**
  - **Early Christian literature**

Latinos (U.S.)
- USE **Hispanic Americans**

Latitude   526; 527
- UF Degrees of latitude and longitude
- BT **Earth**
  - **Geodesy**
  - **Nautical astronomy**

Latter-day Saints
- USE **Church of Jesus Christ of Latter-day Saints**

Laughter   152.4
- BT **Emotions**

Launching of satellites
- USE **Artificial satellites—Launching**

Laundry   648
- UF Ironing
  - Washing
- BT **Cleaning**
  - **Home economics**
  - **Household sanitation**

Law (May subdiv. geog.)   **340**
- UF Jurisprudence
  - Laws
  - Statutes

- SA names of particular legal systems, e.g. **Islamic law**; special branches of law, e.g. **Criminal law**; subjects with the subdivision *Law and legislation*, e.g. **Automobiles—Law and legislation**; and ethnic groups and classes of persons with the subdivision *Legal status, laws, etc.*, e.g. **Handicapped—Legal status, laws, etc.** [to be added as needed]
- BT **Political science**
- NT **Abortion—Law and legislation**
  - **Administration of justice**
  - **Administrative law**
  - **Automobiles—Law and legislation**
  - **Chemical industry—Law and legislation**
  - **Commercial law**
  - **Common law**
  - **Constitutional law**
  - **Constitutions**
  - **Corporation law**
  - **Courts**
  - **Criminal law**
  - **Ecclesiastical law**
  - **Environmental law**
  - **Food—Law and legislation**
  - **Gun control**
  - **Handicapped—Legal status, laws, etc.**
  - **Industrial laws and legislation**
  - **Internal revenue law**
  - **International law**
  - **Islamic law**
  - **Justice**
  - **Law reform**
  - **Lawyers**
  - **Libraries—Law and legislation**
  - **Litigation**
  - **Maritime law**
  - **Martial law**
  - **Medicine—Law and legislation**
  - **Military law**
  - **Natural law**
  - **Power of attorney**
  - **Safety regulations**
  - **Space law**

Law—*Continued*
> Water rights
> RT **Legislation**

Law and legislation
> USE subjects with the subdivision *Law and legislation,* e.g. **Automobiles—Law and legislation** [to be added as needed]

Law, Election
> USE **Election law**

Law enforcement (May subdiv. geog.) 363.2
> BT **Administration of criminal justice**
> NT **Criminal investigation**
> **Police**

Law—Fiction
> USE **Legal stories**

Law of nations
> USE **International law**

Law of nature
> USE **Natural law**

Law of supply and demand
> USE **Supply and demand**

Law of the sea
> USE **Maritime law**

Law reform (May subdiv. geog.) 340
> UF Legal reform
> BT **Law**

Law schools (May subdiv. geog.) 340.071
> BT **Colleges and universities**

Law suits
> USE **Litigation**

Law—United States 349.73
> UF United States—Law

Law—Vocational guidance 340.023
> BT **Professions**
> **Vocational guidance**

Lawmakers
> USE **Legislators**

Lawn tennis
> USE **Tennis**

Lawns 635.9; 712
> BT **Landscape gardening**
> RT **Grasses**

Laws
> USE **Law**
> **Legislation**

Lawsuits
> USE **Litigation**

Lawyers (May subdiv. geog.) 340.092; 920
> UF Attorneys
> Bar
> Barristers
> Jurists
> Legal profession
> Solicitors
> BT **Law**
> NT **Judges**
> RT **Legal ethics**

Lawyers—Fiction
> USE **Legal stories**

Lawyers—Salaries, wages, etc. (May subdiv. geog.) 331.2
> BT **Salaries, wages, etc.**

Lay ministry 253
> UF Volunteers in church work
> BT **Church work**
> RT **Laity**

Laymen
> USE **Laity**

Laziness 179
> UF Indolence
> Sloth
> BT **Personality**

Lead poisoning 615.9
> UF Lead—Toxicology
> BT **Occupational diseases**
> **Poisons and poisoning**

Lead—Toxicology
> USE **Lead poisoning**

Leadership 158; 303.3
> BT **Ability**
> **Executive ability**
> **Social groups**
> **Success**
> NT **Elite (Social sciences)**

League of Nations 341.22
> BT **International arbitration**
> **International cooperation**
> **International organization**
> **World War, 1914-1918—Peace**

Learned institutions and societies
> USE **Learning and scholarship**

Learned societies
> USE **Societies**

Learning and scholarship (May subdiv. geog.) 001.2
> UF Erudition
> Learned institutions and societies

Learning and scholarship—*Continued*
Scholarship
BT   **Civilization**
       Intellectual life
NT   **Humanities**
       Professional education
RT   **Culture**
       Education
       Humanism
       Research

Learning center approach to teaching
USE   **Open plan schools**

Learning disabilities   153.1; 371.9; 616.85
SA   types of learning disabilities [to be added as needed]
BT   **Psychology of learning**
       Slow learning children
NT   **Reading disability**

Learning, Psychology of
USE   **Psychology of learning**

Learning resource centers
USE   **Instructional materials centers**

Learning, Verbal
USE   **Verbal learning**

Lease and rental services   333.5
UF   Lease services
       Rental services
BT   **Service industries**

Lease services
USE   **Lease and rental services**

Leather   675
BT   **Animal products**
RT   **Hides and skins**
       Leather industry
       Tanning

Leather clothing
USE   **Leather garments**

Leather garments   391; 685
UF   Leather clothing
BT   **Clothing and dress**
       Leather work

Leather industry (May subdiv. geog.)   338.4
UF   Leather industry and trade
BT   **Industries**
NT   **Shoe industry**
RT   **Leather**

Leather industry and trade
USE   **Leather industry**

Leather work   745.53

BT   **Decoration and ornament**
       Decorative arts
       Handicraft
NT   **Leather garments**

Leave for parenting
USE   **Parental leave**

Leave of absence (May subdiv. geog.)   331.25
BT   **Hours of labor**
NT   **Parental leave**

Leaves   575.5; 581.4
UF   Foliage
BT   **Plants**

Lebanon   956.92

May be subdivided like **United States** except for *History.*

Lebanon—History   956.92

Lebanon—History—1975-1976, Civil War   956.9204

Lectures and lecturing   808.5

Use for general materials on lectures and the art of delivering speeches on academic subjects. Collections of speeches on several subjects and materials about non-academic speeches are entered under **Speeches**. Collections of lectures on a single subject are entered under that subject.

UF   Addresses
       Speaking
BT   **Public speaking**
       Rhetoric
       Teaching
NT   **Radio addresses, debates, etc.**
RT   **Speeches**

Left and right
USE   **Left and right (Direction)**
       Right and left (Political science)

Left and right (Direction)   152.1

Use for children's materials on left and right as indications of location or direction. Materials on political views or attitudes are entered under **Right and left (Political science)**. Materials on the physical characteristics of favoring one hand or the other are entered under **Left- and right-handedness**.

UF   Left and right
       Right and left
BT   **Direction sense**

Left- and right-handedness   152.3
UF   Handedness
       Right- and left-handedness
BT   **Psychophysiology**

Left (Political science)
USE **Liberalism**
Right and left (Political science)

Legacies
USE **Inheritance and succession**
Wills

Legal aid (May subdiv. geog.)   **362.5**
Use for materials on legal services to the poor, usually provided under the sponsorship of local bar associations or governmental units.
UF   Legal assistance to the poor
Legal representation of the poor
Legal services for the poor
BT   **Public welfare**

Legal assistance to the poor
USE   **Legal aid**

Legal drama (Films)   **791.43**
Use for individual works, collections, or materials about motion pictures dealing with trials or litigations.
UF   Courtroom drama
BT   **Motion pictures**

Legal drama (Radio programs)   **791.44**
Use for individual works, collections, or materials about radio programs dealing with trials or litigations.
UF   Courtroom drama
BT   **Radio programs**

Legal drama (Television programs)   **791.45**
Use for individual works, collections, or materials about television programs dealing with trials or litigations.
UF   Courtroom drama
BT   **Television programs**

Legal ethics (May subdiv. geog.)   **174; 340**
BT   **Ethics**
Professional ethics
RT   **Lawyers**

Legal fiction (Literature)
USE   **Legal stories**

Legal holidays
USE   **Holidays**

Legal medicine
USE   **Medical jurisprudence**

Legal novels
USE   **Legal stories**

Legal profession
USE   **Lawyers**

Legal reform
USE   **Law reform**

Legal representation of the poor
USE   **Legal aid**

Legal responsibility
USE   **Liability (Law)**

Legal services for the poor
USE   **Legal aid**

Legal status, laws, etc.
USE   ethnic groups and classes of persons with the subdivision *Legal status, laws, etc.,* e.g.
Handicapped—Legal status, laws, etc. [to be added as needed]

Legal stories   **808.3; 808.83**
Use for individual works, collections, or materials about fiction dealing with trials or litigations.
UF   Law—Fiction
Lawyers—Fiction
Legal fiction (Literature)
Legal novels
Trials—Fiction
BT   **Fiction**

Legal tender
USE   **Money**

Legations
USE   **Diplomatic and consular service**

Legendary characters   **398.22**
SA   names of individual legendary characters, e.g. **Bunyan, Paul (Legendary character)** [to be added as needed]
BT   **Legends**
Mythology
NT   **Merlin (Legendary character)**
Oedipus (Legendary character)
Scheherazade (Legendary character)

Legends (May subdiv. geog.)   **398.2**
Use for individual works, collections, or materials about tales coming down from the past, especially those relating to actual events or persons. Collections of tales written between the eleventh and fourteenth centuries and dealing with the age of chivalry or the supernatural are entered under **Romances**.
UF   Folk tales
Stories
Tales
Traditions
SA   relgious topics and names of individual persons or sacred works with the subdivision

Legends—*Continued*
    Legends; e.g. **Grail—Legends**; legends of particular ethnic or religious groups, e.g. **Jewish legends**; and names of individual legendary characters, e.g. **Bunyan, Paul (Legendary character)** [to be added as needed]
  BT **Fiction**
      Literature
  NT **Celtic legends**
      Christian legends
      Jewish legends
      Legendary characters
      Norse legends
      Tall tales
  RT **Fables**
      Folklore
      Mythology
      Romances
Legends, Jewish
  USE **Jewish legends**
Legends—United States   398.20973; 973
Legerdemain
  USE **Juggling**
       Magic tricks
Legibility of handwriting
  USE **Handwriting**
Legislation (May subdiv. geog.)   328
    Use for materials on the theory of lawmaking and descriptions of the preparation and enactment of laws.
  UF Laws
  SA subjects with the subdivision *Law and legislation* [to be added as needed]
  BT **Political science**
  NT **Abortion—Law and legislation**
      Automobiles—Law and legislation
      Chemical industry—Law and legislation
      Food—Law and legislation
      Gun control
      Industrial laws and legislation
      Legislative bodies
      Libraries—Law and legislation
      Medicine—Law and legislation
      Parliamentary practice
  RT **Law**

Legislation, Direct
  USE **Referendum**
Legislative bodies (May subdiv. geog.)   328.3
    Use for materials on various law making bodies considered collectively.
  UF Legislatures
      Parliaments
  SA names of individual legislative bodies, e.g. **United States. Congress** [to be added as needed]
  BT **Constitutional law**
      Legislation
      Representative government and representation
  NT **Parliamentary practice**
      Term limits (Public office)
      United States. Congress
      War and emergency powers
Legislative investigations
  USE **Governmental investigations**
Legislative reapportionment
  USE **Apportionment (Election law)**
Legislators (May subdiv. geog.)   328
  UF Lawmakers
      Members of Parliament
  BT **Statesmen**
Legislatures
  USE **Legislative bodies**
Legitimacy (Law)
  USE **Illegitimacy**
Leisure (May subdiv. geog.)   790.01
  UF Free time (Leisure)
      Leisure time
  NT **Hobbies**
      Retirement
  RT **Recreation**
Leisure time
  USE **Leisure**
Lemon
  USE **Lemons**
Lemons   634; 641.3
  UF Lemon
  BT **Citrus fruits**
Lending
  USE **Loans**
Lending institutions
  USE **Financial institutions**
Lending of library materials
  USE **Library circulation**
Lenses   535

Lenses—*Continued*

SA   types of lenses, e.g. **Contact lenses** [to be added as needed]

BT   **Optical instruments**

NT   **Contact lenses**

Lensless photography

USE   **Holography**

Lent   263

BT   **Church year**

NT   **Good Friday**

     Holy Week

     Lenten sermons

RT   **Easter**

Lent—Meditations   242

BT   **Meditations**

Lenten sermons   252

Use for collections of sermons on any subject preached during the season of Lent.

BT   **Lent**

     Sermons

Lepidoptera

USE   **Butterflies**

     Moths

Leprosy (May subdiv. geog.)   **616.9**

UF   Hansen's disease

BT   **Diseases**

Lesbian marriage

USE   **Same-sex marriage**

Lesbian rights

USE   **Gay rights**

Lesbianism (May subdiv. geog.)   **306.76**

BT   **Homosexuality**

RT   **Lesbians**

Lesbians (May subdiv. geog.)   **306.76**

UF   Gay women

     Gays, Female

     Homosexuals, Female

BT   **Women**

NT   **Gay parents**

     Gays and lesbians in the military

RT   **Homosexuality**

     Lesbianism

     Lesbians' writings

Lesbians and gays in the military

USE   **Gays and lesbians in the military**

Lesbians—Civil rights

USE   **Gay rights**

Lesbians in the military

USE   **Gays and lesbians in the military**

Lesbians—Ordination

USE   **Ordination of gays and lesbians**

Lesbians' writings   808.8

Use for collections of lesbians' writings by more than one author and for materials about such writings.

UF   Gay women's writings

     Writings of lesbians

BT   **Literature**

RT   **Lesbians**

Less developed countries

USE   **Developing countries**

Letter-sound association

USE   **Reading—Phonetic method**

Letter writing   383; 808.6

Use for materials on composition, forms, and etiquette of correspondence. Materials limited to business correspondence are entered under **Business letters**. Collections of literary letters are entered under **Letters**.

UF   Correspondence

BT   **Etiquette**

     Literary style

     Rhetoric

NT   **Business letters**

Lettering   745.6

UF   Ornamental alphabets

BT   **Decoration and ornament**

     Industrial painting

     Mechanical drawing

NT   **Monograms**

RT   **Alphabets**

     Initials

     Sign painting

Letters   808.86

Use for collections of literary letters. Materials on the composition, forms, and etiquette of correspondence are entered under **Letter writing**. Materials limited to business correspondence are entered under **Business letters**.

UF   Correspondence

SA   ethnic groups, classes of persons, and names of individual persons and families with the subdivision *Correspondence*, e.g. **Authors—Correspondence** [to be added as needed]

NT   **American letters**

     Authors—Correspondence

Letters—*Continued*
> **English letters**

Letters of credit
> USE **Credit**
> **Negotiable instruments**

Letters of marque
> USE **Privateering**

Letters of recommendation
> USE **Applications for positions**

Letters of the alphabet
> USE **Alphabet**

Leukemia   616.99
> BT **Blood—Diseases**
> **Cancer**

Levant
> USE **Middle East**

Leveraged buyouts   338.8; 658.1
> UF Buyouts, Leveraged
> Management buyouts
> BT **Corporate mergers and acquisitions**

Lewis and Clark Expedition (1804-1806)   973.4
> BT **United States—Exploring expeditions**
> **United States—History—1783-1815**

Liability for environmental damages (May subdiv. geog.)   **344**
> UF Environmental damages, Liability for
> BT **Environmental law**
> **Liability (Law)**

Liability (Law) (May subdiv. geog.)   **346.02**
> UF Accountability
> Legal responsibility
> Responsibility, Legal
> BT **Contracts**
> NT **Liability for environmental damages**
> **Malpractice**

Liability, Professional
> USE **Malpractice**

Libel and slander (May subdiv. geog.)   **346.03**
> UF Character assassination
> Defamation
> Slander (Law)
> BT **Journalism**
> NT **Gossip**

> RT **Freedom of speech**
> **Freedom of the press**

Liberalism (May subdiv. geog.)   **148; 320.5**
> UF Left (Political science)
> BT **Political science**
> **Social sciences**
> RT **Right and left (Political science)**

Liberation movements, National
> USE **National liberation movements**

Liberation theology   261.8
> UF Theology of liberation
> BT **Christianity—Doctrines**
> **Church and social problems**
> **Theology**

Liberty
> USE **Freedom**

Liberty of conscience
> USE **Freedom of conscience**

Liberty of speech
> USE **Freedom of speech**

Liberty of the press
> USE **Freedom of the press**

Liberty of the will
> USE **Free will and determinism**

Librarians (May subdiv. geog.)   **020.92; 920**
> NT **African American librarians**
> **Black librarians**
> **Library technicians**
> RT **Libraries**

Librarians—Collective bargaining
> USE **Collective bargaining—Librarians**

Librarians—Education
> USE **Library education**

Librarians—Ethics   174
> UF Librarians—Professional ethics
> BT **Professional ethics**

Librarians—In-service training   020.71
> BT **Library education**

Librarians—Professional ethics
> USE **Librarians—Ethics**

Librarians—Rating   023

Librarians—Recruiting   023
> BT **Recruiting of employees**

Librarians—Training
> USE **Library education**

Librarians' unions   331.88
> UF Library unions

Librarians' unions—*Continued*
    BT   **Labor unions**
Librarianship
    USE **Library science**
Libraries (May subdiv. geog.)   **027**
    SA   types of libraries, e.g. **Academic libraries**; names of individual libraries, e.g. **Library of Congress**; libraries and particular groups of people, e.g. **Libraries and African Americans**; and libraries and other subjects, e.g. **Libraries and community** [to be added as needed]
    BT   **Documentation**
    NT   **Academic libraries**
         Children's libraries
         Church libraries
         Digital libraries
         Hospital libraries
         Instructional materials centers
         Libraries and community
         Libraries and schools
         Library architecture
         Library catalogs
         Library cooperation
         Library of Congress
         Library resources
         Library services
         Library technical processes
         Public libraries
         School libraries
         Special libraries
         Young adults' libraries
    RT   **Archives**
         Information services
         Librarians
Libraries—Acquisitions   **025.2**
    UF   Acquisitions (Libraries)
         Book buying (Libraries)
         Libraries—Order department
         Library acquisitions
    BT   **Libraries—Collection development**
         Library technical processes
    NT   **Book selection**
Libraries—Administration   **025.1**
    UF   Library administration
         Library policies
    NT   **Library finance**
         Library trustees

Libraries and African Americans   **027.6**
    UF   African Americans and libraries
         Afro-Americans and libraries
         Library services to African Americans
    BT   **African Americans**
         Library services
Libraries and children
    USE **Children's libraries**
Libraries and community   **021.2**
    UF   Community and libraries
    BT   **Libraries**
    NT   **Libraries—Public relations**
Libraries and readers
    USE **Library services**
Libraries and schools   **021**
    UF   Schools and libraries
    BT   **Libraries**
         Schools
    NT   **Students—Library services**
    RT   **Children's libraries**
         School libraries
Libraries and state
    USE **Libraries—Government policy**
Libraries and students
    USE **Students—Library services**
Libraries and the elderly
    USE **Elderly—Library services**
Libraries—Automation   **025.04**
    UF   Library automation
    SA   names of projects, formats, and systems, e.g. **MARC formats** [to be added as needed]
    BT   **Automation**
    NT   **Machine readable bibliographic data**
    RT   **Information systems**
         Online catalogs
Libraries—Boards of trustees
    USE **Library trustees**
Libraries, Business
    USE **Business libraries**
Libraries—Cataloging
    USE **Cataloging**
Libraries—Catalogs
    USE **Library catalogs**
Libraries—Censorship   **025.2**
    BT   **Censorship**
Libraries—Centralization   **021.6**
    UF   Library systems

Libraries—Circulation, loans
USE **Library circulation**
Libraries—Collection development
025.2
UF Collection development (Libraries)
BT **Library technical processes**
NT **Book selection**
Libraries—Acquisitions
Libraries—Collective bargaining
USE **Collective bargaining—Librarians**
Libraries—Cooperation
USE **Library cooperation**
Libraries, Corporate
USE **Corporate libraries**
Libraries—Equipment and supplies
022
UF Library equipment and supplies
Library supplies
BT **Furniture**
Libraries—Federal aid
USE **Federal aid to libraries**
Libraries—Finance
USE **Library finance**
Libraries—Government aid
USE **Government aid to libraries**
Libraries—Government policy (May
subdiv. geog.) **021.8**
UF Libraries and state
BT **Social policy**
NT **Federal aid to libraries**
Government aid to libraries
Libraries, Governmental
USE **Government libraries**
Libraries, Hospital
USE **Hospital libraries**
Libraries—Law and legislation (May
subdiv. geog.) **344**
UF Library laws
Library legislation
BT **Law**
Legislation
Libraries—Lighting **022**
BT **Lighting**
Libraries, Music
USE **Music libraries**
Libraries, National
USE **National libraries**
Libraries—Order department
USE **Libraries—Acquisitions**

Libraries, Presidential
USE **Presidents—United States—Archives**
Libraries—Public relations (May subdiv.
geog.) **021.7**
UF Public relations—Libraries
BT **Libraries and community**
NT **Book talks**
Libraries, Regional
USE **Regional libraries**
Libraries—Special collections **026**
May be subdivided by subject or form, e.g.
Libraries—Special collections—Science fiction; Libraries—Special collections—Videotapes; etc.
UF Special collections in libraries
Libraries—State aid
USE **Government aid to libraries**
Libraries—Statistics **020**
BT **Statistics**
Libraries—Technical services
USE **Library technical processes**
Libraries—Trustees
USE **Library trustees**
Libraries—United States **027.073**
Library acquisitions
USE **Libraries—Acquisitions**
Library administration
USE **Libraries—Administration**
Library architecture (May subdiv. geog.)
727
Use for materials on the design of library
buildings.
BT **Architecture**
Libraries
Library assistants
USE **Library technicians**
Library automation
USE **Libraries—Automation**
Library boards
USE **Library trustees**
Library book fairs
USE **Books—Exhibitions**
Library cataloging
USE **Cataloging**
Library catalogs **017; 025.3**
UF Catalogs
Catalogs, Library
Libraries—Catalogs
SA types of library catalogs, e.g.
Online catalogs [to be added
as needed]
BT **Libraries**

Library catalogs—*Continued*
  NT **Card catalogs**
        Classified catalogs
        Online catalogs
        Subject catalogs
  RT **Cataloging**
Library circulation   025.6
  UF Book lending
        Circulation of library materials
        Lending of library materials
        Libraries—Circulation, loans
  BT **Library services**
  NT **Interlibrary loans**
Library classification   025.4
  May be further subdivided by a type of literature or by the subject of the materials classified.
  UF Books—Classification
        Classification—Books
  BT **Cataloging**
        Classification
        Library technical processes
  NT **Dewey Decimal Classification**
  RT **Classified catalogs**
Library clerks
  USE **Library technicians**
Library consortia
  USE **Library cooperation**
Library cooperation (May subdiv. geog.)
        021.6
  UF Consortia, Library
        Libraries—Cooperation
        Library consortia
  BT **Libraries**
  NT **Interlibrary loans**
        Library information networks
Library education (May subdiv. geog.)
        020.71
  Use for materials on the education of librarians. Materials on the instruction of readers in library use are entered under **Bibliographic instruction**.
  UF Education for librarianship
        Librarians—Education
        Librarians—Training
        Library science—Study and
          teaching
  BT **Education**
        Professional education
  NT **Librarians—In-service training**
        Library schools
Library education—Audiovisual aids
        020.71

  BT **Audiovisual education**
        Audiovisual materials
Library education—Curricula   020.71
  BT **Education—Curricula**
Library equipment and supplies
  USE **Libraries—Equipment and**
          supplies
Library extension   021.6
  BT **Library services**
  NT **Bookmobiles**
Library finance (May subdiv. geog.)
        025.1
  UF Libraries—Finance
  BT **Finance**
        Libraries—Administration
  NT **Government aid to libraries**
  RT **Federal aid to libraries**
Library information networks (May
        subdiv. geog.)   **021.6**
  Use for materials on networks that facilitate the sharing of information resources among several libraries.
  UF Library networks
        Library systems
  BT **Information networks**
        Library cooperation
Library instruction
  USE **Bibliographic instruction**
Library laws
  USE **Libraries—Law and legislation**
Library legislation
  USE **Libraries—Law and legislation**
Library materials
  USE **Library resources**
Library networks
  USE **Library information networks**
Library of Congress   027.573
  UF United States. Library of Congress
  BT **Libraries**
Library orientation
  USE **Bibliographic instruction**
Library policies
  USE **Libraries—Administration**
Library processing
  USE **Library technical processes**
Library reference services
  USE **Reference services (Libraries)**
Library resources (May subdiv. geog.)
        025
  Use for materials on the resources and collections available in libraries for research not limited to a single subject or discipline.

Library resources—*Continued*

UF   Library materials

SA   subjects, ethnic groups, classes of persons, corporate bodies, individual persons, literary authors, and names of countries, cities, etc., with the subdivision *Library resources*, e.g. **United States—History—Library resources** [to be added as needed]

BT   **Libraries**

NT   **Government publications**

Library resources—Conservation and restoration   025.8

UF   Books—Preservation

Library resources—Preservation

Preservation of library resources

Library resources—Preservation

USE   **Library resources—Conservation and restoration**

Library schools (May subdiv. geog.)   020.71

BT   **Library education**

Library science (May subdiv. geog.)   020

Use for general materials on the knowledge and skill necessary for the organization and administration of libraries. Materials on services offered by libraries to patrons are entered under **Library services**.

UF   Librarianship

BT   **Documentation**

Information science

NT   **Cataloging**

Library surveys

Library technical processes

RT   **Bibliography**

Library services

Library science—Study and teaching

USE   **Library education**

Library services (May subdiv. geog.)   025.5

Use for materials on services offered by libraries to patrons. General materials on the knowledge and skill necessary for the organization and administration of libraries are entered under **Library science**.

UF   Libraries and readers

Library services to readers

Reader services (Libraries)

Readers and libraries

SA   libraries and specific types of users or specific activities for which services are provided, e.g. **Elderly—Library services** [to be added as needed]

BT   **Libraries**

NT   **Bibliographic instruction**

Elderly—Library services

Libraries and African Americans

Library circulation

Library extension

Reference services (Libraries)

Students—Library services

RT   **Library science**

Library services to African Americans

USE   **Libraries and African Americans**

Library services to children

USE   **Children's libraries**

Library services to readers

USE   **Library services**

Library services to teenagers

USE   **Young adults' libraries**

Library services to the elderly

USE   **Elderly—Library services**

Library services to young adults

USE   **Young adults' libraries**

Library skills

USE   **Bibliographic instruction**

Library supplies

USE   **Libraries—Equipment and supplies**

Library surveys   020

BT   **Library science**

Surveys

Library systems

USE   **Libraries—Centralization**

Library information networks

Library technical processes   025

Use for materials on the activities and processes concerned with the acquisition, organization, and preparation of library materials for use.

UF   Centralized processing (Libraries)

Libraries—Technical services

Library processing

Processing (Libraries)

Technical services (Libraries)

BT   **Libraries**

Library science

Library technical processes—*Continued*
- NT **Cataloging**
  Libraries—Acquisitions
  Libraries—Collection develop-ment
  Library classification

Library technicians (May subdiv. geog.) **020.92**
- UF Library assistants
  Library clerks
  Paraprofessional librarians
- BT **Librarians**
  Paraprofessionals

Library trustees   021.8
- UF Libraries—Boards of trustees
  Libraries—Trustees
  Library boards
- BT **Libraries—Administration**
  Trusts and trustees

Library unions
- USE **Librarians' unions**

Library user orientation
- USE **Bibliographic instruction**

Librettos   780; 780.26
Use for collections of miscellaneous librettos and for materials on the history and criticism of librettos and on writing librettos. Individual librettos and collections of librettos of a specific type are entered under the specific type of libretto.
- SA types of librettos, e.g. **Opera librettos** [to be added as needed]
- BT **Books**
- NT **Opera librettos**

Libya   961.2
May be subdivided like **United States** except for *History.*

Licenses (May subdiv. geog.)   **352.8**
Use for general works on legal permissions to engage in business or perform other work or activities.
- SA occupational groups, types of industries, and types of vehicles with the subdivision *Licenses,* e.g. **Physicians—Licenses;** which may be further subdivided geographically [to be added as needed]
- BT **Commercial law**
  Public administration

Lie detectors and detection   363.2
- UF Polygraph

- BT **Criminal investigation**
  Medical jurisprudence
  Truthfulness and falsehood

Life   128
Use for materials on philosophical or religious considerations of life. Materials on life from a scientific point of view are entered under **Life (Biology).**
- NT **Death**
  Life expectancy
- RT **Life (Biology)**

Life after death
- USE **Future life**
  Immortality

Life (Biology)   570.1
Use for materials on life from a scientific point of view. Materials on philosophical or religious considerations of life are entered under **Life.**
- BT **Biology**
- NT **Gaia hypothesis**
  Genetics
  Life cycles (Biology)
  Middle age
  Protoplasm
  Reproduction
- RT **Life**

Life care communities (May subdiv. geog.)   **362.61; 363.5**
Use for materials on retirement communities that guarantee services and medical care for the rest of a person's life.
- UF Continuing care communities
  Continuing care retirement communities
- BT **Retirement communities**

Life cycles
- USE **Life cycles (Biology)**
  and types of plants or animals with the subdivision *Life cycles* [to be added as needed]

Life cycles (Biology)   571.8
- UF Life cycles
- SA types of plants or animals with the subdivision *Life cycles* [to be added as needed]
- BT **Biology**
  Cycles
  Life (Biology)

Life expectancy (May subdiv. geog.)   **304.6**
- UF Expectancy of life
  Expectation of life

Life expectancy—*Continued*
- BT **Age**
  - **Life**
  - **Vital statistics**
- NT **Longevity**

Life, Future
- USE **Future life**

Life histories
- USE **Biography**

Life insurance (May subdiv. geog.)
  368.32
- UF Insurance, Life
- BT **Insurance**
- NT **Group insurance**
- RT **Annuities**

Life on other planets   576.8

Use for materials on the possibility of indigenous life in outer space. Materials on the biology of humans or other earth creatures while in outer space are entered under **Space biology**.

- UF Astrobiology
  - Extraterrestrial life
- BT **Astronomy**
  - **Planets**
  - **Universe**
- NT **Extraterrestrial beings**
  - **Interstellar communication**
- RT **Human-alien encounters**

Life—Origin   113
- UF Germ theory
  - Origin of life
- BT **Evolution**

Life quality
- USE **Quality of life**

Life saving
- USE **Lifesaving**

Life sciences (May subdiv. geog.)   570
- UF Biosciences
- BT **Science**
- NT **Agriculture**
  - **Biology**
  - **Medicine**

Life sciences ethics
- USE **Bioethics**

Life skills (May subdiv. geog.)   158; 640

Use for materials on skills needed by an individual to exist in modern society, including skills related to education, employment, finance, etc.

- UF Basic life skills
  - Coping skills
  - Functional competencies
  - Fundamental life skills

Life skills guides
  Living skills
  Personal life skills
- SA groups and classes of persons with the subdivision *Life skills guides*, e.g. **Elderly—Life skills guides** [to be added as needed]
- BT **Interpersonal relations**
  - **Success**
- NT **Conduct of life**
  - **Elderly—Life skills guides**
  - **Self-help techniques**
  - **Self-improvement**
  - **Social skills**
  - **Study skills**
  - **Survival skills**
- RT **Human behavior**

Life skills guides
- USE **Life skills**
  - and groups and classes of persons with the subdivision *Life skills guides*, e.g. **Elderly—Life skills guides** [to be added as needed]

Life span prolongation
- USE **Longevity**

Life styles
- USE **Lifestyles**

Life support systems (Medical environment)   362.1
- BT **Hospitals**
  - **Terminal care**

Life support systems (Space environment)   629.47
- BT **Human engineering**
  - **Space medicine**
- NT **Apollo project**
  - **Lunar bases**
  - **Space suits**

Life support systems (Submarine environment)   627
- BT **Human engineering**

Lifeguards (May subdiv. geog.)   797.21
- BT **Water safety**

Lifelong education
- USE **Adult education**
  - **Continuing education**

Lifesaving   363.1
- UF Life saving
- BT **Rescue work**

Lifesaving—*Continued*
    RT **First aid**
Lifestyles (May subdiv. geog.)   **306**
    UF Life styles
    SA types of lifestyles [to be added
          as needed]
    BT **Human behavior**
          Manners and customs
    NT **Alternative lifestyles**
          Counter culture
          Unmarried couples
Lifts
    USE **Elevators**
           Hoisting machinery
Light   **535**
    BT **Electromagnetic waves**
          Physics
    NT **Color**
          Lasers
          Lighting
          Luminescence
          Refraction
    RT **Optics**
          Photometry
          Radiation
          Spectrum analysis
Light and shade
    USE **Shades and shadows**
Light, Electric
    USE **Electric lighting**
Light production in animals
    USE **Bioluminescence**
Light ships
    USE **Lightships**
Light—Therapeutic use
    USE **Phototherapy**
Light verse
    USE **Humorous poetry**
Lighthouses (May subdiv. geog.)   **387.1;**
        623.89; 627
    BT **Navigation**
    NT **Lightships**
Lighting (May subdiv. geog.)   **621.32**
    UF Illumination
    SA types of lighting and types of
          buildings, structures, rooms,
          installations, etc., with the
          subdivision *Lighting*, e.g. **Li-**
          braries—Lighting [to be add-
          ed as needed]
    BT **Interior design**
          Light

    NT **Candles**
          Electric lighting
          Lamps
          Libraries—Lighting
          Photography—Lighting
          Stage lighting
          Streets—Lighting
Lightning   **551.56**
    BT **Electricity**
          Meteorology
          Thunderstorms
Lightships   **623.89; 627**
    UF Light ships
    BT **Lighthouses**
          Ships
Limbs, Artificial
    USE **Artificial limbs**
Lime   **631.8; 666**
    UF Lime (Mineral)
    BT **Fertilizers**
          Minerals
Lime (Fruit)
    USE **Limes**
Lime (Mineral)
    USE **Lime**
Limericks   **808.1; 808.81**
    Use for collections of limericks by one or
    several authors or for materials about limer-
    icks.
    UF Rhymes
    BT **Humorous poetry**
    RT **Nonsense verses**
Limes   **634**
    UF Lime (Fruit)
    BT **Citrus fruits**
Limitation of armament
    USE **Arms control**
Limited access highways
    USE **Express highways**
Limited companies
    USE **Limited liability companies**
Limited liability companies (May subdiv.
    geog.)   **338.7**
    UF Limited companies
          LLCs (Limited liability compa-
            nies)
          Private companies
          Private limited companies
    BT **Corporation law**
          Corporations
Lincoln, Abraham, 1809-1865   **92; B**
    BT **Presidents—United States**

Lincoln Day
  USE **Lincoln's Birthday**
Lincoln family   920; 929
Lincoln's Birthday   394.261
  UF Lincoln Day
  BT **Holidays**
Line engraving
  USE **Engraving**
Linear algebra   512
  BT **Algebra**
       Mathematical analysis
  RT **Topology**
Linear system theory
  USE **System analysis**
Linen   677
  BT **Fabrics**
       Fibers
  RT **Flax**
Linguistic science
  USE **Linguistics**
Linguistics (May subdiv. geog.)   **410**
   Use for materials on the scientific study of
   speech and for comparative studies of lan-
   guages. General materials on the history, phi-
   losophy, origin, etc., of languages are entered
   under **Language and languages**.
  UF Comparative linguistics
       Comparative philology
       Language and languages—Com-
         parative philology
       Linguistic science
       Philology
       Philology, Comparative
  BT **Language and languages**
  NT **Grammar**
       Semantics
       Sociolinguistics
       Universal language
Linoleum block printing   761
  UF Block printing
  BT **Printing**
       Prints
Linotype   686.2
  BT **Printing**
       Type and type-founding
       Typesetting
Lip-reading
  USE **Lipreading**
Lipreading   418
  UF Lip-reading
  BT **Deaf—Means of communica-
       tion**

Liquefaction of coal
  USE **Coal liquefaction**
Liqueurs
  USE **Liquors**
Liquid fuel
  USE **Petroleum as fuel**
Liquids   532
  BT **Fluid mechanics**
       Physics
  NT **Hydraulics**
       Hydrodynamics
       Hydrostatics
Liquor industry (May subdiv. geog.)
       338.4
  BT **Beverage industry**
  NT **Bars**
  RT **Liquors**
Liquor problem
  USE **Alcoholism**
       Drinking of alcoholic beverages
Liquors   641.2; 663
  UF Cordials (Liquor)
       Drinks
       Intoxicants
       Liqueurs
       Liquors and liqueurs
  SA types of liquors and liqueurs [to
         be added as needed]
  BT **Alcoholic beverages**
       Beverages
  RT **Brewing**
       Distillation
       Liquor industry
Liquors and liqueurs
  USE **Liquors**
List books
  USE **Books of lists**
Listening   153.6; 153.7
  BT **Attention**
       Educational psychology
  RT **Hearing**
Listening devices
  USE **Eavesdropping**
Lists
  USE **Books of lists**
       and topics with the subdivision
         Lists, e.g. **Sports—Lists** [to
         be added as needed]
Literacy (May subdiv. geog.)   **302.2;
       379.2**
  UF Illiteracy

Literacy—*Continued*
   BT   **Education**
   NT   **Computer literacy**
         Functional literacy
         Media literacy
         Technological literacy
         Visual literacy
Literacy, Visual
   USE   **Visual literacy**
Literary awards
   USE   **Literary prizes**
Literary characters
   USE   **Characters and characteristics in literature**
Literary collections
   USE   **Anthologies**
         Literature—Collections
         and form headings for minor literary forms that represent collections of works of several authors, e.g. **Essays; American essays; Parodies; Short stories;** etc.; major literary forms and national literatures with the subdivision *Collections,* e.g. **Poetry—Collections; English literature—Collections;** etc.; and subjects with the subdivision *Literary collections,* for collections focused on a single subject by two or more authors involving two or more literary forms, e.g. **Cats—Literary collections** [to be added as needed]
Literary criticism
   USE   **Criticism**
         Literature—History and criticism
Literary forgeries   098
   UF   Frauds, Literary
   BT   **Counterfeits and counterfeiting**
         Forgery
Literary landmarks (May subdiv. geog.)   809
   UF   Authors—Homes and haunts
         Landmarks, Literary
   BT   **Historic buildings**
         Literature—History and criticism
   NT   **English authors—Homes**

Literary landmarks—United States   810.9
Literary prizes (May subdiv. geog.)   807.9
   UF   Book awards
         Book prizes
         Literary awards
         Literature—Prizes
   SA   names of awards, e.g. **Caldecott Medal** [to be added as needed]
   BT   **Awards**
   NT   **Caldecott Medal**
         Coretta Scott King Award
         Edgar Allan Poe Awards
         Hugo Award
         Literature—Competitions
         Nebula Award
         Newbery Medal
Literary property
   USE   **Copyright**
         Intellectual property
Literary recreations   793.73
   UF   Language games
         Recreations, Literary
   BT   **Amusements**
   NT   **Charades**
         Plot-your-own stories
         Rebuses
         Riddles
         Word games
Literary style   808
   UF   Style, Literary
   BT   **Literature**
   NT   **Letter writing**
   RT   **Criticism**
         Rhetoric
Literary themes
   USE   **Literature—Themes**
Literature   800
   Literatures are described by countries or geographic regions. In countries or regions with more than one major language the literature may be further qualified by the language in parentheses, e.g. **Canadian literature (French).** There is no distinction made in subject headings between literary works in their original languages and in translations.
   UF   Belles lettres
         Modern literature
   SA   literatures of countries or of regions larger than a single country, e.g. **English litera-**

ture; **French literature**;
Scandinavian literature; etc.;
national or regional literatures
qualified if needed by the
language in which the literature was originally written or
subdivided by a sub-set of
authors within the literature,
e.g. **African literature (English); American literature—
African American authors**;
etc.; literatures of particular
religions, e.g. **Christian literature**; literatures of languages
not identified with a particular
country, e.g. **Latin literature**;
and subjects, themes, and sty-
listic features in literature, e.g.
**Bible in literature; Children
in literature; Characters and
characteristics in literature;
Symbolism in literature**; etc.
[to be added as needed]

BT **Humanities**
Language arts

NT **African literature**
African literature (English)
American literature
Arabic literature
Authorship
Ballads
Bible in literature
Biography as a literary form
Black humor (Literature)
Brazilian literature
Campaign literature
Canadian literature
Catholic literature
Chapbooks
**Characters and characteristics
in literature**
Children's literature
Classical literature
Classicism
Communism and literature
Comparative literature
Criticism
Danish literature
Diaries
Drama
Early Christian literature

English literature
Epic literature
Erotic literature
Essay
Fables
Fiction
Folk literature
French literature
Gay men's writings
German literature
Gothic revival (Literature)
Greek literature
Hebrew literature
Humanism
Icelandic literature
Indic literature
Jewish literature
Journalism
Latin American literature
Latin literature
Legends
Lesbians' writings
Literary style
Medieval literature
Mexican literature
Mock-heroic literature
Modern Greek literature
Modernism in literature
Multicultural literature
Music and literature
Native American literature
Norwegian literature
Old Norse literature
Parody
Picaresque literature
Poetry
Portuguese literature
Realism in literature
Religion in literature
Religious literature
Romance literature
Romances
Russian literature
Sagas
Satire
Scandinavian literature
Short story
Soviet literature
Spanish literature
Speeches
Stories, plots, etc.

Literature—*Continued*
>> Swedish literature
>> Symbolism in literature
>> Teenagers' writings
>> West Indian literature (French)
>> Wit and humor
>> World War, 1939-1945—Literature and the war
>> Young adult literature
> RT **Books**

Literature and communism
> USE **Communism and literature**

Literature and music
> USE **Music and literature**

Literature and the war
> USE names of wars with the subdivision *Literature and the war*, e.g. **World War, 1939-1945—Literature and the war** [to be added as needed]

Literature—Bio-bibliography   809
> RT **Authors**

Literature—Collections   808.8
> Use for collections of literary works by several authors not limited to a single literature or literary form or focused on a single subject.
> UF Collected works
>> Collections of literature
>> Literary collections
>> Literature—Selections
> SA form headings for minor literary forms that represent collections of works of several authors, e.g. **Essays**; **American essays**; **Parodies**; **Short stories**; etc.; major literary forms and national literatures with the subdivision *Collections*, e.g. **Poetry—Collections**; **English literature—Collections**; etc.; and subjects with the subdivision *Literary collections*, for collections focused on a single subject by two or more authors involving two or more literary forms, e.g. **Cats—Literary collections** [to be added as needed]

Literature, Comparative
> USE **Comparative literature**

Literature—Competitions   807.9
> BT **Contests**
>> **Literary prizes**

Literature—Criticism
> USE **Literature—History and criticism**

Literature—Dictionaries   803
> BT **Encyclopedias and dictionaries**
> NT **English literature—Dictionaries**

Literature, Erotic
> USE **Erotic literature**

Literature—Evaluation
> USE **Best books**
>> **Book reviewing**
>> **Books and reading**
>> **Criticism**
>> **Literature—History and criticism**

Literature—Film and video adaptations
> USE **Film adaptations**
>> **Television adaptations**

Literature—History and criticism   809
> Use for materials that are themselves histories or criticisms of literature in general. Materials on the history, principles, methods, etc., of literary criticism are entered under **Criticism**.
> UF Appraisal of books
>> Books—Appraisal
>> Evaluation of literature
>> Literary criticism
>> Literature—Criticism
>> Literature—Evaluation
> NT **Literary landmarks**

Literature—Indexes   016.8

Literature, Medieval
> USE **Medieval literature**

Literature—Outlines, syllabi, etc.   802
> NT **English literature—Outlines, syllabi, etc.**

Literature—Prizes
> USE **Literary prizes**

Literature—Selections
> USE **Literature—Collections**

Literature—Stories, plots, etc.
> USE **Stories, plots, etc.—Collections**

Literature—Themes   809
> UF Literary themes
>> Themes in literature
> SA subjects, racial and ethnic groups, and classes of persons in literature, e.g. **Dogs in literature**; **Women in litera-**

Literature—Themes—*Continued*
ture; etc., and names of persons, families, and corporate bodies with the subdivision *In literature*, e.g. **Napoleon I, Emperor of the French, 1769-1821—In literature**, [to be added as needed]

- NT **African Americans in literature**
  Animals in literature
  Blacks in literature
  Children in literature
  Dogs in literature
  Napoleon I, Emperor of the French, 1769-1821—In literature
  Nature in literature
  Travel in literature
  Women in literature
- RT **Characters and characteristics in literature**

Literatures of the Soviet Union
- USE **Soviet literature**

Lithographers (May subdiv. geog.)
763.092; 920
- BT **Artists**

Lithography (May subdiv. geog.)   **686.2; 763; 764**
- UF Lithoprinting
- BT **Color printing**
  Printing
  Prints
- NT **Offset printing**

Lithoprinting
- USE **Lithography**
  Offset printing

Litigation (May subdiv. geog.)   **347**
- UF Actions and defenses
  Civil law suits
  Defense (Law)
  Law suits
  Lawsuits
  Personal actions (Law)
  Suing (Law)
  Suits (Law)
- BT **Law**
- NT **Class actions (Civil procedure)**
  Witnesses
- RT **Arbitration and award**
  Civil procedure

Littering
- USE **Refuse and refuse disposal**

Little League baseball   **796.357**
- BT **Baseball**

Little magazines (May subdiv. geog.)
050
- BT **Periodicals**

Little theater movement   **792**
- UF Community theater
- BT **Theater**
- RT **Amateur theater**

Liturgical year
- USE **Church year**

Liturgics
- USE **Liturgies**

Liturgies   **203; 264**
Use for general materials on the forms of prayers, rituals, and ceremonies used in public worship, including the theological and historical study of liturgies, and for texts of liturgies from more than one religion.
- UF Church service books
  Liturgics
  Liturgy
  Ritual
  Service books (Liturgy)
- SA names of individual religions and denominations with the subdivision *Liturgy* or *Liturgy—Texts*; e.g. **Catholic Church—Liturgy**; **Catholic Church—Liturgy—Texts** etc. [to be added as needed]
- BT **Public worship**
  Rites and ceremonies
- NT **Catholic Church—Liturgy**
  Eucharist
  Hymns
  Judaism—Liturgy
  Mass (Liturgy)
- RT **Church music**
  Worship programs

Liturgy
- USE **Liturgies**
  and names of individual religions and denominations with the subdivision *Liturgy* e.g. **Judaism—Liturgy; Catholic Church—Liturgy;** etc. [to be added as needed]

Live poliovirus vaccine
- USE **Poliomyelitis vaccine**

Livestock
USE **Domestic animals**
     Livestock industry
Livestock breeding (May subdiv. geog.)
    636.08
UF Livestock—Breeding
BT **Breeding**
    Livestock industry
Livestock—Breeding
USE **Livestock breeding**
Livestock industry (May subdiv. geog.)
    636

    Use for materials on stock raising as an industry. General materials on farm and other domestic animals are entered under **Domestic animals**.

UF Animal husbandry
    Animal industry
    Livestock
    Stock raising
BT **Agriculture**
    Economic zoology
NT **Dairying**
    Livestock breeding
    Livestock judging
RT **Domestic animals**
Livestock judging   **636**
UF Stock judging
BT **Livestock industry**
Living earth theory
USE **Gaia hypothesis**
Living skills
USE **Life skills**
Living together
USE **Unmarried couples**
Living trusts (May subdiv. geog.)
    346.05
BT **Trusts and trustees**
Living wills   **344**
BT **Wills**
RT **Right to die**
    Terminal care
Livres à clef
USE **Romans à clef**
Lizards (May subdiv. geog.)   **597.95**
BT **Reptiles**
LLCs (Limited liability companies)
USE **Limited liability companies**
Loan associations
USE **Savings and loan associations**
Loan funds, Student
USE **Student loan funds**

Loans (May subdiv. geog.)   **332.7**
UF Borrowing
    Lending
BT **Finance**
NT **Capital market**
    Government lending
    Home equity loans
    Interest (Economics)
    Microfinance
    Mortgages
    Personal loans
    Public debts
    Savings and loan associations
    Student aid
RT **Credit**
    Investments
Loans, Personal
USE **Personal loans**
Lobbying (May subdiv. geog.)   **328.3**

    Use for materials on groups that promote their own interests with public officials. Materials on special interest groups that support sympathetic candidates for public office through campaign contributions are entered under **Political action committees**.

UF Interest groups
    Lobbying and lobbyists
    Lobbyists
    Pressure groups
SA names of specific lobbying and
    pressure groups [to be added
    as needed]
BT **Politics**
    Propaganda
RT **Political action committees**
Lobbying and lobbyists
USE **Lobbying**
Lobbyists
USE **Lobbying**
Lobsters (May subdiv. geog.)   **595.3**
BT **Crustacea**
    Shellfish
Local area networks   **004.6**
UF LANs (Computer networks)
BT **Computer networks**
Local government (May subdiv. geog.)
    320.8; 352.14

    Use for materials on the government of districts, counties, townships, etc. Materials limited to county government only are entered under **County government**. Materials limited to the government of cities and towns are entered under **Municipal government**.

Local government—*Continued*
- UF Government, Local
  Town meeting
  Township government
- BT **Administrative law**
  Community organization
  Political science
- NT **County government**
  Metropolitan government
  Municipal government
  Public administration
  State-local relations

Local history 907

Use for materials on the writing and compiling of local histories. Collective histories of several localities are entered under the country, state, etc., with the subdivision *Local history*. Individual local histories are entered under the city, county, or other locality with the subdivision *History*.

- UF Community history
  Regional history
- SA names of countries, states, etc., with the subdivision *Local history*, e.g. **United States—Local history**; **Ohio—Local history**; etc.; and names of cities, counties, or other localities with the subdivision *History*, e.g. **Chicago (Ill.)—History** [to be added as needed]
- BT **Historiography**
  History
- NT **Ohio—Local history**
  United States—Local history

Local-state relations
- USE **State-local relations**

Local traffic
- USE **City traffic**

Local transit (May subdiv. geog.) **388.4**

Use for materials on the various modes of local public transportation.

- UF City transit
  Mass transit
  Municipal transit
  Public transit
  Rapid transit
  Transit systems
  Urban transportation
- BT **Traffic engineering**
  Transportation
- NT **Buses**
  Street railroads
  Subways

Taxicabs

Localism
- USE **Regionalism**

Localisms
- USE names of languages with the subdivision *Provincialisms,* e.g. **English language—Provincialisms** [to be added as needed]

Loch Ness monster 001.944
- UF Nessie (Monster)
- BT **Monsters**

Lockouts
- USE **Strikes**

Locks and keys 683
- UF Keys
- BT **Burglary protection**

Locomotion 152.3; 388
- NT **Aeronautics**
  Animal locomotion
  Flight
  Horsemanship
  Human locomotion
  Navigation
  Transportation

Locomotives (May subdiv. geog.) 625.26
- BT **Railroads**
- NT **Steam locomotives**

Locomotives—Models 625.1
- UF Model trains
- BT **Models and modelmaking**

Locusts 595.7; 632
- BT **Insect pests**
  Insects

Log cabins and houses (May subdiv. geog.) **728**
- UF Cabins
- BT **House construction**
  Houses

Logarithms 513.2
- BT **Algebra**
  Mathematics—Tables
  Trigonometry—Tables
- NT **Slide rule**

Logging (May subdiv. geog.) **634.9**

Use for materials on the felling of trees and the transportation of logs to sawmills. Materials on lumber and the preparation of lumber are entered under **Lumber and lumbering**.

- UF Timber—Harvesting
- BT **Forests and forestry**

Logic 160

Logic—*Continued*
    UF   Argumentation
          Deduction (Logic)
          Dialectics
          Fallacies
          Induction (Logic)
    BT   **Intellect**
          Philosophy
          Science—Methodology
    NT   **Certainty**
          Critical thinking
          Probabilities
          Symbolic logic
          Theory of knowledge
    RT   **Reasoning**
          Thought and thinking

Logic, Symbolic and mathematical
    USE **Symbolic logic**
Lone Ranger films   **791.43**
    Use for individual works, collections, or materials about Lone Ranger films.
    BT   **Western films**
Loneliness   **155.9; 158**
    UF   Social isolation
    BT   **Emotions**
    RT   **Solitude**
Long distance running
    USE **Marathon running**
Long distance swimming
    USE **Marathon swimming**
Long distance telephone service (May subdiv. geog.)   **384.6**
    UF   Telephone—Long distance
    BT   **Telephone**
Long life
    USE **Longevity**
Long-term care facilities (May subdiv. geog.)   **362.16**
    UF   Extended care facilities
    BT   **Hospitals**
          Medical care
    NT   **Nursing homes**
          Sanatoriums
Longevity (May subdiv. geog.)   **612.6; 613**
    UF   Life span prolongation
          Long life
    BT   **Age**
          Life expectancy
    NT   **Aging**
    RT   **Middle age**
          Old age

Longitude   **526; 527**
    UF   Degrees of latitude and longitude
    BT   **Earth**
          Geodesy
          Nautical astronomy
Looking glasses
    USE **Mirrors**
Looms   **677; 746.1**
    BT   **Weaving**
Loran   **621.384**
    BT   **Navigation**
Lord's Day
    USE **Sabbath**
Lord's prayer   **226.9; 242**
    BT   **Jesus Christ—Prayers**
Lord's Supper
    USE **Eucharist**
Losing things
    USE **Lost and found possessions**
Lost and found possessions   **330.1**
    UF   Finding things
          Losing things
          Lost possessions
          Lost things
    BT   **Property**
Lost architectural heritage
    USE **Lost architecture**
Lost architecture (May subdiv. geog.)   **720**
    Use for materials on buildings and structures that have been destroyed or demolished.
    UF   Lost architectural heritage
          Lost buildings
    BT   **Architecture**
Lost buildings
    USE **Lost architecture**
Lost children
    USE **Missing children**
Lost continents   **001.94; 398.23; 551.94**
    BT   **Continents**
          Geographical myths
    NT   **Atlantis (Legendary place)**
Lost possessions
    USE **Lost and found possessions**
Lost things
    USE **Lost and found possessions**
Lost tribes of Israel   **909**
    UF   Israel, Ten lost tribes of
          Jews—Lost tribes
          Ten lost tribes of Israel
    BT   **Jews**

Lotteries (May subdiv. geog.)   **336.1**
>BT   **Gambling**

Louisiana Purchase   **973.4; 976.3**
>BT   **United States—History—1783-1815**

Love   **152.4; 177; 306.7**
>UF   Affection
>BT   **Emotions**
>   **Human behavior**
>NT   **Courtship**
>   **Crushes**
>RT   **Friendship**

Love Canal Chemical Waste Landfill (Niagara Falls, N.Y.)   **363.72**
>BT   **Hazardous waste sites**
>   **Landfills**

Love poetry   **808.1; 808.81**
>Use for individual works, collections, or materials about love poetry.
>BT   **Poetry**
>RT   **Erotic poetry**

Love—Religious aspects   **202; 231**
>UF   Love (Theology)
>RT   **Charity**

Love stories   **808.3; 808.83**
>Use for individual works, collections, or materials about love stories.
>UF   Romance novels
>   Romances (Love stories)
>   Romantic fiction
>   Romantic stories
>BT   **Fiction**
>RT   **Erotic fiction**
>   **Gothic novels**
>   **Romantic suspense novels**

Love stories—Technique   **808.3**
>BT   **Authorship**

Love (Theology)
>USE   **Love—Religious aspects**

Low-carbohydrate diet   **613.2**
>BT   **Diet**
>RT   **Carbohydrates**

Low-cholesterol diet   **613.2**
>BT   **Diet**
>RT   **Cholesterol**

Low-fat diet   **613.2**
>BT   **Diet**
>RT   **Oils and fats**

Low income housing
>USE   **Public housing**

Low-sodium diet
>USE   **Salt-free diet**

Low temperature biology
>USE   **Cryobiology**

Low temperatures   **536; 621.5**
>UF   Cryogenics
>BT   **Temperature**
>NT   **Cryobiology**
>RT   **Cold**
>   **Refrigeration**

Loyalists, American
>USE   **American Loyalists**

Loyalty   **172**
>UF   Faithfulness
>BT   **Ethics**
>   **Virtue**
>NT   **Patriotism**

Loyalty oaths
>USE   **Internal security**

LSD (Drug)   **615**
>UF   Acid (Drug)
>   Lysergic acid diethylamide
>BT   **Hallucinogens**

Lubrication and lubricants   **621.8**
>UF   Grease
>BT   **Machinery**
>RT   **Bearings (Machinery)**
>   **Oils and fats**

Lucumi (Religion)
>USE   **Santeria**

Luggage   **685**
>UF   Baggage
>BT   **Containers**

Lullabies   **782.42**
>UF   Cradle songs
>BT   **Bedtime**
>   **Children's poetry**
>   **Children's songs**
>   **Songs**

Lumber and lumbering (May subdiv. geog.)   **634.9; 674**
>Use for general materials on lumber and the preparation of lumber. Materials on the felling of trees and the transportation of logs to sawmills are entered under **Logging**.
>UF   Timber
>   Woods
>BT   **Forest products**
>   **Forests and forestry**
>   **Trees**
>   **Wood**

Luminescence   **535**
>BT   **Light**
>   **Radiation**

Luminescence—*Continued*
  NT   **Bioluminescence**
       Phosphorescence
Luminescent books
  USE **Glow-in-the-dark books**
Luminous books
  USE **Glow-in-the-dark books**
Lunar bases 629.45
  UF   Moon bases
  BT   **Civil engineering**
       Life support systems (Space environment)
Lunar eclipses 523.3
  UF   Eclipses, Lunar
       Moon—Eclipses
  BT   **Astronomy**
Lunar expeditions
  USE **Space flight to the moon**
Lunar exploration
  USE **Moon—Exploration**
Lunar geology 559.9
  UF   Geology, Lunar
       Geology—Moon
       Moon—Geology
  BT   **Astrogeology**
  NT   **Lunar soil**
       Moon rocks
Lunar petrology
  USE **Moon rocks**
Lunar probes 629.43
  UF   Moon probes
  SA   names of specific lunar probe projects [to be added as needed]
  BT   **Space probes**
  NT   **Project Ranger**
Lunar rocks
  USE **Moon rocks**
Lunar soil 523.3; 552.0999; 631.4
  UF   Moon soil
       Soils, Lunar
  BT   **Lunar geology**
  RT   **Moon—Surface**
Lunar surface
  USE **Moon—Surface**
Lunar surface radio communication
  USE **Radio in astronautics**
Luncheons 642
  BT   **Cooking**
       Menus
  RT   **Entertaining**

Lunchrooms
  USE **Restaurants**
Lung cancer 616.99
  UF   Lungs—Cancer
  BT   **Cancer**
       Lungs—Diseases
Lungs 611; 612.2
  BT   **Respiratory system**
Lungs—Cancer
  USE **Lung cancer**
Lungs—Diseases 616.2
  SA   types of lung diseases [to be added as needed]
  BT   **Diseases**
  NT   **Asthma**
       Lung cancer
       Pneumonia
       Tuberculosis
Lying
  USE **Truthfulness and falsehood**
Lyme disease 616.9
  BT   **Diseases**
Lymphatic system 573.1; 612.4; 616.4
  BT   **Physiology**
Lynching (May subdiv. geog.) 364.1
  BT   **Crime**
  RT   **Vigilantes**
Lyricists (May subdiv. geog.) 782.0092; 920
  UF   Songwriters
  BT   **Poets**
Lyrics
  USE **Popular song lyrics**
Lysergic acid diethylamide
  USE **LSD (Drug)**
Machine design 621.8
  UF   Machinery—Construction
       Machinery—Design and construction
  SA   types of machines, equipment, etc., with the subdivision *Design and construction*, e.g. **Airplanes—Design and construction** [to be added as needed]
  BT   **Design**
       Machinery
  NT   **Machinery—Models**
Machine intelligence
  USE **Artificial intelligence**

Machine language
USE **Programming languages**
Machine readable bibliographic data
025.3
UF Bibliographic data in machine
readable form
Cataloging data in machine read-
able form
SA names of projects, formats, and
systems, e.g. **MARC formats**
[to be added as needed]
BT **Cataloging**
Information services
Information systems
Libraries—Automation
NT **MARC formats**
Machine readable catalog system
USE **MARC formats**
Machine readable dictionaries   413
UF Dictionaries, Machine readable
BT **Encyclopedias and dictionaries**
Machine shop practice   670.42
UF Shop practice
NT **Drilling and boring (Metal,**
wood, etc.)
Grinding and polishing
RT **Machine shops**
Machine shops   670.42
RT **Machine shop practice**
Machine tools   621.9
SA types of machine tools [to be
added as needed]
BT **Machinery**
Tools
NT **Planing machines**
RT **Drilling and boring (Metal,**
wood, etc.)
Grinding and polishing
Manufacturing processes
Machinery   621.8
UF Machines
BT **Manufactures**
Mechanical engineering
Power (Mechanics)
Technology
Tools
NT **Agricultural machinery**
Bearings (Machinery)
Belts and belting
Construction equipment
Conveying machinery

Electric machinery
Engines
Gearing
Hoisting machinery
Hydraulic machinery
Industrial equipment
Lubrication and lubricants
Machine design
Machine tools
Mechanical drawing
Metalworking machinery
Robots
Simple machines
Woodworking machinery
RT **Mechanics**
Mills
Power transmission
Machinery—Construction
USE **Machine design**
Machinery—Design and construction
USE **Machine design**
Machinery—Drawing
USE **Mechanical drawing**
Machinery in industry
USE **Industrial equipment**
Machinery in the workplace
Machinery in the workplace   338
Use for materials on the social and econom-
ic aspects of mechanization in the area of
work.
UF Machinery in industry
Technology in the workplace
BT **Work environment**
NT **Automation**
Machinery—Models   621.8
UF Mechanical models
Models, Mechanical
BT **Machine design**
Models and modelmaking
Machines
USE **Machinery**
Machines, Simple
USE **Simple machines**
Macintosh (Computer)   004.165
UF Apple Macintosh (Computer)
BT **Computers**
Macroeconomics   339
BT **Economics**
Made-for-TV movies
USE **Television movies**
Madonna
USE **Mary, Blessed Virgin, Saint**

Magazine editing
USE **Journalism—Editing**

Magazines
USE **Periodicals**

Maghreb
USE **North Africa**

Magic (May subdiv. geog.)   **133.4**

Use for materials on charms, spells, etc., believed to have supernatural power. Materials on types of entertainment involving illusionistic tricks are entered under **Magic tricks**.

UF   Black art (Magic)
Black magic (Witchcraft)
Necromancy
Sorcery
Spells

BT   **Occultism**

RT   **Hallucinations and illusions**
Magic tricks
Witchcraft

Magic lanterns
USE **Projectors**

Magic tricks   793.8

UF   Conjuring
Legerdemain
Prestidigitation
Sleight of hand

BT   **Amusements**
Tricks

NT   **Card tricks**

RT   **Hallucinations and illusions**
Magic

Magna Carta   342; 942.03

BT   **Charters**
Great Britain—History—1154-1399, Plantagenets

Magnet schools (May subdiv. geog.)
373.24

Use for materials on schools offering special courses not available in the regular school curriculum and designed to attract students without reference to the usual attendance zone rules, often as an aid to voluntary school desegregation.

BT   **Public schools**
School integration
Schools

Magnet winding
USE **Electromagnets**

Magnetic needle
USE **Compass**

Magnetic recorders and recording
621.382

Use for general materials on audio, computer, and video recording on a magnetizable medium.

UF   Cassette recorders and recording
Tape recorders

BT   **Electronic apparatus and appliances**

Magnetic resonance accelerator
USE **Cyclotrons**

Magnetic resonance imaging   616.07

UF   Imaging, Magnetic resonance
MRI (Magnetic resonance imaging)
Nuclear magnetic resonance imaging

BT   **Diagnosis**

Magnetism   538

BT   **Physics**

NT   **Compass**
Electromagnetism
Electromagnets
Geomagnetism
Magnets

RT   **Electricity**

Magnets   538; 621.34

BT   **Magnetism**

NT   **Electromagnets**

Mail-order business (May subdiv. geog.)
658.8; 659.13

UF   Mail order catalogs

BT   **Business**
Direct selling
Selling

NT   **Direct marketing**

Mail order catalogs
USE **Commercial catalogs**
Mail-order business

Mail service
USE **Postal service**

Mainstreaming in education (May subdiv. geog.)   **371.9**

BT   **Education**
Exceptional children
Handicapped children

RT   **Special education**

Maintenance and repair
USE **Repairing**
and types of things that require
maintenance with the subdivi-

Maintenance and repair—*Continued*
>sion *Maintenance and repair,* e.g. **Automobiles—Maintenance and repair; Buildings—Maintenance and repair;** etc.; and types of things that require no maintenance with the subdivision *Repairing,* e.g. **Radio—Repairing** [to be added as needed]

Maintenance of biodiversity
>USE **Biodiversity conservation**

Maize
>USE **Corn**

Make-believe playmates
>USE **Imaginary playmates**

Makeup (Cosmetics)
>USE **Cosmetics**

Makeup, Theatrical
>USE **Theatrical makeup**

Making-choices stories
>USE **Plot-your-own stories**

Maladjusted children
>USE **Emotionally disturbed children**

Maladjustment (Psychology)
>USE **Adjustment (Psychology)**

Malaria (May subdiv. geog.) **616.9**
>BT **Diseases**

Male actors (May subdiv. geog.) **791.4; 792; 920**
>Use for materials on several male actors that emphasize their identity as men. General materials on persons of the acting profession, whether male or female, are entered under **Actors**.
>UF Men actors
>BT **Actors**

Male change of life
>USE **Male climacteric**

Male circumcision
>USE **Circumcision**

Male climacteric **612.6**
>UF Change of life in men
>Climacteric, Male
>Male change of life
>Male menopause
>Menopause, Male
>BT **Aging**

Male-female relationship
>USE **Man-woman relationship**

Male impersonators **791.4**
>Use for materials on women who impersonate men for purposes of entertainment or com-

ic effect. Materials on persons, especially men, who assume the dress of the opposite sex for psychological gratification are entered under **Transvestites**.
>BT **Impostors and imposture**

Male menopause
>USE **Male climacteric**

Male role
>USE **Sex role**

Malfeasance in office
>USE **Misconduct in office**

Malformations, Congenital
>USE **Birth defects**

Malignant tumors
>USE **Cancer**

Malls, Shopping
>USE **Shopping centers and malls**

Malnutrition (May subdiv. geog.) **362.1; 616.3**
>BT **Nutrition**
>RT **Starvation**

Malpractice (May subdiv. geog.) **346.03**
>UF Liability, Professional
>Professional liability
>Professions—Tort liability
>Tort liability of professions
>SA types of professional personnel with the subdivision *Malpractice* [to be added as needed]
>BT **Liability (Law)**
>NT **Medical personnel—Malpractice**
>**Physicians—Malpractice**

Malpractice insurance (May subdiv. geog.) **368.5**
>UF Insurance, Malpractice
>Insurance, Professional liability
>Professional liability insurance
>BT **Insurance**

Mammals (May subdiv. geog.) **599**
>SA types of mammals, e.g. **Marine mammals; Primates; Bats;** etc. [to be added as needed]
>BT **Animals**
>NT **Badgers**
>**Bats**
>**Bears**
>**Beavers**
>**Bison**
>**Camels**
>**Cats**
>**Cattle**
>**Chipmunks**

Mammals—*Continued*
>>> **Deer**
>>> **Dogs**
>>> **Elephants**
>>> **Fossil mammals**
>>> **Horses**
>>> **Marine mammals**
>>> **Mice**
>>> **Pigs**
>>> **Primates**
>>> **Rabbits**
>>> **Reindeer**
>>> **Seals (Animals)**
>>> **Sheep**
>>> **Squirrels**
>>> **Whales**
>>> **Wild cats**

Mammals, Fossil
> USE **Fossil mammals**

Man
> USE **Human beings**

Man—Antiquity
> USE **Human origins**

Man in space
> USE **Space flight**

Man—Influence of environment
> USE **Environmental influence on humans**

Man—Influence on nature
> USE **Human influence on nature**

Man—Origin
> USE **Human origins**

Man power
> USE **Manpower**

Man, Prehistoric
> USE **Fossil hominids**
> **Prehistoric peoples**

Man, Primitive
> USE **Primitive societies**

Man (Theology)
> USE **Human beings (Theology)**

Man-woman relationship (May subdiv. geog.) **306.7**
> UF Female-male relationship
> Male-female relationship
> Men—Relations with women
> Men-women relationship
> Relationships, Man-woman
> Woman-man relationship
> Women-men relationship
> Women—Relations with men
> BT **Interpersonal relations**

> RT **Dating (Social customs)**

Management (May subdiv. geog.)   **658**
> Use for materials on the theory of management and on the application of management principles to business and industry.
> UF Administration
> Business administration
> Business management
> Industrial management
> Industrial organization
> Management science
> Organization and management
> Scientific management
> SA types of management, e.g. **Office management**; types of businesses and industries, types of industrial plants and processes, and names of individual corporate bodies, with the subdivision *Management*, e.g. **Information systems—Management**; and types of institutions in the spheres of health, education, and social services, and names of individual institutions with the subdivision *Administration*, e.g. **Libraries—Administration**; **Schools—Administration**; etc. [to be added as needed]
> BT **Business**
> **Industries**
> NT **Conflict management**
> **Crisis management**
> **Factory management**
> **Farm management**
> **Industrial efficiency**
> **Industrial relations**
> **Industrial welfare**
> **Information systems—Management**
> **Inventory control**
> **Job analysis**
> **Knowledge management**
> **Marketing**
> **Materials handling**
> **Natural resources—Management**
> **Occupational health and safety**
> **Office management**
> **Organizational behavior**

Management—*Continued*
> **Organizational change**
> **Personnel management**
> **Planning**
> **Production standards**
> **Purchasing**
> **Sales management**
> **Time management**
> RT **Operations research**

Management buyouts
> USE **Leveraged buyouts**

Management consultants
> USE **Business consultants**

Management—Employee participation
> USE **Participative management**

Management information systems (May subdiv. geog.) **658.4**
> UF Computer-based information systems
> BT **Information systems**

Management of conflict
> USE **Conflict management**

Management of knowledge assets
> USE **Knowledge management**

Management science
> USE **Management**

Managers
> USE **Supervisors**

Mandates (May subdiv. geog.) **321**
> BT **International law**
> **International organization**
> **International relations**

Manga 741.5
> Use for individual works, collections, or materials about manga.
> BT **Graphic novels**
> NT **Gundam (Fictional character)**
> **Josei**
> **Kodomo**
> **Mecha**
> **Neon Genesis Evangelion (Fictional robot)**
> **Seinen**
> **Shojo-ai**
> **Shojo manga**
> **Shonen-ai**
> **Shonen manga**

Mania
> USE **Manic-depressive illness**

Manic depression
> USE **Manic-depressive illness**

Manic-depressive illness 616.89
> UF Bipolar depression
> Bipolar disorder
> Mania
> Manic depression
> Manic-depressive psychoses
> Manic-depressive psychosis
> Melancholia
> BT **Affective disorders**
> **Mental illness**
> RT **Depression (Psychology)**

Manic-depressive psychoses
> USE **Manic-depressive illness**

Manic-depressive psychosis
> USE **Manic-depressive illness**

Manifest destiny (United States)
> USE **United States—Territorial expansion**

Manikins (Fashion models)
> USE **Fashion models**

Manipulative materials
> USE **Manipulatives**

Manipulatives 371.33
> Use for works on educational materials designed to be handled or touched by students in learning mathematical concepts.
> UF Manipulative materials
> Manipulatives (Education)
> BT **Audiovisual materials**
> **Mathematics—Study and teaching**
> **Teaching—Aids and devices**

Manipulatives (Education)
> USE **Manipulatives**

Manned space flight
> USE **Space flight**

Manned undersea research stations
> USE **Undersea research stations**

Mannequins (Fashion models)
> USE **Fashion models**

Manners
> USE **Courtesy**
> **Etiquette**

Manners and customs 390
> UF Ceremonies
> Customs, Social
> Folkways
> Social customs
> Social life and customs
> Traditions
> SA ethnic groups and names of countries, cities, etc., with the subdivision *Social life and*

Manners and customs—*Continued*
> *customs* [to be added as needed]

   BT   **Civilization**
         Ethnology
   NT   **African Americans—Social life and customs**
         Anniversaries
         Blacks—Social life and customs
         Bohemianism
         Caste
         Chicago (Ill.)—Social life and customs
         Chivalry
         Clothing and dress
         Costume
         Country life
         Courts and courtiers
         Dating (Social customs)
         Dueling
         Excuses
         Fads
         Family traditions
         Festivals
         Folklore
         Funeral rites and ceremonies
         Gifts
         Holidays
         Hugging
         Jews—Social life and customs
         Lifestyles
         Marriage customs and rites
         Native Americans—Social life and customs
         Ohio—Social life and customs
         Seafaring life
         Taboo
         Tattooing
         Travel
         United States—Social life and customs
   RT   **Etiquette**
         Rites and ceremonies

Manpower (May subdiv. geog.)   **331.11**
> Use for materials on the strength of a country in terms of available personnel, both military and industrial. Materials on personnel in specific fields are entered under kinds of workers, e.g. **Agricultural laborers**; **Nurses**; etc. Materials on investments of capital in training and educating employees to improve their productivity are entered under **Human capital**.

   UF   Human resources
         Man power
   SA   names of wars with the subdivision *Manpower*; e.g. **World War, 1939-1945—Manpower** [to be added as needed]
   RT   **Labor supply**
         Military readiness

Manpower policy
   USE   **Labor policy**

Manslaughter
   USE   **Homicide**

Manual training
   USE   **Industrial arts education**

Manual workers
   USE   **Labor**
         Working class

Manufactures (May subdiv. geog.)   **338.4; 670**
   SA   types of manufacturing industries, e.g. **Textile industry**, and types of manufactures, e.g. **Glass manufacture** [to be added as needed]
   BT   **Commercial products**
         Industries
   NT   **Brand name products**
         Consumer goods
         Generic products
         Machinery
         Mills
         Papermaking
         Patents
         Prices
         Trademarks
         Waste products
   RT   **Manufacturing industries**

Manufactures—Chicago (Ill.)   **338.4**
   UF   Chicago (Ill.)—Manufactures

Manufactures—Defects
   USE   **Product recall**

Manufactures—Ohio   **338.4**
   UF   Ohio—Manufactures

Manufactures recall
   USE   **Product recall**

Manufactures—United States   **338.4**
   UF   United States—Manufactures

Manufacturing in space
   USE   **Space industrialization**

Manufacturing industries (May subdiv. geog.)   **338.4**

Manufacturing industries—*Continued*

SA types of manufacturing industries, e.g. **Textile industry**,
  and types of manufactures,
  e.g. **Glass manufacture** [to
  be added as needed]

BT **Industries**

RT **Manufactures**

Manufacturing processes (May subdiv.
  geog.) **658.5; 670**

UF Industrial processing
  Production processes

SA types of manufacturing industries, e.g. **Textile industry**,
  and types of manufactures,
  e.g. **Glass manufacture** [to
  be added as needed]

BT **Industrial arts**

NT **Forging**
  Founding
  Turning
  Welding

RT **Machine tools**
  Materials

Manures

USE **Fertilizers**

Manuscripts (May subdiv. geog.) **091**

SA subjects, literatures, groups of
  authors, individual literary authors, literary works entered
  under title, and sacred works
  with the subdivision *Manuscripts* [to be added as need-
  ed]

BT **Archives**
  Bibliography
  Books

NT **Illumination of books and
  manuscripts**

RT **Autographs**
  Charters

Manuscripts, Illuminated

USE **Illumination of books and
  manuscripts**

Map drawing **526**

UF Cartography
  Plans

BT **Drawing**

RT **Topographical drawing**

Maple sugar **641.3; 664**

BT **Sugar**

Maps **912**

Use for general materials about maps and
their history. Materials on the methods of map
making and the mapping of areas are entered
under **Map drawing**. Geographical atlases of
world coverage are entered under **Atlases**.

UF Cartography
  Chartography
  Plans

SA types of maps, e.g. **Road maps**;
  subjects with the subdivision
  Maps, e.g. **Geology—Maps**;
  and names of countries, cities,
  etc., and names of wars with
  the subdivision *Maps* [to be
  added as needed]

BT **Geography**

NT **Atlases**
  Automobile travel—Guidebooks
  Chicago (Ill.)—Maps
  Geology—Maps
  Globes
  Moon—Maps
  Nautical charts
  Ohio—Maps
  Road maps
  United States—Maps
  World War, 1939-1945—Maps

RT **Charts, diagrams, etc.**

Maps, Historical

USE **Historical atlases**

Maps, Military

USE **Military geography**

Marathon running **796.42**

UF Long distance running

BT **Running**

Marathon swimming **797.2**

UF Long distance swimming

BT **Swimming**

Marble **552; 553.5**

BT **Rocks**
  Stone

MARC formats **025.3**

UF Machine readable catalog system
  MARC system

BT **Bibliographic control**
  **Machine readable bibliographic
  data**

MARC system

USE **MARC formats**

Marches (Demonstrations)

USE **Demonstrations**

Marches (Exercises)
USE **Marching drills**
Marches for civil rights
USE **Civil rights demonstrations**
Marches (Music)   783.18
BT **Military music**
Marching
USE **Marching drills**
Marching drills   613.7
UF Drill (Nonmilitary)
Drills, Marching
Marches (Exercises)
Marching
BT **Physical education**
Mardi Gras
USE **Carnival**
Mariculture
USE **Aquaculture**
Marihuana
USE **Marijuana**
Marijuana   362.29; 613.8; 615; 633.7
UF Cannabis
Grass (Drug)
Hashish
Marihuana
Pot (Drug)
BT **Narcotics**
Marinas (May subdiv. geog.)   **387.1**
UF Yacht basins
BT **Boats and boating**
Harbors
Yachts and yachting
NT **Docks**
Marine animals (May subdiv. geog.)
591.77
UF Marine fauna
Sea animals
BT **Aquatic animals**
NT **Corals**
Marine mammals
RT **Marine biology**
Marine aquaculture
USE **Aquaculture**
Marine aquariums   597.073; 639.34
UF Salt water aquariums
Sea water aquariums
SA names of specific marine aquari-
ums [to be added as needed]
BT **Aquariums**
NT **Marineland (Fla.)**

Marine architecture
USE **Naval architecture**
Marine biology   578.77
UF Ocean life
Sea life
BT **Biology**
Oceanography
NT **Marine ecology**
Marine plants
Marine resources
RT **Marine animals**
Marine disasters
USE **Shipwrecks**
Marine drilling platforms
USE **Drilling platforms**
Marine ecology   578.77
BT **Ecology**
Marine biology
Marine engineering (May subdiv. geog.)
623.8
Use for materials on engineering as applied
to ships and their machinery.
UF Naval engineering
BT **Civil engineering**
Engineering
Mechanical engineering
Naval architecture
Naval art and science
Steam navigation
Marine engines   623.87
BT **Engines**
Shipbuilding
Steam engines
Marine fauna
USE **Marine animals**
Marine flora
USE **Marine plants**
Marine geology
USE **Submarine geology**
Marine insurance   368.2
UF Insurance, Marine
BT **Commerce**
Insurance
Maritime law
Merchant marine
Shipping
Marine law
USE **Maritime law**
Marine mammals (May subdiv. geog.)
599.5
SA types of marine mammals [to be
added as needed]

459

Marine mammals—*Continued*
- BT **Mammals**
  Marine animals
- NT **Dolphins**
  Seals (Animals)
  Whales

Marine mineral resources (May subdiv. geog.) **333.8; 553**
- UF Mineral resources, Marine
  Ocean mineral resources
- BT **Marine resources**
  Mines and mineral resources
  Ocean bottom
  Ocean engineering
- NT **Ocean mining**
- RT **Ocean energy resources**

Marine painting **758**
- UF Sea in art
  Seascapes
  Ships in art
- BT **Painting**

Marine plants (May subdiv. geog.) **579**
- UF Aquatic plants
  Marine flora
  Water plants
- BT **Marine biology**
  Plants
- NT **Algae**
- RT **Freshwater plants**

Marine pollution (May subdiv. geog.) **363.739**
- UF Ocean pollution
  Offshore water pollution
  Sea pollution
- BT **Oceanography**
  Water pollution
- RT **Oil pollution of water**

Marine resources (May subdiv. geog.) **333.91; 591.77**
- UF Ocean—Economic aspects
  Ocean resources
  Resources, Marine
  Sea resources
- BT **Commercial products**
  Marine biology
  Natural resources
  Oceanography
- NT **Aquaculture**
  Marine mineral resources
  Ocean energy resources
  Ocean engineering
  Seafood

Marine salvage **387.5; 627**
- UF Ship salvage
- BT **International law**
  Maritime law
  Salvage
- RT **Shipwrecks**

Marine transportation
- USE **Shipping**

Marineland (Fla.) **597.073; 639.34**
- BT **Marine aquariums**

Mariners
- USE **Sailors**

Mariner's compass
- USE **Compass**

Marionettes
- USE **Puppets and puppet plays**

Marital communication
- USE **Communication in marriage**

Marital counseling
- USE **Marriage counseling**

Marital infidelity
- USE **Adultery**

Marital separation
- USE **Separation (Law)**

Maritime discoveries
- USE **Exploration**

Maritime law (May subdiv. geog.) **341.4; 343.09**
- UF Law of the sea
  Marine law
  Merchant marine—Law and legislation
  Naval law
  Navigation—Law and legislation
  Sea laws
- BT **International law**
  Law
  Shipping
- NT **Freight**
  Marine insurance
  Marine salvage
  Merchant marine
  Pirates
  Ships—Safety regulations
- RT **Commercial law**
  Territorial waters

Market gardening
- USE **Truck farming**

Market surveys (May subdiv. geog.) **658.8**

Market surveys—*Continued*

  BT **Advertising**

      Surveys

  RT **Public opinion polls**

Marketing (May subdiv. geog.) **381;**
  658.8

    Use for materials on the principles and
methods involved in the transfer of merchandise from producer to consumer. Materials on
food buying are entered under **Grocery shopping**.

  UF Distribution (Economics)

      Merchandising

  SA subjects with the subdivision

      Marketing, e.g. **Farm pro-
duce—Marketing** [to be added as needed]

  BT **Business**

      Management

  NT **Direct marketing**

      Direct selling

      Farm produce—Marketing

      Internet marketing

      New products

      Sales management

      Telemarketing

  RT **Advertising**

      Selling

Marketing (Home economics)

  USE **Grocery shopping**

      Shopping

Marketing of farm produce

  USE **Farm produce—Marketing**

Markets (May subdiv. geog.) **381; 658.8**

    Use for materials on places where many
buyers and sellers are brought into contract
with one another in order to exhange goods
and services.

  BT **Business**

      Cities and towns

      Commerce

  NT **Flea markets**

      Stock exchanges

  RT **Fairs**

Marking and grading (Education)

  USE **Grading and marking (Education)**

Marks

  USE **Hallmarks**

      and types of things with identi-
fying marks, other than plate,
with the subdivision *Marks,*
e.g. **Pottery—Marks** [to be
added as needed]

Marks on plate

  USE **Hallmarks**

Marriage (May subdiv. geog.) **306.81;**
  346.01

  UF Married life

      Matrimony

  BT **Family**

      Sacraments

  NT **Betrothal**

      Communication in marriage

      Husbands

      Intermarriage

      Marriage contracts

      Marriage counseling

      Marriage customs and rites

      Married people

      Polygamy

      Remarriage

      Same-sex marriage

      Separation (Law)

      Teenage marriage

      Weddings

      Wives

  RT **Courtship**

      Domestic relations

Marriage—Annulment **262.9; 346.01**

  UF Annulment of marriage

Marriage contracts (May subdiv. geog.)
  306.81; 346.01

  UF Antenuptial contracts

      Premarital contracts

      Prenuptial agreements

      Prenuptial contracts

  BT **Contracts**

      Marriage

Marriage counseling **362.82**

  UF Marital counseling

      Premarital counseling

  BT **Counseling**

      Family life education

      Marriage

  RT **Divorce mediation**

Marriage—Cross-cultural studies
  306.81

Marriage customs and rites (May subdiv.
  geog.) **392.5**

  UF Bridal customs

  BT **Manners and customs**

      Marriage

      Rites and ceremonies

      Weddings

Marriage, Interracial
USE **Interracial marriage**
Marriage registers
USE **Registers of births, etc.**
Marriage statistics
USE **Vital statistics**
Married life
USE **Marriage**
Married men
USE **Husbands**
Married people (May subdiv. geog.)
306.872
UF Married persons
BT **Family**
Marriage
NT **Husbands**
Wives
Married persons
USE **Married people**
Married women
USE **Wives**
Mars (Planet)   523.43
BT **Planets**
NT **Mars probes**
Mars (Planet)—Exploration   629.43
BT **Planets—Exploration**
Mars (Planet)—Geology   559.9
BT **Astrogeology**
Mars (Planet)—Pictorial works   523.43;
778.3
BT **Space photography**
Mars (Planet)—Satellites   523.9
UF Satellites—Mars
BT **Satellites**
Mars probes   629.43
UF Martian probes
BT **Mars (Planet)**
Space probes
Marshall Plan
USE **Reconstruction (1939-1951)**
Marshes (May subdiv. geog.)   **551.41**
BT **Wetlands**
Martial arts (May subdiv. geog.)   **796.8**
BT **Athletics**
NT **Archery**
Dueling
Jiu-jitsu
Judo
Karate
Kung fu
Tai chi

RT **Self-defense**
Self-defense for women
Martial law (May subdiv. geog.)   **342**
BT **Law**
NT **Habeas corpus**
RT **Military law**
Martian probes
USE **Mars probes**
Martin Luther King Day   394.261
BT **Holidays**
Martyrs   200.92; 272.092
BT **Church history**
Heroes and heroines
RT **Persecution**
Saints
Marxian theory
USE **Marxism**
Marxism (May subdiv. geog.)   **335.4**
UF Marxian theory
Marxist theory
BT **Economics**
Philosophy
Political science
Sociology
RT **Class consciousness**
Communism
Dialectical materialism
Socialism
Marxist theory
USE **Marxism**
Mary, Blessed Virgin, Saint   232.91
UF Blessed Virgin Mary
Madonna
Virgin Mary
BT **Saints**
Mary, Blessed Virgin, Saint—Art   704.9
BT **Christian art**
Mary, Blessed Virgin, Saint—Prayers
242
BT **Prayers**
Mascots   302.2223
UF School mascots
Sports mascots
Masculine psychology
USE **Men—Psychology**
Masculinity (May subdiv. geog.)   **155.3**
UF Masculinity (Psychology)
BT **Sex (Psychology)**
RT **Men**
Masculinity (Psychology)
USE **Masculinity**

Masers   621.381
    BT   Amplifiers (Electronics)
         Electromagnetism
         Microwaves
Masks (Facial)   391.4
    BT   Costume
Masks (Plays)   808.2; 808.82
    Use for individual works, collections, or
    materials about masks.
    UF   Masques (Plays)
    BT   Drama
         Pageants
         Theater
Masks (Sculpture) (May subdiv. geog.)
         731
    UF   Death masks
    BT   Sculpture
Masonic orders
    USE   Freemasons
Masonry (May subdiv. geog.)   693
    BT   Building
         Stone
    NT   Cement
         Concrete
         Plaster and plastering
         Stonecutting
    RT   Bricklaying
Masons (Secret order)
    USE   Freemasons
Masques (Plays)
    USE   Masks (Plays)
Mass
    USE   Mass (Liturgy)
Mass communication
    USE   Communication
         Mass media
         Telecommunication
Mass culture
    USE   Popular culture
Mass feeding
    USE   Food service
Mass (Liturgy)   264
    UF   Mass
    BT   Liturgies
    RT   Eucharist
Mass media (May subdiv. geog.)   302.23
    UF   Mass communication
         Media
    SA   topics with the subdivision *Press
         coverage*, e.g. Food contami-
         nation—Press coverage [to
         be added as needed]

    BT   Communication
    NT   Motion pictures
         Newspapers
         Periodicals
         Radio broadcasting
         Sex in mass media
         Television broadcasting
         Violence in mass media
    RT   Popular culture
Mass media literacy
    USE   Media literacy
Mass political behavior
    USE   Political participation
         Political psychology
Mass psychology
    USE   Social psychology
Mass spectra
    USE   Mass spectrometry
Mass spectrometry   543; 547
    UF   Mass spectra
         Mass spectrum analysis
    BT   Spectrum analysis
Mass spectrum analysis
    USE   Mass spectrometry
Mass transit
    USE   Local transit
Massacres (May subdiv. geog.)   179.7;
         904
    SA   names of individual massacres,
         e.g. Saint Bartholomew's
         Day, Massacre of, 1572 [to
         be added as needed]
    BT   Atrocities
         History
         Persecution
    NT   Saint Bartholomew's Day,
         Massacre of, 1572
Massage   613.7; 615.8
    BT   Physical therapy
    NT   Acupressure
         Chiropractic
         Electrotherapeutics
    RT   Osteopathic medicine
Mastodon   569
    BT   Extinct animals
         Fossil mammals
Mate selection in animals
    USE   Animal courtship
Materia medica (May subdiv. geog.)
         615

Materia medica—*Continued*
- UF Herbals
     Pharmacopoeias
- SA types of drugs [to be added as needed]
- BT **Medicine**
     Therapeutics
- NT **Anesthetics**
     Narcotics
- RT **Drugs**
     Pharmacology
     Pharmacy

Material culture (May subdiv. geog.) **306; 930.1**

Use for materials on the folk artifacts of a people produced by traditional methods.
- SA ethnic groups with the subdivision *Material culture*, e.g., **Native Americans—Material culture** [to be added as needed]
- BT **Culture**
- RT **Folklore**
     Technology

Materialism (May subdiv. geog.) **146**
- BT **Philosophy**
     Positivism
- RT **Idealism**
     Realism

Materials **620.1**

Use for comprehensive works on the basic processed materials used in engineering and industry. Works on unprocessed minerals and unprocessed animal and vegetable products are entered under **Raw materials**.
- UF Engineering materials
     Industrial materials
     Strategic materials
- SA types of materials, e.g. **Building materials**; **Hazardous substances**; etc.; and scientific and technical disciplines and types of equipment and construction with the subdivision *Materials* [to be added as needed]
- NT **Adhesives**
     Airplanes—Materials
     Artists' materials
     Building materials
     Ceramics
     Finishes and finishing
     Hazardous substances

- RT **Engineering**
     Manufacturing processes

Materials handling **388; 658.7**
- UF Handling of materials
     Mechanical handling
- BT **Management**
- NT **Conveying machinery**
     Freight
- RT **Trucks**

Maternity
- USE **Mothers**

Maternity leave (May subdiv. geog.) **331.44**
- BT **Parental leave**

Mathematical ability **153.9**
- UF Arithmetical ability
     Number ability
- BT **Ability**

Mathematical analysis **515**
- UF Analysis (Mathematics)
- BT **Mathematics**
- NT **Algebra**
     Calculus
     Functions
     Graph theory
     Linear algebra
     Numerical analysis

Mathematical drawing
- USE **Geometrical drawing**
     Mechanical drawing

Mathematical logic
- USE **Symbolic logic**

Mathematical models **511**
- UF Models
     Models, Mathematical
- SA subjects with the subdivision *Mathematical models*, e.g. **Pollution—Mathematical models** [to be added as needed]
- BT **Mathematics**
- NT **Computer simulation**
     Fractals
     Game theory
     Pollution—Mathematical models
     System analysis

Mathematical notation **510**

Use for materials on the system of graphic symbols used in mathematics as well as for materials on the process or method of setting these down.

Mathematical notation—*Continued*
- UF   Mathematical symbols
       Mathematics—Notation
       Mathematics—Symbols
       Notation, Mathematical
       Symbols, Mathematical
- RT   **Mathematics**

Mathematical readiness   372.7
- UF   Arithmetical readiness
       Mathematics readiness
       Number readiness
       Readiness for mathematics
- BT   **Arithmetic—Study and teaching**
       Mathematics—Study and teaching

Mathematical recreations   793.74
- UF   Recreations, Mathematical
- BT   **Amusements**
       Puzzles
       Scientific recreations
- NT   **Number games**

Mathematical sequences
- USE **Sequences (Mathematics)**

Mathematical sets
- USE **Set theory**

Mathematical symbols
- USE **Mathematical notation**

Mathematicians (May subdiv. geog.)
       510.92; 920
- BT   **Scientists**
- RT   **Mathematics**

Mathematics (May subdiv. geog.)   **510**
- SA   subjects with the subdivision
       Mathematics, e.g. **Astronomy—Mathematics** [to be
       added as needed]
- BT   **Science**
- NT   **Algebra**
       Arithmetic
       Astronomy—Mathematics
       Binary system (Mathematics)
       Biomathematics
       Business mathematics
       Calculus
       Dynamics
       Fourth dimension
       Fractions
       Functions
       Game theory
       Geometry
       Group theory

Mathematical analysis
Mathematical models
Measurement
Metric system
Number theory
Patterns (Mathematics)
Probabilities
Sequences (Mathematics)
Set theory
Symbolic logic
Trigonometry
Word problems (Mathematics)
- RT   **Mathematical notation**
       Mathematicians

Mathematics—Computer-assisted instruction   372.7; 510.78
- BT   **Computer-assisted instruction**

Mathematics—Notation
- USE **Mathematical notation**

Mathematics readiness
- USE **Mathematical readiness**

Mathematics—Study and teaching   372.7; 510.7
- NT   **Manipulatives**
       Mathematical readiness

Mathematics—Symbols
- USE **Mathematical notation**

Mathematics—Tables   510
- UF   Ready reckoners
- NT   **Logarithms**
       Trigonometry—Tables

Mating behavior
- USE **Animal courtship**
       Sexual behavior in animals

Matrimony
- USE **Marriage**

Matter   117; 530
- BT   **Dynamics**
       Physics
- NT   **Dark matter (Astronomy)**

Mausoleums
- USE **Tombs**

Maxims
- USE **Proverbs**

Mayas   972.004
- BT   **Native Americans—Central America**
       Native Americans—Mexico

Maze gardens (May subdiv. geog.)   **717**
- UF   Labyrinth gardens
       Mazes

Maze gardens—*Continued*
  BT Gardens
Maze puzzles 793.73
  UF Mazes
  BT Puzzles
Mazes
  USE Maze gardens
       Maze puzzles
Meal planning
  USE Menus
       Nutrition
Meals
  USE types of meals, e.g. Breakfasts;
       Dinners; etc. [to be added as
       needed]
Meals for school children
  USE School children—Food
Meals on wheels programs 362
    Use for materials on programs that deliver
  meals to the homebound.
  UF Home delivered meals programs
  BT Food relief
Meanness
  USE Bad behavior
Measurement 389; 530.8
  UF Metrology
  SA subjects with the subdivision
       Measurement, e.g. Air pollu-
       tion—Measurement [to be
       added as needed]
  BT Mathematics
  NT Air pollution—Measurement
       Geodesy
       Measuring instruments
       Photometry
       Surveying
       Volume (Cubic content)
  RT Weights and measures
Measurements, Electric
  USE Electric measurements
Measures
  USE Weights and measures
Measuring instruments 389; 681
  UF Instruments, Measuring
  BT Measurement
       Weights and measures
Meat 641.3; 664
  SA types of meat [to be added as
       needed]
  BT Food
  NT Beef
       Carving (Meat, etc.)

Cooking—Meat
Meat-eating animals
  USE Carnivorous animals
Meat industry (May subdiv. geog.)
       338.1
  UF Meat industry and trade
       Meat packing industry
       Packing industry
  BT Food industry
  NT Meat inspection
       Stockyards
Meat industry and trade
  USE Meat industry
Meat inspection (May subdiv. geog.)
       363.19
  UF Inspection of meat
  BT Food adulteration and inspec-
       tion
       Meat industry
       Public health
Meat packing industry
  USE Meat industry
Mecha 741.5
    Use for individual works, collections, or
  materials about mecha.
  UF Robot manga
  BT Manga
  NT Fictional robots
       Gundam (Fictional character)
       Neon Genesis Evangelion (Fic-
       tional robot)
Mechanic arts
  USE Industrial arts
Mechanical brains
  USE Cybernetics
Mechanical drawing 604.2
  UF Drafting, Mechanical
       Engineering drawing
       Industrial drawing
       Machinery—Drawing
       Mathematical drawing
       Plans
       Structural drafting
  BT Drawing
       Engineering
       Machinery
       Patternmaking
  NT Blueprints
       Graphic methods
       Lettering
  RT Geometrical drawing

Mechanical engineering (May subdiv. geog.) **621**

Use for materials on the application of the principles of mechanics to the design, construction, and operation of machinery. Materials on the application of the principles of mechanics to engineering structures other than machinery are entered under **Applied mechanics**.

  BT Civil engineering
  NT Electrical engineering
      Machinery
      Marine engineering
      Mechanical movements
      Power (Mechanics)
      Power transmission
  RT Steam engineering
Mechanical handling
  USE **Materials handling**
Mechanical models
  USE **Machinery—Models**
Mechanical movements 531
  UF Mechanisms (Machinery)
  BT **Kinematics**
      Mechanical engineering
      Mechanics
      Motion
  NT **Robots**
      Simple machines
  RT **Gearing**
Mechanical musical instruments 786.6
  UF Musical instruments, Mechanical
  SA types of instruments, e.g. **Music boxes** [to be added as needed]
  BT **Musical instruments**
  NT **Music boxes**
Mechanical properties testing
  USE **Testing**
Mechanical speech recognition
  USE **Automatic speech recognition**
Mechanics 530; 531
  BT **Physics**
  NT **Applied mechanics**
      Dynamics
      Fluid mechanics
      Hydraulics
      Hydrodynamics
      Hydrostatics
      Mechanical movements
      Power (Mechanics)
      Simple machines
      Soil mechanics

      Statics
      Strains and stresses
      Strength of materials
      Vibration
      Viscosity
      Wave mechanics
  RT **Force and energy**
      Kinematics
      Machinery
      Motion
Mechanics, Applied
  USE **Applied mechanics**
Mechanics (Persons) 920
Mechanisms (Machinery)
  USE **Mechanical movements**
Medallions
  USE **Medals**
Medals (May subdiv. geog.) **355.1; 737**
  UF Badges of honor
      Medallions
  SA names of military services and other appropriate subjects with the subdivision *Medals, badges, decorations, etc.* [to be added as needed]
  NT **United States. Army—Medals, badges, decorations, etc.**
      United States. Navy—Medals, badges, decorations, etc.
  RT **Decorations of honor**
      Insignia
      Numismatics
Medals, badges, decorations, etc.
  USE types of armed forces with the subdivision *Medals, badges, decorations, etc.,* e.g. **United States. Army—Medals, badges, decorations, etc.** [to be added as needed]
Media
  USE **Mass media**
Media centers (Education)
  USE **Instructional materials centers**
Media coverage
  USE topics with the subdivision *Press coverage,* e.g. **Food contamination—Press coverage** [to be added as needed]

Media literacy (May subdiv. geog.)
    302.23

Use for materials on a person's knowledge of and ability to use, interpret, and evaluate the mass media.

  UF   Mass media literacy

  BT   **Literacy**

Mediation

  USE **Arbitration and award**

Mediation, Divorce

  USE **Divorce mediation**

Mediation, Industrial

  USE **Industrial arbitration**

Mediation, International

  USE **International arbitration**

Medicaid (May subdiv. geog.)
    362.10973; 368.4

  UF   Medical care for the poor

  BT   **National health insurance**

        Poor—Medical care

        State medicine

  RT   **Medicare**

Medical appointments and schedules

  USE **Medical practice**

Medical botany 581.6

  UF   Botany, Medical

        Drug plants

        Herbal medicine

        Medicinal herbs

        Medicinal plants

        Plants, Medicinal

  BT   **Botany**

        Medicine

        Pharmacy

Medical care (May subdiv. geog.) **362.1**

Use for materials on the organization of services and facilities for medical care. Materials on the technical and scientific aspects of medical care are entered under **Medicine**.

  UF   Delivery of health care

        Delivery of medical care

        Health care

        Health care delivery

        Medical services

        Personal health services

  SA   ethnic groups, classes of persons, and names of wars with the subdivision *Medical care*, e.g. **Native Americans—Medical care**; **Elderly—Medical care**; etc. [to be added as needed]

  BT   **Public health**

  NT   **Access to health care**

        Armies—Medical care

        Dental care

        Elderly—Medical care

        Health facilities

        Health self-care

        Home care services

        Long-term care facilities

        Medical charities

        Mental health services

        Native Americans—Medical care

        Occupational health services

        Poor—Medical care

        Sports medicine

        Terminal care

        United States—History—1861-1865, Civil War—Medical care

        World War, 1939-1945—Medical care

  RT   **Health care reform**

        Medicine

Medical care—Access

  USE **Access to health care**

Medical care—Costs 362.1

  UF   Cost of medical care

        Medical service, Cost of

        Medicine—Cost of medical care

  BT   **Medical economics**

Medical care—Ethical aspects

  USE **Medical ethics**

Medical care facilities

  USE **Health facilities**

Medical care for the elderly

  USE **Elderly—Medical care**

        Medicare

Medical care for the poor

  USE **Medicaid**

        Poor—Medical care

Medical care—Government policy

  USE **Medical policy**

Medical care reform

  USE **Health care reform**

Medical care, Right to

  USE **Right to health care**

Medical care—Social aspects

  USE **Social medicine**

Medical centers (May subdiv. geog.)
    362.11

  RT   **Hospitals**

Medical charities (May subdiv. geog.)
362.1
UF Charities, Medical
BT **Charities**
Medical care
Public health
NT **Institutional care**
RT **Hospitals**
Medical chemistry
USE **Clinical chemistry**
Medical colleges (May subdiv. geog.)
610.71
UF Medical schools
BT **Colleges and universities**
RT **Medicine—Study and teaching**
Medical consultation
USE **Medical practice**
Medical diagnosis
USE **Diagnosis**
Medical drama (Films)   791.43
Use for individual works, collections, or materials about medical films.
UF Doctor films
BT **Motion pictures**
Medical drama (Radio programs)
791.44
Use for individual works, collections, or materials about medical radio programs.
UF Doctor radio programs
BT **Radio programs**
Medical drama (Television programs)
791.45
Use for individual works, collections, or materials about medical television programs.
UF Doctor television programs
BT **Television programs**
Medical economics   338.4
Use for comprehensive materials on the economic aspects of medical service from the point of view of both the practitioner and the public.
SA types of medical services with the subdivision *Costs* [to be added as needed]
BT **Economics**
NT **Medical care—Costs**
Medical education
USE **Medicine—Study and teaching**
Medical electricity
USE **Electrotherapeutics**

Medical errors
USE **Errors**
Medical personnel—Malpractice
Physicians—Malpractice
Medical ethics (May subdiv. geog.)
174.2
UF Medical care—Ethical aspects
Medicine—Ethical aspects
SA types of medical practices and procedures with the subdivision *Ethical aspects*, e.g.
Transplantation of organs, tissues, etc.—Ethical aspects
[to be added as needed]
BT **Bioethics**
Ethics
Professional ethics
NT **Euthanasia**
Human experimentation in medicine
Right to die
RT **Social medicine**
Medical examinations
USE **Periodic health examinations**
and subjects, classes of persons, ethnic groups, and military services with the subdivision *Medical examinations*, e.g.
Children—Medical examinations [to be added as needed]
Medical experimentation on humans
USE **Human experimentation in medicine**
Medical fiction
USE **Medical novels**
Medical folklore
USE **Traditional medicine**
Medical genetics (May subdiv. geog.)
616
UF Clinical genetics
Congenital diseases
Hereditary diseases
Heredity of diseases
SA names of diseases with the subdivision *Genetic aspects* [to be added as needed]
BT **Genetics**
Pathology
NT **Birth defects**
Cancer—Genetic aspects

Medical genetics—*Continued*
> **Genetic counseling**

Medical inspection in schools
> USE   **Children—Medical examinations**

Medical insurance
> USE   **Health insurance**

Medical insurance, National
> USE   **National health insurance**

Medical jurisprudence (May subdiv. geog.)   **614**

> Use for materials on the application of medical knowledge to questions of law. Materials on the law as it affects medicine and the medical profession are entered under **Medicine—Law and legislation**.

> UF   Forensic medicine
> Jurisprudence, Medical
> Legal medicine
> BT   **Forensic sciences**
> NT   **DNA fingerprinting**
> **Lie detectors and detection**
> **Poisons and poisoning**
> **Suicide**
> RT   **Medicine—Law and legislation**

Medical laws and legislation
> USE   **Medicine—Law and legislation**

Medical malpractice
> USE   **Medical personnel—Malpractice**

Medical missions (May subdiv. geog.)   **362.1**

> UF   Missions, Medical
> BT   **Medicine**

Medical novels   808.3

> Use for individual works, collections, or materials about novels with a medical setting.

> UF   Doctor novels
> Medical fiction
> Medicine—Fiction
> BT   **Fiction**

Medical offices
> USE   **Medical practice**

Medical partnership
> USE   **Medical practice**

Medical personnel (May subdiv. geog.)   **610.69**

> UF   Health care personnel
> Health personnel
> Health professions
> Health sciences personnel
> Health services personnel
> Medical profession

> BT   **Employees**
> NT   **Nurses**
> **Physicians**
> **Women in medicine**
> RT   **Medicine**

Medical personnel—Malpractice (May subdiv. geog.)   **346.03**

> UF   Medical errors
> Medical malpractice
> SA   classes of persons in the medical field with the subdivision *Malpractice*; e.g. **Physicians—Malpractice** [to be added as needed]
> BT   **Malpractice**
> **Medicine—Law and legislation**

Medical photography   621.36; 778.3

> BT   **Photography**
> **Photography—Scientific applications**

Medical policy (May subdiv. geog.)   **362.1**

> UF   Government policy
> Health care policy
> Health policy
> Medical care—Government policy
> Medicine and state
> Public health—Government policy
> BT   **Social policy**

Medical practice (May subdiv. geog.)   **610.6**

> Use for materials on the organization and management of medicine as a profession. Scientific materials on the practice of medicine are entered under **Medicine**.

> UF   Clinics
> Group medical practice
> Medical appointments and schedules
> Medical consultation
> Medical offices
> Medical partnership
> Medical profession
> Medicine—Practice
> SA   types of medicine with the subdivision *Practice*, e.g. **Nuclear medicine—Practice** [to be added as needed]
> BT   **Medicine**

Medical practice—*Continued*
   NT   **Health maintenance organizations**
        Nuclear medicine—Practice
Medical profession
   USE **Medical personnel**
        Medical practice
        Medicine
Medical records (May subdiv. geog.)
    651.5
   UF Clinical records
        Health records
        Hospital care records
        Patient care records
Medical research
   USE **Medicine—Research**
Medical schools
   USE **Medical colleges**
Medical sciences
   USE **Medicine**
Medical self-care
   USE **Health self-care**
Medical service, Cost of
   USE **Medical care—Costs**
Medical services
   USE **Medical care**
Medical sociology
   USE **Social medicine**
Medical technologists (May subdiv. geog.)
    610.69
   BT **Allied health personnel**
Medical technology (May subdiv. geog.)
    610.28
   BT **Medicine**
   NT **Stem cell research**
Medical transplantation
   USE **Transplantation of organs, tissues, etc.**
Medical waste disposal
   USE **Medical wastes**
Medical wastes   **363.72**
   UF Disposal of medical waste
        Hospital wastes
        Infectious wastes
        Medical waste disposal
        Wastes, Medical
   BT **Refuse and refuse disposal**
   RT **Hazardous wastes**
Medicare (May subdiv. geog.)   **368.4**
   UF Medical care for the elderly
   BT **Elderly—Medical care**
        National health insurance

        State medicine
   RT **Medicaid**
Medication abuse   **362.29; 613.8; 616.86**
   Use for materials on the abuse or misuse of therapeutic or medicinal drugs, either prescription or non-prescription.
   UF Abuse of medications
        Abuse of medicines
        Pharmaceutical abuse
        Prescription drug abuse
   BT **Drug abuse**
Medicinal chemistry
   USE **Pharmaceutical chemistry**
Medicinal herbs
   USE **Herbs—Therapeutic use**
        Medical botany
Medicinal plants
   USE **Medical botany**
Medicine (May subdiv. geog.)   **610**
   Use for materials on the technical and scientific aspects of medical care. Materials on the organization of services and facilities for medical care are entered under **Medical care**. Materials on the organization and management of medicine as a profession are entered under **Medical practice**.
   UF Medical profession
        Medical sciences
   SA types of medicine, e.g. **Sports medicine**; and names of diseases and groups of diseases, e.g. **AIDS (Disease); Fever; Nervous system—Diseases**; etc., and traditional medicine of particular ethnic groups, e.g. **Native American medicine** [to be added as needed]
   BT **Life sciences**
        Therapeutics
   NT **Alternative medicine**
        Anatomy
        Aviation medicine
        Biochemistry
        Dentistry
        Diagnosis
        Emergency medicine
        Endocrinology
        Family medicine
        First aid
        Health
        Holistic medicine
        Hygiene
        Immunology
        Materia medica

Medicine—*Continued*

> Medical botany
> Medical missions
> Medical practice
> Medical technology
> Military medicine
> Mind and body
> Native American medicine
> Nuclear medicine
> Nursing
> Orthopedics
> Osteopathic medicine
> Pathology
> Periodic health examinations
> Pharmacology
> Pharmacy
> Physiology
> Podiatry
> Popular medicine
> Preventive medicine
> Psychiatry
> Psychosomatic medicine
> Quacks and quackery
> Social medicine
> Space medicine
> Sports medicine
> State medicine
> Submarine medicine
> Surgery
> Therapeutics
> Toxicology
> Traditional medicine
> Tropical medicine
> Veterinary medicine

 RT **Diseases**
> **Medical care**
> **Medical personnel**
> **Physicians**

Medicine and religion
 USE **Medicine—Religious aspects**

Medicine and state
 USE **Medical policy**

Medicine—Biography 610.92; 920
 BT **Biography**

Medicine—Cost of medical care
 USE **Medical care—Costs**

Medicine—Ethical aspects
 USE **Medical ethics**

Medicine—Fiction
 USE **Medical novels**

Medicine—Law and legislation (May subdiv. geog.) **344**

> Use for materials on the law as it affects medicine and the medical profession. Materials on the application of medical knowledge to questions of law are entered under **Medical jurisprudence**.

 UF Medical laws and legislation
 BT **Law**
> **Legislation**

 NT **Medical personnel—Malpractice**
> **Physicians—Licenses**
> **Physicians—Malpractice**
> **Right to die**

 RT **Medical jurisprudence**

Medicine men
 USE **Shamans**

Medicine, Military
 USE **Military medicine**

Medicine—Miscellanea 610.2
 BT **Curiosities and wonders**

Medicine, Pediatric
 USE **Children—Diseases**

Medicine—Physiological effect
 USE **Pharmacology**

Medicine, Popular
 USE **Popular medicine**

Medicine—Practice
 USE **Medical practice**

Medicine, Preventive
 USE **Preventive medicine**

Medicine, Psychosomatic
 USE **Psychosomatic medicine**

Medicine—Religious aspects 201; 261.5; 615.8
 UF Medicine and religion
> Religion and medicine

 NT **Spiritual healing**

Medicine—Research 610.7
 UF Medical research
 BT **Research**
 NT **Experimental medicine**
> **Human experimentation in medicine**
> **Stem cell research**

Medicine—Social aspects
 USE **Social medicine**

Medicine, State
 USE **State medicine**

Medicine—Study and teaching 610.7
 UF Medical education
 RT **Medical colleges**

Medicine—United States   610.973

Medieval architecture (May subdiv. geog.)   **723**

UF   Architecture, Medieval

BT   **Architecture**
  Medieval civilization

NT   **Byzantine architecture**
  Gothic architecture
  Romanesque architecture

RT   **Castles**
  Cathedrals

Medieval art (May subdiv. geog.)   **709.02**

UF   Art, Medieval

BT   **Art**
  Medieval civilization

NT   **Byzantine art**
  Gothic art
  Illumination of books and manuscripts
  Romanesque art

Medieval church history

USE   **Church history—600-1500, Middle Ages**

Medieval civilization   **909.07**

Use for materials on cultural and intellectual developments in the Middle Ages not limited to a single country or region.

UF   Civilization, Medieval

BT   **Civilization**

NT   **Feudalism**
  Medieval architecture
  Medieval art
  Medieval literature
  Medieval philosophy
  Medieval tournaments

RT   **Chivalry**
  Middle Ages

Medieval Greece

USE   **Greece—History—323-1453**

Medieval literature   **809**

May use same subdivisions as for Literature.

UF   Literature, Medieval

BT   **Literature**
  Medieval civilization

NT   **Early Christian literature**
  Old Norse literature

Medieval philosophy   **189**

UF   Philosophy, Medieval

BT   **Medieval civilization**
  Philosophy

Medieval tournaments (May subdiv. geog.)   **394**

Use for materials on medieval contests in which mounted and armored contestants fought for a prize with blunted weapons and in accordance with certain rules, and for materials on modern re-enactments of such events.

UF   Tournaments

BT   **Chivalry**
  Medieval civilization
  Pageants

Meditation   **158; 204; 248.3; 296.7**

Use for materials on spiritual contemplation or mental prayer. Collections of personal reflections or thoughts for use in meditation are entered under **Meditations**.

BT   **Devotional exercises**
  Spiritual life

NT   **Transcendental meditation**

RT   **Meditations**

Meditations   **204; 242**

Use for collections of personal reflections or thoughts for use in meditation. Materials on spiritual contemplation or mental prayer are entered under **Meditation**.

SA   religious topics, names of individual persons, and titles of sacred works with the subdivision *Meditations*, e.g. **Lent—Meditations** [to be added as needed]

BT   **Devotional literature**
  Prayers

NT   **Lent—Meditations**

RT   **Meditation**

Mediterranean Sea   **551.462**

BT   **Seas**

Meetings, Public

USE   **Public meetings**

Melancholia

USE   **Depression (Psychology)**
  Manic-depressive illness

Melodrama   **808.82**

Use for individual works, collections, or materials about melodrama.

BT   **Drama**

Members of Parliament

USE   **Legislators**

Memoirs

USE   **Autobiographies**
  Autobiography
  Biography

Memorabilia

USE   **Collectibles**

Memorial Day   **394.262**

Memorial Day—*Continued*
  UF   Decoration Day
  BT   **Holidays**
Memorizing
  USE subjects, types of literature, and
        titles of sacred works with
        the subdivision *Memorizing,*
        e.g. **Poetry—Memorizing** [to
        be added as needed]
Memory 153.1
  SA   subjects, types of literature, and
        titles of sacred works with
        the subdivision *Memorizing,*
        e.g. **Poetry—Memorizing** [to
        be added as needed]
  BT   **Brain**
       Educational psychology
       Intellect
       Psychology
       Psychophysiology
       Thought and thinking
  NT   **Amnesia**
       Attention
       False memory syndrome
       Forgetfulness
       Psychology of learning
       Recovered memory
  RT   **Mnemonics**
Memory devices (Computers)
  USE **Computer storage devices**
Men (May subdiv. geog.) **305.31**
  SA   men of particular racial, reli-
        gious or ethnic groups, e.g.
        African American men; Jew-
        ish men; and men in various
        occupations and professions,
        e.g. **Male actors** [to be added
        as needed]
  NT   **African American men**
       Brothers
       Fathers
       Gay men
       Husbands
       Jewish men
       Single men
       Sons
       Widowers
       Young men
  RT   **Masculinity**
Men actors
  USE **Male actors**
Men—Biography 920

  BT   **Biography**
Men—Clothing
  USE **Men's clothing**
Men—Diseases 616.0081
  BT   **Diseases**
Men—Education (May subdiv. geog.)
        370.81
  UF   Education of men
  BT   **Education**
  RT   **Coeducation**
Men—Employment 331.11
  BT   **Employment**
Men in business
  USE **Businessmen**
Men—Psychology 155.3
  UF   Masculine psychology
  BT   **Psychology**
Men—Relations with women
  USE **Man-woman relationship**
Men—Social conditions 305.32
  BT   **Social conditions**
  NT   **Men's movement**
Men—Societies 367
  UF   Men's clubs
       Men's organizations
  BT   **Clubs**
       Societies
Men-women relationship
  USE **Man-woman relationship**
Mendel's law 576.5
  BT   **Breeding**
       Variation (Biology)
  NT   **Genetics**
  RT   **Heredity**
Mendicancy
  USE **Begging**
Mendicant orders
  USE **Franciscans**
Mending
  USE **Clothing and dress—Repairing**
       Repairing
Mennonites (May subdiv. geog.) **289.7**
  BT   **Christian sects**
  NT   **Amish**
Menopause 612.6; 618.1
  UF   Change of life in women
       Climacteric, Female
       Female climacteric
  BT   **Aging**
Menopause, Male
  USE **Male climacteric**

Men's clothing   646; 687
- UF   Men—Clothing
- BT   **Clothing and dress**

Men's clubs
- USE   **Men—Societies**

Men's liberation movement
- USE   **Men's movement**

Men's movement   305.32
- UF   Men's liberation movement
- BT   **Men—Social conditions**

Men's organizations
- USE   **Men—Societies**

Menstruation   612.6
- BT   **Reproduction**
- NT   **Premenstrual syndrome**

Mental arithmetic   513
- UF   Mental calculation
- BT   **Arithmetic**

Mental calculation
- USE   **Mental arithmetic**

Mental deficiency
- USE   **Mental retardation**

Mental depression
- USE   **Depression (Psychology)**

Mental diseases
- USE   **Abnormal psychology**
         Mental illness

Mental healing   615.8

Use for materials on psychic or psychological means to treat illness. Materials on the use of faith, prayer, or religious means to treat illness are entered under **Spiritual healing**.

- UF   Healing, Mental
         Mind cure
         Psychic healing
- BT   **Alternative medicine**
- NT   **Hypnotism**
- RT   **Mental suggestion**
         Mind and body
         Psychotherapy
         Spiritual healing
         Subconsciousness
         Suggestive therapeutics

Mental health (May subdiv. geog.)
         362.2
- UF   Mental hygiene
- SA   ethnic groups, classes of persons, and names of individual persons with the subdivision *Mental health*, e.g. **Women—Mental health** [to be added as needed]

- BT   **Happiness**
         Health
- NT   **Burn out (Psychology)**
         Occupational therapy
         Stress (Psychology)
         Women—Mental health
- RT   **Abnormal psychology**
         Mental illness
         Mind and body
         Psychiatry
         Psychology

Mental health care
- USE   **Mental health services**

Mental health services (May subdiv. geog.)   **362.2; 616.89**
- UF   Mental health care
         Psychiatric care
         Psychiatric services
- SA   ethnic groups, classes of persons, and names of individual educational institutions with the subdivision *Mental health services* [to be added as needed]
- BT   **Medical care**
- NT   **Crisis intervention (Mental health services)**

Mental hospitals
- USE   **Psychiatric hospitals**

Mental hygiene
- USE   **Mental health**

Mental illness (May subdiv. geog.)
         362.2; 616.89

Use for popular materials and materials on regional or social aspects of mental disorders. Materials on clinical aspects of mental disorders, including therapy, are entered under **Psychiatry**. Systematic descriptions of mental disorders are entered under **Abnormal psychology**.

- UF   Mental diseases
         Psychoses
- SA   names of specific illnesses, e.g. **Manic-depressive illness** [to be added as needed]
- BT   **Abnormal psychology**
         Diseases
- NT   **Manic-depressive illness**
         Multiple personality
         Neurasthenia
- RT   **Mental health**
         Mentally ill
         Personality disorders

Mental illness—*Continued*
    Psychiatry
Mental illness—Drug therapy   **616.89**
  BT **Drug therapy**
Mental illness—Jurisprudence
  USE **Insanity defense**
Mental illness—Physiological aspects
    616.89
  BT **Physiology**
Mental institutions
  USE **Mentally ill—Institutional care**
Mental patients
  USE **Mentally ill**
Mental retardation (May subdiv. geog.)
    362.3; 616.85
  UF Mental deficiency
  BT **Abnormal psychology**
  NT **Down syndrome**
  RT **Mentally handicapped**
Mental stereotype
  USE **Stereotype (Social psychology)**
Mental stress
  USE **Stress (Psychology)**
Mental suggestion   **131; 154.7; 615.8**
  UF Autosuggestion
      Suggestion, Mental
  BT **Mind and body**
      Parapsychology
      Subconsciousness
  NT **Brainwashing**
  RT **Hypnotism**
      Mental healing
      Suggestive therapeutics
Mental telepathy
  USE **Telepathy**
Mental tests
  USE **Intelligence tests**
      Psychological tests
Mental types
  USE **Typology (Psychology)**
Mentally depressed
  USE **Depression (Psychology)**
Mentally deranged
  USE **Mentally ill**
Mentally handicapped (May subdiv.
    geog.)   **305.9; 362.2; 362.3**
  UF Mentally retarded
  BT **Handicapped**
  NT **Mentally handicapped children**
  RT **Mental retardation**

Mentally handicapped children (May
    subdiv. geog.)   **155.45; 362.2;**
    362.3
  UF Children, Retarded
      Mentally retarded children
      Retarded children
  BT **Child psychiatry**
      Handicapped children
      Mentally handicapped
  RT **Slow learning children**
Mentally handicapped children—Educa-
    tion (May subdiv. geog.)   **371.92**
  BT **Education**
      Special education
Mentally ill (May subdiv. geog.)   **362.2;**
    616.89
  UF Insane
      Mental patients
      Mentally deranged
      Psychotics
  BT **Sick**
  NT **Emotionally disturbed children**
  RT **Mental illness**
Mentally ill children
  USE **Emotionally disturbed children**
Mentally ill—Institutional care   **362.2**
  UF Mental institutions
  BT **Institutional care**
  RT **Psychiatric hospitals**
Mentally retarded
  USE **Mentally handicapped**
Mentally retarded children
  USE **Mentally handicapped children**
Mentoring   **361; 371.102; 658.3**
  BT **Counseling**
Menus   **642**
  UF Bills of fare
      Meal planning
  BT **Cooking**
      Diet
  NT **Breakfasts**
      Dinners
      Luncheons
  RT **Catering**
Mercantile buildings
  USE **Commercial buildings**
Mercantile law
  USE **Commercial law**
Mercenary soldiers (May subdiv. geog.)
    355.3

Mercenary soldiers—*Continued*
  UF   Mercenary troops
         Soldiers of fortune
  BT   **Military personnel**
         Soldiers
Mercenary troops
  USE   **Mercenary soldiers**
Merchandise
  USE   **Commercial products**
         Consumer goods
Merchandising
  USE   **Marketing**
         Retail trade
Merchant marine (May subdiv. geog.)
         387.5
  BT   **Maritime law**
         Sailors
         Ships
         Transportation
  NT   **Harbors**
         Marine insurance
  RT   **Shipping**
Merchant marine—Law and legislation
  USE   **Maritime law**
Merchant marine—Safety regulations
  USE   **Ships—Safety regulations**
Merchant marine—United States
         387.50973
Merchants (May subdiv. geog.)
         380.1092; 920
  BT   **Businesspeople**
Mercury   546; 669
  UF   Quicksilver
  BT   **Chemical elements**
         Metals
Mercury (Planet)   523.41
  BT   **Planets**
Mercy killing
  USE   **Euthanasia**
Mergers
  USE   **Corporate mergers and acqui-
         sitions**
         and types of institutions and
         types of industries and busi-
         nesses with the subdivision
         Mergers, e.g. **Railroads—
         Mergers** [to be added as
         needed]
Merlin (Legendary character)   398.22
  BT   **Legendary characters**
Mermaids and mermen   398.21
  BT   **Mythical animals**

Mesmerism
  USE   **Hypnotism**
Messages
  USE   types of public officials and
         names of individual public of-
         ficials with the subdivision
         Messages, e.g. **Presidents—
         United States—Messages** [to
         be added as needed]
Messages to Congress
  USE   **Presidents—United States—
         Messages**
Messiness   648
  UF   Disorderliness
         Sloppiness
  BT   **Human behavior**
Metabolism   572
  BT   **Biochemistry**
  NT   **Growth disorders**
         Minerals in the body
Metal finishing
  USE   **Metals—Finishing**
Metal work
  USE   **Metalwork**
Metallography   669
         Use for materials on the science of metal
         structures and alloys, especially the study of
         such structures with the microscope. Materials
         on the process of extracting metals from their
         ores, refining them, and preparing them for
         use, are entered under **Metallurgy**.
  UF   Metallurgical analysis
         Microscopic analysis
  BT   **Metals**
Metallurgical analysis
  USE   **Metallography**
Metallurgy (May subdiv. geog.)   **669**
         Use for materials on the process of extract-
         ing metals from their ores, refining them, and
         preparing them for use. Materials on the sci-
         ence of metal structures and alloys, especially
         the study of such structures with the micro-
         scope, are entered under **Metallography**.
  NT   **Electrometallurgy**
  RT   **Alloys**
         Chemical engineering
         Industrial chemistry
         Metals
         Ores
         Smelting
Metals   669
  SA   types of metals [to be added as
         needed]

Metals—*Continued*
  BT **Inorganic chemistry**
      Ores
  NT **Alloys**
      Aluminum
      Brass
      Iron
      Mercury
      Metallography
      Pewter
      Precious metals
      Soldering
      Tin
      Zinc
  RT **Metallurgy**
      Metalwork
Metals—Finishing **671.7**
  UF Metal finishing
  BT **Finishes and finishing**
      Metalwork
Metalwork (May subdiv. geog.) **671;**
      739
  UF Metal work
  BT **Decoration and ornament**
  NT **Architectural metalwork**
      Art metalwork
      Bronzes
      Copperwork
      Dies (Metalworking)
      Electroplating
      Forging
      Founding
      Goldwork
      Ironwork
      Metals—Finishing
      Plate metalwork
      Sheet metalwork
      Silverwork
      Soldering
      Steel
      Tinwork
      Welding
  RT **Metals**
      Metalworking machinery
Metalworking machinery **621.9**
  BT **Machinery**
  RT **Metalwork**
Metamorphosis **571.876**
  SA individual animals and groups of
      animals with the subdivision
      Metamorphosis, e.g. **Insects—**

Metamorphosis [to be added
      as needed]
  BT **Change**
Metamorphosis—Folklore **398.2**
  UF Metamorphosis (in religion, folk-
      lore, etc.)
Metamorphosis (in religion, folklore, etc.)
  USE **Metamorphosis—Folklore**
       Metamorphosis—Religious as-
       pects
Metamorphosis—Religious aspects **291**
  UF Metamorphosis (in religion, folk-
      lore, etc.)
Metaphysics **110**
  BT **Philosophy**
  NT **Causation**
      Change
      Existentialism
      Space and time
      Theory of knowledge
  RT **God**
Meteorites **523.5**
  BT **Astronomy**
      Meteors
Meteorological instruments **551.5028**
  UF Instruments, Meteorological
  SA types of meteorological instru-
      ments [to be added as need-
      ed]
  BT **Scientific apparatus and in-**
      struments
  NT **Barometers**
      Thermometers
Meteorological observatories **551.5028**
  UF Meteorology—Observatories
      Observatories, Meteorological
      Weather stations
  RT **Meteorology**
Meteorological satellites **551.63**
  UF Weather satellites
  SA names of satellites, e.g. **TIROS**
      satellites [to be added as
      needed]
  BT **Artificial satellites**
  NT **TIROS satellites**
Meteorology (May subdiv. geog.) **551.5**
  Use for scientific materials on the atmo-
  sphere, especially weather factors. Materials
  on climate as it relates to humans and to plant
  and animal life, including the effects of
  changes of climate, are entered under **Cli-**
  mate. Materials on the state of the atmosphere

478

Meteorology—*Continued*
at a given time and place with respect to heat or cold, wetness or dryness, calm or storm, are entered under **Weather**.

   BT   **Earth sciences**
   NT   **Air**
        Auroras
        Clouds
        Cyclones
        Droughts
        Floods
        Fog
        Frost
        Humidity
        Lightning
        Meteorology in aeronautics
        Precipitation (Meteorology)
        Rainbow
        Seasons
        Solar radiation
        Storms
        Sunspots
        Thunderstorms
        Tornadoes
        Weather control
        Weather—Folklore
        Weather forecasting
        Winds
   RT   **Atmosphere**
        Climate
        Meteorological observatories
        Weather

Meteorology in aeronautics   **629.132**
   BT   **Aeronautics**
        Meteorology

Meteorology—Observatories
   USE   **Meteorological observatories**

Meteorology—Tables   **551.5**

Meteors   **523.5**
   UF   Falling stars
        Shooting stars
   BT   **Astronomy**
        Solar system
   NT   **Meteorites**

Meter
   USE   **Musical meter and rhythm**
         Versification

Meters, Electric
   USE   **Electric meters**

Meth (Drug)
   USE   **Methamphetamine**

Methamphetamine   **362.29; 615**

   UF   Meth (Drug)
        Speed (Drug)
   BT   **Amphetamines**
   NT   **Crystal meth (Drug)**

Methodology
   USE   subjects with the subdivision *Methodology,* e.g. **Science— Methodology** [to be added as needed]

Metric system   **389; 530.8**
   BT   **Arithmetic**
        Mathematics
   RT   **Decimal system**
        Weights and measures

Metrical romances
   USE   **Romances**

Metrology
   USE   **Measurement**
        Weights and measures

Metropolitan areas (May subdiv. geog.)   **307.76**
   UF   Urban areas
   SA   names of metropolitan areas, e.g. **Chicago Metropolitan Area (Ill.)** [to be added as needed]
   BT   **Cities and towns—Growth**
   NT   **Suburbs**
        Urban renewal

Metropolitan finance   **336**
   Use for general materials on the public finance of metropolitan areas. Materials on the finance of a particular metropolitan area are entered under **Public finance** with the appropriate geographic subdivision.
   BT   **Municipal finance**
        Public finance

Metropolitan government   **320.8; 352.16**
   SA   names of metropolitan areas with the subdivision *Politics and government* [to be added as needed]
   BT   **Local government**
   NT   **Chicago Metropolitan Area (Ill.)—Politics and government**
   RT   **Municipal government**

Metropolitan planning
   USE   **Regional planning**

Mexican American authors   **810.9; 920**
   SA   genres of American literature with the subdivision *Mexican American authors* [to be added as needed]

Mexican American authors—*Continued*
  BT   **Hispanic American authors**
Mexican American literature (English)
  USE   **American literature—Mexican
        American authors**
Mexican American women (May subdiv.
        geog.)   **305.868**
  UF   Chicanas
  BT   **Mexican Americans
        Women**
Mexican Americans (May subdiv. geog.)
        305.868; 973
  Use for materials on American citizens of
  Mexican descent. Materials on noncitizens
  from Mexico are entered under **Mexicans—
  United States**. Use these same patterns for
  other ethnic groups in the U.S. and other
  countries.
  UF   Chicanos
  BT   **Ethnic groups
        Hispanic Americans
        Immigrants—United States
        Minorities**
  NT   **Mexican American women**
  RT   **Mexicans—United States**
Mexican Americans—Ethnic identity
        305.868
Mexican literature   860; M860
  May use same subdivisions and names of
  literary forms as for **English literature**.
  BT   **Latin American literature
        Literature**
Mexican War, 1846-1848   973.6
  UF   United States—History—1845-
        1848, War with Mexico
  BT   **United States—History—1815-
        1861**
Mexicans (May subdiv. geog.)   **305.868;
        920; 972**
Mexicans—United States   305.868
  Use for materials on noncitizens from Mex-
  ico. Materials on American citizens of Mexi-
  can descent are entered under **Mexican
  Americans**. Use these same patterns for other
  ethnic groups in the U.S. and other countries.
  BT   **Aliens—United States
        Minorities**
  RT   **Mexican Americans**
Mexico   972
  May be subdivided like **United States** ex-
  cept for *History*.
Mexico—Presidents
  USE   **Presidents—Mexico**
Mezzotint engraving   766
  BT   **Engraving**

MIAs
  USE   **Missing in action**
Mice   599.35; 636.088
  UF   Mouse
  BT   **Mammals**
Microbes
  USE   **Bacteria
        Germ theory of disease
        Microorganisms
        Viruses**
Microbial drug resistance
  USE   **Drug resistance in microorga-
        nisms**
Microbial energy conversion
  USE   **Biomass energy**
Microbiology   579
  SA   subjects with the subdivision *Mi-
        crobiology* [to be added as
        needed]
  BT   **Biology**
  NT   **Air—Microbiology
        Bacteriology
        Biotechnology
        Cheese—Microbiology
        Fermentation
        Food—Microbiology
        Soil microbiology**
  RT   **Microorganisms**
Microbreweries (May subdiv. geog.)
        663
  UF   Boutique breweries
  BT   **Breweries**
Microchemistry   540
  BT   **Chemistry**
Microcomputers
  USE   **Personal computers**
Microcredit
  USE   **Microfinance**
Microeconomics   338.5
  UF   Price theory
  BT   **Economics**
Microelectronics   621.381
  UF   Microminiature electronic equip-
        ment
        Microminiaturization (Electron-
        ics)
  BT   **Electronics
        Semiconductors**
Microfilming
  USE   **Microphotography**
Microfilms   302.23; 686.4

Microfilms—*Continued*
  BT **Microforms**
Microfinance 332
  UF Microcredit
        Microloans
  BT **Loans**
Microforms 302.23; 686.4
  UF Micropublications
  SA types of microforms [to be add-
        ed as needed]
  NT **Microfilms**
  RT **Microphotography**
Microloans
  USE **Microfinance**
Microminiature electronic equipment
  USE **Microelectronics**
Microminiaturization (Electronics)
  USE **Microelectronics**
Microorganisms 579
  UF Germs
        Microbes
        Microscopic organisms
  NT **Bacteria**
        Drug resistance in microorga-
        nisms
        Probiotics
        Protozoa
        Viruses
  RT **Microbiology**
Microphotography 686.4
    Use for materials on the photographing of
objects of any size to produce minute images.
Materials on the photographing of minute ob-
jects through a microscope are entered under
Photomicrography.
  UF Microfilming
  BT **Photography**
  RT **Microforms**
Microprocessors 004.16
    Use for materials on the silicon chip that
contains the central processing units of a
microcomputer or other electronic device.
  BT **Computers**
Micropublications
  USE **Microforms**
Microscope and microscopy
  USE **Microscopes**
Microscopes 502.8
  UF Microscope and microscopy
        Microscopic analysis
  BT **Optical instruments**
  NT **Electron microscopes**
  RT **Photomicrography**

Microscopic analysis
  USE **Metallography**
        Microscopes
Microscopic organisms
  USE **Microorganisms**
Microsoft Word (Computer software)
    005.5
  UF Word (Computer software)
  BT **Computer software**
Microwave communication systems
    621.381
  BT **Intercommunication systems**
        Shortwave radio
        Telecommunication
  NT **Closed-circuit television**
Microwave cookery
  USE **Microwave cooking**
Microwave cooking 641.5
  UF Microwave cookery
  BT **Cooking**
Microwaves 537.5
  BT **Electric waves**
        Electromagnetic waves
        Shortwave radio
  NT **Masers**
Mid-career changes
  USE **Career changes**
Mid-life crisis
  USE **Midlife crisis**
Middle age 305.24
  BT **Age**
        Life (Biology)
  NT **Aging**
        Midlife crisis
  RT **Longevity**
        Middle aged persons
Middle aged men (May subdiv. geog.)
    305.244
  BT **Middle aged persons**
Middle aged persons (May subdiv. geog.)
    305.24
  BT **Age**
  NT **Middle aged men**
        Middle aged women
  RT **Middle age**
Middle aged women (May subdiv. geog.)
    305.244
  BT **Middle aged persons**
Middle Ages 909.07
    Use for materials on the history of the me-
dieval world not limited to a single country or
region.

Middle Ages—*Continued*
> UF   Dark Ages
> > Middle Ages—History
>
> BT   **World history**
> NT   **Church history—600-1500,**
> > **Middle Ages**
> > **Knights and knighthood**
> > **World history—12th century**
> > **World history—13th century**
> > **World history—14th century**
> > **World history—15th century**
>
> RT   **Europe—History—476-1492**
> > **Medieval civilization**

Middle Ages—History
> USE   **Middle Ages**

Middle Atlantic States
> USE   **Atlantic States**

Middle child
> USE   **Birth order**

Middle class (May subdiv. geog.)   **305.5**
> UF   Bourgeoisie
> BT   **Social classes**

Middle East   **956**
> Use for materials on the region consisting of northeastern Africa and Asia west of Afghanistan. Materials on several Arabic-speaking countries are entered under **Arab countries**.
>
> UF   Levant
> > Near East
> > Orient
>
> BT   **Asia**
> NT   **Arab countries**
> > **Israel**

Middle East—Strategic aspects   **956**
> BT   **Military geography**
> > **Strategy**

Middle East War, 1991
> USE   **Persian Gulf War, 1991**

Middle English language
> USE   **English language—Middle English period**

Middle English literature
> USE   **English literature—Middle English period**

Middle schools (May subdiv. geog.)
>   **373.236**
> UF   Intermediate schools
> BT   **Schools**
> RT   **Elementary schools**
> > **Junior high schools**

Middle West   **977**

> UF   Central States
> > Midwest
> > North Central States
>
> BT   **Mississippi River Valley**
> > **United States**
>
> RT   **Old Northwest**

Midget cars
> USE   **Karts and karting**

Midlife crisis   **305.244**
> UF   Mid-life crisis
> BT   **Middle age**

Midwest
> USE   **Middle West**

Midwifery
> USE   **Midwives**

Midwives (May subdiv. geog.)   **618.2**
> UF   Birth attendants
> > Midwifery
> > Nurse midwives
>
> BT   **Childbirth**
> > **Natural childbirth**
> > **Nurses**

Migraine   **616.8**
> BT   **Headache**

Migrant labor (May subdiv. geog.)
>   **331.5; 362.85**
> Use for materials on casual or seasonal workers who move from place to place in search of employment. Materials on the movement of population within a country for permanent settlement are entered under **Internal migration**.
>
> UF   Migratory workers
> BT   **Employees**
> > **Labor**
>
> RT   **Agricultural laborers**
> > **Alien labor**
> > **Internal migration**

Migration
> USE   **Animals—Migration**
> > **Immigration and emigration**
> > and types of animals with the subdivision *Migration*, e.g.
> > > **Birds—Migration** [to be added as needed]

Migration, Internal
> USE   **Internal migration**

Migration of birds
> USE   **Birds—Migration**

Migratory workers
> USE   **Migrant labor**

Military aeronautics (May subdiv. geog.)
>   **358.4**

Military aeronautics—*Continued*
    UF   Aeronautics, Military
            Air warfare
            Naval aeronautics
    SA   names of wars with the subdivision *Aerial operations*, e.g. **World War, 1939-1945—Aerial operations** [to be added as needed]
    BT   **Aeronautics**
            Military art and science
            War
    NT   **Aerial reconnaissance**
            Air bases
            Air defenses
            Air power
            Aircraft carriers
            Military airplanes
            Parachute troops
            World War, 1939-1945—Aerial operations

Military aid
    USE   **Military assistance**
Military air bases
    USE   **Air bases**
Military airplanes (May subdiv. geog.) **623.74**
    UF   Air warfare
            Airplanes, Military
            Naval airplanes
    SA   types of military airplanes [to be added as needed]
    BT   **Airplanes**
            Military aeronautics
    NT   **Bombers**
Military art and science (May subdiv. geog.) **355**
    UF   Army
            Fighting
            Military power
            Military science
    NT   **Armed forces**
            Armor
            Artillery
            Battles
            Biological warfare
            Camouflage (Military science)
            Chemical warfare
            Civil defense
            Fortification
            Friendly fire (Military science)
            Guerrilla warfare

            Industrial mobilization
            Military aeronautics
            Military camps
            Military transportation
            Ordnance
            Psychological warfare
            Signals and signaling
            Strategy
            Tactics
            Veterans
            War games
    RT   **Armies**
            Drill and minor tactics
            Military personnel
            Naval art and science
            War
            Weapons
Military art and science—Study and teaching
    USE   **Military education**
Military assistance **355**
    UF   Arms sales
            Foreign aid program
            Military aid
            Military sales
            Mutual defense assistance program
    SA   military assistance from particular countries, e.g. **American military assistance** [to be added as needed]
    BT   **Military policy**
    NT   **American military assistance**
    RT   **Arms transfers**
Military assistance, American
    USE   **American military assistance**
Military atrocities
    USE   **Atrocities**
            War crimes
Military bases (May subdiv. geog.) **355.7**
    UF   Army bases
            Army posts
            Military facilities
            Military installations
            Military posts
Military biography
    USE   names of armies and navies with the subdivision *Biography,* e.g. **United States. Army—Biography; United States.**

Military biography—*Continued*
> Navy—**Biography;** etc. [to be added as needed]

Military camps   355.7
- UF   Camps (Military)
- BT   **Military art and science**
- NT   **Concentration camps**

Military conscription
- USE   **Draft**

Military courts
- USE   **Courts martial and courts of inquiry**

Military crimes
- USE   **Military offenses**

Military desertion (May subdiv. geog.) **343; 355.1**
- UF   Army desertion
  - Desertion
  - Desertion, Military
- SA   names of wars with the subdivision *Desertions* [to be added as needed]
- BT   **Military offenses**
- NT   **World War, 1939-1945—Desertions**
- RT   **Draft resisters**

Military desertion—United States   343
Military draft
- USE   **Draft**

Military drill
- USE   **Drill and minor tactics**

Military education (May subdiv. geog.) **355.007; 355.5**
- UF   Army schools
  - Military art and science—Study and teaching
  - Military schools
  - Military training
  - Schools, Military
- SA   names of military schools, e.g. **United States Military Academy** [to be added as needed]
- BT   **Education**
- NT   **Military training camps**

Military engineering (May subdiv. geog.) **623**
- SA   names of wars with the subdivision *Engineering and construction* [to be added as needed]
- BT   **Civil engineering**
  - **Engineering**

- NT   **World War, 1939-1945—Engineering and construction**
- RT   **Fortification**

Military facilities
- USE   **Military bases**

Military forces
- USE   **Armed forces**

Military geography   355.4
- UF   Maps, Military
  - Military maps
- SA   areas of the world with the subdivision *Strategic aspects* [to be added as needed]
- BT   **Geography**
- NT   **Middle East—Strategic aspects**

Military government   341.6; 355.4
> Use for general materials on governments under military regimes, not limited to a single country.
- UF   Government, Military
- SA   names of countries with the subdivision *Politics and government*, or *History*, with appropriate dates as needed, for materials on governments of particular countries under military rule; and names of countries occupied by foreign military governments with the appropriate subdivision under *History*, e.g., **Netherlands—History—1940-1945, German occupation**; **Japan—History—1945-1952, Allied occupation**; etc. [to be added as needed]
- BT   **Public administration**
- RT   **Military occupation**

Military health
- USE   **Military personnel—Health and hygiene**

Military history   355.009
- UF   History, Military
  - Wars
- SA   names of countries with the subhead *Army* or the subdivision *Military history*, e.g. **United States. Army**; **United States—Military history**; and names of wars, battles, sieges, etc. [to be added as needed]
- BT   **History**

Military history—*Continued*
NT   **Battles**
     Military policy
     United States. Army
     United States—Military history
RT   **Naval history**
Military hospitals (May subdiv. geog.)
    355.7
UF   Field hospitals
     Veterans—Hospitals
SA   names of wars with the subdivi-
     sion *Medical care*, e.g. **World**
     War, 1939-1945—Medical
     care [to be added as needed]
BT   **Hospitals**
     Military medicine
RT   **Veterans**
Military installations
USE   **Military bases**
Military intelligence (May subdiv. geog.)
    355.3
SA   names of wars with the subdivi-
     sion *Military intelligence*, e.g.
     World War, 1939-1945—
     Military intelligence [to be
     added as needed]
BT   **Intelligence service**
NT   **World War, 1939-1945—Mili-**
     tary intelligence
Military intervention
USE   **Intervention (International law)**
Military law (May subdiv. geog.)   **343**
UF   Articles of war
     War, Articles of
BT   **International law**
     Law
NT   **Draft**
     Military offenses
     Veterans—Legal status, laws,
     etc.
RT   **Courts martial and courts of**
     inquiry
     Martial law
     War
Military life
USE   **Military personnel**
     and names of countries with the
     subdivision *Armed forces* or
     the subheads *Army* or *Navy;*
     etc., with the subdivision *Mil-*
     itary life, e.g. **United**

     States—Armed forces—Mili-
     tary life; United States.
     Army—Military life; etc. [to
     be added as needed]
Military maneuvers (May subdiv. geog.)
    355.4
BT   **Tactics**
NT   **War games**
Military maps
USE   **Military geography**
Military medicine   **616.9**
UF   Field hospitals
     Medicine, Military
SA   names of wars with the subdivi-
     sion *Medical care*, e.g. **World**
     War, 1939-1945—Medical
     care [to be added as needed]
BT   **Medicine**
NT   **Armies—Medical care**
     Military hospitals
RT   **Military personnel—Health**
     and hygiene
Military music   **781.5**
SA   names of wars with the subdivi-
     sion *Songs* [to be added as
     needed]
BT   **Music**
NT   **Band music**
     Marches (Music)
     World War, 1939-1945—Songs
Military occupation   **341.6; 355.4**
UF   Occupation, Military
     Occupied territory
SA   names of occupied countries
     with the appropriate subdivi-
     sion under *History*, e.g.,
     Netherlands—History—1940-
     1945, German occupation;
     Japan—History—1945-1952,
     Allied occupation; etc. [to be
     added as needed]
BT   **War**
NT   **World War, 1939-1945—Occu-**
     pied territories
RT   **Military government**
Military offenses (May subdiv. geog.)
    343; 355.1
UF   Crimes, Military
     Military crimes
     Naval offenses
     Offenses, Military

Military offenses—*Continued*
  SA types of military offenses, e.g.
      Military desertion [to be
      added as needed]
  BT **Criminal law**
      Military law
  NT **Military desertion**
Military offenses—United States **343;**
355.1
  UF United States—Military offenses
Military pensions (May subdiv. geog.)
331.25
  UF Naval pensions
      Pensions, Naval
      War pensions
  BT **Pensions**
  RT **Veterans**
Military personnel (May subdiv. geog.)
355.3
  UF Military life
      Servicemen
      Servicewomen
  SA names of countries with the sub-
      division *Armed forces* or the
      subheads *Army* or *Navy*, etc.,
      with the subdivision *Military
      life* or *Officers*, e.g. **United
      States—Armed forces—Mili-
      tary life**; **United States.
      Army—Officers**; etc. [to be
      added as needed]
  BT **Armed forces**
      War
  NT **Admirals**
      Armies
      **Gays and lesbians in the mili-
      tary**
      Generals
      Mercenary soldiers
      Navies
      Recruiting and enlistment
      Sailors
      Soldiers
      **United States. Army—Military
      life**
      United States. Army—Officers
      United States. Navy—Officers
      **United States—Armed forces—
      Military life**
      Women in the military
  RT **Military art and science**
      Veterans

Military personnel—Health and hygiene
613.6
  UF Hygiene, Military
      Military health
      Soldiers—Hygiene
  SA names of wars with the subdivi-
      sion *Health aspects* or *Medi-
      cal care*, e.g. **World War,
      1939-1945—Health aspects**;
      **World War, 1939-1945—
      Medical care**; etc. [to be
      added as needed]
  BT **Hygiene**
  RT **Armies—Medical care**
      Military medicine
Military personnel missing in action
  USE **Missing in action**
Military personnel—United States
355.30973
  UF United States—Military person-
      nel
Military policy (May subdiv. geog.) **355**
  UF Defense policy
      Government policy
  BT **Military history**
  NT **Military assistance**
      Military readiness
  RT **National security**
Military policy—United States **355**
  UF United States—Military policy
  NT **Strategic Defense Initiative**
Military posts
  USE **Military bases**
Military power
  USE **Armies**
      Military art and science
      Navies
      Sea power
Military preparedness
  USE **Military readiness**
Military readiness **355**
    Use for materials on military strength, in-
  cluding military personnel, munitions, natural
  resources, and industrial war potential. Materi-
  als on the implements of war are entered un-
  der **Ordnance** or **Military weapons**. Materi-
  als on the industries producing them are entered under **Defense industry**.
  UF Armaments
      Defense readiness
      Military preparedness
      National defenses

Military readiness—*Continued*
 SA names of countries with the sub-
     division *Defenses*, e.g. **United**
     States—Defenses [to be add-
     ed as needed]
 BT **Military policy**
 NT **United States—Defenses**
 RT **Armed forces**
     Arms control
     Arms race
     Defense industry
     Industrial mobilization
     Manpower
Military research (May subdiv. geog.)
     355
 UF Defense research
 BT **Research**
Military sales
 USE **Arms transfers**
     Defense industry
     Military assistance
Military schools
 USE **Military education**
Military science
 USE **Military art and science**
Military service, Compulsory
 USE **Draft**
Military service, Voluntary
 USE **Voluntary military service**
Military signaling
 USE **Signals and signaling**
Military strategy
 USE **Strategy**
Military supplies industry
 USE **Defense industry**
Military tactics
 USE **Tactics**
Military tanks   358; 623.7
 UF Armored cars (Tanks)
     Tanks (Military science)
 BT **Military vehicles**
 RT **Tank warfare**
Military training
 USE **Military education**
Military training camps (May subdiv.
     geog.) **355.7**
 UF Students' military training camps
     Training camps, Military
 BT **Military education**
Military training, Universal
 USE **Draft**
Military transportation   358

 UF Transportation, Military
 SA names of wars with the subdivi-
     sion *Transportation*, e.g.
     World War, 1939-1945—
     Transportation [to be added
     as needed]
 BT **Military art and science**
     Transportation
 NT **Military vehicles**
Military uniforms   355.1
 UF Naval uniforms
     Uniforms, Military
     Uniforms, Naval
 SA names of military services with
     the subdivision *Uniforms*, e.g.
     United States. Army—Uni-
     forms [to be added as need-
     ed]
 BT **Uniforms**
Military vehicles   355.8
 UF Army vehicles
     Vehicles, Military
 BT **Military transportation**
     Vehicles
 NT **Military tanks**
Military weapons (May subdiv. geog.)
     355.8; 623.4
 UF Armaments
     Arms sales
     Munitions
 SA names of wars with the subdivi-
     sion *Equipment and supplies*
     [to be added as needed]
 BT **Ordnance**
     Weapons
 NT **Nuclear weapons**
     Space weapons
     World War, 1939-1945—
     Equipment and supplies
 RT **Arms race**
     Defense industry
Militia
 USE names of countries and states
     with the subdivision *Militia,*
     e.g. **United States—Militia**
     [to be added as needed]
Militia movements (May subdiv. geog.)
     303.48
 Use for materials on anti-government
 paramilitary social movements.
 UF Militias
     Paramilitary militia movements

Militia movements—*Continued*
    BT   **Radicalism**
          Social movements
Militias
    USE **Militia movements**
Milk   637; 641.3
    BT   **Dairy products**
          Dairying
          Food
    NT   **Dried milk**
Milk—Analysis   637; 641.3
Milk supply   338.1
    BT   **Food adulteration and inspection**
          Public health
Milky Way   523.1
    BT   **Galaxies**
Mill and factory buildings
    USE **Factories**
Millenarianism
    USE **Millennium**
Millennialism
    USE **Millennium**
Millennium   236
    UF   Millenarianism
          Millennialism
    BT   **Eschatology**
    RT   **Second Advent**
Millikan rays
    USE **Cosmic rays**
Millinery
    USE **Hats**
Milling (Flour)
    USE **Flour mills**
Millionaires (May subdiv. geog.)   **920**
    BT   **Rich**
Mills (May subdiv. geog.)   **670.42**
    UF   Mills and millwork
    SA   types of mills [to be added as needed]
    BT   **Manufactures**
          Technology
    NT   **Flour mills**
    RT   **Factories**
          Machinery
Mills and millwork
    USE **Mills**
Mime   792.3
    BT   **Acting**
    RT   **Pantomimes**

Mind
    USE **Intellect**
          Psychology
Mind and body   128; 150
    UF   Body and mind
    BT   **Brain**
          Medicine
          Parapsychology
          Philosophy
    NT   **Abnormal psychology**
          Biofeedback training
          Body image
          Consciousness
          Mental suggestion
          Psychosomatic medicine
          Sleep
          Temperament
    RT   **Holistic medicine**
          Human body
          Hypnotism
          Mental healing
          Mental health
          Phrenology
          Psychoanalysis
          Psychophysiology
          Spiritual healing
          Subconsciousness
Mind control
    USE **Brainwashing**
Mind cure
    USE **Mental healing**
Mind reading
    USE **Telepathy**
Mine surveying   622.028
    BT   **Mining engineering**
          Prospecting
          Surveying
Mineral lands
    USE **Mines and mineral resources**
Mineral resources
    USE **Mines and mineral resources**
Mineral resources, Marine
    USE **Marine mineral resources**
Mineralogy
    USE **Minerals**
          Natural history
Minerals (May subdiv. geog.)   **549**
    Use for materials on the chemical and geological aspects of natural compounds extracted from the earth. Materials on mines and mining and the potential economic value of minerals are entered under **Mines and mineral resources**.

Minerals—*Continued*
UF Mineralogy
SA names of minerals, e.g. **Quartz**
[to be added as needed]
BT **Geology**
NT **Asbestos**
Gems
Gypsum
Lime
Minerals in human nutrition
Minerals in the body
Ores
Precious stones
Quartz
RT **Crystals**
Mines and mineral resources
Natural history
Petrology
Minerals in human nutrition   612.3;
613.3
BT **Food**
Minerals
Nutrition
Minerals in the body   612.3; 613.2
SA individual minerals in the body,
e.g. **Iron in the body** [to be
added as needed]
BT **Metabolism**
Minerals
Minerals in the body
NT **Iron in the body**
Minerals in the body
Miners (May subdiv. geog.)   622.092;
920
SA types of miners [to be added as
needed]
BT **Labor**
NT **Coal miners**
Miners—Diseases   616.9
UF Miners' diseases
BT **Occupational diseases**
Miners' diseases
USE **Miners—Diseases**
Mines and mineral resources (May
subdiv. geog.)   **333.8; 338.2**
Use for materials on mines and mining and
the potential economic value of minerals. Ma-
terials on the chemical or geological aspects
of natural compounds extracted from the earth
are entered under **Minerals**.
UF Mineral lands
Mineral resources
Mining

SA types of mines and mining, e.g.
Coal mines and mining [to
be added as needed]
BT **Economic geology**
Natural resources
Raw materials
NT **Coal mines and mining**
Gold mines and mining
Marine mineral resources
Mining engineering
Precious metals
Prospecting
Silver mines and mining
RT **Minerals**
**Mines and mineral resources—United
States**   333.8; 338.2
Miniature gardens   635.9
UF Gardens, Miniature
Tray gardens
BT **Gardens**
Miniature objects
RT **Container gardening**
Indoor gardening
Terrariums
Miniature objects   688; 745.592
UF Miniatures
Tiny objects
SA types of objects with the subdi-
vision *Models* [to be added as
needed]
BT **Art objects**
NT **Doll furniture**
Dollhouses
Miniature gardens
Miniature painting
Models and modelmaking
RT **Toys**
Miniature painting   751.7; 757
UF Miniatures (Portraits)
Portrait miniatures
BT **Miniature objects**
Painting
RT **Portrait painting**
Miniatures
USE **Miniature objects**
Miniatures (Illumination of books and
manuscripts)
USE **Illumination of books and
manuscripts**
Miniatures (Portraits)
USE **Miniature painting**

Minibikes 629.227
  BT **Bicycles**
       Motorcycles
Minimum drinking age
  USE **Drinking age**
Minimum wage (May subdiv. geog.)
      331.2
  BT **Salaries, wages, etc.**
Mining
  USE **Mines and mineral resources**
      Mining engineering
Mining, Electric
  USE **Electricity in mining**
Mining engineering (May subdiv. geog.)
      622
  UF Mining
  BT **Civil engineering**
      Coal mines and mining
      Engineering
      Mines and mineral resources
  NT **Drilling and boring (Earth and rocks)**
      Mine surveying
      Ocean mining
  RT **Electricity in mining**
Mining, Ocean
  USE **Ocean mining**
Ministers (Diplomatic agents)
  USE **Diplomats**
Ministers of state
  USE **Cabinet officers**
Ministers of the gospel
  USE **Clergy**
Ministry 206; 253
  UF Clergy—Office
  SA ministries of particular religions, e.g. **Christian ministry** [to be added as needed]
  BT **Church work**
      Pastoral theology
  NT **Christian ministry**
  RT **Clergy**
Minor arts
  USE **Decorative arts**
Minor planets
  USE **Asteroids**
Minor tactics
  USE **Drill and minor tactics**
Minorites
  USE **Franciscans**

Minorities (May subdiv. geog.) **305.8; 323.1**
  UF Foreign population
      Minority groups
  SA names of particular ethnic and racial minorities and of national groups in a foreign country, e.g. **African Americans**; **Mexican Americans**; **Mexicans—United States**; etc.; names of places with the subdivision *Race relations*, e.g. **United States—Race relations**; names of places with the subdivision *Ethnic relations*, e.g. **United States—Ethnic relations**; and headings for minorities in various industries and fields of endeavor, e.g., **Minorities in broadcasting** [to be added as needed]
  NT **Aliens**
      Immigrants
      Mexican Americans
      Mexicans—United States
      Minorities in broadcasting
      Minorities in television broadcasting
      Minorities on television
      Minority business enterprises
      Minority women
      Minority youth
  RT **Discrimination**
      Ethnic relations
      Race relations
      Segregation
Minorities in broadcasting **384.5; 791.4**
  Use for materials on minority involvement in the broadcasting industry.
  UF Minority groups in broadcasting
  SA names of particular minority groups in broadcasting or in particular broadcast media, e.g. **African Americans in television broadcasting** [to be added as needed]
  BT **Broadcasting**
      Minorities
  NT **Minorities in television broadcasting**
Minorities in engineering **620**

Minorities in engineering—*Continued*
UF   Minority groups in engineering
BT   **Engineering**
Minorities in television
USE   **Minorities on television**
Minorities in television broadcasting
791.45
Use for materials on all aspects of minority involvement in television. Materials on the portrayal of minorities in television programs are entered under **Minorities on television**.
UF   Minorities in the television industry
SA   names of particular minority groups in television broadcasting, e.g. **African Americans in television broadcasting** [to be added as needed]
BT   **Minorities**
Minorities in broadcasting
Television broadcasting
Minorities in the television industry
USE   **Minorities in television broadcasting**
Minorities on television   791.45
Use for materials on the portrayal of minorities in television programs. Materials on all aspects of minority involvement in television are entered under **Minorities in television broadcasting**.
UF   Minorities in television
SA   names of particular minority groups in television, e.g. **African Americans on television** [to be added as needed]
BT   **Minorities**
Television
Minority business enterprises   338.6
UF   Minority businesses
Minority-owned business enterprises
BT   **Business enterprises**
Minorities
Minority business enterprises—Federal aid
USE   **Federal aid to minority business enterprises**
Minority businesses
USE   **Minority business enterprises**
Minority groups
USE   **Minorities**
Minority groups in broadcasting
USE   **Minorities in broadcasting**
Minority groups in engineering
USE   **Minorities in engineering**

Minority-owned business enterprises
USE   **Minority business enterprises**
Minority women   305.48
BT   **Minorities**
Women
Minority youth   305.235
BT   **Minorities**
Youth
Minstrels   791.092; 920
BT   **Poets**
NT   **Troubadours**
Mints   332.4
BT   **Money**
RT   **Coinage**
Miracle plays
USE   **Mysteries and miracle plays**
Miracles   202; 212; 231.7
Use for materials on miracles in any or all religious traditions.
RT   **Spiritual healing**
Supernatural
Mirrors   748.8
UF   Looking glasses
BT   **Furniture**
Miscarriage   618.3
UF   Fetal death
BT   **Pregnancy**
Miscellanea
USE   **Books of lists**
Curiosities and wonders
and subjects with the subdivision *Miscellanea,* e.g. **Medicine—Miscellanea** [to be added as needed]
Miscellaneous facts
USE   **Books of lists**
Curiosities and wonders
Misconduct in office (May subdiv. geog.)
353.4
UF   Malfeasance in office
Official misconduct
SA   names of specific incidents and offenses [to be added as needed]
BT   **Conflict of interests**
Criminal law
NT   **Police corruption**
RT   **Political corruption**
Misdemeanors (Law)
USE   **Criminal law**
Misleading advertising
USE   **Deceptive advertising**

Misrepresentation in advertising
　USE　**Deceptive advertising**
Missiles, Ballistic
　USE　**Ballistic missiles**
Missiles, Guided
　USE　**Guided missiles**
Missing children (May subdiv. geog.)
　　362.82; 363.2
　UF　Lost children
　BT　**Children**
　　　Missing persons
　NT　**Runaway children**
Missing in action　341.6; 355.7
　UF　MIAs
　　　Military personnel missing in action
　SA　names of wars with the subdivision *Missing in action* [to be added as needed]
　BT　**Prisoners of war**
　　　Soldiers
　NT　**World War, 1939-1945—Missing in action**
Missing persons (May subdiv. geog.)
　　363.2
　BT　**Criminal investigation**
　NT　**Missing children**
　　　Runaway adults
　　　Runaway teenagers
Missionaries, Christian
　USE　**Christian missionaries**
Missions
　USE　names of Christian churches, denominations, religious orders, etc., with the subdivision *Missions,* e.g. **Catholic Church—Missions;** and names of peoples evangelized with the subdivision *Christian missions,* e.g. **Native Americans—Christian missions** [to be added as needed]
Missions, Christian
　USE　**Christian missions**
Missions, Medical
　USE　**Medical missions**
Mississippi River Valley　977
　UF　Mississippi Valley
　BT　**United States**
　NT　**Middle West**
Mississippi River Valley—History　977

　UF　New France—History
Mississippi Valley
　USE　**Mississippi River Valley**
Mistakes
　USE　**Errors**
Mixed marriage
　USE　**Interfaith marriage**
　　　Intermarriage
Mixed race people
　USE　**Racially mixed people**
Mixology
　USE　**Bartending**
Mnemonics　153.1
　SA　subjects, types of literature, and titles of sacred works with the subdivision *Memorizing,* e.g. **Poetry—Memorizing** [to be added as needed]
　NT　**Poetry—Memorizing**
　RT　**Memory**
Mobile home living　643; 728.7
　BT　**Home economics**
　　　Mobile homes
　NT　**Trailer parks**
Mobile home parks
　USE　**Trailer parks**
Mobile homes　643; 728.7
　　Use for materials on stationary transportable structures designed for year-round living. Materials on structures mounted upon a truck or towed by a truck or automobile for the purpose of temporary dwelling or cargo hauling are entered under **Travel trailers and campers**.
　UF　House trailers
　　　Trailers
　BT　**Housing**
　NT　**Mobile home living**
　RT　**Travel trailers and campers**
Mobiles (Sculpture)　731
　BT　**Kinetic sculpture**
　　　Sculpture
Mobilization, Industrial
　USE　**Industrial mobilization**
Mobs
　USE　**Crowds**
　　　Riots
Mock epic literature
　USE　**Mock-heroic literature**
Mock-heroic literature　800
　　Use for individual works, collections, or materials about mock-heroic literature.
　UF　Comic epic literature
　　　Mock epic literature

Mock-heroic literature—*Continued*
  BT **Literature**
      Wit and humor
  RT **Epic literature**
      Humorous fiction
Model airplanes
  USE **Airplanes—Models**
Model cars
  USE **Automobiles—Models**
Model making
  USE **Models and modelmaking**
Model ships
  USE **Ships—Models**
Model trains
  USE **Locomotives—Models**
      Railroads—Models
Modeling   731.4; 738.1
  UF Clay modeling
  BT **Clay**
      Sculpture
  NT **Soap sculpture**
  RT **Sculpture—Technique**
Modelmaking
  USE **Models and modelmaking**
Models
  USE **Artists' models**
      Fashion models
      Mathematical models
      Models and modelmaking
      and types of objects with the
        subdivision *Models,* e.g. **Air-**
        planes—Models [to be added
        as needed]
Models and model making
  USE **Models and modelmaking**
Models and modelmaking   688
  UF Model making
      Modelmaking
      Models
      Models and model making
  SA types of objects with the subdi-
        vision *Models*, e.g. **Air-**
        planes—Models [to be added
        as needed]
  BT **Handicraft**
      Miniature objects
  NT **Airplanes—Models**
      Automobiles—Models
      Locomotives—Models
      Machinery—Models
      Motorboats—Models
      Patternmaking

      Railroads—Models
      Ships—Models
Models, Artists'
  USE **Artists' models**
Models, Mathematical
  USE **Mathematical models**
Models, Mechanical
  USE **Machinery—Models**
Models (Persons)
  USE **Artists' models**
      Fashion models
Modern architecture
  USE **Modernism in architecture**
Modern architecture—1600-1799 (17th and
    18th centuries)
  USE **Architecture—17th and 18th**
        centuries
Modern architecture—1800-1899 (19th cen-
    tury)
  USE **Architecture—19th century**
Modern architecture—1900-1999 (20th cen-
    tury)
  USE **Architecture—20th century**
Modern architecture—2000-2099 (21st cen-
    tury)
  USE **Architecture—21st century**
Modern art
  USE **Modernism in art**
Modern art—1800-1899 (19th century)
  USE **Art—19th century**
Modern art—1900-1999 (20th century)
  USE **Art—20th century**
Modern art—2000-2099 (21st century)
  USE **Art—21st century**
Modern church history
  USE **Church history—1500-, Mod-**
        ern period
Modern civilization   306.09; 909
    Use for materials on cultural and intellectu-
    al developments since 1453 not limited to a
    single country or region.
  UF Civilization, Modern
  BT **Civilization**
  NT **Enlightenment**
Modern civilization—1950-   306.09;
    909.82
    Use for materials on cultural and intellectu-
    al developments since 1950 not limited to a
    single country or region.
Modern dance   792.8
  UF Interpretive dance
  BT **Dance**

Modern Greek language   489

May be subdivided like **English language**.

UF   Greek language, Modern

Romaic language

BT   **Language and languages**

RT   **Greek language**

Modern Greek literature   889

May use same subdivisions and names of literary forms as for **English literature**.

UF   Greek literature, Modern

Neo-Greek literature

Romaic literature

BT   **Literature**

Modern history   909.08

Use for materials covering the period after 1453.

UF   History, Modern

BT   **World history**

Modern history—1800-1899 (19th century)

USE   **World history—19th century**

Modern history—1900-1999 (20th century)

USE   **World history—20th century**

Modern history—1945-

USE   **World history—1945-**

Modern history—Study and teaching 907

NT   **Current events**

Modern languages   410

Use for materials dealing collectively with living literary languages. May be subdivided like **English language**.

UF   Languages, Modern

BT   **Language and languages**

Modern languages—Conversation and phrase books   418

Use for instructional materials or for books of convenient conversations and phrases for travelers.

UF   Conversation and phrase books

Conversation in foreign languages

Conversations and phrases

Foreign language phrases

SA   names of languages with the subdivision *Conversation and phrase books*, e.g. **French language—Conversation and phrase books** [to be added as needed]

Modern languages—Study and teaching 418

RT   **Language laboratories**

Modern literature

USE   **Literature**

Modernism in literature

Modern painting—1800-1899 (19th century)

USE   **Painting—19th century**

Modern painting—1900-1999 (20th century)

USE   **Painting—20th century**

Modern painting—2000-2099 (21st century)

USE   **Painting—21st century**

Modern philosophy   190

Use for materials on developments in Western philosophy since the Middle Ages.

UF   Philosophy, Modern

BT   **Philosophy**

NT   **Enlightenment**

Existentialism

Phenomenology

Modern sculpture

USE   **Modernism in sculpture**

Modern sculpture—1900-1999 (20th century)

USE   **Sculpture—20th century**

Modernism

USE   **Modernism (Aesthetics)**

Modernism (Theology)

Modernism (Aesthetics)   700.1

Use for materials on the philosophy and practice of the arts since the nineteenth century characterized by a self-conscious break with the past and a search for new forms of expression.

UF   Modernism

Modernism (Arts)

BT   **Aesthetics**

NT   **Avant-garde (Aesthetics)**

Modernism in architecture

Modernism in art

Modernism in literature

Modernism in sculpture

RT   **Postmodernism**

Modernism (Art)

USE   **Modernism in art**

Modernism (Arts)

USE   **Modernism (Aesthetics)**

Modernism in architecture   724

Use for materials on the theory and practice of modernism in the architecture.

UF   Architecture, Modern

Modern architecture

BT   **Architecture**

Modernism (Aesthetics)

Modernism in art   709.04

Use for materials on the theory and practice of modernism in the visual arts.

UF   Modern art
Modernism (Art)
BT   **Art**
Modernism (Aesthetics)

Modernism in literature   801

UF   Modern literature
Modernism (Literature)
BT   **Literature**
Modernism (Aesthetics)

Modernism in sculpture   735

UF   Modern sculpture
Modernism (Sculpture)
Sculpture, Modern
BT   **Modernism (Aesthetics)**
Sculpture

Modernism (Literature)
USE   **Modernism in literature**

Modernism (Sculpture)
USE   **Modernism in sculpture**

Modernism (Theology)   230; 273

Use for materials on the movement in the Christian churches that applies modern critical methods to biblical study and the history of dogma, and emphasizes the spiritual and ethical side of religion over historic dogmas and creeds.

UF   Modernism
Modernist-fundamentalist controversy
BT   **Christianity—Doctrines**
RT   **Christian fundamentalism**

Modernist-fundamentalist controversy
USE   **Christian fundamentalism**
Modernism (Theology)

Modernization
USE   **Modernization (Sociology)**

Modernization (Sociology) (May subdiv. geog.)   **303.44**

Use for materials on the process by which traditional societies achieve the political, cultural, economic, and social characteristics of modernity.

UF   Development
Modernization
BT   **Social change**
RT   **Industrialization**

Mold (Fungi)
USE   **Molds (Fungi)**

Molding (Metal)
USE   **Founding**

Molds (Botany)
USE   **Molds (Fungi)**

Molds (Fungi)   579.5

UF   Mold (Fungi)
Molds (Botany)
BT   **Fungi**

Molecular biochemistry
USE   **Molecular biology**

Molecular biology   591.6

UF   Biology, Molecular
Molecular biochemistry
Molecular biophysics
BT   **Biochemistry**
Biophysics
NT   **Genetic code**

Molecular biophysics
USE   **Molecular biology**

Molecular cloning   572.8

UF   DNA cloning
BT   **Cloning**
Genetic engineering

Molecular technology
USE   **Nanotechnology**

Molecules   539; 541.2

BT   **Physical chemistry**

Molesting of children
USE   **Child sexual abuse**

Mollusks   594

Use for materials on mollusks and for systematic and comprehensive materials on shells. Popular materials on shells and shell collecting are entered under **Shells**.

BT   **Shellfish**
RT   **Shells**

Monarchs
USE   **Kings and rulers**

Monarchy (May subdiv. geog.)   **321; 321.8**

UF   Royal houses
Royalty
Sovereigns
BT   **Constitutional history**
Constitutional law
Executive power
Political science
NT   **Empresses**
Queens
RT   **Kings and rulers**

Monasteries (May subdiv. geog.)   **255; 271; 726**

UF   Cloisters

Monasteries—*Continued*
  BT **Church architecture**
      Church history
  NT **Abbeys**
      Convents
  RT **Monasticism and religious orders**

Monastic orders
  USE **Monasticism and religious orders**

Monasticism
  USE **Monasticism and religious orders**

Monasticism and religious orders (May subdiv. geog.) **255; 271**

Use for materials on the institution of monasticism and for general materials on religious orders not limited to orders for a single sex. This heading may be subdivided by religion or denomination as needed.

  UF Monastic orders
      Monasticism
      Orders, Monastic
      Religious orders
  SA names of monastic and religious orders, e.g. **Franciscans** [to be added as needed]
  NT **Franciscans**
      Monasticism and religious orders for men
      Monasticism and religious orders for women
  RT **Hermits**
      Religious life

Monasticism and religious orders for men 255; 271

This heading may be subdivided by religion or denomination as needed.

  UF Religious orders for men
  BT **Monasticism and religious orders**
  RT **Monks**

Monasticism and religious orders for women 255; 271

This heading may be subdivided by religion or denomination as needed.

  UF Religious orders for women
      Sisterhoods
  BT **Convents**
      Monasticism and religious orders
  RT **Nuns**

Monetary policy (May subdiv. geog.)
      332.4
  UF Currency devaluation
      Devaluation of currency
      Free coinage
      Government policy
  BT **Economic policy**
  RT **Finance**
      Fiscal policy
      Inflation (Finance)
      Money

Monetary policy—United States 332.4
  UF United States—Monetary policy

Monetary unions (May subdiv. geog.)
      332.4
  UF Common currencies
  BT **Money**

Money (May subdiv. geog.) **332.4**

Use for materials on currency as a medium of exchange or measure of value and for general materials on various types of money.

  UF Currency
      Legal tender
      Standard of value
  BT **Economics**
      Exchange
      Finance
  NT **Barter**
      Children's allowances
      Coinage
      Coins
      Counterfeits and counterfeiting
      Credit
      Euro
      Foreign exchange
      Mints
      Monetary unions
      Paper money
  RT **Banks and banking**
      Gold
      Monetary policy
      Silver
      Wealth

Money-making projects for children 332.024; 650.1
  UF Children's moneymaking projects
      Moneymaking projects for children
  BT **Business enterprises**
  RT **Children's allowances**

Money raising
  USE **Fund raising**

Moneymaking projects for children
　USE **Money-making projects for children**

Monkeys (May subdiv. geog.)　**599.8**
　BT **Primates**

Monkeys—Behavior　**599.8**
　UF Monkeys—Habits and behavior
　BT **Animal behavior**

Monkeys—Habits and behavior
　USE **Monkeys—Behavior**

Monks　**255; 271**
　RT **Monasticism and religious orders for men**

Monograms　**745.6**
　UF Ciphers (Lettering)
　BT **Alphabets**
　　Decoration and ornament
　　Lettering
　RT **Initials**

Monologues　**808.85**
　Use for individual works, collections, or materials about monologues. Monologues with incidental musical background and musical works in which spoken language is an integral part are entered under **Monologues with music**.
　UF Declamations
　　Narrations
　BT **Recitations**
　RT **Monologues with music**

Monologues with music　**808.85; 782.2**
　Use for musical scores and for materials about monologues with incidental musical background and musical works in which spoken language is an integral part. Individual monologues without music, collections, and materials about monologues without music are entered under **Monologues**.
　UF Musical declamation
　　Narration with music
　　Recitations with music
　BT **Recitations**
　RT **Monologues**

Monopolies (May subdiv. geog.)　**338.8**
　BT **Commerce**
　　Economics
　RT **Competition**
　　Corporation law
　　Industrial trusts
　　Restraint of trade

Monorail railroads　**385.5; 625.1**
　UF Railroads, Single rail
　　Single rail railroads
　BT **Railroads**

Monotheism (May subdiv. geog.)　**211**

　BT **Religion**
　　Theism
　RT **God**

Monroe Doctrine　**327.73**
　BT **International relations**
　　Intervention (International law)
　　United States—Foreign relations

Monster films
　USE **Horror films**

Monsters　**001.9; 398.2**
　Use for materials on legendary animals combining features of human and animal form or having the forms of various animals in combination. Materials on human abnormalities are entered under either **Birth defects** or **Growth disorders**.
　BT **Animals—Folklore**
　　Curiosities and wonders
　　Folklore
　　Mythology
　NT **Dragons**
　　Giants
　　Loch Ness monster
　　Sasquatch
　　Yeti

Montessori method of education　**371.39**
　BT **Elementary education**
　　Kindergarten
　　Teaching

Months　**529**
　SA names of the months [to be added as needed]
　BT **Calendars**
　　Chronology
　NT **Special months**

Monumental brasses
　USE **Brasses**

Monuments (May subdiv. geog.)　**725**
　UF Statues
　SA ethnic groups, classes of persons, individual persons, families, and wars with the subdivision *Monuments*, e.g. **World War, 1939-1945—Monuments** [to be added as needed]
　BT **Architecture**
　　Sculpture
　NT **Historic buildings**
　　National monuments
　　Natural monuments
　　Obelisks

Monuments—*Continued*

    Pyramids

    Tombs

    World War, 1939-1945—Monuments

Mood disorders

  USE **Affective disorders**

Moon 523.3

  BT **Astronomy**

    Solar system

Moon bases

  USE **Lunar bases**

Moon—Eclipses

  USE **Lunar eclipses**

Moon—Exploration 629.45

  UF Lunar exploration

  BT **Space flight to the moon**

Moon—Folklore 398.26

Moon—Geology

  USE **Lunar geology**

Moon—Maps 523.3022

  BT **Maps**

Moon—Photographs

  USE **Moon—Pictorial works**

Moon—Pictorial works 523.3; 778.3

  UF Moon—Photographs

  BT **Space photography**

Moon probes

  USE **Lunar probes**

Moon—Religious aspects 299.9

Moon rocks 552.0999

  UF Lunar petrology

    Lunar rocks

  BT **Lunar geology**

    Petrology

Moon soil

  USE **Lunar soil**

Moon—Surface 523.3

  UF Lunar surface

  RT **Lunar soil**

Moon, Voyages to

  USE **Space flight to the moon**

Moon worship 202

  BT **Religion**

Moonlighting

  USE **Supplementary employment**

Moons

  USE **Satellites**

Moorish architecture

  USE **Islamic architecture**

Moors

  USE **Muslims**

Moral and philosophic stories

  USE **Didactic fiction**

    Fables

    Parables

Moral conditions 301; 306; 900

  UF Morals

  SA names of countries, cities, etc., with the subdivision *Moral conditions* [to be added as needed]

  BT **Social conditions**

  NT **Chicago (Ill.)—Moral conditions**

    Ohio—Moral conditions

    United States—Moral conditions

Moral development 155.2; 155.4

  UF Ethical development

  BT **Child psychology**

    Moral education

Moral education (May subdiv. geog.) 370.11

  UF Character education

    Ethical education

  BT **Education**

    Ethics

  NT **Moral development**

  RT **Religious education**

Moral philosophy

  USE **Ethics**

Moral theology, Christian

  USE **Christian ethics**

Morale 152.4

  SA types of morale, e.g. **Employee morale** [to be added as needed]

  BT **Courage**

  NT **Employee morale**

    Psychological warfare

Moralities

  USE **Morality plays**

Morality

  USE **Ethics**

Morality plays 792.1; 808.82

  Use for individual works, collections, or materials about plays in which the chief characters are personifications of abstract qualities.

  UF Moralities

  BT **Drama**

    English drama

    Religious drama

    Theater

Morality plays—*Continued*
    RT   **Mysteries and miracle plays**
Morality stories
    USE **Didactic fiction**
Morality tales
    USE **Parables**
Morals
    USE **Conduct of life**
            Ethics
            Human behavior
            Moral conditions
Moravians (May subdiv. geog.)   **284**
    UF   United Brethren
    BT   **Christian sects**
Mormon Church
    USE **Church of Jesus Christ of Latter-day Saints**
Mormons (May subdiv. geog.)   **289.3092**
    RT   **Church of Jesus Christ of Latter-day Saints**
Morocco 964
       May be subdivided like **United States** except for *History*.
Morphine 362.29; 615
    BT   **Narcotics**
    NT   **Heroin**
    RT   **Opium**
Morphology 571.3
    UF   Biological form
           Biological structure
           Comparative morphology
           Form in biology
           Structure in biology
    SA   animals, languages, plants, and crops with the subdivision *Morphology* [to be added as needed]
    BT   **Comparative anatomy**
Morse code
    USE **Cipher and telegraph codes**
Mortality (May subdiv. geog.)   **304.6**
    UF   Burial statistics
           Death rate
           Mortuary statistics
    SA   ethnic groups, classes of persons, diseases, and animals with the subdivision *Mortality*, for works on the number of deaths during a given time among a particular groups or due to a particular cause, e.g.

Infants—Mortality; Tuberculosis—Mortality; etc. [to be added as needed]
    BT   **Population**
           Vital statistics
    NT   **Children—Mortality**
           Infants—Mortality
    RT   **Death**
Mortar 666; 691
    BT   **Adhesives**
           Plaster and plastering
Mortgage loans
    USE **Mortgages**
Mortgages (May subdiv. geog.)   **332.63; 332.7**
    UF   Home loans
           Mortgage loans
    BT   **Loans**
           Securities
Morticians
    USE **Undertakers and undertaking**
Mortuary customs
    USE **Cremation**
           Funeral rites and ceremonies
Mortuary statistics
    USE **Mortality**
           Vital statistics
Mosaics 729; 738.5; 748.5
    BT   **Decoration and ornament**
           Decorative arts
    RT   **Mural painting and decoration**
Moslems
    USE **Muslims**
Mosques (May subdiv. geog.)   **726**
    BT   **Islamic architecture**
           Religious institutions
           Temples
Mosquitoes 595.77
    BT   **Insects**
Mosquitoes—Control 363.7
    BT   **Pest control**
Mosses (May subdiv. geog.)   **588**
    BT   **Plants**
Motels
    USE **Hotels and motels**
Mother and child
    USE **Mother-child relationship**
Mother-child relationship 306.874
    UF   Child and mother
           Mother and child

Mother-child relationship—*Continued*
   BT   **Children**
        Mothers
        Parent-child relationship
   NT   **Mother-daughter relationship**
        Mother-son relationship
Mother-daughter relationship   305.4;
    306.874
   UF   Daughters and mothers
        Mothers and daughters
   BT   **Daughters**
        Mother-child relationship
        Mothers
Mother Goddess religion
   USE   **Goddess religion**
Mother-son relationship   306.874
   UF   Mothers and sons
        Sons and mothers
   BT   **Mother-child relationship**
        Mothers
        Sons
Motherhood   306.874
   BT   **Parenthood**
   RT   **Mothers**
Mothers (May subdiv. geog.)   306.874
   UF   Maternity
   BT   **Family**
        Women
   NT   **Mother-child relationship**
        Mother-daughter relationship
        Mother-son relationship
        Stepmothers
        Surrogate mothers
        Teenage mothers
        Unmarried mothers
   RT   **Motherhood**
Mothers and daughters
   USE   **Mother-daughter relationship**
Mothers and sons
   USE   **Mother-son relationship**
Mother's Day   394.2628
   BT   **Holidays**
Mothers' pensions
   USE   **Child welfare**
Moths (May subdiv. geog.)   595.78
   UF   Cocoons
        Lepidoptera
   BT   **Insects**
   NT   **Caterpillars**
        Silkworms
   RT   **Butterflies**
Motion   531

   UF   Kinetics
   BT   **Dynamics**
   NT   **Mechanical movements**
        Speed
   RT   **Force and energy**
        Kinematics
        Mechanics
Motion picture actors and actresses
   USE   **Actors**
Motion picture adaptations
   USE   **Film adaptations**
Motion picture cameras   778.5
   UF   Movie cameras
   BT   **Cameras**
        Cinematography
   RT   **Amateur films**
Motion picture cartoons
   USE   **Animated films**
Motion picture direction
   USE   **Motion pictures—Production
        and direction**
Motion picture directors
   USE   **Motion picture producers and
        directors**
Motion picture festivals
   USE   **Film festivals**
Motion picture industry (May subdiv.
    geog.)   384; 791.43
   UF   Film industry (Motion pictures)
   BT   **Industries**
   NT   **African Americans in the mo-
        tion picture industry**
        **Blacks in the motion picture
        industry**
        **Motion picture producers and
        directors**
        **Motion pictures—Production
        and direction**
        **Women in the motion picture
        industry**
   RT   **Motion pictures**
Motion picture musicals
   USE   **Musical films**
Motion picture photography
   USE   **Cinematography**
Motion picture plays
   USE   **Screenplays**
Motion picture plays—Technique   808.2
   UF   Motion pictures—Play writing
        Play writing
        Playwriting

Motion picture plays—Technique—_Continued_

    BT   **Drama—Technique**

Motion picture posters

    USE   **Film posters**

Motion picture producers

    USE   **Motion picture producers and directors**

Motion picture producers and directors

    (May subdiv. geog.)   **791.43; 920**

    UF   Film directors

          Film producers

          Motion picture directors

          Motion picture producers

    BT   **Motion picture industry**

    RT   **Motion pictures—Production and direction**

Motion picture production

    USE   **Motion pictures—Production and direction**

Motion picture projectors

    USE   **Projectors**

Motion picture scripts

    USE   **Screenplays**

Motion picture serials   **791.43**

    Use for individual works, collections, or materials about motion picture serials.

    BT   **Motion pictures**

Motion picture theaters (May subdiv. geog.)   **725**

    UF   Cinemas

          Movie theaters

    BT   **Theaters**

Motion pictures (May subdiv. geog.)   **384; 791.43**

    Use for general materials on motion pictures, including motion pictures as an art form. Materials on the technical aspects of making motion pictures and their projection onto a screen are entered under **Cinematography**. For materials on motion pictures produced by the motion picture industry of an individual country or on the motion pictures shown in a country, subdivide geographically, e.g. **Motion pictures—United States**.

    UF   Cinema

          Films

          Movies

    SA   types of motion pictures, e.g. **Documentary films**; **Horror films**; motion pictures and particular groups of persons, e.g., **Motion pictures and children**; motion pictures as used in various industries or fields of endeavor, e.g. **Motion pictures in education**; subjects and groups of persons portrayed in motion pictures, e.g. **Animals in motion pictures**; **Women in motion pictures**; groups of persons in the motion picture industry, e.g. **Women in the motion picture industry**; and names of individual motion pictures [to be added as needed]

    BT   **Audiovisual materials**

          Mass media

          Performing arts

    NT   **Academy Awards (Motion pictures)**

          Adventure films

          African Americans in motion pictures

          Amateur films

          Animals in motion pictures

          Animated films

          Apocalyptic films

          Bible films

          Biographical films

          Blacks in motion pictures

          Comedy films

          Documentary films

          Epic films

          Erotic films

          Experimental films

          Fantasy films

          Film adaptations

          Film noir

          Gangster films

          Horror films

          Legal drama (Films)

          Medical drama (Films)

          Motion picture serials

          Motion pictures and children

          Motion pictures in education

          Musical films

          Mystery films

          Science fiction films

          Sherlock Holmes films

          Short films

          Silent films

          Sports drama (Films)

          Spy films

Motion pictures—*Continued*
    Star Wars films
    Television movies
    Three Stooges films
    Vampire films
    War films
    Western films
    Women in motion pictures
    World War, 1939-1945—Motion pictures and the war
  RT **Motion picture industry**

Motion pictures, American
  USE **Motion pictures—United States**

Motion pictures and children 305.23; 649; 791.43
    Use for materials on the effect of motion pictures on children and youth.
  UF Children and motion pictures
  BT **Children**
    Motion pictures

Motion pictures and the war
  USE names of wars with the subdivision *Motion pictures and the war,* e.g. **World War, 1939-1945—Motion pictures and the war** [to be added as needed]

Motion pictures—Biography 791.43092; 920
  BT **Biography**

Motion pictures—Catalogs 016.79143
  UF Catalogs, Film
    Film catalogs
    Filmography
  SA types of motion pictures with the subdivision *Catalogs,* e.g. **Science fiction films—Catalogs**; and subjects, classes of persons, corporate entities, and names of individual persons with the subdivision *Filmography,* e.g. **Animals—Filmography**; **Shakespeare, William, 1564-1616—Filmography**; etc. [to be added as needed]

Motion pictures—Censorship (May subdiv. geog.) **791.43**
  BT **Censorship**

Motion pictures—Ethical aspects 791.43

  UF Motion pictures—Moral and religious aspects
  BT **Ethics**

Motion pictures in education 371.33
  UF Educational films
  BT **Audiovisual education**
    Motion pictures
    Teaching—Aids and devices

Motion pictures—Moral and religious aspects
  USE **Motion pictures—Ethical aspects**
    Motion pictures—Religious aspects

Motion pictures—Play writing
  USE **Motion picture plays—Technique**

Motion pictures—Posters
  USE **Film posters**

Motion pictures—Production and direction 384; 791.4302
  UF Film direction
    Film production
    Filmmaking
    Motion picture direction
    Motion picture production
  BT **Motion picture industry**
  RT **Motion picture producers and directors**

Motion pictures—Religious aspects 204; 248.4; 791.43
  UF Motion pictures—Moral and religious aspects

Motion pictures—Reviews 791.43

Motion pictures—Television adaptations
  USE **Television adaptations**

Motion pictures—United States 791.430973
    Use for materials on motion pictures produced by the motion picture industry of the United States or on motion pictures shown in the United States.
  UF American films
    American motion pictures
    Motion pictures, American

Motion study 658.5
  BT **Factory management**
    Industrial efficiency
    Job analysis
    Personnel management
    Production standards
  RT **Time study**

Motivation (Psychology)   153.8
    UF   Incentive (Psychology)
    BT   **Psychology**
    NT   **Achievement motivation**
          Burn out (Psychology)
          Wishes
Motor boats
    USE **Motorboats**
Motor buses
    USE **Buses**
Motor cars
    USE **Automobiles**
Motor coordination
    USE **Movement education**
Motor cycles
    USE **Motorcycles**
Motor trucks
    USE **Trucks**
Motor vehicle industry
    USE **Automobile industry**
Motor vehicles—Drivers' licenses
    USE **Drivers' licenses**
Motorboats   623.82
    UF   Motor boats
          Power boats
    BT   **Boats and boating**
Motorboats—Models   623.82
    BT   **Models and modelmaking**
Motorcycles (May subdiv. geog.)
        629.227
    UF   Motor cycles
    SA   specific makes and models of
          motorcycles [to be added as
          needed]
    BT   **Bicycles**
    NT   **Antique and vintage motorcy-
          cles**
          Minibikes
    RT   **Motorcycling**
Motorcycling (May subdiv. geog.)   **796.7**
    BT   **Cycling**
    RT   **Motorcycles**
Motoring
    USE **Automobile travel**
Motors
    USE **Electric motors**
          Engines
          and types of engines and mo-
          tors, e.g. **Steam engines;
          Electric motors;** etc., and
          types of vehicles and makes

and models of vehicles with
the subdivision *Motors,* e.g.
    Automobiles—Motors [to be
    added as needed]
Motorways
    USE **Express highways**
Mottoes   808.88; 929.8
    Use for collections of mottoes and for ma-
    terials about mottoes.
    UF   Emblems
    BT   **Heraldry**
    RT   **National emblems**
Moulding (Metal)
    USE **Founding**
Mound-builders
    USE **Mounds and mound builders**
Mounds and mound builders (May
        subdiv. geog.)   **930.1; 970.004**
    UF   Barrows
          Graves
          Mound-builders
    BT   **Archeology**
          Burial
          Tombs
    RT   **Excavations (Archeology)**
Mount Rainier (Wash.)   979.7
    BT   **Mountains**
Mountain animals (May subdiv. geog.)
        591.75
    UF   Alpine animals
          Alpine fauna
          Mountain fauna
    BT   **Animals**
Mountain bicycles
    USE **Mountain bikes**
Mountain bikes   629.227
    UF   All terrain bicycles
          Mountain bicycles
    BT   **All terrain vehicles**
          Bicycles
Mountain biking (May subdiv. geog.)
        796.63
    UF   All terrain cycling
    BT   **Cycling**
Mountain climbing
    USE **Mountaineering**
Mountain fauna
    USE **Mountain animals**
Mountain flora
    USE **Mountain plants**
Mountain life (May subdiv. geog.)
        307.72

Mountain life—*Continued*
   BT   **Country life**
Mountain people (May subdiv. geog.)
   307.7
   BT   **Ethnology**
Mountain plants (May subdiv. geog.)
   581.7; 635.9
   UF   Alpine flora
          Alpine plants
          Mountain flora
   BT   **Plant ecology**
          Plants
Mountaineering 796.522
   UF   Mountain climbing
          Rock climbing
   BT   **Outdoor life**
   RT   **Trails**
Mountains (May subdiv. geog.)   **551.43**
   SA   names of mountain ranges and
          of individual mountains [to be
          added as needed]
   BT   **Landforms**
          Physical geography
   NT   **Mount Rainier (Wash.)**
          Rocky Mountains
          Volcanoes
Mourning
   USE   **Bereavement**
Mourning customs
   USE   **Funeral rites and ceremonies**
Mouse
   USE   **Mice**
Mouth 591.4; 612.3
   BT   **Face**
          Head
Mouth—Diseases 617.5
   BT   **Diseases**
   NT   **Bad breath**
Movable books
   USE   **Toy and movable books**
Movement disorders 616.8
   UF   Diskinesia
   BT   **Disabilities**
          Nervous system—Diseases
Movement education 152.3; 153.7;
   372.86
   UF   Creative movement
          Motor coordination
   BT   **Physical education**
Movement, Freedom of
   USE   **Freedom of movement**

Movements of animals
   USE   **Animal locomotion**
Movie cameras
   USE   **Motion picture cameras**
Movie festivals
   USE   **Film festivals**
Movie novelizations
   USE   **Movie novels**
Movie novels 808.3
   Use for individual works, collections, or
   materials about novels based on movies.
   UF   Movie novelizations
          Movie tie-ins
   BT   **Fiction**
   RT   **Radio and television novels**
Movie posters
   USE   **Film posters**
Movie scripts
   USE   **Screenplays**
Movie theaters
   USE   **Motion picture theaters**
Movie tie-ins
   USE   **Movie novels**
Movies
   USE   **Motion pictures**
Moving 648
   Use for materials on changing the location
   of possessions, household, office, etc.
   UF   Household moving
          Moving, household
   BT   **Home economics**
Moving, household
   USE   **Moving**
MP3 players 006.5; 621.389
   BT   **Computer sound processing**
          Sound—Recording and repro-
          ducing
MRI (Magnetic resonance imaging)
   USE   **Magnetic resonance imaging**
Mulattoes
   USE   **Racially mixed people**
Multi-age grouping
   USE   **Nongraded schools**
Multicultural diversity in the workplace
   USE   **Diversity in the workplace**
Multicultural education (May subdiv.
   geog.) **370.117**
   Use for materials on the attempt to eradi-
   cate racial and religious prejudices through the
   study of various races, creeds, and immigrant
   cultures.
   UF   Intercultural education

Multicultural education—*Continued*
- BT **Acculturation**
  Education
  Multiculturalism
- NT **Bilingual education**
- RT **International education**
  Multicultural literature

Multicultural literature   808.8

Use for collections that bring together literatures of various cultures for the purpose of illustrating racial, religious, or ethnic diversity.
- BT **Literature**
  Multiculturalism
- RT **Multicultural education**

Multiculturalism (May subdiv. geog.)
    305.8; 306.44

Use for materials on policies or programs that foster the preservation of various cultures or cultural identities within a unified society. Materials on the coexistence of several distinct ethnic, religious, or cultural groups within one society are entered under **Pluralism (Social sciences)**. Materials on the presence of two distinct cultures within a single country or region are entered under **Biculturalism**.
- UF Diversity movement
- BT **Culture**
  Social policy
- NT **Diversity in the workplace**
  Multicultural education
  Multicultural literature
- RT **Biculturalism**
  Ethnic relations
  Ethnicity
  Pluralism (Social sciences)
  Race relations

Multilingual dictionaries
- USE **Polyglot dictionaries**

Multilingual glossaries, phrase books, etc.
- USE **Polyglot dictionaries**

Multilingualism (May subdiv. geog.)
    306.44
- BT **Language and languages**

Multimedia   006.7

Use for materials on computer systems, software, or data items that allow users to manipulate diverse integrated media, such as text, graphics, sound, etc.
- UF Computer-based multimedia information systems
  Interactive media
  Interactive multimedia
  Multimedia computing
  Multimedia information systems
  Multimedia knowledge systems
  Multimedia systems
- SA subjects with the subdivision *Interactive multimedia*, e.g. **Geology—Interactive multimedia** [to be added as needed]
- BT **Computer software**
  Information systems
- NT **Hypertext**

Multimedia centers
- USE **Instructional materials centers**

Multimedia computing
- USE **Multimedia**

Multimedia information systems
- USE **Multimedia**

Multimedia knowledge systems
- USE **Multimedia**

Multimedia materials
- USE **Audiovisual materials**

Multimedia systems
- USE **Multimedia**

Multinational corporations (May subdiv. geog.)   **338.8; 658**
- UF Business—International aspects
  Corporations, Multinational
  International business enterprises
- BT **Business enterprises**
  Commerce
  Corporations
  International economic relations
- NT **Foreign investments**

Multiple birth   618.2
- UF Birth, Multiple
- SA types of multiple births, e.g. **Twins** [to be added as needed]
- BT **Childbirth**
- NT **Twins**
- RT **Multiple pregnancy**

Multiple personalities
- USE **Multiple personality**

Multiple personality   616.85
- UF Double consciousness
  Multiple personalities
  Personality, Multiple
  Split personality
- BT **Abnormal psychology**
  Mental illness
  Personality disorders
  Psychology

Multiple plot stories

USE **Plot-your-own stories**

Multiple pregnancy   618.25

UF   Plural pregnancy

BT   **Pregnancy**

RT   **Multiple birth**

Multiplication   513.2

BT   **Arithmetic**

Multiracial people

USE   **Racially mixed people**

Mummies (May subdiv. geog.)   **393**

BT   **Archeology**

Burial

Municipal administration

USE   **Municipal government**

Municipal art (May subdiv. geog.)   **711**

UF   Art, Municipal

Civic art

Municipal improvements

BT   **Art**

Cities and towns

RT   **City planning**

Municipal civil service

USE   **Municipal officials and employees**

Municipal employees

USE   **Municipal officials and employees**

Municipal engineering (May subdiv. geog.)   **628**

BT   **Engineering**

Public works

NT   **Drainage**

Refuse and refuse disposal

Sewerage

Street cleaning

RT   **Sanitary engineering**

Municipal-federal relations

USE   **Federal-city relations**

Municipal finance (May subdiv. geog.) **336**

Use for general materials on city finance and, when subdivided by country, state, or region, for general considerations of municipal finance in those places. Materials on the finance of individual cities, towns, or metropolitan areas are entered under **Public finance** with the appropriate geographic subdivision.

UF   Cities and towns—Finance

Finance, Municipal

BT   **Municipal government**

Public finance

NT   **Metropolitan finance**

Municipal government (May subdiv. geog.)   **320.8; 352.16**

Use for materials on the government of cities in general and, when subdivided by country, state, or region, for general consideration of municipal government in those places. Materials on the government of individual cities, towns, or metropolitan areas are entered under the name of the city, town, or area with the subdivision *Politics and government.*

UF   Cities and towns—Government

City government

Government, Municipal

Municipal administration

Municipalities

SA   names of cities, towns, and metropolitan areas with the subdivision *Politics and government* [to be added as needed]

BT   **Local government**

Political science

NT   **Chicago (Ill.)—Politics and government**

Federal-city relations

Municipal finance

Municipal government by city manager

Municipal government by commission

Public administration

State-local relations

RT   **Metropolitan government**

Municipal officials and employees

Municipal government by city manager 320.8; 352.16

UF   City manager

Commission government with city manager

BT   **Municipal government**

Municipal government by commission 320.8; 352.16

UF   Commission government

Government by commission

BT   **Municipal government**

Municipal government—United States 320.8; 352.160973

UF   United States—Municipal government

Municipal improvements

USE   **Cities and towns—Civic improvement**

Municipal art

Municipal officers
  USE **Municipal officials and employees**
Municipal officials and employees 352.16
  UF Municipal civil service
      Municipal employees
      Municipal officers
      Town officers
  SA names of cities with the subdivision *Officials and employees*, e.g. **Chicago (Ill.)—Officials and employees** [to be added as needed]
  BT **Civil service**
  RT **Municipal government**
Municipal ownership 338.9; 352.5
  UF Public ownership
  BT **Corporations**
      Economic policy
      Government ownership
Municipal planning
  USE **City planning**
Municipal transit
  USE **Local transit**
Municipalities
  USE **Cities and towns**
      Municipal government
Munitions
  USE **Defense industry**
      Military weapons
Mural painting and decoration (May subdiv. geog.) **729; 751.7**
  UF Fresco painting
      Wall decoration
      Wall painting
  BT **Decoration and ornament**
      Interior design
      Painting
  RT **Mosaics**
Murder
  USE **Homicide**
Murder mysteries
  USE **Mystery and detective plays**
      Mystery fiction
      Mystery films
      Mystery radio programs
      Mystery television programs
Murder trials
  USE **Trials (Homicide)**
Muscles 611; 612.7

  BT **Musculoskeletal system**
Muscular system
  USE **Musculoskeletal system**
Musculoskeletal system 611; 612.7
  UF Muscular system
  BT **Anatomy**
      Physiology
  NT **Bones**
      Muscles
      Skeleton
  RT **Human locomotion**
Museums (May subdiv. geog.) **069; 708**
  SA appropriate subjects and names of wars and of corporate bodies with the subdivision *Museums*, e.g. **World War, 1939-1945—Museums**; and names of individual galleries and museums [to be added as needed]
  NT **Art museums**
      Museums and schools
      World War, 1939-1945—Museums
Museums and schools 069
  UF Schools and museums
  BT **Museums**
      Schools
Museums—Ohio 708.171
Museums—United States 708.13
Mushrooms 579.6; 635
  UF Toadstools
  BT **Plants**
  RT **Fungi**
Music 780
  UF Classical music
  SA music of particular countries or ethnic groups, e.g. **American music**; **Native American music**; etc.; types of music, e.g. **Vocal music**; and subjects, classes of persons, and names of individual persons, corporate bodies, places, or wars, with the subdivision *Songs* for collections of songs or materials about songs pertaining to the topic or entity named, e.g. **Cowhands—Songs; Surfing—Songs; United States Mili-**

Music—*Continued*

tary Academy—Songs [to be added as needed]

BT **Humanities**

NT **African American music**
American music
Black music
Chamber music
Church music
Composition (Music)
Computer music
Concerts
Conducting
Cowhands—Songs
Dance music
Electronic music
Ensembles (Music)
Folk music
Harmony
Instrumental music
Instrumentation and orchestration
Islamic music
Jazz music
Military music
Music and literature
Musical notation
Musicians
Native American music
Orchestral music
Organ music
Piano music
Popular music
Radio and music
Rock music
Singing
Violin music
Vocal music

Music—Acoustics and physics   781.2

UF Acoustics

BT **Music—Theory**
Physics

RT **Sound**

Music, American

USE **American music**

Music—Analysis, appreciation

USE **Music appreciation**
Music—History and criticism

Music and literature   780

UF Literature and music
Music and poetry
Poetry and music

BT **Literature**
Music

Music and poetry

USE **Music and literature**

Music and radio

USE **Radio and music**

Music—Anecdotes   780

UF Music—Anecdotes, facetiae, satire, etc.

BT **Anecdotes**

Music—Anecdotes, facetiae, satire, etc.

USE **Music—Anecdotes**
Music—Humor

Music appreciation   781.1

UF Appreciation of music
Music—Analysis, appreciation
Musical appreciation

BT **Music—Study and teaching**

RT **Music—History and criticism**

Music box

USE **Music boxes**

Music boxes   786.6

UF Music box

BT **Mechanical musical instruments**

Music—Cataloging

USE **Cataloging of music**

Music, Choral

USE **Choral music**

Music—Composition

USE **Composition (Music)**

Music conductors

USE **Conductors (Music)**

Music—Criticism

USE **Music—History and criticism**

Music—Discography   016.78

Music education

USE **Music—Study and teaching**

Music—Examinations   780.76

UF Music—Examinations, questions, etc.

BT **Examinations**

Music—Examinations, questions, etc.

USE **Music—Examinations**

Music festivals (May subdiv. geog.)
780.79

BT **Festivals**

RT **Concerts**

Music, Gospel

USE **Gospel music**

Music-halls
USE **Concert halls**
Music—History and criticism 780.9
UF Music—Analysis, appreciation
Music—Criticism
Musical criticism
RT **Music appreciation**
Music—Humor 780
UF Music—Anecdotes, facetiae, satire, etc.
BT **Wit and humor**
Music—Instruction and study
USE **Music—Study and teaching**
Music libraries (May subdiv. geog.) **026**
UF Libraries, Music
BT **Special libraries**
Music—Notation
USE **Musical notation**
Music—Psychological aspects 781
UF Psychology of music
BT **Psychology**
Music—Publishing (May subdiv. geog.)
070.5
BT **Publishers and publishing**
Music—Study and teaching 780.7
UF Music education
Music—Instruction and study
Musical education
Musical instruction
School music
NT **Music appreciation**
Music—Theory 781
NT **Composition (Music)**
Counterpoint
Harmony
Music—Acoustics and physics
Musical form
Musical meter and rhythm
Music—Therapeutic use
USE **Music therapy**
Music therapy 615.8; 616.89
UF Music—Therapeutic use
Musical therapy
BT **Therapeutics**
Music videos 384.55; 778.59
Use for individual works, collections, or materials about music videos.
UF Videos, Music
BT **Television programs**
Videodiscs
Videotapes
Musical ability 780.7

UF Musical talent
BT **Ability**
Musical accompaniment 781.47
UF Accompaniment, Musical
BT **Composition (Music)**
Musical appreciation
USE **Music appreciation**
Musical comedies
USE **Musicals**
Musical composition
USE **Composition (Music)**
Musical criticism
USE **Music—History and criticism**
Musical declamation
USE **Monologues with music**
Musical education
USE **Music—Study and teaching**
Musical ensembles
USE **Ensembles (Music)**
Musical films 791.43
Use for individual works, collections, or materials about musical films.
UF Motion picture musicals
Musicals (Motion pictures)
BT **Motion pictures**
RT **Musicals**
Musical form 784.18
SA names of musical forms expressed in the singular, to be used both for musical scores and for materials about the musical form, e.g. **Concerto** [to be added as needed]
BT **Composition (Music)**
Music—Theory
NT **Concerto**
Ensembles (Music)
Fugue
Opera
Operetta
Oratorio
Sonata
Suite (Music)
Symphony
Musical instruction
USE **Music—Study and teaching**
Musical instruments (May subdiv. geog.)
784.19
UF Instruments, Musical
SA types of instruments, e.g. **Percussion instruments** [to be added as needed]

Musical instruments—*Continued*
  NT **Bells**
      Drums
      Electronic musical instruments
      **Mechanical musical instru-
        ments**
      Organs (Musical instruments)
      Percussion instruments
      Stringed instruments
      Wind instruments
  RT **Instrumental music**
      **Instrumentation and orchestra-
        tion**
      Orchestra
      Tuning
Musical instruments, Electronic
  USE **Electronic musical instruments**
Musical instruments, Mechanical
  USE **Mechanical musical instru-
        ments**
Musical meter and rhythm   781.2
  UF Meter
  BT **Music—Theory**
      Rhythm
Musical notation   780.1
  UF Music—Notation
  BT **Music**
Musical revues, comedies, etc.
  USE **Musicals**
Musical talent
  USE **Musical ability**
Musical therapy
  USE **Music therapy**
Musicals (May subdiv. geog.)   **782.1;
      792.6**

  Use for scores and for materials about musical comedies and revues.

  UF Dramatic music
      Musical comedies
      Musical revues, comedies, etc.
  BT **Theater**
  RT **Musical films**
      Operetta
Musicals (Motion pictures)
  USE **Musical films**
Musicians (May subdiv. geog.)   **780.92;
      920**
  SA types of musicians and names of
        individual musicians [to be
        added as needed]
  BT **Music**

  NT **African American musicians**
      Black musicians
      Composers
      Conductors (Music)
      Disc jockeys
      Ensembles (Music)
      Instrumentalists
      Singers
Musicians—Biography   780.92; 920
  BT **Biography**
Musicians, Black
  USE **Black musicians**
Musicians—Portraits   780.92
Musicians—United States   780.92; 920
  UF American musicians
Muslim architecture
  USE **Islamic architecture**
Muslim art
  USE **Islamic art**
Muslim civilization
  USE **Islamic civilization**
Muslim countries
  USE **Islamic countries**
Muslim holy war
  USE **Jihad**
Muslim law
  USE **Islamic law**
Muslim literature
  USE **Islamic literature**
Muslim sermons
  USE **Islamic sermons**
Muslim women (May subdiv. geog.)
      305.48
  UF Islamic women
  BT **Muslims**
      Women
Muslims (May subdiv. geog.)   **297.092**
  UF Moors
      Moslems
  NT **Muslim women**
  RT **Islam**
Muslims—United States   297.092
  NT **Black Muslims**
Mutation (Biology)
  USE **Evolution**
      Variation (Biology)
Mutilation, Female genital
  USE **Female circumcision**
Mutual defense assistance program
  USE **Military assistance**

Mutual funds (May subdiv. geog.)
    332.63
    UF   Investment companies
        Investment trusts
    BT   **Investments**
Mutual support groups
    USE   **Self-help groups**
Mutualism (Biology)
    USE   **Symbiosis**
Myanmar   959.1
    May be subdivided like **United States** except for *History*.
    UF   Burma
Mycology
    USE   **Fungi**
Myocardial infarction
    USE   **Heart attack**
Myotherapy
    USE   **Acupressure**
Mysteries
    USE   **Mysteries and miracle plays**
        Mystery and detective plays
        Mystery fiction
        Mystery films
        Mystery radio programs
        Mystery television programs
Mysteries and miracle plays   792.1;
808.82
    Use for individual plays, collections, or materials about medieval plays depicting the life of Jesus or legends of the saints.
    UF   Miracle plays
        Mysteries
        Mystery plays
    BT   **Bible plays**
        English drama
        Pageants
        Religious drama
        Theater
    NT   **Passion plays**
    RT   **Morality plays**
Mystery and detective comics
    USE   **Mystery comic books, strips, etc.**
Mystery and detective films
    USE   **Mystery films**
Mystery and detective plays   808.82
    Use for individual works, collections, or materials about mystery and detective dramas.
    UF   Crime plays
        Detective and mystery plays
        Murder mysteries
        Mysteries

Mystery plays
Private eye stories
Whodunits
    BT   **Drama**
Mystery and detective radio programs
    USE   **Mystery radio programs**
Mystery and detective stories
    USE   **Mystery fiction**
Mystery and detective television programs
    USE   **Mystery television programs**
Mystery comic books, strips, etc.   741.5
    Use for individual works, collections, or materials about mystery and detective comics.
    UF   Crime comics
        Detective and mystery comic books, strips, etc.
        Detective comics
        Mystery and detective comics
    BT   **Comic books, strips, etc.**
Mystery fiction   808.3; 808.83
    Use for individual works, collections, or materials about mystery fiction.
    UF   Crime stories
        Detective and mystery stories
        Detective fiction
        Detective stories
        Murder mysteries
        Mysteries
        Mystery and detective stories
        Mystery stories
        Private eye stories
        Suspense novels
        Whodunits
    BT   **Fiction**
    NT   **Edgar Allan Poe Awards**
    RT   **Ghost stories**
        Horror fiction
        Romantic suspense novels
        Spy stories
Mystery films   791.43
    Use for individual works, collections, or materials about mystery and detective films.
    UF   Crime films
        Detective and mystery films
        Murder mysteries
        Mysteries
        Mystery and detective films
        Private eye stories
        Suspense films
        Whodunits

Mystery films—*Continued*

 SA particular kinds of detective and mystery films, e.g. **Sherlock Holmes films** [to be added as needed]

 BT **Motion pictures**

 NT **Sherlock Holmes films**

 RT **Film noir**

   Gangster films

   Spy films

Mystery graphic novels 741.5

 Use for individual works, collections, or materials about mystery graphic novels.

 BT **Graphic novels**

Mystery plays

 USE **Mysteries and miracle plays**

   Mystery and detective plays

Mystery radio programs 791.44

 Use for individual works, collections, or materials about mystery and detective radio programs.

 UF Crime programs

   Detective and mystery radio programs

   Murder mysteries

   Mysteries

   Mystery and detective radio programs

   Private eye stories

   Suspense programs

   Whodunits

 BT **Radio programs**

Mystery stories

 USE **Mystery fiction**

Mystery television programs 791.45

 Use for individual works, collections, or materials about mystery and detective television programs.

 UF Crime programs

   Detective and mystery television programs

   Murder mysteries

   Mysteries

   Mystery and detective television programs

   Private eye stories

   Suspense programs

   Whodunits

 BT **Television programs**

 RT **Spy television programs**

Mystical theology

 USE **Mysticism**

Mysticism (May subdiv. geog.) 204; 248.2

 May be subdivided by religion or sect.

 UF Dark night of the soul

   Mystical theology

 BT **Spiritual life**

 NT **Cabala**

   Theosophy

Mysticism—Comparative studies 204; 248.2

Mysticism—Islam (May subdiv. geog.) 297.4

 UF Islamic mysticism

 BT **Islam**

 NT **Sufism**

Mythical animals 398.24

 UF Animal lore

   Animals, Mythical

   Imaginary animals

   Imaginary creatures

 SA types of mythical animals [to be added as needed]

 BT **Mythology**

 NT **Dragons**

   Griffins

   Mermaids and mermen

   Phoenix (Mythical bird)

   Sasquatch

   Unicorns

   Yeti

 RT **Animals—Folklore**

Mythology 201; 398.2

 UF Myths

 SA mythology of ancient peoples, e.g. **Celtic mythology**; themes in mythology, e.g. **Fire in mythology**; and names of individual gods and goddesses, e.g. **Vesta (Roman deity)** [to be added as needed]

 NT **African mythology**

   Art and mythology

   Celtic mythology

   Classical mythology

   Egyptian mythology

   Fire in mythology

   Geographical myths

   Legendary characters

   Monsters

   Mythical animals

   Symbolism

Mythology—*Continued*
>Totems and totemism
RT Folklore
>Gods and goddesses
>Heroes and heroines
>Legends
>Religion
Mythology, Celtic
USE **Celtic mythology**
Mythology, Classical
USE **Classical mythology**
Mythology, Greek
USE **Greek mythology**
Mythology in art
USE **Art and mythology**
Mythology, Roman
USE **Roman mythology**
Myths
USE **Mythology**
Name
USE names of countries, cities, etc., individual persons, dieties, corporate bodies, ethnic groups, wars, etc., with the subdivision *Name,* for materials on the name's origin, history, validity, etc. [to be added as needed]
Names   929.4
UF Epithets
>Proper names
SA types of names, e.g. **Geographic names**; types of objects, domestic animals, events, organization, and institutions with the subdivision *Names*, for materials on the naming of those items, e.g. **Pets— Names**; and names of countries, cities, etc., individual persons, dieties, corporate bodies, ethnic groups, wars, etc., with the subdivision *Name*, for materials on the name's origin, history, validity, etc. [to be added as needed]
NT **Code names**
>**Geographic names**
>**Native American names**
>**Personal names**
>**Pseudonyms**

Terms and phrases
Names, Geographical
USE **Geographic names**
Names, Personal
USE **Personal names**
Names—Pronunciation   421
Nannies   649
UF Nursemaids
BT **Child care**
Nanotechnology (May subdiv. geog.)
>**620**
UF Molecular technology
BT **Technology**
Napkin folding   642
UF Folding of napkins
BT **Table setting and decoration**
Napoleon I, Emperor of the French, 1769-1821—Drama   808.82
>Use for collections of plays about Napoleon. Materials on Napoleon as a character in drama are entered under **Napoleon I, Emperor of the French, 1769-1821—In literature**.
Napoleon I, Emperor of the French, 1769-1821—Fiction   808.83
>Use for collections of fiction about Napoleon. Materials on Napoleon as a character in fiction are entered under **Napoleon I, Emperor of the French, 1769-1821—In literature**.
Napoleon I, Emperor of the French, 1769-1821—In art   704.9
>Use for materials about the depiction of Napoleon in works of art.
UF Napoleon in art
BT **Art—Themes**
Napoleon I, Emperor of the French, 1769-1821—In literature   809
>Use for materials about Napoleon as a character or as he is portrayed in works of fiction, drama, or poetry. Collections in which Napoleon is a character are entered under **Napoleon I, Emperor of the French, 1769-1821— Fiction; Napoleon I, Emperor of the French, 1769-1821—Drama**; or **Napoleon I, Emperor of the French, 1769-1821—Poetry**; as appropriate.
UF Napoleon in fiction, drama, poetry, etc.
BT **Literature—Themes**
Napoleon I, Emperor of the French, 1769-1821—Poetry   808.81
>Use for collections of poetry about Napoleon. Materials on Napoleon as portrayed in poetry are entered under **Napoleon I, Emperor of the French, 1769-1821—In literature**.
Napoleon in art
USE **Napoleon I, Emperor of the French, 1769-1821—In art**

Napoleon in fiction, drama, poetry, etc.
    USE   **Napoleon I, Emperor of the French, 1769-1821—In literature**
Napoleonic Wars, 1800-1815   940.2
    BT   **Europe—History—1789-1815**
          France—History—1799-1815
Narcotic abuse
    USE   **Drug abuse**
Narcotic addiction
    USE   **Drug abuse**
Narcotic addiction counseling
    USE   **Drug abuse counseling**
Narcotic addicts
    USE   **Drug addicts**
Narcotic habit
    USE   **Drug abuse**
Narcotic traffic
    USE   **Drug traffic**
Narcotics   178; 394.1; 615
    Use for materials limited to those drugs that induce sleep or lethargy or deaden pain.
    UF   Opiates
          Soporifics
    SA   types of narcotics [to be added as needed]
    BT   **Drugs**
          Materia medica
          Psychotropic drugs
    NT   **Cocaine**
          Heroin
          Marijuana
          Morphine
          Opium
Narcotics and crime
    USE   **Drugs and crime**
Narcotics and criminals
    USE   **Criminals—Drug use**
Narcotics and teenagers
    USE   **Teenagers—Drug use**
Narcotics and youth
    USE   **Youth—Drug use**
Narnia (Imaginary place)   809
    BT   **Imaginary places**
Narration with music
    USE   **Monologues with music**
Narrations
    USE   **Monologues**
          Recitations
Narrative poetry   808.1; 808.81
    Use for individual works, collections, or materials about narrative poetry. Rhyming sto-

ries for very young children are entered under the form heading **Stories in rhyme**.
    BT   **Poetry**
    NT   **Epic poetry**
          Historical poetry
          Stories in rhyme
Nation of Islam
    USE   **Black Muslims**
National anthems
    USE   **National songs**
National Book Week   021.7
    UF   Book Week, National
    BT   **Books and reading**
National characteristics   305.8
    UF   National images
          National psychology
    SA   national characteristics of particular countries, e.g. **American national characteristics** [to be added as needed]
    BT   **Anthropology**
          Nationalism
          Social psychology
    NT   **American national characteristics**
    RT   **Ethnopsychology**
National characteristics, American
    USE   **American national characteristics**
National community service
    USE   **National service**
National consciousness
    USE   **Nationalism**
National dances
    USE   **Folk dancing**
National debts
    USE   **Public debts**
National defenses
    USE   **Industrial mobilization**
          Military readiness
National emblems (May subdiv. geog.)
        929.9
    UF   Emblems
          National symbols
    SA   types of national emblems and national symbols, e.g. **Flags** [to be added as needed]
    BT   **Signs and symbols**
    RT   **Flags**
          Heraldry
          Insignia
          Mottoes

National emblems—*Continued*
    Seals (Numismatics)
    State emblems
National forests
  USE **Forest reserves**
National Guard (U.S.)
  USE **United States. National Guard**
National health insurance (May subdiv. geog.) **368.4**
  UF Government health insurance
      Medical insurance, National
      National health service
      Socialized medicine
  BT **Health insurance**
  NT **Medicaid**
      Medicare
  RT **State medicine**
National health service
  USE **National health insurance**
      State medicine
National heritage
  USE **Cultural property**
National holidays
  USE **Holidays**
National hymns
  USE **National songs**
National images
  USE **National characteristics**
National interest
  USE **Public interest**
National landmarks
  USE **National monuments**
National languages
  USE **Language and languages—Government policy**
National liberation movements (May subdiv. geog.) **320.5**
  Use for materials on minority or other groups in armed rebellion against a colonial government or against a national government charged with corruption or foreign domination, usually in the period since World War II.
  UF Liberation movements, National
  SA names of individual liberation movements [to be added as needed]
  BT **Nationalism**
      Revolutions
  NT **Guerrillas**
National libraries (May subdiv. geog.) **027.5**
  Use for materials on libraries maintained by government funds that serve a country as a whole, particularly in collecting and preserving that country's publications.
  UF Libraries, National
  SA names of individual national libraries [to be added as needed]
  BT **Government libraries**
National monuments (May subdiv. geog.) **917.3**
  Use for materials on monuments, such as historic sites or geographic areas, that are owned and maintained in the public interest by a country's government.
  UF Landmarks, Preservation of
      National landmarks
  SA names of individual national monuments [to be added as needed]
  BT **Monuments**
      National parks and reserves
  RT **Historic sites**
      Natural monuments
National parks and reserves (May subdiv. geog.) **338.78; 363.6; 719**
  SA names of individual national parks, e.g. **Yosemite National Park (Calif.)** [to be added as needed]
  BT **Parks**
      Public lands
  NT **National monuments**
  RT **Conservation of natural resources**
      Forest reserves
      Natural monuments
      Wilderness areas
National parks and reserves—United States **719; 917.3**
  UF United States—National parks and reserves
  NT **Yosemite National Park (Calif.)**
National patrimony
  USE **Cultural property**
National planning
  USE **Economic policy**
      Social policy
National product, Gross
  USE **Gross national product**
National psychology
  USE **Ethnopsychology**
      National characteristics

National resources
USE **Economic conditions**
Natural resources
United States—Economic conditions
National security (May subdiv. geog.)
355
RT **Economic policy**
International relations
Military policy
National security—United States   **355**
UF United States—National security
National self-determination (May subdiv.
geog.)   **320.1; 341.26**
UF Self-determination, National
BT **Nationalism**
RT **Sovereignty**
National service   **361.2**
UF Alternative military service
National community service
BT **Public welfare**
RT **Volunteer work**
National socialism   **320.5; 335.6**
Use for materials limited to fascism in Germany during the Nazi regime.
UF Nazism
BT **Fascism**
World War, 1939-1945—
Causes
RT **Neo-Nazis**
Socialism
National songs (May subdiv. geog.)
782.42
UF National anthems
National hymns
Patriotic songs
BT **Songs**
NT **War songs**
RT **Folk songs**
Patriotic poetry
National songs—United States   **782.42**
UF American national songs
United States—National songs
BT **American songs**
National symbols
USE **National emblems**
National treasure
USE **Cultural property**
Nationalism (May subdiv. geog.)   **320.5**
UF National consciousness
BT **International relations**
Political science

NT **Ethnocentrism**
National characteristics
National liberation movements
National self-determination
RT **Patriotism**
Regionalism
Nationalism, Black
USE **Black nationalism**
Nationalism—United States   **320.5**
Nationalist China
USE **Taiwan**
Nationality (Citizenship)
USE **Citizenship**
Nationalization
USE **Government ownership**
Nationalization of railroads
USE **Railroads—Government policy**
Nationalized companies
USE **Government business enterprises**
Nations   **900**
UF Countries
BT **Political science**
Native American architecture (May
subdiv. geog.)   **720.97; 970.004**
UF Indians of North America—Architecture
BT **Architecture**
RT **Native Americans—Dwellings**
Native American art (May subdiv. geog.)
704; 709.01
UF Indians of North America—Art
BT **Art**
Native American authors   **810.9; 920**
UF American Indian authors
BT **Authors**
Native American children (May subdiv.
geog.)   **305.23; 970.004**
UF Indians of North America—Children
Native Americans—Children
SA children of specific Native
American groups, e.g. **Navajo**
children [to be added as
needed]
BT **Children**
NT **Navajo children**
Native American costume (May subdiv.
geog.)   **970.004**
UF Indians of North America—Costume

Native American costume—*Continued*
    BT   **Costume**
Native American dance (May subdiv.
    geog.)   **793.3; 970.004**
    UF   Indians of North America—
           Dances
    BT   **Folk dancing**
Native American games (May subdiv.
    geog.)   **790.1; 970.004**
    UF   Indians of North America—
           Games
    BT   **Games**
        **Native Americans—Social life
        and customs**
Native American languages (May subdiv.
    geog.)   **497**
    Use for materials on the several languages
    of Native Americans.
    UF   Indian languages (North Ameri-
           can)
        Indians of North America—Lan-
           guages
    SA   names of individual languages,
           e.g. **Navajo language** [to be
           added as needed]
    BT   **Language and languages**
    NT   **Navajo language**
Native American legends
    USE   **Native Americans—Folklore**
Native American literature (May subdiv.
    geog.)   **897**
    Use for collections or materials about litera-
    ture written in Native American languages by
    several Native American authors. Collections
    or materials about literature written in English
    by several Native American authors are en-
    tered under **American literature—Native
    American authors**.
    UF   Indians of North America—Lit-
           erature
    BT   **Literature**
Native American medicine (May subdiv.
    geog.)   **615.8**
    UF   Indians of North America—Med-
           icine
    BT   **Medicine**
Native American music (May subdiv.
    geog.)   **780.89**
    Use for musical transcriptions or for materi-
    als about the music of the Native Americans.
    UF   Indians of North America—Mu-
           sic
    BT   **Music**

Native American mythology
    USE   **Native Americans—Folklore
           Native Americans—Religion**
Native American names (May subdiv.
    geog.)   **929.4**
    UF   Indians of North America—
           Names
    BT   **Names**
Native American sign language   **419**
    UF   Indians of North America—Sign
           language
    BT   **Sign language**
Native American silverwork   **739.2**
    UF   Indians of North America—Sil-
           verwork
    BT   **Silverwork**
Native American women (May subdiv.
    geog.)   **305.4; 970.004**
    UF   Indians of North America—
           Women
        Native Americans—Women
    SA   women of specific Native Amer-
           ican groups, e.g. **Navajo
           women** [to be added as need-
           ed]
    BT   **Women**
    NT   **Navajo women**
Native Americans (May subdiv. geog.)
    970.004
    Use for general materials on the native peo-
    ples of the Western Hemisphere. Libraries that
    prefer not to subdivide by *United States* may
    also use this heading for materials limited to
    the native peoples of the United States. Phrase
    headings derived from this term may be simi-
    larly established for other ethnic groups and
    for specific Native American peoples and lin-
    guistic families. Topical subdivisions provided
    under this heading may also be used under
    other ethnic groups and under specific Native
    American peoples and linguistic families.
    UF   American Indians
        Indians
        Indians of North America
        Indigenous peoples—America
        Pre-Columbian Americans
    SA   names of particular Native
           American peoples and linguis-
           tic families, e.g. **Aztecs**; **Nav-
           ajo Indians** etc. [to be added
           as needed]
    BT   **Indigenous peoples**
Native Americans—Agriculture (May
    subdiv. geog.)   **338.1; 630**

Native Americans—Agriculture—*Continued*

 UF   Indians of North America—Agriculture

 BT   **Agriculture**

Native Americans—Amusements

 USE   **Native Americans—Social life and customs**

Native Americans—Antiquities (May subdiv. geog.)   **970.004**

 UF   Indians of North America—Antiquities

 BT   **Antiquities**

Native Americans—Canada   **971.004**

 UF   Canadian Indians
       First nations
       Indians of Canada
       Indians of North America—Canada

Native Americans—Captivities (May subdiv. geog.)   **970.004**

 Use for materials on captivities by Native Americans

 UF   Indians of North America—Captivities

 BT   **Frontier and pioneer life**

Native Americans—Central America   **972.8004**

 UF   Indians of Central America

 NT   **Mayas**

Native Americans—Children

 USE   **Native American children**

Native Americans—Christian missions (May subdiv. geog.)   **266**

 UF   Indian missions
       Indians of North America—Christian missions

 BT   **Christian missions**

Native Americans—Chronology

 USE   **Native Americans—History—Chronology**

Native Americans—Claims (May subdiv. geog.)   **323.1197; 970.004**

 UF   Indians of North America—Claims
       Native Americans—Land claims

Native Americans—Customs

 USE   **Native Americans—Social life and customs**

Native Americans—Dwellings (May subdiv. geog.)   **728; 970.004**

 UF   Indians of North America—Dwellings

 NT   **Tepees**

 RT   **Native American architecture**

Native Americans—Economic conditions (May subdiv. geog.)   **970.004**

 UF   Indians of North America—Economic conditions

 BT   **Economic conditions**

Native Americans—Education (May subdiv. geog.)   **371.829; 970.004**

 UF   Indians of North America—Education
       Indians of North America—Schools

 BT   **Education**

Native Americans—Ethnobiology   **578.6**

 BT   **Ethnobiology**

Native Americans—Ethnobotany   **581.6**

 BT   **Ethnobotany**

Native Americans—Ethnozoology   **591.6**

 BT   **Ethnozoology**

Native Americans—First contact with Europeans (May subdiv. geog.)   **970.004**

 UF   Indians of North America—First contact with Europeans

 BT   **Native Americans—History**

 RT   **Native Americans—Relations with early settlers**

Native Americans—Folklore (May subdiv. geog.)   **398**

 Use for collections of Native American legends, myths, tales, etc., and for materials about the folklore and mythology of Native Americans.

 UF   Indians of North America—Folklore
       Native American legends
       Native American mythology

 BT   **Folklore**

Native Americans—Forced removal

 USE   **Native Americans—Relocation**

Native Americans—Government policy

 USE   **Native Americans—Government relations**

Native Americans—Government relations (May subdiv. geog.)   **323.1197; 970.004**

 Use for materials on the Indian policy of the United States government and on relations between North American governments and the Native Americans.

Native Americans—Government rela-
tions—*Continued*
> UF Federal-Indian relations
>> Indians of North America—Gov-
>> ernment relations
>> Native Americans—Government
>> policy
> RT **Native Americans—Relations**
>> **with early settlers**

Native Americans—Guatemala
972.81004
> UF Indians of Central America—
>> Guatemala

Native Americans—History   970.004
> UF Indians of North America—His-
>> tory
> NT **Native Americans—First con-**
>> **tact with Europeans**
>> **Native Americans—Relations**
>> **with early settlers**
>> **Native Americans—Wars**

Native Americans—History—Chronology
970.004
> Use for materials that list events and dates
> in the history of the Native Americans in the
> order of their occurrence.
> UF Indians of North America—His-
>> tory—Chronology
>> Native Americans—Chronology

Native Americans—Housing (May subdiv.
geog.)   **307.3; 363.5**
> BT **Housing**

Native Americans—Hunting (May subdiv.
geog.)   **970.004**
> BT **Hunting**

Native Americans—Industries (May
subdiv. geog.)   **338.4; 680;**
970.004
> UF Indians of North America—In-
>> dustries
> BT **Industries**

Native Americans—Land claims
> USE **Native Americans—Claims**

Native Americans—Material culture
970.004

Native Americans—Medical care (May
subdiv. geog.)   **362.1**
> BT **Medical care**

Native Americans—Mexico   972.004
> UF Indians of Mexico
> NT **Aztecs**
>> **Mayas**

Native Americans—North America
970.004
> UF Indians of North America
> SA names of particular Native
>> American peoples and linguis-
>> tic families, e.g. **Navajo Indi-**
>> **ans** [to be added as needed]

Native Americans—Origin   970.004
> UF Indians of North America—Ori-
>> gin

Native Americans—Peru   985
> UF Indians of South America—Peru

Native Americans—Politics and govern-
ment (May subdiv. geog.)
970.004
> UF Indians of North America—Poli-
>> tics and government
>> Native Americans—Tribal gov-
>> ernment
> BT **Politics**

Native Americans—Psychology   155.8
> UF Indians of North America—Psy-
>> chology
> BT **Ethnopsychology**

Native Americans—Relations with early
settlers (May subdiv. geog.)
970.004
> UF Indians of North America—Rela-
>> tions with early settlers
> BT **Native Americans—History**
> RT **Native Americans—First con-**
>> **tact with Europeans**
>> **Native Americans—Govern-**
>> **ment relations**

Native Americans—Religion (May subdiv.
geog.)   **270.089; 299.7; 299.8**
> UF Indians of North America—Reli-
>> gion
>> Native American mythology
> BT **Religion**

Native Americans—Relocation (May
subdiv. geog.)   **970.004**
> UF Forced removal of Indians
>> Indian removal
>> Native Americans—Forced re-
>> moval
>> Native Americans—Removal
>> Removal of Indians

Native Americans—Removal
> USE **Native Americans—Relocation**

Native Americans—Reservations (May
  subdiv. geog.) **333.1; 970.004**
  UF Indian reservations
      Indians of North America—Res-
        ervations
  SA names of native peoples, tribes,
      etc., with the subdivision *Res-
      ervations* [to be added as
      needed]
Native Americans—Rites and ceremonies
  970.004
  UF Indians of North America—Rites
      and ceremonies
  BT **Rites and ceremonies**
  NT **Powwows**
Native Americans—Social conditions
  (May subdiv. geog.) **970.004**
  UF Indians of North America—So-
      cial conditions
  BT **Social conditions**
**Native Americans—Social life and cus-
  toms** (May subdiv. geog.)
  970.004
  UF Indians of North America—So-
      cial life and customs
      Native Americans—Amusements
      Native Americans—Customs
  BT **Manners and customs**
  NT **Native American games**
      Powwows
Native Americans—South America **980**
  UF Indians of South America
  NT **Incas**
Native Americans—Southwestern States
  979
  NT **Cliff dwellers and cliff dwell-
      ings**
      Navajo Indians
Native Americans—Tribal government
  USE **Native Americans—Politics and
      government**
Native Americans—United States
  973.04
  UF Indians of North America
Native Americans—Wars (May subdiv.
  geog.) **970.004**
  UF Indians of North America—Wars
  BT **Native Americans—History**
  NT **Black Hawk War, 1832**
      King Philip's War, 1675-1676

**Pontiac's Conspiracy, 1763-
      1765**
    **United States—History—1689-
      1697, King William's War**
    **United States—History—1755-
      1763, French and Indian
      War**
Native Americans—West Indies
    972.9004
  UF Indians of the West Indies
Native Americans—Women
  USE **Native American women**
Native peoples
  USE **Indigenous peoples**
Natives
  USE **Indigenous peoples**
Nativity of Jesus Christ
  USE **Jesus Christ—Nativity**
NATO
  USE **North Atlantic Treaty Organi-
      zation**
Natural beauty conservation
  USE **Landscape protection**
Natural childbirth **618.4**
  UF Lamaze method of childbirth
  BT **Childbirth**
  NT **Midwives**
Natural cycles
  USE **Cycles**
Natural disasters (May subdiv. geog.)
      904
  SA types of natural disasters [to be
      added as needed]
  BT **Disasters**
  NT **Earthquakes**
      Environmental degradation
      Floods
      Landslides
      Storms
      Tsunamis
Natural disasters—United States **973**
Natural food cooking
  USE **Cooking—Natural foods**
Natural foods **641.3**
  UF Health foods
      Organically grown foods
  BT **Food**
  RT **Cooking—Natural foods**
Natural gardening
  USE **Organic gardening**

Natural gas (May subdiv. geog.)   553.2;
   665.7
   BT   **Fuel**
      Gases
Natural gas companies
   USE   **Gas companies**
Natural gas utilities
   USE   **Gas companies**
Natural history (May subdiv. geog.)
   508
   Use for materials on the unsystematic study
   of zoology, botany, mineralogy, etc., the collecting of specimens, and, with a geographic
   subdivision, the description of nature in a par-
   ticular place. Materials on the study of ani-
   mals and plants as an elementary school sub-
   ject are entered under **Nature study**. General
   and theoretical materials on the natural world
   are entered under **Nature**.
   UF   Animal lore
      Mineralogy
   BT   **Science**
   NT   **Aquariums**
      Bible—Natural history
      Bird watching
      Fossils
      Nature photography
   RT   **Biogeography**
      Botany
      Minerals
      Nature
      Zoology
Natural history—United States   508.73
   UF   Nature study—United States
Natural law   340
   UF   Law of nature
      Natural rights
   BT   **Ethics**
      Law
   RT   **International law**
Natural monuments (May subdiv. geog.)
   719
   Use for general materials on natural objects
   of historic or scientific interest such as caves,
   cliffs, and natural bridges.
   UF   Landmarks, Preservation of
      Preservation of natural scenery
      Protection of natural scenery
      Scenery
   SA   names of individual natural
      monuments [to be added as
      needed]
   BT   **Landscape protection**
      Monuments

Nature conservation
   RT   **National monuments**
      National parks and reserves
Natural monuments—United States
   719; 917.3
Natural parents
   USE   **Birthparents**
Natural pesticides   668
   BT   **Pesticides**
Natural religion
   USE   **Natural theology**
Natural resources (May subdiv. geog.)
   333.7
   UF   National resources
   SA   types of natural resources [to be
      added as needed]
   BT   **Economic conditions**
   NT   **Conservation of natural re-
      sources**
      Energy resources
      Forests and forestry
      Marine resources
      Mines and mineral resources
      Water resources development
      Water supply
   RT   **Public lands**
Natural resources—Management   333.7
   BT   **Management**
Natural resources—United States   333.7
Natural rights
   USE   **Natural law**
Natural satellites
   USE   **Satellites**
Natural selection   576.8
   UF   Survival of the fittest
   BT   **Genetics**
      Variation (Biology)
   RT   **Evolution**
      Heredity
Natural steam energy
   USE   **Geothermal resources**
Natural theology   210
   Use for materials on the knowledge of
   God's existence obtained by observing the
   visible processes of nature.
   UF   Natural religion
   BT   **Apologetics**
      Theology
   NT   **Creation**
   RT   **Religion and science**
Natural therapy
   USE   **Naturopathy**

Naturalism in art
USE **Realism in art**
Naturalism in literature
USE **Realism in literature**
Naturalists (May subdiv. geog.)
508.092; 920
SA types of naturalists, e.g. **Botanists** [to be added as needed]
BT **Scientists**
NT **Biologists**
Botanists
Naturalization 323.6
BT **Immigration and emigration**
International law
Suffrage
RT **Aliens**
Americanization
Citizenship
Nature 508
Use for general and theoretical materials on the natural world. Materials on the study of animals and plants as an elementary school subject are entered under **Nature study**. Materials on the unsystematic study of zoology, botany, mineralogy, etc., the collecting of specimens, and the description of nature in a particular place are entered under **Natural history**.
RT **Natural history**
Nature study
Nature and nurture (May subdiv. geog.)
155.2
UF Genetics and environment
Heredity and environment
Nurture and nature
BT **Genetics**
Heredity
Nature conservation (May subdiv. geog.)
333.72
UF Conservation of nature
Nature protection
Preservation of natural scenery
Protection of natural scenery
BT **Conservation of natural resources**
NT **Endangered species**
Landscape protection
Natural monuments
Plant conservation
Wildlife conservation
Nature craft 745.5
Use for materials on crafts using objects found in nature, such as leaves, shells, etc.
UF Naturecraft

BT **Handicraft**
NT **Potpourri**
Sand sculpture
Nature—Effect of human beings on
USE **Human influence on nature**
Nature in literature 809
BT **Literature—Themes**
Nature in the bible
USE **Bible—Natural history**
Nature photography 778.9
UF Photography of nature
SA photography of particular subjects in nature, e.g. **Photography of birds** [to be added as needed]
BT **Natural history**
Photography
NT **Photography of animals**
Photography of birds
Photography of fishes
Photography of plants
RT **Outdoor photography**
Nature poetry 808.1; 808.81
Use for individual works or collections of poetry about nature.
UF Nature—Poetry
BT **Poetry**
Nature—Poetry
USE **Nature poetry**
Nature prints 761
BT **Printing**
Prints
Nature protection
USE **Nature conservation**
Nature study 372.35; 508.07
Use for materials on the study of animals and plants as an elementary school subject. Materials on the unsystematic study of zoology, botany, mineralogy, etc., the collecting of specimens, and the description of nature in a particular place are entered under **Natural history**. General and theoretical materials on the natural world are entered under **Nature**.
BT **Education**
Science—Study and teaching
RT **Nature**
Outdoor education
Outdoor life
Nature study—United States
USE **Natural history—United States**
Nature tourism
USE **Ecotourism**
Nature trails (May subdiv. geog.) **508**
BT **Trails**

Naturecraft
  USE **Nature craft**
Naturopathy   615.5
  UF Natural therapy
  BT **Alternative medicine**
      Therapeutics
  RT **Chiropractic**
Nautical almanacs   528
  BT **Almanacs**
      Navigation
Nautical astronomy   527
  BT **Astronomy**
  NT **Latitude**
      Longitude
  RT **Navigation**
      Time
Nautical charts   623.89
  UF Charts, Nautical
      Navigation charts
      Navigation maps
      Pilot charts
  BT **Maps**
      Navigation
Navaho Indians
  USE **Navajo Indians**
Navaho language
  USE **Navajo language**
Navajo children (May subdiv. geog.)
      973.04
  UF Navajo Indians—Children
  BT **Native American children**
      Navajo Indians
Navajo Indians   973.04
  UF Navaho Indians
  BT **Native Americans—Southwest-**
      ern States
  NT **Navajo children**
      Navajo women
Navajo Indians—Children
  USE **Navajo children**
Navajo Indians—Women
  USE **Navajo women**
Navajo language   497
  UF Navaho language
  BT **Native American languages**
Navajo women (May subdiv. geog.)
      973.04
  UF Navajo Indians—Women
  BT **Native American women**
      Navajo Indians

Naval administration
  USE **Naval art and science**
      and names of countries with the
      subhead *Navy,* e.g. **United**
      States. Navy [to be added as
      needed]
Naval aeronautics
  USE **Military aeronautics**
Naval air bases
  USE **Air bases**
Naval airplanes
  USE **Military airplanes**
Naval architecture   623.8
  UF Marine architecture
  BT **Architecture**
  NT **Boatbuilding**
      Marine engineering
      Shipbuilding
      Steamboats
      Warships
Naval art and science (May subdiv.
      geog.) **359**
  UF Fighting
      Naval administration
      Naval science
      Naval warfare
      Navy
  SA names of wars with the subdivi-
      sion *Naval operations,* e.g.
      World War, 1939-1945—Na-
      val operations [to be added
      as needed]
  NT **Camouflage (Military science)**
      Marine engineering
      Navy yards and naval stations
      Privateering
      Sailors
      Sea power
      Signals and signaling
      Strategy
      Submarine warfare
      Torpedoes
      Warships
  RT **Military art and science**
      Navies
      Navigation
      War
Naval art and science—Study and teaching
  USE **Naval education**
Naval bases
  USE **Navy yards and naval stations**

Naval battles   359.4; 904
    UF   Naval warfare
    SA   names of countries with the sub-
          division *Naval history*; names
          of wars with the subdivision
          Naval operations, e.g. **World**
          War, 1939-1945—Naval op-
          erations; and names of spe-
          cific naval battles [to be add-
          ed as needed]
    BT   **Battles**
    RT   **Naval history**
Naval biography
    USE   names of navies with the subdi-
           vision *Biography,* e.g. **United**
           States. Navy—Biography [to
           be added as needed]
Naval education (May subdiv. geog.)
    359.007
    UF   Naval art and science—Study
          and teaching
          Naval schools
    BT   **Education**
Naval engineering
    USE   **Marine engineering**
Naval history   359.009
    UF   Wars
    SA   names of countries with the sub-
          head *Navy* or the subdivision
          Naval history [to be added as
          needed]
    BT   **History**
    NT   **Pirates**
          Privateering
          United States—Naval history
    RT   **Military history**
          Naval battles
          Sea power
Naval law
    USE   **Maritime law**
Naval offenses
    USE   **Military offenses**
Naval operations
    USE   names of wars with the subdivi-
          sion *Naval operations,* e.g.
          World War, 1939-1945—Na-
          val operations [to be added
          as needed]
Naval pensions
    USE   **Military pensions**

Naval personnel
    USE   **Sailors**
Naval power
    USE   **Sea power**
Naval schools
    USE   **Naval education**
Naval science
    USE   **Naval art and science**
Naval shipyards
    USE   **Navy yards and naval stations**
Naval signaling
    USE   **Signals and signaling**
Naval strategy
    USE   **Strategy**
Naval uniforms
    USE   **Military uniforms**
Naval warfare
    USE   **Naval art and science**
          Naval battles
          Submarine warfare
Navies   359.3
    UF   Military power
          Navy
          Sea life
    SA   names of countries with the sub-
          head *Navy,* e.g. **United**
          States. Navy [to be added as
          needed]
    BT   **Armed forces**
          Military personnel
    NT   **Admirals**
          Sailors
          United States. Navy
    RT   **Naval art and science**
          Sea power
          Warships
Navigation (May subdiv. geog.)   **623.89;**
    629.04
    UF   Pilots and pilotage
          Seamanship
    BT   **Locomotion**
    NT   **Compass**
          Global Positioning System
          Harbors
          Inland navigation
          Knots and splices
          Lighthouses
          Loran
          Nautical almanacs
          Nautical charts
          Ocean currents

Navigation—*Continued*
>> **Pilot guides**
>> **Radar**
>> **Shipwrecks**
>> **Signals and signaling**
>> **Steam navigation**
>> **Winds**
> RT **Direction sense**
>> **Nautical astronomy**
>> **Naval art and science**
>> **Sailing**
>> **Ship pilots**

Navigation (Aeronautics)   629.132
> UF   Aerial navigation
>> Aeronautics—Navigation
>> Air navigation
> BT   **Aeronautics**
> NT   **Airplanes—Piloting**
>> **Radio in aeronautics**

Navigation (Astronautics)   629.45
> UF   Astronavigation
>> Space navigation
> BT   **Astrodynamics**
>> **Astronautics**
> NT   **Astronautical instruments**
>> **Radio in astronautics**
>> **Space vehicles—Piloting**
> RT   **Space flight**

Navigation charts
> USE   **Nautical charts**

Navigation—Law and legislation
> USE   **Maritime law**

Navigation maps
> USE   **Nautical charts**

Navigators
> USE   **Explorers**
>> **Sailors**

Navy
> USE   **Naval art and science**
>> **Navies**
>> **Sea power**
>> and names of countries with the subhead *Navy*, e.g. **United States. Navy** [to be added as needed]

Navy Sealab project
> USE   **Sealab project**

Navy yards and naval stations (May subdiv. geog.)   **359.7**
> UF   Naval bases
>> Naval shipyards
> BT   **Naval art and science**

Nazi persecution
> USE   religious groups and classes of persons with the subdivision *Nazi persecution,* e.g. **Handicapped—Nazi persecution** [to be added as needed]

Nazi persecution of the handicapped
> USE   **Handicapped—Nazi persecution**

Nazism
> USE   **National socialism**

Near-death experiences   133.9; 155.9
> Use for materials on the paranormal experiences of those who have survived near death or apparent death.
> BT   **Death**
> RT   **Parapsychology**

Near East
> USE   **Middle East**

Neatness
> USE   **Cleanliness**
>> **Orderliness**

Nebula Award   808.3
> BT   **Literary prizes**
>> **Science fiction**

Nebulae, Extragalactic
> USE   **Galaxies**

Necrologies
> USE   **Obituaries**

Necromancy
> USE   **Divination**
>> **Magic**

Needlepoint   746.44
> UF   Canvas embroidery
> BT   **Embroidery**
>> **Needlework**

Needlework   746.4
> SA   types of needlework [to be added as needed]
> BT   **Decoration and ornament**
>> **Decorative arts**
> NT   **Appliqué**
>> **Crocheting**
>> **Drawn work**
>> **Embroidery**
>> **Hardanger needlework**
>> **Knitting**
>> **Lace and lace making**
>> **Needlepoint**
>> **Patchwork**
>> **Quilting**
>> **Samplers**
>> **Smocking**

Needlework—*Continued*
    Tapestry
  RT **Dressmaking**
    Sewing
Negotiable instruments (May subdiv.
  geog.) **332.7**
  UF Bills and notes
    Bills of credit
    Commercial paper
    Instruments, Negotiable
    Letters of credit
  BT **Banks and banking**
    Commercial law
    Contracts
    Credit
  NT **Bonds**
Negotiation **158; 302.3**
  UF Bargaining
    Discussion
  BT **Applied psychology**
  NT **Collective bargaining**
    Conflict management
    Hostage negotiation
    Industrial arbitration
Negritude
  USE **Blacks—Race identity**
Negro leagues **796.357**
  BT **Baseball**
Negroes
  USE **African Americans**
    Blacks
Neighborhood (May subdiv. geog.)
  307.3
  UF Neighborhoods
  BT **Community life**
    Social groups
Neighborhood centers
  USE **Community centers**
    Social settlements
Neighborhood development
  USE **Community development**
Neighborhoods
  USE **Neighborhood**
Neo-fascism
  USE **Fascism**
    Neo-Nazis
Neo-Greek literature
  USE **Modern Greek literature**
Neo-impressionism (Art)
  USE **Impressionism (Art)**
Neo-Latin languages
  USE **Romance languages**

Neo-Nazis (May subdiv. geog.) **320.5**
  Use for materials on political groups whose
  social beliefs or political agendas are reminis-
  cent of those of Hitler's Nazis.
  UF Neo-fascism
    Neo-nazism
  BT **Fascism**
  RT **National socialism**
Neo-nazism
  USE **Neo-Nazis**
Neolithic period
  USE **Stone Age**
Neon Genesis Evangelion (Fictional ro-
  bot) **741.5**
  BT **Fictional robots**
    Manga
    Mecha
Neon tubes **621.32**
  BT **Electric signs**
Neopaganism (May subdiv. geog.) **299**
  BT **Religions**
Neptune (Planet) **523.48**
  BT **Planets**
Nero, Emperor of Rome, 37-68 **92; B**
  BT **Emperors—Rome**
Nerves **611; 612.8**
  BT **Nervous system**
Nerves—Diseases
  USE **Nervous system—Diseases**
Nervous breakdown
  USE **Neurasthenia**
Nervous exhaustion
  USE **Neurasthenia**
Nervous prostration
  USE **Neurasthenia**
Nervous system **611; 612.8**
  UF Neurology
  BT **Anatomy**
    Physiology
  NT **Abnormal psychology**
    Brain
    Nerves
    Psychophysiology
Nervous system—Diseases **616.8**
  UF Nerves—Diseases
    Neuropathology
  BT **Diseases**
  NT **Communicative disorders**
    Epilepsy
    Movement disorders
    Paralysis

Nessie (Monster)
    USE **Loch Ness monster**
Nest building   591.56
    UF Building nests
         Nesting (Animal behavior)
         Nesting behavior
    SA types of animals and individual
         species on animals with the
         subdivision *Nests*, e.g.
         Birds—Nests [to be added as
         needed]
    BT **Animal behavior**
         Animals—Habitations
Nesting (Animal behavior)
    USE **Nest building**
Nesting behavior
    USE **Nest building**
Nests
    USE types of animals and individual
         species of animals with the
         subdivision *Nests,* e.g.
         Birds—Nests [to be added as
         needed]
Netherlands   949.2
    May be subdivided like **United States** except for *History*.
    UF Holland
Netherlands—History   949.2
Netherlands—History—1940-1945, German occupation   949.207
    UF German occupation of Netherlands, 1940-1945
Network theory
    USE **System analysis**
Networks (Associations, institutions, etc.)
    USE **Associations**
Networks, Computer
    USE **Computer networks**
Networks, Information
    USE **Information networks**
Neurasthenia   616.85
    UF Nervous breakdown
         Nervous exhaustion
         Nervous prostration
    BT **Mental illness**
Neurology
    USE **Nervous system**
Neuropathology
    USE **Nervous system—Diseases**
Neuroses   616.85
    BT **Abnormal psychology**

    NT **Anxiety**
         Depression (Psychology)
         Obsessive-compulsive disorder
         Panic disorders
         Phobias
         Post-traumatic stress disorder
Neurotic children
    USE **Emotionally disturbed children**
Neutrality (May subdiv. geog.)   **327.1; 341.6**
    UF Nonalignment
    BT **International law**
         International relations
         International security
    RT **Intervention (International law)**
         Isolationism
Neutrality—United States   327.73
    UF United States—Neutrality
    RT **United States—Foreign relations**
Neutron bomb   623.4
    UF Neutron bombs
    BT **Bombs**
         Neutron weapons
Neutron bombs
    USE **Neutron bomb**
Neutron weapons   623.4
    UF Enhanced radiation weapons
    BT **Nuclear weapons**
    NT **Neutron bomb**
Neutrons   539.7
    BT **Atoms**
         Particles (Nuclear physics)
New Age movement (May subdiv. geog.)   **130; 131; 299**
    Use for materials on any of various post-1970 cults and organizations that incorporate Eastern or Native American religions, occult beliefs and practices, mysticism, or meditation techniques in an attempt to enhance consciousness and develop human potential.
    UF Aquarian Age movement
    BT **Cults**
         Occultism
         Social movements
New birth (Theology)
    USE **Regeneration (Christianity)**
New business enterprises (May subdiv. geog.)   **338.7**
    UF How to start a business
         Starting a business
    BT **Business enterprises**

New communities
USE **Planned communities**
New countries
USE **New states**
New Deal, 1933-1939   973.917
BT **United States—History—1933-**
1945
New England   974
BT **United States**
New France—History
USE **Canada—History—0-1763 (New**
France)
Mississippi River Valley—His-
tory
New nations
USE **New states**
New Negro Movement
USE **Harlem Renaissance**
New product development
USE **New products**
New products (May subdiv. geog.)
658.5
UF New product development
Product development
BT **Commercial products**
Industrial research
Marketing
New states   321
UF New countries
New nations
States, New
BT **Developing countries**
New Testament
USE **Bible. N.T.**
New words   417
UF Coinage of words
Words, New
BT **Vocabulary**
New York Knicks (Basketball team)
796.323
UF Knicks (Basketball team)
BT **Basketball teams**
New York (N.Y.)—Streets
USE **Streets—New York (N.Y.)**
New Zealand   993
May be subdivided like **United States** ex-
cept for *History*.
Newbery Award
USE **Newbery Medal**
Newbery Medal   028.5
UF Newbery Award
Newbery Prize books

BT **Children's literature**
Literary prizes
Newbery Prize books
USE **Newbery Medal**
News agencies (May subdiv. geog.)
070.4
UF News services
Wire services
BT **Press**
News editing
USE **Journalism—Editing**
News photography
USE **Photojournalism**
News services
USE **News agencies**
Newsletters   070.1
BT **Journalism**
Newspapers
Newspaper advertising   659.13
Use for materials on advertising in newspa-
pers. Materials on the advertising of newspa-
pers are entered under **Advertising—Newspa-**
pers.
UF Advertising, Newspaper
BT **Advertising**
Newspapers
Newspaper clippings
USE **Clippings (Books, newspapers,**
etc.)
Newspaper work
USE **Reporters and reporting**
Newspapers (May subdiv. geog.)   **070**
Use for materials limited to the history, or-
ganization, and management of newspapers.
Materials on writing for the periodical press,
on the editing of such writing, and on journal-
ism as an occupation, are entered under **Jour-**
nalism.
SA names of individual newspapers
[to be added as needed]
BT **Mass media**
Serial publications
NT **Clippings (Books, newspapers,**
etc.)
Newsletters
Newspaper advertising
Reporters and reporting
RT **Journalism**
Periodicals
Press
Newspapers—Advertising
USE **Advertising—Newspapers**
Newspapers—Editing
USE **Journalism—Editing**

Newspapers—Great Britain   072
    UF   English newspapers
Newspapers—Indexes   070.1
Newspapers—Sections, columns, etc.
        070.4
    SA   types of newspaper columns, e.g.
            Advice columns [to be added
            as needed]
    NT   **Advice columns**
Newspapers—United States   071
    UF   American newspapers
Nicene Creed   238
    BT   **Creeds**
Nicknames   929.4
    UF   Epithets
            Sobriquets
    BT   **Personal names**
Nicotine habit
    USE   **Tobacco habit**
Nigeria   966.9
        May be subdivided like **United States** ex-
        cept for *History*.
Night   529
    BT   **Chronology**
            Time
    NT   **Bedtime**
    RT   **Day**
Night clubs, cabarets, etc. (May subdiv.
        geog.)   **725**
    UF   Cabarets
    BT   **Theaters**
Night schools
    USE   **Evening and continuation**
            schools
Nike rocket   623.4
    BT   **Guided missiles**
Nineteen eighties (May subdiv. geog.)
        909.82
    UF   1980s
    BT   **World history—20th century**
Nineteen fifties (May subdiv. geog.)
        909.82
    UF   1950s
    BT   **World history—20th century**
Nineteen forties (May subdiv. geog.)
        909.82
    UF   1940s
    BT   **World history—20th century**
Nineteen nineties (May subdiv. geog.)
        909.82
    UF   1990s
    BT   **World history—20th century**

Nineteen seventies (May subdiv. geog.)
        909.82
    UF   1970s
    BT   **World history—20th century**
Nineteen sixties (May subdiv. geog.)
        909.82
    UF   1960s
    BT   **World history—20th century**
Nineteen thirties (May subdiv. geog.)
        909.82
    UF   1930s
    BT   **World history—20th century**
Nineteen twenties (May subdiv. geog,)
        909.82
    UF   1920s
    BT   **World history—20th century**
Nineteenth century
    USE   **World history—19th century**
Nisei
    USE   **Japanese Americans**
Nitrates   553.6
    BT   **Chemicals**
            Fertilizers
Nitrogen   546; 665
    BT   **Gases**
Nobel Prizes   001.4; 807.9
    BT   **Awards**
Nobility (May subdiv. geog.)   **305.5;**
        929.7
    UF   Peerage
    BT   **Upper class**
    NT   **Knights and knighthood**
    RT   **Aristocracy**
            Heraldry
Noise   363.74
    SA   subjects with the subdivision
            Noise [to be added as needed]
    BT   **Public health**
            Sound
    NT   **Airplanes—Noise**
Noise pollution (May subdiv. geog.)
        363.74
    SA   subjects with the subdivision
            Noise [to be added as needed]
    BT   **Pollution**
    NT   **Airplanes—Noise**
Nomadic peoples
    USE   **Nomads**
Nomads (May subdiv. geog.)   **305.9**
    UF   Nomadic peoples
            Pastoral peoples

Nomads—*Continued*

  BT **Primitive societies**

Nomenclature

  USE types of scientific and technical disciplines and types of substances, plants, and animals with the subdivision *Nomenclature,* for systematically derived lists of names or designations that have been formally adopted or sanctioned, and for discussions of the principles involved in the creation and application of such names, e.g. **Botany—Nomenclature;** scientific and technical disciplines and types of animals, plants, and crops with the subdivision *Nomenclature (Popular),* for lists or materials about popular, nontechnical names or designations of substances, species, etc., e.g. **Trees—Nomenclature (Popular);** and subjects, classes of persons, sacred works, and religious sects with the subdivision *Terminology,* for lists or discussions of words and expressions found in those works or used in those fields, e.g. **Botany—Terminology** [to be added as needed]

Nomenclature (Popular)

  USE types of scientific and technical disciplines and types of animals, plants, and crops with the subdivision *Nomenclature (Popular),* for lists of popular or non-technical names or designations of substances, species, etc., e.g. **Trees—Nomenclature (Popular);** and scientific and technical disciplines and types of substances, plants, and animals with the subdivision *Nomenclature,* for systematically derived lists of names or designations that have been formal-ly adopted or sactioned, and for discussions of the principles involved in the creation and application of such names, e.g. **Botany—Nomenclature** [to be added as needed]

Nomination

  USE types of public officials and names of individual public officials with the subdivision *Nomination,* e.g. **Presidents—United States—Nomination** [to be added as needed]

Nomination of presidents

  USE **Presidents—United States—Nomination**

Non-institutional churches   289.9

  UF Avant-garde churches

      Churches, Non-institutional

      Noninstitutional churches

  BT **Christian sects**

Non-professional theater

  USE **Amateur theater**

Non-proliferation of nuclear weapons

  USE **Arms control**

Non-promotion (School)

  USE **Promotion (School)**

Non-victim crimes

  USE **Crimes without victims**

Non-wage payments

  USE **Fringe benefits**

Nonalignment

  USE **Neutrality**

Nonbook materials

  USE **Audiovisual materials**

Noncitizens

  USE **Aliens**

Nonconformity

  USE **Conformity**

      Counter culture

      Dissent

Nondenominational churches

  USE **Community churches**

Nonfiction films

  USE **Documentary films**

Nonformal schools

  USE **Experimental schools**

Nonfossil fuels

  USE **Synthetic fuels**

Nongraded schools (May subdiv. geog.)
371.2
UF Multi-age grouping
Ungraded schools
BT **Ability grouping in education**
Education—Experimental
methods
Schools
Noninstitutional churches
USE **Non-institutional churches**
Nonlinguistic communication
USE **Nonverbal communication**
Nonnationals
USE **Aliens**
Nonnutritive sweeteners
USE **Sugar substitutes**
Nonobjective art
USE **Abstract art**
Nonprescription drugs   615
UF Drugs, Nonprescription
Over-the-counter drugs
Patent medicines
BT **Drugs**
Nonprint materials
USE **Audiovisual materials**
Nonprofit corporations
USE **Nonprofit organizations**
Nonprofit organizations (May subdiv.
geog.)   **346; 658**
UF Corporations, Nonprofit
Nonprofit corporations
Nonprofit sector
Nonprofits
Not-for-profit organizations
Organizations, Nonprofit
BT **Associations**
Nonprofit sector
USE **Nonprofit organizations**
Nonprofitable drugs
USE **Orphan drugs**
Nonprofits
USE **Nonprofit organizations**
Nonpublic schools
USE **Church schools**
Private schools
Nonsense verses   808.1; 808.81
Use for individual works, collections, or
materials about nonsense verse.
UF Rhymes
BT **Children's poetry**
Humorous poetry
Wit and humor

NT **Tongue twisters**
RT **Limericks**
Nonsupport
USE **Desertion and nonsupport**
Nonverbal communication   153.6; 302.2
UF Nonlinguistic communication
BT **Communication**
NT **Body language**
Hugging
Personal space
RT **Deaf—Means of communica-**
tion
Nonvictim crimes
USE **Crimes without victims**
Nonviolence (May subdiv. geog.)   **179;**
303.6
NT **Hunger strikes**
RT **Pacifism**
Passive resistance
Nonviolent noncooperation
USE **Passive resistance**
Nonwage payments
USE **Fringe benefits**
Nonword stories
USE **Stories without words**
Nordic peoples
USE **Teutonic peoples**
Normal schools
USE **Teachers colleges**
Normandy (France), Attack on, 1944
940.54
UF D Day
BT **World War, 1939-1945—Cam-**
paigns
Normans (May subdiv. geog.)   **941.02**
BT **Great Britain—History—1066-**
1154, Norman period
RT **Vikings**
Norse languages
USE **Old Norse language**
Scandinavian languages
Norse legends   398.20893
BT **Legends**
Norse literature
USE **Old Norse literature**
Scandinavian literature
Norsemen
USE **Vikings**
North Africa   961
Use for materials dealing collectively with
the region of Africa that includes Morocco,
Algeria, Tunisia, and Libya.

North Africa—*Continued*
>   UF   Africa, North
>   Barbary States
>   Maghreb
>   BT   **Africa**

North America   970
>   BT   **America**
>   NT   **Central America**
>   **Northwest Coast of North
>   America**
>   **Pacific Northwest**

**North Atlantic Treaty Organization
341.7**
>   UF   NATO
>   BT   **International organization**

North Central States
>   USE   **Middle West**

North Korea
>   USE   **Korea (North)**

North Pole   910.9163; 998
>   BT   **Polar regions**
>   RT   **Arctic regions**

Northeast Africa   960
>   Use for materials dealing collectively with
>   the region of Africa that includes Sudan, Ethi-
>   opia, Eritrea, Somalia, and Djibouti.
>   UF   Africa, Northeast
>   BT   **Africa**

Northeast Passage   998
>   BT   **Arctic regions**
>   **Exploration**
>   **Voyages and travels**

Northern lights
>   USE   **Auroras**

Northmen
>   USE   **Vikings**

Northwest Africa   964
>   Use for materials dealing collectively with
>   the region of Africa that includes Morocco,
>   Western Sahara, Mauritania, Algeria, Mali,
>   Tunisia, Libya, Niger, and Chad.
>   UF   Africa, Northwest
>   BT   **Africa**

**Northwest Coast of North America
979.5**
>   UF   Northwest, Pacific coast
>   Pacific Northwest coast
>   BT   **North America**

Northwest, Old
>   USE   **Old Northwest**

Northwest, Pacific
>   USE   **Pacific Northwest**

Northwest, Pacific coast
>   USE   **Northwest Coast of North
>   America**

Northwest Passage   971.9
>   BT   **America—Exploration**
>   **Arctic regions**

Northwest Territory
>   USE   **Old Northwest**

Norway   948.1
>   May be subdivided like **United States** ex-
>   cept for *History.*

Norwegian drawn work
>   USE   **Hardanger needlework**

Norwegian language   439.8
>   May be subdivided like **English language.**
>   BT   **Language and languages**
>   **Scandinavian languages**
>   NT   **Danish language**

Norwegian language—0-1350
>   USE   **Old Norse language**

Norwegian literature   839.82
>   May use same subdivisions and names of
>   literary forms as for **English literature.**
>   BT   **Literature**
>   **Scandinavian literature**

Nose   611; 612.2
>   BT   **Face**
>   **Head**
>   RT   **Smell**

Not-for-profit organizations
>   USE   **Nonprofit organizations**

Notation, Mathematical
>   USE   **Mathematical notation**

Novelists   809.3; 920
>   SA   novelists of particular countries,
>   e.g. **American novelists**; and
>   names of individual novelists
>   [to be added as needed]
>   BT   **Authors**
>   NT   **American novelists**

Novelists, American
>   USE   **American novelists**

Novels
>   USE   **Fiction**

Novels in letters
>   USE   **Epistolary fiction**

Nuclear bomb shelters
>   USE   **Air raid shelters**

Nuclear energy (May subdiv. geog.)
333.792; 539.7
>   UF   Atomic energy
>   Atomic power

Nuclear energy—*Continued*
    Nuclear power
  BT **Nuclear physics**
  NT **Nuclear engineering**
      Nuclear propulsion
      Nuclear reactors
  RT **Nuclear industry**
      Nuclear power plants
Nuclear engineering (May subdiv. geog.)
    621.48
  BT **Engineering**
      Nuclear energy
      Nuclear physics
  NT **Nuclear reactors**
      Radioactive waste disposal
      Radioisotopes
Nuclear freeze movement
  USE **Antinuclear movement**
Nuclear industry (May subdiv. geog.)
    333.792
  UF Atomic industry
  BT **Industries**
  RT **Nuclear energy**
Nuclear magnetic resonance imaging
  USE **Magnetic resonance imaging**
Nuclear medicine 616.07
  UF Atomic medicine
  BT **Medicine**
  RT **Radiation—Physiological effect**
Nuclear medicine—Practice 616.07
  BT **Medical practice**
Nuclear non-proliferation
  USE **Arms control**
Nuclear particles
  USE **Particles (Nuclear physics)**
Nuclear physics 539.7
  UF Atomic nuclei
  BT **Physics**
  NT **Cosmic rays**
      Cyclotrons
      Nuclear energy
      Nuclear engineering
      Nuclear reactors
      Particles (Nuclear physics)
      Radiobiology
      Transmutation (Chemistry)
  RT **Physical chemistry**
      Radioactivity
Nuclear pollution
  USE **Radioactive pollution**
Nuclear power
  USE **Nuclear energy**

Nuclear power plants (May subdiv. geog.)
    621.48
  UF Atomic power plants
      Power plants, Nuclear
  BT **Electric power plants**
  RT **Nuclear energy**
Nuclear power plants—Accidents
    363.17
**Nuclear power plants—Environmental
    aspects 333.792; 621.48**
  BT **Environment**
      Environmental health
  NT **Radioactive waste disposal**
  RT **Antinuclear movement**
**Nuclear power plants—Fires and fire
    prevention 363.37; 628.9**
  BT **Fire prevention**
      Fires
**Nuclear power plants—Security mea-
    sures 621.48**
Nuclear propulsion 621.48
  UF Atomic-powered vehicles
  SA specific applications of nuclear
      propulsion, e.g. **Nuclear sub-
      marines** [to be added as
      needed]
  BT **Nuclear energy**
  NT **Nuclear submarines**
  RT **Nuclear reactors**
Nuclear reactors 621.48
  UF Reactors (Nuclear physics)
  BT **Nuclear energy**
      Nuclear engineering
      Nuclear physics
  RT **Nuclear propulsion**
Nuclear submarines (May subdiv. geog.)
    623.825
  UF Atomic submarines
  BT **Nuclear propulsion**
      Submarines
Nuclear test ban
  USE **Arms control**
Nuclear warfare 355.02
  UF Atomic warfare
  BT **War**
  RT **Nuclear weapons**
Nuclear waste disposal
  USE **Radioactive waste disposal**
Nuclear weapons (May subdiv. geog.)
    355.8; 623.4

Nuclear weapons—*Continued*
- UF   Atomic weapons
  - Weapons, Atomic
  - Weapons, Nuclear
- SA   types of nuclear weapons, e.g.
  - **Atomic bomb** [to be added as needed]
- BT   **Military weapons**
- NT   **Antinuclear movement**
  - **Atomic bomb**
  - **Ballistic missiles**
  - **Hydrogen bomb**
  - **Neutron weapons**
- RT   **Nuclear warfare**

Nucleic acids   547; 572.8
- UF   Polynucleotides
- BT   **Biochemistry**
- NT   **DNA**
  - **RNA**

Nucleons
- USE   **Particles (Nuclear physics)**

Nude in art   704.9; 743.4
- UF   Human anatomy in art
  - Human figure in art
- BT   **Art—Themes**
- NT   **Artistic anatomy**

Number ability
- USE   **Mathematical ability**

Number concept   119; 155.4; 372.7

Use for materials on the apperception and conceptualization of numbers. Materials on numbers, numbering, and systems of numeration are entered under **Numbers**. Materials on counting, including counting books, are entered under **Counting**.
- BT   **Apperception**
  - **Psychology**
- RT   **Numbers**

Number games   793.74
- BT   **Arithmetic—Study and teaching**
  - **Counting**
  - **Mathematical recreations**

Number patterns
- USE   **Patterns (Mathematics)**

Number readiness
- USE   **Mathematical readiness**

Number symbolism
- USE   **Numerology**
  - **Symbolism of numbers**

Number systems
- USE   **Numbers**

Number theory   512.7

Use for materials on that branch of mathematics that involves the study of integers and their relation to one another.
- UF   Theory of numbers
- BT   **Algebra**
  - **Mathematics**
  - **Set theory**
- NT   **Group theory**
- RT   **Numbers**

Numbers   119; 513

Use for materials on numbers, numbering, and systems of numeration. Materials on the conceptualization of numbers are entered under **Number concept**. Materials on counting, including counting books, are entered under **Counting**. Materials on the graphic representation of numbers are entered under **Numerals**.
- UF   Number systems
  - Numeration
- SA   names of individual numbers, e.g. **Three (The number)**; and systems of numeration, e.g. **Decimal system** [to be added as needed]
- NT   **Binary system (Mathematics)**
  - **Decimal system**
  - **Three (The number)**
- RT   **Arithmetic**
  - **Counting**
  - **Number concept**
  - **Number theory**
  - **Numerals**
  - **Symbolism of numbers**

Numeral formation
- USE   **Writing of numerals**

Numeral writing
- USE   **Writing of numerals**

Numerals   513

Use for materials on the graphic representation of numbers.
- SA   types of numerals, e.g. **Roman numerals** [to be added as needed]
- NT   **Roman numerals**
  - **Writing of numerals**
- RT   **Numbers**

Numerals, Writing of
- USE   **Writing of numerals**

Numeration
- USE   **Numbers**

Numerical analysis   518
- BT   **Mathematical analysis**

Numerical analysis—*Continued*

   NT   **Approximate computation**

Numerical sequences

   USE   **Sequences (Mathematics)**

Numerology   133.3

   Use for materials on the occult significance of numbers. General materials on the symbolism of numbers, as in philosophy, religion, or literature, are entered under **Symbolism of numbers**.

   UF   Number symbolism

         Sacred numbers

         Symbolic numbers

   BT   **Occultism**

         Symbolism of numbers

Numismatics (May subdiv. geog.)   **737**

   Use for materials on coins, paper money, medals, and tokens considered as works of art, as historical specimens, or as aids to the study of history, archeology, etc.

   BT   **Ancient history**

         Archeology

         History

   NT   **Seals (Numismatics)**

   RT   **Coins—Collectors and collecting**

         Medals

Nunneries

   USE   **Convents**

Nuns (May subdiv. geog.)   **271; 255**

   UF   Sisters (Religious)

   BT   **Women**

   NT   **Ex-nuns**

   RT   **Monasticism and religious orders for women**

Nurse clinicians

   USE   **Nurse practitioners**

Nurse midwives

   USE   **Midwives**

Nurse practitioners (May subdiv. geog.)   **610.73092; 920**

   UF   Nurse clinicians

   BT   **Allied health personnel**

         Nurses

Nursemaids

   USE   **Nannies**

Nurseries, Day

   USE   **Day care centers**

Nurseries (Horticulture) (May subdiv. geog.)   **631.5; 635**

   BT   **Fruit culture**

         Gardening

   NT   **Plant propagation**

Nursery rhymes   398.8

   Use for collections of nursery rhymes or for materials about nursery rhymes.

   UF   Poetry for children

         Rhymes

   BT   **Children's poetry**

         Children's songs

         Folklore

Nursery schools   372.21

   BT   **Elementary education**

         Schools

   RT   **Day care centers**

         Kindergarten

         Preschool education

Nurses (May subdiv. geog.)   **610.73092; 920**

   SA   types of nurses [to be added as needed]

   BT   **Medical personnel**

   NT   **Midwives**

         Nurse practitioners

         Practical nurses

         School nurses

   RT   **Nursing**

Nursing (May subdiv. geog.)   **610.73; 649.8**

   SA   types of nursing, e.g. **Home nursing**; and diseases and medical procedures with the subdivision *Nursing* [to be added as needed]

   BT   **Medicine**

         Therapeutics

   NT   **Cancer—Nursing**

         Cooking for the sick

         First aid

         Heart—Surgery—Nursing

         Home nursing

         Practical nursing

   RT   **Nurses**

         Sick

Nursing homes (May subdiv. geog.)   **362.1**

   BT   **Hospitals**

         Institutional care

         Long-term care facilities

Nursing (Infant feeding)

   USE   **Breast feeding**

Nurture and nature

   USE   **Nature and nurture**

Nutrition (May subdiv. geog.)   **613.2**

   UF   Meal planning

Nutrition—*Continued*

SA   animals, plants and crops, ethnic groups, and classes of persons with the subdivision *Nutrition*, e.g. **Children—Nutrition**; names of diseases with the subdivision *Diet therapy*, e.g. **Cancer—Diet therapy**; and types of foods with the subdivision *Therapeutic use*; e.g. **Herbs—Therapeutic use** [to be added as needed]

BT   **Health**
      Physiology
      Therapeutics

NT   **Astronauts—Nutrition**
      Carbohydrates
      Children—Nutrition
      Dietary supplements
      Eating customs
      Infants—Nutrition
      Malnutrition
      Minerals in human nutrition
      Plants—Nutrition
      Proteins
      Vitamins

RT   **Diet**
      Digestion
      Food

Nutritional supplements
   USE   **Dietary supplements**

Nuts   581.4; 634

Names of specific kinds of nuts may be used for materials on the nut or the tree.

SA   types of nuts, e.g. **Pecans** [to be added as needed]

BT   **Food**
      Seeds

NT   **Pecans**

Nylon   677
   BT   **Synthetic fabrics**

Oak   583
   UF   Oaks
   BT   **Trees**
      Wood

Oaks
   USE   **Oak**

Oats   633.1
   BT   **Feeds**

Obedience   179
   UF   Disobedience
   BT   **Virtue**

Obelisks (May subdiv. geog.)   **721**
   BT   **Archeology**
      Architecture
      Monuments
      Pyramids

Obesity   613.2; 616.3
   UF   Corpulence
      Fatness
      Overweight
   BT   **Body weight**

Obituaries (May subdiv. geog.)   **920**
   UF   Death notices
      Necrologies
   SA   ethnic groups and classes of persons with the subdivision *Obituaries* [to be added as needed]
   BT   **Biography**

Objets d'art
   USE   **Art objects**

Obligation
   USE   **Responsibility**

Obscene materials
   USE   **Obscenity (Law)**
      Pornography

Obscenity (Law) (May subdiv. geog.)   **345**
   UF   Obscene materials
   BT   **Criminal law**
   RT   **Erotica**
      Pornography

Observatories, Astronomical
   USE   **Astronomical observatories**

Observatories, Meteorological
   USE   **Meteorological observatories**

Obsession (Psychology)
   USE   **Obsessive-compulsive disorder**

Obsessive-compulsive disorder   616.85
   UF   Fixed ideas
      Obsession (Psychology)
      Obsessive-compulsive neuroses
   BT   **Neuroses**
   RT   **Compulsive behavior**

Obsessive-compulsive neuroses
   USE   **Obsessive-compulsive disorder**

Obstetrics
   USE   **Childbirth**

Obstinacy
   USE   **Stubbornness**

Occidental civilization
   USE   **Western civilization**

Occult fiction   808.3; 808.83

Use for individual works, collections, or materials about fiction dealing with supernatural powers.

BT **Fiction**

NT **Ghost stories**

Gothic novels

RT **Fantasy fiction**

Occult sciences

USE **Occultism**

Occultism (May subdiv. geog.)   **130**

UF Hermetic art and philosophy

Occult sciences

Sorcery

BT **Religions**

Supernatural

NT **Alchemy**

Astrology

Cabala

Clairvoyance

Demonology

Divination

Magic

New Age movement

Numerology

Oracles

Palmistry

Prophecies

Spiritualism

Witchcraft

RT **Parapsychology**

Occupation, Military

USE **Military occupation**

Occupational accidents

USE **Industrial accidents**

Occupational crimes

USE **White collar crimes**

Occupational diseases (May subdiv. geog.)   **616.9**

UF Industrial diseases

Occupations—Diseases

SA occupational groups with the subdivision *Diseases*, e.g. **Miners—Diseases**; types of industries with the subdivisions *Employees—Diseases*; e.g. **Chemical industry—Employees—Diseases**; and names of occupational diseases [to be added as needed]

BT **Diseases**

NT **Chemical industry—Employees—Diseases**

Lead poisoning

Miners—Diseases

RT **Hazardous occupations**

Occupational health and safety

Occupational forecasting

USE **Employment forecasting**

Occupational guidance

USE **Vocational guidance**

Occupational health and safety (May subdiv. geog.)   **363.11; 658.3**

UF Health, Industrial

Industrial health

Industrial safety

Safety, Industrial

BT **Environmental health**

Management

Public health

NT **Burn out (Psychology)**

RT **Hazardous occupations**

Occupational diseases

Occupational health services

Occupational health services (May subdiv. geog.)   **331.25**

Use for materials on health services for employees, usually provided at the place of work.

UF Employee health services

BT **Medical care**

RT **Occupational health and safety**

Occupational injuries

USE **Industrial accidents**

Occupational literacy

USE **Functional literacy**

Occupational retraining (May subdiv. geog.)   **331.25**

UF Job retraining

Retraining, Occupational

BT **Employees—Training**

Labor supply

Occupational training

Technical education

Unemployed

Vocational education

Occupational stress

USE **Job stress**

Occupational therapy   615.8

BT **Mental health**

Physical therapy

Physically handicapped—Rehabilitation

Occupational therapy—*Continued*
Therapeutics
RT **Handicraft**
Occupational training (May subdiv.
geog.) **331.25; 374**
Use for materials on teaching people a skill
after formal education. Materials on teaching
a skill during the educational process are en-
tered under **Vocational education**. Materials
discussing on-the-job training are entered un-
der **Employees—Training**. Materials on
retraining are entered under **Occupational
retraining**.
UF Job training
Training, Occupational
Training, Vocational
Vocational training
BT **Technical education**
Vocational education
NT **Employees—Training**
Occupational retraining
Occupations (May subdiv. geog.)
331.702
Use for descriptions and lists of occupa-
tions.
UF Careers
Jobs
Trades
Vocations
SA fields of knowledge, professions,
industries, and trades with the
subdivision *Vocational guid-
ance*, and ethnic groups and
classes of persons with the
subdivision *Employment*, e.g.
Women—Employment [to be
added as needed]
NT **Hazardous occupations**
Job analysis
Paraprofessionals
Professions
Vocation
RT **Employment**
Vocational guidance
Work
Occupations—Chicago (Ill.) **331.702**
UF Chicago (Ill.)—Occupations
Occupations—Diseases
USE **Occupational diseases**
Occupations—Ohio **331.702**
UF Ohio—Occupations
Occupations—United States **331.702**
UF United States—Occupations

Occupied territories
USE names of wars with the subdivi-
sion *Occupied territories,* e.g.
**World War, 1939-1945—Oc-
cupied territories** [to be add-
ed as needed]
Occupied territory
USE **Military occupation**
Ocean **551.46**
UF Oceans
BT **Earth**
Physical geography
Water
NT **Atlantic Ocean**
Icebergs
Indian Ocean
Ocean bottom
Ocean currents
Ocean waves
Pacific Ocean
Tides
RT **Oceanography**
Seashore
Ocean bottom **551.46**
UF Ocean floor
Sea bed
BT **Ocean**
Submarine geology
NT **Marine mineral resources**
Ocean cables
USE **Submarine cables**
Ocean currents **551.46**
UF Currents, Ocean
BT **Navigation**
Ocean
NT **El Niño Current**
Ocean drilling platforms
USE **Drilling platforms**
Ocean—Economic aspects
USE **Marine resources**
Shipping
Ocean energy resources **333.91**
BT **Energy resources**
Marine resources
Ocean engineering
NT **Geothermal resources**
RT **Marine mineral resources**
Ocean engineering (May subdiv. geog.)
627
Use for materials on engineering beneath
the surface of the ocean.

Ocean engineering—*Continued*
>   UF Deep sea engineering
>   Submarine engineering
>   Undersea engineering
>   BT **Engineering**
>   **Marine resources**
>   **Oceanography**
>   NT **Drilling platforms**
>   **Marine mineral resources**
>   **Ocean energy resources**
>   **Ocean mining**
>   **Offshore oil well drilling**

Ocean farming
>   USE **Aquaculture**

Ocean fishing
>   USE **Saltwater fishing**

Ocean floor
>   USE **Ocean bottom**

Ocean life
>   USE **Marine biology**

Ocean mineral resources
>   USE **Marine mineral resources**

Ocean mining (May subdiv. geog.)   **622**
>   UF Deep sea mining
>   Mining, Ocean
>   BT **Marine mineral resources**
>   **Mining engineering**
>   **Ocean engineering**

Ocean pollution
>   USE **Marine pollution**

Ocean resources
>   USE **Marine resources**

Ocean routes
>   USE **Trade routes**

Ocean transportation
>   USE **Shipping**

Ocean travel   910.4
>   UF Cruises
>   Sea travel
>   BT **Transportation**
>   **Travel**
>   **Voyages and travels**
>   NT **Steamboats**
>   **Yachts and yachting**

Ocean waves   551.46
>   UF Breakers
>   Sea waves
>   Surf
>   Swell
>   BT **Ocean**
>   **Waves**
>   NT **Tsunamis**

Oceania   995
>   Use for comprehensive materials on the lands and area of the central and southern Pacific Ocean, including Micronesia, Melanesia, and Polynesia. Comprehensive works on all the islands of the Pacific Ocean are entered under **Islands of the Pacific**.
>   UF South Pacific region
>   South Sea Islands
>   South Seas
>   Southwest Pacific region
>   BT **Islands of the Pacific**

Oceanographic research
>   USE **Oceanography—Research**

Oceanography (May subdiv. geog.)
>   **551.46**
>   UF Oceanology
>   BT **Earth sciences**
>   NT **Marine biology**
>   **Marine pollution**
>   **Marine resources**
>   **Ocean engineering**
>   **Submarine geology**
>   **Underwater exploration**
>   RT **Ocean**

Oceanography—Atlantic Ocean   551.46
Oceanography—Computer software
>   **551.46**
>   BT **Computer software**

Oceanography—Research   551.46
>   UF Oceanographic research
>   BT **Research**
>   NT **Bathyscaphe**
>   **Undersea research stations**

Oceanology
>   USE **Oceanography**

Oceans
>   USE **Ocean**

Oddities
>   USE **Curiosities and wonders**

Oedipus (Legendary character)   398.22
>   BT **Legendary characters**

Offenses against property (May subdiv. geog.)   **364.16**
>   UF Crimes against property
>   Property, Crimes against
>   SA types of offenses, e.g. **Vandalism** [to be added as needed]
>   BT **Crime**
>   **Criminal law**
>   NT **Arson**
>   **Extortion**
>   **Fraud**

Offenses against property—*Continued*
> Theft
> Vandalism

Offenses against public safety (May subdiv. geog.) **364.1**
> UF   Crimes against public safety
>   Public safety, Crimes against
> SA   types of offenses, e.g. **Hijacking of airplanes** [to be added as needed]
> BT   **Crime**
>   **Criminal law**
> NT   **Bombings**
>   **Hijacking of airplanes**
>   **Riots**
>   **Sabotage**

Offenses against the person (May subdiv. geog.) **364.15**
> UF   Abuse of persons
>   Assault, Criminal
>   Crimes against the person
>   Criminal assault
> SA   types of offenses, e.g. **Kidnapping** [to be added as needed]
> BT   **Crime**
>   **Criminal law**
> NT   **Homicide**
>   **Identity theft**
>   **Kidnapping**
>   **Rape**
>   **Stalking**

Offenses, Military
> USE   **Military offenses**

Office buildings (May subdiv. geog.) **725**
> UF   Buildings, Office
> BT   **Buildings**

Office employees
> USE   **Office workers**

Office equipment and supplies **651**
> UF   Business machines
>   Office machines
>   Office supplies
> SA   types of office equipment and supplies [to be added as needed]
> BT   **Bookkeeping**
>   **Office management**
> NT   **Calculators**
>   **Copying machines**
>   **Keyboards (Electronics)**
>   **Typewriters**

Office etiquette
> USE   **Business etiquette**

Office machines
> USE   **Office equipment and supplies**

Office management **651.3**
> UF   Office procedures
> BT   **Business**
>   **Factory management**
>   **Industrial efficiency**
>   **Management**
> NT   **Files and filing**
>   **Office equipment and supplies**
>   **Office practice**
>   **Secretaries**
>   **Word processing**
> RT   **Personnel management**

Office practice **651.3**
> UF   Secretarial practice
> BT   **Office management**
> NT   **Keyboarding (Electronics)**
>   **Shorthand**
>   **Typewriting**
>   **Word processing**
> RT   **Office workers**

Office procedures
> USE   **Office management**

Office romance
> USE   **Sex in the workplace**

Office supplies
> USE   **Office equipment and supplies**

Office work—Training
> USE   **Business education**

Office workers (May subdiv. geog.) **331.7; 651.3**
> UF   Clerical employees
>   Clerical personnel
>   Clerks
>   Commercial employees
>   Office employees
> BT   **Employees**
> RT   **Office practice**

Office workers—Salaries, wages, etc. (May subdiv. geog.) **331.2**
> BT   **Salaries, wages, etc.**

Officers
> USE   names of armed forces with the subdivision *Officers,* e.g. **United States. Army—Officers** [to be added as needed]

Official languages
    USE   **Language and languages—Gov-
            ernment policy**
Official misconduct
    USE   **Misconduct in office**
Official publications
    USE   **Government publications**
Officials and employees
    USE   **Civil service
            Public officers**
            and names of countries, states,
            cities, etc., and corporate
            bodies with the subdivision
            Officials and employees, e.g.
            **United States—Officials and
            employees; Ohio—Officials
            and employees; Chicago
            (Ill.)—Officials and employ-
            ees; United Nations—Offi-
            cials and employees;** etc. [to
            be added as needed]
Offset printing   686.2
    UF   Lithoprinting
    BT   **Lithography
            Printing**
Offshore oil industry (May subdiv. geog.)
        338.2
    UF   Oil industry, Offshore
    BT   **Petroleum industry**
    NT   **Offshore oil well drilling**
Offshore oil well drilling (May subdiv.
        geog.)   **622**
    UF   Deep sea drilling (Petroleum)
            Oil well drilling, Offshore
            Oil well drilling, Submarine
            Submarine oil well drilling
            Underwater drilling (Petroleum)
    BT   **Ocean engineering
            Offshore oil industry
            Oil well drilling**
    NT   **Drilling platforms**
Offshore water pollution
    USE   **Marine pollution**
Ohio   977.1
    The subdivisions under **Ohio** may be used
    under the name of any state of the United
    States or province of Canada. The subdivi-
    sions under **United States** may be further
    consulted as a guide for formulating other
    headings as needed.
Ohio—Antiquities   977.1
    BT   **Antiquities**
Ohio—Bibliography   015.771; 016.9771

Ohio—Bio-bibliography   012
Ohio—Biography   920.0771
    BT   **Biography**
**Ohio—Biography—Dictionaries
        920.0771**
Ohio—Biography—Portraits   920.0771
Ohio—Boundaries   977.1
    BT   **Boundaries**
Ohio—Census   317.71
    BT   **Census**
Ohio—Church history   277.71
    UF   Church history—Ohio
            Ohio—Religious history
    BT   **Church history**
    RT   **Ohio—Religion**
Ohio—Civilization   977.1
    BT   **Civilization**
Ohio—Climate   551.69771
    BT   **Climate**
Ohio—Commerce   381
    BT   **Commerce**
Ohio—Constitution
    USE   **Constitutions—Ohio**
Ohio—Constitutional history
    USE   **Constitutional history—Ohio**
Ohio—Constitutional law
    USE   **Constitutional law—Ohio**
Ohio—Description
    USE   **Ohio—Description and travel**
Ohio—Description and travel   917.71
    UF   Ohio—Description
            Ohio—Travel
Ohio—Description and travel—Guidebooks
    USE   **Ohio—Guidebooks**
Ohio—Description and travel—Views
    USE   **Ohio—Pictorial works**
Ohio—Directories   917.710025
    Use for lists of names and addresses. Lists
    of names without addresses are entered under
    Ohio—Registers.
    BT   **Directories**
    RT   **Ohio—Registers**
Ohio—Economic conditions   330.9771
    BT   **Economic conditions**
Ohio—Economic policy
    USE   **Economic policy—Ohio**
Ohio—Employees
    USE   **Ohio—Officials and employees**
Ohio—Executive departments
    USE   **Executive departments—Ohio**

Ohio—Executive departments—Reorganization
USE **Administrative agencies—Reorganization—Ohio**
Ohio—Fiction   808.83; 813
Use for collections of stories about Ohio.
Ohio—Gazetteers   917.71
BT **Gazetteers**
Ohio—Government employees
USE **Ohio—Officials and employees**
Ohio—Government publications
USE **Government publications—Ohio**
Ohio—Guidebooks   917.7104
UF Ohio—Description and travel—Guidebooks
Ohio—Historic buildings
USE **Historic buildings—Ohio**
Ohio—History   977.1
NT **Constitutional history—Ohio**
Ohio—History—Societies   977.106
BT **History—Societies**
Ohio—History—Sources   977.1
Ohio—Industries
USE **Industries—Ohio**
Ohio—Intellectual life   977.1
BT **Intellectual life**
Ohio—Local history   977.1
BT **Local history**
Ohio—Manufactures
USE **Manufactures—Ohio**
Ohio—Maps   912.771
BT **Maps**
Ohio—Militia   355.3
BT **Armed forces**
Ohio—Moral conditions   977.1
BT **Moral conditions**
Ohio—Occupations
USE **Occupations—Ohio**
Ohio—Officials and employees   351.771
UF Ohio—Employees
Ohio—Government employees
Ohio—Officials and employees—Salaries, wages, etc.   331.2
BT **Salaries, wages, etc.**
Ohio—Pictorial works   917.710022
UF Ohio—Description and travel—Views
Ohio—Politics and government   977.1
Ohio—Population   304.609771
BT **Population**

Ohio—Public buildings
USE **Public buildings—Ohio**
Ohio—Public lands
USE **Public lands—Ohio**
Ohio—Public works
USE **Public works—Ohio**
Ohio—Race relations   305.8009771
BT **Race relations**
Ohio—Registers   917.710025
Use for lists of names without addresses. Lists of names that include addresses are entered under **Ohio—Directories**.
RT **Ohio—Directories**
Ohio—Religion   277.71
BT **Religion**
RT **Ohio—Church history**
Ohio—Religious history
USE **Ohio—Church history**
Ohio—Rural conditions   307.7209771
BT **Rural sociology**
Ohio—Social conditions   977.1
BT **Social conditions**
Ohio—Social life and customs   977.1
BT **Manners and customs**
Ohio—Social policy
USE **Social policy—Ohio**
Ohio—Statistics   317.71
BT **Statistics**
Ohio—Travel
USE **Ohio—Description and travel**
Oil
USE **Oils and fats**
Petroleum
Oil burners   697
BT **Heating**
Petroleum as fuel
Oil drilling platforms
USE **Drilling platforms**
Oil engines
USE **Internal combustion engines**
Oil fuel
USE **Petroleum as fuel**
Oil industry
USE **Petroleum industry**
Oil industry, Offshore
USE **Offshore oil industry**
Oil painting
USE **Painting**
Oil pollution of rivers, harbors, etc.
USE **Oil pollution of water**
Oil pollution of water (May subdiv. geog.)   **363.739; 628.1**

Oil pollution of water—*Continued*
> UF   Oil pollution of rivers, harbors,
>   etc.
>   Petroleum pollution of water
>   Water—Oil pollution
> BT   **Water pollution**
> NT   **Oil spills**
> RT   **Marine pollution**

Oil spills (May subdiv. geog.)   **363.738**
> BT   **Oil pollution of water**

Oil well drilling (May subdiv. geog.)
622
> UF   Drilling, Oil well
>   Petroleum—Well boring
>   Well drilling, Oil
> BT   **Drilling and boring (Earth and**
>   **rocks)**
>   **Petroleum industry**
> NT   **Offshore oil well drilling**
>   **Oil wells—Blowouts**
> RT   **Oil wells**

Oil well drilling, Offshore
> USE   **Offshore oil well drilling**

Oil well drilling, Submarine
> USE   **Offshore oil well drilling**

Oil wells (May subdiv. geog.)   **622**
> BT   **Petroleum industry**
> RT   **Oil well drilling**

Oil wells—Blowouts   **622**
> UF   Blowouts, Oil well
> BT   **Oil well drilling**

Oils and fats   **665**
> UF   Animal oils
>   Fats
>   Grease
>   Oil
>   Vegetable oils
> NT   **Essences and essential oils**
>   **Petroleum**
> RT   **Low-fat diet**
>   **Lubrication and lubricants**

Old age (May subdiv. geog.)   **305.26**
> BT   **Age**
> NT   **Aging**
>   **Retirement**
> RT   **Elderly**
>   **Gerontology**
>   **Longevity**

Old age homes
> USE   **Elderly—Institutional care**

Old age pensions (May subdiv. geog.)
331.25; 368.3

> UF   Aged—Pensions
>   Employees—Pensions
> BT   **Pensions**
>   **Retirement income**

Old English language
> USE   **English language—Old English**
>   **period**

Old English literature
> USE   **English literature—Old English**
>   **period**

Old Icelandic language
> USE   **Old Norse language**

Old Norse language   **439**
> UF   Icelandic language—0-1500
>   Norse languages
>   Norwegian language—0-1350
>   Old Icelandic language
>   Old Norwegian language
> BT   **Language and languages**
>   **Scandinavian languages**

Old Norse literature   **839**
> UF   Norse literature
> BT   **Literature**
>   **Medieval literature**
> NT   **Eddas**
>   **Sagas**
> RT   **Icelandic literature**
>   **Scandinavian literature**

Old Northwest   **977**
> Use for materials on the region between the
> Ohio and Mississippi rivers and the Great
> Lakes.
> UF   Northwest, Old
>   Northwest Territory
> BT   **United States**
> RT   **Middle West**

Old Norwegian language
> USE   **Old Norse language**

Old Southwest   **976**
> Use for materials on that section of the
> United States that comprised the southwestern
> part before the cessions of land from Mexico
> following the Mexican War. It included Loui-
> siana, Texas, Arkansas, Tennessee, Kentucky
> and Missouri.
> UF   Southwest, Old
> BT   **United States**

Old Testament
> USE   **Bible. O.T.**

Older persons
> USE   **Elderly**

Oldest child
> USE   **Birth order**

Olympic games   **796.48; 796.98**

Olympic games—*Continued*
    UF   Olympics
    SA   topical headings for Olympic
           events of a particular year,
           e.g. **Olympic games, 1996**
           (Atlanta, Ga.) [to be added
           as needed]
    BT   **Athletics**
         Contests
         Games
         Sports
    NT   **Olympic games, 1996 (Atlanta,**
         Ga.)
         Special Olympics
Olympic games, 1996 (Atlanta, Ga.)
    796.48
    BT   **Olympic games**
Olympics
    USE **Olympic games**
Ombudsman (May subdiv. geog.)   **328.3;**
    342; 352.8
    UF   Citizen's defender
           Grievance procedures (Public ad-
           ministration)
    BT   **Administrative law**
         Public interest
On-line sex
    USE **Computer sex**
One act plays   808.82
    Use for individual works, collections, or
    materials about one-act plays.
    UF   Plays
           Short plays
    BT   **Amateur theater**
         Drama
One parent family
    USE **Single-parent families**
Online auctions
    USE **Internet auctions**
Online books
    USE **Electronic books**
Online catalogs   025.3
    UF   Catalogs, Online
           Online public access catalogs
           OPACs (Online public access
           catalogs)
    BT   **Library catalogs**
    RT   **Libraries—Automation**
Online chat groups   004.69
    Use for materials on services that allow us-
    ers to engage in conversations in real time.
    Materials on services, commonly called elec-

tronic mailing lists, that allow subscribers to
post messages that are then distributed to other subscribers are entered under **Electronic
discussion groups**. Materials on services that
allow users to post messages and retrieve
messages from others who have some common interest are entered under **Computer
bulletin boards**.
    UF   Chat groups, Online
           Chat rooms, Online
           Internet chat groups
           Online chat rooms
    BT   **Conversation**
    RT   **Computer bulletin boards**
         Electronic discussion groups
Online chat rooms
    USE **Online chat groups**
Online commerce
    USE **Electronic commerce**
Online discussion groups
    USE **Electronic discussion groups**
Online gambling
    USE **Internet gambling**
Online journalism (May subdiv. geog.)
    070.4
    UF   Electronic journalism
           Internet journalism
    BT   **Journalism**
    NT   **Weblogs**
Online marketing
    USE **Internet marketing**
Online public access catalogs
    USE **Online catalogs**
Online publishing
    USE **Electronic publishing**
Online reference services
    USE **Electronic reference services**
           (Libraries)
Online selling
    USE **Internet marketing**
Online sex
    USE **Computer sex**
Online shopping
    USE **Internet shopping**
Online social networking
    USE **Social networking**
Only child   155.44; 306.874
    UF   Single child
    BT   **Children**
         Family size
OPACs (Online public access catalogs)
    USE **Online catalogs**
Opaque projectors
    USE **Projectors**

Open access publishing (May subdiv. geog.)   **070.5**
  BT **Electronic publishing**
Open and closed shop (May subdiv. geog.)   **331.88**
  UF Closed shop
      Right to work
      Union shop
  BT **Labor**
      Labor contract
      Labor unions
Open classroom approach to teaching
  USE **Open plan schools**
Open code software
  USE **Open source software**
Open education
  USE **Open plan schools**
Open heart surgery
  USE **Heart—Surgery**
Open housing
  USE **Discrimination in housing**
Open plan schools (May subdiv. geog.)   **371.2**
  Use for materials on schools without interior walls.
  UF Interest centers approach to teaching
      Learning center approach to teaching
      Open classroom approach to teaching
      Open education
  BT **Education—Experimental methods**
  RT **Experimental schools**
      Individualized instruction
Open source software   **005.3**
  UF Open code software
  BT **Computer software**
Open universities
  USE **Free universities**
Opera (May subdiv. geog.)   **782.1; 792.5**
  Use for musical scores and for materials about the opera.
  UF Comic opera
      Dramatic music
      Operas
  BT **Drama**
      Musical form
      Performing arts
      Vocal music
  NT **Operetta**

Opera librettos   **782.1026**
  Use for individual opera librettos and for collections of opera librettos.
  UF Operas—Librettos
  BT **Librettos**
  RT **Opera—Stories, plots, etc.**
Opera plots
  USE **Opera—Stories, plots, etc.**
Opera—Sound recordings   **782.1**
  BT **Sound recordings**
Opera—Stories, plots, etc.   **782.1026**
  UF Opera plots
  RT **Opera librettos**
Operas
  USE **Opera**
Operas—Librettos
  USE **Opera librettos**
Operating systems (Computers)
  USE **Computer operating systems**
Operation Desert Storm
  USE **Persian Gulf War, 1991**
Operational analysis
  USE **Operations research**
Operational research
  USE **Operations research**
Operations research   **658.5**
  UF Operational analysis
      Operational research
  BT **Research**
      System theory
  RT **Management**
      Systems engineering
Operations, Surgical
  USE **Surgery**
Operetta (May subdiv. geog.)   **782.1; 792.5**
  Use for musical scores and for materials on the operetta as a musical form.
  UF Comic opera
      Dramatic music
      Operettas
  BT **Musical form**
      Opera
      Vocal music
  RT **Musicals**
Operettas
  USE **Operetta**
Opiates
  USE **Narcotics**
Opinion polls
  USE **Public opinion polls**

Opinion, Public
   USE **Public opinion**
Opium 615
   BT **Narcotics**
   RT **Morphine**
Opium—Physiological effect 615
   BT **Drugs—Physiological effect**
Opposites 153.2
   UF Antonyms
       Polarity
   BT **Concepts**
   RT **English language—Synonyms
       and antonyms**
**Optical data processing 006.4; 621.36;
   621.39**
   BT **Data processing**
   NT **Laser recording**
Optical discs
   USE **Optical storage devices**
Optical illusions 152.14
   UF Illusions
   BT **Hallucinations and illusions
       Psychophysiology
       Vision**
Optical instruments 681
   UF Instruments, Optical
   BT **Scientific apparatus and in-
       struments**
   NT **Lenses
       Microscopes
       Telescopes**
   RT **Optics
       Space optics**
Optical scanners 006.4; 621.39
   BT **Computer peripherals**
Optical storage devices 004.5; 621.39
   Use for materials on data storage devices in
   which audio, video, or other data are optically
   encoded.
   UF Optical discs
   BT **Computer storage devices**
   NT **CD-I technology
       CD-ROMs
       Compact discs
       DVDs
       Videodiscs**
   RT **Laser recording**
Optics 535; 621.36
   BT **Physics**
   NT **Color
       Perspective
       Radiation**

       **Refraction
       Space optics
       Spectrum analysis
       Vision**
   RT **Light
       Optical instruments
       Photometry**
Optometry 617.7
   RT **Eye**
Oracles 133.3
   BT **Occultism**
   RT **Divination
       Prophecies**
Oral history 907
   Use for materials on recording oral recollec-
   tions of places, events, etc., from persons
   drawing on their own life experiences. Oral
   histories that focus on a particular topic or
   place are entered under that topic or place.
   BT **History**
Oral interpretation
   USE **Recitations**
Orange (Fruit)
   USE **Oranges**
Oranges 634; 641.3
   UF Orange (Fruit)
   BT **Citrus fruits**
Orations
   USE **Speeches**
Oratorio 782.23
   Use for musical scores and for materials on
   the oratorio as a musical form.
   UF Oratorios
   BT **Church music
       Musical form
       Vocal music**
Oratorios
   USE **Oratorio**
Oratory
   USE **Public speaking**
Orbital laboratories
   USE **Space stations**
**Orbital rendezvous (Space flight)
   629.45**
   UF Rendezvous in space
       Space orbital rendezvous
   SA names of projects, e.g. **Apollo
       project; Gemini project**; etc.;
       and names of specific space
       ships [to be added as needed]
   BT **Space flight
       Space stations
       Space vehicles**

Orbital rendezvous (Space flight)—*Continued*
  NT   **Apollo project**
       Gemini project
Orbiting vehicles
  USE **Artificial satellites**
       Space stations
Orchards
  USE **Fruit culture**
Orchestra 784.2
  SA   types of orchestras [to be added
       as needed[
  NT   **Conductors (Music)**
       Instrumentation and orchestration
       Orchestral music
  RT   **Bands (Music)**
       Conducting
       Ensembles (Music)
       Musical instruments
Orchestral music 784.2
  SA   types of orchestral music, e.g.
       Symphony [to be added as
       needed]
  BT   **Instrumental music**
       Music
       Orchestra
  NT   **Concerto**
       String orchestra music
       Suite (Music)
       Symphonic poems
       Symphony
Orchestration
  USE **Instrumentation and orchestration**
Order 117
  NT   **Orderliness**
Orderliness 640; 648
  UF   Neatness
       Tidiness
  BT   **Order**
Orders, Monastic
  USE **Monasticism and religious orders**
Ordination 262; 265
  BT   **Rites and ceremonies**
       Sacraments
  NT   **Ordination of gays and lesbians**
       Ordination of women
  RT   **Clergy**

Ordination of gays and lesbians
      206.108664
  UF   Gay men—Ordination
       Lesbians—Ordination
  BT   **Ordination**
Ordination of women 262
  UF   Women—Ordination
  BT   **Ordination**
  RT   **Women clergy**
Ordnance 355.8; 623.4
    Use for materials on military supplies including weapons, ammunition, and vehicles, and the task of procuring, testing, storing, and issuing such supplies.
  UF   Cannon
       Guns
  SA   types of military ordnance, e.g.
       Bombs; names of armies with
       the subdivision *Ordnance*, e.g.
       United States. Army—Ordnance; and names of wars
       with the subdivision *Equipment and supplies*, e.g. **World War, 1939-1945—Equipment and supplies** [to be added as needed]
  BT   **Military art and science**
  NT   **Ammunition**
       Bombs
       Land mines
       Military weapons
       United States. Army—Ordnance
  RT   **Artillery**
       Defense industry
       Projectiles
Ore deposits (May subdiv. geog.) 553
  SA   types of ores, e.g. **Iron ores** [to
       be added as needed]
  BT   **Geology**
  RT   **Ores**
Ore dressing 622
  UF   Dressing of ores
  BT   **Smelting**
Oregon country
  USE **Pacific Northwest**
Oregon Trail 978
  BT   **Overland journeys to the Pacific**
       United States
Ores 553

Ores—*Continued*

    SA   types of ores, e.g. **Iron ores** [to be added as needed]

    BT   **Minerals**

    NT   **Iron ores**

          Metals

    RT   **Metallurgy**

          Ore deposits

Organ

    USE **Organs (Musical instruments)**

Organ donation

    USE **Donation of organs, tissues, etc.**

Organ music   786.5

    BT   **Church music**

          Instrumental music

          Music

Organ preservation (Anatomy)

    USE **Preservation of organs, tissues, etc.**

Organ transplants

    USE **Transplantation of organs, tissues, etc.**

Organic agriculture

    USE **Organic farming**

Organic chemicals

    USE **Organic compounds**

Organic chemistry   547

    UF   Chemistry, Organic

    BT   **Chemistry**

    NT   **Organic compounds**

Organic chemistry—Synthesis

    USE **Organic compounds—Synthesis**

Organic compounds   547

    UF   Organic chemicals

    SA   types of organic compounds and individual organic substances [to be added as needed]

    BT   **Chemicals**

          Organic chemistry

Organic compounds—Synthesis   547

    UF   Chemistry, Synthetic

          Organic chemistry—Synthesis

          Synthetic chemistry

    NT   **Polymers**

    RT   **Synthetic products**

Organic farming (May subdiv. geog.)   631.5

    UF   Farming, Organic

          Organic agriculture

          Organiculture

    BT   **Agriculture**

Organic gardening (May subdiv. geog.)   635

    UF   Natural gardening

          Organiculture

    BT   **Gardening**

          Horticulture

    RT   **Compost**

Organic waste as fuel

    USE **Waste products as fuel**

Organically grown foods

    USE **Natural foods**

Organiculture

    USE **Organic farming**

          Organic gardening

Organists (May subdiv. geog.)   786.5092; 920

    BT   **Instrumentalists**

Organization and management

    USE **Management**

Organization development

    USE **Organizational change**

Organization (Sociology)

    USE **Organizational sociology**

Organization theory

    USE **Organizational sociology**

Organizational behavior (May subdiv. geog.)   158.2; 302.3; 658

    UF   Behavior in organizations

    BT   **Applied psychology**

          Management

          Social psychology

Organizational change (May subdiv. geog.)   338.7; 658.4

    UF   Change, Organizational

          Organization development

          Organizational development

          Organizational innovation

    BT   **Management**

    NT   **Downsizing of organizations**

Organizational culture

    USE **Corporate culture**

Organizational development

    USE **Organizational change**

Organizational downsizing

    USE **Downsizing of organizations**

Organizational innovation

    USE **Organizational change**

Organizational retrenchment

    USE **Downsizing of organizations**

Organizational sociology   302.3

Organizational sociology—*Continued*
    UF   Organization (Sociology)
            Organization theory
            Sociology of organizations
    BT   **Sociology**
    RT   **Bureaucracy**
Organizational stress
    USE **Job stress**
Organizations
    USE **Associations**
Organizations, Nonprofit
    USE **Nonprofit organizations**
Organized crime (May subdiv. geog.)
    364.106
    UF   Crime syndicates
    SA   types of organized crime, e.g.
            Racketeering [to be added as
            needed]
    BT   **Crime**
    NT   **Gangs**
            Racketeering
Organized labor
    USE **Labor unions**
Organs (Anatomy)—Preservation
    USE **Preservation of organs, tissues,**
            etc.
Organs, Artificial
    USE **Artificial organs**
Organs (Musical instruments) (May
    subdiv. geog.)   **786.5**
    UF   Organ
            Pipe organs
    BT   **Musical instruments**
    NT   **Keyboards (Musical instru-**
            ments)
Orient
    USE **Asia**
           East Asia
           Middle East
Oriental architecture
    USE **Asian architecture**
Oriental art
    USE **Asian art**
Oriental civilization
    USE **Asia—Civilization**
Oriental rugs (May subdiv. geog.) **746.7**
    SA   types of Oriental rugs [to be
            added as needed]
    BT   **Rugs and carpets**

Orientalism (May subdiv. geog.)   **303;**
    950
    Use for materials on the depiction or adop-
    tion of characteristics of Asian and Middle
    Eastern cultures by Westerners.
    BT   **East and West**
Orientation
    USE **Direction sense**
Orienteering   **796.58**
    BT   **Hiking**
            Racing
            Running
            Sports
    RT   **Direction sense**
            Navigation
Origami   **736**
    UF   Japanese paper folding
            Paper folding
    BT   **Paper crafts**
Origin
    USE subjects, ethnic groups, classes
            of persons, animals, plants,
            crops, and religions with the
            subdivision *Origin,* e.g.
            Life—Origin; Native Ameri-
            cans—Origin; etc. [to be
            added as needed]
Origin of life
    USE **Life—Origin**
Origin of man
    USE **Human origins**
Origin of species
    USE **Evolution**
Orlando (Legendary character)
    USE **Roland (Legendary character)**
Ornament
    USE **Decoration and ornament**
Ornamental alphabets
    USE **Alphabets**
            Illumination of books and
            manuscripts
            Lettering
Ornamental plants (May subdiv. geog.)
    635.9; 715
    UF   Plants, Ornamental
    BT   **Cultivated plants**
            Flower gardening
            Landscape gardening
    RT   **Shrubs**
Orphan drugs   **615**
    Use for materials on drugs that appear to be
    useful for the treatment of rare disorders but

Orphan drugs—*Continued*
owing to their limited commercial value have difficulty in finding funding for research and marketing.

UF   Nonprofitable drugs

BT   **Drugs**

Orphanages (May subdiv. geog.)   **362.73**

UF   Charitable institutions

      Homes (Institutions)

BT   **Charities**

      Children—Institutional care

RT   **Child welfare**

Orphans (May subdiv. geog.)
    305.23086; 362.73

UF   Foundlings

BT   **Children**

RT   **Abandoned children**

      Adopted children

Orthodox Eastern Church (May subdiv. geog.)   **281.9**

BT   **Christian sects**

      Eastern churches

NT   **Greek Orthodox Church**

      Russian Orthodox Church

Orthography

USE   names of languages with the subdivision *Spelling,* e.g. **English language—Spelling** [to be added as needed]

Orthopedic apparatus   **617**

UF   Orthotic devices

BT   **Orthopedics**

NT   **Wheelchairs**

Orthopedic surgery

USE   **Orthopedics**

Orthopedics   **616.7; 617.4**

UF   Orthopedic surgery

BT   **Medicine**

      Surgery

NT   **Artificial limbs**

      Orthopedic apparatus

RT   **Physically handicapped**

Orthotic devices

USE   **Orthopedic apparatus**

Oscars (Motion pictures)

USE   **Academy Awards (Motion pictures)**

Osteopathic medicine   **610; 615.5**

Use for materials on the therapeutic system based on the theory that disease is caused by loss of a structural integrity that can be restored by manipulation of the bones and muscles.

UF   Osteopathy

BT   **Medicine**

RT   **Chiropractic**

      Massage

Osteopathy

USE   **Osteopathic medicine**

Osteoporosis   **616.7**

BT   **Bones—Diseases**

Ostrogoths

USE   **Goths**

Out-of-body experiences

USE   **Astral projection**

Out-of-doors education

USE   **Outdoor education**

Out-of-work people

USE   **Unemployed**

Outdoor cooking   **641.5**

UF   Camp cooking

BT   **Camping**

      Cooking

NT   **Barbecue cooking**

Outdoor education   **371.3**

UF   Out-of-doors education

BT   **Education**

RT   **Nature study**

      Outdoor life

Outdoor life (May subdiv. geog.)   **796.5**

UF   Rural life

SA   types of outdoor life, education, or activities [to be added as needed]

NT   **Hiking**

      Mountaineering

      Wilderness survival

RT   **Camping**

      Country life

      Nature study

      Outdoor education

      Sports

Outdoor photography   **778.7**

UF   Field photography

BT   **Photography**

RT   **Nature photography**

Outdoor recreation (May subdiv. geog.)   **796**

SA   types of outdoor recreation, e.g. **Camping** [to be added as needed]

BT   **Recreation**

NT   **Camping**

      Cycling

      Recreational vehicles

Outdoor recreation—*Continued*
> Roller skating
> Safaris

Outdoor survival
> USE **Wilderness survival**

Outer space 523.1
> UF Space, Outer
> BT **Astronautics**
> **Astronomy**
> **Space sciences**
> NT **Space environment**
> **Space warfare**

Outer space and civilization
> USE **Astronautics and civilization**

Outer space—Colonies
> USE **Space colonies**

Outer space—Communication
> USE **Interstellar communication**

Outer space—Exploration 629.4
> UF Exploration of space
> Space exploration (Astronautics)
> Space research
> BT **Exploration**
> **Interplanetary voyages**
> **Space flight**
> NT **Planets—Exploration**
> **Space probes**

Outlaws
> USE **Criminals**
> **Thieves**

Outlines, syllabi, etc.
> USE subjects with the subdivision
> *Outlines, syllabi, etc.,* e.g.
> **English literature—Outlines,**
> **syllabi, etc.** [to be added as
> needed]

Output equipment (Computers)
> USE **Computer peripherals**

Output standards
> USE **Production standards**

Outsourcing 658.723
> UF Contracting for services
> Contracting out
> BT **Contracts**

Over-the-counter drugs
> USE **Nonprescription drugs**

Overland journeys to the Pacific 978
> Use for materials on the pioneers' crossing
> of the American continent toward the Pacific
> by foot, horseback, wagon, etc.
> UF Transcontinental journeys (American continent)

> BT **Frontier and pioneer life**
> **Voyages and travels**
> NT **Oregon Trail**
> RT **West (U.S.)—Exploration**

Overpopulation 363.9; 304.6
> UF Population explosion
> SA names of countries, cities, etc.
> with the subdivision *Population,* e.g. **United States—Population** [to be added as needed]
> BT **Population**

Overseas study
> USE **Foreign study**

Oversize books
> USE **Big books**

Oversized books for shared reading
> USE **Big books**

Overtime
> USE **Hours of labor**

Overweight
> USE **Obesity**

Ownership
> USE **Property**

Oxyacetylene welding
> USE **Welding**

Oxygen 546; 547; 665.8
> BT **Chemical elements**
> **Gases**
> NT **Ozone**

Ozone 665.8
> BT **Oxygen**

Ozone layer 363.738; 551.51
> UF Ozonosphere
> Stratospheric ozone
> BT **Stratosphere**

Ozonosphere
> USE **Ozone layer**

Pacific Islands
> USE **Islands of the Pacific**

Pacific Northwest 979.5
> Use for materials on the old Oregon country, comprising the present states of Oregon, Washington, and Idaho, parts of Montana and Wyoming, and the province of British Columbia.
> UF Northwest, Pacific
> Oregon country
> BT **North America**
> **United States**
> **West (U.S.)**

Pacific Northwest coast
USE **Northwest Coast of North America**

Pacific Ocean   551.465
BT **Ocean**

Pacific Ocean Islands
USE **Islands of the Pacific**

Pacific rim   330.99; 990
Use for materials on the periphery of the Pacific Ocean, especially as a region of interdependent economies.
RT **East Asia**
Islands of the Pacific

Pacific States   979
BT **West (U.S.)**

Pacifism   174; 303.6
Use for materials on the renunciation of offensive or defensive military actions on moral grounds. Materials on social movements adovcating peace are entered under **Peace movements**.
BT **War—Religious aspects**
RT **Conscientious objectors**
Nonviolence
Peace
Peace movements

Pack transportation
USE **Backpacking**

Packaging   658.5
SA types of packaging and packaging materials, and subjects with the subdivision *Packaging*, e.g. **Food—Packaging** [to be added as needed]
BT **Advertising**
Retail trade
NT **Aluminum foil**
Food—Packaging
Gift wrapping
RT **Containers**

Packing industry
USE **Meat industry**

PACs (Political action committees)
USE **Political action committees**

Paganism (May subdiv. geog.)   **292**
BT **Christianity and other religions**
Religions
NT **Goddess religion**
Wicca

Pageants (May subdiv. geog.)   **394; 791.6**
BT **Acting**

NT **Masks (Plays)**
Medieval tournaments
Mysteries and miracle plays
Parades
RT **Festivals**

Pain   152.1; 612.8
BT **Diagnosis**
Emotions
Psychophysiology
Senses and sensation
NT **Chronic pain**
Headache
RT **Anesthetics**
Pleasure
Suffering

Paint   645; 667
BT **Finishes and finishing**
RT **Corrosion and anticorrosives**
Pigments

Paint sniffing
USE **Solvent abuse**

Painted glass
USE **Glass painting and staining**

Painters (May subdiv. geog.)   **759; 920**
BT **Artists**

Painters' materials
USE **Artists' materials**

Painters—United States   759.13; 920
UF American painters

Painting   750
UF Oil painting
Paintings
SA painting of particular countries, e.g. **American painting**; types of painting, e.g. **Landscape painting**; and topics with the subdivision *Painting*; e.g. **Automobiles—Painting** [to be added as needed]
BT **Art**
Graphic arts
NT **American painting**
Animal painting and illustration
China painting
Color
Figure painting
Finger painting
Glass painting and staining
Landscape painting
Marine painting

Painting—*Continued*
> **Miniature painting**
> **Mural painting and decoration**
> **Perspective**
> **Portrait painting**
> **Scene painting**
> **Stencil work**
> **Textile painting**
> **Watercolor painting**
> RT **Composition (Art)**
> **Decoration and ornament**
> **Drawing**
> **Pictures**

Painting—15th and 16th centuries
709.02; 709.03
> UF Painting, Renaissance
> Renaissance painting

Painting—17th and 18th centuries
759.04
> UF Painting, Modern—17th-18th
> centuries

Painting—19th century 759.05
> UF Modern painting—1800-1899
> (19th century)
> Painting, Modern—19th century

Painting—20th century 759.06
> UF Modern painting—1900-1999
> (20th century)
> Painting, Modern—20th century
> SA types of twentieth-century paint-
> ing, e.g. **Cubism** [to be added
> as needed]

Painting—21st century 759.07
> UF Modern painting—2000-2099
> (21st century)
> Painting, Modern—21st century

Painting, American
> USE **American painting**

Painting books
> USE **Coloring books**

Painting—Color reproductions
> USE **Color prints**

Painting—Conservation and restoration
751.6

Painting, Decorative
> USE **Decoration and ornament**

Painting, Finger
> USE **Finger painting**

Painting, Modern—17th-18th centuries
> USE **Painting—17th and 18th centu-
> ries**

Painting, Modern—19th century
> USE **Painting—19th century**

Painting, Modern—20th century
> USE **Painting—20th century**

Painting, Modern—21st century
> USE **Painting—21st century**

Painting, Renaissance
> USE **Painting—15th and 16th centu-
> ries**

Painting, Romanesque
> USE **Romanesque painting**

Painting—Technique 751.4

Paintings
> USE **Painting**

Pair system
> USE **Binary system (Mathematics)**

Pakistan 954.91
> May be subdivided like **United States** ex-
> cept for *History*.

Palaces (May subdiv. geog.) **728.8**
> BT **Buildings**

Paleobotany
> USE **Fossil plants**

Paleolithic period
> USE **Stone Age**

Paleontology (May subdiv. geog.) **560**
> UF Paleozoology
> BT **Historical geology**
> **Zoology**
> RT **Fossils**

Paleozoology
> USE **Paleontology**

Palestine 956.94
> Use for materials on the region on the east-
> ern coast of the Mediterranean Sea that in an-
> cient times was called the Land of Canaan,
> later the kingdoms of Israel and Judah, and in
> modern times comprises the entire state of Is-
> rael, as well as the various disputed territories.
> UF Holy Land
> Palestinian territories
> NT **West Bank**

Palestinian Arabs (May subdiv. geog.)
305.892; 956.94
> UF Arabs—Palestine
> Palestinians
> BT **Arabs**
> RT **Jewish-Arab relations**

Palestinian-Israeli conflict, 1987-1992
> USE **Intifada, 1987-1992**

Palestinian-Israeli conflict, 2000-
> USE **Intifada, 2000-**

Palestinian territories
USE **Palestine**
Palestinian uprising, 1987-1992
USE **Intifada, 1987-1992**
Palestinian uprising, 2000-
USE **Intifada, 2000-**
Palestinians
USE **Palestinian Arabs**
Palmistry 133.6
BT **Divination**
Fortune telling
Occultism
Pamphlets 025.17
UF Street literature
BT **Press**
NT **Chapbooks**
Tracts
Pamphlets—Design 686.2
BT **Design**
Pan-Africanism 320.5; 327
Use for materials on the advocacy of either political alliance or close economic, cultural, and military cooperation among the countries of Africa.
UF African relations
BT **Africa—Politics and government**
Pan-Americanism 320.5; 327
Use for materials on the advocacy of either political alliance or close economic, cultural, and military cooperation among the countries of North and South America.
UF Inter-American relations
BT **America—Politics and government**
Latin America
Pan-Arabism 320.5
Use for materials on the advocacy of either political alliance or close economic, cultural, and military cooperation among the Arab countries.
UF Panarabism
BT **Arab countries—Politics and government**
Panama Canal 972.87
BT **Canals**
Panarabism
USE **Pan-Arabism**
Panel discussions
USE **Discussion groups**
Panel heating
USE **Radiant heating**
Panhandling
USE **Begging**

Panic disorders 362.2; 616.85
BT **Abnormal psychology**
Neuroses
Panics (Finance)
USE **Financial crises**
Pantomimes 792.3
BT **Acting**
Amateur theater
Drama
Theater
NT **Shadow pantomimes and plays**
RT **Ballet**
Mime
Papacy 262
UF Holy See
BT **Catholic Church**
Church history
RT **Popes**
Papal encyclicals 262.9
UF Encyclicals, Papal
BT **Christian literature**
Papal visits (May subdiv. geog.) **262**
UF Popes—Travel
Popes—Voyages and travels
BT **Voyages and travels**
Paper 676
BT **Fibers**
NT **Papermaking**
RT **Paper industry**
Paper airplanes
USE **Airplanes—Models**
Paper bound books
USE **Paperback books**
Paper crafts 745.54
UF Paper folding
Paper sculpture
Paper work
Papier-mâché
SA types of paper crafts [to be added as needed]
BT **Handicraft**
NT **Decoupage**
Gift wrapping
Origami
RT **Papermaking**
Paper folding
USE **Origami**
Paper crafts
Paper hanging
USE **Paperhanging**

Paper industry (May subdiv. geog.)
   338.4
   Use for materials on the business of making and selling paper. Materials on the technology and craft of making paper are entered under **Papermaking**.
   UF   Papermaking industry
   BT   **Industries**
   RT   **Paper**
Paper making
   USE   **Papermaking**
Paper manufacture
   USE   **Papermaking**
Paper money (May subdiv. geog.)   **332.4**
   BT   **Money**
   RT   **Inflation (Finance)**
Paper sculpture
   USE   **Paper crafts**
Paper work
   USE   **Paper crafts**
Paperback books   **070.5**
   UF   Paper bound books
   BT   **Books**
      Editions
Paperhanging   **698**
   UF   Paper hanging
   BT   **Interior design**
   RT   **Wallpaper**
Papermaking (May subdiv. geog.)   **676**
   Use for materials on the technology and craft of making paper. Materials on the business of making and selling paper are entered under **Paper industry**.
   UF   Paper making
      Paper manufacture
   BT   **Manufactures**
      Paper
   RT   **Paper crafts**
Papermaking industry
   USE   **Paper industry**
Papier-mâché
   USE   **Paper crafts**
Parables   **808**
   Use for individual works, collections, or materials about parables.
   UF   Cautionary tales and verses
      Moral and philosophic stories
      Morality tales
   SA   individual parables, e.g. **Prodigal son (Parable)** [to be added as needed]
   NT   **Bible—Parables**
      Jesus Christ—Parables
      Prodigal son (Parable)

   RT   **Allegories**
      Didactic fiction
      Didactic poetry
      Fables
Parachute troops   **356**
   UF   Paratroops
   SA   names of armies with the subdivision *Parachute troops*, e.g. **United States. Army—Parachute troops** [to be added as needed]
   BT   **Military aeronautics**
      Parachutes
   NT   **United States. Army—Parachute troops**
Parachutes   **629.134**
   BT   **Aeronautics**
   NT   **Parachute troops**
Parade floats
   USE   **Parades**
Parades (May subdiv. geog.)   **791.6**
   UF   Floats (Parades)
      Parade floats
      Pomp
      Processions
   BT   **Festivals**
      Pageants
Paradise   **202; 236**
   Use for materials on the earthly paradise or on a blessed intermediate state in the afterlife.
   UF   Earthly paradise
      Eden
      Garden of Eden
   BT   **Future life**
   RT   **Heaven**
      Utopias
Parallel economy
   USE   **Underground economy**
Paralysis   **616.8**
   SA   individual organs and regions of the body with the subdivision *Paralysis* e.g. **Foot—Paralysis** [to be added as needed]
   BT   **Nervous system—Diseases**
   NT   **Foot—Paralysis**
Paralysis, Cerebral
   USE   **Cerebral palsy**
Paramedical personnel
   USE   **Allied health personnel**
      Emergency medical technicians
Paramedics, Emergency
   USE   **Emergency medical technicians**

Paramilitary militia movements
USE **Militia movements**
Paranormal phenomena
USE **Parapsychology**
Paraprofessional librarians
USE **Library technicians**
Paraprofessionals   331.7
    UF   Paraprofessions and
            paraprofessionals
    SA   types of paraprofessional person-
            nel, e.g. **Library technicians;**
            and fields of knowledge, pro-
            fessions, industries, and trades
            with the subdivision *Vocation-*
            al guidance [to be added as
            needed]
    BT   **Occupations**
            Professions
    NT   **Library technicians**
Paraprofessions and paraprofessionals
USE **Paraprofessionals**
Parapsychology (May subdiv. geog.)
        130

Use for materials on investigations of phenomena that appear to be contrary to physical
laws and beyond the normal sense percep-
tions.

    UF   Paranormal phenomena
            Psi (Parapsychology)
            Psychic phenomena
            Psychical research
    BT   **Psychology**
            Research
            Supernatural
    NT   **Apparitions**
            Astral projection
            Extrasensory perception
            Hallucinations and illusions
            Mental suggestion
            Mind and body
            Psychics
            Psychokinesis
            Subconsciousness
            Visions
    RT   **Ghosts**
            Occultism
            Spiritualism
Parasites   577.8; 578.6
    UF   Animal parasites
            Diseases and pests
            Entozoa
            Epizoa

    SA   types of animals and parts of
            the body with the subdivision
            Parasites [to be added as
            needed]
    BT   **Pests**
    NT   **Bacteria**
    RT   **Insect pests**
            Symbiosis
Parasols
USE **Umbrellas and parasols**
Paratroops
USE **Parachute troops**
Parcel post
USE **Postal service**
Pardon   364.6
    BT   **Administration of criminal jus-**
            tice
            Executive power
    RT   **Amnesty**
            Clemency
            Forgiveness
Parent abuse
USE **Elderly abuse**
Parent and child
USE **Parent-child relationship**
Parent-child relationship   306.874

Use for materials on the psychological and
social interaction between parents and their
minor children. Materials on the skills, attributes, and attitudes needed for parenthood are
entered under **Parenting**. Materials on the
principles and techniques of rearing children
are entered under **Child rearing**. Materials restricted to the legal right of parents to visit
their children in situations of separation, divorce, etc., are entered under **Visitation
rights (Domestic relations)**.

    UF   Child and parent
            Parent and child
    BT   **Child-adult relationship**
            Children
            Family
            Parents
    NT   **Adoption**
            Child abuse
            Child custody
            Child rearing
            Children of divorced parents
            Children of working parents
            Conflict of generations
            Father-child relationship
            Mother-child relationship
            Parenting

Parent participation in children's education
  USE **Education—Parent participa-**
      tion
Parent-teacher associations (May subdiv.
    geog.) **371.19**
  UF Parents' and teachers' associa-
      tions
      PTAs
  BT **Community and school**
      Education—Societies
      Parent-teacher relationship
      Societies
  RT **Home and school**
Parent-teacher conferences **371.103**
  UF Conferences, Parent-teacher
      Interviews, Parent-teacher
      Teacher-parent conferences
  BT **Parent-teacher relationship**
Parent-teacher relationship **371.19**
  UF Parent-teacher relationships
      Parents and teachers
      Teacher-parent relationship
      Teachers and parents
  NT **Parent-teacher associations**
      Parent-teacher conferences
  RT **Home and school**
Parent-teacher relationships
  USE **Parent-teacher relationship**
Parental behavior
  USE **Parenting**
Parental custody
  USE **Child custody**
Parental involvement in children's educa-
    tion
  USE **Education—Parent participa-**
      tion
Parental kidnapping (May subdiv. geog.)
    362.82
  UF Child snatching by parents
      Custody kidnapping
      Kidnapping, Parental
  BT **Child custody**
Parental leave (May subdiv. geog.)
    331.25
  UF Family leave
      Infant care leave
      Leave for parenting
  BT **Leave of absence**
  NT **Maternity leave**
Parenthood **306.874; 649**
  BT **Family**

  NT **Fatherhood**
      Motherhood
Parenting (May subdiv. geog.) **306.874;**
    649
    Use for materials on the skills, attributes,
  and attitudes needed for parenthood. Materials
  on the psychological and social interaction be-
  tween parents and their minor children are en-
  tered under **Parent-child relationship**. Mate-
  rials on the principles and techniques of rear-
  ing children are entered under **Child rearing**.
  UF Parental behavior
  BT **Parent-child relationship**
  NT **Grandparenting**
      Grandparents as parents
      Part-time parenting
  RT **Child rearing**
Parenting by grandparents
  USE **Grandparents as parents**
Parenting, Part-time
  USE **Part-time parenting**
Parents (May subdiv. geog.) **306.874**
  SA parents of particular kinds of
      children, e.g. **Parents of**
      handicapped children [to be
      added as needed]
  BT **Family**
      Parents
  NT **Aging parents**
      Birthparents
      Gay parents
      Parent-child relationship
      Parents
      Single parents
      Stepparents
      Teenage parents
Parents and teachers
  USE **Parent-teacher relationship**
Parents' and teachers' associations
  USE **Parent-teacher associations**
Parents, Biological
  USE **Birthparents**
Parents' choice of school
  USE **School choice**
Parents of handicapped children
    306.874
  BT **Handicapped children**
Parents, Unmarried
  USE **Unmarried fathers**
      Unmarried mothers
Parish libraries
  USE **Church libraries**

Parish registers

USE **Registers of births, etc.**

Parks (May subdiv. geog.) **363.6; 712**

BT **Cities and towns**

Landscape architecture

NT **Amusement parks**

Botanical gardens

National parks and reserves

Zoos

RT **Playgrounds**

Parks—United States 363.6; 712; 917.3

Parkways

USE **Express highways**

Parliamentary government

USE **Representative government and representation**

Parliamentary practice 060.4

UF Rules of order

BT **Debates and debating**

Legislation

Legislative bodies

Public meetings

Parliaments

USE **Legislative bodies**

Parochial schools

USE **Church schools**

Parodies 808.87

Use for collections of parodies. Materials on the literary form of parody, that is, satirical or humorous imitation of a serious piece of literature, are entered under **Parody.**

SA types of literature, individual literary works entered under title, and names of prominent authors with the subdivision *Parodies, imitations, etc.,* e.g. **Shakespeare, William, 1564-1616—Parodies, imitations, etc.** [to be added as needed]

NT **Fractured fairy tales**

Parodies, imitations, etc.

USE types of literature, individual literary works entered under title, and names of prominent authors with the subdivision *Parodies, imitations, etc.,* e.g. **Shakespeare, William, 1564-1616—Parodies, imitations, etc.** [to be added as needed]

Parody 808.7

Use for materials about the literary form of parody, that is, satirical or humorous imitation

of a serious piece of literature. Collections of parodies are entered under **Parodies.**

UF Comic literature

Travesty

BT **Literature**

Satire

Wit and humor

NT **Burlesque (Literature)**

Parole (May subdiv. geog.) **364.6**

BT **Administration of criminal justice**

Corrections

Punishment

Social case work

RT **Probation**

Part-time employment 331.25

UF Alternative work schedules

BT **Employment**

Hours of labor

Labor

NT **Job sharing**

Supplementary employment

Part-time parenting 306.874; 649

Use for materials on parenting skills for separated, divorced, or surrogate parents who live apart from their children and spend less than full time with them.

UF Co-parenting

Joint custody of children

Parenting, Part-time

Shared parenting

BT **Parenting**

RT **Children of divorced parents**

Partial hearing

USE **Hearing impaired**

Partially hearing

USE **Hearing impaired**

Participative management 331.89; 658.3

UF Consultative management

Employees' representation in management

Industrial councils

Labor participation in management

Management—Employee participation

Workers' participation in management

Workshop councils

BT **Factory management**

Industrial relations

Personnel management

Participative management—*Continued*
RT **Collective bargaining**
Particles (Nuclear physics) 539.7
UF Elementary particles (Physics)
Nuclear particles
Nucleons
SA names of particles [to be added as needed]
BT **Nuclear physics**
NT **Electrons**
Neutrons
Protons
Quarks
String theory
Parties 793.2
SA types of parties [to be added as needed]
BT **Entertaining**
NT **Children's parties**
Showers (Parties)
Parties, Political
USE **Political parties**
Partisans
USE **Guerrillas**
Partita
USE **Suite (Music)**
Partnership 338.7
UF Companies
Partnership—Law and legislation
BT **Business enterprises**
NT **Joint ventures**
Partnership—Law and legislation
USE **Partnership**
Parts of speech
USE names of languages with the subdivision *Parts of speech,* e.g. **English language—Parts of speech** [to be added as needed]
Passion of Christ
USE **Jesus Christ—Passion**
Passion plays 792.1; 808.82
Use for individual plays, collections, or materials about medieval plays depicting the Passion of Christ.
BT **Bible plays**
Mysteries and miracle plays
Religious drama
Theater
Passions
USE **Emotions**

Passive resistance (May subdiv. geog.) **303.6; 322.4**
UF Nonviolent noncooperation
BT **Resistance to government**
NT **Boycotts**
Hunger strikes
RT **Nonviolence**
Passover (May subdiv. geog.) **296.4; 394.267**
UF Pesach
BT **Jewish holidays**
NT **Seder**
Pastel drawing 741.2
BT **Drawing**
RT **Crayon drawing**
Pastimes
USE **Amusements**
Games
Recreation
Pastoral drama 808.82
Use for individual works, collections, or materials about pastoral drama.
UF Rural comedies
BT **Drama**
Pastoral fiction 808.3; 808.83
Use for individual works, collections, or materials about novels or short stories with a rural setting and a tone of romantic nostalgia.
UF Pastoral romances
Rural comedies
BT **Fiction**
Pastoral peoples
USE **Nomads**
Pastoral poetry 808.1; 808.81
Use for individual works, collections, or materials about pastoral poetry.
UF Bucolic poetry
Eclogues
Idyllic poetry
Rural poetry
BT **Poetry**
Pastoral psychiatry
USE **Pastoral psychology**
Pastoral psychology 206; 253.5
Use for materials on the application of psychology and psychiatry by the clergy to the spiritual problems of individuals.
UF Clerical psychology
Pastoral psychiatry
Psychology, Pastoral
Psychology, Religious
Religious psychology

Pastoral psychology—*Continued*
> BT **Applied psychology**
> **Church work**
> **Psychology of religion**
> RT **Pastoral theology**

Pastoral romances
> USE **Pastoral fiction**

Pastoral theology (May subdiv. geog.)
206; 253
> May be subdivided by sect or denomination.
> UF Pastoral work
> BT **Theology**
> NT **Ministry**
> **Preaching**
> RT **Church work**
> **Clergy**
> **Pastoral psychology**

Pastoral work
> USE **Pastoral theology**

Pastors
> USE **Clergy**
> **Priests**

Pastry **641.8**
> BT **Baking**
> **Cooking**
> RT **Cake**

Pastures (May subdiv. geog.) **333.74**
> BT **Agriculture**
> **Land use**

Patchwork **746.46**
> BT **Needlework**

Patchwork quilts
> USE **Quilts**

Patent medicines
> USE **Nonprescription drugs**

Patents (May subdiv. geog.) **608**
> BT **Manufactures**
> RT **Intellectual property**
> **Inventions**
> **Trademarks**

Pathological psychology
> USE **Abnormal psychology**

Pathology **616.07**
> UF Disease (Pathology)
> BT **Medicine**
> NT **Birth defects**
> **Fever**
> **Medical genetics**
> **Therapeutics**
> RT **Diseases**
> **Preventive medicine**

Patience **179**
> BT **Human behavior**
> **Virtue**

Patience (Game)
> USE **Solitaire (Game)**

Patient care records
> USE **Medical records**

Patients **362.1**
> SA diseases with the subdivision
> *Patients*, e.g. **Cancer—Patients**; and organs or regions
> of the body with the subdivisions *Surgery—Patients*, or
> *Transplantation—Patients* [to
> be added as needed]
> NT **Cancer—Patients**
> RT **Sick**

Patios **643**
> UF Decks (Domestic architecture)
> BT **Landscape architecture**

Patriotic poetry **808.1; 808.81**
> Use for individual works, collections, or
> materials about patriotic poetry.
> BT **Poetry**
> RT **National songs**

Patriotic songs
> USE **National songs**

Patriotism (May subdiv. geog.) **172**
> BT **Citizenship**
> **Human behavior**
> **Loyalty**
> RT **Nationalism**

Patristic philosophy
> USE **Fathers of the church**

Patristics
> USE **Fathers of the church**

Patronage of the arts
> USE **Art patronage**

Pattern making
> USE **Patternmaking**

Pattern perception **152.14**
> UF Design perception
> Pattern recognition
> BT **Perception**

Pattern recognition
> USE **Pattern perception**

Patternmaking **671.2**
> UF Pattern making
> BT **Models and modelmaking**
> NT **Mechanical drawing**
> RT **Design**
> **Founding**

Patterns
USE types of handicrafts and manufactures with the subdivision *Patterns,* e.g. **Dressmaking—Patterns** [to be added as needed]

Patterns (Language arts)
USE **Language arts—Patterning**

Patterns (Mathematics) 372.7
UF Geometric patterns
Number patterns
BT **Mathematics**

Paul Bunyan
USE **Bunyan, Paul (Legendary character)**

Pauperism
USE **Poverty**

Pavements (May subdiv. geog.) 625.8
RT **Roads**
Streets

Pay equity
USE **Equal pay for equal work**

Pay-per-view television
USE **Subscription television**

Pay television
USE **Subscription television**

Payroll taxes
USE **Unemployment insurance**

PC computers
USE **Personal computers**

PCs
USE **Personal computers**

Peace 172; 327.1; 341.7
SA names of wars with the subdivision *Peace* e.g. **World War, 1939-1945—Peace** [to be added as needed]
BT **International relations**
NT **World War, 1914-1918—Peace**
RT **Arms control**
International arbitration
International security
Pacifism
Peace movements
War

Peace keeping forces
USE **United Nations—Armed forces**

Peace movements (May subdiv. geog.) 327.1
Use for materials on social movements advocating peace. Materials on the renunciation of offensive or defensive military actions on moral grounds are entered under **Pacifism**.
UF Antiwar movements
War protest movements
SA names of wars with the subdivision *Protest movements,* e.g. **World War, 1939-1945—Protest movements** [to be added as needed]
BT **Social movements**
RT **Demonstrations**
Peace

Peaceful coexistence
USE **International relations**

Peacocks 598.6
UF Peafowl
Peahens
BT **Birds**

Peafowl
USE **Peacocks**

Peahens
USE **Peacocks**

Pearl fisheries 338.3; 639
UF Pearlfisheries
BT **Commercial fishing**

Pearl Harbor (Oahu, Hawaii), Attack on, 1941 940.54
BT **World War, 1939-1945—Campaigns**

Pearlfisheries
USE **Pearl fisheries**

Peasant art
USE **Folk art**

Peasantry (May subdiv. geog.) 305.5; 307.72
BT **Feudalism**
Labor
RT **Agricultural laborers**
Land tenure
Rural sociology

Pecan
USE **Pecans**

Pecans 583; 634
UF Pecan
BT **Nuts**

Pedagogy
USE **Education**
Education—Study and teaching
Teaching

Peddlers and peddling (May subdiv. geog.) 658.8
UF Door to door selling

Peddlers and peddling—*Continued*
  BT **Direct selling**
      Sales personnel
Pediatric psychiatry
  USE **Child psychiatry**
Pediatric surgery
  USE **Children—Surgery**
Pediatrics
  USE **Children—Diseases**
      Children—Health and hygiene
      Infants—Diseases
      Infants—Health and hygiene
Pedigrees
  USE **Genealogy**
      Heraldry
Peer counseling   158; 361.3
  UF Peer counseling in rehabilitation
      Peer counseling of students
      Peer group counseling
      Rehabilitation peer counseling
      Student to student counseling
  BT **Counseling**
Peer counseling in rehabilitation
  USE **Peer counseling**
Peer counseling of students
  USE **Peer counseling**
Peer group counseling
  USE **Peer counseling**
Peer group influence
  USE **Peer pressure**
Peer pressure   303.3; 364.2
  UF Peer group influence
  BT **Socialization**
Peer pressure in adolescence   303.3
Peerage
  USE **Nobility**
Pelts
  USE **Hides and skins**
Pen drawing   741.2
  UF Ink drawing
  BT **Drawing**
Pen names
  USE **Pseudonyms**
Penal codes
  USE **Criminal law**
Penal colonies (May subdiv. geog.)   **365**
  UF Expulsion
      Transportation of criminals
  BT **Colonies**
      Correctional institutions

Penal institutions
  USE **Correctional institutions**
      Prisons
      Reformatories
Penal law
  USE **Criminal law**
Penal reform
  USE **Prison reform**
Penance (May subdiv. geog.)   **265**
  UF Contrition
      Reconciliation, Sacrament of
      Sacrament of Reconciliation
  BT **Sacraments**
  RT **Confession**
      Forgiveness of sin
      Repentance
Pencil drawing   741.2
  BT **Drawing**
Penicillin   615
  BT **Antibiotics**
Peninsulas (May subdiv. geog.)   **551.41**
  SA names of peninsulas [to be add-
      ed as needed]
  NT **Arabian Peninsula**
Penitence
  USE **Repentance**
Penitentiaries
  USE **Prisons**
Penmanship
  USE **Handwriting**
Pennsylvania Dutch   974.8
  UF Pennsylvania Germans
Pennsylvania Germans
  USE **Pennsylvania Dutch**
Penology
  USE **Corrections**
      Punishment
Pensions (May subdiv. geog.)   **331.25;**
      353.5; 658.3
  UF Compensation
  SA ethnic groups, classes of per-
      sons, and employees in partic-
      ular industries with the subdi-
      vision *Pensions*, e.g. **Teach-**
      ers—Pensions; Chemical in-
      dustry—Employees—Pen-
      sions; etc. [to be added as
      needed]
  BT **Annuities**
      Retirement income

Pensions—*Continued*
- NT **Individual retirement accounts**
  Military pensions
  Old age pensions
  Social security

Pensions, Naval
- USE **Military pensions**

Pentagon (Va.) terrorist attack, 2001
- USE **September 11 terrorist attacks, 2001**

Pentecostal churches (May subdiv. geog.)
289.9

Use for general materials on Christian denominations of the Pentecostal type. Materials on Christian movements that stress the personal experience of the Holy Spirit in daily life, with emphasis on personal holiness and spiritual gifts, especially the gift of tongues, are entered under **Pentecostalism.**
- BT **Christian sects**
  Protestantism
- RT **Pentecostalism**

Pentecostal movement
- USE **Pentecostalism**

Pentecostalism (May subdiv. geog.)
270.8

Use for materials on Christian movements that stress the personal experience of the Holy Spirit in daily life, with emphasis on personal holiness and spiritual gifts, especially the gift of tongues. General materials on Christian denominations of the Pentecostal type are entered under **Pentecostal churches.**
- UF Charismatic movement
  Charismatic renewal movement
  Pentecostal movement
- BT **Christianity**
- RT **Catholic charismatic movement**
  Glossolalia
  Pentecostal churches
  Spiritual gifts

Peonage (May subdiv. geog.) **306.3; 331.5**
- UF Servitude
- BT **Forced labor**
- RT **Contract labor**
  Slavery

People
- USE **Ethnic groups**
  Indigenous peoples
  Persons
  and racial and ethnic groups
  and native peoples, e.g. **African Americans; Mexican**

Americans; Yoruba (African people); etc., and classes of persons, e.g. **Elderly; Handicapped; Explorers; Drug addicts;** etc. [to be added as needed]

People in space
- USE **Space flight**

People's banks
- USE **Cooperative banks**

People's Republic of China
- USE **China**

Pep pills
- USE **Amphetamines**

Percentage **513.2**
- BT **Arithmetic**

Perception **152.1; 153.7**
- UF Feeling
- SA types of concepts and images, e.g. **Size; Shape;** etc. [to be added as needed]
- BT **Intellect**
  Psychology
  Senses and sensation
  Theory of knowledge
  Thought and thinking
- NT **Concepts**
  Consciousness
  Gestalt psychology
  Pattern perception
  Shape
  Size
- RT **Apperception**
  Intuition

Percussion instruments **786.8**
- SA types of percussion instruments, e.g. **Drums** [to be added as needed]
- BT **Musical instruments**
- NT **Drums**
  Pianos

Perennials **635.9**
- BT **Cultivated plants**
  Flower gardening
  Flowers

Perfectionism (Personality trait) **155.2**
- UF Self-expectations, Perfectionist
- BT **Personality**

Performance **155.2; 658.4**
- UF Competence
- BT **Work**

Performance—*Continued*
  NT **Achievement motivation**
      Performance standards
Performance art (May subdiv. geog.)
      700

  Use for materials on live performances by artists, drawing on literature, theater, music, film, etc., and combining elements of the various arts in untraditional ways.

  UF Happening (Art)
  BT **Art**
      Performing arts
Performance motivation
  USE **Achievement motivation**
Performance standards   658.5
  UF Job performance standards
      Rating
      Work performance standards
  SA subjects and classes of persons with the subdivision *Rating*, e.g. **Bonds—Rating; Employees—Rating**; etc. [to be added as needed]
  BT **Performance**
Performing arts (May subdiv. geog.)
      790.2
  UF Show business
  SA specific art forms performed on stage or screen [to be added as needed]
  BT **Arts**
  NT **Ballet**
      Centers for the performing arts
      Dance
      Motion pictures
      Opera
      Performance art
      Theater
Performing arts audiences
  USE **Performing arts—Audiences**
Performing arts—Audiences   791
  UF Performing arts audiences
  BT **Audiences**
Perfumes   391.6; 668
  BT **Cosmetics**
      Essences and essential oils
  NT **Potpourri**
Periodic health examinations   616.07
  UF Health examinations
      Medical examinations
      Physical examinations (Medicine)

  SA subjects, classes of persons, ethnic groups, and military services with the subdivision *Medical examinations*, e.g. **Children—Medical examinations** [to be added as needed]
  BT **Medicine**
Periodic law   546.8
  BT **Physical chemistry**
  RT **Chemical elements**
Periodicals (May subdiv. geog.)   **050**
  UF Annuals
      Journals
      Magazines
  SA subjects with the subdivision *Periodicals*, e.g. **Engineering—Periodicals**; and names of individual periodicals [to be added as needed]
  BT **Mass media**
      Serial publications
  NT **Chapbooks**
      English periodicals
      Fanzines
      Little magazines
  RT **Journalism**
      Newspapers
      Press
Periodicals—Editing
  USE **Journalism—Editing**
Periodicals—Indexes   050
Periodicals—United States   051
  UF American periodicals
Periodicity
  USE **Cycles**
Permanent education
  USE **Continuing education**
Persecution (May subdiv. geog.)   **201; 909**
  UF Persecutions
      Religious persecution
  SA religious groups with the subdivision *Persecutions*, e.g. **Christians—Persecutions; Jews—Persecutions**; etc.; and religious groups and classes of persons with the subdivision *Nazi persecution*, e.g. **Handicapped—Nazi persecution** [to be added as needed]
  BT **Atrocities**

Persecution—*Continued*
  NT   **Christians—Persecutions**
        Handicapped—Nazi persecution
        Jews—Persecutions
        Massacres
  RT   **Freedom of religion**
        Martyrs
Persecutions
  USE **Persecution**
        and religious groups with the
        subdivision *Persecutions,* e.g.
        Christians—Persecutions;
        Jews—Persecutions; etc.; and
        religious groups and classes
        of persons with the subdivi-
        sion *Nazi persecution,* e.g.
        **Handicapped—Nazi persecu-
        tion** [to be added as needed]
Perseverance   179
  BT   **Ethics**
Persia
  USE **Iran**
Persian Gulf War, 1991   956.7044
  UF   Gulf War, 1991
        Middle East War, 1991
        Operation Desert Storm
  BT   **United States—History—1989-**
Persistence   158
  BT   **Personality**
Persistent pain
  USE **Chronic pain**
Personal actions (Law)
  USE **Litigation**
Personal appearance   391.6
  UF   Appearance, Personal
        Beauty, Personal
        Physical appearance
        Self image
  NT   **Body piercing**
        Personal grooming
        Tattooing
  RT   **Clothing and dress**
Personal cleanliness
  USE **Hygiene**
Personal computers   004.16; 621.39
    Use for materials on small, usually desktop-
sized computers that have a self-contained
central processing unit.
  UF   Desktop computers
        Home computers
        Microcomputers [*Former head-
        ing*]

        PC computers
        PCs
  BT   **Computers**
Personal conduct
  USE **Conduct of life**
Personal development
  USE **Personality**
        Self-improvement
        Success
Personal films
  USE **Amateur films**
        Experimental films
Personal finance (May subdiv. geog.)
      332.024
  UF   Budgets, Personal
        Domestic finance
        Family finance
        Finance, Personal
        Financial planning, Personal
  SA   ethnic groups, classes of per-
        sons, and names of individual
        persons with the subdivision
        Personal finance, e.g. **Retir-
        ees—Personal finance** [to be
        added as needed]
  BT   **Finance**
  NT   **Children's allowances**
        Consumer credit
        Estate planning
        Household budgets
        Insurance
        Saving and investment
        Tax planning
Personal freedom
  USE **Freedom**
Personal grooming   391.6; 646.7
  UF   Beauty, Personal
        Good grooming
        Grooming, Personal
  BT   **Hygiene**
        Personal appearance
  NT   **Cosmetics**
        Hair
        Toiletries
  RT   **Clothing and dress**
Personal growth
  USE **Self-improvement**
Personal health
  USE **Health**
Personal health services
  USE **Medical care**

Personal hygiene
　USE **Hygiene**
Personal income tax
　USE **Income tax**
Personal life skills
　USE **Life skills**
Personal loans　332.7
　　Use for materials on loans to individuals for personal rather than business uses.
　UF　Consumer loans
　　　Loans, Personal
　　　Small loans
　BT　**Consumer credit**
　　　Loans
　NT　**Cooperative banks**
　　　Savings and loan associations
Personal names (May subdiv. geog.)
　　929.4
　UF　Baby names
　　　Christian names
　　　Family names
　　　First names
　　　Names, Personal
　　　Surnames
　SA　personal names of particular national or ethnic origins regardless of the place where they are found, e.g. **Scottish personal names** [to be added as needed]
　BT　**Names**
　NT　**Nicknames**
　　　Pseudonyms
　　　Scottish personal names
Personal names—United States
　　929.40973
　UF　American personal names
Personal narratives
　USE　**Autobiographies**
　　　Biography
　　　and subjects with the subdivision *Biography* or *Correspondence;* and names of diseases, events, and wars with the subdivision *Personal narratives,* e.g. **World War, 1939-1945—Personal narratives** [to be added as needed]
Personal space　153.6; 302.2
　　Use for materials on the sense of physical space required for psychological comfort.
　UF　Space, Personal

　BT　**Interpersonal relations**
　　　Nonverbal communication
　　　Space and time
Personal time management
　USE　**Time management**
Personality　155.2
　UF　Identity
　　　Personal development
　BT　**Consciousness**
　　　Psychology
　NT　**Body image**
　　　Bossiness
　　　Character
　　　Eccentrics and eccentricities
　　　Ego (Psychology)
　　　Forgetfulness
　　　Identity (Psychology)
　　　Laziness
　　　Perfectionism (Personality trait)
　　　Persistence
　　　Self
　　　Selfishness
　　　Stubbornness
　　　Typology (Psychology)
　RT　**Individuality**
　　　Persons
Personality disorders　616.85
　BT　**Abnormal psychology**
　NT　**Multiple personality**
　RT　**Hallucinations and illusions**
　　　Mental illness
Personality, Multiple
　USE　**Multiple personality**
Personnel administration
　USE　**Personnel management**
Personnel classification
　USE　**Job analysis**
Personnel management (May subdiv. geog.)　658.3
　UF　Career development
　　　Employment management
　　　Human resource management
　　　Personnel administration
　　　Supervision of employees
　SA　names of corporate bodies and military services and types of industries, services, and organizations with the subdivision *Personnel management,* e.g. **Hospitals—Personnel man-**

Personnel management—*Continued*
　　　agement [to be added as
　　　needed]
　BT　**Industrial relations**
　　　Management
　NT　**Absenteeism (Labor)**
　　　Affirmative action programs
　　　Applications for positions
　　　Counseling
　　　Diversity in the workplace
　　　Employee assistance programs
　　　Employee morale
　　　Employees—Dismissal
　　　Employees—Training
　　　Employment agencies
　　　**Hospitals—Personnel manage-
　　　ment**
　　　Job analysis
　　　Job satisfaction
　　　Job security
　　　Labor turnover
　　　Motion study
　　　Participative management
　　　Recruiting of employees
　　　Supervisors
　　　Time study
　RT　**Employees**
　　　Factory management
　　　Office management
Personnel service in education
　USE　**Educational counseling**
Persons　128
　　Use for materials on human beings as indi-
　viduals. Materials on the human species from
　the point of view of biology or anthropology
　are entered under **Human beings**.
　UF　Categories of persons
　　　Classes of persons
　　　Groups of persons
　　　People
　SA　classes of persons, e.g. **Elderly**;
　　　Handicapped; **Explorers**;
　　　Drug addicts; etc. [to be
　　　added as needed]
　BT　**Human beings**
　NT　**Celebrities**
　　　Exiles
　　　Intellectuals
　　　Psychics
　　　Transvestites
　RT　**Individualism**
　　　Personality

Perspective　701
　UF　Architectural perspective
　BT　**Descriptive geometry**
　　　Geometrical drawing
　　　Optics
　　　Painting
　RT　**Drawing**
Persuasion (Psychology)　153.8
　UF　Psychology, Applied
　BT　**Communication**
　　　Conformity
　RT　**Propaganda**
Persuasion (Rhetoric)
　USE　**Public speaking**
　　　Rhetoric
Perversion, Sexual
　USE　**Sexual deviation**
Pesach
　USE　**Passover**
Pest control　363.7; 628.9; 632
　UF　Extermination of pests
　　　Pest extermination
　　　Pests—Biological control
　　　Pests—Control
　　　Pests—Extermination
　SA　types of pests with the subdivi-
　　　sion *Control*, e.g. **Mosqui-
　　　toes—Control** [to be added
　　　as needed]
　BT　**Agricultural pests**
　　　Economic zoology
　　　Pests
　NT　**Mosquitoes—Control**
　　　Pesticides
Pest extermination
　USE　**Pest control**
Pesticide pollution
　USE　**Pesticides—Environmental as-
　　　pects**
Pesticides (May subdiv. geog.)　**632; 668**
　BT　**Agricultural chemicals**
　　　Pest control
　　　Poisons and poisoning
　NT　**Fungicides**
　　　Herbicides
　　　Insecticides
　　　Natural pesticides
Pesticides and wildlife　590
　UF　Wildlife and pesticides
　BT　**Pesticides—Environmental as-
　　　pects**

Pesticides and wildlife—*Continued*

Wildlife conservation

Pesticides—Environmental aspects
363.7; 632

UF   Environment and pesticides

Pesticide pollution

BT   **Environment**

Pollution

NT   **Pesticides and wildlife**

Pestilences

USE   **Epidemics**

Pests   591.6; 632

Use for materials on detrimental or annoying animals or organisms.

UF   Vermin

SA   types of pests, e.g. **Agricultural pests**; **Flies**; etc.; and names of crops, trees, etc., with the subdivision *Diseases and pests*, e.g. **Fruit—Diseases and pests** [to be added as needed]

BT   **Economic zoology**

NT   **Agricultural pests**

Flies

Fruit—Diseases and pests

Fungi

Household pests

Insect pests

Parasites

Pest control

Pests—Biological control

USE   **Pest control**

Pests—Control

USE   **Pest control**

Pests—Extermination

USE   **Pest control**

Pet-facilitated psychotherapy

USE   **Pet therapy**

Pet therapy   615.8

UF   Animal-facilitated therapy

Companion-animal partnership

Pet-facilitated psychotherapy

BT   **Animals and the handicapped**

Therapeutics

Petrochemicals   661

UF   Petroleum chemicals

BT   **Chemicals**

Petroglyphs

USE   **Rock drawings, paintings, and engravings**

Petroleum (May subdiv. geog.)   **553.2; 665.5**

UF   Coal oil

Crude oil

Oil

BT   **Oils and fats**

NT   **Coal tar products**

Gasoline

RT   **Petroleum geology**

Petroleum industry

Petroleum as fuel   338.4; 665.5

UF   Fuel oil

Liquid fuel

Oil fuel

BT   **Fuel**

NT   **Oil burners**

Petroleum chemicals

USE   **Petrochemicals**

Petroleum engines

USE   **Internal combustion engines**

Petroleum geology (May subdiv. geog.)   **553.2**

UF   Geology, Petroleum

BT   **Economic geology**

Prospecting

RT   **Petroleum**

Petroleum industry (May subdiv. geog.)   **338.2**

UF   Oil industry

Petroleum industry and trade

BT   **Industries**

NT   **Offshore oil industry**

Oil well drilling

Oil wells

Service stations

RT   **Petroleum**

Petroleum industry and trade

USE   **Petroleum industry**

Petroleum industry—Deregulation (May subdiv. geog.)   **338.2**

Petroleum pipelines (May subdiv. geog.)   **338.2; 665.5**

BT   **Pipelines**

Petroleum pollution of water

USE   **Oil pollution of water**

Petroleum—United States   553.2; 665.5

Petroleum—Well boring

USE   **Oil well drilling**

Petrology (May subdiv. geog.)   **552**

SA   types of rocks, e.g. **Granite** [to be added as needed]

Petrology—*Continued*
- BT   **Science**
- NT   **Geochemistry**
       Moon rocks
- RT   **Geology**
       Minerals
       Rocks
       Stone

Pets (May subdiv. geog.)   **636.088**
- SA   types of common pets, e.g.
       Dogs; and types of animals
       not ordinarily kept as pets,
       e.g. **Snakes as pets** [to be
       added as needed]
- BT   **Animals**
- NT   **Snakes as pets**
- RT   **Domestic animals**

Pets and the handicapped
- USE   **Animals and the handicapped**

Pets—Housing   **690**
- BT   **Animal housing**
- NT   **Kennels**

Pets—Names   **636.088**

Petting zoos   **590.73**
- BT   **Zoos**

Pewter   **673; 739.5**
- BT   **Alloys**
       Art metalwork
       Metals

Phantoms
- USE   **Apparitions**
       Ghosts

Pharmaceutical abuse
- USE   **Medication abuse**

Pharmaceutical chemistry   **615**
- UF   Drugs—Chemistry
       Medicinal chemistry
- BT   **Chemistry**
- NT   **Disinfection and disinfectants**
- RT   **Pharmacy**
       Therapeutics

Pharmaceuticals
- USE   **Drugs**

Pharmacies
- USE   **Drugstores**

Pharmacodynamics
- USE   **Pharmacology**

Pharmacology   **615**

   Use for materials on the action and properties of drugs in general. Materials limited to the effect of drugs on the functions of living organisms are entered under **Drugs—Physio-**

logical effect. Materials on the art or practice of preparing, preserving, and dispensing drugs are entered under **Pharmacy**.
- UF   Drugs—Adulteration and analysis
       Medicine—Physiological effect
       Pharmacodynamics
- BT   **Medicine**
- NT   **Drugs—Physiological effect**
       Drugs—Testing
       Toxicology
- RT   **Drug therapy**
       Drugs
       Materia medica
       Pharmacy

Pharmacopoeias
- USE   **Materia medica**

Pharmacotherapy
- USE   **Drug therapy**

Pharmacy   **615**

   Use for materials on the art or practice of preparing, preserving, and dispensing drugs. Materials on the action and properties of drugs are entered under **Pharmacology**. Materials on business establishments that sell drugs are entered under **Drugstores**.
- BT   **Chemistry**
       Medicine
- NT   **Drugs**
       Homeopathy
       Medical botany
- RT   **Materia medica**
       Pharmaceutical chemistry
       Pharmacology

Pheasants   **598.6; 636.5**
- BT   **Birds**
       Game and game birds

Phenomenology   **142**
- BT   **Modern philosophy**
- NT   **Existentialism**

Philanthropists (May subdiv. geog.)
   361.7092; 920
- UF   Altruists
       Humanitarians
- RT   **Philanthropy**

Philanthropy (May subdiv. geog.)   **177; 361.7**
- RT   **Charities**
       Charity organization
       Endowments
       Philanthropists

Philately
- USE   **Stamp collecting**

Philippines 959.9

May be subdivided like **United States** except for *History*.

Philology

USE   **Language and languages**
       Linguistics

Philology, Comparative

USE   **Linguistics**

Philosophers (May subdiv. geog.)   **180;**
    190; 920

RT   **Philosophy**

Philosophers, American

USE   **Philosophers—United States**

Philosophers' stone

USE   **Alchemy**

Philosophers—United States   191; 920

UF   American philosophers
       Philosophers, American

Philosophy   100

SA   movements in philosophy, e.g.
       Positivism; philosophy of particular countries, e.g. **American philosophy**; philosophy associated with particular religions, e.g. **Christian philosophy**; and subjects with the subdivision *Philosophy*, e.g.
       History—Philosophy [to be added as needed]

BT   **Humanities**

NT   **Aesthetics**
       American philosophy
       Ancient philosophy
       Belief and doubt
       Causation
       Christian philosophy
       Comparative philosophy
       Empiricism
       Ethics
       Evolution
       Fate and fatalism
       Free will and determinism
       Gnosticism
       Good and evil
       Hindu philosophy
       History—Philosophy
       Humanism
       Idealism
       Ideology
       Intuition
       Logic
       Marxism
       Materialism
       Medieval philosophy
       Metaphysics
       Mind and body
       Modern philosophy
       Philosophy and religion
       Positivism
       Pragmatism
       Psychology
       Rationalism
       Realism
       Reality
       Skepticism
       Soul
       Tao
       Theism
       Theory of knowledge
       Transcendentalism
       Truth

RT   **Philosophers**

Philosophy, American

USE   **American philosophy**

Philosophy, Ancient

USE   **Ancient philosophy**

Philosophy and religion   210

Use for materials on the reciprocal relationship and influence between philosophy and religion. Materials on the nature, origin, or validity of religion from a philosophical point of view are entered under **Religion—Philosophy**.

UF   Religion and philosophy

BT   **Philosophy**
       Religion

RT   **Religion—Philosophy**

Philosophy—Encyclopedias   103

BT   **Encyclopedias and dictionaries**

Philosophy, Hindu

USE   **Hindu philosophy**

Philosophy—Historiography   109

BT   **Historiography**

Philosophy, Medieval

USE   **Medieval philosophy**

Philosophy, Modern

USE   **Modern philosophy**

Philosophy of history

USE   **History—Philosophy**

Philosophy of religion

USE   **Religion—Philosophy**

Phobias   616.85

SA   types of phobias, e.g. **Agoraphobia** [to be added as needed]

Phobias—*Continued*
  BT **Fear**
      Neuroses
  NT **Agoraphobia**
Phoenix (Mythical bird)   398.2454
  BT **Mythical animals**
Phonetic spelling
  USE **Spelling reform**
Phonetic spelling   411
  BT **Spelling reform**
Phonetics   414
  UF Phonics
      Phonology
  SA names of languages with the
      subdivision *Pronunciation* [to
      be added as needed]
  BT **Language and languages**
      Sound
  NT **English language—Pronuncia-**
      tion
  RT **Reading—Phonetic method**
      Speech
      Voice
Phonics
  USE **Phonetics**
       Reading—Phonetic method
Phonograph   621.389
  UF Gramophone
  NT **Compact disc players**
  RT **High-fidelity sound systems**
      Sound—Recording and repro-
      ducing
Phonograph records
  USE **Sound recordings**
Phonology
  USE **Phonetics**
       and names of languages with
       the subdivision *Pronunciation,*
       e.g. **English language—Pro-**
       nunciation [to be added as
       needed]
Phosphates   546; 553.6; 631.8
  BT **Fertilizers**
Phosphorescence   535
  BT **Luminescence**
      Radioactivity
Photo journalism
  USE **Photojournalism**
Photocopying   686.4
  UF Photocopying processes
      Photoduplication
      Photographic reproduction

Xerography
  BT **Copying processes**
  RT **Copy art**
Photocopying machines
  USE **Copying machines**
Photocopying processes
  USE **Photocopying**
Photoduplication
  USE **Photocopying**
Photoelectric cells   537.5; 621.3815
  UF Electric eye
Photoengraving   686.2
  UF Halftone process
  BT **Engraving**
  RT **Photomechanical processes**
Photographers (May subdiv. geog.)
      770.92
  BT **Artists**
Photographic chemistry   771
      Use for materials on the chemical processes
      employed in photography.
  BT **Chemistry**
  NT **Photography—Processing**
  RT **Photography**
Photographic film
  USE **Photography—Film**
Photographic reproduction
  USE **Photocopying**
Photographic slides
  USE **Slides (Photography)**
Photographic supplies
  USE **Photography—Equipment and**
       supplies
Photographs   770
      Use for materials that discuss photographs
      as objects, including their classification, cata-
      loging, copying, coloring, mounting, etc.
  UF Photos
      Snapshots
  SA subjects, classes of persons,
      names of wars, and names of
      cities, states, countries, and
      named entities, such as indi-
      vidual parks, structures, etc.,
      with the subdivision *Pictorial*
      works, e.g. **Animals—Pictori-**
      al works; United States—
      History—1861-1865, Civil
      War—Pictorial works; etc.;
      and names of persons or
      groups of persons with the

Photographs—*Continued*
  subdivision *Pictorial works*, or
  Portraits [to be added as
  needed]
  BT **Pictures**
  RT **Photography**
Photographs—Conservation and restoration 771
  UF Conservation of photographs
    Preservation of photographs
    Restoration of photographs
Photographs from space
  USE **Space photography**
Photography (May subdiv. geog.) **770**
  SA kinds of photography, e.g. **Portrait photography**; photography of particular subjects, e.g.
    Photography of birds; and subjects, classes of persons, names of wars, and names of cities, states, countries, and named entities, such as individual parks, structures, etc., with the subdivision *Pictorial works* [to be added as needed]
  BT **Graphic arts**
  NT **Aerial photography**
    Artistic photography
    Astronomical photography
    Cameras
    Cinematography
    Color photography
    Commercial photography
    Digital photography
    Filmstrips
    Holography
    Medical photography
    Microphotography
    Nature photography
    Outdoor photography
    Photojournalism
    Photomechanical processes
    Photomicrography
    Portrait photography
    Slides (Photography)
    Space photography
    Telephotography
    Three dimensional photography
    Underwater photography

  RT **Photographic chemistry**
    Photographs
Photography—Aesthetics
  USE **Artistic photography**
Photography, Artistic
  USE **Artistic photography**
Photography, Color
  USE **Color photography**
Photography—Darkroom technique
  USE **Photography—Processing**
Photography—Developing and developers 771
  BT **Photography—Processing**
Photography—Digital techniques
  USE **Digital photography**
Photography—Enlarging 771
  UF Enlarging (Photography)
Photography—Equipment and supplies 771
  UF Photographic supplies
  NT **Cameras**
Photography—Film 771
  UF Photographic film
Photography—Handbooks, manuals, etc. 770.2
Photography in astronautics
  USE **Space photography**
Photography—Lighting 771; 778.7
  BT **Lighting**
Photography—Motion pictures
  USE **Cinematography**
Photography of animals 778.9
  Use for materials on the technique of photographing animals. Materials consisting of photographs and pictures of animals are entered under **Animals—Pictorial works**.
  UF Animal photography
    Animals—Photography
  BT **Nature photography**
  RT **Animal painting and illustration**
    Animals—Pictorial works
Photography of birds 778.9
  UF Bird photography
    Birds—Photography
  BT **Nature photography**
Photography of fishes 778.9
  UF Fishes—Photography
  BT **Nature photography**
Photography of nature
  USE **Nature photography**
Photography of plants 778.9

Photography of plants—*Continued*
UF Plants—Photography
BT **Nature photography**
Photography—Printing processes 771
BT **Photography—Processing**
Photography—Processing 771
UF Darkroom technique in photography
Photography—Darkroom technique
SA types of photographic processing techniques, e.g. **Photography—Developing and developers; Photography—Printing processes**; etc. [to be added as needed]
BT **Photographic chemistry**
NT **Photography—Developing and developers**
Photography—Printing processes
Photography—Retouching 771
UF Retouching (Photography)
Photography—Scientific applications 778.3
SA specific applications, e.g. **Medical photography** [to be added as needed]
NT **Medical photography**
Space photography
Photography, Stereoscopic
USE **Three dimensional photography**
Photojournalism (May subdiv. geog.) **070.4; 779**
UF Journalistic photography
News photography
Photo journalism
BT **Commercial photography**
Journalism
Photography
Photomechanical processes 686.2
SA types of photomechanical processes, e.g. **Photoengraving** [to be added as needed]
BT **Illustration of books**
Photography
RT **Photoengraving**
Photometry 535
UF Electric light
BT **Measurement**
NT **Color**

RT **Light**
Optics
Photomicrography 778.3
Use for materials on the photographing of minute objects through a miscroscope. Materials on the photographing of objects of any size to produce minute images are entered under **Microphotography**.
BT **Photography**
RT **Microscopes**
Photos
USE **Photographs**
Photosynthesis 572
BT **Botany**
Phototherapy 615.8
UF Electric light
Light—Therapeutic use
BT **Physical therapy**
Therapeutics
RT **Radiotherapy**
Ultraviolet rays
Photovoltaic power generation 621.31
UF Solar cells
BT **Solar energy**
NT **Solar batteries**
Phrenology (May subdiv. geog.) **139**
BT **Brain**
Head
Psychology
RT **Mind and body**
Physiognomy
Physical anthropology (May subdiv. geog.) **599.9**
UF Biological anthropology
BT **Anthropology**
Ethnology
NT **Human origins**
Physical appearance
USE **Personal appearance**
Physical chemistry 541
UF Chemistry, Physical and theoretical
Theoretical chemistry
BT **Chemistry**
Physics
NT **Atmospheric chemistry**
Atomic theory
Atoms
Catalysis
Colloids
Crystals
Electrochemistry
Molecules

Physical chemistry—*Continued*
 Periodic law
 Polymers
 Radiochemistry
 Solids
 Thermodynamics
 RT Nuclear physics
 Quantum theory
Physical culture
 USE **Physical education**
Physical disabilities
 USE **Disabilities**
Physical education (May subdiv. geog.)
 613.7; 796.07
 UF Calisthenics
 Physical culture
 Physical education and training
 Physical training
 SA types of sports activities with
 the subdivision *Training*, e.g.
 Soccer—Training; and names
 of sports and types of physi-
 cal exercise [to be added as
 needed]
 BT **Education**
 NT **Coaching (Athletics)**
 Games
 Marching drills
 Movement education
 Physical fitness
 Soccer—Training
 RT **Athletics**
 Exercise
 Gymnastics
 Sports
Physical education and training
 USE **Physical education**
Physical education—Medical aspects
 USE **Sports medicine**
Physical examinations (Medicine)
 USE **Periodic health examinations**
Physical fitness (May subdiv. geog.)
 613.7
 UF Endurance, Physical
 Fitness
 Physical stamina
 Stamina, Physical
 SA classes of persons with the sub-
 division *Physical fitness*, e.g.,
 Women—Physical fitness [to
 be added as needed]

 BT **Exercise**
 Health
 Health self-care
 Physical education
 NT **Bodybuilding**
 Children—Physical fitness
 Kinesiology
 Physical fitness centers
 Posture
 Women—Physical fitness
Physical fitness centers (May subdiv.
 geog.) **613.7**
 UF Health clubs
 Health spas
 Recreation centers
 Spas
 BT **Physical fitness**
Physical geography (May subdiv. geog.)
 910
 Use for materials on the physical features
 of the earth's surface and its atmosphere.
 General materials, frequently school materials,
 describing the surface of the earth and its in-
 terrelationship with various peoples, animals,
 natural products, and industries are entered
 under **Geography**.
 BT **Geography**
 Geology
 NT **Deserts**
 Earthquakes
 Geysers
 Glaciers
 Ice
 Icebergs
 Lakes
 Mountains
 Ocean
 Rivers
 Seas
 Volcanoes
 Winds
 RT **Earth**
Physical geography—United States
 917.3
Physical sciences 500.2
 BT **Science**
 NT **Astronomy**
 Chemistry
 Earth sciences
 Physics
Physical stamina
 USE **Physical fitness**
Physical therapy 615.8

Physical therapy—*Continued*
 UF Physiotherapy
 SA types of physical therapy, e.g.
  Hydrotherapy; and types of
  disabilities, injuries, or diseas-
  es with the subdivision *Physi-
  cal therapy*, e.g. **Arthritis—
  Physicial therapy** [to be add-
  ed as needed]
 BT **Therapeutics**
 NT **Baths**
  Electrotherapeutics
  Hydrotherapy
  Massage
  Occupational therapy
  Phototherapy
  Radiotherapy
Physical training
 USE **Physical education**
Physically handicapped (May subdiv.
  geog.) **362.4**
 UF Crippled people
 SA types of physically handicapped
  persons, e.g. **Blind**; **Deaf**; etc.
  [to be added as needed]
 BT **Handicapped**
 NT **Blind**
  Deaf
  Hearing impaired
  **Physically handicapped chil-
  dren**
 RT **Orthopedics**
Physically handicapped children (May
  subdiv. geog.) **155.45; 362.4**
 UF Children, Crippled
  Crippled children
 BT **Handicapped children**
  Physically handicapped
Physically handicapped—Housing (May
  subdiv. geog.) **362.4**
 UF Housing for the physically hand-
  icapped
 BT **Housing**
Physically handicapped—Rehabilitation
  362.4
 NT **Occupational therapy**
Physicians (May subdiv. geog.) **610.69;
  920**
 UF Doctors
 SA types of medical specialists [to
  be added as needed]
 BT **Medical personnel**

 NT **Radiologists**
  Surgeons
  Women physicians
 RT **Medicine**
Physicians—Directories **610.69**
 BT **Directories**
Physicians—Drug use **362.29; 610.69**
 UF Drug abusing physicians
  Drug addicted physicians
Physicians—Licenses (May subdiv. geog.)
  344
 BT **Medicine—Law and legislation**
Physicians—Malpractice (May subdiv.
  geog.) **346.03**
 UF Medical errors
 BT **Malpractice**
  Medicine—Law and legislation
Physicists (May subdiv. geog.) **530.092;
  920**
 BT **Scientists**
Physics **530**
 BT **Physical sciences**
  Science
 NT **Astrophysics**
  Biophysics
  Electricity
  Electronics
  Gases
  Geophysics
  Gravitation
  Hydraulics
  Hydrostatics
  Light
  Liquids
  Magnetism
  Matter
  Mechanics
  Music—Acoustics and physics
  Nuclear physics
  Optics
  Physical chemistry
  Pneumatics
  Quantum theory
  Radiation
  Radioactivity
  Relativity (Physics)
  Solids
  Sound
  Statics
  Thermodynamics
  Weight

Physics—*Continued*
> **Weights and measures**
> RT **Dynamics**

Physics—Conferences   530
> UF   Physics—Congresses

Physics—Congresses
> USE   **Physics—Conferences**

Physics, Terrestrial
> USE   **Geophysics**

Physiognomy   138
> BT   **Psychology**
> RT   **Face**
> **Phrenology**

Physiological aspects
> USE   types of activities and mental conditions with the subdivision *Physiological aspects,* e.g. **Mental illness—Physiological aspects** [to be added as needed]

Physiological chemistry
> USE   **Biochemistry**

Physiological effect
> USE   types of drugs, chemicals, or environmental phenomena or conditions with the subdivision *Physiological effect,* e.g. **Alcohol—Physiological effect; Radiation—Physiological effect;** etc. [to be added as needed]

Physiological psychology
> USE   **Psychophysiology**

Physiological stress
> USE   **Stress (Physiology)**

Physiology   571; 612
> Use for general materials on physiology and for materials on human physiology. Materials on the physiology of other animals or of plants are entered under the appropriate heading with the subdivision *Physiology.*

> UF   Human physiology
> SA   names of organs and regions of the body, types of plants and animals, and classes of persons with the subdivision *Physiology,* e.g. **Heart—Physiology; Reptiles—Physiology;** etc.; activities and mental conditions with the subdivision *Physiological aspects,* e.g. **Mental illness—Physio-**

logical aspects; and drugs, chemicals, and environmental phenomena or conditions with the subdivision *Physiological effect,* e.g. **Alcohol—Physiological effect; Radiation—Physiological effect;** etc. [to be added as needed]
> BT   **Biology**
> **Medicine**
> **Science**
> NT   **Blood**
> **Body temperature**
> **Cardiovascular system**
> **Cells**
> **Comparative physiology**
> **Digestion**
> **Fatigue**
> **Glands**
> **Growth**
> **Health**
> **Heart—Physiology**
> **Human locomotion**
> **Immune system**
> **Lymphatic system**
> **Mental illness—Physiological aspects**
> **Musculoskeletal system**
> **Nervous system**
> **Nutrition**
> **Psychophysiology**
> **Reproduction**
> **Reproductive system**
> **Reptiles—Physiology**
> **Respiration**
> **Respiratory system**
> **Senses and sensation**
> **Skin**
> **Stress (Physiology)**
> RT   **Anatomy**
> **Human body**

Physiology, Comparative
> USE   **Comparative physiology**

Physiology of plants
> USE   **Plant physiology**

Physiotherapy
> USE   **Physical therapy**

Physique
> USE   **Bodybuilding**

Phytogeography
   USE   **Plants—Geographical distribution**
Pianists (May subdiv. geog.)   **786.2092; 920**
   BT   **Instrumentalists**
Piano
   USE   **Pianos**
Piano music   **786.2**
   BT   **Instrumental music**
         Music
Pianos   **786.2**
   UF   Piano
   BT   **Percussion instruments**
   NT   **Keyboards (Musical instruments)**
Pianos—Tuning   **786.2**
   BT   **Tuning**
Picaresque literature   **800**
   Use for individual works, collections, or materials about episodic accounts of the adventures of an engagingly roguish hero.
   UF   Picaresque novels
         Rogues and vagabonds—Fiction
   BT   **Fiction**
         Literature
Picaresque novels
   USE   **Picaresque literature**
Picketing
   USE   **Strikes**
Pickling
   USE   **Canning and preserving**
Pickup campers
   USE   **Travel trailers and campers**
Pictographs
   USE   **Picture writing**
Pictorial works
   USE   **Pictures**
         and   subjects, classes of persons, names of wars, and names of cities, states, countries, and named entities, such as individual parks, structures, etc., with the subdivision *Pictorial works,* e.g. **Animals—Pictorial works; United States—History—1861-1865, Civil War—Pictorial works; Chicago (Ill.)—Pictorial works; Yosemite National Park (Calif.)—Pictorial works;**

etc.; and names of persons or groups of persons with the subdivisions *Cartoons and caricatures; Pictorial works;* or *Portraits* [to be added as needed]
Picture books
   USE   **Pictures**
Picture books for children
   BT   **Children's literature**
   NT   **Coloring books**
         Glow-in-the-dark books
         Stories without words
         Toy and movable books
   RT   **Illustration of books**
Picture books for children, Wordless
   USE   **Stories without words**
Picture dictionaries   **413**
   UF   Dictionaries, Picture
         Word books
   BT   **Encyclopedias and dictionaries**
Picture frames and framing   **684; 749**
   UF   Framing of pictures
   BT   **Decoration and ornament**
         Handicraft
Picture galleries
   USE   **Art museums**
         Commercial art galleries
Picture postcards
   USE   **Postcards**
Picture puzzles   **793.73**
   BT   **Puzzles**
Picture telephone
   USE   **Video telephone**
Picture writing   **411**
   Use for materials on the recording of events or the expression of messages by pictures representing actions or facts.
   UF   Pictographs
   BT   **Writing**
   RT   **Hieroglyphics**
Pictures   **025.17; 760**
   Use for general materials on the study and use of pictures and for miscellaneous collections of pictures.
   UF   Pictorial works
         Picture books
   SA   subjects, classes of persons, names of wars, and names of cities, states, countries, and named entities, such as individual parks, structures, etc.,

Pictures—*Continued*

with the subdivision *Pictorial works*, e.g. **Animals—Pictorial works**; **United States—History—1861-1865, Civil War—Pictorial works**; **Chicago (Ill.)—Pictorial works**; **Yosemite National Park (Calif.)—Pictorial works**; etc.; and names of persons or groups of persons with the subdivisions *Cartoons and caricatures*; *Pictorial works*; or *Portraits* [to be added as needed]

    BT   **Art**
    NT   **Cartoons and caricatures**
           Engraving
           Etching
           Photographs
           Portraits
           Views
    RT   **Painting**

Pies   641.8652
    BT   **Baking**
           Cooking

Pigments   547; 667; 751.2
    NT   **Dyes and dyeing**
    RT   **Color**
           Paint

Pigs   599.63; 636.4
    UF   Hogs
           Swine
    BT   **Domestic animals**
           Mammals

Pilates method   613.7
    BT   **Exercise**

Pilgrims and pilgrimages (May subdiv. geog.)   203; 263
    BT   **Voyages and travels**
    RT   **Shrines**

Pilgrims (New England colonists)   974.4
    BT   **Puritans**
           United States—History—1600-1775, Colonial period

Pilot charts
    USE   **Nautical charts**

Pilot guides   623.89
    UF   Coast pilot guides
    BT   **Navigation**

Piloting
    USE   types of aircraft with the subdivision *Piloting*, e.g. **Airplanes—Piloting** [to be added as needed]

Piloting (Astronautics)
    USE   **Space vehicles—Piloting**

Pilots
    USE   **Air pilots**
            Ship pilots

Pilots and pilotage
    USE   **Navigation**
            Ship pilots

Piltdown forgery   569.9
    UF   Piltdown man
    BT   **Forgery**
           Fossil hominids

Piltdown man
    USE   **Piltdown forgery**

Pimples (Acne)
    USE   **Acne**

Ping-pong
    USE   **Table tennis**

Pioneer life
    USE   **Frontier and pioneer life**

Pipe fitting   696
    RT   **Plumbing**

Pipe lines
    USE   **Pipelines**

Pipe organs
    USE   **Organs (Musical instruments)**

Pipelines (May subdiv. geog.)   388.5; 621.8
    UF   Pipe lines
    SA   types of pipelines [to be added as needed]
    BT   **Hydraulic structures**
           Transportation
    NT   **Petroleum pipelines**

Pipes, Tobacco
    USE   **Tobacco pipes**

Piracy
    USE   **Pirates**

Pirates (May subdiv. geog.)   364.16; 910.4
    UF   Buccaneers
           Corsairs
           Piracy
    BT   **Criminals**
           International law
           Maritime law

Pirates—*Continued*
>   Naval history
>   NT **Privateering**

Pistols
>   USE **Handguns**

Pity
>   USE **Sympathy**

Place names
>   USE **Geographic names**

Places of retirement
>   USE **Retirement communities**

Places of work
>   USE **Work environment**

Plague (May subdiv. geog.)   **616.9**
>   UF Black death
>   Bubonic plague
>   BT **Communicable diseases**
>   **Epidemics**

Plain chant
>   USE **Chants (Plain, Gregorian, etc.)**

Plainsong
>   USE **Chants (Plain, Gregorian, etc.)**

Plane crashes
>   USE **Aircraft accidents**

Plane geometry   516.22
>   UF Geometry, Plane
>   BT **Geometry**
>   NT **Triangle**

Plane trigonometry
>   USE **Trigonometry**

Planetariums   520.74
>   BT **Astronomy**

Planetary satellites
>   USE **Satellites**

Planetoids
>   USE **Asteroids**

Planets   523.4
>   BT **Astronomy**
>   **Solar system**
>   NT **Earth**
>   **Extrasolar planets**
>   **Jupiter (Planet)**
>   **Life on other planets**
>   **Mars (Planet)**
>   **Mercury (Planet)**
>   **Neptune (Planet)**
>   **Pluto (Planet)**
>   **Saturn (Planet)**
>   **Uranus (Planet)**
>   **Venus (Planet)**
>   RT **Asteroids**

Planets—Exploration   523.4

>   SA names of planets with the subdivision *Exploration* [to be added as needed]
>   BT **Outer space—Exploration**
>   NT **Mars (Planet)—Exploration**

Planets—Satellites
>   USE **Satellites**

Planing machines   621.9
>   BT **Machine tools**

Planned communities (May subdiv. geog.)   **307.76**
>   UF Housing estates
>   New communities
>   Residential developments
>   BT **City planning**

Planned parenthood
>   USE **Birth control**

Planning (May subdiv. geog.)   **338.9; 658.4**
>   SA types of planning, e.g. **Curriculum planning**; and types of activities, facilities, industries, services, and undertakings with the subdivision *Planning*, e.g. **Transportation—Planning** [to be added as needed]
>   BT **Creation (Literary, artistic, etc.)**
>   **Executive ability**
>   **Management**
>   NT **City planning**
>   **Curriculum planning**
>   **Economic policy**
>   **Estate planning**
>   **Regional planning**
>   **Social policy**
>   **Strategic planning**
>   **Tax planning**
>   **Transportation—Planning**

Plans
>   USE **Geometrical drawing**
>   **Map drawing**
>   **Maps**
>   **Mechanical drawing**

Plant anatomy
>   USE **Plants—Anatomy**

Plant breeding   631.5
> Use for materials on attempts to produce new or improved varieties of plants through controlled reproduction. Materials on the continuance or multiplication of plants by successive production are entered under **Plant propagation**.

Plant breeding—*Continued*
UF Hybridization
BT **Agriculture**
Breeding
Horticulture
RT **Plant propagation**
Plant chemistry
USE **Botanical chemistry**
Plants—Analysis
Plant classification
USE **Botany—Classification**
Plant closings
USE **Plant shutdowns**
Plant conservation (May subdiv. geog.)
333.95; 639.9
UF Conservation of plants
Plants—Conservation
Protection of plants
Wild flowers—Conservation
BT **Conservation of natural re-
sources**
Economic botany
Endangered species
Nature conservation
NT **Scarecrows**
RT **Rare plants**
Plant defenses **581.4**
UF Defense mechanisms of plants
Self-defense in plants
Self-protection in plants
BT **Plant ecology**
RT **Poisonous plants**
Plant diseases (May subdiv. geog.)
571.9; 632
UF Botany—Pathology
Diseases and pests
Diseases of plants
Garden pests
Plant pathology
Plants—Diseases
SA types of crops, plants, trees, etc.,
with the subdivision *Diseases
and pests* [to be added as
needed]
BT **Agricultural pests**
Diseases
Fungi
NT **Fruit—Diseases and pests**
Plant distribution
USE **Plants—Geographical distribu-
tion**
Plant ecology (May subdiv. geog.) **581.7**

UF Botany—Ecology
Plants—Ecology
SA types of plants and crops with
the subdivision *Ecology* [to be
added as needed]
BT **Ecology**
NT **Desert plants**
Forest plants
Mountain plants
Plant defenses
RT **Forest influences**
Symbiosis
Plant introduction (May subdiv. geog.)
581.6; 631.5
BT **Economic botany**
Plant lore
USE **Plants—Folklore**
Plant nutrition
USE **Plants—Nutrition**
Plant pathology
USE **Plant diseases**
Plant physiology **571.2**
UF Botany—Physiology
Physiology of plants
BT **Botany**
NT **Fertilization of plants**
Germination
Plants—Growth
Plants—Nutrition
Plant propagation **631.5**
Use for materials on the continuance or
multiplication of plants by successive produc-
tion. Materials on attempts to produce new or
improved varieties of plants through con-
trolled reproduction are entered under **Plant
breeding**.
UF Plants—Propagation
Propagation of plants
BT **Fruit culture**
Gardening
Nurseries (Horticulture)
NT **Grafting**
Seeds
RT **Plant breeding**
Plant shutdowns (May subdiv. geog.)
338.6
UF Closing of factories
Plant closings
BT **Factories**
Unemployment
Plant taxonomy
USE **Botany—Classification**

Plantation life (May subdiv. geog.)
  307.72
  BT   **Country life**
Plantations (May subdiv. geog.)   **307.72**
  BT   **Farms**
Planting
  USE   **Agriculture**
      Gardening
      Landscape gardening
      Tree planting
Plants (May subdiv. geog.)   **580**
  Use for nonscientific materials. Materials on the science of plants are entered under **Botany**. Subdivisions used under this heading may be used under the names of orders, classes, or individual species of plants.
  UF   Flora
      Vegetable kingdom
  SA   types of plants characterized by their physical characteristics, environment, or use, e.g. **Climbing plants; Desert plants; Forage plants;** etc.; and names of botanical categories of plants, e.g. **Ferns** [to be added as needed]
  NT   **Aromatic plants**
      Bulbs
      Carnivorous plants
      Climbing plants
      Cultivated plants
      Desert plants
      Edible plants
      Ferns
      Fertilization of plants
      Flowers
      Forage plants
      Forest plants
      Fossil plants
      Freshwater plants
      Fruit
      Fungi
      Grasses
      Herbs
      Horticulture
      House plants
      Leaves
      Marine plants
      Mosses
      Mountain plants
      Mushrooms
      Poisonous plants
      Popular plant names
      Rare plants
      Seeds
      Shrubs
      Tobacco
      Trees
      Vegetables
      Weeds
  RT   **Botany**
      Gardening
      Herbicides
Plants—Analysis   572
  UF   Plant chemistry
      Plants—Chemical analysis
  BT   **Botanical chemistry**
Plants—Anatomy   571.3
  UF   Anatomy of plants
      Botany—Anatomy
      Botany—Structure
      Plant anatomy
  BT   **Anatomy**
      Botany
Plants—Chemical analysis
  USE   **Plants—Analysis**
Plants—Classification
  USE   **Botany—Classification**
Plants—Collection and preservation   580.75
  UF   Botanical specimens—Collection and preservation
      Collections of natural specimens
      Herbaria
      Preservation of botanical specimens
      Specimens, Preservation of
  BT   **Collectors and collecting**
  NT   **Flowers—Drying**
Plants—Conservation
  USE   **Plant conservation**
Plants, Cultivated
  USE   **Cultivated plants**
Plants—Diseases
  USE   **Plant diseases**
Plants—Ecology
  USE   **Plant ecology**
Plants, Edible
  USE   **Edible plants**
Plants, Extinct
  USE   **Fossil plants**
Plants—Fertilization
  USE   **Fertilization of plants**
Plants—Folklore   398.24

Plants—Folklore—*Continued*
   UF   Plant lore
   BT   **Folklore**
   NT   **Ethnobotany**
         Language of flowers
Plants, Fossil
   USE **Fossil plants**
Plants—Geographical distribution   581.9
   UF   Geographical distribution of
         plants
         Phytogeography
         Plant distribution
   SA   types of plants with the subdivi-
         sion *Geographical distribution*
         [to be added as needed]
   BT   **Biogeography**
Plants—Growth   571.8
   BT   **Plant physiology**
Plants in art   704.9
   SA   types of plants in art, e.g. **Flow-**
         ers in art [to be added as
         needed]
   BT   **Art—Themes**
   RT   **Botanical illustration**
Plants, Industrial
   USE **Factories**
Plants, Medicinal
   USE **Medical botany**
Plants—Names
   USE **Botany—Nomenclature**
         Popular plant names
Plants—Nomenclature
   USE **Botany—Nomenclature**
         Popular plant names
Plants—Nutrition   575.7; 631.5
   UF   Plant nutrition
   BT   **Nutrition**
         Plant physiology
Plants, Ornamental
   USE **Ornamental plants**
Plants—Photography
   USE **Photography of plants**
Plants—Propagation
   USE **Plant propagation**
Plants—Soilless culture
   USE **Hydroponics**
Plants—United States   581.973
   UF   Botany—United States
Plaster and plastering   693
   UF   Plastering
   BT   **Masonry**

   NT   **Cement**
         Concrete
         Mortar
         Stucco
Plaster casts   731.4
   UF   Casting
         Casts, Plaster
   BT   **Sculpture**
Plastering
   USE **Plaster and plastering**
Plastic industries
   USE **Plastics industry**
Plastic materials
   USE **Plastics**
Plastic surgery   617.9
   UF   Cosmetic surgery
         Reconstructive surgery
         Surgery, Plastic
   BT   **Surgery**
Plastics   668.4
   UF   Plastic materials
   SA   names of specific plastics [to be
         added as needed]
   BT   **Polymers**
         Synthetic products
   NT   **Gums and resins**
         Synthetic rubber
   RT   **Plastics industry**
Plastics industry (May subdiv. geog.)
         338.4; 668.4
   UF   Plastic industries
   BT   **Chemical industry**
   RT   **Plastics**
Plate   739.2
   UF   Gold plate
         Silver plate
   BT   **Goldwork**
         Silverwork
   NT   **Hallmarks**
         Sheffield plate
Plate metalwork   671.8
   BT   **Metalwork**
         Sheet metalwork
Plate tectonics   551.1
   BT   **Earth—Crust**
         Geophysics
   RT   **Continental drift**
         Submarine geology
Platforms, Drilling
   USE **Drilling platforms**
Play   790

Play—*Continued*
    BT   **Recreation**
    NT   **Finger play**
          Imaginary playmates
          Sports
    RT   **Amusements**
          Games

Play centers
    USE **Community centers**
          Playgrounds

Play direction (Theater)
    USE **Theater—Production and direction**

Play production
    USE **Amateur theater**
          Theater—Production and direction

Play—Therapeutic use
    USE **Play therapy**

Play therapy   616.89; 618.9
    UF   Play—Therapeutic use
    BT   **Therapeutics**

Play writing
    USE **Drama—Technique**
          Motion picture plays—Technique
          Radio plays—Technique
          Television plays—Technique

Playbills
    USE **Film posters**

Playgrounds (May subdiv. geog.)   796.06
    UF   Play centers
          Public playgrounds
          School playgrounds
    BT   **Recreation**
          Sports facilities
    RT   **Community centers**
          Parks

Playhouses
    USE **Theaters**

Playing cards   795.4
    UF   Cards, Playing
    NT   **Tarot**
    RT   **Card games**

Plays
    USE **Drama—Collections**
          One act plays

Plays for children
    USE **Children's plays**

Playwrights
    USE **Dramatists**

Playwriting
    USE **Drama—Technique**
          Motion picture plays—Technique
          Radio plays—Technique
          Television plays—Technique

Pleasure   152.4
    BT   **Emotions**
          Joy and sorrow
          Senses and sensation
    RT   **Happiness**
          Pain

Plot-your-own stories   808.3
    UF   Choose-your-own story plots
          Making-choices stories
          Multiple plot stories
          Which-way stories
    BT   **Children's literature**
          Fiction
          Literary recreations

Plots (Drama, fiction, etc.)
    USE **Stories, plots, etc.**

Plows   631.3
    BT   **Agricultural machinery**

Plumbing   696
    BT   **Building**
    NT   **Sewerage**
    RT   **House drainage**
          Household sanitation
          Pipe fitting

Plural pregnancy
    USE **Multiple pregnancy**

Pluralism (Social sciences) (May subdiv. geog.)   305.8

    Use for materials on the coexistence of several distinct ethnic, religious, or cultural groups within one society. Materials on the presence of two distinct cultures within a single country or region are entered under **Biculturalism**. Materials on policies or programs that foster the preservation of various cultures or cultural identities within a unified society are entered under **Multiculturalism**.

    UF   Ethnic diversity
    BT   **Culture**
    NT   **Biculturalism**
    RT   **Ethnic relations**
          Ethnicity
          Multiculturalism
          Race relations

Pluto (Planet)   523.48
    BT   **Planets**

Plywood   674
    BT   **Wood**

PMS (Gynecology)
    USE **Premenstrual syndrome**
Pneumatic transmission
    USE **Compressed air**
Pneumatics 533; 621.5
    BT **Physics**
    NT **Aerodynamics**
          Compressed air
          Sound
    RT **Gases**
Pneumonia 616.2
    BT **Lungs—Diseases**
Pocket billiards
    USE **Pool (Game)**
Pocket calculators
    USE **Calculators**
Podiatry 617.5
    UF Chiropody
    BT **Medicine**
    NT **Foot—Care**
    RT **Foot—Wounds and injuries**
Poetics 808.1

    Use for materials on the art and technique of poetry. General materials on the appreciation, philosophy, etc., of poetry are entered under **Poetry**.

    UF Poetry—Technique
    BT **Poetry**
    NT **Rhyme**
          Rhythm
          Versification
Poetry 809.1

    Use for general materials on poetry, not for individual works. Materials on the history and criticism of poetry from more than one literature are entered under **Poetry—History and criticism**. Materials on the art and technique of poetry are entered under **Poetics**. Collections of poetry are entered under **Poetry—Collections; English poetry—Collections;** etc.

    UF Poetry—Philosophy
    SA types of poetry, e.g. **Haiku**; and subjects, historical events, names of places, ethnic groups, classes of persons, and names of individual persons with the subdivision *Poetry*, to express the theme or subject content of collections of poetry, e.g. **Animals—Poetry; World War, 1939-1945—Poetry; Napoleon I, Emperor of the French,**

          1769-1821—Poetry; etc. [to be added as needed]
    BT **Literature**
    NT **American poetry**
          Ballads
          Children's poetry
          Didactic poetry
          Eddas
          Elegiac poetry
          English poetry
          Epistolary poetry
          Erotic poetry
          Fantasy poetry
          Free verse
          French poetry
          Haiku
          Humorous poetry
          Islamic poetry
          Love poetry
          Narrative poetry
          Nature poetry
          Pastoral poetry
          Patriotic poetry
          Poetics
          Religious poetry
          Science fiction poetry
          Sea poetry
          Songs
          War poetry
Poetry and music
    USE **Music and literature**
Poetry—Collections 808.81
    UF Poetry—Selections
          Rhymes
Poetry—Editing 070.5
    BT **Editing**
Poetry for children
    USE **Children's poetry**
          Nursery rhymes
Poetry, Historical
    USE **Historical poetry**
Poetry—History and criticism 809.1
Poetry—Memorizing 153.1
    BT **Mnemonics**
Poetry—Philosophy
    USE **Poetry**
Poetry—Selections
    USE **Poetry—Collections**
Poetry—Technique
    USE **Poetics**

Poets   809.1; 920

Use for materials on the lives of several poets, not limited to a single national literature.

SA   poets of particular countries, e.g. **American poets** [to be added as needed]

BT   **Authors**

NT   **American poets**
Lyricists
Minstrels
Troubadours

Poets, American

USE   **American poets**

Poison ivy   583

BT   **Poisonous plants**

Poisonous animals (May subdiv. geog.) **591.6**

SA   types of poisonous animals, e.g. **Rattlesnakes** [to be added as needed]

BT   **Animals**
Dangerous animals
Economic zoology
Poisons and poisoning

NT   **Rattlesnakes**

Poisonous gases   363.17

UF   Asphyxiating gases
Gases, Asphyxiating and poisonous

BT   **Gases**
Poisons and poisoning

NT   **Radon**

Poisonous gases—War use

USE   **Chemical warfare**

Poisonous plants (May subdiv. geog.) **581.6**

UF   Toxic plants

SA   types of poisonous plants, e.g. **Poison ivy** [to be added as needed]

BT   **Economic botany**
Plants
Poisons and poisoning

NT   **Poison ivy**

RT   **Plant defenses**

Poisonous substances

USE   **Poisons and poisoning**

Poisons and poisoning   363.17; 615.9

Use for materials on poisonous substances and their use. Materials on the science that treats of poisons and their antidotes are entered under **Toxicology**.

UF   Poisonous substances
Toxic substances

SA   types of poisons or poisoning, e.g. **Lead poisoning**; and types of poisonous substances with the subdivision *Toxicology*, for materials on the influence of particular substances on humans and animals, e.g. **Insecticides—Toxicology** [to be added as needed]

BT   **Accidents**
Hazardous substances
Homicide
Medical jurisprudence

NT   **Food poisoning**
Insecticides—Toxicology
Lead poisoning
Pesticides
Poisonous animals
Poisonous gases
Poisonous plants

RT   **Toxicology**

Poker   795.412

BT   **Card games**

Poland   943.8

May be subdivided like **United States** except for *History*.

Polar expeditions

USE   **Antarctica—Exploration**
Arctic regions—Exploration
Scientific expeditions

Polar lights

USE   **Auroras**

Polar regions   998

Use for materials on both the Antarctic and Arctic regions.

NT   **Antarctica**
Arctic regions
North Pole
South Pole

Polarity

USE   **Opposites**

Police (May subdiv. geog.)   **363.2**

UF   Police officers
Policemen

BT   **Administration of criminal justice**
Law enforcement

NT   **Animals in police work**
Border patrols
Detectives

585

Police—*Continued*
>> **Police brutality**
>> **Police corruption**
>> **Policewomen**
>> **Secret service**
>> **State police**
> RT **Crime**
>> **Criminal investigation**

Police brutality (May subdiv. geog.)
363.2
> UF Police—Complaints against
>> Police cruelty
>> Police repression
>> Police violence
> BT **Police**

Police—Complaints against
> USE **Police brutality**
>> **Police corruption**

Police—Corrupt practices
> USE **Police corruption**

Police corruption (May subdiv. geog.)
363.2
> UF Corruption, Police
>> Police—Complaints against
>> Police—Corrupt practices
> BT **Misconduct in office**
>> **Police**

Police cruelty
> USE **Police brutality**

Police, International
> USE **International police**

Police officers
> USE **Police**

Police repression
> USE **Police brutality**

Police, State
> USE **State police**

Police—United States **363.20973**
> UF United States—Police

Police violence
> USE **Police brutality**

Policemen
> USE **Police**

Policewomen (May subdiv. geog.) **363.2**
> UF Women police officers
> BT **Police**
>> **Women**

Polio
> USE **Poliomyelitis**

Poliomyelitis **616.8**
> UF Infantile paralysis
>> Polio

> BT **Diseases**

Poliomyelitis vaccine **614.4; 615**
> UF Live poliovirus vaccine
>> Sabin vaccine
>> Salk vaccine
> BT **Vaccination**

Polishing
> USE **Grinding and polishing**

Politeness
> USE **Courtesy**
>> **Etiquette**

Political action committees (May subdiv. geog.) **322.4; 324**
> Use for materials on special interest groups that support sympathetic candidates for public office through campaign contributions. Materials on groups that promote their own interests with public officials are entered under **Lobbying**.
> UF Interest groups
>> PACs (Political action committees)
>> Pressure groups
> BT **Political participation**
> RT **Lobbying**

Political activity
> USE **Political participation**
>> and classes of persons, types of industries, military services, and religious denominations, and names of corporate bodies and families with the subdivision *Political activity,* e.g. **Women—Political activity** [to be added as needed]

Political aspects
> USE subjects with the subdivision *Political aspects,* e.g. **Ethnic relations—Political aspects** [to be added as needed]

Political asylum
> USE **Asylum**

Political behavior
> USE **Political participation**
>> **Political psychology**

Political boundaries
> USE **Boundaries**

Political campaign literature
> USE **Campaign literature**

Political campaigns
> USE **Politics**

Political conventions **324.5**
> UF Conventions, Political

Political conventions—*Continued*
- BT **Conferences**
- NT **Primaries**
- RT **Political parties**

Political correctness   306
- BT **Ideology**

Political corruption (May subdiv. geog.)
      324; 353.4
- UF Boss rule
      Corruption in politics
      Graft in politics
      Political scandals
      Politics—Corrupt practices
      Spoils system
- BT **Conflict of interests**
      Political crimes and offenses
      Political ethics
      Politics
- NT **Whistle blowing**
- RT **Misconduct in office**

Political crimes and offenses (May
      subdiv. geog.)   **364.1**
- UF Crimes, Political
      Sedition
- BT **Criminal law**
      Political ethics
      Subversive activities
- NT **Anarchism and anarchists**
      Assassination
      Bombings
      Concentration camps
      Political corruption
      Political prisoners
      Terrorism
      Treason

Political defectors
- USE **Defectors**

Political economy
- USE **Economics**

Political ethics (May subdiv. geog.)   **172**
- BT **Ethics**
      Political science
      Politics
      Social ethics
- NT **Citizenship**
      Conflict of interests
      Political corruption
      Political crimes and offenses
      Resistance to government

Political extremism
- USE **Radicalism**

Political geography
- USE **Boundaries**
      Geopolitics

Political participation (May subdiv. geog.)
      323
- UF Citizen participation
      Civic involvement
      Community action
      Mass political behavior
      Political activity
      Political behavior
- SA subjects designating government
      activity with the subdivision
      Citizen participation, e.g.
      **Crime prevention—Citizen
      participation**; and corporate
      bodies, families, classes of
      persons, industries, military
      services, and religious denom-
      inations with the subdivision
      Political activity, e.g. **Wom-
      en—Political activity** [to be
      added as needed]
- BT **Politics**
- NT **African Americans—Political
      activity**
      Blacks—Political activity
      **City planning—Citizen partici-
      pation**
      Clergy—Political activity
      **College students—Political ac-
      tivity**
      **Crime prevention—Citizen par-
      ticipation**
      Jews—Political activity
      Political action committees
      Students—Political activity
      Women—Political activity
- RT **Social action**

Political parties (May subdiv. geog.)
      324.2
- UF Parties, Political
- SA names of parties [to be added as
      needed]
- BT **Political science**
      Politics
- NT **Democratic Party (U.S.)**
      Politics
      Republican Party (U.S.)
      **Right and left (Political sci-
      ence)**

Political parties—*Continued*
    Third parties (United States politics)
  RT **Political conventions**
Political parties—Finance
  USE **Campaign funds**
Political prisoners (May subdiv. geog.)
  365
  UF Prisoners of conscience
  BT **Political crimes and offenses**
       Prisoners
Political psychology **302**
  UF Mass political behavior
       Political behavior
       Politics—Psychological aspects
  BT **Political science**
       Psychology
       Social psychology
  NT **Propaganda**
       Public opinion
Political refugees (May subdiv. geog.)
  325
  UF Displaced persons
       Refugees, Political
  SA refugees of particular countries, geographic regions, or ethnic groups, e.g. **Vietnamese refugees**; **Arab refugees**; etc., and names of wars with the subdivision *Refugees*, e.g. **World War, 1939-1945—Refugees** [to be added as needed]
  BT **Asylum**
       International law
       International relations
       Refugees
  NT **Defectors**
       Exiles
       World War, 1939-1945—Refugees
Political satire **808.7; 808.87**
  BT **Satire**
Political scandals
  USE **Political corruption**
Political science (May subdiv. geog.)
  320
    Use for materials on the science of politics. Materials on the various aspects of practical politics, such as electioneering, political machines, etc., are entered under **Politics**. Materials on the political processes of particular re-
gions, countries, cities, etc., are entered under the place with the subdivision *Politics and government.*
  UF Civics
       Civil government
       Commonwealth, The
       Government
       Political theory
  SA movements in political philosophy, e.g. **Marxism**; topics with the subdivision *Political aspects*, e.g. **Ethnic relations—Political aspects**; and names of continents, areas, countries, cities, etc., and native peoples with the subdivision *Politics and government*, e.g. **United States—Politics and government**; **Native Americans—Politics and government** [to be added as needed]
  BT **Social sciences**
  NT **Anarchism and anarchists**
       Aristocracy
       Authority
       Bureaucracy
       Citizenship
       Civil rights
       Civil service
       Collectivism
       Communism
       Comparative government
       Conservatism
       Democracy
       Equality
       Executive power
       Federal government
       Freedom
       Geopolitics
       Ideology
       Imperialism
       Individualism
       Islam and politics
       Law
       Legislation
       Liberalism
       Local government
       Marxism
       Monarchy
       Municipal government
       Nationalism

Political science—*Continued*
    Nations
    Political ethics
    Political parties
    Political psychology
    Postcolonialism
    Power (Social sciences)
    Progressivism (United States politics)
    Public administration
    Public opinion
    Radicalism
    Representative government and representation
    Republics
    Resistance to government
    Revolutions
    Right and left (Political science)
    Separation of powers
    Social contract
    Socialism
    Sovereignty
    State governments
    State rights
    Suffrage
    Taxation
    Totalitarianism
    Tribal government
    United States—Politics and government
    Utopias
    World politics
  RT Politics
    State, The
Political science—Early works to 1800
    (May subdiv. geog.) **320**
Political science—Religious aspects
  USE **Religion and politics**
Political theory
  USE **Political science**
Political violence
  USE **Sabotage**
    Terrorism
Politicians (May subdiv. geog.)
    324.2092; 920
  BT **Statesmen**
  NT **Women politicians**
Politicians—United States **324.2092; 920**
  UF American politicians
    United States—Politicians

Politics **324.7**
    Use for materials on the various aspects of practical politics, such as electioneering, political machines, etc. Materials on the science of politics are entered under **Political science**.
  UF Campaigns, Political
    Electioneering
    Political campaigns
    Politics, Practical
    Practical politics
  SA subjects with the subdivision *Political aspects*, e.g. **Ethnic relations—Political aspects**; names of continents, areas, countries, cities, etc., and native peoples, with the subdivision *Politics and government*; and ethnic groups and classes of persons with the subdivision *Political activity*, e.g. **College students—Political activity** [to be added as needed]
  BT **Political parties**
  NT **Arab countries—Politics and government**
    Asia—Politics and government
    Business and politics
    Campaign funds
    Campaign literature
    Chicago (Ill.)—Politics and government
    Elections
    Latin America—Politics and government
    Lobbying
    Native Americans—Politics and government
    Political corruption
    Political ethics
    Political participation
    Political parties
    Primaries
    Regionalism
    Religion and politics
    Television and politics
    United States—Politics and government
  RT **Political science**
Politics and business
  USE **Business and politics**

Politics and Christianity
   USE   **Christianity and politics**
Politics and government
   USE   names of continents, areas,
        countries, cities, etc., and na-
        tive peoples with the subdivi-
        sion *Politics and government,*
        e.g. **United States—Politics**
        and government; Arab
        countries—Politics and gov-
        ernment; Native Ameri-
        cans—Politics and govern-
        ment; etc. [to be added as
        needed]
Politics and Islam
   USE   **Islam and politics**
Politics and religion
   USE   **Religion and politics**
Politics and students
   USE   **Students—Political activity**
Politics and television
   USE   **Television and politics**
Politics—Corrupt practices
   USE   **Political corruption**
Politics, Practical
   USE   **Politics**
Politics—Psychological aspects
   USE   **Political psychology**
Politics—Religious aspects
   USE   **Religion and politics**
Polity, Ecclesiastical
   USE   **Church polity**
Pollen as food   641.3
   BT   **Food**
Pollination
   USE   **Fertilization of plants**
Polls
   USE   **Elections**
         Public opinion polls
Pollution (May subdiv. geog.)   **304.2;**
     363.73
   UF   Chemical pollution
        Contamination of environment
        Environmental pollution
   SA   types of pollution, e.g. **Air pol-**
        lution [to be added as need-
        ed]
   BT   **Environmental health**
        Human influence on nature
        Public health
        Sanitary engineering

        Sanitation
   NT   **Air pollution**
        Noise pollution
        Pesticides—Environmental as-
        pects
        Radioactive pollution
        Space debris
        Water pollution
   RT   **Environmental protection**
        Hazardous wastes
        Industrial waste
        Pollution control industry
        Refuse and refuse disposal
Pollution control
   USE   **Pollution control industry**
Pollution control devices (Motor vehicles)
   USE   **Automobiles—Pollution control**
        devices
Pollution control industry (May subdiv.
   geog.)   **338.4; 363.73**
   UF   Pollution control
        Pollution—Prevention
   BT   **Industries**
   NT   **Automobiles—Pollution control**
        devices
        Recycling
        Refuse and refuse disposal
   RT   **Pollution**
Pollution—Mathematical models   304.2;
     363.73
   BT   **Mathematical models**
Pollution of air
   USE   **Air pollution**
Pollution of water
   USE   **Water pollution**
Pollution—Prevention
   USE   **Pollution control industry**
Pollution, Radioactive
   USE   **Radioactive pollution**
Poltergeists
   USE   **Ghosts**
Polygamy (May subdiv. geog.)   **306.84**
   BT   **Marriage**
Polyglot dictionaries   413
   UF   Dictionaries, Multilingual
        Dictionaries, Polyglot
        Multilingual dictionaries
        Multilingual glossaries, phrase
          books, etc.
        Polyglot glossaries, phrase
          books, etc.

Polyglot dictionaries—*Continued*
    BT   **Encyclopedias and dictionaries**
Polyglot glossaries, phrase books, etc.
    USE   **Polyglot dictionaries**
Polygraph
    USE   **Lie detectors and detection**
Polymer clay craft   731.2; 738.1; 745.57
    BT   **Handicraft**
Polymerization
    USE   **Polymers**
Polymers   541; 547; 668.9
    UF   Polymerization
    SA   types of polymers, e.g. **Plastics**
        [to be added as needed]
    BT   **Organic compounds—Synthesis**
        Physical chemistry
    NT   **Plastics**
Polynucleotides
    USE   **Nucleic acids**
Pomp
    USE   **Parades**
Pompeii (Extinct city)   937
    BT   **Extinct cities—Italy**
        Italy—Antiquities
Ponds (May subdiv. geog.)   551.48
    BT   **Water**
Ponies   636.1
    UF   Foals
    BT   **Horses**
Pontiac's Conspiracy, 1763-1765   973.2
    BT   **Native Americans—Wars**
        United States—History—1600-
        1775, Colonial period
Pony express   383
    BT   **Express service**
        Postal service
Pool (Game) (May subdiv. geog.)
    794.73
    UF   Pocket billiards
    BT   **Billiards**
Pools
    USE   **Swimming pools**
Poor (May subdiv. geog.)   305.5; 362.5
    UF   Poor people
        Poor persons
    BT   **Poverty**
        Public welfare
    NT   **Begging**
        Homeless persons
        Tramps
        Unemployed
Poor—Medical care   362.1

    UF   Medical care for the poor
    BT   **Medical care**
    NT   **Medicaid**
Poor people
    USE   **Poor**
Poor persons
    USE   **Poor**
Poor relief
    USE   **Charities**
        Domestic economic assistance
        Public welfare
Pop culture
    USE   **Popular culture**
Pop-up books
    USE   **Toy and movable books**
Popes   262; 920
    UF   Holy See
    BT   **Church history**
    RT   **Papacy**
Popes—Infallibility   262
    UF   Infallibility of the Pope
Popes—Temporal power   262
    UF   Temporal power of the Pope
    BT   **Church history**
Popes—Travel
    USE   **Papal visits**
Popes—Voyages and travels
    USE   **Papal visits**
Popular arts
    USE   **Popular culture**
Popular culture (May subdiv. geog.)
    306.4
    Use for materials on literature, art, music, motion pictures, etc., produced for a mass audience. General materials on learning and scholarship, literature, the arts, etc., are entered under **Intellectual life**.
    UF   Mass culture
        Pop culture
        Popular arts
    BT   **Communication**
        Culture
        Intellectual life
        Recreation
    NT   **Fads**
        Sex in popular culture
        Violence in popular culture
    RT   **Mass media**
Popular culture—Chicago (Ill.)   977.3
    UF   Chicago (Ill.)—Popular culture
Popular culture—United States   973
    UF   United States—Popular culture

Popular culture—United States—*Continued*

NT   **Americana**

      Hip-hop culture

Popular government

  USE **Democracy**

Popular medicine   616.02

   Use for medical books written for the layman.

  UF   Medicine, Popular

  BT   **Medicine**

  NT   **Traditional medicine**

  RT   **Health self-care**

Popular music (May subdiv. geog.)
    781.64; 782.42164

  UF   Popular songs

  SA   types of popular music [to be added as needed]

  BT   **Music**

      Songs

  NT   **Blues music**

      Country music

      Gospel music

      Rap music

      Reggae music

      Rock music

Popular music—Texts

  USE **Popular song lyrics**

Popular music—Writing and publishing
    070.5; 781.3

  UF   Song writing

      Songwriting

  BT   **Composition (Music)**

Popular plant names   580.1

   Use for materials on the common or vernacular names of plants. Systematically derived lists of names or designations of plants and materials about such names are entered under **Botany—Nomenclature**.

  UF   Plants—Names

      Plants—Nomenclature

  SA   types of plants with the subdivision *Nomenclature (Popular)*, e.g. **Trees—Nomenclature (Popular)** [to be added as needed]

  BT   **Plants**

  NT   **Trees—Nomenclature (Popular)**

  RT   **Botany—Nomenclature**

Popular song lyrics   782.42164

  UF   Lyrics

      Popular music—Texts [*Former heading*]

      Popular songs—Texts

      Song lyrics

Popular songs

  USE **Popular music**

Popular songs—Texts

  USE **Popular song lyrics**

Popularity   158

  BT   **Social psychology**

Population   304.6; 363.9

  UF   Demography

      Foreign population

  SA   ethnic groups and names of countries, cities, etc., with the subdivision *Population*, e.g. **United States—Population** [to be added as needed]

  BT   **Economics**

      Human ecology

      Sociology

      Vital statistics

  NT   **Baby boom generation**

      Birth control

      Census

      Chicago (Ill.)—Population

      Cities and towns—Growth

      Eugenics

      Human fertility

      Human settlements

      Immigration and emigration

      Internal migration

      Mortality

      Ohio—Population

      Overpopulation

      United States—Population

  RT   **Birth rate**

Population explosion

  USE **Overpopulation**

Porcelain (May subdiv. geog.)   738.2

   Use for materials on chinaware and porcelain for the table or decorative use. Materials on the technology of fired earthen products or on clay products intended for industrial use are entered under **Ceramics**.

  UF   China (Porcelain)

      Chinaware

      Dishes

  SA   types of porcelain [to be added as needed]

  BT   **Decorative arts**

      Pottery

      Tableware

  NT   **China painting**

Porcelain enamels
USE **Enamel and enameling**
Porcelain painting
USE **China painting**
Pornography (May subdiv. geog.) **176;**
363.4; 364.1
UF Obscene materials
NT **Child pornography**
RT **Erotica**
Obscenity (Law)
Portable computers 004.16
UF Handheld computers
Laptop computers
BT **Computers**
Portrait miniatures
USE **Miniature painting**
Portrait painting 757
UF Portraiture
BT **Painting**
Portraits
RT **Figure painting**
Miniature painting
Portrait photography (May subdiv. geog.)
778.9; 779
UF Portraiture
BT **Photography**
Portraits
Portraits (May subdiv. geog.) **704.9;**
757
SA headings for collective and indi-
vidual biography, classes of
persons, and names of indi-
viduals with the subdivision
Portraits, e.g. **United**
States—Biography—Por-
traits; **Musicians—Portraits**;
Shakespeare, William, 1564-
1616—Portraits; etc. [to be
added as needed]
BT **Art**
Biography
Pictures
NT **Cartoons and caricatures**
Portrait painting
Portrait photography
Portraiture
USE **Portrait painting**
Portrait photography
Ports
USE **Harbors**

Portugal 946.9
May be subdivided like **United States** ex-
cept for *History*.
Portuguese literature 869
BT **Literature**
Romance literature
Position analysis
USE **Topology**
Positivism 146
BT **Philosophy**
Rationalism
NT **Materialism**
Pragmatism
RT **Agnosticism**
Deism
Realism
Post cards
USE **Postcards**
Post-colonialism
USE **Postcolonialism**
Post-impressionism
USE **Postimpressionism (Art)**
Post-modernism
USE **Postmodernism**
Post office
USE **Postal service**
Post-traumatic stress disorder 616.85
UF Posttraumatic stress disorder
Traumatic stress syndrome
BT **Anxiety**
Neuroses
Stress (Psychology)
Postage stamp collecting
USE **Stamp collecting**
Postage stamps (May subdiv. geog.)
383; 769.56
UF Stamps, Postage
BT **Postal service**
RT **Stamp collecting**
Postage stamps—Collectors and collecting
USE **Stamp collecting**
Postal cards
USE **Postcards**
Postal delivery code
USE **Zip code**
Postal service (May subdiv. geog.)
354.75; 383
UF Mail service
Parcel post
Post office
BT **Communication**
Transportation

Postal service—*Continued*
- NT   **Air mail service**
-       **Pony express**
-       **Postage stamps**
-       **Zip code**

Postal service—United States   354.75;
383
- UF   United States—Mail
-       United States—Postal service

Postcards   383; 741.6
- UF   Picture postcards
-       Post cards
-       Postal cards

Postcards—Collectors and collecting
790.1

Postcolonial theory
- USE   **Postcolonialism**

Postcolonialism (May subdiv. geog.)   325
- UF   Post-colonialism
-       Postcolonial theory
- BT   **Political science**

Posters (May subdiv. geog.)   741.6
- SA   types of posters, e.g. **Film posters**; and subjects, ethnic groups, classes of persons, individual persons, corporate bodies, and names of wars with the subdivision *Posters* [to be added as needed]
- BT   **Advertising**
-       **Commercial art**
- NT   **Film posters**
- RT   **Signs and signboards**

Postimpressionism (Art) (May subdiv. geog.)   709.03
- UF   Post-impressionism
- BT   **Art**

Postmodernism (May subdiv. geog.)
190; 700.1
- UF   Post-modernism
- BT   **Aesthetics**
- RT   **Modernism (Aesthetics)**

Postpartum depression   618.7
- BT   **Depression (Psychology)**

Posttraumatic stress disorder
- USE   **Post-traumatic stress disorder**

Posture   613.7
- BT   **Physical fitness**

Pot (Drug)
- USE   **Marijuana**

Potable water
- USE   **Drinking water**

Potash   631.8; 668
- BT   **Fertilizers**

Potatoes   635; 641.3
- BT   **Vegetables**

Potpourri   668; 745.92
- BT   **Herbs**
-       **Nature craft**
-       **Perfumes**

Potters (May subdiv. geog.)   738.092;
920
- BT   **Artists**

Potters' marks
- USE   **Pottery—Marks**

Pottery   666; 738

    Use for materials on pottery for the table or for decorative use. Materials on the technology of fired earthen products or on clay products intended for industrial use are entered under **Ceramics**.
- UF   Crockery
-       Dishes
-       Earthenware
-       Faience
-       Stoneware
- SA   types of pottery and pottery of particular countries, e.g. **American pottery** [to be added as needed]
- BT   **Ceramics**
-       **Clay industry**
-       **Decoration and ornament**
-       **Decorative arts**
-       **Tableware**
- NT   **American pottery**
-       **Art pottery**
-       **Glazes**
-       **Porcelain**
-       **Terra cotta**
- RT   **Vases**

Pottery, American
- USE   **American pottery**

Pottery—Marks   738
- UF   Potters' marks

Poultry   598.6; 636.5
- SA   types of domesticated birds, e.g. **Ducks** [to be added as needed]
- BT   **Birds**
-       **Domestic animals**
- NT   **Chickens**
-       **Cooking—Poultry**
-       **Ducks**
-       **Geese**

Poultry—*Continued*
    Turkeys
Poverty   305.5; 362.5
    UF   Destitution
           Pauperism
    SA   names of countries with the subdivisions *Economic conditions* and *Social conditions* [to be added as needed]
    BT   **Economic conditions**
           Social problems
    NT   **Homelessness**
           Poor
    RT   **Basic needs**
           Domestic economic assistance
           Public welfare
           Subsistence economy
Powder, Smokeless
    USE   **Gunpowder**
Powdered milk
    USE   **Dried milk**
Power blackouts
    USE   **Electric power failures**
Power boats
    USE   **Motorboats**
Power failures
    USE   **Electric power failures**
Power (Mechanics)   531; 621
    Use for materials on the physics and engineering aspects of power. Materials on the available sources of mechanical power in general are entered under **Energy resources**.
    UF   Energy technology
    BT   **Mechanical engineering**
           Mechanics
    NT   **Compressed air**
           Electric power
           Energy resources
           Force and energy
           Machinery
           Power transmission
           Steam
           Water power
           Wind power
Power of attorney (May subdiv. geog.)   346.02
    UF   Durable power of attorney
    BT   **Law**
Power plants
    USE   **Electric power plants**
Power plants, Hydroelectric
    USE   **Hydroelectric power plants**

Power plants, Nuclear
    USE   **Nuclear power plants**
Power politics
    USE   **Balance of power**
                Cold war
Power resources
    USE   **Energy resources**
Power resources conservation
    USE   **Energy conservation**
Power resources development
    USE   **Energy development**
Power (Social sciences) (May subdiv. geog.)   303.3
    BT   **Political science**
    NT   **Elite (Social sciences)**
Power stations
    USE   **Electric power plants**
Power supply
    USE   **Energy resources**
Power tools   621.9
    BT   **Tools**
Power transmission   621.8
    UF   Transmission of power
    BT   **Mechanical engineering**
           Power (Mechanics)
    NT   **Cables**
           Electric power distribution
           Gearing
    RT   **Belts and belting**
           Machinery
Power transmission, Electric
    USE   **Electric lines**
                Electric power distribution
Powers, Separation of
    USE   **Separation of powers**
POWs
    USE   **Prisoners of war**
Powwows   394.2; 970.004
    BT   **Festivals**
           Native Americans—Rites and ceremonies
           Native Americans—Social life and customs
Practical jokes   793
    UF   Pranks
    BT   **Jokes**
           Wit and humor
Practical nurses (May subdiv. geog.)   610.73; 920
    BT   **Nurses**
Practical nursing   610.73; 649.8

Practical nursing—*Continued*
    BT   **Nursing**
Practical politics
    USE   **Politics**
Practical psychology
    USE   **Applied psychology**
Practice
    USE   types of professions with the
            subdivision *Practice,* e.g. **Nu-
            clear medicine—Practice** [to
            be added as needed]
Practice teaching
    USE   **Student teaching**
Pragmatism   144
    BT   **Philosophy**
          Positivism
          Realism
          Theory of knowledge
    RT   **Empiricism**
          Reality
          Truth
          Utilitarianism
Prairies (May subdiv. geog.)   **577.4;
   578.74**
    BT   **Grasslands**
Praise of God   248.3
    UF   God—Praise
    BT   **Worship**
Pranks
    USE   **Practical jokes**
Prayer   204; 248.3
      May be subdivided by religion or sect. Use
    for materials about prayer. Collections of
    prayers are entered under **Prayers**.
    UF   Devotion
          Devotional theology
    BT   **Worship**
    RT   **Devotional exercises**
          Prayers
Prayer-books
    USE   **Prayers**
Prayer-books and devotions
    USE   **Prayers**
Prayer in the public schools (May
   subdiv. geog.)   **379.2**
      Use for materials on the inclusion of
    prayers or a period for silent prayer or medi-
    tation in the daily schedule of public schools.
    Materials on the teaching of religion in the
    public schools or on the religious freedom of
    students and school employees are entered un-
    der **Religion in the public schools**.
    UF   Prayers in the public schools
          School prayer

    BT   **Religion in the public schools**
Jesus Christ—Prayers
    NT   **Lord's prayer**
Prayers   204; 242; 264
      Use for collections of prayers. Materials
    about prayer are entered under **Prayer**.
    UF   Collects
          Prayer-books
          Prayer-books and devotions
    SA   names of religions, denomina-
          tions, religious orders, classes
          of persons for whose use the
          prayers are intended, and
          names of saints and deities to
          whom the prayers are directed
          with the subdivision *Prayers,*
          e.g. **Buddhism—Prayers**;
          **Sick—Prayers; Mary,
          Blessed Virgin, Saint—
          Prayers**; etc. [to be added as
          needed]
    BT   **Devotional literature**
    NT   **Buddhism—Prayers**
          **Mary, Blessed Virgin, Saint—
          Prayers**
          Meditations
          Sick—Prayers
    RT   **Prayer**
Prayers in the public schools
    USE   **Prayer in the public schools**
Pre-Columbian Americans
    USE   **Native Americans**
Pre-Lenten festivities
    USE   **Carnival**
Preachers
    USE   **Clergy**
Preaching (May subdiv. geog.)   **206; 251**
      Use for materials on the art of writing and
    delivering sermons. Collections of sermons
    not limited to a single topic, occasion, or
    Christian denomination are entered under **Ser-
    mons**.
    UF   Speaking
    BT   **Pastoral theology**
          Public speaking
          Rhetoric
    RT   **Sermons**
Precious metals (May subdiv. geog.)
   553.4; 669
    UF   Bullion
    BT   **Metals**
          Mines and mineral resources

Precious metals—*Continued*
   NT   **Gold**
         Silver
Precious stones (May subdiv. geog.)
      553.8
      Use for mineralogical or technological materials on gem stones. Materials on cut and polished precious stones treated from the point of view of art or antiquity are entered under **Gems**. Materials on gems in which the emphasis is on the setting are entered under **Jewelry**.
   UF   Gemstones
         Jewels
   SA   names of precious stones [to be added as needed]
   BT   **Minerals**
   NT   **Diamonds**
   RT   **Gems**
Precipitation forecasting
   USE   **Weather forecasting**
Precipitation (Meteorology) (May subdiv. geog.)   **551.57**
   BT   **Meteorology**
         Water
         Weather
   NT   **Rain**
         Snow
Precocious children
   USE   **Gifted children**
Predators
   USE   **Predatory animals**
Predatory animals   **591.5**
   UF   Predators
   SA   types of predatory animals [to be added as needed]
   BT   **Animals**
   NT   **Birds of prey**
Predestination   **202; 234**
   UF   Election (Theology)
         Foreordination
   BT   **Theology**
   RT   **Fate and fatalism**
         Free will and determinism
Predictions
   USE   **Forecasting**
         Prophecies
Prefabricated buildings   **693**
   UF   Buildings, Prefabricated
   BT   **Buildings**
   NT   **Prefabricated houses**
Prefabricated houses   **693; 728**

   BT   **Domestic architecture**
         House construction
         Houses
         Prefabricated buildings
Pregnancy   **599; 612.6; 618.2**
   BT   **Reproduction**
   NT   **Miscarriage**
         Multiple pregnancy
         Prenatal care
         Teenage pregnancy
   RT   **Childbirth**
Prehistoric animals   **560**
   UF   Animals, Prehistoric
   BT   **Animals**
         Fossils
   NT   **Dinosaurs**
   RT   **Extinct animals**
Prehistoric art (May subdiv. geog.)   **709.01**
   UF   Art, Prehistoric
   BT   **Art**
   NT   **Rock drawings, paintings, and engravings**
Prehistoric man
   USE   **Fossil hominids**
         Prehistoric peoples
Prehistoric peoples (May subdiv. geog.)   **930.1**
   UF   Man, Prehistoric
         Prehistoric man
         Prehistory
   SA   names of prehistoric peoples, e.g. **Cro-Magnons**; etc.; and names of countries, cities, etc., with the subdivision *Antiquities*, e.g. **United States—Antiquities** [to be added as needed]
   BT   **Antiquities**
         Archeology
         Human beings
   NT   **Cave dwellers**
         Cro-Magnons
   RT   **Human origins**
Prehistory
   USE   **Archeology**
         Fossil hominids
         Prehistoric peoples
Prejudice
   USE   **Prejudices**

Prejudice in testing
USE **Test bias**
Prejudice-motivated crimes
USE **Hate crimes**
Prejudices (May subdiv. geog.) **152.4;
177; 303.3**
UF Bias (Psychology)
Bigotry
Prejudice
SA types of prejudice [to be added
as needed]
BT **Attitude (Psychology)**
Emotions
Interpersonal relations
NT **Antisemitism**
Discrimination
Ethnocentrism
Racism
Sexism
Prejudicial publicity
USE **Freedom of the press and fair
trial**
Prelude and fugue
USE **Fugue**
Preludes and fugues
USE **Fugue**
Premarital contracts
USE **Marriage contracts**
Premarital counseling
USE **Marriage counseling**
Premature burial **306.9**
UF Burial, Premature
BT **Burial**
Premenstrual syndrome **618.1**
UF PMS (Gynecology)
Premenstrual tension
BT **Menstruation**
Premenstrual tension
USE **Premenstrual syndrome**
Premiers
USE **Prime ministers**
Prenatal care (May subdiv. geog.) **618.2**
BT **Pregnancy**
Prenatal diagnosis **618.3**
BT **Diagnosis**
NT **Amniocentesis**
Genetic counseling
Prenuptial agreements
USE **Marriage contracts**
Prenuptial contracts
USE **Marriage contracts**

Prepaid group medical practice
USE **Health maintenance organiza-
tions**
Preparation guides for examinations
USE **Examinations—Study guides**
Prepared cereals **641.3; 664**
UF Breakfast cereals
Cereals, Prepared
BT **Breakfasts**
Food
Preprimers
USE **Easy reading materials**
Presbyterian Church (May subdiv. geog.)
285
BT **Christian sects**
Presbyterian Church—Sermons **252**
BT **Sermons**
Preschool children
USE **Children**
Preschool education (May subdiv. geog.)
372.21
UF Children—Education
Education, Preschool
Infants—Education
BT **Education**
NT **Readiness for school**
RT **Kindergarten**
Nursery schools
Preschool reading materials
USE **Easy reading materials**
Prescription drug abuse
USE **Medication abuse**
Presents
USE **Gifts**
Preservation
USE types of foods and other things
preserved with the subdivision
Preservation, e.g. **Fruit—
Preservation; Wood—Preser-
vation;** etc.; antiquities and
types of natural objects, in-
cluding animal specimens and
plant specimens, with the sub-
division *Collection and preservation,* e.g. **Birds—Collection and preservation;** and
types of art objects, library
materials, architecture, and
land vehicles with the subdivision *Conservation and restoration,* e.g. **Automobiles—**

Preservation—*Continued*

> **Conservation and restoration**
> [to be added as needed]

Preservation of antiquities
> USE **Antiquities—Collection and preservation**

Preservation of biodiversity
> USE **Biodiversity conservation**

Preservation of botanical specimens
> USE **Plants—Collection and preservation**

Preservation of buildings
> USE **Architecture—Conservation and restoration**

Preservation of food
> USE **Food—Preservation**

Preservation of forests
> USE **Forest conservation**

Preservation of historical records
> USE **Archives**

Preservation of library resources
> USE **Library resources—Conservation and restoration**

Preservation of natural resources
> USE **Conservation of natural resources**

Preservation of natural scenery
> USE **Landscape protection**
> **Natural monuments**
> **Nature conservation**

Preservation of organs, tissues, etc. 617.9
> UF   Organ preservation (Anatomy)
> Organs (Anatomy)—Preservation
> RT   **Transplantation of organs, tissues, etc.**

Preservation of photographs
> USE **Photographs—Conservation and restoration**

Preservation of specimens
> USE **Taxidermy**

Preservation of wildlife
> USE **Wildlife conservation**

Preservation of wood
> USE **Wood—Preservation**

Preservation of works of art
> USE subjects with the subdivision *Conservation and restoration,* e.g. **Painting—Conservation and restoration** [to be added as needed]

Preservation of zoological specimens
> USE **Zoological specimens—Collection and preservation**

Preservationism (Historic preservation)
> USE **Historic preservation**

Preserving
> USE **Canning and preserving**

Presidential aides
> USE **Presidents—United States—Staff**

Presidential campaigns—United States
> USE **Presidents—United States—Election**

Presidential libraries
> USE **Presidents—United States—Archives**

Presidents (May subdiv. geog.)   352.23; 920
> SA   names of presidents [to be added as needed]
> BT   **Heads of state**
> NT   **Vice-presidents**
> RT   **Executive power**

Presidents—Mexico   920; 972
> UF   Mexico—Presidents

Presidents—Powers
> USE **Executive power**

Presidents' spouses—United States   920
> UF   First ladies—United States
> Presidents—United States—Spouses
> Presidents' wives—United States
> Wives of presidents—United States

Presidents—United States   352.230973; 920

> When applicable, the subdivisions under this heading may be used under names of presidents, prime ministers, and other rulers.

> UF   United States—Presidents
> SA   names of presidents [to be added as needed]
> NT   **Lincoln, Abraham, 1809-1865**

Presidents—United States—Appointment 352.23

Presidents—United States—Archives 026
> UF   Libraries, Presidential
> Presidential libraries
> Presidents—United States—Libraries

Presidents—United States—Archives— *Continued*

SA   names of individual libraries [to be added as needed]

BT   **Archives**

NT   **Harry S. Truman Library (Independence, Mo.)**

Presidents—United States—Assassination 364.15; 973

BT   **Assassination**

Presidents—United States—Burial

USE   **Presidents—United States— Death and burial**

Presidents—United States—Children 920

Presidents—United States—Death and burial 393; 973

UF   Presidents—United States—Burial

Presidents—United States—Funeral and memorial services

Presidents—United States—Memorial services

Presidents—United States—Election 324.973

May further subdivide by date.

UF   Campaigns, Presidential—United States

Electoral college

Presidential campaigns—United States

BT   **Elections**

Presidents—United States—Family 920

Presidents—United States—Fathers 920

Presidents—United States—Funeral and memorial services

USE   **Presidents—United States— Death and burial**

Presidents—United States—Health 352.23; 920

UF   Presidents—United States—Illness

Presidents—United States—Homes 728

Presidents—United States—Illness

USE   **Presidents—United States— Health**

Presidents—United States—Impeachment 342

Presidents—United States—Inability to serve

USE   **Presidents—United States— Succession**

Presidents—United States—Inaugural addresses 352.23

BT   **Speeches**

Presidents—United States—Inauguration 352.23

Presidents—United States—Libraries

USE   **Presidents—United States—Archives**

Presidents—United States—Medals 352.23

Presidents—United States—Memorial services

USE   **Presidents—United States— Death and burial**

Presidents—United States—Messages 352.23

UF   Messages to Congress

Presidents—United States—State of the Union message

State of the Union messages

Presidents—United States—Mothers 920

Presidents—United States—Nomination 324.50973

UF   Nomination of presidents

Presidents—United States—Portraits 973

Presidents—United States—Power

USE   **Executive power—United States**

Presidents—United States—Press relations 070.4; 352.230973

Presidents—United States—Protection 352.23

Presidents—United States—Quotations 818

BT   **Quotations**

Presidents—United States—Relations with Congress 328.73; 352.23

Presidents—United States—Religion 920

Presidents—United States—Resignation 352.23

Presidents—United States—Sports 920

Presidents—United States—Spouses

USE   **Presidents' spouses—United States**

Presidents—United States—Staff 352.23

UF   Presidential aides

BT   **Executive departments—United States**

Presidents—United States—State of the
Union message
    USE   **Presidents—United States—
Messages**
**Presidents—United States—Succession
342; 352.23**
    UF   Presidents—United States—In-
ability to serve
**Presidents—United States—Tombs
917.3**
**Presidents—United States—Travel
352.23**
    UF   Presidents—United States—Voy-
ages and travels
Presidents—United States—Voyages and
travels
    USE   **Presidents—United States—
Travel**
Presidents' wives—United States
    USE   **Presidents' spouses—United
States**
Press (May subdiv. geog.)   **070**
    SA   topics with the subdivision *Press
coverage*, e.g. **Food contami-
nation—Press coverage** [to
be added as needed]
    BT   **Journalism
Propaganda
Publicity**
    NT   **Alternative press
Broadcast journalism
Freedom of the press
Freedom of the press and fair
trial
News agencies
Pamphlets**
    RT   **Newspapers
Periodicals
Public opinion**
Press and government
    USE   **Press—Government policy**
Press censorship
    USE   **Freedom of the press**
Press clippings
    USE   **Clippings (Books, newspapers,
etc.)**
Press coverage
    USE   topics with the subdivision *Press
coverage,* e.g. **Food contami-
nation—Press coverage** [to
be added as needed]

Press—Government policy (May subdiv.
geog.)   **323.44**
    UF   Government and the press
Press and government
    BT   **Freedom of information**
Press relations
    USE   types of public officials and
names of individual public of-
ficials with the subdivision
Press relations, e.g. **Presidents—United States—Press
relations** [to be added as
needed]
Press working of metal
    USE   **Sheet metalwork**
Pressure groups
    USE   **Lobbying
Political action committees**
Prestidigitation
    USE   **Magic tricks**
Pretenders
    USE   **Impostors and imposture**
Prevention
    USE   types of diseases, medical condi-
tions, and situations to be
avoided with the subdivision
Prevention, e.g. **AIDS (Dis-
ease)—Prevention; Acci-
dents—Prevention;** etc. [to
be added as needed]
Prevention of accidents
    USE   **Accidents—Prevention**
Prevention of crime
    USE   **Crime prevention**
Prevention of cruelty to animals
    USE   **Animal welfare**
Prevention of disease
    USE   **Preventive medicine**
Prevention of fire
    USE   **Fire prevention**
Prevention of smoke
    USE   **Smoke prevention**
Preventive medicine   613
    UF   Diseases—Prevention
Medicine, Preventive
Prevention of disease
    SA   names of diseases with the sub-
division *Prevention,* e.g.
AIDS (Disease)—Prevention
[to be added as needed]
    BT   **Medicine**

Preventive medicine—*Continued*
>NT **Communicable diseases—Prevention**
>
>>**Health**
>>
>>**Heart diseases—Prevention**
>>
>>**Hygiene**
>>
>>**Vaccination**
>
>RT **Pathology**

Price controls
>USE **Wage-price policy**

Price indexes, Consumer
>USE **Consumer price indexes**

Price theory
>USE **Microeconomics**

Price-wage policy
>USE **Wage-price policy**

Prices (May subdiv. geog.)   **338.5**
>SA subjects with the subdivision *Prices*, e.g. **Art—Prices** [to be added as needed]
>
>BT **Commerce**
>
>>**Consumption (Economics)**
>>
>>**Economics**
>>
>>**Finance**
>>
>>**Manufactures**
>
>NT **Art—Prices**
>
>>**Books—Prices**
>>
>>**Consumer price indexes**
>>
>>**Farm produce—Marketing**
>>
>>**Stock price indexes**
>>
>>**Wage-price policy**
>
>RT **Cost and standard of living**
>
>>**Salaries, wages, etc.**
>>
>>**Supply and demand**

Pride and vanity   **179**
>UF Vanity
>
>BT **Conduct of life**
>
>>**Sin**
>
>RT **Snobs and snobbishness**

Priests (May subdiv. geog.)   **200.92; 270.092**
>UF Pastors
>
>SA names of church denominations with the subdivision *Clergy*, e.g. **Catholic Church—Clergy** [to be added as needed]
>
>BT **Clergy**
>
>NT **Catholic Church—Clergy**
>
>>**Ex-priests**

Primaries (May subdiv. geog.)   **324.5**
>UF Direct primaries
>
>BT **Elections**
>
>>**Political conventions**
>>
>>**Politics**

Primary education
>USE **Elementary education**

Primates (May subdiv. geog.)   **599.8**
>SA types of primates, e.g. **Monkeys** [to be added as needed]
>
>BT **Mammals**
>
>NT **Apes**
>
>>**Human beings**
>>
>>**Monkeys**

Primates—Behavior   **599.8**
>UF Primates—Habits and behavior
>
>BT **Animal behavior**

Primates—Habits and behavior
>USE **Primates—Behavior**

Prime ministers (May subdiv. geog.)   **352.23; 920**
>May use same subdivisions, following geographic subdivision, as for **Presidents—United States**.
>
>UF Premiers
>
>BT **Cabinet officers**
>
>>**Executive power**

Prime ministers—Great Britain   **352.230941; 920**
>UF Great Britain—Prime ministers

Primers
>USE **Easy reading materials**

Primitive Christianity
>USE **Church history—30-600, Early church**

Primitive man
>USE **Primitive societies**

Primitive societies (May subdiv. geog.)   **305.8; 306**
>Use for materials on nonliterate, nonindustrialized peoples.
>
>UF Man, Primitive
>
>>Primitive man
>>
>>Primitive society
>>
>>Society, Primitive
>
>BT **Civilization**
>
>>**Ethnology**
>
>NT **Nomads**

Primitive society
>USE **Primitive societies**

Princes (May subdiv. geog.)   **920**
>UF Princes and princesses
>
>>Royalty
>
>BT **Courts and courtiers**

Princes and princesses
USE **Princes**
Princesses
Princesses (May subdiv. geog.) 920
UF Princes and princesses
Royalty
BT **Courts and courtiers**
Printing (May subdiv. geog.) 686.2
SA types of printing processes [to
be added as needed]
BT **Bibliography**
Book industry
Graphic arts
Industrial arts
Publishers and publishing
NT **Advertising layout and typography**
Color printing
Electrotyping
Linoleum block printing
Linotype
Lithography
Nature prints
Offset printing
Proofreading
Textile printing
Type and type-founding
Typesetting
Typography
RT **Books**
Prints
Printing—Exhibitions 686.2074
BT **Exhibitions**
Printing—Specimens 686.2
UF Type specimens
BT **Advertising**
Initials
RT **Type and type-founding**
Printing—Style manuals 686.02
UF Style manuals
RT **Authorship—Handbooks, manuals, etc.**
Prints 769
SA prints of particular countries, e.g.
American prints [to be added as needed]
BT **Graphic arts**
NT **American prints**
Bookplates
Color prints
Linoleum block printing

Lithography
Nature prints
Woodcuts
RT **Printing**
Prints, American
USE **American prints**
Prison escapes
USE **Escapes**
Prison labor
USE **Convict labor**
Prison reform 365
UF Penal reform
BT **Social problems**
Prison schools
USE **Prisoners—Education**
Prisoners (May subdiv. geog.) 365
UF Convicts
Prisoners and prisons
BT **Criminals**
NT **Convict labor**
Political prisoners
RT **Prisoners of war**
Prisons
Prisoners and prisons
USE **Prisoners**
Prisoners of war
Prisons
and names of wars with the
subdivision *Prisoners and
prisons,* e.g. **World War,
1939-1945—Prisoners and
prisons** [to be added as needed]
Prisoners—Education (May subdiv. geog.)
365
UF Education of criminals
Education of prisoners
Prison schools
BT **Adult education**
Prisons
Prisoners of conscience
USE **Political prisoners**
Prisoners of war (May subdiv. geog.)
341.6; 355.7
UF Exchange of prisoners of war
POWs
Prisoners and prisons
SA names of wars with the subdivision *Prisoners and prisons,*
e.g. **World War, 1939-**

Prisoners of war—*Continued*
>> 1945—**Prisoners and prisons**
>> [to be added as needed]
> BT **War**
> NT **Missing in action**
>> **United States—History—1861-1865, Civil War—Prisoners and prisons**
>> **World War, 1939-1945—Prisoners and prisons**
> RT **Concentration camps**
>> **Prisoners**
>> **Prisons**

Prisons (May subdiv. geog.) **365**
> UF Imprisonment
>> Jails
>> Penal institutions
>> Penitentiaries
>> Prisoners and prisons
> SA types of prisons, names of individual prisons, and names of wars with the subdivision *Prisoners and prisons*, e.g. **World War, 1939-1945—Prisoners and prisons** [to be added as needed]
> BT **Administration of criminal justice**
>> **Correctional institutions**
>> **Punishment**
> NT **Escapes**
>> **Prisoners—Education**
>> **Probation**
>> **Reformatories**
>> **United States—History—1861-1865, Civil War—Prisoners and prisons**
>> **World War, 1939-1945—Prisoners and prisons**
> RT **Prisoners**
>> **Prisoners of war**

Prisons—United States **365**
> UF United States—Prisons

Privacy **323.44**
> BT **Social psychology**
> RT **Secrecy**
>> **Solitude**

Privacy, Right of
> USE **Right of privacy**

Private art collections
> USE **Art collections**

Private companies
> USE **Limited liability companies**

Private enterprise
> USE **Free enterprise**

Private eye stories
> USE **Mystery and detective plays**
>> **Mystery fiction**
>> **Mystery films**
>> **Mystery radio programs**
>> **Mystery television programs**

Private funding of the arts
> USE **Art patronage**

Private limited companies
> USE **Limited liability companies**

Private property, Right of
> USE **Right of property**

Private schools (May subdiv. geog.) **371.02; 373.2**
> UF Boarding schools
>> Independent schools
>> Nonpublic schools
> BT **Schools**
> NT **Church schools**
>> **English public schools**

Private theater
> USE **Amateur theater**

Privateering (May subdiv. geog.) **359.4**
> UF Letters of marque
> BT **International law**
>> **Naval art and science**
>> **Naval history**
>> **Pirates**

Privatization (May subdiv. geog.) **338.9**
> Use for materials on the transfer of public assets and service functions to the private sector.
> UF Denationalization
> BT **Economic policy**
>> **Industrial policy**
> RT **Government ownership**

Prize fighting
> USE **Boxing**

Prizes (Rewards)
> USE **Awards**

Pro-abortion movement
> USE **Pro-choice movement**

Pro-choice movement **179.7; 363.46**
> UF Abortion rights movement
>> Freedom of choice movement
>> Pro-abortion movement
>> Right to choose movement
> BT **Social movements**

Pro-choice movement—*Continued*
  RT **Abortion—Ethical aspects**
      Abortion—Religious aspects
      Women's rights
Pro-life movement   179.7; 363.46
  UF Anti-abortion movement
      Antiabortion movement
      Right-to-life movement (Anti-
        abortion movement)
  BT **Social movements**
  RT **Abortion—Ethical aspects**
      Abortion—Religious aspects
      Women's rights
Probabilities   519.2
  UF Fortune
      Statistical inference
  BT **Algebra**
      Logic
      Mathematics
      Statistics
  NT **Average**
      Game theory
      Reliability (Engineering)
      Sampling (Statistics)
  RT **Risk**
Probate law and practice (May subdiv.
    geog.)   **346.05**
  BT **Civil procedure**
      Inheritance and succession
Probation (May subdiv. geog.)   **364.6**
  UF Reform of criminals
      Suspended sentence
  BT **Corrections**
      Criminal law
      Prisons
      Punishment
      Reformatories
      Social case work
  RT **Juvenile courts**
      Parole
Probiotics   613.2; 615.1
  BT **Dietary supplements**
      Microorganisms
Problem children
  USE **Emotionally disturbed children**
Problem drinking
  USE **Alcoholism**
Problem families—Counseling of
  USE **Family therapy**
Problem solving   153.4; 510.76
  BT **Psychology**

  NT **Conflict management**
      Crisis management
      Critical thinking
      Group problem solving
  RT **Decision making**
Problems, exercises, etc.
  USE subjects with the subdivision
       Problems, exercises, etc., for
       compilations of practice prob-
       lems or exercises for use in
       the study of a topic, e.g.
       **Chemistry—Problems, exer-
       cises, etc.** [to be added as
       needed]
Procedural due process
  USE **Due process of law**
Processing (Libraries)
  USE **Library technical processes**
Processions
  USE **Parades**
Procurement, Government
  USE **Government purchasing**
Prodigal son (Parable)   226.8
  BT **Parables**
Producers
  USE types of producers and directors
       in specific media, e.g. **Motion
       picture producers and direc-
       tors; Theatrical producers
       and directors;** etc. [to be
       added as needed]
Product development
  USE **New products**
Product recall   658.5
  UF Commercial products recall
      Manufactures—Defects
      Manufactures recall
      Recall of products
  BT **Consumer protection**
Product safety   363.19; 658.5
  UF Unsafe products
  BT **Consumer protection**
Production
  USE **Economics**
       Industries
Production engineering
  USE **Factory management**
Production processes
  USE **Manufacturing processes**

Production standards   658.5

Use for materials on the unit time value for the accomplishment of a work task as determined by work measurement techniques.

    UF   Output standards
          Standards of output
          Time production standards
          Work standards
    SA   types of industries and processes with the subdivision *Production standards*, e.g. **Automobile industry—Production standards** [to be added as needed]
    BT   **Labor productivity**
          Management
    NT   **Automobile industry—Production standards**
          Motion study
          Time study

Productivity of labor
    USE **Labor productivity**

Products, Agricultural
    USE **Farm produce**

Products, Animal
    USE **Animal products**

Products, Commercial
    USE **Commercial products**

Products, Dairy
    USE **Dairy products**

Products, Generic
    USE **Generic products**

Professional associations
    USE **Trade and professional associations**

Professional education (May subdiv. geog.)   **378**
    SA   types of professions with the subdivision *Study and teaching*, e.g. **Medicine—Study and teaching** [to be added as needed]
    BT   **Education**
          Higher education
          Learning and scholarship
    NT   **Colleges and universities**
          Library education
    RT   **Technical education**
          Vocational education

Professional ethics (May subdiv. geog.)   **174**
    SA   types of professional ethics, e.g. **Medical ethics**; professions and types of professional personnel with the subdivision *Ethics*, e.g. **Librarians—Ethics**; and subjects with the subdivision *Ethical aspects* [to be added as needed]
    BT   **Ethics**
    NT   **Business ethics**
          Journalism—Objectivity
          Legal ethics
          Librarians—Ethics
          Medical ethics

Professional liability
    USE **Malpractice**

Professional liability insurance
    USE **Malpractice insurance**

Professional sports (May subdiv. geog.)   **796**
    SA   types of sports [to be added as needed]
    BT   **Sports**

Professions (May subdiv. geog.)   **331.702**
    UF   Careers
          Jobs
          Vocations
    SA   types of professions with the subdivision *Vocational guidance*, e.g. **Law—Vocational guidance** [to be added as needed]
    BT   **Occupations**
          Self-employed
    NT   **College graduates**
          Law—Vocational guidance
          Paraprofessionals
    RT   **Vocational guidance**

Professions—Tort liability
    USE **Malpractice**

Professors
    USE **Educators**
          Teachers

Profit   338.5; 658.15
    BT   **Business**
          Capital
          Economics
          Wealth
    NT   **Capitalism**
    RT   **Income**
          Risk

Profit sharing (May subdiv. geog.)
      331.2; 658.3
  BT **Commerce**
      Salaries, wages, etc.
  RT **Cooperation**
Program evaluation in education
  USE **Educational evaluation**
Programmed instruction   **371.39**
  UF Programmed textbooks
  SA subjects with the subdivision
       Programmed instruction [to
       be added as needed]
  BT **Teaching—Aids and devices**
  NT **Computer-assisted instruction**
      English language—Pro-
      grammed instruction
      Teaching machines
Programmed textbooks
  USE **Programmed instruction**
Programming (Computers)
  USE **Computer programming**
Programming languages   **005.13**
  UF Computer languages
      Computer program languages
      Machine language
      Programming languages (Com-
      puters)
      Programming languages (Elec-
      tronic computers)
  SA names of specific languages, e.g.
      FORTRAN (Computer lan-
      guage) [to be added as need-
      ed]
  BT **Computer software**
      Language and languages
  NT **FORTRAN (Computer lan-**
      guage)
      HTML (Document markup
      language)
  RT **Computer programming**
Programming languages (Computers)
  USE **Programming languages**
Programming languages (Electronic com-
      puters)
  USE **Programming languages**
Programs, Computer
  USE **Computer software**
Programs, Radio
  USE **Radio programs**
Programs, Television
  USE **Television programs**

Programs, Twelve-step
  USE **Twelve-step programs**
Progress   **303.44**
  UF Social progress
  BT **Civilization**
  NT **Science and civilization**
Progressive education
  USE **Education—Experimental**
       methods
Progressivism (United States politics)
      320.973
  BT **Political science**
Prohibited books
  USE **Books—Censorship**
Prohibition (May subdiv. geog.)   **344**
    Use for materials on the legal prohibition of
  liquor traffic and liquor manufacture.
  BT **Criminal law**
  RT **Temperance**
Project Apollo
  USE **Apollo project**
Project Gemini
  USE **Gemini project**
Project method in teaching   **371.3**
  BT **Teaching**
Project Ranger   **629.43**
  UF Ranger project
  BT **Lunar probes**
Project schools
  USE **Experimental schools**
Project Sealab
  USE **Sealab project**
Project Telstar
  USE **Telstar project**
Project Voyager   **629.43**
  UF Voyager project
  BT **Astronautics—United States**
Projectiles   **623.4**
  UF Shells (Projectiles)
  NT **Ammunition**
      Bombs
      Guided missiles
      Rockets (Aeronautics)
  RT **Ordnance**
Projective geometry   **516**
  UF Geometry, Projective
  BT **Geometry**
Projectors   **778.2**
  UF Film projectors
      Magic lanterns
      Motion picture projectors
      Opaque projectors

Projectors—*Continued*
    Slide projectors
    Stereopticon
Proletariat   **305.5**
    BT   **Labor**
       Socialism
       Working class
Proliferation of arms
    USE   **Arms race**
Promises   **170**
    BT   **Ethics**
Promotion in school
    USE   **Promotion (School)**
Promotion (School)   **371.2**
    UF   Grade repetition
       Grade retention
       Non-promotion (School)
       Promotion in school
       Retention, Grade
       School grade retention
       School promotion
       Student promotion
    BT   **Grading and marking (Education)**
Promptness
    USE   **Punctuality**
Pronunciation
    USE   names of languages with the subdivision *Pronunciation,* e.g. **English language—Pronunciation** [to be added as needed]
Proofreading   **070.5; 686.2**
    BT   **Printing**
Propaganda   **303.3; 327.1**
    SA   propaganda of particular countries, e.g. **American propaganda**; and names of wars with the subdivision *Propaganda,* e.g. **World War, 1939-1945—Propaganda** [to be added as needed]
    BT   **Political psychology**
       Public opinion
    NT   **American propaganda**
       Lobbying
       Press
       Psychological warfare
       World War, 1939-1945—Propaganda
    RT   **Advertising**
       Persuasion (Psychology)
       Publicity

Propaganda, American
    USE   **American propaganda**
Propagation of plants
    USE   **Plant propagation**
Propellers, Aerial
    USE   **Aerial propellers**
Proper names
    USE   **Names**
Property (May subdiv. geog.)   **330.1**
    UF   Ownership
    BT   **Economics**
    NT   **Airspace law**
       Cultural property
       Eminent domain
       Income
       Intellectual property
       Lost and found possessions
       Real estate
       Right of property
       Surplus government property
       Timesharing (Real estate)
    RT   **Wealth**
Property, Crimes against
    USE   **Offenses against property**
Property, Right of
    USE   **Right of property**
Property rights
    USE   **Right of property**
Property tax—Assessment
    USE   **Tax assessment**
Prophecies   **133.3; 202**
    UF   Predictions
       Prophecies (Occult sciences)
       Prophecies (Occultism)
       Prophecy
    SA   subjects, titles of sacred works, and names of persons with the subdivision *Prophecies,* e.g. **Bible—Prophecies** [to be added as needed]
    BT   **Occultism**
       Supernatural
    RT   **Divination**
       Oracles
Prophecies (Bible)
    USE   **Bible—Prophecies**
Prophecies (Occult sciences)
    USE   **Prophecies**
Prophecies (Occultism)
    USE   **Prophecies**

Prophecy
USE **Prophecies**
Prophets (May subdiv. geog.)   **200.92**
BT **Religious biography**
Proportion (Architecture)
USE **Architecture—Composition,
proportion, etc.**
Proportional representation (May subdiv.
geog.)   **328.3**
UF Representation, Proportional
BT **Constitutional law
Representative government and
representation**
RT **Elections**
Proprietary rights
USE **Intellectual property**
Prose literature, American
USE **American prose literature**
Prose literature, English
USE **English prose literature**
Prosody
USE **Versification**
Prospecting (May subdiv. geog.)   **622**
BT **Gold mines and mining
Mines and mineral resources
Silver mines and mining**
NT **Mine surveying
Petroleum geology**
Prosthesis
USE **Artificial limbs
Artificial organs**
Prostitution (May subdiv. geog.)   **176;
306.74; 363.4; 364.1**
BT **Sexual ethics
Social problems
Women—Social conditions**
NT **Juvenile prostitution**
Protection
USE subjects with the subdivision
Protection, e.g. **Birds—Pro-
tection** [to be added as need-
ed]
Protection against burglary
USE **Burglary protection**
Protection of animals
USE **Animal welfare**
Protection of birds
USE **Birds—Protection**
Protection of children
USE **Child welfare**

Protection of environment
USE **Environmental protection**
Protection of game
USE **Game protection**
Protection of natural scenery
USE **Landscape protection
Natural monuments
Nature conservation**
Protection of plants
USE **Plant conservation**
Protection of wildlife
USE **Wildlife conservation**
Protectionism (May subdiv. geog.)   **382**
UF Free trade and protection
BT **Commercial policy**
RT **Free trade
Tariff**
Proteins   **547; 572**
BT **Biochemistry
Nutrition**
NT **Enzymes**
Protest
USE **Dissent**
Protest marches and rallies
USE **Demonstrations**
Protest movements (May subdiv. geog.)
303.48
SA names of wars and other objects
of protest with the subdivision
Protest movements, e.g.
**World War, 1939-1945—
Protest movements** [to be
added as needed]
BT **Social movements**
NT **World War, 1939-1945—Pro-
test movements**
RT **Demonstrations**
Protestant churches (May subdiv. geog.)
280
Use for materials on Protestant denomina-
tions treated collectively. Works on Protestant
church buildings are entered under **Church
buildings**.
UF Denominations, Protestant
Protestant denominations
SA names of Protestant churches,
e.g. **Presbyterian Church** [to
be added as needed]
BT **Christian sects
Church history
Protestantism**

Protestant denominations
USE **Protestant churches**
Protestant Episcopal Church in the U.S.A.
USE **Episcopal Church**
Protestant Reformation
USE **Reformation**
Protestant work ethic
USE **Work ethic**
Protestantism (May subdiv. geog.)   **280**
BT **Christianity**
Church history
NT **Evangelicalism**
Pentecostal churches
Protestant churches
RT **Reformation**
Protests, demonstrations, etc.
USE **Demonstrations**
Protons   **539.7**
UF Hydrogen nucleus
BT **Atoms**
Particles (Nuclear physics)
Protoplasm   **571.6**
BT **Biology**
Life (Biology)
RT **Cells**
Embryology
Protozoa   **579.4**
BT **Microorganisms**
Proverbs   **398.9**
UF Adages
Maxims
Sayings
BT **Folklore**
Quotations
RT **Epigrams**
Providence and government of God
202; 214; 231
UF God—Providence and govern-
ment
God—Sovereignty
BT **God**
Provincialism
USE **Regionalism**
Provincialisms
USE names of languages with the
subdivision *Provincialisms,*
e.g. **English language—Pro-
vincialisms** [to be added as
needed]
Pruning   **631.5**

BT **Forests and forestry**
Fruit culture
Gardening
Trees
Pseudonyms   **929.4**
UF Anonyms
Fictitious names
Pen names
BT **Names**
Personal names
Psi (Parapsychology)
USE **Parapsychology**
Psychiatric care
USE **Mental health services**
Psychiatric hospitals (May subdiv. geog.)
362.2
UF Mental hospitals
BT **Hospitals**
RT **Mentally ill—Institutional care**
Psychiatric services
USE **Mental health services**
Psychiatrists (May subdiv. geog.)   **920;**
926
UF Psychopathologists
BT **Psychologists**
Psychiatry (May subdiv. geog.)   **616.89**
Use for materials on clinical aspects of
mental disorders, including therapy. Popular
materials and materials on regional or social
aspects of mental disorders are entered under
Mental illness. Systematic descriptions of
mental disorders are entered under **Abnormal
psychology**.
BT **Medicine**
NT **Adolescent psychiatry**
Child psychiatry
Psychotherapy
RT **Abnormal psychology**
Mental health
Mental illness
Psychic healing
USE **Mental healing**
Psychic phenomena
USE **Parapsychology**
Psychical research
USE **Parapsychology**
Psychics   **133.8092**
UF Clairvoyants
BT **Parapsychology**
Persons
Psychoactive drugs
USE **Psychotropic drugs**

Psychoanalysis (May subdiv. geog.)
150.19; 616.89
BT Psychology
NT Ego (Psychology)
Psychosomatic medicine
RT Abnormal psychology
Hypnotism
Mind and body
Subconsciousness

Psychogenetics
USE Behavior genetics

Psychokinesis 133.8
UF Telekinesis
BT Parapsychology
Spiritualism

Psychological aspects
USE subjects with the subdivision
Psychological aspects, e.g.
Drugs—Psychological aspects; World War, 1939-1945—Psychological aspects;
etc. [to be added as needed]

Psychological stress
USE Stress (Psychology)

Psychological tests 150.28
UF Mental tests
BT Psychology
NT Ability—Testing
RT Educational tests and measurements

Psychological types
USE Typology (Psychology)

Psychological warfare 355.3
Use for materials on methods used to undermine the morale of the civilian population and the military forces of an enemy country.
UF War of nerves
SA names of wars with the subdivision *Psychological aspects* [to be added as needed]
BT Applied psychology
Military art and science
Morale
Propaganda
War
NT Brainwashing
World War, 1939-1945—Psychological aspects

Psychologists (May subdiv. geog.)
150.92; 920
NT Psychiatrists
School psychologists

RT Psychology
Psychology (May subdiv. geog.) 150
UF Mind
SA religions, theological topics, titles of individual sacred works, types of animals, classes of persons, ethnic groups, and names of individual persons, including individual literary authors, with the subdivision *Psychology,* e.g.
Christianity—Psychology; Women—Psychology; Native Americans—Psychology; etc.;
and subjects with the subdivision *Psychological aspects* for materials on the relationship of particular situations, conditions, activities, environments, or objects to the mental condition or personality of the individual, e.g. **Color—Psychological aspects** [to be added as needed]
BT Brain
Philosophy
Soul
NT Adjustment (Psychology)
Adolescent psychology
Aggressiveness (Psychology)
Apperception
Applied psychology
Assertiveness (Psychology)
Attention
Attitude (Psychology)
Behavior genetics
Behaviorism
Bible—Psychology
Child psychology
Choice (Psychology)
Color—Psychological aspects
Consciousness
Criminal psychology
Developmental psychology
Dogs—Psychology
Educational psychology
Ego (Psychology)
Emotions
Ethnopsychology
Genius
Gestalt psychology

Psychology—*Continued*
>   Habit
>   Human behavior
>   Identity (Psychology)
>   Ideology
>   Imagination
>   Individuality
>   Instinct
>   Intellect
>   Intuition
>   Memory
>   Men—Psychology
>   Motivation (Psychology)
>   Multiple personality
>   Music—Psychological aspects
>   Number concept
>   Parapsychology
>   Perception
>   Personality
>   Phrenology
>   Physiognomy
>   Political psychology
>   Problem solving
>   Psychoanalysis
>   Psychological tests
>   Psychology of religion
>   Psychophysiology
>   Reasoning
>   Self-acceptance
>   Self-consciousness
>   Self-control
>   Self-esteem
>   Self-perception
>   Self-realization
>   Senses and sensation
>   Sex (Psychology)
>   Social psychology
>   Stress (Psychology)
>   Subconsciousness
>   Temperament
>   Thought and thinking
>   Typology (Psychology)
>   Values
>   Women—Psychology
>   RT   Mental health
>   Psychologists

Psychology and religion
>   USE   Psychology of religion

Psychology, Applied
>   USE   Applied psychology
>   Persuasion (Psychology)

Psychology, Comparative
>   USE   Comparative psychology

Psychology—Computer simulation   150
>   BT   Computer simulation

Psychology of color
>   USE   Color—Psychological aspects

Psychology of learning   153.1
>   UF   Learning, Psychology of
>   BT   Animal intelligence
>   Child psychology
>   Education
>   Educational psychology
>   Memory
>   NT   Behavior modification
>   Biofeedback training
>   Brainwashing
>   Concept learning
>   Feedback (Psychology)
>   Learning disabilities
>   Reading comprehension
>   Verbal learning

Psychology of music
>   USE   Music—Psychological aspects

Psychology of religion   200.1
>   UF   Psychology and religion
>   Psychology, Religious
>   Religion and psychology
>   Religion—Psychological aspects
>   Religious psychology
>   SA   religious topics, titles of individ-
>   ual sacred works, and names
>   of religions with the subdivi-
>   sion *Psychology* [to be added
>   as needed]
>   BT   Psychology
>   Religion
>   NT   Christianity—Psychology
>   Faith—Psychology
>   Pastoral psychology

Psychology, Pastoral
>   USE   Pastoral psychology

Psychology, Pathological
>   USE   Abnormal psychology

Psychology, Religious
>   USE   Pastoral psychology
>   Psychology of religion

Psychology, Structural
>   USE   Gestalt psychology

Psychopathologists
>   USE   Psychiatrists

Psychopathology
USE **Abnormal psychology**
Psychopathy
USE **Abnormal psychology**
Psychopharmaceuticals
USE **Psychotropic drugs**
Psychophysics
USE **Psychophysiology**
Psychophysiology 152
Use for materials on the relationship between psychological and physiological processes.
UF Behavioral psychology
Physiological psychology
Psychophysics
BT **Nervous system**
Physiology
Psychology
NT **Behaviorism**
Color sense
Emotions
Human engineering
Hypnotism
Left- and right-handedness
Memory
Optical illusions
Pain
Senses and sensation
Sleep
Temperament
RT **Mind and body**
Psychoses
USE **Mental illness**
Psychosomatic medicine 616.08
UF Medicine, Psychosomatic
BT **Abnormal psychology**
Medicine
Mind and body
Psychoanalysis
Psychotherapy (May subdiv. geog.)
616.89
UF Therapy, Psychological
BT **Psychiatry**
Therapeutics
NT **Biofeedback training**
Family therapy
Sex therapy
Transactional analysis
RT **Mental healing**
Suggestive therapeutics
Psychotic children
USE **Emotionally disturbed children**

Psychotics
USE **Mentally ill**
Psychotropic drugs 615
Use for general materials on the group of drugs that act on the central nervous system to affect behavior, mental activity, or perception, including the antipsychotic drugs, antidepressants, hallucinogenic agents, and tranquilizers.
UF Psychoactive drugs
Psychopharmaceuticals
SA types of drugs and names of individual drugs [to be added as needed]
BT **Drugs**
NT **Antidepressants**
Hallucinogens
Narcotics
Stimulants
PTAs
USE **Parent-teacher associations**
Puberty 612.6
BT **Sex (Biology)**
RT **Adolescence**
Public accommodations, Discrimination in
USE **Discrimination in public accommodations**
Public administration 351
Use for general materials on the conduct of public business not limited to a specific place.
UF Administration
SA names of countries, states, cities, etc., with the subdivision *Politics and government*, e.g. **United States—Politics and government** [to be added as needed]
BT **Local government**
Municipal government
Political science
NT **Administrative agencies**
Bureaucracy
Civil service
Intelligence service
Licenses
Military government
United States—Politics and government
RT **Administrative law**
Public officers
Public assistance
USE **Public welfare**

Public buildings (May subdiv. geog.)
    352.5; 725

Use for materials on buildings owned by the public and maintained at public expense, such as government office buildings, public libraries, public schools, etc. Materials on buildings that are privately owned and maintained and are open to the public for business or entertainment are entered under **Buildings** or under the specific type of building.

  UF   Government buildings

  SA   names of individual public
         buildings [to be added as
         needed]

  BT   **Buildings**
        Public works

  NT   **Capitols**

Public buildings, American
  USE **Public buildings—United States**

Public buildings—Chicago (Ill.)
    725.09773

  UF   Chicago (Ill.)—Public buildings

Public buildings—Ohio   **725.09771**

  UF   Ohio—Public buildings

Public buildings—United States   **352.5;**
    725.0973

Use for materials on U.S. federal government buildings located in or outside of the United States, including materials on U.S embassy or consulate buildings abroad.

  UF   Public buildings, American
        United States—Government
         buildings
        United States—Public buildings

Public debts (May subdiv. geog.)   **336.3**

Use for materials on government debts.

  UF   Debts, Public
        Federal debt
        Government debts
        National debts

  SA   names of wars with the subdivi-
         sion *Finance*, e.g. **World**
         War, 1939-1945—Finance [to
         be added as needed]

  BT   **Debt**
        Loans
        Public finance

  RT   **Bonds**
        Deficit financing

Public debts—United States   **336.3**

  UF   United States—Public debts

Public demonstrations
  USE **Demonstrations**

Public documents
  USE **Government publications**

Public domain
  USE **Public lands**

Public domain software
  USE **Free computer software**

Public enterprises
  USE **Government business enter-
         prises**

Public figures
  USE **Celebrities**

Public finance (May subdiv. geog.)   **336**

Use for general materials on the raising and expenditure of funds in the public sector, and, with a geographic subdivision, for materials on the public finance of countries, states, localities, cities, etc.

  UF   Finance, Public

  BT   **Finance**

  NT   **Budget**
        Deficit financing
        Federal aid
        Fiscal policy
        Government aid
        Government lending
        Grants-in-aid
        Metropolitan finance
        Municipal finance
        Public debts
        Tariff
        Taxation

Public health (May subdiv. geog.)
    362.1; 614

  UF   Hygiene, Social
        Public hygiene
        Social hygiene

  BT   **Health**
        Human services
        Social problems
        State medicine

  NT   **Burial**
        Cemeteries
        Communicable diseases
        Community health services
        Cremation
        Disinfection and disinfectants
        Environmental health
        Epidemics
        **Food adulteration and inspec-
         tion**
        Health boards
        Health facilities
        Hospitals

Public health—*Continued*
>> Immunization
>> Meat inspection
>> Medical care
>> Medical charities
>> Milk supply
>> Noise
>> Occupational health and safety
>> Pollution
>> Refuse and refuse disposal
>> School hygiene
>> Sewage disposal
>> Social medicine
>> Street cleaning
>> Vaccination
>> Water pollution
> RT **Sanitation**

Public health boards
> USE **Health boards**

Public health—Evaluation   362.1
> UF Health program evaluation

Public health—Government policy
> USE **Medical policy**

Public health—United States
>> **362.10973; 614**
> UF United States—Public health

Public housing (May subdiv. geog.)
>> **363.5**
> UF Government housing
>> Housing projects, Government
>> Low income housing
> BT **Housing**

Public hygiene
> USE **Public health**

Public interest (May subdiv. geog.)   **172;**
>> **320.01; 344**
> UF National interest
> BT **State, The**
> NT **Ombudsman**
>> **Whistle blowing**

Public lands (May subdiv. geog.)   **333.1**
> UF Crown lands
>> Public domain
> BT **Colonization**
>> **Land use**
> NT **Forest reserves**
>> **Land grants**
>> **National parks and reserves**
> RT **Natural resources**

Public lands—Ohio   333.109771
> UF Ohio—Public lands

Public lands—United States   333.10973

> UF United States—Public lands

Public libraries (May subdiv. geog.)
>> **027.4**
> UF County libraries
> BT **Libraries**
> NT **Regional libraries**

Public meetings   302.3
> UF Meetings, Public
> BT **Freedom of assembly**
> NT **Demonstrations**
>> **Parliamentary practice**

Public officers   320
>> Use for general materials on elected govern-
>> ment officials not limited to a particular juris-
>> diction.
> UF Elected officials
>> Government officials
>> Officials and employees
>> Public officials
> SA names of countries, states, cities,
>> etc., with the subdivision *Offi-*
>> *cials and employees* [to be
>> added as needed]
> NT **Term limits (Public office)**
> RT **Civil service**
>> **Public administration**

Public officials
> USE **Public officers**

Public opinion (May subdiv. geog.)
>> **303.3**
> UF Opinion, Public
> SA subjects with the subdivision
>> *Public opinion*, e.g. **World**
>> **War, 1939-1945—Public**
>> **opinion**; and names of coun-
>> tries with the subdivision *For-*
>> *eign opinion* for materials
>> dealing with foreign public
>> opinion about the country,
>> e.g. **United States—Foreign**
>> **opinion** [to be added as need-
>> ed]
> BT **Freedom of conscience**
>> **Political psychology**
>> **Political science**
>> **Social psychology**
> NT **Propaganda**
>> **Public opinion polls**
>> **Publicity**
>> **United States—Foreign opinion**
>> **World War, 1939-1945—Public**
>> **opinion**

Public opinion—*Continued*
   RT   **Attitude (Psychology)**
        Press
        Public relations
Public opinion polls   303.3
   Use for general materials and for materials on the technique of polling public opinion. Materials on polls on a specific topic are entered under the appropriate heading for the topic with the subdivision *Public opinion*. Materials on polls taken in a specific place are entered **Public opinion** subdivided geographically. Materials on polls limited to a specific class of persons are entered under the appropriate heading for the class of persons with the subdivision *Attitudes*.
   UF   Opinion polls
        Polls
        Straw votes
   BT   **Public opinion**
   RT   **Market surveys**
Public ownership
   USE   **Government ownership**
         Municipal ownership
Public playgrounds
   USE   **Playgrounds**
Public procurement
   USE   **Government purchasing**
Public purchasing
   USE   **Government purchasing**
Public records—Preservation
   USE   **Archives**
Public relations (May subdiv. geog.)
        659.2
   SA   topics with the subdivision *Public relations*, e.g. **Libraries—Public relations** [to be added as needed]
   NT   **Business entertaining**
        Customer relations
   RT   **Advertising**
        Public opinion
        Publicity
Public relations—Libraries
   USE   **Libraries—Public relations**
Public safety, Crimes against
   USE   **Offenses against public safety**
Public schools (May subdiv. geog.)
        371.01
   Use for materials on preschool, elementary, and secondary schools supported by state and local government. Materials on British endowed secondary schools that are open to public admission but are not financed or administered by any government body are entered under **English public schools**.

   BT   **Schools**
   NT   **Evening and continuation schools**
        High schools
        Junior high schools
        Magnet schools
        Religion in the public schools
        Rural schools
        Summer schools
Public schools and religion
   USE   **Religion in the public schools**
Public schools, Endowed (Great Britain)
   USE   **English public schools**
Public schools, English
   USE   **English public schools**
Public schools—United States
        371.010973
   UF   United States—Public schools
Public service commissions (May subdiv. geog.)   **354.72**
   Use for materials on bodies appointed to regulate or control public utilities.
   UF   Public utility commissions
   BT   **Corporation law**
        Corporations
        Industrial policy
Public service corporations
   USE   **Public utilities**
Public shelters
   USE   **Air raid shelters**
Public speaking   808.5
   Use for materials on the art of delivering speeches. Collections of speeches on several subjects and materials about speeches that have already been delivered are entered under **Speeches**. Materials limited to scholarly lectures are entered under **Lectures and lecturing**.
   UF   Elocution
        Oratory
        Persuasion (Rhetoric)
        Speaking
   BT   **Communication**
   NT   **Acting**
        Book talks
        Chalk talks
        Debates and debating
        Lectures and lecturing
        Preaching
        Voice culture
   RT   **Speeches**
        Voice
Public television (May subdiv. geog.)
        384.55

Public television—*Continued*
  UF Educational television
  BT **Television broadcasting**
Public transit
  USE **Local transit**
Public utilities (May subdiv. geog.)
      343.09; 354.72; 363.6
  UF Public service corporations
      Utilities, Public
  NT **Electric utilities**
      Gas companies
      Telegraph
      Telephone
      Water supply
Public utility commissions
  USE **Public service commissions**
Public welfare (May subdiv. geog.)
      361.6
  Use for materials on tax-supported welfare activities. Materials on privately supported welfare activities are entered under **Charities**. Materials on the methods employed in welfare work, public or private, are entered under **Social work**. General materials on the various policies, programs, services, and facilities to meet basic human needs, such as health, education, and welfare, are entered under **Human services**.
  UF Poor relief
      Public assistance
      Relief, Public
      Social welfare
      Welfare, Public
      Welfare reform
  BT **Human services**
      Social work
  NT **Child welfare**
      Disaster relief
      Food relief
      Institutional care
      Legal aid
      National service
      Poor
      Social medicine
      Volunteer work
      Welfare state
  RT **Charities**
      Poverty
Public works (May subdiv. geog.)
      352.7; 363
  BT **Civil engineering**
      Domestic economic assistance
  NT **Infrastructure (Economics)**
      Municipal engineering

Public buildings
  RT **City planning**
Public works—Chicago (Ill.)   **363.09773**
  UF Chicago (Ill.)—Public works
Public works—Ohio   **352.7; 363.09771**
  UF Ohio—Public works
Public works—United States   **352.7;**
      363.0973
  UF United States—Public works
Public worship   **203; 264**
  May be subdivided by religion or sect.
  UF Church attendance
  BT **Worship**
  NT **Liturgies**
      Worship programs
Publicity   **659**
  BT **Public opinion**
  NT **Press**
  RT **Advertising**
      Propaganda
      Public relations
Publishers and authors
  USE **Authors and publishers**
Publishers and publishing (May subdiv.
      geog.)   **070.5**
  UF Book trade
      Publishing
  SA types of literature, types of published materials, and names of individual corporate bodies and religious denominations with the subdivision *Publishing,* e.g. **Music—Publishing** [to be added as needed]
  NT **Authors and publishers**
      Editing
      Electronic publishing
      Music—Publishing
      Printing
      Publishers' catalogs
      Publishers' standard book
          numbers
      Serial publications
  RT **Book industry**
      Books
      Booksellers and bookselling
Publishers and publishing—Exhibitions
  USE **Books—Exhibitions**
Publishers' catalogs   **015**
  Use for catalogs produced by publishers and for materials about such catalogs. Retail book

Publishers' catalogs—*Continued*
catalogs and book auction catalogs and materials about such catalogs are entered under **Booksellers' catalogs**.

    UF   Books—Catalogs
           Catalogs
           Catalogs, Publishers'
    BT   **Publishers and publishing**

**Publishers' standard book numbers
070.5**

    UF   Book numbers, Publishers' standard
           Standard book numbers
    BT   **Publishers and publishing**
    NT   **International Standard Book Numbers**

Publishing
    USE   **Publishers and publishing**
           and types of literature, types of published materials, and names of individual corporate bodies and religious denominations with the subdivision *Publishing,* e.g. **Music—Publishing** [to be added as needed]

Pubs
    USE   **Bars**
Pugilism
    USE   **Boxing**
Pulmonary resuscitation
    USE   **Artificial respiration**
Pulsars   523.8
    UF   Pulsating radio sources
    BT   **Astronomy**
Pulsating radio sources
    USE   **Pulsars**
Pumping machinery   621.6
    UF   Pumps
    SA   types of pumping machinery, e.g. **Heat pumps** [to be added as needed]
    BT   **Engines**
           Hydraulic engineering
    NT   **Heat pumps**
Pumps
    USE   **Pumping machinery**
Punctuality   640
    UF   Lateness
           Promptness
           Tardiness

    BT   **Time**
           Virtue
Punctuation   411; 421
    UF   English language—Punctuation
    BT   **Rhetoric**
Punishment (May subdiv. geog.)   **364.6**
    UF   Discipline
           Penology
    BT   **Administration of criminal justice**
           Corrections
    NT   **Capital punishment**
           Correctional institutions
           Parole
           Prisons
           Probation
           Reformatories
           Torture
    RT   **Crime**
           Criminal law
Punishment in schools
    USE   **School discipline**
Puns   808.88
    Use for collections of puns or for materials about puns.
    UF   Puns and punning
    BT   **Wit and humor**
Puns and punning
    USE   **Puns**
Puppets and puppet plays   791.5
    UF   Marionettes
    SA   types of puppets or puppet plays [to be added as needed]
    BT   **Drama**
           Folk drama
           Theater
    NT   **Shadow pantomimes and plays**
Puppies
    USE   **Dogs**
Purchasing (May subdiv. geog.)   **658.7**
    Use for general materials on buying and materials on buying by commercial enterprises. Materials on consumer buying are entered under **Shopping**.
    UF   Buying
    SA   types of products and services with the subdivision *Purchasing,* e.g. **Automobiles—Purchasing** [to be added as needed]
    BT   **Management**
    NT   **Government purchasing**
           Installment plan

Purchasing—*Continued*
  Shopping
Pure food
  USE **Food adulteration and inspection**
Purgatory   202; 236
  BT **Eschatology**
Purification of water
  USE **Water purification**
Puritans (May subdiv. geog.)   **285**
  BT **Christian sects**
  NT **Pilgrims (New England colonists)**
  RT **Calvinism**
    Church of England—United States
    Congregationalism
Puzzles   793.73
  SA types of puzzles, e.g. **Crossword puzzles** [to be added as needed]
  BT **Amusements**
  NT **Bible games and puzzles**
    Crossword puzzles
    Jigsaw puzzles
    Mathematical recreations
    Maze puzzles
    Picture puzzles
    Rebuses
  RT **Riddles**
Pyramids (May subdiv. geog.)   **722; 909**
  BT **Ancient architecture**
    Archeology
    Monuments
  NT **Obelisks**
Pyrography (May subdiv.geog.)   **745.51**
  UF Fire etching
    Wood-burning
  BT **Etching**
    Woodwork
Quacks and quackery   615.8
  BT **Impostors and imposture**
    Medicine
    Swindlers and swindling
Quakers
  USE **Society of Friends**
Qualitative analysis
  USE **Analytical chemistry**
Quality control   519.8; 658.5

  SA industries, processes, and materials with the subdivision *Quality control* [to be added as needed]
  BT **Reliability (Engineering)**
    Sampling (Statistics)
  NT **Steel industry—Quality control**
Quality of life (May subdiv. geog.)   **303.3**
  Use for materials on the objective standards and subjective attitudes by which individuals and groups assess their life situations.
  UF Life quality
  BT **Economic conditions**
    Social conditions
  NT **Cost and standard of living**
  RT **Basic needs**
Quantitative analysis
  USE **Analytical chemistry**
Quantity cookery
  USE **Quantity cooking**
Quantity cooking   641.5
  Use for materials limited to the preparation and cooking of food in large quantities. Materials on the preparation, delivery, and serving of ready-to-eat foods in large quantities outside of the home are entered under **Food service**.
  UF Cooking for large numbers
    Quantity cookery
  BT **Cooking**
  RT **Food service**
Quantum mechanics
  USE **Quantum theory**
Quantum theory   530.12
  UF Quantum mechanics
  BT **Dynamics**
    Physics
  NT **Wave mechanics**
  RT **Atomic theory**
    Force and energy
    Physical chemistry
    Radiation
    Relativity (Physics)
    Thermodynamics
Quarantine
  USE **Communicable diseases**
Quarks   539.7
  BT **Particles (Nuclear physics)**
Quarries and quarrying (May subdiv. geog.)   **622**
  UF Stone quarries
  BT **Economic geology**
  RT **Stone**

Quartz 549

UF Rock crystal

BT **Crystals**

Minerals

Quasars 523.1

UF Quasi-stellar radio sources

BT **Astronomy**

Radio astronomy

Quasi-stellar radio sources

USE **Quasars**

Québec (Province) 971.4

Québec (Province)—History 971.4

Québec (Province)—History—Autonomy and independence movements 971.4

UF Québec (Province)—Separatist movement

Separatist movement in Québec (Province)

BT **Separatist movements**

Québec (Province)—Separatist movement

USE **Québec (Province)—History—Autonomy and independence movements**

Queens (May subdiv. geog.) **920; 929.7**

Use for materials on women monarchs as well as on wives or consorts of monarchs.

UF Royalty

Rulers

Sovereigns

SA names of queens, e.g. **Elizabeth II, Queen of Great Britain, 1926-** ; ethnic groups with the subdivision *Queens,* and countries, cities, etc., with the subdivision *Kings and rulers* [to be added as needed]

BT **Monarchy**

NT **Elizabeth II, Queen of Great Britain, 1926-**

RT **Courts and courtiers**

Empresses

Kings and rulers

Queens—Great Britain **920; 941**

UF Great Britain—Queens

SA names of British queens [to be added as needed]

Queries

USE **Questions and answers**

Questions and answers 793.73

Use for collections of informal quizzes on various subjects. Informal quizzes on a partic-

ular subject are entered under the subject with the subdivision *Miscellanea.* Materials on formal examinations are entered under **Examinations**. Examination questions on a particular subject are entered under the subject with the subdivision *Examinations*, e.g. **Music—Examinations**. Compilations of practice problems or exercises for use in the study of a topic are entered under the topic with the subdivision *Problems, exercises, etc.,* e.g. **Chemistry—Problems, exercises, etc.**

UF Answers to questions

Queries

Quizzes

Trivia

SA subjects with the subdivision *Miscellanea*, e.g. **Medicine—Miscellanea** [to be added as needed]

NT **Examinations**

Quick and easy cookery

USE **Quick and easy cooking**

Quick and easy cooking 641.5

Use for materials containing recipes or cooking techniques emphasizing economy of preparation time and the use of readily available ingredients.

UF Convenience cooking

Easy and quick cooking

Quick and easy cookery

Quick-meal cooking

Time saving cooking

BT **Cooking**

Quick-meal cooking

USE **Quick and easy cooking**

Quicksilver

USE **Mercury**

Quilt designing

USE **Quilts—Design**

Quilting 746.46

BT **Needlework**

Sewing

RT **Quilts**

Quilts (May subdiv. geog.) 746.46

UF Coverlets

Patchwork quilts

BT **Interior design**

RT **Quilting**

Quilts—Design 746.46

UF Quilt designing

BT **Design**

Quintets 785

BT **Chamber music**

Quislings
  USE **World War, 1939-1945—Col-laborationists**
Quit-smoking programs
  USE **Smoking cessation programs**
Quizzes
  USE **Questions and answers**
Qumran texts
  USE **Dead Sea scrolls**
Quotations 080; 808.88
  UF Sayings
  SA subjects, classes of persons, eth-nic groups, and names of in-dividuals with the subdivision *Quotations* [to be added as needed]
  BT **Epigrams**
  NT **Presidents—United States—Quotations**
      Proverbs
Qur'an
  USE **Koran**
Rabbis (May subdiv. geog.) **296.6; 920**
  BT **Clergy**
      Judaism
Rabbits 599.32; 636
  UF Bunnies
      Bunny rabbits
      Hares
  BT **Mammals**
Rabies 616.9; 636.089
  UF Hydrophobia
  BT **Communicable diseases**
Race 599.97
  BT **Ethnology**
  NT **Ethnocentrism**
Race awareness (May subdiv. geog.)
      305.8
  UF Race identity
      Racial identity
  SA names of racial groups with the subdivision *Race identity* [to be added as needed]
  BT **Race relations**
  NT **African Americans—Race iden-tity**
      Blacks—Race identity
      Racism
Race discrimination (May subdiv. geog.)
      305.8
  Use for materials on the restriction or deni-al of rights, privileges, or choice because of race. Materials on prejudicial attitudes about particular groups because of their race are en-tered under **Racism**.
  UF Racial discrimination
  SA types of discrimination, e.g. **Dis-crimination in education** [to be added as needed]
  BT **Discrimination**
      Race relations
      Racism
      Social problems
Race identity
  USE **Race awareness**
      and names of racial groups with the subdivision *Race identity,* e.g. **Blacks—Race identity; African Ameri-cans—Race identity;** etc. [to be added as needed]
Race prejudice
  USE **Racism**
Race problems
  USE **Race relations**
Race psychology
  USE **Ethnopsychology**
Race relations 305.8
  UF Integration, Racial
      Interracial relations
      Race problems
      Racial integration
  SA names of countries, cities, etc., with the subdivision *Race re-lations*, e.g. **United States—Race relations** [to be added as needed]
  BT **Acculturation**
      Ethnology
      Sociology
  NT **Chicago (Ill.)—Race relations**
      Culture conflict
      Discrimination
      Interracial adoption
      Ohio—Race relations
      Race awareness
      Race discrimination
      Racism
      School integration
      Segregation
      South Africa—Race relations
      United States—Race relations
      White supremacy movements

Race relations—*Continued*
　RT　**Ethnic relations**
　　　Minorities
　　　Multiculturalism
　　　Pluralism (Social sciences)
Race relations and the church
　USE　**Church and race relations**
Races of people
　USE　**Ethnology**
Racial balance in schools
　USE　**School integration**
　　　Segregation in education
Racial bias
　USE　**Racism**
Racial discrimination
　USE　**Race discrimination**
Racial identity
　USE　**Race awareness**
Racial integration
　USE　**Race relations**
Racial intermarriage
　USE　**Interracial marriage**
Racially mixed people (May subdiv.
　　geog.)　**305.8**
　UF　Bi-racial people
　　　Mixed race people
　　　Mulattoes
　　　Multiracial people
　BT　**Ethnic groups**
Racing　**796**
　SA　types of racing and names of
　　　races, e.g. **Indianapolis 500**
　　　[to be added as needed]
　BT　**Sports**
　NT　**Airplane racing**
　　　Automobile racing
　　　Bicycle racing
　　　Boat racing
　　　Horse racing
　　　Orienteering
　　　Soap box derbies
　RT　**Running**
Racism (May subdiv. geog.)　**305.8;**
　　320.5
　　　Use for materials on prejudicial attitudes
　　about particular groups because of their race.
　　Materials on the restriction or denial of rights,
　　privileges, or choice because of race are en-
　　tered under **Race discrimination**.
　UF　Race prejudice
　　　Racial bias
　BT　**Attitude (Psychology)**
　　　Prejudices

　　　Race awareness
　　　Race relations
　NT　**Race discrimination**
　　　White supremacy movements
Racketeering (May subdiv. geog.)
　　364.106
　UF　Crime syndicates
　BT　**Crime**
　　　Organized crime
　NT　**Extortion**
Radar　**621.3848**
　BT　**Navigation**
　　　Radio
　　　Remote sensing
Radar defense networks　**623**
　UF　Defenses, Radar
　BT　**Air defenses**
Radiant heating　**697**
　UF　Panel heating
　BT　**Heating**
Radiation　**539.2**
　BT　**Optics**
　　　Physics
　　　Waves
　NT　**Cosmic rays**
　　　Electromagnetic waves
　　　Gamma rays
　　　Infrared radiation
　　　Luminescence
　　　Radioactivity
　　　Radium
　　　Sound
　　　Spectrum analysis
　　　Ultraviolet rays
　　　X-rays
　RT　**Light**
　　　Quantum theory
Radiation biology
　USE　**Radiobiology**
Radiation—Physiological effect　**612**
　RT　**Atomic bomb—Physiological**
　　　　effect
　　　Nuclear medicine
Radiation—Safety measures　**363.1; 612**
　BT　**Accidents—Prevention**
Radiation, Solar
　USE　**Solar radiation**
Radiation therapy
　USE　**Radiotherapy**

Radicalism (May subdiv. geog.)   **320.5**

Use for materials on extremist social and political movements of either the right or the left.

UF   Extremism (Political science)
Political extremism
Radicals and radicalism

BT   **Political science**
Revolutions
Right and left (Political science)

NT   **Militia movements**

RT   **Counter culture**

Radicals and radicalism

USE   **Radicalism**

Radio   621.384

UF   Wireless

SA   radio and other subjects, e.g.
Radio and music; and radio in various industries or fields of endeavor, e.g. **Radio in aeronautics** [to be added as needed]

BT   **Telecommunication**

NT   **Radar**
Radio and music
Radio frequency modulation
Radio in aeronautics
Radio in astronautics
Radio in education
Shortwave radio

Radio addresses, debates, etc.   384.54; 808.5; 808.85

UF   Radio lectures

BT   **Debates and debating**
Lectures and lecturing
Radio broadcasting
Radio scripts

Radio advertising   659.14

UF   Commercials, Radio
Radio commercials

BT   **Advertising**
Radio broadcasting

Radio and music   780; 781.5

UF   Music and radio

BT   **Music**
Radio

NT   **Disc jockeys**

Radio and television novels   808.3

Use for individual works, collections, or materials about novels based on radio or television programs.

UF   Radio novels
Television novels

BT   **Fiction**

RT   **Movie novels**

Radio astronomy   522

SA   names of celestial radio sources, e.g. **Quasars** [to be added as needed]

BT   **Astronomy**
Interstellar communication

NT   **Quasars**

Radio authorship   808

UF   Radio script writing
Radio writing

BT   **Authorship**
Radio broadcasting

NT   **Radio plays—Technique**

RT   **Radio scripts**

Radio broadcasting (May subdiv. geog.)   **384.54**

UF   Radio industry

SA   radio broadcasting of particular kinds of programs, e.g. **Radio broadcasting of sports** [to be added as needed]

BT   **Broadcasting**
Mass media

NT   **Radio addresses, debates, etc.**
Radio advertising
Radio authorship
Radio broadcasting of sports
Radio programs
Radio stations

Radio broadcasting of sports   070.4

UF   Sports broadcasting
Sports in radio

BT   **Broadcast journalism**
Radio broadcasting

Radio chemistry

USE   **Radiochemistry**

Radio comedies

USE   **Comedy radio programs**

Radio comedy programs

USE   **Comedy radio programs**

Radio commercials

USE   **Radio advertising**

Radio drama

USE   **Radio plays**

Radio—Equipment and supplies   621.384028

Radio—Equipment and supplies—*Continued*

    NT   **Radio—Receivers and reception**

    RT   **Radio supplies industry**

Radio equipment industry

    USE **Radio supplies industry**

Radio frequency modulation   621.384

    UF   FM radio

         Frequency modulation, Radio

    BT   **Radio**

    NT   **Shortwave radio**

Radio in aeronautics   629.135

    BT   **Aeronautics**

         Navigation (Aeronautics)

         Radio

Radio in astronautics   629.4

    UF   Lunar surface radio communication

    BT   **Astronautics—Communication systems**

         Navigation (Astronautics)

         Radio

Radio in education   371.33

    UF   Education and radio

    BT   **Audiovisual education**

         Radio

         Teaching—Aids and devices

Radio industry

    USE **Radio broadcasting**

         Radio supplies industry

Radio journalism

    USE **Broadcast journalism**

Radio lectures

    USE **Radio addresses, debates, etc.**

Radio novels

    USE **Radio and television novels**

Radio operators   621.3841

Radio plays   808.2; 808.82

    Use for individual works, collections, or materials about radio plays.

    UF   Radio drama

         Scenarios

    BT   **Drama**

         Radio programs

    NT   **Soap operas**

    RT   **Radio scripts**

Radio plays—Technique   808.2

    UF   Play writing

         Playwriting

    BT   **Drama—Technique**

         Radio authorship

    RT   **Television plays—Technique**

Radio programs   384.54

    Use for individual works, collections, or materials about radio programs.

    UF   Programs, Radio

    SA   types of programs and names of specific programs [to be added as needed]

    BT   **Radio broadcasting**

    NT   **Adventure radio programs**

         Biographical radio programs

         Comedy radio programs

         Fantasy radio programs

         Horror radio programs

         Legal drama (Radio programs)

         Medical drama (Radio programs)

         Mystery radio programs

         Radio plays

         Radio serials

         Science fiction radio programs

         Sports drama (Radio programs)

         Spy radio programs

         Talk shows

         Variety shows (Radio programs)

         War radio programs

         Westerns (Radio programs)

    RT   **Radio scripts**

Radio—Receivers and reception   621.384

    UF   Radio reception

         Radios

    BT   **Radio—Equipment and supplies**

Radio reception

    USE **Radio—Receivers and reception**

Radio—Repairing   621.384

    UF   Radio repairs

         Radio servicing

Radio repairs

    USE **Radio—Repairing**

Radio script writing

    USE **Radio authorship**

Radio scripts   791.44; 808.88

    Use for individual works, collections, or materials about radio scripts.

    NT   **Radio addresses, debates, etc.**

    RT   **Radio authorship**

         Radio plays

Radio scripts—*Continued*
> **Radio programs**

Radio serials 791.44
> Use for individual works, collections, or materials about radio serials.
> BT **Radio programs**
> RT **Soap operas**

Radio servicing
> USE **Radio—Repairing**

Radio stations (May subdiv. geog.) **384.54**
> SA names of specific radio stations [to be added as needed]
> BT **Radio broadcasting**
> NT **Amateur radio stations**

Radio supplies industry (May subdiv. geog.) **338.4**
> UF Radio equipment industry
> Radio industry
> BT **Industries**
> RT **Radio—Equipment and supplies**

Radio waves
> USE **Electric waves**

Radio writing
> USE **Radio authorship**

Radioactive fallout (May subdiv. geog.) **539.7**
> UF Dust, Radioactive
> Fallout, Radioactive
> BT **Atomic bomb**
> **Hydrogen bomb**
> **Radioactive pollution**

Radioactive isotopes
> USE **Radioisotopes**

Radioactive pollution (May subdiv. geog.) **363.17; 363.73; 621.48**
> UF Environmental radioactivity
> Nuclear pollution
> Pollution, Radioactive
> BT **Pollution**
> **Radioactivity**
> NT **Radioactive fallout**
> RT **Radioactive waste disposal**

Radioactive substances
> USE **Radioactivity**

Radioactive waste disposal (May subdiv. geog.) **363.72; 621.48**
> UF Nuclear waste disposal
> BT **Nuclear engineering**
> **Nuclear power plants—Environmental aspects**

> **Radioactivity**
> **Refuse and refuse disposal**
> RT **Radioactive pollution**

Radioactivity 539.7
> UF Radioactive substances
> BT **Physics**
> **Radiation**
> NT **Cosmic rays**
> **Phosphorescence**
> **Radioactive pollution**
> **Radioactive waste disposal**
> **Radiobiology**
> **Radiochemistry**
> **Radiotherapy**
> **Transmutation (Chemistry)**
> RT **Nuclear physics**
> **Radium**
> **Radon**
> **Uranium**

Radiobiology 571.4
> UF Radiation biology
> BT **Biology**
> **Biophysics**
> **Nuclear physics**
> **Radioactivity**

Radiocarbon dating 539.7
> UF Carbon 14 dating
> Dating, Radiocarbon
> BT **Archeology**

Radiochemistry 541
> UF Radio chemistry
> BT **Physical chemistry**
> **Radioactivity**

Radiography
> USE **X-rays**

Radioisotopes 621.48
> UF Radioactive isotopes
> BT **Isotopes**
> **Nuclear engineering**

Radiologists (May subdiv. geog.) **920**
> BT **Physicians**
> RT **Radiotherapy**

Radios
> USE **Radio—Receivers and reception**

Radiotherapy 615.8
> UF Radiation therapy
> BT **Electrotherapeutics**
> **Physical therapy**
> **Radioactivity**
> **Therapeutics**

Radiotherapy—*Continued*
 RT **Phototherapy**
  Radiologists
  Radium
  Ultraviolet rays
  X-rays
Radium 546; 661; 669
 BT **Chemical elements**
  Radiation
 RT **Radioactivity**
  Radiotherapy
Radium emanation
 USE **Radon**
Radon 363.738; 546
 UF Radium emanation
 BT **Poisonous gases**
 RT **Radioactivity**
Rage
 USE **Anger**
Railroad accidents (May subdiv. geog.)
  363.12
 UF Collisions, Railroad
  Derailments
  Railroads—Accidents
  Train wrecks
 BT **Accidents**
  Disasters
Railroad construction
 USE **Railroad engineering**
Railroad engineering (May subdiv. geog.)
  625.1
 UF Railroad construction
 BT **Civil engineering**
  Engineering
  Railroads
Railroad fares
 USE **Railroads—Rates**
Railroad mergers
 USE **Railroads—Mergers**
Railroad rates
 USE **Railroads—Rates**
Railroad workers
 USE **Railroads—Employees**
Railroads (May subdiv. geog.) **385;**
  625.1
 UF Railways
  Trains
 SA names of individual railroads [to
  be added as needed]
 BT **Transportation**
 NT **Cable railroads**
  Electric railroads

  Express service
  Freight
  Locomotives
  Monorail railroads
  Railroad engineering
  Street railroads
  Subways
Railroads—Accidents
 USE **Railroad accidents**
Railroads and state
 USE **Railroads—Government policy**
Railroads, Cable
 USE **Cable railroads**
Railroads—Consolidation
 USE **Railroads—Mergers**
Railroads—Employees (May subdiv.
  geog.) **331.7**
 UF Railroad workers
 BT **Employees**
Railroads—Fares
 USE **Railroads—Rates**
Railroads—Finance **385**
 BT **Finance**
 NT **Railroads—Rates**
Railroads—Government ownership
 USE **Railroads—Government policy**
Railroads—Government policy (May
  subdiv. geog.) **354.6; 385**
 UF Government ownership of rail-
  roads
  Government regulation of rail-
  roads
  Nationalization of railroads
  Railroads and state
  Railroads—Government owner-
  ship
  Railroads, Nationalization of
  State and railroads
  State ownership of railroads
 BT **Government ownership**
  Industrial policy
 NT **Railroads—Rates**
Railroads—Mergers (May subdiv. geog.)
  338.8
 UF Railroad mergers
  Railroads—Consolidation
 BT **Corporate mergers and acqui-**
  sitions
Railroads—Models **625.1**
 UF Model trains
 BT **Models and modelmaking**

Railroads, Nationalization of
    USE   **Railroads—Government policy**
Railroads—Rates (May subdiv. geog.)
    385
    UF   Railroad fares
          Railroad rates
          Railroads—Fares
    BT   **Railroads—Finance**
          Railroads—Government policy
    RT   **Freight**
Railroads—Safety appliances
    USE   **Railroads—Safety devices**
Railroads—Safety devices   625.10028
    UF   Railroads—Safety appliances
    BT   **Accidents—Prevention**
          Safety devices
    NT   **Railroads—Signaling**
Railroads—Signaling   625.1
    UF   Block signal systems
          Interlocking signals
    BT   **Railroads—Safety devices**
          Signals and signaling
Railroads, Single rail
    USE   **Monorail railroads**
Railroads—Statistics   385
    BT   **Statistics**
Railways
    USE   **Railroads**
Rain (May subdiv. geog.)   **551.57**
    UF   Rain and rainfall
          Rainfall
    BT   **Precipitation (Meteorology)**
    NT   **Acid rain**
          Floods
    RT   **Droughts**
          Forest influences
          Storms
Rain and rainfall
    USE   **Rain**
Rain forests (May subdiv. geog.)
    577.34; 634.9
    Use for materials on forests of broad-leaved, mainly evergreen trees found in moist climates in the tropics, subtropics, and some parts of the temperate zones. Materials on impenetrable thickets of second-growth vegetation replacing tropical rain forests that have been disturbed or degraded are entered under **Jungles**.
    UF   Rainforests
          Tropical rain forests
    BT   **Forests and forestry**
    RT   **Jungles**

Rain making
    USE   **Weather control**
Rainbow   551.56
    BT   **Meteorology**
    RT   **Refraction**
Rainfall
    USE   **Rain**
Rainfall and forests
    USE   **Forest influences**
Rainforests
    USE   **Rain forests**
Rallies (Protest)
    USE   **Demonstrations**
Ramadan (May subdiv. geog.)   **297.3**
    BT   **Islamic holidays**
Ranch life (May subdiv. geog.)   **307.72;**
    636
    BT   **Farm life**
          Frontier and pioneer life
    NT   **Cowhands**
Random sampling
    USE   **Sampling (Statistics)**
Ranger project
    USE   **Project Ranger**
Rank
    USE   **Social classes**
Rap music   782.421649
    UF   Rap songs
          Rapping (Music)
    BT   **African American music**
          Popular music
Rap songs
    USE   **Rap music**
Rape (May subdiv. geog.)   **362.883;**
    364.15
    UF   Assault, Sexual
          Sexual assault
    BT   **Offenses against the person**
          Sex crimes
    NT   **Date rape**
Rapid reading
    USE   **Speed reading**
Rapid transit
    USE   **Local transit**
Rapping (Music)
    USE   **Rap music**
Rare animals (May subdiv. geog.)
    591.68
    SA   names of specific animals, e.g.
          Bison [to be added as needed]

Rare animals—*Continued*
- BT **Animals**
- RT **Endangered species**
   Extinct animals
   Wildlife conservation

Rare books (May subdiv. geog.) **090**
- UF Antiquarian books
   Bibliography—Rare books
   Book rarities
- BT **Books**

Rare plants (May subdiv. geog.) **581.68**
- BT **Plants**
- RT **Endangered species**
   Plant conservation

Rates
- USE types of services, utilities, transportation systems, etc., with the subdivision *Rates,* e.g. **Railroads—Rates** [to be added as needed]

Rating
- USE **Performance standards** and subjects and classes of persons with the subdivision *Rating,* e.g. **Bonds—Rating; Employees—Rating;** etc. [to be added as needed]

Ratio and proportion **513.2**
- BT **Arithmetic**
   Geometry

Rationalism **149; 211**
- BT **Philosophy**
   Religion
   Secularism
   Theory of knowledge
- NT **Empiricism**
   Enlightenment
   Intuition
   Positivism
   Reason
   Skepticism
- RT **Agnosticism**
   Atheism
   Belief and doubt
   Deism
   Free thought
   Realism

Rattlesnakes **597.96**
- BT **Poisonous animals**
   Snakes

Raw materials (May subdiv. geog.) **333.7**
Use for works on unprocessed minerals and unprocessed animal and vegetable products. Comprehensive works on the basic processed materials used in engineering and industry are entered under **Materials**.
- BT **Commercial products**
- NT **Farm produce**
   Forest products
   Mines and mineral resources

Rayon **677**
- BT **Synthetic fabrics**

Rays, Ultra-violet
- USE **Ultraviolet rays**

Re-enlistment
- USE **Recruiting and enlistment**

Reaction (Political science)
- USE **Conservatism**

Reactions, Chemical
- USE **Chemical reactions**

Reactors (Nuclear physics)
- USE **Nuclear reactors**

Reader services (Libraries)
- USE **Library services**

Readers
- USE **Reading materials**

Readers and libraries
- USE **Library services**

Readers' theater **792**
Use for materials on the dramatic reading of plays before an audience.
- BT **Theater**

Readiness for mathematics
- USE **Mathematical readiness**

Readiness for reading
- USE **Reading readiness**

Readiness for school **372.21**
- UF School readiness
- BT **Elementary education**
   Preschool education

Reading **372.4; 418**
Use for materials on methods of teaching reading and for general materials on the art of reading. Materials on teaching slow readers are entered under **Reading—Remedial teaching**. Materials on the cultural or informational aspects of reading and general discussions of books are entered under **Books and reading**.
- UF Children's reading
   Reading—Study and teaching
- BT **Language arts**
- NT **Books and reading**
   Reading comprehension
   Reading disability

Reading—*Continued*
>> **Reading—Phonetic method**
>> **Reading readiness**
>> **Speed reading**
>> **Word recognition**
>> **Word skills**

Reading clinics
> USE **Reading—Remedial teaching**

Reading comprehension   372.48
> BT **Psychology of learning**
> **Reading**
> **Verbal learning**

Reading disability   371.91
> SA types of reading disabilities, e.g.
>> **Dyslexia** [to be added as needed]
> BT **Learning disabilities**
> **Reading**
> NT **Dyslexia**

Reading interests
> USE **Books and reading**

Reading interests of children
> USE **Children—Books and reading**

Reading interests of teenagers
> USE **Teenagers—Books and reading**

Reading interests of young adults
> USE **Teenagers—Books and reading**

Reading materials   372.41; 418

Use for materials in English intended to be used in teaching reading or language skills. Such materials in other languages are entered under the language with the subdivision *Reading materials.*

> UF English language—Reading materials
> Readers
> SA names of languages other than English with the subdivision *Reading materials*, e.g.
>> **French language—Reading materials** [to be added as needed]
> BT **Children's literature**
> NT **Basal readers**
> **Big books**
> **Easy reading materials**
> **Hornbooks**
> **Recitations**
> RT **Books and reading**

Reading—Patterning
> USE **Language arts—Patterning**

Reading—Phonetic method   372.46

> UF Letter-sound association
> Phonics
> BT **English language—Pronunciation**
> **Reading**
> RT **Phonetics**

Reading readiness   372.41
> UF Readiness for reading
> BT **Reading**

Reading—Remedial teaching   372.43
> UF Reading clinics
> Remedial reading

Reading—Study and teaching
> USE **Reading**

Readings and recitations
> USE **Recitations**

Readings (Anthologies)
> USE **Anthologies**

Ready reckoners
> USE **Mathematics—Tables**

Real estate (May subdiv. geog.)   **333.3**

Use for materials on land and buildings considered as property. Materials on the buying and selling of real property are entered under **Real estate business**. General materials on land apart from the aspect of ownership are entered under **Land use**.

> UF Real property
> Realty
> BT **Land use**
> **Property**
> NT **Farms**
> **Landlord and tenant**
> **Real estate business**
> **Real estate investment**
> RT **Land tenure**

Real estate business (May subdiv. geog.)
    333.33; 346.04

Use for materials limited to the buying and selling of real property. General materials on land and buildings considered as property are entered under **Real estate**.

> BT **Business**
> **Real estate**
> NT **Houses—Buying and selling**
> **Timesharing (Real estate)**

Real estate investment (May subdiv. geog.)   **332.63**
> UF Investment in real estate
> Real property investment
> BT **Investments**
> **Real estate**
> **Speculation**

Real estate investment—Taxation
343.05
BT Taxation
Real estate timesharing
USE Timesharing (Real estate)
Real property
USE Real estate
Real property investment
USE Real estate investment
Real property tax—Assessment
USE Tax assessment
Realism 149
BT Philosophy
NT Pragmatism
RT Idealism
Materialism
Positivism
Rationalism
Realism in art 709.03
UF Naturalism in art
BT Art
Realism in literature 809
UF Naturalism in literature
BT Literature
Reality 111
BT Philosophy
Truth
RT Pragmatism
Theory of knowledge
Reality shows (Television)
USE Reality television programs
Reality television programs (May subdiv.
geog.) 791.45
UF Reality shows (Television)
BT Television programs
Realty
USE Real estate
Reapers
USE Harvesting machinery
Reapportionment (Election law)
USE Apportionment (Election law)
Reason 128; 160
BT Intellect
Rationalism
NT Reasoning
Reasoning 153.4; 160
BT Psychology
Reason
Thought and thinking
NT Critical thinking

RT Intellect
Logic
Rebellions
USE Insurgency
Revolutions
Rebels (Social psychology)
USE Alienation (Social psychology)
Rebirth
USE Reincarnation
Rebuses 793.73
BT Literary recreations
Puzzles
Riddles
Recall of products
USE Product recall
Recall (Political science) (May subdiv.
geog.) 324.6
BT Impeachments
Representative government and
representation
Recessions (May subdiv. geog.) 338.5
UF Business recessions
Economic recessions
SA names of countries, states, cities,
etc., with the subdivision *Eco-
nomic conditions* [to be added
as needed]
BT Business cycles
Recipes
USE Cooking
Reciprocity
USE Commercial policy
Recitation of the Koran
USE Koran—Recitation
Recitations 808.85
Use for collections of material written or
selected for oral presentation and for materials
about recitation.
UF Declamations
Narrations
Oral interpretation
Readings and recitations
BT Reading materials
School assembly programs
NT Choral speaking
Koran—Recitation
Monologues
Monologues with music
Recitations with music
USE Monologues with music

Reclamation of land (May subdiv. geog.)
    627; 631.6
    Use for general materials on reclamation, including drainage and irrigation.
    UF   Clearing of land
          Land, Reclamation of
    BT   **Agriculture**
          Civil engineering
          Hydraulic engineering
          Land use
    NT   **Drainage**
    RT   **Irrigation**
Recluses
    USE **Hermits**
Recombinant DNA   572.8
    BT   **DNA**
          Genetic engineering
          Genetic recombination
Recombination, Genetic
    USE **Genetic recombination**
Recommendations for positions
    USE **Applications for positions**
Reconciliation, Sacrament of
    USE **Penance**
Reconnaissance, Aerial
    USE **Aerial reconnaissance**
Reconstruction (1865-1876)   973.8
    UF   Carpetbag rule
          United States—History—1861-
          1865, Civil War—Reconstruc-
          tion
    BT   **United States—History—1865-
          1898**
Reconstruction (1914-1939)   940.3
    UF   World War, 1914-1918—Recon-
          struction
    RT   **Foreign aid**
          International cooperation
          **World War, 1914-1918—Eco-
          nomic aspects**
Reconstruction (1939-1951) (May subdiv.
    geog. except U.S.)   **940.53**
    UF   Marshall Plan
          World War, 1939-1945—Recon-
          struction
    NT   **World War, 1939-1945—Civil-
          ian relief**
          **World War, 1939-1945—Repa-
          rations**
    RT   **Foreign aid**
          International cooperation

**World War, 1939-1945—Eco-
          nomic aspects**
Reconstructive surgery
    USE **Plastic surgery**
Recorded books
    USE **Audiobooks**
Recording, Laser
    USE **Laser recording**
Recordings, Sound
    USE **Sound recordings**
Records of achievement
    USE **World records**
Records of births, etc.
    USE **Registers of births, etc.
          Vital statistics**
Records, Phonograph
    USE **Sound recordings**
Records—Preservation
    USE **Archives**
Records, Sports
    USE **Sports records**
Records, World
    USE **World records**
Recovered memories
    USE **Recovered memory**
Recovered memory   616.85
    UF   Delayed memory
          Recovered memories
          Repressed memory
    BT   **Memory**
    RT   **False memory syndrome**
Recovering addicts   362.29; 616.86
    BT   **Drug addicts**
    RT   **Recovering alcoholics**
Recovering alcoholics   362.292; 616.86
    BT   **Alcoholics**
    RT   **Recovering addicts**
Recovery of space vehicles
    USE **Space vehicles—Recovery**
Recreation (May subdiv. geog.)   **790**
    UF   Pastimes
          Relaxation
    SA   classes of persons with the sub-
          division *Recreation*, e.g. **El-
          derly—Recreation** [to be
          added as needed]
    NT   **Camps**
          Community centers
          Elderly—Recreation
          Games
          Hobbies

Recreation—*Continued*
    Outdoor recreation
    Play
    Playgrounds
    Popular culture
    Resorts
    Sports
    Vacations
  RT Amusements
    Leisure
    Sports facilities
Recreation centers
  USE Community centers
    Physical fitness centers
Recreational vehicles 629.226
  UF RVs
  SA types of recreational vehicles,
    e.g. **Travel trailers and**
    campers [to be added as
    needed]
  BT Outdoor recreation
    Vehicles
  NT Travel trailers and campers
Recreations, Literary
  USE Literary recreations
Recreations, Mathematical
  USE Mathematical recreations
Recreations, Scientific
  USE Scientific recreations
Recruiting
  USE Recruiting and enlistment
    Recruiting of employees
    and types of employees and
    professions with the subdivi-
    sion *Recruiting,* e.g. **Librari-**
    ans—Recruiting; and names
    of armed forces and of armies
    and navies with the subdivi-
    sion *Recruiting, enlistment,*
    etc. [to be added as needed]
Recruiting and enlistment 355.2
  UF Armed forces—Recruiting, enlist-
    ment, etc.
    Enlistment
    Re-enlistment
    Recruiting
    Recruiting, enlistment, etc.
  SA names of armed forces and of
    armies and navies with the
    subdivision *Recruiting, enlist-*
    ment, etc., e.g. **United**

    States—Armed Forces—Re-
    cruiting, enlistment, etc.;
    United States. Army—Re-
    cruiting, enlistment, etc.; etc.
    [to be added as needed]
  BT Armed forces
    Military personnel
  NT Draft
    United States. Army—Recruit-
    ing, enlistment, etc.
    United States. Navy—Recruit-
    ing, enlistment, etc.
    United States—Armed
    Forces—Recruiting, enlist-
    ment, etc.
    Voluntary military service
Recruiting, enlistment, etc.
  USE Recruiting and enlistment
    and names of armed forces and
    of armies and navies with the
    subdivision *Recruiting, enlist-*
    ment, etc., e.g. **United**
    States—Armed Forces—Re-
    cruiting, enlistment, etc.;
    United States. Army—Re-
    cruiting, enlistment, etc.; etc.
    [to be added as needed]
Recruiting of employees 658.3
  UF Recruiting
  SA types of employees and profes-
    sions with the subdivision *Re-*
    cruiting, e.g. **Librarians—Re-**
    cruiting [to be added as
    needed]
  BT Personnel management
  NT Employment agencies
    Librarians—Recruiting
Rectors
  USE Clergy
Recurrent education
  USE Continuing education
Recycling (May subdiv. geog.) 628.4
  UF Conversion of waste products
    Recycling (Waste, etc.)
  SA subjects with the subdivision
    Recycling, e.g. **Aluminum—**
    Recycling [to be added as
    needed]
  BT Energy conservation
    Pollution control industry
    Salvage

Recycling—*Continued*

    NT   **Aluminum—Recycling**

    RT   **Refuse and refuse disposal**

          Waste products

Recycling (Waste, etc.)

    USE   **Recycling**

Red   535.6; 752

    BT   **Color**

Redemption

    USE   **Salvation**

Reducing

    USE   **Weight loss**

Reenactment of historical events

    USE   **Historical reenactments**

Reference books (May subdiv. geog.)
    028.7

> Use for materials about reference books. Reference books themselves are entered under **Encyclopedias and dictionaries**; or under the appropriate subjects with the subdivisions *Dictionaries*; *Bibliography*; etc., as needed.

    BT   **Bibliography**

          Books

          Books and reading

    NT   **Encyclopedias and dictionaries**

Reference books—Reviews   028.1

Reference services (Libraries) (May
    subdiv. geog.)   025.5

> Use for materials on activities designed to make information available to library users, including direct personal assistance.

    UF   Library reference services

          Reference work (Libraries)

    BT   **Information services**

          Library services

    NT   **Electronic reference services**
          (Libraries)

Reference work (Libraries)

    USE   **Reference services (Libraries)**

Referendum (May subdiv. geog.)   **328.2**

    UF   Direct legislation

          Initiative and referendum

          Legislation, Direct

    BT   **Constitutional law**

          Democracy

          Elections

Refinishing furniture

    USE   **Furniture finishing**

Reflexology   615.8

    BT   **Alternative medicine**

Reforestation (May subdiv. geog.)
    333.75; 634.9

    BT   **Forests and forestry**

    RT   **Tree planting**

Reform, Agrarian

    USE   **Land reform**

Reform of criminals

    USE   **Corrections**

          Probation

          Reformatories

Reform of health care delivery

    USE   **Health care reform**

Reform of medical care delivery

    USE   **Health care reform**

Reform schools

    USE   **Reformatories**

Reform, Social

    USE   **Social problems**

Reformation (May subdiv. geog.)   **270.6**

    UF   Protestant Reformation

    SA   names of religious sects, e.g.

          Huguenots [to be added as
          needed]

    BT   **Christianity**

          Church history—1500-, Modern period

    NT   **Calvinism**

          Huguenots

    RT   **Counter-Reformation**

          Protestantism

Reformatories (May subdiv. geog.)   **365**

    UF   Penal institutions

          Reform of criminals

          Reform schools

    BT   **Children—Institutional care**

          Correctional institutions

          Prisons

          Punishment

    NT   **Probation**

    RT   **Juvenile delinquency**

Reformers (May subdiv. geog.)   **920**

> Use for materials about political, social, or religious reformers.

    NT   **Abolitionists**

          Suffragists

Refraction   535

    UF   Dioptrics

    BT   **Light**

          Optics

    RT   **Rainbow**

Refrigeration   621.5

    UF   Cooling appliances

          Freezing

          Refrigeration and refrigerating
          machinery

Refrigeration—*Continued*
Refrigerators
  BT **Frost**
  RT **Air conditioning**
      Cold storage
      Low temperatures
Refrigeration and refrigerating machinery
  USE **Refrigeration**
Refrigerators
  USE **Refrigeration**
Refugees (May subdiv. geog.) **305.9;**
    341.4; 362.87
  UF Displaced persons
  SA refugees of particular countries,
      geographic regions, or ethnic
      groups, e.g. **Vietnamese refu-**
      gees; **Arab refugees**; etc.,
      and names of wars with the
      subdivision *Refugees*, e.g.
      World War, 1939-1945—
      Refugees [to be added as
      needed]
  BT **Aliens**
      Homeless persons
      Immigration and emigration
  NT **Arab refugees**
      Political refugees
      Vietnamese refugees
  RT **Sanctuary movement**
Refugees, Arab
  USE **Arab refugees**
Refugees, Political
  USE **Political refugees**
Refuse and refuse disposal (May subdiv.
  geog.) **363.72; 628.4**
  UF Disposal of refuse
      Garbage
      Garbage disposal
      Incineration
      Littering
      Solid waste disposal
      Waste disposal
  SA types of refuse, e.g. **Industrial**
      waste; types of waste dispos-
      al, e.g. **Radioactive waste**
      disposal; **Sewage disposal**;
      etc.; and types of industries,
      plants, and facilities with the
      subdivision *Waste disposal*,
      e.g. **Chemical industry—**
      Waste disposal [to be added
      as needed]

  BT **Municipal engineering**
      Pollution control industry
      Public health
      Sanitary engineering
      Sanitation
  NT **Chemical industry—Waste dis-**
      posal
      Hazardous wastes
      Industrial waste
      Medical wastes
      Radioactive waste disposal
      Sewage disposal
  RT **Pollution**
      Recycling
      Salvage
      Street cleaning
      Waste products
Regattas
  USE **Boat racing**
Regency novels 808.3
    Use for individual works, collections, or
  materials about historical novels set during or
  around the period when the future George IV
  of England acted as Regent for George III
  (1811-1820).
  BT **Historical fiction**
Regeneration (Christianity) 234; 248.2
  UF Born again Christianity
      New birth (Theology)
      Regeneration (Theology)
  BT **Christianity—Doctrines**
      Salvation
  RT **Conversion**
Regeneration (Theology)
  USE **Regeneration (Christianity)**
Reggae music (May subdiv. geog.)
    781.646
  BT **Popular music**
Regimental histories
  USE names of wars with the subdivi-
      sion *Regimental histories,* e.g.
      World War, 1939-1945—
      Regimental histories [to be
      added as needed]
Regional development
  USE **Community development**
      Regional planning
Regional history
  USE **Local history**

Regional libraries (May subdiv. geog.)
027.4

Use for materials on public libraries serving several communities, counties, or other regions.

UF County libraries
      District libraries
      Libraries, Regional

BT **Public libraries**

Regional planning (May subdiv. geog.)
307.1; 711

UF County planning
      Metropolitan planning
      Regional development
      State planning

BT **Land use**
      Planning

NT **Coastal zone management**
      Rural development

RT **City planning**
      Landscape protection

Regionalism (May subdiv. geog.) **320.4; 330.9**

Use for materials on the political or economic power or interests of geographic areas within nations or beyond national boundaries.

UF Localism
      Provincialism
      Sectionalism

BT **Geography**
      Politics

RT **Nationalism**

Regionalism—United States **917.3; 973**

UF Sectionalism (United States)

Registers

USE **Registers of births, etc.**
     and subjects, ethnic groups, classes of persons, names of countries, cities, etc., and names of families and of corporate bodies, such as colleges and universities, with the subdivision *Registers,* for lists of persons or organizations without addresses or other identifying data, e.g. **United States—Registers; United States Military Academy—Registers;** etc. [to be added as needed]

Registers of births, etc. (May subdiv. geog.) **929**

UF Birth records
      Births, Registers of
      Burial statistics
      Deaths, Registers of
      Marriage registers
      Parish registers
      Records of births, etc.
      Registers
      Vital records

BT **Genealogy**

NT **Wills**

RT **Vital statistics**

Registration of voters

USE **Voter registration**

Regulatory agencies

USE **Administrative agencies**

Rehabilitation

USE classes of persons with the subdivision *Rehabilitation,* e.g. **Drug addicts—Rehabilitation; Physically handicapped—Rehabilitation;** etc. [to be added as needed]

Rehabilitation peer counseling

USE **Peer counseling**

Reign of Terror

USE **France—History—1789-1799, Revolution**

Reincarnation **129**

UF Rebirth

BT **Theosophy**

RT **Soul**

Reindeer (May subdiv. geog.) **599.65; 636.2**

BT **Deer**
      Domestic animals
      Mammals

Reinforced concrete **691**

BT **Building materials**
      Concrete

Relations among ethnic groups

USE **Ethnic relations**

Relations with Congress

USE names of presidents with the subdivision *Relations with Congress* [to be added as needed]

Relationships, Man-woman

USE **Man-woman relationship**

Relative humidity

USE **Humidity**

Relativity (Physics) 530.11
  BT Physics
  RT Gravitation
      Quantum theory
      Space and time
Relaxation
  USE Recreation
      Rest
Reliability (Engineering) 620
  UF Reliability of equipment
      Systems reliability
  BT Engineering
      Probabilities
      Systems engineering
  NT Quality control
      Structural failures
      Testing
Reliability of equipment
  USE Reliability (Engineering)
Relief, Public
  USE Public welfare
Religion 200
  SA names of peoples, ethnic groups, countries, states, etc., and individual persons with the subdivision *Religion*, e.g. **Native Americans—Religion; African Americans—Religion; United States—Religion; Shakespeare, William, 1564-1616—Religion**; etc.; religious subjects subdivided by religion or sect, e.g. **Laity—Catholic Church**; and other subjects with the subdivision *Religious aspects*, e.g. **Ethnic relations—Religious aspects; Love—Religious aspects**; etc., which may be further subdivided by religion or sect [to be added as needed]
  NT African Americans—Religion
      Agnosticism
      Ancestor worship
      Art and religion
      Atheism
      Blacks—Religion
      Communism and religion
      Deism
      Faith
      Heresy

      Monotheism
      Moon worship
      Native Americans—Religion
      Ohio—Religion
      Philosophy and religion
      Psychology of religion
      Rationalism
      Religion and politics
      Religion and science
      Religion and sociology
      Religion in literature
      Religious awakening
      Religious education
      Religious fundamentalism
      Religious institutions
      Religious life
      Santeria
      Sun worship
      Supernatural
      Theism
      United States—Religion
      Visions
      War—Religious aspects
      Worship
  RT God
      Mythology
      Religions
      Theology
Religion and art
  USE Art and religion
Religion and communism
  USE Communism and religion
Religion and education
  USE Church and education
Religion and literature
  USE Religion in literature
      Religious literature
Religion and medicine
  USE Medicine—Religious aspects
Religion and philosophy
  USE Philosophy and religion
Religion and politics (May subdiv. geog.)
      201; 261.7; 322
  UF Political science—Religious aspects
      Politics and religion
      Politics—Religious aspects
      Religion—Political aspects
      Religions—Political aspects
  BT Politics
      Religion

Religion and politics—*Continued*
  NT   **Christianity and politics**
Religion and psychology
  USE   **Psychology of religion**
Religion and science (May subdiv. geog.)
      215
  UF   Science and religion
        Science—Religious aspects
  BT   **Religion**
        Science
  NT   **Bible and science**
  RT   **Creationism**
        Evolution
        Natural theology
Religion and social problems
  USE   **Church and social problems**
Religion and society
  USE   **Religion and sociology**
Religion and sociology (May subdiv.
      geog.)   306.6
  Use for materials on religious sociology in
  general. Materials on the sociology of Chris-
  tian denominations and on social theory from
  a Christian point of view are entered under
  Christian sociology. Materials on the practi-
  cal treatment of social problems from the
  point of view of the church are entered under
  Church and social problems.
  UF   Religion and society
        Religion—Social aspects
        Religious sociology
        Society and religion
        Society—Religious aspects
        Sociology and religion
        Sociology of religion
  SA   sociology associated with partic-
          ular religions, e.g. **Christian
          sociology** [to be added as
          needed]
  BT   **Religion**
        Sociology
  NT   **Christian sociology**
Religion and state
  USE   **Church and state**
Religion and war
  USE   **War—Religious aspects**
Religion—Government policy
  USE   **Church and state**
Religion in literature   809
  UF   Religion and literature
  BT   **Literature**
        Religion
  RT   **Bible in literature**

Religion in the public schools (May
    subdiv. geog.)   379.2
  Use for materials on the teaching of religion in the public schools or on the religious
  freedom of students and school employees.
  Materials on the inclusion of prayers or a pe-
  riod for silent prayer or meditation in the daily schedule of public schools are entered under **Prayer in the public schools**.
  UF   Bible in the schools
        Fundamentalism and education
        Public schools and religion
  BT   **Church and education**
        Church and state
        Public schools
        Religious education
  NT   **Prayer in the public schools**
Religion—Philosophy   210
  Use for materials on the nature, origin, or
  validity of religion from a philosophical point
  of view. Materials on the reciprocal relation-
  ship and influence between philosophy and re-
  ligion are entered under **Philosophy and reli-
  gion**.
  UF   Philosophy of religion
  RT   **Philosophy and religion**
Religion—Political aspects
  USE   **Religion and politics**
Religion—Psychological aspects
  USE   **Psychology of religion**
Religion—Social aspects
  USE   **Religion and sociology**
Religion—Study and teaching
  USE   **Theology—Study and teaching**
Religions   200
  Use for materials on the major world reli-
  gions. Materials on independent religious
  groups whose teachings or practices fall with-
  in the normative bounds of the major world
  religions are entered under **Sects**. Materials on
  groups or movements whose beliefs or prac-
  tices differ significantly from the traditional
  religions, often focused upon a charismatic
  leader, are entered under **Cults**.
  UF   Comparative religion
  SA   names of religions and of sects
          within the major world reli-
          gions [to be added as needed]
  BT   **Civilization**
  NT   **Bahai Faith**
        Brahmanism
        Buddhism
        Christianity
        Christianity and other religions
        Confucianism
        Cults
        Druids and Druidism

Religions—*Continued*
  Gnosticism
  Hinduism
  Islam
  Jainism
  Judaism
  Neopaganism
  Occultism
  Paganism
  Sects
  Shamanism
  Shinto
  Taoism
  Theosophy
  Voodooism
  Zoroastrianism
  RT Gods and goddesses
      Religion
Religions—Biography
  USE Religious biography
Religions—Political aspects
  USE Religion and politics
Religious and ecclesiastical institutions
  USE Religious institutions
Religious art (May subdiv. geog.) 203;
      704.9
  UF Religious art and symbolism
      Religious painting
      Religious sculpture
      Sacred art
  BT Art
  NT Christian art
  RT Art and religion
Religious art and symbolism
  USE Religious art
Religious aspects
  USE subjects with the subdivision *Re-
      ligious aspects,* e.g. **Ethnic
      relations—Religious aspects;
      Love—Religious aspects;** etc.,
      which may be further subdi-
      vided by the names of reli-
      gions or sects [to be added as
      needed]
Religious awakening (May subdiv. geog.)
      204; 269
  Use for materials on a renewal of interest in
  religion.
  UF Awakening, Religious
      Revival (Religion)
  BT Religion

Religious belief
  USE Faith
Religious biography 200.92; 920
  UF Religions—Biography
  SA biography of particular religions,
      e.g. **Christian biography** [to
      be added as needed]
  BT Biography
  NT Christian biography
      Prophets
      Saints
Religious ceremonies
  USE Rites and ceremonies
Religious covenants
  USE Covenants
Religious cults
  USE Cults
Religious denominations
  USE Sects
Religious drama 792.1; 808.82
  Use for collections or materials about reli-
  gious drama, not for individual works.
  BT Drama
      Religious literature
  NT Bible plays
      Easter—Drama
      Jesus Christ—Drama
      Morality plays
      Mysteries and miracle plays
      Passion plays
Religious education (May subdiv. geog.)
      207
  Use for materials on the instruction of reli-
  gion in schools and private life. Materials lim-
  ited to the instruction of Christian religion in
  schools and private life are entered under
  Christian education. Materials on the relation
  of the church to education and on the history
  of the part that the church has taken in secular
  education are entered under **Church and education**. Materials on church supported and
  controlled elementary and secondary schools
  are entered under **Church schools**.
  UF Theological education
  BT Education
      Religion
  NT Christian education
      Religion in the public schools
      Sunday schools
  RT Moral education
      Theology—Study and teaching
Religious festivals
  USE Religious holidays

Religious fiction   808.3; 808.83

Use for individual works, collections, or materials about fiction that promotes religious teachings or exemplifies a religious way of life.

SA   fiction associated with particular religions, e.g. **Christian fiction** [to be added as needed]

BT   **Fiction**

NT   **Christian fiction**

Jewish religious fiction

Religious freedom

USE   **Freedom of religion**

Religious fundamentalism (May subdiv. geog.)   **200**

Use for religious groups opposed to modernity and secularism and seeking a revival of orthodox or conservative beliefs and practices.

UF   Fundamentalism

Fundamentalist movements

SA   fundamentalism of various religions, e.g. **Islamic fundamentalism** [to be added as needed]

BT   **Religion**

NT   **Christian fundamentalism**

Islamic fundamentalism

Religious graphic novels   741.5

Use for individual works, collections, or materials about religious graphic novels.

BT   **Graphic novels**

Religious history

USE   **Church history**

Religious holidays (May subdiv. geog.)   **263; 394.265**

Use for materials on religious holidays in general. Materials on secular holidays are entered under **Holidays**. Materials on secular festivals other than holidays are entered under **Festivals**.

UF   Church festivals

Ecclesiastical fasts and feasts

Fasts and feasts

Feast days

Holy days

Religious festivals

SA   holidays of particular religions, e.g. **Jewish holidays**; and names of specific religious holidays and observances, e.g. **Christmas**; **Lent**; etc. [to be added as needed]

BT   **Holidays**

Rites and ceremonies

NT   **Christian holidays**

Church year

Islamic holidays

Jewish holidays

RT   **Fasting**

Festivals

Religious institutions (May subdiv. geog.)   **206; 260**

UF   Churches

Congregations

Ecclesiastical institutions

Institutions, Ecclesiastical

Institutions, Religious

Religious and ecclesiastical institutions

Religious organizations

BT   **Associations**

Religion

NT   **Mosques**

Synagogues

Temples

Religious liberty

USE   **Freedom of religion**

Religious life   204; 248.4

Use for materials that describe or promote personal or community religious and devotional life.

SA   groups and classes of persons with the subdivision *Religious life* [to be added as needed]

BT   **Religion**

NT   **Asceticism**

Celibacy

Christian life

Family—Religious life

Spiritual life

Teenagers—Religious life

Women—Religious life

Youth—Religious life

RT   **Monasticism and religious orders**

Religious life (Christian)

USE   **Christian life**

Religious literature   800

UF   Religion and literature

SA   literatures of particular religions or denominations, e.g. **Catholic literature** [to be added as needed]

BT   **Literature**

NT   **Christian literature**

Devotional literature

Religious literature—*Continued*
>> Islamic literature
>> Jewish literature
>> Religious drama
>> Religious poetry
>> Sacred books
> RT Bible as literature

Religious music
> USE Church music

Religious orders
> USE Monasticism and religious orders

Religious orders for men
> USE Monasticism and religious orders for men

Religious orders for women
> USE Monasticism and religious orders for women

Religious organizations
> USE Religious institutions

Religious painting
> USE Religious art

Religious pamphlets
> USE Tracts

Religious persecution
> USE Persecution

Religious poetry   808.1; 808.81
> Use for collections or materials about religious poetry, not for individual works.

> BT Poetry
>> Religious literature
> RT Hymns

Religious psychology
> USE Pastoral psychology
>> Psychology of religion

Religious sculpture
> USE Religious art

Religious sociology
> USE Religion and sociology

Religious summer schools (May subdiv. geog.)   **207; 268**
> UF Bible classes
>> Vacation church schools
>> Vacation schools, Religious
> BT Schools
>> Summer schools

Religious tolerance (May subdiv. geog.)   **261.7**
> Use for general materials on religous tolerance. Materials on a particular religion's or denomination's position on religious tolerance are entered under this heading subdivided by the name of the religion or denomination.

> BT Toleration

Relocation
> USE ethnic groups and classes of persons with the subdivision *Relocation,* e.g. **Native Americans—Relocation;** which may be further subdivided geographically [to be added as needed]

Relocation of Japanese Americans, 1942-1945
> USE Japanese Americans—Evacuation and relocation, 1942-1945

Remarriage (May subdiv. geog.)   **306.84**
> BT Marriage

Remedial reading
> USE Reading—Remedial teaching

Remedial teaching
> USE school subjects with the subdivision *Remedial teaching,* e.g. **Reading—Remedial teaching** [to be added as needed]

Remodeling
> USE types of buildings and parts of buildings with the subdivision *Remodeling,* e.g. **Houses—Remodeling; Kitchens—Remodeling;** etc. [to be added as needed]

Remodeling (Architecture)
> USE Houses—Remodeling

Remodeling of houses
> USE Houses—Remodeling

Remodeling of kitchens
> USE Kitchens—Remodeling

Remote sensing (May subdiv. geog.)   **621.36**
> UF Sensing, Remote
>> Terrain sensing, Remote
> BT Aerial photography
> NT Aerial reconnaissance
>> Electronic surveillance
>> Radar
> RT Space optics

Removal of Indians
> USE Native Americans—Relocation

Renaissance (May subdiv. geog.)   **940.2**
> Use for materials on cultural and intellectual developments in the fifteenth and sixteenth centuries not limited to a single country or region.

Renaissance—*Continued*
  BT **Civilization**
  RT **Humanism**
Renaissance architecture
  USE **Architecture—15th and 16th centuries**
Renaissance art
  USE **Art—15th and 16th centuries**
Renaissance decoration and ornament
  USE **Decoration and ornament—15th and 16th centuries**
Renaissance English literature
  USE **English literature—16th and 17th centuries**
Renaissance painting
  USE **Painting—15th and 16th centuries**
Rendezvous in space
  USE **Orbital rendezvous (Space flight)**
Renewable energy resources (May subdiv. geog.) **333.79**
  UF Alternate energy resources
      Alternative energy resources
  SA types of renewable resources [to be added as needed]
  BT **Energy resources**
  NT **Geothermal resources**
      Solar energy
      Water power
      Wind power
Renown
  USE **Fame**
Rental services
  USE **Lease and rental services**
Reorganization of administrative agencies
  USE **Administrative agencies—Reorganization**
Repairing 620
  UF Fixing
      Maintenance and repair
      Mending
      Repairs
  SA types of things that require maintenance with the subdivision *Maintenance and repair*, e.g. **Automobiles—Maintenance and repair; Buildings—Maintenance and repair**; etc.; and types of things that require no maintenance

with the subdivision *Repairing*, e.g. **Radio—Repairing** [to be added as needed]
Repairs
  USE **Repairing**
Reparations
  USE names of wars with the subdivision *Reparations,* e.g. **World War, 1939-1945—Reparations** [to be added as needed]
Reparations for historical injustices 305.8; 341.6
  UF Restitution for historical injustices
Repentance 234
  UF Contrition
      Penitence
  RT **Penance**
Report writing 808
  UF Reports—Preparation
      Research paper writing
      Term paper writing
  BT **Authorship**
  NT **School reports**
Reporters and reporting (May subdiv. geog.) **070.4**
  UF Newspaper work
  BT **Journalism**
      Newspapers
  NT **Interviewing (Journalism)**
Reports—Preparation
  USE **Report writing**
Reports, Teachers'
  USE **School reports**
Representation
  USE **Representative government and representation**
Representation, Proportional
  USE **Proportional representation**
Representative government and representation (May subdiv. geog.) **321.8**
  UF Parliamentary government
      Representation
      Self-government
  BT **Constitutional history**
      Constitutional law
      Political science
  NT **Apportionment (Election law)**
      Legislative bodies
      Proportional representation
      Recall (Political science)

Representative government and representation—*Continued*
    RT **Democracy**
        Elections
        Republics
        Suffrage
Representatives, House of (U.S.)
    USE **United States. Congress. House**
Repressed memory
    USE **Recovered memory**
Reprint editions
    USE **Reprints (Publications)**
Reprints (Publications) **016**
    UF Bibliography—Reprint editions
        Reprint editions
    BT **Books**
        Editions
Reproduction **573.6; 612.6**
    BT **Biology**
        Life (Biology)
        Physiology
    NT **Animal reproduction**
        Artificial insemination
        Breeding
        Cells
        Fertility
        Fertilization in vitro
        Fetus
        Genetics
        Human artificial insemination
        Infertility
        Menstruation
        Pregnancy
    RT **Embryology**
        Reproductive system
        Sex (Biology)
Reproduction processes
    USE **Copying processes**
Reproduction—Technological innovations
    USE **Reproductive technology**
Reproductive behavior
    USE **Sexual behavior in animals**
Reproductive organs
    USE **Reproductive system**
Reproductive system **573.6; 611; 612.6**
    UF Generative organs
        Genitalia
        Reproductive organs
        Sex organs
    BT **Anatomy**
        Physiology
        Sex (Biology)

    RT **Reproduction**
Reproductive technology (May subdiv. geog.) **612.6**
    UF Assisted reproduction
        Reproduction—Technological innovations
    BT **Biotechnology**
Reprographic art
    USE **Copy art**
Reprography
    USE **Copying processes**
Reptiles (May subdiv. geog.) **597.9**
    SA types of reptiles [to be added as needed]
    BT **Animals**
    NT **Alligators**
        Crocodiles
        Fossil reptiles
        Lizards
        Snakes
        Turtles
Reptiles, Fossil
    USE **Fossil reptiles**
Reptiles—Physiology **597.9**
    BT **Physiology**
Republic of China, 1949-
    USE **Taiwan**
Republic of South Africa
    USE **South Africa**
Republic of the Congo
    USE **Congo (Republic)**
Republican Party (U.S.) **324.2734**
    BT **Political parties**
Republics **321.8**
    UF Commonwealth, The
    BT **Constitutional history**
        Constitutional law
        Political science
    NT **Federal government**
    RT **Democracy**
        Representative government and representation
Rescue of Jews, 1939-1945
    USE **World War, 1939-1945—Jews—Rescue**
Rescue operations, Space
    USE **Space rescue operations**
Rescue work (May subdiv. geog.) **363.3**
    UF Search and rescue operations
    BT **Civil defense**

Rescue work—*Continued*
  NT **First aid**
      Lifesaving
      Space rescue operations
  RT **Survival after airplane accidents, shipwrecks, etc.**
Research (May subdiv. geog.) **001.4**
  UF Research and development
  SA subjects with the subdivision *Research* [to be added as needed]
  NT **Agriculture—Research**
      Animal experimentation
      Discoveries in science
      Dissertations
      Industrial research
      Intelligence service
      Medicine—Research
      Military research
      Oceanography—Research
      Operations research
      Parapsychology
      Surveys
  RT **Information services**
      Learning and scholarship
Research and development
  USE **Research**
Research buildings
  USE **Laboratories**
Research paper writing
  USE **Report writing**
Reservations
  USE names of native peoples, tribes, etc., with the subdivision *Reservations,* e.g. **Native Americans—Reservations** [to be added as needed]
Reservoirs (May subdiv. geog.) **627; 628.1**
  BT **Hydraulic structures**
Resettlement
  USE **Land settlement**
Residences
  USE **Domestic architecture**
      Houses
Residential developments
  USE **Planned communities**
Residential security
  USE **Burglary protection**
Residential treatment centers
  USE **Group homes**

Resignation
  USE classes of persons and names of individual persons with the subdivision *Resignation,* e.g. **Presidents—United States—Resignation** [to be added as needed]
Resins
  USE **Gums and resins**
Resistance of materials
  USE **Strength of materials**
Resistance to drugs in microorganisms
  USE **Drug resistance in microorganisms**
Resistance to government (May subdiv. geog.) **322.4**
  UF Government, Resistance to
  BT **Political ethics**
      Political science
  NT **Civil disobedience**
      Hunger strikes
      Passive resistance
  RT **Insurgency**
      Revolutions
Resistance welding
  USE **Electric welding**
Resorts (May subdiv. geog.) **790**
  BT **Recreation**
  NT **Health resorts**
      Summer resorts
      Winter resorts
Resource management
  USE **Conservation of natural resources**
Resources, Marine
  USE **Marine resources**
Respiration **573.2; 612.2**
  UF Breathing
  BT **Physiology**
  RT **Respiratory system**
Respiration, Artificial
  USE **Artificial respiration**
Respiratory organs
  USE **Respiratory system**
Respiratory system **573.2; 611; 612.2**
  UF Respiratory organs
  BT **Anatomy**
      Physiology
  NT **Lungs**
  RT **Respiration**

Respite care
USE **Home care services**
Responsibility **170**
UF Accountability
Obligation
BT **Ethics**
Responsibility, Legal
USE **Liability (Law)**
Rest **613.7**
UF Relaxation
BT **Health**
Hygiene
NT **Sleep**
RT **Fatigue**
Restaurants (May subdiv. geog.) **647.95**
UF Cafes
Coffee shops
Lunchrooms
Restaurants, bars, etc.
SA types of restaurants [to be added
as needed]
BT **Food service**
NT **Coffeehouses**
Fast food restaurants
Tearooms
RT **Bars**
Restaurants, bars, etc.
USE **Bars**
Restaurants
Restitution for historical injustices
USE **Reparations for historical in-
justices**
Restoration of automobiles
USE **Automobiles—Conservation
and restoration**
Restoration of buildings
USE **Architecture—Conservation
and restoration**
Restoration of furniture
USE **Furniture finishing**
Furniture—Repairing
Restoration of photographs
USE **Photographs—Conservation
and restoration**
Restoration of works of art
USE subjects with the subdivision
Conservation and restoration,
e.g. **Painting—Conservation
and restoration** [to be added
as needed]

Restraint of trade (May subdiv. geog.)
338.6
UF Restrictive trade practices
Trade, Restraint of
BT **Commerce**
Commercial law
RT **Boycotts**
Corporation law
Industrial trusts
Monopolies
Unfair competition
Restrictive trade practices
USE **Restraint of trade**
Résumés (Employment) **650.14**
UF Job résumés
BT **Applications for positions**
Job hunting
Resurrection
USE **Future life**
Resurrection of Jesus Christ
USE **Jesus Christ—Resurrection**
Resuscitation, Heart
USE **Cardiac resuscitation**
Resuscitation, Pulmonary
USE **Artificial respiration**
Retail franchises
USE **Franchises (Retail trade)**
Retail stores
USE **Stores**
Retail trade (May subdiv. geog.) **381;
658.8**
UF Merchandising
BT **Commerce**
NT **Advertising**
Chain stores
Department stores
Direct selling
Discount stores
Drugstores
Franchises (Retail trade)
General stores
Inventory control
Packaging
Sales personnel
Selling
Shopping centers and malls
Stores
Supermarkets
Retarded children
USE **Mentally handicapped children**

Retention, Grade
  USE **Promotion (School)**
Retired people
  USE **Retirees**
Retired persons
  USE **Retirees**
Retirees (May subdiv. geog.)   **155.67;
    305.9**
  UF   Retired people
       Retired persons
  RT   **Elderly
       Retirement**
Retirees—Personal finance   332.024
Retirement (May subdiv. geog.)   **305.26;
    306.3**
  BT   **Leisure
       Old age**
  NT   **Retirement income**
  RT   **Elderly—Life skills guides
       Retirees**
Retirement communities (May subdiv.
    geog.)   **307.7; 363.5**
  UF   Places of retirement
  BT   **Elderly—Housing**
  NT   **Life care communities**
Retirement income (May subdiv. geog.)
    331.25; 353.5
  BT   **Income
       Retirement**
  NT   **Annuities
       Individual retirement accounts
       Old age pensions
       Pensions**
Retouching (Photography)
  USE **Photography—Retouching**
Retraining, Occupational
  USE **Occupational retraining**
Retreats   269
    Use for materials on periods of withdrawal
    from daily routine for the purpose of prayer,
    meditation, and study.
  BT   **Spiritual life**
Retrenchment of organizations
  USE **Downsizing of organizations**
Retrieval of information
  USE **Information retrieval**
Return migration (May subdiv. geog.)
    304.8
    Use for materials on the return of emigrants
    to their country of origin.
  BT   **Immigration and emigration**

Reunions, Family
  USE **Family reunions**
Revelation   202; 231.7
  BT   **God
       Supernatural
       Theology**
Revenge
  UF   Vengence
  RT   **Vendetta**
Revenue
  USE **Tariff
       Taxation**
Revenue sharing (May subdiv. geog.)
    336.1
    Use for materials on the practice of return-
    ing a percentage of federal tax money to state
    and local governments for locally directed and
    controlled public service programs.
  UF   Federal revenue sharing
       Tax sharing
  BT   **Intergovernmental tax relations**
Reviewing (Books)
  USE **Book reviewing**
Reviews
  USE   topics and types of books with
        the subdivision *Reviews,* e.g.
        **Motion picture—Reviews;
        Reference books—Reviews;**
        etc.; and topics, types of liter-
        ature, ethnic groups, classes
        of persons, and names of
        places with the subdivision
        Book reviews; e.g. **Sociolo-
        gy—Book reviews; Chil-
        dren's literature—Book re-
        views;** etc., for collections of
        reviews [to be added as need-
        ed]
Revival (Religion)
  USE **Evangelistic work
       Religious awakening
       Revivals**
Revivals (May subdiv. geog.)   **204; 269**
  UF   Revival (Religion)
  BT   **Evangelistic work**
Revivals—Music
  USE **Gospel music**
Revolution, American
  USE **United States—History—1775-
       1783, Revolution**

Revolution, French
  USE **France—History—1789-1799, Revolution**
Revolutions (May subdiv. geog.)   **303.6**
  UF   Coups d'état
       Rebellions
       Sedition
  SA   names of countries with the appropriate subdivision under *History*, e.g. **France—History—1789-1799, Revolution** [to be added as needed]
  BT   **Political science**
  NT   **France—History—1789-1799, Revolution**
       Hungary—History—1956, Revolution
       Insurgency
       National liberation movements
       Radicalism
       Slave revolts
       Soviet Union—History—1917-1921, Revolution
       United States—History—1775-1783, Revolution
  RT   **Resistance to government**
Revolvers
  USE   **Handguns**
Rewards (Prizes, etc.)
  USE   **Awards**
Rh factor
  USE   **Blood groups**
Rhetoric   808
  UF   Composition (Rhetoric)
       English language—Rhetoric
       Persuasion (Rhetoric)
       Speaking
  SA   names of languages with the subdivision *Composition and exercises*, e.g. **English language—Composition and exercises** [to be added as needed]
  BT   **Language and languages**
  NT   **Criticism**
       Debates and debating
       Figures of speech
       Lectures and lecturing
       Letter writing
       Preaching
       Punctuation

Satire
  RT   **English language—Composition and exercises**
       Literary style
Rheumatism   616.7
  BT   **Diseases**
  NT   **Gout**
Rhyme   808.1
  SA   names of languages with the subdivision *Rhyme* [to be added as needed]
  BT   **Poetics**
       Versification
  NT   **English language—Rhyme**
       Stories in rhyme
Rhymes
  USE   **Limericks**
        Nonsense verses
        Nursery rhymes
        Poetry—Collections
Rhythm   808.1
  BT   **Aesthetics**
       Poetics
  NT   **Musical meter and rhythm**
       Versification
  RT   **Cycles**
Ribonucleic acid
  USE   **RNA**
Ribose nucleic acid
  USE   **RNA**
Ribozymes
  USE   **Catalytic RNA**
Rich (May subdiv. geog.)   **305.5; 920**
  UF   Affluent people
       High income people
       Rich people
       Rich persons
       Wealthy people
  BT   **Social classes**
  NT   **Millionaires**
Rich people
  USE   **Rich**
Rich persons
  USE   **Rich**
Riches
  USE   **Wealth**
Riddles   398.6; 793.735; 808.88
  Use for collections of riddles considered as folklore, as games, or as literary exercises, by one or several authors, and for materials about riddles.

Riddles—*Continued*
   UF   Conundrums
          Enigmas
   BT   **Amusements**
          Literary recreations
   NT   **Charades**
          Rebuses
   RT   **Puzzles**
Ride sharing
   USE   **Car pools**
Riding
   USE   **Horsemanship**
Rifles   683.4
   UF   Carbines
          Guns
   BT   **Firearms**
Right and left
   USE   **Left and right (Direction)**
           Right and left (Political science)
Right- and left-handedness
   USE   **Left- and right-handedness**
Right and left (Political science)   320.5
    Use for general materials on political views or attitudes, i.e. conservative, traditional, liberal, radical, etc. Materials on the physical characteristics of favoring one hand or the other are entered under **Left- and right-handedness**. Materials on left and right as indications of location or direction are entered under **Left and right (Direction)**.
   UF   Left and right
          Left (Political science)
          Right and left
          Right (Political science)
   BT   **Political parties**
          Political science
   NT   **Radicalism**
   RT   **Conservatism**
          Liberalism
Right of assembly
   USE   **Freedom of assembly**
Right of association
   USE   **Freedom of association**
Right of asylum
   USE   **Asylum**
Right of privacy (May subdiv. geog.)   **323.44**
   UF   Invasion of privacy
          Privacy, Right of
   BT   **Civil rights**
   NT   **Eavesdropping**
          Trade secrets
          Wiretapping

Right of property   323.4
   UF   Private property, Right of
          Property, Right of
          Property rights
   BT   **Civil rights**
          Property
Right (Political science)
   USE   **Conservatism**
          Right and left (Political science)
Right to a fair trial
   USE   **Fair trial**
Right to bear arms
   USE   **Gun control**
Right to choose movement
   USE   **Pro-choice movement**
Right to die (May subdiv. geog.)   **179.7**
   BT   **Death**
          Medical ethics
          Medicine—Law and legislation
   RT   **Euthanasia**
          Living wills
          Suicide
Right to health care   362.1
   UF   Health care, Right to
          Medical care, Right to
          Right to medical care
   BT   **Human rights**
Right to know
   USE   **Freedom of information**
Right-to-life movement (Anti-abortion movement)
   USE   **Pro-life movement**
Right to medical care
   USE   **Right to health care**
Right to work
   USE   **Open and closed shop**
Righteous Gentiles in the Holocaust (May subdiv. geog.)   **940.53**
   BT   **Holocaust, 1933-1945**
          World War, 1939-1945—Jews—Rescue
Rights, Human
   USE   **Human rights**
Rights of animals
   USE   **Animal rights**
Rights of employees
   USE   **Employee rights**
Rights of gays
   USE   **Gay rights**

Rights of lesbians
USE **Gay rights**
Rights of man
USE **Human rights**
Rights of women
USE **Women's rights**
Rights, Proprietary
USE **Intellectual property**
Riot control (May subdiv. geog.) **303.6**
UF Riots—Control
BT **Crowds**
Riots
Riots (May subdiv. geog.) **303.6**
UF Civil disorders
Mobs
SA names of institutions with the
subdivision *Riots*; and names
of specific riots [to be added
as needed]
BT **Crime**
Freedom of assembly
Offenses against public safety
NT **Riot control**
RT **Crowds**
Demonstrations
Riots—Control
USE **Riot control**
Ripoffs
USE **Fraud**
Risk 338.5; 368
BT **Economics**
RT **Probabilities**
Profit
Rites and ceremonies (May subdiv. geog.)
390
UF Ceremonies
Ecclesiastical rites and ceremo-
nies
Religious ceremonies
Ritual
Traditions
SA classes of persons and ethnic
groups with the subdivision
Rites and ceremonies, e.g.
**Native Americans—Rites
and ceremonies**; and names
of individual religions and de-
nominations with the subdivi-
sion *Liturgy* or *Customs and
practices*, e.g. **Catholic
Church—Liturgy; Judaism—**

Customs and practices; etc.
[to be added as needed]
NT **Canonization**
Catholic Church—Liturgy
Funeral rites and ceremonies
Initiation rites
**Judaism—Customs and prac-
tices**
Liturgies
Marriage customs and rites
**Native Americans—Rites and
ceremonies**
Ordination
Religious holidays
Sacraments
Secret societies
RT **Manners and customs**
Ritual
USE **Liturgies**
Rites and ceremonies
River animals
USE **Stream animals**
River pollution
USE **Water pollution**
Rivers (May subdiv. geog.) **551.48**
SA names of rivers [to be added as
needed]
BT **Physical geography**
Water
Waterways
NT **Stream animals**
Water power
RT **Floods**
Hydraulic engineering
Inland navigation
RNA 572.8
UF Ribonucleic acid
Ribose nucleic acid
BT **Nucleic acids**
NT **Catalytic RNA**
Roaches (Insects)
USE **Cockroaches**
Road construction
USE **Roads**
Road engineering
USE **Highway engineering**
Road machinery 625.7
BT **Construction equipment**
Road maps 912
UF Roads—Maps

Road maps—*Continued*
    SA names of countries, areas, states,
            cities, etc., with the subdivi-
            sion *Maps* [to be added as
            needed]
    BT **Maps**
    RT **Automobile travel—Guidebooks**
Road safety
    USE **Traffic safety**
Road signs
    USE **Signs and signboards**
Roads (May subdiv. geog.) **388.1; 625.7**
    UF Construction of roads
            Highway construction
            Highways
            Road construction
            Thoroughfares
    BT **Civil engineering**
            Transportation
    NT **Alaska Highway (Alaska and**
            Canada)
            Express highways
            Roadside improvement
            Scenic byways
            Street cleaning
            Trails
    RT **Highway engineering**
            Pavements
            Soil mechanics
            Streets
Roads—Maps
    USE **Road maps**
Roadside improvement (May subdiv.
        geog.) **713**
    UF Highway beautification
    BT **Grounds maintenance**
            Landscape architecture
            Roads
Robbers
    USE **Thieves**
Robins **598.8**
    BT **Birds**
Robinsonades **808.3; 808.83**
    Use for individual works, collections, or
    materials about fictional works describing a
    character's survival without the aid of civiliza-
    tion, as on a desert island.
    BT **Adventure fiction**
            Imaginary voyages
Robot manga
    USE **Mecha**

Robotics
    USE **Robots**
Robots **629.8**
    Use for general materials on robots and
    robotics. Materials limited to robots in indus-
    try are entered under **Industrial robots**.
    UF Automata
            Automatons
            Robotics
    BT **Machinery**
            Mechanical movements
    NT **Industrial robots**
Robots, Industrial
    USE **Industrial robots**
Rock and roll music
    USE **Rock music**
Rock climbing
    USE **Mountaineering**
Rock crystal
    USE **Quartz**
Rock drawings
    USE **Rock drawings, paintings, and**
            engravings
Rock drawings, paintings, and engrav-
        ings (May subdiv. geog.) **759.01**
    UF Petroglyphs
            Rock drawings
            Rock engravings
            Rock paintings
    BT **Archeology**
            Prehistoric art
    NT **Cave drawings and paintings**
Rock engravings
    USE **Rock drawings, paintings, and**
            engravings
Rock gardens (May subdiv. geog.)
        635.9
    BT **Gardens**
Rock music (May subdiv. geog.) **781.66;**
        782.42166
    UF Rock and roll music
    BT **Music**
            Popular music
Rock paintings
    USE **Rock drawings, paintings, and**
            engravings
Rock tombs
    USE **Tombs**
Rocket airplanes
    USE **Rocket planes**
Rocket flight
    USE **Space flight**

Rocket planes   629.133
> UF   Airplanes, Rocket propelled
>   Rocket airplanes
> SA   names of rocket planes, e.g.
>   **X-15 (Rocket aircraft)** [to be
>   added as needed]
> BT   **High speed aeronautics**
>   **Space vehicles**
> NT   **X-15 (Rocket aircraft)**

Rocketry   621.43
> BT   **Aeronautics**
>   **Astronautics**
> NT   **Guided missiles**
>   **Rockets (Aeronautics)**
>   **Space vehicles**

Rockets (Aeronautics)   629.133
> UF   Aerial rockets
> SA   types of rockets and missiles
>   and names of specific rockets
>   and missiles [to be added as
>   needed]
> BT   **Aeronautics**
>   **High speed aeronautics**
>   **Projectiles**
>   **Rocketry**
> NT   **Artificial satellites—Launching**
>   **Ballistic missiles**
>   **Guided missiles**
> RT   **Interplanetary voyages**
>   **Jet propulsion**

Rocks (May subdiv. geog.)   **552**
> Use for general materials on naturally oc-
> curring solid minerals. Materials on stone as
> a building material are entered under **Stone.**
> SA   varieties of rock, e.g. **Granite**
>   [to be added as needed]
> NT   **Granite**
>   **Marble**
> RT   **Geology**
>   **Petrology**
>   **Stone**

Rocky Mountains   978
> BT   **Mountains**

Rodeos (May subdiv. geog.)   **791.8**
> BT   **Sports**
> RT   **Cowhands**
>   **Horsemanship**

Roentgen rays
> USE   **X-rays**

Rogues and vagabonds—Fiction
> USE   **Picaresque literature**

Roland (Legendary character)   398.22

> UF   Orlando (Legendary character)
> BT   **Folklore**

**Roland (Legendary character)—Ro-
mances   821**

Role conflict   302.5
> Use for materials on the conflict within one
> person who is being called upon to fulfill two
> or more competing roles.
> BT   **Social conflict**
>   **Social role**

Role playing   302
> BT   **Social role**
> NT   **Fantasy games**

Role playing games
> USE   **Fantasy games**

Role, Social
> USE   **Social role**

Roller coasters (May subdiv. geog.)
>   **791.06**
> BT   **Amusements**

Roller skating   796.2
> UF   Skating
> BT   **Outdoor recreation**
> NT   **In-line skating**
>   **Skateboarding**

Rollerblading
> USE   **In-line skating**

Romaic language
> USE   **Modern Greek language**

Romaic literature
> USE   **Modern Greek literature**

Roman antiquities
> USE   **Classical antiquities**
>   **Rome—Antiquities**
>   **Rome (Italy)—Antiquities**

Roman architecture (May subdiv. geog.)
>   **722**
> UF   Architecture, Roman
> BT   **Ancient architecture**
>   **Architecture**

Roman art (May subdiv. geog.)   **709.37**
> UF   Art, Roman
>   Classical art
> BT   **Ancient art**
>   **Art**
>   **Classical antiquities**

Roman Catholic Church
> USE   **Catholic Church**

Roman civilization
> USE   **Rome—Civilization**

Roman emperors
> USE   **Emperors—Rome**

Roman Empire
USE **Rome**
Roman literature
USE **Latin literature**
Roman mythology   **292.1**
UF   Mythology, Roman
BT   **Classical mythology**
Roman numerals   **513**
BT   **Numerals**
Roman philosophy
USE   **Ancient philosophy**
Romance graphic novels   **741.5**
Use for individual works, collections, or materials about romance graphic novels.
BT   **Graphic novels**
Romance languages   **440**
UF   Neo-Latin languages
SA   names of languages belonging to the Romance group, e.g.
French language [to be added as needed]
BT   **Language and languages**
NT   **French language**
Spanish language
RT   **Latin language**
Romance literature   **840**
SA   names of literatures belonging to the Romance group, e.g.
French literature [to be added as needed]
BT   **Literature**
NT   **French literature**
Portuguese literature
Spanish literature
Romance novels
USE   **Love stories**
Romances   **808.8**
Use for individual works, collections, or materials about medieval tales dealing with the age of chivalry or the supernatural. They may be either in verse or in prose and may or may not have a basis in fact. Contemporary romance novels are entered under **Love stories** or **Romantic suspense novels**.
UF   Chivalry—Romances
Metrical romances
Stories
SA   names of historic persons and legendary characters with the subdivision *Romances*, e.g.
Roland (Legendary character)—Romances [to be added as needed]

BT   **Fiction**
Literature
NT   **Arthurian romances**
RT   **Chivalry**
Epic poetry
Fables
Legends
Romances (Love stories)
USE   **Love stories**
Romanesque architecture (May subdiv. geog.)   **723**
UF   Architecture, Romanesque
BT   **Architecture**
Medieval architecture
Romanesque art (May subdiv. geog.)   **709.02**
UF   Art, Romanesque
BT   **Medieval art**
NT   **Romanesque painting**
Romanesque painting (May subdiv. geog.)   **759.02**
UF   Painting, Romanesque
BT   **Romanesque art**
Romanies
USE   **Gypsies**
Romans à clef   **808.3**
Use for individual works, collections, or materials about novels in which fictional characters and events can be readily identified with real persons and events.
UF   Livres à clef
BT   **Fiction**
Romantic crushes
USE   **Crushes**
Romantic fiction
USE   **Love stories**
Romantic stories
USE   **Love stories**
Romantic suspense novels   **808.3**
Use for individual works, collections, or materials about modern romantic suspense novels. Medieval tales are entered under **Romances**.
UF   Suspense novels
BT   **Adventure fiction**
RT   **Gothic novels**
Love stories
Mystery fiction
Spy stories
Romanticism (May subdiv. geog.)   **141; 709.03; 809**
BT   **Aesthetics**
Romanticism in art   **709.03**

Romanticism in art—*Continued*

    BT   **Art**

Rome   937

    Use for materials about the city of Rome in antiquity or about the Roman Empire. Materials on the modern city of Rome are entered under **Rome (Italy)**. Materials on the ruins and remains of ancient Rome, the city and its environs, are entered under **Rome (Italy)—Antiquities**. Materials on Roman antiquities in several countries are entered under **Rome—Antiquities**. Materials on Roman antiquities limited to one modern country, city, etc., are entered under the place with the subdivision *Antiquities*.

    UF   Roman Empire

Rome—Antiquities   937

    Use for materials on Roman antiquities in several countries. Materials on Roman antiquities limited to one modern country, city, etc., are entered under the place with the subdivision *Antiquities*. Materials on the ruins and remains of ancient Rome, the city and its environs, are entered under **Rome (Italy)—Antiquities**.

    UF   Roman antiquities

    BT   **Classical antiquities**

Rome—Biography   920.037

    UF   Classical biography

    BT   **Biography**

Rome—Civilization   937

    Use for materials on the civilization of ancient Rome. Materials on both ancient Greek and Roman civilizations are entered under **Classical civilization**.

    UF   Roman civilization

    BT   **Classical civilization**

Rome—Description

    USE   **Rome—Description and travel**

Rome—Description and travel   913.7; 937

    Use for descriptive materials on the Roman Empire including accounts by travelers of ancient times.

    UF   Rome—Description

Rome—Geography   913.7

    Use for geographic materials on ancient Rome.

    UF   Classical geography

    BT   **Ancient geography**

          Historical geography

Rome—History   937

Rome (Italy)   945

    Use for materials on the modern city of Rome. Materials about the city of Rome in antiquity or about the Roman Empire are entered under **Rome**.

Rome (Italy)—Antiquities   937

    Use for materials on the ruins and remains of ancient Rome, the city and its environs.

Materials on Roman antiquities in several countries are entered under **Rome—Antiquities**. Materials on Roman antiquities limited to one modern country, city, etc., are entered under the place with the subdivision *Antiquities*.

    UF   Roman antiquities

    BT   **Classical antiquities**

Rome (Italy)—Description and travel   914.5

Rome (Italy)—History   945

Roofs   690; 695; 721

    BT   **Architecture—Details**

          Buildings

Rookwood pottery   738

    BT   **Art pottery**

Rooming houses

    USE   **Hotels and motels**

Roommates   643

    RT   **Shared housing**

Rooms   643; 645

    SA   types of rooms [to be added as needed]

    BT   **Buildings**

          Houses

    NT   **Bathrooms**

          Garden rooms

          Kitchens

    RT   **Interior design**

Root crops   633; 635

    BT   **Vegetables**

    RT   **Feeds**

Rope   677

    NT   **Cables**

          Knots and splices

    RT   **Hemp**

Roses (May subdiv. geog.)   583; 635.9

    BT   **Flowers**

Rosetta stone   493

    BT   **Hieroglyphics**

Rosin

    USE   **Gums and resins**

Rotation of crops

    USE   **Crop rotation**

Roughage

    USE   **Food—Fiber content**

Round stage

    USE   **Arena theater**

Routes of trade

    USE   **Trade routes**

Rowing   797.12

    UF   Crew (Rowing)

          Sculling

Rowing—*Continued*
- BT **Athletics**
  Boats and boating
  Exercise
  Sports
  Water sports

Royal houses
- USE **Kings and rulers**
  Monarchy

Royalty
- USE **Kings and rulers**
  Monarchy
  Princes
  Princesses
  Queens

Rubber   678
- BT **Forest products**

Rubber, Artificial
- USE **Synthetic rubber**

Rubber, Synthetic
- USE **Synthetic rubber**

Rubber tires
- USE **Tires**

Rudeness
- USE **Bad behavior**

Rug cleaning
- USE **Rugs and carpets—Cleaning**

Rugs
- USE **Rugs and carpets**

Rugs and carpets (May subdiv. geog.)
  645; 677; 746.7
- UF Carpets
  Rugs
- BT **Decorative arts**
  Interior design
- NT **Hooked rugs**
  Oriental rugs

Rugs and carpets—Cleaning   677
- UF Carpet cleaning
  Rug cleaning

Ruins
- USE **Antiquities**
  Excavations (Archeology)
  Extinct cities

Rule, Golden
- USE **Golden rule**

Rule of equal time (Broadcasting)
- USE **Equal time rule (Broadcasting)**

Rulers
- USE **Emperors**
  Heads of state
  Kings and rulers

Queens

Rules of order
- USE **Parliamentary practice**

Rummage sales (May subdiv. geog.)
  381.195
- UF Jumble sales
- BT **Secondhand trade**
  Selling

Runaway adults   173; 306.88
- UF Husbands, Runaway
  Runaway husbands
  Runaway wives
  Wives, Runaway
- BT **Desertion and nonsupport**
  Missing persons

Runaway children   305.23086; 362.74
- BT **Children**
  Homeless persons
  Missing children

Runaway husbands
- USE **Runaway adults**

Runaway slaves
- USE **Fugitive slaves**

Runaway teenagers   362.74
- BT **Homeless persons**
  Missing persons
  Teenagers

Runaway wives
- USE **Runaway adults**

Running   796.42
- BT **Track athletics**
- NT **Jogging**
  Marathon running
  Orienteering
- RT **Racing**

Rural architecture
- USE **Farm buildings**

Rural churches (May subdiv. geog.)
  254
- UF Churches, Country
  Churches, Rural
  Country churches
- BT **Church work**

Rural comedies
- USE **Pastoral drama**
  Pastoral fiction

Rural community development
- USE **Rural development**

Rural conditions
    USE   names of countries, states, etc.,
            with the subdivision *Rural
            conditions,* e.g. **United
            States—Rural conditions;
            Ohio—Rural conditions;** etc.
            [to be added as needed]
Rural credit
    USE   **Agricultural credit**
Rural development (May subdiv. geog.)
        307.1
    UF   Rural community development
    BT   **Agriculture—Government poli-
            cy
            Community development
            Economic development
            Regional planning**
Rural education
    USE   **Rural schools**
Rural electrification (May subdiv. geog.)
        621.319
    BT   **Electrification**
    RT   **Electricity in agriculture**
Rural families
    USE   **Farm family**
Rural high schools
    USE   **Rural schools**
Rural life
    USE   **Country life
            Farm life
            Outdoor life**
Rural poetry
    USE   **Pastoral poetry**
Rural schools (May subdiv. geog.)   **371**
    UF   Country schools
            District schools
            High schools, Rural
            Rural education
            Rural high schools
    BT   **Public schools
            Schools**
Rural sociology   307.72
    Use for materials on the discipline of rural
    sociology and the theory of social organiza-
    tion in rural areas. Materials on the rural con-
    ditions of particular regions, countries, cities,
    etc., are entered under the place with the sub-
    division *Rural conditions.* Descriptive, popu-
    lar, and literary materials on living in the
    country are entered under **Country life.**
    UF   Sociology, Rural

    SA   names of countries, states, etc.,
            with the subdivision *Rural
            conditions* [to be added as
            needed]
    BT   **Sociology**
    NT   **Ohio—Rural conditions
            United States—Rural condi-
            tions
            Urbanization**
    RT   **Country life
            Farm family
            Farm life
            Peasantry**
Rural-urban migration
    USE   **Internal migration**
Russia   947
    Use for materials on Russia (including the
    Russian Empire) prior to 1917. Materials on
    the Union of Soviet Socialist Republics from
    its inception in 1917 until its dissolution in
    December 1991 are entered under **Soviet
    Union.** Materials on the independent republic
    of Russia since its establishment in December
    1991 are entered under **Russia (Federation).**
    UF   Russian Empire
    NT   **Russians**
    RT   **Russia (Federation)
            Soviet Union**
Russia (Federation)   947.086
    Use for materials on the independent repub-
    lic, established in December 1991. Materials
    on Russia and the Russian Empire before
    1917 are entered under **Russia.** Materials on
    the Union of Soviet Socialist Republics be-
    tween 1917 and 1991 are entered under **Sovi-
    et Union.**
    NT   **Russians**
    RT   **Russia
            Soviet Union**
**Russia (Federation)—History—1991-
        947.086**
Russia—History   947
    Use for materials on the history of Russia
    and the Russian empire before 1917.
**Russia—History—1905, Revolution
        947.08**
Russian Church
    USE   **Russian Orthodox Church**
Russian communism
    USE   **Communism—Soviet Union**
Russian Empire
    USE   **Russia**
Russian language   491.7
    May be subdivided like **English language.**
    BT   **Language and languages**

Russian literature   891.7

May use same subdivisions and names of literary forms as for **English literature**. Use for materials on literature in the Russian language. Materials on several of the literatures of the Soviet Union are entered under **Soviet literature**.

BT   **Literature**

RT   **Soviet literature**

Russian Orthodox Church (May subdiv. geog.)   **281.9**

UF   Russian Church

BT   **Christian sects**

Orthodox Eastern Church

Russian revolution

USE   **Soviet Union—History—1917-1921, Revolution**

Russians (May subdiv. geog.)   **920; 947**

Use for materials on the dominant Slavic-speaking ethnic group of Russia. Materials on the citizens of the Soviet Union between 1917 and 1991, not limited to a single national or linguistic group, are entered under **Soviets (People)**.

BT   **Russia**

Russia (Federation)

Soviet Union

Russo-Finnish War, 1939-1940   948.9703

UF   Finno-Russian War, 1939-1940

Soviet Union—History—1939-1940, War with Finland

BT   **Europe—History—1918-1945**

Russo-Turkish War, 1853-1856

USE   **Crimean War, 1853-1856**

Rust

USE   **Corrosion and anticorrosives**

Rustless coatings

USE   **Corrosion and anticorrosives**

RVs

USE   **Recreational vehicles**

Sabbath   263; 296.4

UF   Lord's Day

BT   **Judaism**

Sabin vaccine

USE   **Poliomyelitis vaccine**

Sabotage (May subdiv. geog.)   **331.89; 364.16**

UF   Political violence

BT   **Offenses against public safety**

Strikes

Subversive activities

Terrorism

Sacrament of Reconciliation

USE   **Penance**

Sacraments   234; 265

BT   **Church**

Grace (Theology)

Rites and ceremonies

NT   **Anointing of the sick**

Baptism

Confirmation

Eucharist

Marriage

Ordination

Penance

Sacred art

USE   **Religious art**

Sacred books   208

SA   names of sacred books [to be added as needed]

BT   **Religious literature**

NT   **Bible**

Koran

Vedas

Sacred music

USE   **Church music**

Sacred numbers

USE   **Numerology**

Symbolism of numbers

Sacrifice   203

UF   Burnt offering

BT   **Worship**

NT   **Atonement—Christianity**

Safaris (May subdiv. geog.)   **796.5; 910.2**

BT   **Adventure and adventurers**

Outdoor recreation

Scientific expeditions

Travel

RT   **Hunting**

Safe sex

USE   **Safe sex in AIDS prevention**

Sexually transmitted diseases—Prevention

Safe sex in AIDS prevention   613.9; 616.97

Use for materials limited to safe sexual practices in the prevention of AIDS. Materials on AIDS prevention in general not limited to safe sexual practices are entered under **AIDS (Disease)—Prevention**.

UF   Safe sex

BT   **AIDS (Disease)—Prevention**

Sexual hygiene

Safety appliances
USE **Safety devices**
Safety devices   363.19; 620.8
UF   Safety appliances
Safety equipment
SA   subjects with the subdivision
Safety devices, e.g. **Rail-
roads—Safety devices** [to be
added as needed]
NT   **Railroads—Safety devices**
RT   **Accidents—Prevention**
Safety education (May subdiv. geog.)
363.1; 371.7
BT   **Accidents—Prevention**
Safety equipment
USE **Safety devices**
Safety, Industrial
USE **Occupational health and safety**
Safety measures
USE **Accidents—Prevention**
and subjects with the subdivi-
sion *Safety measures,* e.g.
**Aeronautics—Safety mea-
sures** [to be added as needed]
Safety regulations (May subdiv. geog.)
343; 363.1
Use for collections or materials about rules
regarding safety that have the force of law.
SA   subjects with the subdivision
Law and legislation or *Safety
regulations*, e.g. **Food—Law
and legislation**; **Ships—Safe-
ty regulations**; etc. [to be
added as needed]
BT   **Accidents—Prevention**
Law
NT   **Drivers' licenses**
Ships—Safety regulations
Traffic regulations
Sagas   398.22; 839
BT   **Folklore**
Literature
Old Norse literature
Scandinavian literature
Sailboarding
USE **Windsurfing**
Sailing (May subdiv. geog.)   623.88;
797.124
BT   **Ships**
Water sports
NT   **Windsurfing**

RT   **Boats and boating**
Navigation
Yachts and yachting
Sailors (May subdiv. geog.)   387.5092;
623.88092; 920
UF   Mariners
Naval personnel
Navigators
Sailors' life
Sea life
Seamen
SA   names of navies, e.g. **United
States. Navy** [to be added as
needed]
BT   **Military personnel**
Naval art and science
Navies
NT   **Merchant marine**
Ship pilots
RT   **Seafaring life**
Sailors—Fiction
USE **Sea stories**
Sailors' handbooks
USE **United States. Navy—Hand-
books, manuals, etc.**
Sailors' life
USE **Sailors**
Seafaring life
Sailors' song
USE **Sea songs**
Sailplanes (Aeronautics)
USE **Gliders (Aeronautics)**
**Saint Bartholomew's Day, Massacre of,
1572**   944
UF   St. Bartholomew's Day, Massa-
cre of, 1572
BT   **France—History—1328-1589,
House of Valois**
Huguenots
Massacres
Saint Francis, Order of
USE **Franciscans**
Saint Valentine's Day
USE **Valentine's Day**
Saints (May subdiv. geog.)   200.92; 920
SA   saints of particular religions, e.g.
Christian saints; and names
of individual saints [to be
added as needed]
BT   **Religious biography**

Saints—*Continued*
  NT Christian saints
      Mary, Blessed Virgin, Saint
  RT Martyrs
Salads 641.8
  BT Cooking
  RT Cooking—Vegetables
Salamanders 597.6
  BT Amphibians
Salaries
  USE Salaries, wages, etc.
Salaries, wages, etc. (May subdiv. geog.)
      331.2; 658.3
  Use for materials on all forms of compensa-
  tion for work performed or services rendered,
  including salaries, wages, fees, commissions,
  fringe benefits, and pensions.
  UF Compensation
      Employees—Salaries, wages, etc.
      Fees
      Salaries
      Wages
  SA types of professional personnel,
      types of workers, and classes
      of persons with the subdivi-
      sion *Salaries, wages, etc.*, e.g.
      **Lawyers—Salaries, wages,
      etc.; Office workers—Sala-
      ries, wages, etc.; Handi-
      capped—Salaries, wages,
      etc.**; industries and types of
      institutions with the subdivi-
      sions *Employees—Salaries,
      wages, etc.*, e.g. **Chemical in-
      dustry—Employees—Sala-
      ries, wages, etc.; Colleges
      and universities—Employ-
      ees—Salaries, wages, etc.**;
      and countries, states, cities,
      etc., with the subdivisions *Of-
      ficials and employees—Sala-
      ries, wages, etc.*, e.g. **Ohio—
      Officials and employees—
      Salaries, wages, etc.** [to be
      added as needed]
  BT Income
  NT Chemical industry—Employ-
      ees—Salaries, wages, etc.
      Colleges and universities—Em-
      ployees—Salaries, wages, etc.
      Equal pay for equal work
      Fringe benefits

Handicapped—Salaries, wages,
      etc.
      Job analysis
      Lawyers—Salaries, wages, etc.
      Minimum wage
      Office workers—Salaries, wag-
      es, etc.
      Ohio—Officials and employ-
      ees—Salaries, wages, etc.
      Profit sharing
      Wage-price policy
  RT Cost and standard of living
      Prices
Sale of infants
  USE Adoption—Corrupt practices
Sales agents
  USE Sales personnel
Sales, Auction
  USE Auctions
Sales management 658.8
  BT Management
      Marketing
      Selling
Sales personnel (May subdiv. geog.)
      381.092; 658.85
  UF Clerks (Retail trade)
      Sales agents
      Salesmen
      Saleswomen
      Traveling sales personnel
  BT Retail trade
  NT Peddlers and peddling
Sales tax (May subdiv. geog.) 336.2
  BT Taxation
Salesmanship
  USE Selling
Salesmen
  USE Sales personnel
Saleswomen
  USE Sales personnel
Saline water
  USE Sea water
Saline water conversion
  USE Sea water conversion
Salk vaccine
  USE Poliomyelitis vaccine
Salmon 597.5
  BT Fishes
Saloons
  USE Bars

Salt free diet
USE **Salt-free diet**
Salt-free diet   613.2
UF   Low-sodium diet
Salt free diet
BT   **Cooking**
Diet
Salt water
USE   **Sea water**
Salt water aquariums
USE   **Marine aquariums**
Saltwater fishing (May subdiv. geog.)
799.16
UF   Ocean fishing
Sea fishing
BT   **Fishing**
Salutations
USE   **Etiquette**
Salvage (May subdiv. geog.)   **627; 628.4**
Use for materials on the recovery of equip-
ment, parts, cargo, merchandise, structures, or
waste, not limited to ships or shipwrecks.
UF   Salvage (Waste, etc.)
Utilization of waste
Waste reclamation
NT   **Marine salvage**
Recycling
Waste products as fuel
RT   **Refuse and refuse disposal**
Salvage (Waste, etc.)
USE   **Salvage**
Salvation   202; 234
UF   Redemption
BT   **Doctrinal theology**
NT   **Atonement—Christianity**
Conversion
Faith
Grace (Theology)
Regeneration (Christianity)
Sanctification
Salvation Army   287.9
BT   **Christian missions**
Christian sects
Salvation—Biblical teaching   234
Salvation history
USE   **Salvation—History of doctrines**
Salvation—History of doctrines   202;
234
UF   Salvation history
BT   **Doctrinal theology**
Same-sex marriage (May subdiv. geog.)
306.81; 346.01

UF   Gay marriage
Homosexual marriage
Lesbian marriage
BT   **Marriage**
Samplers   746.3
BT   **Embroidery**
Needlework
Sampling (Statistics)   519.5
UF   Random sampling
BT   **Probabilities**
Statistics
NT   **Quality control**
Sanatoriums (May subdiv. geog.)   **362.16**
UF   Sanitariums
BT   **Long-term care facilities**
Sanctification   202; 234
BT   **Salvation**
Sanctions (International law)   327.1;
341.5
UF   Economic sanctions
BT   **Economic policy**
International economic rela-
tions
International law
Sanctuary (Law)
USE   **Asylum**
Sanctuary movement (May subdiv. geog.)
261.8
Use for materials on any network of reli-
gious congregations or churches that shelter
refugees or illegal aliens.
BT   **Asylum**
Church and social problems
Social movements
RT   **Illegal aliens**
Refugees
Sand dunes (May subdiv. geog.)   **551.3**
UF   Dunes
BT   **Seashore**
Sand sculpture (May subdiv.geog.)   **736**
BT   **Nature craft**
Sculpture
Sandwiches   641.8
BT   **Cooking**
Sanitariums
USE   **Sanatoriums**
Sanitary affairs
USE   **Sanitary engineering**
Sanitation
Sanitary engineering (May subdiv. geog.)
628

Sanitary engineering—*Continued*
- UF Environmental health engineering
   Sanitary affairs
- BT **Engineering**
- NT **Drainage**
   Pollution
   Refuse and refuse disposal
   Sewerage
   Soil microbiology
   Street cleaning
- RT **Municipal engineering**
   Sanitation

Sanitary landfills
- USE **Landfills**

Sanitation (May subdiv. geog.) **363.72; 648**
- UF Sanitary affairs
- SA subjects, types of industries, and names of individual corporate bodies with the subdivision *Sanitation*, e.g. **Hospitals—Sanitation** [to be added as needed]
- NT **Cemeteries**
   Cleaning
   Cleanliness
   Cremation
   Disinfection and disinfectants
   Hospitals—Sanitation
   Household sanitation
   Pollution
   Refuse and refuse disposal
   School hygiene
   Smoke prevention
   Ventilation
   Water purification
- RT **Hygiene**
   Public health
   Sanitary engineering

Sanitation, Household
- USE **Household sanitation**

Santa Claus **394.2663**
- BT **Christmas**

Santeria **299.6**
- UF Lucumi (Religion)
- BT **Religion**

Sasquatch **001.9**
- UF Big foot
   Bigfoot
- BT **Monsters**
   Mythical animals

SAT
- USE **Scholastic Assessment Test**

Satan
- USE **Devil**

Satellite communication systems
- USE **Artificial satellites in telecommunication**

Satellites **523.9**
- UF Moons
   Natural satellites
   Planetary satellites
   Planets—Satellites
- SA names of planets with the subdivision *Satellites*, e.g. **Mars (Planet)—Satellites** [to be added as needed]
- BT **Solar system**
- NT **Mars (Planet)—Satellites**

Satellites, Artificial
- USE **Artificial satellites**

Satellites—Mars
- USE **Mars (Planet)—Satellites**

Satire **808.7; 808.87**
- UF Comic literature
- SA satire of particular countries, e.g. **American satire** [to be added as needed]
- BT **Literature**
   Rhetoric
   Wit and humor
- NT **American satire**
   Burlesque (Literature)
   English satire
   Invective
   Parody
   Political satire

Satire, American
- USE **American satire**

Satire, English
- USE **English satire**

Saturn (Planet) **523.46**
- BT **Planets**

Saucers, Flying
- USE **Unidentified flying objects**

Sauces **641.8**
- BT **Cooking**

Saudi Arabia **953.8**
> May be subdivided like **United States** except for *History*.

Saving and investment (May subdiv. geog.) **332.024**

Saving and investment—*Continued*
   UF   Capital accumulation
         Capital formation
         Economy
         Investment and saving
         Saving and thrift
         Thrift
   BT   **Capital**
         Economics
         Personal finance
         Wealth
   NT   **Savings and loan associations**
   RT   **Investments**
Saving and thrift
   USE   **Saving and investment**
Savings and loan associations (May subdiv. geog.)   **332.3**
   UF   Building and loan associations
         Loan associations
   BT   **Banks and banking**
         Cooperation
         Cooperative societies
         Investments
         Loans
         Personal loans
         Saving and investment
   RT   **Cooperative banks**
Savings banks
   USE   **Banks and banking**
Saws   **621.9**
   BT   **Carpentry tools**
         Tools
Sayings
   USE   **Epigrams**
         Proverbs
         Quotations
Scandals   **302.2**
   BT   **History**
Scandinavian languages   **439**
   UF   Norse languages
   BT   **Language and languages**
   NT   **Danish language**
         Icelandic language
         Norwegian language
         Old Norse language
         Swedish language
Scandinavian literature   **839**
   UF   Norse literature
   BT   **Literature**
   NT   **Danish literature**
         Eddas
         Icelandic literature

         Norwegian literature
         Sagas
         Swedish literature
   RT   **Old Norse literature**
Scandinavians (May subdiv. geog.)   **920; 948**
   Use for materials on the people of Scandinavia since the tenth century. Materials on earlier Scandinavians are entered under **Vikings**.
   NT   **Vikings**
Scarecrows   **632**
   BT   **Plant conservation**
Scenarios
   USE   **Radio plays**
         Stories, plots, etc.
         Television plays
Scene painting   **792.02**
   BT   **Painting**
         Theaters—Stage setting and scenery
Scenery
   USE   **Landscape protection**
         Natural monuments
         Views
         Wilderness areas
Scenery (Stage)
   USE   **Theaters—Stage setting and scenery**
Scenic byways (May subdiv. geog.)   **910.2**
   UF   Scenic highways
         Scenic roads
   BT   **Roads**
Scenic highways
   USE   **Scenic byways**
Scenic roads
   USE   **Scenic byways**
Scented gardens
   USE   **Fragrant gardens**
Scepticism
   USE   **Skepticism**
Scheherazade (Legendary character)   **398.22**
   BT   **Legendary characters**
Scholarship
   USE   **Learning and scholarship**
Scholarship funds
   USE   **Scholarships**
Scholarships (May subdiv. geog.)   **371.2; 378.3**

Scholarships—*Continued*
  UF Bursaries
      Fellowships
      Scholarship funds
      Scholarships, fellowships, etc.
  SA fields of study, ethnic groups,
      and classes of persons with
      the subdivision *Scholarships*,
      [to be added as needed]
  BT **Education**
      Endowments
      Student aid
Scholarships, fellowships, etc.
  USE **Scholarships**
Scholastic achievement
  USE **Academic achievement**
Scholastic achievement tests
  USE **Achievement tests**
Scholastic Aptitude Test
  USE **Scholastic Assessment Test**
Scholastic Assessment Test 378.1
  UF SAT
      Scholastic Aptitude Test
  BT **Colleges and universities—Entrance examinations**
      Examinations
School achievement tests
  USE **Achievement tests**
School administration and organization
  USE **Schools—Administration**
School-age fathers
  USE **Teenage fathers**
School-age mothers
  USE **Teenage mothers**
School and community
  USE **Community and school**
School and home
  USE **Home and school**
School architecture
  USE **School buildings**
School assembly programs 371.8
  UF Assembly programs, School
      School entertainments
      Schools—Exercises and recreations
      Schools—Opening exercises
  BT **Student activities**
  NT **Commencements**
      Recitations
  RT **Drama in education**
School athletics
  USE **School sports**

School attendance (May subdiv. geog.)
  371.2
  UF Absence from school
      Absenteeism (Schools)
      Attendance, School
      Compulsory school attendance
  BT **Schools—Administration**
  RT **Compulsory education**
      Dropouts
School boards (May subdiv. geog.)
  353.8
  UF Boards of education
  BT **Schools—Administration**
School books
  USE **Textbooks**
School buildings (May subdiv. geog.)
  371.6; 727
  UF Buildings, School
      School architecture
      School houses
      Schoolhouses
  BT **Buildings**
      Schools
School busing
  USE **Busing (School integration)**
      School children—Transportation
School children (May subdiv. geog.)
  155.42; 305.234
  BT **Children**
      Students
School children—Food 371.7; 642
  UF Food for school children
      Meals for school children
      School lunches
  BT **Children—Nutrition**
      Diet
      Food
School children—Medical examinations
  USE **Children—Medical examinations**
School children—Transportation 371.8
  UF School busing
  BT **Transportation**
  NT **Busing (School integration)**
School choice (May subdiv. geog.) **379.1**
  Use for materials on choosing a school and
  on the right of parents to choose their children's school.
  UF Choice of school
      Parents' choice of school
      Schools—Selection

School choice—*Continued*

    BT   **Education**

    NT   **College choice**

School clubs

    USE   **Students—Societies**

School counseling   371.4

    Use for materials on the assistance given to students by schools, colleges, or universities in understanding and coping with adjustment problems. Materials on the assistance given to students in the selection of a program of studies are entered under **Educational counseling**.

    UF   Guidance counseling, School

    BT   **Counseling**

    RT   **Educational counseling**

         School psychologists

School desegregation

    USE   **School integration**

School discipline   371.5

    UF   Discipline of children

         Punishment in schools

    BT   **Schools—Administration**

         Teaching

    NT   **Classroom management**

         Student government

School dropouts

    USE   **Dropouts**

School entertainments

    USE   **School assembly programs**

School excursions

    USE   **Field trips**

School fiction

    USE   **School stories**

School finance

    USE   **Education—Finance**

School furniture

    USE   **Schools—Equipment and supplies**

School grade retention

    USE   **Promotion (School)**

School houses

    USE   **School buildings**

School hygiene   371.7

    BT   **Children—Health and hygiene**

         Health education

         Hygiene

         Public health

         Sanitation

    RT   **School nurses**

School inspection

    USE   **School supervision**

         Schools—Administration

School integration (May subdiv. geog.)
    379.2

    UF   Desegregated schools

         Desegregation in education

         Education—Integration

         Integrated schools

         Integration in education

         Racial balance in schools

         School desegregation

    BT   **Race relations**

    NT   **Busing (School integration)**

         Magnet schools

    RT   **Segregation in education**

School journalism

    USE   **College and school journalism**

School libraries (May subdiv. geog.)
    027.8

    BT   **Instructional materials centers**

         Libraries

    NT   **Elementary school libraries**

         High school libraries

         Students—Library services

    RT   **Libraries and schools**

School life

    USE   **Students**

School lunches

    USE   **School children—Food**

School management and organization

    USE   **Schools—Administration**

School mascots

    USE   **Mascots**

School media centers

    USE   **Instructional materials centers**

School music

    USE   **Music—Study and teaching**

         School songbooks

         Singing

School newspapers

    USE   **College and school journalism**

School nurses   371.7

    BT   **Nurses**

    RT   **Health education**

         School hygiene

School organization

    USE   **Schools—Administration**

School playgrounds

    USE   **Playgrounds**

School plays

    USE   **Children's plays**

         College and school drama

School prayer
    USE **Prayer in the public schools**
School principals
    USE **School superintendents and principals**
School promotion
    USE **Promotion (School)**
School prose
    USE **Children's writings**
School psychologists (May subdiv. geog.) **371.7**
    BT **Psychologists**
    RT **School counseling**
School readiness
    USE **Readiness for school**
School reports **371.2**
    UF Educational reports
        Reports, Teachers'
        Teachers' reports
    BT **Report writing**
    RT **Grading and marking (Education)**
School shootings (May subdiv. geog.) **371.7**
    UF Shootings in schools
    BT **Crime**
        School violence
School shops **373.2**
    UF Industrial arts shops
    BT **Technical education**
School songbooks **782.42**
    UF School music
    BT **Songbooks**
        Songs
    NT **Children's songs**
School sports (May subdiv. geog.) **371.8**
    UF Interscholastic sports
        School athletics
    BT **Sports**
        Student activities
    RT **College sports**
School stories **808.83**
    Use for individual works, collections, or materials about school stories.
    UF School fiction
        Schools—Fiction
    BT **Fiction**
School superintendents and principals (May subdiv. geog.) **371.2**
    UF School principals
        Superintendents of schools
    BT **Schools—Administration**

    RT **School supervision**
School supervision **371.2**
    Use for materials on the supervision of instruction. Materials on the management and organization of schools and on the administrative duties of educators are entered under **Schools—Administration**.
    UF Inspection of schools
        Instructional supervision
        School inspection
        Supervision of schools
    BT **Schools—Administration**
        Teaching
    RT **School superintendents and principals**
School surveys
    USE **Educational surveys**
School taxes
    USE **Education—Finance**
School teaching
    USE **Teaching**
School trips
    USE **Field trips**
School verse
    USE **Children's writings**
School violence (May subdiv. geog.) **371.7**
    UF Student violence
        Violence in schools
    BT **Juvenile delinquency**
        Violence
    NT **School shootings**
School vouchers
    USE **Educational vouchers**
School yearbooks **371.8**
    UF Annuals
        College yearbooks
        High school yearbooks
        Student yearbooks
    BT **Serial publications**
        Yearbooks
Schoolhouses
    USE **School buildings**
Schools (May subdiv. geog.) **371**
    SA types of schools, e.g. **Church schools**; **Rural schools**; etc.; names of individual schools; and subjects with the subdivision *Study and teaching*, e.g. **Science—Study and teaching** [to be added as needed]
    NT **Business schools**
        Charter schools

Schools—*Continued*
> Church schools
> Colleges and universities
> Correspondence schools and
> courses
> Elementary schools
> Evening and continuation
> schools
> Experimental schools
> High schools
> Junior high schools
> Kindergarten
> Libraries and schools
> Magnet schools
> Middle schools
> Museums and schools
> Nongraded schools
> Nursery schools
> Private schools
> Public schools
> Religious summer schools
> Rural schools
> School buildings
> Single-sex schools
> Summer schools
> Urban schools

RT   Education

Schools—Accreditation (May subdiv.
geog.)   379.1

UF   Accreditation (Education)
Educational accreditation

SA   types of educational institutions
and names of individual institutions with the subdivision
Accreditation, e.g. **Colleges
and universities—Accreditation**; and subjects with the
subdivision *Study and teaching*, for accreditation of programs of study in those subjects, e.g. **Mathematics—
Study and teaching** [to be
added as needed]

Schools—Administration (May subdiv.
geog.)   371.2

Use for materials on the management and
organization of schools and on the administrative duties of educators. Materials on the supervision of instruction are entered under
School supervision.

UF   Educational administration
Inspection of schools

School administration and orga-
nization
School inspection
School management and organi-
zation
School organization
Schools—Management and orga-
nization

NT   **Articulation (Education)**
School attendance
School boards
School discipline
**School superintendents and
principals**
School supervision
Schools—Centralization
Schools—Decentralization
Student government

Schools and libraries
USE   **Libraries and schools**
Schools and museums
USE   **Museums and schools**
Schools—Centralization (May subdiv.
geog.)   379.1

UF   Centralization of schools
Consolidation of schools

BT   **Schools—Administration**

Schools—Curricula
USE   **Education—Curricula**
Schools—Decentralization (May subdiv.
geog.)   379.1

UF   Decentralization of schools

BT   **Schools—Administration**

Schools—Equipment and supplies   371.6

UF   School furniture

BT   **Furniture**

Schools—Exercises and recreations
USE   **School assembly programs**
Schools—Fiction
USE   **School stories**
Schools—Management and organization
USE   **Schools—Administration**
Schools, Military
USE   **Military education**
Schools, Nonformal
USE   **Experimental schools**
Schools—Opening exercises
USE   **School assembly programs**
Schools—Selection
USE   **School choice**
Schools—United States   371.00973

Schools—United States—_Continued_
  UF American schools
Science (May subdiv. geog.) **500**
  NT **Astronomy**
      Bible and science
      Biology
      Botany
      Chaos (Science)
      Chemistry
      Computer science
      Discoveries in science
      Earth sciences
      Environmental sciences
      Forensic sciences
      Fossils
      Fraud in science
      Geology
      Life sciences
      Mathematics
      Natural history
      Petrology
      Physical sciences
      Physics
      Physiology
      Religion and science
      Science and civilization
      Science and the humanities
      Space sciences
      System theory
      Zoology
  RT **Laboratories**
      Scientific apparatus and in-
      struments
      Scientists
Science and civilization **306.4**
  UF Civilization and science
      Science and society
  BT **Civilization**
      Progress
      Science
Science and religion
  USE **Religion and science**
Science and society
  USE **Science and civilization**
Science and space
  USE **Space sciences**
Science and state
  USE **Science—Government policy**
Science and the Bible
  USE **Bible and science**
Science and the humanities **001.3**
  UF Humanities and science

  BT **Humanities**
      Science
Science—Exhibitions **507.4**
  UF Science fairs
  BT **Exhibitions**
  NT **Science projects**
Science experiments
  USE **Science—Experiments**
Science—Experiments **507**
  UF Experiments, Scientific
      Science experiments
      Scientific experiments
  SA branches of science with the
      subdivision _Experiments_, e.g.
      Chemistry—Experiments to
      be added as needed]
  RT **Science projects**
Science fair projects
  USE **Science projects**
Science fairs
  USE **Science—Exhibitions**
Science fiction **808.3; 808.83**
    Use for individual works, collections, or
  materials about fiction based on imagined de-
  velopments in science and technology.
  UF Space flight (Fiction)
  BT **Adventure fiction**
      Fiction
  NT **Dystopias**
      Hugo Award
      Imaginary voyages
      Nebula Award
      Utopian fiction
  RT **Fantasy fiction**
      Interplanetary voyages
Science fiction comic books, strips, etc.
      741.5
    Use for individual works, collections, or
  materials about science fiction comics.
  BT **Comic books, strips, etc.**
Science fiction films **791.43**
    Use for individual works, collections, or
  materials about science fiction films.
  SA types of science fiction films,
      e.g. **Star Wars films** [to be
      added as needed]
  BT **Motion pictures**
  NT **Star Wars films**
  RT **Fantasy films**
Science fiction films—Catalogs
      016.79143

Science fiction graphic novels 741.5
> Use for individual works, collections, or materials about science fiction graphic novels.

BT **Graphic novels**

Science fiction plays 808.82
> Use for individual works, collections, or materials about science fiction plays.

BT **Drama**

Science fiction poetry 808.1; 808.81
> Use for individual works, collections, or materials about science fiction poetry.

BT **Poetry**

Science fiction radio programs 791.44
> Use for individual works, collections, or materials about science fiction radio programs.

BT **Radio programs**

Science fiction television programs 791.45
> Use for individual works, collections, or materials about science fiction television programs.

BT **Television programs**
RT **Fantasy television programs**

Science—Government policy (May subdiv. geog.) **353.7; 500**

UF Science and state
Science policy

Science—Islamic countries 508.53

UF Arab science
Islamic science

Science journalism
USE **Scientific journalism**

Science laboratories
USE **Laboratories**

Science—Methodology 501

UF Scientific method
NT **Logic**

Science policy
USE **Science—Government policy**

Science projects 507.8

UF Science fair projects
BT **Science—Exhibitions**
RT **Science—Experiments**

Science—Religious aspects
USE **Religion and science**

Science—Societies 506

UF Scientific societies
BT **Societies**

Science—Study and teaching 507

UF Scientific education
NT **Nature study**

Science—Study and teaching—Audiovisual aids 507.8

Science—Study and teaching—Evaluation 507.6

Science—United States 509.73

Scientific apparatus and instruments 502.8

UF Apparatus, Scientific
Instruments, Scientific
Scientific instruments

SA types of instruments, e.g. **Aeronautical instruments**; and names of specific instruments [to be added as needed]

NT **Aeronautical instruments**
Astronomical instruments
Chemical apparatus
Electric apparatus and appliances
Electronic apparatus and appliances
Engineering instruments
Meteorological instruments
Optical instruments

RT **Science**

Scientific breakthroughs
USE **Discoveries in science**

Scientific creationism
USE **Creationism**

Scientific discoveries
USE **Discoveries in science**

Scientific education
USE **Science—Study and teaching**

Scientific errors
USE **Errors**

Scientific expeditions 508

UF Expeditions, Scientific
Polar expeditions

SA names of regions explored with the subdivision *Exploration* for materials on scientific expeditions to regions that are unsettled or sparsely settled and largely unknown to the world at large, e.g. **Antarctica—Exploration**; names of countries, states, etc., with the subdivision *Exploring expeditions* for materials on explorations sponsored by those governments; and names of expeditions [to be added as needed]

Scientific expeditions—*Continued*
- BT   **Voyages and travels**
- NT   **Antarctica—Exploration**
        Arctic regions—Exploration
        Safaris
- RT   **Exploration**

Scientific experiments
- USE   **Science—Experiments**

Scientific fraud
- USE   **Fraud in science**

Scientific instruments
- USE   **Scientific apparatus and instruments**

Scientific journalism (May subdiv. geog.) **070.4**
- UF   Journalism, Scientific
        Science journalism
- BT   **Journalism**

Scientific laboratories
- USE   **Laboratories**

Scientific management
- USE   **Management**

Scientific method
- USE   **Science—Methodology**

Scientific names of plants
- USE   **Botany—Nomenclature**

Scientific plant names
- USE   **Botany—Nomenclature**

Scientific recreations **793.8**
- UF   Recreations, Scientific
- BT   **Amusements**
- NT   **Mathematical recreations**

Scientific societies
- USE   **Science—Societies**

Scientific writing
- USE   **Technical writing**

Scientists (May subdiv. geog.) **920; 509.2**
- SA   types of scientists and names of individual scientists [to be added as needed]
- NT   **Astronomers**
        Biologists
        Chemists
        Geologists
        Mathematicians
        Naturalists
        Physicists
- RT   **Science**

Scottish clans
- USE   **Clans—Scotland**

Scottish personal names **929.4**
- BT   **Personal names**

Scottish tartans
- USE   **Tartans**

Scouts and scouting **369.4**
- BT   **Clubs**
        Community life
- NT   **Boy Scouts**
        Girl Scouts

Scrapbook journaling
- USE   **Scrapbooking**

Scrapbooking **745.593**
- UF   Scrapbook journaling
- BT   **Handicraft**

Screen printing
- USE   **Silk screen printing**

Screening for drug abuse
- USE   **Drug testing**

Screenplays
- USE   **Television scripts**

Screenplays **808.2; 808.82**
> Use for individual works, collections, or materials about motion picture plays.
- UF   Film scripts
        Motion picture plays
        Motion picture scripts
        Movie scripts
- BT   **Drama**

Scriptures, Holy
- USE   **Bible**

Scuba diving (May subdiv. geog.) **797.2**
> Use for materials on free diving with the aid of a self-contained underwater breathing apparatus. Materials on free diving with mask, fins, and snorkel are entered under **Skin diving**.
- UF   Free diving
- BT   **Deep diving**

Sculling
- USE   **Rowing**

Sculptors (May subdiv. geog.) **730.92; 920**
- BT   **Artists**

Sculptors—United States **730.92; 920**
- UF   American sculptors

Sculpture **730**
- UF   Statues
- SA   sculpture of particular countries, e.g. **Greek sculpture**; and specific types of sculpture [to be added as needed]
- BT   **Art**
        Decoration and ornament

Sculpture—*Continued*
NT American sculpture
Brasses
Bronzes
Greek sculpture
Kinetic sculpture
Masks (Sculpture)
Mobiles (Sculpture)
Modeling
Modernism in sculpture
Monuments
Plaster casts
Sand sculpture
Soap sculpture
RT Carving (Decorative arts)
Sculpture—20th century 735
UF Modern sculpture—1900-1999
(20th century)
Sculpture, Modern—20th century
Sculpture—21st century 735
Sculpture, Greek
USE Greek sculpture
Sculpture in motion
USE Kinetic sculpture
Sculpture, Modern
USE Modernism in sculpture
Sculpture, Modern—20th century
USE Sculpture—20th century
Sculpture—Technique 731.4
RT Modeling
SDI (Ballistic missile defense system)
USE Strategic Defense Initiative
Sea animals
USE Marine animals
Sea bed
USE Ocean bottom
Sea farming
USE Aquaculture
Sea fisheries
USE Commercial fishing
Sea fishing
USE Saltwater fishing
Sea food
USE Seafood
Sea in art
USE Marine painting
Sea laboratories
USE Undersea research stations
Sea laws
USE Maritime law

Sea life
USE Marine biology
Navies
Sailors
Seafaring life
Sea mosses
USE Algae
Sea poetry 808.1; 808.81
Use for individual works, collections, or materials about poetry about the sea.
BT Poetry
NT Sea songs
Sea pollution
USE Marine pollution
Sea power 359
UF Dominion of the sea
Military power
Naval power
Navy
SA names of countries with the subhead *Navy* or the subdivision *Naval history*, e.g. United States. Navy; United States—Naval history; etc. [to be added as needed]
BT Naval art and science
NT Warships
RT Naval history
Navies
Sea resources
USE Marine resources
Sea routes
USE Trade routes
Sea shells
USE Shells
Sea-shore
USE Seashore
Sea songs 782.42
UF Chanties
Sailors' song
BT Sea poetry
Songs
Sea stories 808.3; 808.83
Use for individual works, collections, or materials about sea stories.
UF Sailors—Fiction
BT Adventure and adventurers
Adventure fiction
Fiction
Sea transportation
USE Shipping

Sea travel
USE **Ocean travel**
Sea water 551.46
UF Saline water
Salt water
BT **Water**
Sea water aquariums
USE **Marine aquariums**
Sea water conversion 628.1
UF Conversion of saline water
Desalination of water
Desalting of water
Saline water conversion
BT **Water purification**
Sea waves
USE **Ocean waves**
Seafaring life 910.4
UF Sailors' life
Sea life
SA names of countries with the sub-
head *Navy*, e.g. **United
States. Navy** [to be added as
needed]
BT **Adventure and adventurers
Manners and customs
Voyages and travels**
RT **Sailors**
Seafood 641.3
UF Sea food
SA names of marine fish, shellfish,
etc., used as food [to be add-
ed as needed]
BT **Food
Marine resources**
NT **Cooking—Seafood**
RT **Fish as food**
Sealab project 551.46
UF Navy Sealab project
Project Sealab
BT **Undersea research stations**
Seals (Animals) (May subdiv. geog.)
599.79
BT **Mammals
Marine mammals**
Seals (Numismatics) (May subdiv. geog.)
737; 929.8
UF Emblems
Signets
BT **Heraldry
History
Inscriptions**

Numismatics
RT **National emblems**
Seamanship
USE **Navigation**
Seamen
USE **Sailors**
Search and rescue operations
USE **Rescue work**
Searching the Internet
USE **Internet searching**
Seas (May subdiv. geog.) 551.46
SA names of seas, e.g. **Mediterra-
nean Sea** [to be added as
needed]
BT **Earth
Physical geography
Water**
NT **Mediterranean Sea**
Seascapes
USE **Marine painting**
Seashore (May subdiv. geog.) 551.45
UF Sea-shore
BT **Landforms**
NT **Beaches
Sand dunes**
RT **Coasts
Ocean**
Seasons (May subdiv. geog.) 508.2; 525
BT **Astronomy
Climate
Meteorology**
NT **Autumn
Spring
Summer
Winter**
Seaweeds
USE **Algae**
Secession (May subdiv. geog.) 973.713
BT **Sovereignty**
RT **Separatist movements**
Secession—Southern States 973.713
BT **United States—History—1861-
1865, Civil War**
NT **United States—History—1861-
1865, Civil War—Causes**
Secessionist movements
USE **Separatist movements**
Seclusion
USE **Solitude**
Second Advent 236
UF Second coming of Christ

Second Advent—*Continued*
    BT   **Eschatology**
    NT   **Judgment Day**
    RT   **Millennium**
Second coming of Christ
    USE   **Second Advent**
Second economy
    USE   **Underground economy**
Second hand trade
    USE   **Secondhand trade**
Second job
    USE   **Supplementary employment**
Second World War
    USE   **World War, 1939-1945**
Secondary education (May subdiv. geog.)
    373
    UF   Education, Secondary
         High school education
         Secondary schools
    BT   **Education**
    NT   **Adult education**
         Evening and continuation
         schools
    RT   **High schools**
         Junior high schools
Secondary employment
    USE   **Supplementary employment**
Secondary school libraries
    USE   **High school libraries**
Secondary schools
    USE   **High schools**
         Junior high schools
         Secondary education
Secondhand trade   **381**
    UF   Second hand trade
         Used merchandise
    SA   types of secondhand trade, e.g.
         Garage sales [to be added as
         needed]
    BT   **Selling**
    NT   **Flea markets**
         Garage sales
         Rummage sales
         Thrift shops
Secrecy   **158.2; 302.5**
    UF   Concealment
    NT   **Children's secrets**
    RT   **Privacy**
Secret service (May subdiv. geog.)
    363.28
    Use for materials on governmental service
of a secret nature.

    SA   names of wars with the subdivi-
         sion *Secret service* [to be
         added as needed]
    BT   **Police**
    NT   **Espionage**
         World War, 1939-1945—Secret
         service
    RT   **Detectives**
         Intelligence service
         Spies
Secret service—United States   **363.28**
    UF   United States—Secret service
Secret societies (May subdiv. geog.)
    366; 371.8
    SA   names of secret societies, e.g.
         Freemasons [to be added as
         needed]
    BT   **Rites and ceremonies**
         Societies
    NT   **Freemasons**
         Ku Klux Klan
    RT   **Fraternities and sororities**
Secret writing
    USE   **Cryptography**
Secretarial practice
    USE   **Office practice**
Secretaries (May subdiv. geog.)   **651.3**
    BT   **Office management**
Secrets, Trade
    USE   **Trade secrets**
Sectionalism
    USE   **Regionalism**
Sectionalism (United States)
    USE   **Regionalism—United States**
Sects (May subdiv. geog.)   **209; 280**
    Use for materials on independent religious
groups whose teachings or practices fall within the normative bounds of the major world
religions. Materials on the major world religions are entered under **Religions**. Materials
on groups or movements whose beliefs or
practices differ significantly from the traditional religions, often focused upon a charismatic leader, are entered under **Cults**.
    UF   Church denominations
         Denominations, Religious
         Religious denominations
    SA   names of churches and sects
         within the major world reli-
         gions, e.g. **Presbyterian**
         Church; **Hasidim**; etc. [to be
         added as needed]
    BT   **Church history**
         Religions

Sects—*Continued*
    NT   **Christian sects**
         Islamic sects
    RT   **Cults**
Secular humanism
    USE **Secularism**
Secularism (May subdiv. geog.)   **171;**
    211
    Use for materials on any intellectual or philosophical movement or set of beliefs that promotes human values as separate and distinct from religious doctrines.
    UF   Humanism, Secular
         Secular humanism
    BT   **Ethics**
         Utilitarianism
    NT   **Atheism**
         Rationalism
    RT   **Humanism**
Securities (May subdiv. geog.)   **332.63**
    UF   Capitalization (Finance)
         Dividends
    SA   types of securities [to be added as needed]
    BT   **Finance**
         Investments
         Stock exchanges
    NT   **Bonds**
         Capital market
         Day trading (Securities)
         Futures
         Insider trading
         Mortgages
         Stocks
Securities exchange
    USE **Stock exchanges**
Securities fraud (May subdiv. geog.)
    345; 364.1
    UF   Stock fraud
         Stock market fraud
    BT   **Fraud**
Securities trading, Insider
    USE **Insider trading**
Security, Internal
    USE **Internal security**
Security, International
    USE **International security**
Security measures
    USE subjects with the subdivision *Security measures*, e.g. **Nuclear power plants—Security measures** [to be added as needed]

Security traders
    USE **Stockbrokers**
Seder   **296.4**
    BT   **Judaism—Customs and practices**
         Passover
Sedition
    USE **Political crimes and offenses**
         Revolutions
Seed capital
    USE **Venture capital**
Seeds   **581.4**
    BT   **Plant propagation**
         Plants
    NT   **Nuts**
Seeds—Germination
    USE **Germination**
Seeing eye dogs
    USE **Guide dogs**
Seeking attention
    USE **Showing off**
Segregation (May subdiv. geog.)   **305.8**
    UF   Desegregation
    SA   segregation in particular areas, e.g. **Segregation in education**; and racial and ethnic groups and classes of persons with the subdivision *Segregation*, e.g. **African Americans—Segregation** [to be added as needed]
    BT   **Race relations**
    NT   **African Americans—Segregation**
         Apartheid
         Blacks—Segregation
         Segregation in education
    RT   **Discrimination**
         Minorities
Segregation in education (May subdiv. geog.)   **379.2**
    UF   Education—Integration
         Education—Segregation
         Integration in education
         Racial balance in schools
    BT   **Segregation**
    RT   **Discrimination in education**
         School integration
Segregation in housing
    USE **Discrimination in housing**

Segregation in public accommodations
USE **Discrimination in public accommodations**

Seinen   741.5

Use for individual works, collections, or materials about manga for men ages 18-30.

BT **Manga**

Seismic sea waves
USE **Tsunamis**

Seismography
USE **Earthquakes**

Seismology
USE **Earthquakes**

Selection, Artificial
USE **Breeding**

Selective service
USE **Draft**

Self   126; 155.2
BT **Consciousness**
Individuality
Personality
NT **Ego (Psychology)**
Human body
Identity (Psychology)

Self-acceptance   155.2
UF Self-love (Psychology)
BT **Psychology**
RT **Self-confidence**
Self-esteem
Self-perception

Self-actualization
USE **Self-realization**

Self-assurance
USE **Self-confidence**
Self-reliance

Self-awareness
USE **Self-perception**

Self-care, Health
USE **Health self-care**

Self-care, Medical
USE **Health self-care**

Self-change techniques
USE **Self-help techniques**

Self-concept
USE **Self-perception**

Self-confidence   155.2
UF Self-assurance
BT **Emotions**
RT **Assertiveness (Psychology)**
Self-acceptance
Self-consciousness
Self-esteem

Self-reliance
Self-consciousness   155.2
UF Embarrassment
BT **Psychology**
RT **Self-confidence**
Self-esteem
Self-perception

Self-control   153.8
UF Self-discipline
Self-mastery
Will power
Willpower
BT **Psychology**

Self-culture
USE **Self-improvement**
Self-instruction

Self-defense   613.6; 796.8
UF Fighting
NT **Boxing**
Jiu-jitsu
Judo
Karate
Self-defense for children
Self-defense for women
RT **Martial arts**

Self-defense for children   613.6; 796.8
UF Children—Defense
Children—Self-defense
BT **Self-defense**

Self-defense for women   613.6; 796.8
UF Fighting
Women—Self-defense
Women's self-defense
BT **Self-defense**
RT **Martial arts**

Self-defense in animals
USE **Animal defenses**

Self-defense in plants
USE **Plant defenses**

Self-determination, National
USE **National self-determination**

Self-development
USE **Self-improvement**
Self-instruction

Self-directed change
USE **Self-help techniques**

Self-discipline
USE **Self-control**

Self-education
USE **Self-instruction**

Self-employed (May subdiv. geog.)
    331.12
    UF   Freelancers
    BT   **Businesspeople**
    NT   **Entrepreneurs**
          Home-based business
          Professions
Self-employed women (May subdiv. geog.)
    331.4
    UF   Women, Self-employed
    BT   **Women—Employment**
Self-esteem   155.2
    UF   Self-love (Psychology)
          Self-respect
    BT   **Psychology**
    RT   **Self-acceptance**
          Self-confidence
          Self-consciousness
          Self-perception
Self-evaluation in education
    USE **Educational evaluation**
Self-examination, Medical
    USE **Health self-care**
Self-expectations, Perfectionist
    USE **Perfectionism (Personality**
          trait)
Self-fulfillment
    USE **Self-realization**
Self-government
    USE **Democracy**
          Representative government and
          representation
Self-government (in education)
    USE **Student government**
Self health care
    USE **Health self-care**
Self-help groups   361.4; 616.85
    UF   Mutual support groups
          Support groups
    BT   **Counseling**
Self-help medical care
    USE **Health self-care**
Self-help techniques   155.2; 158.1
    UF   Self-change techniques
          Self-directed change
    BT   **Applied psychology**
          Life skills
    NT   **Affirmations**
Self image
    USE **Personal appearance**
Self-improvement   158

    UF   Personal development
          Personal growth
          Self-culture
          Self-development
    BT   **Life skills**
    RT   **Self-instruction**
Self-instruction   371.39
    UF   Home education
          Home study courses
          Self-culture
          Self-development
          Self-education
          Teach yourself courses
    SA   subjects with the subdivision
          Programmed instruction, e.g.
          English language—Pro-
          grammed instruction [to be
          added as needed]
    BT   **Education**
          Study skills
    RT   **Correspondence schools and**
          courses
          Self-improvement
Self-love (Psychology)
    USE **Self-acceptance**
          Self-esteem
Self-mastery
    USE **Self-control**
Self-medication
    USE **Health self-care**
Self-mutilation   616.85
    BT   **Abnormal psychology**
Self-perception   155.2
    UF   Self-awareness
          Self-concept
    BT   **Psychology**
    NT   **Body image**
    RT   **Self-acceptance**
          Self-consciousness
          Self-esteem
Self-protection in animals
    USE **Animal defenses**
Self-protection in plants
    USE **Plant defenses**
Self-realization   155.2; 158
    UF   Fulfillment, Self
          Self-actualization
          Self-fulfillment
    BT   **Psychology**
    RT   **Success**
Self-reliance   179

Self-reliance—*Continued*
    UF   Self-assurance
    RT   **Self-confidence**
           Survival skills
Self-respect
    USE **Self-esteem**
Selfishness   179
    BT   **Personality**
Selling   381; 658.8
    UF   Salesmanship
    BT   **Business**
           Retail trade
    NT   **Auctions**
           Direct selling
           Mail-order business
           Rummage sales
           Sales management
           Secondhand trade
    RT   **Advertising**
           Marketing
Selling of infants
    USE **Adoption—Corrupt practices**
Semantics   121; 302.2; 401
    BT   **Language and languages**
           Linguistics
    NT   **Semiotics**
Semiarid regions
    USE **Arid regions**
Semiconductors   621.3815
    BT   **Electric conductors**
           Electronics
    NT   **Microelectronics**
           Transistors
Semiotics   302.2; 401
    Use for materials on the relationship between signs and symbols and whatever it is they stand for.
    BT   **Semantics**
    NT   **Visual literacy**
    RT   **Signs and symbols**
Semitic peoples (May subdiv. geog.)
    305.892
    BT   **Ethnology**
Senate (U.S.)
    USE **United States. Congress. Senate**
Senescence
    USE **Aging**
Senior centers (May subdiv. geog.)
    362.6
    UF   Centers for older people
           Centers for the elderly
           Elderly centers

    BT   **Community centers**
Senior citizens
    USE **Elderly**
Sense of direction
    USE **Direction sense**
Senses and sensation   152.1; 612.8
    BT   **Intellect**
           Physiology
           Psychology
           Psychophysiology
           Theory of knowledge
    NT   **Color sense**
           Gestalt psychology
           Hearing
           Pain
           Perception
           Pleasure
           Senses and sensation in animals
           Smell
           Taste
           Touch
           Vision
Senses and sensation in animals   573.8
    UF   Animal senses
           Animals—Senses and sensation
    SA   particular senses in animals, e.g.
           Hearing in animals [to be added as needed]
    BT   **Senses and sensation**
    NT   **Hearing in animals**
           Vision in animals
Sensing, Remote
    USE **Remote sensing**
Sensitivity training
    USE **Group relations training**
Separate development (Race relations)
    USE **Apartheid**
Separation anxiety in children   155.4
    BT   **Anxiety**
           Child psychology
Separation (Law) (May subdiv. geog.)
    306.89
    UF   Marital separation
    BT   **Divorce**
           Marriage
Separation of church and state
    USE **Church and state**
Separation of powers (May subdiv. geog.)
    320.4; 342

Separation of powers—*Continued*

    UF   Division of powers

           Powers, Separation of

    BT   **Constitutional law**

           Executive power

           Political science

Separation of powers—United States
     320.473

    UF   United States—Separation of
           powers

Separatism, Black

    USE **Black nationalism**

Separatist movement in Québec (Province)

    USE **Québec (Province)—History—**
          Autonomy and independence
          movements

Separatist movements   320.54

    UF   Secessionist movements

    SA   names of regions, countries, etc.
           with the subdivision *History—*
           Autonomy and independence
           movements [to be added as
           needed]

    BT   **Social movements**

    NT   **Québec (Province)—History—**
          Autonomy and independence
          movements

    RT   **Secession**

September 11 terrorist attacks, 2001
     973.931

    UF   Pentagon (Va.) terrorist attack,
           2001

           Terrorist attacks, September 11,
           2001

           World Trade Center (New York,
           N.Y.) terrorist attack, 2001

    BT   **Terrorism—United States**

Sepulchers

    USE **Tombs**

Sepulchral brasses

    USE **Brasses**

Sequences (Mathematics)   510

    UF   Mathematical sequences

           Numerical sequences

    BT   **Algebra**

           Mathematics

Serial killers   364.15

    UF   Serial murderers

    BT   **Criminals**

           Homicide

    NT   **Jack the Ripper murders, Lon-**
          don (England), 1888

Serial murderers

    USE **Serial killers**

Serial publications (May subdiv. geog.)
     050

    Use for general materials on publications in
    any medium issued in successive parts bearing
    numerical or chronological designations and
    intended to be continued indefinitely.

    BT   **Bibliography**

           Publishers and publishing

    NT   **Almanacs**

           Newspapers

           Periodicals

           School yearbooks

           Yearbooks

    RT   **International Standard Serial**
           Numbers

Serigraphy

    USE **Silk screen printing**

Sermon on the mount   226.9

Sermons (May subdiv. geog.)   **204; 252**

    Use for collections of sermons of several
    religions and for collections of Christian ser-
    mons not limited to a single topic, occasion,
    or Christian denomination. Materials on the
    art of writing and delivering sermons are en-
    tered under **Preaching**.

    SA   sermons of particular countries,
           languages, or religions, e.g.
           English sermons; Islamic
           sermons; etc.; sermons
           preached at particular times of
           year or on particular occa-
           sions, e.g. **Lenten sermons**;
           and topics and Christian de-
           nominations with the subdivi-
           sion *Sermons*, e.g. **Christian**
           life—Sermons; Presbyterian
           Church—Sermons; etc. [to
           be added as needed]

    BT   **Christian literature**

    NT   **Christian life—Sermons**

           English sermons

           Islamic sermons

           Lenten sermons

           Presbyterian Church—Sermons

    RT   **Preaching**

Serpents

    USE **Snakes**

Servants

    USE **Household employees**

Service books (Liturgy)

    USE **Liturgies**

Service, Customer
    USE **Customer services**
Service (in industry)
    USE **Customer services**
Service industries (May subdiv. geog.)
      338.4
    SA types of service industries [to be
          added as needed]
    BT **Industries**
    NT **Food service**
          Hospitality industry
          Hotels and motels
          Lease and rental services
          Undertakers and undertaking
Service stations (May subdiv. geog.)
      629.28
    UF Filling stations
         Gas stations
    BT **Automobile industry**
         Petroleum industry
Servicemen
    USE **Military personnel**
Services, Customer
    USE **Customer services**
Services for
    USE classes of persons, ethnic
          groups, animals, and types of
          schools with the subdivision
          Services for, e.g. **Handi-**
          capped—Services for [to be
          added as needed]
Services for the handicapped
    USE **Handicapped—Services for**
Services of worship
    USE **Worship programs**
Servicewomen
    USE **Military personnel**
Servitude
    USE **Peonage**
         Slavery
Servomechanisms **629.8**
    UF Automatic control
    BT **Automation**
         Feedback control systems
Set theory **511.3**
    UF Aggregates
         Classes (Mathematics)
         Ensembles (Mathematics)
         Mathematical sets
         Sets (Mathematics)
    BT **Mathematics**

    NT **Arithmetic**
         Boolean algebra
         Fractals
         Functions
         Number theory
         Topology
    RT **Symbolic logic**
Sets, Fractal
    USE **Fractals**
Sets (Mathematics)
    USE **Set theory**
Sets of fractional dimension
    USE **Fractals**
Settlement of land
    USE **Land settlement**
Settlements, Social
    USE **Social settlements**
Seven Years' War, 1756-1763 **940.2**
    BT **Europe—History—1492-1789**
    NT **United States—History—1755-**
         1763, French and Indian
         War
Seventeenth century
    USE **World history—17th century**
Seville (Spain). World's Fair, 1992
    USE **Expo 92 (Seville, Spain)**
Sewage disposal (May subdiv. geog.)
      628.3
    BT **Public health**
         Refuse and refuse disposal
    RT **Water pollution**
Sewerage (May subdiv. geog.) **628**
    UF Sewers
    BT **House drainage**
         Municipal engineering
         Plumbing
         Sanitary engineering
    RT **Drainage**
Sewers
    USE **Sewerage**
Sewing **646.2**
    BT **Home economics**
    NT **Embroidery**
         Quilting
         Soft toy making
    RT **Dressmaking**
         Needlework
         Sewing machines
Sewing machines **646.2044**
    RT **Sewing**

Sex 306.7

Use for materials on the social and behavioral aspects of sexuality. Materials on the physiological traits that distinguish the male and female of a species and on the physiological aspects of sexuality are entered under **Sex (Biology)**. Materials on the psychology of sexuality are entered under **Sex (Psychology)**.

UF Human beings—Sexual behavior
  Human sexuality
  Sexual behavior [*Former heading*]
  Sexual practices
  Sexuality

SA social groups and classes of persons with the subdivision *Sexual behavior*, e.g. **College students—Sexual behavior** [to be added as needed]

BT **Human behavior**

NT **Bisexuality**
  College students—Sexual behavior
  Computer sex
  Homosexuality
  Sex crimes
  Sex in the workplace
  Sex role
  Sexual abstinence
  Sexual deviation
  Sexual harassment

RT **Sex (Biology)**
  Sex (Psychology)
  Sexual disorders
  Sexual ethics

Sex bias
  USE **Sexism**

Sex (Biology) 571.8; 612.6

Use for materials on the physical traits that distinguish the male and female of a species and on the physiological aspects of sexuality. Materials on the social and behavioral aspects of sexuality are entered under **Sex**. Materials on the psychology of sexuality are entered under **Sex (Psychology)**.

UF Sex—Physiological aspects
  Sexuality

BT **Biology**

NT **Puberty**
  Reproductive system
  Sexual behavior in animals
  Sexual disorders

RT **Reproduction**
  Sex

Sex change
  USE **Transsexualism**

Sex crimes (May subdiv. geog.) 364.15

UF Sexual abuse
  Sexual crimes
  Sexual offenses

SA types of sex crimes [to be added as needed]

BT **Crime**
  Sex

NT **Child sexual abuse**
  Incest
  Rape

Sex differences (Psychology) 155.3

BT **Sex (Psychology)**

NT **Androgyny**
  Sex role

Sex discrimination (May subdiv. geog.) 305.3

Use for materials on the restriction or denial of rights, privileges, or choice because of one's sex. Materials on prejudicial attitudes toward people because of their sex are entered under **Sexism**.

BT **Discrimination**
  Sexism

NT **Equal rights amendments**
  Women's rights

Sex disorders
  USE **Sexual disorders**

Sex education (May subdiv. geog.) 372.37; 613.9071; 649

UF Sex instruction

BT **Family life education**

RT **Sexual hygiene**

Sex in art
  USE **Erotic art**

Sex in mass media 302.23

BT **Mass media**

Sex in popular culture 306.7

BT **Popular culture**

Sex in the office
  USE **Sex in the workplace**

Sex in the workplace 306.7; 658

UF Office romance
  Sex in the office

BT **Sex**

RT **Sexual harassment**

Sex instruction
  USE **Sex education**

Sex organs
  USE **Reproductive system**

Sex—Physiological aspects
　USE　**Sex (Biology)**
Sex—Psychological aspects
　USE　**Sex (Psychology)**
Sex (Psychology)　**155.3**

Use for materials on the psychology of sexuality. Materials on the social and behavioral aspects of sexuality are entered under **Sex**. Materials on the physiological traits that distinguish the male and female of a species and on the physiological aspects of sexuality are entered under **Sex (Biology)**.

　UF　Sex—Psychological aspects
　　　Sexual behavior, Psychology of
　　　Sexual psychology
　　　Sexuality
　BT　**Psychology**
　NT　**Femininity**
　　　Masculinity
　　　Sex differences (Psychology)
　RT　**Sex**
Sex role　**305.3**

Use for materials on the patterns of attitudes and behavior that are regarded as appropriate to one sex rather than the other.

　UF　Female role
　　　Gender identity
　　　Male role
　　　Sexual identity
　BT　**Sex**
　　　Sex differences (Psychology)
　　　Social role
　NT　**Androgyny**
　　　Transsexualism
　RT　**Sexism**
Sex therapy　**616.6; 616.85**
　BT　**Psychotherapy**
　RT　**Sexual disorders**
Sexism (May subdiv. geog.)　**305.3**

Use for materials on prejudicial attitudes toward people because of their sex. Materials on the restriction or denial of rights, privileges, or choice because of one's sex are entered under **Sex discrimination**.

　UF　Sex bias
　BT　**Attitude (Psychology)**
　　　Prejudices
　NT　**Sex discrimination**
　RT　**Sex role**
Sexual abstinence　**176; 306.73**

Use for materials on abstinence from sexual activity. Materials on the virtue that moderates and regulates the sexual appetite in human beings are entered under **Chastity**. Materials on the renunciation of marriage for religious reasons are entered under **Celibacy**.

　UF　Abstinence, Sexual
　BT　**Asceticism**
　　　Sex
　RT　**Birth control**
　　　Celibacy
　　　Chastity
Sexual abuse
　USE　**Child sexual abuse**
　　　Sex crimes
　　　Sexual harassment
Sexual assault
　USE　**Rape**
Sexual behavior
　USE　**Sex**
Sexual behavior in animals　**591.56**
　UF　Animal sexual behavior
　　　Animals—Sexual behavior
　　　Breeding behavior
　　　Mating behavior
　　　Reproductive behavior
　BT　**Animal behavior**
　　　Sex (Biology)
　NT　**Animal courtship**
Sexual behavior, Psychology of
　USE　**Sex (Psychology)**
Sexual crimes
　USE　**Sex crimes**
Sexual deviation　**306.7; 616.85**
　UF　Deviation, Sexual
　　　Perversion, Sexual
　　　Sexual perversion
　BT　**Sex**
　　　Sexual disorders
Sexual disorders　**616.6; 616.85**
　UF　Sex disorders
　BT　**Sex (Biology)**
　NT　**Sexual deviation**
　RT　**Sex**
　　　Sex therapy
Sexual ethics (May subdiv. geog.)　**176**
　BT　**Ethics**
　NT　**Adultery**
　　　Chastity
　　　Free love
　　　Prostitution
　　　Sexual harassment
　RT　**Sex**
Sexual harassment (May subdiv. geog.)　**331.13; 344**
　UF　Harassment, Sexual
　　　Sexual abuse

Sexual harassment—*Continued*
   BT Sex
      Sexual ethics
   RT Sex in the workplace
Sexual hygiene   613.9
   UF Hygiene, Sexual
      Social hygiene
   BT **Hygiene**
   NT **Birth control**
      Safe sex in AIDS prevention
      Sexually transmitted diseases—
         Prevention
   RT Sex education
      Sexually transmitted diseases
Sexual identity
   USE **Sex role**
Sexual offenses
   USE **Sex crimes**
Sexual perversion
   USE **Sexual deviation**
Sexual practices
   USE **Sex**
Sexual psychology
   USE **Sex (Psychology)**
Sexuality
   USE **Sex**
      Sex (Biology)
      Sex (Psychology)
Sexually abused children
   USE **Child sexual abuse**
Sexually transmitted diseases (May
      subdiv. geog.)   616.95
   UF VD
      Venereal diseases
   SA types of sexually transmitted dis-
      eases [to be added as needed]
   BT **Communicable diseases**
   NT **Syphilis**
   RT **Sexual hygiene**
Sexually transmitted diseases—Prevention
   616.95
   UF Safe sex
   BT **Sexual hygiene**
Shade gardens
   USE **Gardening in the shade**
Shades and shadows   741.2
   UF Light and shade
      Shadows
   BT **Drawing**
Shadow economy
   USE **Underground economy**
Shadow pantomimes and plays   791.5

   BT **Amateur theater**
      Pantomimes
      Puppets and puppet plays
      Shadow pictures
      Theater
Shadow pictures   793
   UF Hand shadows
      Shadowplay
   BT **Amusements**
   NT **Shadow pantomimes and plays**
Shadowpact (Fictional characters)
   741.5
   BT **Superheroes**
Shadowplay
   USE **Shadow pictures**
Shadows
   USE **Shades and shadows**
Shady gardens
   USE **Gardening in the shade**
Shaft sinking
   USE **Drilling and boring (Earth and**
      rocks)
Shakers (May subdiv. geog.)   289
   BT **Christian sects**
Shakespeare, William, 1564-1616   822.3
      When applicable, the subdivisions provided
   with this heading may be used for other volu-
   minous authors, e.g. Dante; Goethe; etc. These
   headings are to be used for materials about
   Shakespeare and about his writings. The texts
   of his plays, etc., are not given subject head-
   ings.

Shakespeare, William, 1564-1616—Adap-
      tations   822.3
      May be used for individual works, collec-
   tions, or materials about literary, cinematic,
   video, or television adaptations of Shake-
   speare's works.
   UF Shakespeare, William, 1564-
      1616—Paraphrases
Shakespeare, William, 1564-1616—Allu-
      sions   822.3
Shakespeare, William, 1564-1616—Anni-
      versaries   822.3
Shakespeare, William, 1564-1616—Au-
      thorship   822.3
   UF Bacon-Shakespeare controversy
Shakespeare, William, 1564-1616—Bibli-
      ography   016.8223
Shakespeare, William, 1564-1616—Biogra-
      phy—Psychology
   USE **Shakespeare, William, 1564-**
      1616—Psychology

Shakespeare, William, 1564-1616—Characters 822.3

Shakespeare, William, 1564-1616—Comedies 822.3

Use for materials about the comedies, not for the texts of the plays.

Shakespeare, William, 1564-1616—Concordances 822.303

UF   Shakespeare, William, 1564-1616—Indexes

Shakespeare, William, 1564-1616—Criticism 822.3

Use for materials discussing the criticism of Shakespeare's works, including historical materials. Criticism of Shakespeare's works in general is entered under **Shakespeare, William, 1564-1616**. Criticism of the comedies is entered under **Shakespeare, William, 1564-1616—Comedies**; criticism of the sonnets under **Shakespeare, William, 1564-1616—Sonnets**; etc. Criticism of an individual play is entered under **Shakespeare, William, 1564-1616**, followed by the title of the play.

UF   Shakespeare, William, 1564-1616—Criticism, interpretation, etc.

Shakespeare, William, 1564-1616—Psychological studies

Shakespeare, William, 1564-1616—Criticism, interpretation, etc.

USE   **Shakespeare, William, 1564-1616—Criticism**

Shakespeare, William, 1564-1616—Dictionaries 822.303

BT   **Encyclopedias and dictionaries**

Shakespeare, William, 1564-1616—Discography 016.8223

Shakespeare, William, 1564-1616—Dramatic production 822.3

UF   Shakespeare, William, 1564-1616—Stage setting and scenery

Shakespeare, William, 1564-1616—Ethics 822.3

UF   Shakespeare, William, 1564-1616—Moral ideas

Shakespeare, William, 1564-1616—Religion and ethics

Shakespeare, William, 1564-1616—Filmography 016.8223

Shakespeare, William, 1564-1616—Histories 822.3

Use for materials about the histories, not for the texts of the plays.

Shakespeare, William, 1564-1616—Indexes

USE   **Shakespeare, William, 1564-1616—Concordances**

Shakespeare, William, 1564-1616—Influence 822.3

Use for materials on Shakespeare's influence on national literatures, literary movements, or specific persons.

Shakespeare, William, 1564-1616—Knowledge 822.3

Use for materials on Shakespeare's knowledge or treatment of specific subjects. May be subdivided by subject, e.g. **Shakespeare, William, 1564-1616—Knowledge—Animals**; etc.

Shakespeare, William, 1564-1616—Moral ideas

USE   **Shakespeare, William, 1564-1616—Ethics**

Shakespeare, William, 1564-1616—Paraphrases

USE   **Shakespeare, William, 1564-1616—Adaptations**

Shakespeare, William, 1564-1616—Parodies, imitations, etc. 822.3

UF   Shakespeare, William, 1564-1616—Parodies, travesties, etc.

Shakespeare, William, 1564-1616—Parodies, travesties, etc.

USE   **Shakespeare, William, 1564-1616—Parodies, imitations, etc.**

Shakespeare, William, 1564-1616—Poetic works 822.3

Use for materials about the poetic works, not for the poetic texts themselves.

Shakespeare, William, 1564-1616—Portraits 822.3022

Shakespeare, William, 1564-1616—Psychological studies

USE   **Shakespeare, William, 1564-1616—Criticism**

Shakespeare, William, 1564-1616—Psychology

Shakespeare, William, 1564-1616—Psychology 822.3

UF   Shakespeare, William, 1564-1616—Biography—Psychology

Shakespeare, William, 1564-1616—Psychological studies

Shakespeare, William, 1564-1616—Quotations 822.3

Shakespeare, William, 1564-1616—Religion 822.3

UF Shakespeare, William, 1564-1616—Religion and ethics

Shakespeare, William, 1564-1616—Religion and ethics

USE **Shakespeare, William, 1564-1616—Ethics**

Shakespeare, William, 1564-1616—Religion

Shakespeare, William, 1564-1616—Sonnets 822.3

Use for materials about the sonnets, not for the texts of the sonnets.

Shakespeare, William, 1564-1616—Stage history 792; 822.3

BT **Theater**

Shakespeare, William, 1564-1616—Stage setting and scenery

USE **Shakespeare, William, 1564-1616—Dramatic production**

Shakespeare, William, 1564-1616—Style

USE **Shakespeare, William, 1564-1616—Technique**

Shakespeare, William, 1564-1616—Technique 822.3

UF Shakespeare, William, 1564-1616—Style

Shakespeare, William, 1564-1616—Tragedies 822.3

Use for materials about the tragedies, not for the texts of the plays.

Shamanism (May subdiv. geog.) **291.144; 291.66**

BT **Religions**

RT **Shamans**

Shamans (May subdiv. geog.) **200.92**

UF Medicine men

RT **Shamanism**

Shame 152.4

BT **Emotions**

RT **Guilt**

Shape 516

UF Shapes

Size and shape

SA types of geometric shapes, e.g. **Square** [to be added as needed]

BT **Concepts**

Geometry

Perception

NT **Square**

Shapes

USE **Shape**

Sharecropping (May subdiv. geog.) **333.33**

BT **Farm tenancy**

Shared custody

USE **Child custody**

Shared housing (May subdiv. geog.) **363.5; 643**

Use for materials on two or more single, unrelated adults who live together.

UF Home sharing

House sharing

BT **Housing**

NT **Unmarried couples**

RT **Roommates**

Shared parenting

USE **Part-time parenting**

Shared reading books

USE **Big books**

Shares of stock

USE **Stocks**

Shareware (Computer software) 005.3

Use for materials on computer software offered to consumers on a trial basis with the provision that they pay a voluntary fee if they want to use it.

UF Software for sharing

BT **Computer software**

Sharing of jobs

USE **Job sharing**

Sheep 599.649; 636.3

UF Lambs

BT **Domestic animals**

Mammals

Sheet metalwork 671.8

UF Press working of metal

BT **Metalwork**

NT **Plate metalwork**

Sheffield plate 739.2

BT **Plate**

Shellfish 594; 641.3

BT **Aquatic animals**

NT **Crabs**

Crustacea

Lobsters

Mollusks

Shells (May subdiv. geog.) **591.47; 594.147**

Use for popular materials on seashells and shell collecting. Systematic and comprehensive materials on shells are entered under **Mollusks**.

UF Sea shells

Shells—*Continued*
    RT   **Mollusks**
Shells (Projectiles)
    USE **Projectiles**
Shelterbelts
    USE **Windbreaks**
Shelters, Air raid
    USE **Air raid shelters**
Sherlock Holmes (Fictitious character)
    USE **Holmes, Sherlock (Fictional character)**
Sherlock Holmes films   791.43
    Use for individual works, collections, or materials about Sherlock Holmes films.
    BT   **Motion pictures**
         Mystery films
Shia
    USE **Shiites**
Shiism
    USE **Shiites**
Shiites (May subdiv. geog.)   297.82
    UF   Shia
         Shiism
    BT   **Islamic sects**
Shinto (May subdiv. geog.)   299.5
    BT   **Religions**
Ship building
    USE **Shipbuilding**
Ship models
    USE **Ships—Models**
Ship pilots (May subdiv. geog.)   623.89
    UF   Pilots
         Pilots and pilotage
    BT   **Sailors**
    RT   **Navigation**
Ship safety
    USE **Ships—Safety regulations**
Ship salvage
    USE **Marine salvage**
Shipbuilding (May subdiv. geog.)   623.8
    UF   Ship building
         Ships—Construction
    BT   **Naval architecture**
    NT   **Marine engines**
         Steamboats
    RT   **Boatbuilding**
         Ships
Shipping (May subdiv. geog.)   387.5
    UF   Marine transportation
         Ocean—Economic aspects
         Ocean transportation
         Sea transportation

         Water transportation
    BT   **Transportation**
    NT   **Harbors**
         Inland navigation
         Marine insurance
         Maritime law
         Territorial waters
    RT   **Merchant marine**
Shipping—United States   387.00973
Ships (May subdiv. geog.)   387.2; 623.82
    UF   Vessels (Ships)
    SA   types of ships and vessels and names of individual ships [to be added as needed]
    NT   **Clipper ships**
         Hospital ships
         Lightships
         Merchant marine
         Sailing
         Steamboats
         Submarines
         Warships
         Yachts and yachting
    RT   **Boats and boating**
         Shipbuilding
Ships—Construction
    USE **Shipbuilding**
Ships in art
    USE **Marine painting**
Ships—Models   623.82
    UF   Model ships
         Ship models
    BT   **Models and modelmaking**
Ships—Safety regulations   341.7; 343
    UF   Merchant marine—Safety regulations
         Ship safety
    BT   **Maritime law**
         Safety regulations
Shipwrecks   363.12; 910.4
    UF   Marine disasters
    SA   names of wrecked ships [to be added as needed]
    BT   **Accidents**
         Adventure and adventurers
         Disasters
         Navigation
         Voyages and travels
    RT   **Marine salvage**
         Survival after airplane accidents, shipwrecks, etc.

Shoe industry (May subdiv. geog.)
338.4; 685
　BT　**Clothing industry**
　　　Leather industry
　RT　**Shoes**
Shoes (May subdiv. geog.)　**391.4; 646;**
685
　UF　Boots
　　　Footwear
　BT　**Clothing and dress**
　RT　**Shoe industry**
Shojo-ai　**741.5**
　Use for individual works, collections, or
materials about shojo-ai.
　UF　Girl-love manga
　　　Yuri
　BT　**Manga**
Shojo manga　**741.5**
　Use for individual works, collections, or
materials about manga for girls ages 12-18.
　BT　**Manga**
Shonen-ai　**741.5**
　Use for individual works, collections, or
materials about shonen-ai.
　UF　Boy-love manga
　　　Yaoi
　BT　**Manga**
Shonen manga　**741.5**
　Use for individual works, collections, or
materials about manga for boys ages 12-18.
　BT　**Manga**
Shooting (May subdiv. geog.)　**799.3**
　Use for materials on the use of firearms.
Materials on shooting game are entered under
Hunting.
　NT　**Archery**
　　　Decoys (Hunting)
　RT　**Firearms**
　　　Hunting
Shooting stars
　USE　**Meteors**
Shootings in schools
　USE　**School shootings**
Shop management
　USE　**Factory management**
Shop practice
　USE　**Machine shop practice**
Shop windows
　USE　**Show windows**
Shoplifting　**364.16**
　BT　**Theft**

Shoppers' guides
　USE　**Consumer education**
　　　Shopping
Shopping (May subdiv. geog.)　**381; 640**
　Use for materials on consumer buying.
General materials on buying and materials on
buying by commercial enterprises are entered
under **Purchasing**.
　UF　Buyers' guides
　　　Marketing (Home economics)
　　　Shoppers' guides
　SA　types of products and services
　　　with the subdivision *Purchas-*
　　　ing, e.g. **Automobiles—Pur-**
　　　chasing [to be added as need-
　　　ed]
　BT　**Home economics**
　　　Purchasing
　NT　**Grocery shopping**
　　　Internet shopping
　RT　**Consumer education**
Shopping centers and malls (May subdiv.
geog.)　**381; 658.8**
　UF　Malls, Shopping
　　　Shopping malls
　BT　**Commercial buildings**
　　　Retail trade
　RT　**Stores**
Shopping—Computer network resources
　USE　**Internet shopping**
Shopping—Internet resources
　USE　**Internet shopping**
Shopping malls
　USE　**Shopping centers and malls**
Shops
　USE　**Stores**
Short films　**791.43**
　Use for individual works, collections, or
materials about short films.
　BT　**Motion pictures**
Short plays
　USE　**One act plays**
Short stories　**808.83**
　Use for collections of short stories by one
author or by several authors. Materials on the
short story as a literary form and on the tech-
nique of writing short stories are entered un-
der **Short story**.
　UF　Stories
　BT　**Fiction**
Short stories—Indexes　**016.80883**
Short story　**808.3**
　Use for materials on the short story as a lit-
erary form and on the technique of writing

Short story—*Continued*
short stories. Collections of stories are entered under **Short stories**.

  BT **Authorship**
       Fiction
       Literature
  RT **Storytelling**
Shorthand   653
  UF Stenography
  BT **Business education**
       Office practice
       Writing
  RT **Abbreviations**
Shortwave radio   621.3841
  UF High-frequency radio
       UHF radio
       Ultrahigh frequency radio
       Very high frequency radio
       VHF radio
  BT **Radio**
       Radio frequency modulation
  NT **Amateur radio stations**
       Citizens band radio
       Microwave communication systems
       Microwaves
Shotguns   683.4
  UF Guns
  BT **Firearms**
Show business
  USE **Performing arts**
Show windows   659.1
  UF Shop windows
       Window dressing
  BT **Advertising**
       Decoration and ornament
       Windows
Showers (Parties)   793.2
  UF Baby showers
       Bridal showers
       Wedding showers
  BT **Parties**
Showing off   302.5
  UF Attention-seeking
       Seeking attention
  BT **Human behavior**
Shrines (May subdiv. geog.)   **203; 263; 726**
  NT **Tombs**
  RT **Pilgrims and pilgrimages**
Shroud, Holy
  USE **Holy Shroud**

Shroud of Turin
  USE **Holy Shroud**
Shrubs (May subdiv. geog.)   **582.1; 635.9**
  BT **Plants**
       Trees
  NT **Evergreens**
  RT **Landscape gardening**
       Ornamental plants
Shyness   155.2
  UF Bashfulness
  BT **Emotions**
Sibling rivalry   306.875
  BT **Child psychology**
       Siblings
Sibling sequence
  USE **Birth order**
Siblings   155.44; 306.875
  UF Brothers and sisters
       Sisters and brothers
  BT **Family**
  NT **Brothers**
       Sibling rivalry
       Sisters
       Twins
Sick   305.9; 362.1
  BT **Handicapped**
  NT **Church work with the sick**
       Cooking for the sick
       First aid
       Invalids
       Mentally ill
       Terminally ill
  RT **Diseases**
       Home nursing
       Nursing
       Patients
Sick—Prayers   204; 242
  BT **Prayers**
Sickness
  USE **Diseases**
SIDS (Disease)
  USE **Sudden infant death syndrome**
Sieges
  USE **Battles**
Sight
  USE **Vision**
Sight saving books
  USE **Large print books**
Sign language   419
  UF Deaf—Sign language

Sign language—*Continued*
   BT   **Language and languages**
   NT   **Native American sign language**
   RT   **Deaf—Means of communication**
        Signs and symbols
Sign painting   667
   BT   **Advertising**
        Industrial painting
   NT   **Alphabets**
   RT   **Lettering**
        Signs and signboards
Signaling
   USE   types of transportation and communication with the subdivision *Signaling,* e.g. **Railroads—Signaling** [to be added as needed]
Signals and signaling   388; 621.382
   UF   Coastal signals
        Fog signals
        Military signaling
        Naval signaling
   SA   types of transportation and communication with the subdivision *Signaling,* e.g. **Railroads—Signaling** [to be added as needed]
   BT   **Communication**
        Military art and science
        Naval art and science
        Navigation
        Signs and symbols
   NT   **Railroads—Signaling**
        Sonar
   RT   **Flags**
Signboards
   USE   **Signs and signboards**
Signed editions
   USE   **Autographed editions**
Signets
   USE   **Seals (Numismatics)**
Signs (Advertising)
   USE   **Signs and signboards**
Signs and signboards   659.13
   UF   Billboards
        Road signs
        Signboards
        Signs (Advertising)
   BT   **Advertising**
   NT   **Electric signs**

   RT   **Posters**
        Sign painting
Signs and symbols (May subdiv. geog.)   302.2; 419
   UF   Emblems
        Symbols
   BT   **Communication**
   NT   **Ciphers**
        Cryptography
        Heraldry
        National emblems
        Signals and signaling
        State emblems
   RT   **Abbreviations**
        Semiotics
        Sign language
        Symbolism
Signs and symbols in literature
   USE   **Symbolism in literature**
Silage and silos   633.2
   UF   Silos
   BT   **Feeds**
        Forage plants
Silent films (May subdiv. geog.)   791.43
      Use for individual works, collections, or materials about films made before the development of films with sound.
   UF   Silent motion pictures
   BT   **Motion pictures**
Silent motion pictures
   USE   **Silent films**
Silk (May subdiv. geog.)   677
   BT   **Fabrics**
        Fibers
   RT   **Silkworms**
Silk screen printing (May subdiv. geog.)   764
   UF   Screen printing
        Serigraphy
   BT   **Color printing**
        Stencil work
   RT   **Textile printing**
Silkworms   595.78; 638
   UF   Cocoons
   BT   **Beneficial insects**
        Insects
        Moths
   RT   **Silk**
Silos
   USE   **Silage and silos**
Silver (May subdiv. geog.)   332.4; 669

Silver—*Continued*
- BT **Chemical elements**
  Precious metals
- NT **Silverwork**
- RT **Coinage**
  Money

Silver articles
- USE **Silverwork**

Silver mines and mining (May subdiv. geog.) **622**
- BT **Mines and mineral resources**
- NT **Prospecting**

Silver plate
- USE **Plate**
  Silverware

Silver work
- USE **Silverwork**

Silversmithing
- USE **Silverwork**

Silverware (May subdiv. geog.) **642; 739.2**
- UF Flatware, Silver
  Silver plate
- BT **Decorative arts**
  Silverwork
  Tableware

Silverwork (May subdiv. geog.) **739.2**
- UF Silver articles
  Silver work
  Silversmithing
- BT **Art metalwork**
  Metalwork
  Silver
- NT **Native American silverwork**
  Plate
  Silverware

Simple machines **621.8**
- UF Machines, Simple
- SA types of simple machines, e.g. **Wheels** [to be added as needed]
- BT **Machinery**
  Mechanical movements
  Mechanics
- NT **Wheels**

Simplicity **179; 646.7**
- BT **Conduct of life**

Simulation, Computer
- USE **Computer simulation**

Simulation games **003**
- UF Gaming simulations
- BT **Game theory**
- NT **War games**

Simulation games in education **371.39**
- UF Educational gaming
  Educational simulation games
  Gaming, Educational
- BT **Education**
  Educational games
  Game theory

Sin **205; 241**
- BT **Ethics**
  Good and evil
  Theology
- NT **Avarice**
  Guilt
  Pride and vanity
- RT **Forgiveness of sin**

Sin, Forgiveness of
- USE **Forgiveness of sin**

Sinai Campaign, 1956 **956.04**
- UF Anglo-French intervention in Egypt, 1956
  Arab-Israel War, 1956
  Israel-Arab War, 1956
- BT **Egypt—History**
  Israel-Arab conflicts

Singers **782.0092; 920**
- BT **Musicians**
- NT **African American singers**

Singing **782; 783**
- UF School music
- BT **Music**
- NT **Songbooks**
  Voice culture
- RT **Choirs (Music)**
  Vocal music
  Voice

Singing games **796.1**
- BT **Games**

Singing societies
- USE **Choral societies**

Single child
- USE **Only child**

Single men (May subdiv. geog.) **155.6; 306.81**
- UF Bachelors
  Unmarried men
- BT **Men**
  Single people
- NT **Divorced men**

Single-parent families (May subdiv. geog.)
306.85

Use for materials on households in which a parent living without a partner is rearing children. Materials on parents who were not married at the time of the birth of their children are entered under **Unmarried fathers** or **Unmarried mothers**.

UF   One parent family

Single parent family

BT   **Family**

RT   **Single parents**

Single parent family

USE   **Single-parent families**

Single parents (May subdiv. geog.)
306.85

BT   **Parents**

Unmarried couples

NT   **Children of single parents**

Unmarried fathers

Unmarried mothers

RT   **Single-parent families**

Single parents' children

USE   **Children of single parents**

Single people (May subdiv. geog.)
155.6; 306.81

UF   Unmarried people

NT   **Divorced people**

Single men

Single women

Single rail railroads

USE   **Monorail railroads**

Single-sex education

USE   **Single-sex schools**

Single-sex schools (May subdiv. geog.)
370

UF   Single-sex education

BT   **Schools**

Single women (May subdiv. geog.)
155.6; 306.81

UF   Unmarried women

BT   **Single people**

Women

NT   **Divorced women**

Sirius   **523.8**

BT   **Stars**

Sisterhoods

USE   **Monasticism and religious orders for women**

Sisters   **306.875**

BT   **Siblings**

Women

Sisters and brothers

USE   **Siblings**

Sisters (Religious)

USE   **Nuns**

Sit-down strikes

USE   **Strikes**

Sit-ins for civil rights

USE   **Civil rights demonstrations**

Sitcoms

USE   **Comedy television programs**

Site oriented art

USE   **Earthworks (Art)**

Sitters (Babysitters)

USE   **Babysitters**

Situation comedies

USE   **Comedy television programs**

Six Day War, 1967

USE   **Israel-Arab War, 1967**

Sixteenth century

USE   **World history—16th century**

Size   **530.8**

UF   Large and small

Size and shape

Small and large

BT   **Concepts**

Perception

Size and shape

USE   **Shape**

Size

Skateboarding   **796.22**

BT   **Roller skating**

Skating

USE   **Ice skating**

Roller skating

Skeletal remains

USE   **Anthropometry**

Skeleton   **573.7; 611**

Use for materials limited to the morphology or mechanics of the skeleton, human or animal. Comprehensive and systematic materials on the anatomy of bones are entered under **Bones**.

BT   **Musculoskeletal system**

RT   **Bones**

Skepticism   **149; 186; 211**

UF   Scepticism

Unbelief

BT   **Free thought**

Philosophy

Rationalism

RT   **Agnosticism**

Belief and doubt

Truth

Sketching
USE **Drawing**
Ski resorts (May subdiv. geog.) **796.93**
BT **Winter resorts**
Skidoos
USE **Snowmobiles**
Skiing (May subdiv. geog.) **796.93**
UF Skis and skiing
Snow skiing
BT **Winter sports**
Skill
USE **Ability**
Skilled labor (May subdiv. geog.) **331.7**
BT **Labor**
Skills
USE **Ability**
Skin **611; 612.7**
BT **Anatomy**
Physiology
Skin—Care **616.5; 646.7**
UF Skin care
Skin—Care and hygiene
Skin care
USE **Skin—Care**
Skin—Care and hygiene
USE **Skin—Care**
Skin—Diseases **616.5**
UF Dermatitis
SA types of skin diseases [to be
added as needed]
BT **Diseases**
NT **Acne**
Skin diving (May subdiv. geog.) **797.2**
Use for materials on free diving with mask,
fins, and snorkel. Materials on free diving
with the aid of a self-contained underwater
breathing apparatus are entered under **Scuba
diving**.
UF Free diving
Snorkeling
Underwater swimming
BT **Deep diving**
Skinheads
USE **White supremacy movements**
Skins
USE **Hides and skins**
Skis and skiing
USE **Skiing**
Skits **791**
BT **Amusements**
Theater
Sky **520; 551.5**

BT **Astronomy**
Atmosphere
NT **Constellations**
Sky diving
USE **Skydiving**
Skydiving (May subdiv. geog.) **797.5**
UF Sky diving
BT **Aeronautical sports**
Skyscrapers (May subdiv. geog.) **690;
720**
UF High rise buildings
BT **Buildings**
Skyscrapers—Earthquake effects **690;
725**
BT **Buildings—Earthquake effects**
Earthquakes
Slander (Law)
USE **Libel and slander**
Slang
USE names of languages with the
subdivision *Slang*, e.g. **En-
glish language—Slang** [to be
added as needed]
Slanted journalism
USE **Journalism—Objectivity**
Slapstick comedies
USE **Comedies**
Comedy films
Comedy television programs
Slave insurrections
USE **Slave revolts**
Slave narratives **306.3**
BT **Autobiography**
Slavery
Slave revolts (May subdiv. geog.) **326;
909**
UF Slave insurrections
BT **Revolutions**
RT **Slavery**
Slave trade (May subdiv. geog.) **306.3;
381**
BT **International law**
Slavery
Slavery (May subdiv. geog.) **177; 306.3;
326; 342**
UF Abolition of slavery
Antislavery
Servitude
BT **Crimes against humanity**
NT **Slave narratives**
Slave trade

Slavery—*Continued*
Slaves
  RT **Abolitionists**
      Forced labor
      Peonage
      Slave revolts
      Slaves—Emancipation
Slavery—Emancipation
  USE **Slaves—Emancipation**
Slavery—United States **306.3; 326.0973**
  RT **Southern States—History**
      Underground railroad
Slavery—United States—Fiction **808.83; 813**

Use for collections of stories dealing with slavery in the United States.

Slaves (May subdiv. geog.) **306.3**
  BT **Slavery**
  NT **Fugitive slaves**
Slaves—Emancipation (May subdiv. geog.) **306.3**
  UF Abolition of slavery
      Antislavery
      Emancipation of slaves
      Slavery—Emancipation
  BT **Freedom**
  RT **Abolitionists**
      Slavery
Sled dog racing (May subdiv. geog.) **798.8**
  UF Dog sled racing
  BT **Winter sports**
Sledding **796.9**
  BT **Winter sports**
  RT **Sleds**
Sledges
  USE **Sleds**
Sleds **688.7**
  UF Sledges
      Sleighs and sledges
  BT **Vehicles**
  RT **Sledding**
Sleep **154.6; 612.8; 613.7**
  BT **Brain**
      Health
      Hygiene
      Mind and body
      Psychophysiology
      Rest
      Subconsciousness
  NT **Bedtime**

  RT **Dreams**
      Insomnia
Sleeplessness
  USE **Insomnia**
Sleighs and sledges
  USE **Sleds**
Sleight of hand
  USE **Juggling**
      Magic tricks
Slide projectors
  USE **Projectors**
Slide rule **510.28**
  BT **Calculators**
      Logarithms
Slides (Photography) **778.2**
  UF Color slides
      Lantern slides
      Photographic slides
  BT **Photography**
  RT **Filmstrips**
Sloppiness
  USE **Messiness**
Sloth
  USE **Laziness**
Slovakia **943.73**

May be subdivided like **United States** except for *History*.

  RT **Czechoslovakia**
Slow food movement (May subdiv. geog.) **641.01**
  BT **Gastronomy**
      Social movements
Slow learning children **155.4; 371.92**

Use for materials on children with less than average intelligence and slow social development who can nonetheless be educated and lead a normal life.

  BT **Exceptional children**
  NT **Learning disabilities**
  RT **Mentally handicapped children**
Slum clearance
  USE **Urban renewal**
Small and large
  USE **Size**
Small arms
  USE **Firearms**
Small business (May subdiv. geog.) **338.6; 658.02**

Use for materials on small independent business enterprises.

  BT **Business**
  NT **Entrepreneurship**
      Home-based business

Small business—*Continued*
> **Underground economy**

Small cars
> USE **Compact cars**

Small claims courts (May subdiv. geog.)
> 347
> BT **Civil procedure**
> **Courts**

Small loans
> USE **Personal loans**

Smell 152.1
> BT **Senses and sensation**
> RT **Nose**

Smelting 669
> BT **Furnaces**
> NT **Blast furnaces**
> **Electrometallurgy**
> **Ore dressing**
> RT **Metallurgy**

Smocking 746.44
> BT **Needlework**

Smoke-ending programs
> USE **Smoking cessation programs**

Smoke prevention 363.738; 628.5
> UF **Prevention of smoke**
> BT **Sanitation**

Smoke stacks
> USE **Chimneys**

Smokeless powder
> USE **Gunpowder**

Smoking (May subdiv. geog.) 178;
> 613.85
> NT **Cigarettes**
> **Cigars**
> **Tobacco habit**
> **Tobacco pipes**
> RT **Tobacco**

Smoking cessation programs 613.85
> UF How-to-stop-smoking programs
> Quit-smoking programs
> Smoke-ending programs
> BT **Tobacco habit**

Smuggling 364.1
> UF Contraband trade
> BT **Crime**
> **Tariff**

Smuggling of drugs
> USE **Drug traffic**

Snack foods 641.5; 642
> UF Snacks
> BT **Food**

Snacks
> USE **Snack foods**

Snakes (May subdiv. geog.) 597.96
> UF Serpents
> Vipers
> SA types of snakes, e.g. **Rattle-snakes** [to be added as needed]
> BT **Reptiles**
> NT **Rattlesnakes**
> **Snakes as pets**

Snakes as pets 636.088
> BT **Pets**
> **Snakes**

Snapshots
> USE **Photographs**

Snobbery
> USE **Snobs and snobbishness**

Snobbishness
> USE **Snobs and snobbishness**

Snobbism
> USE **Snobs and snobbishness**

Snobs and snobbishness 303.3
> UF Snobbery
> Snobbishness
> Snobbism
> RT **Pride and vanity**

Snorkeling
> USE **Skin diving**

Snow (May subdiv. geog.) 551.57
> BT **Precipitation (Meteorology)**
> NT **Avalanches**
> RT **Blizzards**
> **Storms**

Snow boarding
> USE **Snowboarding**

Snow skiing
> USE **Skiing**

Snowboarding (May subdiv. geog.)
> 796.939
> UF Snow boarding
> BT **Winter sports**

Snowmobiles 629.22; 796.94
> UF Skidoos
> BT **All terrain vehicles**

Soap 668
> BT **Cleaning compounds**
> RT **Detergents**

Soap box derbies 796.6
> BT **Racing**

Soap carving

USE **Soap sculpture**

Soap operas   791.44; 791.45

Use for individual works, collections, or materials about soap operas.

BT **Radio plays**

Television plays

RT **Radio serials**

Television serials

Soap sculpture   736

UF Soap carving

BT **Modeling**

Sculpture

Soaring flight

USE **Gliding and soaring**

Sobriquets

USE **Nicknames**

Soccer (May subdiv. geog.)   **796.334**

BT **Ball games**

Football

Sports

Soccer—Training   796.334

BT **Physical education**

Social ability

USE **Social skills**

Social action (May subdiv. geog.)   **361.2**

UF Social activism

SA subjects with the subdivision *Citizen participation*, e.g. **City planning—Citizen participation** [to be added as needed]

BT **Social policy**

NT **City planning—Citizen participation**

RT **Political participation**

Social problems

Social work

Social activism

USE **Social action**

Social adjustment   158; 303.3

UF Adjustment, Social

BT **Human behavior**

Interpersonal relations

Social psychology

NT **Socially handicapped**

RT **Deviant behavior**

Social alienation

USE **Alienation (Social psychology)**

Social anthropology

USE **Ethnology**

Social aspects

USE subjects with the subdivision *Social aspects,* e.g. **Genetic engineering—Social aspects** [to be added as needed]

Social behavior

USE **Human behavior**

Social case work   361.3

UF Case work, Social

Family social work

BT **Social work**

NT **Parole**

Probation

RT **Counseling**

Social change (May subdiv. geog.) **303.4; 909**

UF Change, Social

Cultural change

Social evolution

BT **Anthropology**

Social sciences

Sociology

NT **Community development**

Modernization (Sociology)

Urbanization

Social classes (May subdiv. geog.) **305.5; 323.3**

UF Class distinction

Rank

Social distinctions

BT **Caste**

Sociology

NT **Class consciousness**

Elite (Social sciences)

Intellectuals

Middle class

Rich

Upper class

Working class

Social competence

USE **Social skills**

Social conditions   306.09; 909

Use for materials on the social aspects of several of the following topics: labor, poverty, education, health, housing, recreation, moral conditions.

UF Social history

SA racial and ethnic groups, classes of persons, and names of countries, cities, etc., with the subdivision *Social conditions* [to be added as needed]

Social conditions—*Continued*
  BT **Sociology**
  NT **African Americans—Social
       conditions**
       Blacks—Social conditions
       **Chicago (Ill.)—Social condi-
       tions**
       Cost and standard of living
       Counter culture
       Economic conditions
       Jews—Social conditions
       Labor
       Men—Social conditions
       Moral conditions
       **Native Americans—Social con-
       ditions**
       Ohio—Social conditions
       Quality of life
       Social movements
       Social policy
       Social problems
       **United States—Social condi-
       tions**
       Urbanization
       Women—Social conditions
Social conflict (May subdiv. geog.)
     303.6
  UF Class conflict
       Class struggle
       Conflict, Social
  BT **Social psychology**
       Sociology
  NT **Conflict management**
       Conflict of generations
       Role conflict
Social conformity
  USE **Conformity**
Social contract 320.01; 320.1
  BT **Political science**
       Sociology
Social customs
  USE **Manners and customs**
Social democracy
  USE **Socialism**
Social deviance
  USE **Deviant behavior**
Social distinctions
  USE **Social classes**
Social drinking
  USE **Drinking of alcoholic beverages**
Social ecology
  USE **Human ecology**

Social equality
  USE **Equality**
Social ethics (May subdiv. geog.)   **170**
  BT **Ethics**
       Sociology
  NT **Political ethics**
  RT **Social problems**
Social evolution
  USE **Social change**
Social geography
  USE **Human geography**
Social group work   361.4; 362
  UF Group social work
       Group work, Social
       Social work with groups
  BT **Counseling**
       Social work
Social groups   302.3; 305
  UF Group dynamics
       Groups, Social
  BT **Sociology**
  NT **Elite (Social sciences)**
       Leadership
       Neighborhood
       Social psychology
       Teams in the workplace
Social history
  USE **Social conditions**
Social hygiene
  USE **Public health**
       Sexual hygiene
Social identity
  USE **Group identity**
Social insurance
  USE **Social security**
Social isolation
  USE **Loneliness**
Social justice (May subdiv. geog.)   **303.3**
  BT **Equality**
       Justice
Social learning
  USE **Socialization**
Social life and customs
  USE **Manners and customs**
       and names of ethnic groups,
       countries, cities, etc., with the
       subdivision *Social life and
       customs,* e.g. **Native Ameri-
       cans—Social life and cus-
       toms; Jews—Social life and
       customs; United States—So-**

Social life and customs—*Continued*

cial life and customs; etc. [to be added as needed]

Social medicine (May subdiv. geog.) **306.4; 362.1**

Use for materials on the study of social, genetic, and environmental influences on human disease and disability, as well as the promotion of health measures to protect both the individual and the community.

UF Medical care—Social aspects
Medical sociology
Medicine—Social aspects

BT **Medicine**
Public health
Public welfare
Sociology

NT **Hospices**

RT **Medical ethics**

Social movements (May subdiv. geog.) **303.48**

SA types of social movements, e.g.
Environmental movement [to be added as needed]

BT **Social conditions**
Social psychology

NT **Animal rights movement**
Anti-apartheid movement
Antinuclear movement
Environmental movement
Labor movement
Militia movements
New Age movement
Peace movements
Pro-choice movement
Pro-life movement
Protest movements
Sanctuary movement
Separatist movements
Slow food movement
Survivalism
White supremacy movements
Youth movement

Social networking **303.48**

Use for materials on a variety of Internet applications designed to help connect friends, business associates, or other individuals with common interests.

UF Online social networking
Social networks

BT **Communication**

Social networks

USE **Social networking**

Social planning

USE **Social policy**

Social policy (May subdiv. geog.) **361.6**

Use for materials on the ways a society regulates the relationships among individuals, groups, communities, and institutions, and on systematic procedures for achieving social goals and managing available resources to attain social change.

UF Government policy
National planning
Social planning
State planning

SA ethnic groups, classes of persons, and topics with the subdivision *Government policy*, e.g. **Homeless persons—Government policy**; and types of activities, facilities, industries, services, and undertakings with the subdivision *Planning*, e.g. **Transportation—Planning** [to be added as needed]

BT **Planning**
Social conditions

NT **Arts—Government policy**
Education—Government policy
Homeless persons—Government policy
Land reform
Libraries—Government policy
Medical policy
Multiculturalism
Social action
Urban policy
Welfare state

RT **Economic policy**

Social policy—Chicago (Ill.) **361.6; 977.3**

UF Chicago (Ill.)—Social policy

Social policy—Ohio **361.6; 977.1**

UF Ohio—Social policy

Social policy—United States **361.6; 973**

UF United States—Social policy

Social problems (May subdiv. geog.) **361.1**

UF Reform, Social
Social reform
Social welfare

BT **Social conditions**
Sociology

NT **Alcoholism**
Child labor

Social problems—*Continued*

    Church and social problems
    Crime
    Discrimination
    Drug abuse
    Fetal alcohol syndrome
    Homelessness
    Juvenile delinquency
    Poverty
    Prison reform
    Prostitution
    Public health
    Race discrimination
    Solvent abuse
    Suicide
    Unemployment
  RT Social action
    Social ethics

Social problems and the church
  USE **Church and social problems**

Social problems in education
  USE **Educational sociology**

Social progress
  USE **Progress**

Social psychology (May subdiv. geog.)
    302
  UF Mass psychology
  BT **Human ecology**
    Psychology
    Social groups
    Sociology
  NT **Alienation (Social psychology)**
    Ambition
    Audiences
    Class consciousness
    Cooperativeness
    Discrimination
    Empathy
    Interpersonal relations
    Interviewing
    National characteristics
    Organizational behavior
    Political psychology
    Popularity
    Privacy
    Public opinion
    Social adjustment
    Social conflict
    Social movements
    Social role
    Social status
    Stereotype (Social psychology)

    Violence
  RT **Applied psychology**
    Crowds
    Ethnopsychology

Social reform
  USE **Social problems**

Social responsibility of business (May
    subdiv. geog.) **174; 658.4**
  UF Business—Social responsibility
    Corporate accountability
    Corporate responsibility
    Corporations—Social responsibil-
    ity
    Industries—Social responsibility
  BT **Business**
    Business ethics

Social role **302**
  UF Role, Social
  BT **Social psychology**
  NT **Role conflict**
    Role playing
    Sex role

Social sciences (May subdiv. geog.) **300**
    Use for general and comprehensive materi-
    als on the various branches of knowledge
    dealing with human society, such as sociolo-
    gy, political science, economics, etc.
  UF Social studies
  BT **Civilization**
  NT **Anthropology**
    Conservatism
    Cross-cultural studies
    Economics
    Gerontology
    History
    Human behavior
    Liberalism
    Political science
    Social change
    Social surveys
    Sociology

Social security (May subdiv. geog.) **362;
    368.4**
  UF Insurance, Social
    Social insurance
  BT **Pensions**
  NT **Workers' compensation**

Social service
  USE **Social work**

Social settlements (May subdiv. geog.)
    361.7; 362.5

Social settlements—*Continued*
    UF   Church settlements
           Neighborhood centers
           Settlements, Social
    SA   names of settlements, e.g. **Hull House (Chicago, Ill.)** [to be added as needed]
    BT   **Charities**
           Industrial welfare
           Social work
    NT   **Community centers**
           Hull House (Chicago, Ill.)

Social skills   302; 646.7
    UF   Interpersonal competence
           Social ability
           Social competence
    BT   **Interpersonal relations**
           Life skills

Social standing
    USE   **Social status**

Social status (May subdiv. geog.)   302
    UF   Social standing
           Socio-economic status
           Status, Social
    BT   **Social psychology**

Social studies
    USE   **Geography**
          History
          Social sciences

Social surveys (May subdiv. geog.)   300.7
    Use for materials on the methods employed in conducting surveys of social and economic conditions.
    UF   Community surveys
    SA   names of regions, countries, cities, etc., with the subdivision *Social conditions* [to be added as needed]
    BT   **Social sciences**
           Surveys

Social surveys—United States   301

Social systems   301
    BT   **Sociology**
           System theory

Social values (May subdiv. geog.)   303.3
    UF   Group values
    BT   **Values**

Social welfare
    USE   **Charities**
          Public welfare
          Social problems

Social work
Social work (May subdiv. geog.)   361.3
    Use for materials on the methods employed in welfare work, public or private. Materials on privately supported welfare activities are entered under **Charities**. Materials on tax-supported welfare activities are entered under **Public welfare**. General materials on the various policies, programs, services, and facilities to meet basic human needs, such as health, education, and welfare, are entered under **Human services**.
    UF   Social service
           Social welfare
           Welfare work
    SA   social work with particular groups of people, e.g. **Social work with the elderly**; and classes of persons and ethnic groups with the subdivision *Services for*, e.g. **Handicapped—Services for** [to be added as needed]
    BT   **Human services**
    NT   **Charities**
           Child welfare
           Community organization
           Community services
           Crisis centers
           Group homes
           Handicapped—Services for
           Hotlines (Telephone counseling)
           Industrial welfare
           Public welfare
           Social case work
           Social group work
           Social settlements
           Social work with the elderly
    RT   **Social action**

Social work with groups
    USE   **Social group work**

Social work with the elderly   362.6
    BT   **Elderly**
           Social work

Socialism (May subdiv. geog.)   320.5; 335
    UF   Social democracy
    BT   **Collectivism**
           Economics
           Political science
    NT   **Collective settlements**
           Dialectical materialism
           Government ownership
           Proletariat

Socialism—*Continued*
    Utopias
  RT **Communism**
    Marxism
    National socialism
Socialism—United States   **320.5;
335.00973**
Socialization (May subdiv. geog.)   **303.3**
   Use for materials on the process by which individuals acquire group values and learn to function effectively in society.
  UF Children—Socialization
    Social learning
  BT **Acculturation**
    Child rearing
    Education
    Sociology
  NT **Americanization**
    Peer pressure
Socialization of industry
  USE **Government ownership**
Socialized medicine
  USE **National health insurance**
    State medicine
Socially handicapped (May subdiv. geog.)
    362
  UF Culturally deprived
    Culturally handicapped
    Disadvantaged
    Underprivileged
  BT **Handicapped**
    Social adjustment
  NT **Socially handicapped children**
Socially handicapped children (May
    subdiv. geog.)   **362.74**
  UF Culturally deprived children
    Culturally handicapped children
    Disadvantaged children
    Underprivileged children
  BT **Handicapped children**
    Socially handicapped
  RT **At risk students**
Socials
  USE **Church entertainments**
Societies (May subdiv. geog.)   **060**
  UF Learned societies
  SA types of societies, e.g. **Choral
    societies**; subjects, ethnic
    groups, classes of persons,
    corporate bodies, individual
    persons, and sacred works

with the subdivision *Societies*,
    e.g. **Agriculture—Societies**;
    Women—Societies; etc.; and
    names of individual societies
    [to be added as needed]
  BT **Associations**
  NT **Agriculture—Societies**
    Boys' clubs
    Chemistry—Societies
    Choral societies
    Cooperative societies
    Education—Societies
    Elderly—Societies
    Girls' clubs
    History—Societies
    Labor unions
    Men—Societies
    Parent-teacher associations
    Science—Societies
    Secret societies
    Students—Societies
    Women—Societies
  RT **Clubs**
Society and art
  USE **Art and society**
Society and language
  USE **Sociolinguistics**
Society and religion
  USE **Religion and sociology**
Society of Friends (May subdiv. geog.)
    289.6
  UF Friends, Society of
    Quakers
  BT **Christian sects**
Society, Primitive
  USE **Primitive societies**
Society—Religious aspects
  USE **Religion and sociology**
Socio-economic status
  USE **Social status**
Sociobiology   **304.5; 577.8; 591.56**
   Use for materials on the biological basis of social behavior, especially as transmitted genetically.
  UF Biology—Social aspects
  BT **Comparative psychology**
    Sociology
Sociolinguistics (May subdiv. geog.)
    306.44
   Use for materials on the study of the social aspects of language, particularly linguistic behavior, as determined by sociocultural factors.

Sociolinguistics—*Continued*
UF Language and society
Society and language
Sociology of language
BT **Language and languages**
Linguistics
Sociology
Sociology (May subdiv. geog.) **301**
SA sociology of particular religions, e.g. **Christian sociology**; and racial and ethnic groups, classes of persons, and names of countries, cities, etc., with the subdivision *Social conditions*, e.g. **United States—Social conditions** [to be added as needed]
BT **Social sciences**
NT **Christian sociology**
Cities and towns
Communication
Educational sociology
Equality
Ethnic relations
Ethnopsychology
Family
Human ecology
Human settlements
Individualism
Information society
Labor
Marxism
Organizational sociology
Population
Race relations
Religion and sociology
Rural sociology
Social change
Social classes
Social conditions
Social conflict
Social contract
Social ethics
Social groups
Social medicine
Social problems
Social psychology
Social systems
Socialization
Sociobiology
Sociolinguistics
Urban sociology

RT **Civilization**
Culture
Sociology and art
USE **Art and society**
Sociology and religion
USE **Religion and sociology**
Sociology—Book reviews **301**
Sociology, Christian
USE **Christian sociology**
Sociology of language
USE **Sociolinguistics**
Sociology of organizations
USE **Organizational sociology**
Sociology of religion
USE **Religion and sociology**
Sociology, Rural
USE **Rural sociology**
Sociology, Urban
USE **Urban sociology**
Sodium content of food
USE **Food—Sodium content**
Soft toy making **745.592**
UF Stuffed toy making
BT **Sewing**
Toy making
Softball **796.357**
BT **Ball games**
Baseball
Software, Computer
USE **Computer software**
Software for sharing
USE **Shareware (Computer software)**
Software viruses
USE **Computer viruses**
Soil conservation (May subdiv. geog.) **631.4**
UF Conservation of the soil
BT **Conservation of natural resources**
Environmental protection
RT **Erosion**
Soil erosion
Soil engineering
USE **Soil mechanics**
Soil erosion (May subdiv. geog.) **631.4**
UF Top soil loss
BT **Erosion**
RT **Soil conservation**
Soil fertility
USE **Soils**

Soil mechanics   620.1
    UF   Soil engineering
           Soils (Engineering)
    BT   **Mechanics**
           Structural engineering
    RT   **Foundations**
           Roads
           Soils

Soil microbiology   631.4
    UF   Soils—Bacteriology
    BT   **Microbiology**
           Sanitary engineering
    RT   **Agricultural bacteriology**

Soilless agriculture
    USE **Hydroponics**

Soils (May subdiv. geog.)   **631.4**
    UF   Soil fertility
    BT   **Agriculture**
           Economic geology
    NT   **Clay**
           Compost
           Fertilizers
    RT   **Agricultural chemistry**
           Soil mechanics

Soils—Bacteriology
    USE **Soil microbiology**

Soils (Engineering)
    USE **Soil mechanics**

Soils, Lunar
    USE **Lunar soil**

Solace
    USE **Consolation**

Solar batteries   621.31
    UF   Batteries, Solar
           Solar cells
           Sun powered batteries
    BT   **Electric batteries**
           Photovoltaic power generation
           Solar radiation

Solar cells
    USE **Photovoltaic power generation**
          Solar batteries

Solar eclipses   523.7
    UF   Eclipses, Solar
           Sun—Eclipses
    BT   **Astronomy**

Solar energy (May subdiv. geog.)
           333.792; 621.47
    UF   Solar power
    BT   **Energy resources**
           Renewable energy resources

           Solar radiation
           Sun
    NT   **Photovoltaic power generation**
           Solar engines
           Solar heating

Solar engines   621.47
    BT   **Engines**
           Solar energy

Solar heating   621.47; 697
    SA   types of solar heating applica-
           tions, e.g. **Solar homes** [to be
           added as needed]
    BT   **Heating**
           Solar energy
    NT   **Solar homes**

Solar homes   697; 728
    BT   **Domestic architecture**
           Houses
           Solar heating

Solar physics
    USE **Sun**

Solar power
    USE **Solar energy**

Solar radiation   523.7; 621.47
    UF   Radiation, Solar
           Sun—Radiation
    BT   **Meteorology**
           Space environment
    NT   **Greenhouse effect**
           Solar batteries
           Solar energy
           Sunspots

Solar system   523.2
    BT   **Astronomy**
           Stars
    NT   **Asteroids**
           Comets
           Earth
           Meteors
           Moon
           Planets
           Satellites
           Sun

Solder and soldering
    USE **Soldering**

Soldering   671.5
    UF   Solder and soldering
    BT   **Metals**
           Metalwork
    RT   **Welding**

Soldiers (May subdiv. geog.)   **355.0092; 920**

UF   Army life
      Soldiers' life

SA   names of countries with the sub-
      head *Army* and the subdivi-
      sion *Military life*, e.g. **United
      States. Army—Military life**
      [to be added as needed]

BT   **Armies
      Military personnel**

NT   **Mercenary soldiers
      Missing in action
      United States. Army—Military
      life
      United States. Army—Officers**

RT   **Veterans**

Soldiers' handbooks

USE   **United States. Army—Hand-
      books, manuals, etc.**

Soldiers—Hygiene

USE   **Military personnel—Health
      and hygiene**

Soldiers' life

USE   **Soldiers**

      and names of countries with the
      subhead *Army* and the subdi-
      vision *Military life*, e.g. **Unit-
      ed States. Army—Military
      life** [to be added as needed]

Soldiers of fortune

USE   **Mercenary soldiers**

Soldiers' songs

USE   **War songs**

Soldiers—United States   **355.0092; 920**

UF   GIs
      United States—Soldiers

Solicitors

USE   **Lawyers**

Solid geometry   **516.23**

UF   Geometry, Solid

BT   **Geometry**

Solid waste disposal

USE   **Refuse and refuse disposal**

Solids   **530.4; 531; 541**

BT   **Physical chemistry
      Physics**

NT   **Crystals**

Solitaire (Game)   **795.4**

UF   Patience (Game)

BT   **Card games**

Solitude   **155.9**

UF   Seclusion

RT   **Loneliness
      Privacy**

Solvent abuse (May subdiv. geog.)
      362.29

UF   Aerosol sniffing
      Glue sniffing
      Inhalant abuse
      Inhalation abuse of solvents
      Paint sniffing
      Substance abuse

BT   **Social problems**

RT   **Drug abuse**

Somalia   **967.73**

May be subdivided like **United States** except for *History.*

Sonar   **621.389**

UF   Sound navigation

BT   **Signals and signaling**

Sonata   **784.18**

Use for musical scores and for materials on
the sonata as a musical form.

UF   Sonatas

BT   **Musical form**

Sonatas

USE   **Sonata**

Song books

USE   **Songbooks**

Song lyrics

USE   **Popular song lyrics**

Song writing

USE   **Composition (Music)
      Popular music—Writing and
      publishing**

Songbooks   **782.42**

Use for general collections of songs that
contain both words and music. Similar collections limited to sacred songs are entered under
Hymnals. Materials about songs are entered
under **Songs.** Collections of songs on a single
subject are entered under the subject with the
subdivision *Songs.*

UF   Song books

BT   **Singing
      Songs**

NT   **Hymnals
      School songbooks**

Songs   **782.42**

Use for materials about songs. General collections of songs that contain both words and
music are entered under **Songbooks.** Collections of songs that contain the words but not
the music are entered under **Poetry—Collections** for classical songs and under **Popular
song lyrics** for popular songs.

Songs—*Continued*

SA   types of songs, e.g. **Children's songs**; songs of particular countries, e.g. **American songs**; subjects, classes of persons, and names of persons, corporate bodies, places, or wars, with the subdivision *Songs*, for collections or individual songs about the topic or associated with the entity named, e.g. **Cowhands—Songs**; **Surfing—Songs**; **United States Military Academy—Songs**; **World War, 1939-1945—Songs**; etc.; and names of individual songs [to be added as needed]

BT   **Poetry**
      Vocal music

NT   **African songs**
      American songs
      Ballads
      Carols
      Children's songs
      Cowhands—Songs
      Folk songs
      Hymns
      Lullabies
      National songs
      Popular music
      School songbooks
      Sea songs
      Songbooks
      State songs
      Students' songs
      Surfing—Songs
      United States. Army—Songs
      War songs

Songs, African
USE   **African songs**

Songs, African American
USE   **African American music**

Songs and music
USE   music of particular countries or ethnic groups, e.g. **American music; Native American music;** etc.; types of music, e.g. **Vocal music;** and subjects, classes of persons, and names of individual persons, corpo-

rate bodies, places, or wars, with the subdivision *Songs* for collections of songs or materials about songs pertaining to the topic or entity named, e.g. **Cowhands—Songs; Surfing—Songs; United States Military Academy—Songs** [to be added as needed]

Songs for children
USE   **Children's songs**

Songwriters
USE   **Composers**
      Lyricists

Songwriting
USE   **Composition (Music)**
      Popular music—Writing and publishing

Sons   306.874
BT   **Family**
      Men
NT   **Father-son relationship**
      Mother-son relationship

Sons and fathers
USE   **Father-son relationship**

Sons and mothers
USE   **Mother-son relationship**

Soothsaying
USE   **Divination**

Soporifics
USE   **Narcotics**

Sorcery
USE   **Magic**
      Occultism
      Witchcraft

Sororities
USE   **Fraternities and sororities**

Sorrow
USE   **Bereavement**
      Grief
      Joy and sorrow

Soul   128; 233
UF   Spirit
BT   **Future life**
      Human beings (Theology)
      Philosophy
NT   **Immortality**
      Psychology
RT   **Reincarnation**

Sound   534; 620.2
UF   Acoustics

Sound—*Continued*
- BT **Physics**
  - **Pneumatics**
  - **Radiation**
- NT **Architectural acoustics**
  - **Computer sound processing**
  - **Hearing**
  - **Noise**
  - **Phonetics**
  - **Sound effects**
  - **Soundproofing**
  - **Sounds**
  - **Ultrasonics**
  - **Vibration**
- RT **Music—Acoustics and physics**

Sound effects   534; 620.2
- BT **Sound**

Sound insulation
- USE **Soundproofing**

Sound navigation
- USE **Sonar**

Sound processing, Computer
- USE **Computer sound processing**

Sound recording
- USE **Sound—Recording and repro-**
  ducing

Sound—Recording and reproducing
  621.389

Use for materials on the equipment or the process by which sound is recorded. Materials on sound recordings that emphasize the content of the recording rather than the equipment, process, or format are entered under **Sound recordings**. Materials about the format are entered under the format, e.g. **Compact discs**.

- UF Sound recording
- SA methods of recording, e.g. **Mag-**
  netic recorders and record-
  ing [to be added as needed]
- NT **Compact disc players**
  - **High-fidelity sound systems**
  - **MP3 players**
  - **Stereophonic sound systems**
- RT **Phonograph**
  - **Sound recordings**

Sound recordings (May subdiv. geog.)
  621.389; 780.26

Use for general materials and for materials on sound recordings that emphasize the content of the recording rather than the format. Materials about the format are entered under the format, e.g. **Compact discs**. Materials about the equipment or the process by which sound is recorded are entered under **Sound—Recording and reproducing**.

- UF Audio cassettes
  - Audiotapes
  - Cassette tapes, Audio
  - Discography
  - Phonograph records
  - Recordings, Sound
  - Records, Phonograph
  - Tape recordings, Audio
- SA types of sound recordings, e.g.
  Compact discs and types of
  music with the subdivision
  Sound recordings, e.g. **Op-**
  era—Sound recordings [to
  be added as needed]
- BT **Audiovisual materials**
- NT **Audiobooks**
  - **Compact discs**
  - **Grammy Awards**
  - **Opera—Sound recordings**
- RT **Sound—Recording and repro-**
  ducing

Sound recordings—Copyright
- USE **Copyright—Sound recordings**

Sound waves   534; 620.2
- BT **Vibration**
  - **Waves**
- NT **Ultrasonic waves**

Soundproofing   620.2; 693.8
- UF Insulation (Sound)
  - Sound insulation
- BT **Architectural acoustics**
  - **Sound**

Sounds   534; 620.2
- BT **Sound**

Soups   641.8
- BT **Cooking**

Sources
- USE historical subjects, periods of
  history, individual literary and
  sacred works, and names of
  wars with the subdivision
  Sources, e.g. **World War,**
  1939-1945—Sources; and
  subjects, ethnic groups, classes of persons, coporate
  bodies, and names of countries, states, etc., with the
  subdivisions *History—Sources;*
  e.g. **United States—History—**
  Sources [to be added as
  needed]

South Africa 968

Use for materials on the Republic of South Africa.

UF   Republic of South Africa

       Union of South Africa

BT   **Africa**

       Southern Africa

South Africa—History 968

South Africa—Race relations
     305.800968; 968

BT   **Race relations**

NT   **Anti-apartheid movement**

       Apartheid

South African Dutch

USE   **Afrikaners**

South Africans, Afrikaans-speaking

USE   **Afrikaners**

South America 980

BT   **America**

South American literature

USE   **Latin American literature**

South Atlantic States

USE   **Atlantic States**

South Korea

USE   **Korea (South)**

South Pacific region

USE   **Oceania**

South Pole 998

BT   **Polar regions**

RT   **Antarctica**

South Sea Islands

USE   **Oceania**

South Seas

USE   **Oceania**

South (U.S.)

USE   **Southern States**

Southeast Asia 959

Use for materials dealing collectively with the region of Asia that includes Burma, Thailand, Malaysia, Singapore, Indonesia, Vietnam, Cambodia, Laos, and the Philippines.

UF   Asia, Southeastern

BT   **Asia**

NT   **Indochina**

Southern Africa 968

Use for materials dealing collectively with the area south of the countries of Zaire and Tanzania. Southern Africa includes the political entities of Angola, Botswana, Comoros, Lesotho, Madagascar, Malawi, Mozambique, Namibia, South Africa, Swaziland, Zambia, and Zimbabwe. Materials on the Republic of South Africa are entered under **South Africa**.

UF   Africa, Southern

BT   **Africa**

NT   **South Africa**

Southern cooking 641.5975

BT   **Cooking**

Southern lights

USE   **Auroras**

Southern literature

USE   **American literature—Southern States**

Southern States 975

UF   South (U.S.)

BT   **United States**

Southern States—African Americans

USE   **African Americans—Southern States**

Southern States—History 975

BT   **United States—History**

RT   **Slavery—United States**

Southwest, New

USE   **Southwestern States**

Southwest, Old

USE   **Old Southwest**

Southwest Pacific region

USE   **Oceania**

Southwestern States 979

Use for materials on that part of the United States that corresponds roughly with the old Spanish province of New Mexico, including the present Arizona, New Mexico, southern Colorado, Utah, Nevada, and California.

UF   Southwest, New

BT   **United States**

Sovereigns

USE   **Emperors**

       Kings and rulers

       Monarchy

       Queens

Sovereignty (May subdiv. geog.) 320.1

BT   **International law**

       Political science

NT   **Secession**

RT   **National self-determination**

Soviet communism

USE   **Communism—Soviet Union**

Soviet literature 890

Use for materials on several of the literatures of the Soviet Union. Materials on the individual literatures of the republics that made up the Soviet Union are entered with the appropriate adjective, e.g. **Russian literature**; etc.

UF   Literatures of the Soviet Union

       Soviet Union—Literatures

BT   **Literature**

RT   **Russian literature**

Soviet people

USE **Soviets (People)**

Soviet Union   947.084

Use for materials on the Union of Soviet Socialist Republics between 1917 and 1991. Materials on Russia or the Russian empire before 1917 are entered under **Russia**. Materials on the independent republic of Russia since its establishment in December 1991 are entered under **Russia (Federation)**. Materials on several or all of the countries that emerged from the dissolution of the Soviet Union in 1991 are entered under **Former Soviet republics**. Material specifically on the federation of former Soviet republics, which was established in December 1991 and does not include the Baltic states, are entered under **Commonwealth of Independent States**. The Baltic states and the other republics of the former Soviet Union are: Armenia (Republic); Azerbaijan; Belarus; Estonia; Georgia (Republic); Kazakhstan; Kyrgyzstan; Latvia; Lithuania; Moldova; Tajikistan; Turkmenistan; Ukraine; and Uzbekistan; to be added as needed. The adjective Soviet is used to refer to the Soviet Union as a whole between 1917 and 1991, e.g. **Soviet literature**. Materials on the citizens of the Soviet Union between 1917 and 1991 are entered under **Soviets (People)**. Materials on topics pertaining to individual republics, nationalities, or ethnic groups of the former Soviet Union are to be added as needed with the appropriate qualifier, e.g., **Russians**; **Russian language**; etc.

UF   Union of Soviet Socialist Republics

USSR

NT   **Russians**

Soviets (People)

RT   **Former Soviet republics**

Russia

Russia (Federation)

Soviet Union—Communism

USE   **Communism—Soviet Union**

Soviet Union—History   947.084

UF   Soviet Union—History—1917-1991

Soviet Union—History—1917-1921, Revolution   947.084

UF   Russian revolution

BT   **Revolutions**

**Soviet Union—History—1917-1925
947.084**

Soviet Union—History—1917-1991

USE   **Soviet Union—History**

**Soviet Union—History—1925-1953
947.084**

Soviet Union—History—1939-1940, War with Finland

USE   **Russo-Finnish War, 1939-1940**

Soviet Union—History—1953-1985

USE   **Soviet Union—History—1953-1991**

**Soviet Union—History—1953-1991
947.085**

UF   Soviet Union—History—1953-1985

Soviet Union—History—1985-1991

Soviet Union—History—1985-1991

USE   **Soviet Union—History—1953-1991**

Soviet Union—Literatures

USE   **Soviet literature**

Soviets (People)   920; 947.084

Use for materials on the citizens of the Soviet Union between 1917 and 1991, not limited to a single national or ethnic group. Materials on the individual ethnic groups of the former Soviet Union are entered under the name for the ethnic group, e.g. **Russians**; etc.

UF   Soviet people

BT   **Soviet Union**

Soybean   633.3

BT   **Forage plants**

Space age

USE   **Astronautics and civilization**

Space and time   115

UF   Time and space

BT   **Fourth dimension**

Metaphysics

Space sciences

Time

NT   **Cyberspace**

Personal space

Time travel

RT   **Relativity (Physics)**

Space-based weapons

USE   **Space weapons**

Space biology   571.0919; 612

Use for materials on the biology of humans or other earth creatures while in outer space. Materials on the possibility of indigenous life in outer space are entered under **Life on other planets**.

UF   Astrobiology

Cosmobiology

BT   **Biology**

Space sciences

NT   **Space medicine**

Space chemistry   523

UF   Astrochemistry

Cosmochemistry

BT   **Chemistry**

Space colonies   629.44; 999

Use for materials on communities established in space or on natural extraterrestrial bodies. Materials on bases established on natural extraterrestrial bodies for specific functions other than colonization are entered under **Extraterrestrial bases**. Materials on manned installations orbiting in space for specific functions, such as servicing space ships, are entered under **Space stations**.

UF   Colonies, Space

Communities, Space

Outer space—Colonies

BT   **Astronautics and civilization**

RT   **Extraterrestrial bases**

Space commercialization

USE   **Space industrialization**

Space communication

USE   **Astronautics—Communication systems**

Interstellar communication

Space debris   629.4

UF   Debris in space

Junk in space

Space pollution

BT   **Pollution**

Space environment

Space environment   629.4

UF   Environment, Space

Extraterrestrial environment

Space weather

BT   **Astronomy**

Outer space

NT   **Cosmic rays**

Solar radiation

Space debris

Space exploration (Astronautics)

USE   **Outer space—Exploration**

Space flight   629.4

Use for materials on the physics and technical details of flight beyond the earth's atmosphere. General materials and imaginary accounts of travel to other planets are entered under **Interplanetary voyages**.

UF   Humans in space

Man in space

Manned space flight

People in space

Rocket flight

Space travel

SA   names of projects, e.g. **Gemini project**; and space flight to particular places, e.g. **Space flight to the moon** [to be added as needed]

BT   **Aeronautics—Flights**

Astronautics

NT   **Astronauts**

Extravehicular activity (Space flight)

Gemini project

Orbital rendezvous (Space flight)

Outer space—Exploration

Space flight to the moon

RT   **Astrodynamics**

Interplanetary voyages

Navigation (Astronautics)

Space medicine

Space vehicles

Space flight (Fiction)

USE   **Imaginary voyages**

Science fiction

Space flight—Law and legislation

USE   **Space law**

Space flight—Rescue work

USE   **Space rescue operations**

Space flight to the moon   629.45

UF   Flight to the moon

Lunar expeditions

Moon, Voyages to

Voyages to the moon

BT   **Astronautics**

Space flight

NT   **Apollo project**

Moon—Exploration

Space heaters   644; 697

BT   **Heating**

NT   **Fireplaces**

Stoves

Space industrial processing

USE   **Space industrialization**

Space industrialization (May subdiv. geog.)   **629.44**

UF   Commercial endeavors in space

Industrial uses of space

Manufacturing in space

Space commercialization

Space industrial processing

Space manufacturing

Space stations—Industrial applications

BT   **Industrialization**

Space laboratories

USE   **Space stations**

Space law (May subdiv. geog.)   **341.4**

Space law—*Continued*
  UF   Aerospace law
         Artificial satellites—Law and
            legislation
         Astronautics—Law and legisla-
            tion
         Space flight—Law and legisla-
            tion
         Space stations—Law and legisla-
            tion
  BT   **Astronautics and civilization**
         International law
         Law

Space manufacturing
  USE **Space industrialization**

Space medicine   616.9
  UF   Aerospace medicine
         Bioastronautics
  BT   **Medicine**
         Space biology
         Space sciences
  NT   **Life support systems (Space**
         environment)
         Weightlessness
  RT   **Aviation medicine**
         Space flight

Space navigation
  USE **Navigation (Astronautics)**

Space nutrition
  USE **Astronauts—Nutrition**

Space optics   535
  BT   **Optics**
         Space sciences
  NT   **Astronautical instruments**
         Astronomical instruments
  RT   **Optical instruments**
         Remote sensing

Space orbital rendezvous
  USE **Orbital rendezvous (Space**
         flight)

Space, Outer
  USE **Outer space**

Space, Personal
  USE **Personal space**

Space photography   778.3
  UF   Photographs from space
         Photography in astronautics
  SA   celestial bodies or objects in
         space with the subdivision
         Pictorial works [to be added
         as needed]

  BT   **Photography**
         Photography—Scientific appli-
         cations
  NT   **Mars (Planet)—Pictorial works**
         Moon—Pictorial works

Space platforms
  USE **Space stations**

Space pollution
  USE **Space debris**

Space power
  USE **Astronautics and civilization**

Space probes   629.43
    Use for materials on space exploration by
  remote control from earth.
  SA   types of probes, e.g. **Lunar**
         probes; **Mars probes**; etc.;
         and names of space vehicles
         and space projects, e.g. **Proj-**
         ect Voyager [to be added as
         needed]
  BT   **Outer space—Exploration**
         Space vehicles
  NT   **Lunar probes**
         Mars probes

Space rescue operations   629.45
  UF   Rescue operations, Space
         Space flight—Rescue work
         Space vehicles—Rescue work
  BT   **Rescue work**

Space research
  USE **Outer space—Exploration**
         Space sciences

Space rockets
  USE **Space vehicles**

Space sciences (May subdiv. geog.)
     500.5
    Use for general materials and for scientific
  results of space exploration and scientific ap-
  plications of space flight.
  UF   Science and space
         Space research
  BT   **Science**
  NT   **Outer space**
         Space and time
         Space biology
         Space medicine
         Space optics
  RT   **Astronautics**
         Astronomy

Space sciences—International cooperation
     500.5
  BT   **International cooperation**

Space ships
    USE **Space vehicles**
Space shuttles   629.44
    SA   names of individual space shut-
            tles [to be added as needed]
    BT   **Space vehicles**
Space stations   629.44
    Use for materials on manned installations
    orbiting in space for specific functions, such
    as servicing space ships. Materials on bases
    established on natural extraterrestrial bodies
    for specific functions other than colonization
    are entered under **Extraterrestrial bases**. Ma-
    terials on communities established in space or
    on natural extraterrestrial bodies are entered
    under **Space colonies**.
    UF   Orbital laboratories
            Orbiting vehicles
            Space laboratories
            Space platforms
    BT   **Artificial satellites**
            Astronautics
            Space vehicles
    NT   **Orbital rendezvous (Space
            flight)**
Space stations—Industrial applications
    USE **Space industrialization**
Space stations—Law and legislation
    USE **Space law**
Space suits   629.47
    UF   Astronauts—Clothing
    BT   **Life support systems (Space
            environment)**
Space telecommunication
    USE **Interstellar communication**
Space travel
    USE **Interplanetary voyages
            Space flight**
Space vehicle accidents   363.12; 629.4
    UF   Astronautical accidents
            Astronautics—Accidents
            Space vehicles—Accidents
    BT   **Accidents**
Space vehicles   629.47
    UF   Space rockets
            Space ships
            Spacecraft
    BT   **Rocketry**
    NT   **Orbital rendezvous (Space
            flight)
            Rocket planes
            Space probes
            Space shuttles
            Space stations**

    RT   **Artificial satellites
            Astronautics
            Space flight**
Space vehicles—Accidents
    USE **Space vehicle accidents**
Space vehicles—Extravehicular activity
    USE **Extravehicular activity (Space
            flight)**
**Space vehicles—Guidance systems
            629.47**
Space vehicles—Instruments
    USE **Astronautical instruments**
Space vehicles—Piloting   629.45
    UF   Piloting (Astronautics)
    BT   **Astronauts
            Navigation (Astronautics)**
**Space vehicles—Propulsion systems
            629.47**
Space vehicles—Recovery   629.4
    UF   Recovery of space vehicles
Space vehicles—Rescue work
    USE **Space rescue operations**
**Space vehicles—Thermodynamics
            629.47**
    BT   **Thermodynamics**
Space vehicles—Tracking   629.4
    UF   Tracking of satellites
Space walk
    USE **Extravehicular activity (Space
            flight)**
Space warfare   358
    Use for materials on interplanetary warfare,
    attacks on earth from outer space, and warfare
    among the nations of earth in outer space.
    UF   Interplanetary warfare
            Interstellar warfare
            Space wars
    BT   **Outer space
            War**
    NT   **Space weapons
            Strategic Defense Initiative**
Space wars
    USE **Space warfare**
Space weapons   358
    UF   Space-based weapons
            Star Wars weapons
            Weapons, Space
    BT   **Military weapons
            Space warfare**
    RT   **Strategic Defense Initiative**
Space weather
    USE **Space environment**

Spacecraft

USE **Space vehicles**

Spain   946

> May be subdivided like **United States** except for *History*.

Spain—History   946

NT   **Spanish-American War, 1898**

Spanish Armada, 1588

Spain—History—1898, War of 1898

USE   **Spanish-American War, 1898**

Spain—History—1936-1939, Civil War 946.081

Spain—History—1939-1975   946.082

Spain—History—1975-   946.083

Spanish America

USE   **Latin America**

Spanish American literature

USE   **American literature (Spanish)**

Latin American literature

Spanish-American War, 1898   973.8

UF   American-Spanish War, 1898

Spain—History—1898, War of 1898

United States—History—1898, War of 1898

BT   **Spain—History**

United States—History—1865-1898

United States—History—1898-1919

Spanish Armada, 1588   942.05; 946

UF   Armada, 1588

Invincible Armada

BT   **Great Britain—History—1485-1603, Tudors**

Spain—History

Spanish language   460

> May be subdivided like **English language**.

BT   **Language and languages**

Romance languages

Spanish literature   860

> May use same subdivisions and names of literary forms as for **English literature**.

BT   **Literature**

Romance literature

Sparring

USE   **Boxing**

Spas

USE   **Health resorts**

Physical fitness centers

Speaking

USE   **Debates and debating**

Lectures and lecturing

Preaching

Public speaking

Rhetoric

Speech

Voice

Speaking choirs

USE   **Choral speaking**

Speaking in tongues

USE   **Glossolalia**

Speaking with tongues

USE   **Glossolalia**

Spear fishing   799.1

BT   **Fishing**

Special collections in libraries

USE   **Libraries—Special collections**

Special education (May subdiv. geog.) **371.9**

SA   classes of exceptional children with the subdivision *Education* [to be added as needed]

BT   **Education**

NT   **Mentally handicapped children—Education**

RT   **Mainstreaming in education**

Special libraries (May subdiv. geog.) **026; 027.6**

> Use for materials on libraries covering specialized subjects, containing special format materials, or serving a specialized clientele.

SA   types of special libraries, e.g. **Business libraries** [to be added as needed]

BT   **Libraries**

NT   **Business libraries**

Corporate libraries

Government libraries

Music libraries

Special months   394.26

SA   names of particular months of celebration or commemoration, e.g. **Black History Month** [to be added as needed]

BT   **Months**

NT   **Black History Month**

Special Olympics   796.087

BT   **Olympic games**

Sports for the handicapped

Special weeks   394.26

Special weeks—*Continued*

   SA names of particular weeks of celebration or commemoration, e.g. **Holy Week** [to be added as needed]

   BT **Week**

   NT **Holy Week**

Specialists exchange programs

   USE **Exchange of persons programs**

Specie

   USE **Coins**

Specifications

   USE types of engineering, construction, industries, products, and merchandise with the subdivision *Specifications,* for works on the particular qualities prescribed for a product to meet specific requirements [to be added as needed]

Specimens, Preservation of

   USE **Plants—Collection and preservation**

      Taxidermy

      Zoological specimens—Collection and preservation

      and types of natural specimens with the subdivision *Collection and preservation,* e.g. **Birds—Collection and preservation** [to be added as needed]

Spectacles

   USE **Eyeglasses**

Specters

   USE **Apparitions**

      Ghosts

Spectra

   USE **Spectrum analysis**

Spectrochemical analysis

   USE **Spectrum analysis**

Spectrochemistry

   USE **Spectrum analysis**

Spectroscopy

   USE **Spectrum analysis**

Spectrum analysis   535.8

   UF Spectra

      Spectrochemical analysis

      Spectrochemistry

      Spectroscopy

   BT **Astronomy**

      Astrophysics

      Chemistry

      Optics

      Radiation

   NT **Mass spectrometry**

   RT **Light**

Speculation (May subdiv. geog.)   332.64

   BT **Finance**

   NT **Real estate investment**

   RT **Investments**

      Stock exchanges

Speech   302.2; 372.62; 410; 612.7

   UF Speaking

   BT **Language arts**

   NT **Speech disorders**

      Speech processing systems

      Speech therapy

      Voice culture

   RT **Language and languages**

      Phonetics

      Voice

Speech correction

   USE **Speech therapy**

Speech disorders   616.85

   Use for materials on disorders of the physiological mechanisms required for speech. Materials on disorders of the central neurological functions affecting the reception, processing, or expression of language are entered under **Language disorders**.

   UF Defective speech

      Speech pathology

      Stammering

      Stuttering

   BT **Communicative disorders**

      Speech

   NT **Aphasia**

Speech, Freedom of

   USE **Freedom of speech**

Speech pathology

   USE **Speech disorders**

Speech problems

   USE **Aphasia**

Speech processing systems   006.5

   UF Computer speech processing systems

      Electronic speech processing systems

      Speech scramblers

   BT **Speech**

   NT **Automatic speech recognition**

      Speech synthesis

   RT **Computer sound processing**

Speech recognition, Automatic
  USE **Automatic speech recognition**
Speech scramblers
  USE **Speech processing systems**
Speech synthesis   006.5
  BT **Speech processing systems**
Speech therapy   616.85
  UF   Speech correction
  BT **Speech**
Speeches   808.85
  Use for collections of speeches on several
  subjects and materials about speeches that
  have already been delivered. Materials on the
  art of delivering speeches are entered under
  Public speaking or under **Lectures and lec-
  turing**. Collections of speeches on a single
  subject are entered under that subject.
  UF   Addresses
        Orations
        Speeches, addresses, etc.
  SA   speeches of particular countries,
        e.g. **American speeches** [to
        be added as needed]
  BT **Literature**
  NT **After dinner speeches**
     American speeches
     English speeches
     **Presidents—United States—In-
       augural addresses**
     Toasts
  RT **Lectures and lecturing**
     Public speaking
Speeches, addresses, etc.
  USE **Speeches**
Speeches, addresses, etc., American
  USE **American speeches**
Speeches, addresses, etc., English
  USE **English speeches**
Speed   531
  UF   Velocity
  BT **Motion**
Speed (Drug)
  USE **Methamphetamine**
Speed reading   372.45
  UF   Accelerated reading
        Faster reading
        Rapid reading
  BT **Reading**
Speed, Supersonic
  USE **Supersonic aerodynamics**
Speleology
  USE **Caves**
Spellers   418

  BT **English language—Spelling**
Spelling   411
  NT **English language—Spelling**
     Spelling reform
Spelling reform   418
  UF   English language—Spelling re-
        form
        Phonetic spelling
  BT **Spelling**
  NT **Phonetic spelling**
Spells
  USE **Charms**
     Magic
Spherical trigonometry
  USE **Trigonometry**
Spices   641.3
  SA   types of spices [to be added as
        needed]
  BT **Food**
Spider Man (Fictional character)   741.5
  UF   Spider-Man (Fictional character)
  BT **Superheroes**
Spider-Man (Fictional character)
  USE **Spider Man (Fictional charac-
        ter)**
Spiders (May subdiv. geog.)   **595.4**
  BT **Arachnids**
Spies (May subdiv. geog.)   **327.12;
       353.1; 355.3**
  UF   Intelligence agents
        Spying
  BT **Espionage**
     Subversive activities
  RT **Secret service**
Spinning   677; 746.1
  BT **Textile industry**
  RT **Yarn**
Spiral gearing
  USE **Gearing**
Spires   721
  UF   Steeples
  BT **Architecture**
     Church architecture
Spirit
  USE **Soul**
Spiritism
  USE **Spiritualism**
Spirits   133.9
  UF   Invisible world
  BT **Supernatural**

Spirits—*Continued*
>   NT   **Angels**
>   **Apparitions**
>   **Ghosts**
>   RT   **Demonology**
>   **Spiritualism**

Spiritual gifts   234

Use for materials on extraordinary phenomena, such as glossolalia, visions, prophecies and interpretations, healings, discernment of spirits, etc. Materials dealing collectively with ordinary spiritual phenomena, such as faith, hope, love, patience, temperance, etc., are entered under **Virtue**.

>   UF   Charismata
>   Gifts of grace
>   Gifts of the Holy Spirit
>   Gifts, Spiritual
>   BT   **Grace (Theology)**
>   NT   **Glossolalia**
>   **Spiritual healing**
>   **Visions**
>   RT   **Catholic charismatic movement**
>   **Holy Spirit**
>   **Pentecostalism**

Spiritual healing   203; 234; 615.8

Use for materials on the use of faith, prayer, or other religious means to treat illness. Materials on psychic or psychological means to treat illness are entered under **Mental healing**.

>   UF   Divine healing
>   Evangelistic healing
>   Faith cure
>   Faith healing
>   Healing, Spiritual
>   BT   **Medicine—Religious aspects**
>   **Spiritual gifts**
>   RT   **Christian Science**
>   **Mental healing**
>   **Mind and body**
>   **Miracles**
>   **Subconsciousness**
>   **Suggestive therapeutics**

Spiritual life   204; 248

Use for materials on spiritual practices and on the relationship that individuals may attain with the sacred. May be subdivided by religion or sect.

>   BT   **Religious life**
>   NT   **Conversion**
>   **Faith**
>   **Hope**
>   **Meditation**
>   **Mysticism**

Retreats

Spiritualism (May subdiv. geog.)   **133.9**

Use for materials on extraordinary spiritual phenomena, especially contact with the spirits of the dead.

>   UF   Spiritism
>   BT   **Occultism**
>   **Supernatural**
>   NT   **Psychokinesis**
>   RT   **Apparitions**
>   **Parapsychology**
>   **Spirits**

Spirituals (Songs)   782.25

>   BT   **Folk songs—United States**
>   **Hymns**
>   RT   **African American music**
>   **Gospel music**

Splicing
>   USE   **Knots and splices**

Splicing of genes
>   USE   **Genetic engineering**

Split personality
>   USE   **Multiple personality**

Spoils system
>   USE   **Political corruption**

Sponges (May subdiv. geog.)   **593.4**
>   BT   **Aquatic animals**

Sport utility vehicles   629.22
>   UF   SUVs (Vehicles)
>   BT   **Vehicles**

Sporting equipment
>   USE   **Sporting goods**

Sporting goods   796.028
>   UF   Sporting equipment
>   Sports—Equipment and supplies
>   RT   **Sports**

Sports (May subdiv. geog.)   **796**
>   SA   types of sports and names of
>   sports competitions [to be
>   added as needed]
>   BT   **Play**
>   **Recreation**
>   NT   **Aeronautical sports**
>   **Baseball**
>   **Basketball**
>   **Bullfights**
>   **Coaching (Athletics)**
>   **College sports**
>   **Cycling**
>   **Extreme sports**
>   **Field hockey**
>   **Fishing**

Sports—*Continued*
>> Football
>> Gymnastics
>> Olympic games
>> Orienteering
>> Professional sports
>> Racing
>> Rodeos
>> Rowing
>> School sports
>> Soccer
>> Sports cards
>> Sports for women
>> Sports records
>> Sports teams
>> Sports tournaments
>> Sportsmanship
>> Tennis
>> Track athletics
>> Violence in sports
>> Water sports
>> Winter sports
> RT Amusements
>> Athletes
>> Athletics
>> Games
>> Outdoor life
>> Physical education
>> Sporting goods
>> Sports facilities

Sports and drugs
> USE **Athletes—Drug use**

Sports—Audiences
> USE **Sports spectators**

Sports betting (May subdiv. geog.) **796**
> UF Sports handicapping
> BT **Gambling**

Sports broadcasting
> USE **Radio broadcasting of sports**
>> **Television broadcasting of**
>> **sports**

Sports cards **769**
> UF Cards, Sports
> SA types of cards for specific
>> sports, e.g. **Baseball cards** [to
>> be added as needed]
> BT **Sports**
> NT **Baseball cards**

Sports cars (May subdiv. geog.) **629.222**
> SA names of specific sports cars [to
>> be added as needed]
> BT **Automobiles**

Sports coaching
> USE **Coaching (Athletics)**

Sports—Corrupt practices **796**
> UF Cheating in sports
>> Corruption in sports
>> Sports scandals
> BT **Criminal law**

Sports drama (Films) **791.43**
> Use for individual works, collections, or materials about sports drama on film.
> BT **Motion pictures**

Sports drama (Radio programs) **791.44**
> Use for individual works, collections, or materials about sports drama on the radio.
> BT **Radio programs**

Sports drama (Television programs)
>> **791.45**
> Use for individual works, collections, or materials about sports drama on television.
> BT **Television programs**

Sports—Equipment and supplies
> USE **Sporting goods**

Sports events
> USE names of specific sports events,
>> e.g. **Super Bowl (Game)** [to
>> be added as needed]

Sports facilities (May subdiv. geog.)
>> **796.06**
> SA types of sports facilities [to be
>> added as needed]
> NT **Golf courses**
>> **Playgrounds**
>> **Stadiums**
>> **Swimming pools**
> RT **Recreation**
>> **Sports**

Sports fans
> USE **Sports spectators**

Sports—Fiction **808.83**
> Use for collections of sports stories.
> UF Sports stories
> SA types of sports with the subdivi-
>> sion *Fiction*, e.g. **Baseball—**
>> **Fiction** [to be added as need-
>> ed]

Sports for the handicapped **796.01**
> BT **Handicapped**
> NT **Special Olympics**
>> **Wheelchair sports**

Sports for women (May subdiv. geog.)
>> **796**
> UF Women—Sports

Sports for women—*Continued*
    SA   types of sports for women, e.g.,
          Basketball for women [to be
          added as needed]
    BT   **Sports**
    NT   **Basketball for women**
Sports—Graphic novels   741.5
    BT   **Graphic novels**
Sports handicapping
    USE   **Sports betting**
Sports in radio
    USE   **Radio broadcasting of sports**
Sports in television
    USE   **Television broadcasting of
          sports**
Sports—Lists   796
Sports mascots
    USE   **Mascots**
Sports—Medical aspects
    USE   **Sports medicine**
Sports medicine   613.7; 617.1
    UF   Athletic medicine
          Physical education—Medical as-
          pects
          Sports—Medical aspects
    BT   **Medical care**
          Medicine
Sports records (May subdiv. geog.)   **796**
    Use for materials on top performances or
    achievements.
    UF   Records, Sports
    BT   **Sports**
    RT   **Sports—Statistics**
          World records
Sports scandals
    USE   **Sports—Corrupt practices**
Sports spectators (May subdiv. geog.)
          306.4; 796
    UF   Sports—Audiences
          Sports fans
    BT   **Audiences**
Sports—Statistics   796
    SA   types of sports with the subdivi-
          sion *Statistics* [to be added as
          needed]
    BT   **Statistics**
    RT   **Sports records**
Sports stories
    USE   **Sports—Fiction**
Sports teams (May subdiv. geog.)
          796.06

    SA   types of sports teams, e.g. **Base-
          ball teams**, and names of in-
          dividual teams, e.g. **New
          York Knicks (Basketball
          team)** [to be added as need-
          ed]
    BT   **Sports**
    NT   **Baseball teams**
          Basketball teams
Sports tournaments (May subdiv. geog.)
          796
    UF   Tournaments
    SA   types of sports with the subdivi-
          sion *Tournaments*, e.g. **Ten-
          nis—Tournaments**; names of
          sports tournaments, e.g. **Super
          Bowl** [to be added as needed]
    BT   **Contests**
          Sports
    NT   **Super Bowl (Game)**
          Tennis—Tournaments
Sports violence
    USE   **Violence in sports**
Sportsmanship   175
    UF   Bad sportsmanship
    BT   **Human behavior**
          Sports
Spot welding
    USE   **Electric welding**
Spouses
    USE   **Husbands**
          Wives
Spraying and dusting   632
    UF   Dusting and spraying
    BT   **Agricultural pests**
          Fruit—Diseases and pests
    NT   **Aeronautics in agriculture**
    RT   **Fungicides**
          Herbicides
          Insecticides
Spreadsheet software   005.54
    UF   Electronic spreadsheets
    BT   **Computer software**
Spring   508.2; 578.43
    BT   **Seasons**
Spun glass
    USE   **Glass fibers**
Spy films   791.43
    Use for individual works, collections, or
    materials about spy films.
    UF   Espionage films
          Suspense films

Spy films—*Continued*
  BT **Motion pictures**
  RT **Mystery films**
Spy novels
  USE **Spy stories**
Spy radio programs   791.44
    Use for individual works, collections, or
  materials about spy radio programs.
  UF Suspense programs
  BT **Radio programs**
Spy stories   808.3; 808.83
    Use for individual works, collections, or
  materials about spy stories.
  UF Espionage stories
      Spy novels
  BT **Adventure fiction**
  RT **Mystery fiction**
      Romantic suspense novels
Spy television programs   791.45
    Use for individual works, collection, or ma-
  terials about spy television programs.
  UF Espionage television programs
      Suspense programs
  BT **Television programs**
  RT **Mystery television programs**
Spying
  USE **Espionage**
       Spies
Square   516
  BT **Geometry**
      Shape
Square dancing   793.3
  BT **Folk dancing**
Square root   513.2
  BT **Arithmetic**
Squirrels   599.36
  BT **Mammals**
  NT **Chipmunks**
Sri Lanka   954.93
    May be subdivided like **United States** ex-
  cept for *History*.
  UF Ceylon
SST (Supersonic transport)
  USE **Supersonic transport planes**
St. Bartholomew's Day, Massacre of, 1572
  USE **Saint Bartholomew's Day,**
       Massacre of, 1572
St. Francis, Order of
  USE **Franciscans**
St. Valentine's Day
  USE **Valentine's Day**
Stabilization in industry
  USE **Business cycles**

Stadia
  USE **Stadiums**
Stadiums (May subdiv. geog.)   796.06
  UF Ballparks
      Stadia
  BT **Sports facilities**
Staff
  USE types of institutions, types of
       public officials, and names of
       individual public officials with
       the subdivision *Staff,* e.g.
       Presidents—United States—
       Staff [to be added as needed]
Stage
  USE **Acting**
       Drama
       Theater
Stage history
  USE names of dramatists with the
       subdivision *Stage history,* e.g.
       Shakespeare, William, 1564-
       1616—Stage history [to be
       added as needed]
Stage lighting   792.02
  UF Television—Stage lighting
      Theaters—Stage lighting
  BT **Lighting**
Stage scenery
  USE **Theaters—Stage setting and**
       scenery
Stage setting
  USE **Theaters—Stage setting and**
       scenery
Stagecoaches
  USE **Carriages and carts**
Stained glass
  USE **Glass painting and staining**
Stalking (May subdiv. geog.)   364.1
  UF Antistalking laws
      Stalking—Law and legislation
  BT **Offenses against the person**
Stalking—Law and legislation
  USE **Stalking**
Stamina, Physical
  USE **Physical fitness**
Stammering
  USE **Speech disorders**
Stamp collecting (May subdiv. geog.)
       769.56
    Use for materials on the collecting, buying,
  and selling of postage stamps.

Stamp collecting—*Continued*
UF   Philately
       Postage stamp collecting
       Postage stamps—Collectors and
          collecting
       Stamps—Collectors and collect-
          ing
BT   **Collectors and collecting**
RT   **Postage stamps**
Stamps—Collectors and collecting
USE   **Stamp collecting**
Stamps, Postage
USE   **Postage stamps**
Standard book numbers
USE   **Publishers' standard book
          numbers**
Standard of living
USE   **Cost and standard of living**
Standard of value
USE   **Money**
Standard time
USE   **Time**
Standards
USE   subjects, types of school and in-
          stitutions, and types of indus-
          tries with the subdivision
          Standards, e.g. **Environmen-
          tal protection—Standards;**
          which may be further subdi-
          vided geographically [to be
          added as needed]
Standards of output
USE   **Production standards**
Star Wars (Ballistic missile defense sys-
       tem)
USE   **Strategic Defense Initiative**
Star Wars films   791.43
       Use for individual works, collections, or
       materials about Star Wars films.
BT   **Motion pictures**
       Science fiction films
Star Wars weapons
USE   **Space weapons**
Stars   523.8
SA   names of constellations and of
          individual stars, e.g. **Sirius** [to
          be added as needed]
NT   **Black holes (Astronomy)**
       Galaxies
       Sirius
       Solar system
       Supernovas

RT   **Astronomy**
       Constellations
Stars—Atlases   523.8022
UF   Astronomy—Atlases
       Atlases, Astronomical
BT   **Atlases**
Starting a business
USE   **New business enterprises**
Starvation   363.8
NT   **Famines**
RT   **Fasting**
       Hunger
       Malnutrition
State aid to education
USE   **Government aid to education**
State aid to libraries
USE   **Government aid to libraries**
State and agriculture
USE   **Agriculture—Government poli-
          cy**
State and environment
USE   **Environmental policy**
State and railroads
USE   **Railroads—Government policy**
State and the arts
USE   **Federal aid to the arts**
State birds   598
BT   **Birds**
       State emblems
State constitutions
USE   **Constitutions**
       Constitutions—United States
State emblems (May subdiv. geog.)
       929.9
UF   Emblems, State
       State symbols
SA   types of state emblems and state
          symbols, e.g. **State birds;**
          State flowers [to be added as
          needed]
BT   **Signs and symbols**
NT   **State birds**
       State flowers
RT   **National emblems**
State encouragement of science, literature,
       and art
USE   **Cultural policy**
State encouragement of the arts
USE   **Arts—Government policy**
       Federal aid to the arts

State-federal relations
  USE **Federal-state relations**
State flowers   582.13
  BT **Flowers**
      State emblems
State governments   352.13
  Use for general materials on state govern-
  ment not limited to a single state.
  UF United States—State govern-
       ments
  SA names of states with the subdi-
       vision *Politics and govern-*
       ment, e.g. **Ohio—Politics and**
       government [to be added as
       needed]
  BT **Political science**
  NT **Federal-state relations**
      Governors
      State-local relations
  RT **Federal government**
State, Heads of
  USE **Heads of state**
State libraries (May subdiv. geog.)
       027.5
  Use for materials on government libraries,
  maintained by state funds, that preserve state
  records and publications.
  BT **Government libraries**
State-local relations (May subdiv. geog.)
       320.4; 320.8; 352.13
  UF City-state relations
      Local-state relations
  BT **Local government**
      Municipal government
      State governments
State-local tax relations
  USE **Intergovernmental tax relations**
State medicine (May subdiv. geog.)
       362.1; 368.4; 614
  Use for general materials on the relations of
  the state to medicine, public health, medical
  legislation, examinations of physicians by
  state boards, etc.
  UF Medicine, State
      National health service
      Socialized medicine
  BT **Medicine**
  NT **Medicaid**
      Medicare
      Public health
  RT **National health insurance**
State ministries
  USE **Executive departments**

State of the Union messages
  USE **Presidents—United States—**
        Messages
State ownership
  USE **Government ownership**
State ownership of railroads
  USE **Railroads—Government policy**
State planning
  USE **Economic policy**
        Regional planning
        Social policy
State police   363.2
  UF Police, State
  BT **Police**
State regulation of industry
  USE **Industrial policy**
State rights   321.02; 342
  UF States' rights
  BT **Political science**
State songs   782.42
  BT **Songs**
State symbols
  USE **State emblems**
State, The   320.1
  UF Commonwealth, The
  NT **Church and state**
      Public interest
      Welfare state
  RT **Political science**
States, New
  USE **New states**
States' rights
  USE **State rights**
Statesmen (May subdiv. geog.)   **920**
  NT **Diplomats**
      Heads of state
      Legislators
      Politicians
Statesmen—United States   973
  NT **Founding Fathers of the Unit-**
       ed States
Statics   531
  BT **Mechanics**
      Physics
  NT **Hydrostatics**
      Strains and stresses
  RT **Dynamics**
Statistical diagrams
  USE **Statistics—Graphic methods**
Statistical inference
  USE **Probabilities**

715

Statistics   001.4; 310

Use for materials on the theory and methods of statistics.

SA   subjects and names of countries,
cities, etc., with the subdivision *Statistics* [to be added as
needed]

BT   **Economics**

NT   **Agriculture—Statistics**
Average
Census
Chicago (Ill.)—Statistics
Education—Statistics
Gross national product
Libraries—Statistics
Ohio—Statistics
Probabilities
Railroads—Statistics
Sampling (Statistics)
Sports—Statistics
United States—Statistics
Vital statistics

Statistics—Graphic methods   001.4

UF   Statistical diagrams

BT   **Graphic methods**

Statues

USE   **Monuments**
Sculpture

Status, Social

USE   **Social status**

Statutes

USE   **Law**

Stealing

USE   **Theft**

Steam   536; 621.1

BT   **Heat**
Power (Mechanics)
Water

RT   **Steam engineering**

Steam engineering (May subdiv. geog.)
621.1

BT   **Engineering**

NT   **Steam engines**
Steam navigation
Steam power plants

RT   **Mechanical engineering**
Steam

Steam engines   621.1

BT   **Engines**
Steam engineering

NT   **Condensers (Steam)**
Marine engines

Steam turbines

Steam heating   697

BT   **Heating**

Steam locomotives (May subdiv. geog.)
625.26

BT   **Locomotives**

Steam navigation   387; 623.89

BT   **Navigation**
Steam engineering
Transportation

NT   **Marine engineering**
Steam turbines

RT   **Steamboats**

Steam power plants   621.1

BT   **Electric power plants**
Steam engineering

Steam turbines   621.1

BT   **Steam engines**
Steam navigation
Turbines

Steamboats (May subdiv. geog.)   **387.2;
623.82**

UF   Steamships

BT   **Boats and boating**
Naval architecture
Ocean travel
Shipbuilding
Ships

RT   **Steam navigation**

Steamships

USE   **Steamboats**

Steel   669; 672

BT   **Iron**
Metalwork

NT   **Structural steel**

Steel construction (May subdiv. geog.)
693

UF   Building, Iron and steel
Iron and steel building

BT   **Building**
Structural engineering

RT   **Structural steel**

Steel engraving

USE   **Engraving**

Steel industry (May subdiv. geog.)
338.4; 672

UF   Steel industry and trade

BT   **Industries**

RT   **Iron industry**

Steel industry and trade

USE   **Steel industry**

Steel industry—Labor productivity
338.4
  BT Labor productivity
Steel industry—Quality control   338.4;
672
  BT Quality control
Steel industry—Technological innovations
338.4
  BT Technological innovations
Steel, Structural
  USE Structural steel
Steeples
  USE Spires
Steers
  USE Beef cattle
Stem cell research (May subdiv. geog.)
616.007
  BT Medical technology
       Medicine—Research
Stencil work   686.2; 745.7
  BT Decoration and ornament
       Painting
  NT Silk screen printing
Stenography
  USE Shorthand
Step dancing   793.31
  BT Dance
Step-parents
  USE Stepparents
Stepfamilies   306.874
  UF Stepfamily
  BT Family
Stepfamily
  USE Stepfamilies
Stepfathers   306.874
  BT Fathers
       Stepparents
Stepmothers   306.874
  BT Mothers
       Stepparents
Stepparents   306.874
  UF Step-parents
  BT Parents
  NT Stepfathers
       Stepmothers
Stereo photography
  USE Three dimensional photogra-
       phy
Stereo sound systems
  USE Stereophonic sound systems
Stereophonic sound systems   621.389

  UF Stereo sound systems
  BT High-fidelity sound systems
       Sound—Recording and repro-
       ducing
Stereophotography
  USE Three dimensional photogra-
       phy
Stereopticon
  USE Projectors
Stereoscopic photography
  USE Three dimensional photogra-
       phy
Stereotype (Social psychology) (May
subdiv. geog.)   303.3
  UF Mental stereotype
       Stereotyped behavior
  BT Attitude (Psychology)
       Social psychology
       Thought and thinking
Stereotyped behavior
  USE Stereotype (Social psychology)
Sterility in animals
  USE Infertility
Sterility in humans
  USE Infertility
Sterilization (Birth control) (May subdiv.
geog.)   363.9; 613.9
  BT Birth control
  NT Vasectomy
Steroids   572; 612
  UF Anabolic steroids
  BT Biochemistry
       Drugs
  RT Athletes—Drug use
       Hormones
Stewardesses, Airline
  USE Flight attendants
Stewards, Airline
  USE Flight attendants
Stills
  USE Distillation
Stimulants   613.8; 615
  SA types of stimulants, e.g. Am-
       phetamines; and names of in-
       dividual stimulants [to be
       added as needed]
  BT Drugs
       Psychotropic drugs
  NT Amphetamines
       Hallucinogens

Stock averages
USE **Stock price indexes**
Stock brokerage firms
USE **Stockbrokers**
Stock brokers
USE **Stockbrokers**
Stock car racing (May subdiv. geog.)
796.72
BT **Automobile racing**
Stock control
USE **Inventory control**
Stock exchange
USE **Stock exchanges**
Stock exchange crashes
USE **Financial crises**
Stock exchanges (May subdiv. geog.)
332.64
UF Securities exchange
Stock exchange
Stock market
BT **Finance**
Markets
NT **Bonds**
Insider trading
Securities
Wall Street (New York, N.Y.)
RT **Investments**
Speculation
Stocks
Stock fraud
USE **Securities fraud**
Stock indexes
USE **Stock price indexes**
Stock judging
USE **Livestock judging**
Stock market
USE **Stock exchanges**
Stock market fraud
USE **Securities fraud**
Stock market panics
USE **Financial crises**
Stock price indexes   332.63
UF Stock averages
Stock indexes
BT **Prices**
Stock raising
USE **Livestock industry**
Stock yards
USE **Stockyards**
Stockbrokers (May subdiv. geog.)
332.62

UF Brokers (Stocks)
Investment brokers
Security traders
Stock brokerage firms
Stock brokers
BT **Brokers**
Stockings
USE **Hosiery**
Stocks (May subdiv. geog.)   **332.63**
UF Dividends
Shares of stock
BT **Commerce**
Securities
RT **Bonds**
Corporations
Investments
Stock exchanges
Stocks—Insider trading
USE **Insider trading**
Stockyards (May subdiv. geog.)   **338.4**
UF Stock yards
BT **Meat industry**
Stoics   188
BT **Ancient philosophy**
Ethics
Stomach   612.3
BT **Anatomy**
RT **Digestion**
Stone   553.5; 693
Use for materials on stone as a building material. General materials on naturally occurring solid minerals are entered under **Rocks**.
SA types of stone, e.g. **Marble** [to be added as needed]
BT **Building materials**
Economic geology
NT **Granite**
Marble
Masonry
Stonecutting
RT **Petrology**
Quarries and quarrying
Rocks
Stone Age (May subdiv. geog.)   **930.1**
UF Eolithic period
Neolithic period
Paleolithic period
BT **Civilization**
RT **Stone implements**
Stone-cutting
USE **Stonecutting**

Stone implements (May subdiv. geog.)
 930.1
  UF   Flint implements
  BT   **Implements, utensils, etc.**
  RT   **Stone Age**
Stone quarries
  USE   **Quarries and quarrying**
Stonecutting   693
  UF   Stone-cutting
  BT   **Masonry**
       Stone
Stoneware
  USE   **Pottery**
Storage
  USE   types of commodities, foods,
        materials, industrial products,
        etc., with the subdivision
        Storage, e.g. **Grain—Storage**
        [to be added as needed]
Storage batteries   621.31
  UF   Batteries, Electric
  BT   **Electric apparatus and appli-
        ances**
  RT   **Electric batteries**
Storage devices, Computer
  USE   **Computer storage devices**
Storage in the home   648
  UF   Home storage
  BT   **Home economics**
Store buildings
  USE   **Commercial buildings**
Stores (May subdiv. geog.)   **381**
  UF   Retail stores
       Shops
  SA   types of stores, e.g. **Drugstores**
        [to be added as needed]
  BT   **Commercial buildings**
       Retail trade
  NT   **Chain stores**
       Department stores
       Discount stores
       Drugstores
       General stores
       Supermarkets
       Thrift shops
  RT   **Shopping centers and malls**
Stories
  USE   **Anecdotes**
       Bible stories
       Fairy tales
       Fiction

       Legends
       Romances
       Short stories
       Stories in rhyme
       Stories without words
       Storytelling
       and national literatures and lit-
       erary or musical forms with
       the subdivision *Stories, plots,
       etc.,* e.g. **Ballet—Stories,
       plots, etc.; Opera—Stories,
       plots, etc.;** etc. [to be added
       as needed]
Stories for children
  USE   **Children's stories**
Stories in rhyme   808.1; 808.81
   Use as a form heading for narrative poems
   for very young children. Narrative poetry and
   materials about narrative poetry for older children and for adults are entered under **Narrative poetry**.
  UF   Stories
  BT   **Narrative poetry**
       Rhyme
Stories, plots, etc.   808
   Use for materials that analyze plots or discuss the technique of constructing plots. Collections of plots of a specific literary or musical form are entered under that form with the
   subdivision *Stories, plots, etc.* General collections of literary plots are entered under **Stories, plots, etc.—Collections**.
  UF   Dramatic plots
       Fictional plots
       Plots (Drama, fiction, etc.)
       Scenarios
  SA   national literatures and literary
       or musical forms with the
       subdivision *Stories, plots, etc.,*
       e.g. **Ballet—Stories, plots,
       etc.; Opera—Stories, plots,
       etc.** [to be added as needed]
  BT   **Literature**
Stories, plots, etc.—Collections   802
   Use for collections of literary plots. Materi-
   als that analyze plots or discuss the technique
   of constructing plots are entered under **Sto-
   ries, plots, etc.**
  UF   Literature—Stories, plots, etc.
  SA   national literatures and specific
       genres of literature with the
       subdivision *Stories, plots, etc.*
       [to be added as needed]
Stories without words
   Use as a form heading for stories for chil-
   dren told only through a sequence of pictures.

Stories without words—*Continued*
    UF   Nonword stories
          Picture books for children,
            Wordless
          Stories
          Wordless stories
    BT   **Picture books for children**

Storms (May subdiv. geog.)   **551.55**
    SA   types of storms [to be added as
          needed]
    BT   **Meteorology**
          Natural disasters
          Weather
    NT   **Blizzards**
          Cyclones
          Dust storms
          Hurricanes
          Thunderstorms
          Tornadoes
          Typhoons
    RT   **Rain**
          Snow
          Winds

Storytelling   **027.62; 372.67**
    UF   Stories
    BT   **Children's literature**
    RT   **Folklore**
          Short story

Storytelling—Collections   **808.85**
    Use for collections of stories compiled primarily for oral presentation.
    UF   Collected works
          Collections of literature

Stoves   **697**
    BT   **Heating**
          Space heaters

Strain (Psychology)
    USE **Stress (Psychology)**

Strains and stresses   **531; 620.1; 624.1**
    UF   Stresses
    BT   **Mechanics**
          Statics
          Structural analysis (Engineering)
    RT   **Strength of materials**

Strangers and children
    USE **Children and strangers**

Strategic aspects
    USE areas of the world with the subdivision *Strategic aspects,* e.g. **Middle East—Strategic aspects** [to be added as needed]

Strategic Defense Initiative   **358.1**
    UF   SDI (Ballistic missile defense system)
          Star Wars (Ballistic missile defense system)
    BT   **Military policy—United States**
          Space warfare
          United States—Defenses
    RT   **Space weapons**

Strategic management
    USE **Strategic planning**

Strategic materials
    USE **Materials**

Strategic planning (May subdiv. geog.)   **352.3; 658.4**
    UF   Strategic management
    BT   **Planning**

Strategy   **355.4**
    UF   Military strategy
          Naval strategy
    SA   countries and areas of the world with the subdivision *Strategic aspects*, e.g. **Middle East—Strategic aspects** [to be added as needed]
    BT   **Military art and science**
          Naval art and science
    NT   **Middle East—Strategic aspects**
          Tactics

Stratigraphic geology (May subdiv. geog.)   **551.7**
    May be subdivided by geological period.
    UF   Geology, Stratigraphic
    BT   **Geology**
    NT   **Fossils**

Stratosphere   **551.5**
    BT   **Upper atmosphere**
    NT   **Ozone layer**

Stratospheric ozone
    USE **Ozone layer**

Straw votes
    USE **Public opinion polls**

Strawberries   **634**
    BT   **Berries**

Stream animals (May subdiv. geog.)   **578.76**
    UF   River animals
          Stream fauna
    BT   **Animals**
          Rivers

Stream fauna
USE **Stream animals**
Streamlining
USE **Aerodynamics**
Street cars
USE **Street railroads**
Street cleaning   363.72; 628.4
BT **Cleaning**
Municipal engineering
Public health
Roads
Sanitary engineering
Streets
RT **Refuse and refuse disposal**
Street gangs
USE **Gangs**
Street life (May subdiv. geog.)   **307.76**
UF Urban street life
BT **City and town life**
Street lighting
USE **Streets—Lighting**
Street literature
USE **Pamphlets**
Street people
USE **Homeless persons**
Street railroads (May subdiv. geog.)
388.4; 625.6
UF Interurban railroads
Street cars
Trams
Trolley cars
BT **Local transit**
Railroads
RT **Cable railroads**
Electric railroads
Street traffic
USE **City traffic**
Traffic engineering
Streets (May subdiv. geog.)   **388.4; 625.7**
UF Alleys
Avenues
Boulevards
Thoroughfares
BT **Cities and towns**
Civil engineering
Transportation
NT **City traffic**
Street cleaning
RT **Pavements**
Roads
Streets—Chicago (Ill.)   977.3

UF Chicago (Ill.)—Streets
Streets—Lighting (May subdiv. geog.)
628.9
UF Cities and towns—Lighting
Street lighting
BT **Lighting**
Streets—New York (N.Y.)   974.7
UF New York (N.Y.)—Streets
RT **Wall Street (New York, N.Y.)**
Strength of materials   620.1
UF Resistance of materials
SA types of materials with the sub-
division *Testing*, e.g. **Con-
crete—Testing** [to be added
as needed]
BT **Mechanics**
**Structural analysis (Engineer-
ing)**
NT **Concrete—Testing**
RT **Building materials**
Strains and stresses
Testing
Strength training
USE **Weight lifting**
Stress management   155.9
BT **Health**
Stress (Physiology)   612; 616.8
UF Physiological stress
Tension (Physiology)
BT **Adaptation (Biology)**
Physiology
NT **Job stress**
Stress (Psychology)   155.9; 616.89
UF Emotional stress
Mental stress
Psychological stress
Strain (Psychology)
Tension (Psychology)
BT **Mental health**
Psychology
NT **Anxiety**
Burn out (Psychology)
Job stress
Post-traumatic stress disorder
Stresses
USE **Strains and stresses**
Strikes (May subdiv. geog.)   **331.892**
This heading may also be subdivided by in-
dustry or occupation and then geographically,
e.g. **Strikes—Automobile industry—United
States**.

721

Strikes—*Continued*
- UF   Lockouts
  - Picketing
  - Sit-down strikes
  - Strikes and lockouts
  - Work stoppages
- BT   **Industrial relations**
  - **Labor disputes**
- NT   **Sabotage**
- RT   **Collective bargaining**
  - **Industrial arbitration**
  - **Injunctions**
  - **Labor unions**

Strikes and lockouts
- USE   **Strikes**

Strikes—Automobile industry—United States   331.892

Strikes—United States   331.892

String figures   793.9
- UF   Cat's cradle
  - String games
- BT   **Amusements**

String games
- USE   **String figures**

String models
- USE   **String theory**

String orchestra music   784.7
- BT   **Orchestral music**

String theory   530.14; 539.7
- UF   String models
- BT   **Particles (Nuclear physics)**

Stringed instruments   787
- UF   Bowed instruments
- SA   types of stringed instruments [to be added as needed]
- BT   **Musical instruments**
- NT   **Guitars**
  - **Violins**
  - **Violoncellos**

Strip films
- USE   **Filmstrips**

Stroke   616.8
- UF   Apoplexy
  - Cerebrovascular disease
- BT   **Brain—Diseases**

Structural analysis (Engineering)   624
- UF   Architectural engineering
  - Theory of structures
- BT   **Structural engineering**
- NT   **Strains and stresses**
  - **Strength of materials**

Structural drafting
- USE   **Mechanical drawing**

Structural engineering (May subdiv. geog.)   624.1
- UF   Architectural engineering
- BT   **Civil engineering**
  - **Engineering**
- NT   **Building**
  - **Foundations**
  - **Hydraulic structures**
  - **Soil mechanics**
  - **Steel construction**
  - **Structural analysis (Engineering)**

Structural failures   624.1
- UF   Collapse of structures
  - Failures, Structural
- SA   types of structural failures, e.g. **Building failures** [to be added as needed]
- BT   **Reliability (Engineering)**
- NT   **Building failures**

Structural materials
- USE   **Building materials**

Structural psychology
- USE   **Gestalt psychology**

Structural steel   691
- UF   Steel, Structural
- BT   **Building materials**
  - **Civil engineering**
  - **Steel**
- RT   **Steel construction**

Structural zoology
- USE   **Animals—Anatomy**

Structure in biology
- USE   **Morphology**

Structures
- USE   **Buildings**

Structures, Garden
- USE   **Garden structures**

Stubbornness   155.2; 179
- UF   Obstinacy
- BT   **Personality**

Stucco   693
- BT   **Building materials**
  - **Decoration and ornament**
  - **Plaster and plastering**

Student achievement
- USE   **Academic achievement**

Student activities (May subdiv. geog.)   371.8

Student activities—*Continued*
- UF Extracurricular activities
- BT **Students**
- NT **After school programs**
 Cheerleading
 College and school drama
 College and school journalism
 College sports
 Field trips
 School assembly programs
 School sports

Student aid (May subdiv. geog.)   **371.2; 378.3**
- UF Financial aid to students
 Student financial aid
- BT **College costs**
 Loans
- NT **Scholarships**
 Student loan funds

Student busing
- USE **Busing (School integration)**

Student cheating
- USE **Cheating (Education)**

Student clubs
- USE **Students—Societies**

Student councils
- USE **Student government**

Student dishonesty
- USE **Cheating (Education)**

Student dropouts
- USE **Dropouts**

Student evaluation of teachers   **371.14**
- UF Student rating of teachers
 Teachers, Student rating of
- BT **Teacher-student relationship**

Student exchange programs   **370.116**
- UF Exchange of students
 Exchange programs, Student
 International exchange of students
- BT **Exchange of persons programs**
 International education

Student financial aid
- USE **Student aid**

Student government   **371.5**
- UF Self-government (in education)
 Student councils
 Student self-government
- BT **School discipline**
 Schools—Administration

Student guidance
- USE **Educational counseling**

Student life
- USE **College students**
 Students

Student loan funds (May subdiv. geog.)   **371.2; 378.3**
- UF Loan funds, Student
- BT **College costs**
 Student aid

Student movement
- USE **Youth movement**

Student promotion
- USE **Promotion (School)**

Student protests, demonstrations, etc.
- USE **Students—Political activity**
 Youth movement

Student rating of teachers
- USE **Student evaluation of teachers**

Student revolt
- USE **Students—Political activity**
 Youth movement

Student self-government
- USE **Student government**

Student societies
- USE **Students—Societies**

Student songs
- USE **Students' songs**

Student-teacher relationships
- USE **Teacher-student relationship**

Student teaching   **370.71**
- UF Practice teaching
 Teachers—Practice teaching
- BT **Teachers—Training**
 Teaching

Student to student counseling
- USE **Peer counseling**

Student violence
- USE **School violence**

Student yearbooks
- USE **School yearbooks**

Students (May subdiv. geog.)   **371.8**
- UF School life
 Student life
- SA types of students, e.g. **College students** [to be added as needed]
- NT **At risk students**
 College students
 Dropouts
 Foreign students
 High school students
 School children

Students—*Continued*
>> Student activities
>> Underachievers
Students and libraries
> USE Students—Library services
Students—Counseling
> USE Educational counseling
Students, Foreign
> USE Foreign students
Students—Grading and marking
> USE Grading and marking (Education)
Students—Library services 027.62
> UF Libraries and students [*Former heading*]
> > Students and libraries
> BT Libraries and schools
> > Library services
> > School libraries
Students' military training camps
> USE Military training camps
Students—Political activity 324; 371.8
> UF Politics and students
> > Student protests, demonstrations, etc.
> > Student revolt
> BT Political participation
> > Youth movement
Students—Societies 371.8
> UF School clubs
> > Student clubs
> > Student societies
> BT Societies
> NT Fraternities and sororities
Students' songs 782.42
> UF College songs
> > Student songs
> BT Songs
> NT United States Military Academy—Songs
Students—United States 371.80973
Students with problems
> USE At risk students
Studio pottery
> USE Art pottery
Study abroad
> USE Foreign study
Study and teaching
> USE Education
> > and subjects with the subdivision *Study and teaching*, e.g.

Science—Study and teaching
> [to be added as needed]
Study, Foreign
> USE Foreign study
Study guides
> USE named examinations with the subdivision *Study guides,* e.g. Graduate Record Examination—Study guides; and subjects, educational levels, and names of educational institutions with the subdivisions *Examinations—Study guides,* e.g. English language—Examinations—Study guides [to be added as needed]
Study guides for examinations
> USE Examinations—Study guides
Study methods
> USE Study skills
Study overseas
> USE Foreign study
Study skills 371.3028
> UF How to study
> > Study methods
> SA subjects with the subdivision *Study and teaching*, e.g. Art—Study and teaching [to be added as needed]
> BT Education
> > Life skills
> > Teaching
> NT Examinations—Study guides
> > Homework
> > Independent study
> > Self-instruction
Study-work plan
> USE Cooperative education
Stuffed bears (Toys)
> USE Teddy bears
Stuffed toy making
> USE Soft toy making
Stunt flying 797.5
> UF Aerobatics
> BT Airplanes—Piloting
Stunt men
> USE Stunt performers
Stunt performers (May subdiv. geog.)
> 791.4
> UF Stunt men
> BT Actors

Stuttering
    USE   **Speech disorders**
Style in dress
    USE   **Clothing and dress**
           Costume
           Fashion
Style, Literary
    USE   **Literary style**
Style manikins
    USE   **Fashion models**
Style manuals
    USE   **Printing—Style manuals**
Sub-Saharan Africa   960
    UF   Africa, Sub-Saharan
          Black Africa
    BT   **Africa**
Subconsciousness   127; 154.2
    BT   **Parapsychology**
          Psychology
    NT   **Hallucinations and illusions**
          Mental suggestion
          Sleep
    RT   **Consciousness**
          Dreams
          Hypnotism
          Mental healing
          Mind and body
          Psychoanalysis
          Spiritual healing
Subculture
    USE   **Counter culture**
Subgravity state
    USE   **Weightlessness**
Subject catalogs   016; 017
    UF   Catalogs, Subject
    BT   **Library catalogs**
    NT   **Subject headings**
Subject dictionaries
    USE   **Encyclopedias and dictionaries**
Subject headings   025.4
    UF   Thesauri
    BT   **Cataloging**
          Indexes
          Subject catalogs
Submarine boats
    USE   **Submarines**
Submarine cables   384.1; 384.6
    UF   Cables, Submarine
          Ocean cables
    BT   **Telecommunication**
          Telegraph

Submarine diving
    USE   **Deep diving**
Submarine engineering
    USE   **Ocean engineering**
Submarine exploration
    USE   **Underwater exploration**
Submarine geology (May subdiv. geog.)
    551.46
    UF   Marine geology
          Underwater geology
    BT   **Geology**
          Oceanography
    NT   **Ocean bottom**
    RT   **Plate tectonics**
Submarine medicine   616.9
    UF   Underwater medicine
          Underwater physiology
    BT   **Medicine**
Submarine oil well drilling
    USE   **Offshore oil well drilling**
Submarine photography
    USE   **Underwater photography**
Submarine research stations
    USE   **Undersea research stations**
Submarine vehicles
    USE   **Submersibles**
Submarine warfare   359.9
    UF   Naval warfare
          Warfare, Submarine
    BT   **Naval art and science**
          War
    NT   **Submarines**
          Torpedoes
          World War, 1939-1945—Naval
             operations—Submarine
Submarines (May subdiv. geog.)   **359.9;**
    623.82

    Use for materials on submarines only. Materials on other underwater craft are entered under **Submersibles**.

    UF   Submarine boats
    BT   **Ships**
          Submarine warfare
          Submersibles
          Warships
    NT   **Nuclear submarines**
Submersibles   623.82
    UF   Submarine vehicles
          Undersea vehicles
    SA   types of submersibles [to be
            added as needed]
    BT   **Vehicles**

Submersibles—*Continued*
  NT **Bathyscaphe**
      Submarines
Subscription television   384.55
  UF Pay-per-view television
      Pay television
      Television, Subscription
  BT **Television broadcasting**
Subsidies (May subdiv. geog.)   **338.9**
  Use for materials on financial or other aid given, without equivalent recompense, by governments or governmental agencies to private enterprises.
  UF Corporate welfare
      Government subsidies
      Grants
      Subventions
  SA types of subsidies, e.g. **Agricultural subsidies**; and federal aid to specific endeavors, e.g. **Federal aid to minority business enterprises** [to be added as needed]
  BT **Domestic economic assistance**
      Economic policy
  NT **Agricultural subsidies**
      Federal aid to minority business enterprises
      Transfer payments
Subsistence economy (May subdiv. geog.)   **330.9**
  BT **Cost and standard of living**
  NT **Barter**
  RT **Poverty**
Substance abuse
  USE **Drug abuse**
       Solvent abuse
Substantive due process
  USE **Due process of law**
Substitute products   338
  SA types of substitute products, e.g. **Sugar substitutes** [to be added as needed]
  BT **Commercial products**
  NT **Sugar substitutes**
  RT **Synthetic products**
Subterfuge
  USE **Deception**
Subterranean water
  USE **Groundwater**
Subtraction   513.2
  BT **Arithmetic**

Suburban areas
  USE **Suburbs**
Suburban life (May subdiv. geog.)
      307.74
  BT **Suburbs**
Suburbs (May subdiv. geog.)   **307.76**
  UF Suburban areas
      Suburbs and environs
  SA names of suburban areas, e.g. **Chicago Suburban Area (Ill.)** [to be added as needed]
  BT **Cities and towns—Growth**
      City planning
      Metropolitan areas
  NT **Suburban life**
Suburbs and environs
  USE **Suburbs**
Subventions
  USE **Subsidies**
Subversive activities (May subdiv. geog.)
      322.4; 327.12
  Use for materials on any attempt to subvert, overthrow, or cause the destruction of any established or legally constituted government. Materials on the offense of acting to overthrow one's own government or to harm or kill its sovereign are entered under **Treason**.
  UF Fifth column
  BT **Insurgency**
  NT **Espionage**
      Political crimes and offenses
      Sabotage
      Spies
      Terrorism
      Treason
  RT **Internal security**
Subways (May subdiv. geog.)   **388.4; 625.4**
  UF Underground railroads
  BT **Local transit**
      Railroads
Success   158; 650.1
  UF Fortune
      Personal development
  BT **Business ethics**
      Wealth
  NT **Academic achievement**
      Leadership
      Life skills
  RT **Ability**
      Self-realization

Succession
 USE presidents, prime ministers, and other rulers with the subdivision *Succession,* e.g. **Presidents—United States—Succession** [to be added as needed]
Sudan 962.4
 May be subdivided like **United States** except for *History.*
Sudden death in infants
 USE **Sudden infant death syndrome**
Sudden infant death syndrome 618.92
 UF Cot death
 Crib death
 Infant sudden death
 SIDS (Disease)
 Sudden death in infants
 BT **Infants—Death**
Suffering 128; 152.1; 214
 UF Affliction
 RT **Joy and sorrow**
 Pain
Suffrage (May subdiv. geog.) **324.6**
 UF Franchise
 Voting
 SA ethnic groups and classes of persons with the subdivision *Suffrage* [to be added as needed]
 BT **Citizenship**
 Constitutional law
 Democracy
 Elections
 Political science
 NT **African Americans—Suffrage**
 Blacks—Suffrage
 Naturalization
 Voter registration
 Women—Suffrage
 RT **Representative government and representation**
Suffragettes
 USE **Suffragists**
Suffragists (May subdiv. geog.) **324.6; 920**
 UF Suffragettes
 BT **Reformers**
 RT **Feminism**
 Women—Suffrage
Sufism (May subdiv. geog.) **297.4**
 BT **Mysticism—Islam**
 RT **Dervishes**

Sugar 641.3; 664
 SA types of sugar [to be added as needed]
 BT **Food**
 NT **Maple sugar**
 Syrups
Sugar substitutes 641.3; 664
 UF Artificial sweeteners
 Nonnutritive sweeteners
 BT **Substitute products**
Suggestion, Mental
 USE **Mental suggestion**
Suggestive therapeutics 615.8
 UF Therapeutics, Suggestive
 BT **Therapeutics**
 RT **Hypnotism**
 Mental healing
 Mental suggestion
 Psychotherapy
 Spiritual healing
Suicidal behavior
 USE **Suicide—Psychological aspects**
Suicide (May subdiv. geog.) **179.7; 362.28**
 UF Attempted suicide
 Suicide attempts
 SA classes of persons and ethnic groups with the subdivision *Suicide,* e.g. **Teenagers—Suicide** [to be added as needed]
 BT **Medical jurisprudence**
 Social problems
 NT **Teenagers—Suicide**
 RT **Homicide**
 Right to die
Suicide attempts
 USE **Suicide**
Suicide bombers (May subdiv. geog.) **303.6**
 BT **Terrorism**
Suicide—Psychological aspects 616.85
 UF Suicidal behavior
 BT **Human behavior**
Suing (Law)
 USE **Litigation**
Suite (Music) 784.18
 Use for musical scores and for materials on the suite as a musical form.
 UF Partita
 Suites
 BT **Musical form**
 Orchestral music

727

Suites
    USE   **Suite (Music)**
Suits (Law)
    USE   **Litigation**
Suits of armor
    USE   **Armor**
Sulfa drugs
    USE   **Sulfonamides**
Sulfonamides   615
    UF   Sulfa drugs
    BT   **Drugs**
Sulfur
    USE   **Sulphur**
Sulphur   546; 553.6; 661
    UF   Sulfur
    BT   **Chemical elements**
Summer   508.2; 578.43
    BT   **Seasons**
Summer camps
    USE   **Camps**
Summer cottages
    USE   **Vacation homes**
Summer employment   331.1
    BT   **Employment**
    RT   **Teenagers—Employment**
         Youth—Employment
Summer homes
    USE   **Vacation homes**
Summer resorts   790
    BT   **Resorts**
Summer schools (May subdiv. geog.)
         371.2
    UF   Vacation schools
    BT   **Public schools**
         Schools
    NT   **Religious summer schools**
Summer theater (May subdiv. geog.)
         792.0224
    BT   **Theater**
Sun   523.7
    UF   Solar physics
    BT   **Astronomy**
         Solar system
    NT   **Solar energy**
         Sunspots
Sun-dials
    USE   **Sundials**
Sun—Eclipses
    USE   **Solar eclipses**
Sun—Folklore   398.26

Sun powered batteries
    USE   **Solar batteries**
Sun—Radiation
    USE   **Solar radiation**
Sun—Religious aspects   299.9
Sun-spots
    USE   **Sunspots**
Sun worship (May subdiv. geog.)   **202**
    BT   **Religion**
Sunday schools (May subdiv. geog.)   **268**
    UF   Bible classes
    BT   **Church work**
         Religious education
    NT   **Bible—Study and teaching**
Sundials   681.1
    UF   Horology
         Sun-dials
    BT   **Clocks and watches**
         Garden ornaments and furni-
           ture
         Time
Sunken cities
    USE   **Extinct cities**
Sunken treasure
    USE   **Buried treasure**
Sunnis (May subdiv. geog.)   **297.82**
    UF   Sunnites
    BT   **Islamic sects**
Sunnites
    USE   **Sunnis**
Sunspots   523.7
    UF   Sun-spots
    BT   **Meteorology**
         Solar radiation
         Sun
Super Bowl (Game)   796.332
    BT   **Football**
         Sports tournaments
Super markets
    USE   **Supermarkets**
Supercomputers   004.1
      Use for materials on extraordinarily power-
    ful computers.
    BT   **Computers**
Superconducting materials
    USE   **Superconductors**
Superconductive devices
    USE   **Superconductors**
Superconductivity
    USE   **Superconductors**
Superconductors   537.6; 621.3

Superconductors—*Continued*
  UF Superconducting materials
      Superconductive devices
      Superconductivity
  BT **Electric conductors**
      Electronics
Superhero comic books, strips, etc.
      741.5
  Use for individual works, collections, or materials about superhero comics.
  BT **Comic books, strips, etc.**
Superhero films 791.43
  Use for individual works, collections, or materials about superhero films.
  SA films with particular superheroes,
      e.g. **Superman films** [to be added as needed]
  BT **Adventure films**
  NT **Superman films**
Superhero graphic novels 741.5
  Use for individual works, collections, or materials about superhero graphic novels.
  SA names of individual superheroes,
      e.g. **Superman (Fictional character)** [to be added as needed]
  BT **Graphic novels**
Superhero radio programs 791.44
  Use for individual works, collections, or materials about superhero radio programs.
  BT **Adventure radio programs**
Superhero television programs 791.45
  Use for individual works, collections, or materials about superhero television programs.
  BT **Adventure television programs**
Superheroes 808.3
  SA names of superheroes, e.g. **Superman (Fictional character)** or groups of superheroes, e.g. **Justice League (Fictional characters)** [to be added as needed]
  NT **Justice League (Fictional characters)**
      Shadowpact (Fictional characters)
      Spider Man (Fictional character)
      Superman (Fictional character)
      Wonder Woman (Fictional character)
Superhighways
  USE **Express highways**

Superintendents of schools
  USE **School superintendents and principals**
Superman (Fictional character) 741.5
  BT **Superheroes**
Superman films 791.43
  Use for individual works, collections, or materials about Superman films.
  BT **Superhero films**
Supermarket shopping
  USE **Grocery shopping**
Supermarkets (May subdiv. geog.)
      658.8
  UF Super markets
  BT **Grocery trade**
      Retail trade
      Stores
Supernatural 133; 202; 398.2
  BT **Religion**
  NT **Exorcism**
      Occultism
      Parapsychology
      Prophecies
      Revelation
      Spirits
      Spiritualism
  RT **Miracles**
Supernatural graphic novels 741.5
  Use for individual works, collections, or materials about supernatural graphic novels.
  BT **Graphic novels**
Supernovae
  USE **Supernovas**
Supernovas 523.8
  UF Supernovae
  BT **Stars**
Supersonic aerodynamics 629.132
  UF Aerodynamics, Supersonic
      High speed aerodynamics
      Speed, Supersonic
  BT **Aerodynamics**
      High speed aeronautics
  NT **Aerothermodynamics**
Supersonic airliners
  USE **Supersonic transport planes**
Supersonic transport planes 629.133
  UF SST (Supersonic transport)
      Supersonic airliners
  BT **Jet planes**
Supersonic waves
  USE **Ultrasonic waves**

729

Supersonics
USE **Ultrasonics**
Superstition (May subdiv. geog.)   **001.9;**
398
UF   Folk beliefs
Traditions
BT   **Folklore**
NT   **Charms**
RT   **Errors**
Supervision of employees
USE   **Personnel management**
Supervision of schools
USE   **School supervision**
Supervisors   331.7; 658.3
UF   Foremen
Managers
BT   **Factory management**
Personnel management
Supplementary employment   331.1
UF   Employment, Supplementary
Moonlighting
Second job
Secondary employment
BT   **Labor**
Part-time employment
Supply and demand   332; 338.5; 658.8
UF   Law of supply and demand
SA   occupational groups and types of
employees with the subdivi-
sion *Supply and demand*, e.g.
Unskilled labor—Supply and
demand; Chemical indus-
try—Employees—Supply and
demand [to be added as
needed]
BT   **Economics**
NT   **Chemical industry—Employ-**
ees—Supply and demand
Unskilled labor—Supply and
demand
RT   **Competition**
Exchange
Prices
Support groups
USE   **Self-help groups**
Support of children
USE   **Child support**
Supreme Court—United States
USE   **United States. Supreme Court**
Surf
USE   **Ocean waves**

Surf riding
USE   **Surfing**
Surface of the earth
USE   **Earth—Surface**
Surfboarding
USE   **Surfing**
Surfing (May subdiv. geog.)   **797.3**
UF   Body surfing
Surf riding
Surfboarding
BT   **Water sports**
Surfing—Songs   782.42
UF   Surfing—Songs and music
BT   **Songs**
Surfing—Songs and music
USE   **Surfing—Songs**
Surgeons (May subdiv. geog.)   **617.092;**
920
BT   **Physicians**
Surgery (May subdiv. geog.)   **617**
UF   Operations, Surgical
SA   classes of persons, names of dis-
eases, and names of organs
and regions of the body with
the subdivision *Surgery* [to be
added as needed]
BT   **Medicine**
NT   **Artificial organs**
Cancer—Surgery
Children—Surgery
Cryosurgery
Heart—Surgery
Orthopedics
Plastic surgery
Transplantation of organs, tis-
sues, etc.
Vivisection
RT   **Anesthetics**
Antiseptics
Surgery, Plastic
USE   **Plastic surgery**
Surgical transplantation
USE   **Transplantation of organs, tis-**
sues, etc.
Surnames
USE   **Personal names**
Surplus government property (May
subdiv. geog.)   **352.5**
UF   Excess government property
Government property, Surplus
BT   **Property**

Surrealism (May subdiv. geog.) **709.04; 759.06; 809**

Use for the movement or style of surrealism in literature or in the visual arts.

BT **Arts**

Surrogate mothers **176; 306.874; 346.01**

BT **Mothers**

Surveillance, Electronic

USE **Electronic surveillance**

Surveying (May subdiv. geog.) **526.9**

UF Land surveying

Land surveys

SA names of countries, cities, etc., with the subdivision *Surveys*, for works containing the results of land surveys in those places, e.g. **United States—Surveys** [to be added as needed]

BT **Civil engineering**

Geography

Measurement

NT **Mine surveying**

Topographical drawing

RT **Geodesy**

Surveys **001.4**

UF Government surveys

SA types of surveys, e.g. **Market surveys**; and names of countries, cities, etc., with the subdivision *Surveys*, for works containing the results of land surveys in those places, e.g. **United States—Surveys** [to be added as needed]

BT **Research**

NT **Educational surveys**

Library surveys

Market surveys

Social surveys

Survival after airplane accidents, shipwrecks, etc. **613.6**

UF Castaways

RT **Aircraft accidents**

Rescue work

Shipwrecks

Wilderness survival

Survival of the fittest

USE **Natural selection**

Survival skills **613.6**

Use for materials on skills needed to survive in a hazardous environment, usually stressing self-reliance and economic self-sufficiency.

UF Emergency survival

Human survival skills

SA types of survival, e.g. **Wilderness survival** [to be added as needed]

BT **Civil defense**

Environmental influence on humans

Human ecology

Life skills

NT **Wilderness survival**

RT **Self-reliance**

Survivalism (May subdiv. geog.) **320.5; 613.6**

UF Survivalist movements

BT **Social movements**

Survivalist movements

USE **Survivalism**

Suspended sentence

USE **Probation**

Suspense films

USE **Adventure films**

Mystery films

Spy films

Suspense novels

USE **Adventure fiction**

Mystery fiction

Romantic suspense novels

Suspense programs

USE **Mystery radio programs**

Mystery television programs

Spy radio programs

Spy television programs

Sustainable architecture (May subdiv. geog.) **720**

UF Environmentally friendly architecture

BT **Architecture**

Sustainable development (May subdiv. geog.) **333.71; 338.9**

Use for materials on economic development that satisfies the needs of the present generation without depleting natural resources for the future or having adverse environmental effects. General materials on the environmental impact of economic development are entered under **Economic development—Environmental aspects**.

Sustainable development—*Continued*
UF   Economic sustainability
       Sustainable economic develop-
          ment
BT   **Economic development**

Sustainable economic development
USE **Sustainable development**

SUVs (Vehicles)
USE **Sport utility vehicles**

Swamp animals (May subdiv. geog.)
    578.768
UF   Swamp fauna
BT   **Animals**

Swamp fauna
USE **Swamp animals**

Swamps (May subdiv. geog.)   **551.41**
BT   **Wetlands**

Swashbucklers
USE **Adventure fiction**
       Adventure films

Sweden   **948.5**
May be subdivided like **United States** except for *History.*

Swedish language   **439.7**
May be subdivided like **English language**.
BT   **Language and languages**
       Scandinavian languages

Swedish literature   **839.7**
May use same subdivisions and names of
literary forms as for **English literature**.
BT   **Literature**
       Scandinavian literature

Sweets
USE **Candy**
       Confectionery

Swell
USE **Ocean waves**

Swimming   **797.2**
BT   **Water sports**
NT   **Diving**
       Marathon swimming
       Synchronized swimming

Swimming pools   **690; 725; 797.2**
UF   Pools
BT   **Sports facilities**

Swindlers and swindling (May subdiv.
   geog.)   **364.16**
UF   Con artists
       Con game
       Confidence game
BT   **Crime**
       Criminals

NT   **Counterfeits and counterfeiting**
       Credit card fraud
       Quacks and quackery
RT   **Fraud**
       Impostors and imposture

Swine
USE **Pigs**

Switchboard hotlines
USE **Hotlines (Telephone counseling)**

Switzerland   **949.4**
May be subdivided like **United States** except for *History.*

Swords (May subdiv. geog.)   **623.441;**
    739.722
BT   **Weapons**

Symbiosis   **577.8**
UF   Mutualism (Biology)
BT   **Biology**
       Ecology
RT   **Parasites**
       Plant ecology

Symbolic logic   **511.3**
UF   Logic, Symbolic and mathemati-
          cal
       Mathematical logic
BT   **Logic**
       Mathematics
NT   **Boolean algebra**
RT   **Set theory**

Symbolic numbers
USE **Numerology**
       Symbolism of numbers

Symbolism (May subdiv. geog.)   **203;**
    302.2; 700
SA   symbolism of particular reli-
       gions, e.g. **Christian symbol-**
       ism; and symbolism in partic-
       ular subjects, e.g. **Symbolism**
       in literature [to be added as
       needed]
BT   **Art**
       Mythology
NT   **Christian symbolism**
       Figures of speech
       Heraldry
       Symbolism in literature
       Symbolism of numbers
RT   **Signs and symbols**

Symbolism in literature   **809**
UF   Signs and symbols in literature
BT   **Literature**
       Symbolism

Symbolism in literature—*Continued*
  RT **Allegory**
Symbolism of numbers   203; 246; 809
  Use for general materials on the symbolism of numbers, as in philosophy, religion, or literature. Materials on the occult significance of numbers are entered under **Numerology**.
  UF Number symbolism
      Sacred numbers
      Symbolic numbers
  BT **Symbolism**
  NT **Numerology**
  RT **Cabala**
      Numbers
Symbols
  USE **Signs and symbols**
Symbols, Mathematical
  USE **Mathematical notation**
Sympathy   177
  UF Pity
  BT **Conduct of life**
      Emotions
Symphonic poems   784.2
  BT **Orchestral music**
Symphonies
  USE **Symphony**
Symphony   784.18; 784.2
  Use for musical scores and for materials on the symphony as a musical form.
  UF Symphonies
  BT **Musical form**
      Orchestral music
Symptoms
  USE **Diagnosis**
Synagogues (May subdiv. geog.)   296.6; 726
  BT **Buildings**
      Religious institutions
      Temples
  RT **Judaism**
Synchronized swimming   797.2
  UF Water ballet
  BT **Swimming**
Synods
  USE **Councils and synods**
Synonyms and antonyms
  USE names of languages with the subdivision *Synonyms and antonyms,* e.g. **English language—Synonyms and antonyms** [to be added as needed]

Synthesizer music
  USE **Electronic music**
Synthesizer (Musical instrument)
  USE **Synthesizers (Musical instruments)**
Synthesizers (Musical instruments) 786.7
  UF Synthesizer (Musical instrument)
  BT **Electronic musical instruments**
Synthetic chemistry
  USE **Organic compounds—Synthesis**
Synthetic detergents
  USE **Detergents**
Synthetic drugs of abuse
  USE **Designer drugs**
Synthetic fabrics   677
  SA types of synthetic fabrics [to be added as needed]
  BT **Fabrics**
      Synthetic products
  NT **Nylon**
      Rayon
Synthetic foods
  USE **Artificial foods**
Synthetic fuels   662
  UF Artificial fuels
      Nonfossil fuels
  BT **Fuel**
      Synthetic products
Synthetic products   670
  SA types of synthetic products and names of specific products [to be added as needed]
  BT **Industrial chemistry**
  NT **Artificial foods**
      Plastics
      Synthetic fabrics
      Synthetic fuels
      Synthetic rubber
  RT **Organic compounds—Synthesis**
      Substitute products
Synthetic rubber   678
  UF Rubber, Artificial
      Rubber, Synthetic
  BT **Plastics**
      Synthetic products
Syphilis (May subdiv. geog.)   616.95
  BT **Sexually transmitted diseases**
Syria   956.91
  May be subdivided like **United States** except for *History.*
Syrups   641.3

Syrups—*Continued*
  BT   **Sugar**
System analysis   003; 004.2; 658.4
  UF   Flow charts
       Flowcharting
       Linear system theory
       Network theory
       Systems analysis
  BT   **Cybernetics**
       Mathematical models
       System theory
  NT   **Fuzzy systems**
       System design
       Systems engineering
System design   003; 004.2; 621.39
  UF   Systems design
  BT   **System analysis**
  NT   **Database design**
System engineering
  USE   **Systems engineering**
System theory   003
  UF   Systems, Theory of
       Theory of systems
  BT   **Science**
  NT   **Chaos (Science)**
       Cybernetics
       Operations research
       Social systems
       System analysis
       Systems engineering
Systematic botany
  USE   **Botany—Classification**
Systematic theology
  USE   **Doctrinal theology**
Systems analysis
  USE   **System analysis**
Systems, Database management
  USE   **Database management**
Systems design
  USE   **System design**
Systems engineering   620
  UF   System engineering
  BT   **Automation**
       Cybernetics
       Engineering
       Industrial design
       System analysis
       System theory
  NT   **Bionics**
       Reliability (Engineering)
  RT   **Operations research**

Systems, Fuzzy
  USE   **Fuzzy systems**
Systems reliability
  USE   **Reliability (Engineering)**
Systems, Theory of
  USE   **System theory**
T groups
  USE   **Group relations training**
T-shirts   391; 687
  UF   Tee shirts
  BT   **Clothing and dress**
Table decoration
  USE   **Table setting and decoration**
Table etiquette   395.5
  BT   **Eating customs**
       Etiquette
  RT   **Dining**
Table setting and decoration   642
  UF   Table decoration
  BT   **Decoration and ornament**
  NT   **Flower arrangement**
       Napkin folding
       Tableware
Table talk
  USE   **Conversation**
Table tennis   796.34
  UF   Ping-pong
  BT   **Ball games**
Tables   645; 749
  BT   **Furniture**
Tables (Systematic lists)
  USE   subjects with the subdivision *Tables,* e.g. **Meteorology—Tables; Trigonometry—Tables** etc. [to be added as needed]
Tableware (May subdiv. geog.)   **642**
  UF   Dishes
  BT   **Table setting and decoration**
  NT   **Glassware**
       Porcelain
       Pottery
       Silverware
Taboo (May subdiv. geog.)   **390**
  BT   **Manners and customs**
Tactics   355.4
  UF   Military tactics
  BT   **Military art and science**
       Strategy
  NT   **Biological warfare**
       Drill and minor tactics
       Guerrilla warfare

Tactics—*Continued*

  Military maneuvers

  War games

Tadpoles

 USE **Frogs**

Tai chi 613.7; 796.815

 UF Tai ji quan

   Taichi

 BT **Exercise**

   Martial arts

Tai ji quan

 USE **Tai chi**

Taichi

 USE **Tai chi**

Tailoring 646.4; 687

 UF Garment making

 BT **Clothing and dress**

   Clothing industry

 RT **Dressmaking**

Taiwan 951.24

  Use for materials dealing with the island of Taiwan, regardless of time period, or with the post-1948 Republic of China. Materials dealing with mainland China, regardless of time period, or with the People's Republic of China and comprehensive materials on China including Taiwan are entered under **China**. May be subdivided like **United States** except for *History*.

 UF China (Republic)

   Formosa

   Nationalist China

   Republic of China, 1949-

Takeovers, Corporate

 USE **Corporate mergers and acquisitions**

Talebearing

 USE **Tattling**

Talent

 USE **Ability**

   Genius

Talents

 USE **Ability**

Tales

 USE **Fables**

   Fairy tales

   Folklore

   Legends

Talismans

 USE **Charms**

Talk shows (May subdiv. geog.) **791.44; 791.45**

 BT **Interviewing**

   Radio programs

   Television programs

Talking

 USE **Conversation**

Talking books

 USE **Audiobooks**

Tall tales 398.2; 808.83

  Use for individual works, collections, or materials about tall tales.

 BT **Folklore**

   Legends

   Wit and humor

Talmud 296.1

 BT **Hebrew literature**

   Jewish literature

   Judaism

Tank tactics

 USE **Tank warfare**

Tank warfare 358

 UF Antitank warfare

   Tank tactics

 SA names of individual wars with the subdivision *Tank warfare* e.g. **World War, 1939-1945—Tank warfare** [to be added as needed]

 BT **War**

 NT **World War, 1939-1945—Tank warfare**

 RT **Military tanks**

Tanks (Military science)

 USE **Military tanks**

Tanning 675

 BT **Industrial chemistry**

 RT **Hides and skins**

   Leather

Tantrums, Temper

 USE **Temper tantrums**

Tao 181

 UF Dao

   Way (Chinese philosophy)

 BT **Philosophy**

 RT **Taoism**

Taoism (May subdiv. geog.) **299.5**

 BT **Religions**

 RT **Tao**

Tap dancing 792.7

 BT **Dance**

Tap water

 USE **Drinking water**

Tape recorders

 USE **Magnetic recorders and recording**

Tape recordings, Audio
USE **Sound recordings**
Tape recordings, Video
USE **Videotapes**
Tapestry (May subdiv. geog.) **677;
746.3**
BT **Decoration and ornament
Decorative arts
Interior design
Needlework**
Tardiness
USE **Punctuality**
Tariff (May subdiv. geog.) **336.2; 382**
UF Custom duties
Customs (Tariff)
Duties
Revenue
BT **Commercial policy
Economic policy
Public finance**
NT **Smuggling**
RT **Free trade
Protectionism**
Tariff—United States 382; 336.2
UF United States—Tariff
Tarot 133.3; 795.4
Use for materials on the cards and the
game.
UF Tarot (Game)
BT **Card games
Fortune telling
Playing cards**
Tarot (Game)
USE **Tarot**
Tartans 391; 929.6
UF Highland costume
Scottish tartans
BT **Clans—Scotland**
Taste 152.1
BT **Senses and sensation**
Taste (Aesthetics)
USE **Aesthetics**
Tatting 746.43
BT **Lace and lace making**
Tattling 177; 302.3
UF Talebearing
BT **Gossip**
Tattooing (May subdiv. geog.) **391.6**
UF Tattoos (Body markings)
BT **Manners and customs
Personal appearance**

Tattoos (Body markings)
USE **Tattooing**
Taverns
USE **Bars**
Tax assessment (May subdiv. geog.)
336.2
Use for general materials on the valuation
of property for determining tax liability. Mate-
rials on the assessment of property for tax
purposes in a particular place are entered un-
der **Taxation** followed by the appropriate geo-
graphical subdivision.
UF Appraisal
Assessment
Assessment, Tax
Property tax—Assessment
Real property tax—Assessment
BT **Taxation
Valuation**
NT **Tax exemption**
Tax avoidance
USE **Tax evasion
Tax planning**
Tax credits (May subdiv. geog.) **336.2**
BT **Income tax**
Tax evasion 345
UF Tax avoidance
Tax fraud
BT **Criminal law
White collar crimes**
Tax exempt status
USE **Tax exemption**
Tax exemption (May subdiv. geog.)
336.2
UF Exemption from taxation
Tax exempt status
BT **Tax assessment**
Tax fraud
USE **Tax evasion**
Tax planning (May subdiv. geog.)
343.04
UF Tax avoidance
Tax saving
BT **Personal finance
Planning
Taxation**
RT **Estate planning**
Tax relations, Intergovernmental
USE **Intergovernmental tax relations**
Tax saving
USE **Tax planning**

Tax sharing
USE **Intergovernmental tax relations**
Revenue sharing
Taxation (May subdiv. geog.) **336.2**
UF Direct taxation
Duties
Revenue
Taxes
SA subjects with the subdivision
Taxation, e.g. **Real estate in-
vestment—Taxation** [to be
added as needed]
BT **Political science**
Public finance
NT **Income tax**
Inheritance and transfer tax
Intergovernmental tax relations
Internal revenue
**Real estate investment—Taxa-
tion**
Sales tax
Tax assessment
Tax planning
Tithes
Taxation of legacies
USE **Inheritance and transfer tax**
Taxation—United States **336.200973**
UF United States—Taxation
Taxes
USE **Taxation**
Taxicabs (May subdiv. geog.) **338.34232**
UF Cabs
Taxis (Vehicles)
BT **Local transit**
Vehicles
Taxidermy **590.75**
UF Preservation of specimens
Specimens, Preservation of
SA types of specimens with the sub-
division *Collection and pres-
ervation*, e.g. **Birds—Collec-
tion and preservation** [to be
added as needed]
RT **Zoological specimens—Collec-
tion and preservation**
Taxis (Vehicles)
USE **Taxicabs**
Taxonomy (Botany)
USE **Botany—Classification**

Tea **633.7; 641.8**
Use for materials on the plant or on the
beverage. Materials on the meal are entered
under **Afternoon teas**.
BT **Beverages**
RT **Afternoon teas**
Tea industry
Tea houses
USE **Tearooms**
Tea industry (May subdiv. geog.) **338.1;
338.4**
UF Tea trade
BT **Beverage industry**
NT **Tearooms**
RT **Tea**
Tea rooms
USE **Tearooms**
Tea shops
USE **Tearooms**
Tea trade
USE **Tea industry**
Teach yourself courses
USE **Self-instruction**
Teacher exchange programs **370.116**
UF Exchange of teachers
BT **Exchange of persons programs**
International education
Teacher-parent conferences
USE **Parent-teacher conferences**
Teacher-parent relationship
USE **Parent-teacher relationship**
Teacher-student relationship **371.1;
378.1**
UF Student-teacher relationships
Teacher-student relationships
BT **Child-adult relationship**
Interpersonal relations
Teaching
NT **Student evaluation of teachers**
Teacher-student relationships
USE **Teacher-student relationship**
Teacher training
USE **Teachers—Training**
Teachers (May subdiv. geog.) **371.1;
920**
Use for materials on educators engaged in
classroom or other instruction. Materials on
people engaged professionally in the field of
education in general are entered under **Educa-
tors**.
UF College teachers
Faculty (Education)
Professors

Teachers—*Continued*
   BT   **Educators**
   NT   **Colleges and universities—Faculty**
   RT   **Teaching**
Teachers and parents
   USE   **Parent-teacher relationship**
Teachers colleges (May subdiv. geog.) **378.1**

Use for general and historical materials about teachers colleges. Materials on their educational functions are entered under **Teachers—Training**.

   UF   Normal schools
          Training colleges for teachers
   SA   names of teachers colleges [to be added as needed]
   BT   **Colleges and universities**
          Education—Study and teaching
   RT   **Teachers—Training**
Teachers' institutes
   USE   **Teachers' workshops**
Teachers—Pensions (May subdiv. geog.) **331.25**

   SA   types of educational institutions and names of individual educational insititutions with the subdivisions *Faculty—Pensions*, e.g. **Colleges and universities—Faculty—Pensions** [to be added as needed]
Teachers—Practice teaching
   USE   **Student teaching**
Teachers' reports
   USE   **School reports**
Teachers, Student rating of
   USE   **Student evaluation of teachers**
Teachers—Training (May subdiv. geog.) **370.71**

Use for materials on the history and methods of training teachers, including the educational functions of teachers colleges. Materials on the study of education as a discipline are entered under **Education—Study and teaching**. Materials on the art of teaching and methods of teaching are entered under **Teaching**.

   UF   Teacher training
          Teachers—Training of
   BT   **Education—Study and teaching**
          Teaching
   NT   **Student teaching**
          Teachers' workshops
   RT   **Teachers colleges**

Teachers—Training of
   USE   **Teachers—Training**
Teachers' workshops   **371.1**
   UF   Teachers' institutes
          Workshops, Teachers'
   BT   **Teachers—Training**
Teaching (May subdiv. geog.)   **371.102**

Use for materials on the art of teaching and methods of teaching. Materials on the study of education as a discipline are entered under **Education—Study and teaching**. Materials on the history and methods of training teachers, including the educational functions of teachers colleges, are entered under **Teachers—Training**.

   UF   Instruction
          Pedagogy
          School teaching
   SA   subjects with the subdivision *Study and teaching*, e.g. **Science—Study and teaching** [to be added as needed]
   BT   **Education**
   NT   **Classroom management**
          Cooperative learning
          Educational psychology
          Examinations
          Lectures and lecturing
          Montessori method of education
          Project method in teaching
          School discipline
          School supervision
          Student teaching
          Study skills
          Teacher-student relationship
          Teachers—Training
          Teaching teams
          Tutors and tutoring
   RT   **Teachers**
Teaching—Aids and devices   **371.33**
   UF   Educational media
          Instructional materials
          Teaching materials
   NT   **Audiovisual materials**
          Bulletin boards
          Flannel boards
          Manipulatives
          Motion pictures in education
          Programmed instruction
          Radio in education
          Teaching machines
          Television in education

Teaching—Aids and devices—*Continued*
  RT **Educational technology**
Teaching—Data processing
  USE **Computer-assisted instruction**
Teaching—Experimental methods
  USE **Education—Experimental
       methods**
Teaching, Freedom of
  USE **Academic freedom**
Teaching machines   371.33
  BT **Programmed instruction
      Teaching—Aids and devices**
Teaching materials
  USE **Teaching—Aids and devices**
Teaching teams   371.14
  UF Team teaching
  BT **Teaching**
Teachings of Jesus Christ
  USE **Jesus Christ—Teachings**
Teahouses
  USE **Tearooms**
Team problem solving
  USE **Group problem solving**
Team teaching
  USE **Teaching teams**
Team work in the workplace
  USE **Teams in the workplace**
Teams in the workplace (May subdiv.
      geog.)   **658.4**
  UF Team work in the workplace
      Teamwork in the workplace
      Work groups
      Work teams
  BT **Social groups
      Work environment**
Teamwork in the workplace
  USE **Teams in the workplace**
Tearooms (May subdiv. geog.)   **647.95**
    Use for materials on public establishments
    devoted primarily to serving tea.
  UF Tea houses
      Tea rooms
      Tea shops
      Teahouses
      Teashops
  BT **Restaurants
      Tea industry**
Teas
  USE **Afternoon teas**
Teashops
  USE **Tearooms**
Teasing   158.2; 302.3

  BT **Aggressiveness (Psychology)
      Interpersonal relations**
Technical assistance (May subdiv. geog.)
      338.91; 361.6
    Use for materials on foreign aid in the form
    of technical expertise. Materials on the trans-
    fer of innovations in technology from one
    country to another are entered under **Technol-
    ogy transfer**.
  UF Aid to developing areas
      Assistance to developing areas
      Foreign aid program
  SA technical assistance from particu-
      lar countries, e.g. **American
      technical assistance** [to be
      added as needed]
  BT **Foreign aid
      International economic rela-
      tions**
  NT **American technical assistance**
  RT **Community development
      Technology transfer**
Technical assistance, American
  USE **American technical assistance**
Technical chemistry
  USE **Industrial chemistry**
Technical education (May subdiv. geog.)
      370.11; 373.246; 374
  UF Industrial education
      Industrial schools
      Technical schools
      Trade schools
  SA technical subjects with the sub-
      division *Study and teaching*,
      e.g. **Engineering—Study and
      teaching** [to be added as
      needed]
  BT **Education
      Higher education
      Technology**
  NT **Apprentices
      Correspondence schools and
      courses
      Engineering—Study and teach-
      ing
      Evening and continuation
      schools
      Occupational retraining
      Occupational training
      School shops**
  RT **Employees—Training
      Industrial arts education
      Professional education**

Technical education—*Continued*
>   **Vocational education**
Technical schools
>   USE   **Technical education**
Technical service
>   USE   **Customer services**
Technical services (Libraries)
>   USE   **Library technical processes**
Technical terms
>   USE   **Technology—Dictionaries**
Technical writing   808
>   UF   Scientific writing
>   BT   **Authorship**
>   **Technology—Language**
Technique
>   USE   subjects and names of authors
>   and artists with the subdivi-
>   sion *Technique,* e.g. **Fiction—**
>   **Technique; Painting—Tech-**
>   **nique; Shakespeare, William,**
>   **1564-1616—Technique;** etc.
>   [to be added as needed]
Technological change
>   USE   **Technological innovations**
Technological innovations (May subdiv.
>   geog.)   **338**

Use for materials on technological improvements in materials, production methods, processes, organization, or management. Works
on original devices or processes are entered
under **Inventions**.

>   UF   Innovations, Technological
>   Technological change
>   SA   subjects with the subdivision
>   *Technological innovations,* e.g.
>   **Automobiles—Technological**
>   **innovations; Steel industry—**
>   **Technological innovations** [to
>   be added as needed]
>   BT   **Inventions**
>   **Technology**
>   NT   **Agricultural innovations**
>   **Automobiles—Technological in-**
>   **novations**
>   **Steel industry—Technological**
>   **innovations**
>   RT   **Industrial research**
Technological literacy (May subdiv.
>   geog.)   **302.2**

Use for materials on a person's comprehension of technological innovation and the ability to use particular innovations appropriately.

>   BT   **Literacy**

Technological transfer
>   USE   **Technology transfer**
Technology (May subdiv. geog.)   **600**
>   UF   Applied science
>   High tech
>   High technology
>   SA   technology and other subjects,
>   e.g. **Technology and civiliza-**
>   **tion** [to be added as needed]
>   NT   **Distillation**
>   **Electronics**
>   **Engineering**
>   **Green technology**
>   **Industrial chemistry**
>   **Information technology**
>   **Inventions**
>   **Machinery**
>   **Mills**
>   **Nanotechnology**
>   **Technical education**
>   **Technological innovations**
>   **Technology and civilization**
>   **Technology transfer**
>   RT   **Industrial arts**
>   **Material culture**
Technology and civilization   303.4
>   UF   Civilization and technology
>   BT   **Civilization**
>   **Technology**
>   NT   **Computers and civilization**
>   RT   **Industrial revolution**
Technology—Dictionaries   603
>   UF   Technical terms
>   BT   **Encyclopedias and dictionaries**
Technology in the workplace
>   USE   **Machinery in the workplace**
Technology—Language   601; 603
>   NT   **Technical writing**
Technology transfer (May subdiv. geog.)
>   **338.9**

Use for materials on the transfer of innovations in technology from one country to another. Materials on foreign aid in the form of
technical expertise are entered under **Technical assistance**. May be subdivided by the region or country receiving the technology.
Where applicable, make an additional entry
under this heading subdivided by the region
or country transferring the technology.

>   UF   Technological transfer
>   Transfer of technology
>   BT   **Inventions**
>   **Technology**

Technology transfer—*Continued*

    RT   **International cooperation**

          International relations

          Technical assistance

Teddy bears (May subdiv. geog.)   **790.1**

    UF   Stuffed bears (Toys)

    BT   **Toys**

Tee shirts

    USE   **T-shirts**

Teen age

    USE   **Adolescence**

Teen suicide

    USE   **Teenagers—Suicide**

Teenage behavior

    USE   **Adolescent psychology**

          Etiquette for children and

             teenagers

          Teenagers—Conduct of life

Teenage consumers

    USE   **Young consumers**

Teenage drinking

    USE   **Teenagers—Alcohol use**

Teenage dropouts

    USE   **Dropouts**

Teenage fathers (May subdiv. geog.)

        306.874; 362.7

    Use for materials focusing on fathers who are teenagers. Materials on fathers who at the time of a child's birth were not married to the child's mother are entered under **Unmarried fathers**. Materials focusing on fathers rearing children without a partner in the household are entered under **Single-parent families**.

    UF   Adolescent fathers

          School-age fathers

    BT   **Fathers**

          Teenage parents

Teenage gangs

    USE   **Gangs**

Teenage literature

    USE   **Young adult literature**

Teenage marriage (May subdiv. geog.)

        306.81

    BT   **Marriage**

Teenage mothers (May subdiv. geog.)

        306.874; 362.7; 362.83

    Use for materials focusing on mothers who are teenagers. Materials on mothers who at the time of giving birth were not married to the child's father are entered under **Unmarried mothers**. Materials focusing on mothers rearing children without a partner in the household are entered under **Single-parent families**.

    UF   Adolescent mothers

          School-age mothers

    BT   **Mothers**

          Teenage parents

    RT   **Teenage pregnancy**

Teenage parents (May subdiv. geog.)

        306.874; 362.7

    BT   **Parents**

          Teenagers

    NT   **Teenage fathers**

          Teenage mothers

Teenage pregnancy (May subdiv. geog.)

        362.7; 618.2

    UF   Adolescent pregnancy

    BT   **Pregnancy**

    RT   **Teenage mothers**

Teenage prostitution

    USE   **Juvenile prostitution**

Teenage suicide

    USE   **Teenagers—Suicide**

Teenagers (May subdiv. geog.)   **305.235**

    Use for materials about teen youth. Materials on the time of life extending from thirteen to twenty-five years, as well as on people in that general age range, are entered under **Youth**. Materials limited to people in the general age range of eighteen through twenty-five years of age are entered under **Young men** or **Young women**. Materials on the process or state of growing up are entered under **Adolescence**.

    UF   Adolescents

          Teens

          Young adults

          Young people

          Young persons

    BT   **Age**

          Youth

    NT   **Runaway teenagers**

          Teenage parents

    RT   **Boys**

          Girls

Teenagers—Alcohol use (May subdiv. geog.)   **362.292; 613.81; 616.86**

    UF   Alcohol and teenagers

          Drinking and teenagers

          Teenage drinking

          Teenagers and alcohol

    NT   **Drinking age**

Teenagers and alcohol

    USE   **Teenagers—Alcohol use**

Teenagers and drugs

    USE   **Teenagers—Drug use**

Teenagers and narcotics
USE **Teenagers—Drug use**
Teenagers—Attitudes   155.5; 305.235
BT **Attitude (Psychology)**
**Teenagers—Books and reading   011.62;
028.5**

Use for materials on the reading interests of
teenagers and for lists of books for teenagers.
Collections or materials about literature published for teenagers are entered under **Young
adult literature**.

UF Books and reading for teenagers
Books and reading for young
adults
Reading interests of teenagers
Reading interests of young
adults
Young adults—Books and read-
ing
BT **Books and reading**
Teenagers—Conduct of life   173
UF Behavior of teenagers
Teenage behavior
BT **Conduct of life**
NT **Etiquette for children and
teenagers**
Teenagers—Development
USE **Adolescence**
Teenagers—Drug use (May subdiv. geog.)
362.29; 613.8; 616.86
UF Drugs and teenagers
Narcotics and teenagers
Teenagers and drugs
Teenagers and narcotics
BT **Youth—Drug use**
RT **Juvenile delinquency**
Teenagers—Employment (May subdiv.
geog.)   **331.3**
BT **Age and employment
Employment
Youth—Employment**
RT **Summer employment**
Teenagers—Etiquette
USE **Etiquette for children and
teenagers**
Teenagers—Literature
USE **Young adult literature**
Teenagers—Psychiatry
USE **Adolescent psychiatry**
Teenagers—Psychology
USE **Adolescent psychology**
Teenagers—Religious life   204; 248.4

BT **Religious life
Youth—Religious life**
Teenagers—Suicide   362.28; 616.85
UF Teen suicide
Teenage suicide
BT **Suicide**
Teenagers—United States   305.2350973
UF American teenagers
BT **Youth—United States**
Teenagers' writings   818.8
UF Writings of teenagers
BT **Literature**
Teens
USE **Teenagers**
Teepees
USE **Tepees**
Teeth   611; 612.3; 617.6
BT **Head**
RT **Dentistry**
Teeth—Diseases   617.6
BT **Diseases**
Telecommunication (May subdiv. geog.)
384; 621.382
UF Mass communication
SA subjects with the subdivision
Communication systems, e.g.
**Astronautics—Communica-
tion systems** [to be added as
needed]
BT **Communication**
NT **Artificial satellites in telecom-
munication
Astronautics—Communication
systems
Broadcasting
Computer networks
Data transmission systems
Electronic mail systems
Fax transmission
Intercommunication systems
Interstellar communication
Microwave communication sys-
tems
Radio
Submarine cables
Telecommuting
Telegraph
Telephone
Television
Wireless communication sys-
tems**

Telecommuting (May subdiv. geog.)
 331.25; 658.3

Use for materials on employment at home
with computers, word processors, etc., connected to a central work site, permitting employees to substitute telecommunications for
transportation.

  UF   Alternate work sites

         Work at home

         Working at home

  BT   **Automation**

         Telecommunication

Teleconferencing   **384; 658.4**

  UF   Conference calls

          (Teleconferencing)

         Telephone—Conference calls

  BT   **Telephone**

Telegraph   **384.1; 621.383**

  BT   **Public utilities**

         Telecommunication

  NT   **Cipher and telegraph codes**

         Submarine cables

Telegraph codes

  USE   **Cipher and telegraph codes**

Telekinesis

  USE   **Psychokinesis**

Telemarketing (May subdiv. geog.)   **381;
 658.8**

Use for materials on the use of electronic
media as a form of marketing that bypasses
retail outlets in the advertising and selling of
goods.

  UF   Electronic marketing

  BT   **Direct selling**

         Marketing

Telepathy   **133.8**

  UF   Mental telepathy

         Mind reading

  BT   **Extrasensory perception**

  RT   **Clairvoyance**

Telephone   **384.6; 621.385**

  BT   **Public utilities**

         Telecommunication

  NT   **Cellular telephones**

         **Long distance telephone ser-
  vice**

         Teleconferencing

         Video telephone

Telephone—Conference calls

  USE   **Teleconferencing**

Telephone counseling

  USE   **Hotlines (Telephone counseling)**

Telephone directories

  USE   names of countries, cities, etc.,
  corporate bodies, classes of
  persons, ethnic groups, and
  types of organizations and industries with the subdivision
  Telephone directories, e.g.
  **Chicago (Ill.)—Telephone di-
  rectories** [to be added as
  needed]

Telephone—Long distance

  USE   **Long distance telephone service**

Telephotography   **778.3**

  BT   **Photography**

Telescope

  USE   **Telescopes**

Telescopes   **522; 681**

  UF   Telescope

  BT   **Astronomical instruments**

         Optical instruments

  NT   **Hubble Space Telescope**

Teletext systems   **004.692; 384.3**

Use for materials on the one-way transmission of computer-based data, such as weather
forecasts or stock quotations, from a central
source to a television set.

  BT   **Data transmission systems**

         Electronic publishing

         Information systems

         Television broadcasting

  RT   **Videotex systems**

Televangelists   **269.2092**

  UF   Television evangelists

  BT   **Clergy**

         Television personalities

Television (May subdiv. geog.)   **302.23;
 384.55; 621.388**

Use for materials on the technology of television. Materials on what is seen on television
are entered under **Television programs**.

  UF   TV

  SA   television and particular groups
  of people, e.g. **Television and
  children**; and television in
  various industries or fields of
  endeavor, e.g. **Television in
  education** [to be added as
  needed]

  BT   **Telecommunication**

  NT   **African Americans on television**

         Closed caption television

Television—*Continued*
>> **Closed-circuit television**
>> **Color television**
>> **High definition television**
>> **Home video systems**
>> **Minorities on television**
>> **Television and children**
>> **Television and politics**
>> **Television and youth**
>> **Television broadcasting**
>> **Television in education**
>> **Video art**
>> **Video telephone**
>> **Violence on television**
>> **Women on television**
> RT **Videodiscs**
>> **Videotapes**

Television actors
> USE **Actors**

Television adaptations   791.45
> Use for individual works, collections, or materials about television adaptations of material from other media.
> UF   Adaptations
>> Literature—Film and video adaptations
>> Motion pictures—Television adaptations
> SA   names of authors, titles of anonymous literary works, types of literature, and types of musical compositions with the subdivision *Adaptations*, for individual works, collections, or criticism and interpretation of literary, cinematic, video, or television adaptations, e.g., **Shakespeare, William, 1564-1616—Adaptations**; **Beowulf—Adaptations**; **Arthurian romances—Adaptations**; etc. [to be added as needed]
> BT   **Television plays**
>> **Television programs**
>> **Television scripts**

Television advertising (May subdiv. geog.) **659.14**
> UF   Commercials, Television
>> Television commercials
> BT   **Advertising**
>> **Television broadcasting**

Television and children   305.23; 384.55; 791.45
> Use for materials on the effect of television on children.
> UF   Children and television
> BT   **Children**
>> **Television**

Television and infrared observation satellite
> USE   **TIROS satellites**

Television and politics (May subdiv. geog.)   **324**
> UF   Politics and television
>> Television in politics
> BT   **Politics**
>> **Television**
> NT   **Equal time rule (Broadcasting)**
>> **Fairness doctrine (Broadcasting)**

Television and youth (May subdiv. geog.) **305.235; 384.55; 791.45**
> UF   Youth and television
> BT   **Television**
>> **Youth**

Television—Audiences
> USE   **Television viewers**

Television authorship   808
> UF   Television writing
> BT   **Authorship**
> NT   **Television plays—Technique**

Television broadcasting (May subdiv. geog.)   **384.55**
> UF   Television industry
> SA   television broadcasting of particular kinds of programs, e.g. **Television broadcasting of sports** [to be added as needed]
> BT   **Broadcasting**
>> **Mass media**
>> **Television**
> NT   **African Americans in television broadcasting**
>> **Cable television**
>> **Emmy Awards**
>> **Minorities in television broadcasting**
>> **Public television**
>> **Subscription television**
>> **Teletext systems**
>> **Television advertising**
>> **Television broadcasting of news**

Television broadcasting—*Continued*
> Television broadcasting of
> sports
> Television—Production and di-
> rection
> Television programs
> Television scripts
> Television stations
> Videotex systems
> Women in television broadcast-
> ing

Television broadcasting of news   070.4
    UF   Television coverage of news
           Television journalism
           Television news
    BT   **Broadcast journalism**
           Television broadcasting

Television broadcasting of sports   070.4
    UF   Sports broadcasting
           Sports in television
           Television sports
    BT   **Broadcast journalism**
           Television broadcasting

Television broadcasting—Vocational guidance   384.55
    BT   **Vocational guidance**

Television cartoons
    USE   **Animated television programs**

Television—Censorship (May subdiv. geog.)   **384.55**
    BT   **Censorship**
    NT   **V-chips**

Television, Closed-circuit
    USE   **Closed-circuit television**

Television comedies
    USE   **Comedy television programs**

Television comedy programs
    USE   **Comedy television programs**

Television commercials
    USE   **Television advertising**

Television coverage of news
    USE   **Television broadcasting of news**

Television drama
    USE   **Television plays**

Television—Equipment and supplies   621.388
    NT   **Television—Receivers and reception**
           Videodisc players
    RT   **Television supplies industry**
           Video recording

Television equipment industry
    USE   **Television supplies industry**

Television evangelists
    USE   **Televangelists**

Television fans
    USE   **Television viewers**

Television films
    USE   **Television movies**

Television games
    USE   **Video games**

Television in education (May subdiv. geog.)   **371.33**
    UF   Education and television
           Educational television
    BT   **Audiovisual education**
           Teaching—Aids and devices
           Television

Television in politics
    USE   **Television and politics**

Television industry
    USE   **Television broadcasting**
           Television supplies industry

Television journalism
    USE   **Broadcast journalism**
           Television broadcasting of news

Television movies   791.45
    Use for individual works, collections, or materials about television movies.
    UF   Made-for-TV movies
           Television films
    BT   **Motion pictures**
           Television programs

Television news
    USE   **Television broadcasting of news**

Television novels
    USE   **Radio and television novels**

Television personalities (May subdiv. geog.)   **791.45**
    UF   TV personalities
    BT   **Celebrities**
    NT   **Televangelists**

Television plays   808.2; 808.82
    Use for individual works, collections, or materials about television plays.
    UF   Scenarios
           Television drama
    BT   **Drama**
           Television programs
    NT   **Soap operas**
           Television adaptations

Television plays—*Continued*
   RT   **Television scripts**
Television plays—Technique   808.2
   UF   Play writing
          Playwriting
   BT   **Drama—Technique**
          Television authorship
   RT   **Radio plays—Technique**
Television—Production and direction
   384.55; 791.4502
   BT   **Television broadcasting**
Television programs (May subdiv. geog.)
   791.45
Use for materials on what is seen on television. Materials on the technology of television are entered under **Television**.
   UF   Programs, Television
   SA   types of television programs and
          names of specific programs
          [to be added as needed]
   BT   **Television broadcasting**
   NT   **Adventure television programs**
          Animated television programs
          Biographical television programs
          Comedy television programs
          Fantasy television programs
          Horror television programs
          Legal drama (Television programs)
          Medical drama (Television programs)
          Music videos
          Mystery television programs
          Reality television programs
          Science fiction television programs
          Sports drama (Television programs)
          Spy television programs
          Talk shows
          Television adaptations
          Television movies
          Television plays
          Television serials
          Variety shows (Television programs)
          Violence on television
          War television programs
          Westerns (Television programs)
   RT   **Television scripts**

Television—Receivers and reception
   621.388
   UF   Television reception
          Television sets
   BT   **Television—Equipment and supplies**
   NT   **V-chips**
Television reception
   USE   **Television—Receivers and reception**
Television—Repairing   621.388
Television scripts   791.45; 808.88
Use for individual works, collections, or materials about television scripts.
   UF   Screenplays
   BT   **Television broadcasting**
   NT   **Television adaptations**
   RT   **Television plays**
          Television programs
Television serials   791.45
Use for individual works, collections, or materials about television serials.
   BT   **Television programs**
   RT   **Soap operas**
Television sets
   USE   **Television—Receivers and reception**
Television sports
   USE   **Television broadcasting of sports**
Television—Stage lighting
   USE   **Stage lighting**
Television stations   384.55
   BT   **Television broadcasting**
Television, Subscription
   USE   **Subscription television**
Television supplies industry (May subdiv. geog.)   **338.4; 384.55**
   UF   Television equipment industry
          Television industry
   RT   **Television—Equipment and supplies**
Television viewers (May subdiv. geog.)   **302.23; 791.4**
   UF   Television—Audiences
          Television fans
          Television watchers
   BT   **Audiences**
Television watchers
   USE   **Television viewers**
Television writing
   USE   **Television authorship**

Telstar project   621.382
    UF   Bell System Telstar satellite
            Project Telstar
    BT   **Artificial satellites in telecom-
          munication**
Temper tantrums   152.4
    UF   Tantrums, Temper
    BT   **Emotions**
         Human behavior
Temperament   155.2
    BT   **Mind and body**
         Psychology
         Psychophysiology
    NT   **Typology (Psychology)**
    RT   **Character**
Temperance   178; 241; 613.81
    Use for materials on the virtue of temper-
  ance or on the temperance movement.
    UF   Abstinence
         Drunkenness
         Intemperance
         Intoxication
         Total abstinence
    BT   **Virtue**
    RT   **Alcoholism**
         Drinking of alcoholic beverages
         Prohibition
Temperature   536
    NT   **Low temperatures**
    RT   **Cold**
         Heat
         Thermometers
Temperature, Animal and human
    USE **Body temperature**
Temperature, Body
    USE **Body temperature**
Temples (May subdiv. geog.)   **203; 726**
    BT   **Buildings**
         Religious institutions
    NT   **Mosques**
         Synagogues
Temporal power of the Pope
    USE **Popes—Temporal power**
Temporary employment   331.25
    UF   Employment, Temporary
    BT   **Employment**
Ten commandments   222
    UF   Decalogue
    BT   **Bible. O.T.**
Ten lost tribes of Israel
    USE **Lost tribes of Israel**

Tenant and landlord
    USE **Landlord and tenant**
Tenant farming
    USE **Farm tenancy**
Tenement houses (May subdiv. geog.)
       647
    UF   Tenements (Apartment houses)
    BT   **Apartment houses**
Tenements (Apartment houses)
    USE **Tenement houses**
Tennis (May subdiv. geog.)   **796.342**
    UF   Lawn tennis
    BT   **Sports**
Tennis—Tournaments (May subdiv.
    geog.)   **796.342**
    BT   **Sports tournaments**
Tenpins
    USE **Bowling**
Tension (Physiology)
    USE **Stress (Physiology)**
Tension (Psychology)
    USE **Stress (Psychology)**
Tents   796.54
    BT   **Camping**
Tenure of land
    USE **Land tenure**
Tenure of office
    USE **Civil service**
Tepees   728; 970.004
    UF   Teepees
         Wigwams
    BT   **Native Americans—Dwellings**
Term limitations (Public office)
    USE **Term limits (Public office)**
Term limits (Public office) (May subdiv.
    geog.)   **328**
    UF   Term limitations (Public office)
    BT   **Legislative bodies**
         Public officers
**Term limits (Public office)—United
    States   328.73**
    UF   United States—Term limits
         (Public office)
Term paper writing
    USE **Report writing**
Terminal care (May subdiv. geog.)
       362.17; 616; 649.8
    UF   Care of the dying
    BT   **Medical care**

Terminal care—*Continued*
  NT Hospices
      Life support systems (Medical
        environment)
  RT Death
      Living wills
      Terminally ill
Terminally ill (May subdiv. geog.)
    362.17; 649.8
  UF Dying patients
      Fatally ill patients
  BT Sick
  NT Terminally ill children
  RT Death
      Terminal care
Terminally ill children (May subdiv.
    geog.) 362.17; 649.8
  UF Dying children
      Fatally ill children
  BT Terminally ill
  RT Children—Death
Terminals, Computer
  USE Computer terminals
Termination of pregnancy
  USE Abortion
Terminology
  USE Terms and phrases
      and subjects, classes of persons,
        sacred works, and religious
        sects with the subdivision
        Terminology, for lists or dis-
        cussions of words and expres-
        sions found in those works or
        used in those fields, e.g. **Bot-
        any—Terminology;** names of
        languages with the subdivision
        Terms and phrases, e.g. **En-
        glish language—Terms and
        phrases;** scientific and techni-
        cal disciplines and types of
        substances, plants, and ani-
        mals with the subdivision *No-
        menclature,* for systematically
        derived lists of names or des-
        ignations that have been for-
        mally adopted or sanctioned,
        and for discussions of the
        principles involved in the cre-
        ation and application of such
        names, e.g. **Botany—Nomen-
        clature;** and scientific and

technical disciplines and types
of animals, plants, and crops
with the subdivision *Nomenclature (Popular),* for lists or
materials about popular, non-
technical names or designations of substances, species,
etc., **Trees—Nomenclature
(Popular)** [to be added as
needed]
Terms and phrases   030
  UF Commonplaces
      Terminology
  SA names of languages with the
        subdivision *Terms and
        phrases,* e.g. **English lan-
        guage—Terms and phrases;**
        subjects, classes of persons,
        sacred works, and religious
        sects with the subdivision
        Terminology, for lists or dis-
        cussions of words and expres-
        sions found in those works or
        used in those fields, e.g. **Bot-
        any—Terminology;** scientific
        and technical disciplines and
        types of substances, plants,
        and animals with the subdivi-
        sion *Nomenclature,* for sys-
        tematically derived lists of
        names or designations that
        have been formally adopted
        or sanctioned, and for discus-
        sions of the principles in-
        volved in the creation and ap-
        plication of such names, e.g.
        Botany—Nomenclature; and
        scientific and technical disci-
        plines and types of animals,
        plants, and crops with the
        subdivision *Nomenclature
        (Popular),* for lists or materi-
        als about popular, non-
        technical names or designa-
        tions of substances, species,
        etc., **Trees—Nomenclature
        (Popular)** [to be added as
        needed]
  BT Names
  RT Allusions
Terns 598.3

Terns—*Continued*
    BT   **Birds**
         Water birds
Terra cotta   620.1; 691
    BT   **Building materials**
         Decoration and ornament
         Pottery
Terrain sensing, Remote
    USE **Remote sensing**
Terrapins
    USE **Turtles**
Terrariums   635.9
    BT   **Indoor gardening**
    RT   **Miniature gardens**
Terrestrial physics
    USE **Geophysics**
Territorial expansion
    USE names of countries, regions, etc.,
           with the subdivision *Territori-*
           al expansion, e.g. **United**
           States—Territorial expansion
           [to be added as needed]
Territorial questions
    USE names of wars with the subdivi-
           sion *Territorial questions,* e.g.
           World War, 1939-1945—
           Territorial questions; which
           may be further subdivided
           geographically [to be added
           as needed]
Territorial waters (May subdiv. geog.)
         341.4; 342
    UF   Economic zones (Maritime law)
         Three-mile limit
    BT   **Shipping**
    RT   **Continental shelf**
         Maritime law
Territorial waters—United States
         341.4; 342
    UF   United States—Territorial waters
Territories and possessions
    USE names of countries with the sub-
           division *Territories and pos-*
           sessions, or *Colonies,* e.g.
           United States—Territories
           and possessions; Great Brit-
           ain—Colonies; etc. [to be
           added as needed]
Terror, Reign of
    USE **France—History—1789-1799,**
           Revolution

Terror tales
    USE **Ghost stories**
         Horror fiction
Terrorism (May subdiv. geog.)   **303.6**
    UF   Political violence
         Terrorist acts
    BT   **Insurgency**
         Political crimes and offenses
         Subversive activities
    NT   **Bombings**
         Domestic terrorism
         Ecoterrorism
         Hostages
         Sabotage
         Suicide bombers
    RT   **Anarchism and anarchists**
Terrorism—Prevention   363.32
    UF   Anti-terrorism
         Counter-terrorism
Terrorism—United States   303.6; 322.4
    NT   **September 11 terrorist attacks,**
         2001
Terrorist acts
    USE **Terrorism**
Terrorist attacks, September 11, 2001
    USE **September 11 terrorist attacks,**
         2001
Terrorist bombings
    USE **Bombings**
Test bias   371.2601
    UF   Bias in testing
         Prejudice in testing
    BT   **Discrimination in education**
         Educational tests and measure-
         ments
Test pilots
    USE **Air pilots**
         Airplanes—Testing
Test preparation guides
    USE **Examinations—Study guides**
Test tube babies
    USE **Fertilization in vitro**
Test tube fertilization
    USE **Fertilization in vitro**
Testing   620
    UF   Mechanical properties testing
    SA   things tested with the subdivi-
         sion *Testing,* e.g. **Ability—**
         Testing; Airplanes—Testing;
         Concrete—Testing; etc [to be
         added as needed]

Testing—*Continued*
  BT **Reliability (Engineering)**
  NT **Electric testing**
  RT **Strength of materials**
Testing for drug abuse
  USE **Drug testing**
Tests
  USE **Educational tests and measure-
       ments
       Examinations**
Teutonic peoples (May subdiv. geog.)
       305.83
  UF Nordic peoples
       Teutonic race
  SA names of particular Teutonic
       peoples, e.g. **Goths** [to be
       added as needed]
  NT **Anglo-Saxons
       Goths**
Teutonic race
  USE **Teutonic peoples**
Textbooks **371.3**
  UF School books
  SA branches of study with the sub-
       division *Textbooks*, e.g. **Arith-
       metic—Textbooks** [to be add-
       ed as needed]
  BT **Books**
Textile chemistry **677**
  UF Chemistry, Textile
  BT **Industrial chemistry
       Textile industry**
  NT **Dyes and dyeing**
Textile design (May subdiv. geog.) **746**
  UF Fabric design
  BT **Commercial art
       Decoration and ornament
       Design**
  NT **Textile painting**
  RT **Textile printing**
Textile fibers
  USE **Fibers**
Textile industry (May subdiv. geog.)
       338.4; 677
  SA types of articles manufactured,
       e.g **Rugs and carpets; Ho-
       siery**; etc. [to be added as
       needed]
  BT **Industries**
  NT **Bleaching
       Cotton manufacture
       Dyes and dyeing**

**Hosiery
Spinning
Textile chemistry
Textile printing
Weaving**
Textile painting **746.6**
  BT **Painting
       Textile design**
Textile printing **746.6**
  UF Block printing
  BT **Printing
       Textile industry**
  RT **Silk screen printing
       Textile design**
Textiles
  USE **Fabrics**
Texts
  USE types of lesser-known languages,
       dialects, early periods of lan-
       guages, liturgies, and types of
       vocal music with the subdivi-
       sion *Texts,* e.g. **Catholic
       Church—Liturgy—Texts** for
       individual texts or collections
       of texts [to be added as need-
       ed]
Thankfulness
  USE **Gratitude**
Thanksgiving Day 394.2649
  BT **Holidays**
Theater (May subdiv. geog.) **792**
    Use for materials on drama as acted on the
  stage. Materials on drama as a literary form
  are entered under **Drama; American drama;
  English drama;** etc. Collections of plays are
  entered under **Drama—Collections; Ameri-
  can drama—Collections**; etc. Materials on
  theater buildings are entered under **Theaters.**
  UF Stage
  SA names of wars with the subdivi-
       sion *Theater and the war* e.g.
       **World War, 1939-1945—
       Theater and the war** [to be
       added as needed]
  BT **Amusements
       Performing arts**
  NT **Amateur theater
       Arena theater
       Ballet
       Burlesque (Theater)
       Children's plays
       Experimental theater
       Little theater movement**

Theater—*Continued*
    Masks (Plays)
    Morality plays
    Musicals
    Mysteries and miracle plays
    Pantomimes
    Passion plays
    Puppets and puppet plays
    Readers' theater
    Shadow pantomimes and plays
    Shakespeare, William, 1564-1616—Stage history
    Skits
    Summer theater
    Vaudeville
    World War, 1939-1945—Theater and the war
  RT **Acting**
    Drama
    Dramatic criticism
    Theaters
Theater and the war
  USE names of wars with the subdivision *Theater and the war,* e.g. **World War, 1939-1945—Theater and the war** [to be added as needed]
Theater criticism
  USE **Dramatic criticism**
Theater-in-the-round
  USE **Arena theater**
Theater—Japan   792.0952
  NT **Kabuki**
Theater—Production and direction   792
  UF Direction (Theater)
    Play direction (Theater)
    Play production
    Theatrical direction
    Theatrical production
  RT **Theatrical producers and directors**
Theater—United States   792.0973
Theaters (May subdiv. geog.)   **725**
    Use for materials on theater buildings, their architecture, technical fixtures, decoration, etc. Materials on drama as a literary form are entered under **Drama**. Materials on drama as acted on the stage are entered under **Theater**.
  UF Playhouses
  SA types of theaters [to be added as needed]

  BT **Buildings**
    Centers for the performing arts
    Theaters
  NT **Motion picture theaters**
    Night clubs, cabarets, etc.
    Theaters
  RT **Theater**
Theaters—Conservation and restoration (May subdiv. geog.)   **725**
  BT **Historic preservation**
Theaters—Stage lighting
  USE **Stage lighting**
Theaters—Stage setting and scenery   792.02
  UF Scenery (Stage)
    Stage scenery
    Stage setting
    Theatrical scenery
  NT **Scene painting**
Theatrical costume
  USE **Costume**
Theatrical direction
  USE **Theater—Production and direction**
Theatrical directors
  USE **Theatrical producers and directors**
Theatrical makeup   791.43; 791.45; 792
  UF Makeup, Theatrical
  BT **Cosmetics**
    Costume
Theatrical producers
  USE **Theatrical producers and directors**
Theatrical producers and directors (May subdiv. geog.)   **792; 920**
  UF Theatrical directors
    Theatrical producers
  RT **Theater—Production and direction**
Theatrical production
  USE **Theater—Production and direction**
Theatrical scenery
  USE **Theaters—Stage setting and scenery**
Theft   364.16
  UF Larceny
    Stealing

Theft—*Continued*
  BT **Crime**
        Offenses against property
  NT **Art thefts**
        Bank robberies
        Identity theft
        Shoplifting
  RT **Thieves**
Theism (May subdiv. geog.)   **211**
  BT **Philosophy**
        Religion
        Theology
  NT **Monotheism**
  RT **Atheism**
        Deism
        God
Theme parks
  USE **Amusement parks**
Themes in art
  USE **Art—Themes**
Themes in literature
  USE **Literature—Themes**
Theological education
  USE **Religious education**
        Theology—Study and teaching
Theology (May subdiv. geog.)   **202; 230**
  NT **Apologetics**
        Atheism
        Church
        Covenants
        Deism
        Doctrinal theology
        Eschatology
        Faith
        Feminist theology
        Good and evil
        Immortality
        Liberation theology
        Natural theology
        Pastoral theology
        Predestination
        Revelation
        Sin
        Theism
        Worship
  RT **God**
        Religion
Theology, Doctrinal
  USE **Doctrinal theology**
Theology of liberation
  USE **Liberation theology**

Theology—Study and teaching   **202;**
        230.07
  UF Education, Theological
        Religion—Study and teaching
        Theological education
  NT **Catechisms**
  RT **Religious education**
Theoretical chemistry
  USE **Physical chemistry**
Theory of games
  USE **Game theory**
Theory of graphs
  USE **Graph theory**
Theory of knowledge   **001.01; 121**
        Use for materials on the origin, nature,
        methods, and limits of human knowledge.
  UF Cognition
        Epistemology
        Knowledge, Theory of
        Understanding
  BT **Consciousness**
        Logic
        Metaphysics
        Philosophy
  NT **Belief and doubt**
        Certainty
        Cognitive styles
        Empiricism
        Gestalt psychology
        Ideology
        Intuition
        Perception
        Pragmatism
        Rationalism
        Senses and sensation
  RT **Apperception**
        Intellect
        Reality
        Truth
Theory of numbers
  USE **Number theory**
Theory of structures
  USE **Structural analysis (Engineer-**
        ing)
Theory of systems
  USE **System theory**
Theosophy (May subdiv. geog.)   **299**
  BT **Mysticism**
        Religions
  NT **Reincarnation**
        Vedanta
        Yoga

Therapeutic systems
USE **Alternative medicine**
Therapeutic use
USE subjects with the subdivision
Therapeutic use, e.g. **Cold—
Therapeutic use; Herbs—
Therapeutic use** etc. [to be
added as needed]

Therapeutics   615.5
UF Diseases—Treatment
Therapy
Treatment
Treatment of diseases
SA types of therapies, e.g. **Hydro-
therapy**; diseases with the
subdivision *Treatment,* e.g.
AIDS (Disease)—Treatment;
subjects with the subdivision
Therapeutic use, e.g. **Cold—
Therapeutic use; Herbs—
Therapeutic use**; etc.; diseas-
es with the subdivision *Diet
therapy,* e.g. **Cancer—Diet
therapy**; and types of drugs
and names of specific drugs
[to be added as needed]
BT **Medicine
Pathology**
NT **AIDS (Disease)—Treatment
Antiseptics
Aromatherapy
Art therapy
Cold—Therapeutic use
Diet in disease
Diet therapy
Drug abuse—Treatment
Drug therapy
Drugs
Electrotherapeutics
Gene therapy
Healing
Herbs—Therapeutic use
Hydrotherapy
Materia medica
Medicine
Music therapy
Naturopathy
Nursing
Nutrition
Occupational therapy
Pet therapy**

**Phototherapy
Physical therapy
Play therapy
Psychotherapy
Radiotherapy
Suggestive therapeutics**
RT **Pharmaceutical chemistry**
Therapeutics, Suggestive
USE **Suggestive therapeutics**
Therapy
USE **Therapeutics**
Therapy, Gene
USE **Gene therapy**
Therapy, Psychological
USE **Psychotherapy**
Thermal insulation
USE **Insulation (Heat)**
Thermal waters
USE **Geothermal resources
Geysers**
Thermoaerodynamics
USE **Aerothermodynamics**
Thermodynamics   536
SA subjects with the subdivision
Thermodynamics, e.g. **Space
vehicles—Thermodynamics**
[to be added as needed]
BT **Dynamics
Physical chemistry
Physics**
NT **Aerothermodynamics
Entropy
Heat engines
Heat pumps
Space vehicles—Thermodynam-
ics**
RT **Heat
Heat engines
Quantum theory**
Thermometers   536
UF Thermometry
BT **Heat
Meteorological instruments**
RT **Temperature**
Thermometry
USE **Thermometers**
Thesauri
USE **Subject headings**
and names of languages with
the subdivision *Synonyms and
antonyms,* e.g. **English lan-**

Thesauri—*Continued*

        guage—Synonyms and antonyms [to be added as needed]

Theses
    USE   **Dissertations**

Thieves (May subdiv. geog.)   **364.3**
    UF   Bandits
          Brigands
          Burglars
          Highwaymen
          Outlaws
          Robbers
    BT   **Criminals**
    RT   **Theft**

Think tanks
    USE   **Group problem solving**

Thinking
    USE   **Thought and thinking**

Third parties (United States politics)
    324.273
    BT   **Political parties**
          United States—Politics and government

Third World
    USE   **Developing countries**

Third World War
    USE   **World War III**

Thirteenth century
    USE   **World history—13th century**

Thirty Years' War, 1618-1648   **909.08; 940.2**
    BT   **Europe—History—1492-1789**
          Germany—History—1517-1740

Thoroughfares
    USE   **Roads**
          Streets

Thought and thinking   **153.4**
    UF   Thinking
    BT   **Educational psychology**
          Psychology
    NT   **Attention**
          Critical thinking
          Ideology
          Memory
          Perception
          Reasoning
          Stereotype (Social psychology)
    RT   **Intellect**
          Logic

Thought control
    USE   **Brainwashing**

Threatened species
    USE   **Endangered species**

Three dimensional photography   **778.4**
    UF   3-D photography
          Photography, Stereoscopic
          Stereo photography
          Stereophotography
          Stereoscopic photography
    BT   **Photography**
    RT   **Holography**

Three-mile limit
    USE   **Territorial waters**

Three Stooges films   **791.43**
    Use for individual works, collections, or materials about Three Stooges films.
    BT   **Comedy films**
          Motion pictures

Three (The number)   **513**
    BT   **Numbers**

Thrift
    USE   **Saving and investment**

Thrift shops (May subdiv. geog.)   **381.19**
    UF   Charity shops
    BT   **Secondhand trade**
          Stores

Thrillers
    USE   **Adventure fiction**
          Adventure films

Throat   **611; 612; 617.5**
    BT   **Anatomy**
    NT   **Voice**

Thunderstorms (May subdiv. geog.)   **551.55**
    BT   **Meteorology**
          Storms
    NT   **Lightning**

Tiananmen Square Incident, Beijing (China), 1989   **951.05**
    UF   Beijing Massacre, 1989
          China—History—1989,
              Tiananmen Square Incident

Ticks   **595.4**
    BT   **Arachnids**

Tidal waves
    USE   **Tsunamis**

Tides (May subdiv. geog.)   **551.46**
    BT   **Ocean**

Tidiness
    USE   **Orderliness**

Tie dyeing   **746.6**
    BT   **Dyes and dyeing**

Tiles (May subdiv. geog.)   666; 693;
    738.6
    UF   Ceramic tiles
    BT   **Building materials**
         Ceramics
Timber
    USE   **Forests and forestry**
          Lumber and lumbering
          Trees
          Wood
Timber—Harvesting
    USE   **Logging**
Time   529
    UF   Horology
         Standard time
    NT   **Calendars**
         Chronology
         Clocks and watches
         Day
         Night
         Punctuality
         Space and time
         Sundials
         Time management
    RT   **Cycles**
         Nautical astronomy
Time and space
    USE   **Space and time**
Time management   640; 650.1
    UF   Allocation of time
         Personal time management
    BT   **Management**
         Time
Time production standards
    USE   **Production standards**
Time saving cooking
    USE   **Quick and easy cooking**
Time sharing (Real estate)
    USE   **Timesharing (Real estate)**
Time study   658.5
    BT   **Factory management**
         Industrial efficiency
         Job analysis
         Personnel management
         Production standards
    RT   **Motion study**
Time travel   115
    BT   **Fourth dimension**
         Space and time
Timesharing (Real estate) (May subdiv.
    geog.)   333.3; 333.5; 643

    UF   Condominium timesharing
         Real estate timesharing
         Time sharing (Real estate)
         Vacation home timesharing
    BT   **Condominiums**
         Housing
         Property
         Real estate business
Tin   669
    BT   **Chemical elements**
         Metals
Tinsmithing
    USE   **Tinwork**
Tinwork (May subdiv. geog.)   673
    UF   Tinsmithing
    BT   **Metalwork**
Tiny objects
    USE   **Miniature objects**
Tires   678
    UF   Rubber tires
    BT   **Wheels**
Tiros (Meteorological satellite)
    USE   **TIROS satellites**
TIROS satellites   551.5
    UF   Television and infrared observa-
         tion satellite
         Tiros (Meteorological satellite)
    BT   **Meteorological satellites**
Tissue donation
    USE   **Donation of organs, tissues,**
          etc.
Tissues—Transplantation
    USE   **Transplantation of organs, tis-**
          sues, etc.
Tithes (May subdiv. geog.)   248; 254
    BT   **Church finance**
         Ecclesiastical law
         Taxation
Toadstools
    USE   **Mushrooms**
Toasts   808.5; 808.85
    UF   Healths, Drinking of
    BT   **Epigrams**
         Speeches
    RT   **After dinner speeches**
Tobacco (May subdiv. geog.)   633.7
    BT   **Plants**
    NT   **Cigarettes**
         Cigars
    RT   **Smoking**

Tobacco habit (May subdiv. geog.)   **178;**
  613.85; 616.86
  UF Addiction to nicotine
      Addiction to tobacco
      Nicotine habit
  BT **Habit**
      Smoking
  NT **Smoking cessation programs**
Tobacco industry (May subdiv. geog.)
  338.17371
  BT **Industries**
Tobacco pipes   688
  UF Pipes, Tobacco
  BT **Smoking**
Toilet preparations
  USE **Toiletries**
Toilet training   649
  BT **Child rearing**
Toiletries   646.7
  UF Toilet preparations
  BT **Personal grooming**
  RT **Cosmetics**
Tolerance
  USE **Toleration**
Toleration (May subdiv. geog.)   **179;**
  323
  UF Bigotry
      Intolerance
      Tolerance
  BT **Interpersonal relations**
  NT **Academic freedom**
      Freedom of conscience
      Freedom of religion
      Religious tolerance
  RT **Discrimination**
Toll roads
  USE **Express highways**
Tombs (May subdiv. geog.)   **726**
  UF Graves
      Mausoleums
      Rock tombs
      Sepulchers
      Vaults (Sepulchral)
  SA classes of persons, and names of
      families, royal houses,
      dynasties, etc., with the subdi-
      vision *Tombs*, e.g. **Presi-
      dents—United States—
      Tombs** [to be added as need-
      ed]

  BT **Archeology**
      Architecture
      Burial
      Monuments
      Shrines
  NT **Brasses**
      Catacombs
      Epitaphs
      Mounds and mound builders
  RT **Cemeteries**
Tomography   616.07; 621.36
  UF CAT scan
      Computerized tomography
  BT **X-rays**
Tongue twisters   398.8
  BT **Children's poetry**
      Folklore
      Nonsense verses
Tools (May subdiv. geog.)   **621.9**
  SA types of tools [to be added as
      needed]
  BT **Implements, utensils, etc.**
  NT **Agricultural machinery**
      Carpentry tools
      Machine tools
      Machinery
      Power tools
      Saws
      Weapons
Top soil loss
  USE **Soil erosion**
Topographical drawing   526
  BT **Drawing**
      Surveying
  RT **Map drawing**
Topology   514
  UF Position analysis
  BT **Geometry**
      Set theory
  NT **Fractals**
      Graph theory
  RT **Linear algebra**
Tories, American
  USE **American Loyalists**
Tornadoes (May subdiv. geog.)   **551.55**
  UF Twisters (Tornadoes)
  BT **Meteorology**
      Storms
      Winds
Torpedoes   623.4

Torpedoes—*Continued*
  BT **Explosives**
      Naval art and science
      Submarine warfare
Tort liability of professions
  USE **Malpractice**
Tortoises
  USE **Turtles**
Torture (May subdiv. geog.)   **365**
  BT **Criminal procedure**
      Cruelty
      Punishment
Total abstinence
  USE **Temperance**
Totalitarianism (May subdiv. geog.)
      321.9
  UF Authoritarianism
  BT **Political science**
  NT **Communism**
      Dictators
      Fascism
Totem poles (May subdiv. geog.)   **299.7;**
      704.9; 731
  BT **Totems and totemism**
Totems and totemism (May subdiv.
      geog.)   **202**
  BT **Ethnology**
      Mythology
  NT **Totem poles**
Touch   **152.1; 612**
  UF Feeling
  BT **Senses and sensation**
  NT **Hugging**
Touring, Bicycle
  USE **Bicycle touring**
Tourism
  USE **Tourist trade**
      Travel
Tourist accommodations
  USE **Hotels and motels**
      Youth hostels
Tourist industry
  USE **Tourist trade**
Tourist trade (May subdiv. geog.)   **338.4**
  UF Tourism
      Tourist industry
      Tourists
      Travel industry
  BT **Commerce**
  NT **Cultural tourism**
      Ecotourism
  RT **Travel**

Tourists
  USE **Tourist trade**
      Travelers
Tournaments
  USE **Medieval tournaments**
      Sports tournaments
      and types of sports and games
      with the subdivision *Tourna-
      ments,* e.g. **Tennis—Tourna-
      ments** [to be added as need-
      ed]
Town life
  USE **City and town life**
Town meeting
  USE **Local government**
Town officers
  USE **Municipal officials and em-
      ployees**
Town planning
  USE **City planning**
Towns
  USE **Cities and towns**
Towns, Abandoned
  USE **Ghost towns**
Township government
  USE **Local government**
Toxic dumps
  USE **Hazardous waste sites**
Toxic plants
  USE **Poisonous plants**
Toxic substances
  USE **Hazardous substances**
      Poisons and poisoning
Toxic wastes
  USE **Hazardous wastes**
Toxicology   **571.9; 615.9**
  Use for materials on the science that treats
  of poisons and their antidotes. Materials on
  poisonous substance and their use are entered
  under **Poisons and poisoning**.
  UF Chemicals—Toxicology
  SA types of poisons or poisoning,
      e.g. **Lead poisoning**; and
      types of poisonous substances
      with the subdivision *Toxicolo-
      gy,* for materials on the influ-
      ence of particular substances
      on humans and animals, e.g.
      Insecticides—Toxicology [to
      be added as needed]
  BT **Medicine**
      Pharmacology

Toxicology—*Continued*
   RT   **Poisons and poisoning**
Toy and movable books
   UF   Movable books
         Pop-up books
   BT   **Picture books for children**
   NT   **Glow-in-the-dark books**
Toy making (May subdiv. geog.)
       745.592
   BT   **Handicraft**
   NT   **Soft toy making**
         Wooden toy making
   RT   **Toys**
Toys (May subdiv. geog.)   **688.7; 790.1**
   SA   types of toys [to be added as
         needed]
   BT   **Amusements**
   NT   **Doll furniture**
         Dollhouses
         Dolls
         Electric toys
         Electronic toys
         Teddy bears
   RT   **Miniature objects**
         Toy making
Track and field
   USE **Track athletics**
Track athletics (May subdiv. geog.)
       796.42
   UF   Field athletics
         Track and field
   SA   types of track sports [to be add-
         ed as needed]
   BT   **Athletics**
         Sports
   NT   **Running**
Tracking and trailing (May subdiv.
     geog.)   **799.2**
   UF   Trailing
   BT   **Hunting**
   NT   **Animal tracks**
   RT   **Animal behavior**
Tracking of satellites
   USE **Artificial satellites—Tracking**
         Space vehicles—Tracking
Tracks of animals
   USE **Animal tracks**
Traction engines
   USE **Tractors**
Tractors   **629.225; 631.3**
   UF   Traction engines
   BT   **Agricultural machinery**

Tracts   **243**
   Use for collections, individual works or ma-
   terials about religious pamphlets.
   UF   Religious pamphlets
   BT   **Chapbooks**
         Pamphlets
Trade
   USE **Business**
         Commerce
Trade agreements (Labor)
   USE **Industrial arbitration**
         Labor contract
Trade and professional associations (May
     subdiv. geog.)   **381; 650**
   UF   Professional associations
         Trade associations
   BT   **Associations**
Trade associations
   USE **Trade and professional associa-
         tions**
Trade, Balance of
   USE **Balance of trade**
Trade barriers
   USE **Commercial policy**
Trade, Boards of
   USE **Chambers of commerce**
Trade catalogs
   USE **Commercial catalogs**
Trade deficits
   USE **Balance of trade**
Trade expositions
   USE **Trade shows**
Trade fairs
   USE **Trade shows**
Trade, International
   USE **International trade**
Trade marks
   USE **Trademarks**
Trade, Restraint of
   USE **Restraint of trade**
Trade routes (May subdiv. geog.)   **387**
   UF   Ocean routes
         Routes of trade
         Sea routes
   BT   **Commerce**
         Commercial geography
         Transportation
Trade schools
   USE **Technical education**
Trade secrets   **346.04; 658.4**
   UF   Business secrets
         Commercial secrets

Trade secrets—*Continued*
 Industrial secrets
 Secrets, Trade
 BT **Right of privacy**
 Unfair competition
Trade shows (May subdiv. geog.) **659.1**
 UF Industrial exhibitions
 Trade expositions
 Trade fairs
 BT **Exhibitions**
 Fairs
Trade surpluses
 USE **Balance of trade**
Trade-unions
 USE **Labor unions**
Trade waste
 USE **Industrial waste**
 Waste products
Trademarks (May subdiv. geog.)
 346.04; 929.9
 UF Company symbols
 Corporate symbols
 Trade marks
 SA types of industries and products
 with the subdivision *Trade-marks*, for materials on the
 words, letters, or symbols
 used by the manufacturers or
 dealers of those goods to dis-
 tinguish them from the goods
 of others, e.g. **Glassware—
 Trademarks** [to be added as
 needed]
 BT **Commerce**
 Manufactures
 NT **Glassware—Trademarks**
 RT **Brand name products**
 Patents
Trades
 USE **Industrial arts**
 Occupations
Trading card games
 USE **Collectible card games**
Trading cards **741.6**
 BT **Collectibles**
Traditional medicine (May subdiv. geog.)
 615.8
 UF Folk medicine
 Folklore, Medical
 Medical folklore

 SA traditional medicine of particular
 ethnic groups, e.g. **Native
 American medicine** [to be
 added as needed]
 BT **Medicine**
 Popular medicine
Traditions
 USE **Folklore**
 Legends
 Manners and customs
 Rites and ceremonies
 Superstition
Traffic accidents (May subdiv. geog.)
 363.12
 UF Automobile accidents
 Automobiles—Accidents
 Car accidents
 Car wrecks
 Highway accidents
 BT **Accidents**
Traffic, City
 USE **City traffic**
Traffic control
 USE **Traffic engineering**
 Traffic regulations
Traffic engineering (May subdiv. geog.)
 388.4
 Use for materials on the planning of the
 flow of traffic and related topics, largely as
 they concern street transportation in cities and
 metropolitan areas.
 UF Street traffic
 Traffic control
 BT **Engineering**
 Highway engineering
 Transportation
 NT **Car pools**
 City traffic
 Express highways
 Local transit
 Traffic safety
 RT **Traffic regulations**
Traffic regulations (May subdiv. geog.)
 388.4
 UF Traffic control
 BT **Safety regulations**
 RT **Automobiles—Law and legisla-
 tion**
 Traffic engineering
Traffic safety **363.12**
 UF Highway safety
 Road safety

Traffic safety—*Continued*

    BT   **Highway transportation**

          Traffic engineering

Trafficking in drugs

    USE **Drug traffic**

Trafficking in narcotics

    USE **Drug traffic**

Tragedies   808.82

    Use for individual works or for collections. Materials about tragedy as a literary form are entered under **Tragedy**.

    BT   **Drama**

Tragedy   792.1; 809.2

    Use for materials on tragedy as a literary form. Individual works and collections of tragedies are entered under **Tragedies**.

    BT   **Drama**

    RT   **Tragicomedy**

Tragicomedy   809.2

    BT   **Drama**

    RT   **Comedy**

          Tragedy

Trail riding (May subdiv. geog.)   **798.2**

    BT   **Horsemanship**

Trailer camps

    USE **Trailer parks**

Trailer parks (May subdiv. geog.)   **647; 796.54**

    UF   Mobile home parks

          Trailer camps

    BT   **Campgrounds**

          Mobile home living

Trailers

    USE **Mobile homes**

          Travel trailers and campers

Trailing

    USE **Tracking and trailing**

Trails (May subdiv. geog.)   **796.51**

    BT   **Roads**

    NT   **Nature trails**

    RT   **Hiking**

          Mountaineering

Train wrecks

    USE **Railroad accidents**

Training

    USE types of sports activities, plants and crops, animals, and classes of persons with the subdivision *Training,* e.g. **Soccer—Training; Horses—Training; Teachers—Training;** etc. [to be added as needed]

Training camps, Military

    USE **Military training camps**

Training colleges for teachers

    USE **Teachers colleges**

Training, Occupational

    USE **Occupational training**

Training of animals

    USE **Animals—Training**

Training of children

    USE **Child rearing**

Training of employees

    USE **Employees—Training**

Training, Vocational

    USE **Occupational training**

Trains

    USE **Railroads**

Traitors (May subdiv. geog.)   **364.1**

    NT   **Collaborationists**

    RT   **Treason**

Tramps (May subdiv. geog.)   **305.5**

    Use for materials on homeless persons who travel about from place to place and work in occasional jobs.

    UF   Hoboes

          Vagabonds

          Vagrants

    BT   **Homeless persons**

          Poor

    RT   **Begging**

          Unemployed

Trams

    USE **Street railroads**

Transactional analysis   158

    BT   **Psychotherapy**

Transatlantic flights

    USE **Aeronautics—Flights**

Transcendental meditation   158

    BT   **Meditation**

Transcendentalism   141

    BT   **Philosophy**

    RT   **Idealism**

Transcontinental journeys (American continent)

    USE **Overland journeys to the Pacific**

Transcultural studies

    USE **Cross-cultural studies**

Transfer of technology

    USE **Technology transfer**

Transfer payments (May subdiv. geog.)   **339.5**

    UF   Government transfer payments

Transfer payments—*Continued*
 BT **Domestic economic assistance**
  Economic policy
  Subsidies
Transfer tax
 USE **Inheritance and transfer tax**
Transformation (Genetics)
 USE **Genetic transformation**
Transformers, Electric
 USE **Electric transformers**
Transgenics
 USE **Genetic engineering**
Transistor amplifiers 621.3815
 UF Amplifiers, Transistor
  Audio amplifiers, Transistor
  Transistor audio amplifiers
 BT **Amplifiers (Electronics)**
  Transistors
Transistor audio amplifiers
 USE **Transistor amplifiers**
Transistors 621.3815
 BT **Electronics**
  Semiconductors
 NT **Transistor amplifiers**
Transit systems
 USE **Local transit**
Translating and interpreting (May
  subdiv. geog.) **418**
 UF Interpreting and translating
 BT **Language and languages**
Transmission of data
 USE **Data transmission systems**
Transmission of power
 USE **Electric lines**
  Electric power distribution
  Power transmission
Transmissions, Automobile
 USE **Automobiles—Transmission de-
  vices**
Transmutation (Chemistry) 539.7
  Use for materials on the transmutation of
  metals in nuclear physics. Materials on medi-
  eval attempts to change base metals into gold
  are entered under **Alchemy**.
 UF Transmutation of metals
 BT **Atoms**
  Nuclear physics
  Radioactivity
 NT **Cyclotrons**
 RT **Alchemy**

Transmutation of metals
 USE **Alchemy**
  Transmutation (Chemistry)
Transplantation
 USE **Transplantation of organs, tis-
  sues, etc.**
  and organs of the body with
  the subdivision *Transplanta-
  tion,* e.g. **Heart—Transplan-
  tation** [to be added as need-
  ed]
**Transplantation of organs, tissues, etc.
  617.9**
 UF Medical transplantation
  Organ transplants
  Surgical transplantation
  Tissues—Transplantation
  Transplantation
 SA organs of the body with the
  subdivision *Transplantation,*
  e.g. **Heart—Transplantation**
  to be added as needed]
 BT **Surgery**
 NT **Heart—Transplantation**
 RT **Donation of organs, tissues,
  etc.**
  **Preservation of organs, tissues,
  etc.**
**Transplantation of organs, tissues, etc.—
  Ethical aspects 174**
 UF Transplantation of organs, tis-
  sues, etc.—Moral and reli-
  gious aspects
 BT **Bioethics**
Transplantation of organs, tissues, etc.—
  Moral and religious aspects
 USE **Transplantation of organs, tis-
  sues, etc.—Ethical aspects**
  **Transplantation of organs, tis-
  sues, etc.—Religious aspects**
**Transplantation of organs, tissues, etc.—
  Religious aspects 201; 241**
 UF Transplantation of organs, tis-
  sues, etc.—Moral and reli-
  gious aspects
Transportation (May subdiv. geog.) **388**
 SA subjects, classes of person, and
  names of wars with the sub-
  division *Transportation,* e.g.
  **Hazardous substances—
  Transportation**; **School chil-**

Transportation—*Continued*
> dren—**Transportation**;
> **World War, 1939-1945—**
> **Transportation**; etc. [to be
> added as needed]

BT **Locomotion**
NT **Air travel**
 Automobile travel
 Bridges
 Canals
 Car pools
 Commercial aeronautics
 Express service
 Freight
 Harbors
 Hazardous substances—Trans-
 portation
 Highway transportation
 Inland navigation
 Local transit
 Merchant marine
 Military transportation
 Ocean travel
 Pipelines
 Postal service
 Railroads
 Roads
 School children—Transporta-
 tion
 Shipping
 Steam navigation
 Streets
 Trade routes
 Traffic engineering
 Trucking
 Vehicles
 Waterways
 World War, 1939-1945—Trans-
 portation
RT **Commerce**
Transportation, Highway
 USE **Highway transportation**
Transportation, Military
 USE **Military transportation**
Transportation of criminals
 USE **Penal colonies**
Transportation—Planning (May subdiv.
 geog.) **338**
 BT **Planning**
Transsexualism **305.3; 616.85**
 UF Change of sex
 Sex change

Transsexuality
 BT **Sex role**
Transsexuality
 USE **Transsexualism**
Transvestites **306.77**
> Use for materials on persons, especially
> men, who assume the dress of the opposite
> sex for psychological gratification. Materials
> on men who impersonate women for purposes
> of entertainment or comic effect are entered
> under **Female impersonators**. Materials on
> women who impersonate men for purposes of
> entertainment or comic effect are entered un-
> der **Male impersonators**.

 UF Crossdressers
 BT **Persons**
Trapping (May subdiv. geog.) **639**
 NT **Fur trade**
 RT **Game and game birds**
 Hunting
Traumatic stress syndrome
 USE **Post-traumatic stress disorder**
Travel **910**
> Use for materials on the art and enjoyment
> of travel and advice for travelers. Descriptions
> of actual voyages are entered under **Voyages**
> **and travels** or under the name of a place with
> the subdivision *Description and travel*. An ac-
> count of an extinct city or town by a traveler
> in ancient times is entered under the name of
> the extinct city or town, without further subdi-
> vision, e.g. **Delphi (Extinct city)**.

 UF Group travel
 Journeys
 Tourism
 SA names of cities (except extinct
 cities), countries, states, etc.,
 with the subdivision *Descrip-*
 tion and travel, e.g. **United**
 States—Description and
 travel; and ethnic groups,
 classes of persons, and names
 of individuals with the subdi-
 vision *Travel*, e.g. **Handi-**
 capped—Travel [to be added
 as needed]
 BT **Manners and customs**
 NT **Adventure travel**
 Air travel
 Automobile travel
 Bicycle touring
 Handicapped—Travel
 Ocean travel
 Safaris
 Travel in literature
 Voyages around the world

Travel—*Continued*
   RT   **Tourist trade**
          Voyages and travels
Travel—Authorship
   USE **Travel writing**
Travel books
   USE **Voyages and travels**
          Voyages around the world
Travel guides
   USE **Automobile travel—Guidebooks**
          and names of cities (except an-
          cient cities), countries, states,
          etc., with the subdivision
          Guidebooks, e.g. **Chicago**
          (Ill.)—Guidebooks; United
          States—Guidebooks; etc. [to
          be added as needed]

Travel in literature   809
   Use for materials about the theme of travel in literature. Materials about non-fiction travel writing, collections of travel writings, and accounts of voyages and travels not limited to a single place are entered under **Voyages and travels**. Accounts of voyages and travels limited to a single place are entered under the name of the place with the subdivision *Description and travel.*
   UF Voyages and travels in literature
   BT **Literature—Themes**
          Travel
   RT **Voyages and travels**
Travel industry
   USE **Tourist trade**
Travel trailers and campers   629.226; 796.7
   Use for materials on structures mounted upon a truck or towed by a truck or automobile for the purpose of temporary dwelling or cargo hauling. Materials on stationary transportable structures designed for year-round living are entered under **Mobile homes**.
   UF Automobiles—Trailers
          Campers and trailers
          House trailers
          Pickup campers
          Trailers
   BT **Camping**
          Recreational vehicles
   NT **Vans**
   RT **Mobile homes**
Travel writing   808
   Use for materials about the art of travel writing. Materials about a particular place are entered under the name of the place with the subdivision *Description and travel,* e.g. **Chicago (Ill.)—Description and travel**.
   UF Travel—Authorship

   BT **Authorship**
Travelers (May subdiv. geog.)   910.92; 920
   UF Tourists
          Voyagers
   SA travelers from particular countries, e.g. **American travelers**; and ethnic groups, classes of person, and names of individuals with the subdivision *Travel*, e.g. **Presidents—United States—Travel** [to be added as needed]
   BT **Voyages and travels**
   NT **American travelers**
   RT **Explorers**
Traveling sales personnel
   USE **Sales personnel**
Travels
   USE **Voyages and travels**
Travesty
   USE **Burlesque (Theater)**
          Parody
Tray gardens
   USE **Miniature gardens**
Treason (May subdiv. geog.)   364.1
   Use for materials on the offense of acting to overthrow one's own government or to harm or kill its sovereign. Materials on any attempt to subvert, overthrow, or cause the destruction of any established or legally constituted government are entered under **Subversive activities**.
   UF High treason
   BT **Crime**
          Political crimes and offenses
          Subversive activities
   RT **Traitors**
Treasure trove
   USE **Buried treasure**
Treaties   341; 341.3
   SA names of countries with the subdivision *Foreign relations—Treaties*, and names of wars with the subdivision *Treaties* [to be added as needed]
   BT **Diplomacy**
          International law
          International relations
   NT **International arbitration**
          United States—Foreign relations—Treaties

Treaties—*Continued*
>> **World War, 1939-1945—Treaties**

Treatment
>> USE **Therapeutics**
>> and types of diseases with the subdivision *Treatment,* e.g.
>> **AIDS (Disease)—Treatment**
>> [to be added as needed]

Treatment of diseases
>> USE **Therapeutics**

Tree houses   690
>> BT **Buildings**

Tree planting (May subdiv. geog.)   **635.9**
>> UF Planting
>> BT **Forests and forestry**
>> NT **Windbreaks**
>> RT **Reforestation**
>> **Trees**

Trees (May subdiv. geog.)   **582.16; 635.9**
>> Names of nuts and tree fruits may be used for either the nut or fruit or the tree.
>> UF Arboriculture
>>   Timber
>> SA types of trees, e.g. **Oak** [to be added as needed], in the singular form
>> BT **Plants**
>> NT **Christmas trees**
>> **Dwarf trees**
>> **Evergreens**
>> **Fruit culture**
>> **Lumber and lumbering**
>> **Oak**
>> **Pruning**
>> **Shrubs**
>> **Wood**
>> RT **Forests and forestry**
>> **Landscape gardening**
>> **Tree planting**

Trees—Nomenclature (Popular)   582.16
>> BT **Popular plant names**

Trees—United States   582.160973

Trent Affair, 1861   973.7
>> BT **United States—History—1861-1865, Civil War**

Trial by jury
>> USE **Jury**

Trial by publicity
>> USE **Freedom of the press and fair trial**

Trial marriage
>> USE **Unmarried couples**

Trials (May subdiv. geog.)   **345; 347**
>> May be qualified by topic, e.g. **Trials (Homicide)**.
>> BT **Criminal law**
>> NT **Courts martial and courts of inquiry**
>> **Trials (Homicide)**
>> **War crime trials**
>> **Witnesses**
>> RT **Crime**

Trials—Fiction
>> USE **Legal stories**

Trials (Homicide) (May subdiv. geog.)   **345**
>> UF Homicide trials
>>   Murder trials
>>   Trials (Murder)
>> BT **Homicide**
>> **Trials**

Trials (Murder)
>> USE **Trials (Homicide)**

Triangle   516.15
>> BT **Plane geometry**

Tribal government (May subdiv. geog.)   **306.2**
>> BT **Political science**
>> **Tribes**

Tribes (May subdiv. geog.)   **305.8**
>> UF Tribes and tribal system
>> BT **Clans**
>> **Family**
>> NT **Tribal government**

Tribes and tribal system
>> USE **Tribes**

Tricks   793.5
>> SA types of tricks [to be added as needed]
>> BT **Amusements**
>> NT **Card tricks**
>> **Juggling**
>> **Magic tricks**

Tricycles   629.227; 796.6
>> UF Trikes
>> BT **Vehicles**
>> RT **Cycling**

Trigonometry   516.24
>> UF Plane trigonometry
>>   Spherical trigonometry
>> BT **Geometry**
>> **Mathematics**

Trigonometry—Tables   516.24
   BT   **Mathematics—Tables**
   NT   **Logarithms**
Trikes
   USE   **Tricycles**
Trinity   231
   BT   **Christianity—Doctrines**
         God—Christianity
   NT   **Holy Spirit**
Tripoline War, 1801-1805
   USE   **United States—History—1801-**
         1805, Tripolitan War
Tripolitan War, 1801-1805
   USE   **United States—History—1801-**
         1805, Tripolitan War
Trivia
   USE   **Curiosities and wonders**
         Questions and answers
Trolley cars
   USE   **Street railroads**
Tropes
   USE   **Figures of speech**
Tropical conditions
   USE   subjects with the subdivision
         Tropical conditions, e.g.
         Building—Tropical condi-
         tions or the subdivision *Trop-*
         ics, e.g. **Agriculture—Tropics**
         [to be added as needed]
Tropical diseases
   USE   **Tropical medicine**
Tropical fish   597.17
   BT   **Fishes**
Tropical hygiene
   USE   **Tropical medicine**
Tropical jungles
   USE   **Jungles**
Tropical medicine (May subdiv. geog.)
         614
   UF   Diseases, Tropical
         Tropical diseases
         Tropical hygiene
   SA   types of tropical diseases, e.g.
         Yellow fever [to be added as
         needed]
   BT   **Medicine**
   NT   **Yellow fever**
Tropical rain forests
   USE   **Rain forests**
Tropics   910.913

   SA   subjects with the subdivision
         Tropics, e.g. **Agriculture—**
         Tropics or *Tropical condi-*
         tions, e.g. **Building—Tropical**
         conditions [to be added as
         needed]
   BT   **Earth**
   NT   **Agriculture—Tropics**
Troubadours   849.1; 920
   BT   **French poetry**
         Minstrels
         Poets
Trout fishing (May subdiv. geog.)   **799.1**
   BT   **Fishing**
Troy (Extinct city)   939
   UF   Ilium (Extinct city)
   BT   **Extinct cities—Turkey**
         Turkey—Antiquities
Truck crops
   USE   **Truck farming**
Truck farming (May subdiv. geog.)   **635**
   UF   Garden farming
         Market gardening
         Truck crops
         Truck gardening
   BT   **Agriculture**
         Gardening
         Horticulture
   RT   **Vegetable gardening**
Truck freight
   USE   **Trucking**
Truck gardening
   USE   **Truck farming**
Trucking (May subdiv. geog.)   **388.3**
   UF   Truck freight
   BT   **Freight**
         Transportation
Trucks (May subdiv. geog.)   **629.224**
   UF   Motor trucks
   SA   types of trucks and names of
         specific makes and models [to
         be added as needed]
   BT   **Automobiles**
         Highway transportation
   RT   **Materials handling**
Trucks—Weight   629.224
Trust   158.2
   BT   **Attitude (Psychology)**
         Emotions
Trust companies (May subdiv. geog.)
         332.2

Trust companies—*Continued*
　BT　**Business**
　　　Corporations
　RT　**Banks and banking**
　　　Trusts and trustees
Trust funds
　USE　**Trusts and trustees**
Trustees
　USE　**Trusts and trustees**
Trusts and trustees (May subdiv. geog.)
　　346.05
　UF　Boards of trustees
　　　Fiduciaries
　　　Trust funds
　　　Trustees
　SA　types of trustees, e.g. **Library**
　　　trustees [to be added as
　　　needed]
　BT　**Contracts**
　NT　**Library trustees**
　　　Living trusts
　RT　**Estate planning**
　　　Executors and administrators
　　　Inheritance and succession
　　　Trust companies
Trusts, Industrial
　USE　**Industrial trusts**
Truth　**121**
　BT　**Belief and doubt**
　　　Philosophy
　NT　**Reality**
　　　Truthfulness and falsehood
　RT　**Certainty**
　　　Pragmatism
　　　Skepticism
　　　Theory of knowledge
Truth in advertising
　USE　**Deceptive advertising**
Truthfulness and falsehood　**177**
　UF　Credibility
　　　Falsehood
　　　Lying
　　　Untruth
　BT　**Human behavior**
　　　Truth
　NT　**Deception**
　　　Lie detectors and detection
　RT　**Honesty**
Tsunamis (May subdiv. geog.)　**551.46**
　UF　Earthquake sea waves
　　　Seismic sea waves
　　　Tidal waves

　BT　**Natural disasters**
　　　Ocean waves
Tuberculosis (May subdiv. geog.)　**616.9**
　BT　**Lungs—Diseases**
Tuberculosis—Mortality (May subdiv.
　　geog.)　**616.9**
Tuberculosis—Vaccination (May subdiv.
　　geog.)　**614.4**
　BT　**Vaccination**
Tugboats　**623.82**
　BT　**Boats and boating**
Tuition
　USE　**College costs**
　　　Colleges and universities—Fi-
　　　nance
　　　Education—Finance
Tumbling　**796.47**
　BT　**Acrobats and acrobatics**
Tumors　**616.99**
　NT　**Cancer**
Tuning　**784.192**
　SA　types of instruments with the
　　　subdivision *Tuning* [to be
　　　added as needed]
　NT　**Pianos—Tuning**
　RT　**Musical instruments**
Tunnels (May subdiv. geog.)　**388; 624.1**
　BT　**Civil engineering**
　NT　**Excavation**
　RT　**Drilling and boring (Earth and**
　　　rocks)
Turbines　**621.406**
　BT　**Engines**
　　　Hydraulic machinery
　NT　**Gas turbines**
　　　Steam turbines
Turin Shroud
　USE　**Holy Shroud**
Turkey　**956.1**
　　May be subdivided like **United States** ex-
　cept for *History.*
Turkey—Antiquities　**956.1**
　BT　**Antiquities**
　NT　**Troy (Extinct city)**
Turkeys　**598.6; 636.5**
　BT　**Birds**
　　　Poultry
Turncoats
　USE　**Defectors**
Turning　**621.9**
　UF　Lathe work
　　　Wood turning

766

Turning—*Continued*
> BT **Carpentry**
> **Manufacturing processes**
> RT **Lathes**
> **Woodwork**

Turnpikes (Modern)
> USE **Express highways**

Turtles (May subdiv. geog.)   **597.92**
> UF Terrapins
> Tortoises
> BT **Reptiles**

Tutoring
> USE **Tutors and tutoring**

Tutors
> USE **Tutors and tutoring**

Tutors and tutoring (May subdiv. geog.)
371.39
> Use for general materials on one-on-one instruction. Materials on the adaptation of instruction to meet individual needs within a group are entered under **Individualized instruction**.

> UF Tutoring
> Tutors
> BT **Teaching**
> NT **Independent study**
> **Individualized instruction**

TV
> USE **Television**

TV personalities
> USE **Television personalities**

Twelfth century
> USE **World history—12th century**

Twelve-step programs   **362.29**
> UF Programs, Twelve-step
> Twelve steps (Self-help)
> SA names of specific twelve-step programs [to be added as needed]
> BT **Behavior modification**
> RT **Alcoholism**
> **Compulsive behavior**
> **Drug abuse**

Twelve steps (Self-help)
> USE **Twelve-step programs**

Twentieth century
> USE **World history—20th century**

Twenty-first century
> USE **World history—21st century**

Twins   **155.44; 306.875**
> BT **Multiple birth**
> **Siblings**

Twisters (Tornadoes)
> USE **Tornadoes**

Two-career couples
> USE **Dual-career families**

Two-career families
> USE **Dual-career families**

Two-career family
> USE **Dual-career families**

Two-income families
> USE **Dual-career families**

Two-year colleges
> USE **Junior colleges**

Type and type-founding (May subdiv. geog.)   **686.2**
> UF Type and type founding
> BT **Founding**
> **Printing**
> NT **Computer fonts**
> **Linotype**
> RT **Initials**
> **Printing—Specimens**
> **Typesetting**
> **Typography**

Type and type founding
> USE **Type and type-founding**

Type design
> USE **Typography**

Type-setting
> USE **Typesetting**

Type specimens
> USE **Printing—Specimens**

Typefaces
> USE **Typography**

Types, Psychological
> USE **Typology (Psychology)**

Typesetting   **686.2**
> UF Composition (Printing)
> Type-setting
> BT **Printing**
> NT **Linotype**
> RT **Type and type-founding**

Typewriters   **652.3; 681**
> BT **Office equipment and supplies**

Typewriting   **652.3**
> UF Typing
> BT **Business education**
> **Office practice**
> **Writing**
> RT **Keyboarding (Electronics)**

Typhoid fever   **616.9**
> UF Enteric fever

Typhoid fever—*Continued*
  BT **Diseases**
Typhoons (May subdiv. geog.) **551.55**
  Use for cyclonic storms originating in the region of the China Seas and the Philippines.
  BT **Cyclones**
      Storms
      Winds
  RT **Hurricanes**
Typing
  USE **Typewriting**
Typography 686.2
  UF Type design
      Typefaces
  BT **Graphic arts**
      Printing
  NT **Advertising layout and typography**
  RT **Type and type-founding**
Typology (Psychology) 155.2
  UF Mental types
      Psychological types
      Types, Psychological
  BT **Personality**
      Psychology
      Temperament
  NT **Enneagram**
UFO abduction
  USE **Alien abduction**
UFOs
  USE **Unidentified flying objects**
UHF radio
  USE **Shortwave radio**
Ultrahigh frequency radio
  USE **Shortwave radio**
Ultrasonic waves 534.5
  UF Supersonic waves
      Waves, Ultrasonic
  BT **Sound waves**
      Ultrasonics
Ultrasonic waves—Industrial applications 620.2
Ultrasonics 534.5
  UF Inaudible sound
      Supersonics
  BT **Sound**
  NT **Ultrasonic waves**
Ultraviolet rays 535.01; 621.36
  UF Rays, Ultra-violet
  BT **Electromagnetic waves**
      Radiation

  RT **Phototherapy**
      Radiotherapy
Umbrellas and parasols 391.4; 685
  UF Parasols
  BT **Clothing and dress**
UN
  USE **United Nations**
Unbelief
  USE **Skepticism**
Unborn child
  USE **Fetus**
Uncles (May subdiv. geog.) **306.87**
  BT **Family**
Unconventional warfare
  USE **Guerrilla warfare**
Undenominational churches
  USE **Community churches**
Underachievers (May subdiv. geog.)
      371.28
  BT **Students**
Underdeveloped areas
  USE **Developing countries**
Undergraduates
  USE **College students**
Underground architecture (May subdiv. geog.) **624.1; 690; 720**
  UF Underground design
  BT **Architecture**
  NT **Basements**
      Earth sheltered houses
Underground design
  USE **Underground architecture**
Underground economy (May subdiv. geog.) **381**
  Use for materials on goods and services that are produced and sold legally but not reported or taxed. Materials on illegal trade aimed at avoiding government regulations, such as fixed prices or rationing, are entered under **Black market**.
  UF Economy, Underground
      Hidden economy
      Informal sector (Economics)
      Parallel economy
      Second economy
      Shadow economy
      Untaxed income
  BT **Economics**
      Small business
  NT **Barter**
      Illegal aliens
  RT **Black market**

Underground films
  USE **Experimental films**
Underground houses
  USE **Earth sheltered houses**
Underground literature
  USE **Alternative press**
Underground movements
  USE names of wars with the subdivision *Underground movements,* e.g. **World War, 1939-1945—Underground movements** [to be added as needed]
Underground press
  USE **Alternative press**
Underground railroad (May subdiv. geog.) **326**
  RT **Slavery—United States**
Underground railroads
  USE **Subways**
Underground water
  USE **Groundwater**
Underprivileged
  USE **Socially handicapped**
Underprivileged children
  USE **Socially handicapped children**
Underprivileged students
  USE **At risk students**
Undersea engineering
  USE **Ocean engineering**
Undersea exploration
  USE **Underwater exploration**
Undersea research stations **551.46**
  UF Manned undersea research stations
      Sea laboratories
      Submarine research stations
      Underwater research stations
  SA names of special research projects and stations, e.g. **Sealab project** [to be added as needed]
  BT **Oceanography—Research**
      Underwater exploration
  NT **Sealab project**
Undersea vehicles
  USE **Submersibles**
Understanding
  USE **Intellect**
      Theory of knowledge

Undertakers and undertaking (May subdiv. geog.) **363.7; 393**
  UF Funeral directors
      Morticians
  BT **Service industries**
Underwater diving
  USE **Deep diving**
Underwater drilling (Petroleum)
  USE **Offshore oil well drilling**
Underwater exploration (May subdiv. geog.) **551.46; 627**
  UF Submarine exploration
      Undersea exploration
  BT **Exploration**
      Oceanography
  NT **Buried treasure**
      Deep diving
      Undersea research stations
Underwater geology
  USE **Submarine geology**
Underwater medicine
  USE **Submarine medicine**
Underwater photography **778.7**
  UF Deep-sea photography
      Submarine photography
  BT **Photography**
Underwater physiology
  USE **Submarine medicine**
Underwater research stations
  USE **Undersea research stations**
Underwater swimming
  USE **Skin diving**
Undocumented aliens
  USE **Illegal aliens**
Unemployed (May subdiv. geog.) **331.13**
  UF Jobless people
      Out-of-work people
  BT **Labor supply**
      Poor
      Unemployment
  NT **Food relief**
      Occupational retraining
  RT **Domestic economic assistance**
      Tramps
Unemployment (May subdiv. geog.) **331.13**
  UF Joblessness
  BT **Employment**
      Labor supply
      Social problems

Unemployment—*Continued*
  NT   **Employment agencies**
       Plant shutdowns
       Unemployed
Unemployment insurance (May subdiv.
       geog.)   **368.4**
  UF   Insurance, Unemployment
       Labor—Insurance
       Payroll taxes
  BT   **Insurance**
Unfair competition   338.6
  UF   Competition, Unfair
       Fair trade
       Unfair trade practices
  BT   **Commercial law**
  NT   **Trade secrets**
  RT   **Restraint of trade**
Unfair trade practices
  USE **Unfair competition**
Ungraded schools
  USE **Nongraded schools**
Unicorns   398.2454
  BT   **Mythical animals**
Unidentified flying objects   001.9
  UF   Flying saucers
       Saucers, Flying
       UFOs
  BT   **Aeronautics**
       Astronautics
  RT   **Human-alien encounters**
Uniforms (May subdiv. geog.)   **391**
  SA   classes of persons and names of
       individual corporate bodies
       and military services with the
       subdivision *Uniforms*, e.g.
       United States. Army—Uni-
       forms [to be added as need-
       ed]
  BT   **Clothing and dress**
       Costume
  NT   **Military uniforms**
Uniforms, Military
  USE **Military uniforms**
Uniforms, Naval
  USE **Military uniforms**
Union churches
  USE **Community churches**
Union of South Africa
  USE **South Africa**
Union of Soviet Socialist Republics
  USE **Soviet Union**

Union shop
  USE **Open and closed shop**
Unions, Labor
  USE **Labor unions**
Unison speaking
  USE **Choral speaking**
Unitarianism   289.1
  BT   **Christian sects**
       Congregationalism
United Brethren
  USE **Moravians**
United Nations   341.23
  UF   UN
  BT   **International arbitration**
       International cooperation
       International organization
United Nations—Armed forces   341.23;
       355.3
  UF   Peace keeping forces
  BT   **Armed forces**
United Nations—Employees
  USE **United Nations—Officials and**
       employees
United Nations—Finance   336.09;
       341.23
  BT   **Finance**
United Nations—Information services
       341.23
  BT   **Information services**
United Nations—Officials and employees
       341.23
  UF   United Nations—Employees
United States   973
       The subdivisions under **United States**, with
       the exception of the period divisions of histo-
       ry, may be used under the name of any coun-
       try or region. The subdivisions under **Ohio**
       may be used under names of states, and those
       under **Chicago (Ill.)** under cities. Corporate
       name headings for corporate entities within
       the United States government, such as govern-
       ment agencies and departments, which are
       used either as authors or as subjects, have a
       period rather than a dash between the parts,
       e.g. **United States. Army**; and may be added
       as needed.
  UF   US
       USA
  SA   regions of the United States and
       groups of states, e.g. **New**
       England; Southern States;
       etc. [to be added as needed]
  NT   **Appalachian Region**
       Atlantic States
       Gulf States (U.S.)

United States—*Continued*
>   Middle West
>   Mississippi River Valley
>   New England
>   Old Northwest
>   Old Southwest
>   Oregon Trail
>   Pacific Northwest
>   Southern States
>   Southwestern States
>   West (U.S.)
> RT   **Americans**

United States. Army   355
>   Subdivisions used under this heading may be used under armies of other countries as appropriate.
> BT   **Armies**
>   **Military history**
>   **United States—Armed forces**
> NT   **United States Military Academy**

United States. Army—Appointments and retirements   355.1
> UF   United States. Army—Retirements

United States. Army—Biography   920
> BT   **Biography**

United States. Army—Chaplains   355.3; 920
> BT   **Chaplains**

United States. Army—Demobilization 355.2

United States. Army—Enlistment
> USE   **United States. Army—Recruiting, enlistment, etc.**

United States. Army—Examinations 355.1
> UF   Army tests
> BT   **Examinations**

United States. Army—Handbooks, manuals, etc.   355
> UF   Soldiers' handbooks
>   United States. Army—Officers' handbooks
>   United States. Army—Soldiers' handbooks

United States. Army—Insignia   355.1
> BT   **Insignia**

United States. Army—Medals, badges, decorations, etc.   355.1
> BT   **Insignia**
>   **Medals**

United States. Army—Military life 355.1
> BT   **Military personnel**
>   **Soldiers**

United States. Army—Music
> USE   **United States. Army—Songs**

United States. Army—Officers   355.3
> BT   **Military personnel**
>   **Soldiers**

United States. Army—Officers' handbooks
> USE   **United States. Army—Handbooks, manuals, etc.**

United States. Army—Ordnance   355.8
> UF   United States. Army—Ordnance and ordnance stores
> BT   **Ordnance**

United States. Army—Ordnance and ordnance stores
> USE   **United States. Army—Ordnance**

United States. Army—Parachute troops 356
> UF   United States—Parachute troops
> BT   **Parachute troops**

United States. Army—Recruiting, enlistment, etc.   355.2
> UF   United States. Army—Enlistment
> BT   **Recruiting and enlistment**

United States. Army—Retirements
> USE   **United States. Army—Appointments and retirements**

United States. Army—Soldiers' handbooks
> USE   **United States. Army—Handbooks, manuals, etc.**

United States. Army—Songs   782.42
> UF   United States. Army—Music
>   United States. Army—Songs and music
> BT   **Songs**

United States. Army—Songs and music
> USE   **United States. Army—Songs**

United States. Army—Uniforms   355.1
United States. Congress   328.73
> UF   Congress (U.S.)
> BT   **Legislative bodies**
> NT   **United States. Congress. House**
>   **United States. Congress. Senate**

United States. Congress. House   328.73
> UF   House of Representatives (U.S.)
>   Representatives, House of (U.S.)
> BT   **United States. Congress**

United States. Congress. Senate 328.73
>UF   Senate (U.S.)
>BT   **United States. Congress**

United States. Constitution 342.73
>Use for the text of the United States Constitution and for materials about that document.
>UF   American constitution
>Constitution (U.S.)

United States. Constitution. 1st-10th amendments 342.73
>Use for the text of the United States Bill of rights and for materials about that document.
>UF   American Bill of rights
>Bill of rights (U.S.)
>United States—Bill of rights

United States. Library of Congress
>USE   **Library of Congress**

United States. National Guard 355.3
>UF   National Guard (U.S.)
>BT   **United States—Militia**

United States. Navy 359
>Subdivisions used under **United States. Army** may be used under this heading and under navies of other countries as appropriate.
>BT   **Navies**
>**United States—Armed forces**

United States. Navy—Biography 920
>BT   **Biography**

United States. Navy—Enlistment
>USE   **United States. Navy—Recruiting, enlistment, etc.**

United States. Navy—Handbooks, manuals, etc. 359
>UF   Sailors' handbooks
>United States. Navy—Officers' handbooks
>United States. Navy—Sailors' handbooks

United States. Navy—Insignia 359.1
>BT   **Insignia**

United States. Navy—Medals, badges, decorations, etc. 359.1
>BT   **Insignia**
>**Medals**

United States. Navy—Officers 359.3
>BT   **Military personnel**

United States. Navy—Officers' handbooks
>USE   **United States. Navy—Handbooks, manuals, etc.**

United States. Navy—Recruiting, enlistment, etc. 359.2
>UF   United States. Navy—Enlistment
>BT   **Recruiting and enlistment**

United States. Navy—Sailors' handbooks
>USE   **United States. Navy—Handbooks, manuals, etc.**

United States. Supreme Court 347.73
>UF   Supreme Court—United States
>BT   **Courts**

United States. Supreme Court—Biography 920
>BT   **Biography**

United States—Annexations
>USE   **United States—Territorial expansion**

United States—Antiquities 973
>BT   **Antiquities**

United States—Appropriations and expenditures 352.4
>UF   Federal spending policy
>Government spending policy
>BT   **Budget—United States**

United States—Archives
>USE   **Archives—United States**

United States—Armed forces 355.00973
>SA   official names and branches of the armed forces, e.g. **United States. Army; United States. Navy**; etc. [to be added as needed]
>BT   **Armed forces**
>NT   **United States. Army**
>**United States. Navy**

United States—Armed forces—Gays
>USE   **Gays and lesbians in the military**

United States—Armed forces—Military life 355.10973
>BT   **Military personnel**

United States—Armed Forces—Recruiting, enlistment, etc. 355.2
>BT   **Recruiting and enlistment**

United States—Atlases
>USE   **United States—Maps**

United States—Bibliography 015.73; 016.973

United States—Bicentennial celebrations
>USE   **American Revolution Bicentennial, 1776-1976**

United States—Bill of rights
>USE   **United States. Constitution. 1st-10th amendments**

United States—Bio-bibliography 012

United States—Biography 920.073

United States—Biography—*Continued*
  BT **Biography**
United States—Biography—Dictionaries
    920.073
United States—Biography—Portraits
    920.073
  UF United States—History—Portraits
United States—Boundaries 973
  BT **Boundaries**
United States—Budget
  USE **Budget—United States**
United States—Campaign funds
  USE **Campaign funds—United
      States**
United States—Census 317.3; 352.7
  BT **Census**
United States—Centennial celebrations,
    etc. 973
  NT **American Revolution Bicenten-
      nial, 1776-1976**
United States—Church and state
  USE **Church and state—United
      States**
United States—Church history 277.3
  UF Church history—United States
      United States—Religious history
  BT **Church history**
  RT **United States—Religion**
United States—Cities and towns
  USE **Cities and towns—United
      States**
United States—Civil defense
  USE **Civil defense—United States**
United States—Civil service
  USE **Civil service—United States**
United States—Civilization 973
  BT **Civilization**
  NT **Americana**
United States—Civilization—1960-1970
    973.92
United States—Civilization—1970-
    973.92
United States—Civilization—Foreign in-
    fluences 973
United States—Climate 551.6973
  BT **Climate**
United States—Commerce 381;
    382.0973
  BT **Commerce**
United States—Commerce—Japan 382

United States—Commercial policy
  USE **Commercial policy—United
      States**
United States—Constitutional history
  USE **Constitutional history—United
      States**
United States—Constitutional law
  USE **Constitutional law—United
      States**
United States—Constitutions
  USE **Constitutions—United States**
United States—Courts
  USE **Courts—United States**
United States—Cultural policy
  USE **Cultural policy—United States**
United States—Declaration of indepen-
    dence 973.3
  UF Declaration of independence
      (U.S.)
United States—Defenses 355.4
  BT **Military readiness**
  NT **Strategic Defense Initiative**
United States—Description
  USE **United States—Description and
      travel**
United States—Description and travel
    917.3
  UF United States—Description
      United States—Travel
  BT **Geography**
United States—Description and travel—
    Guidebooks
  USE **United States—Guidebooks**
United States—Description and travel—
    Views
  USE **United States—Pictorial works**
United States—Diplomatic and consular
    service
  USE **American diplomatic and con-
      sular service**
United States—Directories 917.30025
    Use for lists of names and addresses. Lists
    of names without addresses are entered under
    United States—Registers.
  BT **Directories**
  RT **United States—Registers**
United States—Economic conditions
    330.973
  UF National resources
  BT **Economic conditions**
United States—Economic policy
  USE **Economic policy—United States**

United States—Elections
  USE **Elections—United States**
United States—Emigration and immigration
  USE **United States—Immigration
       and emigration**
United States—Employees
  USE **United States—Officials and
       employees**
United States—Environmental policy
  USE **Environmental policy—United
       States**
United States—Ethnic relations   305.8
United States—Ethnology
  USE **Ethnology—United States**
United States—Executive departments
  USE **Executive departments—United
       States**
United States—Executive departments—Re-
  organization
  USE **Administrative agencies—Reor-
       ganization—United States**
United States—Executive power
  USE **Executive power—United
       States**
United States—Exploration   973
  UF Exploration—United States
  BT **America—Exploration
       Exploration**
  NT **West (U.S.)—Exploration**
**United States—Exploring expeditions
  910.973; 973**
  Use for materials on exploring expeditions
  sponsored by the United States. Materials on
  early exploration of a particular place are en-
  tered under the name of the place with the
  subdivision *Exploration*.
  UF American exploring expeditions
  SA names of expeditions, e.g. **Lewis
       and Clark Expedition (1804-
       1806)** [to be added as need-
       ed]
  BT **Explorers**
  NT **Lewis and Clark Expedition
       (1804-1806)**
United States—Fiscal policy
  USE **Fiscal policy—United States**
United States—Flags
  USE **Flags—United States**
**United States—Foreign economic rela-
  tions   337.73**
  UF Foreign economic relations—
       United States

  BT **International economic rela-
       tions**
United States—Foreign opinion (May
  subdiv. geog.)   **303.3; 973**
  Use for materials on foreign public opinion
  about the United States. May be further subdi-
  vided by the country holding the opinion, e.g.
  United States—Foreign opinion—France.
  UF Anti-Americanism
       Antiamericanism
       United States—Foreign public
       opinion
  BT **Public opinion**
**United States—Foreign opinion—France
  303.3; 973**
  Use for materials on French public opinion
  about the United States.
United States—Foreign policy
  USE **United States—Foreign rela-
       tions**
United States—Foreign population
  USE **Aliens—United States
       Immigrants—United States**
United States—Foreign public opinion
  USE **United States—Foreign opinion**
United States—Foreign relations (May
  subdiv. geog.)   **327.73**
  When further subdividing geographically,
  provide an additional subject entry with the
  two places in reversed positions, i.e. **United
  States—Foreign relations—Iran** and also
  Iran—Foreign relations—United States.
  UF United States—Foreign policy
  BT **Diplomacy
       International relations
       World politics**
  NT **Monroe Doctrine**
  RT **Neutrality—United States**
**United States—Foreign relations—Iran
  327.73055**
  NT **Iran hostage crisis, 1979-1981**
**United States—Foreign relations—Trea-
  ties   327.73; 341.3**
  UF United States—Treaties
  BT **Treaties**
United States—Gazetteers   917.3003
  BT **Gazetteers**
United States—Geographic names
  USE **Geographic names—United
       States**
United States—Geography   917.3
  BT **Geography**

United States—Government
  USE **United States—Politics and
       government**
United States—Government buildings
  USE **Public buildings—United States**
United States—Government employees
  USE **United States—Officials and
       employees**
United States—Government publications
  USE **Government publications—
       United States**
United States—Governmental investigations
  USE **Governmental investigations—
       United States**
United States—Guidebooks   917.304
  UF   United States—Description and
       travel—Guidebooks
United States—Historic buildings
  USE **Historic buildings—United
       States**
**United States—Historical geography
  911**
  BT   **Historical geography**
**United States—Historical geography—
  Maps   911**
  BT   **United States—Maps**
United States—Historiography   973.07
  UF   United States—History—Histori-
       ography
  BT   **Historiography**
United States—History   973
  UF   American history
  NT   **Americana**
       **Constitutional history—United
       States**
       Southern States—History
       West (U.S.)—History
**United States—History—1600-1775, Colo-
  nial period   973.2**
  Use for materials on American history from
  the earliest permanent English settlements on
  the Atlantic coast up to the American Revolu-
  tion. Materials on the period of discovery are
  entered under **United States—Exploration**.
  UF   American colonies
       Colonial history (U.S.)
  NT   **Bacon's Rebellion, 1676**
       King Philip's War, 1675-1676
       **Pilgrims (New England colo-
       nists)**
       **Pontiac's Conspiracy, 1763-
       1765**

**United States—History—1689-
  1697, King William's War**
**United States—History—1755-
  1763, French and Indian
  War**
United States—History—1675-1676, King
  Philip's War
  USE **King Philip's War, 1675-1676**
**United States—History—1689-1697, King
  William's War   973.2**
  UF   King William's War, 1689-1697
  BT   **Native Americans—Wars**
       **United States—History—1600-
       1775, Colonial period**
**United States—History—1755-1763,
  French and Indian War   973.2**
  UF   French and Indian War
  BT   **Native Americans—Wars**
       Seven Years' War, 1756-1763
       **United States—History—1600-
       1775, Colonial period**
**United States—History—1775-1783, Rev-
  olution   973.3**
  May be subdivided like **United States—
  History—1861-1865, Civil War**.
  UF   American Revolution
       Revolution, American
       War of the American Revolution
  BT   **Revolutions**
  NT   **American Loyalists**
       Canadian Invasion, 1775-1776
       Fourth of July
United States—History—1775-1783, Revo-
  lution—Centennial celebrations, etc.
  USE **American Revolution Bicenten-
       nial, 1776-1976**
United States—History—1783-1809
  USE **United States—History—1783-
       1815**
**United States—History—1783-1815
  973.3; 973.4**
  UF   Confederation of American colo-
       nies
       United States—History—1783-
       1809 [*Former heading*]
  NT   **Lewis and Clark Expedition
       (1804-1806)**
       Louisiana Purchase
       War of 1812
United States—History—1783-1865   973
**United States—History—19th century
  973.5**

United States—History—1801-1805, Tripolitan War 973.4

UF Tripoline War, 1801-1805
Tripolitan War, 1801-1805

United States—History—1812-1815, War of 1812

USE **War of 1812**

United States—History—1815-1861 973.5; 973.6

NT **Black Hawk War, 1832**
Mexican War, 1846-1848

United States—History—1845-1848, War with Mexico

USE **Mexican War, 1846-1848**

United States—History—1861-1865, Civil War 973.7

UF American Civil War
Civil War—United States

NT **Confederate States of America**
Secession—Southern States
Trent Affair, 1861

United States—History—1861-1865, Civil War—Biography 920; 973.7092

BT **Biography**

United States—History—1861-1865, Civil War—Campaigns 973.7

SA names of battles, e.g. **Gettysburg (Pa.), Battle of, 1863**
[to be added as needed]

NT **Gettysburg (Pa.), Battle of, 1863**

United States—History—1861-1865, Civil War—Causes 973.7

BT **Secession—Southern States**

United States—History—1861-1865, Civil War—Centennial celebrations, etc. 973.7

United States—History—1861-1865, Civil War—Drama 808.82; 812

Use for collections of plays dealing with the Civil War.

BT **Historical drama**

United States—History—1861-1865, Civil War—Fiction 808.83; 813

Use for collections of stories dealing with the Civil War.

United States—History—1861-1865, Civil War—Health aspects 973.7

United States—History—1861-1865, Civil War—Historiography 973.7

BT **Historiography**

United States—History—1861-1865, Civil War—Medical care 973.7

BT **Medical care**

United States—History—1861-1865, Civil War—Naval operations 973.7

United States—History—1861-1865, Civil War—Personal narratives 973.7

Use for collective or individual eyewitness reports or autobiographical accounts of the war in general. Accounts limited to a specific topic are entered under that topic.

BT **Autobiographies**
Biography

United States—History—1861-1865, Civil War—Pictorial works 973.7022

United States—History—1861-1865, Civil War—Prisoners and prisons 973.7

BT **Prisoners of war**
Prisons

United States—History—1861-1865, Civil War—Reconstruction

USE **Reconstruction (1865-1876)**

United States—History—1861-1865, Civil War—Sources 973.7

United States—History—1865-1898 973.8

NT **Reconstruction (1865-1876)**
Spanish-American War, 1898

United States—History—1898-1919 973.9; 973.91

NT **Spanish-American War, 1898**

United States—History—1898, War of 1898

USE **Spanish-American War, 1898**

United States—History—20th century 973.9

United States—History—1914-1918, World War

USE **World War, 1914-1918—United States**

United States—History—1919-1933 973.91

United States—History—1933-1945 973.917

NT **New Deal, 1933-1939**

United States—History—1939-1945, World War

USE **World War, 1939-1945—United States**

United States—History—1945- 973.92

United States—History—1945-1953
973.918

United States—History—1953-1961
973.921

United States—History—1961-1974
973.92

    NT   **Vietnam War, 1961-1975**

          Watergate Affair, 1972-1974

United States—History—1974-1989
973.92

United States—History—1989-   973.928

    NT   **Persian Gulf War, 1991**

United States—History—21st century
973.9

United States—History—Bibliography
016.973

United States—History—Chronology
973

United States—History—Dictionaries
973.03

    BT   **History—Dictionaries**

United States—History—Drama   808.82;
812

Use for collections of plays dealing with American history.

    BT   **Historical drama**

United States—History—Examinations
973.076

    UF   United States—History—Examinations, questions, etc.

    BT   **United States—History—Study and teaching**

United States—History—Examinations, questions, etc.

    USE   **United States—History—Examinations**

United States—History—Fiction   808.83;
813

Use for collections of stories dealing with American history.

United States—History—Historiography

    USE   **United States—Historiography**

United States—History—Library resources   973.07

United States—History—Outlines, syllabi, etc.   973.02

    BT   **United States—History—Study and teaching**

United States—History—Periodicals
973.05

United States—History—Poetry   808.81;
811

Use for collections of poetry dealing with American history.

    BT   **Historical poetry**

United States—History—Portraits

    USE   **United States—Biography—Portraits**

United States—History—Societies
973.06

    BT   **History—Societies**

United States—History—Sources   973

United States—History—Study and teaching   973.07

    NT   **United States—History—Examinations**

          United States—History—Outlines, syllabi, etc.

United States—Immigration and emigration   325; 325.73

    UF   United States—Emigration and immigration

    SA   names of immigrant groups, e.g. **Mexican Americans; Mexicans—United States** [to be added as needed]

    BT   **Americanization**

          Immigration and emigration

    RT   **Aliens—United States**

          Immigrants—United States

United States—Industrial policy

    USE   **Industrial policy—United States**

United States—Industries

    USE   **Industries—United States**

United States—Insular possessions

    USE   **United States—Territories and possessions**

United States—Intellectual life   973

    BT   **Intellectual life**

United States—Intelligence service

    USE   **Intelligence service—United States**

United States—Internal security

    USE   **Internal security—United States**

United States—Land settlement

    USE   **Land settlement—United States**

United States—Land surveys

    USE   **United States—Surveys**

United States—Languages   306.44
> Use for materials on the several languages spoken in the United States.

United States—Law
> USE **Law—United States**

United States—Local history   973
> BT **Local history**

United States—Mail
> USE **Postal service—United States**

United States—Manufactures
> USE **Manufactures—United States**

United States—Maps   912.73
> UF   United States—Atlases
> BT **Atlases**
>   **Maps**
> NT **United States—Historical geography—Maps**

United States Military Academy 355.0071
> UF   USMA
>   West Point (Military academy)
> BT **Colleges and universities**
>   **United States. Army**

United States Military Academy—Registers   355.0071

United States Military Academy—Songs 782.42
> UF   United States Military Academy—Songs and music
> BT **Students' songs**

United States Military Academy—Songs and music
> USE **United States Military Academy—Songs**

United States—Military history 355.00973; 973
> BT **Military history**

United States—Military offenses
> USE **Military offenses—United States**

United States—Military personnel
> USE **Military personnel—United States**

United States—Military policy
> USE **Military policy—United States**

United States—Militia   355.3
> BT **Armed forces**
> NT **United States. National Guard**

United States—Monetary policy
> USE **Monetary policy—United States**

United States—Moral conditions   973
> BT **Moral conditions**

United States—Municipal government
> USE **Municipal government—United States**

United States—National characteristics
> USE **American national characteristics**

United States—National parks and reserves
> USE **National parks and reserves—United States**

United States—National security
> USE **National security—United States**

United States—National songs
> USE **National songs—United States**

United States—Naval history   359.00973
> BT **Naval history**

United States—Neutrality
> USE **Neutrality—United States**

United States—Occupations
> USE **Occupations—United States**

United States—Officials and employees 351.73
> UF   United States—Employees
>   United States—Government employees
> RT **Civil service—United States**

United States—Parachute troops
> USE **United States. Army—Parachute troops**

United States—Peoples
> USE **Ethnology—United States**

United States—Pictorial works 917.30022
> UF   United States—Description and travel—Views

United States—Police
> USE **Police—United States**

United States—Politicians
> USE **Politicians—United States**

United States—Politics
> USE **United States—Politics and government**

United States—Politics and government 973
> UF   American government
>   American politics
>   United States—Government
>   United States—Politics
> BT **Political science**
>   **Politics**
>   **Public administration**

United States—Politics and government— *Continued*

    NT   **Third parties (United States politics)**

United States—Popular culture

    USE   **Popular culture—United States**

United States—Population   304.60973

    BT   **Population**

United States—Postal service

    USE   **Postal service—United States**

United States—Presidents

    USE   **Presidents—United States**

United States—Prisons

    USE   **Prisons—United States**

United States—Public buildings

    USE   **Public buildings—United States**

United States—Public debts

    USE   **Public debts—United States**

United States—Public health

    USE   **Public health—United States**

United States—Public lands

    USE   **Public lands—United States**

United States—Public schools

    USE   **Public schools—United States**

United States—Public works

    USE   **Public works—United States**

United States—Race relations 305.800973

    BT   **Race relations**

United States—Registers   917.30025

    Use for lists of names without addresses. Lists of names that include addresses are entered under **United States—Directories**.

    RT   **United States—Directories**

United States—Religion   200.973; 277.3

    BT   **Religion**

    RT   **United States—Church history**

United States—Religious history

    USE   **United States—Church history**

United States—Rural conditions 307.720973

    BT   **Rural sociology**

United States—Secret service

    USE   **Secret service—United States**

United States—Separation of powers

    USE   **Separation of powers—United States**

United States—Social conditions   973

    BT   **Social conditions**

United States—Social life and customs 973

    BT   **Manners and customs**

United States—Social policy

    USE   **Social policy—United States**

United States—Soldiers

    USE   **Soldiers—United States**

United States—State governments

    USE   **State governments**

United States—Statistics   317.3

    BT   **Statistics**

United States—Surveys   972

    Use for materials containing the results of land surveys of the United States.

    UF   United States—Land surveys

United States—Tariff

    USE   **Tariff—United States**

United States—Taxation

    USE   **Taxation—United States**

United States—Term limits (Public office)

    USE   **Term limits (Public office)— United States**

United States—Territorial expansion 973

    UF   Expansion (United States politics)

           Manifest destiny (United States)

           United States—Annexations

           Westward movement

United States—Territorial waters

    USE   **Territorial waters—United States**

United States—Territories and possessions   325; 973

    UF   United States—Insular possessions

United States—Travel

    USE   **United States—Description and travel**

United States—Treaties

    USE   **United States—Foreign relations—Treaties**

United States—Vice-presidents

    USE   **Vice-presidents—United States**

United States—World War, 1914-1918

    USE   **World War, 1914-1918—United States**

United States—World War, 1939-1945

    USE   **World War, 1939-1945—United States**

United States—World War, 1939-1945—Casualties

    USE   **World War, 1939-1945—Casualties—United States**

United States—World War, 1939-1945—
　　Casualties—Statistics
　　USE　**World War, 1939-1945—Casu-
　　　　　alties—United States—Statis-
　　　　　tics**
United Steelworkers of America　331.88
　　BT　**Labor unions**
Universal bibliographic control
　　USE　**Bibliographic control**
Universal history
　　USE　**World history**
Universal language　401
　　UF　International language
　　　　Language, International
　　　　Language, Universal
　　　　World language
　　BT　**Language and languages**
　　　　Linguistics
　　NT　**Esperanto**
Universal military training
　　USE　**Draft**
Universe　113; 523.1
　　　　Use for materials limited to the physical de-
　　　　scription of the universe. General and theoreti-
　　　　cal materials on the science or philosophy of
　　　　the universe are entered under **Cosmology**.
　　UF　Cosmogony
　　　　Cosmography
　　NT　**Astronomy**
　　　　Cosmology
　　　　Life on other planets
　　RT　**Creation**
Universities
　　USE　**Colleges and universities**
Universities and colleges
　　USE　**Colleges and universities**
University degrees
　　USE　**Academic degrees**
University extension (May subdiv. geog.)
　　　　378.1
　　BT　**Colleges and universities**
　　　　Distance education
　　　　Higher education
　　NT　**Adult education**
　　　　Correspondence schools and
　　　　　courses
University graduates
　　USE　**College graduates**
University libraries
　　USE　**Academic libraries**
University students
　　USE　**College students**

Unmarried couples (May subdiv. geog.)
　　　　306.84
　　UF　Cohabitation
　　　　Common law marriage
　　　　Living together
　　　　Trial marriage
　　　　Unmarried people
　　BT　**Lifestyles**
　　　　Shared housing
　　NT　**Single parents**
Unmarried fathers (May subdiv. geog.)
　　　　306.874; 362.82
　　　　Use for materials on fathers who at the time
　　　　of childbirth were not married to the child's
　　　　mother. Materials on fathers rearing children
　　　　without a partner in the household are entered
　　　　under **Single-parent families**. Materials on fa-
　　　　thers who are teenagers are entered under
　　　　Teenage fathers.
　　UF　Parents, Unmarried
　　　　Unmarried parents
　　　　Unwed fathers
　　BT　**Fathers**
　　　　Single parents
　　RT　**Illegitimacy**
Unmarried men
　　USE　**Single men**
Unmarried mothers (May subdiv. geog.)
　　　　306.874; 362.83
　　　　Use for materials on mothers who at the
　　　　time of giving birth were not married to the
　　　　child's father. Materials on mothers rearing
　　　　children without a partner in the household
　　　　are entered under **Single-parent families**. Ma-
　　　　terials on mothers who are teenagers are en-
　　　　tered under **Teenage mothers**.
　　UF　Parents, Unmarried
　　　　Unmarried parents
　　　　Unwed mothers
　　BT　**Mothers**
　　　　Single parents
　　RT　**Illegitimacy**
Unmarried parents
　　USE　**Unmarried fathers**
　　　　　Unmarried mothers
Unmarried people
　　USE　**Single people**
　　　　　Unmarried couples
Unmarried women
　　USE　**Single women**
Unsafe products
　　USE　**Product safety**
Unselfishness
　　USE　**Altruism**

Unskilled labor (May subdiv. geog.)
331.7
UF Unskilled workers
BT **Labor**
Unskilled labor—Supply and demand
331.12
BT **Supply and demand**
Unskilled workers
USE **Unskilled labor**
Untaxed income
USE **Underground economy**
Untruth
USE **Truthfulness and falsehood**
Unwed fathers
USE **Unmarried fathers**
Unwed mothers
USE **Unmarried mothers**
Upholstery   684.1; 747
BT **Interior design**
NT **Draperies**
RT **Furniture**
Upper atmosphere   551.5
UF Atmosphere, Upper
BT **Atmosphere**
NT **Stratosphere**
Upper class (May subdiv. geog.)   **305.5**
UF Fashionable society
High society
Upper classes
BT **Social classes**
NT **Aristocracy**
Nobility
Upper classes
USE **Upper class**
Uranium   669
BT **Chemical elements**
RT **Radioactivity**
Uranus (Planet)   523.47
BT **Planets**
Urban areas
USE **Cities and towns**
Metropolitan areas
Urban development
USE **Cities and towns—Growth**
City planning
Urbanization
Urban education
USE **Urban schools**
Urban-federal relations
USE **Federal-city relations**

Urban fiction   808.83
Use for individual works, collections or materials about fiction dealing with the harsh, often violent, side of contemporary city life.
UF Hip-hop fiction
BT **Fiction**
Urban folklore (May subdiv. geog.)
398.2
UF Urban legends
BT **Folklore**
Urban homesteading (May subdiv. geog.)
363.5
BT **Houses—Buying and selling**
Housing
Urban renewal
Urban housing
USE **Housing**
Urban legends
USE **Urban folklore**
Urban life
USE **City and town life**
Urban planning
USE **City planning**
Urban policy (May subdiv. geog.)
307.76; 320.8
UF Urban problems
BT **City and town life**
Economic policy
Social policy
Urban sociology
RT **City planning**
Urban renewal
Urban problems
USE **Urban policy**
Urban renewal (May subdiv. geog.)
307.3
Use for materials on the economic, sociological, and political aspects of urban redevelopment. Materials on the architectural and engineering aspects are entered under **City planning**.
UF Slum clearance
BT **Metropolitan areas**
Urban sociology
NT **Community development**
Urban homesteading
RT **City planning**
Community organization
Urban policy
Urban renewal—Chicago (Ill.)   307.3
UF Chicago (Ill.)—Urban renewal
Urban renewal—United States   307.3

Urban-rural migration
USE **Internal migration**
Urban schools (May subdiv. geog.) **371**
UF City schools
Inner city schools
Urban education
BT **Schools**
Urban sociology (May subdiv. geog.)
307.76
UF Sociology, Urban
BT **Sociology**
NT **City and town life**
Urban policy
Urban renewal
Urbanization
RT **Cities and towns**
Urban street life
USE **Street life**
Urban traffic
USE **City traffic**
Urban transportation
USE **Local transit**
Urbanization (May subdiv. geog.)
307.76
Use for materials on the process by which town and communities acquire urban characteristics.
UF Cities and towns, Movement to
Urban development
BT **Cities and towns**
Rural sociology
Social change
Social conditions
Urban sociology
RT **Cities and towns—Growth**
US
USE **United States**
USA
USE **United States**
Usage
USE names of languages and groups of languages with the subdivision *Usage*, e.g. **English language—Usage** [to be added as needed]
Used merchandise
USE **Secondhand trade**
Useful insects
USE **Beneficial insects**
USMA
USE **United States Military Academy**

USSR
USE **Soviet Union**
Utensils
USE **Implements, utensils, etc.**
Utensils, Kitchen
USE **Kitchen utensils**
Utilitarianism 144
BT **Ethics**
NT **Secularism**
RT **Pragmatism**
Utilities (Computer programs)
USE **Utilities (Computer software)**
Utilities (Computer software) 005.4
Use for materials on software used to perform standard computer system operations such as sorting data, searching for viruses, copying data from one file to another, etc.
UF Computer utility programs
Computers—Utility programs
Utilities (Computer programs)
Utility programs (Computer software)
BT **Computer software**
Utilities, Public
USE **Public utilities**
Utility programs (Computer software)
USE **Utilities (Computer software)**
Utilization of waste
USE **Salvage**
Utopian fiction 808.3; 808.83
Use for individual works, collections, or materials about imaginative accounts of ideal societies. Theoretical materials about ideal societies and accounts of practical attempts to create such societies are entered under **Utopias**.
UF Ideal states
Utopian literature
BT **Fantasy fiction**
Science fiction
RT **Dystopias**
Utopias
Utopian literature
USE **Utopian fiction**
Utopias
Utopias 321; 335
Use for theoretical materials on ideal societies and for accounts of practical attempts to create such societies. Imaginative accounts of ideal societies are entered under **Utopian fiction**.
UF Ideal states
Utopian literature
BT **Political science**
Socialism

Utopias—*Continued*
    RT   **Collective settlements**
          Paradise
          Utopian fiction
V-chips   363.3
    UF   Violence chips
    BT   **Television—Censorship**
          Television—Receivers and re-
            ception
Vacation church schools
    USE **Religious summer schools**
Vacation home timesharing
    USE **Timesharing (Real estate)**
Vacation homes (May subdiv. geog.)
          643.2; 728.72
    UF   Summer cottages
          Summer homes
          Vacation houses
    BT   **Houses**
Vacation houses
    USE **Vacation homes**
Vacation schools
    USE **Summer schools**
Vacation schools, Religious
    USE **Religious summer schools**
Vacations (May subdiv. geog.) **331.25;**
          658.3
    BT   **Recreation**
    RT   **Holidays**
Vaccination (May subdiv. geog.)   **614.4**
    Use for materials on active immunization
    with a vaccine. Materials on any process, ac-
    tive or passive, that leads to increased immu-
    nity are entered under **Immunization**.
    UF   Inoculation
    SA   types of animals and types of
          diseases with the subdivision
          Vaccination, e.g. **Cattle—**
          Vaccination; Tuberculosis—
          Vaccination [to be added as
          needed]
    BT   **Immunization**
          Preventive medicine
          Public health
    NT   **Cattle—Vaccination**
          Poliomyelitis vaccine
          Tuberculosis—Vaccination
Vacuum tubes   **537.5; 621.3815**
    UF   Electron tubes
    BT   **Electronic apparatus and ap-**
          pliances
    NT   **Cathode ray tubes**

    RT   **X-rays**
Vagabonds
    USE **Tramps**
Vagrants
    USE **Tramps**
Valentine's Day   **394.2618**
    UF   Saint Valentine's Day
          St. Valentine's Day
    BT   **Holidays**
Valuation   **338.5**
    Use for general materials on the appraisal
    of property. Materials on valuation of particu-
    lar types of property are entered under the
    type of property, e.g. **Real estate**. Materials
    on valuation for taxing purposes are entered
    under **Tax assessment**.
    UF   Appraisal
          Capitalization (Finance)
    NT   **Tax assessment**
Values   **121; 170; 303.3**
    Use for materials on moral and aesthetic
    values.
    UF   Axiology
          Human values
          Worth
    BT   **Aesthetics**
          Ethics
          Psychology
    NT   **Social values**
Vampire films   **791.43**
    Use for individual works, collections, or
    materials about vampire films.
    UF   Vampires in motion pictures
    BT   **Horror films**
          Motion pictures
Vampires (May subdiv. geog.)   **398.21**
    BT   **Folklore**
Vampires in motion pictures
    USE **Vampire films**
Van pools
    USE **Car pools**
Vandalism   **364.16**
    UF   Destruction of property
    BT   **Offenses against property**
    NT   **Graffiti**
Vanishing species
    USE **Endangered species**
Vanity
    USE **Pride and vanity**
Vans   **728.7**
    BT   **Travel trailers and campers**
Variation (Biology)   **576.5**
    UF   Mutation (Biology)

Variation (Biology)—*Continued*
    BT   **Biology**
          Genetics
          Heredity
    NT   **Adaptation (Biology)**
          Mendel's law
          Natural selection
    RT   **Evolution**
Variety shows (Radio programs)
    791.44

    Use for individual works, collections, or materials about variety shows on the radio.

    BT   **Radio programs**
Variety shows (Television programs)
    791.45

    Use for individual works, collections, or materials about variety shows on television.

    BT   **Television programs**
Varnish and varnishing   667; 698
    BT   **Finishes and finishing**
Varsity sports
    USE **College sports**
Vascular system
    USE **Cardiovascular system**
Vasectomy   613.9
    BT   **Sterilization (Birth control)**
Vases (May subdiv. geog.)   **731; 738**
    RT   **Glassware**
          Pottery
Vassals
    USE **Feudalism**
Vatican City   945.6

    Use for geographical and descriptive materials on the independent papal state in Rome. Materials on the central administration of the Roman Catholic Church are entered under **Catholic Church**.

Vatican City—Foreign relations
    USE **Catholic Church—Foreign relations**
Vatican Council (2nd: 1962-1965)   262
    BT   **Councils and synods**
Vaudeville (May subdiv. geog.)   **792.7**
    BT   **Amusements**
          Theater
Vaults (Sepulchral)
    USE **Tombs**
VCRs
    USE **Video recording**
VD
    USE **Sexually transmitted diseases**
Vedanta   294.5

    BT   **Hinduism**
          Theosophy
Vedas   294.5
    BT   **Hinduism**
          Sacred books
Vegetable gardening (May subdiv. geog.)
    635
    UF   Kitchen gardens
    BT   **Gardening**
          Horticulture
    RT   **Truck farming**
          Vegetables
Vegetable kingdom
    USE **Botany**
          Plants
Vegetable oils
    USE **Essences and essential oils**
          Oils and fats
Vegetables (May subdiv. geog.)   **635;**
    641.3
    SA   types of vegetables [to be added as needed]
    BT   **Food**
          Plants
    NT   **Celery**
          Cooking—Vegetables
          Potatoes
          Root crops
    RT   **Vegetable gardening**
Vegetables—Canning
    USE **Vegetables—Preservation**
Vegetables—Preservation   641.4
    UF   Vegetables—Canning
    BT   **Canning and preserving**
Vegetarian cookery
    USE **Vegetarian cooking**
Vegetarian cooking (May subdiv. geog.)
    641.5
    UF   Vegetarian cookery
    BT   **Cooking**
    RT   **Cooking—Vegetables**
Vegetarianism (May subdiv. geog.)
    613.2
    BT   **Diet**
Vehicles   388; 629.2
    SA   types of vehicles and names of specific makes and models of vehicles [to be added as needed]
    BT   **Transportation**

Vehicles—*Continued*
- NT **Air-cushion vehicles**
  All terrain vehicles
  Automobiles
  Bicycles
  Carriages and carts
  Military vehicles
  Recreational vehicles
  Sleds
  Sport utility vehicles
  Submersibles
  Taxicabs
  Tricycles

Vehicles, Military
- USE **Military vehicles**

Velocity
- USE **Speed**

Vendetta (May subdiv. geog.)   **364.256**
- UF Blood feuds
  Feuds
- RT **Revenge**

Veneers and veneering   674; 698
- BT **Cabinetwork**
  Furniture

Venereal diseases
- USE **Sexually transmitted diseases**

Venezuela   987

May be subdivided like **United States** except for *History.*

Vengence
- USE **Revenge**

Ventilation   697.9
- SA types of buildings with the subdivision *Heating and ventilation*, e.g. **Houses—Heating and ventilation** [to be added as needed]
- BT **Air**
  Home economics
  Household sanitation
  Hygiene
  Sanitation
- RT **Air conditioning**
  Heating

Ventriloquism   793.8
- BT **Amusements**
  Voice

Venture capital   332
- UF Seed capital
- BT **Capital**

Venus (Planet)   523.42
- BT **Planets**

Verbal abuse
- USE **Invective**

Verbal learning   153.1; 370.15

Use for materials on the process of learning and understanding written or spoken language, ranging from learning to associate two nonsense syllables to solving problems presented in verbal terms.
- UF Learning, Verbal
- BT **Language and languages**
  Psychology of learning
- NT **Reading comprehension**

Vermin
- USE **Household pests**
  Pests

Vers libre
- USE **Free verse**

Verse epistles
- USE **Epistolary poetry**

Versification   808.1
- UF English language—Versification
  Meter
  Prosody
- BT **Authorship**
  Poetics
  Rhythm
- NT **Rhyme**

Vertebrates (May subdiv. geog.)   **596**
- BT **Animals**

Very high frequency radio
- USE **Shortwave radio**

Vessels (Ships)
- USE **Ships**

Vesta (Roman deity)   292.2
- BT **Gods and goddesses**

Veterans (May subdiv. geog.)   **305.9; 920**
- UF War veterans
- SA names of wars with the subdivision *Veterans*, e.g. **World War, 1939-1945—Veterans** [to be added as needed]
- BT **Military art and science**
  Veterans
- NT **Veterans**
  World War, 1939-1945—Veterans
- RT **Military hospitals**
  Military pensions
  Military personnel
  Soldiers

Veterans Day   394.264
- UF Armistice Day

Veterans Day—*Continued*
  BT **Holidays**
Veterans—Education (May subdiv. geog.)
    362.86
  UF Education of veterans
  BT **Education**
Veterans—Employment 331.5
  BT **Employment**
Veterans—Hospitals
  USE **Military hospitals**
Veterans—Legal status, laws, etc. 343
  BT **Military law**
Veterans—United States 305.9;
    353.5380973; 920
Veterinary medicine (May subdiv. geog.)
    636.089
  SA types of animals with the subdi-
      vision *Diseases*, e.g. **Horses—**
      Diseases; or with the subdivi-
      sion *Wounds and injuries*, e.g.
      Horses—Wounds and inju-
      ries [to be added as needed]
  BT **Medicine**
  RT **Animals—Diseases**
VHF radio
  USE **Shortwave radio**
Viaducts
  USE **Bridges**
Vibration 531; 620.3
  BT **Mechanics**
      Sound
  NT **Sound waves**
      Waves
Vicarious atonement
  USE **Atonement—Christianity**
Vice 170
  UF Vices
  SA types of vices [to be added as
      needed]
  BT **Conduct of life**
      Ethics
      Human behavior
  RT **Crime**
Vice-presidents (May subdiv. geog.)
    352.23; 920
  BT **Presidents**
Vice-presidents—United States 352.23;
    920
  UF United States—Vice-presidents
Vices
  USE **Vice**

Victimless crimes
  USE **Crimes without victims**
Victims of atomic bombings
  USE **Atomic bomb victims**
Victims of crime
  USE **Victims of crimes**
Victims of crimes (May subdiv. geog.)
    362.88
  UF Crime victims
      Victims of crime
  BT **Crime**
  NT **Abused women**
      Adult child abuse victims
Victorian architecture (May be subdiv.
    geog.) **724**
  BT **Architecture—19th century**
      Gothic revival (Architecture)
Victorian literature
  USE **English literature—19th centu-**
      ry
Victoriana 745.1; 747.0942
  BT **Antiques**
      Collectibles
Video art (May subdiv. geog.) **700;**
    791.45
    Use for materials on works of art created
    with the use of television and video recording
    technology.
  UF Electronic art
  BT **Art**
      Television
      Video recording
Video cameras, Home
  USE **Camcorders**
Video cassette recorders and recording
  USE **Video recording**
Video cassettes
  USE **Videotapes**
Video disc players
  USE **Videodisc players**
Video discs
  USE **Videodiscs**
Video display terminals
  USE **Computer monitors**
Video games 688.7; 794.8
  UF Electronic games
      Television games
  SA types of video games and names
      of individual games [to be
      added as needed]
  BT **Electronic toys**
      Games

Video recording 384.55; 621.388; 778.59

Use for materials on either the equipment or the process by which video or video and audio materials are recorded.

UF VCRs

Video cassette recorders and recording

Videorecorders

Videotape recorders and recording

NT **Camcorders**

Video art

Videodiscs

Videotapes

RT **Home video systems**

Television—Equipment and supplies

Video recordings

USE **Videodiscs**

Videotapes

Video recordings, Closed caption

USE **Closed caption video recordings**

Video recordings for the hearing impaired

USE **Closed caption video recordings**

Video tapes

USE **Videotapes**

Video telephone 384.6; 621.386

UF Picture telephone

Videophone

BT **Data transmission systems**

Telephone

Television

Videocassettes

USE **Videotapes**

Videodisc players 384.55; 621.388

UF Video disc players

BT **Television—Equipment and supplies**

Videodiscs 384.55; 621.388

UF Video discs

Video recordings

BT **Audiovisual materials**

Optical storage devices

Video recording

NT **Closed caption video recordings**

Music videos

RT **Television**

Videophone

USE **Video telephone**

Videorecorders

USE **Video recording**

Videos, Music

USE **Music videos**

Videotape recorders and recording

USE **Video recording**

Videotapes 384.55; 778.59

UF Tape recordings, Video

Video cassettes

Video recordings

Video tapes

Videocassettes

BT **Audiovisual materials**

Home video systems

Video recording

NT **Closed caption video recordings**

Music videos

RT **Television**

Videotex systems 004.69; 384.3

Use for materials on the transmission of computer-based data from a central source to a television set or personal computer allowing for two-way interactions, such as with home shopping or home banking.

UF Interactive videotex

Viewdata systems

BT **Data transmission systems**

Information systems

Television broadcasting

RT **Teletext systems**

Vietnam 959.7

May be subdivided like **United States** except for *History*.

Vietnam War, 1961-1975 959.704

May use appropriate subdivisions under **World War, 1939-1945**.

UF Vietnamese Conflict, 1961-1975

Vietnamese War, 1961-1975

BT **United States—History—1961-1974**

Vietnamese Conflict, 1961-1975

USE **Vietnam War, 1961-1975**

Vietnamese refugees (May subdiv. geog.) 305.9

BT **Refugees**

Vietnamese War, 1961-1975

USE **Vietnam War, 1961-1975**

Viewdata systems

USE **Videotex systems**

Views 910.22

Use for collections of pictures of many places.

UF Scenery

SA countries, states, cities, etc., and named entities, such as individual parks, structures, etc., with the subdivision *Pictorial works*, e.g. **Chicago (Ill.)—Pictorial works**; **United States—Pictorial works**; **Yosemite National Park (Calif.)—Pictorial works**; etc. [to be added as needed]

BT **Pictures**

Vigilance committees

USE **Vigilantes**

Vigilantes (May subdiv. geog.) **364.1; 364.4**

UF Vigilance committees [*Former heading*]

BT **Crime**

   Criminal law

RT **Lynching**

Vikings (May subdiv. geog.) **948**

Use for materials on early Scandinavian people. Materials on the people since the tenth century are entered under **Scandinavians**.

UF Norsemen

   Northmen

BT **Scandinavians**

RT **Normans**

Villages (May subdiv. geog.) **307.76**

BT **Cities and towns**

Vines

USE **Climbing plants**

Vineyards (May subdiv. geog.) **634.8**

UF Viticulture

BT **Farms**

RT **Grapes**

   Wine and wine making

Vintage automobiles

USE **Antique and classic cars**

Vintage cars

USE **Antique and classic cars**

Vintage motorcycles

USE **Antique and vintage motorcycles**

Violence (May subdiv. geog.) **303.6**

SA types of violence [to be added as needed]

BT **Aggressiveness (Psychology)**

   Social psychology

NT **Domestic violence**

   Hate crimes

   School violence

   Violence in mass media

   Violence in popular culture

   Violence in sports

   Violence in the workplace

   Violence on television

Violence chips

USE **V-chips**

Violence in mass media **302.23**

BT **Mass media**

   Violence

Violence in popular culture **306.4**

BT **Popular culture**

   Violence

Violence in schools

USE **School violence**

Violence in sports **796**

UF Sports violence

BT **Sports**

   Violence

Violence in television

USE **Violence on television**

Violence in the workplace **658.4**

UF Workplace violence

BT **Violence**

   Work environment

Violence on television **302.23; 791.45**

UF Violence in television

BT **Television**

   Television programs

   Violence

Violin

USE **Violins**

Violin music **787.2**

BT **Music**

Violin players

USE **Violinists**

Violinists (May subdiv. geog.) **787.2092; 920**

UF Violin players

BT **Instrumentalists**

Violins **787.2**

UF Fiddle

   Violin

BT **Stringed instruments**

Violoncellists (May subdiv. geog.) **787.4092**

Violoncellists—*Continued*
 UF Cellists
   Cello players
   Violoncello players
 BT **Instrumentalists**
Violoncello
 USE **Violoncellos**
Violoncello players
 USE **Violoncellists**
Violoncellos 787.4
 UF Cello
   Violoncello
 BT **Stringed instruments**
Vipers
 USE **Snakes**
Virgin Mary
 USE **Mary, Blessed Virgin, Saint**
Virtual libraries
 USE **Digital libraries**
Virtual reality 006.8
 UF Artificial reality
 BT **Computer simulation**
 RT **Computer graphics**
Virtue 170
 UF Virtues
 SA types of virtues [to be added as needed]
 BT **Conduct of life**
   Ethics
   Human behavior
 NT **Charity**
   Chastity
   Courage
   Courtesy
   Faith
   Forgiveness
   Gratitude
   Hope
   Justice
   Loyalty
   Obedience
   Patience
   Punctuality
   Temperance
Virtues
 USE **Virtue**
Viruses 579.2
 UF Microbes
 BT **Microorganisms**
 NT **Chickenpox**
Viruses, Computer
 USE **Computer viruses**

Visceral learning
 USE **Biofeedback training**
Viscosity 532; 620.1
 BT **Hydrodynamics**
   Mechanics
Vision 152.14; 573.8; 612.8; 617.7
 UF Sight
 BT **Optics**
   Senses and sensation
 NT **Color sense**
   Optical illusions
   Vision disorders
 RT **Eye**
Vision disorders 362.4; 617.7
 UF Defective vision
   Impaired vision
   Visual handicaps
   Visual impairments
 BT **Vision**
 NT **Blindness**
   Color blindness
Vision in animals 573.8
 UF Animals—Vision
 BT **Senses and sensation in animals**
Visions 133.8; 204; 248.2
 BT **Parapsychology**
   Religion
   Spiritual gifts
 NT **Dreams**
   Hallucinations and illusions
 RT **Apparitions**
Visitation rights (Domestic relations)
  (May subdiv. geog.) 306.8
 BT **Domestic relations**
 RT **Child custody**
Visitors' exchange programs
 USE **Exchange of persons programs**
Visual handicaps
 USE **Vision disorders**
Visual impairments
 USE **Vision disorders**
Visual instruction
 USE **Audiovisual education**
Visual literacy 153; 707
  Use for materials on the ability to interpret and evaluate visual objects and symbols, such as television, motion pictures, art works, etc.
 UF Literacy, Visual
 BT **Arts**
   Literacy
   Semiotics

Vital records
USE **Registers of births, etc.**
Vital statistics   304.6; 310
UF Burial statistics
Death rate
Marriage statistics
Mortuary statistics
Records of births, etc.
SA names of countries, cities, etc.,
and names of ethnic groups
with the subdivision *Vital sta-
tistics*, for compilations of
birth, marriage, and death sta-
tistics; and names of wars
with the subdivision
Casualities—Statistics, e.g.
**World War, 1939-1945—Ca-
sualties—Statistics**; **World
War, 1939-1945—Casual-
ties—United States—Statis-
tics**; etc. [to be added as
needed]
BT **Statistics**
NT **Birth rate**
Census
Life expectancy
Mortality
Population
RT **Registers of births, etc.**
Vitamins   572; 613.2; 615
BT **Food**
Nutrition
NT **Dietary supplements**
Viticulture
USE **Grapes**
Vineyards
Wine and wine making
Vivisection   179
BT **Animal experimentation**
Surgery
Vocabulary   418
UF English language—Vocabulary
Languages—Vocabulary
Words
BT **Language and languages**
NT **New words**
Word recognition
Vocal culture
USE **Voice culture**
Vocal ensembles
USE **Ensembles (Music)**

Vocal music (May subdiv. geog.)   **782**
BT **Music**
NT **Cantatas**
Carols
Choral music
Folk songs
Hymns
Opera
Operetta
Oratorio
Songs
RT **Singing**
Vocation   158.6; 253
BT **Duty**
Ethics
Occupations
Work
Vocation, Choice of
USE **Vocational guidance**
Vocational education (May subdiv. geog.)
370.113; 373.246; 374
Use for materials on teaching a skill during
the educational process. Materials on teaching
people a skill after formal education are en-
tered under **Occupational training**. Materials
discussing on-the-job training are entered un-
der **Employees—Training**. Materials on
retraining are entered under **Occupational
retraining**.
UF Career education
SA types of industries, professions,
etc., with the subdivision
Study and teaching, e.g. **Agri-
culture—Study and teaching**
[to be added as needed]
BT **Education**
NT **Agriculture—Study and teaching**
Cooperative education
Employees—Training
Industrial arts education
Occupational retraining
Occupational training
Vocational guidance
RT **Professional education**
Technical education
Vocational guidance (May subdiv. geog.)
331.702; 371.4
Use for materials on the activities and pro-
grams designed to help people plan, choose,
and succeed in their careers. Materials on the
assistance given to students by schools, col-
leges, or universities in the selection of a pro-
gram of studies suited to their abilities, inter-

Vocational guidance—*Continued*
ests, future plans, and general ·circumstances
are entered under **Educational counseling**.

UF Career counseling
Career development
Career guidance
Careers
Choice of profession, occupation, vocation, etc.
Employment guidance
Guidance, Vocational
Job placement guidance
Occupational guidance
Vocation, Choice of

SA vocational guidance for particular classes of persons, e.g. **Vocational guidance for the handicapped**; and fields of knowledge, corporate bodies, military services, professions, and industries and trades with the subdivision *Vocational guidance* [to be added as needed]

BT **Counseling**
Vocational education

NT **Career changes**
Job hunting
Law—Vocational guidance
Television broadcasting—Vocational guidance
Vocational guidance for the handicapped

RT **Educational counseling**
Employment
Occupations
Professions

Vocational guidance for the handicapped (May subdiv. geog.) **371.4**

BT **Handicapped**
Vocational guidance

Vocational training
USE **Occupational training**

Vocations
USE **Occupations**
Professions

Vodun
USE **Voodooism**

Voice 783

UF Speaking

BT **Language and languages**
Throat

NT **Automatic speech recognition**
Ventriloquism

RT **Phonetics**
Public speaking
Singing
Speech

Voice culture 808.5

UF Vocal culture
Voice training

BT **Public speaking**
Singing
Speech

Voice training
USE **Voice culture**

Volatile oils
USE **Essences and essential oils**

Volcanoes (May subdiv. geog.) **551.21**

SA names of volcanoes [to be added as needed]

BT **Geology**
Mountains
Physical geography

Volleyball 796.325

BT **Ball games**

Volume (Cubic content) 389; 530.8

UF Cubic measurement

BT **Geometry**
Measurement
Weights and measures

Volume feeding
USE **Food service**

Voluntarism
USE **Volunteer work**

Voluntary associations
USE **Associations**

Voluntary military service (May subdiv. geog.) **355.2**

UF Military service, Voluntary
Volunteer military service

BT **Armed forces**
Recruiting and enlistment

Voluntary organizations
USE **Associations**

Volunteer military service
USE **Voluntary military service**

Volunteer work (May subdiv. geog.) **361.3**

UF Voluntarism
Volunteering
Volunteerism
Volunteers

Volunteer work—*Continued*
    SA   types of volunteer work and
           names of volunteer programs,
           e.g. **Meals on wheels pro-**
           grams [to be added as need-
           ed]
    BT   **Public welfare**
    NT   **Caregivers**
          Foster grandparents
    RT   **Charities**
          National service
Volunteering
    USE   **Volunteer work**
Volunteerism
    USE   **Volunteer work**
Volunteers
    USE   **Volunteer work**
Volunteers in church work
    USE   **Lay ministry**
Voodoo
    USE   **Voodooism**
Voodooism (May subdiv. geog.)   **299.6**
    UF   Vodun
          Voodou
          Voudou
          Voudouism
    BT   **Religions**
Voter registration (May subdiv. geog.)
    324.6
    UF   Registration of voters
    BT   **Elections**
          Suffrage
Voting
    USE   **Elections**
          Suffrage
Vouchers, Educational
    USE   **Educational vouchers**
Voudou
    USE   **Voodooism**
Voudouism
    USE   **Voodooism**
Voyager project
    USE   **Project Voyager**
Voyagers
    USE   **Explorers**
          Travelers
Voyages and travels   910.4
    Use for materials about non-fiction travel
writing, for collections of travel writings, and
for accounts of voyages and travels not limit-
ed to a single place. Materials about the
theme of travel in literature are entered under

Travel in literature. Materials on the art and
enjoyment of travel and advice for travelers
are entered under **Travel**.
    UF   Journeys
          Travel books
          Travels
    SA   names of cities (except extinct
          cities), states, countries, conti-
          nents, etc., with the subdivi-
          sion *Description and travel*;
          e.g. **United States—Descrip-**
          tion and travel; names of ex-
          tinct cities or towns, without
          further subdivision, for ac-
          counts of those places by
          travelers in ancient times, e.g.
          Delphi (Extinct city); names
          of individual ships; names of
          regions, e.g. **Arctic regions**;
          ethnic groups, classes of per-
          sons, and names of individu-
          als with the subidivision
          Travel, e.g. **Handicapped—**
          Travel; names of countries
          sponsoring exploring expedi-
          tions with the subdivision *Ex-*
          ploring expeditions; e.g. **Unit-**
          ed States—Exploring expedi-
          tions; and names of places
          that were unsettled or sparsely
          settled and largely unknown
          to the world at large at the
          time of exploration, with the
          subdivision *Exploration*, e.g.
          America—Exploration [to be
          added as needed]
    BT   **Geography**
    NT   **Adventure travel**
          Aeronautics—Flights
          Air travel
          Automobile travel
          Northeast Passage
          Ocean travel
          Overland journeys to the Pa-
          cific
          Papal visits
          Pilgrims and pilgrimages
          Scientific expeditions
          Seafaring life
          Shipwrecks
          Travelers
          Voyages around the world

Voyages and travels—*Continued*
      Whaling
      Yachts and yachting
   RT **Adventure and adventurers**
      Exploration
      Explorers
      Travel
      Travel in literature
Voyages and travels in literature
   USE **Travel in literature**
Voyages around the world   910.4
   UF Circumnavigation
      Travel books
   BT **Travel**
      Voyages and travels
Voyages to the moon
   USE **Imaginary voyages**
      Space flight to the moon
Wage-price controls
   USE **Wage-price policy**
Wage-price policy (May subdiv. geog.)
   331.2
   UF Government policy
      Price controls
      Price-wage policy
      Wage-price controls
   BT **Inflation (Finance)**
      Prices
      Salaries, wages, etc.
Wages
   USE **Salaries, wages, etc.**
Wagons
   USE **Carriages and carts**
Waiters and waitresses (May subdiv.
   geog.) **642**
   UF Waitresses
   BT **Food service**
Waitresses
   USE **Waiters and waitresses**
Wakefulness
   USE **Insomnia**
Walking (May subdiv. geog.) **796.51**
   BT **Aerobics**
      Athletics
      Human locomotion
   RT **Hiking**
Walking in space
   USE **Extravehicular activity (Space
      flight)**
Wall decoration
   USE **Mural painting and decoration**

Wall painting
   USE **Mural painting and decoration**
Wall Street (New York, N.Y.)   332.6
   Use for materials on the activities of Wall
   Street as a financial district. Historical and de-
   scriptive materials on Wall Street as a street
   are entered under **Streets—New York (N.Y.)**.
   BT **Stock exchanges**
   RT **Streets—New York (N.Y.)**
Wallpaper   676; 747
   BT **Interior design**
   RT **Paperhanging**
Walls   690; 721
   BT **Buildings**
      Civil engineering
Walt Disney World (Fla.)   791.06
   UF Disney World (Fla.)
   BT **Amusement parks**
War   172; 303.6; 355.02
   UF Fighting
      Wars
   SA names of wars, battles, etc., e.g.
      **United States—History—
      1861-1865, Civil War**; **Get-
      tysburg (Pa.), Battle of,
      1863**; and war and other sub-
      jects, e.g. **War and civiliza-
      tion** [to be added as needed]
   NT **Arms control**
      Battles
      Chemical warfare
      Children and war
      Guerrilla warfare
      Intervention (International law)
      Military aeronautics
      Military occupation
      Military personnel
      Nuclear warfare
      Prisoners of war
      Psychological warfare
      Space warfare
      Submarine warfare
      Tank warfare
      War and civilization
      War and emergency powers
      War casualties
      War crimes
      War—Religious aspects
      World War III
   RT **Armed forces**
      International law
      Military art and science

War—*Continued*
    Military law
    Naval art and science
    Peace
War and children
  USE **Children and war**
War and civilization **172; 303.4**
  UF Civilization and war
  BT **Civilization**
      War
War and emergency powers (May subdiv.
  geog.) **342**
  UF Emergency powers
      War powers
  BT **Constitutional law**
      Executive power
      Legislative bodies
      War
War and industry
  USE **War—Economic aspects**
War and religion
  USE **War—Religious aspects**
War, Articles of
  USE **Military law**
War—Casualties
  USE **War casualties**
War casualties (May subdiv. geog.)
  363.3498
  UF War—Casualties
  SA names of wars with the subdivi-
      sion *Casualties*, e.g. **World
      War, 1939-1945—Casualties**
      [to be added as needed]
  BT **War**
  NT **World War, 1939-1945—Casu-
      alties**
War crime trials (May subdiv. geog.)
  341.6; 345
  BT **Trials**
War crimes (May subdiv. geog.) **341.6;
  345; 364.1**
  UF Military atrocities
  SA names of wars with the subdivi-
      sion *Atrocities*, e.g. **World
      War, 1939-1945—Atrocities**;
      and names of specific atroci-
      ties [to be added as needed]
  BT **Crimes against humanity**
      International law
      War

War—Economic aspects (May subdiv.
  geog.) **303.6**
  Use for materials discussing the economic
  causes of war and the effect of war on indus-
  try and trade.
  UF Economics of war
      Industry and war
      War and industry
  SA names of wars with the subdivi-
      sion *Economic aspects* [to be
      added as needed]
  NT **Industrial mobilization**
      **World War, 1939-1945—Eco-
      nomic aspects**
  RT **International competition**
War films **791.43**
  Use for individual works, collections, or
  materials about war films in general, not lim-
  ited to a particular war.
  UF Anti-war films
  SA names of wars with the subdivi-
      sion *Motion pictures and the
      war*; e.g. **World War, 1939-
      1945—Motion pictures and
      the war** [to be added as
      needed]
  BT **Historical drama**
      Motion pictures
  NT **World War, 1939-1945—Mo-
      tion pictures and the war**
War games (May subdiv. geog.) **355.48;
  793.92**
  UF War—Simulation games
      Wargames
  BT **Military art and science**
      Military maneuvers
      Simulation games
      Tactics
War of 1812 **940.2; 973.5**
  UF United States—History—1812-
      1815, War of 1812
  BT **Great Britain—History—1714-
      1837**
      **United States—History—1783-
      1815**
War of nerves
  USE **Psychological warfare**
War of the American Revolution
  USE **United States—History—1775-
      1783, Revolution**
War pensions
  USE **Military pensions**

War poetry   808.1; 808.81

Use for individual works or collections of war poetry, or for materials about war poetry in general, not confined to a particular war.

UF   Anti-war poetry

SA   names of wars with the subdivision *Poetry* [to be added as needed]

BT   **Poetry**

NT   **World War, 1939-1945—Poetry**

RT   **War songs**

War powers

USE   **War and emergency powers**

War protest movements

USE   **Peace movements**

War radio programs   791.44

Use for individual works, collections, or materials about war radio programs.

BT   **Radio programs**

War—Religious aspects   201; 261.8

May be subdivided by religion or sect.

UF   Religion and war
War and religion

SA   names of wars with the subdivision *Religious aspects*, e.g. **World War, 1939-1945—Religious aspects** [to be added as needed]

BT   **Religion**
War

NT   **Conscientious objectors**
Pacifism

War reparations   364.15; 364.16

SA   individual wars with the subdivision *Reparations*, e.g. **World War, 1939-1945—Reparations** [to be added as needed]

BT   **War reparations**

NT   **War reparations**

War ships

USE   **Warships**

War—Simulation games

USE   **War games**

War songs   782.42

UF   Battle songs
Soldiers' songs

BT   **National songs**
Songs

NT   **World War, 1939-1945—Songs**

RT   **War poetry**

War stories   808.3; 808.83

Use for individual works, collections, or materials about war stories.

UF   Anti-war stories

SA   names of wars and battles with the subdivision *Fiction*, e.g. **World War, 1939-1945—Fiction** [to be added as needed]

BT   **Fiction**
Historical fiction

War television programs   791.45

Use for individual works, collections, or materials about war television programs.

BT   **Television programs**

War use

USE   subjects with the subdivision *War use,* e.g. **Dogs—War use** [to be added as needed]

War use of animals

USE   **Animals—War use**

War use of dogs

USE   **Dogs—War use**

War veterans

USE   **Veterans**

War work

USE   names of wars with the subdivision *War work,* e.g. **World War, 1939-1945—War work** [to be added as needed]

Warfare, Submarine

USE   **Submarine warfare**

Wargames

USE   **War games**

Warm air heating

USE   **Hot air heating**

Wars

USE   **Military history**
Naval history
War

and ethnic groups with the subdivision *Wars,* e.g. **Native Americans—Wars** [to be added as needed]

Wars of the Roses, 1455-1485

USE   **Great Britain—History—1455-1485, Wars of the Roses**

Warships (May subdiv. geog.)   **359.8; 623.825**

UF   Battle ships
Battleships
War ships

SA   names of countries with the subhead *Navy,* e.g. **United States. Navy**; and names of

Warships—*Continued*
          individual warships [to be
          added as needed]
  BT   **Naval architecture**
         Naval art and science
         Sea power
         Ships
  NT   **Aircraft carriers**
         Submarines
  RT   **Navies**

Washing
  USE **Laundry**

Wasps 595.79
  BT   **Insects**

Waste as fuel
  USE **Waste products as fuel**

Waste disposal
  USE **Refuse and refuse disposal**
       and types of waste disposal,
       e.g. **Radioactive waste dis-**
       posal; Sewage disposal; etc.;
       and types of industries, plants,
       and facilities with the subdivi-
       sion *Waste disposal,* e.g.
       Chemical industry—Waste
       disposal [to be added as
       needed]

Waste (Economics) 339.4
  BT   **Economics**

Waste products 628.4
  UF   By-products
        Junk
        Trade waste
  BT   **Industrial chemistry**
        Manufactures
  NT   **Industrial waste**
  RT   **Recycling**
        Refuse and refuse disposal

Waste products as fuel 333.793; 662
  UF   Energy conversion from waste
        Organic waste as fuel
        Waste as fuel
  BT   **Salvage**
  RT   **Biomass energy**

Waste reclamation
  USE **Salvage**

Wastes, Hazardous
  USE **Hazardous wastes**

Wastes, Medical
  USE **Medical wastes**

Watches
  USE **Clocks and watches**

Water 551.4; 553.7
  UF   Hydrology
  BT   **Earth sciences**
        Hydraulics
  NT   **Drinking water**
        Floods
        Frost
        Geysers
        Groundwater
        Hydrotherapy
        Ice
        Lakes
        Ocean
        Ponds
        Precipitation (Meteorology)
        Rivers
        Sea water
        Seas
        Steam
  RT   **Hydraulic engineering**
        Water rights

Water—Analysis 546; 628.1
  BT   **Analytical chemistry**
  RT   **Water pollution**

Water animals
  USE **Aquatic animals**

Water ballet
  USE **Synchronized swimming**

Water birds (May subdiv. geog.)
         598.176
  UF   Aquatic birds
        Water fowl
        Wild fowl
  SA   types of water birds [to be add-
        ed as needed]
  BT   **Birds**
  NT   **Geese**
        Terns

Water conduits
  USE **Aqueducts**

Water conservation (May subdiv. geog.)
         333.91
  UF   Conservation of water
  BT   **Conservation of natural re-**
        sources
  NT   **Xeriscaping**
  RT   **Water supply**

Water cure
  USE **Hydrotherapy**

Water farming
  USE **Hydroponics**

Water flow
USE **Hydraulics**
Water fluoridation   628.1
UF   Fluoridation of water
Water—Fluoridation
BT   **Water supply**
Water—Fluoridation
USE   **Water fluoridation**
Water fowl
USE   **Water birds**
Water—Oil pollution
USE   **Oil pollution of water**
Water plants
USE   **Freshwater plants**
Marine plants
Water pollution (May subdiv. geog.)
363.739; 628.1
UF   Detergent pollution of rivers,
lakes, etc.
Pollution of water
River pollution
SA   types of pollution, e.g. **Oil pol-
lution of water** [to be added
as needed]
BT   **Environmental health**
Pollution
Public health
NT   **Acid rain**
Marine pollution
Oil pollution of water
RT   **Industrial waste**
Sewage disposal
Water—Analysis
Water power   333.9; 621.2
UF   Hydroelectric power
Water-power
BT   **Energy resources**
Hydraulics
Power (Mechanics)
Renewable energy resources
Rivers
Water resources development
NT   **Hydraulic engineering**
Hydraulic machinery
Hydroelectric power plants
Water-power
USE   **Water power**
Water—Purification
USE   **Water purification**
Water purification   628.1

UF   Purification of water
Water—Purification
BT   **Sanitation**
Water supply
NT   **Sea water conversion**
Water resources development (May
subdiv. geog.)   **333.91**
BT   **Energy development**
Natural resources
NT   **Irrigation**
Water power
RT   **Water supply**
Water rights (May subdiv. geog.)
333.91; 346.04
BT   **Law**
RT   **Water**
Water safety   363.14; 797.028
UF   Aquatic sports—Safety measures
Drowning prevention
Water sports—Safety measures
BT   **Accidents—Prevention**
NT   **Lifeguards**
Water skiing   797.3
BT   **Water sports**
Water sports (May subdiv. geog.)   **797**
UF   Aquatic sports
SA   types of water sports [to be add-
ed as needed]
BT   **Sports**
NT   **Boats and boating**
Canoes and canoeing
Deep diving
Diving
Rowing
Sailing
Surfing
Swimming
Water skiing
Yachts and yachting
Water sports—Safety measures
USE   **Water safety**
Water supply (May subdiv. geog.)
363.6; 628.1
UF   Waterworks
BT   **Natural resources**
Public utilities
NT   **Aqueducts**
Dams
Drinking water
Forest influences
Irrigation

Water supply—*Continued*
>> Water fluoridation
>> Water purification
> RT Water conservation
>> Water resources development
>> Wells

Water supply engineering (May subdiv. geog.) **628.1**
> BT Civil engineering
>> Engineering
> NT Drilling and boring (Earth and rocks)
> RT Hydraulic engineering

Water transportation
> USE Shipping

Watercolor painting (May subdiv. geog.) **751.42**
> UF Watercolors
> BT Painting

Watercolors
> USE Watercolor painting

Watergate Affair, 1972-1974 **973.924**
> BT United States—History—1961-1974

Watering places
> USE Health resorts

Waterways (May subdiv. geog.) **386**
> Use for materials on rivers, lakes, and canals used for transportation.
> BT Transportation
> NT Canals
>> Lakes
>> Rivers
> RT Inland navigation

Waterwise gardening
> USE Xeriscaping

Waterworks
> USE Water supply

Wave mechanics **530.12; 531**
> BT Mechanics
>> Quantum theory
>> Waves

Waves **531**
> BT Hydrodynamics
>> Vibration
> NT Electric waves
>> Ocean waves
>> Radiation
>> Sound waves
>> Wave mechanics

Waves, Electromagnetic
> USE Electromagnetic waves

Waves, Ultrasonic
> USE Ultrasonic waves

Way (Chinese philosophy)
> USE Tao

Wealth (May subdiv. geog.) **330.1**
> UF Distribution of wealth
>> Fortunes
>> Riches
> BT Economics
>> Finance
> NT Cost and standard of living
>> Economic conditions
>> Gross national product
>> Income
>> Inheritance and succession
>> Profit
>> Saving and investment
>> Success
> RT Capital
>> Money
>> Property

Wealthy people
> USE Rich

Weaponry
> USE Weapons

Weapons (May subdiv. geog.) **355.8; 623.4**
> UF Arms and armor
>> Weaponry
> SA types of weapons, e.g. **Swords** [to be added as needed]
> BT Tools
>> Weapons
> NT Bow and arrow
>> Firearms
>> Knives
>> Military weapons
>> Swords
>> Weapons
> RT Armor
>> Military art and science

Weapons, Atomic
> USE Nuclear weapons

Weapons industry
> USE Defense industry
>> Firearms industry

Weapons, Nuclear
> USE Nuclear weapons

Weapons, Space
> USE Space weapons

Weariness
  USE **Fatigue**
Weather 551.6

  Use for materials on the state of the atmosphere at a given time and place with respect to heat or cold, wetness or dryness, calm or storm. Scientific materials on the atmosphere, especially weather factors, are entered under **Meteorology**. Materials on climate as it relates to humans and to plant and animal life, including the effects of changes of climate, are entered under **Climate**.

  SA names of countries, cities, etc.,
         with the subdivision *Climate*,
         e.g. **United States—Climate**
         [to be added as needed]
  NT **Humidity**
       Precipitation (Meteorology)
       Storms
       Weather control
       Weather forecasting
       Winds
  RT **Climate**
       Meteorology
Weather control 551.68
  UF Artificial weather control
       Cloud seeding
       Rain making
       Weather modification
  BT **Meteorology**
       Weather
Weather—Folklore 398.26
  UF Weather lore
  BT **Folklore**
       Meteorology
       Weather forecasting
Weather forecasting (May subdiv. geog.)
         551.63
  UF Precipitation forecasting
  BT **Forecasting**
       Meteorology
       Weather
  NT **Weather—Folklore**
Weather lore
  USE **Weather—Folklore**
Weather modification
  USE **Weather control**
Weather satellites
  USE **Meteorological satellites**
Weather stations
  USE **Meteorological observatories**
Weaving (May subdiv. geog.) **677;**
         746.1; 746.41
  UF Hand weaving

  SA types of woven articles, e.g.
         Rugs and carpets [to be added as needed]
  BT **Handicraft**
       Textile industry
  NT **Basket making**
       Lace and lace making
       Looms
  RT **Fabrics**
Web databases 005.75; 025.04
  BT **Databases**
Web logs
  USE **Weblogs**
Web pages
  USE **Web sites**
Web publishing
  USE **Electronic publishing**
Web search engines 005.75; 025.04
  UF Web searching
       World Wide Web searching
  SA names of individual Web search
         engines [to be added as needed]
  BT **Internet searching**
       World Wide Web
Web searching
  USE **Internet searching**
       Web search engines
Web servers 004.67
  UF World Wide Web servers
  BT **World Wide Web**
Web sites 005.7
  UF Web pages
       Websites
       World Wide Web pages
       World Wide Web sites
  SA names of individual web sites;
         and topics, geographic names,
         categories of persons, ethnic
         groups, etc., with the subdivision *Internet resources* [to be
         added as needed]
  BT **Internet resources**
  NT **Wikis (Computer science)**
Web sites—Design 005.7
  BT **Design**
Weblogs 006.7
  UF Blogs
       Web logs
  BT **Diaries**
       Online journalism

Websites
USE **Web sites**
Wedding showers
USE **Showers (Parties)**
Weddings (May subdiv. geog.) **392.5; 395.2**
BT **Marriage**
NT **Marriage customs and rites**
Weed killers
USE **Herbicides**
Weeds (May subdiv. geog.) **632**
BT **Agricultural pests**
Economic botany
Gardening
Plants
Week 529
BT **Calendars**
Chronology
NT **Special weeks**
RT **Days**
Weight 530.8
UF Weight (Physics)
SA types of objects and substances
with the subdivision *Weight*,
e.g. **Trucks—Weight** [to be
added as needed]
BT **Physics**
NT **Body weight**
RT **Weights and measures**
Weight control
USE **Weight loss**
Weight gain 613.2
UF Gaining weight
BT **Body weight**
RT **Diet**
Weight lifting 796.41; 613.7
UF Strength training
Weight training
Weightlifting
BT **Athletics**
Exercise
RT **Bodybuilding**
Weight loss 613.2
UF Dieting
Diets, Reducing
Reducing
Weight control
BT **Body weight**
RT **Diet**
Exercise

Weight (Physics)
USE **Weight**
Weight training
USE **Weight lifting**
Weightlessness 531
UF Free fall
Gravity free state
Subgravity state
Zero gravity
BT **Environmental influence on
humans**
Space medicine
Weightlifting
USE **Weight lifting**
Weights and measures (May subdiv.
geog.) **389; 530.8**
UF Measures
Metrology
SA types of objects and substances
with the subdivision *Weight*,
e.g. **Trucks—Weight** [to be
added as needed]
BT **Physics**
NT **Electric measurements**
Measuring instruments
Volume (Cubic content)
RT **Measurement**
Metric system
Weight
Welding 671.5
UF Oxyacetylene welding
BT **Blacksmithing**
Forging
Ironwork
Manufacturing processes
Metalwork
NT **Electric welding**
RT **Soldering**
Welding, Electric
USE **Electric welding**
Welfare agencies
USE **Charities**
Welfare, Public
USE **Public welfare**
Welfare reform
USE **Public welfare**
Welfare state (May subdiv. geog.)
330.12; 361.6
BT **Economic policy**
Public welfare
Social policy

Welfare state—*Continued*
    State, The
Welfare work
  USE **Charities**
        Social work
Welfare work in industry
  USE **Industrial welfare**
Well boring
  USE **Drilling and boring (Earth and rocks)**
Well drilling, Oil
  USE **Oil well drilling**
Wells (May subdiv. geog.)   **551.49; 628.1**
  BT **Hydraulic engineering**
  RT **Drilling and boring (Earth and rocks)**
       Water supply
West Africa   **966**
    Use for materials dealing collectively with the southern half of the western bulge of the African continent, bounded on the north by the Sahara and on the south and west by the Atlantic Ocean. The term usually includes Benin, Burkina Faso, Cameroon, Gambia, Ghana, Guinea, Guinea-Bissau, Ivory Coast, Liberia, Nigeria, Senegal, Sierra Leone, and Togo, and sometimes Mali, Mauritania, and Niger as well.
  UF Africa, West
  BT **Africa**
  NT **French-speaking West Africa**
West Bank   **956.95**
  UF Judea and Samaria
       West Bank of the Jordan River
  BT **Palestine**
West Bank of the Jordan River
  USE **West Bank**
West Germany
  USE **Germany (West)**
West Indian literature (French)   **840**
    Use for collections and for materials on West Indian literature written originally in French.
  BT **Literature**
West Indies Region
  USE **Caribbean Region**
West Point (Military academy)
  USE **United States Military Academy**
West (U.S.)   **978**
    Use for the region west of the Mississippi River.
  UF Western States

  SA names of individual states in this region [to be added as needed]
  BT **United States**
  NT **Pacific Northwest**
       Pacific States
West (U.S.)—Exploration   **978**
  BT **United States—Exploration**
  RT **Overland journeys to the Pacific**
West (U.S.)—History   **978**
  UF Westward movement
  BT **United States—History**
Western civilization   **306.09; 909**
    Use for materials on the culture and society stemming from the Greco-Roman traditions of the occident rather than those of Islam, India, or the Far East.
  UF Civilization, Western
       Occidental civilization
  BT **Civilization**
       East and West
Western comic books, strips, etc.   **741.5**
    Use for individual works, collections, or materials about Western comics.
  BT **Comic books, strips, etc.**
Western Europe
  USE **Europe**
Western films   **791.43**
    Use for individual works, collections, or materials about Western films.
  UF Westerns
  SA types of Western films, e.g.
       Lone Ranger films [to be added as needed]
  BT **Adventure films**
       Historical drama
       Motion pictures
  NT **Lone Ranger films**
Western Hemisphere
  USE **America**
Western States
  USE **West (U.S.)**
Western stories   **808.3; 808.83**
    Use for individual works, collections, or materials about post-19th-century fiction set in the 19th-century American West.
  UF Westerns
  BT **Adventure fiction**
       Fiction
       Historical fiction
Westerns
  USE **Western films**
       Western stories

Westerns—*Continued*

· **Westerns (Radio programs)**
Westerns (Television programs)
Westerns (Radio programs)   **791.44**
Use for individual works, collections, or materials about Westerns on the radio.
UF   Westerns
BT   **Radio programs**
Westerns (Television programs)   **791.45**
Use for individual works, collections, or materials about Westerns on television.
UF   Westerns
BT   **Television programs**
Westminster Abbey   726.5
BT   **Abbeys**
Church buildings
Westward movement
USE   **Land settlement—United States**
United States—Territorial expansion
West (U.S.)—History
Wetlands (May subdiv. geog.)   **551.41**
SA   types of wetlands, e.g. **Marshes** [to be added as needed]
BT   **Landforms**
NT   **Bogs**
Marshes
Swamps
Whales (May subdiv. geog.)   **599.5**
BT   **Mammals**
Marine mammals
Whaling (May subdiv. geog.)   **639.2**
BT   **Commercial fishing**
Hunting
Voyages and travels
Wheat (May subdiv. geog.)   **633.1**
BT   **Grain**
Wheel chairs
USE   **Wheelchairs**
Wheelchair basketball   796.32
BT   **Basketball**
Wheelchair sports
Wheelchair sports   796.04
BT   **Sports for the handicapped**
NT   **Wheelchair basketball**
Wheelchairs   617
UF   Wheel chairs
BT   **Chairs**
Orthopedic apparatus
Wheels   621.8; 629.2
UF   Car wheels
BT   **Simple machines**

NT   **Gearing**
Tires
Which-way stories
USE   **Plot-your-own stories**
Whistle blowing (May subdiv. geog.)
174; 342; 353.4
Use for materials on the practice of calling public attention to corruption, mismanagement, or waste in government, business, the military, etc.
UF   Blowing the whistle
Whistleblowing
BT   **Political corruption**
Public interest
Whistleblowing
USE   **Whistle blowing**
White collar crimes (May subdiv. geog.)
364.16
UF   Occupational crimes
BT   **Crime**
NT   **Fraud**
Tax evasion
White supremacist movements
USE   **White supremacy movements**
White supremacy movements (May subdiv. geog.)   **320.5**
UF   Skinheads
White supremacist movements
BT   **Race relations**
Racism
Social movements
Whitechapel murders, 1888
USE   **Jack the Ripper murders, London (England), 1888**
Whittling
USE   **Wood carving**
Whodunits
USE   **Mystery and detective plays**
Mystery fiction
Mystery films
Mystery radio programs
Mystery television programs
Whole language   372.62
Use for materials on the integration of listening, speaking, writing, and reading skills in meaningful situations in which children participate actively.
UF   Integrated language arts (Holistic)
Language arts (Holistic)
Language experience approach in education

Whole language—*Continued*
  BT **Education—Experimental
      methods
      Language arts**
Wholistic medicine
  USE **Holistic medicine**
Wica
  USE **Wicca**
Wicca 133.4
  UF Wica
  BT **Paganism**
  RT **Goddess religion
      Witchcraft**
Wickedness
  USE **Good and evil**
Widowers (May subdiv. geog.) **306.88**
  BT **Men**
Widows (May subdiv. geog.) **306.88**
  BT **Women**
Wife abuse (May subdiv. geog.) **362.82**
  UF Abuse of wives
      Abused wives
      Battering of wives
      Wife battering
      Wife beating
  BT **Domestic violence**
  RT **Abused women**
Wife battering
  USE **Wife abuse**
Wife beating
  USE **Wife abuse**
Wigs 391.5
  BT **Clothing and dress
      Costume
      Hair**
Wigwams
  USE **Tepees**
Wikis (Computer science) 004.693
  BT **Web sites**
Wild animal dwellings
  USE **Animals—Habitations**
Wild animals
  USE **Animals
      Wildlife**
Wild cats (May subdiv. geog.) **599.75;
  636.8**
  Use for materials on non-domesticated spe-
  cies of cats or domestic cats living in a wild
  state. Materials on domestic cats are entered
  under **Cats**.
  UF Felidae
      Feral cats

  Wildcats
  SA types of wild cats [to be added
      as needed}]
  BT **Mammals**
  RT **Cats**
Wild children (May subdiv. geog.)
  155.45
  Use for materials on children who have
  been raised by animals or have lived their
  formative years in the wild without contact
  with human society.
  UF Feral children
      Wolf children
  BT **Exceptional children**
Wild flowers (May subdiv. geog.)
  582.13
  UF Wildflowers
  BT **Flowers**
Wild flowers—Conservation
  USE **Plant conservation**
Wild fowl
  USE **Game and game birds
      Water birds**
Wildcats
  USE **Wild cats**
Wilderness areas (May subdiv. geog.)
  333.78
  UF Scenery
  BT **Forest reserves**
  RT **Conservation of natural re-
      sources
      National parks and reserves**
Wilderness survival (May subdiv. geog.)
  613.6; 796.5
  UF Bush survival
      Outdoor survival
  BT **Camping
      Outdoor life
      Survival skills**
  RT **Survival after airplane acci-
      dents, shipwrecks, etc.**
Wildflowers
  USE **Wild flowers**
Wildlife (May subdiv. geog.) **333.95;
  639**
  Use for materials on wild animals in their
  natural environment, especially mammals,
  birds, and fishes that are hunted for sport or
  food.
  UF Feral animals
      Wild animals

Wildlife—*Continued*
    SA   types of wildlife, e.g. **Desert animals** [to be added as needed]
    BT   **Animals**
    NT   **Game and game birds**
    RT   **Wildlife conservation**
Wildlife and pesticides
    USE   **Pesticides and wildlife**
Wildlife attracting   **639.9**
    UF   Attracting wildlife
    BT   **Animals**
    NT   **Bird attracting**
Wildlife conservation (May subdiv. geog.)   **639.9**
    UF   Conservation of wildlife
            Preservation of wildlife
            Protection of wildlife
    BT   **Conservation of natural resources**
            Economic zoology
            Endangered species
            Environmental protection
            Nature conservation
    NT   **Birdbanding**
            Birds—Protection
            Game protection
            Game reserves
            Pesticides and wildlife
            Wildlife refuges
    RT   **Rare animals**
            Wildlife
Wildlife refuges (May subdiv. geog.)   **639.9**
    UF   Wildlife sanctuaries
    SA   names of specific refuges [to be added as needed]
    BT   **Wildlife conservation**
Wildlife sanctuaries
    USE   **Wildlife refuges**
Will
    USE   **Brainwashing**
            Free will and determinism
Will power
    USE   **Self-control**
Willpower
    USE   **Self-control**
Wills   **346.05**
    UF   Bequests
            Legacies
    BT   **Genealogy**
            Registers of births, etc.

    NT   **Living wills**
    RT   **Executors and administrators**
            Inheritance and succession
Wind
    USE   **Winds**
Wind instruments   **788**
    SA   types of wind instruments [to be added as needed]
    BT   **Musical instruments**
    NT   **Brass instruments**
            Flutes
            Woodwind instruments
Wind power (May subdiv. geog.)   **333.9; 621.4**
    BT   **Energy resources**
            Power (Mechanics)
            Renewable energy resources
    RT   **Windmills**
Windbreaks   **634.9**
    UF   Shelterbelts
    BT   **Tree planting**
Windmills (May subdiv. geog.)   **621.4**
    RT   **Wind power**
Window dressing
    USE   **Show windows**
Window gardening   **635.9**
    UF   Windowbox gardening
            Windowsill gardening
    BT   **Gardening**
            Indoor gardening
    NT   **House plants**
    RT   **Container gardening**
            Flower gardening
Windowbox gardening
    USE   **Window gardening**
Windows   **721**
    BT   **Architecture—Details**
            Buildings
    NT   **Show windows**
Windows, Stained glass
    USE   **Glass painting and staining**
Windowsill gardening
    USE   **Window gardening**
Winds   **551.51**
    UF   Gales
            Wind
    BT   **Meteorology**
            Navigation
            Physical geography
            Weather

Winds—*Continued*
  NT **Cyclones**
      Hurricanes
      Tornadoes
      Typhoons
  RT **Storms**
Windsurfing (May subdiv. geog.) **797.3**
  UF Board sailing
      Sailboarding
  BT **Sailing**
Wine and wine making (May subdiv.
      geog.) **641.2; 663**
  UF Viticulture
  BT **Alcoholic beverages**
  RT **Grapes**
      Vineyards
Wing chun
  USE **Kung fu**
Winter **398.33; 578.43**
  BT **Seasons**
Winter gardening **635.9; 712**
      Use for materials on the culture of decora-
      tive plants that bloom outdoors in winter.
  BT **Gardening**
Winter resorts (May subdiv. geog.)
      796.9
  BT **Resorts**
  NT **Ski resorts**
Winter sports (May subdiv. geog.)
      796.9
  UF Ice sports
  SA types of winter sports [to be
      added as needed]
  BT **Sports**
  NT **Hockey**
      Ice skating
      Skiing
      Sled dog racing
      Sledding
      Snowboarding
Wire services
  USE **News agencies**
Wireless
  USE **Radio**
Wireless communication systems **384.5**
  UF Communication systems, Wire-
      less
      Wireless information networks
  BT **Telecommunication**
Wireless information networks
  USE **Wireless communication sys-
      tems**

Wiretapping **363.25**
  BT **Criminal investigation**
      Right of privacy
  RT **Eavesdropping**
Wiring, Electric
  USE **Electric wiring**
Wishes **153.8**
  BT **Motivation (Psychology)**
Wit and humor **808.7; 808.87**
      Use for individual works, collections, or
      materials about wit and humor.
  UF Facetiae
      Humor
  SA wit and humor of particular
      countries or ethnic groups,
      e.g. **American wit and hu-
      mor**; **Jewish wit and humor**,
      etc., and subjects with the
      subdivision *Humor*, e.g. **Mu-
      sic—Humor** [to be added as
      needed]
  BT **Literature**
  NT **American wit and humor**
      Black humor (Literature)
      Cartooning
      Chapbooks
      Comedies
      Comedy
      Comic books, strips, etc.
      English wit and humor
      Epigrams
      Humorists
      Humorous fiction
      Humorous poetry
      Jewish wit and humor
      Jokes
      Mock-heroic literature
      Music—Humor
      Nonsense verses
      Parody
      Practical jokes
      Puns
      Satire
      Tall tales
      **World War, 1939-1945—Hu-
      mor**
  RT **Anecdotes**
Witchcraft (May subdiv. geog.) **133.4**
  UF Black art (Magic)
      Black magic (Witchcraft)
      Sorcery

Witchcraft—*Continued*
- BT **Folklore**
-     **Occultism**
- NT **Witches**
- RT **Magic**
-     **Wicca**

Witches (May subdiv. geog.)   **133.4**
- UF Covens
- BT **Witchcraft**

Witnesses (May subdiv. geog.)   **345; 347**
- UF Cross-examination
- BT **Litigation**
-     **Trials**

Wives (May subdiv. geog.)   **306.872**
- UF Married women
-     Spouses
- BT **Family**
-     **Marriage**
-     **Married people**
-     **Women**

Wives of presidents—United States
- USE **Presidents' spouses—United States**

Wives, Runaway
- USE **Runaway adults**

Wok cooking   **641.7**
- BT **Cooking**

Wolf children
- USE **Wild children**

Woman
- USE **Women**

Woman-man relationship
- USE **Man-woman relationship**

Women (May subdiv. geog.)   **305.4**
- UF Woman
- SA women of particular racial, religious or ethnic groups, e.g. **Mexican American women**; **Jewish women**; women in various occupations and professions, e.g. **Women artists**; **Policewomen**; **Women in the motion picture industry**; etc.; and names of wars and military services with the subdivision *Women*, e.g. **World War, 1939-1945—Women** [to be added as needed]
- NT **Abused women**
-     **African American women**
-     **Black women**
-     **Businesswomen**
-     **Daughters**
-     **Jewish women**
-     **Lesbians**
-     **Mexican American women**
-     **Minority women**
-     **Mothers**
-     **Muslim women**
-     **Native American women**
-     **Nuns**
-     **Policewomen**
-     **Single women**
-     **Sisters**
-     **Widows**
-     **Wives**
-     **Women air pilots**
-     **Women artists**
-     **Women astronauts**
-     **Women athletes**
-     **Women authors**
-     **Women clergy**
-     **Women in medicine**
-     **Women in the military**
-     **Women in the motion picture industry**
-     **Women judges**
-     **Women physicians**
-     **World War, 1939-1945—Women**
-     **Young women**
- RT **Femininity**

Women actors
- USE **Actresses**

Women air pilots (May subdiv. geog.)   **629.13092; 920**
- BT **Air pilots**
-     **Women**

Women artists (May subdiv. geog.)   **709.2; 920**

  Use for materials on the attainments of several women in the area of art.
- BT **Artists**
-     **Women**

Women astronauts (May subdiv. geog.)   **629.450082**
- BT **Astronauts**
-     **Women**

Women athletes (May subdiv. geog.)   **796.082**
- BT **Athletes**
-     **Women**

Women authors 809; 920

Use for collections and for materials on the attainments of several women authors not limited to a single national literature or literary form.

SA   literary forms and national literatures with the subdivision *Women authors*, e.g. **American literature—Women authors** [to be added as needed]

BT   **Authors**

      Women

Women—Biography   920

BT   **Biography**

Women—Biography—Dictionaries

   920.72

Women, Black

USE   **Black women**

Women—Civil rights

USE   **Women's rights**

Women clergy (May subdiv. geog.)

   200.92; 270.092

BT   **Clergy**

      Women

RT   **Ordination of women**

Women—Clothing

USE   **Women's clothing**

Women—Clubs

USE   **Women—Societies**

Women—Diseases   616.0082; 618.1

UF   Diseases of women

      Gynecology

BT   **Diseases**

NT   **Breast cancer**

RT   **Women—Health and hygiene**

Women—Dress

USE   **Women's clothing**

Women—Education (May subdiv. geog.)

   371.822

UF   Education of women

BT   **Education**

RT   **Coeducation**

Women—Emancipation

USE   **Women's rights**

Women—Employment (May subdiv. geog.)   **331.4**

UF   Girls—Employment

      Working women

SA   women in various occupations and professions, e.g. **Women artists; Policewomen; Women in the motion picture industry**; etc. [to be added as needed]

BT   **Employment**

NT   **Equal pay for equal work**

      Self-employed women

Women—Enfranchisement

USE   **Women—Suffrage**

Women—Equal rights

USE   **Women's rights**

Women—Health and hygiene   613

UF   Gynecology

      Women—Hygiene

BT   **Health**

      Hygiene

NT   **Women—Mental health**

      Women—Physical fitness

RT   **Women—Diseases**

Women—History   305.409

Use for comprehensive materials on the history of women, their socio-economic, political, and legal position, their participation in historical events, and their contributions to society. Materials dealing specifically with women's social condition and status, including historical discussions of the same, are entered under **Women—Social conditions**.

BT   **Feminism**

      History

Women—Hygiene

USE   **Women—Health and hygiene**

Women—Identity   305.4

UF   Female identity

      Feminine identity

BT   **Identity (Psychology)**

Women in art   704.9

Use for materials on women depicted in works of art. Materials on the attainments of several women in the area of art are entered under **Women artists**.

BT   **Art—Themes**

Women in business

USE   **Businesswomen**

Women in literature   809

Use for materials on the theme of women in works of literature. Collections and materials on several women authors not limited to a single national literature or literary form are entered under **Women authors**.

BT   **Literature—Themes**

Women in medicine (May subdiv. geog.)

   610.82

BT   **Medical personnel**

      Women

Women in motion pictures   791.43

Use for materials discussing the portrayal of women in motion pictures. Materials discussing all aspects of women's involvement in motion pictures are entered under **Women in the motion picture industry**.

BT   **Motion pictures**

Women in television

USE   **Women on television**

Women in television broadcasting   384.55; 791.45

Use for materials on all aspects of women's involvement in the television industry. Materials on the portrayal of women in television programs are entered under **Women on television**.

UF   Women in the television industry

BT   **Television broadcasting**

Women in the armed forces

USE   **Women in the military**

Women in the Bible   220.8

UF   Bible—Women

Women in the military (May subdiv. geog.)   **355.0082**

UF   Armed forces—Women

Women in the armed forces

BT   **Military personnel**

Women

Women in the motion picture industry   791.43

Use for materials discussing all aspects of women's involvement in motion pictures. Materials discussing the portrayal of women in motion pictures are entered under **Women in motion pictures**.

BT   **Motion picture industry**

Women

Women in the television industry

USE   **Women in television broadcasting**

Women judges (May subdiv. geog.)   **347; 920**

BT   **Judges**

Women

Women-men relationship

USE   **Man-woman relationship**

Women—Mental health   362.2

BT   **Mental health**

Women—Health and hygiene

RT   **Women—Psychology**

Women on television   791.45

Use for materials on the portrayal of women in television programs. Materials on all aspects of women's involvement in the televi-

sion industry are entered under **Women in television broadcasting**.

UF   Women in television

BT   **Television**

Women—Ordination

USE   **Ordination of women**

Women—Physical fitness   613.7

BT   **Physical fitness**

Women—Health and hygiene

Women physicians (May subdiv. geog.)   **610.69; 920**

BT   **Physicians**

Women

Women police officers

USE   **Policewomen**

Women—Political activity (May subdiv. geog.)   **324**

BT   **Political participation**

NT   **Women politicians**

Women politicians (May subdiv. geog.)   **324.2092; 920**

BT   **Politicians**

Women—Political activity

Women—Psychology   155.3

UF   Feminine psychology

BT   **Psychology**

RT   **Women—Mental health**

Women—Relations with men

USE   **Man-woman relationship**

Women—Religious life   204; 248.4

BT   **Religious life**

Women—Self-defense

USE   **Self-defense for women**

Women, Self-employed

USE   **Self-employed women**

Women—Social conditions (May subdiv. geog.)   **305.42**

Use for materials dealing specifically with women's social condition and status, including historical discussions of the same. Comprehensive materials on the history of women are entered under **Women—History**.

BT   **Social conditions**

NT   **Prostitution**

Women's movement

Women—Societies (May subdiv. geog.)   **367**

UF   Women—Clubs

Women's clubs

Women's organizations

BT   **Clubs**

Societies

Women—Sports
USE **Sports for women**
Women—**Suffrage** (May subdiv. geog.)
324.6
UF Women—Enfranchisement
Women's suffrage
BT **Suffrage**
Women's rights
RT **Suffragists**
Women—United States 305.40973
Women's clothing (May subdiv. geog.)
646
UF Women—Clothing
Women—Dress
BT **Clothing and dress**
Women's clubs
USE **Women—Societies**
Women's friendship
USE **Female friendship**
Women's liberation movement
USE **Women's movement**
Women's movement (May subdiv. geog.)
305.42; 323.3
Use for materials on activities aimed at ob-
taining equal rights and opportunities for
women. Materials on the theory of the politi-
cal and social equality of the sexes and wom-
en's perspectives on various subjects are en-
tered under **Feminism**.
UF Women's liberation movement
BT **Women—Social conditions**
Women's rights
RT **Feminism**
Women's organizations
USE **Women—Societies**
Women's rights (May subdiv. geog.)
323.3; 342
UF Emancipation of women
Rights of women
Women—Civil rights
Women—Emancipation
Women—Equal rights
BT **Civil rights**
Sex discrimination
NT **Women—Suffrage**
Women's movement
RT **Feminism**
Pro-choice movement
Pro-life movement
Women's self-defense
USE **Self-defense for women**
Women's suffrage
USE **Women—Suffrage**

Wonder Woman (Fictional character)
741.5
BT **Superheroes**
Wonders
USE **Curiosities and wonders**
Wood (May subdiv. geog.) **620.1; 674**
UF Timber
Woods
SA types of wood, e.g. **Oak** [to be
added as needed]
BT **Building materials**
Forest products
Fuel
Trees
NT **Lumber and lumbering**
Oak
Plywood
Woodwork
RT **Forests and forestry**
Wood block printing
USE **Wood engraving**
Woodcuts
Wood-burning
USE **Pyrography**
Wood carving 731.4; 736
UF Carving, Wood
Whittling
BT **Carving (Decorative arts)**
Decoration and ornament
Woodwork
Wood engraving 761
UF Block printing
Wood block printing
BT **Engraving**
Wood finishing 698
BT **Finishes and finishing**
NT **Furniture finishing**
Wood—Preservation 674
UF Preservation of wood
Wood toy making
USE **Wooden toy making**
Wood turning
USE **Turning**
Woodcuts 761
UF Block printing
Wood block printing
BT **Prints**
Wooden toy making 745.592
UF Wood toy making
BT **Toy making**
Woodwork

Woods
USE   **Forests and forestry**
       Lumber and lumbering
       Wood
Woodwind instruments   877.2
    BT   **Wind instruments**
Woodwork (May subdiv. geog.)   **684**
    BT   **Architecture—Details**
          Decorative arts
          Wood
    NT   **Furniture making**
          Pyrography
          Wood carving
          Wooden toy making
    RT   **Cabinetwork**
          Carpentry
          Turning
Woodworking machinery   621.9; 684
    SA   types of woodworking machines
          [to be added as needed]
    BT   **Machinery**
    NT   **Lathes**
Wool (May subdiv. geog.)   **677**
    BT   **Animal products**
          Fabrics
          Fibers
Word books
    USE   **Picture dictionaries**
Word building
    USE   **Word skills**
Word (Computer software)
    USE   **Microsoft Word (Computer**
           software)
Word games   793.734
    SA   types of word games, e.g.
          Crossword puzzles [to be
          added as needed]
    BT   **Games**
          Literary recreations
    NT   **Crossword puzzles**
Word histories
    USE   **Language and languages—Ety-**
           mology
Word problems (Mathematics)   510
    BT   **Mathematics**
Word processing   005.52
    BT   **Office management**
          Office practice
    RT   **Desktop publishing**
          Word processing software
Word processing software   005.52

    BT   **Computer software**
    RT   **Word processing**
Word processor keyboarding
    USE   **Keyboarding (Electronics)**
Word recognition   372.46
    BT   **Reading**
          Vocabulary
Word skills   372.4; 418
    Use for educational materials on conso-
    nants, blends, vowels, prefixes and suffixes,
    digraphs, syllables, root words, rhyming, and
    alphabet, etc.
    UF   Word building
          Words
    BT   **Reading**
    RT   **English language—Spelling**
Wordless stories
    USE   **Stories without words**
Words
    USE   **Vocabulary**
           Word skills
Words, New
    USE   **New words**
Work   158.7; 306.3
    Use for materials on the physical or mental
    exertion of individuals to produce or accom-
    plish something. Materials on the collective
    human activities involved in the production
    and distribution of goods and services in an
    economy, as well as materials on the group of
    workers who render these services for wages,
    are entered under **Labor**.
    NT   **Job satisfaction**
          Performance
          Vocation
          Work and family
          Work environment
          Work ethic
    RT   **Labor**
          Occupations
Work addiction
    USE   **Workaholism**
Work and family (May subdiv. geog.)
          306.3; 306.87; 646.7
    Use for materials on the conflict or balance
    in people's lives between the demands of
    work and family.
    UF   Family and work
    BT   **Family**
          Work
    RT   **Dual-career families**
Work at home
    USE   **Home-based business**
           Telecommuting

Work-based learning
    USE **Cooperative education**
Work environment (May subdiv. geog.)
        331.25; 620.8
    UF Places of work
        Work places
        Working environment
        Workplace environment
        Worksite environment
    BT **Environment**
        Work
    NT **Machinery in the workplace**
        Teams in the workplace
        Violence in the workplace
Work ethic (May subdiv. geog.)   **174**
    UF Protestant work ethic
    BT **Ethics**
        Work
Work groups
    USE **Teams in the workplace**
Work—Law and legislation
    USE **Labor laws and legislation**
Work performance standards
    USE **Performance standards**
Work places
    USE **Work environment**
Work satisfaction
    USE **Job satisfaction**
Work standards
    USE **Production standards**
Work stoppages
    USE **Strikes**
Work stress
    USE **Job stress**
Work teams
    USE **Teams in the workplace**
Workaholic syndrome
    USE **Workaholism**
Workaholism   **155.2; 616.85**
    UF Addiction to work
        Compulsive working
        Work addiction
        Workaholic syndrome
    BT **Compulsive behavior**
Workers
    USE **Employees**
        Labor
        Working class
Workers' compensation (May subdiv.
    geog.)   **368.4**

    UF Compensation
        Employers' liability
        Insurance, Workers' compensa-
        tion
        Workmen's compensation
    BT **Accident insurance**
        Health insurance
        Social security
Workers' participation in management
    USE **Participative management**
Workforce diversity
    USE **Diversity in the workplace**
Working animals   **636.088**
    SA animals in specific working situ-
        ations [to be added as need-
        ed]
    BT **Animals**
        Domestic animals
        Economic zoology
    NT **Animals in police work**
        Animals—War use
        Working dogs
Working at home
    USE **Home-based business**
        Telecommuting
Working children
    USE **Child labor**
Working class (May subdiv. geog.)
        305.5
    Use for materials on the social class com-
    posed of persons who work for wages, usually
    in manual labor.
    UF Blue collar workers
        Factory workers
        Industrial workers
        Labor and laboring classes
        Laborers
        Laboring class
        Laboring classes
        Manual workers
        Workers
        Working classes
    BT **Social classes**
    NT **Proletariat**
    RT **Labor**
Working classes
    USE **Working class**
Working couples
    USE **Dual-career families**
Working day
    USE **Hours of labor**
Working dogs   **362.4; 636.73**

Working dogs—*Continued*
   BT   **Dogs**
         Working animals
   NT   **Guide dogs**
         Hearing ear dogs
Working environment
   USE **Work environment**
Working hours
   USE **Hours of labor**
Working parents' children
   USE **Children of working parents**
Working robots
   USE **Industrial robots**
Working women
   USE **Women—Employment**
Workmen's compensation
   USE **Workers' compensation**
Workplace environment
   USE **Work environment**
Workplace violence
   USE **Violence in the workplace**
Workshop councils
   USE **Participative management**
Workshops, Teachers'
   USE **Teachers' workshops**
Worksite environment
   USE **Work environment**
World
   USE **Earth**
World economics
   USE **Commercial geography**
         Commercial policy
         Economic conditions
         International competition
World government
   USE **International organization**
World history   **909**
   UF   Universal history
   BT   **History**
   NT   **Ancient history**
         Geography
         Middle Ages
         Modern history
World history—12th century   **909**
   UF   Twelfth century
   SA   names of regions, countries, cities, etc., with the subdivision *History—12th century* [to be added as needed]
   BT   **Middle Ages**
World history—13th century   **909**
   UF   Thirteenth century

   SA   names of regions, countries, cities, etc., with the subdivision *History—13th century* [to be added as needed]
   BT   **Middle Ages**
World history—14th century   **909**
   UF   Fourteenth century
   SA   names of regions, countries, cities, etc., with the subdivision *History—14th century* [to be added as needed]
   BT   **Middle Ages**
World history—15th century   **909**
   UF   Fifteenth century
   SA   names of regions, countries, cities, etc., with the subdivision *History—15th century* [to be added as needed]
   BT   **Middle Ages**
World history—16th century   **909**
   UF   History, Modern—16th century
         Sixteenth century
   SA   names of regions, countries, cities, etc., with the subdivision *History—16th century* [to be added as needed]
World history—17th century   **909**
   UF   History, Modern—17th century
         Seventeenth century
   SA   names of regions, countries, cities, etc., with the subdivision *History—17th century* [to be added as needed]
World history—18th century   **909.7**
   UF   Eighteenth century
         History, Modern—18th century
   SA   names of regions, countries, cities, etc., with the subdivision *History—18th century* [to be added as needed]
World history—19th century   **909.81**
   UF   History, Modern—19th century
         Modern history—1800-1899 (19th century)
         Nineteenth century
   SA   names of regions, countries, cities, etc., with the subdivision *History—19th century* [to be added as needed]
World history—20th century   **909.82**

World history—20th century—*Continued*

> UF History, Modern—20th century
> Modern history—1900-1999
> (20th century)
> Twentieth century
> SA names of regions, countries, cities, etc., with the subdivision *History—20th century* [to be added as needed]
> NT **Nineteen eighties**
> **Nineteen fifties**
> **Nineteen forties**
> **Nineteen nineties**
> **Nineteen seventies**
> **Nineteen sixties**
> **Nineteen thirties**
> **Nineteen twenties**
> **World War, 1914-1918**
> **World War, 1939-1945**

World history—1945-   909.82

> UF History, Modern—1945-
> Modern history—1945-

World history—21st century   909.83

> UF History, Modern—21st century
> Twenty-first century
> SA names of regions, countries, cities, etc., with the subdivision *History—21st century* [to be added as needed]

World language

> USE **Universal language**

World order

> USE **International relations**

World organization

> USE **International organization**

World politics   909

> Use for historical accounts of international political affairs. Materials on the theory of international relations are entered under **International relations**.
>
> UF International politics
> SA names of countries with the subdivisions *Foreign relations* and *Politics and government* [to be added as needed]
> BT **Political science**
> NT **United States—Foreign relations**
> **World War, 1914-1918**
> **World War, 1939-1945**
> **World War III**

> RT **Geopolitics**
> **International organization**
> **International relations**

World politics—1945-   909.82

World politics—1945-1965   909.82

World politics—1945-1991   909.82

> NT **Cold war**

World politics—1965-   909.82

World politics—1991-   909.82

World records   030

> UF Human records
> Records of achievement
> Records, World
> World's records
> BT **Curiosities and wonders**
> RT **Sports records**

World Trade Center (New York, N.Y.) terrorist attack, 2001

> USE **September 11 terrorist attacks, 2001**

World War I

> USE **World War, 1914-1918**

World War II

> USE **World War, 1939-1945**

World War, 1914-1918 (May subdiv. geog.)   **940.3; 940.4**

> May be subdivided like **World War, 1939-1945**.
>
> UF First World War
> World War I
> BT **Europe—History—1871-1918**
> **World history—20th century**
> **World politics**

World War, 1914-1918—Chemical warfare   940.4

> UF World War, 1914-1918—Gas warfare
> BT **Chemical warfare**

World War, 1914-1918—Economic aspects   940.3

> RT **Reconstruction (1914-1939)**

World War, 1914-1918—Gas warfare

> USE **World War, 1914-1918—Chemical warfare**

World War, 1914-1918—Peace   940.3

> BT **Peace**
> NT **League of Nations**

World War, 1914-1918—Reconstruction

> USE **Reconstruction (1914-1939)**

World War, 1914-1918—Territorial questions (May subdiv. geog.)   **940.3**

> BT **Boundaries**

World War, 1914-1918—United States
940.3; 940.4; 973.91

UF   United States—History—1914-1918, World War

      United States—World War, 1914-1918

World War, 1939-1945 (May subdiv. geog.) 940.53; 940.54

Subdivisions used under this heading may be used under other wars.

UF   Second World War

      World War II

SA   names of battles, campaigns, sieges, etc., e.g. **Ardennes, Battle of the, 1944-1945; Pearl Harbor (Oahu, Hawaii), Attack on, 1941**; etc. [to be added as needed]

BT   **Europe—History—1918-1945**

      World history—20th century

      World politics

World War, 1939-1945—Aerial operations 940.54

UF   World War, 1939-1945—Battles, sieges, etc.

BT   **Military aeronautics**

World War, 1939-1945—African Americans 940.53; 940.54

BT   **African Americans**

World War, 1939-1945—Amphibious operations 940.54

BT   **World War, 1939-1945—Naval operations**

World War, 1939-1945—Antiwar movements

USE   **World War, 1939-1945—Protest movements**

World War, 1939-1945—Armistices 940.53

World War, 1939-1945—Arms

USE   **World War, 1939-1945—Equipment and supplies**

World War, 1939-1945—Art and the war 940.53

UF   World War, 1939-1945—Iconography

      World War, 1939-1945, in art

BT   **Art**

World War, 1939-1945—Atrocities 940.54

SA   names of specific atrocities and crimes [to be added as needed]

BT   **Atrocities**

NT   **Handicapped—Nazi persecution**

World War, 1939-1945—Battlefields 940.54

World War, 1939-1945—Battles, sieges, etc.

USE   **World War, 1939-1945—Aerial operations**

      World War, 1939-1945—Campaigns

      World War, 1939-1945—Naval operations

World War, 1939-1945—Biography 920

BT   **Biography**

World War, 1939-1945—Blockades 940.54

World War, 1939-1945—Campaigns (May subdiv. geog.) 940.54

UF   World War, 1939-1945—Battles, sieges, etc.

SA   names of battles, campaigns, sieges, etc., e.g. **Ardennes (France), Battle of the, 1944-1945** [to be added as needed]

NT   **Ardennes (France), Battle of the, 1944-1945**

      Normandy (France), Attack on, 1944

      Pearl Harbor (Oahu, Hawaii), Attack on, 1941

World War, 1939-1945—Cartoons and caricatures 940.53

BT   **Cartoons and caricatures**

World War, 1939-1945—Casualties (May subdiv. geog.) 940.54

BT   **War casualties**

World War, 1939-1945—Casualties—Statistics 940.54

World War, 1939-1945—Casualties—United States 940.54

UF   United States—World War, 1939-1945—Casualties

World War, 1939-1945—Casualties—United States—Statistics 940.54

UF   United States—World War, 1939-1945—Casualties—Statistics

World War, 1939-1945—Causes   940.53
  NT   National socialism
World War, 1939-1945—Censorship
    940.54
  BT   Censorship
World War, 1939-1945—Charities
  USE   World War, 1939-1945—Civil-
      ian relief
      World War, 1939-1945—War
      work
World War, 1939-1945—Chemical war-
    fare   940.54
  BT   Chemical warfare
World War, 1939-1945—Children
    940.53
  BT   Children and war
World War, 1939-1945—Civilian evacua-
    tion
  USE   World War, 1939-1945—Evac-
      uation of civilians
World War, 1939-1945—Civilian relief
    940.54
  UF   World War, 1939-1945—Chari-
      ties
  BT   Charities
      Food relief
      Foreign aid
      Reconstruction (1939-1951)
      World War, 1939-1945—War
      work
  RT   World War, 1939-1945—Refu-
      gees
World War, 1939-1945—Collaborationists
    940.53
  UF   Fifth column
      Quislings
  BT   Collaborationists
World War, 1939-1945—Conferences
    940.53
  UF   World War, 1939-1945—Con-
      gresses
  BT   Conferences
World War, 1939-1945—Congresses
  USE   World War, 1939-1945—Con-
      ferences
World War, 1939-1945—Conscientious
    objectors   940.53
  BT   Conscientious objectors
World War, 1939-1945—Correspondents
  USE   World War, 1939-1945—Jour-
      nalists

World War, 1939-1945—Desertions
    940.54
  BT   Military desertion
World War, 1939-1945—Destruction and
    pillage   940.54
World War, 1939-1945—Diplomatic his-
    tory   940.53
  NT   World War, 1939-1945—Gov-
      ernments in exile
World War, 1939-1945—Displaced persons
  USE   World War, 1939-1945—Refu-
      gees
World War, 1939-1945—Draft resisters
    940.54
  BT   Draft resisters
World War, 1939-1945—Economic as-
    pects   940.53
    Use for materials on the economic causes
    of the war and the effect of the war on com-
    merce and industry.
  BT   War—Economic aspects
  NT   World War, 1939-1945—Fi-
      nance
      World War, 1939-1945—
      Manpower
      World War, 1939-1945—Repa-
      rations
  RT   Reconstruction (1939-1951)
World War, 1939-1945—Education and
    the war   940.53
  BT   Education
World War, 1939-1945—Engineering and
    construction   940.54
  BT   Military engineering
World War, 1939-1945—Equipment and
    supplies   940.54
  UF   World War, 1939-1945—Arms
      World War, 1939-1945—Military
      supplies
      World War, 1939-1945—Military
      weapons
      World War, 1939-1945—Ord-
      nance
      World War, 1939-1945—Sup-
      plies
      World War, 1939-1945—Weap-
      ons
  BT   Military weapons
World War, 1939-1945—Ethical aspects
    940.53
  UF   World War, 1939-1945—Moral
      and religious aspects

World War, 1939-1945—Ethical aspects—
Continued
  BT **Ethics**
**World War, 1939-1945—Evacuation of
  civilians 940.54**
  UF Civilian evacuation
      World War, 1939-1945—Civilian
        evacuation
  BT **Civil defense**
      **World War, 1939-1945—Refu-
        gees**
  NT **Japanese Americans—Evacua-
        tion and relocation, 1942-
        1945**
World War, 1939-1945—Fiction 808.83
  Use for collections of stories dealing with
  the Second World War. Materials about the
  depiction of the war in literature are entered
  under **World War, 1939-1945—Literature
  and the war**.
**World War, 1939-1945—Finance
  940.53**
  Use for materials on the cost and financing
  of the war, including war debts, and the effect
  of the war on financial systems, including in-
  flation.
  BT **World War, 1939-1945—Eco-
        nomic aspects**
**World War, 1939-1945—Food supply
  940.53**
  BT **Food relief**
**World War, 1939-1945—Forced repatria-
  tion 940.53**
  RT **World War, 1939-1945—Refu-
        gees**
**World War, 1939-1945—Governments in
  exile 940.53**
  BT **World War, 1939-1945—Diplo-
        matic history**
World War, 1939-1945—Guerrillas
  USE **World War, 1939-1945—Un-
        derground movements**
**World War, 1939-1945—Health aspects
  940.54**
World War, 1939-1945—Hospitals
  USE **World War, 1939-1945—Medi-
        cal care**
World War, 1939-1945—Human resources
  USE **World War, 1939-1945—
        Manpower**
World War, 1939-1945—Humor 940.53
  BT **Wit and humor**

World War, 1939-1945—Iconography
  USE **World War, 1939-1945—Art
        and the war**
World War, 1939-1945, in art
  USE **World War, 1939-1945—Art
        and the war**
World War, 1939-1945, in literature
  USE **World War, 1939-1945—Liter-
        ature and the war**
World War, 1939-1945, in motion pictures
  USE **World War, 1939-1945—Mo-
        tion pictures and the war**
**World War, 1939-1945—Influence
  940.53**
World War, 1939-1945—Jews 940.53
  BT **Jews**
  RT **Holocaust, 1933-1945**
**World War, 1939-1945—Jews—Rescue
  940.54**
  UF Rescue of Jews, 1939-1945
  BT **Jews—Persecutions**
  NT **Righteous Gentiles in the
        Holocaust**
**World War, 1939-1945—Journalists
  940.54**
  UF World War, 1939-1945—Corre-
        spondents
      World War, 1939-1945—War
        correspondents
  BT **Journalists**
**World War, 1939-1945—Literature and
  the war 809; 940.53**
  Use for materials on the depiction of the
  war in literature. Collections of stories dealing
  with the Second World War are entered under
  World War, 1939-1945—Fiction.
  UF World War, 1939-1945, in litera-
        ture
  BT **Literature**
**World War, 1939-1945—Manpower
  940.54**
  UF World War, 1939-1945—Human
        resources
  BT **World War, 1939-1945—Eco-
        nomic aspects**
World War, 1939-1945—Maps 940.53
  BT **Maps**
**World War, 1939-1945—Medical care
  940.54**
  UF World War, 1939-1945—Hospi-
        tals
  BT **Medical care**

World War, 1939-1945—Military intelligence   940.54
   BT   **Military intelligence**
World War, 1939-1945—Military supplies
   USE   **World War, 1939-1945—Equipment and supplies**
World War, 1939-1945—Military weapons
   USE   **World War, 1939-1945—Equipment and supplies**
World War, 1939-1945—Missing in action   940.54
   BT   **Missing in action**
       World War, 1939-1945—Prisoners and prisons
World War, 1939-1945—Monuments   725
   BT   **Monuments**
World War, 1939-1945—Moral and religious aspects
   USE   **World War, 1939-1945—Ethical aspects**
       World War, 1939-1945—Religious aspects
World War, 1939-1945—Motion pictures and the war   791.43; 940.53

Use for materials about films dealing with the Second World War or about the use of motion pictures in the war effort.

   UF   World War, 1939-1945, in motion pictures
   BT   **Motion pictures**
       War films
World War, 1939-1945—Museums   940.53
   BT   **Museums**
World War, 1939-1945—Naval operations   940.54
   UF   World War, 1939-1945—Battles, sieges, etc.
   NT   **World War, 1939-1945—Amphibious operations**
World War, 1939-1945—Naval operations—Submarine   940.54
   UF   World War, 1939-1945—Submarine operations
   BT   **Submarine warfare**
World War, 1939-1945—Occupied territories   940.54
   SA   names of occupied countries with the appropriate subdivision under *History*, e.g.,

Netherlands—History—1940-1945, German occupation; Japan—History—1945-1952, Allied occupation; etc. [to be added as needed]
   BT   **Military occupation**
       World War, 1939-1945—Territorial questions
World War, 1939-1945—Ordnance
   USE   **World War, 1939-1945—Equipment and supplies**
World War, 1939-1945—Peace   940.53
World War, 1939-1945—Personal narratives   940.53; 940.54

Use for collective or individual eyewitness reports or autobiographical accounts of the war in general. Accounts limited to a specific topic are entered under that topic.

   BT   **Autobiographies**
       Biography
World War, 1939-1945—Pictorial works   940.53022
World War, 1939-1945—Poetry   808.81

Use for collections of poetry dealing with the Second World War.

   BT   **Historical poetry**
       War poetry
World War, 1939-1945—Prisoners and prisons   940.54
   BT   **Concentration camps**
       Prisoners of war
       Prisons
   NT   **World War, 1939-1945—Missing in action**
World War, 1939-1945—Propaganda   940.54
   BT   **Propaganda**
World War, 1939-1945—Protest movements   940.53
   UF   World War, 1939-1945—Antiwar movements
       World War, 1939-1945—Protests, demonstrations, etc.
   BT   **Protest movements**
World War, 1939-1945—Protests, demonstrations, etc.
   USE   **World War, 1939-1945—Protest movements**
World War, 1939-1945—Psychological aspects   940.53
   BT   **Psychological warfare**
World War, 1939-1945—Public opinion   940.53

World War, 1939-1945—Public opinion—
Continued
- BT **Public opinion**

World War, 1939-1945—Railroads
- USE **World War, 1939-1945—Transportation**

World War, 1939-1945—Reconstruction
- USE **Reconstruction (1939-1951)**

World War, 1939-1945—Refugees
940.53
- UF World War, 1939-1945—Displaced persons
- BT **Political refugees**
- NT **World War, 1939-1945—Evacuation of civilians**
- RT **World War, 1939-1945—Civilian relief**
  World War, 1939-1945—Forced repatriation

World War, 1939-1945—Regimental histories 940.54

World War, 1939-1945—Religious aspects 940.53
- UF World War, 1939-1945—Moral and religious aspects

World War, 1939-1945—Reparations
940.53
- BT **Reconstruction (1939-1951)**
  World War, 1939-1945—Economic aspects

World War, 1939-1945—Resistance movements
- USE **World War, 1939-1945—Underground movements**

World War, 1939-1945—Secret service
940.54
- BT **Secret service**

World War, 1939-1945—Social aspects
940.53

World War, 1939-1945—Social work
- USE **World War, 1939-1945—War work**

World War, 1939-1945—Songs 782.42
- UF World War, 1939-1945—Songs and music
- BT **Military music**
  War songs

World War, 1939-1945—Songs and music
- USE **World War, 1939-1945—Songs**

World War, 1939-1945—Sources
940.53

World War, 1939-1945—Submarine operations
- USE **World War, 1939-1945—Naval operations—Submarine**

World War, 1939-1945—Supplies
- USE **World War, 1939-1945—Equipment and supplies**

World War, 1939-1945—Tank warfare
940.54
- BT **Tank warfare**

World War, 1939-1945—Territorial questions (May subdiv. geog.) **940.53**
- BT **Boundaries**
- NT **World War, 1939-1945—Occupied territories**

World War, 1939-1945—Theater and the war 792; 940.53
- BT **Theater**

World War, 1939-1945—Transportation
940.54
- UF World War, 1939-1945—Railroads
- BT **Transportation**

World War, 1939-1945—Treaties
940.53
- BT **Treaties**

World War, 1939-1945—Underground movements 940.54
- UF Anti-fascist movements
  Anti-Nazi movement
  World War, 1939-1945—Guerrillas
  World War, 1939-1945—Resistance movements

World War, 1939-1945—United States
940.53; 940.54; 973.917
- UF United States—History—1939-1945, World War
  United States—World War, 1939-1945

World War, 1939-1945—Veterans (May subdiv. geog.) **305.9**
- BT **Veterans**

World War, 1939-1945—War correspondents
- USE **World War, 1939-1945—Journalists**

World War, 1939-1945—War work
940.53
- UF World War, 1939-1945—Charities

World War, 1939-1945—War work—*Continued*

World War, 1939-1945—Social work

NT **World War, 1939-1945—Civilian relief**

World War, 1939-1945—Weapons

USE **World War, 1939-1945—Equipment and supplies**

World War, 1939-1945—Women
940.53; 940.54

BT **Women**

World War III   355

UF Third World War

BT **War**

World politics

World Wide Web   004.67

UF World Wide Web (Information retrieval system)

BT **Internet**

NT **Web search engines**

Web servers

World Wide Web (Information retrieval system)

USE **World Wide Web**

World Wide Web pages

USE **Web sites**

World Wide Web searching

USE **Internet searching**

Web search engines

World Wide Web servers

USE **Web servers**

World Wide Web sites

USE **Web sites**

World's Fair (1992: Seville, Spain)

USE **Expo 92 (Seville, Spain)**

World's fairs

USE **Exhibitions**

Fairs

World's records

USE **World records**

Worms   592

BT **Animals**

Worry   152.4

BT **Emotions**

RT **Anxiety**

Worship   203; 248.3; 264

UF Devotion

BT **Religion**

Theology

NT **Church year**

Devotional exercises

Interfaith worship

Praise of God

Prayer

Public worship

Sacrifice

Worship of the dead

USE **Ancestor worship**

Worship programs   264

Use for individual works or collections of services of any type for use in public worship other than authorized standard liturgies.

UF Services of worship

Worship services

BT **Public worship**

RT **Liturgies**

Worship services

USE **Worship programs**

Worth

USE **Values**

Wounded, First aid to

USE **First aid**

Wounds and injuries   617.1

UF Injuries

SA classes of persons, animals, organs of the body, and plants and crops with the subdivision *Wounds and injuries*, e.g. **Horses—Wounds and injuries**; **Foot—Wounds and injuries**; etc. [to be added as needed]

BT **Accidents**

NT **Disabilities**

Fractures

Wrapping of gifts

USE **Gift wrapping**

Wrath

USE **Anger**

Wrecks

USE **Accidents**

Wrestling (May subdiv. geog.)   **796.812**

BT **Athletics**

Writers

USE **Authors**

Writing   411

Use for materials on the process or result of recording language in the form of conventionalized visible marks or signs on a surface. Materials limited to writing with a pen or pencil and practical or prescriptive guides to penmanship or the art of writing are entered under **Handwriting**. Materials on handwriting as an expression of the writer's character are entered under **Graphology**. Materials on the

Writing—*Continued*

alphabet or writing of a particular language are entered under the name of the language with the subdivisions *Alphabet* and *Writing*.

   BT   **Communication**
         Language and languages
         Language arts
   NT   **Abbreviations**
         Alphabet
         Autographs
         Braille
         Calligraphy
         Cryptography
         Graphology
         Handwriting
         Hieroglyphics
         Picture writing
         Shorthand
         Typewriting
         Writing of numerals
   RT   **Ciphers**

Writing (Authorship)
   USE   **Authorship**
          Creative writing

Writing of numerals   513
   UF   Numeral formation
         Numeral writing
         Numerals, Writing of
   BT   **Handwriting**
         Numerals
         Writing

Writing—Patterning
   USE   **Language arts—Patterning**

Writing—Study and teaching
   USE   **Handwriting**

Writings of gay men
   USE   **Gay men's writings**

Writings of lesbians
   USE   **Lesbians' writings**

Writings of teenagers
   USE   **Teenagers' writings**

Wrought iron work
   USE   **Ironwork**

X-15 (Rocket aircraft)   629.133
   BT   **Rocket planes**

X-rays   539.7
   UF   Radiography
         Roentgen rays
         X rays
   BT   **Electromagnetic waves**
         Radiation

   NT   **Gamma rays**
         Tomography
   RT   **Radiotherapy**
         Vacuum tubes

X rays
   USE   **X-rays**

Xeriscaping   635.9
   UF   Waterwise gardening
   BT   **Landscape gardening**
         Water conservation

Xerographic art
   USE   **Copy art**

Xerography
   USE   **Photocopying**

YA literature
   USE   **Young adult literature**

Yacht basins
   USE   **Marinas**

Yachting
   USE   **Yachts and yachting**

Yachts and yachting (May subdiv. geog.)
            797.1
   UF   Yachting
   BT   **Boatbuilding**
         Boats and boating
         Ocean travel
         Ships
         Voyages and travels
         Water sports
   NT   **Marinas**
   RT   **Sailing**

Yaoi
   USE   **Shonen-ai**

Yard sales
   USE   **Garage sales**

Yarn   677
   NT   **Cotton**
         Flax
   RT   **Spinning**

Yearbooks   050
   UF   Annuals
   SA   subjects with the subdivision *Periodicals*, e.g. **Engineering—Periodicals** [to be added as needed]
   BT   **Serial publications**
   NT   **School yearbooks**
   RT   **Almanacs**

Yeast   641.3
   BT   **Fungi**

Yellow fever   616.9

Yellow fever—*Continued*
  BT **Tropical medicine**
Yeti 001.9
  UF Abominable snowman
  BT **Monsters**
      Mythical animals
Yiddish language 439
    May be subdivided like **English language**.
  UF Jewish language
      Jews—Language
  BT **Language and languages**
Yiddish literature 839
    May use same subdivisions and names of literary forms as for **English literature**.
  BT **Jewish literature**
Yoga 181; 613.7
  BT **Hindu philosophy**
      Hinduism
      Theosophy
  NT **Chakras**
      Hatha yoga
Yoga exercises
  USE **Hatha yoga**
Yoga, Hatha
  USE **Hatha yoga**
Yom Kippur 296.4
  UF Atonement, Day of
      Day of Atonement
  BT **Jewish holidays**
Yom Kippur War, 1973
  USE **Israel-Arab War, 1973**
Yoruba (African people) 305.896
  BT **Africans**
      Indigenous peoples
Yosemite National Park (Calif.) 719; 979.4
  BT **National parks and reserves— United States**
Yosemite National Park (Calif.)—Pictorial works 979.4
Young adult literature 808; 808.8; 809
    Use for collections or materials about literature published for teenage readers. Materials on the reading interests of teenagers and lists of books for teenagers are entered under **Teenagers—Books and reading**.
  UF Books for teenagers
      Teenage literature
      Teenagers—Literature
      YA literature
      Young adults' literature
  BT **Literature**

Young adults
  USE **Teenagers**
       Youth
Young adults—Books and reading
  USE **Teenagers—Books and reading**
Young adults' libraries (May subdiv. geog.) 027.62
  UF Library services to teenagers
      Library services to young adults
      Young adults' library services
  BT **Libraries**
Young adults' library services
  USE **Young adults' libraries**
Young adults' literature
  USE **Young adult literature**
Young consumers 640.73; 658.8
  UF Children as consumers
      Teenage consumers
      Youth market
  BT **Consumers**
Young men (May subdiv. geog.) 305.31
    Use for materials on men in the general age range of eighteen through twenty-five years. Materials on the time of life between thirteen and twenty-five, as well as on people in that greater age range are entered under **Youth**.
  BT **Men**
      Youth
  RT **Boys**
Young people
  USE **Teenagers**
       Youth
Young persons
  USE **Teenagers**
       Youth
Young women (May subdiv. geog.) 305.4
    Use for materials on women in the general age range of eighteen through twenty-five years. Materials on the time of life between thirteen and twenty-five, as well as on people in that greater age range are entered under **Youth**.
  BT **Women**
      Youth
  RT **Girls**
Youngest child
  USE **Birth order**
Youth (May subdiv. geog.) 305.235
    Use for materials on the time of life between thirteen and twenty-five years, as well as on people in this general age range. Materials limited to teen youth are entered under **Teenagers**. Materials limited to people in the general age range of eighteen through twenty-

Youth—*Continued*

five years of age are entered under **Young men** or **Young women**. Materials on the process or state of growing up are entered under **Adolescence**.

> UF Young adults
> Young people
> Young persons
> SA youth of particular racial or ethnic groups [to be added as needed]
> BT **Age**
> NT **African American youth**
> **Church work with youth**
> **Dropouts**
> **Minority youth**
> **Teenagers**
> **Television and youth**
> **Young men**
> **Young women**

Youth—Alcohol use (May subdiv. geog.)
  616.86; 613.81

> UF Alcohol and youth
> Drinking and youth
> NT **Drinking age**

Youth and drugs
> USE **Youth—Drug use**

Youth and narcotics
> USE **Youth—Drug use**

Youth and television
> USE **Television and youth**

Youth—Drug use (May subdiv. geog.)
  613.8; 616.86

> UF Drugs and youth
> Narcotics and youth
> Youth and drugs
> Youth and narcotics
> NT **Teenagers—Drug use**
> RT **Juvenile delinquency**

Youth—Employment (May subdiv. geog.)
  331.3

> UF Boys—Employment
> Girls—Employment
> BT **Age and employment**
> **Employment**
> NT **Teenagers—Employment**
> RT **Summer employment**

Youth hostels (May subdiv. geog.)
  910.46

> UF Hostels, Youth
> Tourist accommodations
> BT **Community centers**
> **Hotels and motels**

Youth market
> USE **Young consumers**

Youth movement (May subdiv. geog.)
  322.4

> UF Student movement
> Student protests, demonstrations, etc.
> Student revolt
> BT **Social movements**
> NT **Students—Political activity**

Youth—Religious life **204; 248.4**

> BT **Religious life**
> NT **Teenagers—Religious life**

Youth—United States **305.230973**

> UF American youth
> NT **Teenagers—United States**

Yuri
> USE **Shojo-ai**

Zaire
> USE **Congo (Democratic Republic)**

Zen Buddhism (May subdiv. geog.)
  294.3

> BT **Buddhism**

Zeppelins
> USE **Airships**

Zero gravity
> USE **Weightlessness**

Zeus (Greek deity) **292.2**

> BT **Gods and goddesses**

Zinc **669**

> BT **Chemical elements**
> **Metals**

Zines
> USE **Fanzines**

Zionism (May subdiv. geog.) **320.5**

> UF Zionist movement
> RT **Jews—Restoration**

Zionist movement
> USE **Zionism**

Zip code (May subdiv. geog.) **383**

> UF Postal delivery code
> BT **Postal service**

Zodiac **133.5; 523**

> BT **Astrology**
> **Astronomy**

Zoning (May subdiv. geog.) **346.04; 354.3**

> UF City planning—Zone system
> Districting (in city planning)
> BT **City planning**

Zoological gardens
USE **Zoos**

Zoological specimens—Collection and preservation **590.75**
UF Collections of natural specimens
Preservation of zoological specimens
Specimens, Preservation of
SA types of specimens with the subdivision *Collection and preservation*, e.g. **Birds—Collection and preservation** [to be added as needed]
BT **Collectors and collecting**
NT **Birds—Collection and preservation**
RT **Taxidermy**

Zoology **590**
Use for materials on the science of animals. Nonscientific materials on animals are entered under **Animals**.
UF Animal kingdom
Animal physiology
Fauna
SA names of divisions, classes, etc., of the animal kingdom, e.g. **Invertebrates**; **Vertebrates**; **Birds**; **Mammals**; etc.; and names of animals [to be added as needed]
BT **Biology**
Science
NT **Animal behavior**
Animals—Anatomy
Comparative anatomy
Comparative psychology
Economic zoology
Embryology
Paleontology
RT **Animals**
Natural history
Zoos

Zoology—Anatomy
USE **Animals—Anatomy**

Zoology, Economic
USE **Economic zoology**

Zoology of the Bible
USE **Bible—Natural history**

Zoology—United States
USE **Animals—United States**

Zoos (May subdiv. geog.) **590.73**
UF Zoological gardens
SA names of individual zoos [to be added as needed]
BT **Parks**
NT **Petting zoos**
RT **Animals**
Zoology

Zoroastrianism (May subdiv. geog.) **295**
BT **Religions**